THE
CHICANO
HERITAGE

This is a volume in the Arno Press collection

THE CHICANO HERITAGE

Advisory Editor
Carlos E. Cortés

Editorial Board
Rodolfo Acuña
Juan Gómez-Quiñones
George F. Rivera, Jr.

*See last pages of this volume
for a complete list of titles.*

U.S. President, 1849-1850 (Taylor)

CALIFORNIA
AND
NEW MEXICO

Message From The
President Of The United States
Communicating Information Called For
By A Resolution
Of The Senate

ARNO PRESS

A New York Times Company

New York — 1976

LEARNING RESOURCES CENTER
NAZARETH COLLEGE

Editorial Supervision: LESLIE PARR

———◆———

Reprint Edition 1976 by Arno Press Inc.

Reprinted from a copy in the State
   Historical Society of Wisconsin Library

THE CHICANO HERITAGE
ISBN for complete set: 0-405-09480-9
See last pages of this volume for titles.

Manufactured in the United States of America

———◆———

Library of Congress Cataloging in Publication Data

United States. President, 1849-1850 (Taylor)
   California and New Mexico.

   (The Chicano heritage)
   Reprint of the 1850 ed. which was issued as
Executive document no. 17 of the United State Congress, 1st session, House of Representatives.
   Documents furnished by the War Department: p.
   1. California--History--1846-1850--Sources.
2. New Mexico--History--War with Mexico, 1845-1848--
Sources. I. United States. War Department.
II. Title. III. Series. IV. Series: United
States. 31st Congress, 1st session 1849-1850.
House. Executive document ; no. 17.

F864.U59   1976   979.4'03   76-1618
ISBN 0-405-09530-9

31st Congress, [SENATE.] Rep. Com.
1st *Session.* No. 18.

MESSAGE

FROM

THE PRESIDENT OF THE UNITED STATES,

COMMUNICATING

Information called for by a resolution of the Senate of the 17th instant, in relation to California and New Mexico.

January 24, 1850.
Ordered to be printed.

To the Senate of the United States:

I transmit to the Senate, in answer to a resolution of that body passed on the 17th instant, the accompanying reports of heads of departments, which contain all the official information in the possession of the Executive asked for by the resolution.

On coming into office, I found the military commandant of the department of California exercising the functions of civil governor in that Territory; and left, as I was, to act under the treaty of Guadalupe Hidalgo, without the aid of any legislative provision establishing a government in that Territory, I thought it best not to disturb that arrangement, made under my predecessor, until Congress should take some action on that subject. I therefore did not interfere with the powers of the military commandant, who continued to exercise the functions of civil governor as before; but I made no such appointment, conferred no such authority, and have allowed no increased compensation to the commandant for his services.

With a view to the faithful execution of the treaty, so far as lay in the power of the Executive, and to enable Congress to act, at the present session, with as full knowledge and as little difficulty as possible, on all matters of interest in these Territories, I sent the honorable Thomas Butler King as bearer of despatches to California, and certain officers to California and New Mexico, whose duties are particularly defined in the accompanying letters of instruction addressed to them severally by the proper departments.

I did not hesitate to express to the people of those Territories my desire that each Territory should, if prepared to comply with the requisitions of the constitution of the United States, form a plan of a State constitution and submit the same to Congress, with a prayer for admission into the Union as a

State; but I did not anticipate, suggest, or authorize the establishment of any such government without the assent of Congress; nor did I authorize any government agent or officer to interfere with or exercise any influence or control over the election of delegates, or over any convention, in making or modifying their domestic institutions or any of the provisions of their proposed constitution. On the contrary, the instructions given by my orders were, that all measures of domestic policy adopted by the people of California must originate solely with themselves; that while the Executive of the United States was desirous to protect them in the formation of any government republican in its character, to be, at the proper time, submitted to Congress, yet it was to be distinctly understood that the plan of such a government must, at the same time, be the result of their own deliberate choice, and originate with themselves, without the interference of the Executive.

I am unable to give any information as to laws passed by any supposed government in California, or of any census taken in either of the Territories mentioned in the resolution, as I have no information on those subjects.

As already stated, I have not disturbed the arrangements which I found had existed under my predecessor.

In advising an early application by the people of these Territories for admission as States, I was actuated principally by an earnest desire to afford to the wisdom and patriotism of Congress the opportunity of avoiding occasions of bitter and angry dissensions among the people of the United States.

Under the constitution, every State has the right of establishing, and, from time to time, altering its municipal laws and domestic institutions, independently of every other State and of the general government; subject only to the prohibitions and guaranties expressly set forth in the constitution of the United States. The subjects thus left exclusively to the respective States were not designed or expected to become topics of national agitation. Still, as, under the constitution, Congress has power to make all needful rules and regulations respecting the Territories of the United States, every new acquisition of territory has led to discussions on the question whether the system of involuntary servitude which prevails in many of the States should or should not be prohibited in that Territory. The periods of excitement from this cause which have heretofore occurred have been safely passed; but during the interval, of whatever length, which may elapse before the admission of the Territories ceded by Mexico as States, it appears probable that similar excitement will prevail to an undue extent.

Under these circumstances, I thought, and still think, that it was my duty to endeavor to put it in the power of Congress, by the admission of California and New Mexico as States, to remove all occasion for the unnecessary agitation of the public mind.

It is understood that the people of the western part of California have formed a plan of a State constitution, and will soon submit the same to the judgment of Congress, and apply for admission as a State. This course on their part, though in accordance with, was not adopted exclusively in consequence of, any expression of my wishes, inasmuch as measures tending to this end had been promoted by the officers sent there by my predecessor, and were already in active progress of execution before any communication from me reached California. If the proposed constitution shall, when submitted to Congress, be found to be in compliance with the requisitions of the constitution of the United States, I earnestly recommend that it may receive the sanction of Congress.

The part of California not included in the proposed State of that name is believed to be uninhabited, except in a settlement of our countrymen in the vicinity of Salt Lake.

A claim has been advanced by the State of Texas to a very large portion of the most populous district of the Territory commonly designated by the name of New Mexico. If the people of New Mexico had formed a plan of a State government for that Territory as ceded by the treaty of Guadalupe Hidalgo, and had been admitted by Congress as a State, our constitution would have afforded the means of obtaining an adjustment of the question of boundary with Texas by a judicial decision. At present, however, no judicial tribunal has the power of deciding that question, and it remains for Congress to devise some mode for its adjustment. Meanwhile, I submit to Congress the question whether it would be expedient, before such adjustment, to establish a territorial government, which, by including the district so claimed, would practically decide the question adversely to the State of Texas, or, by excluding it, would decide it in her favor. In my opinion, such a course would not be expedient, especially as the people of this Territory still enjoy the benefit and protection of their municipal laws, originally derived from Mexico, and have a military force stationed there to protect them against the Indians. It is undoubtedly true that the property, lives, liberties, and religion of the people of New Mexico are better protected than they ever were before the treaty of cession.

Should Congress, when California shall present herself for incorporation into the Union, annex a condition to her admission as a State affecting her domestic institutions, contrary to the wishes of her people, and even compel her, temporarily, to comply with it, yet the State could change her constitution, at any time after admission, when to her it should seem expedient. Any attempt to deny to the people of the State the right of self-government, in a matter which peculiarly affects themselves, will infallibly be regarded by them as an invasion of their rights; and, upon the principles laid down in our own Declaration of Independence, they will certainly be sustained by the great mass of the American people. To assert that they are a conquered people, and must submit, as a State, to the will of their conquerors in this regard, will meet with no cordial response among American freemen. Great numbers of them are native citizens of the United States, not inferior to the rest of our countrymen in intelligence and patriotism; and no language of menace, to restrain them in the exercise of an undoubted right, substantially guarantied to them by the treaty of cession itself, shall ever be uttered by me, or encouraged and sustained by persons acting under my authority. It is to be expected that, in the residue of the territory ceded to us by Mexico, the people residing there will, at the time of their incorporation into the Union as a State, settle all questions of domestic policy to suit themselves. No material inconvenience will result from the want, for a short period, of a government established by Congress over that part of the territory which lies eastward of the new State of California; and the reasons for my opinion that New Mexico will, at no very distant period, ask for admission into the Union, are founded on unofficial information, which, I suppose, is common to all who have cared to make inquiries on that subject.

Seeing, then, that the question which now excites such painful sensations in the country will, in the end, certainly be settled by the silent effect of causes independent of the action of Congress, I again submit to your wisdom the policy recommended in my annual message, of awaiting the salutary operation of those causes, believing that we shall thus avoid the creation of geographical parties, and secure the harmony of feeling so necessary to the beneficial action of our political system. Connected as the Union is with the remembrance of past happiness, the sense of present blessings, and the hope of future peace and prosperity, every dictate of wisdom, every feeling of duty, and every emotion of patriotism, tend to inspire fidelity and devotion to it, and admonish us cautiously to avoid any unnecessary controversy which can either endanger it or impair its strength, the chief element of which is to be found in the regard and affection of the people for each other.

Z. TAYLOR.

WASHINGTON, *January* 23, 1850.

DEPARTMENT OF STATE.

Department of State,
Washington, January 19, 1850.

The Secretary of State, to whom has been referred a resolution of the Senate of the 17th instant, requesting the President of the United States to inform that body, as early as practicable, "whether any person has been by him appointed civil or military governor of California since the 4th day of March last; and, if so, who has been so appointed, and what compensation has been allowed him; also, that he be requested to inform the Senate whether any agent has been appointed by the Executive, or any of the departments of the government, and sent to California with instructions or authority to organize a State government for that Territory, or to aid and advise the people within its limits in such organization; and further, that he be requested to inform the Senate how the delegates recently assembled in California, calling themselves a convention, were elected; by whom the qualifications of the voters were fixed and determined; what those qualifications were; and by what law the time, places, and manner of holding said election were regulated; and further, that he be requested to inform the Senate whether any census of the inhabitants of said territory has been taken, and if so, by what law and under what authority; and further, that he be requested to communicate to the Senate all orders, (written or verbal,) instructions, or correspondence with any person as civil or military Governor of California, or as agent on the part of the United States government in California by the preceding administration and the present administration; and further, that he be requested to inform the Senate whether any steps have been taken by the Executive, or any department of the government, to assemble a convention in New Mexico for the purpose of adopting a constitution and making application for admission into the Union, and if so, that he be requested to communicate to the Senate all orders, instructions, and papers in relation thereto; and further, that he be requested to inform the Senate upon what ground he bases the opinion expressed in his annual message of December 4, 1849, that the people of New Mexico will 'at no very distant period present themselves for admission into the Union,'"—has the honor to report to the President the accompanying papers, on file in his department, embraced by the resolution. Copies of so much of the correspondence of this department during the last administration with officers and agents in California, after the treaty of Guadalupe, as was deemed proper or useful to be communicated to Congress, will be found among the papers accompanying the message of President Polk of December 5, 1848, from page 45 to page 69, inclusive. (See volume 1 Executive Documents, 2d session 30th Congress.) Prior to that period, T. O. Larkin, esq., was appointed confidential agent of the department in California, and received for his services the sum of $6,107. The sum of $1,000 has been paid to Mr. King.

The Secretary of State has the honor to add, that no official report has yet been received at this department from Mr. King, who, on the 3d day of

April last, was appointed bearer of despatches to California and agent to collect information necessary to the proper execution of the treaty with Mexico, as well as to communicate information to the people of that Territory, as is fully stated in the copy of his instructions herewith sent. Private advices from California have informed us that he was confined by severe illness, not long after his arrival at San Francisco, but that he had recovered; and his arrival in the United States may, therefore, soon be expected. A report will then, doubtless, be made by him, in obedience to his instructions.

Respectfully submitted.

JOHN M. CLAYTON.

To the PRESIDENT OF THE UNITED STATES.

DEPARTMENT OF STATE,
Washington, October 7, 1848.

SIR: Previous to your departure for California, the President has instructed me to make known, through your agency, to the citizens of the United States inhabiting that Territory, his views respecting their present condition and future prospects. He deems it proper to employ you for this purpose, because the Postmaster General has appointed you an agent, under the "Act to establish certain post routes," approved August 14, 1848, " to make arrangements for the establishment of post offices, and for the transmission, receipt, and conveyance of letters in Oregon and California."

The President congratulates the citizens of California on the annexation of their fine province to the United States. On the 30th of May, 1848, the day on which the ratifications of our late treaty with Mexico were exchanged, California finally became an integral portion of this great and glorious republic; and the act of Congress to which I have already referred, in express terms recognises it to be " within the territory of the United States."

May this union be perpetual!

The people of California may feel the firmest conviction that the government and people of the United States will never abandon them or prove unmindful of their prosperity. Their fate and their fortunes are now indissolubly united with that of their brethren on this side of the Rocky mountains. How propitious this event both for them and for us! Whilst the other nations of the world are distracted by domestic dissensions, and are involved in a struggle between the privileges of the few and the rights of the many, Heaven has blessed our happy land with a government which secures equal rights to all our citizens, and has produced peace, happiness, and contentment throughout our borders. It has combined liberty with order, and all the sacred and indefeasible rights of the citizens with the strictest observance of law. Satisfied with the institutions under which we live, each individual is therefore left free to promote his own prosperity and happiness in the manner most in accordance with his own judgment.

Under such a constitution and such laws, the prospects of California are truly encouraging. Blessed with a mild and salubrious climate and a fertile soil, rich in mineral resources, and extending over nearly ten degrees of latitude along the coast of the Pacific, with some of the finest harbors in the world, the imagination can scarcely fix a limit to its future wealth and prosperity.

We can behold in the not distant future one or more glorious States of this confederacy springing into existence in California, governed by institutions similar to our own, and extending the blessings of religion, liberty, and law over that vast region. Their free and unrestricted commerce and intercourse with the other States of the Union will confer mutual benefits and blessings on all parties concerned, and will bind us all together by the strongest ties of reciprocal affection and interest. Their foreign trade with the west coast of America, with Asia, and the isles of the Pacific, will be protected by our common flag, and cannot fail to bear back to their shores the rich rewards of enterprise and industry.

After all, however, the speedy realization of these bright prospects depends much upon the wise and prudent conduct of the citizens of California in the present emergency. If they commence their career under proper auspices, their advance will be rapid and certain; but should they become entangled in difficulties and dissensions at the start, their progress will be greatly retarded.

The President deeply regrets that Congress did not at their late session establish a territorial government for California. It would now be vain to enter into the reasons for this omission. Whatever these may have been, he is firmly convinced that Congress feel a deep interest in the welfare of California and its people, and will at an early period of the next session provide for them a territorial government suited to their wants. Our laws relating to trade and intercourse with the Indians will then be extended over them, custom-houses will be established for the collection of the revenue, and liberal grants of land will be made to those bold and patriotic citizens who amidst privations and dangers have emigrated or shall emigrate to that Territory from the States on this side of the Rocky mountains.

The President, in his annual message, at the commencement of the next session, will recommend all these great measures to Congress in the strongest terms, and will use every effort, consistently with his duty, to insure their accomplishment.

In the mean time, the condition of the people of California is anomalous, and will require, on their part, the exercise of great prudence and discretion. By the conclusion of the treaty of peace, the military government which was established over them under the laws of war, as recognised by the practice of all civilized nations, has ceased to derive its authority from this source of power. But is there, for this reason, no government in California? Are life, liberty, and property under the protection of no existing authorities? This would be a singular phenomenon in the face of the world, and especially among American citizens, distinguished as they are above all other people for their law abiding character. Fortunately, they are not reduced to this sad condition. The termination of the war left an existing government, a government *de facto*, in full operation; and this will continue, with the presumed consent of the people, until Congress shall provide for them a territorial government. The great law of necessity justifies this conclusion. The consent of the people is irresistibly inferred from the fact that no civilized community could possibly desire to abrogate an existing government, when the alternative presented would be to place themselves in a state of anarchy, beyond the protection of all laws, and reduce them to the unhappy necessity of submitting to the dominion of the strongest.

This government *de facto* will, of course, exercise no power inconsistent with the provisions of the constitution of the United States, which is the supreme law of the land. For this reason, no import duties can be levied in California on articles the growth, produce, or manufacture of the United States, as no such duties can be imposed in any other part of our Union on the productions of California. Nor can new duties be charged in California upon such foreign productions as have already paid duties in any of our ports of entry, for the obvious reason that California is within the territory of the United States. I shall not enlarge upon this subject, however, as the Secretary of the Treasury will perform that duty.

The President urgently advises the people of California to live peaceably and quietly under the existing government. He believes that this will promote their lasting and best interests. If it be not what they could desire and had a right to expect, they can console themselves with the reflection that it will endure but for a few months. Should they attempt to change or amend it during this brief period, they most probably could not accomplish their object before the government established by Congress would go into operation. In the mean time, the country would be agitated, the citizens would be withdrawn from their usual employments, and domestic strife might divide and exasperate the people against each other; and this all to establish a government which in no conceivable contingency could endure for a single year. During this brief period, it is better to bear the ills they have than fly to others they know not of.

The permanent prosperity of any new country is identified with the perfect security of its land titles. The land system of the general government has been a theme of admiration throughout the world. The wisdom of man has never devised a plan so well calculated to prevent litigation and place the rights of owners of the soil beyond dispute. This system has been one great cause of the rapid settlement and progress of our new States and Territories. Emigrants have been attracted there, because every man knew that when he had acquired land from the government, he could sit under his own vine and under his own fig tree, and there would be none to make him afraid. Indeed, there can be no greater drawback to the prosperity of a country, as several of the older States have experienced, than disputed land titles. Prudent men will be deterred from emigrating to a State or Territory where they cannot obtain indisputable title, and must consequently be exposed to the danger of strife and litigation in respect to the soil on which they dwell. An uncertainty respecting the security of land titles arrests all valuable improvement, because no prudent man will expend his means for this purpose while there is danger that another may deprive him of the fruit of his labors. It is fortunate, therefore, that Congress alone, under the constitution, possesses " the power to dispose of and make all needful rules and regulations respecting the territory or other property belonging to the United States." In the exercise of this power, the President is convinced that the emigrants will receive liberal donations of the public land.

Although Congress have not established a territorial government for the people of California, they have not been altogether unmindful of their interests. The benefit of our Post Office laws has been extended to them; and you will bear with you authority from the Postmaster General to provide for the conveyance of public information and private correspondence among themselves, and between them and the citizens of Oregon, and of our States east of the Rocky mountains. The monthly steamers on the line from Panama to Astoria have been required "to stop and deliver and take mails at San Diego, San Francisco, and Monterey." These steamers, connected by the isthmus of Panama with those on the Atlantic, between New York and Chagres, will keep up a regular communication with California, and afford facilities to all those who may desire to emigrate to that Territory.

The necessary appropriations have also been made by Congress to maintain troops in California to protect its inhabitants against all attacks from a civilized or savage foe; and it will afford the President peculiar pleasure to perform this duty promptly and effectively.

But, above all, the constitution of the United States, the safeguard of all our civil rights, was extended over California on the 30th May, 1848, the day on which our late treaty with Mexico was finally consummated. From that day its inhabitants became entitled to all the blessings and benefits resulting from the best form of civil government ever established amongst men. That they will prove worthy of this inestimable boon, no doubt is entertained.

Whilst the population of California will be composed chiefly of our own kindred, of a people speaking our own language, and educated for self-government under our own institutions, a considerable portion of them were Mexican citizens before the late treaty of peace. These, our new citizens, ought to be, and, from the justice and generosity of the American character, the President is confident that they will be, treated with respect and kindness, and thus be made to feel that by changing their allegiance they have become more prosperous and happy.

Yours, very respectfully,

JAMES BUCHANAN.

WILLIAM V. VORHIES, Esq.,
Washington city.

DEPARTMENT OF STATE,
Washington, April 3, 1849.

SIR: The President, reposing full confidence in your integrity, abilities, and prudence, has appointed you an agent for the purpose of conveying important instructions and despatches to our naval and military commanders in California. It is his desire that you should lose no time in repairing thither, by the best and most expeditious route, in the prosecution of the duties devolved upon you, which I shall proceed to explain in the following instructions.

The situation of the people of California and New Mexico has already, at this early period of his administration, attracted his attention. By the late treaty with Mexico, provision was made for the future admission of these Territories into the Union as States; and, in the mean time, the government of the United States is bound to protect the inhabitants residing in them in the free and entire enjoyment of their lives, liberty, and property, and in the exercise of their civil and religious rights. Owing to causes with which you are fully acquainted, the Congress of the United States failed to assist the Executive by the passage of a law establishing a government in either of the new Territories. You are aware, however, that an act was passed, at the last session, to extend the revenue laws of the United States over the territory and waters of Upper California. This act creates a collection district in California. And you also know that, by another previous act, certain mail facilities have been extended to the same Territory. Whatever can be done, by the aid of the constitution of the United States, the treaty with Mexico, and the enactments of Congress, to afford to the people of the Territories the benefits of civil government and the protection that is due them, will be anxiously considered and attempted by the Executive.

You have been selected by the President to convey to them these assurances, and especially the assurance of his firm determination, so far as his constitutional power extends, to omit nothing that may tend to promote and secure their peace and happiness. You are fully possessed of the President's views, and can, with propriety, suggest to the people of California the adoption of measures best calculated to give them effect. These measures must, of course, originate solely with themselves. Assure them of the sincere desire of the Executive of the United States to protect and defend them in the formation of any government, republican in its character, hereafter to be submitted to Congress, which shall be the result of their own deliberate choice. But let it be, at the same time, distinctly understood by them that the plan of such a government must originate with themselves, and without the interference of the Executive.

The laws of California and New Mexico, as they existed at the conclusion of the treaty of Guadalupe Hidalgo, regulating the relations of the inhabitants with each other, will necessarily remain in force in those Territories. Their relations with their former government have been dissolved, and new relations created between them and the government of the United States; but the existing laws regulating the relations of the people with each other will continue until others, lawfully enacted, shall supersede them. Our naval and military commanders on those stations will be fully instructed to co-operate with the friends of order and good government, so far as their co-operation can be useful and proper.

An important part of your duty will be to acquire, and to transmit to this department, the best and fullest information in regard to the population, the productions, and the resources of the country; the extent and character of all grants of land made by Mexico prior to the late treaty; the quantity and condition of the public domain, and especially of those portions which are rendered valuable by their metallic and mineral wealth; and the general fitness and capacity of these new acquisitions for the great purposes of agriculture, commerce, and manufactures. The development of the resources of this vast and interesting region, in all that concerns the interest and welfare of its present and future occupants, is a cherished object of this government; and all information which you can obtain in relation to these subjects will be most acceptable to this department.

It is desirable to know the numbers of the various Indian tribes which form a portion of the population of the Territories; their power, character, and modes of life; and the number of Mexicans held as captives there by any savage tribes, whose release and restoration to their own country this government is bound to exact by the 4th and 11th articles of the treaty: also, as nearly as may be, the number of Mexicans who, within the year after the exchange of the ratifications of the treaty, have withdrawn from the Territories; and the number of those who have declared their intention to preserve the character of citizens of the Mexican republic, agreeably to the 8th article of the treaty.

It is not credited by this government that any attempt will be made to alienate either of these portions of the Territories of the United States, or to establish an independent government within their limits. But should the existence of any such project be detected, you will not fail to bring it to the immediate notice of your government, that proper measures for the protection of the interests of the people of the United States may be promptly adopted.

You are fully authorized to confer with our military and naval commanders within these Territories, who will be instructed to assist you in the accomplishment of the objects of your mission.

Your compensation will be at the rate of eight dollars per diem, from the time of your departure on the business of your mission until your return home; and you will be allowed your travelling and other expenses during your absence, for which you will be careful to take vouchers in all cases where they can be obtained.

The sum of one thousand dollars is advanced to you on account.

I am, sir, very respectfully, your obedient servant,
JOHN M. CLAYTON.

Hon. THOMAS BUTLER KING,
Appointed agent of the United States to California.

DEPARTMENT OF THE TREASURY.

TREASURY DEPARTMENT, *January* 21, 1850.

SIR: I have the honor to acknowledge the receipt of the resolution of the Senate of the United States of the 17th instant, referred by you to this department, requesting the President of the United States to communicate certain information in reference to the appointment of a civil and military governor for the Territory of California, and the organization of a government for said Territory.

In answer thereto, I herewith transmit all the information in this department called for by said resolution.

I have the honor to be, very respectfully, your obedient servant,
W. M. MEREDITH,
Secretary of the Treasury.

To the PRESIDENT.

TREASURY DEPARTMENT, *April* 2, 1849.

SIR: This will be handed to you by the Hon. T. Butler King, if there should be in his opinion occasion for so doing. The object of this letter is to impress upon you the desire of the President that you should, in all matters connected with Mr. King's mission, aid and assist him in carrying out the views of the government as expressed in his instructions from the Department of State, and that you should be guided by his advice and counsel in the conduct of all proper measures within the scope of those instructions.

I am, very respectfully, your obedient servant,
W. M. MEREDITH,
Secretary of the Treasury.

JAMES COLLIER, Esq.,
Collector of the Customs Upper California.

WASHINGTON CITY, *March* 29, 1849.

SIR: Myself and associate will build ten fire-proof stores at San Francisco, California; provided the government of the United States will rent them for a period of fifteen years, at an annual rent of seven thousand dollars per store, payable quarterly. The stores to be four stories high, twenty-five feet wide, and one hundred long, to be built entirely of brick and iron, and in the strongest and most approved manner; the stores to be received as finished; and all to be completed within two years from the date of the contract.

Very respectfully, your obedient servant,
DANL. SAFFARRANS.

Hon. W. M. MEREDITH, *Secretary of the Treasury.*

TREASURY DEPARTMENT, *April* 3, 1849.

SIR: In view of your departure for California, to enter upon your duties, in pursuance of your commission as collector of the customs for the district of Upper California and inspector of the revenue for the port of San Francisco, it is deemed expedient and proper to furnish you with the following preliminary instructions for your information and government: When you shall have executed your official bond as collector, and the same shall have been accepted and approved by the First Comptroller of the Treasury, your compensation, as fixed by the fourth section of the act of 3d of March, 1849, entitled "An act to extend the revenue laws of the United States over the territory and waters of Upper California, and to create a collection district therein," will commence on the date of the approval of your bond. Your compensation, as provided by the act referred to, is "fifteen hundred dollars per annum, and the fees and commissions allowed by law." The official fees are enumerated in the second section of the compensation act of 2d March, 1799—see Compilation of Revenue Laws, by Gordon, page 136—and those specified in the thirty-fourth section of the coasting act of the 20th February, 1793—same book, page 39. You will also be entitled to receive a commission of three per centum, as authorized by the second section of the compensation act before mentioned, on all moneys received on account of duties accruing on all goods, wares, and merchandise imported into the district of Upper California, and duly accounted for by authorized disbursements or deposites; and out of the emoluments that would accrue to you as aforesaid in your capacity of collector, you cannot be allowed to retain more than at the maximum rate of three thousand dollars per annum, to be computed from the beginning of your official year, as prescribed by the tenth section of the act "further to establish the compensation of officers of the customs," &c., approved 7th May, 1822; nor out of the emoluments that shall accrue to you for services performed in other capacities than *collector*, can you receive more than at the maximum rate of four hundred dollars per annum. The compensations of the deputy collectors authorized by the act in question to be stationed at the ports of delivery—to wit: San Diego, Monterey, and at a point to be selected by the department near the junction of the rivers Gila and Colorado, at the head of the gulf of California—are fixed by the act at one thousand dollars each per annum, "and the fees and commissions allowed by law."

As vessels and cargoes arriving from foreign ports cannot, under existing provisions of law, enter and land cargo and pay or secure the duties at any other place than at a port of entry, and the ports before designated being ports of delivery merely, no duties can legally be paid or secured at either of said ports. All vessels from foreign ports must enter and the duties be paid or secured at San Francisco, the port of entry for the district. On this being done, the vessel may proceed with her cargo, or any portion thereof, and land the same at either of the ports of delivery mentioned, on due compliance being had with the requirements of law, as prescribed in the general collection act of 2d March, 1799. The fees accruing to the deputy collectors for services enjoined by law upon them in such cases will be found specified in the compensation acts before mentioned. As no moneys can, for the reasons before stated, be received by these deputies on account of duties on imported merchandise, no commissions can accrue to them in the capacity of deputy collectors. Commissions, however, may accrue to them, at the rate of two and a half per centum, as agents for the disbursements of moneys placed in their hands for the relief of sick and disabled seamen, under the marine hospital laws, as also for disbursements for light house establishments, should it be found necessary hereafter to constitute them such agents. These officers are by law made subject to your control and direction, and should be required to report to you in regard to their official acts, and make such periodical statements and returns as may be found needful. You will, from time to time, furnish them with funds to pay their salaries, and such public expenses incurred at their ports as may be authorized by law and the instructions of the department, they accounting to you for all moneys thus placed in their hands.

Upon the execution and approval of the bonds, in the penal sum prescribed by the Solicitor of the Treasury, given under the independent treasury act, approved the 6th of August, 1846, you become authorized to discharge the duties of a designated depositary of public moneys under said act. This service being incidental to your office as collector of the customs and revenue, no compensation can legally be allowed for services performed in that capacity.

Should you propose to appoint the deputy collectors for the ports of delivery enumerated in the act before reaching your collection district, they should be submitted for the approval of the department, in pursuance of the seventh section of the act of 3d March, 1817. (See Compilation of Revenue Laws, page 226.) When the approval is given, they may qualify by taking the oath of office; and their compensations will commence with the date of their oaths respectively. In pursuance of the same act, you are authorized to appoint, subject to approval as aforesaid, a deputy collector and inspector; to aid you in the discharge of your official duties at the port of San Francisco, who will be allowed the maximum pay of an inspector of the customs—viz: at a rate not to exceed three dollars per day.

Upon entering on the discharge of your duties at San Francisco, should it become necessary to employ subordinate officers of the customs, you may, in pursuance of the 2d section of the compensation act of 2d March, 1799, as modified by the act of 26th April, 1816, employ such temporary or occasional inspectors as may be found indispensably necessary for the protection and security of the revenue, to be paid, when actually employed, a sum not exceeding three dollars per day each. Should the employment of *permanent* subordinate officers of the customs be deemed necessary, you will, in pursuance of the 21st section of the general collection act of 2d March, 1799, nominate, for the approval of the department, competent and trustworthy persons to perform the respective duties mentioned in said section, or such of them as may be needed—taking care to furnish reasons to show the necessity for their employment, and stating the rate of compensation proposed to be allowed, which in no case can, for inspectors of the customs, exceed three dollars per day. These officers cannot be employed or paid until the approval of the department is received; but occasional or temporary inspectors may be employed and paid at the commencement of your duties, as before intimated, without awaiting such approval.

As authorized by the 21st section of the act of 2d March, 1799, you are authorized to provide at the port of San Francisco, at the public expense, storehouse accommodations for the safe-keeping of goods, &c., in which building the collector's office may be held. In providing such public store, it is expected that you will exercise proper economy, and pay no higher rent than the rate usual at the port for similar accommodations.

You will take care to advise the department on this subject, and state the rate of rent proposed to be allowed. Should it become necessary to provide stores for warehousing foreign imported goods under bonds, under the warehousing act of 6th August, 1846, you will be governed by the instructions and regulations issued by the department under said act, which have been supplied you.

Copies of the laws, with proper forms and instructions, in reference to the safe-keeping and rendition of your accounts, together with the periodical returns to be made, and instructions to govern you in the assessments and collection of duties, have been furnished you. The First Comptroller has been instructed to furnish you with the necessary articles appertaining to the custom-house, for the use of the collector's office at San Francisco, and also for the offices of the deputies at their respective ports.

It being ascertained that expenses will be necessarily incurred in your district before funds are likely to come into your hands from duties, it is deemed proper, to prevent delay and embarrassment on this account, to advance to you out of the revenue, to be carried with you to your destination, a sum of money deemed to be adequate to defray such expenses. The First Comptroller has accordingly been directed to furnish you, by an order on the collector of New York, with the sum of six thousand dollars, together with the additional sum of five hundred dollars to defray your own actual travelling expenses incurred in proceeding hence to San Francisco.

With these sums you will be duly charged and held accountable, and will receive due credits in the settlement of your official accounts for such disbursements, properly vouched, as may be made in pursuance of law and instructions. No travelling expenses can be allowed to your deputies or any other subordinate officers who may accompany you to California. Should it become necessary, in the enforcement of the revenue laws, to call for additional aid and assistance beyond that afforded by the regular officers of the customs, you are authorized by law to employ the revenue cutter C. W. Lawrence, assigned to that station, as provided in the 99th section of the general collection act of 2d March, 1799, to which your attention is specially called.

It is proper to advise you that you can only receive, in payment of duties, coins of the United States, and such foreign coins as are recognised and their values established by acts of Congress.

In conclusion, I would add that, in view of the great distance of your district from the seat of government, and the consequent infrequency and uncertainty of regular communications, much must be left to your good judgment and discretion, which the department confidently expects will, within the limits of law, be judiciously exercised.

You will be expected to furnish returns and other official statements with the utmost punctuality practicable, and will communicate by letter with the department as often as opportunities shall occur, offering such suggestions for its consideration as the interests of the revenue and the general condition of things in your district may, in your opinion, render expedient.

              W. M. MEREDITH,
               Secretary of the Treasury.

JAMES COLLIER, Esq.,
 Collector of the Customs for port of San Francisco,
  District of Upper California, now in Washington.

WASHINGTON, *April* 3, 1849.

SIR: I respectfully nominate William Prentiss to be an inspector of the customs for the district of Upper California.

I am, sir, very respectfully, your obedient servant,
J. COLLIER,
Collector of the Customs for district of Upper California.

Hon. WM. M. MEREDITH,
Secretary of the Treasury.

TREASURY DEPARTMENT, *April* 4, 1849.

SIR: Your nomination, under date the 3d inst., of William Prentiss to be an inspector of the customs for the district of California, is approved.

I am, very respectfully, your obedient servant,
W. M. MEREDITH,
Secretary of the Treasury.

J. COLLIER, Esq.,
Collector, &c., for Upper California.

WASHINGTON, *April* 3, 1849.

SIR: I respectfully nominate for the district of Upper California:

Alexander Irvin, of Pennsylvania, to be deputy collector at Monterey.

Williamson Ferrel, of South Carolina, to be deputy collector at San Diego.

Alexander Bradford, of Mississippi, to be deputy collector at the point near the junction of the Gila and Colorado hereafter to be designated by the Secretary of the Treasury.

Edwin D. Collier, to be deputy collector at San Francisco.

Also, John Caperton, Thomas Harvey, Augustus Richards, Amos Adams, and John A. Collier, to be inspectors of the customs, to be stationed as the public interests may require.

I am, sir, very respectfully, your obedient servant,
J. COLLIER,
Collector for district of Upper California.

Hon. WM. M. MEREDITH,
Secretary of the Treasury.

TREASURY DEPARTMENT, *April* 3, 1849.

SIR: The following nominations made by you for the district of Upper California, under date of to-day, are approved, viz:

Alexander Irvin, to be deputy collector at Monterey.

Williamson Ferrel, to be deputy collector at San Diego.

Alexander Bradford, to be deputy collector at junction of Gila and Colorado.

Edwin D. Collier, to be deputy collector at San Francisco.

Also, John Caperton, Thomas Harvey, Augustus Richards, Amos Adams, and John A. Collier, to be inspectors of the customs.

I am, very respectfully, your obedient servant,
W. M. MEREDITH,
Secretary of the Treasury.

J. COLLIER, Esq., *Collector of Customs,*
Port of San Francisco, District of Upper California.

WASHINGTON CITY, *April* 4, 1849.

SIR: During my stay in the city, and while making the necessary arrangements for my early departure for Upper California, I have felt no little anxiety as to what might be the state of things on my arrival at San Francisco, and what facilities might be found on the spot to enable me to carry into execution the revenue laws of the country. I must have, in the first place, a suitable building, or buildings, to protect the public property committed to my care ; and there ought to be warehouses sufficient to store the goods that may and no doubt will be imported. Shall I find these indispensable buildings on my arrival? Upon this subject I have endeavored to inform myself, by conversation with persons who have been upon the spot, and by communication with others who have friends now residing there. All concur in saying that it will be next to impossible to find a building suitable for an office, or for a warehouse, should one be required. I take it for granted that the government desires to extend to the people of California all the facilities which the commerce, now rapidly increasing, of the country, may require. The cities upon the Atlantic seaboard have been greatly favored in this particular, and millions have been expended for that purpose. As yet, nothing has been done for California. The question, then, which I desire to submit to your consideration, is this : " Ought not some measures to be adopted, previous to my departure for so distant a point, for the purpose of securing the erection of suitable buildings for the accommodation of the collector, and for the convenience of shippers of merchandise to that coast?" Upon this subject I cannot withhold the expression of my own opinion. Something ought to be done. Good policy seems to require that I should be enabled to say to those people on my arrival, The government are making the necessary preparations for all these things, and they will be forwarded as speedily as the nature of the business will permit. In looking over my instructions, I find that upon the subject of warehouses I am to be governed by the instructions heretofore issued from the department to the various collectors in the United States. These instructions require the collectors in all cases to give a preference to fire-proof buildings, and such as are particularly described by the department. Acting upon these instructions, I cannot, in view of all the information I have been enabled to collect, hesitate to recommend that arrangements be made for the erection of such buildings as are deemed indispensable by the collector, at the earliest period possible. It is true, I cannot say to what extent these buildings may be required. Judging, however, from the amount of shipments already reported, and the number of vessels advertised to leave the several seaports, large buildings must and will be required.

I respectfully submit these suggestions to the consideration of the department. The necessity of my immediate departure will excuse the haste in which they have been drawn up. I desire to discharge my whole duty, but it is evident that this cannot be done unless the necessary means are provided.
Very respectfully,
J. COLLIER,
Collector of Customs for the district of Upper California.
Hon. WM. M. MEREDITH,
Secretary of the Treasury.

WASHINGTON,
Wednesday evening, April 4, 1849.

SIR: I have just received the enclosed letter, containing propositions to erect buildings for the accommodation of the customs at San Francisco. I have, of course, made no reply, but desire to submit it to your consideration, presuming, however, that nothing will be determined upon until you shall hear from me, on my arrival at San Francisco. I could do no less than submit it to you.
Very respectfully,
J. COLLIER,
Collector, &c., &c.
Hon. W. M. MEREDITH,
Secretary of the Treasury.

WASHINGTON, *April* 4, 1849.

SIR: Understanding that it is the opinion of the Secretary of the Treasury that the government of the United States may not want as many stores at San Francisco as I offered to rent in my proposition to the department, and that the power to contract for such stores has been delegated by law to the collectors, I proceed to make such modifications in my original proposition as may meet the demands of government.

Myself and associate are willing to build eight stores of the character we first proposed, following the plans as submitted by Geo. Law, esq., of New York, (for stores in that city,) which were left with the late Secretary of the Treasury, and approved by him.

Of the stores I propose to build, five must be taken by the government the moment they are finished, at an annual rent of seven thousand dollars, payable quarterly—it being distinctly understood that, as soon as the increasing commerce of San Francisco shall require more store room, the collector shall rent the additional stores, upon the same terms.

We stipulated for two years' time in which to complete the building of the stores; but our own interest is a sufficient guaranty that they will be built at the earliest practicable moment. Yet it must be borne in mind that we will have to ship all our material from the Atlantic cities, (a six months' voyage,) and a single accident to a vessel bearing the material, which no insurance could prevent, might delay us six or eight months; but, should no unforeseen difficulty arise, we confidently believe that we will have the stores ready for use within twelve months.

The plans of Mr. Law, by which we purpose to be governed, were made out with great care, and are on file in the Treasury Department.

Very respectfully, your obedient servant,
DANL. SAFFARRANS.

Col. Jas. Collier,
Collector, San Francisco.

Treasury Department, *April* 7, 1849.

Sir: The confirmation of "William Prentiss," under date the 1st instant, nominated by you to be an "inspector of the customs for the district of Upper California," is hereby revoked; and you are requested to withdraw said nomination.

I am, very respectfully, your obedient servant,
W. M. MEREDITH,
Secretary of the Treasury.

J. Collier, Esq., *Collector district U. California,*
Now at Steubenville, Ohio.

Treasury Department, *April* 10, 1849.

Sir: It is deemed proper to call your attention to the subject of the deputy collectors and inspectors of the customs recently appointed by you, with the approval of the department; and to state that, before those officers can, in pursuance of law, enter upon the discharge of their respective duties, or be allowed compensation, they must qualify by taking the oath or affirmation prescribed by law—such oath or affirmation to be taken before yourself, as collector of the district to which they respectively belong, and transmitted to the department. For your information, a form of the oath or affirmation to be taken by the deputy collectors, as well as by the inspectors of the customs, has been prepared, and will be found on the opposite page of this letter.

Very respectfully,
C. B. PENROSE,
Acting Secretary of the Treasury.

James Collier, Esq.,
Collector of district of Upper California, now at Steubenville, O.

Steubenville, *April* 12, 1849.

Sir: Yours of the 7th instant, revoking the confirmation of William Prentiss, (nominated by myself as inspector of the customs for the district of Upper California,) was received on yesterday. In accordance with your request, I withdraw said nomination. I regret that I am unadvised as to his location in Illinois, and that I cannot, therefore, give him notice of what has transpired.

As I shall have occasion, before leaving, of submitting several nominations for your consideration, I shall defer making any at this date to fill the vacancy which has thus occurred.

I am making every exertion to leave at the earliest possible moment. My business affairs, of course, require some attention previous to my departure. I will advise you from Cincinnati or St. Louis of my movements.

Very respectfully,
J. COLLIER, *Collector, &c.*

Hon. WM. M. MEREDITH,
Secretary of the Treasury.

TREASURY DEPARTMENT, *April* 20, 1849.

SIR: I have to acknowledge the receipt of your several letters of the 4th instant and that of the 12th instant, from Steubenville, Ohio. Should you have arrived at any definite conclusion on the subject of procuring proper warehousing accommodations at San Francisco, Upper California, and for the custom-house referred to in your letters, you will find the enclosed form an aid in enabling you to put any agreement you may make on the subject in proper form for submission to this department for its sanction.

I am, very respectfully, your obedient servant,
W. M. MEREDITH,
Secretary of the Treasury.

JAMES COLLIER, Esq.,
Collector of Customs, district of Upper California,
Now at St. Louis, Missouri.

Articles of agreement made and concluded this twenty-eighth day of April, in the year eighteen hundred and forty-nine, by and between Daniel Saffarrans of the first part, and the United States of America, by James Collier, collector of the district of San Francisco, California, acting by the direction and authority of William M. Meredith, Secretary of the Treasury, of the second part.

The said party of the first part, for the considerations hereinafter mentioned, doth, for himself, his heirs, executors, and administrators, hereby covenant with the said party of the second part, that he will well and substantially erect, build, and finish a store or building in said San Francisco, of the dimensions and description hereinafter mentioned, the whole subject to such modifications and alterations as the said collector of San Francisco shall require or approve, to wit: Said stores to be four stories high, twenty-five feet wide, and one hundred feet long, to be constructed of iron and brick, so far as may be necessary to make them strictly fire-proof, and to be built in the strongest and most approved manner, the said collector reserving to himself the sole power and privilege of selecting the site or ground upon which said store or stores shall be erected. It is further understood that said collector is to lease said store or stores of said party of the first part for the term of fifteen years. The rent per annum to be determined upon and fixed by the collector, at the time said store or stores shall be erected and received by said collector.

And the said party of the first part doth further covenant, that he will erect and finish said store in such manner as the said collector shall require or approve, so that the said store shall be ready for occupancy on or before the first day of September, eighteen hundred and fifty.

And the said party of the first part doth further covenant, that whenever the said store shall be erected and finished and ready for occupancy to the acceptance of said collector, he will lease, and he doth hereby lease, the said store to the said party of the second part for a term commencing on the day when the said collector shall approve and accept of said store, and terminating on the expiration of the term aforesaid, to wit: fifteen years from the time they are received by said collector, upon the terms and conditions and for the rent hereinafter mentioned.

And the said party of the first part doth further covenant, that the said store is free from all incumbrance, and that the United States shall not be liable for any lien upon said store during the term aforesaid, or any other claim of any nature whatsoever, except only the rent hereinafter stipulated, and that he will keep the said store in good order and sufficient repair—injuries arising from the misconduct of officers of the government only excepted.

And the said party of the second part do hereby covenant with the said party of the first part, his heirs, executors, and administrators, that whenever the said store shall be ready for the occupancy to the acceptance of the said collector, they will hire and lease of the said party of the first part the said store, upon the terms and conditions and for the period herein mentioned; that they will pay rent for the said store, at the rate of   dollars per annum, said rent to be paid quarter-yearly on the first of January, April, July, and October; and that the said rent on said store shall commence as soon as the same be ready for occupancy and accepted by the said collector as aforesaid.

And it is further agreed by the said parties of the first and second parts, that should the said store be destroyed or injured by fire, or the action of any of the elements, so that the same shall become untenantable, the said party of the first part shall rebuild and repair the same as soon as practicable; and the rent of said store shall cease and remain discontinued during all the time the occupancy of said store shall be interrupted or prevented from the causes aforesaid, or any other cause not arising from the act or default of the Secretary of the Treasury or the collector aforesaid.

In testimony whereof, the said parties to these presents, on the day and year first above written, have hereunto, and to two other copies of the same, interchangably set their hands and seals, the said party of the first part in person, and the United States by James Collier, collector, acting as aforesaid; and William M. Meredith, Secretary of the Treasury, in evidence of the authority aforesaid and of his approval of the premises, has hereunto affixed his official signature.

DANIEL SAFFARRANS. [L. S.]
JAMES COLLIER, [L. S.]
Collector of the District of Upper California.

Signed, sealed, and delivered in presence of
SAML. T. WYLIE,
N. HEADINGTON.

STATE OF OHIO, *Hamilton county, sct:*

Personally appeared before me, the undersigned, a notary public in and for the county and State aforesaid, on this twenty-eighth day of April, A. D. eighteen hundred and forty-nine, Daniel Saffarrans and James Collier, the parties to the foregoing instrument, and severally acknowledged the same to be their voluntary act and deed, for the uses and purposes therein mentioned.

In testimony whereof, I have hereunto set my hand and affixed my notarial seal, this twenty-eighth day of April, eighteen hundred and forty-nine.
[L. S.]

SAML. T. WYLIE,
Notary Public.

The foregoing articles of agreement are approved, on the following express reservations and conditions only, to wit:

First. That wherever the name of James Collier, collector of the district of San Francisco, California, is mentioned, or where the words collector or said collector are used, they shall be deemed and understood to mean and apply to the collector of the district aforesaid in his official capacity for the time being.

Second. That this agreement is understood and intended to apply to the construction and renting of *one* " store or building" only, and to no more, unless hereafter deemed necessary, and then rented with the approbation of the Secretary of the Treasury.

Third. The rate of rent to be paid for the building to be agreed upon by the collector, subject expressly to the approval of the Secretary of the Treasury.

Fourth. The rent stipulated for to depend upon and be paid out of appropriations expressly made by Congress for the purpose, and from no other source, or according to the existing laws at the times of payment.

In witness whereof, I, William M. Meredith, Secretary of the Treasury, have hereunto signed my name and affixed the seal of the Treasury Department, this eighth day of May, in the year of our Lord one thousand eight hundred and forty-nine.
[L. S.]

W. M. MEREDITH,
Secretary of the Treasury.

I, William M. Meredith, Secretary of the Treasury, do hereby certify the within to be a correct and true copy of the original on file in this department.

In witness whereof, I have hereunto signed my name, and affixed the seal of the Treasury Department, this fourteenth day of May, in the year of our Lord one thousand eight hundred and forty-nine.
[L. S.]

W. M. MEREDITH,
Secretary of the Treasury.

CINCINNATI, *April* 26, 1849.

SIR: Having reached this city several days since, and. after some delay, completed my arrangements, I shall leave this afternoon for St. Louis.

Considering it necessary to take with me a reliable force, I respectfully nominate the following gentlemen as *inspectors*, who will, on our arrival at San Francisco, be located at the several ports of entry, or delivery, as may be thought advisable after looking over the ground, to wit: Abraham Bartol, Sheldon W. McDonnell, William Smyth, Alexander A. Marshall, Andrew Randal, John C. Fulton, Charles Pixley, Heland R. Hulburd, Jesse O. Goodwin, John A. McDonnell, Edward S. Tremain, John Myers, Joseph Adams, jr., Albert G. Lawrence, W. N. Jackson, Levi Beardsley, jr., Abraham Kentzing, jr., William Wood.

Should you approve of these nominations, may I ask you to say by telegraph at St. Louis, "*approved.*"

I enclose the oaths of office administered to E. D. Collier and John A. Collier.

I will advise you previous to our departure from Fort Leavenworth.

Very respectfully,

J. COLLIER, *Collector, &c.*

Hon. W. M. MEREDITH,
Secretary of the Treasury.

TREASURY DEPARTMENT, *May* 2, 1849.

SIR: Your letter of the 26th ultimo, dated at Cincinnati, Ohio, submitting a list of nominations of inspectors of the customs for the district of Upper California, is received.

The nomination of Abraham Kentzing, jr., as inspector of the customs for the district mentioned, is approved. It is not deemed expedient to approve the other nominations submitted, for the following reasons:

The act of 3d March, 1849, "requiring all money receivable from customs and from all other sources to be paid immediately into the treasury, without abatement or reduction, and for other purposes," prohibits the expenses of collecting the entire revenue from customs from exceeding a certain specified sum per annum. It consequently becomes the duty of the department to take care that the expenses of the respective districts shall be placed on such a footing as to preclude any probable excess of expenditure for collecting the revenue beyond the sum designated and appropriated for the object by the act referred to. The appointment of the complement of subordinate officers, already sanctioned, to accompany you hence to California, was authorized by the department in view of the peculiar circumstances connected with this new district, and in order to avoid any embarrassment or delay, on reaching your destination, to a prompt entry on the discharge of your official duties. Whatever additional inspectors or other subordinate officers of the customs, after entering on the discharge of your duties, you shall find necessary for the due collection and security of the revenue in your district, may be selected from suitable persons residing in said district; as likewise in regard to filling any vacancies that may occur in the complement already authorized. In making such appointments you will be governed by the directions given in my instructions to yourself under date of the 3d ultimo.

Very respectfully,

W. M. MEREDITH,
Secretary of the Treasury.

JAMES COLLIER, Esq.,
Collector of district of Upper California, now at St. Louis, Mo.

COLLECTOR'S OFFICE, SAN FRANCISCO,
October 30, 1849.

SIR: This office has never as yet been supplied with any locks for ships' hatches, nor with any gauging or weighing machines, nor measures of any kind; and, this being a new country, it is impossible to purchase such things here. There should be sent here from three to five hundred locks for ships' hatches and storehouses: these should be of various sizes; some fifty pair of scales and balances, of different kinds and sizes; and a quantity of measures, of different kinds, &c., and sizes; and also a quantity of gauging rods, &c. All of these articles are much wanted. Also, want a few copies each of the different revenue laws, tariffs, &c., and all blanks, such as registers, crew lists, &c., that are furnished by the government; and also sea letters. The business of this office is of much more importance than the department at Washington has any conception of; and there are many things here that need regulating and advising about, and which I should have addressed the department about long since, but have been expecting the collector (Col. Collier) daily for the last three months. If Col. Collier does not arrive before the departure of the next steamer, I shall take the liberty to report upon many points of importance. The present system adopted here makes it impossible to conform with the law in many respects. Shall the mail steamers, running from this to Panama, be allowed to purchase coal, intended for consumption on the route from this to Panama, *free of duty?* So far they have been doing so, but I can find no law which will justify the course pursued.

The department here is suffering much for the want of the articles I have asked for in this letter.

Very respectfully, your obedient servant,
J. D. CARR, *Acting Deputy Collector.*
ABRAHAM KENTZING, JR., *Appraiser.*

Hon. W. M. MEREDITH,
Secretary of the Treasury, Washington city, D. C.

SAN FRANCISCO, *November* 13, 1849.

SIR: I am at last at my post. The delay attendant upon my arrival has been to me a source of great anxiety, and given me much trouble. I can only say that I have been in the hands of others, over whose movements I had no control. Remonstrances and importunities were alike disregarded. I have suffered much of hardship, of privation, and toil, and encountered no little of peril. We were compelled, for several days in succession, to fight our way through hostile bands of Indians, but escaped without the loss of life on our part, and with but one man wounded, he having both bones of his arm broken. It is with great regret that I have to state, also, that in crossing the Colorado four persons were drowned, and that one of the number was Captain Thorn, of New York, who was in command of the dragoons. At some future period I hope to give you some account of my pilgrimage, and of the miserable country we have passed over. At present, owing to the early departure of the steamer, I have barely sufficient time to advise you of the condition of things in the " State of California," and of the business of this office.

You are no doubt already advised that the people of California, in convention, have adopted a constitution of State government; and the election for governor and for other officers is this day being held. Our friend T. Butler King is a candidate for the United States Senate, with some prospect of being elected by the legislature. He has been, I am informed, quite ill. I have not had the pleasure of seeing him, as he is at present located at Benicia.

I am perfectly astounded at the amount of business in this office. I took possession of it on yesterday, and during so short a period have been unable to make all the inquires and examination necessary to put me in possession of all the information desirable. The amount of tonnage, however, on the 10th instant, in port, was 120,317 tons; of which 87,494 were American, and 32,823 were foreign.

Number of vessels in the harbor on that day, 10th instant, 312, and the whole number of arrivals since the first of April, 697; of which 401 were American, and 296 foreign. This state of things, so unexpected, has greatly surprised me. Desirous as I am of conforming to the instructions received from the Treasury Department, yet you will see, from what follows, that so far as the salaries of the various officers employed in this office is concerned it will be wholly impossible. The clerks, for instance, are receiving from $1,800 to $3,000 per annum, and there is not a sufficient number to transact the business. More must be employed, and that, too, with like salaries. The inspectors are receiving four dollars per day, and a large number are employed. The necessity for the payment of such salaries arises from the fact that the expenses of living justify the payment. For example: Flour is this day selling for forty dollars per barrel, and pork at $60. For boarding the average is $5 per day, without rooms or lodging. A small room, barely sufficient to contain a single bed, rents readily at $150 per month. Wood is $40 per cord, and every article of food is at a like rate. It is impossible, therefore, to retain clerks or other officers without the payment of salaries corresponding with the expenses of living. So much for the expenses of the office. The business is now daily on the increase, and my whole attention day and night will be required. I shall be compelled also to employ additional clerks. One difficulty, however, presents itself; and that is, where to put them. I am occupying what was the old Mexican custom-house, constructed of unburnt brick. It is a long, dark, one-story building, in miserable condition. The roof leaks so badly, that during a rain our papers are liable to be wet. The doors are some of them off the hinges, and all are insecure. I have no vault for the safe-keeping of the public money. Owing to the rates for rent, I am afraid to lease a building. One for myself, containing four rooms, two below and two above, without fireplaces, was offered to me on yesterday at $2,400 per month. I am so remote from Washington, that under these circumstances I shall be compelled to "take the responsibility" of making repairs, even at present prices, to wit: shingles at $60 per thousand, and lumber at $300, and shall have to pay the carpenters from $12 to $16 per day. These facts may startle you; but such is the true state of things. I hope, therefore, that in ordering these indispensable repairs, without waiting for these instructions, I shall not be censured. A custom-house must be built, and ought to be immediately contracted for and sent around. One of cast iron will be the best, if it can be built. There should be no delay. The business will justify it, and it is indispensable. Great inconvenience is felt, and no little risk incurred, from the fact that we have not a house nor a room for stowing goods. I have been compelled to continue a practice which I found existing, of stowing goods and warehousing on board of vessels. There are now *nineteen thus employed.* This is a hazardous and most inconvenient practice, and opens a broad door for smuggling. Several warehouses (not less than four) should be immediately sent out. You will see from a paper addressed to me by the merchants of this city (containing thirty thousand people) that they deem it indispensable. I may, nay, I probably shall be compelled, before I can hear from you, to rent a building for a warehouse. Should I do so, it will be at a price that may astonish you, and yet the government will not be the loser. The charge for storage must correspond with the price paid, and in the end the building or buildings thus employed will be a source of revenue. I have written by the steamer to Messrs. Saffarrans & Co., urging them to push forward, without delay, the building already contracted for, and desiring them to call upon you in relation to the construction of four others of the same dimensions. We have not now a room for the appraisers or inspectors. Goods that have to be appraised are either exposed on board the ship, or deposited in the store of the owner or consignee. When it is known that, in a commercial point of view, this port is equal to that of Philadelphia, the necessity of providing suitable buildings without delay must be seen and acknowledged. I should be doing great injustice, not only to the government, but to all concerned in commerce, were I to refrain from expressing my opinion frankly upon these important subjects.

On my voyage to this port from San Diego, I had an opportunity of visiting some of the points on the coast, which, in a commercial point of view, are of no little importance, and to which your attention is solicited. One of them is San Pedro. I am fully of opinion that more goods are landed at San Pedro than at any other point, excepting only San Francisco. A large amount of smuggling is carried on at that place. It is distant from Los Angeles some twenty-five miles, and from the latter the Mexicans obtain all their goods for trade in the interior of Mexico. These goods are generally of high price and rich fabric. I met several large parties of these traders on my way to the Pacific, and in every instance was advised by them that they purchased their goods at Los Angeles. I saw, while at San Pedro, (which contains but three buildings,) in a warehouse, a large amount of goods from China. I have been unable to ascertain where they were entered. The *collector* resides at Los Angeles; and these goods, together with most if not all that have been landed, have escaped the payment of duties. I recommend that it should be made a port of delivery, and that a deputy should be stationed there. Santa Barbara is also a place of some importance, and should be made a port of delivery. As a town, the latter is far superior to San Diego. These are the only points where I landed on the coast.

To enforce the revenue laws in this district, and to cut up and prevent smuggling, which has been and is now carried to a great extent, it seems to be necessary that an additional cutter should be sent out, or that the Ewing, now in this port, should be assigned to that duty. Do all that you can, I fear it cannot be prevented; but it may be greatly curtailed. In connexion with this service, permit me to suggest the propriety, nay, the necessity, of shipping, as soon as possible, a sufficient amount (for at least one year) of supplies for the Lawrence, and for any other vessel that may be assigned to the revenue service. I have advertised for proposals for furnishing provisions, but cannot take the responsibility of entering into a contract at the present prices. It would be an immense saving to the government to despatch forthwith an ample supply from the Atlantic.

I presume that no proposal will be offered at less than $50 or $60 per barrel for pork, and not less than $30 per barrel for flour. Under these circumstances, I must purchase a temporary supply, and wait your instructions upon the subject. You are aware that the duties collected on this coast have been hitherto collected under military authority, and that the money has been paid over to the pay and quartermaster's departments. I have already been inquired of, whether I would cash the drafts of these departments. This I cannot do without your instructions. Situated as I am, I should like to be relieved from the responsibility of retaining the money in my hands for any considerable length of time. The duties will amount to a large sum; and I have no secure or safe place of keeping it. There is another subject to which I desire to call your attention—that of the establishment of a marine hospital. Almost daily applications are made for relief or assistance by sick and disabled seamen. I do not know anything that I can do without your instructions. A suitable building, even could one be procured, could not be rented for any reasonable sum. And yet humanity requires that this class should be provided for. A physician could not be procured by the offer of three times the present fees.

I had hoped to have found on my arrival letters from the department, but was disappointed. It is extremely difficult to institute and carry on a suit commenced against a vessel seized for violating the revenue laws. Two seizures have been made since I took possession of the office. These suits are to be instituted in Oregon or Louisiana. How is process to be served? Can the marshal in either district serve process without special authority to do so by act of Congress? Can he appoint a deputy for California? It seems to me that great difficulty will be found in carrying out the law in this particular. The act of Congress making California a collection district requires the Secretary of the Treasury to establish a port of delivery as near as may be to the junction of the rivers Gila and Colorado, at the head of the gulf of California. The establishment of such an office I do not consider as at all practicable. The Colorado will never, in my opinion, become navigable to the point. It is far off from civilization, on the borders of the great desert, and in the midst of numerous tribes of Indians. The line between the United States and Mexico will not be more than two or three miles from the junction of the rivers. The valley of the Gila is utterly worthless, and I would not take a deed of the whole country to-morrow. It is true that here and there a spot may be found susceptible of cultivation, but they are "few and far between." I presume that no white man could be found willing to become deputy collector in a port where a flag would never flutter. I have had possession of this office but two days, and have hardly yet recovered from the toils of my long and weary pilgrimage. What I have written has been done in great haste. The early departure of the steamer, however, will be my excuse. I beg you to be assured that this port is of the first importance to the country, and deserves, and will no doubt receive, the prompt attention of the department.

In the discharge of the responsible duties of this office, I may, and no doubt shall, commit many errors. Situated as I am, without the aid of courts, and remote from Washington, I shall be called upon to exercise discretionary powers. The rights of our countrymen and the interests of commerce seem to require it. I hope to so discharge the trust confided to me as to secure your approval. By the next steamer I hope to address you, if not more fully, at least with less haste.

Before closing this communication, permit me to say that the articles directed to be shipped from New York for this office have not as yet arrived. I have, consequently, been compelled to purchase such books as were to be provided here. They are not, however, what they ought to be. May I ask you to have forwarded without delay, by the steamer, a supply of sea-letters for vessels, coasting licenses for vessels both under and above 20 tons, both for steam and sail vessels, registers and records for vessels, crew lists, and two dozen copies of the tariff of 1846. The price of printing here is enormous, and I must look to the department for a supply. Since writing the foregoing, I have to add that I caused the publication of notice in the papers in this city soliciting proposals for supplies for the revenue service. I enclose copies of two that have been received, in order that you may the better judge what course should be pursued, and of the propriety of my purchasing temporary supplies, looking to a decline in present prices.

Very respectfully, yours,
J. COLLIER, *Collector.*

Hon. W. M. MEREDITH,
Secretary of the Treasury.

SAN FRANCISCO, *November* 13, 1849.

SIR: The undersigned, merchants of the port of San Francisco, Upper California, take leave to congratulate you on your safe arrival at this port; and whilst, for the better protection of their interests in lawful trade, they ask of you the strict enforcement of the revenue laws of the United States of America, they also desire that the usual facilities afforded to their fellow-merchants on the Atlantic coast shall likewise be extended to them, particularly the warehousing system in public stores.

The very fact that San Francisco is daily becoming the grand depot for the whole trade of the Pacific ocean, is sufficient evidence that their wants imperatively demand of our government warehouses for bonded goods.

The undersigned are, sir, your most obedient servants,
MELLUS, HOWARD, & CO.,
ALFRED ROBINSON,
TESCHEMACHER & CO.,
CROSS, HOBSON, & CO.,
GILLESPIE & CO.,
FINLEY, JOHNSON, & CO.,
LEMOND, HUTCHINSON, & CO.,
E. MICKLE & CO.,
T. M. Z. DEHON,
ROBT. SMITH & CO.,
SAML. MOSS & CO.,

THOMAS O. LARKIN,
ROBERT WELLS & CO.,
WARD, & CO.,
SHERMAN, RUCKLE, & CO.,
OSBORN & SHANNAN,
MACONDRAY & CO.

To Col. COLLIER,
Collector of the port of San Francisco, U. C.

CUSTOM-HOUSE, SAN FRANCISCO,
November 29, 1849.

SIR: The departure of the steamer so soon after my assuming the duties of this office prevented me from calling your attention to several important questions which I had been called upon to decide, and which I now beg leave to submit to your consideration.

Previous to my arrival, the then collector, acting under the instructions of the military commander from whom he received his appointment, with the sanction of Commodore Jones, the commander-in-chief of the naval forces on the Pacific, had issued licenses to *foreign vessels* to engage in the coasting trade in the bay of San Francisco and its tributaries. This practice was introduced, as they claim, from necessity. There were but few American vessels in the bay or on the coast, and the large number of persons employed at the mines looked to this port alone for their supplies. In order to afford them *relief*, this practice was introduced. On assuming the duties of the office, I *revoked* all the licenses granted to foreign vessels to engage in the coasting trade, and have refused to grant licenses to *all* vessels other than American. This has been the subject of complaint on the part of some American citizens who have purchased *foreign* vessels with the expectation that the former practice would be continued. Upon this subject I received a letter from Commodore Jones, a copy of which, marked A, together with my reply, marked B, I herewith enclose. I *think* I am right, and shall carry out the law, as I understand it, until I am otherwise directed. Another practice, as I suppose, in direct violation of law, had been sanctioned and approved of by the same authority—that of permitting brandy and other spirituous liquors to be imported in bottles and cases of less quantity than fifteen gallons. The law, as I suppose, was violated in two particulars: First. According to my understanding, brandy can only be imported in "*casks* of a capacity not less than fifteen gallons." By importing in bottles of less capacity they violate that law, and escape the duty also upon the bottles.

If I am right, (and I shall act upon that supposition until otherwise advised,) the vessels and cargoes are *forfeited* for an infraction of the law in that particular.

Still another practice prevailed here—that of permitting French vessels, for instance, clearing from a port in France for San Francisco, and taking on board a part of their cargo at Valparaiso, the product of the latter country, to enter. This I have supposed to be contrary to law.

I desire to call your attention to a case where I felt called upon to seize a vessel having a valuable cargo on board. The facts are as follows: The British barque Collooney cleared from this port on the 6th of August for Vancouver's island, within the possessions of Great Britain; from thence she went to Puget's sound in *Oregon*, within our *waters* and the jurisdiction of this collection district, took on board a quantity of lumber, the product of the United States, and left that port *without a clearance*, and proceeded to *Fort Victoria*, Vancouver's island, taking on board the product of the British possessions to complete her cargo, and from thence sailed for this port, where she arrived a few days since.

She brings with her a *clearance* from Fort Victoria, purporting to be signed by Mr. Douglass, as *factor for the Hudson's Bay Company*. The papers are without seal, though purporting to be attested. I have assumed that the Hudson's Bay Company, through their agent or otherwise, have not the power to receive or collect duties, grant clearances, or to do any other act relative to the revenue laws of Great Britain; that the power to collect duties, &c., is an act of *sovereignty*, and cannot be delegated to a *corporation;* and that if it be true, as is claimed, that the factor of that company is in fact the collector, commissioned by his government, he must act in *that* capacity, and not as *factor* of the Hudson's Bay Company. Taking this view of it, I determined that this vessel was engaged in the *coasting trade*, contrary to law; that she sailed from an American port with the product of the United States, and entered an American port with that cargo. I have treated the papers purporting to be signed by Mr. Douglass, as factor of that corporation, as nugatory, and decided that the voyage from Oregon to this port was a continuous voyage. I beg leave to call your attention to this case, and ask that I may be fully instructed as to the position and powers of the Hudson's Bay Company in that particular. They assume high powers, and have had heretofore almost the entire control of everything in this distant region. The rapidly-increasing business of Oregon, especially in the lumber trade, (lumber being worth this day in this city $450 per thousand,) requires full instructions upon this and like cases. May I ask, as in a former letter, for instructions also as to the course to be pursued to bring this case, as well as other cases of seizure, before the court in Oregon or Louisiana.

I have been called upon to decide another question which seems to have caused the *Californians* some trouble. Prior to the ratification of the treaty of peace with Mexico, and while California was within her dominion, vessels had been built, and were engaged in the coasting trade, &c. During our *military* occupation, vessels were also built for like purposes. It is claimed that by the provisions of the treaty these vessels have become *naturalized*, and are to be regarded as American, and entitled to all the privileges of American ships. I have decided otherwise, and regarded California as a *foreign* territory until the ratification of the treaty. If I am correct, then there will be an immediate necessity for the action of Congress, as in the case of Louisiana and Florida. In looking to the future, it is hardly possible to anticipate the *destiny* of California. There is something so peculiar in her present position, that I cannot refrain from offering you my views and opinions; and in doing so, I trust they will be taken with all allowances, and as the opinion of one whose views are based in a great degree upon first impressions. Her position is peculiar, in the first place, from the fact that here *labor* controls *capital*. In other words, the mechanic and artisan fixes his own price, and the capitalist is compelled from *necessity* to submit to that price, whatever it may be. The pressing wants of the thousands now in the country, and the anticipated wants of those on their way hither, (and their name is legion,) require the immediate construction and erection of buildings to shelter them. Hence the carpenter charges and receives from $12 to $17 per day, and other mechanics in the same ratio. Rents are consequently at such rates as startle a sober, sedate man; and this state of things must continue for a long time to come. Her position is peculiar in another respect. California now is, and for all time to come must be, essentially *commercial*. There *is* gold in *California*. She *is* rich in mineral wealth: that is a "fixed fact." The extent of her resources is not known, it is true, and time and science can only ascertain the value of the precious metals in her mountains and valleys. So long as the search for gold shall continue, just so long will agriculture be neglected. It will not pay, for the obvious reason that labor will command higher prices than can be paid for growing grain. For these and for various other reasons, her commercial interest will be the great interest of the State. Owing to the many advantages which San Francisco possesses over all other ports on the Pacific, it must become to the nation what New York is to the Atlantic. This very fact will keep up the present high prices for labor and building materials. It is impossible to estimate the extent to which her commerce may reach. It is now large, and will be constantly on the increase. These facts are stated for the double purpose of putting you in possession of what may be anticipated from duties, and of impressing upon Congress the necessity of doing something—doing *much* for California, and that without delay. The responsibilities that rest upon the collector, in the absence of any legal tribunal, any *legal* adviser to which he might resort for redress or advice, weigh heavily upon me. My decision may almost be regarded as final, owing to the absence of a tribunal to which resort might be had for revision. In another respect, also, are the responsibilities of a grave character. It becomes a matter of *absolute necessity* on the part of the collector to appoint s*ubordinates*, and to place them immediately upon duty, without waiting for the approval of the Secretary, as required by law. Men resort to the custom-house for *temporary* employment, and for that only. They will continue only just so long as is necessary to seek something more profitable. An instance has occurred this morning to illustrate this. I have a clerk acting as cashier, to whom I was compelled to pay (what you might regard as a high salary) $3,000 per annum. He was offered from a banking-house $5,000, with the promise of a future interest, and has consequently given notice that he shall leave the office.

The situation of the bay, there being no wharves, renders it necessary for vessels to anchor some distance from the shore, and goods are landed by lighters and small boats employed for that purpose. This, together with the fact that the high price of storage, three dollars per month per barrel, and the price of drayage, three or four dollars per load, either induces or compels the owners or consignees to keep their cargoes on board, (the same being bonded,) and consequently an officer must remain for sometimes weeks, perhaps months, on board;—this will account for the large number of inspectors. Nor can this be avoided until the department authorize the leasing of warehouses. Under these circumstances, is it too much to ask that the collector of this district be vested with *discretionary* power, not only as to salaries, but as to the appointment of subordinate officers? There must be some law or authority of this sort, or the collector will be involved in difficulty. Upon the subject of salaries, I need not say that no man can afford to hold office at the present rate. The deputy ought to receive at least six thousand dollars per annum. No competent man can be found who will with integrity discharge its duties for a less sum. Upon this subject, however, I refer to the members of the Senate and House from this State. They are well advised as to the state of affairs here.

Will you permit me to again urge upon your consideration the subject of warehouses, and the power to rent a sufficient number, and authorizing the construction of cast iron, as stipulated in the contract heretofore *made* for the one, and with the persons contracted with. They are, I think, entitled to the preference. The interest of the government will be, I think, amply protected by this arrangement, and it will be a source of revenue. But I must again say, so far as California is concerned, you must give the collector a large discretion. If you impose too many restrictions, or require him to postpone his appointments, or to await the approval of the department, the business of this office will be greatly embarrassed. I ask this for myself and for those who will come after me.

I have written, as usual, in great haste, and in the midst of constant interruption. My time, from early in the morning until midnight, has been occupied in the business of the office, and in the examination of various and important questions I have been called upon to investigate and determine.

Since writing the foregoing, I have felt constrained to trouble you still further, and to call your attention to another subject, which the growing importance of our commercial affairs in this quarter seems to require should be investigated by the government of the United States. We have with Chili a treaty of reciprocity, by the provisions of which I am to be governed, as it is the law between the two nations, and binding upon both. As collector of customs, I cannot take notice of any infractions of that treaty on the part of the government of Chili, that being the subject-matter of discussion and adjustment between the two powers; and yet I am advised by the United States consul, Mr. Moorhead, resident at Valparaiso, that little or no regard is paid to it by the government of Chili. It is notorious that such is the fact here; and the merchants having knowledge that such is the fact, have inquired whether this office will still regard it (the treaty) as in full force. My answer has been in the affirmative, until otherwise directed. I am convinced that great injustice is being practised upon our commerce by the government of Chili in this particular. I submit the subject to your consideration. You will receive herewith a copy of a letter from Mr. Moorhead addressed to a former collector, marked C.

In relation to the brandy and other spirits which I have taken possession of, I desire to say that, under the peculiar circumstances of the case, and from the fact that this practice had obtained the approval of the military government, I have refrained from interfering with the vessel and the balance of the cargo, with the conviction that it would operate as a *fraud* upon the importer, were I to seize the ship and cargo. The importer, though he knew the law and was bound to know it, had knowledge also that the law was disregarded by the authorities here. I have, therefore, required that the spirits imported contrary to law should be placed in the custody of the collector. And it is stipulated that, should the Secretary decide that brandy and other spirits not entered for exportation, and in casks of less capacity than is provided for by law, are subject to forfeiture, then they shall be sold as forfeited, and no further litigation is to follow. Your opinion, therefore, will be conclusive upon all the parties.

A case has this day occurred, which I beg leave also to submit. There is between the United States and the Hanseatic republic of Lubec, Bremen, and Hamburg, a reciprocal treaty of commerce and navigation, under which the ships of those cities claim an exemption from *tonnage* duties; and they are no doubt exempt, provided the vessels of the United States are not in their ports charged with like duties. But the act of Congress of the 31st of May, 1830, declares that the President of the United States must be satisfied that foreign nations do not require our ships to pay tonnage duties, before the ships of such foreign nation can claim this exemption. I am unadvised as to what nations this law applies to. It may include the ones referred to, and also others from whom the fees are exacted. Will you have the goodness to advise me. You will pardon the infliction of this long epistle. I am a *young* beginner, but desire to learn my duty. I send you herewith a monthly summary, commencing on the 12th instant, the day I assumed the duties of this office.

Very respectfully, your obedient servant,

J. COLLIER, *Collector.*

Hon. W. M. MEREDITH,
  Secretary of the Treasury.

SAN FRANCISCO, *November* 14, 1849.

SIR: We propose to furnish the revenue cutter C. W. Lawrence with provisions for the rations as enumerated in your schedule, and subject to your approval, at the following prices, for one year:

Beef, per barrel, fifteen dollars.
Pork, per barrel, fifty dollars.
Flour, per barrel, thirty-five dollars.
Rice, per pound, twelve and one-half cents.
Raisins, per box, four dollars.
Dried apples or peaches, thirty-five cents per pound.
Pickles, per dozen, twenty dollars.
Cranberries, none in market.
Biscuit, per pound, twelve and one-half cents.
Sugar, per pound, twenty cents.
Tea, per pound, fifty cents.
Coffee, per pound, ten cents.
Cocoa, none.
Butter, per pound, one dollar.
Cheese, per pound, twenty-five cents.
Beans, per barrel, five dollars.
Molasses, per gallon, seventy-five cents.
Vinegar, per gallon, fifty cents.

Your obedient servants,

BURGOYNE & CO.

J. COLLIER, Esq.,
  Collector of the port, San Francisco.

A.

FLAG-SHIP SAVANNAH,
Bay of San Francisco, November 12, 1849.

SIR: Permit me to congratulate you on your safe arrival at your post—an event which I have anxiously looked for, both officially and individually; and to add, that at all times it will afford me pleasure to co-operate with you, should the naval authority be needed to aid you in the arduous duties of the office upon which you have just entered.

Mr. Harrison, your predecessor, will doubtless make you fully acquainted with all that has been done by the naval and military commanders on this station for the collection of duties, and for the relief of the suffering community, whose wants and necessities were of that urgent nature as to compel the ruling authorities to adopt their measures to meet the urgent wants of the in-pouring emigrants, rather than strict obedience to legislative enactment; this course has been fully approved by both the late and present administrations at Washington.

By the enclosed extract No. 1, you will perceive upon what grounds foreign-built boats and crafts were allowed to participate in the inland trade within the bay of San Francisco. From the daily applications, all of which are refused since June, and the still exorbitant high freights on the rivers, I cannot too earnestly recommend to you, as I have done to the Executive, *to continue the licenses now in force*, until Congress, by the passage of a law, shall legalize such licenses. Were the craft in question suddenly thrown out of the trade, not only would the owners thereof be great losers, but the now ill-supplied emigrants, and the population of the great valleys of the Sacramento and San Joaquin, would be subjected to the greatest extortion for all the necessaries of life, already frightfully deficient in the mining district.

I also enclose an extract from another of my letters to the honorable Secretary of the Navy, in reference to the non-payment of duties, encouraged by the transhipping of foreign goods from sea-going vessels to river craft in the port of San Francisco. I have reason now to believe that the frauds thus practised on the revenue can only be prevented by manifesting and clearing each and every craft, and by the appointment of deputy collectors at each of the ports of Benicia, Sacramento city, and Stockton, where alone vessels should be allowed to discharge, except launches and small steamers plying between those towns and headwaters of the Sacramento and San Joaquin rivers.

The accompanying extract No. 3, from one of the Secretary of the Navy's letters to me, will show in what light the Executive, at Washington, regards the interest and protection of the countless emigrants pouring into California by every avenue of approach.

I have the honor to be, &c., &c., &c., very respectfully,
THOS. AP C. JONES,
Commander-in-Chief U. S. naval forces, Pacific ocean.

Col. COLLIER,
Collector of Customs, San Francisco.

B.

Custom-house,
San Francisco, November 15, 1849.

Dear Sir: The pressure of business arising from the departure of the steamer will plead my excuse for not having more promptly acknowledged the receipt of your favor of the 12th instant. For the kindly feelings manifested towards myself personally, and for the generous offer to co-operate with me in the discharge of the important and responsible duties I have assumed as collector of this district, accept, I pray you, my sincere thanks. Much shall I stand in need of the counsel and advice of one whose large experience in the commercial concerns of the nations of the world has made him familiar with the various and important questions arising out of the execution and enforcement of the revenue laws of the country.

My worthy predecessor has made known to me what has been done by himself, under the advice of the military and naval commanders on this station, in relation to the granting of licenses to vessels, other than those built in the United States, to trade within the bay of San Francisco and its tributaries. I am aware also of the necessity which seemed to justify the exercise of that discretion. It must be admitted, however, that it was in violation of the revenue laws.

I should exceedingly regret that the strict enforcement of those laws should inflict injury upon any portion of my countrymen; but I am not vested with *discretionary* powers upon such subjects. I must abide by the law, whatever it may be. When those licenses were granted, no collection district had been created in California by act of Congress, and that discretion might be properly exercised by the then authorities. It may be, and no doubt is true, that freights must necessarily advance by the revoking of the licenses granted to foreign vessels to engage in the coasting trade. But, while I may lament that any portion of our countrymen who are engaged in the mining district should feel the effects in the increased price of provisions, we have, on the other hand, the satisfaction of knowing that another class, that of the American ship-builders and ship-owners, will enjoy that protection which the law intended to give them, that the great interests of our *own* commerce will be promoted, and that the law of the land is respected and maintained.

Entertaining these views, I must abide by the decision I have already made upon the subject. Congress will soon assemble, and to that tribunal must these questions be submitted.

With high regard, I am your obedient servant,

J. COLLIER, *Collector.*

Thos. Ap C. Jones,
Commander-in-Chief, &c.

Consulate of the United States of America,
Valparaiso, December 8, 1848.

Dear Sir: Understanding that our government has not provided you with the acts of Congress containing the treaties with foreign nations, I take the liberty of sending you the acts of the 23d Congress, which contain the treaty between the United States and Chili, and also with Russia. You will perceive that Chili has not a full and free treaty of commercial reciprocity. The conventions with Chili were officially ratified on the 29th April, 1844, and the 2d article of the first of these conventions provides, among other stipulations, that

"The United States of America and the republic of Chili, desiring to live in peace and harmony with all the other nations of the earth—by means of a policy frank and friendly with all—engage mutually not to grant any particular favor to other nations, in respect to commerce and navigation, which shall not immediately become common to the other party, who shall enjoy the same freely, if the concession were freely made, or on allowing the same compensation, if the concession were conditional, &c."

In somewhat more than two years after the ratification of the conventions with Chili, to wit: on the 21st of May, 1836, a treaty was ratified between the United States and Venezuela, the fourth article of which provides: "They likewise agree that whatever kind of produce, manufactures, or merchandise of *any foreign country*, can be, from time to time, lawfully imported into the United States in her own vessels, may be also imported in vessels of the republic of Venezuela, and that no higher or other duties upon the tonnage of the vessels and their cargoes shall be levied and collected, whether the importation be made in the vessels of the one country or of the other; and, in like manner, that whatever kind of produce, manufacture, or merchandise of *any foreign country*, can be, from time to time, lawfully imported into the republic of Venezuela in its own vessels, may be also imported in vessels of the United States, and that no other or higher duties upon the tonnage of their vessels and their cargoes shall be levied or collected, whether the importation be made in the vessels of one country or of the other; and they agree that, whatever may be lawfully exported or re-exported from the one country, in its own vessels, to any foreign country, may, in like manner, be exported or re-exported in the vessels of the other country. And the same bounties, duties, and drawbacks shall be collected, whether such exportation or re-exportation be made in the vessels of the United States or of the republic of Venezuela."

Provisions, either exactly the same or of precisely similar import, are to be found in a number of the treaties made between the United States and other nations, at subsequent dates, as these references will show.

* * * * * * * * *

Under these references, the question—as far as Chili is interested—recurs: May Chili avail herself of the privileges and immunities which these treaties reciprocally confer on the contracting parties? Without a doubt she may, upon precisely the terms under which Venezuela and the other contracting parties enjoy the same; that is to say, by Chili's reciprocally conferring the like privileges and immunities upon the commerce and navigation of the United States in her ports. This is all that is exacted, and all that is conferred; and though the condition is not to be dispensed with, a compliance with its terms is all that can be required. The conditions which these treaties mutually impose upon the contracting parties thereto consist in the reciprocities they exact, in consideration of the advantages they bestow. Now, Chili has granted nothing to the flag of the United States which she withholds from that of any other nation upon earth, and reserves to her own vessels the exclusive right of commerce at a fixed rate of duties. As, for instance, a vessel built in the United States, owned by a citizen of Chili, pays 10 per cent. more upon the duties than is charged to a vessel, owned by the same parties, built in Chili. A vessel built in and owned by citizens of the United States is charged 20 per cent. upon the duties charged upon Chilian vessels. This, of course, is upon foreign products, and does not apply to American goods. It amounts to this: that our vessels employed in the China trade are required to pay 20 per cent. upon the duties charged to Chilian vessels employed in the same trade in the ports of Chili.

Therefore, I conclude that the Chilian flag is not entitled to any special privileges in the ports of the United States, and, if permitted to enter at all, should be subject to a discriminating duty; otherwise, those nations who concluded a perfect treaty of reciprocity with the United States would not be fairly treated.

I offer this for your consideration, and only regret that I am so much occupied that I could not go more into detail.

With sentiments of respect and esteem, I remain your obedient servant,

WM. G. MOORHEAD,
Consul of the United States of America.

Captain J. L. FOLSOM,
Collector of the port of San Francisco, &c.

MONTHLY SUMMARY STATEMENT.

The United States in account with James Collier, collector of the port of San Francisco, California, from 12th to 30th November, 1849.

DR.					CR.
4th quarter, 1849.			4th quarter, 1849.	
November	30	To amount of receipts for duties, hospital dues, tonnage, and light dues, &c., &c....	$113,942 60	November	30	By amount of disbursements made to clerks, inspectors, contingent expenses, &c., &c....	$10,075 47
				November	30	Balance due the United States....	103,867 13
			113,942 60				113,942 60

I certify, on honor, that the above exhibits a true account of all moneys received by me during the month of November; that the disbursements have been faithfully made; and that the balance due the United States is now in my hands.

COLLECTOR'S OFFICE, *San Francisco, November 30, 1849.*

Coast Survey Office,
Washington, March 16, 1849.

Dear Sir: Under date of August 17, 1848, I received from the Secretary of the Treasury the letter of which the following is a copy:

Treasury Department, *August* 17, 1848.

Sir: Enclosed you will find a bill, passed during the last session of Congress, extending the laws of the United States over the Territory of Oregon, to which I invite your attention, with a view to the commencement of a survey of the coast of the United States on the Pacific.

Very respectfully, your obedient servant,
R. J. WALKER,
Secretary of the Treasury.

Prof. A. D. Bache,
Superintendent U. S. C. S.

In conference with the Secretary of the Treasury, the plans for commencing the survey were submitted, and I received oral directions to mature them, and to take the preparatory steps. These executed, I communicated with the department on the 21st October, and received the following reply:

Treasury Department, *October* 23, 1848.

Sir: Your letter of the 21st instant, communicating the execution of my oral instructions of August last, is received, and the arrangements which you have made approved. The department also approves of the following recommendations:

1. The detail of assistant Jas. S. Williams and sub-assistant Geo. Davidson for section X of the coast survey, to commence such work as may be designated in the instructions of the superintendent, and the furnishing of the parties with all instruments needful to the work.

2. The employment of such aids and such hands in the parties as may be necessary, and the allowance of the requisite outfits. The persons to receive the pay and allowances fixed by the department for the Gulf of Mexico, or as may be necessary and usual on the western coast to secure good hands, and as may be approved by the superintendent. The officers to receive the allowances which apply to the sections on the Gulf of Mexico.

3. The general disbursing agent of coast survey is authorized to advance for the expenses and pay of this party, up to July 1, 1849, a sum not to exceed eight thousand dollars, which sum he shall receive from the treasury in addition to the usual advance.

4. The organization of a hydrographical party, under the command of Lieutenant W. P. McArthur, United States navy, assistant in the coast survey, to accompany, or to follow as soon as practicable, the land party.

A copy of a letter relating to light-houses, beacons, buoys, &c., on the western coast, from the Fifth Auditor, is herewith transmitted.

The department requests that you will further the views of that officer, as far as practicable, by directing immediately such surveys as may be necessary for placing buoys and beacons, or locating light houses, as may not interfere with the general plan of the work—reporting the results to this department; and that you will report, as early as convenient, in regard to the location of light houses, buoys, &c., at the entrance of Columbia river, referred to in section 27 of the law to establish a territorial government in Oregon. The accounts for necessary expenditures in the execution of this duty will be rendered to and paid by the collector at Astoria, who will be the superintendent of lights for the district of Oregon. (*Note*.—Subsequently modified, as far as relates to light-houses at entrance to Columbia river.)

Instructions will be given to the commander of the revenue brig Lawrence to furnish such facilities to the persons and parties of the coast survey, by the use of the vessel, boats, or crew, as may not seriously interfere with the revenue duties. The revenue cutter Ewing will be loaned to the coast survey, to be temporarily replaced by one of the coast survey vessels, until the alterations directed in the schooner Polk have been completed. Directions will be immediately given for the transfer of that vessel to such person as you may designate.

The department favorably considers your suggestion in regard to the land surveys, and proposes to act upon it, at a later date.

The department has communicated with the War and Navy Departments in reference to the arrangements for the survey of the western coast, and has offered to carry out any suggestions which may be made not interfering with the general design of the coast survey.

Should further instructions be necessary, in consequence of any suggestions which may be made, you will be duly advised of them.

Very respectfully, your obedient servant,
R. J. WALKER,
Secretary of the Treasury.
Prof. A. D. BACHE,
Superintendent U. S. Coast Survey, Washington, D. C.

The whole of the arrangements for the execution of the work have been carried out.
Yours, respectfully and truly,
A. D. BACHE.
Hon. McCLINTOCK YOUNG.

COAST SURVEY OFFICE,
Washington, March 19, 1849.

SIR: In compliance with your oral request, I send herewith a copy of the instructions issued by me to the two parties of the coast survey detailed under the direction of the Treasury Department for the survey of section X—the coast of Oregon.

The party for the land work of the survey consists of assistant James S. Williams, Brevet Captain D. P. Hammond, United States army, and sub assistant Joseph S. Ruth.

The hydrographic party consists of Lieutenant Commanding W. P. McArthur, United States navy, Lieutenant W. A. Bartlett, and four other officers.

The instructions to assistant Williams bear date August 28 and September 22, 1848, and January 25, 1849, and are numbered 1 and 2. Those to Lieutenant Commanding McArthur are dated October 27, 1848, and March 10, 1849, and are numbered 3 and 4.

An abstract of the instructions precedes them.

Very respectfully, yours,

A. D. BACHE.

Hon. W. M. Meredith,
Secretary of the Treasury.

Unkonoonuc Station, near Manchester, N. H.,
August 28, 1848—*September* 22, 1848.

Sir: Having received oral directions from the Secretary of the Treasury to commence the survey of the coast of the United States on the Pacific by the survey of Oregon, section X, you will make all the necessary preparations to set out as early as transportation can be procured and the instruments collected, and other arrangements can be made.

It is desirable as a preparation:

1. That you repair to West Point and assist Captain T. J. Lee, United States topographical engineers, assistant in the coast survey, in the astronomical observations in which he is engaged, so as to become versed in the practice and renew the theory.

2. That you proceed to the station of my party at Unkonoonuc, N. H., which I will make an astronomical and magnetic station, and where twin instruments to those which you will take for astronomical purposes to Oregon will be mounted. You will there obtain practice with these instruments, and provide yourself with memoranda on all points relating to their use and computation of results. (If there is time, magnetic observations here—dip, variation, intensity.)

3. That you proceed to the office, to collect there, or on your way, the equipage, instruments, books, &c., which you will need, and obtain forms for computing the geodetic, astronomical, magnetic, and other results used by the parties of the survey; and with Captain Humphreys go over the computations of the geodetic work.

4. To proceed to South Carolina, to turn over the work in section V to the assistant who may be appointed to take charge of it, and to give him any information necessary to begin.

5. That you proceed to Bodie's island, in North Carolina, and remain some days with me, assisting in measuring the base there. The time for this will be about November 20.

6. That in Washington you provide yourself, from assistant S. C. Walker, with the blank forms for computing occultations and moon culminations, and practise in the reductions which they indicate.

7. This will leave the review of no part of the land work, of which you have not had recent practice, unmade, except the magnetic observations.

I expect you to attend personally to the execution of all directions which I may give to others for your preparations; to send as much of the equipage and part of the instruments as can be prepared by the steamer Massachusetts, under charge of a careful hand, and the rest in the following month—November—by the mail steamer, or otherwise, as may be found expedient, under special charge of a trusty hand; to proceed yourself, with the assistants of your party, to Chagres, and overland thence in time to meet the instruments, &c., at Panama, and to proceed with them to Oregon.

1. *Équipage.*—You are authorized to order five wall tents and an instrument tent of suitable dimensions, and with tarpaulins, from Fenton of Philadelphia. They should be soaked in a weak solution of corrosive sublimate, and thoroughly dried before packing—the tarpaulins to be made *very dry*—the whole to be packed, marked, and numbered under your personal direction. Of the soldiers' tents belonging to the survey at Fenton's, you are authorized to take two. The copper bands, &c., for the tent-poles should be taken. Tool chest and tools, (carpenter's,) carpenter's levels, mess furniture for men and aids, who receive their board from the survey; stoves, &c., for cooking, &c.; portable tables and camp stools. Equipage connected with transportation will have to be obtained in the country. The mechanics whom Captain Alexander V. Fraser takes out in connexion with the revenue marine may, no doubt, be available for work of this sort.

Stationery.—Ordinary supplies of writing and drawing materials, and all blank forms used in the coast survey; lithographed tables, con. for barometer, printed regulations, copy of superintendent's reports, all printed instructions, forms of reports, forms of accounts, maps of Atlantic coast of coast survey, as specimens, &c.; books for recording geodetic, astronomical, transit, latitudes, culminations, occultations, magnetic observations, miscellanea, duplicates, &c.; tin cases for maps. You will make your own rules about the amount of baggage to be allowed to your assistant, aid, and men. I will endeavor to have the wages put on the footing of those of the gulf coast, but, as contingencies may be extraordinary, will make every allowance possible for them.

Books.—Pearson's Astronomy, (not indispensable;) Francœur's Astr. Pratique; Francœur's Geodesie; Bailey's Tables and Formula; Simms on Transit Instruments; Trans. Am. Phil. Society, vol. 2, new series, (for Mr. Hassler's paper on Zenith Telescope;) Callet's or Bajuet's Logarithms; Bowditch's Useful Tables, or Bowditch's Navigator; Galbraith's Mathematical and Astronomical Tables; De Mafra's California and Oregon; British Nautical Almanac, as far ahead as published; American Almanac, 1849; Downe's Tables, if out. Such other books, bearing directly on the work, as you may deem advisable to purchase. Examine a set of Vancouver's charts at Blunt's, and, if you deem it advisable, purchase. Any charts of Pacific coast which may be obtained at a reasonable cost, purchase. I have written for the British admiralty charts, and will again try, through a private source, to obtain the published results of all the British surveys. Wilkes's Narratives and Charts; letters in Intelligencer from longitude discussions with Frémont; transit results.

Instruments, geodetic.—Base apparatus; duplicate set of base bars in office to be cleaned, remeasured, and carefully packed—four two-metre bars in the set; clamps to attach them to each other; sector for inclination of apparatus; eight thermometers; rough level; heavy plumb bobs, carefully centred; two small plumb bobs, well centred; microscopes, at least five, with stands; friction rollers on which bars move; large iron screws for trestles, (New York or Philadelphia;) rough levels for trestles, small and large, (office;) small transit for alignment of base. The wooden rod for supporting the bars and the covering box and the wooden parts of the trestles will be made in the country. I suggest that rough levelling screws may be desirable for the feet of the trestles, specimens of which you will see in Washington, as also of supporting plates, which may be made of wood, the joints crossing and the middle cut out. Comparing apparatus for bars, (Saxton's pyrometer;) simple miciem and spring; scale; small telescope, with cross hairs—abutting piece of metal, with screw; stonecutter's tools, mason's ditto; ten-inch Gambey theodolite; six-inch also, if disposable, but not essential; reconnoitring telescope, with divided stand and heliotrope fixtures, (my party;) auxiliary heliotrope, (from my party.)

Topographical.—Plane table and fixture, two standard chains, level, compass, and stand; reconnoitring compass.

Astronomical.—Transit instrument, (C. S., from Professor Kendall, Philadelphia, 45 inch transit, value of level;) zenith telescope from my party; two large lamps; small ditto, with instrument; two extra for marks, (bull's eye;) screw-drivers, wrenches, pins, stops, (send to office containing sizes;) chronometers, six—four by one opportunity, two by the other; two rated to sidereal time, four mean solar, (procured;) sextant, and artificial horizon.

Meteorological instruments.—Barometers, two, "transportable"—one of Alexander, at Green's in Baltimore, (inquire of Mr. Boutelle or Captain Lee;) one of Hassler from office, to be placed in cabin of vessel; four small thermometers for barometer; two small ditto; naked bulbs for evaporating point; four for temperature of air, in cases.—(See Professor Henry about supply of meteorological instruments for stations.)

Nails, iron, (cast and wrought,) and copper; screws, glass, leather, hinges.

Magnetic instruments.—Declenometer at office; (must be examined and used first and coefficients obtained—Davidson;) as also a magnetometer for intensity; dip circle, (Gambey, if it comes, or Robinson, now in my camp.) Tent for magnetics, with copper—Mr. Ruth's.

Let me have an estimate of the cost of articles to be purchased, at your earliest convenience, the approval of which will put you in funds for your purchases. The estimate may be in part only, or in whole, as suits you best.

Party.—Sub-assistant Davidson, who is well versed in the practice of astronomical and magnetic observations, and has a general acquaintance with the work of the survey, will be detailed as your assistant; Mr. William Humphreys will accompany you as aid. You should take two or three men from this side, two to go out with the instruments; and perhaps unavoidable delays may require the three to be so sent. The number of your party on the other side must depend upon circumstances. I rely upon your exercising great economy. It will be better to use men of the country than to take out men, except a nucleus for the party, which should be of the better sort, and of men who had been trained in our parties on this side. Lavalle will be a good person to send round with the astronomical instruments and equipage. Moore will also serve you well, and is a seaman besides. The persons and instruments sent by the mail-boat will probably reach Panama before the others.

About times and opportunities for sending, I expect further information from you. As much as can be ready by the 15th October should be collected at New York and sent out by the quartermaster's steamer. If any official steps are necessary, you will advise me.

Equipage and astronomical instruments (including four of the chronometers) can certainly be ready, and perhaps base apparatus or theodolite.

Reconnoitring telescope, level, compass, plane table, chain, tools, stationery, books, can certainly be ready; leaving only a small *bulk* of articles behind.

I want your suggestions in regard to supplies of articles of provisions or others from this side—say, Unkonoonuc to October 1, to New York. Philadelphia office—say, 5th. New York again, 12th; (articles all collected.) Magnetic observations with Davidson. Articles collected for November 1, New York base; to South Carolina, to assist replacing.

Mr. Davidson is now at New Harmony; will leave there on the 1st of October and proceed to Philadelphia; his address is Frankford Road, above Oxford street, Kensington. He will receive directions from me to be at your disposal. Mr. Humphreys is in Washington. Lavalle is also in Washington. Moore with Mr. Boutelle, with whom communicate, as he is employed in his party.

The work in section X will be executed upon the same principles and by the same methods with that in the sections with which you are already familiar on the eastern coast. Important positions will be fixed by astronomical observations. It will be desirable at once, perhaps, to fix upon a site or sites for astronomical observations, such as will certainly come into connexion with the triangulation. There should be as few and small reductions to the station as practicable. The site to be determined by importance of locality, or by probable beginning of regular work there; or, if needs be, by facilities for working latitudes by zenith telescope. Time by transits. Moon culminations, by transit, for longitude. Occultations, with reconnoitring telescope, for ditto. Azimuths by theodolite and elongations of polaris or other circumpolar star. By azimuths of stars at rising and setting. Difference longitude, where admits of it, of distant points by chronometer.

Magnetic observations should be made in common with the astronomical.

A general reconnoissance of the coast of Oregon should be made as soon as practicable; the minute reconnoissance to follow the base and triangulation which it develops. As it is exceedingly important to produce *results*, you are authorized to invert the usual process when you think it desirable. To measure a suitable local base and make a local survey, which will come into the general plan—subsequently determining the local latitude and longitude by the best means in your power—a hydrographic party will follow you closely, if my expectations in regard to appropriations and facilities for the work are realized. I can hardly venture to sketch a plan of operations; but suppose that you reach Columbia river in the spring, proceed to Puget's sound, (I will endeavor to procure letters for the authorities of the Hudson's Bay and Puget's Sound Company, and will procure letters to the revenue marine establishment to furnish you facilities,) examine shores, establish observatory, make reconnoissance, and perhaps measure local base and survey; a general reconnoissance. It will be an advantage to have several astronomical points which are well connected by $\triangle'$u to eliminate errors of locality. The longitudes are the most tedious part, as a year's culminations and occultations will not do more than give an approximate result. If these are made at points well connected geodetically or by chronometers, they will do as well as if made at one station; indeed better, as eliminating local action. I say nothing now about chronometer expeditions across, because we know so little of the facilities or difficulties of communicating, and the facilities are increasing every day. Keep this subject in mind, however.

Furnish Mr. Downes the latitudes and longitudes of several points—say Columbia river, Puget's sound, *perhaps others*—and request him to compute the predictions for occultations for the next two years for you, from April 1, 1849. His address is John Downes, Walnut street, Philadelphia.

Write to him as soon as you can, in my name, and ask him to let you have results by December 1.

The sooner we can have some harbor maps and sketches of general reconnoissance and information of interest to communicate to Congress and the public, the better. Much of your ultimate success depends upon timely communication. Let me hear from you by every opportunity; and besides the regular formal reports, write very freely, public letters or private ones, at my disposal. I do not wish you to confine your remarks to matters relating to the land work until the hydrographers are with you, but to give any information which may be of interest, and when no regular authority has got charge of procuring it. Of course, when the regular system of division of labor in the survey, or out of it, obtains, I do not desire to suggest interference. Your known qualities make me leave this an open subject, only limited by your discretion. You will forward your accounts in the usual forms as frequently as practicable—monthly when practicable, and not passing over a quarter if it can be avoided without great inconvenience.

Take your vouchers in triplicate, and send two sets by different opportunities, and keep one by you in case of accident to the others. I await your information in regard to the best mode of transmission of funds, the amount you wish to take with you, based upon your estimates and expenses, the form in which you wish it to be furnished. If an estimate to the close of the fiscal year, July, 1849, will carry you certainly through, it would be best to present that for my action before you leave here; then a provisional estimate for the next year, upon which I can act later; and if I should not hear from you, Mr. Hein will make such arrangements in regard to account for salary, &c., as you desire for yourself and Mr. Davidson. For note of books to be kept, and of copies to be made and sent to the office, and of disposal of originals, see paper A.

With hearty wishes for your success, yours, truly and respectfully,

A. D. BACHE,
Superintendent, &c.

JAMES S. WILLIAMS, Esq.,
Assistant U. S. Coast Survey.

[INSTRUCTIONS.]

Coast Survey Office,
Washington, January 25, 1849.

Sir: Your first duty in section X, to which you have been directed to repair in the instructions of August and September last, will be to determine whether a survey, or merely a reconnoissance, will be necessary at the mouth of the Columbia river. This you will execute in connexion with Lieutenant Commanding W. P. McArthur, jointly with whom you will also decide the question whether the light-houses on Cape Disappointment and Point Adams, provided for in the territorial bill relating to Oregon, shall be constructed or not, their location, character, and advantages, accessories required, and any other points of interest, reporting to me your results in regard to light-houses, or of reconnoissance or survey, as early as practicable.

The movement of trade in Oregon, the facilities for entrance to the ports, and other relative local advantages, will determine the question of the point to begin the survey, and I refer this to the joint decision of Lieutenant Commanding McArthur and yourself.

Should Columbia river or Puget's sound be selected, you will establish an astronomical and magnetic station there, and proceed with the measurement of a local base, with a secondary triangulation, and furnish shore line for the hydrography as early as practicable.

I will expect to hear from you by every opportunity. I enclose a letter from the Secretary of the Treasury, directing the officers of the revenue, and others connected with the department, to furnish you such facilities as may not interfere with the discharge of their regular duties. I have applied for a letter from the Secretary of the Treasury to Governor Lane, one from the chargé d'affaires of Great Britain to the officers of the Hudson's Bay Company, and for a copy of so much of the instructions of Captain Alexander V. Fraser, in command of the revenue brig Lawrence, as refers to facilities to the coast survey. When they are received, they will be forwarded to you at New York.

Captain R. P. Hammond, United States army, and Sub-assistant Joseph S. Ruth, have been directed to report to you for duty.

I expect you to take with you the most authentic maps and charts of the western coast, and to make such corrections in them as your opportunities may permit, and as will not interfere with the instructions for work in Oregon.

I will write to you in New York in regard to twin day observations in connexion with Toronto, Cambridge, and Chili.

Yours, respectfully and truly,
A. D. BACHE,
Superintendent, &c.

James S. Williams, Esq.,
Assistant U. S. Coast Survey.

[INSTRUCTIONS.]

NORFOLK, *October* 27, 1848.

SIR: I have been directed by the Treasury Department to make arrangements for commencing the survey of the western coast of the United States. A land party has been for some time organizing under the charge of assistant James S. Williams. I am directed also to organize a hydrographic party to accompany or speedily to follow the land party, and you have been assigned to the command of the party. You will please, therefore, make all preliminary arrangements in conformity with oral instructions already received, or such as may suggest themselves as proper to you under circumstances, observing the usual routine in regard to estimates, &c. If no more suitable vessel for your purpose can be obtained, the schooner Ewing, the transfer of which from the revenue service has been directed by the Secretary of the Treasury, will be assigned to you. The fitting out of this vessel and her despatch at as early a moment as practicable is desirable—say before the last week of November. I do not deem it desirable that you should make the voyage in the vessel, as you cannot complete work now in hands, nor so well seize the most prominent objects of the western work, as by making the journey over the isthmus and joining the vessel at Panama or San Francisco.

The specific duties required of you will be stated later in instructions.

You are authorized to go to New York, in connexion with the transfer of the Ewing, at such time as you may deem best.

I leave to a later day directions in regard to the closing of the work on Albemarle sound, having already communicated my views orally to you.

Very respectfully,
A. D. BACHE,
Superintendent, &c.

Lt. Com. W. P. MCARTHUR,
U. S. Navy, Assistant Coast Survey.

[INSTRUCTIONS.]

COAST SURVEY OFFICE,
Washington, March 10, 1849.

SIR: Under the preliminary instructions of October 27, 1848, you have already attended to the organization of a hydrographic party of the coast survey for section X, to the preparation of the schooner Ewing for sailing, to her despatch, to instruments, books, &c., to estimates, and similar preliminary matters. It remains to give more special instructions in regard to localities and objects of work. All the general instructions, scientific and business, for the coast survey, will be in full force as far as they apply to the circumstances of the service in which you will be engaged. The frequent communications which I expect to receive from you will develop a system of operations which may take the place of the temporary one now necessary.

Your first duty in section X will be to determine whether a survey, or merely a reconnoissance, will be necessary at the mouth of the Columbia river: this you will execute in connexion with assistant James S. Williams, jointly with whom you will also decide the question whether the lighthouses on Cape Disappointment and Point Adams, provided for in the territorial bill of 1848, relating to Oregon, shall be constructed or not, their location, character, and advantages, accessories required, and any other points of interest; reporting to me jointly your results in regard to light-houses, or of reconnoissance, or survey, as early as practicable.

The movement of trade in Oregon, the facilities for entrance to the ports, and other relative local advantages, will determine the question of the points to begin the survey, and I refer this to the joint decision of assistant James S. Williams and yourself.

The work in section X will be executed upon the same principles and by the same method with that in the sections with which you are already familiar on the eastern coast.

The land party under assistant James S. Williams will furnish you latitudes and longitudes in the usual way; and when a reconnoissance merely is required, points determined by directions and distances.

I wish you to give every facility, which may not interfere with the general progress of the work, to the land parties, who may be dependent on you for means of transportation, for the use of boats, and of men at particular times, and other facilities. In this even a closer co-operation is desirable than between the parties on the Atlantic coast, as the parties must be comparatively isolated. In deciding, therefore, in reference to facilities, I would prefer that you should consider the general progress of the work, rather than the advance of any particular department of it.

In the same spirit I entrust to assistant James S. Williams and yourself the decision of any unforeseen questions which may arise, and give you jointly authority where you agree in reference to a measure relating to the progress of the work, locality, arrangements, and the like.

It will be important to establish permanent tidal registers at such points as may furnish facilities in regard to observations and observers, the number to be limited by the expenditure which you find necessary. With these, full series of meteorological observations should be combined, including the pressure (barometer's) of the air, temperature, (thermometer's,) direction and force of the wind, quantity of rain, temperature of a thermometer with a blackened bulb in the sun, and temperature of the surface of the ground. On these subjects I recommend to you the instructions of the Royal Society for meteorological observations for the magnetic observatories. Mr. Williams may furnish parts of these observations, and the subject should be matter for understanding between you.

In regard to preparing preliminary sketches or charts, views of the coast, and the like, I leave the arrangement of the work to Mr. Williams and you jointly, whether to follow the usual mode of returning the land maps and hydrographical charts separately, or to unite in the return.

The sooner we can have some harbor maps, and sketches of general reconnoissance, and information of interest to communicate to Congress and the public, the better. Much of your ultimate success depends upon timely communication. Let me hear from you by every opportunity; and besides the regular formal reports, write very freely, public letters or private ones, at my disposal.

I expect you to take with you the most authentic charts or maps of the western coast, and to make such corrections in them as your opportunities may permit, and as will not interfere with the instructions for work in Oregon.

You will forward your accounts in the usual form, as frequently as practicable—monthly when practicable, and not passing over a quarter if it can be avoided without great inconvenience. Take your vouchers in triplicate, and send two sets by different opportunities, and keep one by you in case of accident to the others. Send an estimate for funds required at least four months in advance.

I will expect to hear from you by every opportunity. You have been furnished with a letter from the Secretary of the Treasury, directing the officers of the revenue, and others connected with the department, to furnish you such facilities as may not interfere with the discharge of their regular duties. I enclose a letter from the Secretary of the Treasury to General Lane, one from the chargé d'affaires of Great Britain to the officers of the Hudson's Bay Company, and a copy of the instructions to Captain Alexander V. Fraser, in command of the revenue brig Lawrence, containing a reference to facilities to the coast survey.

Yours, respectfully and truly,

A. D. BACHE,
Superintendent United States Coast Survey.

Lieut. Com'g W. P. McArthur,
U. S. Navy, Assistant Coast Survey.

Exeter, N. H., *August* 22, 1849.

Sir: The extraordinary expenses which the officers of the coast survey party on the western coast of the United States have met with, induce me to make the recommendation that there be allowed to the chief and assistants of the parties there, instead of the sums already authorized by the department, two dollars and fifty cents per day for subsistence, to take effect from the first of January, 1849, when the Oregon party had nearly completed its preparations to leave the Atlantic coast.

Very respectfully, yours,

A. D. BACHE,
Superintendent U. S. Coast Survey.

W. M. Meredith,
Secretary of the Treasury.

Treasury Department,
August 31, 1849.

Sir: Before acting on the recommendation contained in your letter of the 22d inst. on the subject of an increased allowance for subsistence to the chief and assistants of the coast survey parties on the western coast of the United States, in consideration of the extraordinary expenses to which they are subjected in California, I desire to be informed of the number of persons to whom it is proposed to make this allowance, specifying the navy or army, and civilians. I cannot learn that any of the civil or military officers of the United States stationed in California have had any additional allowances made them on account of the expenses before referred to, and hence it becomes questionable in regard to the propriety of making any distinction in this respect between the different branches of the public service in California.

Very respectfully, your obedient servant,
W. M. MEREDITH,
Secretary of the Treasury.

Prof. A. D. BACHE,
Superintendent Coast Survey, Exeter, N. H.

COAST SURVEY STATION,
Near Portland, Maine, Sept. 5, 1849.

SIR: In reply to yours of August 31st, relating to the allowances recommended by me to be made for subsistence to the chiefs of parties and assistants now employed on the western coast, I beg leave to submit the following:

1. In the instructions from the Treasury Department, dated October 23, 1848, the following paragraph refers to the compensation of persons employed:

"2d. The employment of such aids and such hands in the parties as may be necessary, and the allowance of the requisite outfits," (are authorized.) "The persons to receive the pay and allowances fixed by the department for the Gulf of Mexico, or as may be usual on the western coast to secure good hands, and as may be approved by the superintendent. *The officers to receive the allowances which apply to the sections on the Gulf of Mexico.*" It is for this latter clause that I proposed a substitute in my letter of August 22d, using the same phraseology, but proposing a different amount of allowance.

2. Great advantage has resulted to the survey from the allowances made to civil assistants depending upon work to be done in particular localities, instead of an increase of salary, independent of the place of working, and received whether in the field or office. It has rendered service acceptable, for which otherwise it would have been difficult to obtain willing agents. Men of the requisite capacity, science, and other qualities necessary for this work, are not easily procured nor trained, and *willing* service is the only kind which is profitable to us.

3. The officers whom I had in view in my recommendation to the department as having been subjected to extraordinary expenses were the civil assistants James S. Williams, esq., and Mr. Joseph S. Ruth, sub-assistant. Mr. Williams receives a salary of $1,600, and Mr. Ruth one of $800. The personal expenses of each at San Francisco, with the severest economy, amounted to $3 per day for board and $100 per month for lodging.

4. In general, officers of the army and navy are furnished with quarters, fuel, and rations *in kind,* where the cost exceeds the allowance in money made by the government. It may be that Captain Hammond, of the army, assistant to Mr. Williams, and Lieutenant Commanding McArthur, of the navy, commanding the hydrographic party of the coast survey, have been subjected to extraordinary expenses; but no representations from either have yet reached me. Should they have been involved

in any such expenses, I would deem it my duty to submit their case to your consideration.

5. I would most earnestly advise an additional emolument in the way of subsistence, rather than an increase of regular salary to the assistants, at *the present time*. Without an increase of emolument, they can probably not remain in Oregon; and if it be an increase of salary which does not cease on leaving the western coast, the stimulus to work there, as far as such a consideration would act, is withdrawn. It was not easy to find an assistant exactly suited to send upon this work, and Mr. Williams's compensation is now less than that of any other assistant in charge of work of similar responsibility. We should lose much by his withdrawal.

6. The peculiar attainments required by assistants in the coast survey have always been held to place them on a different footing as to compensation from ordinary civil employés of the government. Mr. Williams, for example, has received four thousand dollars for his services as chief engineer of one of the States; and the offers in California which have been made to induce him to leave our service, and which he has, most honorably to himself, declined, have been large.

7. The commission which an officer of the army and navy holds is an advantage which separates his case from that of civilians employed in the work. He is insured regular promotion as he advances in life; is not exposed to the contingency of an annual appropriation by Congress; is employed during life, whether sick or well—whether the coast survey is finished or in progress; his family receive a pension if he dies from the results of service; he is furnished *in kind*, if necessary, quarters and fuel; is supplied with medical attendance at the cost of the government; and enjoys other advantages which do not attend the position of a civilian on the coast survey.

These considerations will, I trust, serve to separate the case of assistants in the coast survey from those of other civil and military or naval officers, and to warrant the approval of the allowances requested in my former letter, and which I believe are important to the successful prosecution of the work on the western coast at the present time.

Very respectfully, yours,
A. D. BACHE,
Superintendent U. S. Coast Survey.

Hon. W. M. MEREDITH,
Secretary of the Treasury.

TREASURY DEPARTMENT, *September* 27, 1849.

SIR: Your report of the 5th instant, in explanation of your recommendation of the 22d ultimo, respecting an additional allowance to the chief and assistants of the coast survey parties employed on the western coast of the United States, has received due consideration.

In view of the existing condition of things, and the extraordinary expenses to which these officers are subjected in the prosecution of their duties, especially in California, it is deemed expedient and proper to make the allowance proposed. The chief and assistants of the coast survey parties operating on the western coast of the United States will therefore be allowed, in addition to their present compensations, two dollars and fifty cents per day each for subsistence, to commence on their arrival in California, and continue while employed in the discharge of their public duties in California, and cease when engaged elsewhere.

Very respectfully,
W. M. MEREDITH,
Secretary of the Treasury.

Prof. A. D. BACHE,
Superintendent Coast Survey, Washington.

TREASURY DEPARTMENT, *November* 16, 1849.

SIR: Referring you to the instructions of the department of the 17th of August, 1848, in regard to the coast survey operations on the western coast of the United States, and particularly to so much of said instructions as relates to an examination and survey of the entrance to Columbia river, with the view to the location thereat of light-houses, buoys, &c., authorized by the 27th section of the act "to establish the territorial government of Oregon," approved 14th August, 1848, I have to request that the coast survey party assigned to this duty may be urged to an early completion and report of the result of the work, in order that the intention of Congress may be carried into effect by the establishment of light-houses, buoys, &c., at the points indicated, at as early a period as practicable.

So soon as this work shall have been completed, it is the desire of the department, in view of the important commercial interests of the United States on the coast of the Pacific, that reconnoissance should first be made of the headlands, bays, rivers, &c., of the coast of California embraced within the limits of the United States, for the indication of suitable points for the location of light-houses, beacons, buoys, &c.

Your attention, therefore, is called to this subject, in order that the necessary instructions may be given by you to the coast survey parties in California.

Very respectfully, your obedient servant,
W. M. MEREDITH,
Secretary of the Treasury.

Prof. A. D. BACHE,
Superintendent Coast Survey, Washington.

COAST SURVEY OFFICE,
Washington, D. C., December 21, 1849.

SIR: I would respectfully request that, in lieu of the present regulations applying to payment for subsistence of chiefs of parties and assistants in the coast survey work on the western coast, the following regulations be adopted, viz:

Chiefs and assistants of land parties on the western coast of the United States shall receive, while in the field on that coast, an allowance for subsistence of $2 50 per day

I would respectfully request that, in the case of assistant J. S. Williams, and sub-assistant J. S. Ruth, and Captain Hammond, the allowance may take effect from January 1, 1849, when their preparations for the work were made.

Very respectfully, yours,
A. D. BACHE,
Superintendent U. S. Coast Survey.

Hon. W. M. MEREDITH,
Secretary of the Treasury.

TREASURY DEPARTMENT,
October 24, 1848.

SIR: The United States revenue brig C. W. Lawrence, under your command, being fully equipped and ready, you will proceed to sea, and with all prudent despatch, stopping first at San Diego, on the Pacific coast, on your way to Oregon, where you will enter upon your duties as an officer of the revenue.

Your own experience, and the laws which are placed in your possession, will render any detailed explanation of those legitimate duties unnecessary.

You will, however, enter and examine all the different harbors which are now, or which may be, under the jurisdiction of the United States, and exercise the greatest vigilance in the prevention and detection of illicit trade, and in bringing offenders against the revenue service to justice.

At present you will consider the collector of the customs for the district of Oregon as the superintendent to whom your reports and accounts are to be rendered.

Should you, however, be officially notified of the extension of the revenue laws over California, and the appointment of a collector of customs for that district—that being the point where the greatest amount of commerce will most probably be directed—you will transfer your accounts to that collector, and make the point of his location your principal rendezvous for supplies.

When the funds now placed in your possession, and for which you have furnished sureties, shall have been exhausted, and when you shall have deposited with said collector or collectors your accounts in the prescribed form, accompanied by the requisite vouchers showing that said money has been faithfully disbursed, you will present all future accounts, duly authenticated, to said collectors for settlement as they become due.

You will report regularly to this department, and transmit the usual transcripts from the journals, and study the most rigid economy in your expenditures. Should vacancies occur among the officers by casualties or resignations, you will make temporary provision from the officers next in grade, reporting the same forthwith to this department. Incidental to the duties before enumerated will be those of the protection of the commercial interests of the country, particularly in relieving the distresses of merchant vessels when such relief may be necessary, and in making such examination of the various harbors you may visit as your means will permit, and as will not interfere with your legitimate duties. All information on these points is highly important, and will be transmitted to the superintendent of the coast survey through this department. The department has directed the commencement of the survey of the western coast by the superintendent of the coast survey, and one or more assistants of this work will speedily be despatched for this purpose. To these officers you will afford every facility in your power, by conveying them to such points as they may indicate, and by such assistance with your vessel, boats, and crew, as they may desire, and as may not seriously interfere with your revenue duties. They will, of course, be expected to bear their proportion of the expenses of the mess while on board of your vessel. Should letter bags from the other departments of the government be confided to your care, you will receive and deliver them as directed. In the event of your determination to locate your family permanently on the west coast, you will at the expiration of twelve months have permission to absent yourself from the vessel, for a period not to exceed three months, to attend to their removal.

You will be permitted to employ the services of a pilot until you shall become familiar with the different harbors, at the rate of compensation prescribed by the regulations, viz: fifty dollars per month and ration per diem.

In consideration of the peculiar character of your cruising grounds, the absence of marine hospitals, and the exposure of yourself, officers, and crew to casualties, you will be permitted to employ a medical practitioner, provided his compensation shall not exceed that allowed to a pilot.

It only now remains to commit you to the care of Him who controls the elements, and to wish you a safe and prosperous voyage.

I am, sir, very respectfully, your obedient servant,
R. J. WALKER,
Secretary of the Treasury.

Capt. ALEX. V. FRASER,
  United States Revenue Service,
    Commanding U. S. Revenue Brig C. W. Lawrence.

TREASURY DEPARTMENT,
December 28, 1848.

SIR: This department deeming it expedient to send a special messenger to Oregon with official despatches relating to the revenue service, you are hereby directed to proceed without delay to the port of San Francisco, California, where you will obtain such information as may be necessary to enable you to report yourself at the earliest practicable date to Captain Fraser, of the revenue cutter Cornelius W. Lawrence.

It is important that you should immediately communicate to Captain Fraser all the information which you may be able to obtain at San Francisco in relation to the desertion of seamen and the best means of preventing desertion ; also, such information of a general nature connected with our commercial interest as you may obtain in your incidental inquiries. In view of the expected adoption by Congress, during its present session, of laws for the protection of our revenue on the coast of California, it is desirable that you should avail yourself of the opportunity which your visit to San Francisco may offer to acquire such useful knowledge on the subject as will facilitate the future operations of the revenue cutter stationed on the coast of Oregon. You will remain no longer at San Francisco, or any other point in California which it may be found necessary to touch at, than will be requisite for the prompt discharge of your duty; when you will proceed to Astoria, and await further orders from Captain Fraser, to whom you will report yourself.

In consideration of the probable delay and expense arising from the great number of passengers now assembled at the isthmus of Panama and pressing towards that point, and the uncertainty of obtaining any speedy conveyance on the Pacific side, you are at liberty to choose such other route as you may ascertain to be most advantageous and reliable. Your actual expenses to Oregon, not exceeding the usual cost of passage and incidental charges, will be paid, but no compensation in addition to your salary can be allowed you by this department.

Respectfully, R. J. WALKER,
Secretary of the Treasury.

Lieut. JOHN ROSS BROWN,
United States Revenue Marine.

U. S. REVENUE BRIG LAWRENCE,
San Francisco, Nov. 1, 1849.

SIR: I have barely time before the departure of the steamer to announce my arrival at this port, in thirty days from the Sandwich islands, and find the presence of the vessel very necessary for the proper enforcement of the revenue laws.

All the particulars shall be communicated by the next mail from this place; and have the honor to subscribe myself, very respectfully, your obedient servant,

ALEX. V. FRASER, *Captain.*

Hon. WM. M. MEREDITH,
Secretary of the Treasury, Washington, D. C.

UNITED STATES REVENUE BRIG LAWRENCE,
San Francisco, November 6, 1849.

SIR: I had the honor on the 1st instant, per steamer of that date, to report to you merely the arrival of this vessel under my command from the Sandwich islands, where I landed the despatches for the United States commissioner. I regret to inform you that I was compelled to leave Third Lieutenant R. H. Bowlin at Honolulu, who had been suffering during a great portion of the voyage from rheumatism, contracted while serving upon our southern Atlantic coast, and which was greatly aggravated by exposure on board a small vessel during such a passage as we have experienced. He was desirous of keeping the deck, notwithstanding the severity of his disease; and I judged it prudent to submit his case to Dr. Addison, of the United States ship St. Mary's, at Valparaiso, who gave, as his opinion, that the winter months in Chili or California would jeopard his recovery. Under these circumstances, and actuated by a desire that he should recover his health, and be ready at the earliest possible time to resume his duties, I left him, at his own solicitation, at the before-mentioned place. His case, as with all others in the same service, is peculiarly hard and unjust. The law makes no provision for the employment of a medical officer on board of the revenue vessels, although the officers and men contribute to the hospital fund. Consuls refuse to receive them, because their perquisites are not increased by their presence; and, as in the case of three seamen left at Valparaiso, and three at the Sandwich islands, they have been obliged to supply themselves with medical advice and maintenance from their own scanty earnings; while in the merchant service, as well as in the navy, seamen are provided for. I have directed Lieutenant Bowlin, as well as the men who were left, to present to me, on the coast, triplicate bills for their reasonable expenses, which I shall have the honor of presenting to the honorable Secretary, not doubting the liberality and justice of his decision.

Subsequent to the date of my last communication, I have the honor to acknowledge the receipt of the letters from the department of April 14, 1849, relative to clothing procured from the navy agent at Norfolk for the use of the crew; and of the 25th July, 1849, relative to the contract for ship chandlery for the New York station in the years 1847–'48. To the first of these communications I have only to state, that I reported the fact, with the amount, to the department prior to leaving Norfolk; and that the amount, one hundred and forty-six dollars and seventy two cents, ($146 72,) was at that time credited in my accounts, as subsequently has been that received from Mr. Parks, consul at Rio de Janeiro, and that from the navy agent at the same place.

In reply to the latter inquiry, I have to state that every communication received at the revenue bureau, from my connexion with it in April, 1843, until July 1, prior to my departure, was left upon file, bound, indexed, and registered; and that, what was not known prior to my arrival at the department, a full index and register of all papers issued and received was constructed by me, from the burning of the Treasury buildings, in 1833, until the above named period.

The inquiry appears to convey a suspicion of neglect, or of intentional error. I do recollect distinctly, that on one occasion there was but one bid received, and that through the custom house at New York, from C. A. Secor & Co.; that it was referred to the honorable Secretary of the Treasury; and that he, at my suggestion, took the responsibility of delaying the opening of it for two days, in consequence of the uncertainty of the mails during the winter season; that none other was received; and that this one was accepted, because, on comparison with those received from other stations, from New Orleans to Maine, the prices were found to be fair and reasonable. Lieutenant Pierce, fortunately on board of this vessel, was at the department at the time. All bids were first received by the Secretary, endorsed and opened in the presence of the chief clerk and the officer who was my assistant. If there be any person at the department who can place his hand upon the records as I could have done, the facts of this case will require no time to develop themselves, as all cases of doubt were referred by me to the Secretary in writing. I recollect, likewise, that in numerous cases bidders had offered so low as to defy all competition.

I am likewise in receipt of the new regulations for the government of the service, the provisions of which, from my own interpretation, must go into effect at the end of the present month. On this subject, however, I shall confer with the new collector, who has not yet arrived, but who is expected daily.

If it is the expectation of the department to maintain a supervision over the interests of the revenue, under the restrictions thereby conveyed, it will be disappointed. It will only be necessary to state that the services of a steward are worth $150, and seaman $100 per month; and that the present pay of an officer will not furnish him with the absolute necessaries of life. No medical officer is allowed; and at this place a physician would charge from $50 to $100 for a single visit afloat. I have taken the responsibility of serving to the officers, as well as to my own mess, the proper ration, charging the same. It is the only means in our reach for support.

Congress having refused to extend the naval laws over the service, I have neither the power to arrest nor punish deserters. The officers have intimated to me their intention to resign; to which course they will be impelled by the most urgent necessity, in order to support themselves. Pork is $50, beef $30, flour $35 per barrel; sugar 25 cents, potatoes 40 cents, butter $1 50 per pound; and we are compelled to do our own washing on board.

There is no question that a great amount of illicit trade is prosecuted in this bay, and that the most vigilant measures are necessary to prevent it. I shall remain at my post until fairly starved out, trusting that the department may make some provision for our maintenance, and to secure to us, in this climate, medical treatment. At present, I rely entirely upon the kindness of Commodore Jones, who has done all in his power to assist us.

November 25.—Since writing the above, the new collector has arrived, to whom, as the proper officer, I have made known my views upon the prevention of smuggling on this coast, which will be communicated to you. In addition, I would merely state that the revenue boatmen at this port receive one hundred dollars per month, and can scarcely live.

Lieutenant Chaddock, upon whom all my reliance was placed, has been compelled, in self-defence, to resign his commission; and I am left with three officers, and not a seaman among them. Awaiting some action of the department, I have the honor to be, sir, very respectfully, your obedient servant,

ALEX. V. FRASER, *Captain.*

Hon. Secretary of the Treasury,
Washington.

United States Revenue Brig Lawrence,
San Francisco, November 25, 1849.

Sir: I have the honor to transmit a copy of the resignation of J. S. S. Chaddock, esq., first lieutenant in the United States revenue marine, the reasons for which are therein expressed.

I am, sir, very respectfully, your obedient servant,

ALEX. V. FRASER, *Captain.*

Hon. Wm. W. Meredith,
Secretary of the Treasury, Washington.

UNITED STATES REVENUE BRIG LAWRENCE,
Sansolito, November 25, 1849.

SIR: Your several letters applying for leave of absence from this time to the expiration of the present month, and tendering your resignation as first lieutenant in the United States revenue marine, to take effect the 30th instant, are received.

Your request for leave of absence is granted, and a copy of your tender of resignation shall be transmitted, through the collector of the customs, for the consideration of the honorable Secretary of the Treasury; the appointment of a collector of the customs at this port having, in my opinion, annulled my power to accept it.

If you desire it, leave will be granted to you until the decision of the department be known, provided it meets with the approbation of the collector.

I am, sir, very respectfully, your obedient servant,
ALEX. V. FRASER, *Captain.*
Lt. J. S. S. CHADDOCK,
United States Revenue Marine.

U. S. REVENUE BRIG LAWRENCE,
San Francisco, November 26, 1849.

SIR: I have the honor to transmit the resignation of Second Lieutenant E. C. Kennedy, of the United States revenue marine, to take effect on the 15th day of January next, 1850; and an application for relief from this station from Second Lieutenant Wm. R. Pierce, with a qualified tender of his resignation, to take effect on the 1st day of March next, 1850; by which the department will perceive that I shall be entirely unassisted in the discharge of my duties, or in the care of the vessel.

I am, sir, very respectfully, your obedient servant,
ALEX. V. FRASER, *Captain.*
Hon. SECRETARY OF THE TREASURY,
Washington.

U. S. REVENUE BRIG LAWRENCE,
Bay of San Francisco, November 26, 1849.

SIR: Finding it impossible, almost, even to subsist on my compensation as second lieutenant in the revenue service at this place, in consequence of the very high prices charged for the actual necessaries of life, I would respectfully request that I may be relieved from duty here.

I regret to be compelled to pursue this course, after having left home in the vessel with the intention of remaining; but I feel it to be a duty which I owe to myself, and to others who are in a measure dependent on me, to ask; and the request is a reasonable one, when I ask to be relieved for the reasons above stated.

If, however, I cannot be relieved, I must then request that this may be accepted as my resignation from the service, to take effect from and after the first day of March next; but this I would have by no means construed into a threat, being too well aware what effect that would have.

Trusting that the request to be relieved may be granted, I shall remain by the vessel, discharging my duties, until a reasonable time to hear from Washington shall have elapsed.

I am, sir, very respectfully, your obedient servant,
W. R. PIERCE,
Second Lieut. U. S. Revenue Service.

Hon. Secretary of the Treasury,
Washington.

U. S. Revenue Brig C. W. Lawrence,
San Francisco, Upper California, Nov. 27, 1849.

Sir: My pay being insufficient to support myself and others, I have the honor to resign my commission as a second lieutenant in the revenue service of the United States, to take effect from and after the 15th of January.

Respectfully, your obedient servant,
EDMD. C. KENNEDY,
Second Lieut. U. S. Revenue Service.

Hon. Wm. M. Meredith,
Secretary of the Treasury, Washington, D. C.

U. S. Revenue Brig Lawrence,
Sansolito, California, November 30, 1849.

Sir: In consequence of my pay being inadequate for my support on this station, and the precarious situation of the officers of the revenue service, (a number of them having already been dismissed without warning,) I am compelled to tender my resignation for your acceptance as first lieutenant in the revenue service of the United States.

I am, respectfully, your obedient servant,
J. S. S. CHADDOCK,
First Lieut. U. S. Revenue Service.

Capt. Alex. V. Fraser,
Com. U. S. Revenue Brig Lawrence,
Bay of San Francisco, California.

A true copy of the original.
ALEX. V. FRASER, *Captain.*

DEPARTMENT OF THE INTERIOR.

Department of the Interior,
Washington, January 12, 1850.

Sir: In compliance with your directions, accompanying a copy of the resolution of the Senate of the 17th instant, I send herewith a list of all the officers and agents appointed and in the employment of this department in California and New Mexico, together with the letters of instructions under which they have severally acted, and all letters addressed to them by this department, and also all the communications, of whatsoever nature, received from them, in writing or in print, by this department.

I have the honor to be, with great respect, your obedient servant,
T. EWING, *Secretary.*

To the President of the United States.

No. 1.

List of persons appointed and in the employment of the Department of the Interior in California and New Mexico.

IN CALIFORNIA.

John Wilson, Indian agent at the Great Salt Lake.
Adam Johnston, Indian sub-agent for the valley of the San Joachim.
John A. Sutter, Indian sub-agent on the Sacramento river.

IN NEW MEXICO.

James S. Calhoun, Indian agent at Santa Fe.
John C. Hays, Indian sub-agent on the Rio Gila.
Special agent.—William Carey Jones, special agent of the government to examine and report upon claims and titles to land in California and New Mexico.
Mexican Boundary Commission.—John C. Frémont has been appointed commissioner on the part of the United States under the treaty of Guadalupe Hidalgo, in place of John B. Weller, but has not yet entered upon duty.

The persons employed in this commission are as follows:

A. B. Gray, surveyor. (Salary not fixed.)
Wm. R. Rinder, in the employ of Commissioner - $400 00 per annum.
Wm. T. De Bree, heliotropeman - - - 400 00 do
C. J. Whiting, principal assistant to surveyor - 1,800 00 do
Francis Stone, in the employ of Commissioner - 400 00 do
Edward Ingraham, Major Emory's corps - - 400 00 do
O. S. Witherby, in the employ of Commissioner - 400 00 do
O. S. Witherby, as quartermaster - - - 1,000 00 do

Charles C. Parry, assistant computer	600 00	per annum.
Moses C. Conner, carpenter, at $1 50	1 50	per day.
Urbano Idalgo, laborer, at $12	12 00	per month.
Wm. Harney, servant, and employé at $30	30 00	do
W. R. Coleman, employé at $400	400 00	per annum.
James Mooney, principal computer Major Emory	1,000 00	do
Mary Kirk, washerwoman, at $1 50	1 50	per day.
G. C. Gardner, assistant to Major Emory	400 00	per annum.
F. M. Holley, servant to Major Emory	25 00	per month.
H. H. Robinson, secretary to Commissioner	1,500 00	per annum.
Gilbert Murdock, employ Major Emory	400 00	do
E. K. Chamberlin, surgeon	1,200 00	do
Henry Clayton, draughtsman	1,000 00	do
John H. Foster, sub-assistant surveyor	800 00	do
Dennis Gahagan, employé	1,000 00	do
George F. Hooper, sub-assistant	800 00	do
Frederick Emory, sub-assistant	800 00	do
James M. Robinson, employé	400 00	do
William H. Taylor, sub assistant surveyor	800 00	do
Louis Kzouzewski, servant and cook	30 00	per month.
D. Gahagan, interpreter and translator	1,000 00	per annum.
Gilbert Murdock, employé	400 00	do
Wm. D. Miller, employé	30 00	do

C. L. Weller, claiming to be attached to the commission. (Salary not known.)

No. 2.

Correspondence between the United States and the Mexican Boundary Commission.

WASHINGTON, *January* 3, 1848.

SIR: I think it proper that you should be informed that a very considerable portion of the most valuable instruments used on the northeastern boundary survey, and now in possession of Major J. D. Graham, do not belong to the Department of State; and that it is exceedingly probable that, under arrangements in progress, they will be needed by the Topographical Bureau for other surveys; and I think it will not be practicable for the State Department, without inconvenience to other branches of the public service, to obtain the use of them. The instruments that do belong to the State Department are insufficient in number, and many of them not adapted to the nature of the service to which they are to be applied—the survey of the boundary between the United States and Mexico.

Army order No. 65 assigns me to the command of the party to be detailed from the army to run that boundary. Under that order, I had the honor to report to you in person, the day following the date of that order. I then stated my impression that immediate steps should be taken to see that proper instruments were procured for the survey. A more exact knowledge subsequently derived from Major Graham of the number and condition of the instruments which he designs to turn over to the department, makes it my duty to inform you that, unless immediate steps are taken, it is probable the instruments cannot be had, in order to enable the commission to meet agreeably to the terms of the treaty.

I beg leave respectfully to suggest, as I am already assigned to duty under your orders, that such of the instruments as may belong to the State Department may be immediately turned over to me, that I may proceed to put them in condition for service; to make such alterations in them as may be required to meet the peculiarities of the service, and to prepare the information by which you will be enabled to supply the deficiencies when the appropriation for running and marking the boundary becomes available. This recommendation, if adopted, need involve no immediate expenditure. The propriety of this work being confided to the officer who is to use the instruments, I am sure, need not be dwelt upon. He will be held responsible for the results, and should, therefore, be allowed the selection, within reasonable limits, of the means by which he is to attain them.

I have the honor to be your obedient servant,
W. H. EMORY,
Brevet Major U. S. Army.

Hon. JAMES BUCHANAN,
Secretary of State.

ENGINEER DEPARTMENT,
Washington, January 10, 1849.

SIR: On the receipt of your letter of the 3d instant, asking for the loan of the zenith telescope belonging to this department, that had been for some time in the hands of Major Graham, of the topographical engineers, I referred it to the superintendent of the Military Academy, requesting him "to report forthwith whether the instrument can be spared from the course of instruction in the department of philosophy, Major Graham having notified that it is ready, with the other instruments loaned to him, to be returned if wanted at the academy."

The superintendent, in his reply just received, says, after consulting with the Professor of Philosophy, "that the particular instrument referred to by Major Emory would be very useful in the department of philosophy." This being the case, and knowing that the instrument was sent, in the first instance, to the academy, at the request of Professor Bartlett, for use in practical instruction in astronomy, I am under the necessity of declining the proposed loan.

Very respectfully, your obedient servant,
JOS. G. TOTTEN,
Brevet Brigadier General, and Chief Engineer.

Major W. H. EMORY,
U. S. Army, Washington.

WASHINGTON, *January* 11, 1849.

DEAR SIR: As far as I have been able to ascertain, the two instruments mentioned in the enclosed letter of General Totten were purchased for the use of the Ohio and Michigan boundary, in 1835, but, the appropriation having been expended under the War Department, the instruments may be considered as belonging to that department. They are both of great value, and one of them, the zenith telescope, was used by me on the northeastern boundary. It will appear, by the letter of General Totten, they are now both required in the department to which they belong.

I have the honor to be, with great regard, your obedient servant,

W. H. EMORY.

Hon. JAMES BUCHANAN,
 Secretary of State.

NEW YORK, *February* 4, 1849.

SIR: In compliance with instructions of the Department of State, January 19, 1849, I have the honor to report, that I have received from Major J. D. Graham such instruments as were deemed "necessary for correctly running and marking the boundary line" between the United States and Mexico. Two invoices—one dated New York, January 29, 1849, the other dated Boston, February 1, 1849—exhibit the character and condition of these instruments, and are herewith enclosed.

I have been compelled to adopt, in a great measure, Major Graham's report of the condition of the instruments, as it would take more time than I am allowed to set up each instrument and examine it in detail.

The character of the higher class of astronomical instruments, such as the Troughton & Semmes telescope, the transit, and the altitude and azimuth instrument, though admirably adapted for service on the northeastern boundary, intersected, as that boundary was at many points, by the great thoroughfares of travel, are, in consequence of their size, unsuited for general use on the Mexican boundary, and can only be used at or near points accessible by sea—San Diego and the mouth of the Del Norte. At these points, however, they can be profitably used.

The repacking such of the instruments as required it, and were of convenient size to carry into the interior on the backs of animals, was completed yesterday: many of these could have been rendered still more portable by placing the different parts of the same instrument in different boxes; but this is a nice operation, involving the skill of the best instrument makers, and would take one or two months to complete; it has, therefore, not been attempted.

The region in which we operate being destitute of trees of sufficient size to afford stands for the instruments, I have ordered castings to be made for portable stands. I have also ordered the observing tents put in condition for service. Both the castings and the fixtures for the tents will be completed in the course of the week.

I now proceed, in further pursuance of your instructions, to "report what other instruments" are deemed necessary for the survey, together with their probable cost, and where they may be obtained the most speedily and upon the best terms.

Instruments.	Price.	Where to be obtained.
1 pocket chronometer*	$200	W. C. Bond, Boston.
1 box chronometer	285	Do do
2 heliotropes, at $100	200	E. & G. W. Blunt, New York.
2 reconnoitring glasses, at $50	100	Do do
1 portable astronomical telescope	190	Do do
4 Nautical Almanacs, 1849	10	Do do
4 do 1850	10	Do do
1 copy Catalogue Stars, Br. Ass'n	20	Do do
1 set of charts, coast of California	2	Do do
1 Daniels's hygrometer	15	Do do
4 Hassler's Logarithms, at $1	4	Do do
6 thermometers, each $4	24	Do do
2 artificial horizons, at $20, (with boxes for mercury)	40	Do do
6 observing lamps	15	Do do
1 36-inch transit	400	Troughton & Semmes, London.
1 36-inch zenith telescope	700	Do do
4 cases drawing instruments, at $10	40	E. & G. W. Blunt, New York.
4 bottles of ether (sulphuric.)		
½ bushel plaster of Paris.		
2 observing tents, at $40	80	

*Mr Bond has one by Park & Frodsham, No. 648, of tried excellence.

1 equatorial stand, price estimated at $100.

If an arrangement could be made by which the use can be obtained of the transit and the zenith telescopes mentioned in my letter to you of the 11th January last, the two corresponding instruments estimated for in the above list, respectively at 400 and 700 dollars, would not be needed.

These instruments are now at the store of Messrs. E. & G. W. Blunt, New York, awaiting transportation to West Point. The object of sending these instruments there being for the purposes of instruction, as stated in General Totten's letter enclosed in mine of the 11th, I would propose, if no other means could be adopted, to place these instruments at the disposal of the State Department, (where they have been for many years,) to exchange for them the large and valuable altitude and azimuth instrument, by Troughton & Semmes. This is one of the best instruments of the kind in the country, and combines all the parts of both the other instruments; but, unfortunately, it is too large for use on the Mexican boundary. The instrument referred to is the first named on the invoice herewith sent.

A letter received from the Hon. John B. Weller, commissioner, &c., requests that all the instruments intended to go overland may be sent to New Orleans before the 23d.

I return herewith the list of instruments furnished me from the records of the Department of State.

I have the honor to be, with great respect, your obedient servant,

W. H. EMORY, *Bt. Major U. S. Army.*

Hon. JAMES BUCHANAN, *Secretary of State.*

NEW ORLEANS, *March* 7, 1849.

SIR: I received half the amount of draft sent me for three thousand dollars by United States commissioner, upon Secretary of the Treasury, for purposes necessary to outfit and expenses of party, &c., in the boundary line service. When I left Washington ten days ago, immediately after receiving the certificate to a copy of the treaty map, it was supposed that I would meet the commissioner here, and in that event would not require the balance of the amount of draft charged to me.

I advised Mr. Weller that we were coming, but, from the irregularity of the telegraph, presume he did not receive my despatch. I found on my arrival to-day that three of the other officers attached to the survey, from unavoidable detention, (frozen state of the Ohio river,) did not reach this city, either, until two days after the departure of Mr. Weller, who sailed on the 2d instant. I therefore found it necessary to advise you of my want of the other fifteen hundred dollars, and to save time I sent the despatch by telegraph, asking permission to draw on the department for the same.

A vessel will leave this for Chagres in a short time, and I apprehend there will be no delay to prevent our reaching San Diego almost as soon as the commissioner.

With the highest esteem, I remain, very respectfully, your obedient servant,

ANDREW B. GRAY,
Surveyor under 5th article of treaty with Mexico.

Hon. Mr. CLAYTON,
Secretary of State, Washington city.

PANAMA, NEW GRENADA,
March 20, 1849.

SIR: I have the honor to report that, under instructions from your department of the 24th January last, I embarked from New Orleans with the necessary number of employés, on the 2d instant, and reached this city on the 16th. On the 30th January, at my request, a letter was addressed to the American consul in this city, directing him to have transportation ready for me and the party by the 12th instant at Cruces. And although this letter had been duly received, the transportation had not been provided, nor could I hear of the consul in any way until I reached Panama. His conduct here, generally, has given much dissatisfaction to the citizens of the United States emigrating to California; but I have not given such investigation to the various charges made against him as to enable me to say how far they are true.

The charges for transportation over the isthmus are enormous, and there is but little prospect at present of a diminution.

The steamer "Irus" navigates the Chagres river only fifteen miles, and passengers and freight are carried from thence to Gorgona, about thirty-five miles, in canoes. The greater portion of my party will remain at Gorgona until all the supplies reach this place. I have with me four months' supplies for the whole party—six months' supplies having been shipped, previous to my leaving the United States, from New York to San Diego direct.

There is no transportation here now, and from present indications it is exceedingly doubtful whether the party can be gotten to San Diego for months to come, unless a government vessel should touch at this point. I intend, however, to obtain transportation for myself by the first steamer which comes in, so as to comply with the 5th article of the treaty. It is probable I will have to go to San Francisco, and travel by land thence to San Diego.

It is important, in my opinion, that the appropriation made by the act of Congress of the 12th of August, 1848, to defray the expenses, &c., of running the boundary, should be placed in a position where my drafts upon it will be duly honored. The employés generally will desire to receive their pay in the United States; and I have to request, if consistent with the views of the department, that the funds may be drawn from the treasury and placed to my credit in New York—say the Bank of America; I will then be enabled to discharge the demands against the commission without difficulty or delay. The amount now in my hands will be wholly inadequate to pay the expenses here and transportation to San Diego. Major Emory, chief of the topographical engineers, reached this city on yesterday. Mr. Gray, the surveyor, has not yet arrived. As his presence at San Diego previous to the 30th May is indispensable, I may possibly be detained by his movements. At all events, the department may be assured that all in my power will be done to carry out the provisions of the treaty.

In the meanwhile, I have the honor to be, most respectfully, your obedient servant,

JOHN B. WELLER,
U. S. Commissioner.

Hon. SECRETARY OF STATE.

PANAMA, *March* 25, 1849.

SIR: I have the honor to report to you that I joined the commission for "running and marking the boundary between the United States and Mexico," at this place, on the 17th instant, in charge of all the astronomical apparatus and surveying instruments for the use of the commission, except those sent by the steamers Northerner and Senator *via* Cape Horn, of which you have been heretofore advised.

The commissioner reached here one day before me. I exhibited to him my instructions from the State and War Departments, and informed him of the condition and place of the apparatus confided to my care, and the steps taken, under instructions of the Department of State, in regard to it.

It was not possible, as those instructions contemplated, to leave New York before the 1st March; nor was it practicable to carry the instruments overland to New Orleans, to ship on board the steamer Alabama, which sailed from that port for Chagres on the 2d instant; and I was compelled to ship them, and take passage for myself and party, in the steamer Northerner, which sailed direct from New York to Chagres.

Everything has arrived here in safety, and in good condition for immediate service, except some of the astronomical books and tables, left with one of my assistants and my servant in New Orleans.

The means of getting from this place to San Diego are left to the commissioner. It may be proper, however, to inform you that, being charged, in addition to my other duties, with the command of the military escort intended to protect the commission, I will make the attempt to reach San Diego in time to report the escort in readiness as soon as the commission assembles, so that no delay will happen from that cause.

I have the honor to be your obedient servant,
W. H. EMORY,
Brevet Major United States Army, &c.

Hon. Secretary of State.

Steamship Falcon,
At Sea, March 26, 1849.

Sir: Up to the last moment before leaving New Orleans, I waited with anxious expectation a despatch from your department; but, receiving none, I finally sailed, early on the morning of the 21st instant, for Chagres, which latter port we expect to reach in all to-morrow.

At Panama I hope to join the commissioner, and to proceed with him to San Diego. I should have waited till hearing from you; but, finding that little reliance is to be placed in the present system of conducting telegraphic communications, and fearing lest no other favorable opportunity would again occur in some time for me to proceed on my mission, I deemed it advisable to take the responsibility of at once embarking. I hope it will have met with your approval, and that of the President.

I forward a few papers, which I had withdrawn for the purpose of making copies, and which I beg leave to ask may be filed for reference in your department. They are the originals.

I have the honor to remain, very faithfully, your obedient servant,
ANDREW B. GRAY,
United States Surveyor under treaty with Mexico.

Hon. J. M. Clayton,
Secretary of State, Washington city.

Panama, *May* 9, 1849.

Sir: The enclosed package, addressed to Mr. Wm. Cranch Bond, director of the observatory at Cambridge, contains a series of astronomical and other observations, intended for review by the A. academy of Boston. These observations, and the objects in sending them to the academy, being connected directly with the service on the boundary, with which I have been honored by the Department of State, induces me to request that they may be forwarded under the frank of the department.

I have the honor to be your obedient servant,
W. H. EMORY,
Brevet Major United States Army, Chief Astronomer and Topographical Engineer Mexican boundary survey.

Hon. J. M. Clayton,
Secretary of State.

PANAMA, *May* 23, 1849.

SIR: Colonel Weller informed me that he left "a quartermaster behind," and that when this quartermaster sailed for San Diego, funds would be left to defray all the necessary expenses of those of my party remaining. Should I be right in supposing you to be the quartermaster referred to by Colonel Weller, I have to request you to inform me in whose hands funds will be left after your departure in the Oregon, and who will be responsible for the payment of the necessary expenses here, and transportation hence, of those now under my charge. At the same time, while I must, for the want of funds, submit, I strongly protest against your decision of yesterday, in refusing to pay for the passage of those young gentlemen of the commission whom the United States consul, at my request, agreed to add to the number of those designated by you for passage to San Diego in the steamer Oregon.

Very respectfully, your obedient servant,
A. W. WHIPPLE.

O. S. WITHERBY, Esq., &c., &c., *Panama*.

PANAMA, *May* 23, 1849.

DEAR SIR: Mr. Kaufman will act as quartermaster from this time, and will defray all necessary expenses of the members of the commission. He will assign quarters to Messrs. Ingraham, Gardner, and Parry. Your accounts up to this day will be paid by me. You are *right* in supposing I am quartermaster. I should suppose you would have found it out before. Mr. Kaufman will have the full control of all matters hereafter.

Your obedient servant,
O. S. WITHERBY

Lieutenant WHIPPLE.

PANAMA, *May* 17, 1849.

SIR: Under instructions from Major Emory, I have been left here in charge of that portion of his party which cannot obtain passage to San Diego in the steamer Panama.

From the instructions above mentioned, the following is an extract: "I have this day requested the commissioner to place you in funds for the purpose of defraying the expense of detention in Panama and the transportation to San Diego."

Having heard that you are to sail this day in the Panama, I take the liberty of asking to be supplied at once with the funds necessary for the subsistence and transportation of my party. I feel assured, that to one with your knowledge of military discipline, I need only call your attention to the fact that I have orders which must be executed, and that, for the pecuniary means necessary to enable me to accomplish that with which I am charged, I can look to no one but the commissioner himself.

I have the honor to be, with high respect, your obedient servant,
A. W. WHIPPLE.

Hon. JNO. B. WELLER,
United States Commissioner, &c., &c.

PANAMA, N. G., *May* 17, 1849.

SIR: In answer to your note of this date, I have to say that, although I expect to sail to-day on the Panama, I leave a quartermaster behind, whose duty it is to provide subsistence, transportation, &c., for those of the party who may be detained. He will leave, under my instructions, on the Oregon; and up to that time he will see that all the necessary expenses of the party are paid. If you and those placed under your charge are detained beyond that time, funds will be left to defray all the necessary expenses.

Very respectfully, your obedient servant,
JOHN B. WELLER,
United States Commissioner.

Lieut. WHIPPLE, U. S. A.

PANAMA, *May* 13, 1849.

SIR: The commissioner having informed me that he could obtain passage in the steamer Panama for only a small portion of the force intended to aid me in my duties on the boundary, I leave you in the city of Panama, in charge of that portion which remains.

I have this day requested the commissioner to place you in funds for the purpose of defraying the expense of detention in Panama and the transportation to San Diego, where it is desirable, indeed all important, you should be with the whole party as speedily as possible. To effect this, and preserve order, I delegate to you full authority to act according to your judgment.

Very respectfully, yours,
W. H. EMORY,
Brevet Major United States Army, Chief Astronomer and Topographical Engineer boundary commission.

Lieut. A. W. WHIPPLE,
Corps Topographical Engineers.

PANAMA, N. G., *May* 14, 1849.

SIR: A detachment of Major Emory's party having been left at this place under my charge, I beg leave to submit the following estimate for its subsistence during our probable detention in Panama:

For board and quarters for six persons attached to the boundary commission, 30 days, at two dollars each per day	$360 00
For funds to cover contingent expenses, the purchase of candles, cooking utensils, &c., necessary for the use of my party while engaged upon boundary service in the field	140 00
Amount	500 00

A requisition for the above is respectfully submitted by me.

Your obedient servant,
A. W. WHIPPLE,
Lieut. U. S. A., and attached to the U. S. Boundary Commission.

Hon. JOHN B. WELLER,
United States Commissioner.

PANAMA, N. G., *May 23, 1849.*

SIR: Being obliged to embark at once upon the steamer Oregon, leaving behind me the assistants who have been employed for service, under Major W. H. Emory, upon the boundary between the United States and Mexico, I deem it my duty to myself and to the government of the United States to transmit to the department at Washington the enclosed correspondence.

It will, I hope, in some degree, explain why those most important to the service for which Major Emory and myself have been detailed are obliged to remain in Panama. As I must this moment go on board the steamer, I have no time for explanations which I desire to make.

I have the honor to be, very respectfully, your obedient servant,
A. W. WHIPPLE,
Lieut. U. S. Top. Eng., and attached to U. S. B. C.

Hon. SECRETARY OF STATE
of the United States.

PANAMA, *May 23, 1849.*

SIR: Your note of the 22d instant has been received. An arrangement had previously been made between Mr. O. S. Witherby and myself, by which it was determined that a certain number of persons attached to the boundary commission could be accommodated upon the steamer Oregon; that number was designated by Mr. Witherby, and the list arranged to his satisfaction.

Upon the strength of your recommendation, and the apparent necessity to the commission for the services of those designated by you, their names were added by me to the number already upon the list, although much against my desire, the boat being already too much crowded, and his list, with the prices of passage attached, was sent to Mr. Witherby, for a draft to cover the amount. This he refused, alleging he was the person designated by the commissioner to make the selection of those who were to go, and that a Mr. Conner, carpenter, and others, were more necessary to the service of the commission than those designated by you. He was willing to pay for their extra tickets, provided he could select the persons to receive them; but when informed that the steamer was already crowded, that tickets for the persons in question were only issued upon the supposed necessity of their presence in San Diego being indispensable, he preferred detaining the whole until the arrival of the steamer California, rather than any should go other than those selected by himself. For yourself and servant I have secured passage.

In haste, respectfully, your obedient servant,
W. NELSON.

Lieutenant WHIPPLE,
United States Army, &c., &c.

PANAMA, *May 17, 1849.*

DEAR SIR: I send herewith a copy of a letter to Colonel Weller, and his reply, that you may understand the condition in which I am left by the commissioner

In the first place, several days since, I made up my accounts for transportation and per diem allowance, according to the expressed desire of the commissioner, which, when presented, he was willing to take and send to the department at home, but refused to pay.

At the same time, I presented, at his request, an estimate and requisition for the subsistence of those left under my charge. This requisition he never answered. Finding myself about to be left penniless, and absolutely out of the reach of assistance, the correspondence of this date followed. I sent to him, also, a message by Mr. Gardner, with a request that he would send me $400, and take a receipt, such as follows: "Received of the Hon. John B. Weller, United States commissioner, the sum of $400, which sum is designed to pay for subsistence and transportation for myself to San Diego, and is to be refunded to the commissioner, or covered by proper vouchers." This he returned without comment. I then wrote a note to Major Vinton, desiring to know from what appropriation my transportation should be paid, under the circumstances stated. He returned a verbal message merely, referring me to Major McKinstry, who is now on the steamer, out of my reach.

Should I, therefore, be left here without funds to pay my expenses here, and obtain transportation for myself and servant to San Diego; and should my communication with you, my commanding officer, be cut off, I shall be compelled to write the circumstances to Colonel Abert, and have the matter brought before the government, that the responsibility may fall where it belongs. In case the person designated by the commissioner as a quartermaster promptly pays the expenses which I may deem necessary, I shall acquiesce. Otherwise, it will be necessary to inquire from higher authority whether an officer of the army must be subject to the control of an irresponsible person, without a commission and unknown to the government of the United States.

I am, respectfully, yours, &c.,
A. W. WHIPPLE.

Major EMORY,
Chief Astronomer and Top. Eng. Boundary Survey.

PANAMA, *May* 17, 1849.

DEAR SIR: In Washington I was detailed for duty upon the boundary between the United States and Mexico. Will you please to inform me from what appropriation I am to receive my mileage or travelling expenses to San Diego? If from the appropriation for the boundary survey, please refer me to the regulation which authorizes it. If from the quartermaster's department, I would be glad to know whether you are prepared to pay it. Necessity is my excuse for troubling you so soon after your illness.

Very truly, yours, &c.,
A. W. WHIPPLE,
Lieutenant United States Army.

Major VINTON,
Quartermaster United States Army.

PANAMA, *May* 22, 1849.

SIR: The enclosed copy of instructions from Major Emory to myself will show you the position I occupy with reference to the United States and to the boundary commission.

The plan of operations upon the boundary line, submitted by Major Emory to the Secretary of State, requires immediately, at San Diego, the presence of not only myself, but also the civil assistants who have been assigned to duty in his department. I therefore, as an officer of the army of the United States, feel it my duty to look to you, as consul for the same government, for assistance in obtaining passage for myself and servant in the first steamer which sails hence for San Diego. The civil assistants referred to above, are: Dr. Charles Parry, computer; Mr. Edward Ingraham, recorder and assistant computer; Mr. G. Clinton Gardner, do.; Mr. B. B. Ludlum, do.; Mr. R. Rust; Mr. Francis Holly, employé.

The services of the six persons above mentioned are important to the commission, and I shall much regret to leave any of them behind. But should it be impossible to obtain passage immediately for all, I would designate Assistants Parry, Ingraham, and Gardner, and employé Holly, as indispensable for the performance of the astronomical duty, on which the commencement of the survey of the United States and Mexican boundary line depends; and must, therefore, in behalf of the boundary commission, request your influence to secure for them a passage to San Diego in the steamer Oregon, which is about to sail from this place.

I have the honor to be, sir, very respectfully, your obedient servant,
A. W. WHIPPLE.

WM. NELSON, Esq.,
Consul of the U. S., Panama, New Grenada.

SAN DIEGO, CALIFORNIA, *June* 16, 1849.

SIR: I have the honor to report my arrival at this place on the 1st instant, with ten of my party. I regret that the *unnecessary* detention of the steamer at Panama, by the agent of Messrs. Aspinwall & Co., prevented me from complying with the requisitions of the treaty. Another portion of those engaged upon the survey came in a few days since on the Oregon, and the balance still remain at Panama.

In consequence of this division, I have been subjected to much trouble and a good deal of expense, which otherwise would not have been incurred. General Garcia Condé, who, I understand, is the commissioner appointed by the republic of Mexico, has not yet arrived. I received, however, a few days since, a letter from our consul at San Blas, advising me that he sailed from that port in a British vessel for San Diego, on the 24th ultimo, with his suite and one hundred and seventy soldiers. His arrival, therefore, is daily expected. No time will be lost on our part in organizing the commission, and placing the parties in the field. In the absence of instructions, (if agreeable to the Mexican commissioner,) we will proceed with the work as if the meeting had taken place within the time prescribed by the treaty. It will require some time to secure the necessary transportation to pass from the Pacific to the Colorado, and it may be found wholly impracticable to prosecute the work from this direction beyond that point. In the existing state of military discipline here, I apprehend the necessary escort could not be easily obtained beyond that river. Two companies have been reported to me by the commanding officer of the escort—one company of sixty-one dragoons; the other, twenty-two infantry, effective and non effective. I have no information as to the number agreed upon by the respective governments, but in my opinion this force will be entirely too small. Our expenses have already been so great, that I fear the appropriation made by the act of Congress of August 12, 1848, will be quite exhausted soon after the work is commenced. Our limited means will retard our progress very much, and in the end subject us to expenses which otherwise might have been avoided.

The Congress of 1848, I am sure, could not have anticipated the state of affairs in this country, else the appropriation would have been much more liberal. As it is, I can only promise to use the means at my command to the best advantage.

I have the honor to be, very respectfully, your obedient servant,
JOHN B. WELLER,
U. S. Commissioner.

Hon. JOHN M. CLAYTON,
Secre ary of State, Washington, D. C.

PUEBLO OF SAN JOSE, *August*, 1849.

SIR: I have had the honor to receive, by the hands of Mr. Beale, United States navy, your letter conferring upon me the post of commissioner of the United States for the determination of our boundary line with Mexico.

I feel much gratification in accepting the appointment, and beg to offer through you to the President my acknowledgments for the mark of confidence bestowed upon me, and which he may be assured is fully appreciated.

Colonel Weller is now at San Francisco, having just arrived from the south. His reports of the actual state of the survey will probably suggest instructions for me. I will see him within a few days, and, after having made myself acquainted with the condition of the work, shall be able to communicate understandingly with the department.

I have the honor to be, with much respect, your obedient servant,
J. C. FREMONT.

To the Hon. JOHN M. CLAYTON,
Secretary of State.

CAMP RILEY, CALIFORNIA, *September* 15, 1849.

SIR: General Order No. 65, dated Adjutant General's office, Washington, December 27, 1848, placed me in command of the escort to the United States boundary commission, and directed me to report for further instructions to the Secretary of State. I did so report, and received an order transferring to my custody all the astronomical and surveying instruments destined for service on the boundary between the United States and Mexico; I received at the same time information that I was to be the chief astronomer and topographical engineer on the work. In the instructions to the United States commissioner, dated Washington, February 13, 1849, (a copy of which I obtained at my own request,) I am designated as the chief astronomer and topographical engineer.

Beyond this, I have received from the Department of State no instructions, nor have I received a letter of appointment. Being on the ground as commander of the escort, I have retained the custody of these instruments, and have performed the duties above designated. It is questionable in my mind whether the Department of State has followed up its intention, conveyed in the preliminary instructions of February 13. But if it has done so, and I am considered as occupying the position of chief astronomer and topographical engineer, I now desire, for reasons which in my judgment form an insurmountable obstacle to the proper performance of these duties, to be released from all duty with this commission. I request the person may be designated to whom the instruments in my custody shall be turned over; they are at present distributed between Captain Hardcastle, Lieutenant Whipple, Mr. A. B. Gray, and myself. In due season an account will be rendered of my astronomical determinations on this work, as well as those of the officers under my command, and the commission will be furnished with the results. By the time of receiving my recall, I hope to have finished the determination of the astronomical line forming the boundary between the Pacific and the mouth of the Gila river; and it will be a convenient point for the transfer of the work to other hands.

The commissioner has been absent on business since the 16th August, and I am without the means of knowing what is to be done with the civil assistants brought out by me; but I respectfully ask consideration for them, more particularly for the two scientific gentlemen, Professor James Nooney and Dr. C. C. Parry, and that, should their services be no longer required, directions may be given to have their expenses paid back to their homes.

I am, very respectfully, your obedient servant,
W. H. EMORY,
Brevet Major Corps Top. Eng., &c., &c.

Hon. J. M. Clayton,
Secretary of State.

San Diego, California, *October* 4, 1849.

Sir: The sketch which accompanies this note will show you the position of the initial point of boundary between our country and that of the Mexican republic, as fixed by the survey of the southern part of the port of San Diego and measurement of the marine league, agreeably to the decision of the joint commission of July 9, and in conformity with the fifth article of the treaty with Mexico. It will also show approximately the direction that the line will take over the ridge of high lands which come down to the Pacific and across the valley of the river "Tia Juan"—the same valley up which we travelled on our recent reconnoissance—to the mountains separating the desert from the ocean. I had advised the surveyor on the part of Mexico of my having completed the surveys necessary for me to determine the southernmost point of the port, as called for in the treaty; and a few days after your departure to San Francisco, we exhibited to each other small plans of our triangulations, &c., which agreed without any difference. But the changes from local causes by time, &c., which have taken place in that portion of the port, and the peculiar features which it now presents, caused Mr. Jalayer to think the southernmost point to be further to the north than I had believed was represented on the map accompanying the treaty. A difference in the season of the year, which possibly may have been the case in which the two surveys were made, (that of 1782 and that of our own,) might also make a difference in its appearance. I pointed the position of one or two points in the range of bluffs bordering the low salt flats, and in which time seemed to have made no change, and found the identity of this range very nearly with the black curve line, representing the boundary of the port, of the map of Don Juan Pantoja. He desired to make a few more measurements, which he did, and advised me of his being induced to believe that the line of coast on the treaty map was the same very nearly with the high lands, or line of bluffs, mentioned. The difference between the point agreed upon by us and that first supposed by him was some 3,500 feet, and which places the initial point that distance further south. The parallel from which we commenced the measurement of the marine league was that of the highest point at which indications were noticed of the overflow of salt water, or the water of the port. Every degree of accuracy was pursued in the marine league measurement; and the number of metres taken for its length was 5564.6, according to the authority of "Francœur." The double red line upon the sketch will show that two efforts were necessary to avoid inequalities and irregularities in the surface of the ground, and to obtain a level plain as far as practicable. The initial point, as will be seen by the sketch, falls upon the sand beach within a hundred metres of a plain triangularly shaped, and elevated by a bluff bank about fifty feet above the level of the sea. It is also backed by a mountainous spur which puts out from the great chain reaching from Upper to Lower California, and is an excellent natural position for a monument to fix the limits of the two countries.

My parties are now actually engaged in the field; and when I will have returned from the reconnoissance to the mouth of the Gila river along the line, and which I am desirous of accomplishing within the next twenty days, I will then, I hope, have made the requisite triangulation to fix the mouth and vicinity of that river for mapping; also, have obtained in that time sufficient topography, and notes enough of the line between the Pacific and that point. This will enable us, as soon as the latitudes and longitudes of the two extremes are determined by the astronomical party engaged upon that duty, to make out a very correct plan of this whole line between said points, sufficient for the purpose of demarcation, and for the erection of such monuments at those points decided upon at any time by the joint commission hereafter.

I remain, very respectfully, your obedient servant,
ANDREW B. GRAY, *U. S. Surveyor.*

Hon. JOHN B. WELLER,
United States Commissioner, &c., &c.

SAN DIEGO, CALIFORNIA, *October* 5, 1849.

SIR: I have the honor to inform you that, since my despatch of the 28th July last, the commission has been actively engaged in executing the important duties imposed by the treaty. The boundary line, from the initial point on the Pacific to the junction of the Gila with the Colorado, will be an astronomical line connecting the two points. To obtain the azimuth of this line, the determination of latitude and longitude of its extremities was necessary. The determination of this line is nearly completed. Major Emory, the chief astronomer of the commission, finding no suitable point for an observatory at the initial point on the Pacific, established one at "Camp Riley," and determined its geographical position in latitude and longitude by no less than three hundred observations on stars near the zenith, and its longitude by observations on every culmination of the moon and the moon-culminating stars which were observable since the establishment of his observatory on the 20th July last; and these results have been carried from his observatory to the initial points by a single triangle. In a very few days all the necessary computations will be completed.

On the 8th ultimo, Lieutenant Whipple, of the astronomical party, with a suitable escort, was sent to the Gila, and is now at the junction of that river with the Colorado, for the purpose of observing with a view to determine the latitude and longitude of that point. Captain Hardcastle, of the same corps, in the mean time, has been despatched to the mountains, this side of the desert, between the two points, to conduct the signals; by means of which Major Emory will be enabled to connect the two extremes of the line in longitude. In the event this fails, the absolute determinations in longitude made respectively by Major Emory and Lieutenant Whipple will be resorted to, and the azimuth of the line forming the boundary completed and marked on the ground. I will in a few days send a detachment of the surveying party along the line to make a topographical sketch of the country between the two points; and I have no doubt, within twenty or thirty days, this great work on the west side of the Colorado will be completed, and nothing will remain except to fill in a few intermediate points. This, with the placing of suitable monuments on the Pacific and at the intersection of the Gila with the Colorado, will complete what has always been regarded the most difficult portion of the work. The distance will be about one hundred and thirty miles. As a natural boundary (the Gila and the Rio Grande) constitutes a large portion of the remainder of the line, it is thought no difficulty will be found in establishing it.

I must again repeat, that unless Congress, at an early day in its next session, appropriates the necessary means, the work must be suspended. My movements have already been much retarded for the want of funds; and I trust the commission may not be thus embarrassed in future. If the joint commission is broken up from any cause, the work is inevitably suspended for an indefinite period.

I send herewith a map prepared by the surveyor, Mr. Gray, with an explanatory note, showing his operations in determining the initial point in the boundary. No communication whatever has been received from your department since the 15th March last.

I have the honor to be, very respectfully, your obedient servant,
JOHN B. WELLER,
U. S. Commissioner.

Hon. JOHN M. CLAYTON,
Secretary of State.

SAN DIEGO, CALIFORNIA,
November 3, 1849.

SIR: The forms and ceremonies necessary to fix and determine, upon the face of the earth, the initial point in the boundary between the United States and the republic of Mexico, on the Pacific, were gone through with on the 10th ultimo, in presence of various members of the joint commission and numerous other witnesses.

In consequence of some changes which have evidently taken place in the southern part of the port of San Diego since the survey of Don Juan Pantoja in 1782, it became necessary to make an accurate survey of that part of the harbor. This was executed, by the surveyors on each side, some weeks since. A difference of a few feet was found to exist between the representatives of the two governments, as to the precise point which ought to be regarded as "the southernmost point of the port of San Diego." This, however, was soon adjusted, in the spirit of compromise, by the commissioners on the ground, and a point selected, from which "a marine league due south" was measured.

At the place thus selected as the initial point a temporary monument has been erected, until suitable materials for the construction of a permanent one can be obtained. The monument will be placed five hundred feet from the ocean, and on a point of land forty-two feet above the level of the sea. Its precise latitude, as agreed upon, is $32° 31' 59''.58$, which will make it about eighteen miles south of this town. A small portion of the computation necessary to determine the exact longitude has not yet been completed, and, consequently, I am not now able to give it with precision.

The astronomical detachment, under the charge of Lieutenant Whipple, referred to in my last communication, is still at the mouth of the Gila, having nearly completed the observations necessary to determine the geographical position of that point. His return is expected in a few days.

On the 12th ultimo the surveyor, with a portion of his corps, left here for the Gila, with the view to examine the point at which that river empties into the Colorado. For reasons perhaps satisfactory to himself, he returned without having reached that river. As to the extent or character of the information elicited by that expedition, I have no knowledge.

Our movements have been much retarded for the want of the necessary means to purchase transportation, &c. If the department had seen proper to provide me even with the funds parsimoniously appropriated by Congress, the work from the Pacific to the Gila would have been finished before this.

Although the steamers arrive here regularly from the northern as well as the southern portion of this coast, I have not had the honor to receive any communication whatever from your department, excepting your very kind note of the 15th March, sent by way of the city of Mexico.

I have the honor to be, very respectfully, your obedient servant,
JOHN B. WELLER,
United States Commissioner.

Hon. JOHN M. CLAYTON,
Secretary of State, Washington.

SAN DIEGO, CALIFORNIA, *November* 17, 1849.

SIR: I have the honor to address the department, and ask permission to have filed the accompanying copies of letters which have passed between Mr. Weller and myself.

My late reconnoissance towards the Gila river along the boundary does not appear to give him satisfaction, although I contend that everything was accomplished that could have been expected—under not the most favorable circumstances, either.

I cannot but believe that other influences than those of an impartial nature now induce him to judge of my actions upon this line; and, therefore, I hope the department will permit me to refer my work, or such portion of it as is unsatisfactory to the present commissioner, to the government at Washington. The most amicable relations exist between the Mexican commission and myself, and I am happy to state that every accommodation and feelings of reciprocity pass between the surveyor on the part of Mexico and myself, consistent with our duties to our respective governments.

I have the honor to remain, very respectfully, your obedient servant,
ANDREW B. GRAY,
U. S. Surveyor.

Hon. JOHN M. CLAYTON,
Secretary of State, Washington city, D. C.

SAN DIEGO, CALIFORNIA, *November* 7, 1849.

SIR: Having returned from my recent reconnoissance in the direction of the Gila river and the vicinity of the boundary, I have to report to you that I find there will be little or no difficulty in the demarcation of the line almost entire from the Pacific to the junction of said river, where it unites with the Colorado, and with sufficient accuracy for all the purposes required by the treaty, such as mapping, &c.

I procured such Indian guides as were supposed to have the best knowledge of the country over which I designed passing, and proceeded along one of their trails until I thought we had gone sufficiently far northward to preclude all doubt of the line in its true course reaching beyond that latitude. Here the Indians, in order to descend the mountains to cross the portion of country which has been termed the desert, (a part of which the line must pass over,) wished to take us a long distance round, and still further north. I determined to make an examination and ascertain if it was not practicable to go down at a much nearer point to where I supposed the line would intersect this desert. For a day and a half we now remained encamped at the base of a prominent peak, the southernmost part very nearly of a conspicuous range of mountains rising greatly above even the elevated region we had thus far reached. I ascended this peak and made a panoramic sketch of the topographical features of the surrounding country, also obtained a good observation for determining its barometic height. Some miles distant was another mountain, apparently similarly situated, and which I supposed might be about equally far to the southward. Between these two peaks or mountains I believe the line must pass; and the one nearest our encampment I consider an important feature in the topography of the line for mapping, on account of its conspicuous position, as seen from the travelled road across the country from Sonora to California. Very nearly east, now, I directed our examination, and found that I could descend with the animals and packs, with apparently but little detention, to a level with the plain or "desert." We descended without accident of any kind, and, on arriving at the bottom of the pass, found a cañon extending northerly and southerly. I had not time to examine the latter direction just then, or follow it very far, though I believe it runs some distance—possibly to where the line may cross; but I decided from various reasons to proceed northerly and easterly. Our guides affecting to know nothing of the country we were now in, in about eight or ten miles we struck a road, which proved to be the main road from San Diego, and near where it crosses the bed of what is called "Cane creek." We continued on this road, and reached the "Agua Nueva" encampment, which I estimated to be about two-thirds of the entire distance to the mouth of the Gila, or more.

At this point I met a large party of government officers and men, who had been a long time on their way to their place of destination. It was the party of Colonel Collier, consisting of himself, the collector for San Francisco, assistants, &c. They had learned of my having crossed the mountains and into the desert by a different route from the old road, and were very anxious to proceed to the settlements in the shortest possible time consistent with the safety of their packs, &c. They were on reduced rations, and their animals almost exhausted.

The officer commanding the company of dragoons, (the escort,) and others, came to my camp to obtain from me any information in my power to give relative to the country we had gone over. I showed my rough notes and sketches, but did not advise, under the circumstances, their going by this pass. They, however, decided to attempt it, believing it almost impossible for them to reach San Diego by the wagon-road route in safety to their animals, &c.; and, at their earnest solicitation, I agreed to return to guide them in. I felt it my duty to do so, although I was particularly desirous to reach the mouth of the Gila, to observe myself its situation, and to make a reconnoissance of it, preparatory to a decision of the point where its middle unites with the Colorado, and the mapping of the same.

I would not send my assistant back to guide this party, because I wished to be there myself, in case of any accident or obstacle occurring, it being the first time that I believed its ascent had ever been attempted with packs, &c. I therefore gave directions to Mr. Forster, my assistant, to continue on to make the reconnoissance of the remainder of the line, and, on arriving at the Gila, to make such a survey and exploration of its mouth as the time would admit of, and which would enable me to decide what further course to pursue in fixing its position, &c.

On returning from the "Agua Nueva" encampment, I followed for a long distance the direction I supposed the boundary would take, (from all the data we had to go upon,) leaving the road some distance to the northward. Being by myself, and night overtaking me before I had completed the reconnoissance to connect with the point where I thought the line would come down the mountains, I unfortunately became entangled amid some precipitous cliffs; before I could extricate myself entirely, it being dark, my animal fell, and left me afoot. I, however, fortunately came up with the party the next day. This was the only accident occurring of any note on our expedition.

Mr. Forster returned within the time our escort was asked for (twenty days) from the Gila; and everything has been accomplished that the circumstances occurring would permit, and much information obtained relative to the topography of the country in the vicinity of the line, and the practicability of a very correct map being made of it.

From the report of my assistant of the reconnoissance and survey made by him under my direction, particularly of the mouth of the Gila, I find that it may be probable that a difference of opinion might arise as to the position of the precise point of the junction of the river Gila, where it unites with the Colorado.

The surveyor on the part of Mexico having now gone over, and expressing to me his desire that I should be upon, the ground at the same time with himself, I respectfully request that I may be furnished with the requisite animals, &c., and that you agree with me in a continuance of the survey and exploration of this line. It can be followed from the river to its intersection with the mountains on the side of the plain or "desert," and notes accurately taken without any difficulty, and in comparatively a short space of time, and before the rains shall have set in sufficiently to drive us from the field.

I deem it important that this should be accomplished, because it is not entirely a barren plain, but in parts capable of sustaining a strong vegetation.

It is also cut up with dry arroyas and beds of streams, which at times may flow with water; and in the vicinity is a heavily-travelled highway for our own people, as well as those of the adjoining republic. The expenses would be comparatively little, knowing now the exact character of the country it passes through—what facilities we can depend upon at the various points in the neighborhood; and the result would be in direct conformity with the treaty.

If the azimuth of the line has been determined from the results of the latitude and longitude of the extremes, as agreed by the joint commission should be made, and I am furnished with the same from the party having that duty to perform, I will be better enabled to pursue the precise direction; or, if the result of the observations made to fix these points geographically are given me, I will determine the azimuth myself.

I shall expect to take but a small party with me; and with what we now have of notes and surveys made, and what may yet be accomplished, I believe all might be obtained requisite for mapping and planning the line.

I remain, very respectfully, your obedient servant,
A. B. GRAY, *U. S. Surveyor.*
Hon. JOHN B. WELLER, *U. S. Commissioner.*

SAN DIEGO, CALIFORNIA, *November* 8, 1849.

SIR: Your communication of yesterday has been received. Without entering into any discussion upon the subject, I must be permitted to say that your reasons for returning without making the personal examination of the mouth of the Gila river (for which your expedition was started) are far from being satisfactory to my mind.

I have felt, and still feel, the necessity for an accurate survey of the point at which the Gila empties into the Colorado; but as you have failed to furnish it, I presume I will be able to obtain the necessary information from Lieut. Whipple, on his return.

For the present, at least, I decline, for various reasons, sending out a detachment from your party.

Respectfully, your obedient servant,
JNO. B. WELLER, *U. S. Comm'r.*
A. B. GRAY, Esq., *U. S. Surveyor.*

SAN DIEGO, CALIFORNIA, *November* 9, 1849.

SIR: Last evening I received your communication in answer to mine of the 7th instant. I am not desirous of entering into a discussion relative to my recent reconnoissance, believing myself to have been the best judge of the proper disposition of my party while in the field, &c. Still I regret that you do not seem pleased at what has been done by the expedition, when every exertion was used by myself and party to accomplish all that was expected. It was but for twenty days; and we had to pass from the Pacific to the Colorado river and back in this time, to sketch in the topography of the country along the boundary, as near as practicable, and to fix the mouth and vicinity of the Gila for mapping, &c. A desert and an impassable descent from mountains, it was supposed, we would encounter; and great precaution was necessary for the safety of the party.

You will agree with me, I am sure, in this, that the situation of the mouth of the river Gila, as regards a difference of opinion arising relative to the exact position of the boundary at that point, is different from what we had understood, as will be seen by reference to your letter to me of the 14th of August, wherein you state that you are "informed that the precise point at which the Gila empties into the Colorado is so distinctly marked that there will be no difficulty whatever in fixing it;" and this was the only data we had to go upon when we started out. I did not know to the contrary until my assistant, Mr. Forster, reported to me his reconnoissance of the mouth of that river. Everything has been accomplished of the surveys and reconnoissances that I expected when we left, and I am now preparing a sketch of the triangulations made of the mouth of the Gila. I will here state that, the time being limited (a few days only) for my party to remain there, my assistant, Mr. Forster, made a joint reconnoissance and survey, in connexion with Lieutenant Whipple; and so soon as the plan of the same is made out, I will present it to you, with reports, &c.

I hope this will meet with your approval.

Very respectfully, your obedient servant,
A. B. GRAY,
U. S. Surveyor Mexican Boundary.
Hon. JOHN B. WELLER, *U. S. Commissioner.*

SAN DIEGO, *November* 14, 1849.

SIR: I herewith submit to you a sketch or plan of the junction of the Rio Gila, where it unites with the Colorado, as referred to in my communication of the 9th instant. It is made from the notes and topography of the reconnoissance and survey of that point by my assistant, Mr. Forster, (aided by Lieutenant Whipple,) in our late expedition.

B and C are two points, which, at present, might be considered the ends of the banks which form the Gila, at its embouchee into the Colorado. The latter river now being low, the current is swiftest between the island and main land, and strikes the water of the Gila at A; but when higher, the two waters may join or mingle some distance further north.

The land on the west side of the Gila at B is constantly wearing away by the action of the currents, being low and soft; consequently, the position of that point changes, as also the configuration of the mouth of the Gila; and the point D may very shortly (if not now considered) be the end of the southern or western bank of that river; the middle, therefore, to-day, may not be the same as yesterday.

The waters, after mingling, converge and break through a dyke of feltzspatic rock, about seven hundred feet across; and if it is decided that the point where the middle of the river Gila unites with the Colorado is at A, the line of boundary, in its course from the Pacific, will probably fall to the southward of the bluffs, and thus include in our territory both sides of the Colorado, at the present emigrants' crossing. These elevated heights may be considered important, not only in a civil but military point of view.

The rains and weather having been so severe for some days, I have been prevented from drawing, &c., in my tent, or the accompanying plan would have been submitted earlier. I am preparing my notes and sketches now for mapping our further reconnoissances along the boundary line; and, when completed, they will be properly submitted.

Very respectfully, your obedient servant,
A. B. GRAY,
United States Surveyor under treaty with Mexico.
Hon. JOHN B. WELLER, *U. S. Comm'r.*

WASHINGTON CITY, D. C.,
December 15, 1849.

SIR: As an authorized agent and attorney for John B. Weller, commissioner to run and mark the boundary line between the United States and Mexico, I had the honor some months since to apply, through you, for additional funds to enable said commissioner to proceed with said service; and believing now that your refusal at that time was induced principally by the belief that Mr. Weller would be relieved from the duties of commissioner, by a successor, before additional funds were actually needed, and conceiving that such belief has not been borne out by the facts, and learning that the new appointee (Col. Fremont) declines entering upon the duties of commissioner, I beg leave, most respectfully, to renew my application.

Up to the latest day of our last advices from California, the 5th of November, Mr. Weller was still acting in the capacity of commissioner, and was vigorously prosecuting the business of that office—having received no official information regarding a discharge therefrom. He has succeeded in completing the establishment of the initial point on the Pacific coast; has finished the survey and demarcation of the line from the Pacific coast to the Colorado, (a very considerable portion of the work;) and has ascertained the latitude and longitude of each of the two extreme points. In short, I will refer you to the correspondence and documents in your department, received from him, for the amount and nature of the service he has performed; and then ask whether it is not altogether likely that, in order thereto, he has been compelled to incur liabilities greater in amount than the funds that have been directly furnished him.

I think it cannot be said, when all the facts are known, that he ought to have, or possibly can have, funds to any considerable amount remaining in his hands out of the advances heretofore made him.

The vouchers returned by him, and now in the Fifth Auditor's office, will show that all he has had advanced him has been expended for subsistence stores for his party for six months, and for the necessary expenses in getting his party out to the field of labor.

The department, with the ample data in its possession, is able to form a correct estimate of the probable cost of the work completed by Mr. Weller, and therefore, also, of the probable sum now actually needed by the commissioner. The department is also able, no doubt, to fix the probable time at which Mr. Weller will leave the service, and can, therefore, form a tolerably correct estimate of the amount of funds it will take to keep up the service to that time; and here the assumption that the department is unwilling to suffer the entire suspension of the service for any limited period, I hope, is correct, as it is natural and justifiable. And it is quite certain that, unless funds are furnished the commissioner soon, he will be compelled to suspend the work, let the consequences be what they may—the nature of which, I am glad to believe, the department can sufficiently estimate to induce it to avert them.

I sincerely hope, sir, you will see the necessity as well as the justice of furnishing Mr. Weller more funds, and that I shall have the pleasure of conveying the same to him, as I am fully authorized by him to do—the evidence of which I will exhibit to you, at any time you shall name.

I have now only to inform you that, being a subaltern of the commissioner, I have received orders to repair to San Diego, but am unable to do so for want of the necessary means; and unless you can and will furnish me the necessary amount of funds, on account of the commission, I shall remain totally unable to execute the orders of the commissioner.

I have received no payment upon my salary since I first entered the commission; and if you cannot furnish me funds, as just intimated, but will have the goodness to allow me to draw from the treasury (as I am authorized by the commissioner to do) a sufficient portion of my salary to enable me to obey the orders of the commissioner to repair to San Diego, I can and will execute a voucher which shall secure the accounting officer against any charge of wrong-doing, as well as secure the public treasury against any possible loss.

I shall feel greatly obliged to you for an early answer; and in the mean time,

I have the honor to be, your obedient servant,
C. L. WELLER,
Disbursing officer U. S. & M. B. Commission,
and agent and attorney for John B. Weller.

Hon. JOHN M. CLAYTON, *Secretary of State.*

WASHINGTON CITY, D. C.,
December 24, 1849.

SIR: Your favor of the 20th instant, in answer to mine of the 15th, has been received. It informs me that "the commissioner is charged with the disbursement of the appropriation made by Congress for the boundary service," and that "my application for pay on account of my salary as a subaltern in the commission should be made to him." And what I now wish to say in reply is, that all the commissioner desires is, that you will not intervene between him and the strict discharge of his duty, as set forth in your letter. He cannot disburse said appropriation so long as the department refuses to allow it to pass into his hands, or dishonors his requisitions upon the department, given in discharge of liabilities incurred on account of the service. I am the disbursing officer of the commission, as will be seen in the commissioner's report on the organization of the commission, now in the State Department, and as such hold a requisition of the commissioner upon the department for a portion of said appropriation, which I am to disburse, agreeably to directions, on account of the service. And, in the name and on behalf of the commissioner, I only ask that the discharge of his duty, as set forth in your letter, may be rendered possible, by having placed under his control the appropriation made by Congress.

Your reference of me back to the commissioner for my pay is useless, since he cannot be allowed to draw from the treasury funds for the purpose. The commissioner, in recognition and part payment of my claim, put into my hands a draft upon the department, which has not yet been honored. If the commissioner's requisitions are to be dishonored, and yet it be made his duty to defray the expenses of the service, how, I ask, with all due deference, is it proposed he shall accomplish his mission? Whilst so much time is being consumed in getting a successor to Mr. Weller installed, is it expected of him to keep up the service, or is a suspension desired? If the former, it cannot be done without funds; and if the latter, would it not be a saving to the government, and just and magnanimous towards Mr. Weller, to relieve him from the service unconditionally?

The commissioner asks you, through me, to be allowed to pay a portion of the salary of his disbursing officer, and for that purpose has drawn a draft for $500, which I will present at any time you may have the kindness to allow its payment.

With no desire to become importunate, but with a sincere belief that there has been some misconception of the facts of the case, my object in addressing you now is to give you a clear statement in regard to the draft I hold, hoping thereby to overcome your objections to its payment here.

With a respectful request to be informed, as soon as convenient, whether or not you still adhere to your former decision regarding the payment here, in part, of my salary, agreeably to the requisition of the commissioner,
I have the honor to be your obedient servant,

C. L. WELLER.

Hon. THOMAS EWING,
Secretary of Interior Department.

DEPARTMENT OF STATE,
Washington City, January 19, 1849.

GENTLEMEN: You will receive herewith the list of instruments belonging to this department, furnished by Major Graham on the 29th December last.

Major Graham and Major Emory will proceed immediately to New York, and, if they should deem it advisable, to the other cities where these instruments are deposited; and Major Graham, in whose custody they now are, will deliver such of them to Major Emory, the chief of the corps of topographical engineers designated to accompany the commissioner and surveyor under the 5th article of the late treaty with Mexico, as he may deem necessary for correctly running and marking the boundary line between the two republics, taking duplicate receipts for the same. Major Graham will deliver one of these receipts to the department, and preserve the other.

Major Emory will then proceed at once to cause any or all of the instruments so delivered to him to be repaired, if need be, and fitted for the survey of the Mexican boundary, and to be packed and placed in boxes for transportation on mules.

All the actual expenses incurred in executing these instructions, as well as the personal expenses of Majors Graham and Emory, will be paid out of the appropriation made on the 12th August last, not exceeding $50,000, " for the expenses of running and marking the boundary line between the United States and Mexico, and paying the salaries of the officers of the commission." Accounts of these expenses, properly vouched, will be settled by the Fifth Auditor.

Major Emory, after having received and examined such instruments as he may require, will report immediately to this department what other instruments he may deem necessary for the survey, together with their probable cost, and where they may be obtained the most speedily and upon the best terms.

I am, gentlemen, respectfully, your obedient servant,
JAMES BUCHANAN.

Maj. J. D. GRAHAM and Maj. WM. H. EMORY,
Of the Topographical Engineers of the U. S. Army.

DEPARTMENT OF STATE,
Washington, January 24, 1849.

SIR: The fifth article of the treaty requiring that the commissioner and surveyor of the United States and Mexico, respectively, should meet at San Diego before the 30th May, 1849, no time should be lost in organizing the commission on our part, preparatory to its departure for the place of destination.

As you will be held responsible for the able and faithful execution of the important public trust confided to you by this article of the treaty, the President deems it proper to leave to you the organization of the commission, enjoining it upon you, at the same time, to employ as few persons to assist you as may be compatible with the successful and efficient performance of your duties, and to study economy, as far as practicable, in all your expenditures.

The organization will be effected solely with a view to run and mark the boundary line between the two republics; although the selection of individuals for this purpose may be made with reference to the incidental collection of information relative to the construction of "a road, canal, or railway," along the river Gila, as provided for by the sixth article of the treaty.

In organizing the commission, you are referred, for any information which you may deem necessary, to Andrew B. Gray, esq., who has been appointed surveyor under the treaty, and Major William H. Emory, of the topographical engineers, whom the President has designated to be " chief astronomer and head of the topographical scientific corps of the commission."

Congress, by the civil and diplomatic act of August 12, 1848, has appropriated, "for the expenses of running and marking the boundary line between the United States and Mexico, and paying the salaries of the officers of the commission, a sum not exceeding fifty thousand dollars," and the President considers that he will best effectuate the intentions of Congress by directing that the expenses of the commission for one year shall be so graduated as not to exceed this appropriation. You will be charged exclusively with the disbursements of the money thus appropriated, with the exception of the sum which may be necessary to execute my instructions of the 19th instant, to Majors Graham and Emory, relative to the delivery of astronomical instruments from the former to the latter, for the use of the commission.

Your salary as commissioner, as well as that of the surveyor, will commence from this date. In case Congress should not declare by law what these salaries shall be, they will be fixed by the President before the departure of the commission from the United States. Under the head of contingent expenses of the commission will be embraced your reasonable personal expenses while in service, and those of the surveyor, chief astronomer, and other officers of the topographical engineers who may be detailed to assist you in the field, the pay and subsistence of assistant surveyors, chain carriers, and laborers, and the incidental and necessary expenses of exploring parties, the purchase of stationery, of tents and camp equipage, and the purchase or hire of horses, mules, and vehicles for the transportation of the same. Of all these expenses you will keep a regular account, which, together with the necessary vouchers, you will render and transmit quarterly to the Fifth Auditor of the Treasury for settlement. And to meet the same, as likewise the payment of the salaries, you will from time to time, as occasion may require, draw upon the department, taking care not to exceed in the amount drawn at any one time the sum which will be required to meet the actual and necessary expenses of the commission.

After the commission on the part of the United States shall have been properly organized under your direction, and before your departure from the country, you will receive further instructions.

I am, sir, respectfully, your obedient servant,

JAMES BUCHANAN.

To John B. Weller, Esq.,
    " *Commissioner for running the boundary line between the United States and the republic of Mexico, under the fifth article of the treaty with that republic, concluded on the 2d February, 1848.*"

DEPARTMENT OF STATE,
Washington, February 13, 1849.

SIR: In my instructions of the 24th ultimo I promised to send you further instructions before your departure from the United States. I now proceed to perform this duty.

The fifth article of our treaty with Mexico of the 2d February, 1848, as amended by the Senate, (two copies of which are herewith transmitted,) clearly prescribes your duties. This article places you in a highly responsible position; because it declares that the boundary line between the two republics which shall be run and marked by the joint commission shall be deemed a part of the treaty, " and shall have the same force as if it were inserted therein." The action of the commission, therefore, will be final and conclusive; and the President has full confidence that in the discharge of your important duties your conduct will be characterized by prudence, firmness, and a conciliatory spirit.

Whilst he desires no advantage over the Mexican government, you will take care, in running the boundary, that all our just rights, under the treaty, shall be maintained.

Your first duty will be to run and mark that part of the boundary consisting of a straight line from a " point on the coast of the Pacific ocean distant one marine league due south of the southernmost point of the port of San Diego" to " the middle of the Rio Gila, where it unites with the Colorado."

It is not apprehended that you will encounter much difficulty in determining either of these points. This southernmost point of the port of San Diego is to be ascertained, by the treaty, " according to the plan of said port made in the year 1782 by Don Juan Pantoja, second sailing-master of the Spanish fleet, and published at Madrid, in the year 1802, on the atlas to the voyage of the schooners *Sutil* and *Mexicana*, of which plan a copy is hereunto added, signed and sealed by the respective plenipotentiaries." You are furnished with a certified copy of this plan, which appears to fix precisely what is the southern limit of the port of San Diego; and a point on the Pacific " one marine league due south of" this is the place of beginning.

The middle of the Rio Gila, where it unites with the Colorado, being a natural object, there can be but little difficulty in ascertaining this point.

The duties of the surveyor are sufficiently indicated by the treaty itself; those of Major William H. Emory, the chief astronomer, will be to determine all astronomical points, and to direct the mode of running all astronomical lines on the boundary. Lieutenant J. W. Whipple and Brevet Captain E. L. F. Hardcastle, of the corps of topographical engineers, have been designated, under the authority of the President, to accompany Major Emory as his assistants.

The remainder of the boundary runs along the middle of the Rio Gila and the Rio Grande, with the exception of that portion of it between " the point where the Rio Grande strikes the southern boundary of New Mexico; thence westwardly along the whole southern boundary of New Mexico (which runs north of the town called Paso) to its western termination; thence northward, along the western line of New Mexico until it intersects the first branch of the river Gila, (or, if it should not intersect any branch of that river, then to the point on the said line nearest to such branch, and thence in a direct line to the same.")

In regard to this latter portion of the line it is impossible to give you specific instructions, for the want of accurate geographical information. It can only be ascertained by examinations and surveys upon the ground. Besides, the treaty itself declares that "the southern and western limits of New Mexico mentioned in this article are those laid down on the map" of the United Mexican States, published at New York, in 1847, by J. Disturnell, of which a copy was added to the treaty, bearing the signatures and seals of the plenipotentiaries. You are now furnished with a certified copy of this map.

You are also furnished, as bearing upon this subject, with the copy of a map of New Mexico which was attached to the atlas to Thompson's edition of the Geographical and Historical Dictionary of America and the West Indies, by Col. Don Antonio de Alcedo, published at London in 1812—a work of the highest authority.

My successor in office will, most probably, obtain further information in regard to this portion of the line, and, as the work progresses, will doubtless deem it proper to give you further instructions.

I deem it unnecessary, therefore, to say more at present upon the subject.

I need scarcely add, that the President expects you will perform your duties under the treaty with as little delay as practicable consistently with accuracy.

As it is indispensable that each government should be furnished with a full and circumstantial record of the proceedings of the commissioners, they will doubtless order such record to be kept in duplicate. This duty will naturally devolve upon the clerks appointed on both sides, under the supervision of the respective commissioners, who will be responsible for the accuracy of such records, and for their safe delivery, properly certified, to the respective governments, at the expiration of the commission. You will, with that view, provide the clerk appointed on the part of the United States with suitable instructions respecting this and any other duty which it shall be deemed proper to assign to him.

As soon as the boundary shall have been ascertained and marked, you will cause a true and accurate map to be made of the country through which it passes, in its entire extent. A duplicate copy of said map, certified by the commissioners and surveyors on both sides, will accompany the records of the proceedings of the commission. The joint report or declaration by the commissioners of "the final result agreed upon by them," under the fifth article of the treaty, will also be transmitted to the department, to be filed with the journal or record of their proceedings and the map.

As soon as the commission shall be organized, you will transmit to this department a list containing the names of the several persons composing it; the nature of the duties assigned to each individual, and the compensation allowed to them respectively; and will also, from time to time, inform the Secretary of State of any change which you may, by circumstances, be induced to make in its organization.

The sixth article of the treaty provides that "if, by the examinations which may be made, it should be ascertained to be practicable and advantageous to construct a road, canal, or railway, which should in whole or in part run upon the river Gila, or upon its right or its left bank, within the space of one marine league from either margin of the river, the governments of both republics will form an agreement regarding its construction, in order that it may serve equally for the use and advantage of both countries."

Although you are not required to make the examinations referred to in this article under the appropriation made by Congress on the 12th August last, which is limited to "the expenses of running and marking the boundary line," yet the President would be gratified if you could cause these examinations to be made incidentally, without seriously interfering with your appropriate duties. The inquiry is one of great importance to the country; and any information which you can communicate to the department on the subject will be highly appreciated by our fellow-citizens.

Major Emory has received from Major Graham, under my instructions, all the instruments belonging to the department which he believed to be suitable for running the boundary line between the two republics. In a report which he made to the department, dated at New York on the 4th instant, he states that these are not sufficient, and furnishes a list of those which will be required. Several of the latter he deems indispensable that he should carry with him, to wit:

1 box chronometer	$285 00
1 heliotrope	100 00
1 reconnoitring glass	50 00
1 portable astronomical telescope	190 00
4 nautical almanacs, 1849	10 00
1 copy catalogue stars, B. Association	20 00
1 set of charts, coast of California	2 00
1 Daniels's hygrometer	15 00
4 Hassler's logarithms, at $1 each	4 00
6 thermometers, at $4 each	24 00
6 observing lamps	15 00
4 cases drawing instruments, at $10 each	40 00
4 bottles ether (sulphuric.)	
½ bushel plaster of Paris.	
2 observing tents, at $40 each	80 00
1 equatorial stand, price estimated at	100 00

In your absence, the President has not hesitated to advise him to purchase these instruments, not doubting that you would promptly pay for them out of the appropriation. As it will be impossible for him to reach New Orleans before the 28th instant, you will not take your departure thence until after his arrival.

The President has determined that your salary shall be at the rate of $—— per annum, and that of the surveyor at the rate of $—— per annum; but should Congress, before its adjournment, fix your salaries at different rates, this will be the guide in settling your accounts from the beginning.

The military escort, on the part of the United States, to accompany the commission, has been placed by the President under the direction of the Secretary of War.

I am, sir, very respectfully, your obedient servant,
JAMES BUCHANAN.

To JOHN B. WELLER, Esq.,
Commissioner, &c.

DEPARTMENT OF STATE,
Washington, March 15, 1849.

SIR: I have to inform you that Congress, at its late session, omitted to pass any act prescribing the amounts of the salaries of the civilians attached to the commission of which you are the head. Consequently, until this omission be remedied, compensation for your services as commissioner, and for those of Mr. Gray as surveyor, cannot be lawfully paid; and no charge for salary, on the part of either of you, can properly form an item in the statement of your account to the treasury. It will, therefore, be necessary, in any draft which you may have occasion to make on this department for the purpose of carrying your instructions into effect, to make them, on their face, chargeable solely to the appropriation for the "*expenses* of running and marking the boundary between the United States and Mexico," leaving the salaries to be settled at some future day by Congress.

I am, sir, respectfully, your obedient servant,
JNO. M. CLAYTON.

To J. B. WELLER, Esq.,
Commissioner of the United States under the
5th article of the treaty of Guadalupe Hidalgo.

DEPARTMENT OF STATE,
Washington, June 26, 1849.

SIR: The President having thought proper to appoint you the commissioner on the part of the United States for running and marking the boundary line under the 5th article of the treaty of Guadalupe Hidalgo, I transmit your commission in that character. You will also receive herewith a copy of the several instructions which this department has addressed to your predecessor. It is not considered that you will need any further instructions at this time. I would, however, invite your special attention to the necessity of the regular transmission of your accounts and vouchers for settlement at the Treasury Department, as those instructions require. Any drafts, also, which you may have occasion to draw on account of the expenses of the commission, must be addressed to the Secretary of State, and not to the Secretary of the Treasury. You will also forward to this department a full list of the persons (other than military or naval) in the service of the commission on our part, with the rates of compensation allowed to each, and will apprize the department of any changes therein which may from time to time take place.

Your compensation, as well as that of your predecessor, will be settled by Congress at their next session.

I am, sir, respectfully, your obedient servant,
JNO. M. CLAYTON.

To J. C. FREMONT, Esq.,
San Francisco, California.

DEPARTMENT OF STATE,
Washington, June 26, 1849.

SIR: Your letter from Panama, under date of the 20th March last, marked No. 1, has been received.

It is to be regretted that you should have omitted to comply with that part of your instructions which requires you to furnish the department with a list of the persons employed to assist you in the discharge of your duties. In the absence of such a list, and of a statement of the compensation stipulated to be allowed to each person, it is impossible for the department to form an estimate of the probable expenses of the commission. Your instructions also direct you to transmit your account of those expenses at the close of every quarter, with the vouchers requisite for the adjustment of the account at the treasury. The first quarter since your appointment expired on the 31st of March last; but, although large sums had been advanced to you previously to that time, no account or vouchers in support thereof have yet been received from you. Under these circumstances, the department has deemed it necessary to suspend the payment of your drafts, of which a memorandum is subjoined.

The President having thought proper to appoint Mr. J. C. Frémont the commissioner on the part of the United States to run and mark the boundary line under the treaty of Guadalupe Hidalgo, you will transfer to him all the papers and other public property in your custody relating to the duties of that office.

I am, respectfully, your obedient servant,
JNO. M. CLAYTON.

To JOHN B. WELLER, Esq.

DEPARTMENT OF STATE,
Washington, June 28, 1849.

SIR: In a letter from this department, under date the 26th instant, you were informed of your appointment as commissioner of the United States under the 5th article of the treaty of Guadalupe Hidalgo.

With that letter, one addressed to your predecessor was also transmitted, which, however, it is deemed advisable you should not deliver or forward to him until you are about to enter upon the duties of the office. The letter for him which is herewith transmitted, you will consider as addressed to yourself, when you shall have communicated to him that above referred to.

I am, respectfully, your obedient servant,
JNO. M. CLAYTON.

J. C. FREMONT, Esq.

DEPARTMENT OF STATE,
Washington, June 28, 1849.

SIR: Your letter from Panama of the 15th ultimo, with the accompanying lists of persons in the service of the commission, was received at this department on yesterday, the 27th instant.

The difficulties which you anticipate in regard to running and marking the boundary line *from* the Pacific towards the Rio Grande may be realized; but, without actual experience of them, it would be premature even to take into consideration your suggestion as to reversing that course, and beginning the demarcation at the eastern end of the line.

Inasmuch, however, as the starting point for tracing the boundary, as well as the proceedings of the joint commission with reference thereto, is prescribed by the treaty, it would seem that the Executive of neither government has any discretion in regard to them, or any more right to change them than they would have to change the direction of the line itself.

If it should be found to be impracticable to execute the duties of the commission as the treaty contemplates and enjoins, a supplementary article will be necessary to impart validity to any deviations therefrom.

It may, as you suggest, be advisable occasionally to make presents to the Indians who may be met with along the route of the commission. Careful discrimination, however, will be necessary in selecting articles for this purpose. They should be acceptable to the Indians, but not such as would enable them to injure the commission, in case their permanent good will should not be secured. The cost of the presents, also, should be moderate, and our share thereof should bear a just proportion to the fund appropriated by Congress for the expenses of the commission.

Upon this subject, however, you had better consult and make some arrangement with the Mexican commissioner. If presents should be indispensable, they would be for the common benefit of both parties, and both should equally share the expense.

I am, respectfully, your obedient servant,
JNO. M. CLAYTON.

JOHN B. WELLER, Esq.

DEPARTMENT OF STATE,
Washington, July 20, 1849.

SIR: I have received your letter of this morning, and have to inform you, in reply, that by the act of 28th August last, a sum of $50,000 was appropriated "for the expenses of running and marking the boundary line between Mexico and the United States, and paying the salaries of the officers of the commission;" that of this sum, Commissioner Weller has received, in a payment in advance, and accepted drafts drawn on the Department of State - - - - - - - $33,325 00
That vouchers in support of his disbursements have been received (but have not yet been passed by the Fifth Auditor) for - - - - - - - 24,849 32

Leaving overpaid, and wholly unaccounted for, a balance of 8,475 68

You will perceive, from this statement, that the whole sum appropriated for the service of the current year was $50,000, and that *more* than two-thirds of this amount has already been drawn by the commissioner, before and since his removal from office. Under these circumstances, the department must decline to pay any further drafts of Mr. Weller, until his vouchers have been received, and his accounts adjusted at the proper office of the treasury.

I have only to state, with reference to your bill for travelling expenses, as bearer of despatches from Panama to Washington, that it is inadmissible, and cannot be allowed. Your employment in that character was neither warranted by the instructions of Mr. Buchanan to the commissioner, nor by the usages of the department in such cases.

I am, sir, respectfully, your obedient servant,
JNO. M. CLAYTON.
C. L. WELLER, Esq., *Washington, D. C.*

DEPARTMENT OF STATE,
Washington, November 21, 1849.

SIR: Your letter of the 15th of September last has been received. I learn from it, with regret, that you wish to be relieved from your duties as astronomer and topographical engineer in connexion with the commission on the part of the United States for marking the boundary, pursuant to the treaty of Guadalupe Hidalgo. Your claims and peculiar aptitude for that service were so generally acknowledged, that there was every reason to hope you might not be severed from the commission until the close of the business confided to it. Entertaining no doubt, however, that the reasons to which you allude are sound, and that the public will derive advantage from your employment in any other professional duty which may be assigned to you, your request is acceded to; and, in a letter of this date, I have requested the Secretary of War to designate your successor. In regard to the civil assistants to whom you refer, it is presumed that it would be best for them to remain, with a view to aid your successor in the discharge of his duties.

I am, sir, very respectfully, your obedient servant,
JNO. M. CLAYTON.
Brevet Major W. H. EMORY,
Topographical Engineers, San Diego, California.

DEPARTMENT OF STATE,
Washington, November 28, 1849.

SIR: The letter addressed to you by this department, under date of the 21st instant, has been detained for the purpose of being sent by the officer whom the Secretary of War might appoint as your successor. It appears, however, from the communication of Mr. Crawford, of this date, a copy of which is enclosed, that the order for your relief which had been requested of him would be so greatly inconvenient to the military service, that he deems himself constrained to deny the request. Under these circumstances, it is hoped that you will continue to discharge the duties of commander to the escort and chief astronomer to the commission with the same fidelity and ability by which you have attained your high professional and personal character.

I am, sir, very respectfully, your obedient servant,
JNO. M. CLAYTON.
Brevet Major W. H. EMORY,
Topographical Engineers, San Diego, California.

DEPARTMENT OF THE INTERIOR,
Washington, December 17, 1849.

SIR: In a communication from yourself to Col. John B. Weller, United States commissioner, under date of June 28, 1849, reference is made to a letter from said commissioner, dated at Panama, May 15, 1849, and received at your department June 27, 1849. As no such letter appears among the papers transferred by you to this department, I have to request that you will transmit the same to me, at your earliest convenience.
Very respectfully, &c.,

T. EWING.

Hon. JOHN M. CLAYTON,
Secretary of State.

DEPARTMENT OF THE INTERIOR,
Washington, December 19, 1849.

SIR: I have the honor to transmit to you the enclosed duplicate of a communication to the Hon. John B. Weller, and to request that, in accordance with the terms of the same, you will at once receive and take care of all the books, papers, and other property, which he is therein directed to turn over to you.

I am, very respectfully, your obedient servant,

T. EWING.

Major W. H. EMORY,
San Diego, California.

DEPARTMENT OF THE INTERIOR,
Washington, December 19, 1849.

SIR: The direction of the commission for running and marking the boundary line between the United States and Mexico having been transferred to this department, I have to inform you, in case, on the receipt of this, Colonel Fremont shall not have entered upon duty as your successor, that your services are no longer required in said commission; and to request that you will immediately turn over to Major W. H. Emory all the books, papers, and other property in your possession belonging to the United States and pertaining to the boundary service; for which you will take receipt in duplicate, the one to be forwarded to this department, and the other to be preserved by yourself.

You were advised by the Secretary of State, under date of the 26th of June last, that, on account of your failure to comply with your instructions to render to the Fifth Auditor quarterly accounts of your expenditures, with the necessary vouchers, payment of your drafts was suspended. As this barrier to payment still exists, I desire to call your attention to the importance of an early adjustment of your accounts.

I have the honor to be, &c.,

T. EWING.

Hon. JOHN B. WELLER,
San Diego, California.

DEPARTMENT OF THE INTERIOR,
Washington, December 20, 1849.

SIR: Your communication of the 15th, addressed to the Secretary of State, has been transmitted to this department for answer. You were advised by the Secretary of State, under date of July 20, 1849, that the payment of the drafts of John B. Weller, United States commissioner, had been suspended; and I need only to remark that the reasons which induced the suspension, and which were set forth to you, still exist in full force. As to your application for pay on account of your salary as a subaltern in the commission, I have to state that it should be made to the commissioner, he being charged with the disbursement of the appropriation made by Congress for the boundary service.

I am, very respectfully, your obedient servant,

T. EWING.

C. L. WELLER, Esq., *Present.*

DEPARTMENT OF THE INTERIOR,
Washington, December 28, 1849.

SIR: I have received your communication of the 24th instant, and have to state, in reply, that in the official instructions given by the Department of State to commissioner Weller, under date of January 24th, 1849, he was required to keep a regular account of the expenses of the commission, and to render and transmit the same quarterly, with the necessary vouchers, to the Fifth Auditor for settlement.

The amount received by Mr. Weller, prior to July 20, 1849, in a payment in advance and accepted drafts drawn on the Department of State, was..........................	$33,325 00
Vouchers in support of his disbursements had been received (only a part of which have been passed by the Fifth Auditor) for..	24,849 32
Leaving overpaid and wholly unaccounted for a balance of	8,475 68

Under these circumstances, you were apprized, July 20, 1849, that further payment of Mr. Weller's drafts would be refused until his vouchers were received and his accounts adjusted at the proper office of the Treasury. As no additional vouchers or accounts have yet been received from him, I must still decline to make additional payments. I desire, however, to express the hope that Mr. Weller will, by an early settlement, enable the department to meet all the lawful expenses of the commission.

It is understood that you consider yourself officially connected with the commission, under an appointment from the late commissioner. But, the department being unable to perceive that you have rendered or can render any aid in the execution of the duty required of this commission by a protracted residence in this city, your services will be no further required therein.

I am, very respectfully, your obedient servant,

T. EWING.

C. L. WELLER, Esq., *present.*

DEPARTMENT OF THE INTERIOR,
Washington, January 8, 1850.

SIR: Mr. John B. Weller having been relieved from duty as head of the commission to survey the boundary line between the United States and Mexico, and the direction of said commission having therefore fallen temporarily upon you, I have to request that the persons employed on the work may be reduced to the lowest number consistent with the proper, though economical, management of the business confided to you, by the discharge of all such as are not indispensable to the proper performance of the work, and whose services can, therefore, be dispensed with without detriment.

I am, sir, very respectfully, your obedient servant,
T. EWING, *Secretary.*
Maj. WM. H. EMORY,
San Diego, California.

The number of surveyors ought not to exceed three; and in reducing your force, you will have a view to the suggestions of Col. Abert and Lieut. Col. McClellan, a copy of which is enclosed.

DEPARTMENT OF THE INTERIOR,
Washington, January 9, 1850.

SIR: I have to request that you will, as early as may be practicable, furnish this department a statement, showing—

1st. The names of all persons employed by the late commissioner, Mr. Weller, on the Mexican boundary, their compensation and duties respectively.

2d. The names of all such as you may discharge in pursuance of my letter of yesterday, their compensation and duties.

3d. The names, compensation, and duties of all persons who may compose the commission after its reduction by you.

You will also keep the department advised of whatever changes may from time to time be made.

I am, sir, very respectfully, your obedient servant,
T. EWING, *Secretary.*
Maj. WM. H. EMORY,
San Diego, California.

No. 3.

Correspondence with agents and officers of the United States in California and New Mexico.

DEPARTMENT OF THE INTERIOR,
Office of Indian Affairs, January 11, 1850.

SIR: In compliance with the directions in your letter of the 3d instant, I have the honor to transmit, herewith, a copy of all the correspondence

that has been had between this office and " any agent of the government of the United States in California or New Mexico."
Respectfully, your obedient servant;

ORLANDO BROWN.

Hon. THOMAS EWING,
   Secretary of the Interior.

DEPARTMENT OF THE INTERIOR,
Office of Indian Affairs, April 7, 1849.

SIR: I have the honor to enclose, herewith, a commission constituting you Indian agent at Salt Lake, California, to include the Indians at or in the vicinity of that place, and any others that may hereafter be designated by this department.

Your compensation will be at the rate of $1,500 per annum, in full of salary and all emoluments whatever, to commence as soon after the execution of your bond as a notification can reach the person now holding the appointment and receiving the salary, advising him of the change which has been made in the location of the agency, and of the discontinuance of his service and salary.

I enclose, also, the form of a bond to be executed by you, in the penal sum of $5,000, with two or more sureties, whose sufficiency must be certified by a United States district judge or district attorney.

So little is known here of the condition and situation of the Indians in that region that no specific instructions relative to them can be given at present; and the department relies on you to furnish it with such statistical and other information as will give a just and full understanding of every particular relating to them—embracing the names of the tribes, their locations, the distance between the tribes, the probable extent of territory owned or claimed by each respectively, and the tenure by which they hold or claim it; their manners and habits; their disposition and feelings towards the United States, Mexico, and whites generally, and towards each other; whether hostile or otherwise; whether the several tribes speak different languages, and, when different, the apparent analogies between them; and, also, what laws and regulations for their government are necessary, and how far the law regulating trade and intercourse with the Indian tribes (a copy of which I enclose) will, if extended over that country, properly apply to the Indians there, and to the trade and intercourse with them, and what modification, if any, will be required to produce the greatest degree of efficiency.

You are authorized to employ one interpreter permanently, by the year, and such others, from time to time, as you may find necessary in the discharge of your duties. As the law limits the compensation of interpreters to $300 per annum, that amount cannot be exceeded; but, in the case of those employed temporarily, you will engage their services on the best terms you can, and employ them for as short periods and as seldom as possible consistent with a proper discharge of your duties. You will be allowed a horse for yourself and one for your interpreter, to be held as public property, and accounted for as such.

As you will doubtless avail yourself of the military escort which will leave St. Louis shortly, funds will be placed in the hands of the superintendent of Indian affairs at that place, to be turned over to you.

The remote position of the scene of your operations has induced the Secretary of the Interior to authorize an advance of one year's salary to yourself and your interpreter, together with other sums for other objects, as follows, viz:

One year's salary for yourself	$1,500
Do do for interpreter	300
Pay of additional interpreter	200
Contingent expenses, including presents to Indians, purchase of two horses, forage for the same, house rent, fuel, stationery, collection of statistical information, together with your travelling expenses to your agency	1,500
	3,500

It has been represented to this department that there is a Mexican boy in captivity among the Indians, either in New Mexico or California, and for whose release the Mexican minister has made a demand on this government; but as the department is as yet unacquainted with the particulars of the case, it will be made the subject of a special communication to you as soon as they can be ascertained.

After obtaining all the information you can collect with regard to any captives, you will report their names, ages, whether they are Mexicans or Americans, the length of time they have been held in captivity; and if they are Mexicans, whether they were taken prior to the termination of the war and treaty with Mexico, or subsequently.

In dispensing presents to the Indians, you will be as economical as possible, and confine the disposition of them to cases where some important end is to be accomplished.

You will report directly to this office, and will lose no opportunity of doing so, as it is extremely desirable that the department be kept well advised of the state of affairs in that region.

I enclose blank forms to guide you in rendering your accounts, which must be done quarter-yearly, or as nearly so as possible.

In rendering your accounts you will account for the money placed in your hands under the following heads of appropriation, viz:

Pay of superintendents and Indian agents	$1,500
Pay of interpreters	500
Contingencies, Indian department	1,500
	3,500

Very respectfully, your obedient servant,

W. MEDILL.

JOHN WILSON, Esq., *Indian Agent, Salt Lake, California.*

P. S. I enclose a copy of the late treaty with Mexico, and also copies of the reports of Messrs. Frémont, Emory, Abert, and Cook.

W. M.

FORT BRIDGER, ON BLACK'S FORK OF
GREEN OR COLORADO RIVER, *August* 22, 1849.

SIR: We arrived here yesterday. Messrs. Vasques and Bridger are the proprietors, and have resided here and in these mountains for more than 25 years. They are engaged as traders, belonging to the American Fur Company. They are gentlemen of integrity and intelligence, and can be fully relied on in relation to any statement they make in regard to the different tribes, claims, boundaries, and other information in relation to the Utah and Sho-sho-nie tribes and a small band of Pummacks, as they have during all their residence been engaged in trade with them.

Among the Sho-sho-nies there are only two bands, properly speaking. The principal or better portion are called Sho-sho-nies, (or Snakes) who are rich enough to own horses. The others, the Sho-sho-coes, (or Walkers) are those who cannot or do not own horses. The principal chiefs of the Sho-sho-nies are *Mono*, (about 45 years old,) so called from a wound in his face or cheek from a ball, that disfigures him; *Wiskin*, (Cut-hair,) *Washikick*, (Gourd Rattle,) with whom I have had an interview; and *Oapichi*, (Big man.)

Of the Sho-sho-coes, *Augutasipa* is the most noted. Both bands number, probably, over 1,000 lodges of four persons each. Of the relative portion of each band, no definite account can be given; for so soon as a Sho-sho-nie becomes too poor to, or does not, own a horse, he is at once called a Sho-sho-coe; but as soon as a Sho-sho-coe can or does own a horse he is again a riding Indian, and therefore a Sho-sho-nie.

Their language, with the exception of some *Patois* differences, is said to be that of the Comanche tribe. Their claim of boundary is to the east from the Red Buttes, on the north fork of the Platte, to its head in the Park, (decayague,) in Buffalo Bull Pen, in the Rocky mountains; to the south, across the mountains, over to the Yom-pa-pa, till it enters Green or Colorado river, and then across to the Back-Bone, or ridge of mountains called the Bear River mountains, running nearly due west towards the Salt Lake, so as to take in most of the Salt Lake; and thence on to the Sinks of Mary's or Humboldt's river; thence north to the fisheries on the Snake river in Oregon; and thence south (their northern boundary) to the Red Buttes, including the sources of Green river—a territory probably 300 miles square, most of which has too high an elevation ever to be useful for cultivation of any sort. In most of these mountains and valleys it freezes every night in the year, and is in summer quite warm at noon and to half-past three p. m. Nothing whatever will grow of grain or vegetables; but the most luxurious and nutritious grasses grow with the greatest luxuriance, and the valleys are the richest meadows. The part of the Salt Lake valley included in this boundary, the Cache valley, 50 by 100 miles, and part of the valley near and beyond Fort Hall, down Snake river, can be cultivated, and with good results; but this forms a very small part of this country. How these people are to live or ever exist for any great length of time, I cannot by any means determine. Their support has heretofore been mostly game and certain roots, which, in their native state, are rank poison, (called the tobacco root,) but, when put in a hole in the ground and a large fire burnt over them, become wholesome diet. The Mormon settlement in the Salt Lake valley has not only greatly diminished their former very great resource of obtaining fish out of the Utah lake and its sources, which to them was an important resource, but their settlement, with the great emigration to California, has already nearly driven away all the game, and will, unquestionably, soon deprive them almost entirely of the only chances they have for food. This will in a few years produce a result not only disastrous to them, but must inevitably engage the sympathies of the nation. How this is to be avoided is a question of much difficulty, but it is nevertheless the more imperative on the government not only to discuss but to put in practice some mode of relief for these unfortunate people, the outside barriers or enclosing mountains of whose whole country are not only covered in their constant sight with perpetual snow, but in whose lodges *every night in the year* ice is made, over water left in a basin, of near seven-eighths of an inch in thickness. Except in three small places already named as exceptions—and two of these, the Salt Lake valley and Snake river, are already taken from them by the whites—there is but little doubt the *Cache* valley will soon be so occupied.

The *Utahs* probably amount to from two to three thousand lodges, and are divided into many bands—as the *Taos*, 300 lodges; *Yom-pa-pa Utahs*, 500 lodges; *Ewinte*, 50 lodges; *Ten-penny Utahs*, 50 lodges, (this band are about all who reside in the Salt Lake valley;) *Pavant Utahs*, not estimated. Pahnutes (or Paynutes) Utahs and the Sampiche Utahs of these last bands, numbers not known. Their claim of boundaries is all south of that of the Sho-sho-nies, embracing the waters of the Colorado, going most probably to the gulf of California.

This is a much more fortunate location, and large portions of it are rich and fertile lands and a good climate. Their language is essentially Comanche; and although not technically, yet it supposed to be substantially the same as that of the Sho-sho-nies; for although, on first meeting, they do not fully understand each other, yet I am informed four or five days' association enables them to converse freely together. Some of the people are already engaged in the cultivation of the soil, and large tracts of the country afford ample rewards to those who thus expend the sweat of their brow. Portions of these bands have always been at war with the Mexicans, constantly making inroads into New Mexico and California to steal horses. Portions of them are at present at variance with the Sho-sho-nies; and, indeed, the manners and customs of the Yom-pa-pas render an association on the part of the whites with them dangerous, for should one be found amongst them when a sudden death, from either accident or common sickness, takes place amongst them, the relatives of the dead man are at liberty, and are sure to exercise it, of killing any stranger who may happen to be amongst them. Thus, until this custom is abandoned, no safe intercourse can be carried on with them. Their country being more south and out of the range of white settlements or emigrants, the game is not likely to be so scarce for many years to come as it is in the Sho-sho-nie country even now, for already it has nearly all left their boundaries, except a small corner in the northeast corner of their claim; and as they are at war with the Utahs, near whose lines it is, they are afraid to go there to hunt.

Supposing the government will be prepared next summer to take some decided steps towards a regular system of intercourse with them, and with a view of enabling the government as effectually as possible to guard against the unfortunate results in operation for their entire starvation, a few only of which I have mentioned, for want of time, I have concluded to so arrange matters before I leave that both these nations will be able to send large delegations, if not most of the principal bands of their tribes, to a great council to be held *here* next summer, being by far the most convenient place for such a council, but is also where the principal agency ought to be established; and here also ought to be established the leading military post of these mountains, for which hereafter I shall give my views more at large.

I have suggested the matter of the great council to Washikick, the only principal chief I have seen, and he highly approves of the plan. I have already made such arrangements, through the assistance of Mr. Vasques, (Mr. Bridger not being at home) that all of both tribes will be notified of my design to hold such a council; and so soon as I shall hear your pleasure on the subject, which I hope will be at an early day after I get to San Francisco, in November, I will then fix a time which will best suit the views of the department, (if it shall meet with your approbation, as I hope it will,) and will then cause them to be notified of the day, which must, of necessity, not be later than August, and not earlier than July, as any other month would not be convenient for them to attend. The Sho-sho-nies are reputed an honest and sober people, decidedly friendly to the whites; and if proper agents are kept among them, they will be easily managed, if a fair support can be provided for them. Some of the objects which I have supposed might be gained by such a council, you will easily perceive from what I have said above; and many others of perhaps equal importance may also be accomplished. It is of great importance that these Utahs should be laid under obligations to cease their accustomed depredations on the whites and their property; and it is of greater importance to adopt some mode or other to save the Snakes from utter destitution, which, in a year or two, must inevitably take place if things remain as they now are.

I write this in great haste; and, having broken my spectacles, I have to go it blind nearly. This, with the shortness of my stay here, is my excuse for not writing more; but I have touched on all the subjects most important at the present moment. When I get to Salt Lake, I shall have more time and better eyes, and will go more into detail; till when, I remain your obedient servant,

JOHN WILSON.

Hon. T. EWING,
Secretary of the Department of the Interior.

GREAT SALT LAKE VALLEY,
Salt Lake Indian Agency, September 4, 1849.

SIR: Referring you to my letter dated at *Fort Bridger* for what I said in relation to the Indians east of the Sierra Nevada, as to nations, bands, numbers, *claimed* boundaries, as well as some few items as to their manners and customs, my opportunities since have been such as not to add much to the information I then had the honor to communicate. All subsequent information received strongly confirms my then impressions, that the Sho-sho-nies, as a nation, must soon perish for want of food, unless the philanthropy of individuals, or the wisdom and energy of the government, shall devise some method of staying the march of causes which inevitably must produce such a distressing result. You will observe that their claim of boundaries gives them a vast territory, not far from being square—perhaps, however, a little the longer east and west. Our route has, thus far, led us transversely across their territory from the Red Buttes (their southeast corner) in a pretty direct line towards the southwest corner, (somewhere west of the Salt lake.) Hereafter we shall turn more north till we strike the road which leads from Fort Hall to San Francisco, and this will thus cause us to pass through the entire length and almost centre of their country. This valley, a very small portion of the country about Fort Hall, probably a part of *Cache* valley, and it may be New Park, (which latter, you will observe, is the valley of the head of the north fork of the Platte,) are the only portions of all their *claim* which can ever be applied to the purposes of agriculture, on account of the high altitude of its position. Their whole country is essentially a fine grazing country during the summer and fall; and, in many places in the valleys, stock (I mean cattle, horses, mules, &c.) sustain themselves all the year round; and this I am informed they can always do, except when the snows are too deep. Indeed, with the exception of this valley, the snows always fall too deep; but the face of the country is so covered with high mountains and deep valleys, which produce so many currents of the winds as to almost insure that much of the land is left bare by the drifting, in the deepest snows, so that the cattle, &c., can still get access to the grass which remains upon the land all winter; and, although dry, it is good hay, because it is cured without much if any rain; so little of it falls in this country as to leave the grass cured for hay. This valley has been already taken up by the *Latter-Day Saints*, who will soon spread to Cache and Bear river valleys, if they shall be found to produce grain and vegetables, which is exceedingly doubtful; and the government have already occupied the most favored portion about Fort Hall; and then the Indians will have only the New Park, (if indeed it will answer for agricultural pursuits,) and this is a very small piece of country for so many people to attempt the cultivation of the soil, if it should be the policy of the government to attempt to draw the attention of the Indians to that pursuit, to enable them to sustain the simplest but imperative calls of nature. The valley along Black's fork and Harn's fork of Green river and their tributaries (in which is Fort Bridger,) is, perhaps, next to this valley, (and you will see the Sho-sho-nies do not claim all this,) the most extensive and most beautiful, and as to *pasturage* is perhaps little behind this; but yet it is conceived to be entirely beyond the power of the most approved cultivation to raise either grain or vegetables so as to pay for the labor of the husbandman, for there is frost nearly every *night* in the year, as it is reported by those who have long resided therein. The elevation of Fort Bridger is 6,665 feet above the level of the sea; that of the South Pass, 7,085 feet; that of Bear river, (where we crossed it,) 6,836 feet; while the elevation of this valley is only 4,300 feet, and is enclosed in, entirely surrounded by mountains about one and a half mile high. Even in this valley there are light frosts many nights during all the summer months, as I am informed; and indeed, in last month several have fallen while we have been here. There only remain, then, to be mentioned, New Park and *Brown's Hole*, (see Fremont's map, by Colonel J. J. Abert,) if, indeed, that belongs to the Sho-sho-nies (or Snakes,) in which we can expect to find land within their reach and claim fit for cultivation, and it is very questionable whether "*the play would be worth the candle*" in either.

Under the present statute policy of the government, it will unquestionably become its duty, at as early a day as possible, to extinguish by treaty their title to this and the Cache valleys and the adjacent country, and a portion near Fort Hall, and at least negotiate for a highway through their country to this valley and Fort Hall, and, I think, to the country about Fort Bridger, where, in my opinion, without delay, there ought to be established a military post. In a very short time (next year) all the emigration to Oregon and California, as all to this valley does now, will pass that place, and from thence diverge into separate roads, which will lead to their respective destinations. There is a road, already opened by partial travel, almost in a direct line from Fort Bridger to Fort Laramie, (see the map before quoted,) which crosses Green river below the mouth of Harn's fork, and, perhaps, above the mouth of Mary's river, and thence pretty directly across to one of the forks of Laramie river, (perhaps the right hand one,) and thence down to Fort Laramie, which will cut off more than 150 miles in the distance; and Mr. Vasques, one of the firm of Bridger & Vasques, who reside at and own Fort Bridger, and who have both resided in this country about 28 years, says it is a much better road, and passes the Rocky mountains by a pass considerably *lower* than the South Pass, and affords a far better supply of both water and grass the whole road; and as proof that his statement is made upon a complete knowledge of the country, he (Mr. Vasques) is now upon his journey on that road with 7 or 8 ox teams to Fort Laramie for their fall supply of goods, which are already at Fort Laramie; and he intends returning that way with his loaded wagons, thus avoiding a most barren, and, indeed, to cattle, mules, &c., a disastrous road, now travelled from Fort Laramie to the South Pass, called (and properly) the road through the *black hills*, which we found for many long distances without both water and grass. The country in general through which the present travel goes, between Fort Laramie and the South Pass, is a desert in every sense of the term. Captain Stansbury, under the guidance of Mr. Bridger, has already traced out and reviewed a road direct from Fort Bridger, so as to cross Bear river just above where it flows into the Great Salt lake, thus making the road almost straight from Laramie to the north end of the Salt lake, which is the direct course towards where the road crosses the Sierra Nevada to California—not only bettering the road for water and grass, but shortening it to this valley 150 miles, and to the Sierra Nevada more than 300 miles on the one at present travelled by Fort Hall, leaving the latter place more than 100 miles to the north. If Mr. Vasques is not deceived (and he cannot be, as he has often travelled it) in relation to the improvement this cut-off will make in the road between Forts Bridger and Laramie, all the travel hereafter to Oregon, California, and this valley, which comes up the Platte, will unquestionably pass by Fort Bridger; even this year more than half the California emigrants passed by Bridger, and those who did not are said to have nearly perished for want of water and grass. Thus, if the above information proves to be correct, (and I have taken all the pains in my power to have it so,) you will see at once the great importance of the position of Fort Bridger, and the inevitable propriety of making it *the great military post* of this country. Aside from its peculiar propriety, when the facility of the department over which you preside, as regards its intercourse with both the Snake and Utah tribes of Indians, is considered, it is unquestionably the most convenient of all others, so far as I am informed, for the *centre* of your operations with all the Indians in California east of the Sierra Nevada. To come to this valley, is entirely too much to the west; to stop short of Bridger, would be too far to the east. Were there any direct communication with the Middle or Old Park, (where the Grand river takes its rise,) it might be more central for a communication with both Snakes and Utahs, and still more central would the South Park be for a direct communication with the Utahs alone. From the best information I can obtain, (and I hope you will appreciate what I say, when I state that my opportunities have been very limited, and yet nearly all the sources of information, except that of personal examination, have been within my reach that the country affords,) to gain anything like a personal knowledge of the actual situation of these tribes, less than five years' travel on pack mules would scarcely justify the attempt to answer the many questions, with any degree of certainty and accuracy, which are propounded to me in the instructions which were furnished me for my official guidance. I think it probably certain that the two nations, not very far back in their history, were one, and that they originally were a branch of the Comanches. I suppose it is true that the Snake and Utah languages are now somewhat different, although not essentially so, and yet agree more nearly than either does with that of the Comanches, and that probably the Utah language more nearly resembles the original than the Snakes' does; and one evident cause of this is, (if the supposition be true,) they have remained nearer the parent nation than the Snakes. The Green (or Colorado) river, which rises in the Wind River mountains, the sources of which interlock with those of Lewis's fork of the Columbia, northwest of the South Pass, is, where we cross it on the present road from the latter place to Fort Bridger, a fine stream, nearly of the size of the Ohio at Pittsburg at low water; and, as far as we travelled along it, (only 8 or 10 miles,) continued to be so, with a regular but very rapid current. Its valley, however, did not present any signs to encourage the husbandman to make that his home, nor to entice the herdsman to drive his flocks there for pasturage; and it is not till we arrive at *Brown's Hole*, if then, that it becomes very valuable for either. After that, it is said to furnish in its own, as well as the valleys of its tributaries, (as the Yam-pah, the White, and Grand rivers,) fine and extended bottoms, in many places, that will prove fruitful, and will amply reward the labors of both the agriculturist and herdsman. This, including the New, the Middle, and South Parks, (the two latter, and perhaps the first, are fine valleys for cultivation,) would make *a large and fertile country* amongst and surrounded by mountains, not desirable for settlements for white people, and perhaps better fitted than any other portion of the United States, now to be had, for the settlement and collocation of a large number of the original inhabitants of the wilderness; and, indeed, if my information be correct, it is the only large and proper space of country within the reach of the government, and suitable for such a purpose, beyond and out of the reach of the millions of Anglo-Saxons who are pressing towards the setting sun with almost race-horse speed, and *will soon* cover every reasonably inhabitable spot within our very extended national boundaries, especially towards the west and south. The country spoken of, including the valley of the Green, parts and of the headwaters of the Platte and the Arkansas rivers, is the only *fitting* and sufficiently secluded spot that seems to be left in which to attempt to extend that national philanthropy to the Indians of the mountains which has so many years engaged the attention and expended such vast sums of the treasure of the nation, and which has unquestionably fallen far short of the end expected by those who originated and put in motion this system for civilizing the aborigines of the forest, which has been for many years the business of the Indian bureau to carry out and perfect. The philanthropy which originated the measure was certainly correct; whether the system was founded on the best basis was then a question of division, and which perhaps still divides the opinions of some of its best wishers; but I suppose all agree that no very satisfactory results have been attained. When I say all agree, I mean all true philanthropists; for the greedy and land-hungry politicians, many of whom went eagerly for the system, have been amply repaid for their support in the vast territories that have been purchased, perhaps extorted, from these natives of the forest, and who, by this system, are supposed to be entirely capable of managing their own affairs; while in practice they have been either cajoled or menaced out of the soil that contained the bones of their fathers for many generations past, for which, in fact, they only have to show, as the price they have received in exchange, gewgaws and other worthless articles, at the most enormous and unreasonable prices, which the giving consciences of those licensed sharpers chose to ask into whose hands these simple and inexperienced people have been suffered to fall, until their all is spent, and they left a thousand times worse off than they were when the system began. The true philanthropist may well exclaim that scarcely any of the benefits of the civilization intended by its original framers have been imparted to these suffering and receding people. The fault is either in the system, or fails of its benefits by the incompetence or corruption of its administrators, or grows out of both; and to them both I attribute the unquestionable failure to impart any of the substantial benefits of civilization, except in very few and isolated cases. The system I have always considered radically wrong, in supposing the untutored Indian to be capable of dealing with the Anglo-Saxon race, especially those who have descended from the first settlers of America. My idea is, they ought to be treated entirely as wards of the government, and that the execution of the law ought to be confided to the true philanthropist, and not intrusted to the brawling and often bankrupt politician, who seeks the office to restore by speculation, out of these uninstructed people, what he has spent in aiding in the political intrigues and caucuses in his township or county; and as soon as he is thus fully indemnified, which he is almost sure to secure in an incredibly short time, he leaves them, and, instead of teaching them the beauties and benefits of civilization, leaves amongst them disgusting evidences that he has, by his example, encouraged them to continue in their basest immoralities.

The answer to these charges, which cannot be denied by any, is often given by those who uphold the unparalleled scenes of corruption and peculation that have so generally attended the whole system, with a few honorable exceptions, by declaring that men cannot be found honest enough to carry out a system founded on the presumption of the entire inability of the Indian to act for himself; and therefore the present system, say they, is better managed, where the Indian is allowed to make his own bargain, than one would be where men were appointed to bargain for him. This declaration is founded upon the presumption that honest men cannot be found to manage such a system; but if, indeed, this is true, then we ought to be blotted out as a nation, and branded as degenerate sons of worthy ancestors. This cannot be true. We have thousands of virtuous, and self-sacrificing, and philanthropic persons, who, for a fair but moderate salary, which the government could easily afford to pay, would devote their whole time and talents for the benefit, not only of the poor, unfortunate tenants of the forest, but of true philanthropy, which teaches us to wish the civilization of all mankind.

If the system was changed to the one I suppose—of considering the Indians minors in relation to all their interests, subject to be released, under some prescribed rule, when they *come of age* in their progress towards civilization—the government would only have to turn their attention to that part of the community, in making their appointments, (and we have such a class,) who would look with anxious care to the elevation of the morals and character of the red men of the forest. Whether the present system is to be changed or not, I feel bound to say to the department that the best plan to manage and conduct the affairs of the nations of Indians over which, for the present, I hold, by appointment of the government, the direction and management, is, if possible, to unite the Sho-sho-nies and Utahs into *one* nation, and which I believe can be done; and then endeavor, if possible, to turn their attention, *to some extent at least*, to the cultivation of the soil; for I do believe no other employment will civilize a wild man of the forest. There is no part of the Snake country (except, indeed, exceeding small portions, entirely inadequate) that they can *now* occupy for such a purpose, whilst that of the Utahs contains (if I am correctly informed) an ample space, and perhaps prolific soil, to answer all the demands of both nations—in parts, too, now wholly appropriated to the red men and beasts of the forest, and to which region the latter are constantly receding from the advance of the Anglo-Saxon on the south, the east, and northeast, as well as from the west and northwest. The upper end of the valley of the Arkansas, and the south and middle Parks, are said to be splendid valleys of the richest lands and finest pasturage, and that, although perpetual snows cap the high and rugged mountains by which these valleys are, for the greater part, hemmed in, still these valleys are of an altitude low enough to produce fine rewards to the husbandman, and these hills and mountains ample space for the herdsman, and for a long series of years the hunter also; while the climate is supposed to be comparatively mild and pleasant.

The larger portion of the Snake tribe are called Sho-sho-*coes*, or Walkers—that is, they are too poor to have horses. They usually draw most of their subsistence from roots and the black-mountain cricket, and are usually called root-diggers—(not *gold*-diggers)—which costs them very considerable labor; and it is supposed that this portion of the tribe, at least, could be easily trained, *by the right sort of men*, to engage in the labors of husbandry, while some of the Utahs are already engaged in raising corn and potatoes.

The only way in which any such attempt can be made with success, it seems to me, is to call a great council of both nations, and see what can be done, and, if present policy with other Indians is to be pursued, buy of them such parts of their country as we need, including, at all events, this valley, now settled by the whites, its adjacent country, as also a highway through their country, and such places as will be wanted for forts and other public agencies, and agree to pay them in useful implements of husbandry and clothing at the net cost and carriage of such articles, which they should not be allowed to re-sell to any white man; and then send proper men amongst them, who should, out of parts of the annuity coming to them, if any, establish farms—model farms—not models of extravagance in fine buildings and fine enclosures, but plain, simple, and well-conducted farms, with inducements held out to the Indians to work upon them, the avails of which to be appropriated to the nations' use; and then with directions to aid all such as should attempt to establish a farm of their own. In this way, if a few honest and self-sacrificing men were sent amongst them, it seems to me in a few years a beneficial change would be perceptible in the condition of the Indians. It is true, in the Snake claim of boundaries there are many large valleys, where I believe cattle could be reared even with profit; and, therefore, it may be said that it would be good policy to endeavor to turn them into herdsmen and teach them to raise and herd stock. This, if accomplished, would perhaps better their condition, because thus they might secure for themselves and families meat enough for food, which now they do not get; but I very much question whether their moral condition would in any way be bettered, whilst their physical constitution would unquestionably be enervated in the lazy habits of the herdsman. But, while you may easily and rapidly cause a civilized man to approximate towards the savage life by turning him out a herdsman, alone, to eat the beef he tends for his support, still it will be absolutely impossible to make a civilized man out of a savage by teaching him the idle and lazy employment of herding cattle in a barren wilderness amongst the mountains. There is no employment like that of agriculture, which ties them to a local spot of land, to cultivate the feelings of virtue and social intercourse, which are essential ingredients of civilization even in a savage. To attempt an accomplishment, or rather an initiation of such a policy, I have given notice already that I will, if approved of by the department, next summer hold a grand council of the two nations at Fort Bridger, when I will endeavor to carry out these or such other views as the department shall direct me, with these two nations. The council is not only essential to settle difficulties between themselves—for they often go to war with each other—but it is the only way in which the government can, with any probability, expect to become acquainted with their wants; for their country is too extensive, their bands too numerous and widely scattered, to enable any one, or even half a dozen agents and their assistants, to even see them; and when he should do so in relation to one band, the next nearest would probably be several hundred miles distant, without whose assent they could not finally act; and by the time you had seen half a dozen bands and got their consent to any proposed measure, it would be needful to go back, for some of them by this time will have rued their bargain.

In fact, it were as well to say at once that nothing but a great council of both nations together promises any probable favorable result in negotiation with them. Under all the circumstances of the case, I suppose Fort Bridger to be the most proper place, as it is unquestionably the easiest of access to them; and besides, it has for a long period been the principal place where they have traded. And then the vast valleys of the finest grass on the very many fine small streams and brooks in that vicinity, which abound in fine fish, make it the most fit place for such an assemblage. And then there are no settlements of whites in the vicinity, to corrupt them with spirits and other things, to annoy; for such traders as may be there will be subject to the law, and can be restrained under proper regulations. And then it will be within a reasonable distance of Fort Hall, or Bear river, from which a company or two of troops could easily attend, to keep proper regulations; and it will be quite within reach of this place to obtain *there* such supplies of provisions as may be wanted to give a feast, and such like affairs, to facilitate the intercourse with them. Whether the whole system, as at present practised with the Indians under the present statute regulations of the nation, is to be changed or not, so far as these tribes are concerned it ought to be greatly modified. As this is their first intercourse with us, some wholesome regulations may easily be adopted with them, that perhaps could not so easily be introduced amongst those already accustomed to the old mode: for instance, I would exclude all matters of ornament, such as beads, rings, rattles, paints, and a thousand other gewgaws which have been invented expressly for the purpose of cheating these poor people out of whatever little they may have to dispose of, and thus impose upon them articles not only worthless in themselves, but calculated expressly to deceive them as to their intrinsic value. Heretofore the Utahs have driven a large trade in horses, the larger number of which they have stolen from the Mexicans. Some check should be placed on this traffic, which now forms much the larger item of the trade between them and the traders, who have heretofore enjoyed a monopoly of this traffic: either to forbid a sale of a horse altogether, except the consent of some proper man, duly appointed for that purpose, was first had, or unless it could be shown satisfactorily that the Indian had raised or purchased fairly the horse he offered for sale; for it will be exceedingly hard to induce them to quit stealing horses, as long as traders are at liberty to purchase all they bring them. And it cannot be possible that the government can discharge its duty so as to fairly satisfy that philanthropy which unquestionably gave rise to the Indian system under our government, unless traders are regulated both as to *kind* and *prices* of the goods they are allowed to vend to them.

The plan, however, which my judgment dictates as the most proper is, that the government itself should be their *sole factors,* and allow no private trader to go amongst them.

Let the government receive, transmit, and dispose of all they have to spare, and furnish them with all that their produce could pay for, and such other gifts as the government may see proper to add, without charging commission for goods sold for them, or levying per cents on those sold to them—charging only actual costs and charges. This system adopted and placed under the charge of the proper class of men, and I will venture the opinion that in a few years you will see a corresponding improvement of the Indians; and if the previously-formed opinions in favor of the old system are too strong to allow a change of the whole, let it be tried with these unfortunate people within the bounds of Mexican California, and I venture the assertion that these wild and degraded Indians will be greatly improved, more than half of whom already are reduced to the necessity of living upon roots and the mountain black cricket, somewhat resembling, only larger than, the grasshopper, and which in this country is far more destructive on vegetation than the latter.

That portion of the Sho-sho-nies called Sho-sho-coes, (or Walkers,) being without horses, cannot now even go to where a buffalo is to be killed, and consequently are not only deprived of the meat so necessary for their support, but also of their skins, which are equally indispensable to make lodges and clothes to keep them from freezing in these mountains, where the perpetual snows forever are within their sight; and the consequence is, they are obliged to seek such holes and caves in the declivities of these "everlasting hills" as they can find, to keep them and their children from freezing. There are many warm and hot springs throughout this country, and it is said to be no uncommon thing to see them sheltering themselves and their children from the bleak and terrible storms which prevail in these grand and rugged mountains by lying during the greater part of the day (and perhaps night too) in their waters.

It were useless for me to say more at present. The above views appear to me to be correct; and, although the miserable condition of these poor Indians furnishes many other facts and reasons to enforce the necessity of the changes recommended to be made, still I have not time or room to place them before you now: at some future period I may do so. I hope to have your response to these views as early as possible, directed to San Francisco, that I may have ample time, if you approve, to call the tribes together as I propose.

Your obedient servant,
JOHN WILSON,
Indian Agent at the Salt Lake, California.

Hon. THOMAS EWING,
Secretary of the Department of the Interior.

DEPARTMENT OF THE INTERIOR,
Office Indian Affairs, April 14, 1849.

SIR: I have the honor to enclose herewith an appointment for you as sub-Indian agent on the Sacramento and San Joachim rivers, in California, to include the Indians at or in the vicinity of those places, and any others that may hereafter be designated by this department. Your compensation will be at the rate of $750 per annum, to be in full for pay and all emoluments whatsoever. You will execute a bond in the penal sum of $2,000, with two or more sureties, whose sufficiency must be certified by a United States district judge or district attorney.

So little is known here of the condition and situation of the Indians in that region, that no specific instructions relative to them can be given at present; and the department relies on you to furnish it with such statistical and other information as will give a just understanding of every particular relating to them, embracing the names of the tribes; their location; the probable extent of territory owned or claimed by each respectively; the tenure by which they claim it; their manners, habits, disposition, and feelings towards the United States and whites generally, and towards each other; whether hostile or otherwise; whether the tribes speak different languages; and where different, the apparent analogies between them; and also what laws and regulations for their government are necessary, and how far the law regulating trade and intercourse with the Indian tribes (a copy of which I enclose) will, if extended to that country, properly apply to the Indians there, and to the trade and intercourse with them; and what modification, if any, will be required to produce the greatest degree of efficiency.

You are authorized to employ one or more interpreters—not exceeding more than one at the same time, unless otherwise absolutely necessary—to aid you in the discharge of your duties, whose compensation, if employed by the year, will be at the rate of $300 per annum. It is very desirable that the greatest economy shall be observed; and it is therefore hoped that the employment of one permanent interpreter will be sufficient, and that the services of any others will be but temporary, and for as short periods as possible consistent with a proper discharge of your duties.

You will report direct to this office, and will lose no opportunity of doing so, as it is extremely desirable that the department be kept well advised of the state of affairs in that region.

It is possible you will wish to avail yourself of the military escort about to leave St. Louis, and funds will therefore be placed in the hands of the superintendent at that place, to be turned over to you as follows:

One year's salary for self	$750
One year's salary for interpreter	300
Pay of interpreter temporarily employed	100
Contingent expenses, including presents to Indians; purchase of two horses for yourself and your interpreter; collection of statistical information; forage for horses; house rent, fuel, stationery, &c., together with your travelling expenses	1,200
	2,350

You are authorized to purchase two horses, one for yourself and one for your interpreter, for which you will be held accountable as public property. In making presents to Indians, you will be as economical as possible, and confine yourself to such cases only as will effect some important object. It is supposed that there are captives or prisoners—either Mexicans or Americans—among some of the Indians of California or New Mexico. If you should find such to be the case among the Indians of your sub-agency, you will demand and endeavor to procure their release and surrender, whether Americans or Mexicans; but it must, if possible, be done without any compensation whatever, as to make compensation would but encourage a continuance of the practice of making captives; and any demand must be made under circumstances not calculated to produce mischief or hostile feelings on the part of the Indians.

I enclose blank forms to guide you in rendering your accounts, which must be done quarter-yearly, or as nearly so as possible. In rendering your accounts, you will account for the money placed in your hands under the following heads of appropriation, viz:

Pay of sub-agents	$750
Pay of interpreters	400
Contingencies Indian department	1,200
	2,350

I also herewith enclose a copy of the late treaty with Mexico; and also copies of the reports of Messrs. Frémont, Emory, Abert, and Cook, which will be useful to you.

Very respectfully,

W. MEDILL.

ADAM JOHNSTON, Esq., *Present.*

DEPARTMENT OF THE INTERIOR,
April 14, 1849.

SIR: This will be handed to you by the Hon. T. Butler King, if there should be, in his opinion, occasion for so doing. The object of this letter is to impress upon you the desire of the President that you should in all matters connected with Mr. King's mission aid and assist him in carrying out the views of the government, as expressed in his instructions from the Department of State, and that you should be guided by his advice and counsel in the conduct of all proper measures within the scope of those instructions.

I am, very respectfully, your obedient servant,

T. EWING, *Secretary.*

ADAM JOHNSTON, Esq., *Indian Sub-agent for the*
Sacramento and San Joachim rivers, California.

DEPARTMENT OF THE INTERIOR,
Office Indian Affairs, May 2, 1849.

SIR: Your bond as sub-Indian agent, transmitted with your letter of the —— ultimo, has received the approval of the Secretary of the Interior.

Very respectfully, &c.,

W. MEDILL.

ADAM JOHNSTON, Esq.,
Sub-Indian Agent, St. Louis, Mo.

DEPARTMENT OF THE INTERIOR,
Office Indian Affairs, November 24, 1849.

SIR: I enclose you a number of circulars requiring to be filled up for the tribes of Indians under your care, and will thank you for the replies.

I also transmit you a copy of a bibliographical catalogue, by which you will perceive that this office is desirous of obtaining copies of any publication in the Indian tongues, or upon their principle.

Very respectfully, &c.,

ORLANDO BROWN.

ADAM JOHNSTON, Esq.,
Sacramento, California.

A similar letter sent to JOHN A. SUTTER, Esq.

DEPARTMENT OF THE INTERIOR,
Office Indian Affairs, November 24, 1849.

SIR: The Secretary of the Interior has directed that two sub-agencies be formed out of the one now held by you, and has appointed John A. Sutter, Esq., of California, sub-agent for all the Indians on the Sacramento river—your own to be confined to those in the valley of San Joachim. Mr. Sutter's commission has been forwarded to him, and he has been requested to communicate with you as to the dividing line between your agencies, so that the relative boundaries may be perfectly understood between you.

Very respectfully, &c.,
ORLANDO BROWN.

ADAM JOHNSTON, Esq.,
San Francisco, California.

DEPARTMENT OF THE INTERIOR,
Office Indian Affairs, November 24, 1849.

SIR: I have the honor to enclose herewith a commission constituting you sub-Indian agent on the Sacramento river in California, to include the Indians there or in the vicinity thereof, and any others that may hereafter be designated by this department.

Your compensation will be at the rate of $750 per annum; to be in full for pay and all emoluments whatsoever.

You will execute a bond in the penal sum of $2,000, with two or more sureties, whose sufficiency must be certified by a district judge or United States attorney, or by the commandant of a military post.

This sub-agency lately included the valley of the San Joachim, but is now separated, and two distinct sub-agencies formed out of it; the one on the Sacramento to be held by you, and that on the San Joachim by the present incumbent, Adam Johnston, esq. It would be well for you to communicate with Mr. Johnston, and have an understanding as to the relative boundaries of separation between the two.

Very little is known here of the condition, situation, and locality of these Indians, and the department looks to you to furnish it with such statistical and other information as will give any particulars relating to them, embracing the names of the tribes; their location; the probable extent of country owned by each respectively; the tenure by which they claim it; their manners, habits, and disposition towards the United States and whites generally, and towards each other—whether hostile or otherwise; whether the tribes speak different languages, and, where different, the apparent analogies between them; and also what laws and regulations for their government are necessary, and how far the law regulating trade and intercourse with the Indian tribes (a copy of which I enclose) will, if extended to that country, properly apply to the Indians there, and to trade and intercourse with them; and what modification, if any, will be required to produce the greatest degree of efficiency.

You are authorized to employ one or more interpreters, but it is supposed more than one will not be required at any one time, and no more should be employed unless it is absolutely necessary to aid you in the discharge of your duties. The compensation of the interpreters, if employed by the year, will be at the rate of $300 per annum; but where employed temporarily, you will procure their services on the best terms you can, and for the shortest possible periods.

You are authorized to purchase two horses, one for your own use and one for the use of your interpreter, for which you will be held accountable as public property. Two hundred dollars will be allowed for this object.

The sum of three hundred dollars per annum will be allowed you for contingent expenses and such small presents as you may from time to time find it proper to make; but in these you will confine yourself to cases where some object is to be effected of importance to the government or to the Indians.

As the country of California is under military law, it will be proper for you to confer with the military governor or the commandants of the military posts in your vicinity, and obtain their co-operation in all cases where you find assistance necessary either in obtaining the restitution of captives among the Indians, whether Americans or Mexicans, or in any other manner. There being no appropriation out of which payment can be made for the restoration of captives, of course you will incur no expense on that account.

I enclose blank forms to guide you in rendering your accounts, which must be done quarter-yearly, or as nearly so as possible.

You are authorized to draw for the following sums, after your bond shall have been approved, and will account for them under the following heads of appropriation, viz:

Pay of sub-agent one year	$750 00
Pay of interpreters one year	400 00
Contingencies, to include purchase of two horses and presents	500 00
	1,650 00

Very respectfully, &c.,

ORLANDO BROWN.

John A. Sutter, Esq.,
   San Francisco, California.

P. S.—Copies of this letter have been forwarded to Sacramento and to Sutter's Mills. Your commission and accompanying papers are forwarded with this to San Francisco.

O. B.

General Land Office, *July* 5, 1849.

Sir: By a communication of the 29th ultimo, the Secretary of the Interior advised this office of your appointment as confidential agent of the government to visit Mexico and California, in order to obtain information, " as early as practicable, of the character and extent of the titles and claims to lands within the limits of the tract of country acquired by the United States by the late treaty with Mexico, purporting to have emanated from the former authorities of that country." At the same time, the Secretary has requested that such instructions and information may be given to you as the objects in view may render necessary. It is a principle of public law, now acknowledged and recognised by the usage of modern nations, that, though the sovereignty changes, private rights remain unaffected by that change; and consequently that the relation of the people to each other under such circumstances, and "their rights of property, remain undisturbed." This principle is explicitly recognised and sanctioned in the treaty between the United States and Mexico, as ratified on the 4th July, 1848, which in the most solemn form, and as the supreme law of the land, makes it obligatory upon our government to respect the valid and *bona fide* titles of individuals, and, in reference to the future management of the public domain within the limits of our newly acquired territories, makes it incumbent upon us to take such measures as will enable our government to separate from the mass of the public lands all private property resting upon such titles derived from the former governments. To this end, therefore, and in view of the directions from the Secretary, you are hereby instructed:

1. To proceed without delay to Upper California, and to visit such places as Monterey on the Pacific, San Francisco, San Diego, or any other points you may deem necessary, in order to obtain full and authentic information to enable you to have access to all the provincial, departmental, or other records and archives connected with titles and claims to land in California, seeking facilities and aid from the United States military officers in command there, or from such persons as may be officiating judicially or in other civil capacities, for the time being, under the existing customs of the community.

2. Having gained access to those archives, you will then, after a careful and thorough examination of them, prepare a complete and perfect *abstract*, in such a form, as to arrangement and classification, as will exhibit the particulars—

First. As to all grants or claims in the territories derived from the government of Spain when her authorities held dominion over the country, showing the dates of such; the names of the original grantees; the area of each claim, with its front and depth; the name of the watercourse, or other natural object indicating locality; whether or not surveyed; the date of survey, with the name of the officer making the grant, stating whether such grants have been sanctioned; and if so, when and by what officer or authority under the *Mexican* government, designating such as are in regular and legal form and appear *prima facie* to be *bona fide* valid titles, and such as are fraudulent or suspicious, reporting the reasons and grounds of the discrimination you may make.

Second. A similar abstract of such titles as were derived from the authorities of *Mexico* since the separation of that country as an independent republic from Old Spain, indicating the names of the granting officers in each case; dates, &c., of each element of title from the inceptive to the survey, and to the concession or title in form, showing whether the same emanated direct from the supreme government of Mexico, or from the departmental authorities, with information as to the titles and powers of the granting officers; dates of their commissions and periods of incumbency, with such data as you may be able to procure touching their powers, and how derived, for alienating the national property; specifying such grants as appear to be regular and valid, and such as are of an opposite character. You will be pleased to discriminate between such as are perfect titles, clothed with all legal formalities, and such as are inceptive or inchoate, and in all cases designating the names of the parties appearing in the archives, land or judicial records, as " present claimants," or whom, from authentic and reliable sources, you may find to be so, with a reference to the evidence you may have before you of present proprietorship.

Third. You will also make a separate classification and abstract of all grants or titles made about the time of the *revolutionary* movements in California—say in the months of June and July, 1846—and up to the period when actual hostilities between the United States and Mexico were known in California, and also of any which may have been subsequently made; showing the dates of sales; area of tracts; names of original grantees; when and by whom made; whether surveyed or not; whether to residents, non-residents, or foreigners; whether or not allotted with the usual legal formalities; and specifying such as may have been made without legal authority, with an abstract of the evidence of transfer by the grantors, and of such evidence to others from the grantees.

Fourth. You will obtain a copy of all the different authentic forms of title, from the first element up to the consummation of the grant—such as the petition, decree, order of survey, return of actual survey, concession grant, with the denomination of the various allotments, from a square league "*un sitio de gañado mayor*," or square league of 4,428 acres, down to the smallest farm, or village, or town lot, with the ratios usual between the fronts and depths, and will prepare a comparative statement of the land measures formerly used in California under Spain and Mexico, and those now employed in the United States.

3. You will direct particular attention to the extensive tracts or bodies of land covered by what are known as "*missions.*" You will ascertain as fully as possible the extent, locality, and value of each of them, and of the buildings or improvements thereon; will trace out their early history, origin, and date of the establishment of them, respectively, and their transition, and under what authority from the ecclesiastical to the civil power, or national authorities; their condition as to title and possession at the commencement of hostilities between the two republics; the dates of any sales made about that time, previously or subsequently; the circumstances under which, to whom and by whom made, and under color of what authority, with the dates of subsequent sales by parties claiming under grants from the California authorities; with the particulars in each case as to date, consideration, &c., accompanied by plats or sketches exhibiting their actual location and relative position to places now laid down on maps of the country.

4. You will carefully examine and report all the information you can obtain as to whether any titles were granted to "*mines,*" either of the precious metals, quicksilver, or other minerals; when and to whom made; the considerations; conditions; whether or not surveyed; localities; and all matters in regard to the same, particularly in respect to the validity or invalidity of any individual titles or claims which may be alleged to the same.

5. You will also extend your researches so as to ascertain whether any claim has been set up or alleged to the *islands* or *keys,* or any other point on the coast, or in the bays or harbors; and if so, the nature of such claims; whether or not in legal form and from competent

authorities of the former governments, or whether invalid, as against the title of the United States to all the public property under treaty—this inquiry being special, in view of the importance which some of these islands may be to the United States for fortifications and light-houses.

6. You will make an inquiry into the nature of the "*Indian rights*" as existing under the Spanish and Mexican governments, and as subsisting when the United States obtained the sovereignty, indicating from authoritative data the difference between the privileges enjoyed by the wandering tribes and those who have made "actual settlements" and established "rancherias;" and will report their general form, extent, and locality, their probable number, and the manner and form in which such rights have been recognised by the Spanish and Mexican governments.

7. In returning, you are authorized, if you can do so without protracting too long your stay, to proceed to Santa Fe, the capital of New Mexico, and there obtain access to the archives of that country, and to furnish similar information as to all titles which have emanated from the authorities when New Mexico was a province of Spain, and subsequently under the government of the Mexican republic.

Information has reached here that the prefecto at El Paso del Norte, since we acquired the country, had been actually engaged in disposing, for his own benefit, of the most valuable lands on the Rio Grande bottom, antedating titles to purchasers. You will, therefore, make a thorough inquiry and report in this matter, and prepare a complete abstract of such fraudulent grants.

An important object in your appointment is to obtain for our government reliable and authentic information in regard to the whole land system of the former governments while operating in the country comprised within the limits of our new acquisitions; and to this end, you are authorized, either in going or returning, to visit the city of Mexico, for the purpose of examining the archives and obtaining the data desired, and will regard the points specified as intended to guide, but not confine your powers, which you will consider sufficiently expansive to accomplish all the purposes contemplated.

You will keep a journal of all your proceedings as the confidential agent of the government, noting the places in which the archives are deposited, and in whose custody, with minutes of every transaction or incident connected with the subject which you think would be important or useful to the government in determining upon an enlightened and just policy, not only in respect to individual titles, but in the management and disposal of the public domain.

Very respectfully, your obedient servant,

J. BUTTERFIELD,
Commissioner.

Wm. Carey Jones, Esq., *Confidential Agent, &c.*

Department of the Interior,
July 11, 1849.

Sir: That I may be enabled to lay before Congress, at their next session, something reliable as to the condition of land titles in California, it is important that the archives in that Territory, and also in the city of Mexico, (so far as they touch those titles,) be examined and reported upon by a competent person.

To this end, I desire that such person be sent, with official authority to make the necessary examination, to collect and secure the original archives in California, and to procure the necessary copies in the city of Mexico. This latter duty must necessarily be performed under authority from the State Department.

For this mission I propose William Carey Jones, esq., well known to you as an adept in the Spanish language, and, as a lawyer, well skilled in the Spanish colonial titles. I propose, if it meet your approbation, that you commission him to visit the city of Mexico for this purpose, and that he be permitted to go by San Francisco, Monterey, and San Diego, and other places in California, and make at those points the necessary investigations for his government while engaged in California. I have caused the accompanying instructions to be prepared at the General Land Office; and I propose, if you approve it, that he be governed by them, so far as they may be applicable, in his examination at the city of Mexico also.

I am, very respectfully, yours,

T. EWING.

Hon. JOHN M. CLAYTON,
Secretary of State.

DEPARTMENT OF THE INTERIOR,
July 12, 1849.

SIR: I have examined and approved the instructions prepared for you in the General Land Office, and I desire information on all the matters therein named; but it is important that your report should come in prior to the termination of the next session of Congress; and you are charged with duties so extended and diversified, that you will probably not be able to make, in time, the detailed examination contemplated by those instructions.

You will, however, obtain all the information in your power on all the subjects referred to therein; but direct your attention, in the first place, to the mode of creating titles to land, from the first inception to the perfect title, as practised by Mexico within the province of California; what kind of paper issued in the first instance, from what officer, when filed, and how and by whom recorded. So also with the subsequent steps, embracing the proceedings as to survey up to the perfecting of the title; and if there be record books, files, or archives of any kind whatsoever, showing the nature, character, and extent of these grants, endeavor to find and secure them, so that they may be placed in the hands of the acting governor of the Territory for safe custody and future reference. In descending to details, you will examine chiefly the larger grants, as the missions, and find whether the title to them be in assignees, or whether they have reverted and vested in the sovereign.

It is also understood that there are large grants, and grants of islands, keys, and promontories, points of great value to the public, which purport to have emanated just prior to the occupation of the territory by the United States, but which are probably fictitious and really entitled to a later date.

These you will examine carefully, and note down fully all the information which can be had on the spot which will throw light on them when they shall be hereafter the subjects of investigation, stating the nature of the alleged title, whether purporting to be inchoate or complete. If there be any alleged grants of lands covering a portion of the gold mines, you will also give to that your careful consideration. It will be a question worthy of examination, when in the city of Mexico, whether in all grants in general, or in California in particular, there are not conditions and limitations, and whether there is not a reservation of mines of gold and silver, and a similar reservation as to quicksilver and other minerals.

It is also important in all large grants, or grants of important or valuable sites, or of mines, to ascertain whether or not they were actually surveyed and occupied under the government of Spain, or Mexico, and when publicity was first given to such grants, particularly as to such as are of a suspicious or doubtful character.

This department has no authority to pay you anything on account of your services; but you will be paid out of the contingent fund of the General Land Office a sum sufficient to cover your expenses while in California, and also your necessary expenditures in procuring information, and finding and putting in a place of security any books of records of land titles or other archives relating thereto, for which your drafts, not exceeding twenty-five hundred dollars in the whole, accompanied by a letter stating the special objects to which it has been, or is about to be, applied, will be duly honored.

You will be pleased to keep an account of your personal expenses, and also of the expenditures required in the execution of your duties, and make a rendition of the same to this department, to which, as to titles, &c., in California, you will make your report; and in reference to your examinations in Mexico you will make a separate communication to the State Department, a notice of which should be given in your report to this department. An application will be made by this department to Congress for an appropriation as an allowance to you of a fair compensation for your services.

Wishing you a pleasant voyage, and health and success in your arduous undertaking,

I am, very respectfully, your obedient servant,

T. EWING.

Wm. Carey Jones, Esq.

Monterey, California,
September 30, 1849.

Dear Sir: I arrived here on Monday night two weeks since, after a passage of twenty days from Panama. The old archives are here, and I commenced immediately the investigations with which I am charged. Gen. Riley promptly gave directions for all the archives to be open to me; and I hope to be able to make a pretty full report, and with as much despatch as we had originally supposed possible. The archives, however, are very imperfect, and in utter confusion: so much so, that I think a competent person ought to be employed to go over them, sheet by sheet, and collate and arrange them. I do not find any book of records earlier than 1839. The two which I understood from you Col. Mason spoke of, extend from that year to the close of 1845. Whether any book was commenced for 1846 I have not learned; but hope to do so when at Los Angeles, where all the records were at that time kept, and the persons who were employed in the public offices reside   In the hurried reading which I gave to Mr. Halleck's report previous to leaving, I did not observe what is stated in a note of Col. Stevenson's in the appendix, namely: that " two large boxes, said to contain the archives of the Departmental Assembly," were delivered to Commodore Stockton in August, 1846, and " supposed to have been put on board the Congress." The records of the Departmental Assembly are particularly deficient, and the above suggestion may account for it. I would suggest that Commodore Stockton be applied to for information. His reply might possibly reach me from the department and be of use to me before 1 shall be ready to leave.

There is one thing in regard to grants in this country which will call for more liberal legislation than Congress has hitherto accorded, in confirming grants in territories acquired from foreign powers. I allude to the *size* of the grants. They are nearly all large. The Mexican colonization laws, under which the bulk of the grants have been made here, allow as high as *eleven sitios* (eleven leagues square) to be granted to individuals. In many instances the full privilege has been used, and there are very few grants, under those laws, of less than *two sitios*, while four, five, six, eight, and ten, are quite common.

Touching politics, I found a convention in session here, engaged on precisely the work which I suppose will meet your views—forming a State constitution. The convention will finish its work this week, and, I believe, hope to have their Senators and Representatives elected ready to send everything up to you by the steamer which leaves the 1st December. I find there is no lack of candidates for the high offices. A number of persons seem to have come out during the past summer, with no other view than to go back with a title to four thousand miles of *mileage* in their pockets.

If I should find a good opportunity to exchange the bill, I shall take the liberty of drawing upon you, by the present steamer, for the sum of one thousand dollars. I hope still to keep within the sum (fifteen hundred dollars) for which you originally proposed to give me authority to draw.

Very respectfully, sir, your obedient servant and friend,
WM. CAREY JONES.
Hon. Mr. EWING,
Secretary of the Interior.

OCTOBER 1.

DEAR SIR: I have only drawn by this steamer for two hundred dollars, in favor of my wife. Having received the money here and appropriated it, I shall have to draw in the course of this month for probably eight hundred more.

Yours, truly,
WM. CAREY JONES.

[18]

Report on the laws and regulations relative to grants or sales of public lands in California, by H. W. Halleck.

STATE DEPARTMENT OF THE TERRITORY OF CALIFORNIA,
Monterey, March 1, 1849.

SIR: In compliance with your instructions, I have collected together and examined all archives of the government of California which can be found, and have the honor to report as follows:

1st. On the laws and regulations which govern the granting or selling of public lands in California.

2d. On the laws and regulations respecting the lands and other property belonging to the missions of California.

3d. On the titles of lands in California which may be required for fortifications, arsenals, or other military structures, for the use of the general government of the United States.

The translations of the laws are made by Mr. W. E. P. Hartwell, the government translator, and are almost literal versions of the original.

Very respectfully, your obedient servant,
H. W. HALLECK,
Brevet Captain and Secretary of State.

Colonel R. B. MASON,
Commanding 10*th military department, and Governor of California.*

I. *Laws and regulations governing grants or sales of public lands in California.*—The first authority for granting land in Upper California is contained in the viceroy's instructions to the commandant of the "New Establishments of San Diego and Monterey," dated August 17, 1773. By articles 12, 13, 14 and 15 of these instructions, the commandant is empowered both to designate common lands, and to grant titles to individuals, whether Indians or new settlers, in the vicinity of the missions or pueblos. He might also, if he deemed it expedient, change any mission into a pueblo, and subject it to the same civil and economical laws as governed the other pueblos of the kingdom.—(Vide appendix No. 1.)

On the 21st of September, 1774, the viceroy wrote to the commandant in Upper California, granting permission to the soldiers of the garrisons to marry the baptized Indian girls of the missions, and authorizing the assignment of lands to the soldiers so marrying. The first grant of this kind was that of a piece of land in Carmel Valley, of one hundred and forty varas, to Manuel Butron, who had married an Indian girl of the mission of San Carlos.

In order better to carry out the wishes of the Spanish government in reference to the establishment of depots of provisions, &c., in Upper California, for refreshing the Spanish vessels from the East Indies, and to furnish supplies to the garrison of the presidios, directions were sent by the viceroy to Governor Neve in June, 1777, to establish two pueblos, one on the "Rio Guadalupe," and the other on the "Rio Porcincula," and to portion out ground to the new *pobladores,* or colonists.

On the 1st of June, 1779, the governor drew up a new set of regulations for the government of California, which was approved by the King in a royal order of October 24, 1781. Title 14 of these regulations contains instructions respecting colonization, and the government of the new colonists. Each publador was to receive a bounty of $116 44 per annum for the first two years, and $60 per annum for the next three years; and also was to have the loan of horses, mules, cattle, farming utensils, &c. The streets, squares, municipal and common lands of the pueblos, and the *solares* or house-lots, and *suertes* of sowing lands of the *pobladores*, were to be designated by the government.

Discharged soldiers were to receive building and planting lots, the same as the colonists. All the *pobladores* were to possess the right of pasturing their cattle and of cutting wood on the common lands of the pueblos. Certain conditions were to be attached to these grants of land, such as the building of houses, planting of trees, &c., within a specified period of time.—(Vide appendix No. 2.)

These regulations, with slight modifications, have formed the basis of the laws which have ever since governed the pueblos of California.

On the 22d of October, 1791, orders were sent to Governor Romen authorizing the captains of the presidios to grant and distribute house-lots and lands to the soldiers and citizens within the extent of two common leagues in every direction from the centre of each presidio square.—(Vide appendix No. 3.)

Immediately after the independence of Mexico, and during the government of Iturbide, a system of laws were established for colonization, dated April 11, 1823; but as these laws were suspended almost immediately afterwards, it is believed no grants of land were made under them in Upper California. On the 18th of August, 1824, the constituent congress passed a decree for the colonization of the territories of the republic, which decree was limited and defined by a series of regulations, dated Nov. 21, 1828.

By these laws and regulations the governors (gefes politicos) of territories were authorized to grant (with certain specified exceptions) vacant lands to contractors, *(empressarios,)* heads of families, and private persons. The grants to *empressarios* for colonies or towns were not to be valid till approved by the supreme government.

No grants were made to individuals or single families to be held as definitively valid, till approved by the territorial deputation; and if the territorial deputation should not give its approval, the governor was to refer the documents to the supreme government for its action.

But, without the previous approval of the supreme government, no territorial governor could make grants of land within ten leagues of the sea-coast, nor within twenty leagues of the boundaries of any foreign power. Moreover, the general government reserved to itself the right to make use of any portion of these lands for the purpose of constructing warehouses, arsenals, or other public edifices which it might deem expedient for the defence or security of the nation. The maximum and minimum amounts of land which could be given to any one person were specified, and also the circumstances under which the grant should become void.—(Vide appendix Nos. 4 and 5.)

These laws and regulations are believed to be still in force, as they are referred to in the titles to lands granted in Upper California as late as July 8, 1846. The usual form of a confirmation of a grant of land by the territorial legislature is as follows: "The grant made to N, of the place called ——, in the jurisdiction of ——, comprising —— sitios of large cattle, (square leagues,) is approved according to the title given to him on the —— day of ——, 184—, in conformity with the law of the 18th of August, 1824, and the 5th article of the regulations of the 21st of November, 1828.

"A. B., *President of the Departmental Assembly.*

"C. D., *Secretary.*"

The restriction contained in paragraph 4 of the decree of August 18, 1824, is also fully recognised in the proceedings of the territorial legislature. For example: in the instructions of the territorial junta to the deputy from Upper California to the general congress of Mexico, dated July 25, 1836, (paragraph 4,) it is expressly conceded that the general government of Mexico alone had power to dispose of islands on the coast of California; and (paragraph 19) the deputy is directed to solicit from the general government an absolute confirmation of the grants of lands made in California under the colonization decree of August 18, 1824, and the regulations of November 21, 1828, releasing the proprietors from the restrictions contained in these laws and regulations.

Again: in 1840, the territorial deputation made a representation to the general government, asking that the law of colonization be extended so as to include lands lying within ten leagues of the coast of California, and that the grants already made by the territorial government within these limits be confirmed by Mexico. It is believed, however, that the general government never acted on this representation, and that the aforementioned laws and regulations remain unchanged.

The restriction contained in paragraph 7 of the regulations of November 21, 1828, is also recognised in the proceedings of the territorial legislature, and has been announced and enforced by the supreme government. In 1845, when the supreme government confirmed the grant made to Don Estenare Smith of lands situated at and near the port of Bodega, orders were issued that no more grants of that kind be made by the territorial government, without obtaining the necessary authority from the supreme government of Mexico.—(Vide Governor Alvarado's certificate, appendix No. 6.)

Again this restriction is alluded to and recognised in a letter from the Department of Relations, dated Mexico, August 11, 1845, and signed Louis G. Cuenas; and in a letter from the Minister of Foreign Affairs, Government, and Policy, dated Mexico, January 19, 1846, and signed Costillo Lauras—both of these letters having reference to the Macnamara colonization grant—and even in the grant itself, which was given by Governor Pico, and dated July 4, 1846, it is expressly stated that the approval of the supreme government is necessary to make it valid.—(Vide Senate Doc. No. 75, 1st session 30th Congress.)

The territorial governments were originally prohibited from making grants of public lands of the islands of the coast, as well as of those in the bays, without the consent or approbation of the general government of Mexico; but the consent of the supreme executive power was given in 1838 to make grants of islands on the *coast* of California. The islands in the bays, however, are not included in this permission.—(Vide appendix No. 7.)

The general government of Mexico has also reserved to itself the right to take, and use for the purpose of fortifications or arsenals, lands belonging to any *State*, by indemnifying the State for the value of the lands so taken. This law was passed by Congress the 6th of April, 1830, and is in the following words:

"ART. 4. The Executive may take such lands as it considers useful for fortifications or arsenals, and for the new colonies, indemnifying the States for the value thereof out of the amount due by them (the different States) to the federation."

This same law repealed the 7th article of the law of August 18, 1824, in the following words:

"Art. 11. In virtue of the power which the general Congress reserved to itself in the 7th article of the law of the 18th of August, 1824, foreigners belonging to nations whose possessions are bounded by the States and territories of the federation are prohibited from colonizing such adjoining lands; consequently, all contracts opposed to this law which may not as yet have been fulfilled shall be suspended."

A large number of land titles in California are very indefinite with respect to boundaries, the grants being for so many "sitios," "creaderos," &c., lying between certain hills, streams, &c., as shown by rough sketches attached to the petitions. These sketches frequently contain double the amount of land included in the grants; and even now very few of these grants have been surveyed or their boundaries definitely fixed. The usual form of these titles is shown in appendix No. 8.

Some of the land titles given by the California government contain conditions respecting their sale, &c., which are not only onerous to the holders, but contrary to the spirit of our laws. These onerous conditions should be removed by act of Congress. A number of the grants of land made by the governors of California have never been confirmed by the territorial legislature. In some cases that body has positively refused its approbation; in other cases it has merely declined to act until furnished with certain information respecting the amount asked for, its boundaries, &c.; in others again, the petition, though before the legislature, was not reached previous to its final adjournment in July, 1846; and it is probable that some of these titles through carelessness were never submitted to that body for approval. Again: it has been alleged, by very respectable authority, that certain titles to land were given by Governor Pico *after* the United States had taken possession of the country, and made to bear dates prior to the 7th of July, 1846. These grants have of course never been confirmed by the territorial legislature, for that body adjourned on the 8th of July, the day after our flag was raised at Monterey; nor have they been recorded in any book of records among the government archives, although it is said they purport to be so recorded. In settling land titles in this country, a broad distinction should be made between titles of this kind and those which were given in good faith by the California governors previous to our taking possession of this country, but which have failed to receive the requisite confirmation for want of action on the part of the territorial legislature. In appendix No. 9 I have given a description of the different land measures adopted by the Mexican government. The description and table are translated from the "Ordenanzas de Tierras y Aguas," by Mariaus Galvan, edition of 1844.

Where grants of land have been made by the territorial government for towns, (*fundos legal para pueblos*,) in conformity to the provisions of articles 10, 11, 12, and 13 of the regulations of November 21, 1828, the land lying within the limits of such grants may be disposed of by the founders or municipal authorities, agreeably to the general laws regulating the government of such towns. The spirit of these laws in California may be judged of by the following extracts from an act of the territorial deputation, dated August 6, 1834:

"Art. 1. The ayuntamientos will make application through the ordinary channels, requesting lands to be assigned to each pueblo for *egidos* (common lands,) and *proprios* (municipal lands.)

"Art. 2. The lands assigned to each pueblo for *proprios* shall be subdivided into middling-sized and small portions, and may be rented out or given at public auction, subject to an emphitennic rent or tax—*en senso enfitentico*. The present possessors of lands belonging to the *proprios* will pay an annual tax, to be imposed by the ayuntamiento, the opinion of three intelligent men of honor being first taken.

"Art. 3. For the grant of a household lot for building on, the parties interested shall pay six dollars, and two rials for each lot of one hundred varas square, and in the same manner for a larger or smaller quantity, at the rate of two rials for each vara front."

All grants, however, of land lying within ten leagues of the coast, whether made for towns or for any other purpose, must be approved by the supreme executive power of Mexico in order to make them valid; moreover, they are all subject to the reservation contained in article 5 of the law of August 18, 1824; that is, general government has reserved to itself the right to make use of any portion of these lands for the purpose of constructing warehouses, arsenals, and other public edifices.

These town grants are usually not only definitively limited in their extent, but are made with certain conditions respecting the sale or division of these municipal lands, the price being fixed by law.

It appears from the documents and laws which have been referred to—

1st. That no grants of land made by the governors of California, after the 21st of November, 1828, are valid without the approval of the territorial legislature, or of the supreme government of Mexico.

2d. That the governor and legislature of California could, without the approval of the supreme government, make no grants whatever of land within ten leagues of the seacoast, nor within twenty leagues of the boundaries of any foreign power; nor could they anywhere grant to any one person more than one league square *(una legua cuadrada)* of five thousand varas of irrigable land, *(tierra de regadio,)* four superficial ones of land dependent on the seasons, *(cuatro de superficie de temporal,)* and six superficial ones for rearing cattle, *(sers de superficie de abrenado.)*

3d. That where grants are made and properly approved for towns, all municipal lands lying within the limits of such grants may be disposed of by the municipal authorities in *solares* or building lots, in conformity to the laws applicable to such cases, except such lands as may be required by the general government for constructing warehouses, arsenals, or other public edifices, for the defence or security of the nation.

4th. That all lands in California not included within the limits of grants made in conformity to law, and prior to July 7, 1846, formed a part of the public domain of Mexico at the moment when the United States took possession of this territory.

Since the conquest no material change has taken place in the legal condition of land titles in this country.

Numerous applications have been made to the governor to decide upon the validity of these titles; but all questions of this kind have been postponed until some competent tribunal shall be formed for their adjudication, the several claimants being advised in the mean time to have their lands surveyed by some competent surveyor.

Soon after General Kearny became governor of this country, representations were made to him that it was important to the growth and prosperity of the town of San Francisco that the general government of the United States should immediately designate what land within the limits of that town was required for its use, (as pointed out in article 5 of the colonization law of August 18, 1824,) the town being permitted to dispose of the remainder as municipal lands. General Kearny, acting in the double capacity of civil governor of California and legal representative of the United States, made a decree, dated March 10, 1847, directing the selection of such land as was required for government purposes, and surrendering on the part of the United States all claim to the remainder within certain defined limits.

If the beach and water lots "included between the points known as the Rincon and *Fort Montgomery*" are actually included within the original limits of the town, this decree of General Kearny can hardly be regarded as an ordinary *land grant* made by a territorial governor; it was rather the act of an agent of the supreme executive power of the general government, designating the lands required for the purposes contemplated in article 5 of the law of August 18, 1824, and releasing the remaining lands within such limits from the action of the general reservation contained in that article.—(Vide appendix No. 10.)

Representations having been made in 1847 to the governor that the former alcalde of the town of Sonoma had been guilty of fraud in the grants and records of sale of municipal lands, a board of commissioners was appointed to examine into these charges, with powers to settle questions of title to these lands according to equity and justice. The proceedings and findings of these commissioners were approved by the governor, and, on the 9th of October, 1847, returned to the alcalde of Sonoma for file in his office.—(Vide appendix No. 11.)

Representations were also made to the governor that the municipal authorities of the pueblo of San José de Guadalupe had exceeded their powers in selling lands not belonging to, or at the disposal of, the town, and that they had divided up and granted or distributed to individuals all the common lands of the pueblo, the use of which had been conceded to the people of that place for the common purposes of pasture, wood, and sowing, but which had never been placed at the disposal of the municipal authorities either for distribution or sale. The opinion and action of the Executive on these proceedings are given in appendix No. 12.

It has also been alleged that the local authorities of other towns have not only disposed of municipal lands in a manner contrary to the provisions of the territorial laws, but in some instances have even gone beyond the limits of the town grants, and made sale of lands which properly belong to the national domain. But, as has already been said, there being no tribunals in the country competent to decide upon questions of this kind, they have been left for adjudication till the proper courts shall be established. And inasmuch as these questions touching the validity of land titles are exceedingly numerous, and as disputes are daily arising respecting the rights of the different claimants, it is deemed exceedingly important to the peace and prosperity of the country that measures be taken without delay for the speedy and final settlement of these titles upon principles of equity and justice.

II. *Laws and regulations respecting the lands and other property belonging to the missions of California.*—The first law relating to the secularization of the religious establishments of the missionary priests in America was passed by the Spanish cortes the 13th of September, 1813. This law was made with respect to the missions of Buenos Ayres, and the first five articles refer merely to the transfer of the establishments from one class of priests to another. The final article is as follows:

"The religious missionaries shall immediately cease from the government and administration of the property (haciendas) of said Indians, it being left to the care and election of these (Indians) to appoint amongst themselves, by means of their ayuntamientos, and with the intervention of the governor, persons to their satisfaction, capable of administering it, distributing the lands, and reducing them to private property, agreeably to the decree of the 4th of January, 1813, respecting the reduction of vacant and other lands to private dominion."

Basing themselves on the authority of this law, the governor and territorial deputation of California, under the pretence of ameliorating the condition of the natives, prepared a project for secularizing the missions of this province, and for converting them into pueblos or towns. Accordingly a *bando* or decree was issued on the 6th of January, 1831, designating the particular manner of parcelling out the lands and property of the several missions, and of regulating the government and police of the proposed towns. But the whole project (which, being without the approbation or authority of Mexico, was in itself illegal) was defeated by the new governor, who had arrived at Santa Barbara the 31st of December, 1830. The latter immediately recalled the bando of his predecessor, and forbade all attempts to carry it into execution.

The question of secularization was afterwards agitated in the general congress of Mexico; and on the 17th of August, 1833, a law for this object was passed by that body, and received the executive sanction. By this law the missions of Upper and Lower California were *secularized*, and became the property of the government. Each mission was to constitute a parish, and to be placed under the charge of a parish priest of the secular clergy, with a fixed salary. The churches of the several missions, with the sacred vessels, ornaments, and other appurtenances, and such adjacent buildings as the government might deem necessary, were to be assigned for the use of the parish. The most appropriate building of each mission was to be assigned for the habitation of the curate, with a lot of ground not exceeding two hundred varas square. The remaining edifices were to be designated for court-houses, preparatory schools, workshops, &c. A lot of ground was also to be laid out in each parish for a burial-ground. All the expenses of this law were to be provided for out of the "product of the estates, capitals, and revenues at present recognised as the pious fund of the missions of California."—(Vide appendix No. 13.)

The missions of both Upper and Lower California were thus made public property, and the lands which formerly belonged to these establishments could be disposed of, after the date of this law, only under the provisions of the decree of August 18, 1824, and the regulations of November 21, 1828. The case was anticipated and provided for in article 17 of these regulations.

Acting under the authority of these laws, the governor of California, (Figueroa,) on the 9th of August, 1834, issued "provisional regulations," converting ten of these missions into pueblos. By these regulations, the duties of the priests were confined to the spiritual affairs of the missions, while the territorial government assumed to itself the administration of all their temporal affairs. To each head of family, and to all over the age of twenty-one years even when having no family, was to be assigned a lot of land not exceeding four hundred varas square, nor less than one hundred varas, out of the common lands of the missions. Common lands, (*egidos*,) and, when convenient, municipal lands (*proprios*) also, were to be assigned to each pueblo. One-half of the stock, seeds, and agricultural implements of the missions was to be distributed to individuals in the same way; all other lands and property to remain at the disposal and direction of the governor. The fiscal affairs of these new pueblos were to be under the direction of ayuntamientos, while the legal matters were to be decided by the primary judges of the nearest towns. The emancipated Indians were to assist in the cultivation of the common grounds of the new pueblos, but were prohibited from selling any of the lots or stock assigned to them by the government. All contracts made by them were declared null and void, and the property sold by them was to be reclaimed by the government as national property—the purchasers losing their money. If these Indians died without heirs, their property reverted to the nation.—(Vide appendix No. 14.) In the extraordinary session of the legislature at Monterey, November 3, 1834, these provisional regulations (except that relating to the personal services of the Indians to the priests) were confirmed, and others formed marking out the different curacies, defining the salaries of the priests, &c.—(Vide appendix No. 15.) The whole direction of the temporal affairs of these missions was transferred from the priests to civil officers, called administrators, who were stationed in the missions, and who, under the general direction of the government, were to manage the property of these establishments for the benefit of the Indians. They, however, were prohibited from making any sales of mission property without the express orders of the government.

On the 7th of November, 1835, a decree of the supreme government directed that the execution of the law of August 17 be suspended until the curates mentioned in article 2 should take possession.—(Vide appendix No. 16.)

Governor Alvarado's regulations of January 17, 1839, declare null and void all debts contracted by these administrators without the previous consent of the government. On the 1st of March, 1840, he made new regulations for the government of the missions—replacing the administrators by mayordomos, and defining the powers and duties of the latter over these establishments. Both these sets of regulations seemed designed merely to carry out the provisions of the previous laws and decrees.—(Vide appendix Nos. 17 and 18.)

On the 29th of March, 1843, Governor Micheltorena ordered twelve of these missions to be delivered up to the direction and management of the priests—the same as formerly. The mission lands which had been granted previous to that date, and in accordance with the law, were not to be reclaimed; but all the cattle, property, and utensils of the missions which had been let out were to be restored to these establishments. One-eighth part of the total annual produce of these missions was to be paid into the public treasury for the support of the government troops and civil officers.—(Vide appendix No. 19.) By a decree of the departmental assembly of May 28, 1845, it was directed that certain missions (four in number) be considered as having already been converted into pueblos, and that their premises (except the reservations already mentioned) be sold at public auction. It was also directed that if the Indians of five other missions mentioned in the decree did not, after one month's public notice by proclamation, unite for the purpose of occupying and cultivating the said missions, these missions also should be declared unoccupied, and be disposed of as the assembly and departmental government should deem best for the general good; the remainder of the missions in Upper California (with the exception of the principal edifice at Santa Barbara) to be rented out at the option of the government—care being taken to secure their prosperity; one-half of the total rent of the mission of Santa Barbara was to be invested for the benefit of the church and the support of of its ministers, and the other half for the benefit of its Indians. Of the rents of the other missions, one-third was to go to the priests and churches, one-third to go to the benefit of the Indians, and one-third to be devoted to education and public beneficence, as soon as the legal debts of each mission were paid.—(Vide appendix No. 20.)

On the 28th of October, 1845, Governor Pico advertised for sale, to the highest bidder, five of the missions, and directed that, as soon as certain edifices of four other missions were selected for specified objects, the remaining edifices of those four establishments should also be sold at public auction. The day of sale and the manner of giving notice are specified in the regulations. Four other missions were to be rented to the highest bidder for the term of nine years. All the lands, vineyards, orchards, workshops, implements of agriculture, and other property of these missions, were to be included in the renting; but the principal edifice of the mission of Santa Barbara, and the churches, with the appurtenances, the court-houses, curates' houses, school houses, and the small portions of land occupied by certain Indians in each of the missions, were excepted in the order for renting. The proceeds of these rents were to be divided into three parts, and disposed of as has already been mentioned.

The renters were to pay their rents punctually and quarterly; and, at the expiration of the nine years, were to deliver back, with improvements, and in a serviceable order, the property of the missions. They were to return the same number and description of cattle as received, and of such an age as not to embarrass the procreation of the following year. Before they could receive these establishments they were to give bonds to the satisfaction of the government, conditioned on the fulfilment of their obligations, and the payment of such damages as the government should find against them. The government reserved to itself the right of taking care that these establishments should prosper; in virtue of which right, it would take such measures as might be necessary to prevent their distribution, ruin, or decline, during the period of their renting. Six other missions, whose names are given, were to be rented in the same manner, as soon as their debts could be arranged.—(Vide appendix No. 21.)

A decree of the departmental assembly of April 3, 1846, authorized the application of the laws of bankruptcy to certain missions, and, if necessary to prevent their total ruin, their sale at public auction, the customary notice being previously given. A portion of the lands and other property of these missions was to be set apart for the maintenance of the priests and the support of public worship. But this act was in no way to interfere with what had already been done under the previous decrees of the assembly. Six months at furthest were allowed for its fulfilment.—(Vide appendix No. 22.)

In 1846, after the adjournment of the departmental assembly for want of a quorum, and the flight of Governor Pico from the country, Captain Flores, who assumed to be governor *ad interim*, organized a kind of provisional legislature, which body, on the 30th of October, passed a decree annulling the sales of missions made by Pico, and authorizing the governor *ad interim* to mortgage these establishments for the purpose of raising loans of money to carry on the war. But, as these proceedings took place several months after the United States had taken possession of the country, they were evidently illegal, and of no force.—(Vide appendix No. 23.)

It appears from the documents and laws to which I have referred—

1. That since the 17th of August, 1833, the missions of California have been regarded as national property, and held at the disposal of the government.

2. That, when thus made the property of the nation, they could be disposed of by the territorial government only in accordance with the colonization laws of 1824 and 1828, or under the authority of some special law of the Mexican Congress.

3. That the territorial or departmental legislature, basing its authority on the laws of the Mexican Congress, has authorized the governor, on specified conditions, to convert certain of these missions into pueblos, to sell some, and rent others.

4. That the territorial or departmental governors, acting under the authority of the legislature, have converted certain of these missions into pueblos, and sold and rented others, establishing certain conditions or regulations for the conversion, sale, or renting of these establishments.

5. That where any of these missions have been regularly converted into pueblos, the municipal lands, or lands lying within the limits of the town grant, (*fundo legal para pueblo*,) are to be disposed of in *solares*, or building lots, according to the provisions of the law applicable to such cases. The *common* lands granted to these towns must remain as such until the legislature converts them into municipal lands, or otherwise authorizes their sale; and all lands lying without these town limits can be disposed of only in accordance with the laws and regulations of 1824 and 1828.

6. That the land set apart for the priest, in each mission, could not exceed two hundred varas square; nor could more than four hundred varas square be granted to any one individual.

7. That the lands granted to Indians were merely for the use of themselves and of their descendants; that they could in no way be disposed of by them, but when abandoned they reverted to government.

8. That all sales of mission property by the Indians are null and void.

9. That no civil agent or administrator could dispose of mission property, or contract debts in the name of the missions, without the previous authority of the government.

10. That no lease of a mission or of mission property is made in conformity to law, unless bonds have been given to the satisfaction of the government, conditioned for the fulfilment of the obligations of the lessee.

12. That the renters of the missions are bound by certain regulations respecting the care and preservation of the mission property.

13. That the rents are to be paid punctually and quarterly, one-third

(in Santa Barbara one-half) to the padres, prefects, or their authorized agents, and the other two-thirds into the public treasury, to be expended for certain specified objects.

14. That government has reserved to itself the right to take such measures as may be necessary *to prevent "the destruction, ruin, or decline" of the missions during the period of their renting*, and that, therefore, if the renters, previous to the expiration of their leases, be found injuring or destroying the mission property, the government may eject them.

15. That the mission lands and other property which have not been sold in accordance with the provisions of law are still the property of government, and may be disposed of accordingly. Such was the legal condition of the missions of California when, on the 7th of July, 1846, the American flag was raised in Monterey, and the country taken formal possession of in the name of the United States. Nor has this condition been in any way changed by the American authorities since the conquest. Soon after General Kearny assumed the civil government in California, representations were made to him, from the most respectable sources, that the grants and sales of mission property by Governor Pico, just as he was leaving the country, were without the authority of law, and that, though actually made after the 7th of July, 1846, they had been antedated, in order to give them the semblance of legality. These titles were not recorded in the usual book of records in the government archives, but purported to be recorded in some other book, which, as yet, has never been found. Speculators had bought up these doubtful titles, and now demanded to be put in possession of their property. Under these circumstances, General Kearny issued a decree, on the 22d of March, 1847, directing that certain missions, so claimed, be left in the hands of the priests until the proper tribunal should be organized to determine on the validity of these titles.—(Vide appendix No. 24.) In other cases, where the claimants were in actual possession, they were allowed to remain, but with the express understanding that this permission should in no way affect the legality of their titles. Those, also, who were found holding mission property on lease were left in quiet possession, except the renter of the mission of San Buenaventura, who, being detected in selling and destroying the property of the mission, to its injury and almost total ruin, was ejected by the commanding officer of the southern military district. Towards the close of 1847, it was reported to the governor that the priest of the mission of Santa Clara was selling the lands of that mission. He was immediately called upon for his authority for making such sales, and being unable to give any that was deemed satisfactory, the governor declared all sales made by him of mission lands to be illegal, null, and void.—(Vide appendix No. 25.)

Again, in 1848, it being reported that the alcalde of Santa Barbara had attempted to give legal possession to some of the owners of doubtful titles to mission property, notice was given both to the alcalde and the claimants that this act of the alcalde was null and void— no alcalde in California having authority to give any legal force to claims to public lands in this territory.—(Vide appendix No. 26.)

III. *Titles to lands which will probably be required for fortifications, arsenals, or other military structures for the use of the general government of the United States.*—The board of officers for determining sites for permanent fortifications, arsenals, navy-yards, &c., on this coast, has not yet completed its examinations, and the only accessible official information on this subject is a report of a military reconnoissance of the coast of California ordered by General Kearny in the winter of 1847. The most southern point in Upper California there recommended for occupation by permanent works of defence is the entrance to the bay of San Diego. On the north side of this entrance, which is probably the most favorable position for works of military defence, are the remains of old "Fort Guejarro," built by the Spaniards some seventy years ago. This fort, though never of much value in itself, was occupied nearly up to the time the United States took possession of the country; and all the ground in the vicinity is still regarded as public property—no person, so far as is known, having any claim to it.

Monterey is the next point on the coast deemed of sufficient importance at the present time for permanent works. The old battery (San Carlos) at that place was built soon after the establishment of the mission of the same name, (1770,) and, though much dilapidated, was maintained up to about the time the Americans took possession of the country. Another battery in rear of and auxiliary to this was begun by the Mexicans previous to July 7, 1846, and afterwards enlarged by the Americans, and occupied by them, without intermission, to the present time. Copies of the several claims to the land on which these batteries are situated, or which lie so immediately in the vicinity as to be necessary for the public service, if the batteries themselves are retained, are given in appendix No. 27, papers 1, 2, 3, 4, and 5, and the accompanying letters of the alcalde, dated March 23, June 14, and August 10, 1848. It appears from these papers that titles Nos. 1, 2, 3, and 4 were given while Monterey was in possession of the American troops, and by an alcalde who was an officer in the United States navy; that Nos. 1 and 2 were given while the troops were occupying and holding the ground so deeded away, and after both seller and buyers had been informed that the land would be required for government purposes.—(Vide appendix No. 28.) With regard to the extension of the town limits, said by the alcalde to have been made by the territorial legislature some twelve years since, I would remark that no trace of it is found in the recorded proceedings of that body, nor in the archives of this office, although these records of legislative proceedings seem to be quite perfect from about the year 1823 to July 8, 1846; nor can I find any verbal testimony to prove the existence of such decree of extension. The alcalde's right to sell or deed away the lands alluded to will therefore rest most probably upon the "rule of Rob Roy," as given at the close of his letter of June 14, and which he seems to think constitutes the only legal authority which has governed in these matters.

Unfortunately for the plea set up by the alcalde, the laws relating to the granting of lands in California are, as has already been shown, very minute and perfect, resting upon no such doubtful authority as that of Rob Roy, but upon positive and definite decrees of the Mexican Congress, and the subordinate but no less distinct enactments of the territorial legislature—laws which seem to have been perfectly understood and pretty generally obeyed here previous to the irregular proceedings springing out of the mania for land speculations which followed the conquest of the country by the Americans. By a review of these laws, it will be seen that no municipal authority can dispose of lands beyond the limits of a town grant, (*fundo legal, para pueblo;*) nor can they sell any lands within this grant which may be required for the erection of warehouses, arsenals, or structures of any kind for the defence or security of the nation. Moreover, the grant itself, even if signed by both the governor and territorial legislature, inasmuch as it lies within ten leagues of the coast, is utterly invalid until confirmed by the general government, which confirmation it is well known has never been given. Nor is the alcalde more accurate in his opinion that the Mexican government has never designated any particular spot or site for forts or batteries. If he had examined the subject with care, he would have found that the ground which he sold has been occupied by works of military defence from about the year 1772 to the present moment; that when, in 1775, it was proposed by the authorities here to remove these works to a point on the bay further north, the viceroy positively forbade the removal; that there are in the government archives numerous orders, both from the viceroys of New Spain and the ministers of the Mexican republic, for the repair of these identical works, for the mounting of guns in them, &c.; that these are the very works which were captured by the insurgents under Alvarado and Graham in 1836, by the naval forces under Commodore Jones in 1842, and, though greatly dilapidated, constituted the only defences for the harbor and town of Monterey on the 7th of July, 1846. Mr. Little's claim, a part of which lies between the ravines "A" and "B," rests upon no other authority than that of a title given by the alcalde of Monterey some time in the winter of 1846-'7. It may be proper to remark here, that previous to the capture of Monterey, the town limits were not supposed to extend beyond the ravine marked "A" in the plan; and the grant made to Mr. Green, in the summer of 1845, it is believed, was never intended to cross the ravine; if so, no legal possession has ever been given, and the grant was afterwards covered by No. 1 in the appendix. All the ground covered by these claims is still in the possession of the United States, and has never been occupied or built upon by either of the claimants; it is therefore important to have it determined without delay whether the land is wanted for government use, and if so, whether any or all these claims are to be recognised as valid.

The next point which it is proposed to occupy with permanent works is the bay of San Francisco. The position first in importance on this bay is at or near the old battery, ("Fort San Joaquin" of the Spaniards,) on the south side of the narrows. The nature of Mr. Larkin's claim to this land is set forth in his letter, and the accompanying copies of title papers, given in appendix No. 29. The character of this title is pretty fully discussed in the papers given in appendix Nos. 30 and 31; and it is only necessary to remark here, that "Fort San Joaquin," (begun in 1776,) the "Presidio," (begun in 1776,) and "Yerba Buena battery," on Yerba Buena point, (a little west of the present town of San Francisco, and built in 1797,) as well as the intervening lands, have been occupied by the military forces of Spain and Mexico for nearly three-quarters of a century, and are now in possession of the troops of the United States; and it is believed to be susceptible of positive proof that Pio Pico was not in Los Angeles between the 17th of June and about the middle of July, 1846. There are to be found in the miscellaneous correspondence and the manuscript proceedings of the territorial legislature, (now in the archives of this office,) letters and orders from Pio Pico, dated San Buenaventura, June 19, and Santa Barbara, June 21, 23, 24, 27, 28, 29, and 30, and

July 2, 3, and 4; in Santa Fuez, July 7 and 8; in San Luis Obispo, July 11; and again in Santa Barbara, July 16 and 17; which renders it quite certain that he was *not* in Los Angeles the 25th of June, the day on which this title to Benito Diaz purports to have been given. But even supposing this title paper to have been given in good faith, and perfectly in accordance with the territorial laws, and that the land so granted did not include forts and barracks recognised and occupied for more than half a century as the property of the general government, still, under the general laws of Mexico, the grant is not valid until approved by the general government, and is subject to the reservation contained in article 5 of the law of August, 1824.

The position next in importance is most probably Alcatrazas island, (sometimes called White or Bird island,) granted by Pio Pico to Don Francis Plinio Temple. This title is subject to the same suspicions and objections as that of Benita Diaz, and neither has ever been confirmed by the territorial legislature or the general government, nor are they recorded in any book of records in the government archives.

"Punto de los Canallas," on the north side of the narrows, is included in a claim of Guillermo Antonio Richardson, founded on a grant said to have been made to him by Governor Echeandia in the year 1828. This title is not recorded in the archives of the government, and it is not known that it has ever been confirmed by the territorial legislature or the general government; it is believed, however, to be subject to the reservation made in article 5 of the law of 1824. A fort was designed for this point by the Spaniards previous to the revolution in Mexico, and orders were issued by the viceroy for the construction and arming of a battery; but the order, it is believed, was never executed.

Angel island was granted by Governor Alvarado to José Maria Osio, first on the 19th of February, 1838, and again on the 11th of June, 1839.— (Vide appendix Nos. 32 and 33.) It has never been confirmed by the territorial legislature, the claimant not deeming such confirmation necessary, as the grant, in his opinion, comes within the order of the supreme executive relating to islands on the coast.—(Vide appendix No. 7.) The claim to Yerba Buena island has not been examined, but is said to rest upon the same ground as that to Angel island.

What other points (if any) on the coast of California should be occupied by permanent works of defence, it is now difficult to determine; nor is it possible to say what points on the frontiers are most suitable for temporary military posts, in order, on the one hand, to check the depredations of the Indians, and, on the other, to protect the Indians themselves from the encroachments and abuse of the whites. As there are no barracks at San Diego, it will probably be necessary to station troops at San Luis Rey, where they will serve the double purpose of a garrison at San Diego and a lookout to guard the several passes from Lower California and Sonoma by the Colorado and Gila rivers. It is said that Don Antonio José Cot has a claim to this mission under a grant of Pio Pico; but as titles of this kind have already been discussed, it is unnecessary to resume their examination here.

At Sonoma, on the north side of San Francisco bay, there are barracks, which, with little expense, could be made comfortable for a single company. It is not known that the right of the United States to these barracks has ever been disputed.

Military posts should be established somewhere in the great valleys of the San Joaquin and Sacramento rivers; but further examinations are required before fixing definitively the positions of these posts. Most of the lands in these valleys belong to the public domain, and, it is believed, are generally unencumbered by private claims.

H. W. HALLECK,
Brevet Captain and Secretary of State.

MONTEREY, *California, March* 1, 1849.

APPENDIX No. 1.

Extracts from "the instructions to be observed by the commandant appointed to the new establishments of San Diego and Monterey," given by El. Bailio Frior Don Antonio Bucarele y Uruza, dated Mexico, 17th August, 1773.

ARTICLE 2. The confusion which has reigned in the accounts, and the want of order which I have observed in everything else, have compelled me to establish this new method, and to appoint Captain Don Fernando Rivera y Moncada commandant of San Diego and Monterey, because I am well informed of his good conduct or manner of proceeding, and of his knowledge of the new establishments, acquired in the employments and offices which he has therein obtained and in the presidios of California for many years.

ARTICLE 12. With the desire to establish population more speedily in the new establishments, I for the present grant the commandant the power to designate common lands, and also even to distribute lands in private to such Indians as may most dedicate themselves to agriculture and the breeding of cattle, for, having property of their own, the love of it will cause them to radicate themselves more firmly; but the commandant must bear in mind that it is very advisable not to allow them to live dispersed—each one on the lands given to them—but that they must necessarily have their house and habitation in the town or mission where they have been established or settled.

ARTICLE 13. I grant the same faculty to the commandant with respect to distributing lands to the other founders (pobladores) according to their merit and means of labor—they also living in the town and not dispersed, declaring that in the practice of what is prescribed in this article and the preceding 12th, he must act in every respect in conformity with the provisions made in the collection of the laws respecting newly-acquired countries and towns, (*reducciones y poblaciones,*) granting them legal titles for the owner's protection, without exacting any remuneration therefor or for the act of possession.

ARTICLE 14. The commandant must be carefully attentive that the founders who go to the new establishments have the requisite arms for their defence and for assisting the garrisons of the presidios or missions in case of necessity, binding them to this obligation as a thing necessary for their own safety and that of all their neighbors.

ARTICLE 15. When it becomes expedient to change any mission into a pueblo, the commandant will proceed to reduce it to the civil and econominal government which, according to the laws, is observed in the other pueblos of this kingdom, giving it a name, and declaring for its patron the saint under whose auspices and venerable protection the mission was founded.

APPENDIX No. 2.

Extracts from the regulations for the government of the province of California, by Don Felipe De Neve, governor of the same, dated in the royal presidio of San Carlos de Monterey, 1st June, 1779, and approved by his Majesty in a royal order of the 24th October, 1781.

TITLE THE FOURTEENTH.—POLITICAL GOVERNMENT, AND INSTRUCTIONS RESPECTING COLONIZATION.

1st. The object of the greatest importance towards the fulfilment of the pious intentions of the King, our master, and towards securing to his Majesty the dominion of the extensive country, which occupies a space of more than two hundred leagues, comprehending the new establishment of the presidios, and the respective ports of San Diego, Monterey, and San Francisco, being to forward the reduction of. and as far as possible to make this vast country (which, with the exception of seventeen hundred and forty-nine Christians of both sexes in the eight missions on the road which leads from the first to the last-named presidio, is inhabited by innumerable heathens) useful to the State, by erecting pueblos of which people, (*gente de razon*—literally, *people of reason*,) who, being united, may encourage agriculture, planting, the breeding of cattle, and successively the other branches of industry, so that some years hence their produce may be sufficient to provide garrisons of the presidios with provisions and horses, thereby obviating the distance of transportation and the risks and losses which the royal government suffers thereby,—with this just idea, the pueblo of San José has been founded and peopled; and the erection of another is determined upon, in which the colonists and their families, from the provinces of Sonora and Sinaloa, will establish themselves, the progressive augmentation of which, and of the families of the troops, will provide for the establishment of other towns, and furnish recruits for the presidio companies, thus freeing the royal revenue from the indispensable expenses at present required for these purposes; and, it being necessary to establish rules for carrying all this into effect, the following instructions will be observed:

2d. As an equivalent for the $120 and rations which hitherto have been assigned yearly to each poblador (founder or colonist) for the first two years, and the rations alone for the following one, calculated at a rial and a half per diem, free, for the three following ones, they will hereafter receive for each of the first two years $116 and $3\frac{1}{2}$ rials, the rations to be understood as comprehended in this amount; and in lieu of rations for the next three years, they will receive $60 yearly, by which arrangement they will be placed on more favorable terms than formerly, taking into consideration the advance that was charged on what they were paid with, and the discount on the rations furnished, which article they will in future receive at cost from the moment that these regulations be approved and declared to be in force, it being understood that the forementioned term of five years, as regards this emolument, is to be recovered from the day on which the possession of the house-lots and pieces of land, (*solares y suertes de tierras,*) which are to be distributed to each poblador in the manner hereafter mentioned, be given; and the previous time, from the period of their enrolment, must be regulated according to the terms of the respective contracts, and, in order to avoid this expense, measures will be taken to have the new pobladores collocated, and put into possession immediately on their arrival.

3d. To each poblador, and to the community of the pueblo, there shall be given, under condition of repayment in horses and mules fit to be given and received, and in the payment of the other large and small cattle, at the just prices which are to be fixed by tariff, and of the tools and implements at cost as it is ordained, two mares, two cows and one calf, two sheep and two goats, all breeding animals, and one yoke of oxen or steers, one plough-share or point, one hoe, one *coa*, (a kind of wooden spade with a steel point,) one axe and one sickle, one wood-knife, one musket, one leather shield, two horses, and one cargo mule. To the community there shall likewise be given the males corresponding to the total number of cattle of different kinds distributed amongst all the inhabitants, one seed jackass, another common one and three she asses, one boar and three sows, one forge with its corresponding anvil and other necessary tools, six crowbars, six iron spades or shovels, and the necessary tools for carpenter and cast work.

4th. The house-lots to be granted to the new pobladores are to be designated by government, in the situations, and of the extent, corresponding to the locality on which the new pueblos are to be established, so that a square and streets be formed agreeably to the provisions of the laws of the kingdom; and, conformably to the same, competent common lands (egidos) shall be designated for the pueblo and pasture grounds, with the sowing lands that may be necessary for municipal purposes, (proprios.)

5th. Each suerte of land, whether capable of irrigation or dependent on the seasons, (de riego de temporal,) shall consist of two hundred varas in length and two hundred in breadth, this being the area generally occupied in the sowing of one fanega of Indian corn. The distribution which is to effected of these house-lots and pieces of land to the new colonists must be made in the name of the King, our master, by the government, with equality, and a proportion to the ground which admits the benefit of being watered; so that, after making the necessary demarcation, and reserving vacant the fourth part of the number which may result, counting with the number of pobladores, should there be sufficient, each one shall have two suertes of irrigable land, and other two of dry ground, delivered to him: and of the royal lands, (*realengas,*) as many as may be considered necessary shall be separated for the proprios of the pueblo; and the remainder of these, as well as of the house-lots, shall be granted, in the name of his Majesty, by the governor, to those who may hereafter come to colonize, and particularly to those soldiers who, having fulfilled the term of their engagement, or on account of advanced age, may have retired from service; and likewise to the families of those who may die; but those persons must work at their own expense, out of the funds which each of them ought to possess, and will not be entitled to receive from the royal revenue either salary, rations, or cattle, this privilege being limited to those who leave their own country for the purpose of settling this country.

6th. The houses built on the lots granted and designated to the new pobladores, and the parcels of land comprehended in their respective gifts, shall be perpetually hereditary to their sons and descendants, or to their daughters who marry useful colonists who have received no grants of land for themselves, provided the whole of them comply with the obligations to be expressed in these instructions; and in order that the sons of possessors of these gifts observe the obedience and respect which they owe to their parents, these shall be freely authorized, in the case of having two or more sons, to choose which of them they please, being a layman, to succeed to the house and suertes of the town; and they may likewise dispose of them amongst their children, but not so as to divide a single suerte, because each and all of these are to remain indivisible and inalienable forever.

7th. Neither can the pobladores, nor their heirs, impose on the house or parcel of land granted to them, either tax, entail, reversion, mortgage, *(cento, vinculo, fianza, hipoteca,)* or any other burden, although it be for pious purposes; and should any one do so, in violation of this just prohibition, he shall irremissibly be deprived of his property, and his grant shall *ipso facto* be given to another colonist who may be useful and obedient.

8th. The new colonists shall enjoy, for the purpose of maintaining their cattle, the common privilege of the water and pasturage, fire-wood and timber, of the common forest and pasture-lands, to be designated according to law to each new pueblo; and, besides, each one shall privately enjoy the pasture of his own lands, but with the condition that as they have to possess and breed all kinds of large and small cattle, and it not being possible that each one can dedicate himself to the taking care of the small stock consigned to them—as by so doing they would be unable to attend to agriculture and the public works—for the present, the small cattle, the sheep and goats of the community, must feed together, and the shepherd must be paid by such community; and with respect to collecting together the large cattle, and bringing them to the corral, such as mares and asses, as may be required, this must be done by two of the pobladores, whom they must appoint amongst themselves, or as they may see fit, to look after this business; and thus the cattle of different kinds will be taken care of, and freed from the risk of running wild, at the same time that agriculture and the other works of the community will be attended to; and each individual must take care to mark his respective small cattle and brand the large, for which purpose the records of the necessary branding irons will be made without any charge; but it is ordained that henceforward no colonist is to possess more than fifty head of the same kind of cattle, so that the utility produced by cattle be distributed amongst the whole of them, and that the true riches of the pueblo be not monopolized by a few inhabitants.

9th. The new colonists shall be free and exempt from paying tithes, or any other tax, on the fruits and produce of the lands and cattle given to them, provided that within a year from the day on which the house-lots and parcels of land be designated to them they build a house, in the best way they can, and live therein, open the necessary trenches for watering their lands, placing at the boundaries, instead of landmarks, some fruit trees, or wild ones of some utility, at the rate of ten to each suerte; and likewise open the principal drain or trench, form a dam, and the other necessary public works, for the benefit of cultivation, which the community is bound particularly to attend to; and said community will see that the government buildings (casas reales) be completed within the fourth year, and during the third a storehouse sufficiently capacious for a public granary, in which must be kept the produce of the public sowing, which, at the rate of one almud (the twelfth of a fanega) of Indian corn per inhabitant, must be made from said third year to the fifth, inclusive, in the lands designated for municipal purposes, (proprios)—all the labor of which, until harvesting the crop and putting it in the granary, must be done by the community for whose benefit alone it must serve; and for the management and augmentation thereof, the necessary laws to be observed will, in due time, be made.

10th. After the expiration of the five years, they will pay the tithes to his Majesty, for him to dispose of agreeably to his royal pleasure, as belonging solely to him, not only on account of the absolute royal patronage which he possesses in these dominions, but also because they are the produce of uncultivated and abandoned lands, which are about to become fruitful at the cost of the large outlays and expenses of the royal treasury. At the expiration of the said term of five years, the new pobladores and their descendants will pay, in acknowledgment of the direct and supreme dominion which belongs to the sovereign, one-half of a fanega of Indian corn for each irrigable suerte of land; and for their own benefit, they shall be collectively under the direct obligation of attending to the repair of the principal trench, dam, auxiliary drains, and other public works of their pueblos, including that of the church.

11th. When the hogs and asses shall have multiplied, and the sufficient number of seed asses for covering the mares become adopted, and it be found practicable to distribute these two kinds of animals amongst the pobladores, it must be done with all possible equality, so that of the first kind each one may receive one boar and one sow, and of the second one one ass, which the owners will mark and brand.

12th. Within the five years stipulated, the new pobladores shall be obliged to possess two yoke of oxen, two ploughs, two points or ploughshares for tilling the ground, two hoes, and the other necessary implements of agriculture; and by the end of the first three years their houses must be entirely finished, and furnished each with six hens and one cock; and it is expressly forbidden that any one shall, during the forementioned period of five years, alienate, by means of sale, exchange, or other pretext, or kill any of the cattle granted to them, or the respective increase thereof, excepting sheep and goats, which, at the end of four years, it is necessary to dispose of, or else they would die; and therefore they may, at their discretion, dispose of as many of these animals as arrive at that age, but not of any younger ones, under the penalty that whoever shall violate this order, made for his own benefit and for the increase of his prosperity, shall forfeit *ipso facto* the amount of the rations granted to him for one year; and whoever shall receive one or more head of such cattle during the same time, in whatever state or condition they may be, shall be obliged to return them.

13th. At the expiration of said five years—the female breeding animals of every kind, excepting swine and asses, of which each poblador is only obliged to possess one sow and one ass, male or female, being preserved, the yokes of oxen or steers designated for their agricultural purposes being provided, and they being furnished with a cargo mule and necessary horses—they shall be at liberty to sell their bulls, steers, foals or horses, asses, sheep, castrated goats, and pigs and sows; it being forbidden to kill cows, (except old or barren, and consequently unproductive ones,) sheep or she-goats which are not above three years old, and to sell mares or useful breeding females, until each poblador be possessed of fifteen mares and one stallion, fifteen cows and one bull, twelve sheep and one ram, and ten she-goats with one buck.

14th. No poblador or resident shall sell a foal horse or mule, or exchange the same, except amongst each other, after they are provided with the necessary number; for the remainder must be dedicated solely to the purpose of remounting the cavalry of the presidio troops, and will be paid for at the just prices to be established, excepting all particularly fine horses or mules of said pueblos, under the penalty of twenty dollars, to be forfeited by whosoever may violate this order. For every animal disposed of in any other manner than what is here stipulated, the half to be given to the informer, and the other half to be applied to municipal expenses, (gasta de republica.)

15th. The Indian corn, beans, chick-peas, and lentils, produced by the pueblo, after the residents have separated what may be necessary for their own subsistence and for seed, must be bought and paid for in ready money at the prices established, or which may hereafter be established, for provisioning the presidio; and from the amount of the same there must be deducted from the amount of each poblador such provident sums as may be considered proper towards refunding the royal revenue the advances made in money, horses, cattle, implements, seeds, and other articles, so that within the first five years the total amount must be paid.

16th. Each poblador and resident head of a family to whom house-lots or parcels of land may have been, or in future shall be granted, and their successors, shall be obliged to hold themselves equipped with two horses, a saddle complete, a musket, and the other arms already mentioned, which are to be furnished them at first cost, for the defence of their respective districts, and in order that they may (without abandoning this first obligation) repair to where the governor may, in cases of urgency, order them.

17th. The corresponding titles to house-lots, lands, and waters, granted to the new pobladores, or which may hereafter be granted to other residents, shall be made out by the governor, or commissary whom he may appoint for this purpose—records of which, and of the respective branding irons, must be kept in the general book of colonization, to be made and kept in the government archives, as a heading to which a copy of these instructions shall be placed.

18th. And whereas it is expedient for the good government and police of the pueblos, the administration of justice, the direction of public works, the distribution of water privileges, and the carrying into effect the orders given in these instructions, that they should be furnished with ordinary alcaldes and other municipal officers, in proportion to the number of inhabitants, the governor shall appoint such for the first two years; and for the following ones, they shall appoint some ones from amongst themselves to the municipal offices which may have been established, which elections are to be forwarded to the governor for his approbation, who, if he sees fit, may continue said appointment for the three following years.

APPENDIX No. 3.

In conformity with the opinion of the assessor of the *commandancia general*, I have determined in a decree of this date that, notwithstanding the provisions made in the 81st article of the ordinance of the *intendentes*, the captains of presidios are authorized to grant and distribute house-lots and lands to the soldiers and citizens who may solicit them to fix their residences on.

And considering the extent of four common leagues, measured from the centre of the presidio square, viz: two leagues in every direction, to be sufficient for the new pueblos to be formed under the protection of said presidios, I have likewise determined, in order to avoid doubts and disputes in future, that said captains restrict themselves henceforward to the quantity of house-lots and lands within the four leagues already mentioned, without exceeding in any manner said limits, leaving free and open the exclusive jurisdiction belonging to the *intendentes* of the royal hacienda, respecting the sale, composition, and distribution of the remainder of the land in the respective districts.

And that this order may be punctually observed and carried into effect, you will circulate it to the captains and commandants of the presidios of your province, informing me of having done so.

God preserve you many years.
CHIHUAHUA, *March* 22, 1791.
PEDRO DE NAVA.
Señor Don JOSEPH ANTONIO ROMEN.

APPENDIX No. 4.

Decree of the 18th August, 1824, respecting colonization.

The sovereign general constituent Congress of the United Mexican States has been pleased to decree—

1st. The Mexican nation promises to those foreigners who may come to establish themselves in its territory security in their persons and property, provided they subject themselves to the laws of the country.

2d. The objects of this law are those national lands which are neither private property nor belong to any corporation or pueblo, and can therefore be colonized.

3d. To this end the Congress of the States will form, as soon as possible, the laws and regulations of colonization of their respective demarcation, with entire conformity to the constitutive act, the general constitution, and the rules established in this law.

4th. Those territories comprised within twenty leagues of the boundaries of any foreign nation, or within ten leagues of the seacoast, cannot be colonized without the previous approval of the supreme general executive power.

5th. If, for the defence or security of the nation, the federal government should find it expedient to make use of any portion of these lands for the purpose of constructing warehouses, arsenals, or other public edifices, it may do so, with the approbation of the general Congress, or during its recess with that of the government council.

6th. Before the expiration of four years after the publication of this law, no tax or duty (direcho) shall be imposed on the entry of the persons of foreigners who come to establish themselves for the first time in the nation.

7th. Previous to the year 1840, the general Congress cannot prohibit the entry of foreigners to colonize, except compelled to do so, with respect to the individuals of some nation, by powerful reasons.

8th. The government, without prejudicing the object of this law, will take the precautionary measures which it may consider necessary for the security of the federation, with respect to the foreigners who may come to colonize. In the distribution of lands, Mexican citizens are to be attended to in preference; and no distinction shall be made amongst these, except such only as is due to private merit and services rendered to the country, or, in equality of circumstances, residence in the place to which the lands distributed belong.

10th. Military persons who are entitled to lands by the promise made on the 27th of March, 1821, shall be attended to in the States, on producing the diplomas granted to them to that effect by the supreme executive power.

11th. If, by the decrees of capitulization, according to the probabilities of life, the supreme executive should see fit to alienate any portions of land in favor of any military or civil officers of the federation, it may so dispose of the vacant lands of the territories.

12th. No one person shall be allowed to obtain the ownership of more than one league square, of five thousand varas, (5,000 v.) of irrigable land, (de regadio,) four superficial ones of land dependent on the seasons, (de temporal,) and six superficial ones for the purpose of rearing cattle, (de abrevadéso.)

13th. The new colonists cannot transfer their possessions in mortmain, (manos muertas.)

14th. This law guaranties the contracts which the grantees (empresarios) may make with the families which they may bring out at their expense; provided they be not contrary to the laws.

15th. No one who, by virtue of this law, shall acquire the ownership of lands, shall retain them if he shall reside out of the territory of the republic.

16th. The government, in conformity with the principles established in this law, will proceed to the colonization of the territories of the republic.

APPENDIX No. 5.

General rules and regulations for the colonization of territories of the republic.—Mexico, November 21, 1828.

It being stipulated in the 16th article of the general law of colonization of the 18th of August, 1824, that the government, in conformity with the principles established in said law, shall proceed to the colonization of the territories of the republic; and it being very desirable, in order to give to said article the most punctual and exact fulfilment, to dictate some general rules for facilitating its execution in such cases as may occur, his excellency has seen fit to determine on the following articles:

1st. The governors (gefes politicos) of the territories are authorized (in compliance with the law of the general Congress of the 18th of August, 1824, and under the conditions hereafter specified) to grant vacant lands in their respective territories to such contractors, (empressarios,) families, or private persons, whether Mexicans or foreigners, who may ask for them, for the purpose of cultivating and inhabiting them.

2d. Every person soliciting lands, whether he be an *empressario*, head of a family, or private person, shall address to the governor of the respective territory a petition, expressing his name, country, profession; the number, description, religion, and other circumstances of the families or persons with whom he wishes to colonize; describing as distinctly as possible, by means of a map, the land asked for.

3d. The governor shall proceed immediately to obtain the necessary information whether the petition embraces the requisite conditions required by said law of the 18th of August, both as regards the land and the candidate, in order that the petitioner may at once be attended to; or, if it be preferred, the respective municipal authority may be consulted, whether there be any objection to making the grant or not.

4th. This being done, the governor will accede or not to such petition in exact conformity to the laws on the subject, and especially to the beforementioned one of the 18th of August, 1824.

5th. The grants made to families or private persons shall not be held to be definitively valid without the previous consent of the territorial deputation, to which end the respective documents (espedientes) shall be forwarded to it.

6th. When the governor shall not obtain the approbation of the territorial deputation, he shall report to the supreme government, forwarding the necessary documents for its decision.

7th. The grants made to *empressarios* for them to colonize with many families shall not be held to be definitively valid until the approval of the supreme government be obtained; to which the necessary documents must be forwarded, along with the report of the territorial deputation.

8th. The definitive grant asked for being made, a document signed by the governor shall be given, to serve as a title to the party interested, wherein it must be stated that said grant is made in exact conformity with the provisions of the laws, in virtue whereof possession shall be given.

9th. The necessary record shall be kept, in a book destined for the purpose, of all the petitions presented, and grants made, with the maps of the lands granted; and the circumstantial report shall be forwarded quarterly to the supreme government.

10th. No *capitulization* shall be admitted for a new town, except the *capitulizator* bind himself to present, as colonists, at least twelve families.

11th. The governor shall designate to the new colonist a proportionate time within which he shall be bound to cultivate or occupy the land on the terms and with the number of persons or families which he may have *capitulized* for, it being understood that if he does not comply, the grant of the land shall remain void; nevertheless, the governor may revalidate it in proportion to the part which the party may have fulfilled.

12th. Every new colonist, after having cultivated or occupied the land agreeably to his *capitulization*, will take care to prove the same before the municipal authority, in order that, the necessary record being made, he may consolidate and secure his right of ownership, so that he may dispose freely thereof.

13th. The reunion of many families into one town shall follow, in its formation, interior government, and policy, the rules established by the existing laws for the other towns of the republic, special care being taken that the new ones are built with all possible regularity.

14th. The *minimum* of irrigable land to be given to one person for colonization shall be 200 varas square; the *minimum* of land called *de temporal* shall be 800 varas square; and the *minimum* for breeding cattle (*de abrevadéso*) shall be 1,200 varas square.

15th. The land given for a house-lot shall be 100 varas.

16th. The spaces which may remain between the colonized lands may be distributed among the adjoining proprietors who shall have cultivated theirs with the most application, and have not received the whole extent of land allowed by the law, or to the children of said proprietors who may ask for them to combine the possessions of their families; but on this subject particular attention must be paid to the morality and industry of the parties.

17th. In those territories where there are missions, the lands occupied by them cannot be colonized at present, nor until it be determined whether they are to be considered as the property of the establishments of the neophytes, catechumens, and Mexican colonists.

APPENDIX No. 6.

Certificate of Don Juan B. Alvarado, respecting the Mexican government having approved of the grant of land made to Stephen Smith at the Bodega.

I hereby certify, on my word of honor, that towards the end of the year 1845, when Colonel Don Jose Castro was commandant general of California, a mail was received in this port from Mexico, in which I saw and read an official communication from the supreme government, in answer to another of the same character addressed by General Don Manuel Micheltorena, predecessor of Señor Castro in said commandancy, in which it was manifested that the supreme government had approved the grant made to Mr. Stephen Smith of the lands situated in the port of Bodega, ordering at the same time that no more grants of that kind should be made without obtaining the necessary authority from the supreme government.

This I certify, because at that time I was employed in opening and arranging the official correspondence with the ministers in the secretary's office of said commander.

In testimony whereof, I give the present, in Monterey, the 21st of August, one thousand eight hundred and forty-seven.

JUAN B. ALVARADO.

APPENDIX No. 7.

Translation of the copy of an official letter from the Minister of the Interior to the governor of California, respecting the granting of certain islands to Mexican citizens.

MOST EXCELLENT SIR: His Excellency the Minister of the Interior, under date of the 12th of July, 1838, says to me that which I copy:

"MOST EXCELLENT SIR: His Excellency the President, being desirous on the one hand to protect the population of the desert islands adjacent to that department, which form a part of the national territory, and on the other to hinder the many foreign adventurers from benefiting themselves with these considerable portions, from whence they may do great injury to our fisheries, commerce, and interests, has been pleased to resolve that your excellency, in conjunction with the departmental junta, proceed with activity and prudence to grant and distribute lands on said islands to the Mexicans who may solicit them, recommending to you in particular the citizens Antonio and Carlos Carrillo, for their useful and patriotic services, in order that you may attend to them in preference, and grant them exclusively one of said islands, which they themselves may select. I have the honor to communicate this to you for your knowledge and corresponding effect."

And I inform your excellency thereof for your intelligence, &c.

God and liberty. Monterey, February 27, 1840.

JUAN B. ALVARADO.

Most Excellent DEPARTMENTAL JUNTA
of California.

APPENDIX No. 8.

Manuel Micheltorena, brigadier general of the Mexican army, adjutant general of the staff of the same, governor, commandant, and general, and inspector of the department of California:

Whereas Don ———, a naturalized citizen of Mexico, has solicited for his personal benefit five sitios of large cattle, (five square leagues,) between the river Cosumnes on the north side, the rancheria of the Omuchumnes, the strong hills, and the pass which leads to Mr. Sutter's eslishment, where the measurement must commence towards the direction of NNW., the previous measures and investigations having been made, agreeably to the laws and regulations on the subject, I have, in the name of the Mexican nation, granted to him the before-mentioned land, declaring to him the ownership thereof by these presents, subject to the approbation of the most excellent departmental assembly, and to the following conditions:

1st. He cannot sell, alienate, or mortgage it, impose land-rent, (*censo*,) entail, (*miculo*,) reversion, (*fianza*,) or any other burden.

2d. He may enclose it without prejudice to the crossing highways and privileges, (*servidumbres;*) he shall enjoy it freely and exclusively, destining it to the use or cultivation which best may suit him; but within a year he shall build a house, and it shall be inhabited.

3d. He shall solicit the respective magistrate to give him legal possession in virtue of this title, by whom the boundaries shall be traced out, in the limit of which he shall put, beside the landmarks, some fruit trees, or wild ones of some utility.

4th. The land of which donation is made consists of five sitios, (square leagues,) as the respective map explains. The magistrate who gives possession shall cause it to be measured according to law, and the overplus shall remain to the nation for the necessary uses.

5th. If he shall violate these conditions, he shall forfeit his right to the land, and it may be denounced by another.

I consequently command that, these presents being held as firm and valid, a record thereof be made in the respective book, and they be delivered to the party interested, for his security and further ends.

Given in Monterey, on the 8th of January, 1844.

MANUEL MICHELTORENA.
MANUEL JIMENO, *Gov't Secretary.*

[18]

APPENDIX No. 9.

Table of land measures adopted in the Mexican republic.

Names of the measures.	Figures of the measures.	Length of the figures expressed in varas.	Breadth, in varas.	Areas, in square varas.	Areas, in caballerias.
Sitio de ganado mayor	Square	5,000	5,000	25,000,000	41.023
Criadero de ganado mayor	Square	2,500	2,500	6,250,000	10.255
Sitio de ganado menor	Square	3,333$\frac{1}{3}$	3,333$\frac{1}{3}$	11,111,111$\frac{1}{9}$	18.232
Criadero de ganado menor	Square	1,666$\frac{2}{3}$	1,666$\frac{2}{3}$	2,777,777$\frac{7}{9}$	4.558
Caballeria de tierra	Rightangled parallelogram	1,104	552	609,408	1
Media caballeria	Square	552	552	304,704	$\frac{1}{2}$
Cuarto caballeria ò suerte de tierra	Rightangled parallelogram	552	276	152,352	$\frac{1}{4}$
Fanega de sembradura de maiz	Rightangled parallelogram	376	184	50,784	$\frac{1}{12}$
Salar para casa	Square	50	50	2,500	0.004
Fundo legal para pueblos	Square	1,200	1,200	1,440,000	2.036

The Mexican vara is the unit of all the measures of length, the pattern and size of which are taken from the Castilian vara of the mark of Burgos, and is the legal vara used in the Mexican republic. Fifty Mexican varas make a measure which is called cordel, which instrument is used in measuring lands.

The legal league contains 100 cordels or 5,000 varas, which is found by multiplying by 100 the 50 varas contained in a cordel. The league is divided into two halves and four quarters—this being the only division made of it. Half a league contains 2,500 varas, and a quarter of a league 1,250 varas.

Anciently, the Mexican league was divided into three miles, the mile into a thousand paces of Solomon, and one of these paces into five thirds of a Mexican vara; consequently, the league had 3,000 paces of Solomon. This division is recognised in legal affairs, but has been a very long time in disuse—the same as the pace of Solomon, which in those days was called vara, and was used for measuring lands. The mark was equivalent to two varas and seven-eighths—that is, eight marks contained twenty-three varas—and was used for measuring lands.

APPENDIX No. 10.

I, Brigadier General S. W. Kearny, governor of California, by virtue of authority in me vested by the President of the United States of America, do hereby grant, convey, and release unto the town of San Francisco, the people, or corporate authorities thereof, all the right, title, and interest of the government of the United States and of the Territory of California in and to the beach and water-lots on the east front of said town of San Francisco, included between the points known as the "Rincon" and "Fort Montgomery," excepting such lots as may be selected for the use of the government by the senior officers of the army and navy now there: Provided the said grant hereby ceded shall be divided into lots, and sold at public auction, to the highest bidder, after three months' notice previously given; the proceeds of said sale to be for the benefit of the town of San Francisco.

Given at Monterey, capital of California, this 10th day of March, 1847, in the 71st year of the independence of the United States.

S. W. KEARNY,
Brig. Gen. and Governor of California.

APPENDIX No. 11.

Know all men by these presents, that I, Richard B. Mason, colonel 1st regiment of dragoons United States army, and governor of California, by virtue of authority in me vested, do hereby appoint J. R. Snyder, of Monterey, and Timothy Murphy, of San Rafael, commissioners with full power to examine into and correct certain alleged irregularities in the proceedings and records of the office of the late alcalde of Sonoma, J. H. Nash, and to settle according to equity and justice all questions of title to town lots sold or granted by said Nash.

Done at Monterey, capital of California, this 26th day of August, 1847, and the 72d of the independence of the United States.

R. B. MASON,
Colonel 1st Dragoons, and Governor of California.

STATE DEPARTMENT OF THE TERRITORY OF CALIFORNIA,
Monterey, August 26, 1847.

MESSRS: By a decree of the governor of this date, you have been appointed commissioners to examine into certain alleged irregularities in the sales of town lots in the town of Sonoma, by J. H. Nash, late alcalde of said town, and also to settle all questions of title to said lots sold by Nash according to equity and justice, so that innocent purchasers shall not suffer.

It has been alleged that deeds for public lands were made out and signed by said Nash in May and June last, after he (Nash) ceased to be alcalde, (which was on the 10th of April, 1847,) and that these titles have been recorded prior to titles given by the same authority in December and January last; that titles have not been given in comformity with the petitions of applicants and the established rules or usages of sale; that certain petitions and titles have been antedated; that lots have been sold which were previously granted or sold to other persons, and the same recorded; that the original plan or survey of the town has been changed, and also the manner of numbering the lots; and, in addition to other irregularities, that the said alcalde has failed to turn over to his successor in office a full account of his sales and expenditures, and the public funds in his hands. You are empowered by the governor to examine into all these alleged irregularities and defalcations, and to correct the proceedings and records of the said alcalde, (Nash,) and to settle questions to titles to town lots sold or granted by said Nash. You have full power to call for persons and papers, and to examine witnesses.

A full record of your proceedings will be signed by each commissioner, and turned over to the alcalde of Sonoma, to be transmitted by him, with his remarks, to the governor of the territory for approval.

You will examine thoroughly into the receipts and expenditures of said Nash as alcalde, touching the sale, &c., of lots in Sonoma, with a view of showing in what manner and for what purposes expenditures have been made, and to determine the amount of public money arising from said sales still unaccounted for, and yet to be turned over to his successor in office.

Should you find any irregularities in the numbering of lots, or any unauthorized change in the original plan or survey of the town of Sonoma, you will restore the original plan, or take such other measures as in your judgment may be best calculated to secure the just rights of all the parties interested.

You will assemble at Sonoma on the 10th day of September next, or as soon thereafter as practicable. You will each be entitled to four dollars per diem for every day you are in session, and for every day's travel going to and returning from Sonoma, (estimating a day's travel at forty miles,) which will be paid to you by the alcalde of Sonoma from any funds in his hands belonging to the said town.

Very respectfully, your obedient servant,
H. W. HALLECK,
*Lieut. of Engineers and Secretary of State
for the Territory of California.*

Messrs. J. R. SNYDER, *Monterey,*
and TIMOTHY MURPHY, *San Rafael.*

APPENDIX No. 12.

HEADQUARTERS 10TH MILITARY DEPARTMENT,
Monterey, California, March 10, 1848.

SIR: Since writing my letter of yesterday I have found your mislaid letter of the 29th of February.

An alcalde has no right or authority whatever to sell or in any other way to dispose of pueblo lands; and, without touching the question of the legality of the case—proceedings which resulted in the division of the lands of your pueblo, in which division some of them were set apart for the benefit of public schools—I say neither has he any power or authority to give, grant, or sell any of the lands so set apart; and such grant, gift, or sale is utterly null and void, and of no sort of force or effect.

I remark what you say in relation to the sale of some of the pueblo lands alluded to above being entered on the records after transactions of a subsequent date to that which purports to be the sale. This evidently shows there has been something wrong; but in this case it is a matter of no moment, because any sale of those lands made by your predecessor in office, even if not antedated and recorded at the proper time, is utterly void, and of no sort of force or effect.

You will please enter this letter on your record, and file and preserve the original in your office; also, preserve on the files of your office my official letter of the 19th January last, addressed to Mr. James W. Weeks, at that time alcalde of your town.

I am, respectfully, your obedient servant,
R. B. MASON,
Colonel 1st Dragoons, and Governor of California.

CHARLES WHITE,
First Alcalde, Pueblo de San José.

APPENDIX No. 13.

Mexican law of the 17th August, 1833.

ARTICLE 1. Government will proceed to secularize the missions of Upper and Lower California.

ART. 2. In each of said missions a parish shall be established under the charge of a parish priest of the secular clergy, with a salary of from $2,000 to $2,500 per annum, at the discretion of the government.

ART. 3. These parish curates shall exact no emolument for marriages, baptisms, burials, or any other religious functions. With respect to fees of pomp, they may receive such as shall be expressly stipulated in the tariff to be formed for this object, with as little delay as possible, by the reverend bishop of the diocess, and approved by the supreme government.

ART. 4. The churches which have hitherto served the different missions, with the sacred vessels, ornaments, and other appurtenances now belonging to them, shall be assigned to these new parishes, and also such buildings annexed to the said churches as the government may deem necessary for the most decent use of said parish.

ART. 5. The government will order a burial-ground to be erected outside of each parish.

ART. 6. There are $500 per annum assigned to each parish as a donation for religious worship and servants.

ART. 7. Of the buildings belonging to each mission, the most appropriate shall be designated for the habitation of the curate, with the addition of a ground lot which shall not exceed 200 varas square; and the remaining edifices shall be specially adjudicated for a court-house, preparatory schools, public establishments, and workshops.

ART. 8. In order to provide quickly and efficaciously for the spiritual necessities of both Californias, a vicar-generalship shall be established in the capital of Upper California, the jurisdiction of which shall extend to both territories; and the reverend diocesan shall confer upon its incumbent the necessary faculties, with the greatest amplitude possible.

ART. 9. For the donation of this vicar-generalship $3,000 per annum shall be assigned; but the vicar shall be at all the expense of his office, and not exact under any title or pretext any fee whatever, not even for paper.

ART. 10. If by any motive the vicar-generalship should be filled by the parish curate of the capital of any other parish in those districts, said curate shall receive $1,500 yearly, in addition to the donation of his curacy.

ART. 11. No custom obliging the inhabitants of California to make oblations, however pious they may be, although they may be called necessary ones, can be introduced; and neither time nor the consent of the citizens themselves can give them any force or virtue.

ART. 12. The government will efficaciously take care that the reverend diocesan himself concur in carrying into effect the object of this law.

ART. 13. When these new curates are named, the supreme government will gratuitously furnish a passage by sea for them and their families; and besides that, may give to each one from $400 to $800 for their journey by land, according to the distance, and the family they take with them.

ART. 14. Government will pay the passage of the missionary priests who return to Mexico; and in order that they may comfortably reach their convents by land, it may give to each one from $200 to $300, and, at its discretion, what may be considered necessary for those to leave the republic who have not sworn to the independence.

ART. 15. The supreme government will provide for the expenses comprehended in this law out of the product of the estates, capitals, and revenues at present recognised as the pious fund of the missions of California.

APPENDIX No. 14.

Provisional regulations for the secularization of the missions of Upper California promulgated by Governor José Figueroa on the 9th of August, 1834.

ARTICLE 1. The governor, agreeably to the spirit of the law of the 17th August, 1833, and to the instructions which he has received from the supreme government, will, with the co-operation of the prelates of the missionary priests, partially convert into pueblos the missions of this territory, beginning in the next month of August, and commencing at first with ten missions and afterwards with the remainder.

ART. 2. The missionary priests will be exonerated from the administration of temporalities, and will only exercise the functions of their ministry in matters appertaining to the spiritual administration until the formal division of parishes be made, and the supreme government and diocesan provide curates.

ART. 3. The territorial government will reassume the administration of temporalities in the directive part, according to the following bases:

ART. 4. The supreme government will, by the quickest route, be requested to approve of these provisional regulations.

Distribution of property and lands.

Art. 5. To every individual head of a family, and to all those above twenty-one years of age, although they have no family, a lot of land, whether irrigable or otherwise, of not exceeding 400 varas square, nor less than one hundred, shall be given out of the common lands of the missions; and in conformity a sufficient quantity of land shall be allotted them for waterin their cattle. Common lands shall be assigned to each pueblo, and, when convenient, municipal lands also.

Art. 6. One-half of the self-moving property (cattle) shall be distributed among the said individuals, in a proportionable and equitable manner, at the discretion of the governor, taking as a basis the last accounts of all kinds of cattle presented by the missionaries.

Art. 7. One-half or less of the chattels, instruments, and seeds on hand, and indispensable for the cultivation of the ground, shall be divided proportionably among them.

Art. 8. The remainder of all the lands, landed property, cattle, and all other property on hand, will remain under the care and responsibility of the mayordomos, or other officers whom the governor may name, at the disposal of the supreme federal government.

Art. 9. From the common mass of this property, the subsistence of the missionary padres, the pay of the mayordomos and other servants, the expenses of religious worship, schools, and other objects of policy and ornament, shall be provided.

Art. 10. The governor, having under his charge the direction of temporal affairs, will determine and regulate, according to circumstances, all the expenses necessary to be laid out, as well for the execution of this plan as for the conservation and augmentation of this property.

Art. 11. The missionary minister will select the locality in the mission which may best suit him for his own habitation and that of his servants and attendants; and he shall be furnished with the necessary furniture and implements.

Art. 12. The library, sacred dresses, ornaments, and furniture of the church, shall be put in charge of the missionary padre, under the responsibility of the person who acts as subscriber, and whom the priest himself shall elect, and a reasonable salary be given for his trouble.

Art. 13. General inventories shall be made of all property on hand in each mission, with due separation and explanation of the different branches; of the books of debit and credit, and all kinds of papers; of the amount owing by and to the missions; which document and account shall be forwarded to the supreme government.

Political government of the pueblos.

Art. 14. The political government of the pueblos shall be organized in perfect conformity with the existing laws; the governor will give the necessary instructions to have ayuntamientos established and elections made.

Art. 15. The economical government of the pueblos shall be under the charge of the ayuntamientos; but as far as regards the administration of justice in contentious affairs, they will be subject to the primary judges of the nearest towns constitutionally established.

ART. 16. The emancipated Indians will be obliged to assist at the indispensable common labor which, in the opinion of the governor, may be judged necessary for the cultivation of the vineyards, orchards, and cornfields, which, for the present, remain undisposed of until the resolution of the supreme government.

ART. 17. Said emancipated Indians will render to the missionary priest the necessary personal service for the attention of his person.

Restrictions

ART. 18. They cannot sell, burden, or alienate, under any pretext, the lands which may be given to them; neither can they sell their cattle. Whatever contracts may be made against these orders shall be of no value: the government will reclaim the property as belonging to the nation, and the purchasers shall lose their money.

ART. 19. The lands whose owners shall die without heirs shall revert to the possession of the nation.

General orders.

ART. 20. The governor will name such commissioners as he may see fit to carry this plan and its incidents into effect.

ART. 21. The governor is authorized to resolve any doubt or matter which may arise relative to the execution of these regulations.

ART 22. Until these regulations be put in force, the reverend missionary padres are prohibited from slaughtering cattle in large quantities, except the common and ordinary number accustomed to be killed for the subsistence of the neophytes, without allowing any waste.

ART. 23. The debts of the mission shall be paid in preference, out of the common mass of the property, at the time and in the manner that the governor shall determine.

And in order that these regulations be exactly complied with, the following order shall be observed:

As soon as the commissioners receive the order and their appointment, they will present themselves in the respective missions, and commence the execution of the plan, conforming themselves in all respects to the tenor thereof and to these orders. They will manifest their respective credentials to the priest in charge of the missions, and act in concert with him, behaving towards him with the harmony, politeness, and respect which are his due.

Second. The priests will immediately deliver, and the commissioners receive, the cash books, accounts, and other documents relative to property and debts owing by and to the missions. They will afterwards proceed to make out the general inventories (agreeable to article 13 of these regulations) of all property on hand, including the buildings, church, workshops, and other premises, with distinction of what belongs to each department; that is, the utensils, instruments, or ornaments which belong to each. After enumerating all that belongs to the establishment, they will continue with the things belonging to the country; that is, landed property, such as vineyards, orchards, with the number of trees if possible, mills, fences, &c.; after this the cattle and all thereunto belonging. But, as it will be difficult to count said cattle, on account of the number, and want of horses, they shall be examined by two intelligent persons of probity, who will calculate as near as they can the number of each kind; and this shall be put in the inventory. As soon as anything is put into the inventory, it shall be taken out of the charge of the priest and placed at the disposal of the commissioner or mayordomo; but no innovation shall be made in the order of labor and servants until experience may render it necessary, excepting in such common matters as are commonly varied whenever it may be necessary.

Third. The commissioner, in conjunction with the mayordomo, will see that all superfluous expenses cease, and that a well-regulated economy be established in everything which merits reform.

Fourth. Before making an inventory of the outside or country property, the commissioners will endeavor to explain to the Indians, with suavity and patience, that the missions are going to be converted into pueblos; that they will only remain subordinate to the priest in matters in relation to the spiritual administration; that the lands and property will be divided out among them, so that each one may work, maintain, and govern himself without dependence on any one; that the houses in which they live will become their own property; and that, in order to this, they must submit to what is commanded in these regulations and orders, which must be explained to them in the best possible manner. They will likewise have immediately divided out to them the lots for cultivation, agreeable to the fifth article of these regulations. The commissioner, padre, and mayordomo, will select the locality where this is to be, choosing the best and nearest to the mission; and they will give to each the quantity of land which they can cultivate, according to their aptness and family, without exceeding the maximum stipulated. They will likewise see that each person marks his land, in the manner most convenient to him.

Fifth. The debts (of the mission) shall be paid out of the common mass of the property on hand; but neither the commissioner nor the mayordomos shall do this without an express order from the government, which must be informed in preference respecting the matter, in order that it may resolve, and in view thereof determine, the number of cattle which is to be divided out amongst the neophytes, in order that it may take effect as soon as possible, according to what is stipulated in article sixth.

Sixth. The implements and tools necessary for cultivating the soil shall be divided out in the quantity mentioned in article 7, either in community or individually, as may appear best to the commissioner and the priest. The grain shall remain undivided, and be served out to the Indians in the usual rations.

Seventh. What is called the nunnery shall immediately be abolished, and the girls therein shall be delivered over to their parents, recommending to them the care which they ought to take of them, and explaining to them their obligations as parents. The same shall be done with respect to the boys.

Eighth. The commissioner, after having acquired the necessary information and acquaintance, will, as soon as may be proper, report to this government one or more individuals whom he may consider apt and honest for mayordomos, according to article 8, whether they be the same who are actually employed in the missions or others. He will likewise suggest the amount of salary which he thinks they ought to receive, according to the labor of each mission.

Ninth. The rancherias situated at a distance from the missions, and containing more than twenty-five families, may, if they choose, form a separate pueblo, and the distribution of lands and property shall there take place in the manner pointed out for the rest. The rancherias which do not contain twenty-five families, although they remain where they now reside, will form a district or ward, and belong to the nearest pueblo.

Tenth. The commissioner will make known the number of souls in each pueblo, in order to designate the number of municipal officers, and to order the elections to be made, which shall be carried on, as far as possible, in the manner prescribed by the law of 12th June, 1830.

Eleventh. The commissioners will take all such executive measures as the state of affairs may demand, and inform the government; and in doubtful or grave affairs they will consult it.

Twelfth. In all other respects, the commissioners, the padres, the mayordomos, and Indians, will act in conformity with these regulations.

APPENDIX No. 15.

In the extraordinary session of the most excellent California deputation, held in Monterey on the 3d of November, 1834, the following regulations were made respecting the missions which had been secularized agreeably to the supreme order of the 17th August, 1833, and the provisional regulations of Governor Figueroa of the 9th August, 1834:

ARTICLE 1. In accordance with the 2d article of the law of the 17th August, 1833, the amount of $1,500 per annum is assigned to the priests who exercise the functions of parish priest in the curacies of the first class, and $1,000 to those of the second class.

ART. 2. As curacies of the first class, shall be reputed San Diego, San Dieguito, San Luis Rey, Las Flores, and ranches annexed; San Gabriel and Los Angeles; Santa Barbara, the mission and presidio annexed; San Carlos, united to Monterey; Santa Clara, joined to San José de Guadalupe, and San José, San Francisco Solano, San Rafael, and the colony. And the following shall be reputed of the second class: San Juan Capistrano, San Fernando, San Buenaventura, Santa Fuez and la Purissima, San Luis Obispo, San Miguel, San Antonio and La Solidad, San Juan Bautista, Santa Cruz, San Francisco de Asis, and the presidio.

ART. 3. Agreeably to the 8th and 9th articles of said law, the reverend father commissary prefect, Father Francisco Garcia Diego, shall establish his residence in the capital, and the governor (gefe politico) shall request the reverend diocesan to confer upon said prelate the faculties appertaining to a foraneous vicar. He shall enjoy the salary of $3,000 assigned to him by said law.

ART. 4. The foraneous vicar and the curates shall be judged in all other respects by said law of the 17th August, 1833.

ART. 5. Until the government can furnish permanent parish priests, the respective prelates of the missionaries (religiosos) shall do so provisionally, with the approbation of the governor.

ART. 6. With respect to article 6th of said law, the $500 per annum shall be paid for public worship and for servants in each parish.

ART. 7. From the common stock of the property of the extinguished missions, the salaries of the foraneous vicar, the curates, and for religious worship, shall be paid either in cash (should there be any) or in produce or other articles at current prices. The governor will give the necessary orders to have this carried into effect.

ART. 8 The 17th article of the provisional regulations of secularization, which imposed upon Indians the duty of giving personal service to the priests, is annulled.

ART. 9. With respect to the 7th article of said law, the governor will order localities to be appointed for the habitation of the curates, for the court-house, schools, public establishments, and workshops.

ART. 10. The other matters to which the observations of the reverend padre, Fr. Narciso Daran, extend, as they are of easy resolution, will be settled by the governor, who is authorized to do so by the provisional regulations.

ART. 11. This law, together with the opinion of the committee appointed to examine the observations of Padre Daran on the provisional regulations, shall be communicated to the prelates for them to make it known to their subordinates.

ART. 2, (addition to.) The curacies which embrace two or more inhabited places will recognise the first one mentioned as the principal, and there the parish priest will reside; and in San Diego and Santa Barbara the missions will be the places of residence.

APPENDIX No. 16.

Mexican decree of the 7th November, 1835.

The President *ad interim* of the Mexican republic to the inhabitants thereof. Know ye that the general Congress has decreed the following:

"Until the curates mentioned in the 2d article of the law of August, 1833, shall take possession, the government will suspend the execution of the other articles of said law, and maintain things in the state they were in before said law was enacted."

APPENDIX No. 17.

Governor Alvarado's regulations respecting missions, January 17, 1839.

The fact of there not having been published in due season a set of regulations, to which the management of the administrators of the missions ought to have been subject from the moment that the so-called secularization was attempted, having caused evils of great transcendency to this Upper California—as these officers, authorized to dispose without limit of the property under their charge, do not know how to act in regard to their dependence upon the political government—and that of the most excellent departmental junta not being at present in session to consult with respecting the necessary steps to be taken under such circumstances, since the regulations of said secularization neither could nor can take effect, on account of the positive evils attending the fulfilment thereof, as experience itself has demonstrated,—has induced this government, in consideration of the pitiful state in which said establishments at present are, to dictate these provisional regulations, which shall be observed by said administrators, who will subject themselves to the following articles:

ARTICLE 1. All persons who have acted as administrators of missions will, as soon as possible, present to the government the accounts corresponding to their administration for due inspection, excepting those persons who may have already done so.

ART. 2. The present administrators who, at the delivery of their predecessors, may have received said documents as belonging to the archives, will return them to the parties interested, who, in virtue of the foregoing article, will themselves forward them to government, they being solely responsible.

ART. 3. Said officers will likewise remit those belonging to their administration up to the end of December of last year, however long they may have been in office.

ART. 4. Said officers will remit, as soon as possible, an exact account of the debts owing by and to the missions, which may at different times have been contracted.

ART. 5. Under no title or pretext whatever shall they contract debts, whatever may be the object of their inversion, nor make sales of any kind, either to foreign merchants or to private persons of the country, without the previous knowledge of government; for whatever may be done to the contrary shall be null and without effect.

ART. 6. The amounts owed by the establishments to merchants and private persons cannot be paid without an express order from government, to which must likewise be sent an account of all such property of each mission as it has been customary to make such payments with.

ART. 7. Without previous permission from said government, no kind of slaughtering of cattle shall take place, except what is necessary for the maintenance of the Indians, and the ordinary consumption of the house; and even with respect to this, the persons in charge will take care that, as far as possible, no female animals be killed.

ART. 8. The traffic of mules and horses for woollen manufactures, which has hitherto been carried on in the establishments, is hereby absolutely prohibited; and in lieu thereof, the persons in charge will see that the looms are got into operation, so that the wants of Indians may thus be supplied.

ART. 9. At the end of each month, they will send to government a statement of the ingress and egress of all kinds of produce that may have been warehoused or distributed, it being understood that the Indians at all times are to be provided for in the customary manner with such productions; to which end the administrators are empowered to furnish them with those which are manufactured in the establishment.

ART. 10. The administrators will in this year proceed to construct a building, on account of the establishment, to serve them for a habitation, and they may choose the locality which they may deem most convenient, in order that they may vacate the premises which they now occupy.

Art. 11. They shall not permit any individual of those called *de razon* (white people) to settle themselves in the establishments while the Indians remain in community.

Art. 12. They will at an early period present a census of all the inhabitants, distinguishing their classes and ages, in order to form general statistics; and they will likewise mention those who are emancipated and established on the lands of said establishments.

Art. 13. The establishments of San Carlos, San Juan Bautista, and Sonoma are not comprehended in the orders of this regulation. The government will regulate them in a different manner; but the administrators, who at different times may have had the management of their property, will be subject to the orders contained in articles 1 and 2.

Art. 14. They will likewise remit an account of all persons employed under them, designating their monthly pay, according to the orders which may have been given, including that of the reverend padres, with the object of regulating them according to the means of each establishment; and these salaries shall not be paid now nor hereafter with self-moving property.

Art. 15. The administrators will, under the strictest responsibility, fulfil these orders, with the understanding that, in the term of one month, they shall send the information required of them.

Art. 16. Government will continue making regulations respecting everything tending to establish the police to be observed in the establishments, and the manner to be observed in making out the accounts.

Art. 17. For the examination of these accounts, and everything thereto relating, the government will appoint a person with the character of inspector, with a competent salary, to be paid out of the funds of said establishments; and this person will establish his office where the government shall appoint, and have regulations given therefor in due time.

Instructions to be observed by Mr. W. E. Hartwell in the inspection of the establishments of the missions of Upper California.

Article 1. It being a matter of the greatest importance that the missions be regulated as intended when I published my provisional regulations of the 17th of January last, you will methodize the order which you consider best adapted to obtain the monthly information required, and have the annual accounts of the missions kept; and you will instruct the administrators how they shall organize them.

Art. 2. You will, with prudence and foresight, take an exact account of the self-moving property, and all other property on hand, calculating as near as possible the number of cattle, if it cannot be exactly got at.

Art. 3. In order to examine and count said cattle, you will take along with you a person of probity and information, who will attend to this business; and you will offer him the compensation which you may deem just for his services while the inspection may last.

Art. 4. On presenting yourself at each of the establishments, you will inform the administrator of the object of your arrival, referring to him or manifesting to him the respective orders, so that there may be no legal pretext for not punctually observing them.

ART. 5. If any of the administrators of the missions should make known to you any palpable wants which in your opinion ought to be immediately remedied, you will take the proper steps to do so, although it may be necessary to dispose of some of the produce on hand in the stores.

ART. 6. Should any of the reverend padres, or other persons employed, make any complaints to you relating to the management of the administrators, you will, with due prudence make the decision which you think most just, and use your utmost endeavors to keep up harmony among all classes.

ART. 7. You will exhort the administrators to use all possible economy in the use of provisions, weekly and annual slaughtering of cattle, and crops of all kinds of eatables, in order by all these means to further the progress of these establishments.

ART. 8. You are authorized to regulate the weekly and annual slaughtering which it has been customary to make in the missions, taking into consideration the number of calves marked, (annually,) so that the stock of cattle may not diminish.

ART. 9. You will likewise recommend the administrators to be affable in their treatment of Indians, and that the punishment they inflict be moderate and proportioned to their state of uncivilization; and that they (the administrators) see that they frequent divine service, agreeably to the education which they have received.

ART. 10. If any of the administrators should disobey the orders of this government and not fulfil them duly, in spite of the good treatment you give them, you will inform the government by a courier, that it may determine what is to be done; and in case that circumstances should require it, you are authorized to suspend such officer for the time that you may consider necessary, and put the mayordomos in charge in the mean time, in order that the labors of your commission be not paralyzed; and you will likewise inform the government, in order that it may determine what may be convenient.

ART. 11. The government expects, from your zeal, that you will be diligent in your commission, collect all kinds of information, and make the necessary observations for the formation of the police regulations which were promised in those of the 17th already cited.

APPENDIX No. 18.

Regulations of Governor Alvarado respecting the missions of California, obligations of the mayordomos, inspectors, &c., dated March 1, 1840.

Experience having proved in an undoubted manner that the missions of Upper California, for want of regulations organizing the management of the persons in charge of them, have in a short time suffered reverses and losses of great moment, the many abuses which were found to exist in the administration of the property of said missions obliged this government to issue the regulation of 17th January last year; but as it has been found that those have not been sufficient to root out the evils which are experienced, particularly on account of the high salaries with which the establishments are burdened, and which they cannot support, and being desirous to establish economy and a regular administration until the supreme government determine what it may deem proper, I publish the present regulations, which are to be strictly observed:

ARTICLE 1. The situations of administrators in the missions of Upper California are abolished, and in their stead mayordomos are established.

ART. 2. These mayordomos will receive the following salaries: Those of San Diego and San Juan Capistrano, $180; those of Santa Barbara, San Luis Obispo, San Francisco de Asis, and San Rafael, $240; those of San Buenaventura, la Purissima, San Miguel, and San Antonio, $300; those of San Fernando and Santa Fuez, $400; those of San Luis Rey and San Gabriel, $420; the one of Santa Clara, $480; and the one of San José, $600.

ART. 3. The former administrators may occupy said situations, provided that they be proposed in the manner pointed out by these regulations.

ART. 4. The situation of inspector, and the office established agreeably to the 17th article of the regulations of the 17th January last year, shall continue, with a salary of $3,000 per annum, and his powers will be hereafter designated.

Obligations of the mayordomos.

ART. 5. To take care of everything relative to the advancement of the property under their charge, acting in concert with the reverend padres in the difficult cases which may occur.

ART. 6. To compel the Indians to assist in the labors of the community, chastising them moderately for the faults they may commit.

ART. 7. To see that said Indians observe the best morality in their manners, and oblige them to frequent the church at the days and hours that have been customary, in which matter the reverend padres will intervene in the manner and form determined in the instructions given by the inspector to the administrators.

ART. 8. To remit to the inspector's office a monthly account of the produce they may collect into the storehouses, and an annual one of the crops of grain, liquors, &c., and of the branding of all kinds of cattle.

ART. 9. Said account must be authorized by the reverend padres.

ART. 10. To take care that the reverend padres do not want for their necessary aliment, and furnish them with everything necessary for their personal subsistence, as likewise to vaqueros and servants which they may request for their domestic service.

ART. 11. To provide the ecclesiastical prelates all the assistance which they may stand in need of when they make their accustomed visits to the missions through which they pass; and they are obliged under the strictest responsibility to receive them in the manner due to their dignity.

ART. 12. In the missions where the said prelates have their fixed residence, they will have the right to call upon the mayordomos at any hour when they may require them, and said mayordomos are required to present themselves to them every day at a certain hour, to know what they may require in their ministerial functions.

Art. 13. To furnish the priests of their respective missions all necessary assistance for religious worship; but in order to invest any considerable amount in this object, they will solicit the permission to do so from government, through the medium of the inspector.

Art. 14. To take care that in the distribution of goods received from the respective office to the Indians, the due proportion be observed amongst the different classes and description of persons, to which end the reverend padres shall be called to be present, and they will approve of the corresponding list of distribution.

Art. 15. To observe all the orders which they receive from the inspector's office emanating from the government, and to pay religiously all drafts addressed to them by said conduct and authorized by said government.

Art. 16. They will every three months send to the respective office a list of the goods and necessaries they may stand in greatest need of, as well for covering the nakedness of the Indians and carrying on the labor of the establishment, as to provide for the necessities of the priests and religious worship, so that, comparing these requisitions with the stock on hand, the best possible remedy may be applied. They will take care to furnish the necessary means of transport and provisions to the military or private persons who may be travelling on the public service; and they will provide said necessaries as well for the before-mentioned persons as for the commandants of stations who may ask for assistance for the troops; and send in a monthly account to the inspector, that he may recover the amount from the commissariat.

Art. 18. They will likewise render assistance to all other private individuals who may pass through the establishments, charging them for food and horses an amount proportioned to their means.

Art. 19. They will take care that the servants under them observe the best conduct and morality, as well as others who pass through or remain in the establishments; and in urgent cases they are authorized to take such steps as they may consider best adapted to preserve good order.

Art. 20. They may without any charge make use of the provisions produced by the establishments for their own subsistence and that of their families.

Art. 21. They may employ as many servants as they consider necessary for carrying on the work of the community; but their situations must be filled entirely by natives of the establishments themselves.

Art. 22. Said mayordomos are merely allowed to request the appointment of a clerk to carry on their correspondence with the inspector's office.

Art. 23. After the mayordomos have for one year given proofs of their activity, honesty, and good conduct in the fulfilment of their obligations, they shall be entitled (in times of little occupation) to have the government allow the Indians to render them some personal services in their private labors; but the consent of the Indians themselves must be previously obtained.

Art. 24. The mayordomos cannot make any purchase of goods from merchants, nor make any sale of the produce or manufactures of the establishments, without previous authority from government; (Second,) dispose of the Indians in any case for the service of private persons without a positive superior order; (Third,) make any slaughtering of cattle, except what shall be ordered by the inspector to take place weekly, extraordinarily, or annually.

Obligations of the Inspectors.

ART. 25. To make all kinds of mercantile contracts with foreign vessels and private persons of the country for the benefit of the missions.

ART. 26. To provide said establishments with the requisite goods and necessaries mentioned in the lists of the mayordomos, taking into consideration the stock of each establishment.

ART. 27. To draw bills for the payment of the debts contracted by his office and those already due by the establishments.

ART. 28. He shall be the ordinary conductor of communication between the government and the subaltern officers of said missions, as well as between all other persons who may have to apply to government respecting any business relative to said establishments.

ART. 29. He will pay the salaries of the mayordomos and other servants, take care that they fulfil their obligations, and propose to government, in conjunction with the reverend padres, the individuals whom they may consider best qualified to take charge of the missions.

ART. 30. He will determine the number of cattle to be killed weekly, annually, or on extraordinary occasions.

ART. 31. He will form the interior regulations of his office, and propose to government the subalterns which he may judge necessary for the proper management thereof.

General orders.

ART. 32. All merchants and private persons who have any claims on said missions will in due time present to the inspector an account of the amounts due to them, with the respective vouchers, in order that the government may determine the best manner of settling them, as the circumstances of said mission may permit.

ART. 33. With respect to the missions of San Carlos, San Bautista, Santa Cruz, La Solidad, and San Francisco Solano, the general government will continue regulating them as circumstances may permit.

ART. 34. Officers and magistrates of all kinds are at liberty to manifest to government the abuses they may observe in those charged with fulfilling these regulations, so that a quick remedy may be applied.

ART. 35. The government, after previously hearing the opinions of the reverend padres, will arrange matters respecting the expenses of religious worship and the subsistence of said padres, either by fixing a stated amount for both objects, or in some other manner which may be more convenient towards attending to their wants.

ART. 36. All prior regulations and orders conflicting with the present are annulled; and if any doubt occur respecting their observance, the government will be consulted through the established channel.

ART. 37. During the defect or temporary absence of the mayordomos, the reverend padres will in the mean time take charge of the establishments.

APPENDIX No. 19.

Extracts from General Micheltorena's proclamation of the 29th of March, 1843, ordering the majority of the missions to be again placed in charge of the priests, in consequence of an arrangement entered into between said governor and the different prelates of said missions.

ARTICLE 1. The government of the department will order the missions of San Diego, San Luis Rey, San Juan Capistrano, San Gabriel, San Fernando, San Buenaventura, Santa Barbara, Santa Fuez, La Purissima, San Antonio, Santa Clara, and San José, to be delivered up to the very reverend padres whom the respective prelate may appoint to each of them; and said missions shall in future continue to be administered by the very reverend padres, as tutors to the Indians, in the same manner as they held them formerly.

ART. 2. As policy makes irrevocable what has hitherto been done, the missions will not claim any lands already granted up to this date; but they will collect the cattle, property, and utensils, which may have been lent by the priests or administrators, settling the time and manner in a friendly way with debtors or holders.

ART. 3. They will likewise take care to gather together the dispersed Indians, excepting, *first*, those legally emancipated by the superior departmental government; *second*, those who, at the date of this decree, are in the service of private persons—it being understood that even both these classes, if they voluntarily wish it and prefer returning to their missions, shall be admitted and protected, with the knowledge of their masters and of the reverend missionaries.

ART. 4. The departmental government, in whose possession the missions have been up to this date, in virtue of the very ample faculties with which it is invested, authorizes the reverend padres to provide out of the produce of the missions for the indispensable expenses of the conversion, aliment, clothing, and other temporal necessities of the Indians, and to take from the same funds the moderate part which they may require for their own sustenance, for the economical salary of the mayordomos, and for the maintenance of divine worship, on the condition that they oblige themselves on their honor and conscience to deliver to the public treasury, (notice first being given to this government by the reverend padres, and an express order in writing, signed by the undersigned, governor, commandant general, and inspector,) for assistance, aliment, clothing for the troops, and wants of the civil officers, the eighth part of the total annual produce of every description; and they will take care to present, at the end of the year, an exact and true account of the number of neophytes' cattle, property, and all kinds of fruits, or its representative value, belonging to each mission.

ART. 5. The departmental government, which prides itself in being religious, and at the same time entirely Californian, and, as such, interested in the same manner as each and every one of the inhabitants of both Californias in the progress of the holy Catholic faith and prosperity of the country, offers all its power for the protection of the missions, and, as commandant general, the force of arms to escort, defend, and sustain them, as it will likewise do in respect to individual and particular property and guaranties, securing to the owners thereof the possession and preservation of the lands which they this day hold; and promises not to make any new grants without the information of said authorities, of the reverend padres, notorious unoccupancy, want of cultivation, or necessity.

APPENDIX No. 20.

Decree of the Departmental Assembly of 28th May, 1845, respecting the renting of some of the missions, and converting others into pueblos, &c.

ARTICLE 1. The departmental government shall call together the Indians of the missions of San Rafael, Dolores, Solidad, San Miguel, and la Purissima, which are abandoned by them, by means of a proclamation, which it will publish, allowing them the term of one month from the day of its publication in their respective missions, or in those nearest to them, for them to reunite for the purpose of occupying and cultivating them; and they are informed that, if they fail to do so, said missions will be declared to be without owners, (mostreneas,) and the assembly and departmental government will dispose of them as may best suit the general good of the department.

2. The Carmelo, San Juan Bautista, San Juan Capistrano, and San Francisco Solano, shall be considered as pueblos, which is the character they at present have; and the government, after separating a sufficient locality for the curate's house, for churches and appurtenances, and a court-house, will proceed to sell the remaining premises at public auction, in order to pay their respective debts; and the overplus, should there be any, shall remain for the benefit and preservation of divine worship.

3. The remainder of the missions, as far as San Diego, inclusive, may be rented out at the option of the government, which will establish the manner and form of carrying this into execution, taking care in so doing that the establishments move prosperously onward. These respective Indians will consequently remain in absolute liberty to occupy themselves as they may see fit, either in the employment of the renter himself, or in the cultivation of their own lands, which the government must necessarily designate for them, or in the employ of any other private person.

4. The principal edifice of the mission of Santa Barbara is excepted from the renting mentioned in the foregoing article; and the government will arrange, in the most suitable manner, which part thereof shall be destined for the habitation and other conveniences of his grace the bishop and his suite, and which for the reverend missionary padres who at present inhabit said principal edifice. And likewise one-half of the total rent of the other property of the mission shall be invested for the benefit of the church, and for the maintenance of its minister, and the other half for the benefit of its respective Indians.

5. The product of the rents, mentioned in article 3, shall be divided into three equal parts, and the government shall destine one of them for the maintenance of the reverend padre minister and the conservation of divine worship; another for the Indians; and the last shall necessarily be dedicated by government towards education and public beneficence, as soon as the legal debts of each mission be paid.

6. The third part mentioned in the fifth article as destined for the

maintenance of the priests and help towards divine worship shall be placed at the disposal of the reverend prelates, for them to form a general fund, to be distributed equitably in the before-mentioned objects.

7. The authorities or ecclesiastical ministers, should there be any, in the missions referred to in article 1, or those in the nearest missions, or persons who may merit the confidence of government, will be requested by said government to see that the proclamation above mentioned be published, and to give information immediately whether the said neophytes have presented themselves or not within the period fixed, in order that, in view of such documents, the necessary measures may be taken.

8. Government will, in the strictest manner, exact the amount owing by various persons to all the missions in general, as already ordered by the most excellent assembly in its decree of the 24th of August, 1844, and dispose of the same for the object mentioned in the last part of the 5th article.

APPENDIX No. 21.

Governor Pico's regulations for the alienation and renting of the missions, dated October 28, 1845.

OF ALIENATION.

ARTICLE 1. There will be sold in this capital, to the highest bidder, the missions of San Rafael, Dolores, Solidad, San Miguel, and la Purissima, which are abandoned by their neophytes.

ART. 2. Of the existing premises of the pueblos of San Luis Obispo, Carmelo, San Juan Bautista, and San Juan Capistrano, and which formerly belonged to the missions, there shall be separated the churches and appurtenances—one part for the curate's house, another for a court-house and a place for a school, and the remainder of said edifices shall be sold at public auction, where an account of them will be given.

ART. 3. In the same manner will be sold the property on hand belonging to the missions—such as grain, produce, or mercantile goods—giving the preference for the same amount to the renters, and deducting previously that part of said property destined for the food and clothing of the reverend padre minister and the neophytes until the harvest of next year.

ART. 4. The public sale of the missions of San Luis Obispo, Purissima, and San Juan Capistrano shall take place on the first four days of the month of December next, notices being previously posted up in the towns of the department inviting bidders, and three publications being made in the capital at intervals of eight days one from the other before the sale. In the same manner will be sold what belongs to San Rafael, Dolores, San Juan Bautista, Carmelo, and San Miguel, on the 23d and 24th of January next year.

ART. 5. From the date of the publication of these regulations, proposals will be admitted in this capital to be made to government, which will take them into consideration.

ART. 6. The total proceeds of these sales shall be paid into the departmental treasury, to pay therewith the debts of said missions; and should anything remain, it will be placed at the disposal of the respective prelate, for the maintenance of religious worship, agreeably to article 2 of the decree of the departmental assembly.

OF RENTING.

ART. 7. The missions of San Fernando, San Buenaventura, Santa Barbara, and Santa Fuez shall be rented out to the highest bidder for the term of nine years.

ART. 8. To this end, bidders shall be convoked in all the departments, by fixing advertisements in the towns, in order that by the 5th December next they may appear in this capital, either personally or by their legal agents.

ART. 9. Three publications shall be made in this capital at intervals of eight days each before the day appointed for the renting, and proposals will be admitted on the terms expressed in article 5.

ART. 10. There shall be included in said renting all the lands, outdoor property, implements of agriculture, vineyards, orchards, workshops, and whatever, according to the inventories made, belongs to the respective missions, with the mere exception of those small portions of land which have always been occupied by some of the Indians of the missions.

ART. 11. The buildings are likewise included, excepting the churches and their appurtenances, the part destined for the curate's house, the court-house, and place for a school. In the mission of Santa Barbara no part of the principal edifice shall be included which is destined for the habitation of his grace the bishop and suite, and the reverend padres who inhabit it; and there shall be merely placed at the disposal of the renter the cellars, movables, and workshops, which are not applied to the service of said prelates.

ART. 12. As the proceeds of the rent are to be divided into three parts, to be distributed according to article 5 of said decree, the renter may himself deliver to the respective padre, prefect, or to the person whom he may appoint, the third part destined for the maintenance of the minister and the religious worship; and only in the mission of Santa Barbara, the half of said rent-money shall be paid for the same object, in conformity with the 4th article of the decree of the departmental assembly.

ART. 13. The government reserves to itself the right of taking care that the establishments prosper; in virtue of which it will prevent their destruction, ruin, or decline, should it be necessary, during the period of renting.

ART. 14. The renting of the missions of San Diego, San Luis Rey, San Gabriel, San Antonio, Santa Clara, and San José shall take place when the difficulties shall be got over which at present exist with respect to the debts of those establishments, and then the government will inform the public; and all shall be done agreeably to these regulations.

ADVANTAGES AND OBLIGATIONS OF THE RENTERS.

ART. 15. The renters shall have the benefit of the usufruct of everything delivered to them on rent according to these regulations.

Art. 16. The obligations of the renters are: 1st. To pay promptly and quarterly, when due, the amount of the rent. 2d. To deliver back, with improvements, at the expiration of the nine years, whatever they may receive on rent, with the exception of the stills, movables, and implements of agriculture, which must be returned in a serviceable state. 3d. They shall return at the same time the number of cattle which they receive, and of the same description, and of such an age as not to embarrass the procreation of the following year. 4th. They shall give bonds to the satisfaction of government before they receive the establishments, conditioned for the fulfilment of the obligations of the renters—one of which is the payment of the damages which the government may be obliged to find against them, agreeably to article 13.

OF THE INDIANS.

Art. 17. The Indians are free from their neophytism, and may establish themselves in their missions or wherever they choose. They are not obliged to serve the renters, but they may engage themselves to them on being paid for their labor; and they will be subject to the authorities and to the local police.

Art. 18. The Indians radicated in each mission shall appoint from amongst themselves, on the 1st of January in each year, four overseers, who will watch and take care of the preservation of public order, and be subject to the justice of the peace to be named by government in each mission, agreeably to the decree of 4th July last. If the overseers do not perform their duty well, they shall be replaced by others, to be appointed by the justice of the peace, with previous permission from government, who will remain in office for the remainder of the year in which they were appointed.

Art. 19. The overseers shall appoint every month, from amongst the rest of the Indians, a sacristan, a cook, a tortilla maker, a vaquero, and two washer-women, for the service of the padre minister, and no one shall be hindered from remaining in this service as long as he choose. In the mission of Santa Barbara, the overseers will appoint an Indian, to the satisfaction of the priest, to take care daily of the reservoir and water conduits that lead to the principal edifice, and he shall receive a compensation of four dollars per month out of the part of the rent belonging to the Indians.

Art. 20. The Indians who possess portions of land, in which they have their gardens and houses, will apply to this government for the respective title, in order that the ownership thereof may be adjudicated to them, it being understood that they cannot alienate said lands, but they shall be hereditary amongst their relatives, according to the order established by the laws.

Art. 21. From the said Indian population three boys shall be chosen as pages for the priest, and to assist in the ceremonies of the church.

Art. 22. The musicians and singers who may establish themselves in the missions shall be exempted from the burdens mentioned in article 18, but they shall lend their services in the churches, at the masses and the *functions* which may occur.

OF THE JUSTICES OF THE PEACE.

ART. 23. The justices of the peace shall put in execution the orders communicated to them by the nearest superior authority; they will take care that veneration and respect be paid to matters appertaining to our religion and its ministers, and that the 18th and 20th articles, inclusive, of these regulations, be punctually fulfilled; they will see that no one be hindered in the free use of his property; they will quiet the little disturbances that may occur, and, if necessary, impose light and moderate correction; and if the occurrences should be of such a nature as to belong to the cognizance of other authorities, they will remit to such authorities the criminals and antecedents.

APPENDIX No. 22.

Decree of the Departmental Assembly of the 3d of April, 1846, respecting missions.

ARTICLE 1. The government is authorized to carry into effect the object of the decree of 28th May last, published by this honorable assembly, respecting missions; to which end, seeing the impracticability of renting mentioned in article 3 of said decree, the departmental government will act in the manner which may appear most conducive to obviate the total ruin of the missions of San Gabriel, San Luis Rey, San Diego, and the remainder which are in similar circumstances.

ART. 2. As most of these establishments are owing large amounts, if the property on hand should not be sufficient to satisfy their acknowledged debts, attention shall be had to what the laws determine respecting bankruptcies, and steps shall be taken accordingly.

ART. 3. Should government, by virtue of this authority, find that, in order to prevent the total ruin which threatens said missions, it will be necessary to sell them to private persons, this shall be done at public auction, the customary notice being previously given.

ART. 4. In case of sale, if, after the debts be paid, any surplus should remain, this shall be divided among the Indians of the premises sold, government taking care to make the most just distribution possible.

ART. 5. In any case, care must be taken to secure a sufficient amount for the maintenance of the padres and the expenses of public worship, the government being at liberty to separate a part of the whole establishments, whether in lands for cultivation, landed or other property, at its discretion, which will be sufficient to secure both objects, the respective priest being previously heard and attended to.

ART. 6. The premises set apart according to the foregoing article shall be delivered as a sale at a perpetual interest of four per cent.; and the proceeds shall be applied precisely to the objects mentioned in said article 5.

ART. 7. What has hitherto been done agreeably to what was ordained in the decree of the honorable assembly of the 28th May, before cited, remains in full force; and these presents shall in no manner alter the contracts made and measures taken by government in accordance with said decree of May, 1845; nor shall they in future put any obstacle in the way of what may be done in accordance thereto.

ART. 8. The government will remove any obstacles not foreseen in this decree; and within six months at furthest will notify this honorable assembly of the result of its fulfilment.

APPENDIX No. 23.

Decree of the Departmental Assembly of the 31st October, 1846, annulling the sale of missions and other acts of Don Pio Pico.

The citizen José Maria Flores, captain of cavalry in the Mexican army, governor and commandant general *ad interim* of this department, to its inhabitants:

Know ye that the honorable departmental assembly, in an extraordinary session of yesterday, has decreed the following:

The most excellent departmental assembly, taking into consideration the urgent necessity of providing resources for carrying on the war against the invading forces of the United States of North America, and finding that the only way of obtaining them in a sure and prompt manner is to solicit a loan, has, in this day's session, found it expedient to decree the following, viz:

1. The sales of missions made by Don Pio Pico as governor, as well as all other acts done by him on the same subject beyond his authority, are entirely annulled.

2. His excellency the governor *ad interim* is authorized to solicit a loan of such amount as he may consider necessary for the object indicated, it being stipulated that, in accomplishing this act in the most equitable and just manner, he may mortgage one or more of the missions for the corresponding security.

3. These establishments shall continue with the character of being rented and in possession of the renters who shall have fulfilled the conditions stipulated in the proclamation upon that subject.

4. The missions which exist under the circumstances of the preceding article shall suffer no alteration until the term of their lease shall expire, even should they be of those mortgaged; and with respect to the others the government will take care that the regulations formerly given on the subject be duly complied with.

His excellency the governor *ad interim* will be made acquainted herewith, for his government and further ends.

Hall of sessions of the honorable assembly of California, in the city of Los Angeles, October 30, 1846.

FRANCIS FIGUEROA,
President.
AUGUSTIN OLVERA,
Deputy Secretary.

I therefore command it to be published, circulated, and posted up in the usual places, for the knowledge of the public.

Given in the city of Los Angeles, October 31, 1846.

JOSE MARIA FLORES.

NARCISO BOTELLO, *Secretary.*

APPENDIX No. 24.

Know all men by these presents, that I, Brigadier General S. W. Kearny, governor of California, by virtue of authority in me vested, considering that, inasmuch as there are various claimants to the missions of San José, Santa Clara, Santa Cruz, and San Juan, and the houses, gardens, vineyards, &c., around and near them, do hereby decree that, until the proper judicial tribunals to be established shall decide upon the same, the above named missions and property appertaining thereto shall remain under charge of the Catholic priests, as they were when the United States flag was first raised in this territory, it being understood that this decree is not to affect the rights of any claimant, and that the priests are to be responsible for the preservation of said missions and property while under their charge. The alcaldes of the jurisdictions in which the above-named missions are situated will, upon the application of the priests, take the proper measures to remove therefrom all persons trespassing or intruding upon them.

Given at Monterey, capital of California, this 22d day of March, 1847.

S. W. KEARNY,
Brigadier General, and Governor of California.

APPENDIX No. 25.

HEADQUARTERS 10TH MILITARY DEPARTMENT,
Monterey, California, January 3, 1848.

REVEREND SIR: I have the honor to acknowledge the receipt of your letter of the 29th December, and its accompanying documents, purporting to give you authority to sell mission lands, bearing date 25th May and 16th June, 1846, signed by José Castro, and addressed to yourself.

This document certainly could give you no authority to sell any part of the mission lands after the 7th July, 1846, the day on which the United States flag was hoisted in California, if, indeed, it could legally have conferred such authority before. Since that date, the mission lands can only be disposed of by virtue of authority from the United States government. I am therefore obliged to declare, and do hereby declare, all sales of any part of the mission lands made by your reverence to be illegal, null and void, and that the purchasers of such lands hold no legal title to them whatever by virtue of any sale made by your reverence.

I am, respectfully, your obedient servant,

R. B. MASON,
Colonel 1st Dragoons, Governor of California.

Rev. Padre FR. JOSE MARIA DEL R. S. DEL REAL,
Minister of the mission of Santa Clara.

APPENDIX No. 26.

STATE DEPARTMENT, TERRITORY OF CALIFORNIA,
Monterey, August 18, 1848.

SIR: It is reported that you have recently put Dr. R. Den in judicial possession of the rancho or farm of San Marcos, belonging to the mission of Santa Barbara.

The governor therefore directs me to inform you that this act of yours is utterly null and void, no alcalde in California having authority to give any legal force whatever to any existing claims or titles to the missions or other public lands in this territory.

Very respectfully, your obedient servant,
H. W. HALLECK,
Lieutenant of Engineers, and Secretary of State.

DON PEDRO C. CARRILLO,
First Alcalde of Santa Barbara.

NOTE.—A similar notice was served by Colonel Stevenson on Dr. R. Den.

APPENDIX No. 27.

ALCALDE'S OFFICE, MONTEREY,
March 23, 1848.

SIR: My apology for a seeming neglect is, that I have been under the impression that the information called for by your note of this morning had been given as desired.

The only titles which fall within the survey of Lt. Halleck are those of T. H. Green, James Doyle, a small triangle of the land of David Spence, and a claim of some twenty varas by Bernard McKenzie.

Very respectfully, sir, your obedient servant,
WALTER COLTON, *Alcalde.*

Colonel R. B. MASON,
Governor of California.

ALCALDE'S OFFICE, MONTEREY,
June 14, 1848.

SIR: It is not in my power to give very definitive and satisfactory answers to the inquiries proposed in your communication of the 5th instant.

You desire to be informed which are the limits of Monterey, and what law fixes the limits? The limits of the town were formerly, as I am told, restricted to half a league from the church, but that the legislature of the territory, some twelve years since, extended these to the summits of the surrounding hills.

The act involving this extension, like most others emanating from the same body, has been lost in the successive revolutions which have swept over the country; it was passed in compliance with a memorial sent in by the inhabitants of the town.

You ask who has the right to sell or deed away lots within the town? This right vests in the municipal authority, and is exercised by the alcalde, under the advice of the ayuntamientos—such at least has been the usage in Monterey; all lots have been granted or sold in this form.

You inquire for the right of an alcalde to sell the site of a Mexican fort or battery. No Mexican law or decree, as I can find, designates any particular spots as sites of forts or batteries. Each military chief put up a fort where he chose, or demolished those put up by his predecessors. He asked no leave to build, and none to abandon. When guns were mounted, no alcalde ventured with his right to sell, but eagerly extended that right over an abandoned position.

The only rule which appears to have governed the military and civil authorities in these matters seems to have been that of Rob Roy—

————"The simple plan,
That they shall take who have the power,
And they shall keep who can."

Copies of the titles called for shall be made out on the return of the clerk to the office.

I am, very respectfully, sir, your obedient servant,

WALTER COLTON, *Alcalde.*

Colonel R. B. MASON,
   Governor of California.

ALCALDE'S OFFICE, MONTEREY,
August 10, 1848.

SIR: I have the honor to acknowledge your communication desiring certified copies of the land titles which fall within, or trench upon, the lines of Mr. Halleck's survey. They are herewith enclosed, as taken verbatim from the records of this office.

I am, very respectfully, sir, your obedient servant,

WALTER COLTON, *Alcalde.*

Colonel R. B. MASON,
   Governor of California.

NOTE.—The copies of titles forwarded by Alcalde Colton are the following, marked 1, 2, 3, 4, and 5. No copy of Bernard McKenzie's claim was received.

No. 1.

Whereas Commodore W. Branford Shubrick has applied to this court for a building lot in the municipality of Monterey, situated as follows, viz: Beginning at the southwest corner of a lot owned by Theodorus Bailey, esq., and running in a direct line with said lot south twenty-five degrees east the distance of one hundred and thirty yards to a red-wood stake on the northern border of the ravine above the dam; thence crossing the said ravine to an oak tree on the southern side of the said dam, east five degrees south and a half north, sixty-three yards; thence east twenty-two degrees south, one hundred and thirty-three yards to low-water mark; thence along low-water mark with its windings and turnings two hundred yards to the northeast angle of the said Theodorus Bailey's lot; thence along the aforesaid Theodorus Bailey's southern line of boundary, west ten degrees south from low-water mark to the place of beginning: whereas the said building lot is now vacant and at the disposal of the municipality: and whereas the said Commodore W. Branford Shubrick has paid the sum per yard required by law,—he becomes therefore fully and justly entitled to the same, to be held and owned by him in fee simple, to the preclusion of all other claims whatever. In testimony whereof, I hereto set my hand and seal, this 27th day of February, A. D. 1847.

         WALTER COLTON, *Alcalde.* [L. S.]
WILLIAM R. GARNER, *Secretary.*

I certify the above to be a true and faithful copy of the original title in the archives of the alcalde's office of this town.

         WALTER COLTON, *Alcalde.*
MONTEREY, *August* 10, 1848.

No. 2.

Whereas Theodorus Bailey has applied to this court for a building lot, consisting of two hundred and seventeen yards of front line, and two hundred yards depth, situated as follows, viz: Commencing at a point of land on the shore of the bay, opposite a large stone, marked with a cold chisel with the letter B, and at the southeast corner of a lot of land claimed by David Spence, esq., and recorded in the magistrate's office, running from thence west ten degrees south along the line of said Spence's lot of land, two hundred yards to a red-wood stake on the roadside; from thence south twenty-five degrees east along the said road two hundred and seventeen yards, more or less, to another red-wood stake on the same roadside; from thence east ten degrees north two hundred yards, more or less, passing north of but near the old magazine, and south of the old fort, and the house near the same, to the low-water mark on the shore of the bay, opposite to a red-wood stake driven in, on, or near the bank as it winds and turns, to the place of beginning; with the privilege of wharfing and improving the same by erecting piers to extend into the bay—the above land-marks being placed and fixed upon according to a survey of the said plot by Dr. Robert Semple, of San Francisco, and William R. Garner, secretary to the town of Monterey—the above lot to be held and owned by said Theodorus Bailey in fee simple:

Whereas said building lot is now vacant, and at the disposal of the municipality; and whereas said Theodorus Bailey has paid the sum per yard required by law,—he becomes therefore fully and justly entitled to the same, to the preclusion of all other claims whatever.

In testimony whereof, I hereto set my hand and seal, this 11th day of February, A. D. 1847.

         WALTER COLTON, *Alcalde.* [L. S.]
WILLIAM R. GARNER, *Secretary.*

I certify the above to be a true and faithful copy of the original title in the archives of the alcalde's office of this town.

         WALTER COLTON, *Alcalde.*
MONTEREY, *August* 10, 1848.

No. 3.

Whereas James Doyle has applied to this office for a building lot, consisting of one hundred yards square, and situated as follows, viz: On the northern side of the gulsh which runs by the fort of Monterey, the front line running nearly north-northwest and south-southeast on the western side of the main road which goes from the town of Monterey towards Muscle point, and distant from said gulsh about one hundred yards to the northward:

Whereas said lot is now vacant, and at the disposal of the municipality; and whereas said Doyle has paid the sum per yard required by law,—he is therefore recognised by this court as the owner and proprietor of the same building lot herein mentioned.

In testimony of which, I hereunto set my hand and seal, this 14th day of October, 1846.

WALTER COLTON, *Alcalde.* [L. S.]
WILLIAM R. GARNER, *Secretary.*

I certify the above to be a true and faithful copy of the original title in the archives of the alcalde's office of this town.

WALTER COLTON, *Alcalde.*
MONTEREY, *August* 10, 1848.

No. 4.

Whereas David Spence, esq., has applied to this court for a building lot, consisting of two hundred and thirty-nine yards square, and situated as follows, viz: The front line running along the coast about north-northwest and south-southeast from the first point that makes into the sea from the house on the hill, which house was occupied by the Mexican government as a fort; and extending from said point to the next point to the northward, being the distance of two hundred and thirty-nine yards, the last point mentioned on the northernmost one being designated as having held, some twenty-five years back, one or two guns for the better defence of this harbor:

The front line being as above described, the back line will run parallel with the front line, and distant from it two hundred and thirty-nine yards; the whole of this lot forming a square containing fifty-seven thousand one hundred and twenty-one square yards:

Whereas said lot is now vacant, and at the disposal of the municipality; and whereas said David Spence has paid the sum per yard required by law,—he becomes therefore fully and justly entitled to the same, to the preclusion of all other claims whatever.

In testimony of which, I hereto set my hand and seal, this twenty-seventh day of October, A. D. 1846.

WALTER COLTON, *Alcalde.* [L. S.]
WILLIAM R. GARNER, *Secretary.*

I certify the above to be a true and faithful copy of the original title in the archives of the alcalde's office of this town.

WALTER COLTON, *Alcalde.*
MONTEREY, *August* 10, 1848.

No. 5.

Monterey, *Abril* 23 *de* 1846.

Se dio titulo de propiedad al referido Talbot H. Green de un solar de 399 v. cuadradas al oeste del castillo de este puerto de Monterey y del camino real que va para la Punta de Pinos segun se esplica en su solicitad que obra en poder de dicho señor.

J. S. ESCAMILLA.

[Translation.]

A title of ownership was given to said Talbot H. Green of a lot of 399 square varas on the east of the castle of this port of Monterey, and of the high road which leads to Point Pinos, as is explained in his petition in the possession of said gentleman.

Monterey, *Junio* 13 *de* 1846.

Se dio titulo en propiedad al espresado señor del solar que comienza desde la punta del muelle al noroeste hasta en contrar el solar de Señor Deleissegues en estension de noventa y cuatro varas, y ciento y tres v. frente al solar de los S. S. Serrano y Arias, hasta abajo en la canada del castillo cuyos derechos pago.

J. S. ESCAMILLA.

Talbot H. Green.

[Translation.]

A title of ownership was given to the said gentleman of the lot which begins from the point of the mole to the northwest, until joining the lot of Señor Deleissegues, the length of ninety-four varas, and one hundred and three varas in front to the lot of Señores Serrano and Arias, until below the ravine of the castle; the duties of which he paid.

I, William R. Garner, clerk of the first alcalde's court within and for the jurisdiction of Monterey, Upper California, do hereby certify that the two above instruments of writing are each of them a true, complete and faithful copy of the original notes of the titles as they are recorded in the (libro de solares) book of register for building lots in the town of Monterey, on pages fifty-nine (vuelta) and sixty.

In testimony whereof, I have hereunto set my hand and affixed the seal of said court, at office, this twenty-ninth day of September, A. D. eighteen hundred and forty-eight.

[L. S.]

WILLIAM R. GARNER,
Clerk of the Court.

APPENDIX No. 28.

Monterey, California, *June* 20, 1848.

I certify that, on the 28th day of January, 1847, I pointed out to Commodore W. Branford Shubrick, Lieutenant Commanding Theodorus

Bailey, United States navy, Chaplain Walter Colton, United States navy, then acting in the capacity of alcalde of Monterey, and Captain C. Q. Tompkins, United States army, the land situated between the ravines marked A and B in the accompanying field map of Fort Hill, Monterey, California, by Lieutenant W. H. Warner, United States army, and did then inform the aforementioned persons that such land would be required for government purposes in the defence, by fortifications, of the port of Monterey, and that no part of it ought to be sold or otherwise disposed of.

And I do further certify that, between the 28th of January aforesaid and the 11th of February, 1847, on several occasions I informed the said Commodore W. Branford Shubrick and the said Theodorus Bailey that the land about Monterey redoubt and the old Mexican fort, near the beach, lying within the limits aforesaid, was absolutely essential to government for the purposes of fortifying the port of Monterey, and ought not to be sold to, or purchased by, any private individual.

And I do further certify that, on the 27th day of February, 1847, being told by the said Lieutenant Commanding Bailey that he was "about to purchase" certain lands near the old Mexican fort, I informed him that such lands were required for government purposes, and, if legally sold to him, government would afterwards be obliged to purchase them back, and that, therefore. I thought such purchase ought not to be made.

And I do further certify that, on the 27th of February aforesaid, I called the attention of Brigadier General Kearny to the fact that sales of public lands which would eventually be required for public purposes were about to be made by the alcalde of Monterey, notwithstanding that he, the alcalde, had been informed that such lands were required for the public service, and did then request the said General Kearny to use his authority to prevent the completion of such sales, to which General Kearny replied that he would forbid the sales.

H. WAGER HALLECK,
Lieutenant of Engineers.

NOTE.—The survey referred to in the accompanying letters of Alcalde Colton, dated March 23 and August 10, 1848, was a copy of that portion of the field map of Lieutenant Warner bounded by the strong red lines in the attached map.

H. WAGER HALLECK,
Lieutenant of Engineers.

MONTEREY, CALIFORNIA, *August* 10, 1848.

APPENDIX No. 29.

UPPER CALIFORNIA,
Monterey, June 16, 1847.

SIR: I am, by purchase from Don Benito Diaz, of this town, owner of a certain piece or tract of land near the town of San Francisco, formerly called Yerba Buena; which tract of land, containing two leagues, more or less, running from the lagoon de "Loma Alta" to Punta de Lobos, embracing the old presidio and old castle, for many years abandoned, was deeded and granted on the 25th day of June, 1846, to said Diaz by Pio Pico, at that time governor of California; and on the nineteenth day of September, same year, sold and conveyed to me by said Diaz, for a valuable consideration; and by the alcalde of the jurisdiction of San Francisco I was put into possession of the same; and at this present time a part of the land is occupied by my agent.

All the deeds, transfers, and papers of possession relative to said land, are in my hands, subject to your inspection.

In the month of May last, while at San Francisco, I went over this land with Jasper O. Farrel, surveyor, and found that some of the troops of the government of the United States were in possession of the above-mentioned presidio; that they were living there; that they had torn down some of the buildings to repair others, and in some cases were putting new roofs on the houses.

I therefore take this opportunity to inform you of the state of affairs respecting my said land, and personally protest against my said property being used by person or persons privately, or for the government, without a due consideration being paid to me; and further protest against any of the same in case of damages that may be sustained by me now or hereafter.

Your attention as governor of California to this subject is respectfully solicited by your most obedient servant,

THOMAS O. LARKIN.

Col. R. B. MASON,
Governor of the Territory of California.

NOTE.—The following documents, numbered 1, 2, 3, and 4, are copies of the papers presented by Mr. Larkin in proof of the legality of his claim:

No. 1.

Pio Pico, first member of the departmental assembly, and constitutional governor of the Californias.

Whereas D. Benito Diaz has solicited for his personal benefit, and that of his family, the land known by the name of *Punta de Lobos*, situated in the port of San Francisco, the necessary investigations having been previously made, I have, in virtue of the faculties conferred upon me, granted to him, in the name of the Mexican nation, by a decree of this day, the said land, declaring to him the ownership thereof by these presents, in conformity with the law of 18th August, 1824, and the regulation of 21st November, 1828, subject to the approval of the most excellent departmental assembly, and to the following conditions:

1st. He may fence it in, without prejudice to the highways, roads, and privileges, destining it to the use or cultivation which may best suit him.

2d. He shall ask for the judicial possession from the respective magistrate in virtue of this despatch, and the boundary shall be marked by this authority with the respective landmarks.

3d. The land of which donation is made to him consists of two square leagues, (dos sitios de ganado mayor,) a little more or less, comprehending from the lagoon of the high hill to the Punta de Lobos, and the same which is shown by the map which accompanies the documents. The magistrate who gives possession shall have it measured according to law. I consequently command that, holding the present title as firm and valid, a record be kept thereof in the corresponding book, and it be delivered to the party interested, for his security and other ends.

Given in the city of Los Angeles on the twenty-fifth day of June, eighteen hundred and forty-six, on this common paper, for want of sealed paper.

PIO PICO. [L. S.]

MATIAS MORENO,
   Secretary ad interim.

This title has been recorded in the corresponding book.

MORENO.

No. 2.

In the port of Monterey, Upper California, on the nineteenth day of September, eighteen hundred and forty-six, before me, Walter Colton, justice of the peace of this district, and before the undersigned witnesses, appeared Don Benito Diaz, and said, that, in his own name and in that of his wife, Doña Luisa Soto de Diaz, and other heirs and successors, and whoever, through them, may have any kind of title, voice, or fame, he sells and gives in public sale and perpetual alienation, in right of inheritance, and forever and ever, to Mr. Thomas O. Larkin, resident of this place, a land of which he is owner, in virtue of a grant made to him by his Excellency the governor of the department, Don Pio Pico, according to the title which accompanies the present writing, dated the twenty-fifth of June of the present year, which land is composed of two square leagues, a little more or less, situated in the entrance and port of San Francisco, with the boundaries mentioned in said title, which are from the lagoon of the high hill to the Punta de Lobos. The seller declares that he has neither alienated nor mortgaged it, and that it is free from all public burdens; and, as such, he sells it for the price of one thousand dollars in common silver coin, which he has received to his entire satisfaction; that, from this time, he renounces, and separates himself from the dominion, ownership, and every other right which he may have to said land, renouncing and transferring it to the buyer, that he may dispose of it as of a thing which belongs to him, the seller binding himself that this sale shall be to the purchaser certain, sure, and effective, and that no lawsuit shall molest or move him.

In testimony whereof, he signed it with me and the two subscribing witnesses.

WALTER COLTON,
   Chief Magistrate, Monterey.
BENITO DIAZ,
J. DE CASTANEDA,
JOSE JOAQUIN GOMEZ.

GUILLERMO R. GARNER,
   Magistrate's Secretary.

In said day, month, and year, likewise appeared before me, and the witnesses already mentioned, Doña Luisa Soto de Diaz, and said, that in her own name, and in that of the children which she at present has, and of those which she may have in future, she consents to the sale of the beforementioned place, and that she spontaneously and voluntarily renounces whatever right she or her said children may have thereto.

WALTER COLTON,
Chief Magistrate, Monterey.
LUISA SOTO,
J. DE CASTANEDA,
JOSE JOAQUIN GOMEZ.

Guillermo R. Garner,
Magistrate's Secretary.

This instrument of writing was sealed, signed, and delivered in this office, and in my presence, this nineteenth day of September, one thousand eight hundred and forty six.

WALTER COLTON,
Alcalde of Monterey.
William R. Garner, *Secretary.* [L. S.]

No. 4.

Territory of California, District of San Francisco,
Chief Magistrate's Office, Yerba Buena, October 6, 1846.

This is to certify, that Thomas O. Larkin, esq., for himself, and as the representative of Don Benito Diaz, has presented at this office the title to the farm called "Punta de Lobos," on San Francisco bay, as described in said title or grant to the said Don Benito Diaz, and transfer from said Diaz to the said Thomas O. Larkin, esq. He, the said Thomas O. Larkin, claims ownership of said farm, and asks possession thereof, with permission to survey and occupy the land (as described in the title) at the earliest practicable moment. This is, therefore, to order that, in accordance with the aforesaid titles, the aforesaid Thomas O. Larkin can enter upon said premises, and be held to be and considered in legal possession thereof, according to the terms and conditions of the original grant, the boundaries whereof to be fixed as soon as a competent surveyor can be obtained to survey the same.

WASHINGTON A. BARTLETT,
Chief Magistrate.

Note.—The following endorsement was placed on the foregoing documents, marked Nos. 1, 2, 3, and 4:

" The United States troops are in possession of the presidio and old fort at the entrance of the bay of San Francisco, which are claimed by Mr. Thomas O. Larkin as his property.

" Without making any decision for or against the soundness of Mr. Larkin's title, as exhibited by this paper, the possession held by the United

States will not operate to the prejudice of any just claim to said property held by Mr. Larkin.

"MONTEREY, September 3, 1847.

"R. B. MASON,
"Colonel 1st Dragoons, Governor of California."

APPENDIX No. 30.

ASSISTANT QUARTERMASTER'S OFFICE,
San Francisco, California, June 6, 1847.

SIR: In compliance with your instructions, the following report is submitted in relation to Mr. T. O. Larkin's land, in the vicinity of San Francisco. I am forced to believe that Mr. Larkin's title is not good, for the following reasons:

1st. The old fort, at the narrows, was built and has had guns mounted upon it for the last seventy or eighty years, it being the only work commanding the entrance to this bay.

The presidio or barracks hard by were built thirty five years since, by the Mexican soldiery, and have been occupied by a Mexican garrison for upwards of thirty years, they being the only quarters for troops on this side of the bay. It is but four or five years since the military commandant resided there; and, even at this moment, one or more old Mexican soldiers continue to reside there. Both these works are on the land claimed by Mr. Larkin.

2d. I am assured by General Vallejo and Colonel Prudhomme, (the latter a Mexican lawyer,) that it is contrary to the *organic laws of Mexico* to sell or convey away any lands which might be wanted for " forts, barracks, field-works, and public purposes for defence ;" and also that grants of land for farms, according to the Mexican colonization laws, are not to be made to come nearer than ten leagues of the seacoast. Mr. Larkin's land is all within one league of the coast; consequently, under both these laws, his claim is illegal.

Again, no land title is good in California until it has been approved by the departmental assembly, and Mr. Larkin's has no such approval.

It is also required that the alcalde of the town or district shall certify that each *particular grant can be made without any prejudice to the public interests,* or to private claims, *before the grant can be made.*

No such certificate was or could have been made with reference to the grant in question.

3d. Repeated instructions, I am assured on the best authority, have been given from Mexico not to sell or grant any of the lands in or about this bay which might be required for public purposes. Several attempts have been made by Senor Pina and Madam Briones, of this town, in the years 1843, 1844, and 1845, to obtain a grant of this same land, but they were all without success. When Angel island was granted to Senor Osio, such portions as might be required for public purposes were expressly reserved in the grant.

4th. Mr. Larkin's claim has signs of irregularity about it which militate strongly against its validity:

1st. It is dated at the Pueblo de los Angeles, June 25, 1846, and is signed by Pio Pico, as governor. Governor Pico left the pueblo on the 17th or 18th of June, and did not return until the 15th or 20th of July. On the 25th of June, Governor Pico was at Santa Barbara or further north.

2d. It is upon unstamped, and therefore *illegal*, paper. If the governor's signature has the effect of making it legal, I am still informed that it is a strong indication of informality, if not fraud.

3d. There is but little more than half the land within its boundaries which his claim entitles him to.

4th. His claim comes within one mile of the custom-house or public buildings of the town of San Francisco; and this, I am told, is irregular and hitherto unknown, if not positively illegal.

Had my time permitted, this report would have been made at an earlier date, and would have been more complete.

I am, sir, respectfully, your most obedient servant,
J. L. FOLSOM,
Captain, and Assistant Quartermaster.

Major Thos. Swords,
Quartermaster U. S. Army,
Sutter's Fort, Sacramento, California.

APPENDIX No. 31.

Headquarters S. M. District, California,
Ciudad de los Angeles, September 7, 1847.

Sir: The enclosed is all the information I can give in answer to the inquiries contained in your letter of the 23d August last, except that it is perfectly well understood, and can be proved, I am informed, that Governor Pico left here not later than the 17th of June, and did not return for at least four weeks; and that the deeds alluded to in the within were all signed the night before Pico left the pueblo, and when the United States were in possession of California, and Commodore Stockton's forces between here and San Pedro, and were all antedated, which, of course, renders them void; besides, the proper forms were never complied with, and no departmental assembly has ever sat since to confirm the grants.

I have the honor to be, very respectfully, your obedient servant,
J. D. STEVENSON,
Colonel commanding S. M. District.

H. W. Halleck,
Lieut. of Engineers, and Secretary of State
for the Territory of California.

[Memorandum accompanying the foregoing letter.]

Query 1. Cannot answer, but from the best oral information think there is no such prohibition.

Query 2. An exceptional decree said to exist respecting California; date probably 1830, more or less.

Queries 3 and 4. Vide "La ley de Colonizacion," 18th August, 1824, volume iii. orders and decrees of the Mexican Congress, edition 1829, and the "Reglamento" of 1828, defining the manner of granting vacant lands; both of which must exist in the archives of Monterey.

Translation of portion of a deed for land granted according to said law and regulations, date 1840: "Conceding to him said land, declaring it his property by these presents, he subjecting himself to the following conditions, and to the approbation or disapprobation of the honorable junta departmental:

"ARTICLE 1. He can enclose it, without prejudice to the crossing roads and obligations, (servidumbres;) shall enjoy it freely and exclusively, putting it to the use or cultivation most suitable thereto; but within one year he shall build a house, and it shall be inhabited.

"ART. 2. He shall solicit the proper justice to give him judicial possession, in virtue of this decree, which justice shall define the limits, in which limits, besides the landmarks, he shall set out some fruit or useful forest trees.

"ART. 3. The land referred to (asked for) being of —— extent, more or less, according to the plan accompanying said petition, the justice who may give possession shall cause it to be measured according to regulations, the overplus (if any) remaining to the nation, for such uses as may seem fit.

"ART. 4. In case he should violate any of the foregoing conditions, he shall lose his right to said land, and it may be denounced by any other."

Query 5. No such special instructions known of. If any, they can be found in the archives. General Vallejo, or ex-Governor Alvarado, most likely may be able to throw some light on the subject.

Query 6. From the testimony of divers residents in this pueblo, ex-Governor Pio Pico left here June 18, 1846, and did not return till on or about July 21, 1846. References, Manuel Requena, A. Stearns, A. Bell, and Ygnacio Valle.

It is a matter of common notoriety here, that grants of land were made by Pio Pico to the following individuals: Pliny F. Temple, W. Workman, Antonio Cota, R. Den, Bery Wilson, H. Reid, and others, the deeds being made out and signed on or about August 9, 1846. Reference, A. Bell.

Two large boxes, said to contain the archives of the departmental assembly during its sessions in this place, were delivered by Don Luis Vigues, of this place, to the order of Commodore Stockton, in August last, supposed to have been put on board the Congress.

APPENDIX No. 32.

SENOR SUPERIOR POLITICAL CHIEF: Antonio Maria Osio, with the greatest respect, before you says, that since the year 1830 I have petitioned to have the island of Los Angeles, in San Francisco, granted to me for the purpose of putting a house thereon and breeding horses or mules. I now again do the same, hoping that you will be pleased to grant it to me—requesting at the same time that you will please to admit this petition on common paper, for want of the corresponding sealed paper. I swear, &c.

ANTONIO MARIA OSIO.

MONTEREY, *October* 7, 1837.

MONTEREY, *February* 18, 1838.
Let the military commandant of the frontier to the north of San Francisco report.

ALVARADO.

SENOR SUPERIOR POLITICAL CHIEF: The island of Los Angeles, mentioned in the present petition, may be granted to Don Antonio Maria Osio, as I know that he asked for it in the year 1830; but it will be well to make the provision, that when government wish to establish a fortress on the top or principal height thereof, no impediment shall be put in the way.

MARIANO G. VALLEJO.

MONTEREY, *February* 18, 1838.

{ Gov't seal of office. } In view of the preceding petition, the report of the military commandant of the frontier of the north of San Francisco, and all the rest which was borne in mind, to facilitate by all possible means the furtherance of the mercantile interests of our ports, as is recommended by the existing laws, I have by this decree granted to Don Antonio Maria Osio the occupation of the lands comprehended in the island called Los Angeles, situated within the port of San Francisco, that he may put it to the use which best suits him, establish a house, put on cattle, and do everything respecting the furtherance of his mercantile and agricultural interests, on condition that the government shall be allowed to establish a military fortification there whenever it may see fit.

The party interested shall present himself, with this decree, to the respective military commandancy, where it shall be recorded, for the necessary purposes.

Given in Monterey, department of California, the 19th of February, 1838.

JUAN B. ALVARADO.

APPENDIX No. 33.

Juan Bautista Alvarado, governor *ad interim* of the department of the Californias:

Being mindful of the merits of Don Antonio Maria Osio, and having in view the order addressed to this government by the supreme government of the nation, under date of the 20th of July last, authorizing the granting of the islands adjacent to the coast of this soil to natives, I have, in virtue thereof, granted to him the one which is within the port of San Francisco, known by the name of Los Angeles, with the boundaries which it naturally has, the limits of which are therefore not pointed out, as being sufficiently known.

I consequently command that these presents serve the said Senor Osio for a title; and, holding it to be firm and valid, it be recorded in the corresponding book, and be delivered to the party interested, for his protection and further ends.

Given in Monterey, on the 11th June, 1839.

JUAN B. ALVARADO.
MAN'L ZIMENO,
Gov't Secretary.

This title has been recorded in the book of records of titles upon the adjudication of lands, on the 2d page of folio 8.

ZIMENO.

SANTA FE, NEW MEXICO,
November 10, 1846.

SIR: Having been appointed by Brigadier General Kearny governor of the Territory of New Mexico, and by virtue of that appointment *ex officio* superintendent of Indian affairs for said Territory, it becomes my duty to lay before you the following information in regard to the different tribes of Indians inhabiting and frequenting this Territory:

First. I will mention the Apaches or Jicarillas, a band of about 100 lodges, or 500 souls. The Jicarillas have no permanent residence, but roam through the northern settlements of New Mexico. They are an indolent and cowardly people, living principally by theft committed on the Mexicans, there being but little game in the country through which they range, and their fear of other Indians not permitting them to venture on the plains for buffalo. Their only attempt at manufacture is a species of potter's ware, capable of tolerable resistance to fire, and much used by them and the Mexicans for culinary purposes. This they barter with the Mexicans for the necessaries of life, but in such small quantities as scarcely to deserve the name of traffic. The predatory habits of these Indians render them a great annoyance to the New Mexicans.

Second. The Apaches proper, who range through the southern portion of this Territory, through the country of the Rio del Norte and its tributaries, and westward about the headwaters of the river Gila, are a warlike people, numbering about 900 lodges and from 5,000 to 6,000 souls; they know nothing of agriculture or manufactures of any description, but live almost entirely by plundering the Mexican settlements. For many years past they have been in the habit of committing constant depredations upon the lives and property of the inhabitants of this and the adjoining provinces, from which they have carried off an incredible amount of stock of all kinds. The only article of food that grows in their general range is the magney plant, and that spontaneously and in very small quantities. Several bands of the Apaches have for some years past received a bounty of so much per head per diem from the government of the State of Chihuahua, with the object of inducing the Indians to cease their depredations, but without having the desired effect.

Third. The Navajoes are an industrious, intelligent, and warlike tribe of Indians, who cultivate the soil, and raise sufficient grain and fruits of various kinds for their own consumption. They are the owners of large flocks and herds of cattle, sheep, horses, mules, and asses. It is estimated that the tribe possesses 30,000 head of horned cattle, 500,000 head of sheep, and 10,000 head of horses, mules, and asses, it not being a rare instance for one individual to possess 5,000 to 10,000 sheep, and 400 to 500 head of other stock. Their horses and sheep are said to be greatly superior to those reared by the New Mexicans. A large portion of their stock has been acquired by marauding expeditions against the settlements of this Territory. They manufacture excellent coarse blankets and coarse woollen goods for wearing apparel. They have no permanent villages or places of residence, but roam over the country between the river San Juan on the north and the waters of the Gila on the south. The country between these two rivers is about 150 miles wide, consisting of high table mountains, difficult of access, and affording them as yet effectual protection against their enemies. Water is scarce and difficult to be found by those not acquainted with the country, affording another natural safeguard against invasion. Their numbers are variously estimated from 1,000 to 2,000 families, or from 7,000 to 14,000 souls. The Navajoes, so far as I am informed, are the only Indians on the continent, having intercourse with white men, that are increasing in numbers. They have in their possession many prisoners, men, women, and children, taken from the settlements of this Territory, whom they hold and treat as slaves.

Fourth. The Moques are neighbors of the Navajoes, and live in permanent villages, cultivate grain and fruits, and raise all the varieties of stock. They were formerly a very numerous people, the possessors of large flocks and herds, but have been reduced in numbers and possessions by their more warlike neighbors and enemies the Navajoes. The Moques are an intelligent and industrious people; their manufactures are the same as those of the Navajoes. They number about 350 families, or about 2,450 souls.

Fifth. The Utahs inhabit the country north of the Navajoes, and west of the northern settlements of this Territory. They number 800 lodges, and about 4,000 to 5,000 souls. Their range extends from the Navajo country, in about latitude 35° to 40° north. Their range of country is very mountainous and broken, abounding in deer, elk, bear, and other wild game, which serve them for food and raiment. They are a hardy, warlike people, subsisting by the chase. Several bands of them have been carrying on a predatory war with the New Mexicans for the last two years, and have killed and taken prisoners many of the people, and driven off large amounts of stock. Since General Kearny's arrival, these Indians have sued for peace, and measures are now taking to effect a permanent treaty.

Sixth. The Cheyennes and Arapahoes range through the country of the Arkansas and its tributaries, to the north of this Territory. They live almost entirely on the buffalo, and carry on a considerable trade, both with the Americans and Mexicans, in buffalo robes, for which they obtain all the necessaries not derived from the buffalo. They are a roving people, and have for many years been on friendly terms with the New Mexicans. The Arapahoes number about 400 lodges, or 2,000 souls; the Cheyennes 300 lodges, or 1,500 souls.

Seventh. The Comanches range east of the mountains of New Mexico—a numerous and warlike people, subsisting entirely by the chase. Their different bands number in all about 2,500 lodges, or 12,000 souls. They have been at peace for many years with the New Mexicans, but have carried on an incessant and destructive war with the States of Chihuahua,

Durango, and Coahuila, from which they have carried off and still hold as slaves a large number of women and children, and immense herds of horses, mules, and asses.

Eighth. The Cayugas range through a part of the same country, and are similar in habits and customs, and are considered a more brave people than the Comanches. They number about 400 lodges, or 2,000 souls.

Below I give a tabular statement of the population of the tribes of Indians ranging the country within the Territory of New Mexico and its borders, made up from the most reliable information that I have been able to obtain during a residence of many years in New Mexico and its vicinity.

Tribe	Lodges	Souls
Apaches or Jicarillas	100 lodges	500 souls.
Apaches proper,	800 or 900 "	5,500 "
Utahs, Grande Unita rivers,	600 "	3,000 "
Utahs, (southern,)	200 "	1,400 "
Navajoes,	1,000 families	7,000 "
Moques	350 "	2,450 "
Comanches,	2,500 lodges	12,000 "
Cayugas,	400 "	2,000 "
Cheyennes,	300 "	1,500 "
Arapahoes,	400 "	1,600 "
Total		36,950 "

You will perceive by the above statement that with New Mexico nearly 40,000 Indians will fall under the immediate superintendence of the United States government; and it becomes a subject of serious import how these numerous and savage tribes are to be controlled and managed.

As it becomes my duty, by virtue of my office, to lay before you all the information I possess in regard to these tribes of Indians, I will also venture to make a few suggestions for your consideration.

Agents and sub-agents are absolutely necessary for the regulation and control of the various tribes of Indians above named.

A very desirable effect might be produced upon these Indians by sending a delegation from each tribe to Washington. They have no idea at this time of the power of the United States, and have been so long in the habit of waging war and committing depredations against the Mexicans with impunity, that they still show a disposition to continue the same kind of warfare, now that the Territory is in possession of the United States. I am convinced that a visit to our capital by some of the principal men of each of these nations would secure future peace and quiet to the inhabitants of this Territory.

I would also suggest the propriety of sending with this delegation of uncivilized Indians a delegation from the "Pueblos," or civilized Indians, who are by law citizens of this Territory and of the United States. They compose a very considerable portion of the population of New Mexico, and, if excited so to do, might cause a good deal of difficulty. A small expenditure by the government in this manner now, might be the means of avoiding bloodshed hereafter.

You are doubtless aware that presents of goods are indispensable in all friendly communications with Indians. I would respectfully suggest the necessity of goods of that kind, or the means wherewith to purchase them, being placed at the disposition of the superintendent of Indian affairs for this Territory.

I deem it highly necessary to establish stockade forts in the Utah and Navajo countries, with sufficient troops to keep these Indians in check, and from continuing their long-accustomed inroads in this Territory. One should also be established at some suitable point on the Arkansas river, for the purpose of protecting travellers between this Territory and Missouri and the settlements that may be extended in that direction from the Indians of that vicinity. Another establishment of the kind will be required in the southern part of this territory, to serve as a safeguard against both the Apaches and Mexicans on the frontiers of the adjoining Mexican States, who, it may be confidently expected, will continue to make inroads on this Territory from that quarter for many years to come.

I neglected to mention, in the proper place, that Colonel A. W. Doniphan received orders from General Kearny, before leaving the territory for California, to march his regiment against the Navajoes. Overtures of peace had been made to them without effect: they have continued their depredations up to this time. General Kearny, after leaving Santa Fe, wrote to me, advising that full permission should be given to the citizens of New Mexico to march in independent companies against these Indians, for the purpose of making reprisals and for the recovery of property and prisoners. In conformity with his suggestions, I issued a proclamation to that effect. Colonel Doniphan left here a few days ago with his command for the Navajo country; and I feel confident that, with the aid of the auxiliary war parties, he will soon compel the nation to sue for peace, and to make restitution of property and prisoners taken since the entrance of the American forces on the 18th August last.

The existing laws of the United States regulating trade and intercourse with the Indians are doubtless amply sufficient as applied to the Indians referred to in this communication; and, at your earliest convenience, I earnestly solicit your full and particular instructions in reference to the application of these laws in the regulation of the various Indian tribes above mentioned. By so doing you will greatly oblige your truly obedient servant,

CHARLES BENT.

To the Hon. Wm. Medill,
   Commissioner of Indian Affairs.

Department of the Interior,
Office of Indian Affairs, April 7, 1849.

Sir: I have the honor to enclose herewith a commission constituting you Indian agent at Santa Fe, to include the Indians at or in the vicinity of that place, and any others that may hereafter be designated by this department.

Your compensation will be at the rate of $1,500 per annum, in full of salary and all emoluments whatever, to commence as soon after the execution of your bond as a notification can reach the person now holding the appointment and receiving the salary, advising him of the change which has been made in the location of the agency, and of the discontinuance of his services and salary.

I enclose, also, the form of a bond to be executed by you, in the penal sum of $5,000, with two or more sureties, whose sufficiency must be certified by a United States district judge or district attorney.

So little is known here of the condition or situation of the Indians in that region, that no specific instructions relative to them can be given at present; and the department relies on you to furnish it with such statistical and other information as will give a just and full understanding of every particular relating to them, embracing the names of the tribes; their location; the distance between the tribes; the probable extent of territory owned or claimed by each respectively, and the tenure by which they hold or claim it; their manners and habits; their disposition and feelings towards the United States, Mexico, and whites generally, and towards each other; whether hostile or otherwise; whether the several tribes speak different languages, and, where different, the apparent analogies between them; and also what laws and regulations for their government are necessary, and how far the law regulating trade and intercourse with the Indian tribes (a copy of which I enclose) will, if extended over that country, properly apply to the Indians there and to the trade and intercourse with them; and what modification, if any, will be required to produce the greatest degree of efficiency.

You are authorized to employ one interpreter permanently, by the year, and such others from time to time as you may find necessary in the discharge of your duties. As the law limits the compensation of interpreters to $300 per annum, that amount cannot be exceeded; but, in case of those employed temporarily, you will engage their services on the best terms you can, and employ them for as short periods and as seldom as possible consistent with a proper discharge of your duties.

You will be allowed a horse for yourself and one for your interpreter, to be held as public property, and accounted for as such.

As you will doubtless avail yourself of the military escort which will leave St. Louis shortly, funds will be placed in the hands of the superintendent of Indian affairs at that place to be turned over to you.

The remote position of the scene of your operations has induced the Secretary of the Interior to authorize an advance of one year's salary to yourself and your interpreter, together with other sums for other objects, as follows, viz:

One year's salary for yourself - - - - -	$1,500
Do do for interpreter - - - - -	300
Pay of additional interpreters - - - - -	200
Contingent expenses, including presents to Indians, purchase of two horses, forage for the same, house rent, fuel, stationery, collection of statistical information, together with your travelling expenses to your agency - - - - -	1,500
For the release of such Mexican captives as may be found among the Indians, and for which a demand may be made on the government of the United States - - - - -	300
	3,800

It has been represented to the department that there is a Mexican boy in captivity among the Indians either in New Mexico or California, and for whose release the Mexican minister has made a demand on this government; but as the department is, as yet, unacquainted with the particulars of the case, it will be made the subject of a special communication to you, as soon they can be ascertained.

After obtaining all the information you can collect with regard to any captives, you will report their names, ages, whether they are Mexicans or Americans, the length of time they have been held in captivity, and, if they are Mexicans, whether they were taken prior to the termination of the war and treaty with Mexico or subsequently.

In dispensing the presents to the Indians, you will be as economical as possible, and confine the disposition of them to cases where some important end is to be accomplished.

You will report directly to this office, and will lose no opportunity of doing so, as it is extremely desirable that the department be kept well advised of the state of affairs in that region.

I enclose blank forms to guide you in rendering your accounts, which must be done quarterly-yearly, or as nearly so as possible.

In rendering your accounts, you will account for the money placed in your hands under the following heads of appropriation, viz:

Pay of superintendents and Indian agents	$1,500
Pay of interpreters	500
Contingencies for Indian department	1,800
	3,800

I enclose a copy of a communication from Charles Bent, esq., governor of New Mexico, in which you will find a good deal of information that will be useful to you.

Very respectfully, your obedient servant,

W. MEDILL.

Jas. S. Calhoun, Esq.,
Indian Agent, Santa Fe.

P. S. I enclose a copy of the late treaty with Mexico, and also copies of the reports of Messrs. Frémont, Emory, Abert, and Cook.

W. M.

Department of the Interior,
Office of Indian Affairs, July 16, 1849.

Sir: I have had the honor to receive your official bond as Indian agent at Santa Fe. On examination, I find it is defective in several particulars, viz: the omission to fill in the names of the sureties in the body of the bond, the date of its execution and of the oath of office, and also the official character of the officer who certifies the sufficiency of the security. These defects must be supplied, and I therefore enclose the form of a new bond, to be executed by you, and forwarded to this office with as little delay as possible. In the mean time, the bond forwarded by you will be retained, and placed on file.

Very respectfully, your obedient servant,

ORLANDO BROWN.

James S. Calhoun, Esq.,
Indian Agent, Santa Fe,
Care D. D. Mitchell, *Superintendent, &c., St. Louis, Mo.*

DEPARTMENT OF THE INTERIOR,
Office of Indian Affairs, November 7, 1849.

SIR: I have the honor to acknowledge the receipt of your letter of the 25th of September, with a copy of the treaty with the Navajoes, made by Colonel Washington, of the army, and yourself, and also of your interesting report, dated the 1st ultimo, in relation to the military expedition which led to that treaty, and on our Indian affairs generally in New Mexico.

Very respectfully, your obedient servant,

ORLANDO BROWN.

JAMES S. CALHOUN, Esq.,
Indian Agent, Santa Fe,
Care D. D. Mitchell, Esq , Superintendent, &c.,
St. Louis, Mo.

DEPARTMENT OF THE INTERIOR,
Office of Indian Affairs, December 28, 1849.

SIR: I have the honor to acknowledge the receipt of your several communications, numbered from 1 to 17 inclusive, in relation to Indian affairs in New Mexico, and the necessity that exists for prompt and effective measures of a military character, to put a stop to the continued outrages perpetrated upon our citizens by the Indians of that Territory. That portion of them relating to this subject will immediately be laid before the Secretary of War, for his information, and for such action as the means at his control will admit; and such as relate to organization in this branch of the service, and to the proper mode of conducting our intercourse and relations with those Indians, will be communicated to Congress, for the consideration of that body, and its early action upon the subject solicited.

The department has received, with much pain, the intelligence of the attack, by a band of Apaches, upon the party of Mr. White, resulting in the murder of himself and others, and the capture and carrying off of his wife and child, whose situation, as captives among this barbarous and merciless people, has excited the most painful solicitude. The department cannot, however, but entertain the hope that, through the prompt measures which you have so commendably adopted, and those doubtless also taken by the military, she and her child have ere this been rescued, and are now in safety. Should this, however, not be the case, you will continue to exert yourself to the utmost to effect it, and the military will be required to do the same, by instructions which will immediately be sent out by the Secretary of War.

The measures you have already taken are approved, as will be any others you may think advisable to adopt, to deliver the captives, or secure their safety—early intelligence of which being accomplished, I need not say, will not only afford the highest gratification, but relieve the department, as well as their friends and relatives, from a most painful state of saspense.

There not yet having been time for appropriations by Congress for the purposes of the department in our distant territories, the only mode of obtaining funds to meet the expenses which you have incurred or may incur in your efforts to relieve Mrs. White, which can now be suggested, will be, to draw drafts upon this office, payable as soon as the appropriations shall have been made. It is presumed that you will find no difficulty in cashing such drafts, as they will, of course, be very desirable as remittances east.

Enclosed is a section of a map of New Mexico, embracing, it is supposed, the portion of territory occupied by the Indians, or the greater part of it, on which I will thank you to designate, as accurately as may be in your power, the locations of the several tribes, and the extent of country severally claimed by them, and return it to this office by the first opportunity. You will also please to indicate the proper locations for agents and sub-agents, informing the department by letters in detail of the number of each class you deem necessary to aid in a proper administration of Indian affairs in New Mexico, the salaries which should be allowed them, the objects for which expenditures will generally be necessary in connexion with the different agencies, and the amount that will be required for each. It is hoped that this, and such other information having a bearing on the subject of a proper organization for the Indian branch of the service, will be received in time to be considered and acted upon before Congress rises, so that there will be no unavoidable delay in adopting such a course of policy and such measures as are necessary to a prompt and effective administration of the affairs of this department in that quarter.

This communication will be handed to you by Mr. Isaac B. Dunn, a brother of Mrs. White, who proceeds to New Mexico as bearer of despatches, under an escort furnished by the War Department, but the object of whose journey is to seek to aid in rescuing his sister and her child, or to afford her protection in her destitute and bereaved situation, if their rescue shall have happily been effected.

Very respectfully, your obedient servant,
ORLANDO BROWN.

J. S. CALHOUN, Esq.,
   Indian Agent, Santa Fè.

CHATTANOOGA, TENNESSEE, *April* 17, 1849.

SIR: I am here on my way to St. Louis, and will speed forward with all practicable despatch. I have with me fourteen persons, all told—four females among them of my family. Six others will join me at St. Louis.

From Independence I shall have with me twenty bold and enterprising adventurers, several of whom served in the war against Mexico, as volunteers under my command. These young gentlemen will do faithful service in Mexico. For them I desire arms, &c., &c. I have asked for rations and transportation for baggage for twenty—not less than fourteen, the number now with me. I would be glad to include the gentlemen referred to above, for I regard them as absolutely necessary to the entire success of my efforts to discharge my duties in New Mexico.

The Commissioner of Indian Affairs, Colonel Medill, required of me a memorandum of the number of my family before I left Washington, to the end, as I understood, to have the necessary orders issued from the proper bureaus. I gave the number twelve; two others have come with me. I mention these matters to say, this morning, at the moment of my departure for this place, I received a letter from General John Wilson, saying it was necessary to address separate papers to each bureau, for arms, &c., rations, and transportation. I have done so in general terms. I have only to inquire whether it would be improper to cause orders to issue in general terms to the proper officers to furnish arms, transportation, and rations upon my requisition to such only as should be present.

I hope to hear from you at St. Louis.

Wishing you entire success in the administration of your department, I have the honor to be your obedient servant,

JAMES S. CALHOUN.

Hon. T. Ewing,
    Secretary of the Interior,
        Washington city, D. C.

---

28 MILES WEST OF FORT LEAVENWORTH,
May 24, 1849.

SIR: I write only to repeat what I addressed to you two or three days ago, that we are still halted at this point, awaiting orders from General Brooke, from whom we have no certain intelligence as to his arrival; and when he does arrive, in consequence of the feebleness of our oxen, our progress must be slow. For obvious reasons, this state of things is to be regretted; for I apprehend it is important that I should be at Santa Fe at the earliest practicable moment.

I am, with great respect, your obedient servant,

J. S. CALHOUN,
Indian Agent, Santa Fe.

To the COMMISSIONER OF INDIAN AFFAIRS.

This note was written to the Secretary of the Interior before I remembered it should be addressed to you.

J. S. C.

IN CAMP NEAR SANTA FE,
July 29, 1849.

SIR: You are already advised of my departure from Fort Leavenworth on the 16th of May, and I have now to inform you that we reached Santa Fe on the 22d of the present month, having been employed in marching forty-nine days—our halting days numbering nineteen, a greater portion of which was six miles west of Kaw river, in obedience to an order issued by General Brooke to Colonel Alexander, commanding the troops. This, you will perceive, is the eighth day in camp at this place, not having been able to procure quarters elsewhere. I have the promise, however, of an adobe building at the enormous rent of $100 per month, to which an additional expenditure must be made to Americanize it, so that it may be inhabited with any degree of comfort. This excessive rent I was compelled to submit to, or remain in camp. All the buildings in Santa Fe are of mud, with floors and coverings for the roof of the same material. Until our government established a saw-mill near this place, sawed lumber could not be had at any price; since then it has been sold as high as $80 per thousand.

The foregoing statement of facts is submitted to the department to explain the apparent tardiness of my movements, and the extravagant, if not unusual and unreasonable expenditures to be incurred, and altogether unavoidable in Santa Fe. Before the meeting of the ensuing Congress I hope to be able to communicate to the department information more precise and in detail on this subject. While en route, and during the few days I have been in camp here, I have omitted no opportunity that has offered to procure such information as might enable me to execute discreetly the important trusts confided to me by the President of the United States. The obstacles to be overcome in adjusting our Indian relations in New Mexico and its borders are of a much more formidable character than has been anticipated. At and near the Arkansas crossing we found several thousand Indians of various tribes assembled, awaiting the return of Mr. Fitzpatrick from Washington. Their expectations in relation to presents to be received by them, on the return of Mr. Fitzpatrick, were so extravagant as to cause emigrants and others to have fearful apprehensions on account of those who were expected to be on the plains after the 15th of July, the day named by the Indians for the return of Mr. Fitzpatrick. Being ignorant of Mr. Fitzpatrick's authority to enter into stipulations with these Indians, and his means to quiet their expectations, I did not feel at liberty to communicate with them in any official capacity. The Arapahoes, Cheyennes, Kioways, Comanches, and Utahs were the principal tribes in lodges at the Arkansas crossing. It will be readily perceived, if it were practicable at this time to visit the tribes in this Territory and in its borders, the influence which a government agent should exercise over beings guided chiefly by animal instincts would be completely ineffective, were I to attempt it, without definite information in relation to what Mr. Fitzpatrick may have accomplished.

Without visiting them, the information, precise and definite, which I am instructed to lay before the department, cannot be accurately gathered. Yet the nearest possible and reliable approximation shall be transmitted at an early day.

The Pueblo Indians, it is believed, are entitled to the early and especial consideration of the government of the United States. They are the only tribe in perfect amity with the government, and are an industrious, agricultural, and pastoral people, living principally in villages, ranging north and west of Taos south, on both sides of the Rio Grande, more than 250 miles. By a Mexican statute, these people, as I am informed by Judge Houghton, of Santa Fe, to whom I am greatly indebted for much valuable information, were constituted citizens of the republic of Mexico, granting to all of mature age, who could read and write, the privilege of voting. But this statute has had no practical operation. Since the occupancy of this Territory by the government of the United States, the territorial legislature of 1847 passed the following act, which is now in force:

"*Be it enacted by the General Assembly of the Territory of New Mexico:*

"Section 1, That the inhabitants within the Territory of New Mexico known by the name of Pueblo Indians, and living in towns or villages built on lands granted to such Indians by the laws of Spain or Mexico, and conceding to such inhabitants certain land and privileges, to be used for the common benefit, are severally hereby created and constituted bodies politic and corporate, and shall be known in law by the name of the 'Pueblo,' &c., (naming it,) and by that name they and their successors shall have perpetual succession, sue and be sued," &c., &c.

These Indians are anxious to have schools established amongst them, and to receive agricultural information, which, if granted on a liberal scale, could not fail to produce marked and beneficial results, not only upon them, but upon all the tribes of the Territory. So soon as it may be attempted with propriety, it is my intention to visit the principal villages of this tribe, that I may from personal observation ascertain their true state and condition, and from them glean such information as they may be able to afford in relation to other tribes. At present, it is the opinion of Colonel Washington, the military commander of this division, that any attempt to conciliate the tribes who have caused the recent and present troubles in this Territory would have a very injurious tendency. The Indians, presuming upon their knowledge of safe retreats in the mountains, and our entire ignorance of all avenues except established military roads and well-known trails, are not to be subjected to just restraints until they are properly chastised. When they shall feel themselves so chastised, they will sue for peace; and it is respectfully suggested that the government of the United States ought to be prepared to meet them without delay. It may not be amiss to invite, for a moment, the attention of the department to perhaps the very gravest subject connected with our Indian affairs in this Territory.

There are wandering tribes, who have never cultivated the soil, and have supported themselves alone by depredations. This is the only labor known to them. The thought of annihilating these Indians cannot be entertained by an American public; nor can the Indians abandon their predatory incursions, and live and learn to support themselves by the sweat of their own brows, unsustained by a liberal philanthropy. This subject, I humbly conceive, should engage the earnest and early consideration of the Congress of the United States; for it is respectfully submitted, that no earthly power can prevent robberies and murders, unless the hungry wants of these people are provided for, both physically and mentally.

I am, with great respect, your obedient servant,
JAMES S. CALHOUN,
Indian Agent.

Colonel MEDILL, *Commissioner, &c.*

SANTA FE, NEW MEXICO,
August 15, 1849.

SIR: I had hoped by the mail of to-day to have transmitted to you some agreeable intelligence. The Utah Indians promised to come in for the purpose of suing for peace. They have disappointed us. On to-morrow we leave for the Navajo territory, intending to return by way of the Utah country.

The Indians, generally, are in bad temper. The number of troops is not sufficient here to keep upon them a proper check; and infantry are useful only to protect posts, stations, and property. Mounted troops are the only military arm of this country that can be effectively used against the Indian tribes of this remote region.

Colonel Washington goes in person in command of the expedition.

With great respect, your obedient servant,
JAMES S. CALHOUN,
Indian Agent, Santa Fe.

Colonel W. MEDILL,
Commissioner, &c., &c.

SANTA FE, NEW MEXICO,
September 25, 1849.

SIR: With this note I transmit to you a *copy* of a treaty, the character of which will be elucidated by a reference to it.

With Governor Washington and others I returned to Santa Fe on the afternoon of the 23d instant.

During the expedition against the Navajoes, my health was all that I could desire; but I am seriously threatened this morning—resulting, as I suppose, from occupying a room where the air is more confined than I have been accustomed to of late. I trust, however, my recuperative energies will come to the rescue in time to enable me to make you a more elaborate report before our mail is ordered to the United States.

I have no communication from the Department of the Interior of a later date than the 14th of May last.

Is it possible that no plan can be adopted to remedy the want of mail facilities of which we now complain?

I am, with great respect, your obedient servant,
JAMES S. CALHOUN,
Indian Agent, Santa Fe.

W. MEDILL, Esq.,
Commissioner of Indian Affairs, Washington city.

P. S. The great cañon, which we have spelt "Cheille" in the treaty, is pronounced "Chey." I am not at all satisfied as to the correct spelling, nor have I yet met with any one who could enlighten me in reference thereto.

J. S. C.

Copy of a Treaty between the United States of America and the Navajo tribe of Indians.

The following acknowledgments, declarations, and stipulations have been duly considered, and are now solemnly adopted and proclaimed by the undersigned, that is to say:

John M. Washington, governor of New Mexico and lieutenant colonel commanding the troops of the United States in Mexico, and James S. Calhoun, Indian agent, residing at Santa Fé, in New Mexico, representing the United States of America; and Mariance Martinez, head chief, and Chapitone, second chief, on the part of the Navajo tribe of Indians.

1. The said Indians do hereby acknowledge that by virtue of a treaty entered into by the United States of America and the United Mexican States, signed on the second day of February, in the year of our Lord eighteen hundred and forty-eight, at the city of Guadalupe Hidalgo, by N. P. Trist, of the first part, and Luis G. Cuevas, Bernardo Couto, and Migl. Atristain, of the second part, the said tribe was lawfully placed under the exclusive jurisdiction and protection of the government of the said United States, and that they are now and will forever remain under the aforesaid jurisdiction and protection.

2. That from and after the signing of this treaty, hostilities between the contracting parties shall cease, and perpetual peace and friendship shall exist; the said tribe hereby solemnly covenanting that they will not associate with, or give countenance or aid to, any tribe or band of Indians, or other persons or powers, who may be at any time at enmity with the people of the United States; that they will remain at peace, and treat honestly and humanely all persons and powers at peace with the said States; and all cases of aggression against said Navajoes by citizens or others of the United States, or by other persons or powers in amity with the said States, shall be referred to the government of said States for adjustment and settlement.

3. The government of the said States having the sole and exclusive right of regulating the trade and intercourse with the said Navajoes, it is agreed that the laws now in force regulating the trade and intercourse, and for the preservation of peace with the various tribes of Indians under the protection and guardianship of the aforesaid government, shall have the same force and efficacy, and shall be as binding and as obligatory upon the said Navajoes, and executed in the same manner, as if said laws had been passed for their sole benefit and protection; and to this end, and for all other useful purposes, the government of New Mexico, as now organized, or as it may be by the government of the United States, or by the legally constituted authorities of the people of New Mexico, is recognised and acknowledged by the said Navajoes. And for the due enforcement of the aforesaid laws, until the government of the United States shall otherwise order, the territory of the Navajoes is hereby annexed to New Mexico.

4. The Navajo Indians hereby bind themselves to deliver to the military authority of the United States in New Mexico, at Santa Fé, New Mexico, as soon as he or they can be apprehended, the murderer or murderers of Micenti Garcia, that said fugitive or fugitives from justice may be dealt with as justice may decree.

5. All American and Mexican captives, and all stolen property taken from Americans or Mexicans, or other persons or powers in amity with the United States, shall be delivered by the Navajo Indians to the aforesaid military authority at Jemez, New Mexico, on or before the ninth day of October next ensuing, that justice may be meted out to all whom it may concern; and, also, all Indian captives and stolen property of such tribe or tribes of Indians as shall enter into a similar reciprocal treaty, shall, in like manner, and for the same purposes, be turned over to an authorized officer or agent of the said States by the aforesaid Navajoes.

6. Should any citizen of the United States, or other person or persons subject to the laws of the United States, murder, rob, or otherwise maltreat any Navajo Indian or Indians, he or they shall be arrested and

tried, and, upon conviction, shall be subjected to all the penalties provided by law for the protection of the persons and property of the people of the said States.

7. The people of the United States of America shall have free and safe passage through the territory of the aforesaid Indians, under such rules and regulations as may be adopted by authority of the said States.

8. In order to preserve tranquillity, and to afford protection to all the people and interests of the contracting parties, the government of the United States of America will establish such military posts and agencies, and authorize such trading houses, at such time, and in such places, as the said government may designate.

9. Relying confidently upon the justice and the liberality of the aforesaid government, and anxious to remove any possible cause that might disturb their peace and quiet, it is agreed by the aforesaid Navajoes that the government of the United States shall, at its earliest convenience, designate, settle, and adjust their territorial boundaries, and pass and execute in their territory such laws as may be deemed conducive to the prosperity and happiness of said Indians.

10. For and in consideration of the faithful performance of all the stipulations herein contained by the said Navajo Indians, the government of the United States will grant to said Indians such donations, presents, and implements, and adopt such other liberal and humane measures, as said government may deem meet and proper.

11. This treaty shall be binding upon the contracting parties from and after the signing of the same, subject only to such modifications and amendments as may be adopted by the government of the United States. And, finally, this treaty is to receive a liberal construction at all times, and in all places, to the end that the said Navajo Indians shall not be held responsible for the conduct of others, and that the government of the United States shall so legislate and act as to secure the permanent prosperity and happiness of said Indians.

In faith whereof, we, the undersigned, have signed this treaty and affixed thereunto our seals, in the valley of Cheille, this the ninth day of September, in the year of our Lord one thousand eight hundred and forty-nine.

J. M. WASHINGTON,
Brvt. Lt. Colonel Commanding, &c.
JAMES S. CALHOUN,
Indian Agent, residing at Santa Fe.

MARIANA ✕ MARTINEZ, *Head Chief.*
his mark.

CHAPITONE, ✕ *Second Chief.*
his mark.

J. S. COLLINS.
JAMES CONKLIN.
LORENZO TOREY.

ANTONIO ✕ SANDOVAL.
his mark.

FRANCISCO ✕ SOETA, *Gov. of Jemez,*
his mark.

Witnesses:
H. L. KENDRICK, *Brevet Major U. S. Army.*
J. N. WARD, *Brevet 1st Lieutenant, Third Infantry.*
JOHN J. PECK, *Brevet Major U. S. Army.*
J. F HAMMOND, *Assistant Surgeon U. S. Army.*
H. S. DODGE, *Captain Commanding Ent. Rgs.*
RICHARD H. HERN.
J. H. NONES, *Second Lieutenant Second Artillery.*
CYRUS CHOICE.
JOHN H. DICKERSON, *Second Lieutenant First Artillery.*
W. E. LOVE.
JOHN G. JONES.
J. H. SIMPSON, *First Lieutenant Corps Top. Engineers.*

SANTA FE, NEW MEXICO,
October 1, 1849.

SIR: You were advised by my note of the 15th of August last, that on the ensuing day we were to leave on an expedition against the Navajoes, with the intention of returning through the Utah country. Governor Washington was so obliging as to extend to me an invitation to accompany him, which was readily accepted. Our rendezvous was Jemez, an Indian pueblo, 57.47 miles from Santa Fe, as indicated by Major Kendrick's viameter, and in a direction nearly due west.

We marched from Jemez on the 22d of August for the *cañon of Cheille*, the capitol *spot* of the Navajo tribe of Indians, and by them supposed, or rather reported to be, entirely impracticable of approach by an American army. Passing over an exceedingly rugged country, checkered occasionally by beautiful, fertile, and extensive valleys, and encamping sometimes where we could not obtain wood, water, or grass, we pitched our tents in a cornfield in the cañon of Cheille, on the evening of the 6th day of September last, apparently to the utter amazement of several hundred Navajoes, who, during the evening, and until a treaty was concluded with them, continued to occupy the surrounding heights, dashing with great speed from point to point, evidently in great perturbation.

It is proper here to mention an incident that occurred on the east side of the mountain range from Cheille.

On the afternoon of the 30th of August we encamped near extensive cornfields belonging to the Navajoes, in the valley of Tunicha, where we were met by several hundreds of their tribe. They asked for permission to confer with the governor, which was conceded to the chiefs. The governor frankly stated to them that his purpose was to chastise them for their bad conduct in committing murders and stealing horses, sheep, and everything else they could put their hands upon. The chiefs replied that lawless men were to be found everywhere; that such secreted themselves during the day, and prowled about at night; that their utmost vigilance had not rendered it possible for the chiefs and good men to apprehend the guilty, or to restrain the wicked; but that they were ready to make every possible restitution by returning an equal number of animals stolen, returning certain captives, and delivering the murderer or murderers of Micento Garcia, to be dealt with as justice might decree. In short, they were ready to submit themselves and their interests to the authorities of the United States, as the best means of securing the prosperity and happiness of all concerned. A skeleton of a treaty, in substance the same as the treaty concluded at Cheille, was immediately submitted and thoroughly discussed and agreed to, and certain chiefs named to accompany us to Cheille, the residence, so far as he has one, of the head chief, and the seat of the supreme power of the Navajo tribe of Indians. As an earnest of their intentions they delivered to us one hundred and thirty sheep, and some four or five mules and horses. This accomplished, orders were given to prepare to resume our march. In the mean time the Indians were all permitted to descend from the heights, and to occupy a level space, commencing within fifty paces of the governor's quarters. The actings and doings of the parties were duly explained to them by a long and noisy harangue from a Navajo. They were further informed that a certain horse, which was pointed out to them, was the property of a Pueblo Indian then present, and that the horse must be delivered to the proper owner at once. The fact of having stolen the horse was not denied; but a statute of limitation was suggested by the reply that the horse had been ridden back to the country from whence the animal was taken, and that that was the time to have claimed him; and ended by the inquiry, why he was not then claimed? This conversation was reported to Governor Washington in the presence of several chiefs, who were distinctly notified by him that he required the immediate delivery of the horse. The chiefs, among them the senior chief on the east side of the beforementioned mountain range, left the governor's tent, as was supposed, to instruct their people what they should do. The governor, having waited a sufficient length of time without the return of a single chief, or any report from them, ordered a small detachment of the guard to proceed to the crowd, with instructions to the officer of the guard to demand the immediate surrender of the horse, and walked out in person to superintend the execution of the order. The demand not producing the desired effect, Lieutenant Pore, the officer of the guard, was directed by the governor to seize the horse and his rider, and to bring them before him. The moment the guard was ordered forward, every Navajo Indian in the crowd, supposed to number from three to four hundred, all mounted and armed, and, their arms in their hands, wheeled, and put spur to their horses; upon which, the governor ordered the guard to fire. The senior chief, Narbone, was left lifeless upon the ground, and several others were found dead in the vicinity. The Indians did not attempt to fire until their own and our forces were scattered, when feeble efforts to kill and cut off small parties were unsuccessfully made. Except the killing of a few horses, and the loss of a few mules, we sustained no injury. The distance from Santa Fe to Tunicha is 198.99 miles.

In pursuance of orders previously given, we marched during the afternoon of that day about six miles in the direction of Cheille, and encamped adjoining cornfields belonging to Narbone, the chief killed at Tunicha. During the same afternoon, and every day thereafter, on our march to Cheille, Indians of the tribe would come within hallooing distance, and renew expressions of their desire for peace, and of their intention to comply with the terms which their chiefs had agreed to. On the evening that we entered the cañon of Cheille we were again spoken to from the heights, when it was announced they were ready to comply with the governor's demands; and as the governor did not order a halt, they said the governor did not want peace, or why persist in going into the cañon? The governor ordered our Indians who were talking to the Navajoes to be silent, and we quietly entered the much-talked-of cañon, 284 miles from Santa Fe—rich in its valleys, rich in its fields of grain, and rich in its vegetables and peach orchards. Water at this season of the year may be had in any desirable quantity by digging a few feet, and wood in abundance—pine, juniper, and cedar—a few miles off. The quantity of water that runs through and under the surface of the cañon is immense; and in many places above Cheille there is a bold and continuous stream of pure water; but as it reaches the debouching point, the earth becomes quite porous, and the water sinks a few feet.

Early on the day after our arrival at Cheille, the head chief of the tribe, having ascertained by what process he could approach the governor, presented himself at headquarters, heard the demands of the governor, and, after a rather long talk, pledged himself to a compliance, and appointed the second day thereafter as the time to consummate the agreement. At the appointed time, the head chief, with the second, appeared, and announced their readiness and their full authority to redeem the pledge of the head chief, at the same time bringing forward 104 sheep, 4 mules and horses, and delivering 4 captives.

Mexican captives delivered.—1st. Anto. Josea, about ten years old: taken from Jemez, where his parents now live, by the Navajo who delivered him. A flock of goats and sheep were stolen at the same time. He says he was well treated.

2d. Teodosia Gonzales, twelve years of age: was taken, about six years ago, from a corral near the Rio Grande, where he supposes his parents now live. He was stolen while herding goats, but no effort was made to take the goats. He was well treated.

3d. Marceta, eighteen years of age: was taken from Socorro, and knows nothing of his parents, nor how long he has been a captive. He has evidently been a captive many years, as he has entirely forgotten his native tongue. The novelty of a home, as explained to him, seemed to excite him somewhat.

4th. Josea Ignacio Anañe: became a prisoner seventeen years ago: taken when quite a boy, by a roving band of Navajoes, at Tuckolotoe. His parents then lived at Santa Fe, where he supposes they now reside. He is the fortunate possessor of two wives and three children, living at Mecina Gorda, (Big Oak,) north of Cheille two and a half days' travel. He was originally sold to an Indian named Waro, to whom he yet belongs. I do not think he is under many restraints, for he prefers most decidedly to remain with the Navajoes, notwithstanding his peonage.

Subsequently, at Zunia, the Navajoes brought to us Manuel Lucina, taken from Del Mansiña, two years since, while herding sheep. The Indians took only such sheep as were needed at the moment. He is about fourteen years of age, and has been sold several times, and badly treated, by flogging, &c. His parents are said to be living near the place where he was stolen from. At the same time, a brother of Manuel's was taken; but he was returned last year.

These captives, except the one so fortunately married, have been placed in the hands of the friends and acquaintances of their parents.

The treaty, a copy of which I have already addressed to you, having been duly executed, on the 10th of September we marched for Zunia, a distance of 106.17 miles, in a southeastern direction, instead of returning by way of the Utah country. Governor Washington, previous to marching from Santa Fe, ordered about three hundred mounted troops into the Utah country, for the purpose of repressing disturbances, checking depredations, and to recover lost and stolen property. Two of the companies were ordered, if p acticable, to effect a junction with the troops under the governor's immediate command before they reached Cheille. It is matter of regret that this could not be done. The governor, having no reliable information as to what had been done against the Utahs, and hearing (what was believed to be true, and which proved to be false) that the Apaches had entered Zunia, killed a number of its inhabitants, and driven off a great many horses, mules, and sheep, changed the route of his return march, as before stated.

The pueblo of Zunia contains, in my opinion, more than five hundred Indians—a hardy, well-fed, and well-clothed race; and, their location being more than two hundred miles from Santa Fe, and one hundred and thirty miles from Albuquerque, on a good road in every respect, now growing into favor as the best route to California, are subjected to serious annoyances from Navajoes north and northwest, and the Apaches south and southeast. But, what is shockingly discreditable to the American name, emigrants commit the grossest wrongs against these excellent Indians, by taking, in the name of the United States, such horses, mules, and sheep, and grain, as they desire, carefully concealing their true names, but assuming official authority and bearing. A wrong of this kind had been perpetrated a few days previous to our arrival there.

About the same time, the Navajoes descended from the mountains, and made an unsuccessful attempt to drive off a number of sheep, &c. A battle ensued, and several Navajoes are said to have been wounded, and one, whose undried flesh was food for carrion crows as we passed his remains, was left dead on the field, within half a mile of the village. The inhabitants of this pueblo gave us a hearty reception, manifesting their gratification in the most uproarious, wild, and indescribable manner, offering to us large quantities of fruit and bread—all of which was becomingly received.

Passing over a distance of 88.30 miles, wild in its mountains and cañons, beautiful and rich in its extensive valleys, highlands, and lowlands, affording superior grazing, the purest and most delightful water, excellent pine timber, and a superabundant supply of the finest rock, (limestone,) and plaster of paris, for building purposes, we encamped in the valley of Laguna on the afternoon of the 19th instant, within view of the pueblo of that name, containing some four hundred inhabitants. The outrages committed against these Indians, by emigrants to California *and others*, are as frequent and as flagrant as those mentioned of Zunia. Indeed, the last outrage was of an infinitely more aggravated character. Near the hour of 12 m., the day not remembered, the valley was entered, and sheep and other things demanded; to which the governor of the village replied, no sheep could be furnished at that hour, as their flocks were regularly, every morning, sent off, that they might graze during the day. The emigrants, if such they were, assuming official importance, in their anger, threatened to lynch the alcalde, tied the governor, and in that condition carried him from his home, Laguna, to Zunia, the next pueblo west.

The distance between Laguna and Albuquerque is 46.84 miles. The road between the two places is good, water scarce and bad, with but little timber, and less grass. No settlements and no cultivation after passing east from Laguna six miles, on the road to Albuquerque.

About ten miles northwest of Laguna, there is a small Spanish village, called ———.

At one of these points, I venture to say, our government should establish a military post; and I understand Governor Washington will station, at an early day, two companies in that neighborhood. The Navajoes and Apaches are exceedingly troublesome in that neighborhood. At or near Sundia, an Indian pueblo, some fifteen miles on the road from Albuquerque to Santa Fe, five Mexicans were killed by a straggling band of Navajoes, and some property taken off, on the 24th of the preceding month, the second day after we passed, on our return to Santa Fe. Numerous bands of thieving Indians, principally Navajoes, Apaches, and Comanches, are straggling in every direction, busily employed in gathering their winter supplies where they have not sown. Not a day passes without hearing of some fresh outrage, and the utmost vigilance of the military force in this country is not sufficient to prevent murders and depredations; and there are but few so bold as to travel alone ten miles from Santa Fe. How are these wrongs to be remedied? I answer, by a compulsory enlightenment, and the imposition of just restraints, both to be enforced at the point of the bayonet. You are already advised, if not before, by my letter of the 29th of July last, that there were wandering bands of Indians who did not cultivate the soil, and lived *alone* by depredations. The language I used on the occasion alluded to should have been so modified as to have excepted the sustenance which they derive from their *sometimes* successful hunting of buffaloes, the bear, deer, and other game. It is now stated, upon a more intimate knowledge of the various tribes of Indians in this region, that a vast majority of the Apaches and Comanches live chiefly by depredations; that they look upon the cultivators of the soil with contempt, as inferior beings, the products of whose labor legitimately belong to power—the strongest arm; and that labor, except in war, and in love, and in the chase, is degradation; and the man who has not stolen a horse or scalped an enemy is not worthy of association with these lords of the woods.

The wild Indians of this country have been so much more successful in their robberies since General Kearny took possession of the country, that they do not believe we have the power to chastise them. Is it not time to enlighten them upon this subject, and to put an end to their ceaseless depredations? At this moment, above our *established* Indian country on the Arkansas, these people are committing every depredation within their power, as far up as Bent's Fort. These, with the Navajoes and Kioways, are known to be in every section of the Territory. Indeed, we are in a state of war; and their disappointment in Mr. Fitzpatrick's promises is their excuse for their conduct. Concerning Mr. F.'s actings and doings, and his promises and authority to act, I am, as yet, wholly ignorant.

The Navajoes commit their wrongs from a pure love of rapine and plunder. They have extensive fields of corn and wheat, fine peach orchards, and grow quantities of melons, squashes, beans, and peas, and have immense flocks of sheep, and a great number of mules and horses of a superior breed. They have nothing of the cow kind. This statement, I know, is antagonistical to official reports made by others; but I report to you from personal knowledge, obtained during Governor Washington's expedition against the Navajoes.

Distance and numbers, by red men, are matters of fact not to be comprehended and understood by Indians of this country as they are elsewhere. Distance is measured by time, at their pace, which is never slow; and as far as their population is concerned, the governor of the smallest pueblo cannot accurately, rarely approximately, give you the number of its inhabitants.

It is a still much more impracticable matter to ascertain the extent of the population of such a tribe as the Navajoes, the whereabouts of their local habitations depending solely upon the seasons of the year and their apprehensions of danger, not one of them having a permanent abiding place. Their only houses are mere lodges, square or circular, brought to a point about fifteen feet from the ground, and sometimes the outer covering is mud—one room only.

The stone walls which are built and inhabited by them are in the shape, or nearly so, of a square, and sometimes have more than one room from eight to twelve feet in height, and not one that I saw was covered in any way.

The number of Indians of this tribe I do not think can exceed five thousand, and they claim from about 35° to 38° north latitude, and 29° to 33° longitude west from Washington. The conflicting claims of the Utahs east and north, to some extent, must indent their supposed borders; and they are barred on the southeast, south, and west, by special Spanish and Mexican grants to their then Christian Indian allies, all of whom live in pueblos, holding lands in common, the boundaries of which, they say, are distinctly defined by original grants now in existence. They complain of many encroachments upon their boundaries, and hope the United States government will restore them their ancient rights. Wicked men—some Americans, but chiefly Mexicans—for their own mischievous purposes, have awakened the apprehensions of the Pueblos by declaring the Americans would take from them their lands, and remove them to an unknown region. The fears of many on this point I think I have quieted by the assurance that the President had no designs of that character; instead of which, if their population required it, he would add to their grants rather than narrow their limits.

But to return to the Navajoes. They derive their title to the country over which they roam from mere possession, not knowing from whence they came or how they were planted upon its soil; and its soil is easy of cultivation, and capable of sustaining nearly as many millions of inhabitants as they have thousands. I respectfully suggest, these people should have their limits circumscribed and distinctly marked out, and their departure from said limits should be under certain prescribed rules, at least for some time to come. Even this arrangement would be utterly ineffective unless enforced by the military arm of the country.

These Indians are hardy and intelligent; and it is as natural for them to war against all men, and to take the property of others, as it is for the sun to give light by day.

In reference to a majority of the Apaches and Comanches, they should be learned and made to cultivate the soil, and should have prescribed limits, under the rules and regulations, and to be enforced as suggested above.

The Pueblos, by many, are regarded as a *tribe*. A more decided error in reference to these Indians could not be suggested. The number of pueblos, each containing inhabitants from 300 to 600, is about twenty, not including the Indians west or south of the Moques. Of these twenty pueblos, the languages of at least ten of them are altogether different; and it is said by some who claim to be judges, there is not the slightest analogy in language existing between any two of them, and they communicate with each other through the instrumentality of Mexican interpreters, or pantomimic action. The same may be said of the Apaches and Comanches, with the qualification which follows. I have seen but a few of either of these last-named tribes, and I cannot say there is as much dissimilarity in their languages as exists with the various Pueblos. As to the number of either of these tribes, I cannot even venture a guess; and in reference to the extent of territory claimed by them, no satisfactory information has yet been acquired, nor can it be until a sufficient number of troops are sent here to afford escorts to those who may be charged with such investigations. It may be remarked, however, that the Comanches range principally between 32° and 36° N. latitude, and longitude west from Washington 22° and 27°. From thence west, two or three hundred miles *across* the Rio Grande, the Apaches are found on both sides of the dividing line between the United States and the United Mexican States; and this circumstance will be fruitful of some trouble, because those on either side of the line will charge upon the others the wrongs they themselves commit. I am not prepared to say the evils alluded to would have no existence if the article 11th of the late treaty were *reciprocal.*

The terms by which they hold the country over which they roam is a mere possessory title, which the God of nature has permitted to them; and one-tenth of the country would be more than sufficient to satisfy all the wants of a much more consuming people. The disposition of the Utahs is rather equivocal. They have committed no wrongs recently against Americans proper. These Indians met Colonel Beall, who had charge of the expedition ordered against them at the same time Governor Washington marched upon the Navajoes, and agreed to all his demands—an impossibility among them, as I have reason to believe—to wit: the restoration of ALL the Frémont property lost during the past winter. That was out of the question, as a portion of it, as I am informed, has long since been consumed. This fact was seized upon by worthless Mexicans to frighten the Indians off; for they made the Indians believe, if every article was not restored, Colonel Beall would cause every one within his reach to be put to death; therefore it was, as I am informed by Colonel Beall, the Utahs did not come up at the appointed time to consummate the treaty agreed upon.

From the facts herein stated, it must be evident to reflecting minds—

1st. That an additional mounted regiment, full and complete, should be in service in New Mexico. I repeat what I have said in a former communication, infantry are useful only in taking care of public stores and isolated places.

2d. Without an additional force, not a single interest of the country can be fully protected.

3d. Military stations ought to be established at Tunicha, and the cañon of Cheille, in the Navajo county; at or near Jemez, Zunia, and Laguna; and perhaps in other places in the direction of El Paso, and within the Pueblo region.

4th. To every pueblo there ought to be sent at once an Indian agent, to protect the Indians, and to preserve the character of the United States.

Such agents should be continued at each pueblo for the next year or two.

5th. Unless this be done, emigrants and others claiming to be officers of the United States will disaffect these people by their lawless conduct.

6th. It is but fair to presume that in a year or two such improvements in public morals will take place as to justify the discontinuance of most of the agencies that ought *now* to be in existence in each pueblo. Just at this moment the Pueblo Indians (in number 54) who accompanied Governor Washington in his expedition against the Navajoes are complaining that they are not paid for their services. In New Mexico a better population than these Pueblo Indians cannot be found, and they must be treated with great delicacy. The slightest disappointment in their expectations, no matter how created, they regard as a deliberate deceit practised upon them. If properly cared for and instructed, in all Indian wars these Pueblos would be very important auxiliaries. Even now, notwithstanding the discontent mentioned above, at least two hundred of them could be readily raised for mounted service; and, if I had the military command of this Territory, I should regard them as necessary adjuncts.

In compliance with one of the stipulations of the treaty entered into by Governor Washington with the Navajoes, they are to deliver at Jemez, on the ninth of next month, certain captives and stolen property. Although they have delivered to us sheep, horses, mules, and captives, as an earnest of their intentions, we do not feel confident that they will comply with the terms of the treaty. They may not be there at the time. And on the occasion alluded to, the governors, captains, and alcaldes of most of the pueblos east and north of Moques, it is supposed, will be at Jemez. It is my intention to be there too, and, if permitted, what shall then and there occur shall be immediately thereafter reported to you.

The mail leaves to-morrow morning, and I have not been able to-day to complete the labor that belongs to my position, nor have I been able to revise with care what I have caused to be recorded in the foregoing pages.

It is sincerely hoped I may yet, and in due time, cure my omissions of to-day. No opportunity for the transmission of intelligence shall pass me by without my advising you of my actings and doings, and my whereabouts.

I am, with great respect, your obedient servant,
JAMES S. CALHOUN,
Indian Agent, Santa Fe, New Mexico.

Colonel MEDILL,
Commissioner of Indian Affairs, Washington city, D. C.

INDIAN AGENCY, SANTA FE, NEW MEXICO,
October 4, 1849.

SIR: Without having recovered from the prostration occasioned, as I suppose, by the occupancy of a room more confined than I have been accustomed to of late, I will attempt to-day to cure some of the omissions which you will have noted in my communication of the first of the present month.

It is with pleasure I bring to your notice several Indians from different pueblos, who accompanied Governor Washington in his late expedition against the Navajoes. They, as a matter of course, know but little if anything about the military discipline of the United States; yet their deportment and bearing were such as to justify high expectations of their effectiveness in expeditions against their implacable enemies, the wild tribes of New Mexico.

Of the fifty-four Pueblos with us, the following-named Indians were the most prominent and influential:

From Jemez.—Francisco Soste, civil governor and alcalde.
San Felipe.—Mariano Chavis, war captain.
Santa Ana.—Salvadore, war captain.

Hosea Beheale, selected captain to command all the Indians engaged in the expedition. This excellent man is without official position in the pueblo to which he belongs, and there are but few who have such a decided influence over these people generally.

Zia.—Francisco, war captain.
Santa Domingo.—Quandiego, civil governor.

These men are all deserving of favorable consideration. When they were about to part with us to return to their homes, occasion was seized to compliment them upon their gallantry and general good conduct, which was received with lively demonstrations of gratification, and an expression of the desire that the President of the United States should be made acquainted with the estimate in which we held them as men and as soldiers.

In this connexion, I may be pardoned, I trust, for commending, in terms of decided praise, *Henry Linn Dodge*, captain commanding a volunteer company, also with us in the late Navajo expedition. He was at all times efficient and prompt, and commanded the admiration of Governor Washington, as well as others. If I mistake not, Captain Dodge has a father and brother now senators in Congress.

It may be useless to add, the officers and soldiers fully sustained the character of the American army.

Zunia is an isolated Indian pueblo, one hundred and six miles from the cañon of Cheille, (or Chey,) and eighty-eight miles west of Laguna. At Zunia we met with its governor, Pedro Piero; the captain of war, Salvadore; and the alcalde, Mariana Vaca; all intelligent men. Indeed, the citizens of this pueblo, it is believed, are, in every sense of the word, *excellent* people, and ought to be immediately protected as well against the lawless conduct of emigrants and others, as against the treacherous Navajoes.

At Laguna the men were out gathering pine moss. Martio Conchi, the alcalde, was at home, and did the honors of the pueblo, and manifested every disposition to oblige us. This village, and another some ten or fifteen miles to its south, (Acoma,) from their locations, will continue to suffer gross wrongs, until they are protected by the laws of the United States and the presence of an agent.

I have been kindly furnished with the following statement by the Hon. Joab Houghton, one of the supreme judges of this Territory. If the number of Indians in each pueblo was accurately ascertained, I am of the opinion, from actual examinations in the villages I have visited, the aggregate would be more than ten thousand. Be that as it may, it is desirable to know their entire strength, and this cannot be done until agencies are duly established.

The pueblos or civilized towns of Indians of the Territory of New Mexico are the following:

In the county of Taos.—Taos, Picoris—283 inhabitants.
In the county of Rio Arriba.—San Juan, Santa Clara—500 inhabitants.
In the county of Santa Fe.—San Ildefonso, Mambé, Pojoaque, Tezuque—590 inhabitants.
In the county of Santa Ana.—Cochiti, Santa Domingo, San Felipe, Santa Ana, Zia, Jemez—1,918 inhabitants.
In the county of Bernalillo.—Sundia, Gleta—883 inhabitants.
In the county of Valencia.—Laguna, Acoma, Zunia—1,800 inhabitants.
Opposite El Paso.—Socorro, Islettas—600.

Recapitulation—"Pueblos of New Mexico."

County of Taos	283	over 5 years of age.
Rio Arriba	500	do.
Santa Fe	590	do.
Santa Ana	1,918	do.
Bernalillo	833	do.
Valencia	1,800	do.
District of Fontero, opposite El Paso del Norte	600	do.
	6,524	

The above enumeration was taken from the census ordered by the legislature of New Mexico, convened December, 1847, which includes only those of five years of age and upwards.

It is well to remember these pueblos are located from ten to near one hundred miles apart, commencing north at Taos and running south to near El Paso, some four hundred miles or more, and running east and west two hundred miles. This statement has no reference to pueblos west of Zunia.

It must be remembered, too, but a few of these Pueblos speak the same language; and, so far as a majority are concerned, they are so decidedly ignorant of each other's language, they are compelled to call to their aid Spanish and Mexican interpreters. I have not found a single individual in the country who can render any one of the languages of the Pueblos or Navajoes into English.

The protection of these Indians in their persons and property is of great importance. In addition to the obligation which the government of the United States has assumed for their protection, it may be suggested, as a matter of government economy, their property should be protected, and their industry properly stimulated and directed. These people can raise immense quantities of corn and wheat, and have large herds of sheep and goats. The grazing for cattle, generally, is superior, and the reason why they have so few of the cow kind is to be found in the ease with which they may be driven off by the Navajoes and others. The average price paid for corn in this Territory by our government cannot be less than two dollars per bushel; and since I have been in Santa Fe, public horses have not received half the forage allowed to them by the regulations of the army. The exorbitant price now paid for corn and the insufficient quantity grown in this country, and other inconveniences, may be remedied in one year—certainly in two years.

For reasons herein suggested, I venture respectfully to say—

1st. The Pueblos, for the present, ought to be divided into six or seven districts, and an agent conveniently located in each.

2d. Blacksmiths, implements of husbandry, and other implements, ought to be sent to them. Also, some fire-arms, powder and lead, and other presents, should be given to them.

3d. None of the Indians of this Territory have a just conception of the American power and strength; and many of them think, as we have associated with us the Mexicans, for whom they have no respect, we may not have a more efficient government for the protection of the people here than they afforded to them. Therefore it is I add to the recommendations above the propriety of allowing, or rather inviting, some fifteen or twenty of these—and perhaps it would be well to select a few other Indians—to visit Washington city at an early day during the session of the approaching Congress. Unless my powers are enlarged, or other duties assigned me, I may, without detriment to the public service, leave here for a short period; and, if agreeable to the department, I should be pleased to receive orders to take a certain number to Washington city, as one among the best means of securing order and quiet in this Territory.

In January or February we might with safety take the southern route by El Paso, and through Texas, passing by and through the country inhabited by the Apaches and Comanches.

We continue to complain that we are without a mail or proper mail facilities.

I am, with great respect, your obedient servant,
JAMES S. CALHOUN,
Indian Agent, Santa Fe, New Mexico.

Col. W. MEDILL,
Commissioner of Indian Affairs, Washington city, D. C.

P. S. Since the foregoing was written, I have been informed an arrangement with a merchant has been effected, by which the Pueblo Indians who accompanied Governor Washington in his late Navajo expedition have been satisfied for their services.

J. S. C.

INDIAN AGENCY, SANTA FE,
October 5, 1849.

SIR: Since my letter of yesterday's date, I regret to say, rumors of Indian troubles have increased, and received some confirmation by the murder of a Mexican within three miles of this place. The surgeon who examined the murdered man on yesterday says he was shot with sixteen arrows in the back and two in front; that he found arrows upon the ground, and that the trail indicated the number of Indians as unusually large. Several Indians from Ildefonso came to me yesterday, also, saying the Navajoes were impudent, troublesome, and dangerous, and that they were in every nook and corner of the country.

A few moments since, the governor and others of Santa Domingo, thirty-one miles west of Santa Fe, came to give me similar intelligence. One of the owners of Bent's Fort has removed all property from it, and caused the fort to be burnt. Mr. St. Vrain, long a citizen here, every way reliable and intelligent, says a worse state of things has not existed in this country since he has been an inhabitant of it. This fact is sustained by Mr. Folger and others—among them Mr. Smith, who will be in Washington at an early day, as the delegate of a convention assembled here on the 24th of last month to consider of the public good.

The number of discontented Indians in this Territory is not small; and I regret to add, they are not the only evil people in it.

This whole country requires a thorough purging, which can be accomplished only by a thorough exploration of every hole and corner in it. The entire country should be immediately examined and surveyed, and military roads should be opened, and posts and depots established.

This policy would render it absolutely necessary to send out one or two additional regiments, (mounted,) as the surest and only plan of economizing in this branch of the public service; and with this branch, should one or more additional regiments be raised, I should be pleased to be associated, as I have written to you and to the Secretary of War heretofore.

Governor Washington left for Taos on yesterday morning, to be absent for a few days only. I am arranging to leave for Jemez on to-morrow, where, it is understood, a number of the chief officials of several pueblos are to be on the 8th of the present month.

Colonel Monroe has not arrived. No report of troops approaching from the States; and we are yet without a mail.

I am your obedient servant,

JAMES S. CALHOUN,
Indian Agent, Santa Fe, New Mexico.

Col. MEDILL, *Commissioner, &c., Washington city.*

[No. 7.]

INDIAN AGENCY, SANTA FE, NEW MEXICO,
October 13, 1849.

SIR: For obvious reasons, my communications to the department should have been numbered. To remedy the omission, as far as practicable, is now my purpose.

Since my arrival at Santa Fe, on the 22d of July last, the following is the order of my letters to the department:

No. 1	July	29, 1849.
" 2	August	15, "
" 3	September	25, "
" 4	October	1, "
" 5	October	4, "
" 6	October	5, "

Will you oblige me so far as to cause the foregoing numbers and dates to be appropriately endorsed on my letters, which you will have received before this my seventh.

I am, with great respect, your obedient servant,

JAMES S. CALHOUN,
Indian Agent, Santa Fe.

Col. W. MEDILL, *Commissioner of Indian Affairs.*

[No. 8.]

INDIAN AGENCY,
Santa Fe, New Mexico, October 13, 1849.

SIR: My intention to visit Jemez was announced to you in my letter of the 5th instant, which should have been numbered 6. I reached Jemez on the afternoon of the 7th instant, and departed therefrom on the morning of the 10th.

In the first place, it is proper to state, during my stay at Jemez not one word of reliable information was received from the Navajo tribe of Indians, who, through their *first* and *second* chiefs, had bound themselves, by the fifth article of a treaty, a copy of which was forwarded to you on the 25th of last month, (No. 3,) to be there in such a way as to comply with certain stipulations contained in said treaty. Whether they failed to be there by design, or were operated upon and kept away by the artful misrepresentations of thieves and robbers, and *their associates*, is not yet revealed. It is a matter of no little import, in my opinion, to ascertain the cause of their absence, and I have put in requisition everything at my command for the purpose of ascertaining the facts in the case. In a very few days, I trust, I shall be able to afford you some light upon this subject.

While at Jemez, I met with the governors, war captains, alcaldes, and other controlling individuals, from twelve pueblos, viz: Jemez, Laguna, Acoma, Santa Domingo, San Juan, Santa Clara, San Ildefonso, Namba, Pojoaque, Zia, Santa Ana, Sundia. No information, of a perfectly satisfactory character, can be obtained as to the number of pueblos, the number of inhabitants in each, and their respective languages. If, as far as it goes, the information in these particulars transmitted to you in my letter of the 4th instant, (No. 5,) and the statements made to me at Jemez by the most intelligent Indians, be correct, there are *twenty-three* pueblos east of Zunia; inclusive of these, I am informed by intelligent Indians, five use a language in common, without having sprung from a common tribe. Two of these are near Taos, two near Albuquerque, and one below El Paso. There are six who have a common language, peculiar to themselves, and altogether unknown to others. To seven others the same remarks are applicable, as their language differs from all others. Jemez has its own peculiar language, and so has Zunia. In relation to the languages of the pueblos of Gleta, Socorro, and Seneca, I have found no one who could give me information upon the subject.

It must be remembered, the Indians using the same language are not confined to the same section of country. For instance, of the five pueblos first spoken of, Taos and Picoris are near Taos, seventy-five miles north of Santa Fe; Sundia and Isletta are from sixty to eighty miles south of Santa Fe; and another Isletta, near El Paso, more than four hundred miles from the two first named. All the others lie between the extremes mentioned, running west about two hundred miles.

The Indians informed me at Jemez there were seven pueblos of Moques, six having a language of their own, and differing from all others, and one the language of the six first before mentioned.

The best information I could obtain in relation to these people induces me to locate them about one hundred miles west of Zunia, in an excellent country, through which a road must run to the Pacific. Indeed, it is said a large number of emigrants selected that route this season. They are supposed to be decidedly pacific in their character, opposed to all wars, quite honest, and very industrious. It is said, in years gone by, these Indians abandoned a village because its soil had been stained with the blood of a human being. I deeply regret that I have not been able to visit these and all other pueblos in this country, that I might be able to lay before you information of a character more precise and accurate.

The Indians at Jemez, with one voice, renewed their complaints of gross wrongs to which they have been compelled to submit; and they are such, too, as require immediate remedial measures. The lawlessness, the outrages of *roving associations*, comprising all colors and dialects, cannot be seen, and felt, and appreciated in Washington as the truth would sanction. And even here, so much of it comes to our knowledge, we become more indifferent to our own possible fate every day.

But a short time since, a band said to be commanded by an Englishman, well known in Santa Fe, ordered, in the name of the United States, he pueblo of Laguna to furnish them with twenty-five horses, and to call upon the quartermaster in Santa Fe for payment. The order was promptly obeyed, and the Indians do not yet understand the contrivance by which they lost their horses.

The frauds and impositions of certain alcaldes, unknown to their laws, ought not to be endured, if their various statements are correct; and these Indians have not given me one reason to question their veracity.

It is a matter of no moment whether an Indian is in debt or not; a judgment can be obtained against him, which must be paid in cash, or the spirit of the 6th article of the ordinance of 1787 is immediately violated.

Again: the prefects, who, to some extent, govern each a district, the alcaldes being subordinate, and their jurisdictions, so far as the Indians are concerned, confined to the pueblos to which they are appointed, do not, in my opinion, use their authority, whatever it may be, without abusing it. Contributions upon their labor and property are frequently made by the law, or laws, which alcaldes and prefects *manufacture* to suit the occasion. Many facts of this character were mentioned to me, that it is useless to record for your reading.

There are clever alcaldes and prefects in this Territory, who are not to be subjected to the above condemnatory suggestions.

To understand the condition of these people, it must not be forgotten they hold possession of the lands which they occupy and till by special grants from the government of Spain or Mexico.

The extent of these grants is not well understood here.

Checkered throughout the whole country of which I have any knowledge, old Spanish villages are yet to be found, inhabited by a prying people almost in utter seclusion. The extent of the grants and privileges to the proprietors of these villages is not yet known; and the spurious claims will be in proper *form* in time to meet the legislation of the Congress of the United States.

Let me add, these Pueblo Indians pride themselves upon their Catholicism, without having abandoned the queer ceremonials of a very remote and superstitious parentage, and they make no prisoners in war.

To the Indians of Jemez I explained the relation in which they stood to the United States, and to the powers controlling in New Mexico. They were made to comprehend the laws enacted by Congress for the government of our Indian relations; and, as they understood the design and effect of said laws, they foreshadowed a better state of things; and they urged, with much emphasis, the application of these remedial measures to their present wants and necessities. To this end four of the pueblos have signified their wish to make a treaty. *What ought to be done?*

In a day or two I may again have occasion to renew this subject, and will, if possible, condense and present in one view all the suggestions I have heretofore made, in compliance with your instructions to me.

I am, with very great respect, your obedient servant,

J. S. CALHOUN,
Indian Agent, Santa Fe, New Mexico.

Colonel W. MEDILL,
Commissioner Indian Affairs, Washington city, D. C.

[No. 9.]

Santa Fe, New Mexico,
October 14, 1849.

Sir: It may not be amiss to advise you that your letter of instruction, with accompanying papers, of May the 14th, 1849, is the last and only communication I have received from the department since my departure from St. Louis to this place. This information may be important to the department, inasmuch as I am aware it was intended to give me special instructions in relation to Mexican captives, so soon as the Mexican minister should be more precise in compliance with the terms of the treaty between the respective governments.

Some time during the latter part of August, while we were out on the Navajo expedition, a mail was received here, and despatched for Governor Washington's headquarters. The carrier and his guide were intercepted, killed, and the mail distributed to suit the fancy of the Indians then present; and it is said they lost eight men before they succeeded in overpowering Mr. Charles Malone, the carrier, and his Mexican guide.

These murders were committed about the 5th of September last, near forty miles east of Tunicha, and one hundred and fifty west of Santa Fe, by Navajo Indians. These facts have been elicited by inquiries instituted by Governor Washington, whose agent returned some eight or ten days since, and encourages the hope that a large portion of the mail may yet be recovered. Let me add, however, by the last mail none came to this place to my address; a large package of newspapers was received, and despatched as before said.

During my absence at Jemez a mail was received here, and by it I received nought but a solitary letter from the States. Colonel Monroe is expected in six or eight days, when it is hoped we may have some intelligence from home.

With great respect, I am your obedient servant,

J. S. CALHOUN,
Indian Agent, Santa Fe, New Mexico.

Colonel W. MEDILL,
Commissioner of Indian Affairs, Washington city, D. C.

[No. 10.]

INDIAN AGENCY,
Santa Fe, New Mexico, October 15, 1849.

SIR: Before I proceed to the consideration of the primary objects of this communication, let me first premise Governor Washington has afforded me every possible facility in the execution of your instructions of the 7th of April last.

Where I have in my former letters (or may in this) referred to ascertained distances, I am indebted to Brevet Major Kendrick, of the artillery a gentleman of distinguished merit.

General Cyrus Choice, William E. Love, and John G. Jones, have accompanied me in all my trips to the Indian country, and were especially useful in the Navajo expedition.

During my absence, Mr. John H. Davis had charge of my office and its affairs, and conducted matters to my entire satisfaction.

Andrew Lee and Benjamin F. Lee, both from South Carolina, have rendered me very efficient aid in various ways in the discharge of my duties. I may make the same remark of William H. Mitchell, whose general health has somewhat interfered with his efficiency.

I may here state I am under increased obligations to Judge Joab Houghton for valuable information, and for pointing out to me avenues through which I might glean more. I may be pardoned, I trust, for saying my efforts have been unceasing, and that I have avoided no exposure, either by night or day, in order to comply with your instructions; and although the compliance is not precise and accurate in every particular, yet I am emboldened to say, with such aids and such assistance as I have named above, there must be a near approximation to a compliance, where a compliance has been possible; and that it is sufficiently so, or will be when this paper is completed, to enable the government at Washington to legislate and order wisely in the premises.

Recent information has confirmed me in opinions heretofore gravely impressed upon my mind; and I now the more readily proceed to lay before you a summary, or rather a condensation of the suggestions contained in my previous letters, and such other suggestions and *facts* as may possibly serve to some extent to guide you in the management of our Indian affairs in this country, under such laws as the Congress of the United States may be pleased to enact in relation thereto.

On yesterday or the preceding afternoon, as I am informed, a part of the lost mail, concerning which I wrote you on yesterday, (No. 9,) was received by Governor Washington.

It appears that Chapitone, the second in rank among the Navajoes, was found by the governor, and others of Zunia, at Pagnati, a small pueblo belonging to and about two leagues from Laguna. This occurred about the 8th of the present month. Chapitone stated that he and his people had gathered all the stolen property, collected together the captives, and had prepared themselves in every way to comply with the terms of the late treaty, and would have done so but for the statements of Mexican *traders*, representing that all the Pueblo Indians, the Spaniards from the villages near the Pueblos, and American troops, were marching to their country for the purpose of exterminating them, and taking possession of all that belonged to them. Under the impressions made by the statements of these traders, they were frightened from their purpose of being at Jemez on the day appointed. It was then he resolved to ascertain from actual observation whether the reports of the *traders* were true or false, and therefore it was he was at Pagnati. He accompanied the Zunias to Jemez, sent out a messenger, who brought in the recovered portion of the lost mail, and sent word to Governor Washington and myself that he and others would be at San Isidora on the 28th or 29th of this month, prepared to comply with the terms of the treaty. These are the facts as gathered by my agents, who were charged to go and inquire into this matter.

Some time about the 5th of this month, at and near the Spanish village Le Bugarito, not more than fifteen miles northwest of Laguna, Navajoes and others unknown attacked the people of said village in the day time, killed two Spaniards and wounded one, and succeeded in carrying off as a captive a woman.

This morning an Indian came in from Cochiti, a pueblo on the west side of the Rio Grande, a few miles north of Santa Domingo, and informed Governor Washington in my presence that he and his friends had killed *three* Apaches the preceding day, overtaken in "the manner" of driving off sheep belonging to their village. He further said there were a number of Apaches in the mountains beyond Cochiti, who gave them much trouble by driving off their stock, killing their men, and making captives of their women and children.

This Indian, in behalf of the people of Cochiti, *asked for munitions of war.*

The governor, the grand captain, and the captain of war, from Zunia, an Indian pueblo, which you will remember is 201.07 miles west of Santa Fe, have been with me to-day. These are intelligent, active, and athletic Indians, and stated their grievances with great energy, and were especially vehement and vindictive in their denunciations of the faithlessness of all Navajoes. They represented they had been greatly harassed since we left their village on the 16th of September last; that wheresoever they went, they were under the necessity of going guarded and armed, and that they had to watch their horses, mules, and sheep during every hour of the twenty-four.

These people asked for arms and ammunition, and permission to make a war of extermination against the Navajoes.

The deputation from Zunia also stated there were five hundred and fifty-five able-bodied men in their village, and only thirty-two fire-arms, and less than twenty rounds each for said arms.* They spoke confidently of their ability to protect and defend themselves against the aggressions of the Navajoes and Apaches; and if permitted to form a combination of Pueblos, they could and would exterminate these tribes, especially every Navajo who should be so unfortunate as to be caught south of the high mountains north of the San Juan, a supposed tributary to the western Colorado, provided the government of the United States would furnish the necessary fire-arms, ammunition, and subsistence. That a combination as suggested above could accomplish the end so desired *by them*, admits not of the slightest doubt, notwithstanding the ties existing between the Navajoes, Utahs, and Apaches, backed as they might be by

---

*Mr. F. Brown, an American, assisted in taking this census, and says there are 597 men, and 42 muskets and rifles, and 555 men without *fire-arms.*

the Comanches, provided that Mexicans from either side of the line between the United States and Mexico, and all others, were effectually prevented from the indiscriminate and vicious commerce now open to them, and against which there seems to be at this time not the slightest impediment.

While at Zunia I saw several Mexican *traders*, who hailed from various places; all, however, on *our* side of the supposed boundary line between the United States and Mexico. They informed me they had travelled hrough the Apache country from the Rio Grande, west, a great distance, on the Gila river, in the direction of the Colorado. They spoke of the Apaches as good people, who had treated them kindly, which fact is not to be doubted; and although it was true that these Indians had a number of Mexican captives, they were nevertheless friendly with and peaceably disposed towards the people of the United States, and guiltless of outrages generally.

So long as these wandering merchants are permitted a free and unrestrained access to the wild and roving Indians of this country, just so long are we to be harassed by them and their allies, the various bands of robbers and other disturbers of the peace to be found east, west, north, and south, and whose agents these merchants may be. It is through the medium of these traders that arms and ammunition are supplied to the Indians who refuse submission to our authority. These traders go where they please, without being subjected to the slightest risk; but one not of the fraternity dare not advance an inch abroad, without risking life and property. Why is it that these traders have no fears, no apprehensions, and pass in every direction through the country roamed over by the Comanches, Apaches, Navajoes, and Utahs, unharmed in person or property, when these same Indians show by their conduct a determined and eternal hostility to all Mexicans and others who remain quietly at home, and whose wives and children, and property of every kind, are unsafe beyond the shadow of their own domicils?

The question cannot be answered in such a way as to justify a further toleration of these travelling merchants, who are daily creating much anxiety among and bewildering many of the Indians of the various pueblos, by attempting the impression that the government of the United States are unable to hold possession of this country; that the Mexican government, at this time, has twenty-five thousand troops marching, or ready to march, into New Mexico, for the purpose of reconquering and repossessing the ceded domain; and that extermination will be the fate of all Indians who are found in alliance with or claiming the protection of the United States; and further, if it were possible (and none but a very wild imagination can think it possible) that the Americans should continue to hold the country, the fate of all Indians is fixed, as nothing will satisfy the American people short of the entire possession of their whole country and their utter extermination. To this may be added, the crafty misrepresentations of *wicked* priests, aided by the robbing and thieving instincts of others, have also continued to give circulation to falsehoods of every hue, for the purpose of alienating these people, and causing them to believe the Americans were more heartless and untruthful than their former oppressors, and more insatiable in their purposes upon their property than the banded robbers of the mountains.

The whole object of these people is, to keep American settlers out of the country as long as possible; for their presence might lessen the power of some, and throw impediments in the way of others, so as to check their present impositions and frauds upon the Indians, and put an earlier end to their designs upon the lands of this country, in covering the most desirable spots with fictitious grants. I do not assert that all these mischievous people are under preconcerted arrangements; but the tendency of their efforts points to a common end.

There is scarcely a day passes, that a deputation from some one or more of the pueblos does not come to me with statements confirmatory of what is herein stated, and the facts noted in my previous communications; and the question comes up, Ought not some effective remedial measures to be adopted at once? Before I conclude this letter I will show, what to me is very plain, the measures that should be adopted for the government of the Indian tribes in this far-off region.

First, then, the Pueblos. You are already apprized of the fact, if we include the Mochies, only, beyond Zunia, these people of various tongues, each unknown to the tribes of their respective origins, are to be found in villages (pueblos) at uncertain distances from each other, in an extent of country near four hundred miles square. Their pueblos are built with direct reference to defence, and their houses are from one to six stories high, and not one is reached in the ordinary way, except by ladders *These and all other Indians of this country* send out mounted warriors only; foot soldiers remain at home, and fight on foot only when their pueblos are assaulted.

The rapidity of the movements of all Indian warriors or robbers shows the utter worthlessness of infantry, except to take care of localities and property.

To remove and consolidate the Indians of the various pueblos at a common pint, is out of the question. The general character of their houses is superior to those of Santa Fe. They have rich valleys to cultivate, grow quantities of corn and wheat, and raise vast herds of horses, mules, sheep, and goats, all of which may be immensely increased by properly stimulating their industry, and instructing them in the agricultural arts. For the reasons, in an economical point of view, heretofore given, the government of the United States should instruct these people in their agricultural pursuits. They are a valuable and available people, and as firmly fixed in their homes as any one can be in the United States. Their lands are held by Spanish and Mexican grants—to what extent is unknown; and in their religion they are Catholics, with a certain admixture of an early superstition, with its ceremonials; all of which attaches them to the soil of their fathers—the soil upon which they came into existence, and the soil upon which they have been reared; and their concentration is not advisable.

But, in considering this subject, it must not be forgotten there are a few old Spanish villages to be found in the vicinity of perhaps all the pueblos; and the extent of their grants and privileges is not yet known; and judicial proceedings only can reveal the truth in relation to these matters. In this way is the Indian country of the pueblos checkered, and the difficulties in relation to a disposition of them suggested.

Santa Anna (as Major Weightman, a gentleman and a very intelligent lawyer, informs me) decreed in 1843 that one born in Mexico was a Mexican citizen, and, as such, was a voter; and therefore all the pueblo Indians are voters. But still the exercise of this privilege was not known prior to what is termed an election, the last one in this Territory. I understand this was a hurried affair, and manageable voters picked up at whatever place found; and this arose from their extreme anxiety to secure the services of an exceedingly clever man, the Hon. Hugh N. Smith, as the delegate of certain influential citizens of this Territory. Under this view of the subject, what will you do with them?

They must become citizens, sooner or later, of the United States; and, if there was a State or Territory to be formed immediately west of the Rio Grande, I should not hesitate to say these Pueblo Indians are entitled to all the rights and privileges of citizens of the United States *as mere voters.* As to the rights which it may have been designed to confer upon them under the 9th article of the late treaty, I venture not an opinion. If Congress must give to this country a territorial government, they must, of necessity, include the Spanish, and, if there be such, Mexican villages too, that are found in the neighborhood of the pueblos. If the Pueblo Indians are to be taxed, *they are, from their general intelligence and probity, as much entitled to select their agents* as the mass of New Mexico. But, for the present, unless a Territory or State is to be organized on the western side of the Rio Grande, these people should be subjected only to the laws passed by the Congress of the United States. *The Mexicans and the Pueblo Indians have not one feeling in common.*

It is a subject of great delicacy; yet I apprehend it is easier to dispose of the tribes of roving Indians than the better and more civilized Pueblo Indians.

In disposing of the "savage" Indians, the most vexatious, troublesome, and delicate questions will arise from our obligations as recorded in the 11th article of the before-referred-to treaty. At all hazards, and without reference to cost, the government of the United States will, to the letter and to the spirit, comply with our every pledge, and redeem our every undertaking.

It is not necessary to repeat to you that, although the Apaches frequently rove east of the Rio Grande, their conceded localities, and the great mass of them, *when at home,* are to be found on the west side of the aforesaid river, and on both sides of the boundary line between the United States and Mexico, as indicated by the maps, running west several hundred miles to or near the Pimo villages. Here are to be found a majority of the *captives* to be delivered up under the before mentioned treaty. Here are a people who feed on game, the spontaneous products of the soil, and the fruit of other people's labor. Here it is the boundary line will present a barrier to the castigations which these Indians should receive. Here you will find about an equal number upon each side of the boundary line, and alike committing depredations; and it may be we shall be called upon to pay millions on account of the doings of the *Mexican Apaches,* whose bad deeds will be charged to those on our side of the line—the one not being better than the other.

Here, too, the most delicate questions will arise. How are these people to subsist, if you *effectually* check and stop their depredations? How are you to comply with your obligations under the aforesaid 11th article, without invading foreign territory?

To establish a proper state of affairs in this country, with the economy which the government of the United States should and will ever observe, requires a strong arm, and a prompt arm, guided by an enlightened patriotism and a generous spirit of humanity.

Expend your *million now*, if necessary, that you may avoid the expenditure of *millions* hereafter.

The Comanches and Apaches, with all the adjacent fragments of other tribes, must be penned up; and this should be done at the earliest possible day.

If the Navajoes comply with the treaty as entered into with Governor Washington and myself, it is believed the Utahs will ask for a similar treaty. There are strong indications of a disposition to yield upon their part, independently of the course which the Navajoes may pursue. But suppose these tribes continue to withhold their submission to our authority, and to war upon our interest: it will be absolutely necessary to remove and concentrate these people.

To what localities should these wild tribes be confined?

Can the foregoing question be discreetly answered without a thorough knowledge of this country? And can such thorough knowledge be obtained without a thorough exploration? I affirm that it cannot be done; and without an additional number of mounted troops, such an exploration cannot be made at an early day.

If I had authority to do so, I could make treaties with all these tribes; and they would comply with every stipulation, just so long as you have an arm raised to strike them, and no longer—provided they are permitted to roam as heretofore. But confine them to certain limits, restrict intercourse with them, and instruct them, and compel them to cultivate the soil: when you have thus subjugated them, and caused them to feel and appreciate your power, then the proper time will have arrived when presents, to a limited extent, will have a salutary influence, in awakening their pride of person, and creating a love or desire for some of the luxuries of life; for, until a man has reached that point, he has made but a slight advance in civilization.

Let it be remembered, the Navajoes have all the *necessaries* of life, and grow large quantities of corn and wheat, raise immense flocks of sheep and goats, and a great number of fine horses and mules; and rob and murder, and seize captives, because it is a business of life in which they delight.

In reference to the number of Pueblo Indians east of the Mochies, which includes the Pueblos named in No. 5, I have come to the conclusion it cannot be put down at less than twelve thousand, and it would not surprise me if it should reach fifteen thousand. We ventured to guess, while at Zunia, at the number of its people; and no one supposed it to exceed six hundred, all told. It now appears they have five hundred and fifty-five warriors, which does not include boys under sixteen years of age, or old men. If this be true—and I do not question the fact—the aggregate number of inhabitants in Zunia will reach two thousand; and I have no reason to believe the estimates as to other pueblos are more correct than was the estimate for Zunia.

I do not feel at liberty, at present, to disturb the estimates as forwarded to your office by the late Governor Bent. I will remark, however, it is advisable to reduce the number of tribes, in any general classification which may be made by authority of the government of the United States; for there are a number of fragments of tribes, being the product of amalgamations, who are not entitled to the consideration of distinct tribes, and they should be compelled to an association with one or the other of the amalgamating parties, and located and considered accordingly. Without alluding to the Indians of the Arkansas, I would reduce all the roving tribes of New Mexico to four—the Comanches, Apaches, Navajoes, and Utahs.

It would ill become me to venture an opinion as to the proper disposition of the United States military force now in this country: that duty is confided to an abler head. But, as preventive measures, and as measures, too, of a defensive character, allow me to submit, with all due respect, the following suggestions and recommendations:

I repeat the suggestions to be found in my previous letters:

The presence of agents in various places in the Indian country is indispensably necessary. Their presence is demanded by every principle of humanity, by every generous obligation of kindness, of protection, and of good government, throughout this vast Territory. These agents should be intrusted with ordnance and ordnance stores, to be used as emergencies might require, under the direction of a general superintendent; and should be selected, not only with regard to their prudence and discretion, but with a view to the proper training of the Pueblo Indians in the efficient use of our arms.

I design preparing, to accompany this communication, a diagram exhibiting my views of the Indian localities, and pointing out the most appropriate places for the residence of agents; and from which you will perceive how easily the depredations of Utahs, Navajoes, and a portion of the Apaches, may be checked, by a proper use of the arms which I have recommended to be placed in charge of Indian agents.

By keeping up a proper line of communication between the pueblos and other places in this Territory, it will be no difficult matter to intercept roving bands of robbers, no matter what their color may be, so soon as it is ascertained from what quarter they proceed; and that may be done unerringly by an examination of their trail.

That I may be distinctly understood upon this point, look at the locations of Laguna, Zunia, Jemez, and other places. Now, the ordnance and ordnance stores, under the control as before suggested, would enable these people effectually to protect themselves against their implacable enemies; and, at the same time, a vigorous and rapid movement along the line of communication between the pueblos and other points would give them the additional and important power of intercepting those who should dare to penetrate towards the heart of New Mexico.

The rough diagram which will be hereto appended will show why it is, with the views herein expressed, I recommend—

1st. The establishing of a full agency at Taos, or near that place, for the *Utahs* and Pueblos of that neighborhood;

2d. Also, a full agency at and for Zunia and the Navajoes;

3d. A full agency at Socorro, a military post south of Albuquerque, now being established—the agent of this place to look after the Apaches and Comanches, and the pueblo of Isletta, north.

Sub-agents should be sent to San Ildefonso, or near there; to Jemez, Laguna, and the military post near El Paso.

These agents and sub-agents are absolutely necessary to an economical administration of our Indian affairs in this Territory. It is my honest opinion, that for the ensuing year, at least, a sub-agent should be in every pueblo, the whole to be under the direction of a general superintendent, who would be compelled to have one or more clerks.

I am aware that, possibly, I may be twitted concerning my notions of economy in these recommendations, but it will be by no one who has maturely considered the subject in all its various bearings. Adopt my suggestions in all their breadth, especially those in reference to the appointing of agents and depositing with them ordnance and ordnance stores, and properly stimulating and directing the industry of the Pueblos, and it will give quiet and tranquillity to this entire Territory, and materially reduce the now necessary expenditures of the government here. The labor of the country will be protected, the quantity of subsistence stores will be annually increased and the prices greatly diminished, and *millions* will be saved to the government that must be expended as at present conducted; and this I say after due deliberation, and without intending the slightest disrespect to any human being.

The powers here have neither the authority nor the means to reduce to order the chaotic mass in this Territory, and the government at Washington has not thoroughly comprehended the diversity and the magnitude of the difficulties to be overcome.

In conclusion, I still think it important to allow a few of the Pueblo Indians to visit Washington city—some of them are extremely anxious to do so.

Commending this communication to your indulgent criticisms, and referring you to the appendix,

I have the honor to be, your very obedient servant,
JAMES S. CALHOUN,
Indian Agent, Santa Fe, New Mexico.

Colonel W. MEDILL,
Commissioner of Indian Affairs, Washington city.

[No. 11.]

SANTA FE, NEW MEXICO,
October 16, 1849.

SIR: I forward to you, for the information of whom it may concern, the printed "Journal of the Convention of the Territory of New Mexico." It is stated that the election for delegates to the convention was held "in conformity with the proclamation of Lieutenant Colonel Beall, civil and military commandant," &c., &c. I have not been able to procure a copy of the proclamation; therefore, one is not enclosed to you.

Before the honorable Hugh N. Smith left for Washington, he informed me that Governor Washington had refused to approve, or rather to recognise officially, the actings and doings of the convention.

All of which I submit to you without an additional remark.

I am, with great respect, your obedient servant,
J. S. CALHOUN.

Hon. T. EWING,
Secretary of the Interior, Washington city, D. C.

[The department is unable to furnish a copy of the journal above alluded to—there being but one copy received, and that having been sent to the House of Representatives.]

[No. 12.]

SANTA FE, NEW MEXICO,
October 18, 1849.

SIR: It may be important to the government of the United States, undoubtedly important to many of the inhabitants of said States, that the accompanying "table of marches, &c.,' should be made public.

For the "table," &c., as will be seen by a reference to it, I am indebted to that liberal and enlightened officer, H. L. Kendrick, Brevet Major U. S. A., who on every occasion, so far as I have seen, or believe, has manifested every becoming disposition to furnish all the information which he could command, for the general good; and I know of no gentleman who could surpass him in successfully advancing the general good.

With great respect, your obedient servant,
J. S. CALHOUN.

Hon. T. EWING,
Secretary of the Interior, Washington city, D. C.

Table of marches made in the summer of 1849, from Fort Leavenworth to Santa Fe, by a command composed of companies D and B, 2d artillery, and a portion of the 3d infantry.

[DISTANCES MEASURED BY THE VIAMETER.]

Date.	Encampments.	Distances. Per day.	Total from Fort Leavenworth.
		Miles.	*Miles*
May 16	Left Fort Leavenworth.........	....	00.00
19	At Black Hoof (a.)............	....	30.00
31	Lone Elm.....................	14.00	44.00
June 1	Bull creek....................	10.91	54.91
2	Black Jack Point..............	9.28	64.19
3	Sunday, Miller's Spring........	12.33	76.52
4	Pelican creek.................	14.70	91.22
5	One-hundred-and-ten-mile creek.	11.20	102.42
6	Waldo creek, Big creek, &c., (b.)	12.12	114.54
7	One-hundred-and-forty-mile creek	15.27	129.81
8	Rock creek...................	13.15	142.96
9	One mile beyond Council Grove (c.)	9.08	152.04
11	Diamond spring...............	16.50	168.54
12	Lost spring...................	15.75	184.29
13	Cotton wood spring...........	16.95	201.24
14	Little Turkey creek............	18.98	220.22
15	Little Arkansas...............	26.00	246.22
16	Owl creek....................	11.20	257.42
17	Sunday, Big Cow creek.........	10.50	267.92
18	Arkansas river (d.)............	18.00	285.92
19	Ash creek....................	28.15	314.07
20	Pawnee fork..................	7.10	321.17
21	On the Arkansas (e.)..........	16.57	337.74
22	....do....do..................	16.91	354.65
23	....do....do..................	18.65	373.30
24	Sunday...do (f.)..............	22.30	395.60
25	Crossing of Arkansas..........	22.99	418.59
26	Crossing Arkansas to camp (g.).	1.50	420.09
28	At a water hole...............	15.68	435.77
29	Found two water holes.........	30.02	465.79
30	Lower Cimarron springs (h)....	14.14	479.93
July 2	Some pools of water...........	20.00	499.93
3	Middle springs of Cimarron.....	19.02	518.95
4	Little crossings of Cimarron....	12.93	531.88
5	Near upper Cimarron springs...	14.10	545.98
6	Cold spring...................	19.05	565.03
7	Cedar creek..................	16.13	581.16
8	Sunday, Cotton-wood creek.....	21.99	603.15
9	Near Round Mound...........	13.86	617.01
10	Left bank Rabbit-ear creek.....	1.31	618.32
11	Whetstone creek..............	26.40	644.72
12	Points of rocks...............	14.13	658.85
13	Succession of water holes in prairies.	16.62	675.47
14	Ocate creek...................	10.05	685.52
15	Sunday, Wagon Mound........	19.69	705.21
16	Creek, 3 miles from the Mora...	21.62	726.83
17	Las Vegas....................	21.78	748.61
18	Tacalote......................	13.05	761.66
19	4 miles beyond San Miguel.....	18.00	779.66
20	Ruins of Pecos................	17.81	797.47
21	Stone Corral..................	13.41	810.88
22	One mile from Santa Fe........	9.80	820.68
	Santa Fe.....................	1.00	821.68

(*a*.) Camp Kanzas. (*b*.) "Dragoon creek," "Independence," &c. (*c*.) June 10, Sunday. (*d*.) Two miles above Osage camping ground. (*e*.) Guide called this "Love's defeat." (*f*.) Near Fort Mann. (*g*.) Remained in camp on the 27th. (*h*.) Remained in camp July 1, Sunday.

H. L. KENDRICK, *Brevet Major U. S. A.*

[No. 13.]

INDIAN AGENCY,
Santa Fe, New Mexico, October 25, 1849.

SIR: My communication, No. 5, of the 4th of this month, stated in a postscript that " the Pueblo Indians who accompanied Governor Washington in his late Navajo expedition" had been satisfied for *their* services by an arrangement with a merchant.

When the foregoing statement was made to you, I supposed it was an arrangement effected by the government chief in this Territory. To-day I have learned otherwise; and further, that all had not become parties to the mercantile arrangement into which some of their associates had voluntarily entered. But it is said, all of said Indians will after a while come into terms.

The *complainings* of these Indians are exceedingly unpleasant to me; but they are not unjust, and such wrongs should be remedied.

I am, with great respect, your obedient servant,
J. S. CALHOUN,
Indian Agent.

Col. MEDILL, *Washington city, D. C.*

[No. 14.]

INDIAN AGENCY,
Santa Fe, New Mexico, October 27, 1849.

SIR: Colonel Monroe, our new governor, came into this city a few days ago, and assumed the command of this military department. By him I had hoped to receive some additional light—such additional instructions as my earlier communications might have suggested as necessary.

I am yet without the slightest intelligence from the States; and I must repeat, the mail facilities are not such as we are entitled to, and that it is infinitely of more importance to the government at Washington than to us. The controlling powers should be advised more promptly in reference to the various sinuosities daily perpetrated in this far-off region.

The truth in relation to governmental affairs here is not understood at Washington; and until we are brought more immediately under the proper supervisory eye, nothing of a highly reputable character may be expected to transpire in this Territory; and how can a proper supervision be had without certain means of receiving early intelligence, and promptly transmitting orders?

I am, very respectfully, your obedient servant,
J. S. CALHOUN, *Indian Agent.*

Colonel MEDILL,
Commissioner Indian Affairs, Washington city, D. C.

[No. 15.]

INDIAN AGENCY,
Santa Fe, New Mexico, October 28, 1849.

SIR: The quartermaster having arranged to despatch a mail for the States on to-morrow, my agent at Jemez was directed to advise me as to the compliance of the Navajoes with their promise to be at San Isidora on the 27th, (yesterday,) in time to give you by the mail whatever might have transpired.

This evening. at about 8 o'clock, the courier came in with the intelligence that, up to the moment of his leaving San Isidora, this morning, not one word had been heard from the Navajoes. He brought to me a note from my agent, confirmatory of his statement.

The reports of robberies and murders continue to come in upon us.

I am, with great respect, your obedient servant,
J. S. CALHOUN, *Indian Agent.*
Colonel W. MEDILL,
Commissioner Indian Affairs, Washington city, D. C.

[No. 16.]

INDIAN AGENCY, SANTA FE, NEW MEXICO,
October 29, 1849.

SIR: The arrival of an express during the past night brought to us such intelligence as to cause the issuing of an order by Colonel Monroe postponing the departure of the mail for the United States.

Four or five days ago, Mr. Spencer, an American merchant of this city, on his return from a recent visit to the United States, accompanied by a gentleman whose name I do not remember at this moment, in passing a well-known camping ground, "Points of Rocks," saw the dead bodies of Mr. White and five or six others of his party, recently from St. Louis. They also noticed a baggage wagon upset and broken into pieces; and, what is yet more horrible, some Pueblo Indians were met the ensuing day, who stated they were just from the camp of the Apaches. and there saw an American female, with her little daughter, supposed to have been the wife and daughter of Mr. White. It is known that they were of the party; and no trace of a f-male was discovered by Mr. Spencer or his companion at the Points of Rocks. But it is not to be presumed that these gentlemen remained long enough upon the ground to have ascertained accurately all the facts the horrible scene might have disclosed. What they saw was by the light of the moon; and the perpetration was of so recent a moment as to admonish them that the hot breath of the Indians might be near enough to be scented; they therefore hastened on to Las Vegas, and were seventy-eight hours without rest. From Las Vegas Mr. Spencer transmitted a communication by express, which I read a few moments since, announcing the facts as stated above.

As you will perceive by an examination of the schedule of distances forwarded to you in my No. 12, the Points of Rocks are 162.83 miles northeast of Santa Fe, 89.76 miles from Las Vegas, and about twenty miles in the same direction from Red river, and 240.26 southwest of the Arkansas crossing.

The cañons and valleys of Red river afford the usual route through which these Indians pass a very considerable distance in making for the Rio del Norte. When they suppose American troops are in vigorous pursuit of them, they at once make for the Rio del Norte, cross it, and push on to or near the boundary line between the United States and Mexico, ready to rest for a time on the discreet side of it.

Colonel Monroe has not disclosed his purposes yet; but one thing is certain—the most vigorous measures should be pushed forward without one moment's delay; and when this is done, as it doubtless will be by Colonel Monroe, the government of the United States will have sustained its ancient reputation for protecting its citizens and chastising their enemies. The military force in this Territory is not sufficient.

The liberation of Mrs. White and her daughter is to me a matter of the deepest concern; but being entirely destitute of the means necessary to an efficient and prompt action in the premises, I am left to lament the impotency of my arm; and if the two captives are not to be liberated, it is to be hoped they are dead. An effort must and shall be made for their liberation, and I regret that I cannot push it forward at this moment. A purely military effort, in my opinion, cannot be successfully made; and I had determined to select an Indian and a Mexican *trader*, and send them forthwith in the supposed direction of the retreat of the Apaches—offering such inducements to them as would secure the end, if that end be attainable; but Colonel Monroe designs a move of some kind, and is unwilling to do so without further and more precise information; and that further information, I apprehend, cannot be acquired during this day, and every moment's delay lessens the probability of a successful effort. I was, a moment since, in consultation with the Colonel upon this subject, and he is determined to do all in his power to rescue the captives, the moment the facts in the case are sufficiently ascertained. Conflicting efforts must not be attempted

I have just secured the services of a *Mexican trader* who knows the Apaches well, their haunts and trails. This man is well known to respectable people here, as a daring, fearless, and withal a discreet man. I promised to pay him one thousand dollars and other gratuities, if he succeeds in bringing in to me Mrs. White and her daughter. He goes out quietly, but rapidly, as a trader, and, if he finds the objects of his search, will doubtless secure them. I made him understand the same inducements would be held out to other parties, and that the reward should be paid promptly to the successful; and, relying upon the just action of the government of the United States, I shall most certainly and cheerfully redeem my every promise in this matter. And I may be pardoned for adding, if the money promised was the last cent I could command on earth, and I without the slightest hope of its reimbursement, it should not be the less promptly paid, upon the happening of the contingency which induced the reward.

In less than one hour from the time I had an interview with this trader, he was off, manifesting the greatest confidence in his ability to command success. If I can quietly, and in a way that cannot by the remotest possibility conflict with Colonel Monroe's efforts, I will induce other parties to go out, and hope to send another off in a different direction on to-morrow morning.

The sad event at the Points of Rocks has caused the delay of several of my communications to you, as the Hon. H. N. Smith, the delegate to Congress selected by a convention in this city, had them in charge, and, hearing of the murder of Mr. White and the male portion of his party, before progressing so far as the Points of Rocks on his journey to Washington city, has returned to Las Vegas to await further developments. I exceedingly regret the delay, on account of the various important suggestions and recommendations contained in my letters, and which I desired you to receive before the President's message should be sent to Congress; for, if there ever was a time for energetic and prompt action in this Territory, this is the time; and the winter should not prevent campaigns.

One word more: if my recommendations contained in No. 10, which I earnestly renew, in reference to agents and ordnance, and ordnance stores, should be adopted, a larger number of the troops now in the Territory might be usefully and successfully employed in a winter expedition against the Apaches and their allies.

Give me four companies of dragoons, and allow me to organize a force from the Pueblo Indians, with the means to subsist them and to pay them, and, my life for it, in less than six months I will so tame the Navajoes and Utahs that you will scarcely hear of them again. In such an expedition I should desire authority to conduct it, without being controlled by any one in this department, and no other government officers except the proper commanders of the dragoons. I should desire to select my own quartermasters and commissaries, and to give to them such directions as would stimulate to the utmost extent the energies of the Pueblo Indians. I will only add, by adding *four* companies of infantry to guard posts and public stores, and sending out proper scientific men, that whole country should at the same time be thoroughly explored.

The foregoing is respectfully submitted, with an earnest request that it be immediately placed before the chief of the department.

And I have the honor to be your obedient servant,

JAMES S. CALHOUN,
Indian Agent.

Colonel W. MEDILL,
Commissioner of Indian Affairs, Washington, D. C.

[No. 17.]

INDIAN AGENCY, SANTA FE, NEW MEXICO,
October 30, 1849.

SIR: At the last moment before the closing of the mail for the United States, I ask for permission to say that I have to day sent out *three* additional parties in search of Mrs. White and her daughter; and I have offered to each party rewards that they hesitated not to say were entirely satisfactory. They did not intimate a desire that the reward for their services should be increased, and I know of nothing more that I can do, as the representative of your department, for the recovery of Mrs. White and her daughter; but I will not sleep, and, if I see what more I may accomplish, or rather attempt, no matter at what cost, it shall be done.

What Colonel Monroe has done, if anything, or what he may design to do, I know not—nor is it my privilege to know.

Very respectfully, your obedient servant,

J. S. CALHOUN, *Indian Agent.*

Colonel W. MEDILL,
Commissioner Indian Affairs, Washington city, D. C.

[No. 18.]

INDIAN AGENCY,
Santa Fe, New Mexico, November 1, 1849.

SIR: I am this moment in receipt of your communications of the 13th and 16th of July last—the first instructing in reference to a census of Indian tribes, and the latter enclosing a blank bond; both of which shall receive my earliest possible attention.

This is sent to Las Vegas, with the hope of there overtaking the mail that left here on yesterday morning.

In great haste, your obedient servant,
J. S. CALHOUN,
Indian Agent.

ORLANDO BROWN, Esq.,
Commissioner of Indian Affairs, Washington city, D. C.

[No. 19.]

SANTA FE, *New Mexico, November* 1, 1849.

SIR: Not until last evening was I aware of the existence of executive document No. 60, ordered to be published on the 28th of April, 1848; otherwise the labor of preparing my communication of the 25th of September last would have been saved, and you the trouble of its receipt.

At the time the document was ordered to be printed, I was in Cuernavaca, Mexico, to which fact I attribute my ignorance of the publication. In addition to which, the secretary of state for this Territory could give me no information as to the transmission of copies of *the papers* to Washington city—such as I forwarded to you.

With great respect, your obedient servant,
J. S. CALHOUN.

Hon. T. EWING,
Secretary of Interior, Washington city.

DEPARTMENT OF THE INTERIOR,
Office Indian Affairs, April 11, 1849.

SIR: I have the honor to enclose herewith a commission constituting you sub-Indian agent on the Rio Gila, in New Mexico, to include the Indians at or in the vicinity of that place, and any others that may hereafter be designated by this department.

Your compensation will be at the rate of $750 per annum, to be in full for all pay and emoluments whatever.

You will execute a bond, in the penal sum of $2,000, with two or more sureties, whose sufficiency must be certified by a United States district judge or district attorney.

So little is known here of the condition and situation of the Indians in that region, that no specific instructions relative to them can be given at present; and the department relies on you to furnish it with such statistical and other information as will give a just understanding of every particular relating to them, embracing the names of the tribes; their locations; the probable extent of territory owned or claimed by each respectively; the tenure by which they claim it; their manners and habits; disposition and feelings towards the United States and whites generally, and towards each other; whether hostile or otherwise; whether the tribes speak different languages, and, when different, the apparent analogies between them; and also what laws and regulations for their government are necessary; and how far the law regulating trade and intercourse with the Indian tribes (a copy of which I enclose) will, if extended to that country, properly apply to the Indians there, and to the trade and intercourse with them; and what modification, if any, will be required to produce the greatest degree of efficiency.

You are authorized to employ one or more interpreters—not exceeding more than one at the same time, unless otherwise absolutely necessary to aid you in the discharge of your duties—whose compensation, if employed by the year, will be at the rate of $300 per annum. It is very desirable that the greatest economy shall be observed; and it is therefore hoped that the employment of one permanent interpreter will be sufficient, and that the services of any others will be but temporary, and for as short periods as possible, consistent with a proper discharge of your duties.

You will report direct to this office, and will lose no opportunity of doing so, as it is extremely desirable that the department be kept well advised of the state of affairs in that region.

In consequence of the remote position of your sub-agency, the Secretary of the Interior has directed that one year's salary be advanced to you, and the same to your interpreter, together with funds for other objects, which you will find explained as follows. These funds will be remitted, to be paid over to you, as soon as the necessary arrangements can be made:

One year's salary for self..	$750
One year's salary for interpreter.............................	300
Pay of interpreters temporarily employed................	100
Contingent expenses, including presents to Indians, purchase of two horses for yourself and your interpreter, collection of statistical information, forage for horses, house rent, fuel, stationery, &c., &c., together with your travelling expenses...	$1,200
	2,350

You are authorized to purchase two horses—one for yourself and one for your interpreter—which you will be held accountable for as public property.

In making presents to Indians, you will be as economical as possible, and confine yourself to such cases only as will effect some important object.

It is supposed that there are captives, or prisoners, either Mexican or American, among some of the Indians of California or New Mexico. If you should find such to be the case among the Indians of your sub-agency, you will demand, and endeavor to procure, their release and surrender, whether American or Mexican; but it must, if possible, be done without any compensation whatever, as to make compensation would but encourage a continuance of the practice of making captives. And any demand must be made under circumstances not calculated to produce mischief or hostile feelings on the part of the Indians.

I enclose blank forms to guide you in rendering your accounts, which must be done quarter-yearly, or as nearly so as possible.

In rendering your accounts, you will account for the money placed in your hands under the following heads of appropriation, viz:

Pay of sub agents	$750
Pay of interpreters	400
Contingencies Indian department	1,200
	2,350

Very respectfully, your obedient servant,
W. MEDILL.

John C. Hays, Esq.,
   Care of Harvey T. Hays, Esq., New Orleans.

P. S. I enclose copy of the late treaty with Mexico, and also copies of the reports of Messrs. Fremont, Emory, Abert, and Cook. I also enclose a copy of a report from his Excellency Governor Bent, which you will find to contain much useful information in relation to the Indians in New Mexico.

W. M.

Department of the Interior,
   Office Indian Affairs, April 17, 1849.

Sir: You were apprized, in your instructions of the 11th instant, that arrangements would be made for the transmission of the funds for your sub-agency; but, finding it impracticable to adopt any better course, the Secretary of the Interior has directed that you be authorized to draw for the amount allowed for the year's expenses, in conformity with your instructions.

To preserve uniformity, I annex the form of the draft to be used by you:

(Place and date.)

Sir: At sight, please pay to the order of ——— ——— two thousand three hundred and fifty dollars, value received, and charge the same to account of the expenses of my sub-agency on the Rio Gila, New Mexico.

Very respectfully,
J. C. H., *Sub-agent.*

Wm. Medill, Esq.,
   Commissioner of Indian Affairs, Washington city, D. C.

Very respectfully, your obedient servant,
WM. MEDILL, *Commissioner.*

John C. Hays, Esq.,
   Care of Harvey T. Hays, Esq., New Orleans, La.

SAN ANTONIO, TEXAS,
June 5, 1849.

SIR: I have had the honor to receive your favor of the 17th April, and am now prepared to embark for my destination on the Rio Gila, to enter upon the duties assigned me under your instructions, and shall leave here to-morrow, intending to reach my post with the least practicable delay.

I have made much inquiry respecting the Indians with whom my duties will associate me, and have been able, I think, to procure much valuable information, and would report now what I considered most important for your information, but, fearing I might mislead the department, I have concluded to defer even facts, of which I myself am satisfied, until confirmed by personal observation and knowledge. I shall, however, lose no time after my arrival to be correctly informed of all that should be known, and take at once such measures as humanity should always dictate in our delicate relations to the Indians, with a steady eye to their civilization and the best interests of the government. And you may rest assured of being constantly advised of all matters of interest; and my best efforts shall be dedicated to promote the wishes of the government.

I cannot doubt that this agency must be one of the most important in our country, and I would respectfully suggest the propriety of an increased allowance for the expenses of the agency. Its very remote position, and the enormous expense necessarily attending it, must be apparent to you as far above that of any other at present established in the United States; and my own outfit has already far exceeded the allowance your instructions have established; and I do most respectfully urge your favorable consideration of this matter.

Immediately on my arrival, I shall report in detail, and constantly after keep you advised of everything of interest to the department, and hope to reach my point towards the end of July; sooner, if practicable.

I shall hope, from time to time, to receive additional instructions from you by such conveyance as may offer; and will also thank you to forward to me such documents as will keep me constantly informed of the wishes of the government on all Indian matters, and very particularly such as may relate to my agency.

I have, in conformity to your instructions, drawn on you this day, in favor of Major L. G. Capers, for the sum of $2,350, (two thousand three hundred and fifty dollars,) which will be presented in due course.

With high considerations of respect and regard, I have the honor to be, sir, your obedient servant,

JOHN C. HAYS,
Sub-Indian Agent, River Gila.

Hon. WM. MEDILL,
  Commissioner of Indian Affairs,
    Department of the Interior, Washington, D. C.

SAN ANTONIO, *June* 8, 1849.

DEAR SIR: Enclosed you have an official bond, duly approved, together with oath of office. The blank bond enclosed to me from the department was signed and forwarded to Galveston, about ten days ago, for approval by Judge Watrous, but unfortunately was lost on the route. Not having retained a copy of the bond, I do not know the precise form, nor have I been able to procure the form of a bond at this place. I presume, however, that the accompanying bond is sufficient. But if it should not be, I leave a power of attorney authorizing Franklin S. Paschal, of this place, to execute in my name a more formal bond, if it should be deemed necessary by the department, as I shall leave here in a day or two for the Gila. The great distance of the district judge and district attorney, both residing at Galveston, two hundred and fifty miles from this place, and no great facilities of intercommunication, has produced more delay in this matter than was desirable. The last bond was intrusted to the private hands of a person of known responsibility, (Doctor Thomas F. Foster, of Louisville, Kentucky,) and he informs me that there is no prospect of its recovery.

Very respectfully, your obedient servant,
JOHN C. HAYS.

Hon. Thomas Ewing.

Galveston, Texas,
July 7, 1849.

Sir: At the request of George W. Paschal, to whom the enclosed bond was sent by the obligor, I have examined and formally approved said bond. The letter, also enclosed, from Colonel Hays, will give an explanation of the transaction, which may or may not be satisfactory. I am well aware that the act of Congress requires a bond from a sub-agent in the sum of one thousand dollars; the fact that the bond enclosed is for two thousand dollars, I presume, will not render it illegal. I find no act of Congress or rule of your department, or of any other, requiring either the district judge or attorney to approve such bonds. But as a bond has to be executed, I have given it an approval.

I have the honor to be your obedient servant,
ROBERT HUGHES.

Hon. Thomas Ewing,
Secretary of the Interior.

Department of the Interior,
Office Indian Affairs, July 26, 1849.

Sir: I have the honor to acknowledge the receipt of your letter of 8th June last, and to inform you that your official bond as Indian sub-agent, received therewith, has been submitted to the Secretary of the Interior, and by him approved.

Very respectfully, your obedient servant,
ORLANDO BROWN, *Commissioner.*

Col. John C. Hays,
Indian Sub agent, River Gila, New Mexico,
Care of Harvey T. Hays, Esq., New Orleans, La.

DEPARTMENT OF WAR.

War Department,
Washington, January 23, 1850.

Sir: I have the honor of placing before you the accompanying documents from this department, asked for by the resolution of the Senate of the 17th instant, and beg leave to submit a full extract from a communication relating to the same subject which was addressed to you on the 18th instant:

"I beg leave to remark that the exercise of civil authority by any military officer in California, since the termination of the war with Mexico, was first assumed by Brevet Brigadier General Mason, under his proclamation, which was issued on the 7th of August, 1848—the next day after the intelligence reached him that peace had been restored between the United States and Mexico. This proclamation was communicated to the department on the 22d of November, 1848, and its receipt acknowledged by the proper bureau on the 27th of January, 1849, without any comment.

"On the 13th of April, 1849, this officer was relieved of his command in California, and was succeeded by Brevet Brigadier General Riley. At this period, it appears to have been the purpose of this latter officer, with the advice of his predecessor, to have secured to the people of that Territory a fuller enjoyment of the laws, customs, and usages applicable to their condition and wants; and, at the same time, to have provided for the organization of a government, such as is contemplated by the ninth article of the treaty of Guadalupe Hidalgo and the constitution of the United States. The cause of delay in executing the purpose of this officer is fully explained by the following extract from a communication from the commanding general of the Pacific division, dated June 20, 1849, to this department:

" 'Under the hope that some act of the last Congress had provided, or at least defined, the government of California, it was thought prudent to await intelligence of the close of the session; and then, if nothing had been done at Washington, to put in action the machinery of the laws already existing here, and at the same time propose to the people of California to form a State constitution and present it at the next session of Congress, when their admission into the Union as a State would at once solve so many difficulties, and, while it removed a cause of disagreement at home, would give them an opportunity of legislating for themselves. The steamer Edith had been sent to Mazatlan for the necessary intelligence; and, on her arrival with information that no other than a revenue law had been passed, General Riley issued a proclamation for the election of the necessary executive and judicial officers under the existing laws, and recommending, at the same time, the election of delegates to a convention to form a State constitution. Mr. King arrived at the time these proclamations were about being issued; and it was matter of great congratulation that the government, by anticipation, had approved of the latter measure. Every means will be used to give the people of California an opportunity of expressing their wishes on this point, and of bringing the matter to a happy conclusion.'

" The necessity of a civil government in California, adequate to protect and control its increased population, composed of persons who had flocked from all quarters of the globe, was daily rendered more apparent. The common employment in which every interest was directly or remotely connected, and of a mass so dissimilar in habits and language, and probably a part not without a lively sense of an exclusive enjoyment, showed the absolute want of an authority capable of upholding public and private rights. Indeed, this want was so obvious and urgent, that legislative assemblies were established in several districts of California; and by their authority the existing customs and laws, already adverted to, were attempted to be superseded. The whole plan was considered as irregular, and would in the end have been dangerous to the public peace and the public interests.

"The first duty of the army was to execute the order of March 15, 1848, 'to take measures with a view to its (California's) permanent occupation;' and the second, in my opinion, was to separate, as far as practicable, the citizens from the control of martial law. The executive powers exercised by the two commanding officers in California were varied only by the emergencies as they arose, which may be seen by their several reports on the civil affairs of that Territory. In their respective administrations, each has endeavored to avoid the application of the principles and practices of military law."

Respectfully submitted.

GEO. W. CRAWFORD,
Secretary of War

To the PRESIDENT.

Instructions, &c., from the War Department.

1846, May 14. To Col. S. W. Kearny.
   27. To the same.
 June 3. To the same.
   5. To the same.
   18. To the same.
   18. To the same.
 Sept. 12. To the same.
 Nov. 5. To the same.
 Dec. 10. To the same.
1847, Jan. 11. To Colonel Richard B. Mason.
   11. To General Stephen W. Kearny.
 June 12. To the same.
   12. To the same.
 Oct. 13 To Colonel R. B. Mason.
   27. To the same.
   28. To the same.
 Dec. 24. To the same.
1848, Jan. 20. To the same.
 Oct. 9. To the same.
   10. To General Bennet Riley.
   12. To Colonel R. B. Mason.
   13. To General B. Riley.
   13. To the same.

1848, Oct. 13. To General B. Riley.
     Nov. 30. To joint board of army and navy officers.
          15. To General Persifor F. Smith.
1849, April 3. To the same.
          4. To the same.
     June 26. To General B. Riley.
     July 13. To the commanding officer in California.
     Aug. 10. To General R. B. Mason.
          24. To General B. Riley.
     Nov. 12. To Colonel George A. McCall.
          19. To the same.
          28. To General B. Riley.
     Dec. 11. To the same.

WAR DERARTMENT, *May* 14, 1846.

SIR: Mr. G. T. Howard, who will hand you this, is the bearer of a communication to the caravan of traders *en route* for Santa Fe. It is important that he should overtake that caravan with the least possible delay; and you are required to furnish him with a detachment of mounted dragoons of sufficient strength to insure his safety through the country, provided, in your judgment, it can be done consistently with other calls upon your command.

Very respectfully, your obedient servant,
W. L. MARCY,
Secretary of War.

Colonel S. W. KEARNY,
   First regiment of dragoons, or
      Officer commanding Fort Leavenworth, Missouri.

WAR DEPARTMENT,
Washington, May 27, 1846.

SIR: The President has been informed that much pains has been taken to alarm the religious prejudices of the Mexican inhabitants of Santa Fe and its vicinity against the United States. He deems it important that their misapprehensions in this respect should be corrected, as far as it can be done; and, for that purpose, he has caused arrangements to be made for a person of high character and good repute in the Roman Catholic church to accompany your forces in the expedition you are about to conduct to that place. You are directed to receive and treat with respect and courtesy any person who shall present himself to you with a letter of introduction from Bishop Kenrick, of Missouri, the Rev. J. Vandervelde, or the Rev. J. Simon. Though the President cannot commission him as chaplain, yet he requests that the person so recommended to you should be received as of that character by you and your officers, and be respected as such; that he should be permitted to have intercourse with the soldiers of the Catholic faith, and to administer to them religious instruction, and to perform divine service, whenever it can be done without interfering with their military duties.

It is understood that the person who will be invited to attend you will understand and speak the Spanish language; and it is hoped that he will, without departing from the path of his duties as a clergyman, be useful in removing the false impressions of the Mexicans in relation to the United States and their objects in taking possession of New Mexico, and inducing them to confide in the assurance you will make that their religious institutions will be respected, the property of the church protected, their worship undisturbed—in fine, that all their religious rights will be in the amplest manner preserved to them. It is confidently believed that such a person will, besides performing the usual duties of chaplain to your troops, facilitate your entrance into that country, and be eminently serviceable in reconciling the people to the change in their political situation which may result from your occupation of it. You are also requested to provide for him such accommodations as will render his abiding with you comfortable to him. It is understood that when chaplains were allowed by law to the army, they received, in pay and emoluments, about one thousand to twelve hundred dollars per annum. This amount will be paid to the person who will attend you.

Very respectfully, your obedient servant,

W. L. MARCY,
Secretary of War.

Colonel S. W. KEARNY,
First dragoons, Fort Leavenworth, Missouri.

[Confidential.]

WAR DEPARTMENT,
Washington, June 3, 1846.

SIR: I herewith send you a copy of my letter to the governor of Missouri for an additional force of one thousand mounted men.

The object of thus adding to the force under your command is not, as you will perceive, fully set forth in that letter, for the reason that it is deemed prudent that it should not, at this time, become a matter of public notoriety; but to you it is proper and necessary that it should be stated.

It has been decided by the President to be of the greatest importance in the pending war with Mexico to take the earliest possession of Upper California. An expedition with that view is hereby ordered, and you are designated to command it. To enable you to be in sufficient force to conduct it successfully, this additional force of a thousand mounted men has been provided, to follow you in the direction of Santa Fe, to be under your orders, or those of the officer you may leave in command at Santa Fe.

It cannot be determined how far this additional force will be behind that designed for the Santa Fe expedition, but it will not probably be more than a few weeks. When you arrive at Santa Fe with the force already called, and shall have taken possession of it, you may find yourself in a condition to garrison it with a small part of your command, (as the additional force will soon be at that place,) and with the remainder press forward to California. In that case you will make such arrangements, as to being followed by the reinforcement before mentioned, as in your judgment may be deemed safe and prudent. I need not say to you that in case you conquer Santa Fe, (and with it will be included the department or state of New Mexico,) it will be important to provide for retaining safe possession of it. Should you deem it prudent to have still more troops for the accomplishment of the objects herein designated, you will lose no time in communicating your opinion on that point, and all others connected with the enterprise, to this department. Indeed, you are hereby authorized to make a direct requisition for it upon the governor of Missouri.

It is known that a large body of Mormon emigrants are *en route* to California, for the purpose of settling in that country. You are desired to use all proper means to have a good understanding with them, to the end that the United States may have their co-operation in taking possession of and holding that country. It has been suggested here that many of these Mormons would willingly enter into the service of the United States, and aid us in our expedition against California. You are hereby authorized to muster into service such as can be induced to volunteer—not, however, to a number exceeding one-third of your entire force. Should they enter the service, they will be paid as other volunteers; and you can allow them to designate, so far as it can be properly done, the persons to act as officers thereof. It is understood that a considerable number of American citizens are now settled on the Sacramento river, near *Sutter's* establishment, called "Nueva Helvetia," who are well disposed towards the United States. Should you, on your arrival in the country, find this to be the true state of things there, you are authorized to organize and receive into the service of the United States such portion of these citizens as you may think useful to aid you to hold the possession of the country. You will in that case allow them, so far as you shall judge proper, to select their own officers. A large discretionary power is invested in you in regard to these matters, as well as to others, in relation to the expedition confided to your command.

The choice of routes by which you will enter California will be left to your better knowledge and ampler means of getting accurate information. We are assured that a southern route (called the caravan route, by which the wild horses are brought from that country into New Mexico) is practicable, and it is suggested as not improbable that it can be passed over in the winter months, or at least late in autumn. It is hoped that this information may prove to be correct.

In regard to the routes, the practicability of procuring needful supplies for men and animals, and transporting baggage, is a point to be well considered. Should the President be disappointed in his cherished hope that you will be able to reach the interior of Upper California before winter, you are then desired to make the best arrangement you can for sustaining your forces during the winter, and for an early movement in the spring. Though it is very desirable that the expedition should reach California this season, (and the President does not doubt you will make every possible effort to accomplish this object,) yet if, in your judgment, it cannot be undertaken with a reasonable prospect of success, you will defer it, as above suggested, until spring. You are left unembarrassed by any specific directions in this matter.

It is expected that the naval forces of the United States which are now, or will soon be, in the Pacific, will be in possession of all the towns on the seacoast, and will co-operate with you in the conquest of California.

Arms, ordnance, munitions of war, and provisions, to be used in that country, will be sent by sea to our squadron in the Pacific, for the use of the land forces.

Should you conquer and take possession of New Mexico and Upper California, or considerable places in either, you will establish temporary civil governments therein—abolishing all arbitrary restrictions that may exist, so far as it may be done with safety. In performing this duty, it would be wise and prudent to continue in their employment all such of the existing officers as are known to be friendly to the United States and will take the oath of allegiance to them. The duties at the custom-house ought at once to be reduced to such a rate as may be barely sufficient to maintain the necessary officers, without yielding any revenue to the government. You may assure the people of those provinces, that it is the wish and design of the United States to provide for them a free government, with the least possible delay, similar to that which exists in our Territories. They will then be called on to exercise the rights of freemen in electing their own representatives to the territorial legislature. It is foreseen that what relates to the civil government will be a difficult and unpleasant part of your duty, and much must necessarily be left to your own discretion. In your whole conduct you will act in such a manner as best to conciliate the inhabitants and render them friendly to the United States.

It is desirable that the usual trade between the citizens of the United States and the Mexican provinces should be continued, as far as practicable, under the changed condition of things between the two countries. In consequence of extending your expedition into California, it may be proper that you should increase your supply for goods to be distributed as presents to the Indians. The United States superintendent of Indian affairs at St. Louis will aid you in procuring these goods. You will be furnished with a proclamation in the Spanish language, to be issued by you and circulated among the Mexican people on your entering or approaching their country. You will use your utmost endeavors to have the pledges and promises therein contained carried out to the utmost extent.

I am directed by the President to say that the rank of brevet brigadier general will be conferred on you as soon as you commence your movement towards California, and sent round to you by sea, or over the country, or to the care of the commandant of our squadron in the Pacific. In that way, cannon, arms, ammunition, and supplies for the land forces will be sent you.

Very respectfully, your obedient servant,
W. L. MARCY,
Secretary of War.

Colonel S. W. KEARNY,
Fort Leavenworth, Missouri.

WAR DEPARTMENT,
Washington, June 5, 1846.

SIR: I enclosed you a few copies of a proclamation prepared for General Taylor to issue to the Mexicans. I discover that there are parts of it that will not answer our purpose for Santa Fe or Upper California. You will not, therefore, use these copies. It is intended to make the needful alterations in it, and, thus altered, send on copies to you; and I trust I may get them to you before you will have occasion to distribute them. I must, however, urge you not to use those which have been forwarded.

Very respectfully, your obedient servant,

W. L. MARCY,
Secretary of War.

Colonel S. W. KEARNY.

WAR DEPARTMENT,
Washington, June 18, 1846.

SIR: At the request of the President, I commend to your favorable consideration the bearer hereof, Colonel James N. Magoffin. Mr. M. is now and has been for some years a resident of Chihuahua, and extensively engaged in trade in that and other settlements of Mexico. He is well acquainted with the people of Chihuahua, Santa Fe, and the intermediate country. He was introduced to the President by Colonel Benton, as a gentleman of intelligence and most respectable character. The President has had several interviews with him, and is favorably impressed with his character, intelligence, and disposition to the cause of the United States. His knowledge of the country and of the people is such as induces the President to believe he may render important services to you in regard to your military movements in New Mexico. He will leave here for Santa Fe immediately, and will probably overtake you before you arrive at that place. Considering his intelligence, his credit with the people, and his business capacity, it is believed he will give important information, and make arrangements to furnish your troops with abundant supplies in New Mexico. Should you apprehend difficulties of this nature, it is recommended to you to avail yourself in this respect, and others, of his services, for which he will, as a matter of course, be entitled to a fair consideration.

Very respectfully, your obedient servant,

W. L. MARCY,
Secretary of War.

Colonel S. W. KEARNY.

WAR DEPARTMENT,
Washington, June 18, 1846.

SIR: By direction of the President, I have given to the bearer hereof, Colonel Magoffin, a letter of introduction to you, and trust you will derive advantage from his knowledge of the country in which you are to carry on military operations, and the assistance he may afford in securing supplies, &c.

I have nothing of importance to add to the despatches which have been already forwarded to you. Since my last letter, it has been determined to send a small force round Cape Horn to California. The arms, cannon, and provisions to be sent to the Pacific, will be accompanied by one company of artillery of the regular army. Arrangements are now on foot to send a regiment of volunteers by sea. These troops, and such as may be organized in Upper California, will be under your command.

More than common solicitude will be felt here in regard to the expedition committed to you, and it is desired that you should avail yourself of all occasions to inform the government of your progress and prospects. The President desires your opinion, as early as you are in a situation to favor him with it, of the practicability of your reaching California in the course of this autumn or in the early part of next winter. I need not repeat the expression of his wishes that you should take military possession of that country as soon as it can be safely done.

Very respectfully, your obedient servant,
W. L. MARCY,
Secretary of War.

Colonel S. W. KEARNY.

WAR DEPARTMENT,
Washington, September 12, 1846.

SIR: A volunteer regiment raised in the State of New York, engaged to serve during the war with Mexico, and to be discharged wherever they may be at its termination, if in a Territory of the United States, has been mustered into service, and is about to embark at the port of New York for California. This force is to be a part of your command; but as it may reach the place of its destination before you are in a condition to subject it to your orders, the colonel of the regiment, J. D. Stevenson, has been furnished with instructions for his conduct in the mean time. I herewith send you a copy thereof, as well as a copy of the instructions of the Navy Department to the commander of the naval squadron in the Pacific; a copy of a letter to General Taylor, with a circular from the Treasury Department; a copy of a letter from General Scott to Captain Tompkins; and a copy of general regulations relative to the respective rank of naval and army officers. These, so far as applicable, will be looked upon in the light of instructions to yourself. The department is exceedingly desirous to be furnished by you with full information of your progress and proceedings, together with your opinions and views as to your movements into California, having reference to time, route, &c. Beyond the regiment under command of Colonel S. Price, and the separate battalion called for at the same time by the President from the governor of Missouri, a requisition for another regiment of infantry was issued on the 18th of July last, but the information subsequently received here induced the belief that it would not be needed; and the difficulty of passing it over the route at so late a period in the season, with the requisite quantity of supplies, &c., was deemed so great that the orders to muster it into service have been countermanded. It will not be sent. Your views as to the sufficiency of your force, and the practicability of sustaining a larger one, &c., are desired.

I am, with great respect, your obedient servant,
W. L. MARCY,
Secretary of War.

Gen. S. W. KEARNY,
Fort Leavenworth, Missouri.

WAR DEPARTMENT,
Washington, November 5, 1846.

SIR: You are hereby authorized to draw on the Quartermaster General of the army at Washington for such sums of money as you may need, which drafts will be paid on presentation, and charged to the appropriations to be therein designated.

You are also authorized to receive from the disbursing officers of the Pay, Quartermaster, and Subsistence departments, such sums of money as you may require; and for sums so received, and the amount of drafts drawn by you under this authority, you will account according to law.

Very respectfully, your obedient servant,
W. L. MARCY,
Secretary of War.

Col. R. B. MASON,
1st Dragoons.

WAR DEPARTMENT,
Washington, December 10, 1846.

SIR : The information received at the department renders it almost certain that the force sent by sea to California, and that which has been there organized, will be sufficient to hold possession of that country, and successfully defeat any effort which it will be in the power of Mexico to make to recover it.

It is presumed that you will not find a state of things in California requiring you to remain in that country, but that you will deem it proper to leave affairs there in charge of Colonel Mason, recently sent out, and return to Santa Fe. It is not improbable that you will have arrived at that place by the time this communication will be there received.

The department is satisfied, from the information contained in your despatches, and from other sources, that the force at Santa Fe will be greater than will be necessary to retain and secure possession of it and of the province of New Mexico.

The object of this communication is to make some suggestions in relation to the employment of that portion of the forces under your command which may not be needed for that purpose; but, before presenting these suggestions, it may be proper to apprize you of what is now, and probably will be, the state of things on the lower Rio Grande.

General Wool reached Monclova about the last of October. If Mexico had attempted to retain Chihuahua, he would have marched into that department, with a view to conquer and hold possession of it; but as the enemy has no organized force in Chihuahua, and as the invading column under General Taylor has moved from Monterey upon Saltillo, and will doubtless hold the latter place, Chihuahua is, in effect, subjected to our arms, and the forces under General Wool may join General Taylor's column without going into the department of Chihuahua.

It is suggested for your consideration, that you should move with your disposable force towards the positions occupied by General Taylor, passing into Chihuahua and Durango, or some part of it. It is hoped that there will exist no sufficient cause to prevent you from pursuing this course.

Much is left to your discretion in regard to your operations; for it cannot be anticipated what will be the condition of things in those provinces.

I am satisfied that it is the policy of Mexico to carry on a guerrilla warfare, and to seek occasion to fall, with vastly superior force, upon small detachments of our troops.

You will, as a matter of course, take every precaution to ascertain the state of things about you, the condition of the country through which you propose to pass, in regard to the resistance that can be made to your progress. A movement may be made upon the capital of Mexico; if so, the principal column will probably advance from some point on the gulf. In that event your force should be employed in the most effective way to create a diversion. Whether you can render most aid to the principal movements by operating separately, or by joining and strengthening the forces penetrating the enemy's country in the direction of Monterey and Saltillo, cannot be determined here, but must be left to yourself. Should you approach near to these forces, you will naturally fall under the orders of the commander of them.

It will be important that you should unfold to him the plans of your operations, and keep him advised of all your movements.

Very respectfully, your obedient servant,
W. L. MARCY,
Secretary of War.

Brigadier General S. W. KEARNY,
Commanding, &c.

WAR DEPARTMENT,
January 11, 1847.

SIR: The enclosed papers have been addressed jointly to General Kearny and yourself, under the uncertainty whether they will find him in California. Should he have left there before their arrival, you will consider the communication as intended for your guidance, and you will conform your conduct to the views therein presented, so far as relates to the government of that country.

Very respectfully, your obedient servant,
W. L. MARCY,
Secretary of War.

Colonel RICHARD B. MASON,
First regiment U. S. Dragoons, commanding in California.

WAR DEPARTMENT,
Washington, January 11, 1847.

SIR: Your communication from Santa Fe of the 22d of September, accompanied by a copy of the laws prepared for the government of New Mexico, and established in that Territory, was received at this department on the 23d of November last.

Soon after the meeting of Congress, the President was called on by a resolution of the House of Representatives for the *orders and instructions* issued to the officers of the army and navy by him for the civil government of the territories which had been, or might be, acquired by our arms.

I herewith send you a copy of the President's message, with the documents sent to Congress in answer to that resolution. By this you will learn the President's views as to the power and authority to be exercised in the territories conquered and occupied by our forces. These views are presented more in detail in instructions prepared under his directions by the Secretary of the Navy, bearing date this day, an extract of which is herewith transmitted for your information, and particularly for the guidance of your conduct. This document is so full and clear on all points in regard to which you may desire the directions of the government, that I do not deem it necessary to enlarge upon it.

It is proper to remark that the provisions of the laws which have been established for the government of the Territory of New Mexico go, in some few respects, beyond the line designated by the President, and propose to confer upon the people of the Territory political rights under the constitution of the United States: such rights can only be acquired by the action of Congress. So far as the code of laws established in New Mexico by your authority attempts to confer such rights, it is not approved by the President; and he directs me to instruct you not to carry such parts into effect.

Under the law of nations, the power conquering a territory or country has a right to establish a civil government within the same, as a means of securing the conquest, and with a view to protecting the persons and property of the people; and it is not intended to limit you in the full exercise of this authority. Indeed, it is desired you should exercise it in such a manner as to inspire confidence in the people that our power is to be firmly sustained in that country. The territory in our military occupation acquired from the enemy by our arms cannot be regarded, the war still continuing, as permanently annexed to the United States, though our authority to exercise civil government over it is not, by that circumstance, the least restricted.

It is important that the extent and character of our possessions in the territories conquered from the enemy should not be open to question or cavil. This remark, though having reference to all our aquisitions, is in an especial manner applicable to the Californias. As to Upper California, it is presumed no doubt can arise; but it may not be so clear as to Lower California. It is expected that our flag will be hoisted in that part of the country, and actual possession taken, and continuously held, of some place or places in it, and our civil jurisdiction there asserted and upheld.

A copy of this communication will be sent to the commanding officer at Santa Fe, with instructions to conform his conduct to the views herein presented.

Very respectfully, your obedient servant,

W. L. MARCY,
Secretary of War.

Brigadier General STEPHEN W. KEARNY,
Commanding U. S. Army in California, Mexico.

[18]

Extract of a despatch to Commodore Stockton.

NAVY DEPARTMENT, *January* 11, 1847.

SIR: Your communications dated at Monterey on the 18th and 19th of September were received at the department on the 26th December ultimo, by the hands of Mr. Norris, whose activity and intelligence in executing his orders entitle him to my thanks.

You will probably have received, before this can reach you, my despatches which were intrusted to Lieutenant Watson, of the United States navy, under date of the 5th of November, in which, as commander in-chief of the United States naval forces in the Pacific, you were informed that the President "has deemed it best for the public interests to invest the military officer commanding with the direction of the operations on land, and with the administrative functions of government over the people and territory occupied by us."

Accompanying this, I send you copies of the President's annual message, trasmitted to Congress on the 8th of December ultimo, with the accompanying documents, including the annual reports of the War and Navy Departments. I also send you a printed copy of the document No. 19 of the House of Representatives.

You will perceive, from these papers, the view taken by the Executive of the measures which have been adopted by the military and naval commanders in those States of Mexico of which we have acquired possession by military conquest.

I see no reason to qualify the opinion which I expressed in my report, that "your measures in regard to the conquered territory are believed to be warranted by the laws of war;" and in answer to your suggestions that "a general approval by the government of the United States of your conduct, if they do approve, to be published in the Californian, would have a good effect," I have been directed by the President to communicate a more full statement of his views of the principles which govern the conduct of our officers in the circumstances in which you have been placed, and on which the instructions heretofore given were based.

By the constitution of the United States, the power to declare war is vested in Congress. The war with Mexico exists by her own act and the declaration of the Congress of the United States. It is the duty of the Executive to carry on the war, with all the rights and subject to all the duties imposed by the laws of nations—a code binding on both the billigerents.

The possession of portions of the enemy's territory, acquired by justifiable acts of war, gives to us the right of government during the continuance of our possession, and imposes on us a duty to the inhabitants who are thus placed under our dominion. This right of possession, however, is temporary, unless made absolute by subsequent events. If, being in possession, a treaty of peace is made and duly ratified on the principle of *uti possidetis*—that is, that each of the belligerent parties shall enjoy the territory of which it shall be in possession at the date of the treaty—or if the surrender of the territory is not stipulated in the treaty so ratified, then the imperfect title acquired by conquest is made absolute, and the inhabitants, with the territory, are entitled to all the benefits of the federal constitution of the United States, to the same extent as the citizens of any other part of the Union.

The course of our government in regard to California, or other portions of the territory of Mexico now or hereafter to be in our possession by conquest, depends on those on whom the constitution imposes the duty of making and carrying treaties into effect. Pending the war, our possession gives us only such rights as the laws of nations recognise; and the government is military, performing such civil duties as are necessary to the full enjoyment of the advantages resulting from the conquest, and to the due protection of the rights of persons and of property of the inhabitants.

No political right can be conferred on the inhabitants thus situated, emanating from the constitution of the United States. That instrument establishes a form of government for those who are within our limits, and owe voluntary allegiance to it. Unless incorporated with the assent of Congress, by ratified treaty or by legislative act, as in the case of Texas, our rights over enemies' territory in our possession are only such as the laws of war confer, and theirs no more than are derived from the same authority. They are therefore entitled to no representation in the Congress of the United States.

Without anticipating what may be the terms of a treaty which, it is hoped, will be entered into between the two republics, there will be no revocation of the orders given in my despatch of the 5th of November last, " that under no circumstances will you voluntarily lower the flag of the United States or relinquish the actual possession of California," with all the rights which it confers.

In the discharge of the duty of government in the conquered territory during our military possession, it has not been deemed improper or unwise that the inhabitants should be permitted to participate in the selection of agents to make or execute the laws to be enforced. Such a privilege cannot fail to produce ameliorations of the despotic character of martial law, and constitute checks voluntarily and appropriately submitted to by officers of the United States, all whose instructions are based on the will of the governed.

I have regarded your measures in authorizing the election of agents charged with making laws, or in executing them, as founded on this principle; and so far as they carry out the rights of temporary government under existing rights of possession, they are approved. But no officers created or laws or regulations made to protect the rights or perform the duties resulting from our conquests can lawfully continue beyond the duration of the state of things which now exists, without authority of future treaty or act of Congress.

At present it is needless, and might be injurious to the public interests, to agitate the question in California as to how long those persons who have been elected for a prescribed period of time will have official authority. If our right of possession shall become absolute, such an inquiry is needless; and if, by treaty or otherwise, we lose the possession, those who follow us will govern the country. The President, however, anticipates no such result. On the contrary, he foresees no contingency in which the United States will ever surrender or relinquish the possession of the Californias. The number of official appointments, with civil or military duties other than those devolved on our navy and army by our own laws, should be made as small as possible, and the expenses of the local government should be kept within the limits of the revenues received within the territory, if it can be done without detriment to the public interests.

WAR DEPARTMENT, *June* 11, 1847.

SIR: The latest communication from you is your letter of the 30th of January.

Although Commodore Shubrick, who sailed from Boston in August, had arrived at Monterey a few days before your letter was written, it does not appear that the despatch from this department sent out by him had been received by you. It is sincerely to be hoped that the Commodore's instructions from the Navy Department, and those from this department to yourself, put an end to the much-regretted misunderstanding which had arisen between yourself and the commander of the squadron in the Pacific. These instructions bore date as early as August last, before it was known that you had left the United States, and were prepared in great uncertainty whether you would be able to go beyond Santa Fe until this spring, and what would be the condition of affairs there on your arrival. It was then anticipated that the naval force might take possession of important places on the coast of California some time before a land force could arrive in that country to co-operate with it; and the early instructions to that branch of the service were framed with only a very remote expectation of the presence of a land force. The relative powers and duties of the commanders of the land and naval forces were not so particularly considered and defined in these instructions as in those of November, sent out by Colonel Mason, of the army, and by Lieutenant Watson, of the navy. In these latter despatches, the views of the government in relation to the operations of the two branches of the service are clearly set forth, and, when received, (as they must have been several months since,) it is presumed that all conflict of authority ceased. To the senior naval officer all military operations on water were confided, and with them the officers of the army were not to interfere, except when the enterprise required the co-operation of the land forces. So, on the other hand, to the senior officer of the army in that country all the operations on land were intrusted, and by him were to be conducted, assisted, if the exigency of the occasion required, by the naval force. When brought together and co-operating for any particular object, the superior in rank, according to regulations furnished in previous instructions, would have command for the time being.

The views of the President in relation to the temporary civil government of California, in case our arms in that quarter should be so far successful as to render such government expedient, were clearly presented in the despatch of the 5th of November from the Navy Department, and in that of the 3d of the same month from Major General Scott. Though copies of these documents have been forwarded to you since the originals were despatched by Colonel Mason, they are again herewith transmitted in the accompanying document of the House of Representatives of the last session, No. 19. Presuming that the difficulties in California have long since been settled in conformity to these instructions, it is not now proposed to make any modification of them. The temporary civil government in California results from the conquest of that country by our arms; the authority for it is not derived directly from the constitution of the United States or any act of Congress, but is the right of war. By the law of nations, the conqueror has the right to govern the place or territory of which he has acquired military possession. While in California, occupying the position of an officer of the army of the United States highest in rank, you are charged by the instructions heretofore sent to you, and here repeated, with the functions of civil governor of the country, as well as with the command of the land forces, either sent out or there organized. When you return—as you are at liberty to do, if the condition of affairs warrants it—both the command of the troops and the functions of the civil governor will devolve on Colonel Mason, the officer of the army next in rank to yourself, or on such other officer of the army as may be highest in rank for the time being. It is not intended, by what is before said in regard to the functions of the temporary civil governor being in the officer of the army highest in rank, to deny or question his right to invest any other person with the powers and duties of temporary civil governor, should such officer find it inexpedient or inconvenient to exercise these powers and perform these duties in person; but, in case of such delegation of the functions of temporary civil governor, the person exercising them must be subordinate to the commander of the land forces, and removable at his will. The responsibility, as to the military and civil affairs, is with the officer in chief command of the military force.

In relation to the collection of revenue at the several Mexican ports in our military occupancy, there are duties devolved on each branch of the public service, or rather a co-operation by them in regard to this matter. It is not deemed requisite that anything more explicit should be said to indicate the respective duties of each than what is contained in the despatches before referred to, of the 3d and 5th of November last.

The moneys collected at the ports are to be applied to the purposes of the war, and among these purposes is the support of the temporary civil government. It is expected that this government should be simple and economical, and the expenses be brought, if practicable, within the revenues which may be collected in the country; for there are no funds now at the control of the government here which can be devoted to the civil expenses; and whether there will be such hereafter, will depend upon the action of Congress.

A communication, dated at Ciudad de los Angeles, the 3d of February, addressed by Lieutenant Colonel Fremont to the Secretary of State, has been referred to this department. By this communication it appears that considerable sums of money are needed for the temporary civil government of California, and other purposes than for the pay, subsistence, &c., of the military force; and that the necessity for them is urgent in regard to the interest of the United States in that country. Congress has made no provision for such a case, and without it the government here cannot meet such a demand. The only resource to meet such an emergency is the one before indicated—the revenues which may be collected in the country. A similar state of things, I presume, exists in New Mexico. It is quite probable that the President will consider it to be his duty to call the attention of Congress to this subject, and ask for appropriations to meet these cases; but it is not reasonable to expect any relief of this kind can reach California much within a year from this time.

When the despatch from this department was sent out in November last, there was reason to believe that Lieutenant Colonel Fremont would desire to return to the United States, and you were then directed to conform to his wishes in that respect. It is not now proposed to change that direction; but since that time it has become known here that he bore a conspicuous part in the conquest of California; that his services have been very valuable in that country, and doubtless will continue to be so should he remain there.

Impressed, as all engaged in the public service must be, with the great importance of harmony and cordial co-operation in carrying on military operations in a country so distant from the seat of authority, the President is persuaded that when his definite instructions were received, all questions of difficulty were settled, and all feelings which had been elicited by the agitation of them had subsided. Should Lieutenant Colonel Fremont, who has the option to return or remain, adopt the latter alternative, the President does not doubt you will employ him in such a manner as will render his services most available to the public interest, having reference to his extensive acquaintance with the inhabitants of California, and his knowledge of their language—qualifications, independent of all others, which it is supposed may be very useful in the present and prospective state of our affairs in that country.

It is probable that, before this communication is delivered to you, my despatch of the 10th of May last, with the accompanying documents, in relation to the collection of duties as contributions at the Mexican port in our military possession, will have been received. Some modifications in the scale of duties, &c., have since been made. The copy of an order of the President of this date, and a copy of a letter of the Secretary of the Treasury of the 10th instant, which are herewith furnished, will inform you of the character and extent of these modifications, and of the President's approval thereof, which you will cause to be observed and carried into effect.

I transmit herewith a copy of a communication addressed to you on the 10th of May, and sent by Mr. Toler, who proceeded to California by the route across the isthmus of Panama.

Very respectfully, your obedient servant,
W. L. MARCY, *Secretary of War.*

Brig. Gen. S. W. KEARNY,
 *or officer of the U. S. Army highest
  in rank in California, Mexico.*

WAR DEPARTMENT,
Washington, June 12, 1847.

SIR: Herewith I enclose a triplicate of the orders of the Secretary of the Navy to the commanding officer of the naval forces in the Pacific ocean, dated June 11, 1847.

I am, very respectfully, your obedient servant,
W. L. MARCY, *Secretary of War.*

Brigadier General S. W. KEARNY.

WAR DEPARTMENT,
Washington, October 13, 1847.

SIR: In instructions dated 10th May last, sent to General Kearny, then in California, it was stated that vessels engaged in the trade with California, *which left home in the United States before the commercial regulations of April last issued*, would be required to pay duties at each port on only so much of their respective cargoes as might be landed at such port. It has been determined that this permission should extend to vessels, American or foreign, without regard to the time when they sailed. You will, therefore, direct those who are employed by the authority of the commanding officer of the land forces in California to conform to the above modification.

I herewith send you an extract of a letter from the Secretary of the Treasury to the United States collector at Boston, directing the manner of executing the regulation in regard to this subject:

Extract of a letter from the Secretary of the Treasury to the United States Collector at Boston, dated May 10, 1847.

"In respect to the coasting trade between the ports in California, it is to be remarked that the regulations confine the privilege to *American* vessels only. This coastwise trade is to be understood as authorizing *American* vessels only to take in at one or more ports foreign merchandise on which duty under the regulations has been paid, as also articles of the growth or production of California or Mexico, and carry the same to be landed at any other port in our possession in said country.

"Any vessel, American or foreign, arriving at a port in California, that may not be able to dispose of her entire cargo at said port, may enter and pay duty and charges on any part of the same landed thereat, and may then proceed to one or more ports in said country in the actual possession of the United States forces, and land the residue of her cargo, on due entry and payment of duties thereon. In all such cases, the military officers in command at the ports where portions of the cargo may be landed, and the duties paid, should certify on the manifest the quantity, character, and description of goods landed at their respective ports, and the amount of duties collected thereon.

"All export duties being abolished under the regulations, it follows that any vessel making up a cargo for exportation from California to the United States ports, or the ports of any foreign country in amity with the same, may proceed from one or more ports within said country to collect and take in her cargo free of duty or charges."

I am, with great respect, your obedient servant,
W. L. MARCY,
Secretary of War.

Colonel R. B. MASON,
Commanding U. S. Army in California.

WAR DEPARTMENT,
Washington, October 27, 1847.

SIR: You will receive herewith a copy of a letter from the Secretary of State to this department, dated July 23, with a copy of the papers therein referred to; also, a copy of the correspondence between this department and Lieutenant Colonel Frémont, on the subject of the complaints set forth in the letter of the French minister. They are sent to you in order that an investigation may be made into the transaction referred to. You will, therefore, institute a board, to consist of one or more officers, not exceeding three, to examine into the facts, and report the same to this department at the earliest practicable day.

Very respectfully, your obedient servant,

W. L. MARCY,
Secretary of War.

Colonel R. B. MASON,
 Commanding U. S. Army in California,
  Monterey, California.

[Memorandum.]

WAR DEPARTMENT, *October* 28, 1847.

Sent him six copies of pages 19 and 20, addition to regulations relative to contributions, and twenty copies of page 21 of the same, relating more particularly to California.

COL. R. B. MASON, *California.*

WAR DEPARTMENT,
December 24, 1847.

SIR: I have just learned that a messenger will leave here this afternoon, via New York, for California, with despatches from the Navy Department. I avail myself of the occasion to send you a copy of the President's message, and the report of this department. Should the messenger be detained in New York for a day or two, which it is hoped he may be, there will be time to send you a further communication.

Very respectfully, your obedient servant,

W. L. MARCY,
Secretary of War.

Colonel R. B. MASON,
 Commanding U. S. troops in California.

WAR DEPARTMENT, *January* 20, 1848.

SIR: Your communication of the 18th of June has been received. By a reference to the annual report of the department herewith, you will learn its views in respect to an augmentation of the force under your command. A bill to raise additional troops for the war is now before Congress, and, should it become a law, a portion of the force therein provided for will be sent to California. But in order to increase the force there as soon as practicable, part of the troops now in Santa Fe will be sent into that country. Accordingly instructions have been given to the commanding officer in that quarter to detach from his command such of the volunteers as may be safely spared for this service, with directions to proceed by the route taken by General Kearny or Major Cook in 1846. This increase, with the two hundred recruits sent by sea some months since, and such volunteers as may be raised in the country, and which you are authorized to receive, to the extent you may deem necessary, under the act of the 13th of May, 1846, will, it is hoped, be sufficient for present exigencies. Should the state of the country render it hazardous to keep the troops too much dispersed, it may be advisable to concentrate them in larger bodies, by reducing the number of military stations, and maintaining such only as may be deemed essential.

The officers requested in your letter will be ordered to report to you as soon as they can be spared from other duties; and the proper cavalry equipments for the mounted men, as recommended by you, have been ordered, and will be sent by the first opportunity.

The department indulges the hope that its recommendation in respect to the unsettled claims in California, reported in your communication, will receive the favorable action of Congress at an early day, in order that arrangements may be made for their prompt payment.

Very respectfully, your obedient servant,
W. L. MARCY,
Secretary of War.
Col. RICHARD B. MASON,
1st *Reg't of Dragoons, comd'g U. S. A. in California.*

WAR DEPARTMENT,
Washington, March 15, 1848.

SIR: This despatch is committed to Major General Butler, commander-in-chief of our armies in Mexico, and will be transmitted to you in case the pending negotiations for peace are successfully concluded.

By the treaty now pending, Upper California is ceded to the United States. The limits between the United States and the republic of Mexico will be communicated to you by General Butler, with the despatch. You will, therefore, immediately on receiving this communication, and a notification from Major General Butler that peace is definitively settled between the two nations, withdraw your troops to that part of the country which falls within the limits of the United States as defined by the treaty, and take proper measures with a view to its permanent occupation.

Very respectfully, your obedient servant,
W. L. MARCY,
Secretary of War.
Colonel R. B. MASON,
Commanding U. S. forces, California.

WAR DEPARTMENT,
Washington, October 9, 1848.

SIR: Although the regiment of volunteers in California under the command of Colonel J. D. Stevenson entered the service under an agreement to receive their discharge at the end of the war in that country, if it should then be a part of the United States, and that they should not have a claim to be brought home at the expense of the government, yet it is understood that many are anxious to return. The President has deemed it proper to offer facilities for returning to those who cannot be prevailed on to remain in California.

You will, on the receipt of this communication, discharge such of the volunteers in California as are willing to be there discharged, and retain in service such as are unwilling to take their discharge, until they can be conveniently sent to the United States. The authority to retain them is conferred by a joint resolution of Congress passed the 16th day of June last, with a copy of which you are herewith furnished. The Quartermaster General will be directed to furnish such of the volunteers as insist on returning to their homes with the means of doing so. If the navy now in the Pacific shall have the means of bringing them home, directions will be given for that purpose.

Under a late law of Congress, the men, when discharged, will be entitled to three months' extra pay. Herewith instructions will be sent out to the paymaster to make such payments to them. The soldiers who have been employed in California will also be entitled to a bounty in land. Congress will undoubtedly make provision that the lands may be located in California, should the soldiers desire it; but this cannot be done immediately, because our land system has not yet been put in operation in that Territory. It will be necessary that the certificates or warrants for lands should be issued here. The soldiers will be informed what is necessary to be done in order to procure their certificates for land by the papers herewith enclosed from the Pension office. You are desired to have the information communicated to them.

Orders have been issued from the Adjutant General's office for your guidance in military matters. The general duties of the officer in chief command of the United States military force in California are, to protect and defend this Territory, now a part of the United States, from foreign invasion, and to secure its internal tranquillity.

The views of the President in relation to the civil government of California are clearly presented in a letter from Mr. Buchanan, Secretary of State, to Mr. Voorhies, the agent of the Post Office Department, dated the 7th instant, who is charged with making these views known to the people of that Territory. You are herewith furnished with a copy of that letter, and will, in case Mr. Voorhies shall not have arrived in California and made its contents known to the people, cause it to be published and extensively circulated throughout the Territory. The general positions therein maintained are, that at the conclusion of the treaty of peace between the United States and Mexico, the military government which was established in California under the laws of war ceased to derive its authority from this source of power; but the termination of the war left an existing government—a government *de facto*—in full operation; and this will continue, with the presumed consent of the people, until Congress, which has full and exclusive power under the constitution to organize governments for Territories, shall provide a government for them. The consent of the people is irresistibly inferred from the fact that no civilized community could possibly desire to abrogate an existing government, when the alternative presented would be to place them in a state of anarchy, beyond the protection of all law, and reduce them to the unhappy necessity of submitting to the dominion of the strongest. But the government *de facto* can of course exercise no powers inconsistent with the provisions of the constitution of the United States, which is the supreme law for all the States and Territories of our Union. For this reason, no import duties can be levied in California on articles the growth, produce, or manufacture of any State or Territory of the United States; and no such duties can be imposed in any part of the Union on the productions of California; nor can duties be charged on such foreign productions as have already paid duties in any port of the United States. The views of your government on this point are fully presented in a circular from the Secretary of the Treasury to collectors and officers of the customs, dated the 7th instant, a copy of which is herewith sent to you. This you are also requested to make known to the people of California.

Congress will be in session within sixty days, and their attention will be at once directed by the President to the subject of providing an adequate civil government for this Territory; and it is reasonable to expect that such provision will be made before this communication can be received by you. In the mean time, it will be the duty of the commander of our military force to recognise the present government *de facto*, to respect the officers of it, and to lend the aid of the military power to protect the rights of persons and property of the inhabitants of the Territory. Though he has not the right to change or modify the existing civil government, it will be his duty to regard it as an existing government until it is changed by competent authority. He is directed to quiet any uneasiness which may arise in the minds of the people on account of their present anomalous state, by assurances that the Executive of the United States will do what appertains to him to remedy any inconveniences which they may now experience, to secure their rights, and to extend to them in the amplest manner all the benefits of our political institutions. No doubt that upon such assurances they will remain quiet, under the existing state of things, until the proper authority shall have time to interpose and provide them with a new civil organization, securing to them the advantages of a liberal territorial government, with such encouragements as will facilitate the settlement and promote the prosperity of California.

Great difficulty and embarrassment have been here experienced in regard to the expenses and the payment of the battalion which was organized in California. No muster-rolls have been transmitted to Washington; and without them, and without an account of payments made in California, it is impossible to settle the claims presented to the department by the officers and men who served in that corps. It is represented that there are muster-rolls in California. You are desired to cause them to be transmitted as expeditiously as practicable to the Adjutant General here, with such other information as you may be able to obtain in relation to payments and expenses on account of this battalion.

Very respectfully, your obedient servant,
W. L. MARCY, *Secretary of War.*

Colonel R. B. MASON,
Commanding United States forces in California.

WASHINGTON, *October* 10, 1848.

SIR: You will receive with this a copy of the order which has been issued by direction of the President, forming into a third military geographical division the territories of the United States lying beyond the Rocky mountains and along the Pacific. This only modifies, but does not supersede, the provisions of order No. 49. The condition of things in those distant territories, it was apprehended, might require a junction and co-operation of the troops in the two departments No 10 and No. 11; but, without the modification of the general order No. 49, such junction and co-operation could not be effected without orders from Washington; and the length of time which it would require to communicate with general headquarters and receive instructions therefrom might and probably would prove, on a critical emergency, highly detrimental to the public service. It is not proposed, at present at least, to make any further change than to give to the senior in rank of the officers commanding the departments the right to supervise and exercise general command in the division.

The President has determined to assign you to command, according to your brevet rank—the assignment to take effect when you relieve Colonel Mason. The order for this purpose will be sent to you with the instructions with which you will be furnished. Whether your command in California will be such as will entitle you, under the existing laws, to the pay of a brigadier general, is yet under consideration. I shall be able, I trust, to furnish you with the views of the department on this point before your departure from the United States.

Very respectfully, your obedient servant,
W. L. MARCY, *Secretary of War.*

Brev. Brig. Gen. BENNET RILEY, *New York.*

WAR DEPARTMENT,
Washington, October 12, 1848.

SIR: Commodore Jones is directed to take a supply of arms and ammunition from California to Oregon. You will deliver to him such quantity as he may require in the present emergency for that Territory.

Very respectfully, your obedient servant,
W. L. MARCY, *Secretary of War.*

Colonel R. B. MASON,
Commanding United States forces in California.

WAR DEPARTMENT,
Washington, October 12, 1848.

SIR: The enclosed despatch to Colonel Mason is left unsealed for your perusal. Duplicates having been sent him by way of Mazatlan and Santa Fe, they will probably be received long before you reach Monterey. You are requested, however, to present this copy to him; and, after you have relieved him from command, it will be turned over to you, as a matter of course, as instructions for your guidance.

Very respectfully, your obedient servant,
W. L. MARCY, *Secretary of War.*

Brev. Brig. Gen. BENNET RILEY,
United States Army.

WAR DEPARTMENT,
Washington, October 13, 1848.

SIR: In compliance with your request of the 10th instant, I have the honor to forward you the following books, for the use of the commander of the land forces in California, viz:

Kent's Commentaries, 4 volumes.
Blackstone's Commentaries, 2 volumes.
Senate document No. 52, containing copy of the recent treaty with Mexico, &c.
Wheaton's Elements of International Law, 1 volume.
Fremont's First and Second Expeditions, in 1 volume.
Emory's Journal, 1 volume.

Copies of the Constitution of the United States and of the several States cannot now be found in a form convenient for transmission.

Very respectfully, your obedient servant,
W. L. MARCY,
Secretary of War.

General BENNET RILEY,
New York city.

WAR DEPARTMENT,
Washington, October 13, 1848.

SIR: After a consultation with the Attorney General as to the true construction of the act of Congress in relation to the regimental quartermasters, it has been determined that they are not affected by the 5th section of the act of the 11th February, 1847, and that each regiment may have one as well since as before the termination of the war with Mexico.

Very respectfully, your obedient servant,
W. L. MARCY,
Secretary of War.

Brevet Brig. Gen. BENNET RILEY.

WAR DEPARTMENT,
Washington, November 15, 1848.

SIR: By direction of the President, you are hereby assigned, under and by virtue of your rank of brevet brigadier general of the army of the United States, to the command of the third geographical or Pacific division, and will proceed by way of New Orleans, thence to Chagres and across the isthmus of Panama, to California, and assume the command of the said division.

You will establish your headquarters either in California or Oregon, and change them, from time to time, as the exigencies of the public service may require.

Besides the general duties of defending the Territories of California and Oregon, and of preserving peace and protecting the inhabitants from Indian depredations, you will carry out the orders and instructions contained in the letter from this department to Colonel R. B. Mason, a copy of which you are herewith furnished, and such other orders and instructions as you may receive from your government. On arriving in California, you will lose no time in ascertaining the condition of Oregon; and, if not well assured that the Indian disturbances therein have ceased, you will take the earliest and most efficient measures to render the people of Oregon the necessary assistance, so far as is in your power, to repress the Indian hostilities, and afford them complete protection and security.

Very respectfully, your obedient servant,

W. L. MARCY,
Secretary of War.

Brevet Maj. Gen. PERSIFOR F. SMITH,
  United States Army, Washington, D. C.

By direction of the President of the United States, a joint commission of navy and engineer officers has been constituted for the purpose of making an examination of the coast of the United States lying upon the Pacific ocean, with reference to points of defence and occupation for the security and accommodation of trade and commerce, and for military and naval purposes.

The commission—composed of Major J. L. Smith, (colonel by brevet,) Major Cornelius A. Ogden, and Lieutenant Danville Leadbetter, of the corps of engineers, on the part of the army; and Commander Lewis M. Goldsborough, Commander G. J. Van Brunt, and Lieutenant Simon F. Blunt, on the part the navy—will proceed as they may be ordered, and without delay explore the whole extent thereof within the limits of the United States, with a view—

1. To ascertain what harbors, roadsteads, rivers, sounds, &c., will need defence by fortifications and other means.

In relation to this subject, the commissioners will specify in their report the several positions which they deem it necessary to occupy by military defences in each of the harbors, roadsteads, &c., designating such fortifications, if any, as may be of a temporary nature. They will maturely consider the order in which the several parts of the system of defence should be brought to completion—giving a statement of the proposed works, arranged in three classes, according to the order of importance or need: the first class consisting of fortifications, to be erected with the least delay practicable; the second class, of works necessary to a good defence, but of less urgency; the third class, of defences that may be deferred, without serious danger, till the objects to be covered shall have expanded into an importance likely to provoke the cupidity of an enemy. Within each class, moreover, the respective works will be arranged among themselves in the order of importance as to time.

It is not expected that the commission will be able, in their first report, to offer plans for the military defences they may deem necessary, much less that they can make detailed estimates of the probable cost of each or any; still it is hoped they may be able to give, as to the first class of works, approximate estimates, which would be of equal service to the government. The circumstances of the locality and the value of the point to be covered will generally enable them to decide that a fort must be large and strong, or that it need be only of moderate size and strength, or that it may be small and of simple and cheap construction; and it is expected that considerations of this nature may enable the report to convey information sufficiently definitive as to the expense to which the government must go in the first instance, and for the first few years.

The commission will also take into consideration, and report particularly upon, the means of constructing the proposed defensive works, particularly those of the first class; that is to say, they will endeavor to ascertain whether suitable materials can be procured in the neighborhood of the works respectively, and what will be the best sources of supply of such means as are not to be found at hand.

They will, moreover, look particularly into the various modes of supplying labor to these constructions, and will make it part of their duty to present, for the information and consideration of the government, such a project for the prosecution of labor on the fortifications recommended to be first undertaken as they shall deem best adapted to the circumstances. Within the means would fall any idea of transporting from the United States mechanics and laborers, organized as a military body, to be returned to this part of the country on the expiration of the term of enlistment, or to be discharged upon that coast, with grants of land, in order to their becoming settlers. Should means of this nature be regarded by the board as necessary or expedient, they will give particular attention to the details of the process.

2. The commission will take into view, in the second place, the subject of immediate or early occupation of harbors and military posts, for the purpose of fixing the authority of the government over the newly-acquired territory and along the coast, maintaining tranquillity, and securing a free and safe interior and coastwise communication. They will go into all details necessary to elucidate their views, as to the places to be thus occupied; the strength and composition of the garrisons; the nature and position of any temporary defence that may be thought necessary to throw up in the first instance; the source and channels of supply and reinforcement—presenting a particular estimate of the expense to be incurred by such occupation, over and above the cost of pay, subsistence, clothing, and other ordinary and necessary cost of troops.

This view will embrace, of course, all existing posts.

3. The commission will, in the third place, consider the question of establishing upon the Pacific coast or islands a place or places of depot, rendezvous, and repair, for the navy, as connected with conditions of security from attacks by land or naval forces, or by both, for deposite of stores, and for repairs and fitting out ships of war.

Entire security to an establishment of this nature, upon a coast so distant and thinly peopled, and where, consequently, reliance must depend mainly on inherent strength, will probably in all cases involve the use of fortifications to some extent, greater or less, according to local circumstances. In other words, naval strength alone may not be a security against all the dangers to which such establishments must for many years remain exposed.

On the one hand, there should be taken into consideration the wants of the naval service, as regards local accommodation; facility of access and egress; certainty and ease of supply and relief; the influence of position on a vigilant and effective watch over the interests and safety of trade and commerce; security to be derived from means exclusively naval, &c., &c.: while, on the other, there must be duly weighed the strength to be derived from position, mutual support, and the art of fortification.

It is obvious that the selection of points for defensive works, and the other investigations enjoined under the first branch of duties of the commission, must be subject to the considerations arising under the present head; because the planting of a naval establishment in any port will at once greatly enhance the importance of the trust confided to the fortifications of that harbor. In like manner, it is probable that the views of the commission as to the places to be forthwith occupied will be influenced by the necessity or advantage of having, at an early day, a convenient place of resort for our cruisers on that ocean.

If it be in the power of the commission, they will hand in estimates of expenses which must unavoidably be incurred in the commencement of any such naval establishment, or preparatory thereto. Such estimates, although merely approximate, would be of great service to the government.

The commission, while on this part of their duty, will carefully study the means of that country as to naval supplies of all kinds—their sources and amounts, and the mode of supply. Among these, coal, or other fuel, for steamers, will demand special attention.

4. The commission are requested to devote a portion of their examination and report to the subject of communication along that coast by vessels carrying the mail—steamers or others; designating the places to be touched for delivery of letters, for refreshment, repairs, or supplies; and communicating all information they can collect bearing upon that important service.

5. It is directed that the commission, besides stating, in the body of their report, what surveys, for military or naval purposes, general or particular, will be wanted in reference to the subjects of their examination, will make, in a separate communication, a specific call for each survey, arranging them severally in the order of their importance, as to time, and giving a memorandum for each, which will suffice as instructions for the complete execution thereof.

6. The Secretary of the Treasury has notified the War Department of his having made arrangements for the immediate commencement of the survey of the western coast, and for the establishment there of agencies intrusted with the placing of light-houses, beacons, buoys, landmarks, &c. He has, moreover, kindly proposed, in case the survey at an early day of particular portions of the coast or harbors be deemed desirable, to give the necessary directions, so far as they will not interfere with what is deemed essential to the purposes of his department. In reply to this communication, it was stated that the commission would, in consequence, be instructed to avail themselves, in the course of their examination, and afterwards in preparing their report, of any useful information that the persons acting under the authority of the Treasury Department may have collected, in surveys or otherwise, and may make accessible; that valuable information may no doubt be thus afforded, as had been experienced on several occasions of like aid given by the coast survey to the system of defence on the Atlantic coast; and that, if the first labors of the coast-surveying parties should be applied to such harbors as afford the best

places of resort and shelter to navigation, material aid might thereby be given to the investigation of this commission, in every case where these surveys shall have been somewhat advanced before their arrival. The commission will accordingly, in conformity with the spirit of this correspondence, take the steps necessary to derive, in this important public duty, every advantage from these obliging offers of the Secretary of the Treasury.

To give the greatest efficiency to the joint board, and to guard against the possibility of any misunderstanding as to the principle of their association and the rules of proceeding on the part of the officers composing the commission, the following instructions are given, by order of the President:

1st. The relative position or place of precedence of the army and navy officers composing the board, as well as the authority such precedence confers, to be determined by the regulations established by the Secretaries of War and Navy, with the approbation of the President of the United States. They are in the words following:

"The military officers of the land and sea services of the United States shall rank together as follows:

"1. A lieutenant of the navy with captains of the army.

"2. A master commandant with majors.

"3. A captain of the navy, from the date of his commission, with lieutenant colonels;

"4. Five years thereafter, with colonels;

"5. Ten years thereafter, with brigadier generals; and

"6. Fifteen years after the date of his commission, with major generals.

"But, should there be created in the navy the rank of rear admiral, then such rank only shall be considered equal to that of major general.

"Nothing in the preceding paragraph shall authorize a land officer to command any United States vessel or navy yard, nor any sea officer to command any part of the army on land; neither shall an officer of the one service have a right to *demand* any compliment, on the score of rank, from an officer of the other service.

"Land troops *serving* on board a United States vessel as marines shall be subject to the orders of the sea officer in command thereof. Other land troops, embarked on board such vessel for transportation merely, will be considered, in respect to the naval commanders, as passengers—subject, nevertheless, to the internal regulations of the vessels."

2d. The senior in precedence shall preside at the meetings of the board; but, in case of his sickness or absence, the one next in precedence shall do so. If both these officers be prevented from serving, then the third in precedence shall preside; and so on with regard to the rest.

3d. In the deliberations of the board, the voice of any one member is to be regarded as equal, in every respect, to that of any other member.

4th. Every subject or point presented to the board for its action shall be decided by a majority of the votes of the members present; and, in case of a tie vote on any question, it is to be considered as lost for the time being, or until subsequent reflection induce an affirmative decision.

5th. All the duties to be discharged, or movements made, either by the board, collectively, or by its members, in part or individually, are to be determined and directed by the decision of the board itself.

6th. A regular journal is to be kept of the proceedings of the board, in which, if anything be entered that is deemed objectionable by a majority of the members, it is to be forthwith erased. The journal is to be at all times subject to the inspection of any member of the board; but nothing is to be copied from it, nor from any record, drawing, plan, paper, calculation, &c., &c., pertaining to the board, for either public circulation or private disposition, unless the sanction of a majority of the members be previously obtained, and the said publication or disposition be approved by the Secretaries of War and of the Navy.

7th. Should any member or members, who may have voted in the minority on any question, wish to present to the government his or their reasons for so voting, he or they shall be allowed to do so in a separate paper, to be transmitted with the report of the board.

8th. All reports of the board to the government, or public communications of any sort in behalf of the board, are to receive the sanction of a majority of its members; and to all such reports or communications, dissenting members may append their reasons for non-concurrence.

9th. The senior in precedence of the members present, and not disabled from duty, may assemble the board, for purposes of business, whenever he may think fit; but the adjournment of every sitting of the board is to be decided by vote. Also, whenever as many as three of the members may express to the senior in precedence, acting, their desire for a meeting of the board, it shall be incumbent upon him to call such meeting forthwith, or without unnecessary delay.

10th. Should experience develop the necessity or advantage of prescribed rules relative to the order to be observed at meetings of the board—the conduct of details, the apportionment of duties, &c., &c.—the same may be established by the sense of the board, provided they do not obviously conflict with the purport or spirit of the above.

The board will be expected, from time to time, as opportunity may offer, to make succinct reports to the War and Navy Departments of their progress in execution of this order.

W. L. MARCY,
Secretary of War.

WAR DEPARTMENT, *November* 30, 1848.

J. Y. MASON,
Secretary of the Navy.

NAVY DEPARTMENT, *November* 30, 1848.

WAR DEPARTMENT,
Washington, April 3, 1849.

SIR: Your despatch from Mazatlan, dated the 15th of February last, has just been received.

The want of information concerning the internal condition of California at the present time almost excludes the idea that any special instructions can be given to you applicable to the emergencies existing or that may exist there. The President relies with great confidence on your ability and judgment to meet such emergencies when they arise.

Touching the internal regulations of California, it is presumed that a government *de facto* remains or has been established in it; that it rests on the consent of the inhabitants under it; and that its chief authority is exercised for the protection and security of the rights of persons and property. California, being a part of the territory of the United States, must be regarded as subject to the constitution and all laws made in pursuance thereof; and hence any regulation in opposition to them will be considered as having no binding effect. With this limitation, such a government will be respected and aided by you in the exercise of its functions.

The defence of the Territory against foreign invasion, and the preservation of internal tranquillity from civil commotion, will be objects of your care, and may require the exercise of your authority.

The duty of regarding the obligations of the treaty lately concluded with the republic of Mexico is now superadded, especially those provisions which relate to the time when the resident Mexicans are required to make their election of citizenship, and others who may choose to remove with their property beyond the limits of the United States into Mexico. The promise to incorporate the first class into the Union, with all its attendant privileges and blessings, may, and doubtless will, be a subject of deep concern to Congress, which alone can admit them as a component part of our confederacy. Your observation and intercourse will furnish ample opportunities of knowing their probable number, habits of life, and capability to receive and maintain our republican institutions.

The plan of establishing an independent government in California cannot be sanctioned, no matter from what source it may come. The Territory belongs to the United States, and should be defended against all attempts to weaken or overthrow their authority. Already have the revenue laws and those pertaining to the post office been extended over them, and appropriate officers appointed to execute them. An independent government, as contemplated by your letter, would either suspend or set aside the force of these laws and the functions of these officers. The President cannot permit the exercise of any authority in conflict with that which he is bound to maintain, by taking care that the laws be faithfully executed.

Desertions from the army in California appear to be without remedy. In other localities, where the temptation is not so great as in California, desertions are frequently occurring. Without the pride of the soldier in his corps has been awakened, the usual restraints and penalties have proved ineffectual. The proposed separation of detachments, to be sent forward as far as may be practicable, consistently with the public service, from the scene of attraction, as well as all other legal measures of precaution, in preserving the efficiency of the forces under your command, cannot fail to meet the approval of this department.

It is believed that the trespasses by gathering and carrying away gold from "the placers" on the tributaries of the Sacramento river have been committed, in a great measure, by foreigners on lands that are claimed by or are in the occupancy of Indians. The necessary control which the United States exercise over all savage tribes in their territory cannot be diminished or exposed to the hazard of diminution by permitting foreigners to enjoy an unrestricted intercourse with them. The act of Congress, passed in 1834, "to regulate trade and intercourse with the Indian tribes and preserve peace on the frontiers," was intended to prevent, in part, the evils supposed to arise from foreign influence. The form of the remedy will appear sufficiently clear by an examination of the several provisions of this act.

By a recent act of Congress, the Bureau of Indian Affairs has been separated from this department and placed under the control of the Secretary of the Interior. The proper officers for the management of Indian affairs in California have been appointed by that department, who will repair with convenient despatch to the scene of their duties. With them you will consult and co-operate in all matters relating to cases requiring joint action.

Your attention is directed to a copy of a communication lately received at this department from the Secretary of State, in which the resident consul of Peru, at Washington, has complained of certain acts of those charged with the collection of the customs at San Francisco, in June last. A copy of a communication submitted by Mr. Osma is herewith transmitted, and will furnish the necessary data for the inquiry into the cause and extent of the alleged wrong. The relation that California then occupied to the United States, as a conquered province, and subjected to military powers, presents a case fit for your inquiry. The result you will communicate to this department, to the end that the Secretary of State may reply definitely to the Peruvian consul.

Very respectfully, your obedient servant,
GEO. W. CRAWFORD,
Secretary of War.

Gen. Persifor F. Smith, *U. S. A.*,
Commanding Pacific Division, California.

War Department,
Washington, April 4, 1849.

Sir: The bearer hereof, Mr. John Wilson, has been appointed Indian agent for California. I take pleasure in introducing him to you as a gentleman of worth and respectability, whose intercourse with you personally, as well as officially, I doubt not, will be of an agreeable character.

Very respectfully, your obedient servant,
GEO. W. CRAWFORD.

Brevet Major Gen. P. F. Smith,
United States Army, California.

War Department,
Washington, June 26, 1849.

Sir: The latest despatch received from the Pacific is dated the 1st ultimo. Under the belief that Brevet Major General Smith will be absent on the arrival of this communication, I have addressed it to you, as the military commander of the tenth department.

From all the information derived from your department, it is manifest that your command will be surrounded by temptations to insubordination and desertion which will be most difficult to resist. It has heretofore been suggested that the forces should be kept separated from the mines, as far as the public service would justify; and yet it seems manifestly proper that a military force should be stationed near the mines, to quell those occasional disturbances which may arise in that region, where such an immense population is flocking, and the rights of property and person are so insecure. To preserve the tranquillity of the Territory, and repel Indian and other invasion, will be the chief duties of your command.

In connexion with this subject, it is deemed proper that I should say that any plan or scheme calculated to weaken the authority of the United States in the Territory will not be tolerated. Whatever of force may be levied or used to put aside this authority will be resisted.

The revenue and post office laws of the United States have been extended over California; so, also, it is believed that the act of Congress, of 1834, " to regulate trade and intercourse with the Indians," is of force there.

It is equally true, that all laws existing and of force in California at the period of the conquest are still operative, with the limitation that they are not repugnant to the constitution and laws of the United States. In my opinion, these constitute the whole code of laws now in force in California. I should add, that this opinion does not infringe on the rights of communities to make necessary regulations for the police and security of persons and property. Such regulations must necessarily be temporary, as they are presumed to be voluntary, and designed to meet emergencies and difficulties which the sovereign power will take the earliest occasion to remove.

The United States are doubly bound to admit the newly-acquired Territories—California and New Mexico—into the confederacy of the States. It is not necessary to inquire whether the first step, in view of the proposed incorporation, should be taken by the people of the Territories or by the invitation of Congress. In either case, the final judgment rests with Congress. Hence, the opinion is advanced that it is the right of the people of California to assemble by their delegates and adopt a form of government, which, if approved by Congress, may lead to their admission into the federal Union as one of the confederated States.

The Adjutant General has received the necessary instructions to communicate with you on the subjects embraced in General Smith's and your despatches.

I am, very respectfully, your obedient servant,
GEO. W. CRAWFORD,
Secretary of War.

Bt. Brig. Gen. BENNET RILEY,
Monterey, California.

WAR DEPARTMENT,
Washington, July 13, 1849.

SIR: It has been deemed proper to despatch William Carey Jones, esq., as confidential agent of the government, to California, with a view to obtain accurate and full information respecting grants or alleged titles to lands in the territories recently acquired from Mexico; and I have therefore to request that you will extend him such facilities as may be in your power, to aid him in obtaining access to the archives, in prosecuting his investigations, and accomplishing the objects contemplated by his appointment.

Very respectfully, your obedient servant,
GEO. W. CRAWFORD,
Secretary of War.

To the OFFICER COMMANDING IN CALIFORNIA.

WAR DEPARTMENT,
Washington, August 10, 1849.

SIR: I have received your letter of the 7th instant, requesting tha compensation be made to yourself and Brevet Captain Halleck for civil services in California, and also submitting a question with regard to the disposition to be made of the profits of the specimens of gold purchased by your order and converted into coin by this department.

The claim to compensation by yourself and Captain Halleck for services in connexion with the collecting, safe-keeping, and accounting for the revenue levied as military contributions, will be with others submitted to the President, under the act of 3d March last in relation to that subject. Neither the President nor the department, so far as I am aware, is authorized to entertain claims for compensation for any other extra services: Congress only could provide for them.

I have fully considered the question with regard to the disposition to be made of the profits of the gold sent by you to the War Department. The gold was purchased by your order with public money, to accompany an official despatch, in illustration of a subject to which it relates, and was received and treated as public property before it was ascertained whether its value would be more or less than the cost. Being thus considered public property by both parties, it follows that its entire proceeds must be accounted for to the treasury, and for this purpose directions were given some time since. If, indeed, you were correct in stating that had any loss occurred you would have been charged with it, the case would be different, and such a liability on your part would entitle you to corresponding advantage; but I do not apprehend that under the circumstances any such liability attached, or that you could have been charged with the loss had the purchase turned out to be valueless when sent by the department to be tested at the mint.

Very respectfully, your obedient servant,
GEO. W. CRAWFORD,
Secretary of War.

Gen. R. B. MASON, *Washington city.*

WAR DEPARTMENT, *August* 24, 1849.

SIR: Your letters to the Adjutant General of the 11th and 19th June, together with copies of your military correspondence, have been received, and carefully considered.

The department is gratified to learn that the desertions among your command, though they still continue, are becoming less frequent; and it encourages the hope that by your judicious arrangements the evil will be greatly checked, if not entirely eradicated. The disposition you propose to make of the deserters who have been convicted and sentenced by courts-martial is approved; and they can be either sent to the Atlantic posts in our armed vessels returning from the Pacific, if arrangements to that effect can be made with the commander of the squadron, or they may be employed on the public works either in California or Oregon.

A further increase of troops in California, under the circumstances represented in your communication, is no doubt desirable; but the exigencies of the service in other quarters, more particularly in Florida and Texas, have weakened the means of the department to this end, and no assurance can be now given that additional troops will be speedily sent to you beyond what may be required to keep up the present companies to their legal establishment.

There should be a limit as to time in which the New York volunteers may avail themselves of the provisions of the instructions of this department in October, 1848. Such as may not already have signified their determination to return home will be precluded from doing so at the public expense.

Your application for topographical officers, and for additional medical officers, cannot be complied with. It appears, from information in the appropriate bureaus, that six topographical engineers are now in California, three of whom are engaged upon the boundary, and that one surgeon and seven assistant surgeons are also in that country, besides Acting Assistant Surgeon Booth, not yet discharged by you.

Your arrangements for the purpose of controlling the Indians and preventing unauthorized interference with them appear judicious; and it is hoped that the several positions of the troops, as indicated by you, will greatly contribute to preserve order and prevent future collisions. The department cannot too strongly urge the importance of so disposing your command as to be prepared promptly to check any efforts of this kind which may be likely to take place between the whites and Indians, as well as to prevent, as far as possible, any combination between the different tribes for a hostile purpose.

Nor should I omit to state, that the Indians are placed in a state of pupilage to the general government by the constitution and the decisions of the Supreme Court. In my opinion, by the act of annexation the constitution was extended over the Territory of California, and became the supreme law in all cases to which its provisions are applicable. Indeed, a careful examination will show, that even in a Territory anomalously situated like California, a large mass of personal and political rights is secured and protected by the constitution.

In view of the exercise of the most important political right which appertains to the people of California—that of forming a constitution and asking admission into the Union of these States—this department has watched with great care and solicitude the steps already taken to effect these objects. Regarding your proclamation of the 3d June last as a notice intended, in part, to render popular action uniform in respect to the desired organization of California into a more perfect government, it is seen with great satisfaction that your propositions had been accepted with great cheerfulness and alacrity, except in a few instances, where it is supposed selfish and unpatriotic motives prevailed.

I am, very respectfully, your obedient servant,
GEO. W. CRAWFORD, *Secretary of War.*
Brevet Brigadier General RILEY,
　　Monterey, California.

WAR DEPARTMENT,
Washington, November 12, 1849.

SIR: By a recent order from general headquarters, I am informed that, having reported for duty, you have been ordered to your regiment in

New Mexico. I desire, before you proceed to join your command, that you will do me the favor to pass through or come to Washington, where I hope to have an interview with you.

Your obedient servant,
GEO. W. CRAWFORD,
Secretary of War.

Brevet Lieut. Col. GEORGE A. MCCALL,
U. S. A., Philadelphia.

WAR DEPARTMENT,
Washington, November 19, 1849.

SIR: As you are about to join your regiment, now on duty in New Mexico, it has occurred to me as proper to make some observations on the peculiar condition of that and another Territory of the United States.

Since the annexation, these Territories, in respect to their civil governments, have in a great measure depended on the officers of the army there in command—a duty it is considered as falling beyond their appropriate spheres of action, and to be relieved from which cannot be more desired by them than by this department. This condition has arisen from the omission of Congress to provide suitable governments; and in regard to the future, there is reason to believe that the difficulties of the past are still to be encountered. In every possible aspect, it is important both to New Mexico and the United States that these embarrassments should be quickly removed.

It is not doubted that the people of New Mexico desire and want a government organized with all proper functions for the protection and security of their persons and property.

The question readily occurs, how that government can be supplied? I have already adverted to past and still existing difficulties, that have retarded, and may continue to retard, the action of the United States in respect to this necessary and first want. To remove it may, in some degree, be part of the duty of the officers of the army, on whom, under the necessities of the case, has been devolved a partial participation in their civil affairs. It is therefore deemed proper that I should say, that it is not believed that the people of New Mexico are required to await the movements of the federal government in relation to the plan of a government proper for the regulation of their own internal concerns.

The constitution of the United States and the late treaty with Mexico guaranty their admission into the Union of our States, subject only to the judgment of Congress. Should the people of New Mexico wish to take any steps towards this object, so important and necessary to themselves, it will be your duty, and the duty of others with whom you are associated, not to thwart but advance their wishes. It is their right to appear before Congress and ask for admission into the Union.

Other and complicated questions may arise, which are considered as merged in this essential right of these people, and for the decision of which we must look beyond the authority of the Executive.

It will be instructive and probably necessary information, when the people of New Mexico form a constitution and seek admission into the confederacy of the States, to have your observation and views on their probable numbers, habits, customs, and pursuits of life.

I have the honor to be, very respectfully, your obedient servant,
GEO. W. CRAWFORD,
Secretary of War.
Brevet Lieut. Col. GEORGE A. MCCALL,
Philadelphia, Pennsylvania.

WAR DEPARTMENT,
Washington, November 28, 1849.

SIR: The Adjutant General has submitted to this department your letter of the 1st of October, on the subject of the civil affairs of California, in which you propose, should it be the wish of the people to put the new government into operation without waiting the action of Congress, to surrender your civil powers into the hands of the new executive of that Territory, unless specially ordered to the contrary. As the arrangement contemplated by you may already have been made, any instructions from this department contrary to your views on the subject might militate against the peace and quiet of the community, and be productive of evil. The first consideration is a due observance of law and order; and this, it is hoped and believed, will be attained under the new state of things. It is not doubted that Congress will either recognise the constitution which it is supposed the people of California have formed and probably adopted, or provide a territorial government for them. In either event, the officers of the army will be relieved of the necessity of participating in civil matters, so inconsistent with their appropriate public duties, and under circumstances so embarrassing, by the absence of legislative authority to guide and control.

In respect to the disposition to be made of the civil funds in your hands derived from collections, a part of which has been used in defraying the expenses of the government, whatever opinions may be entertained as to the propriety of their transfer to the executive authority of the Territory, it is deemed proper, as these funds were collected through the agency of the general government, that they should be held subject to the final action of Congress. To that end, therefore, you will cause them to be placed in safe-keeping of the proper officers of the Treasury Department, and submit to this department an account, with vouchers, of such disbursement as may have been made by you from the funds collected.

Very respectfully, your obedient servant,
GEO. W. CRAWFORD,
Secretary of War.
Brevet Brigadier General B. RILEY,
Commanding 10*th Department, Monterey, California.*

WAR DEPARTMENT,
Washington, December 11, 1849.

SIR: Your letter of the 1st ultimo has been received.

In calling attention, in my letter of the 24th of August, to the number of topographical and medical officers in California, it was intended to show that the details from those branches of the staff for service in that Territory were as large as could at that time be made with a proper regard to the wants of the service in other quarters; and it was believed that the three topographical officers then in California, and not attached to the boundary commission, would be sufficient for the reconnoissance contemplated in general orders No. 49 of 1848. It is still thought that this number of officers, properly distributed, will fulfil the requirements of your letter on this subject; at least, they are as many as can at this time be spared from other pressing duties. In consequence of the death of Captain Warner, another officer of that corps has been ordered to report to you. Instructions have also been given for two additional medical officers to repair to your headquarters for service in California.

It having been determined to relieve Brevet Major Emory from duty with the boundary commission, the necessary orders will be given for such relief, to take effect as soon as that officer shall have completed his calculations of the survey of the line between the Pacific and the junction of the Colorado and Gila rivers, so as to obtain the action of the commission thereon, when he will turn over the command of the escort to the senior officer of the line with it. Brevet Major Emory will be replaced in his duties with the commission by Brevet Lieutenant Colonel McClellan, of the same corps.

I transmit herewith a copy of my letter to you of the 28th ultimo, on the subject of the disposition to be made of the civil funds in your hands.

Very respectfully, your obedient servant,
GEO. W. CRAWFORD,
Secretary of War.

Brevet Brig. Gen. BENNET RILEY,
Commanding 10th Military Dept., Monterey, California.

List of reports from General Kearny.

1847, January 14. Report.
           16. Report with enclosures.
    March 15. Report.
    April 26. Correspondence to this date.
           28. Report with general order.
    May 1. Report with civil correspondence.
           13. Report.
           30. Report with enclosures.
           31. Report with enclosures.

HEADQUARTERS ARMY OF THE WEST,
Ciudad de los Angeles, U. California, January 14, 1847.

SIR: This morning, Lieutenant Colonel Frémont, of the regiment of mounted riflemen, reached here with 400 volunteers from the Sacramento. The enemy capitulated with him yesterday, near San Fernando, agreeing to lay down their arms; and we have now the prospect of having peace and quietness in this country, which I hope may not be interrupted again.

I have not yet received any information of the troops which were to come from New York, nor of those to follow me from New Mexico, but presume they will be here before long. On their arrival, I shall, agreeably to the instructions of the President of the United States, have the management of affairs in this country, and will endeavor to carry out his views in relation to it.

Very respectfully, your obedient servant,
S. W. KEARNY, *Brigadier General.*
Brigadier General R. JONES,
   Adjutant General United States Army.

HEADQUARTERS ARMY OF THE WEST,
Ciudad de los Angeles, January 16, 1847.

SIR: I enclose herewith a copy of two communications of this date: one from myself to Commodore R. F. Stockton, United States navy, on the subject of forming a civil government for California; the other, his reply to the same.

Very respectfully, your obedient servant,
S. W. KEARNY, *Brigadier General.*
Brigadier General R. JONES,
   Adjutant General United States Army, Washington.

HEADQUARTERS ARMY OF THE WEST,
Ciudad de los Angeles, January 16, 1847.

SIR: I am informed that you are now engaged in organizing a civil government, and appointing officers for it in this Territory. As this duty has been specially assigned to myself by orders of the President of the United States, conveyed in letters to me from the Secretary of War of June 3 and 18, 1846—the originals of which I gave to you on the 12th instant, which you returned to me on the 13th, and copies of which I furnished you with on the 24th December—I have to ask if you have any authority from the President, from the Secretary of the Navy, or from any other channel of the President, to form such government and make such appointments?

If you have such authority, and will show it to me, or furnish me with a certified copy of it, I will cheerfully acquiesce in what you are doing. If you have not such authority, I then demand that you cease all further proceeding relating to the formation of a civil government for this Territory, as I cannot recognise in you any right in assuming to perform duties confided to me by the President.

Very respectfully, your obedient servant,
S. W. KEARNY, *Brigadier General U. S. A.*
Commodore R. F. STOCKTON,
   United States Navy, Acting Governor of California.

A true copy:
A. S. TURNER, *Captain Dragoons.*

HEADQUARTERS, CIUDAD DE LOS ANGELES,
January 16, 1847.

SIR: In answer to your note, received this afternoon, I need say but little more than that which I communicated to you in a conversation at San Diego—that California was conquered and a civil government put into successful operation; that a copy of the laws made by me for the government of the Territory, and the names of the officers selected to see them faithfully executed, were transmitted to the President of the United States before your arrival in the Territory.

I will only add that I cannot do anything, nor desist from doing anything, nor alter anything, on your demand—which I will submit to the President, and ask for your recall. In the mean time, you will consider yourself suspended from the command of the United States forces in this place.

Faithfully, your obedient servant,
R. F. STOCKTON,
Commander-in-chief.

Brevet Brigadier General S. W. KEARNY.

A true copy:
A. S. TURNER, *Captain Dragoons.*

HEADQUARTERS 10TH MILITARY DEPARTMENT,
Monterey, California, March 15, 1847.

SIR: As the ship Savannah is getting ready to leave here for New York, I avail myself of the opportunity to write by her.

Accompanied by Captain Turner, 1st dragoons, and Lieutenant Warner, topographical engineers, I left San Diego on the 31st January, as I informed you I should do in my letter of the day previous; and reaching this post on the 8th of February, I was much gratified in finding the ship Independence, with Commodore Shubrick, and the ship Lexington, which had brought out Captain Tompkins's company 3d artillery.

On my showing to Commodore Shubrick my instructions from the War Department of June 3d and 18th, 1846, he was at once prepared to pay all proper respect to them; and, being at that time the commander-in-chief of the naval forces on this station, he acknowledged me as the head and commander of the troops in California, which Commodore Stockton and Lieutenant Colonel Fremont had hitherto refused. He then showed me the instructions to Commodore Sloat of July 12, from the Navy Department, received by the Lexington at Valparaiso on the 2d December, and which he had brought with him from there; and as they contained directions for Commodore Sloat to take charge of the civil affairs in California, I immediately told Commodore Shubrick that I cheerfully acquiesced, and was ready to afford him any assistance in my power. We agreed upon our separate duties, and I then went to the bay of San Francisco, taking with me Lieutenant Halleck, of the engineers, besides Captain Turner and Lieutenant Warner, when was made a reconnoissance of the bay, with a view to the selection of sites for fortifications, for the protection of the shipping in the harbor, and security of the land forces.

Colonel Mason, 1st dragoons, arrived at the bay February 12, with letters and instructions to me from Washington as late as November 5; and was accompanied by Lieutenant Watson, of the navy, with instructions to Commodore Shubrick. On my return here, and on my showing to Commodore S. my instructions, and seeing his, we deemed it advisable to inform the people in California at once of the President's instructions to us; and we jointly issued a circular on the 1st of March; and I, with his approval and that of Commodore Biddle, (who arrived on the 2d,) issued a proclamation on the 4th, (dated the 1st,) a copy of which papers in print is enclosed herewith.

Upon Commodore Biddle's arrival I had a full understanding with him relating to our duties; and I take pleasure here to acknowledge the great courtesy I have received from both these gentlemen, and to add that, so long as either continues in the command of the naval forces on this station, there is no possibility of any other than a cordial and harmonious co operation between us.

On the 2d instant I sent Captain Turner to the Ciudad de los Angeles, carrying with him department orders No. 2, and my letter to Lieutenant Colonel Fremont, both of March 1, a copy of which is enclosed. I have not heard of his arrival there.

On the 5th instant Colonel Stevenson, with three companies of his regiment, (the 7th New York volunteers,) arrived at the bay of San Francisco; on learning which, I issued orders No. 4, a copy of which is enclosed. The heavy ordnance and stores brought out by that regiment will be landed at San Francisco, and be protected by the command to be stationed there; that brought out by the Lexington is still on board of her in this harbor, as at present there is no place on shore where I am willing to trust it.

From the large amount of ordnance and stores sent to California by the department, I presume the territory will never be restored to Mexico; and it should not be. Should it be restored, Mexico could not possibly hold it three months. The people in the Territory (Californians as well as emigrants) would resist Mexican authority, and then would follow dissensions, quarrels, and fighting between them, till humanity would compel our government to interpose a strong arm to put a stop to such civil war, and to take the country again under her protection.

The Californians are now quiet, and I shall endeavor to keep them so by mild and gentle treatment. Had they received such treatment from the time our flag was hoisted here, in July last, I believe there would have been but little or no resistance on their part. They have been most cruelly and shamefully abused by our own people—by the volunteers (American emigrants) raised in this part of the country and on the Sacramento. Had they not resisted, they would have been unworthy the name of men. If the people remain quiet, and California continues under our flag, it will ere long be a bright star in our Union. The climate is pure and healthy—physicians meeting with no encouragement, as its inhabitants are never sick; the soil is rich, and there is much unsettled land that will admit of a dense population. California, with Oregon, is destined to supplant the Sandwich islands, and will furnish our 600 whaling vessels, and our 20,000 sailors in them, besides our navy and our troops, with their breadstuffs and most of the other articles they are to consume.

At present the population is small, most probably not exceeding 12,000, of which about one-fifth are emigrants. A very few years will add greatly to the latter class. Besides, there are about 15,000 Indians, nearly one-third being called Christian Indians, who speak the Spanish language; the remainder are the wild Indians, who live in the mountains, and subsist in a great measure on the horses and cattle they steal from the farms. The Christian Indians are the laborers and servants of the country, and are held, if not in bondage like our own slaves, at least very much like it.

For the preservation of the peace and quiet now so happily existing in California, and to protect the people from the Indians depredating on them, there should be kept in the Territory, for some years to come, about 1,000 soldiers; they should be enlisted expressly to serve here, as I suggested in my letter to you of the 16th September last. We can get no recruits here.

The bays of San Francisco, Monterey, and Diego afford excellent harbors, and they should be protected by permanent fortifications. I have directed the old Spanish fort at the entrance of the bay of San Francisco to be put in good order, and guns to be mounted there; it will be a barbette battery. Its position is a highly important one, as no vessel can enter without passing under its guns, the distance from it to the opposite shore being less than one mile; the work will cost but a few thousand dollars. There are other places in the bay where extensive fortifications should be erected, and which will cost much money; these will not be commenced till an appropriation is made, or orders received for it. The subject will be fully presented to you after the engineer officers have made a careful examination and report upon it.

I have not heard of Colonel Price and his Missouri regiment since I eft New Mexico, and presume he must have passed the winter there. I, of course, cannot know if he intends this spring to avail himself of the authority to come here which I gave him on the 2d of October last, a copy of which I furnished you.

I have to acknowledge the receipt by Colonel Mason of the following papers:

Letters from Secretary of War to General Kearny, September 12, with papers referred to.

Letter from Secretary of War to Colonel Stevenson, September 11.
Letter from Secretary of War to Colonel Stevenson, September 15.
Letter from General-in-chief to General Kearny, November 3.
Letter from Adjutant General to General Kearny, November 4.
Letter from Secretary of Navy to Commodore Shubrick, August 17.
Letter from Secretary of Navy to Commodore Stockton, November 5.
Circular of Secretary of War of October 15, and "general orders" Nos. 34, 43, 45, 48, 49.

Agreeably to directions in yours of November 4, I have numbered this letter 7 of this year: mine to you of January 12th would be No. 1; January 14, No. 2; January 16, No. 3; January 17, No. 4; January 23, No. 5; January 30, No. 6.

I enclose a copy of the rough notes of the journal of our march from New Mexico to California, kept by my ate aid-de-camp, Captain Johnston, 1st dragoons. When I receive the journal of the Mormon battalion, I will forward it to you. Lieutenant Emory, of the topographical engineers, having gone to Washington, will there prepare for your office his notes and map of the country passed over by us.

I enclose letter of March 14, from Captain Tompkins, 3d artillery, stating that he had "concluded to resign his commission in the army of the United States, and requesting its acceptance at the earliest convenient date;" and I recommend that he be gratified, on the close of the war.

Very respectfully, your obedient servant,
     S. W. KEARNY, *Brigadier General.*
Brigadier General R. JONES,
 Adjutant General United States Army, Washington.

HEADQUARTERS TENTH MILITARY DEPARTMENT,
Monterey, March 27, 1847.

SIR: You will proceed to the southern military district of this Territory, and inspect the troops in that quarter. You are hereby clothed with full authority to give such orders and instructions in that country, upon all matters whatever, both civil and military, as in your judgment you may think conducive to the public interest. You will then return to this place.

I am, sir, very respectfully, &c.,
     S. W. KEARNY,
 Brigadier General, and Governor of California.
Col. R. B. MASON,
 First Dragoons.

HEADQUARTERS TENTH MILITARY DEPARTMENT,
Monterey, California, March 28, 1847.

SIR: This will be handed to you by Colonel Mason, 1st dragoons, who goes to the southern military district clothed by me with full authority to give such orders and instructions upon all matters, both civil and military, in that section of country, as he may deem proper and necessary. Any instructions he may give to you will be considered as coming from myself.

I deem it proper to suggest to you, that, should there be at the pueblo any unsettled accounts or demands against the government, incurred by your orders or approval, which you may not have already authenticated and completed for the action of the disbursing officers, you at once do so, as it may be necessary for you to proceed from here to Washington city; and, should there be any of the party which accompanied you from Missouri still with you, and under pay from the Topographical Department, you will cause them to come to this place, that they may be returned home and discharged, and be of no further expense to the United States, unless they prefer being discharged at once in this country.

In twelve days after you have embarked the volunteers at San Pedro, I desire to see you in this place.

Very respectfully, your obedient servant,
     S. W. KEARNY,
 Brigadier General, and Governor of California.
Lieut. Col. J. C. FREMONT,
 Regiment of Mounted Riflemen,
  Com'g Bat'n Cal. Volunteers, Ciudad de los Angeles.

Monterey, California,
April 26, 1847.

Sir: In obedience to your instructions of the 27th March, directing me to proceed to the southern military district of this Territory for the purpose of inspecting the troops and looking into both the civil and military affairs in that quarter, and giving such orders and instructions as 1 might deem necessary, I have the honor to make the following report:

The battalion of Mormons, under Lieutenant Colonel Cooke, encamped near the Ciudad de los Angeles, as might be expected after their long and arduous march from Missouri, are in a miserable condition for the want of clothing; their arms and accoutrements are in good serviceable order; they are daily undergoing a course of instruction by Lieutenant Colonel Cooke, who exhibits a praiseworthy zeal in his efforts to perfect them in a knowledge of the drill and camp duties.

I saw the battalion go through the manual and the firings, without cartridges. They acquitted themselves with a good deal of credit. This battalion is in great want of musket flints and cartridges, having on hand only *thirty-one rounds*. Company " C," first dragoons, stationed at the Angeles, is inefficient for the want of horse equipage; their saddles and bridles are entirely worn out, and no material can be obtained in the country to repair them; their carbines, many of them, are much damaged by rough service, and the company are in want of a speedy supply of percussion caps, carbine and pistol cartridges. The horses that they have received from the late California battalion will fill up the company in point of numbers; but they, as well as those heretofore on hand, are the California horses, which a few days' active service soon knocks up. My letter to Captain Turner, acting assistant adjutant general, of the 10th instant, and its accompanying papers, will have informed you of my official acts at the Ciudad de los Angeles up to that date.

I failed to obtain from Lieutenant Colonel Fremont any record or papers of any description touching the civil affairs of the country during the time he claimed to be governor of California, and only received the papers, &c., mentioned in the accompanying list, marked A, purporting to be a few of the papers that he could then find of the California battalion of volunteers whilst under his command. The papers herewith, marked from 1 to 4, inclusive, is the correspondence between Lieutenant Colonel Fremont and myself on the subject of the records. Whilst at the Ciudad de los Angeles, I learned that the master or supercargo of certain vessels had been buying up the claims of individual members of the California battalion of volunteers on the United States government, as certified to by the staff officers of that corps, at a discount of about 30 per cent., for the purpose of paying custom-house dues at San Pedro. Upon making inquiry of Mr. Alexander, the custom-house officer at San Pedro, whom I fell in with at the Angeles, he informed me that he had been instructed by Colonel Fremont to receive such certificates, called "government payment," in payment of custom-house dues.

The paper marked B is the original order to Mr. Alexander to receive the above-mentioned certificates. Mr. Alexander has received, in accordance with said instructions, about seventeen hundred dollars of that kind of paper, in payment of duties at his port.

That it may more fully appear what is the character of the certificates given by the staff officers of the California battalion, so called—for the corps has refused to be mustered into service, and therefore have never been lawfully a corps in the pay of the United States—I have made a memorandum of some of the certificates in the hands of Mr. Alexander, which he has received in payment for duties, and some I copied in full. (See paper marked C.)

The Indians have been committing extensive depredations upon the persons and property of the citizens, both above and below the Ciudad de los Angeles. The papers marked D, E, and F, will show the steps I deemed it proper to take while in the south to check their invasion of the country. I herewith enclose the original order, marked G, from Lieutenant Colonel Fremont, of the 15th March, 1847, to Captain Richard Owens, of the California battalion of volunteers, directing him not to obey the order of any officer that did not emanate from him, Lieutenant Colonel Fremont, nor to turn over the public arms, &c , to any corps without his special order. I received from Lieutenant Colonel Cooke a copy of his letter of the 14th March to Lieutenant Colonel Frémont, the lieutenant colonel's reply thereto, dated on the next day, which I also enclose, marked H and I.

From the papers purporting to be a portion of the records of the battalion of California volunteers, put into my hands by Lieutenant Colonel Fremont, through his adjutant, I made a copy of some of his orders, &c., which is enclosed herewith, marked K.

The list marked L will show the amount of property pertaining to the quartermaster's department turned over by J. R. Snyder, quartermaster California battalion, to Lieutenant Davidson, 1st dragoons. There were other horses to be turned over, but which had not been delivered at the date of the said list.

I am, very respectfully, your obedient servant,
R. B. MASON,
Colonel 1st Dragoons.
Brig. Gen. S. W. KEARNY,
 U. S. Army, com'g 10th Military Department,
  and Governor of California.

CIUDAD DE LOS ANGELES, *April* 13, 1847.

SIR: I have the honor to be in receipt of your communication of last evening, requiring from me a list of civil appointments made by me in this Territory, and further demanding to be put in possession of such official records as I may have, civil or military.

In compliance with your order, I send by the hands of the former or late adjutant of the California battalion, Mr. R. N. Loker, the few papers pertaining to that battalion which I can at present find. These I request to be returned to me.

Such brief records of my official acts as governor of the Territory as were preserved by me have been forwarded to the United States.

My position here having been denounced as usurpation by General Kearny, I could not anticipate from him any call for these papers; and in requiring, myself, from the general government, means and authority to comply with my engagement, it became necessary that these and their objects should be thoroughly made known.

The permanent civil appointments made by me are two, viz: Don Santiago Arguillo to be collector of the customs for the port of San Diego; Don Pedro Carrillo to be collector of the customs for the port of Santa Barbara.

I am, very respectfully, your obedient servant,
         J. C. FREMONT,
        Lieut. Col. Rifle Regiment.

Col. R. B. MASON,
 First Dragoons.

      CIUDAD DE LOS ANGELES, *March* 21, 1847.

SIR: You are hereby ordered and permitted, in the case of F. Huttman, to receive government payments in payment of his custom-house dues.
     Very respectfully,
        J. C. FREMONT,
         Governor of California.
     By WM. H. RUSSELL,
         Secretary of State.

DAVID W. ALEXANDER,
 Collector of the port of San Diego.

N. B. Mr. Huttman will be entitled to the usual discount by prompt payment.
      W. H. R.
     For J. C. FREMONT, *Governor.*

      PUEBLO DE LOS ANGELES, *April* 12, 1847.

SIR: Be pleased to furnish me with a list of such civil appointments as you have made in this Territory, setting forth the names of the individuals appointed, to what office, and when.

I would prefer seeing myself, as I told you in conversation to-day, such of the official records as you have, civil and military, that I may judge whether they contain any information that may be useful to me, or influence me in the discharge of those duties with which General Kearny, the governor of the Territory, has charged me. I therefore desire that you submit the whole of them, civil and military, to me, early in the day to-morrow, as I am making efforts to leave here the next day for Monterey.

I am, very respectfully, your obedient servant,
         R. B. MASON,
        Colonel 1st Dragoons.

Lieutenant Colonel J. C. FREMONT,
 Mounted Riflemen.

   HEADQUARTERS TENTH MILITARY DEPARTMENT,
     Monterey, California, April 28, 1847.

SIR: Paymaster Rich arrived here on the 23d instant, and brought me your communication of 11th January, in which I find instructions to have our flag hoisted in Lower California, possession of some place in it taken and continuously held, and our civil jurisdiction asserted.

These are the first instructions I have received either from your department or the general-in-chief in relation to that country, and I lost no time in attending to them. I called upon Commodore Biddle, commanding the Pacific squadron, and concerted with him all the necessary measures to carry your instructions into effect, by sending a company or two of the New York volunteers, in one of the public ships of war, to take possession of La Paz, or some other place on the gulf of California, and not far from Cape St. Lucas. We are now compelled to stop all further proceedings in the above matter, and turn our attention to the southern section of this Territory—Upper California. Reports and rumors from Los Angeles reached here yesterday, brought by a few Mexicans from Sonora, that General Bustamente had been appointed commander-in-chief of Chihuahua, Sonora, and California, and that, at the time of their leaving Sonora, he was expected there with 1,500 men on his way to California. I do not place much credit in the latter part of the above, but it has much excited these excitable Californians; and it becomes necessary to reinforce the command at Los Angeles, as will be seen by department orders No. 13, of this date, a copy of which is herewith enclosed.

We have now in this Territory the following troops, viz:

1 company 1st dragoons	- - -	88 total.
1 do 3d artillery	- - -	107
10 companies New York volunteers	- -	550
5 do Mormon battalion	- -	314
17		1,059

And as I consider the security of this Territory all important, and that of the other to be but secondary, I must wait till quiet is again restored here before attempting to execute your instructions in relation to it, and which I hope will soon be. The regiment of New York volunteers are enrolled for *during the war;* the Mormon battalion for twelve months, and will be entitled to their discharge in July. We cannot rely upon any of them re-entering the service, as wages for mechanics and laborers are so enormously high in this country. I consider it important that more troops should be sent here, to preserve quiet and to secure possession of the two Californias. We cannot enrol any of the emigrants under the laws of May and June, 1846; they consider the pay, &c., allowed, entirely inadequate to their services. The late California battalion refused to a man to be mustered into service under those laws, and have been, by my order, discharged by Lieutenant Colonel Fremont. When they entered the service they were promised from $25 to $35 each per month; their horses and equipments to be furnished by the public, and rations to the families left behind, some of which have received as many as 11 per day, at 25 or 30 cents per ration each.

The wild Indians, by the frequent incursions of their small parties, are very troublesome to the frontier inhabitants, driving off much of their stock, cattle, and horses. These, as well as the Christian Indians, have been badly treated by most of the Californians; they think they are entitled to what they can steal and rob from them. I am of the opinion that much good might be done by making a few presents to them, and I recommend that there should be sent here for that purpose some medals, beads, (white stones,) red flannel, colored handkerchiefs, tobacco, &c.; a few colored blankets would be much prized by them.

Very respectfully, your obedient servant,
S W. KEARNY, *Brigadier General.*

Hon. W. L. MARCY,
 Secretary of War, Washington.

HEADQUARTERS TENTH MILITARY DEPARTMENT,
Monterey, California, April 28, 1847.

I. Colonel J. D. Stevenson, 7th regiment New York volunteers, will conduct two of the companies of his regiment, now stationed here, to the Pueblo de los Angeles, and there take post; on his arrival at Pueblo, Colonel Stevenson will relieve Liuetenant Colonel Cooke in the command of the southern military district, and use the utmost vigilance in preserving quiet and order therein.

II. Major J. A. Hardie, 7th regiment New York volunteers, now stationed at San Francisco, will assume command of the northern military district, and make such disposition of the troops under his command as shall be most conducive to the public tranquillity and protection from Indian depredations.

III. Captain H. M. Nagle, 7th regiment New York volunteers, will, with his mounted command, move out and take post at Felipe; from thence he will make frequent excursions along the frontier the valley of the San Joachim, &c., with the view of giving protection to the persons and property of the inhabitants, and preventing further depredations on the part of the Indians.

By order of Brigadier General S. W. Kearny:
H. S. TURNER,
Captian A. A. Adjt. General.

MONTEREY, CALIFORNIA, *May* 1, 1847.

SIR: I enclose herewith a copy of all communications and papers issued by me relating to the civil department of Upper California up to this date.

Very respectfully, your obedient servant,
S. W. KEARNY,
Brigadier General and Governor of California.

Brigadier General R. JONES,
 Adjutant General United States Army, Washington

Edwin Bryant, esq., is hereby appointed alcalde of the town of Yerba Buena and of the district of San Francisco, *vice* Lieutenant W. A. Bartlett, who returns to his naval duties.

Given at Yerba Buena, Upper California, this 22d of February, 1847, and in the 71st year of the independence of the United States.

S. W. KEARNY,
Brigadier General United States Army.

CIRCULAR.

To all whom it may concern, be it known :

That the President of the United States, desirous to give and secure to the people of California a share of the good government and happy civil organization enjoyed by the people of the United States, and to protect them at the same time from the attack of foreign foes and from internal commotions, has invested the undersigned with separate and distinct powers, civil and military, a cordial co operation in the exercise of which, it is hoped and believed, will have the happy results desired.

To the commander-in-chief of the naval forces the President has as signed the regulation of the import trade; the conditions on which vessels of all nations, our own as well as foreign, may be admitted into the ports of the Territory; and the establishment of all port regulations.

To the commanding military officer the President has assigned the direction of the operations on land, and has invested him with administrative functions of government over the people and territory occupied by the forces of the United States.

Done at Monterey, capital of California, this 1st day of March, A. D. 1847.

W. BRANFORD SHUBRICK,
Commander in-chief of the Naval Forces.
S. W. KEARNY,
Brigadier General United States Army, and Governor of California.

PROCLAMATION.

To the people of California.

The President of the United States having instructed the undersigned to take charge of the civil government of California, he enters upon his duties with an ardent desire to promote, as far as he is able, the interests of the country and the welfare of its inhabitants.

The undersigned has instructions from the President to respect and protect the religious institutions of California, and to see that the religious rights of the people are in the amplest manner preserved to them, the constitution of the United States allowing every man to worship his Creator in such a manner as his own conscience may dictate to him.

The undersigned is also instructed to protect the persons and property of the quiet and peaceable inhabitants of the country against all or any of their enemies, whether from abroad or at home; and when he now assures the Californians that it will be his duty and his pleasure to comply with those instructions, he calls upon them all to exert themselves in preserving order and tranquillity, in promoting harmony and concord, and in maintaining the authority and the efficacy of the laws.

It is the wish and design of the United States to provide for California, with the least possible delay, a free government similar to those in her own territories; and the people will soon be called upon to exercise their rights as freemen, in electing their own representatives, to make such laws as may be deemed best for their interests and welfare. But until this can be done, the laws now in existence, and not in conflict with the constitution of the United States, will be continued until changed by competent authority; and those persons who hold office will continue in the same for the present, provided they swear to support that constitution and faithfully perform their duty.

The undersigned hereby absolves all the inhabitants of California from any further allegiance to the republic of Mexico, and will consider them as citizens of the United States. Those who remain quiet and peaceable will be respected in their rights, and protected in them. Should any take up arms against or oppose the government of the Territory, or instigate others to do so, they will be considered as enemies, and treated accordingly.

When Mexico forced a war upon the United States, time did not permit the latter to invite the Californians as friends to join her standard, but compelled her to take possession of the country to prevent any European power from seizing upon it; and in doing so, some excesses and unauthorized acts were no doubt committed by persons employed in the service of the United States, by which a few of the inhabitants have met with a loss of property. Such losses will be duly investigated, and those entitled to remuneration will receive it.

California has for many years suffered greatly from domestic troubles; civil wars have been the poisoned fountains which have sent forth trouble and pestilence over her beautiful land. Now, those fountains are dried up; the star-spangled banner floats over California; and as long as the sun continues to shine upon her, so long will it float there, over the natives of the land, as well as others who have found a home in her bosom; and under it, agriculture must improve, and the arts and sciences flourish, as seed in a rich and fertile soil.

The Americans and Californians are now but one people; let us cherish one wish, one hope, and let that be for the peace and quiet of our country. Let us as a band of brothers unite and emulate each other in our exertions to benefit and improve this our beautiful, and which soon must be our happy and prosperous home.

Done at Monterey, capital of California, this first day of March, A. D. 1847, and in the 71st year of the independence of the United States.

S. W. KEARNY,
Brigadier General U. S. A., and Governor of California.

HEADQUARTERS TENTH MILITARY DEPARTMENT,
Monterey, California, March 1, 1847.

SIR: By department orders No. 2 of this date, which will be handed to you by Captain Turner, first dragoons, acting assistant adjutant general for my command, you will see that certain duties are there required of you as commander of the battalion of California volunteers.

In addition to the duties above referred to, I have now to direct that you will bring with you, and with as little delay as possible, all the archives and public documents and papers which may be subject to your control, and which appertain to the government of California, that I may receive them from your hands at this place, the capital of the Territory.

Very respectfully, your obedient servant,
S. W. KEARNY,
Brigadier General, and Governor of California.
Lt. Col. J. C. FREMONT,
Regiment Mounted Riflemen, commanding battalion
California Volunteers, Ciudad de los Angeles.

MONTEREY, *March 3, 1847.*

SIR: I have this day received yours of the 26th ultimo, asking me to provide for your office an interpreter and translator of the Spanish language; and in reply I have to observe that the Territorial government cannot make an appointment of such an officer, nor furnish funds for the payment of one. If an interpreter is indispensable, (as you say,) I know of no other way in which you can obtain him than by your selecting one and paying him from the fees of your office.

I have also received a copy of the proceedings of a meeting of the people of Sonoma, at which L. W. Boggs presided, relating to their being represented in the legislative council; and I will thank you to inform all concerned that I have not called for any such council, nor at present do I contemplate doing so.

Very respectfully, your obedient servant,
S. W. KEARNY,
Brigadier General, and Governor of California.
JOHN H. NASH, Esq.,
Alcalde, &c., Sonoma.

MONTEREY, *March 4, 1847.*

DEAR SIR: I yesterday received a copy of the proceedings of meetings of the people held at Yerba Buena and at Sonoma, at which Mr. S. Cooper and L. W. Boggs presided, relating to the representation in the legislative council; and I will thank you, in reply, to say to those gentlemen, and all others interested and concerned in the matter, that I have not called for any such council, nor do I at present contemplate doing so.

Very respectfully, your obedient servant,
S. W. KEARNY,
Brigadier General, and Governor of California.
EDW. BRYANT, Esq.,
Alcalde, Yerba Buena.

William Edward Petty Hartwell is hereby appointed translator and interpreter of the Spanish language for the governor and military commandant of California.

Done at Monterey, this 10th day of March, 1847, and of the independence of the United States the 71st.

S. W. KEARNY,
Brigadier General, and Governor of California.

The above named Hartwell is employed at a salary at the rate of fifteen hundred dollars per year.

S. W. KEARNY, *Brigadier General.*

I, Brigadier General S. W. Kearny, governor of California, by virtue of authority in me vested by the President of the United States of America, do hereby grant, convey, and release unto the town of San Francisco, the people or corporate authorities thereof, all the right, title, and interest of the government of the United States, and of the Territory of California, in and to the beach and water lots, on the east front of said town of San Francisco, included between the points known as the "Rincon" and "Fort Montgomery," excepting such lots as may be selected for the use of the general government by the senior officers of the army and navy now there; provided the said ground hereby ceded shall be divided into lots, and sold by public auction to the highest bidder, after three months' notice previously given; the proceeds of said sale to be for the benefit of the town of San Francisco.

Given at Monterey, capital of California, this 10th day of March, 1847, and in the 71st year of the independence of the United States.

S. W. KEARNY,
Brigadier General, and Governor of California.

Know all men by these presents, that I, Brigadier General S. W. Kearny, governor of California, by virtue of authority in me vested, considering that, inasmuch as there are various claimants to the missions of San José, Santa Clara, Santa Cruz, and San Juan, to the houses, grounds, gardens, vineyards, &c., around and near them, do hereby decree, that until the proper judicial tribunals to be established shall decide upon the same, the above named missions and property appertaining thereto shall remain under charge of the Catholic priests, as they were when the United States flag was first raised in this Territory—it being understood that this decree is not to affect the rights of any claimant, and that the priests are to be responsible for the preservation of said missions and property whilst under their charge.

The alcaldes of the jurisdiction in which the above-named missions are situated will, upon the application of the priests, take the proper measures to remove therefrom all persons trespassing or intruding upon them.

Given at Monterey, capital of California, this 22d day of March, 1847.

S. W. KEARNY,
Brigadier General, and Governor of California.

Know all men by these presents, that I, S. W. Kearny, Brigadier General United States army, and governor of California, by virtue of authority in me vested by the President of the United States, do hereby appoint

Walter Colton judge of the court of admiralty in and for the Territory of California.
Given at Monterey, capital of California, this 24th day of March, 1847.
S. W. KEARNY,
Brigadier General, and Governor of California.

MONTEREY, CALIFORNIA, *March* 26, 1847.

SIR: It has been represented to me that Antonio Hernano, a resident in the district of San Juan, has been summoned to appear before you, the alcalde, to answer to a complaint of one Gabriel Castro, in which he claims from the former the sum of five hundred dollars, or thereabouts, said to be due by his winning that amount at a horse race. It has further been represented to me, that the aforesaid claim was instituted three or four years since, before the then existing authorities, and that it was, according to the laws and custom then existing, decided by the authorities adverse to the claimant. Assuming the above representations to be true, I have now to direct that you dismiss the said suit, claim, or demand of Gabriel Castro against Antonio Hernano, and without costs to said Hernano.

I have further to direct that you will not entertain any suit before your court which has been decided by the former courts of the country.

Very respectfully, your obedient servant,
S. W. KEARNY,
Brigadier General, and Governor of California.
JOHN BURTON, Esq.,
Alcalde, &c., Pueblo de San José.

HEADQUARTERS TENTH MILITARY DEPARTMENT,
Monterey, California, March 27, 1847.

SIR: You will proceed to the southern military district of this Territory, and inspect the troops in that quarter. You are hereby clothed with full authority to give such orders and instructions in that country, upon all matters whatever, both civil and military, as in your judgment you may think most conducive to the public interest. You will then return to this place.

I am, respectfully, your obedient servant,
S. W. KEARNY,
Brigadier General, and Governor of California.
Colonel R. B. MASON,
1st regiment Dragoons.

MONTEREY, CALIFORNIA, *March* 29, 1847.

SIR: You will please pay over to Captain J. L. Folsom, assistant quartermaster United States army stationed at San Francisco, such money as you may have in possession collected from custom-house duties. His receipt will be your voucher for the same.

Very respectfully, your obedieut servant,
S. W. KEARNY,
Brigadier General, and Governor of California.
Mr. W. A. RICHARDSON,
Collector, San Francisco, California.

MONTEREY, CALIFORNIA, *March* 29, 1847.

SIR: I have received yours of the 4th instant, calling my attention to a case before you, the civil magistrate of Sonoma, as follows, viz: "The Catholic church, plaintiff, *vs.* Colonel Victor Prudon, defendant, for holding possession of a house belonging to the priest." That on the trial of the cause it appeared to you by documentary proof that the house in dispute belonged to the church; that judgment was rendered by you against defendant, to give possession to the church, and damages awarded of $420; that you have issued a writ of restitution, requiring the sheriff to remove the defendant, and have arrested proceedings for forty days, and you now ask me for instructions in the case; that you have the proclamation of the governor of California, dated in 1845, that the house (in dispute) should be reserved for the use of the priest, and the supreme prefect's decree to the same effect; and that the defendant relies alone on a title derived from General José Castro, June 9, 1846, which title you think, for reasons stated, General Castro had no right to give. Withholding my opinion of the right of General Castro to grant the house in dispute, and without intending to effect the rights of the parties, (the priest and Colonel Prudon)—for that must be left to the judicial tribunals yet to be established in the Territory—I have now to direct, from the premises stated by yourself, that, inasmuch as Colonel Prudon is at this time in possession of the house by decree of General José Castro of June, 1846, he continue the possession of it; that the damages awarded against him be annulled; and that you dismiss all further proceedings in the matter, without cost to said Prudon.

Very respectfully, your obedient servant,
S. W. KEARNY,
Brigadier General, and Governor of California.
JOHN H. NASH, Esq.,
Alcalde, &c., Sonoma, California.

MONTEREY, CALIFORNIA, *April* 6, 1847.

SIR: I have to acknowledge the receipt of yours of yesterday, enclosing a copy of two communications to you from the former governor, Don José Figueroa, each of June 24, 1845, being instructions to build a town in the valley of Sonoma, and to colonize the frontier on the northern side of the bay of San Francisco and Sacramento river, by granting lands to such persons as may wish to settle there, said grants to be confirmed by the territorial government, upon proper application to it.

In relation to the subject above referred to I have only to remark, that, though the instructions to you from Don José Figueroa may no longer be exercised, yet there is no doubt that whatever has been done under his instructions, and which he was authorized to give, will be fully recognised and confirmed by the government of the United States.

With great respect, your obedient servant,
S. W. KEARNY,
Brigadier General, and Governor of California.

Señor DON MARIANO G. VALLEJO,
Monterey.

MONTEREY, CALIFORNIA, *April* 7, 1847.

SIR: I enclose herewith an appointment for you of sub-agent for the Indians living on and near the Sacramento and San Joaquin rivers.

In sending this appointment, I deem it necessary to remind you that those Indians have of late given great trouble to the frontier inhabitants in the upper part of California, by driving off horses and cattle, and attacking small parties at the ranches and on the road. This conduct on the part of the Indians must cease. I am in hopes that, by good advice and prudent counsel, which your perfect acquaintance with them will enable you to give, they will be induced to abstain from giving further cause of complaint against them. Should they not do so, they will most assuredly be punished by an armed force, which I will send among them, and which I wish you to inform them of.

I wish you to explain to the Indians the change in the administration of public affairs in this Territory; that they must now look to the President of the United States as their great father; that he takes good care of his good children; that the officers now here are acting under his orders and instructions; that the Americans and Californians are now one people, and any offences which they may commit against the latter will be punished in the same way as if committed against the former.

I will endeavor to obtain and furnish you with a quantity of Indian goods, to be given as presents to such chiefs and bands as may conduct themselves peaceably and honestly. You can tell the Indians of this.

You will please report, from time to time, to me or the future governor of the Territory, any occurrence which you may deem worthy of attention, and offer such suggestions relating to the Indians and Indian affairs as you may think proper.

Your salary will be $750 per year.

You will please not to expend any public money, or contract any debt against the United States or Territory of California, under virtue of your appointment of Indian sub-agent.

Very respectfully, your obedient servant,
S. W. KEARNY,
Brigadier General, and Governor of California

Captain JOHN A. SUTTER,
Indian Sub-agent, New Helvetia.

Know all men by these presents, that I, S. W. Kearny, brigadier general United States army and governor of California, by virtue of authority in me vested, do hereby appoint John A. Sutter sub-agent for the Indians on and near the Sacramento and San Joaquin rivers.

Given at Monterey, capital of California, this 7th day of April, 1847.
S. W. KEARNY,
Brigadier General, and Governor of California.

Know all men by these presents, that Lilburn W. Boggs is hereby appointed alcalde of the district of Sonoma, *vice* John H. Nash, esq.

Given at Monterey, capital of California, this 10th day of April, 1847.
S. W. KEARNY,
Brigadier General, and Governor of California.

MONTEREY, CALIFORNIA, *April* 10, 1847.

SIR: I have received yours of the 31st March, in which you state that one James Stokes, of the pueblo de San José, has lately caused notice to be given to Juan Sepulveda and Anselmo Garcia to leave the premises they occupy forthwith, the said Stokes claiming the property as his own. You further state that the said Stokes entered a suit in your office, on the 15th January last, against the above-named persons, for forcibly holding possession of his property; that they were cited and appeared before you with their witnesses; that Stokes had a jury of six men, by his own choice, who, after hearing testimony, decided that the persons in possession of the property had all the rights and interests in said land; and you now wish me to settle the question.

In reply to the above, it is only necessary for me to say, that this case, having once been decided in your court, cannot again be brought up before it; and if Mr. Stokes is not satisfied with that decision, he must wait until higher judicial tribunals are established in the country, to which he may make an appeal.

Very respectfully, your obedient servant,
S. W. KEARNY,
Brigadier General, and Governor of California.

JOHN BURTON, Esq.,
Alcalde, &c., Pueblo de San José.

MONTEREY, CALIFORNIA,
April 11, 1847.

SIR: I have received your communication of this date, enclosing a copy of a license to the brig Primavera, under Mexican colors, " to trade on any portion of the coast of California, on terms and with the same immunities as merchant vessels of the United States," granted on the 9th of March, by Lieutenant Colonel Frémont, United States army, who signs himself " Governor of California."

In reference to the license, I have only to remark that I claim for myself, as governor of California, by virtue of instructions from the President of the United States, no such power as is attempted to be exercised by Lieutenant Colonel Frémont, the President having assigned "to the commander-in-chief of the naval forces the regulation of the import trade, and the conditions on which vessels of all nations, our own as well as foreign, may be admitted into the ports of the Territory."

Lieutenant Colonel Frémont has no authority for considering himself governor of California, and attempting to perform the duties of that office, except what he may have derived from Commodore R. F. Stockton, of the navy; and he well knows that the President of the United States has assigned that duty to myself, having been officially informed of that fact by a circular of March 1st, signed by Commodore Shubrick and myself, before your arrival here, (a copy of which was sent to him,) and by letter from Commodore Shubrick, of February 3, a copy of which is enclosed herewith.

Very respectfully, your obedient servant,

S. W. KEARNY,
Brigadier General, and Governor of California.
Com. JAMES BIDDLE,
U. S. Navy, com'g Pacific squadron.

Know all men by these presents, that I, Brigadier General S. W. Kearny, United States army, and governor of California, by virtue of authority in me vested, do hereby appoint Don Manuel G. Vallejo sub-agent for the Indians on the north side of the bay of San Francisco, including those on Cash creek and the lakes.

Given at Monterey, capital of California, this 14th day of April, 1847.

S. W. KEARNY,
Brigadier General, and Governor of California.

MONTEREY, CALIFORNIA, *April* 14, 1847.

SIR: I enclose herewith an appointment for you of sub-agent for the Indians on the north side of the bay of San Francisco, including those on Cash creek and on the lakes.

In offering this appointment to you, it may be proper for me to remind you that the Indians have lately assumed a threatening attitude, and given some alarm to the inhabitants, not only near Sonoma, but to those north and east of it. I am in hopes that by good advice and prudent counsel, and the well-known influence which you possess over these Indians, they may be induced by you to remain quiet and refrain from committing any further acts of depredation or hostility upon the people or their property. Should they not do so, they will most assuredly be punished by an armed force sent among them, and which you will please inform them of.

Will you explain to the Indians and to their chiefs the change which has taken place in the government of this country; that they must now look upon the Californians and the Americans as one people, and any offences they may commit upon the one will be punished in the same manner as if committed upon the other.

I will endeavor to obtain and furnish you with a quantity of Indian goods, to be given as presents to such chiefs and bands as may conduct themselves peaceably and quietly.

You will please report to me, from time to time, any occurrence which you may deem worthy of notice, and offer such suggestions relating to the Indians and Indian affairs as may appear expedient to you.

Your salary will be $750 per year.

Very respectfully, your obedient servant,
S. W. KEARNY,
Brigadier General, and Governor of California.
Don MARIANO G. VALLEJO,
Indian Sub-agent, Monterey.

MONTEREY, CALIFORNIA, *April* 16, 1847.

SIR: I learn that you have under your charge a number of horses, mares, cattle, and other public property appertaining to the mission of San Rafael. I wish you to send as early as possible an inventory of the same to Captain Folsom, assistant quartermaster at San Francisco, and comply with his instructions relating thereto.

Very respectfully, your obedient servant,
S. W. KEARNY,
Brigadier General, and Governor of California.
Mr. TIMOTHY MURPHY,
San Rafael, California.

MONTEREY, CALIFORNIA, *April* 19, 1847.

SIR: Your letter of the 16th was delivered to me by Mr. Wm. S. Clarke, of the town of San Francisco, who at the same time laid before me his application or petition of February 1, 1847, to the alcalde of the district of San Francisco, for the privilege to build a public wharf in front of the city or town, ending as follows:

"*Third.* That your petitioner shall have possession given of the fractional lot of the northeast corner of Broadway and Battery streets, of 50 varas fronting on said Battery-place street, with the privilege of extending the same so far as the said wharf may or shall be completed; your petitioner reserving the right, in preference to all others, to obtain a grant of the said lot, to him and his heirs forever, from the proper authorities, when constituted."

Mr. Clarke also laid before me a deed of possession, granted to him on the same date, (February 1,) by "Washington A. Bartlett, chief magistrate," "of the land, lot, or plot asked for as described in his petition and this instrument, and with the conditions thereof." I presume copies of both these papers are on file in your office.

Having on the 10th of March, 1847, given up to the town of San Francisco all claim on the part of the United States and Territory of California to the beach and water lots within certain described limits, which I believe include the lot referred to in the petition and deed of possession,

I do not feel authorized at this time to make any decision in this matter of Mr Clarke, but cannot refrain from recommending it to the most favorable consideration of all the constituted authorities of your town, and adding that justice and good faith require that we should, as far as in our power, assist in fulfilling the engagements entered into by authorities which have preceded us, without inquiring into their expediency, provided they are not contrary to law.

Very respectfully, your obedient servant,
S. W. KEARNY,
Brigadier General, and Governor of California.
Edwin Bryant,
Alcalde, &c., San Francisco, California.

Monterey, California, *April* 19, 1847.

The undersigned has the honor to acknowledge the receipt of the communication addressed to him on the 8th instant by Don Cesareo Sataillade, vice consul of her Catholic Majesty, and to state, in reply, that as the vice consul prefers a residence in Santa Barbara, it affords the undersigned great pleasure in acceding thereto, and to add that instructions will be given that the vice consul may receive all the privileges his office and high standing so justly entitle him to.

The undersigned offers to the vice consul the assurance of his esteem and consideration.

S. W. KEARNY,
Brigadier General, and Governor of California.
Don Cesareo Sataillade,
Vice Consul de España, Santa Barbara, California.

Monterey, California, *April* 21, 1847.

Sir: As you have been appointed collector of the port and harbor-master at San Francisco, I have to direct that you receive for the customs and fees nothing but specie, treasury notes, or drafts. You will please settle your accounts quarterly with Captain Folsom, assistant quartermaster at San Francisco, turning over to him all money, &c., received by you for customs and fees under your two appointments of collector and harbor-master. You have a deputy collector at Sansolito, and, as his services can be dispensed with, you will please do so. Your compensation for performing the duties at San Francisco of collector of the port and harbor-master will be twelve hundred dollars ($1,200) per year.

Very respectfully, your obedient servant,
S. W. KEARNY,
Brigadier General, and Governor of California.
Mr. Wm. A. Richardson,
Collector, &c., Monterey.

MONTEREY, CALIFORNIA, *April* 21, 1847.

SIR: I learn that you have been appointed collector of the customs for the port of San Diego, which appointment is hereby confirmed to you. I enclose herewith a printed circular of March 1st, signed by Commodore Shubrick and myself, announcing the duties confided by the President of the United States to the senior officers of the land and naval forces; a proclamation of my own of the same date; and instructions to you, of March 29, from Commodore James Biddle, commanding the Pacific squadron.

You will please send to me copies of such instructions as you may have received relating to your duties as collector, and inform me what salary has been allowed you, and what public funds you may have received and have on hand.

Very respectfully, your obedient servant,

S. W. KEARNY,
Brigadier General, and Governor of California.

Don SANTIAGO ARGUILLO,
Collector, &c., San Diego, California.

MONTEREY, CALIFORNIA,
April 24, 1847.

SIR: I have received yours of the 21st relating to a room in the public buildings at San Francisco, now occupied by you as an office; and, taking all things into consideration, I am of opinion that the municipal authorities of the town should provide a room elsewhere, so that the military may have the exclusive control and management of that building.

Very respectfully, your obedient servant,

S. W. KEARNY,
Brigadier General, and Governor of California.

EDWIN BRYANT, Esq.,
Alcalde, &c., San Francisco.

MONTEREY, CALIFORNIA,
April 24, 1847.

SIR: Your communications of the 17th March and 7th April have been duly received.

During the existence of the present war between the United States and Mexico, there must of necessity arise many cases of great hardship and injustice, which for the time being are without remedy. This state of affairs is inseparable from a state of war; and your case, as represented by you, may be considered as one of that class. I sincerely hope that ere long the restoration of peace will lead to the establishment of a permanent civil government for this Territory, which will secure to all their just rights.

Very respectfully, your obedient servant,

S. W. KEARNY,
Brigadier General, and Governor of California.

Mr. GEORGE W. BELLAMY,
Santa Clara, California.

MONTEREY, CALIFORNIA,
April 26, 1847.

SIR: I learn that you have been appointed collector of the port and harbor-master at San Pedro, which appointments are hereby confirmed to you. I enclose herewith a printed circular of March 1, signed by Commodore Shubrick and myself, announcing the duties confided by the President of the United States to the senior officers of the land and naval forces; a proclamation of my own of same date; and instructions to you of March 29 from Commodore Biddle, commanding the Pacific squadron. You will please send me, as early as possible, copies of such instructions as you may have received relating to your duties as collector and harbor-master, and inform me what salary has been allowed you, and what amount of funds you may have received, and how much on hand.

You will please settle your accounts quarterly with Lieutenant Colonel Cooke, at the City of the Angels, or with such officer as he may designate, turning over to him all money, &c., received by you for customs and fees under your appointment of collector and harbor-master. His receipt will be your voucher for the same. You will receive nothing but *specie, treasury notes,* or *drafts.*

I have received from Colonel Mason, 1st dragoons, the instructions to you of 21st March, signed "J. C. Fremont, governor of California, by William H. Russell, secretary of State," ordering and permitting you to receive from Mr. S. Hultman "government payment," (that is, as I understand, due-bills of the paymaster and quartermaster of the late battalion of California volunteers,) in payment of his custom-house duties; and I learn that you have received seventeen hundred dollars of that paper, bought up by Mr. H. at 25 or 30 per cent. discount. As you have by the act of others been led into this mistake, what you have received from Mr. H. must be passed to your credit.

Very respectfully, your obedient servant,
S. W. KEARNY,
Brigadier General, and Governor of California.
Mr. DAVID W. ALEXANDER,
Collector, &c., San Pedro, California.

MONTEREY, CALIFORNIA,
April 26, 1847.

SIR: In addition to the instructions sent to you by me on the 21st instant, I have to direct that you will receive in payment for duties and fees, under your appointments of collector of the port and harbor-master at San Diego, nothing but specie, treasury notes, or drafts; and that you will please settle your accounts quarterly with Lieutenant Colonel Cooke, (commanding the southern military district,) or with such officer as he may designate, turning over to him all money received by you for customs and fees; and his receipt will be your voucher for the same.

Very respectfully, your obedient servant,
S. W. KEARNY,
Brigadier General, and Governor of California.
Don SANTIAGO ARGUILLO,
Collector and Harbor-master, San Diego, California.

MONTEREY, CALIFORNIA,
April 26, 1847.

SIR: In addition to the instructions of Commodore James Biddle of March 29, which I have forwarded to you, I have to direct that you will receive for customs and fees, as collector of the port and harbor-master at Santa Barbara, nothing but specie, treasury notes, and drafts; and tha you will please settle your accounts quarterly with Lieutenant Colone Burton, commanding at Santa Barbara, or with such officer as he may designate, turning over to him all money received by you. His receipt will be your voucher for the same.

You will please send me a copy of such instructions as you may have received (which have not passed through my hands) relating to your duties as collector, and inform me what salary has been allowed you, and what money you have received as collector, and how much on hand.

I am of opinion that I have written to you a letter similar to this, but it has not been copied in my letter-book. Should you have received one from me, please send me a copy.

Very respectfully, your obedient servant,
S. W. KEARNY,
Brigadier General, and Governor of California.

Don PEDRO CARRILLO,
Collector, &c., Santa Barbara, California.

MONTEREY, CALIFORNIA,
April 27, 1847.

SIR: I have received your communication of the 30th March, relating to a decree made by me on the 26th of that month, in the case of Gabriel Castro *vs.* Antonio Hernano; and I have since learned that you have, contrary to that decree, "given judgment and issued an execution, to be levied by a sheriff, against various portions of the property of the defendant, A. Hernano."

I have now to decree that you stay all further proceedings in this case until you hear further from me on the subject.

Very respectfully, your obedient servant,
S. W. KEARNY,
Brigadier General, and Governor of California.

JOHN BURTON, Esq.,
Alcalde, &c., Pueblo de San José.

MONTEREY, CALIFORNIA, *April* 27, 1847.

SIR: I consider the order of Captain Montgomery in the case of the Russian American Company against J. A. Sutter as having been given by competent authority, and as still remaining in full force. All steps in disobedience of that order, until it is repealed by the proper authority, must therefore be considered void. As Captain Montgomery was no doubt as well or better acquainted with the facts of the case above mentioned than myself, I do not feel disposed, for the present at least, to interfere with his order in reference to it. You will consequently please to restore that case to the situation it occupied at the time Captain Montgomery issued his aforesaid order.

Very respectfully, your obedient servant,
S. W. KEARNY,
Brigadier General, and Governor of California.
EDWIN BRYANT, Esq.,
Alcalde, &c., San Francisco.

MONTEREY, CALIFORNIA, *April 27, 1847.*

SIR: Yours of the 22d instant has been received. By my decree of the 10th ultimo, I conveyed all the right of the United States and of this Territory in the lots mentioned in your communication to the town of San Francisco. By that act I lost all power and control over those lots. Having already relinquished all claim to those lots to another, I have no right now to recall, annul, or modify that relinquishment in any manner whatever, and am unable, therefore, to do anything for your relief, but must refer you to the authorities of the town, who, I hope, will do you full justice.

Very respectfully, your obedient servant,
S. W. KEARNY,
Brigadier General, and Governor of California.
Mr. WM. PETTIT, San Francisco.

MONTEREY, CALIFORNIA, *April 27, 1847.*

SIR: Your communications relating to the cases of Thomas Russell and John Warner have been received. I regret to learn that Mr. Warner refuses obedience to your decree. If he remain refractory, you are authorized to call upon the military officer most convenient to you for men to enforce your decree. This authority is also delegated to you in any other case in which the military may be required to give effect to your dicial acts. In the case of Thomas Russell, I see no difficulty. You can either fine Russell or imprison him, or both fine and imprison him. The amount of the fine and the duration of the imprisonment are left to your discretion.

Very respectfully, your obedient servant,
S. W. KEARNY,
Brigadier General, and Governor of California.
H. D. FITCH, Esq.,
Alcalde, &c., San Diego.

MONTEREY, CALIFORNIA, *April 27, 1847.*

SIR: Your communication of April 16 has been received. You will obey the order of the alcalde at San Diego with regard to the property in your possession. You will return to the owners all the property you may have, and which was taken by the Indians.

Very respectfully, your obedient servant,
        S. W. KEARNY,
    Brigadier General, and Governor of California.
Mr. J. J. Warner,
 San Diego, or Agua Calienta.

    Monterey, California, *April* 30, 1847.

Sir: Your communication of the 15th April has been received. I desire that you continue to discharge the duties of alcalde; and it is hoped that a sufficient number of good citizens will be found, who, in the absence of the military, will be ready to assist you in carrying into effect your decrees.

I have not abolished the duty "established for the sale of aguardiente," nd your informant had no authority for saying that I have done so; I have made no decree on the subject.

Very respectfully, your obedient servant,
        S. W. KEARNY,
    Brigadier General, and Governor of California.
Don J. Mariano Bonillo,
 Alcalde, &c., San Luis Obispo.

    Monterey, California, *April* 30, 1847.

Sir: I have received a communication from W. E. P. Hartwell, in which he states that the mission of San Rafael, under the charge of Mr. Timothy Murphy, has long been owing him (Hartwell) " the amount of $267 33½, and that the former governor of California, Don Manuel Micheltorena, sent to said Murphy, in the year 1844, two separate written orders for him to pay the said amount out of whatever property the mission might have." Hartwell also requests that I should give you an order to pay the same. In order that I may understand this matter, and the nature of the debt in particular, I have to request that you will at the earliest opportunity furnish me with a full statement of the subjects mentioned in the extract from Mr. Hartwell's note above quoted.

Very respectfully, your obedient servant,
        S. W. KEARNY,
    Brigadier General, and Governor of California.
Mr. Timothy Murphy, *San Rafael, California.*

  Headquarters Tenth Military Department,
   Ciudad de los Angeles, California, May 13, 1847.

Sir: My letter (No. 10) of May 3, informed you of my intention of coming to this place with Colonel Stevenson and two companies of his regiment, (7th New York volunteers.) We reached here on the 9th; and

I find the people of this part of California quiet, notwithstanding some rumors to the contrary, circulated (and I fear originated) by some of our own officers, to further their own wicked purposes.

I leave here to-morrow for Monterey, and will close my public business there as soon as possible, and then proceed to St. Louis, (via the South Pass,) where I hope to be by the 20th of August, and where, if this reaches you in time, (it will go by Santa Fe,) I shall expect to receive orders for my further movements. I shall be prepared to go at once wherever it is deemed my services may be needed.

I this morning started Lieutenant Colonel Frémont to Monterey to close his public business there before he leaves for Washington. His conduct in California has been such that I shall be compelled, on arriving in Missouri, to arrest him, and send him under charges to report to you.

I shall be accompanied from Monterey by Lieutenant Colonel Frémont; Major Swords, (quartermaster,) who goes to settle his accounts and bring his family here; Captains Cooke and Turner, 1st dragoons, who go to join their companies; and Assistant Surgeon Sanderson, who has resigned. My escort will be the men of the topographical parties who came to this country with Lieutenant Colonel Frémont and Lieutenant Emory, and thirteen of the Mormon battalion.

Very respectfully, your obedient servant,
S. W. KEARNY,
Brigadier General.

The ADJUTANT GENERAL *U. S. A.*

HEADQUARTERS TENTH MILITARY DEPARTMENT,
Monterey, California, May 30, 1847.

SIR: I enclose herewith a copy of department orders, including No. 19- which have been issued by my directions, and a copy of my letter of instructions of this date to Lieutenant Colonel Burton, 7th New York volunteers, for him and two companies of his regiment to proceed to Lower California.

I shall leae here to-morrow for Missouri and Washington city, where I hope to be by the last of August, and when I shall be ready for any duty which may be assigned to me. The officers and party which accompany me from here you were informed of in my letter (No. 11) of the 13th instant.

Colonel Mason, 1st dragoons, succeeds to the command of the 10th military department.

Very respectfully, your obedient servant,
S. W. KEARNY,
Brigadier General.

The ADJUTANT GENERAL *U. S. A.*

HEADQUARTERS TENTH MILITARY DEPARTMENT,
Monterey, California, May 30, 1847.

SIR: I enclose herewith an extract of a letter to me from the Secretary of War, of January 11, 1847, in which you will find directions that our flag be hoisted in Lower California, and actual possession taken and continuously held of some place or places in it, and our civil jurisdiction there asserted and upheld.

I also enclose a copy of letters to Commodores Biddle and Shubrick, of April 27 and May 24, with other papers from Captain Montgomery, United States navy, who, in the months of March and April, took possession of San Lucas, San José, and La Paz, (being on the cape and eastern shore of the gulf of California,) with the sailors under his command, in the ship Portsmouth.

In compliance with the instructions of January 11 from the Secretary of War, I have now to direct that you, with two companies of your regiment, now under your command, taking six months' provisions with them, embark on board the ship Lexington, Commander Bailey, who is directed by Commodore Biddle to carry you and your command to the Gulf of California, and to remain there with you. Upon your arrival in the gulf, you will, after having consulted freely with Commander Bailey, decide where to land your command, and establish yourself with it. I recommend that it should be at La Paz or San José, or at both places; but of this you will be better able to judge after your arrival there, and ascertaining the number of the inhabitants, &c., of the country.

It is understood that the people of Lower California have not the power, if they possessed the disposition, to resist your command; but you must not on that account allow the discipline of your soldiers to relax, but hold them at all times ready to resist or make an attack. The best means of preserving peace is to be prepared for war.

I have most strongly to urge upon you the necessity of the utmost cordiality on the part of our land forces towards those of our navy, in the joint service on the coast of California. Reciprocity may be confidently expected; and, towards that end, frequent conferences between commanders of the two arms are recommended. Harmony in co-operation, and success cannot but follow. You will, as often as opportunities offer, report the state and condition of your command and of affairs in Lower California to Colonel Mason, 1st dragoons, who succeeds, on my departure from here, (to-morrow,) to the command of the tenth military department.

I enclose a copy of instructions to the collectors of ports in California, dated March 29, from Commodore James Biddle, commanding the Pacific squadron, which you will see are enforced at the ports under your control.

The collectors of the ports will be appointed by yourself, and the customs received will be subject to your orders.

The money should go towards paying the collectors moderate salaries— say about $600 or $700 per year—and for such other purposes as may be found necessary.

Very respectfully, your obedient servant,
S. W. KEARNY,
Brigadier General.

Lieut. Col. H. S. BURTON,
7th New York Volunteers, Santa Barbara.

MONTEREY, CALIFORNIA, *May* 31, 1847.

SIR: I enclose herewith a copy of all communications and papers issued by me relating to the civil department of Upper California since the 1st instant, the date of my letter to you, (No. 9,) transmitting a copy of those previously issued by me.

I shall leave here to-morrow for Washington city, leaving Colonel Mason, 1st dragoons, in command of the troops in California, and consequently in charge of the civil department in the Territory.

Very respectfully, your obedient servant,
S. W. KEARNY,
Brigadier General, and Governor of California.

Brig. Gen. R. JONES,
Adjutant General U. S. A., Washington.

MONTEREY, CALIFORNIA, *May* 3, 1847.

SIR: In addition to the instructions from Commodore J. Biddle of March 29, which you have received, I have to direct that you will receive for customs and fees, as collector of the port and harbor-master at this place, nothing but specie, treasury notes, and drafts; and that you will settle your accounts quarterly with Major Swords, (quartermaster,) turning over to him what money you may have on hand, taking his receipts for the same; which receipts and settlement, as certified by him, will be full and sufficient vouchers for you. Your salary as collector and harbor-master will be $1,000 (one thousand dollars) per year, commencing from January 28, 1847.

Very respectfully, your obedient servant,
S. W. KEARNY,
Brigadier General, and Governor of California.

Mr. T. H. GREEN,
Collector, &c., Monterey.

MONTEREY, CALIFORNIA, *May* 4, 1847.

SIR: The instructions to you from Commodore Biddle, of March 29, and from me, April 26, will be sufficient for your government for the present. I have now to state that your salary as collector of the port and harbor-master at Santa Barbara will be $1,000 (one thousand dollars) per year, provided the duties of impost collected there cover that allowance.

Very respectfully, your obedient servant,
S. W. KEARNY,
Brigadier General, and Governor of California.

Don PEDRO CARRILLO,
Collector, &c., Monterey.

MONTEREY, CALIFORNIA, *May* 5, 1847.

SIR: General Kearny, before leaving this place for the south, turned over to me, for such action as I think proper, the complaint made to him by Maria Roza Archuleta against her husband, Francisco Rochin. The parties must refer their case to the decision of arbitrators: that is the course most likely to give satisfaction. Let Francisco Rochin choose one arbitrator, and Maria Roza Archuleta another, and the two thus chosen must choose a third. Then let the three arbitrators in your presence hear what both parties have to say, and decide whether Francisco Rochin and his wife, Maria Roza Archuleta, shall be separated for *three, six,* or *twelve* months, if separated at all.

Very respectfully, your obedient servant,
R. B. MASON,
Colonel 1st Dragoons, commanding.

JOHN BARTON, Esq.,
Alcalde, &c., San José.

LOS ANGELES, CALIFORNIA, *May* 12, 1847.

SIR: Your salary for performing the duty of collector of the port and harbor-master at San Pedro will be $1,000 (one thousand dollars) per year, commencing from the 25th August, 1846, the date of your appointment, the same to be paid half-yearly. You report to me that you have on hand $1,731 "government paper," and $766 in specie. You will be allowed to retain your half year's salary ($500) from the specie; the balance, with the "government paper," you will turn over to Lieutenant Davidson, 1st dragoons, acting assistant quartermaster at this place, and in future settle quarterly with him, or with such officer as the commanding officer of this district may designate.

Very respectfully, your obedient servant,
S W. KEARNY,
Brigadier General, and Governor of California.

Mr. D. W. ALEXANDER,
Collector, &c., San Pedro.

Know all men by these presents, that I, S. W. Kearny, brigadier general United States army, and governor of California, by virtue of authority in me vested, do hereby appoint George Hyde alcalde of the district of San Francisco, vice Edwin Bryant, resigned.

Given at Monterey, capital of California, this 28th May, 1847.
S. W. KEARNY,
Brigadier General, and Governor of California.

List of Reports from Colonel R. B. Mason.

1847, June   18. Report with correspondence.
       June   21. Report with correspondence.
       July   21. Civil correspondence to date.
       July   21. Report.
       Sept.   18. Report with correspondence to September 6.
       Oct.   7. Report.
       Sept.   24. Correspondence from July 12 to date.

1847, Oct.   6. Correspondence from September 24 to date.
      Oct.   21. Correspondence from October 11 to date.
      Nov.   11. Correspondence from October 14 to date.
      Nov.   11. Report with enclosures.
      Nov.   13. Report with enclosures.
1848, Jan.   27. Correspondence from November 11, 1847.
      April   12. Report with enclosures.
      April   15. Report to Secretary of War.
      April   18. Correspondence from January 28.
      Aug.   16. Report with enclosures.
      Aug.   17. Report with enclosures.
      Aug.   18. Report with enclosures.
      Aug.   19. Report with correspondence from April 18.
      Aug.   23. Report with enclosures.
      Aug.   26. Correspondence from May 22.
      Aug.   28. Report with enclosures.
      Sept.   12. Report with enclosures.
      Nov.   20. Report.
      Nov.   24. Report.
      Dec.   27. Report with enclosures.
1849, March   8. Report.
      March   28. Report.
      April   9. Correspondence from 7th August.

HEADQUARTERS TENTH MILITARY DEPARTMENT,
Monterey, California, June 18, 1847.

SIR: I enclose herewith copies of department orders, including No. 26, and copies of correspondence, (such as are of any consequence,) to include the 16th instant, the proceedings of a general court-martial convened by virtue of department order No. 21, a department return for the month of March, and post returns of Monterey up to include May.

I am not sure that the department return and post returns are critically correct. I have been obliged to make some guess-work in them, owing to the faulty returns of the volunteers; but they cannot vary more than some two or three men, if indeed they vary at all.

The term of service of the Mormon battalion will expire about the middle of July. I do not think they will re-enter the service.

The country still continues to be quiet, and I think will remain so, though the people dislike the change of flags, whatever may be said or written to the contrary, and in the southern part of Upper California would rise immediately if it were possible for Mexico to send even a small force into the country; nothing keeps them quiet but the want of a proper leader and a rallying-point.

I send you a map showing the positions occupied by the troops, the number at each station, and the estimated distance between the posts. You will perceive they are pretty well stretched out; but, under existing circumstances, it cannot well be avoided. We must keep up a show of troops, however small in numbers, at the different points occupied.

The United States ship Lexington will sail in a few days for Santa Barbara, to take Lieutenant Colonel Burton and two companies of the

New York volunteers from that post to La Paz, the capital of Lower California, in obedience to instructions from the War Department.

The very large amount of ordnance and ordnance stores brought out by the Lexington and Colonel Stevenson's three ships are landed at San Francisco and Monterey. They greatly embarrass me and cause me some uneasiness, being from necessity stored in different insecure buildings until places of greater security can be constructed.

I cannot too strongly impress upon the department the absolute necessity of sending an ordnance officer to report to me, as also an officer of the Adjutant General's department. Mounted troops are greatly wanted in California, both to hold the country, preserve order, sustain the laws, and to keep in check the Indians, who are committing extensive depredations upon persons and property of both foreigners and natives—burning, killing, &c. Mounted troops can alone operate to advantage in this country.

A part of Captain Nagle's company, New York volunteers, have been mounted and sent out, but it is badly equipped. The proper equipage is not to be had in the country. I would respectfully ask that a full and complete set of cavalry equipage, including spurs and valises, to mount 150 men, may be sent to me as early as possible. The saddles, if not on hand, should be made by Grimsby, in St. Louis.

The Indians from the different missions have mostly fled to the mountains and joined the wild tribes, and from their knowledge of the country are enabled to do great mischief. They might be reclaimed and placed between the settlements (which are very sparse) and the wild Indians, and thus be used as a barrier, by entering into some treaty stipulations with them, and placing among them some discreet sub-agents; but without a supply of Indian presents it is useless at this time to attempt anything of the kind. The Indians are very numerous. It would be good policy to send to this place a large supply of Indian presents, such as will be really useful—not trinkets and baubles—and enter into a treaty with them.

There is one subject that I desire to bring to the serious consideration of the department and the Executive; and that is, the speedy payment of the various claims in California against the United States created since the hoisting of our flag in this country. These claims are for horses and other property taken, and supplies furnished, for the use of the troops that were at the time hastily collected, as well as for the payment now due to the men themselves, and the various other debts that were necessarily contracted in carrying on operations.

The troops thus hastily got together were discharged in April last; but, from bad counsel or from some other cause, they refused to be mustered into service under the volunteer acts of May and June, 1846, and therefore could not be paid by the army paymasters at all.

The claimants, natives and foreigners, are loud and clamorous, and excite a great deal of dissatisfaction and bad feeling in the country towards our government; they charge it with a want of good faith, violation of promises, &c., &c.

A speedy payment of these claims will do more towards reconciling the Californians to the change of flags, and be worth more to the United States, than ten times the money it will take to pay the debt.

I would most earnestly recommend that some discreet *citizen*, who is in no way interested in those claims, be appointed, with a secretary, to investigate and adjudicate upon all claims presented against the United States. Those upon which he puts a favorable endorsement, authorize the disbursing officers, who should be supplied with ample funds, to pay at once.

Many of these claims, perhaps a great majority of them, are only evidenced by the receipt or certificate given for the property taken or amount claimed by persons not in the service of the United States, but who were sent out, by the authority of the land or naval commander at the time, to collect horses, saddles, &c., &c.; and I believe all the claims of the officers and men of the late California battalion of volunteers are evidenced by the due bills given and signed by the pay and quartermaster of that corps; and a very great many claimants assert, and I believe truly, that their property was taken and no receipt or certificate given.

Treasury drafts, or the drafts of disbursing officers, are here twenty per cent. below par. Remove these claims—pay them off—and the disbursing officers can obtain money here for their drafts at par, and the people will become reconciled and satisfied.

I am, respectfully, your obedient servant,
R. B. MASON,
Colonel 1st Dragoons, commanding.

Brig. Gen. R. JONES,
Adjutant General U. S. Army, Washington, D. C.

HEADQUARTERS TENTH MILITARY DEPARTMENT,
Monterey, California, June 1, 1847.

SIR: The Lexington transport will soon be at Santa Barbara to take yourself and two companies of your command to Lower California. I have no instructions for you in addition to those written by the General, who left here yesterday for the United States, except that you will take your surgeon with you and such supplies of medicines and hospital stores as may be deemed necessary, taking care to leave a sufficiency for the company that remains.

You will give up the house that you rented for the use of the camp women, as there will be ample room for all in the quarters now occupied when the two companies embark.

The funds derived from the custom-houses in Lower California are to be applied exclusively to civil purposes.

The custom-house officers should not receive as salary more than from five to seven hundred dollars per year, (to be paid half-yearly,) provided that they collect as much revenue at their respective ports.

The quartermasters, should you occupy more than one place, nearest the custom-houses will audit the accounts of the collector, and receive from him all funds arising from the customs, port charges, &c., &c., and render to you a quarterly account of the same, a copy of which you will send to this office.

The civil officers (collectors of customs, alcaldes, &c.) now in Lower California should be continued in office, if they are suitable and well-disposed towards our cause; if not, remove them and appoint others.

Take care, in appointing officers entitled to a salary, to keep your appointments within the receipts from the customs.

Let me know if a suitable physician can be obtained in Santa Barbara for the company you will leave there, and at what price. [See Regulations, 309 and 310.] If I sanction the employment of one, he will be paid before sending his accounts to the Surgeon General, as directed in paragraph 1,222, Army Regulations.

The two companies that you take with you to Lower California should not be encumbered with much, if any, private baggage; it should be securely boxed up, marked, and left in store at Santa Barbara. You might indulge your camp women a little, by not restricting them too closely.

Very respectfully, your obedient servant,

R. B MASON,
Colonel 1st Dragoons.

Lieut. Col. H. S. Burton, *Santa Barbara, California.*

Headquarters Tenth Military Department,
Monterey, California, June 2, 1847.

Sir: You will, in accordance with the enclosed order, No. 23, of this date, afford Mr. L. W. Boggs, the alcalde of Sonoma district, such assistance with the force under your orders as may be necessary to enable him to obtain the public records and papers appertaining to his office from the possession of Mr. Nash, the late alcalde of said district, who refuses to give them up. Should you be obliged to arrest Mr. Nash with your guard, do it firmly, but at the same time with as much civility and courtesy as the circumstances of the case will admit of, and continue the arrest no longer than, after a conference with the alcalde, it may be deemed necessary.

I am, respectfully, your obedient servant,

R. B. MASON,
Colonel 1st Dragoons, commanding.

Captain J. E. Bracket,
7th Regiment New York Volunteers,
Commanding at Sonoma, California.

Headquarters Tenth Military Department,
Monterey, California, June 4, 1847.

Sir: I have the honor to acknowledge the receipt of your two letters of the 30th May, as also the one of the 26th.

In a few days I will give you instructions in relation to the San Rafael property, &c.

The course pursued by yourself relative to the public meeting recently held in San Francisco meets my approval.

I cannot at this time relieve you from duty with the regiment of volunteers of which you are the major—the interests of the service will not admit of it; and were you to retire now, I think it would seriously affect **your standing as** a military man.

I well know the perplexities and difficulties you have to encounter at San Francisco, but a firm and determined perseverance will overcome them after a while.

I am, respectfully, your obedient servant,
R. B. MASON,
Colonel 1st Dragoons, commanding.

Major J. A. HARDIE,
7th Regiment New York Volunteers, San Francisco.

P. S.—Send me, as early as practicable, an inventory of all ordnance and ordnance stores at San Francisco.

R. B. M., *Colonel, commanding.*

HEADQUARTERS TENTH MILITARY DEPARTMENT,
Monterey, California, June 5, 1847.

COLONEL: I enclose you a copy of a letter I have this day written to Captain Hunt, of the Mormon battalion, and beg of you to use your best efforts to accomplish the object I have therein proposed, and to carry out my views.

You will order up the company from San Diego in season to join the battalion at the Angeles some several days before the expiration of their service, both with a view of being paid and mustered out of service at the same time, as well as to give those who may choose to do so an opportunity of re-entering, reorganizing, and being mustered in for another term of twelve months, unless sooner discharged.

The reorganization and mustering in, upon the new term, must take place on the same day that they are mustered out of service on their present term.

Should you be able to get three companies to re-enter the service, you will send one of them back to San Diego or San Luis Rey, as you may think proper; or you may keep the whole of them at the Angeles for a short time to assist in completing the fort, but say nothing of working on the fort until after they are mustered into service.

I have been informed that one of the objections some of the Mormons express against continuing in service another year is, that it brings them to the middle of summer before they are discharged, when it is too late to begin farming; and that if they could be discharged say at the end of March, many would re-enter who otherwise would not.

The law of the 13th May last requires that the volunteers should enter for twelve months; and, therefore, I could not muster them in for a less time; but I will pledge that they shall be discharged at the end of March next, if they desire it.

I am, sir, very respectfully, your obedient servant,
R. B. MASON,
Colonel 1st Dragoons, commanding.

Colonel J. D. STEVENSON,
Commanding Southern Military District,
Pueblo de los Angeles.

HEADQUARTERS TENTH MILITARY DEPARTMENT,
Monterey, June 7, 1847.

SIR: I have sent to Colonel Stevenson an order for you to muster out of service the Mormon battalion when their time shall have expired, as also to muster into service any companies that may wish to re-enter. As there will have to be an entire reorganization of the companies that re-enter, it had better be commenced several days beforehand, so that the officers can be elected, and all the rolls made out, and they be mustered in on the very same day that their time expires—muster out and muster into service all on the same day.

Captain Jefferson Hunt will be mustered in as the major or lieutenant colonel, according to the number of companies, if he wishes the command; but if an election for the field officers is insisted upon, he must be elected by the officers of the new battalion.

I wish you would converse freely with Captain Hunt upon the subject, and urge upon him to accept the command with the increased rank and pay.

I am, respectfully, your obedient servant,
R. B. MASON,
Colonel 1st Dragoons, commanding.
Lieutenant J. H. SMITH,
 1*st Dragoons, Angeles, California.*

HEADQUARTERS TENTH MILITARY DEPARTMENT,
Monterey, California, June 12, 1847.

SIR: Your letter of the 7th May, from Wallock, Sacramento, has been received.

Colonel Mason, governor of California, says that you should at once collect all the evidence you can from competent persons as to the number, description, and value of the horses for which you claim remuneration, by whom they were taken, and that they were received into actual service of the United States; all which should be laid before whatever person the United States may hereafter appoint to settle up and pay off such claims.

It is expected that Congress will, at an early date, make provision for the payment of all good claims in California against the government.

I am, with great respect, your most obedient servant,
W. T. SHERMAN,
First Lieutenant 3d Artillery, A. A. A. G.
Mr. THOMAS M. HARDY.

HEADQUARTERS TENTH MILITARY DEPARTMENT,
Monterey, California, June 12, 1847.

SIR: Your letter of May 25 reached this place after General Kearny had started for the United States. Colonel Mason, who succeeds him in the office of governor of California, has examined it and the statement of your account against the government of the United States.

He says that if you will send him copies of the receipts of Major Swords and Lieutenant Davidson, he will examine them and see if they can be paid.

But he has no authority to pay any claim at present, such as you hold the receipt of Mr. Snyder for; but you should keep that receipt and procure other written evidence of the delivery to Lieutenant Gillespie of the five mules, so as to be prepared to lay your claim before such person as may hereafter be appointed to examine and pay off the claims against the United States.

I am, with great respect, your most obedient servant,
W. T. SHERMAN,
First Lieutenant 3d Artillery, A. A. A. G.

Mr. J. J. WARNER,
Care of the Quartermaster, Los Angeles, California.

HEADQUARTERS TENTH MILITARY DEPARTMENT,
Monterey, California, June 14, 1847.

SIR: Colonel Mason has received your letter, enclosing a requisition for ordnance and ordnance stores for the fort at Los Angeles. He directs me to inform you that there are no 24 or 32-pounder howitzers here, and that at a fort so far inland, where there is no danger of an attack from heavy guns, he considers 6 or 9-pounder guns of sufficiently heavy calibre for its defence.

He directs that you select from among the guns you now have at the pueblo such as are best suited to the purpose, and cause them to be placed in the battery in the fort, with their own carriages mounted on platforms.

The United States ship Lexington will carry for you to San Pedro a field battery of two guns and two howitzers, with caissons, battery wagon, forge, and all the necessary harness and equipments complete, with a full supply of ammunition.

These, together with such of the old guns as you may erect in battery in the fort, are supposed to be as many as you can use to advantage.

If you know of any artillery in the country, you will cause it to be rendered useless to an enemy, or conveyed to the pueblo.

I have the honor to be, sir, your most obedient servant,
W. T. SHERMAN,
First Lieutenant 3d Artillery, A. A. A. G.

Colonel J. D. STEVENSON,
Los Angeles, California.

HEADQUARTERS TENTH MILITARY DEPARTMENT,
Monterey, June 16, 1847.

SIR: Colonel Mason has sent the battery of field artillery from Monterey to Pueblo de los Angeles and Lower California, and directs it to be replaced by the one now at San Francisco.

You will therefore cause that battery, with all the harness, equipments, fixed ammunition, and whatever else belongs to it, to be sent to Monterey by the first opportunity; the whole to be invoiced and marked to Lieutenant E. O. C., ordnance, commanding company F, 3d artillery.

I have the honor to be your most obedient servant,

W. T. SHERMAN,
First Lieutenant 3d Artillery, A. A. A. G.

Major J. A. HARDIE,
Commanding, San Francisco.

HEADQUARTERS TENTH MILITARY DEPARTMENT,
Monterey, California, June 1, 1847.

SIR: Your two communications of the 15th and 19th ultimo, addressed to Brigadier General Kearny, have been turned over to me for official action by that officer, who left here yesterday on his return to the United States.

Enclosed is an appointment of *alcalde* for Louis Robideau, of the district of San Bernadeno, which be pleased to forward to him.

Notify the alcalde at Los Angeles that the appointment has been officially made, so that the jurisdiction of the two districts may not clash.

I enclose a blank appointment for a collector of customs and harbormaster at San Diego. I wish the blank filled with the name of Don Juan Baudini, if he will accept the appointment. If he declines it, then fill the blank with the name of any one whom you think the most proper person.

The present collector must settle all his accounts, and turn over to the quartermaster at Los Angeles all custom-house funds, and to his successor all the property and records of his office, together with all orders and instructions that he has received. When that is done, his resignation will be considered as having taken effect.

The new collector should be required to give security for the faithful performance of his duties.

I transmit herewith for Don Santiago Arguillo, the custom-house officer at San Diego, a copy of General Kearny's letter to him of the 21st April, which it appears he has never received.

Very respectfully, your obedient servant,

R. B. MASON,
Colonel 1st Dragoons, and Governor of California.

Colonel J. D. STEVENSON,
Seventh Regiment New York Volunteers,
commanding at Los Angeles, California.

Know all men by these presents, that I, Richard B. Mason, colonel 1st regiment dragoons United States army, and governor of California, by virtue of authority in me vested, do hereby appoint *Louis Robideau* alcalde for and in the district of San Bernadeno, Upper California.

Given at Monterey, the capital of California, this first day of June, in the year of our Lord eighteen hundred and forty-seven, and the 71st of the independence of the United States.

R. B. MASON,
Colonel 1st Dragoons, Governor of California.

CIRCULAR.

HEADQUARTERS TENTH MILITARY DEPARTMENT,
Monterey, California, June 1, 1847.

The military officers in Upper California who have been directed to settle the accounts of the custom-house officers, and to receive from them the funds arising from the customs, will keep and account to these headquarters for those funds at the end of each regular quarter of the year, commencing with the first quarter of 1847, separate and apart from all other public funds in their possession. These funds are to be applied only upon the order of the governor to the civil department in California.

R. B. MASON,
Colonel 1st Dragoons, Governor of California.

MONTEREY, CALIFORNIA, *June 2, 1847.*

SIR: Your letters to General Kearny of the 26th and 28th of April, and of the 6th of May, reached here during his absence to Los Angeles, which will account to you why the subjects to which they refer have not been attended to at an earlier date.

The General left here on the 31st ultimo, on his way to the United States, and turned the above-named letters over to me for official action.

I have issued an order directing the commanding officers at all posts and stations to aid, with the troops under their command, the civil magistrates, when called upon, in executing the laws and carrying into effect their judicial decrees, where they cannot otherwise do it, directing the officers at the same time to perform this duty in a civil and courteous manner, and to use no more harshness than is absolutely necessary for effecting their purpose. The military officer near you will therefore give you his aid in obtaining the records of your office from Mr. Nash, the late alcalde in your district. The proper manner to proceed will be to make an official call, in writing, upon the military officer near you, for force to assist you in searching the premises of Mr. Nash, and taking from him, wherever they can be found, all public papers appertaining to the office of alcalde in the district of Sonoma; and this search you are hereby authorized to make. It would be well to take with you two disinterested persons to be present as witnesses.

Having been only two days in office as governor, I am not at this time prepared to say what is the extent of your powers and jurisdiction as alcalde; you must, for the time being, be governed by the customs and laws of the country, as far as you can ascertain them, and by your own good sense and sound discretion.

In relation to an interpreter, be pleased to refer to the letter of my predecessor to the alcalde of the Sonoma district, dated March 3, 1847.

I regret that it is not in my power to afford the people in California any greater mail facilities at this time than the military express that has been established, once in two weeks, between San Francisco and San Diego, which carries the letters and papers for all persons free of charge.

Your letter of the 6th May I will reply to in a short time.

This is a military government, and the supreme power, as you say, is vested in the senior military officer of the Territory.

My instructions tell me it is the duty of the Executive to carry on the war with all the rights and subject to all the duties imposed by the laws of nations, a code binding on both belligerents.

The possession of portions of the enemy's territory, acquired by justifiable acts of war, gives to us the right of government during the continuance of our possession, and imposes on us a duty to the inhabitants who are thus placed under our dominion.

This right of possession, however, is temporary, unless made absolute by subsequent events. If, being in possession, a treaty of peace is made and duly ratified on the principle of " *uti possidetis*"—that is, that each of the belligerent parties shall enjoy the territory of which it shall be in possession at the date of the treaty—or if the surrender of the territory is not stipulated in the treaty so ratified, then the imperfect title acquired by conquest is made absolute, and the inhabitants, with the territory, are entitled to all the benefits of the federal constitution of the United States, to the same extent as the citizens of any other part of the Union.

The course of our government in regard to California, or other portions of the territory of Mexico, now or hereafter to be in our possession by conquest, depends on those on whom the constitution imposes the duty of making and carrying treaties into effect.

Pending the war, our possession gives only such rights as the laws of nations recognise; and the government is military, performing such civil duties as are necessary to the full enjoyment of the advantages resulting from the conquest, and to the due protection of the rights of persons and of property of the inhabitants.

No political rights can be conferred on the inhabitants thus situated emanating from the constitution of the United States. That instrument established a form of government for those who are within our limits, and owe voluntary allegiance to it, unless incorporated, with the assent of Congress, by ratified treaty or by legislative act, as in the case of Texas. Our rights over enemies' territory in our possession are only such as the laws of war confer, and theirs no more than are derived from the same authority.

I am, respectfully, your obedient servant,
R. B. MASON,
Colonel 1st Dragoons, Governor of California.

L. W. BOGGS, Esq.,
Alcalde at Sonoma, California.

MONTEREY, CALIFORNIA, *June* 3, 1847.

SIR: I find among the papers turned over to me by General Kearny, when he left this place on his return to the United States, the proceedings of a public meeting held at Sonoma on the 21st of the last month, of which you were the chairman, requesting the General to recall his order for the removal of Mr. J. H. Nash from the office of alcalde of Sonoma district.

I know not the reasons that influenced the General in his removal of Mr. Nash, but am bound to presume they were good and sufficient, and therefore I cannot feel justified in revoking his order.

It may not be improper to remark, that many of my countrymen in

California labor under a mistake in believing that, because we are in possession of the country, we are under the constitution and laws of the United States.

Pending a war with a foreign country, a possession of any of the enemy's territories acquired by conquest gives only such rights as are recognised by the laws of nations, and theirs no more than are derived from the same authority.

I have little doubt but that in a very short time we shall have the good tidings of peace; then to a *certainty*, to a great and *moral certainty*, California will forever belong to the United States, and we all shall enjoy the blessings of our own constitution and laws.

In the mean time it behooves every good man, each in his respective sphere, as far as in him lies, both by precept and example, to preserve the quiet of the country that now so happily exists, and to abstain from all things that might have a tendency to produce an excitement through the country, or an irritation in the minds of the native citizens.

Let the Californians, when they come under the constitution and laws of the United States, *as they inevitably must*, be as favorably impressed as possible towards our people and our institutions.

I am, sir, very respectfully, your obedient servant,
R. B. MASON,
Colonel 1st Dragoons, Governor of California.

Mr. JOHN GRIGSBY,
   Sonoma, California.

MONTEREY, CALIFORNIA, *June* 3, 1847.

SIR: Your communication of the 20th ultimo, and its enclosure, addressed to General Kearny, was turned over to me unacted upon by that officer when he left here on his return to the United States.

In that communication you say: "I deem my title perfectly valid before the Mexican government, but I am desirous that it should be ratified by the United States government, and that I have now the honor respectfully to solicit your excellency's approbation to the same, in order to its perfect security."

The United States can ratify no land titles in California until her laws and courts are established in the country; at present she pretends to the exercise of no right that is not authorized by the laws of nations and the laws of war.

I am, respectfully, your obedient servant,
R. B. MASON,
Colonel 1st Dragoons, Governor of California.

NATHAN SPEAR,
   San Francisco, California.

MONTEREY, CALIFORNIA, *June* 3, 1847.

SIR: Your letter of the 10th May, addressed to the governor of Upper California, was turned over to me by General Kearny when he left here on his return to the United States.

It is not proper that I should exercise the power of granting lands in California to individuals; that can only be done by the Congress of the United States, when she establishes her laws over the country.

At present I pretend to exercise no right that is not authorized by the laws of nations and the laws of war.

I am, respectfully, your obedient servant,
R. B. MASON,
Colonel 1st Dragoons, Governor of California.

Mr. GABRIEL ALBISU, *Santa Clara, California.*

MONTEREY, CALIFORNIA, *June 4,* 1847.

SIR: I find among the official papers left here by General Kearny two communications from you to that officer, dated on the 28th May, to which I have the honor now to reply.

The case which you present of the claim of Mr. Oliver to the garden at the mission of San Juan has already been disposed of by my predecessor in office, by his decree bearing date the 22d of March last.

The various claims which exist in California to mission property can only be settled by the proper judicial tribunals, when they are established in the country. I regret that it is beyond the reach of my authority or power to cause the pension which has heretofore been paid by the government of California, from the custom-house funds at this port, to be continued to Pedro Atillan.

The funds now collected at the custom-house in Monterey belong to the United States, and cannot be paid in the way of pension to any person whatever, until that person's name has been placed upon the pension list by an act of the Congress of the United States.

I have the honor to be, sir, with high regard and esteem, your obedient servant,
R. B. MASON,
Colonel 1st Dragoons, Governor of California.

Mr. J. S. MOERENHOUT,
Consul of France, Monterey, California.

MONTEREY, CALIFORNIA, *June 7,* 1847

SIR: You will, upon the receipt of this communication, deliver over to Mr. L. W. Boggs, the alcalde at Sonoma, all the books, papers, and records of every description appertaining to the alcalde's office at that place.

Be pleased also to turn over to Mr. Boggs all funds or obligations for funds arising from the sale of lots in Sonoma, together with a schedule of all lots that you have sold, and an account current of the proceeds, &c.

I am, respectfully, your obedient servant,
R. B. MASON,
Colonel 1st Dragoons, Governor of California.

Mr. NASH,
At Sonoma, California.

NOTE.—The original of this letter this day enclosed to L. W. Boggs in the letter addressed to him and dated on the 2d instant.
JUNE 7, 1847.

Know all men by these presents, that I, Richard B. Mason, colonel first regiment dragoons, United States army, and governor of California, by virtue of authority in me vested, do hereby appoint William B. Ide *land surveyor* for and in the northern department of Upper California. Done at Monterey, Upper California, this 7th day of June, 1847, and the seventy-first of the independence of the United States.

R. B. MASON,
Colonel 1st Dragoons, Governor of California.

MONTEREY, CALIFORNIA, *June* 7, 1847.

SIR: I have reflected upon the subject presented in your letter of the 6th May, addressed to General Kearny, my predecessor in office.

I possess no authority to make or authorize the grants of land in California; my authority here is that of a belligerent, which gives only the right acquired by conquest to establish a temporary government during the time the province is held by a miliary force. Any grant of land that I might make or authorize to be made would therefore be null and void, if, at the definitive treaty of peace, Mexico were to retain California.

I do not mean by this that there is the slightest possibility that Mexico will ever again recover California, by treaty or otherwise.

It being the practice and custom of the country for the alcaldes to sell lots within the limits of their town, as I know is done both here and at San Francisco, you are hereby authorized to carry out so much of General Vallejo's instructions from the Mexican government as relates to the *sale* of lots in the town of Sonoma; the proceeds, after paying expenses, to be applied for benefiting and improving the town.

I see that in the instructions to General Vallejo above mentioned, as published in the Californian of the 10th of April, the word "*grant*" is used, and not the word "*sell*" or "*sale.*" That word "*grant,*" as applied to town lots, I construe, for your guide, to mean *sale* of town lots, to *sell* town lots, town lots *sold;* and in view of that construction, I have used the word "*sale*" in the authority above given you.

The town lots sold by the former alcalde, Mr. Nash, must stand, as to title, on the same footing as those sold, or to be sold, by yourself.

Congress will unquestionably confirm all titles so given when our title to California is made absolute by a definitive treaty of peace, if the title as it stands is not deemed sound and good without such confirmation.

I am, respectfully, your obedient servant,

R. B. MASON,
Colonel 1st Dragoons, Governor of California.

Mr. L. W. BOGGS,
Alcalde at Sonoma, California.

P. S.—I have inadvertently spoken of General Vallejo's instructions as instructions from the Mexican government. In this I was wrong. The instructions were from José Figueroa, the governor of Upper California in 1835. June 8, 1847.

MONTEREY, CALIFORNIA, *June* 14, 1847.

GENTLEMEN: I have the honor to acknowledge the receipt of your communication of the 5th of the present month, addressed to General Kearny, my predecessor in office. I admire and applaud the feelings of patriotism which dictated your letter.

In the present condition of affairs in California, the alcaldes are not "authorities of the United States," nor are they Mexican authorities. They are the civil magistrates of California, and therefore the "authorities of California" within their respective jurisdictions, subject to removal from office by the authority of the governor, and, from the circumstances in which the country is at present placed, must necessarily be so.

It is so essentially necessary to the preservation of law and order that the offices of alcalde at Santa Barbara should be filled by good men, that I fondly cherish the hope you will continue to California those good services which I know you are so capable of performing.

I am, gentlemen, with sentiments of great respect and esteem, your obedient servant,

R. B. MASON,
Colonel 1st Dragoons, Governor of California.

Señores Don PABLO DE LA GUERRA, and
Don LUIS CARRILLO,
Alcaldes at Santa Barbara.

Know all men by these presents, that I, Richard B. Mason, colonel 1st regiment dragoons United States army, and governor of California, by virtue of authority in me vested, do hereby appoint James F. Reed sheriff of the district of Sonoma, on the north side of the bay of San Francisco.

Given at Monterey, the capital of California, this 14th day of June, in the year of our Lord eighteen hundred and forty-seven, and the 71st of the independence of the United States.

R. B. MASON,
Colonel 1st Dragoons, Governor of California.

MONTEREY, CALIFORNIA, *June* 14, 1847.

SIR: I should have done myself the honor to have answered your note of the 7th instant at an earlier date, but that it was kept until Saturday by Lieutenant Maddox, into whose hands I placed it, that he might have the opportunity of offering anything he had to say touching the subject to which it refers. The accompanying papers, marked 1, 2, 3, and 4, will show you the lieutenant's version of the subject. It is expected that our Congress at their next meeting will make an early appropriation for the purpose of satisfying the just claims existing in California against the United States.

The demands of Richards and Maube will then have to be submitted to such person or persons as may be appointed to adjudicate and pay off such claims.

I have the honor to be, sir, with great respect and esteem, your obedient servant,

R. B. MASON,
Colonel 1st Dragoons, Governor of California.

Mr. J. S. MOERENHOUT,
Consul of France, Monterey, California.

MONTEREY, CALIFORNIA, *June* 16, 1847.

Your communications of the 6th of the present month, respecting the recent acts of lawless violence committed in San Luis Obispo, have been received.

I have to desire that you will, with as little delay as circumstances will admit, come to Monterey. You will bring with you Vincente Feliz, Francisco Abbisu, and Soluy, who are charged with taking part in the aforesaid acts of violence.

You will bring with you Gaudalupe Cantua, Thomas Olivera, and Joaquin Valenzuela, as witnesses summoned by Faustino Garcia and José Rodriguez, alias Lerta, who are now in confinement at this place.

And I have also to desire that you will bring some three or four witnesses who are thoroughly cognizant of all the facts attending the outrages said to have been committed, whose evidence will be required in prosecuting the investigation which public justice demands against the persons implicated.

For the execution of this order, you are at liberty to use the authority of my name, and employ any force that may be necessary.

The promptitude with which you have acted in this affair merits commendation.

Very respectfully, your obedient servant,
R. B. MASON,
Colonel 1*st Dragoons, Governor of California.*

J. MARIANO BONILLO,
Alcalde of San Luis Obispo.

To all whom it may concern:

Know ye, that I, Richard B. Mason, colonel of the 1st regiment United States dragoons, and governor of California, do hereby grant unto Colonel José Castro, late commandant general of California, a free passport to return to Monterey, in Upper California, where he will be kindly and well received by the undersigned and all United States authorities.

All United States naval officers on the western coast of Mexico and California are requested to aid in facilitating the return of the said Castro to Monterey.

Given at Monterey, the capital of California, this 17th day of June, in the year of our Lord eighteen hundred and forty-seven, and the 71st of the independence of the United States.
R. B. MASON,
Colonel 1*st Dragoons, Governor of California.*

HEADQUARTERS TENTH MILITARY DEPARTMENT,
Monterey, California, June 1, 1847.

SIR: If there are any muskets or rifles at your post that have been *collected from the people* living in the southern part of Upper California, they may be returned to *such few individuals* as you may think can be safely trusted; but be very cautious into whose hands you place them.

Should any such arms—those taken from the people to the southward—be *borne upon* the *returns* of the ordnance sergeant, he must have a written order to turn them over, so as to enable him to account for them.

Inform me of the name and date with which you will fill the blanks in the appointment for the collector at San Diego.

Very respectfully, your obedient servant,

R. B. MASON,
Colonel 1st Dragoons, Governor of California.

Colonel J. D. STEVENSON,
7th Regiment New York Volunteers,
Com'g at Los Angeles, California.

HEADQUARTERS TENTH MILITARY DEPARTMENT,
Monterey, California, June 21, 1847.

SIR: An opportunity offering to San Francisco, I send off this letter in the hope that it will overtake my despatch to you of the 18th instant at that place, and that both will reach you at the same time.

A claim has to-day been presented to me against the United States of so extraordinary a nature that I deem it proper to send it to you for the information of the department.

You will perceive it is for money borrowed at an enormous rate of interest by Lieutenant Colonel Fremont, from one Antonio José Cot, and, too, in the official character of governor of California, when he knew that General Kearny, his superior and commanding officer, was here in the country.

In the same manner, the Lieutenant Colonel gave orders and caused the collector of customs at San Pedro to receive in payment of custom-house dues a large amount, say about $1,700, of depreciated paper, signed by individuals in no way responsible to the government.

General Kearny has gone home prepared to lay all the facts attending that transaction before the War Department.

The object that I now have in view is to request that Lieutenant Colonel Fremont may be required to refund immediately the seventeen hundred dollars that the treasury of California has thus lost by his illegal order.

The money is wanted to defray the expenses of the civil department in this country.

I am, respectfully, your obedient servant,

R. B. MASON,
Colonel 1st Dragoons, commanding.

Brigadier General R. JONES,
Adjutant General U. S. A., Washington, D. C.

I, the undersigned, governor of California for the United States of North America, acknowledge that I have received from Don Antonio José Cot, merchant of this city, *two thousand dollars* in hard cash, which he has furnished this government for the public service. And I bind myself, in the name of the United States government, to return the said sum within the term of two months from this date, paying for interest three per cent. per month, or one hundred and twenty dollars. But if, at the expiration

of this term, the government should see fit still to make use of these two thousand dollars, Mr. Cot agrees that the interest shall run for four months longer at two per cent. per month, or one hundred and sixty dollars for the four months. And for the fulfilment of what has been stipulated I bind myself, as governor of California.
For $2,000. J. C. FREMONT.
ANGELES, *February* 4, 1847.

I have furthermore received from the said Mr. Cot the sum of one thousand dollars, in the terms expressed above.
For $1,000. J. C. FREMONT.
ANGELES, *February* 20, 1847.

I have received from Mr. Fremont the sum of one hundred and eighty dollars for the interest of two months on the three thousand dollars mentioned in this obligation.
ANTONIO JOSE COT.
A copy of the original:
ANTONIO JOSE COT.
ANGELES, *April* 12, 1847.

HEADQUARTERS TENTH MILITARY DEPARTMENT,
Monterey, California, July 21, 1847.

SIR: I herewith transmit the post return of Monterey for the month of June, 1847, and in other packages, by the same opportunity, the muster-rolls of company F, 3d artillery, companies D and I, 7th regiment New York volunteers, and of the company of California volunteers, copies of orders of the tenth military department up to June 28, 1847, and the original proceedings of general courts-martial at Ciudad de los Angeles and San Francisco, California.

Lieutenant Colonel Burton, 7th regiment New York volunteers, sailed from Santa Barbara for Lower California, in the United States storeship Lexington, about the 3d or 4th of July. No official intelligence has yet been received of the exact date. He took with him companies A and B of that regiment—an aggregate of 115.

I also send copies of letters and decrees relating to the civil affairs of California up to July 13, 1847.

I have the honor to be your most obedient servant,
R. B. MASON,
Colonel 1st Dragoons, commanding.
To General R. JONES,
Adjutant General United States Army,
Washington, D. C.

To all whom it may concern:

Be it known, that, Brigadier General S. W. Kearny having been permitted to return to the United States, the undersigned, by virtue of the authority and orders of the President of the United States, this day enters upon the duties of governor and commander-in-chief of all the United States land forces in California.

Done at Monterey, the capital of California, this 31st day of May, in the year of our Lord 1847, and the 71st of the independence of the United States.

R. B. MASON,
Colonel 1st Dragoons, Governor and Commander-in-chief of the United States land forces in California.

To all whom it may concern:

Know ye, that I, Richard B. Mason, colonel 1st regiment United States dragoons, and governor of California, do hereby grant unto Colonel José Castro, late commandant general of California, a free passport to return to Monterey, in Upper California, where he will be kindly and well received by the undersigned and all United States authorities.

All United States naval officers on the western coast of Mexico and California are requested to aid in facilitating the return of the said Castro to Monterey.

Given at Monterey, the capital of California, this 17th day of June, in the year of our Lord 1847, and the 71st of the independence of the United States.

R. B. MASON,
Colonel 1st Dragoons, Governor of California.

Know all men by these presents, that I, Richard B. Mason, colonel 1st regiment dragoons United States army, and governor of California, by virtue of authority in me vested, do hereby appoint *William Blackburn* an alcalde within the jurisdiction of Santa Cruz, Upper California.

Given at Monterey, the capital of California, this 21st day of June, 1847, and the 71st of the independence of the United States.

R. B. MASON,
Colonel 1st Dragoons, Governor of California.

HEADQUARTERS TENTH MILITARY DEPARTMENT,
Monterey, California, June 21, 1847.

SIR: Herewith I send you an appointment of alcalde within the jurisdiction of Santa Cruz.

I have complaints made to me that certain foreigners are intruding upon the lands and trespassing upon the property of Mr. Pierre Sainsevain, a Frenchman, who has exhibited his title papers to me. They appear to be full, clear, and beyond dispute.

I request that in all cases you will cause the just rights of the citizens to be duly respected. This we are bound to do. The lands of this Frenchman will be soon surveyed, and his boundaries duly marked. In the mean time, those persons who have *no claim* to land adjoining this

Frenchman should not be permitted to intrude within his claimed boundaries because his lines happen not to be distinctly marked. Emigrants coming into the country who wish their own rights respected should not violate the rights of others—the natives and adopted citizens.

I am, respectfully, your obedient servant,
R. B. MASON,
Colonel 1st Dragoons, Governor of California.

Mr. WILLIAM BLACKBURN,
Alcalde, jurisdiction of Santa Cruz.

HEADQUARTERS TENTH MILITARY DEPARTMENT,
Monterey, California, June 21, 1847.

SIR: I have reflected well upon the subject you presented in the case of B. R. Buckalew *versus* the town of San Francisco. If the report of the commissioners, Messrs. Sempel and Pettit, be carried into effect, and the one-half of the fractional lot immediately south of lot No. 208 be given to Mr. Buckalew, in consideration of the damages he has sustained by a change made in Battery street, a change must necessarily be made in the conditions contained in the grant made by my predecessor, General Kearny, to the town of San Francisco, before the town authorities can make Buckalew a legal title; for without such change in the conditions of the grant, the town authorities can only dispose of said fractional lot at public auction, and not then until public notice has been given for a certain length of time.

I do not feel disposed to interfere with any of the conditions imposed by General Kearny affecting the sale of water lots in the town of San Francisco, and therefore decree that any damage sustained by individuals consequent upon the change of streets is a just charge against the town, and may very properly be paid out of the funds arising from the sale of said lots.

I am, respectfully, your obedient servant,
R. B. MASON,
Colonel 1st Dragoons, Governor of California.

GEORGE HYDE, Esq.,
First Alcalde, San Francisco, California.

MONTEREY, CALIFORNIA,
June 24, 1847.

ANTONIO ROUBIDOUX
    vs. } Trover and conversion.
JACOB P. LEASE.

The plaintiff in the above-entitled cause makes an affidavit and files a petition for a change of venue. The venue is accordingly changed from San Francisco to Monterey.

In granting this change of venue, it is not to be construed as at all affecting the question of jurisdiction.

Done at Monterey, the capital of California, this 24th day of June, 1847, and the 71st of the independence of the United States.

R. B. MASON,
Colonel 1st Dragoons, Governor of California.

To all whom it may concern:

All persons occupying any of the mission buildings at Santa Clara and San José without the permission of the Catholic priest, (Padre Real,) are hereby required to vacate immediately said buildings.

Ample and sufficient time has been afforded the occupants of the above-mentioned mission buildings to seek other places of abode since the decree of General Kearny, concerning said missions, dated March 22, 1847.

The alcalde at the Pueblo de San José will take measures—if rendered necessary by the said occupants continuing to remain in the mission buildings—to carry the aforesaid decree of the 22d March into effect, as the latter clause thereof directs. If required, a military force will be sent to the pueblo to enforce the judicial acts of the alcalde.

Done at Monterey, the capital of California, this 24th day of June, 1847, and the 71st of the independence of the United States.

R. B. MASON,
Colonel 1st Dragoons, Governor of California.

Know all men by these presents, that I, Richard B. Mason, colonel 1st regiment dragoons United States army, and governor of California, by virtue of authority in me vested, do hereby appoint Jasper O'Farrel an additional land surveyor for and in the northern department of Upper California.

Done at Monterey, the capital of California, this 6th day of July, 1847, and the 71st of the independence of the United States.

R. B. MASON,
Colonel 1st Dragoons, Governor of California.

HEADQUARTERS TENTH MILITARY DEPARTMENT,
Monterey, California, July 12, 1847.

REVEREND SIR: I have the honor to acknowledge the receipt of your two letters, both of the 14th June, together with their accompanying papers.

The account for loss of property at the missions of Santa Clara and San José I will lay before such commission as may be appointed by the United States government to adjudicate and pay off the various claims in California against the United States. I very much regret to learn that those missions have suffered so great a loss.

You having called my attention to the non-observance of General Kearny's decree of the 22d March, I had prepared instructions for Captain Nagle's command, which left here for Pueblo yesterday, to cause that decree to be enforced; but I changed those instructions in consequence of the understanding I had with you through Mr. Hartwell, the official interpreter.

I send you a copy of the instructions above mentioned as changed, by which you will see that if the occupants of the missions of Santa Clara and San José remain longer than is necessary to gather their crops, it must be by a special agreement with yourself.

I have duly considered your complaint against the alcalde at Pueblo de San José. I will instruct that officer not again to perform the marriage ceremony during the military occupation of California, where either party is a member of the Catholic church.

I am, sir, with high respect and esteem, your obedient servant,
R. B. MASON,
Colonel 1st Dragoons, Governor of California.

To the Rev. Father JOSE MARIA DEL REAL,
now in Monterey, California.

HEADQUARTERS TENTH MILITARY DEPARTMENT,
Monterey, California, July 13, 1847.

SIR: I desire that, during the existing state of affairs in California, you will not perform the marriage ceremony in any case where either of the parties is a member of the Catholic church of this country.

I am induced to give these instructions from the fact that the United States government are exceedingly desirous, and indeed make it obligatory upon their authorities here, to secure to the Californians the full enjoyment of their religion and security in all their church and church privileges.

As their canonical laws, and I believe their civil laws also, prohibit any but their own priests from uniting members of their church in marriage, it is not proper that we should break in upon those laws, or customs, as the case may be, and particularly as it is the wish of the President that when the country is subjected to our laws the people may be as favorably disposed towards our government as possible.

It is therefore good policy for us to abstain from doing anything that will have a tendency to give them offence in matters wherein it may be thought their religion or church privileges are encroached upon.

I am, respectfully, your obedient servant,
R. B. MASON,
Colonel 1st Dragoons, Governor of California.

JOHN BURTON, Esq.,
Alealde, Pueblo de San José.

HEADQUARTERS TENTH MILITARY DEPARTMENT,
Monterey, California, July 21, 1847.

SIR: I have this moment received the original of which the enclosed is a copy. Being almost in the act of sealing my package for the United States that an express is now ready to take to San Francisco, to put on board the Columbus, I have had but a few moments to converse with Mr. Sparks, the gentleman mentioned in Captain Lippett's letter. From what I can learn from him, the expected attack on Santa Barbara is confined mostly to the people of the town and its vicinity, and altogether owing to the lawless acts of violence committed upon the people by the New York volunteers at that post. The officers, he tells me, have no control over the men, now that Lieutenant Colonel Burton has sailed for

Lower California. I shall immediately proceed to Santa Barbara, and take the most prompt and decisive measures that circumstances may call for.

I am, respectfully, your obedient servant,
R. B. MASON,
Colonel 1st Dragoons, commanding.

Brigadier General R. JONES,
Adjutant General U. S. A., Washington.

BARRACKS AT SANTA BARBARA, *July* 16, 1847.

SIR: I have the honor to state that, according to information derived from the most reliable sources, an attack will shortly be made by the Californians on this post.

If it is deemed proper to reinforce the post in consequence, I respectfully suggest that *regulars only* be sent, and that they be accompanied by a couple of field-pieces. Of regulars, *one-half* of a company would be amply sufficient.

The number of non-commissioned officers, musicians, and privates for duty by this morning's report, is fifty.

We have no other ammunition than about 3,700 rounds of ball cartridge, (percussion.)

The bearer, Mr. Sparks, who has obligingly volunteered to convey this communication express, is a gentleman in whose statements the most implicit reliance may be placed, and in whom Lieutenant Colonel Burton instructed me to place *peculiar* confidence. I beg to refer you to him for further particulars, not detailed in this letter.

With the greatest respect, your obedient servant,
FRANCIS J. LIPPETT,
Capt. Comp'y F, 7th reg't N. Y. volunteers,
comd'g, Santa Barbara.

Lieut. W. T. SHERMAN,
Acting Assistant Adjutant General.

HEADQUARTERS TENTH MILITARY DEPARTMENT,
Monterey, September 18, 1847.

SIR: My last letter to you was addressed on the 21st of July last, when I was preparing to embark in the sloop of war Dale for Santa Barbara. I reached that place on the evening of the 25th July, and took quarters with Captain Lippett, in the same building with the garrison of the town. I remained there eight days, and became fully satisfied that there were no just grounds to apprehend a popular outbreak, and that if threats to that effect had been made, they were nothing more than the expression of the natural feelings resulting from the bad conduct of some of the men composing the garrison. These I caused to be tried by a general court-martial or military commission, and to be punished as their cases merited. Since my return to Monterey, I have frequently heard from Santa Barbara, and have reason to believe my visit was of material service.

Colonel Stevenson, the commanding officer of Ciudad de los Angeles, met me at Santa Barbara, to consult upon the affairs of that section of California. He assured me that quiet and order prevailed, that all the natives seemed to be engaged in their customary pursuits, and that he asked no increase of force to maintain our supremacy at that place, hitherto and still to be considered the centre of disaffection. A small field-work had been constructed overlooking the town, in which is posted a strong guard daily, whilst the balance of the garrison is quartered in the town itself.

The town of San Diego, the southernmost one of Upper California, is now garrisoned by a company of Mormons, under the command of Captain D. C. Davis. The company was organized on the 20th of July at Los Angeles, and on the 25th of the same month marched to occupy the town of San Diego, which had been necessarily left without a garrison when Captain Hunter's company, of the Mormon battalion, was withdrawn to be discharged. During this temporary abandonment, the good people of the town expressed great terror of the Indians and of their own countrymen; but since the return of the company, not a word of fear or apprehension has reached me, and I infer they are perfectly satisfied.

The time for which the battalion of Mormons had agreed to serve expired on the 16th of July, on which day they were formally mustered out of service by First Lieutenant A. J. Smith, first dragoons, at Los Angeles, California; and as General Kearny had promised them their arms and accoutrements, I caused this promise to be redeemed, and in addition ordered to be given to such as really intended to return towards the United States to meet their families a small quantity of ammunition. Of the services of this battalion, of their patience, subordination, and general good conduct, you have already heard; and I take great pleasure in adding, that, as a body of men, they have religiously respected the rights and feelings of these conquered people, and not a syllable of complaint has reached my ears of a single insult offered, or outrage done, by a Mormon volunteer. So high an opinion did I entertain of the battalion, and of their especial fitness for the duties now performed by the garrison in this country, that I made strenuous efforts to engage their services for another year; but succeeded in engaging but one company, which, as before stated, is now at San Diego. Certain promises or pledges were made to this company, which you will find amongst the military correspondence sent to you by this same mail. Some few of the discharged Mormons are scattered throughout the country, but the great mass of them have gone to meet their families, supposed to be somewhere in the vicinity of the Great Salt Lake. Captain J. D. Hunter, late of the Mormon battalion, has been appointed sub-Indian agent, to take charge of the mission of San Luis Rey, and the mission Indians in that neighborhood. The mass of the Indians that formerly belonged to the prosperous missions of the country have either returned to their original habits and country or sunk into a most debased condition. It will be one of Captain Hunter's first duties to attempt to bring the lazy and thriftless Indians under his charge into habits of order and industry, not for the immediate benefit of himself or government, but for the improvement of the condition of the Indians themselves. Nearly all the missions of California, once so rich, are now in a state of decay, and, with few exceptions, are held by private individuals, either as claimants or tenants, under the late Mexican government. To these missions are attached large tracts of land, to which the titles are in dispute. The late emigrants from the United States looked to these missions for shelter, and to their lands for farms, under the belief that they belonged to the United States, and were subject to her laws concerning public lands. In many cases emigrants have taken forcible possession; but in every instance I have caused restitution to the individual holding possession at the time of the hoisting the American flag, either actual or by the payment of a small rent; and I shall in no way interfere with the titles to such property, but leave them to the future tribunals that shall be established in this country.

The headquarters of this department have been for some time past at this place, (Monterey,) on account of its central position.

The garrison of the place being of a mixed character, I have exercised the command myself, and caused the construction, under the immediate superintendence of Lieutenant Halleck, of the engineers, of a redoubt in the form of a bastion, on a hill overlooking the town and anchorage. It has twenty 24-pounders mounted, and four 8-inch mortars on platforms. All the shot and shells brought out by the Lexington are piled within the redoubt. Across the gorge has been constructed, by company F, 3d artillery, a two-story substantial log house, 100 feet by 17, giving comfortable and ample room to quarter that company. It is nearly complete; and near it another two-story log house, containing six rooms, as quarters for officers. These buildings have been constructed exclusively by the labor of the artillery company. In the rear of the redoubt, I have caused to be constructed, mostly by contract labor, a stone house, 75 feet by 25, with an excellent shingle roof, containing ample room to store all the valuable ordnance stores sent out in the Lexington. An ordnance officer is very much needed in the country; and in the absence of one, I have been compelled to assign Lieut. Warner, of the topographical engineers, to that duty. He is now engaged in storing, in the new building, the ordnance property; so that, when the rainy season sets in, every particle of it will be well stored and sheltered. Two companies of New York volunteers are stationed in the barracks of the town; and at present, Captain Nagle, with a strong detachment of his company, mounted, is out in pursuit of some Indians lately engaged in robbing and stealing horses; but the want of suitable equipments and good horses is so great at this time, that pursuit is almost useless. I trust that, long since, proper saddles, bridles, and more especially *saddle blankets*, have been shipped for California. Those used by the natives are coarse, very severe to the horse, and exorbitantly dear. During last winter this region of country was thoroughly stripped of horses for public service, and where they have gone it is impossible to say. At present, but few are owned by the quartermaster's department, and I do not feel disposed to order the purchase of more, as the want of forage, and miserable grazing, would soon reduce them to the condition of what are on hand. Still, if California is to be held permanently by us, these aggressions of the horse-thieving Indians must be checked and thoroughly put down. To do this will require one or more posts in the valley of the San Joaquin, garrisoned by horsemen well mounted and equipped. At San Francisco, Major Hardie, of the 7th New York volunteers, commands two companies of that regiment, which have been engaged principally during the past summer in repairing the old presidio, about three miles from the town and one from the fort, and in removing the great quantity of ordnance and ordnance stores from the town to the presidio: no efforts shall be spared in completing this removal before the rainy season sets in. Little or nothing has been done to the fort there, and as yet not one of the guns has been placed in battery there. I propose going myself in a few days to inspect the post and condition of affairs in and about San Francisco.

At the town of Sonoma, at the head of the bay of San Francisco, has been stationed part of a company of New York volunteers, under command of Captain Brackett, the balance of the company being detached to Sutter's Fort, on the Sacramento. This latter detachment has lately been withdrawn and ordered to Sonoma, on account of the great amount of sickness prevailing at Sutter's. Thus you will perceive that, with the exception of the discharge of the Mormon battalion, no material change has taken place in the disposition of the troops under my command since my last letter, nor do I contemplate any unless circumstances require it; but I must call your attention to the fact, that in the whole of the two Californias there are but two companies of regular troops, both of which are being rapidly diminished in strength by deaths and desertions: all other troops will claim and must receive their discharge the moment peace with Mexico is declared. When you remember the extent of the coast and frontier; the great number of Indians upon the immediate border, who know that a change of government has been effected in this country, and are watching its effects upon the character of the people, as to whether it is better for them to live on as thieves and robbers or as friendly tribes; and also the immense amount of property in deposite,—you can readily appreciate my anxiety in contemplating that event. There are other dangers in this country I must point out. The numbers of natives and foreigners in the country are nearly balanced, and of course a strong jealousy exists between them, not only on the score of which government shall prevail, but as to ideas of personal liberty, property, and all the every-day dealings of life. There are subordinate jealousies, too, between the foreigners of different nations, the old settlers and the new; and, indeed, when you remember that the great part of these foreigners are deserters from ships, and men who have been accustomed to lead a lawless life, you can see what confusion would result from the sudden withdrawal of strong authority, well backed by force. I do not conceive a less force than a good regiment of infantry, a battalion of dragoons, and a battalion of artillery, adequate to the duties that must necessarily devolve upon the military authorities in California. A less force would do if it were possible to receive succor upon short notice, but it must be remembered that it requires now six months to send to the United States, and as long to receive an answer. I conceive it highly impolitic to depend upon the emigrants for military service, as the best interests of this country demand their entire attention and industry to develop its resources. In connexion with this subject, I would mention that our latest dates from Washington are the 22d of February, by the storeship Southampton, and no safe means are offered of sending despatches to the United States, except occasionally by one of the national vessels returning home. A regular and more speedy communication is absolutely requisite.

Before closing, it becomes my painful duty to report to you that Major J. H. Cloud, additional paymaster, when travelling on duty, was thrown from his horse, near Sutter's Fort, on the 3d of August, 1847, and died eight hours after. He received every attention, but it was fruitless. He was in vigorous manly health at the time, had just completed the payment of the small garrison, and, in company with Captain Folsom and Mr. Sutter, started to return to San Francisco. It appears he had sent back for a pair of spurs, which overtook him; he dismounted, fixed his spurs and remounted, but his saddle bags prevented him from securing his seat in the saddle, and his horse, starting at a gallop, threw him forward, so that his head struck upon the hard sun-burnt ground. He never spoke again. He was a faithful officer, very attentive to his duties, and of sterling integrity. The funds and papers in his possession have been turned over to Major William Rich; and Captain H. M. Nagle, 7th regiment New York volunteers, has been ordered to make the necessary inventory of his private effects.

Death has also been among the small circle of our officers here, and taken one of its brightest ornaments, Lieutenant C. J. Minor, of the artillery, who died of fever on the 17th of August, 1847. He is a severe loss to the service. A favorite alike to soldiers and citizens, his death was deeply lamented.

In commemoration of Major Cloud and Lieutenant Minor, the officers at this post adopted appropriate resolutions, copies of which will be sent to you.

To-morrow I shall start for the bay of San Francisco, and close this letter to be ready for any opportunity that may occur during my absence. I subjoin a list of papers, sent by the same opportunity.

I have the honor to be your obedient servant,
R. B. MASON,
Colonel 1st Dragoons, commanding.

General R. JONES,
Adjutant General U. S. A., Washington city, D. C.

HEADQUARTERS TENTH MILITARY DEPARTMENT,
Monterey, California, June 23, 1847.

SIR: Colonel Mason has not yet officially learned that any selections have been made of lots in the town of San Francisco known as the beach and water lots granted to the said town for sale, excepting such as should be selected for the use of the general government by the senior officers of the army and navy.

The time of sale, under the decree of General Kearny of March 16, 1847, renders it necessary that the selection be made soon; and Colonel Mason wishes you to consult with Commodore Biddle, or other senior naval officer that may be on the station, and to select, in accordance with the terms of the grant, if it has not already been done, the lots best suited for wharves, both for army and navy purposes, with space enough for all the buildings that it may be necessary to erect hereafter.

A suitable lot should also be selected for a custom-house, with the storehouses that it may require.

Colonel Mason wishes these selections to be made, so far as the army is concerned, and officially communicated to the alcalde of the town before the day of sale.

I have the honor to be your most obedient servant,
W. T. SHERMAN,
1st Lieut. 3d Artillery, A. A. Adj. General.
Major JAMES A. HARDIE,
Commanding, San Francisco, California.

HEADQUARTERS TENTH MILITARY DEPARTMENT,
Monterey, California, June 24, 1847.

SIR: The United States ship Lexington will convey to San Pedro, at the same time with this letter, a battery of four field-pieces, three caissons, a forge and battery-wagon, together with some wagons, carts, and other stores.

It is greatly to be desired that the ship should not be detained at San Pedro longer than is absolutely necessary to land the stores on the beach; and Colonel Mason directs that you send there a sufficient number of men to receive and convey these stores to the Ciudad de los Angeles.

I am, with great respect, your most obedient servant,
W. T. SHERMAN,
1st Lieutenant 3d Artillery, A. A. A. General.
Colonel J. D. STEVENSON,
Commanding Los Angeles.

HEADQUARTERS TENTH MILITARY DEPARTMENT,
Monterey, California, June 25, 1847.

SIR: Your letter of the 16th instant is received; and in answer thereto, Colonel Mason directs me to inform you that such of the Mormon battalion as, after their discharge, desire to remove towards Council Bluffs, will be supplied with twenty rounds of musket-cartridge each. You are authorized to make a requisition upon Colonel Stevenson accordingly, who has instructions to supply you with ammunition.

I have the honor to be your most obedient servant,
W. T. SHERMAN,
1st Lieutenant 3d Artillery, A. A. A. General.
Captain HUNT,
Commanding Mormon battalion, Los Angeles.

HEADQUARTERS TENTH MILITARY DEPARTMENT,
Monterey, California, June 25, 1847.

SIR: At the same time with this I send you some blank certificates of ordinary disability. Please have one of them filled up in the case of private Charles Brown, and sent here, as a substitute for the manuscript one just received, which is incomplete.

Colonel Mason has well considered the subject of the commutation of rations to the mail-carriers, and has ordered the practice to be discontinued, and that the men carry their own provisions with them from station to station.

This order was conveyed to your adjutant in a letter dated June 2, 1847, the same day on which it was sent to all the other posts. Colonel Mason wishes it carried into effect.

In answer to your letter upon the subject of erecting quarters at Peublo de los Angeles, Colonel Mason directs me to inform you that you may employ your whole command in erecting suitable quarters, within the fort now under construction, for one full company with its officers, with the necessary magazines and storehouses, and that when it is completed you cause it to be occupied by one company, and withdraw the balance of your command to the mission of San Gabriel.

Colonel Mason wishes you to see that, where the mission is occupied by a part of your command, the buildings, vineyards, fences, and all other property at the mission be preserved and taken the best care of.

The ordnance, wheelbarrows, wagons, carts, and tools, to which your letter of the 16th instant refers, are all on board the Lexington, and will be landed at San Pedro as soon as the Lexington can take on board Lieutenant Colonel Burton's command at Santa Barbara.

You are informed that General Kearny promised the Mormon battalion their arms and accoutrements upon being discharged. Colonel Mason wishes that promise to be respected, and each member of that battalion will be permittted to retain in his possession the arms and accoutrements he received from the United States.

A letter has been received from Captain J. Hunt requesting that ammunition be supplied to those of his battalion who propose going towards Council Bluffs, Missouri, to meet their families. Colonel Mason orders that you cause such as are going towards the United States for that purpose to be supplied with twenty-one rounds of musket-cartridge each.

Colonel Mason wishes you to impress upon the acting assistant quartermaster the absolute necessity of the most rigid economy in all disbursements at the posts, and that you will not sanction any expenditures that are not strictly required.

The scarcity of funds in the Territory now, and the difficulty of procuring more, renders this the more imperative.

I have the honor to be your most obedient servant,
W. T. SHERMAN,
1st Lieutenant 3d Artillery, A. A. A. General.

Colonel J. D. STEVENSON,
Commanding Los Angeles, California.

HEADQUARTERS TENTH MILITARY DEPARTMENT,
Monterey, California, June 25, 1847.

SIR: Your letter of the 18th instant is just received, and Colonel Mason directs me, in answer, to inform you that you can take with you in the Lexington to San Pedro private George F. Carter, of company B, where, if he be duly accepted and enlisted in the dragoons, you may discharge him from the service in the volunteer regiment.

I send you herewith enclosed a manuscript copy of the forms of accounts and reports used by the collector of this port. They are made quarterly to the quartermaster, who is ordered to audit them carefully.

They appear to be the only accounts rendered by the collector of the port.
I am, sir, with great respect, your obedient servant,
W. T. SHERMAN,
1st Lieut. 3d Artillery, A. A. Adj. General.
Lieutenant Colonel H. S. BURTON,
Commanding, Santa Barbara, California.

HEADQUARTERS TENTH MILITARY DEPARTMENT,
Monterey, California, June 29, 1847.

SIR: I enclose herewith the post return for Ciudad de los Angeles for the month of May, 1847.

It is not signed, and is otherwise inaccurate. Upon the face of the return you will find the notes of Colonel Mason pointing out the errors, and an examination of the printed note on the back of the return will show you the order in which the names of the commissioned officers should be arranged. You have arranged them by companies, merely making a remark to show those who are absent. The proper way is to place the name of the commanding officer immediately under the words "present at the post;" opposite it, in the column of remarks, record the date of his assuming the command, provided he did so during the month. After the commanding officer's name place those of the general and regimental staff; and then those of the company officers, in the order of *their exact rank*, without regard to the corps or company to which they belong. Officers present at the post should be numbered in one series, and the whole number should correspond with the *"total present"* on the face of the return. The absent officers belonging to a post should then be accounted for in the order indicated on the back of the return, taking care that in every instance the number of names correspond with the figures on the face of the return.

I have made out a post return in pencil, which is as near right as the date we have in the office will permit, and send it with the post return first referred to, as a guide in making out a correct return. I may not have arranged the officers' names right; but you must know the rank of every officer at the post, and can make the corrections necessary. It is also possible that among the men of your regiment, at your post, there may be some that belong to companies stationed elsewhere. If such be the case, their number will be reported on separate lines, one for each company, just below where E and G companies are reported; and the names of these men should be written in the blank space prepared for that purpose upon the face of the return.

The strength of the band, of which in your return no notice was taken, should be included on the same line with E and G companies.

I have been thus minute, as it is very important that the post returns should be correct upon first being received, as otherwise they are necessarily sent back, causing much trouble and delay. In this instance a good opportunity has been lost of sending reports required from this office to the Adjutant General of the army at Washington city, by the inaccuracies in post returns.

I have the honor to be your obedient servant,
W. T. SHERMAN,
First Lieut. 3d Artillery, A. A. A. G.
Col. J. D. STEVENSON,
Com'g Cuidad de los Angeles, California.

HEADQUARTERS TENTH MILITARY DEPARTMENT,
Monterey, California, July 1, 1847.

SIR: Colonel Mason has received a letter from Mr James A. Griffiths, of Sonoma, in which he applies for the payment of one thousand dollars due him on a contract entered into, on the 10th day of December, 1846, between himself and Lieutenant William L. Murray, commandant of the district of Sonoma, for roofing a certain building, then and still occupied by the garrison stationed at Sonoma. Colonel Mason wishes you to inquire, through Captain Brackett, if the work has been done agreeably to that contract, and whether it is a public building to which the United States will have a title when the country is ceded.

If you become satisfied that the building is public property, and that the contract has been fulfilled on the part of Mr. Griffiths, you are authorized to pay him the thousand dollars, taking from him the necessary vouchers, including the original contract.

I am, sir, very respectfully, your obedient servant,
W. T. SHERMAN,
First Lieut. 3d Artillery, A. A. A. G.

Captain J. L. FOLSOM,
A. Quartermaster, San Francisco, California.

HEADQUARTERS TENTH MILITARY DEPARTMENT,
Monterey, California, July 2, 1847.

SIR: It is reported here that the mail-carriers that arrived from San Francisco still receive commutation money for their rations, in violation of the order contained in my letter to you of June 9, 1847.

Colonel Mason wishes you to inquire into it, and give to the acting assistant commissary of subsistence at your post the necessary orders, so that mail-carriers or express-men will carry with them the provisions they require from one post to another. Between San Francisco and Monterey are required but three days' provisions, which can easily be carried on horseback.

The petition for discharge of private Livingston, of K company, 7th regiment of New York volunteers, endorsed by yourself, has been received; and, in relation to it, Colonel Mason directs me to inform you that he can only grant discharges from service under the authority of the army regulations now in force, which require that the soldier be examined by the surgeon of the post, who makes a certificate, according to the forms sent you by a previous mail. Upon the same blank, the commanding officer of the soldier's company makes another certificate, when it is sent to the general headquarters. But as we are so distant from Washington city, Colonel Mason is willing to grant discharges, provided all the requirements of the regulations are complied with; and if private Livingston is unfit for service from physical causes, you can have him examined by the surgeon. Let the captain of his company fill his certificate, and then forward it, with such remark as you deem requisite, to these headquarters. This same course should be pursued in all cases "when any non-commissioned officer or soldier shall be incapable of discharging his duties in consequence of his wounds, disease, or infirmity."

Colonel Mason directs that you send by the first opportunity all men of

Colonel Stevenson's regiment now at San Francisco, whose companies are not there, to their proper companies. This will include private Harris of G company, whose certificate of ordinary disability has been received here.

I am, sir, very respectfully, your most obedient servant,
W. T. SHERMAN,
First Lieut. 3d Artillery, A. A. A. G.

Major J. A. HARDIE,
Commanding, San Francisco, California.

HEADQUARTERS TENTH MILITARY DEPARTMENT,
Monterey, California, July 3, 1847.

SIR: I herewith send you an order which is in force at all the military stations in California, by which you will see that you have authority to call for military aid, should it become necessary in order to enforce your decrees, and to execute the laws of the country.

I have the honor to be your most obedient servant,
W. T. SHERMAN,
1st Lieut. 3d Artillery, A. A. Adj. General.

To the ALCALDES of *San Francisco, Monterey, Santa Barbara, Los Angeles, and San Diego, California.*

HEADQUARTERS TENTH MILITARY DEPARTMENT,
Monterey, California, July 5, 1847.

SIR: By direction of Colonel Mason, I make the following extract from the 2d volume of McArthur's treatise upon the Principles and Practice of Naval and Military Courts-martial, page 221, edition of 1813, which he wishes you to lay before the general court-martial of which you are the president, as illustrative of the principle of law involved in the case of William Leggett, of company H, 7th regiment New York volunteers, which case is referred back to the court for a reconsideration:

"But supposing a prisoner to be tried for a crime said to have been committed on a particular day of the month, and that it is proved on the trial to have happened on a day different to what the indictment or accusation sets forth, this is not a ground to acquit him. An instance to the contrary occurred (2d January, 1759) in the trial of Richard Bird, seaman, belonging to the Norwich, who was accused of having attempted to desert, by swimming on shore, 14th November, 1758; but it was proved to have been attempted on the 15th of November. He was acquitted. This is not, however, to be adopted as a precedent.

"In all criminal cases, without distinction, both by law and by practice, the precise day laid in the indictment is not so very material upon the evidence, unless an *alibi* has been attempted to be proved by the prisoner; and there can be no reason why a different rule should be followed in courts-martial. With a view to the prisoner's defence, it is right to be as explicit as propriety will admit; but the only absolute requisite is to prove that the offence was committed previous to the charge or indictment, and within the time limited for the prosecution, where such limitation is assigned under the authority of an act of Parliament."

The principle laid down by McArthur is the law and practice of the present day, that where a crime is clearly proven to have been committed, and the perpetrators identified with that crime, the date is not material, provided that the date be subsequent to the time when the crime was actually committed.

I send herewith the original proceedings of the court in the case of private Leggett, which, together with this letter, you will be pleased to lay before the court when it has reconvened under orders No. 33 of this date.

Very respectfully, your obedient servant,

W. T. SHERMAN,
1st *Lieutenant 3d Artillery, A. A. A. General.*

Major J. A. HARDIE,
7th regiment New York Volunteers, San Francisco.

HEADQUARTERS TENTH MILITARY DEPARTMENT,
Monterey, California, July 10, 1847.

SIR: By the decree of General Kearny of the 22d March last, and my public notice of the 24th June, (both herewith enclosed,) you will see that certain persons have been required to vacate the mission buildings at Santa Clara and San José.

These persons, emigrants from the United States, hold possession of some of the buildings contrary to the consent of the Catholic priest, and have much damaged and injured the premises, as I know from personal observation. At San José, so entirely are the emigrants in possession, to the exclusion of the priest, that when he visits that mission upon duties connected with his church he has not even one room at his disposal.

I desire that you proceed to the Pueblo de San José with your command, and offer any assistance to the alcalde at that place that he may require to eject the aforesaid occupants from the mission buildings at Santa Clara and San José, who are in the occupancy of them without the permission of the Catholic priest, Padre Real.

If the alcalde does not act promptly and efficiently in this matter, then you must remove the intruders yourself. Use mild and persuasive means to induce them to vacate the premises before resorting to force. Say to those people they have no right whatever to dispossess the priest, and occupy those missions contrary to his consent, any more than they have to dispossess the rancheros and occupy their ranches; that they must respect the rights of others before they can claim any respect for their own; that we are bound to protect, and will protect, the priests in the quiet possession of the missions at Santa Clara and San José, and not suffer their premises to be wrested from them even by the Californians, much less by a people who have just come into the country, who have not a shadow of claim to the premises, and who, in the first place, were permitted from motives of charity to occupy them temporarily, to shield them from the last winter's rains.

You will return to this place by the end of the month, unless you find the presence of your command is required for a longer time in the vicinity of the aforesaid missions.

You will preserve good order and discipline in your command—suffer no officer or soldier to leave your column or camp without your special permission.

Your horses at all times require great care and attention, both on the part of the *officers* as well as the men. They should be inspected by an *officer*, preferably by yourself, every morning before they are saddled; and any man who neglects his horse, or from carelessness injures his back, should be dismounted and made to walk.

Great care should be paid to the pack animals, to see that the saddles are properly fitted and the packs properly put on.

Your camp in the vicinity of the mission should be selected where the best grazing can be had for the horses.

When on the march, the horses should graze at least one hour in the day, *and longer* where the grass was not good at the camp the overnight.

I am, respectfully, your obedient servant,
R. B. MASON,
Colonel 1st Dragoons, commanding.

Capt. H. M. NAGLE,
7th New York Volunteers, present.

HEADQUARTERS,
Monterey, California, July 11, 1847.

SIR: Since writing my letter of instructions of yesterday's date, I have seen Padre Real, the Catholic priest of the missions of Santa Clara and San José.

I proposed to him that he should permit the occupants of the said missions to remain in them until they harvested their crops, and until they could procure shelter elsewhere. This he has consented to do.

He further consented for them to remain for a longer time, if they desire to do so, (say another year,) provided they will further agree to pay something in the way of rent for the benefit of the church—this to be a matter of special agreement between themselves and the priest.

I am much pleased that the padre has given this consent; for it has spared me the performance of a very disagreeable and unpleasant duty—one that he has heretofore insisted on my performing.

I am sure the occupants of the missions cannot fail to see the propriety of paying something to the priest for the benefit of his church, if they wish to continue another year in the missions. All this you will communicate to them, and not carry into execution your instructions for removing them.

Take some good position in the vicinity of the pueblo of Santa Clara, where your horses can have plenty to eat; and let the people know that you have come there for the purpose of seeing what was going on, and to sustain the civil magistrates in the execution of the laws, if it becomes necessary.

I am told you are going into a bad neighborhood; it will therefore be necessary that you keep up a good discipline and a close watch upon your horses, lest they be stolen.

I am, respectfully, your obedient servant,
R. B. MASON,
Colonel 1st Dragoons, commanding.

Capt. NAGLE, *7th New York Volunteers, present.*

[18]

HEADQUARTERS TENTH MILITARY DEPARTMENT,
Monterey, California, July 14, 1847.

SIR: I learn from Captain Frisby that the quarters of the men and officers at the presidio cannot be made comfortable for the want of lumber.

If your saw-mill (if you have one) cannot furnish the quantity necessarily required, you must purchase it, using the most rigid economy in the purchase as well as in the application of the lumber.

I am, respectfully, your obedient servant,

R. B. MASON,
Colonel 1st Dragoons, commanding.

Captain FOLSOM,
Assistant Quartermaster, San Francisco, California.

HEADQUARTERS TENTH MILITARY DEPARTMENT,
Monterey, California, July 14, 1847.

SIR: Your communication of the 28th, and three of the 29th ultimo, together with the accompanying papers, are received.

I am fully aware there should be a show of force, at least, at San Diego; and if I cannot get one of the ships of war there, I must send a company from here.

I approve of your views, as expressed in your letter of the 28th June, relative to San Luis Rey, the Indian Samuel, and the propriety of an Indian agent at or near San Luis Rey, and will make the appointment as soon as you can find me a proper person.

Any person put in charge of the missions must be put in possession by a written instrument, expressly setting forth that they are in charge by the authority of the military, and that the person or persons are merely the *tenants at will* of the military government of California, and that no pre-emption rights are to be acquired by such possession.

I send you the appointment for Mr. Foster. Fill up the blank in his appointment with his given name, which let me know; as also the names of the other ranches referred to in your above-named letter of the 28th ultimo.

I enclose a blank bond, to be executed by the securities of the customhouse officer at San Diego, Don Miguel de Pedrovena. Similar bonds I desire you to cause to be given by the custom-house officers at San Pedro and Santa Barbara. I cannot find that any such have been given.

The salary of the collector of customs at Santa Barbara will be at the rate of $1,000 per annum, provided as much revenue is collected at his port as will pay it—the expenses of his office being first paid from the revenue received.

Should you not succeed in mustering in a Mormon company, you will send an officer and twenty men to San Diego to take charge of the public property until I can get a ship of war or a land force there.

I regret to hear that any "prominent Californians" should make a threat to cut down your flag-staff. Such an act will be considered an act of war, and punished accordingly. Such threats, if they can be clearly proven, should be visited by prompt arrests, and the individuals sent out of the country, and not suffered to return. It will be well to intimate to the suspected individuals that, upon sufficient proof, such a course will be pursued.

Should any men of your regiment wish to enlist in company "C," 1st dragoons, you will discharge them from your corps, upon the enlistment being completed.

I am, respectfully, your obedient servant,
R. B. MASON,
Colonel 1st Dragoons, commanding.

Col. J. D. STEVENSON,
Commanding, Cuidad de los Angeles, California.

HEADQUARTERS TENTH MILITARY DEPARTMENT,
Monterey, California, July 14, 1847.

SIR: Your communication of the 29th ultimo is received. I have heard nothing of Streeter.

I have instructed Colonel Stevenson to discharge any soldier from his regiment upon the completion of his enlistment in the dragoons.

I am, sir, very respectfully, your obedient servant,
R. B. MASON,
Colonel 1st Dragoons, com'g.

Lieut. A. J. SMITH,
1st Dragoons, Los Angeles, California.

HEADQUARTERS TENTH MILITARY DEPARTMENT,
Monterey, California, July 19, 1847.

SIR: I received, last evening, your letter of the 17th. The priest consented that the people at the missions should remain until they harvested their crops, and could procure shelter elsewhere, they to make use of reasonable exertions to do so. When they have harvested and secured their crops, they will then have to remove from the mission and mission land, unless they obtain the sanction of the priest to remain.

The United States government fully recognise and will sustain the rights of the priests at the missions, and to all mission property, against all those who cannot, in due course of law, show a just and sound legal title; and my instructions from the President require me to sustain him.

Show this letter and your instructions of the 11th instant to the occupants of the missions.

I am, respectfully, your obedient servant,
R. B. MASON,
Colonel 1st Dragoons, commanding.

Capt. H. M. NAGLE,
7th New York Volunteers, Pueblo de San José.

HEADQUARTERS TENTH MILITARY DEPARTMENT,
Monterey, California, July 20, 1847.

SIR: It has come indirectly to the knowledge of Colonel Mason that the volunteers of the 7th New York regiment intend to claim and insist upon their discharge from service in August next.

By the terms of their engagement with the United States they bind themselves to serve till the termination of the present war with Mexico, and to these terms they will be held.

Should anything like a mutinous disposition in this matter be shown, on the part of any one, or a resistance to the lawful authority of their officers, it must be put down at once by the most prompt and decisive measures.

I have the honor to be your most obedient servant,
W. T. SHERMAN,
1st. Lieut. 3d Artillery, A. A. A. G.

Major J. A. HARDIE,
Com'g, San Francisco, California.

HEADQUARTERS TENTH MILITARY DEPARTMENT,
Monterey, California, July 21, 1847.

SIR: From the information derived from a letter just received from Captain Lippett, New York volunteers, commanding at Santa Barbara, (a copy of which is enclosed,) I deem my presence of the utmost importance at that place.

Can you send me there in one of the public ships?

I shall wish to take with me a few boxes of ammunition.

I am, respectfully, your obedient servant,
R. B. MASON,
Col. 1st Dragoons, com'g.

Captain J. B. HULL,
U. S. Navy, Monterey, California.

HEADQUARTERS TENTH MILITARY DEPARTMENT,
Monterey, California, July 21, 1847.

SIR: You will afford every assistance with your command to Mr. Sutter, the sub-Indian agent, to arrest the persons charged with the recent outrages committed upon the unoffending Indians on the Sacramento, and to restore to their people those Indians that the same persons have captured and now hold in bondage.

The perpetrators, when arrested, must be safely kept until they can be brought to trial before such a tribunal as shall be organized. I shall, therefore, hold you to a strict responsibility for their safe-keeping.

I am informed there are a number of United States horses in your neighborhood; if so, collect them and send them to Captain Folsom. Retain a few to mount any of your men that you may find it necessary to mount in executing these instructions.

I will direct Captain Folsom to furnish you with money to purchase six or eight saddles and bridles. Be careful in expending the public money; use the most rigid economy, even in the smallest expenditures.

I am, sir, very respectfully, your obedient servant,
R. B. MASON,
Col. First Dragoons, commanding.

Lieutenant ANDERSON,
7th New York Volunteers, Sutter's Fort.

P. S.—Receive and obey Captain Folsom's instructions relative to collecting public horses.

R. B. M., *Colonel, commanding.*

HEADQUARTERS TENTH MILITARY DEPAREMENT,
Monterey, California, July 21, 1847.

SIR: I have just received your letter of the 18th instant, and its enclosure of the 20th November last, being a communication from Lieutenant Revere, of the navy, to General Vallejo, on the subject of keeping government horses.

Have collected all the public horses that can be found, both in the country about Sonoma and Sutter's, or elsewhere. Keep as many as you require and send the remainder here. Such as are unfit for service, have condemned and sold.

In collecting the horses, be careful to take none but those that are clearly recognised and admitted to be public property.

Perhaps none of those horses have been paid for, and but few for which receipts have been given. It is, therefore, more than probable that many will be reclaimed by their original owners when brought to San Francisco; if so, and they can produce good presumptive evidence of ownership, give them up, and take a receipt from them, acknowledging that their horse or horses have been restored to them, so as to guard against any further claim against the United States.

The claim of General Vallejo for keeping public horses I cannot order paid. It must be settled when the other accounts created by the navy in the country are paid off. The army officers cannot with propriety interfere with accounts created by the navy.

The horses should at once be received from General Vallejo, so as to stop any further charge on the United States; or perhaps it will be more to the interest of the public to give him the horses to pay for keeping them. Examine the matter, and do that which you may think most for the interest of the government.

I wish you to furnish Lieutenant Anderson, at or near Sutter's, with six or eight saddles and bridles. Perhaps he had better buy them in the country where he is, for which purpose he should be furnished with money. Give him such instructions as to making the purchase, and taking for you the necessary vouchers, as you think proper. Also, give Lieutenant A. particular instructions relative to collecting horses and sending them to you; or perhaps it would be well to employ some experienced person to collect them, and direct Lieutenant A. to furnish assistance.

Seal the enclosed letters, (I have left them open for you and Major Hardie to read,) addressed to Lieutenant Anderson and Sutter, and send by the first opportunity.

I am, respectfully, your obedient servant,

R. B. MASON,
Col. 1st Dragoons, com'g.

Captain J. L. FOLSOM,
Asst. Quartermaster, San Francisco, California.

HEADQUARTERS TENTH MILITARY DEPARTMENT,
Monterey, California, July 22, 1847.

SIR: When Mr. Nash, the late alcalde at Sonoma, arrives at San Francisco, I wish you to send him back to Sonoma—the expense to be paid out of the civil fund. The old gentleman appears fully sensible of his error, and has made me every promise that I could ask of him.

I am, respectfully, your obedient servant,
R. B. MASON,
Col. First Dragoons, commanding.

Captain J. L. FOLSOM,
Assistant Quartermaster, San Francisco, California.

HEADQUARTERS TENTH MILITARY DEPARTMENT,
Santa Barbara, California, July 25, 1847.

SIR: Colonel Mason arrived here this evening in the sloop-of-war Dale, and has ordered a special express to carry this to you as soon as possible.

He orders that you come to Santa Barbara as soon as you possibly can, to meet him upon business, and that you bring with you one of the lieutenants of your regiment, as a general court-martial will probably be ordered here upon your arrival.

Colonel Mason wishes to return to the north as soon as he can, and wishes you to use despatch in coming to this place.

I have the honor to be your most obedient servant,
W. T. SHERMAN,
1st Lieut. 3d Artillery, A. A. A. G.

Col. J. D. STEVENSON,
Com'g, Los Angeles, California.

HEADQUARTERS TENTH MILITARY DEPARTMENT,
Santa Barbara, California, August 1, 1847.

SIR: I enclose to you herewith the appointment as sub-Indian agent for the lower district of Upper California, and more especially for the district of country in and about the mission of San Luis Rey. This appointment invests you with a wide range of discretionary powers, and Colonel Mason wishes me to impress upon you the great importance of your office, and the great good that will result to the people of that district from a prudent and mild, yet determined, course of conduct.

You will establish yourself at or near the mission of San Luis Rey, and at the earliest moment practicable make a correct inventory of property belonging to that mission—such as farms, horses, cattle, and every species of property; a copy of which inventory you will send to headquarters.

You will then consider yourself the agent for that property, so as effectually to guard it from abuse or destruction, and more especially to see that no damage or desecration is offered the church or any other religious fixture.

You will take a protective charge of all the Indians living at the mission, and in the neighborhood, to draw them gradually to habits of order and industry, and maintain them from the proceeds of the mission property.

You will likewise endeavor to reclaim such as formerly belonged to the mission, and persuade them to return, to restore it to its former prosperity. To do this, you can maintain them and their families at the mission, but in no event contract a debt, or go beyond the resources of the property of which you have the charge.

You will make such rules for the government of the Indians as you deem suitable to their condition, so as to prevent their committing any depredations on others, or leading an idle, thriftless life. You will endeavor to prevent their going about in crowds, and make them receive from yourself a written paper when they desire to go any distance from their houses or rancherias, setting forth that they are under your protection, &c., &c. Much, however, is left to your own good sense and judgment to reclaim the old mission Indians to habits of industry, and, if possible, to draw in the wild ones too, and protect them in their lives and true interests, and to prevent them from encroaching in any way upon the peaceable inhabitants of the land.

Frequent communication upon all subjects of interest is requested, both to the commanding officer at Los Angeles and to these headquarters. A small force will probably be sent to assist you in maintaining effectually your authority.

Your salary will be seven hundred and fifty dollars a year, payable quarterly to yourself by the quartermaster at Los Angeles.

I have the honor to be your most obedient servant,
W. T. SHERMAN,
First Lieutenant Third Artillery, A. A. A. G.

J. D. HUNTER,
Late Captain Mormon Battalion, Santa Barbara, California.

HEADQUARTERS TENTH MILITARY DEPARTMENT,
Santa Barbara, California, August 2, 1847.

SIR: Your several communications of the 21st, two of 23d, 24th, and two of 27th ultimo, have been duly received.

The southern military district embraces the port of Santa Barbara.

I return to you the proceedings of the council of administration in the case of sutler Haight, with my approval, though I do not deem any action in the matter necessary. Mr. H. has already been appointed sutler to your regiment by the Secretary of War.

I approve of the conditions upon which the Mormon company have been engaged to serve, except that I would rather not have stipulated to give them travelling allowance to Salt Lake, at the expiration of their service, unless they serve out the full period of twelve months; otherwise to get travelling allowances only to the bay of San Francisco. Perhaps you may yet prevail upon them to accept these terms by making known to them my views, as you are not at all committed in the agreement you have signed. If they insist upon the terms as they stand, I must yield; the necessities of the service compel me to it.

I will examine the records when I return to Monterey, and write you fully on the subject of the salary, &c., of the collector at San Diego. I wish you at all times to give the officers in your district, who audit the accounts of the collectors, such instructions as you may deem proper for more effectually guarding the public interests, &c., and to let the collector of the customs have one or two competent persons from among the troops as a guard to be placed on boards of vessels while discharging cargo, to assist him in his duties, and to prevent frauds upon the revenue.

I am, sir, very respectfully, your obedient servant,
R. B. MASON,
Colonel 1st Dragoons, commanding.

Colonel J. D. STEVENSON,
7th N. Y. Volunteers, commanding Southern District.

P. S.—Enclosed is a letter of this date for Captain J. D. Hunter, sub-Indian agent.
R. B. M.

HEADQUARTERS SOUTHERN MILITARY DISTRICT, CALIFORNIA,
Ciudad de los Angeles, July 27, 1847.

COLONEL: Before the company of Mormons under the command of Captain Davis would consent to be mustered into the service of the United States, they required that the conditions, a copy of which is enclosed, should be signed by me. The only condition upon which I had any hesitation was that agreeing to discharge or pay transportation or rations for the time it would take them to reach Bear river or San Francisco after they were discharged; but upon reflection I became satisfied that it would be much cheaper to obtain them on these terms than to transport a company from the north to San Diego, to supply their place, and that, by way of saving transportation, they could be ordered to Bear river or San Francisco time enough to enable them to reach there before their term of service expired. The promise to disband them in March you had previously made to Hunt; I therefore had no difficulty on that point. There was a strong effort made to obtain for them other arms, that their own might, no doubt, be sent forward or disposed of to the Mormon association; but I positively refused to receive them without arms, except those who were formerly musicians and had now entered the ranks: these, together with some muskets unfit for service, in all about ten, five bayonets, and some few belts, and four non-commissioned officers' swords, were all the arms issued by the ordnance sergeant, and they were receipted for by the captain. I have promised to send them a garrison flag, which you will oblige me by directing the quartermaster to send me, of a medium size, to that post, by the first opportunity. But for the necessity of having troops to garrison San Diego, I should not have subscribed to the enclosed conditions, but have forwarded them to you. The exigency of the case, however, will, I trust, justify the act. The company left here early on the morning of the 25th, and will reach San Diego by Saturday next. The names of the officers are D. C. Davis, captain; 1st lieutenant, C. C. Canfield; 2d lieutenants, Inel Barras, and Robert Clift, who performed the duties of acting assistant quartermaster and commissary while that post was garrisoned by Captain Hunter's company; and as he is a good accountant, and has the reputation of being a very correct man, I have directed him to perform those duties at that post, under the command of Captain Davis.

The christian name of Foster, alcalde at San Juan, is *John*, which I have inserted in the appointment and forwarded. I have also sent the bond to the collector at San Diego for execution, and I will see that the collectors at Santa Barbara and San Pedro both execute similar ones. In your letter of the 14th instant you name the amount of salary the collector at Santa Barbara is to receive, but omit San Diego. As neither the rate of compensation, nor the office expenses that will be allowed, have yet been fixed for that post, I would respectfully request that you will fix them at your earliest convenience. The mail before last I requested advice as to the extent of my jurisdiction as commander of the southern military district. As your last communication was silent on that subject, I presume it was overlooked. May I request an answer at your earliest convenience.

All is quiet here as when I last wrote you.

I have the honor to be, very respectfully, your obedient servant,

J. D. STEVENSON,
Colonel commanding Southern Military District, California.

Colonel R. B. MASON,
1st *U. S. Dragoons, Governor of California.*

True copy.
W. T. SHERMAN,
1st *Lt.* 3d *Art., A. A. A. G.*

CUIDAD DE LOS ANGELES, *July* 23, 1847.

DEAR SIR: By the same hand you receive this, I send an official communication announcing the reorganization of one company of Mormons, and their having been mustered into service. Captain Hunt, late in command of the battalion, starts to-day for the north. He will stop at Monterey and proffer his services to raise a battalion of Mormons from those that are coming into the country, and I have given him a letter to you on that subject, a copy of which is enclosed. My intercourse with the Mormons has satisfied me that the great mass of them are a simple-minded, ignorant people, entirely under the control of their leaders, and that in every community or association there is some one man who is the controlling spirit, and that all are under the direction and control of some one master-spirit. In the battalion were two men, one of whom was a private soldier, who were the chief men; and but for them, at least three companies would have re-entered; but they opposed, and not a man would enter; and I do not believe we should have succeeded in getting one company, if they had not given it their countenance, or at least made no formal objection. Both before and since they were mustered out of the service, I have consulted with Captain Hunt and some other leaders, and am satisfied they desire to get the military control of the country, and that from time to time they will supply from 100 to 1,000 men for the service, until their whole community shall have had some experience as soldiers, and become furnished with arms; which, by the time the civil government shall be organized, will give them control as well of the ballot-box by their numerical strength, as physically, being corps of many hundred soldiers, well armed and equipped for service in the field. They look forward to the disbanding of any regiment of volunteers, at the close of the war, as an event that will throw the military defence and control of this country entirely in their own hands. This I know to be their calculation, for Hunt and his officers have so expressed themselves to me. This may account for the opposition a re-enlistment of the entire battalion has met from some of their society leaders, as I am well assured they regard an order or instruction from them as paramount to any other power; for at all times I have been told that if a messenger should arrive with but five lines from one of their chief leaders now on the road to this country, all would have re-entered, and all the officers here feel confident that Hunt can raise a battalion if you require it. I deemed it my duty to give you my views of what I conceive to be the Mormon plan of action in California, and you can no doubt judge of the propriety of giving them the military control.

The company that is ordered to San Diego will be sufficient for all military purposes at that post and the surrounding country; and I have no hesitation in saying that the force I have here, dragoons and New York volunteers, will be sufficient to keep this place against any force that can be brought against us, especially if you will authorize the filling up of the two companies of my regiment stationed here. Our discipline is strict, drills regular and rigid, and every point is strictly and vigilantly guarded day and night; and therefore, unless you require them for some other purpose, an additional force will not be necessary here. This place is at the present time quite unhealthy; two of our men have recently died of fever. Our sick list has not, however, increased since my last communication.

It may not be improper for me to remark, that many of our disbanded men are now selling their arms to any that will purchase them. This should prevent any further donation of arms to a company or battalion of Mormons, if mustered into the service.

Very respectfully, your obedient servant,

J. D. STEVENSON,
Colonel, commanding Southern Military District.

Colonel R. B. MASON,
Commanding 1st Reg't Dragoons, Gov. of California.

We, of the Mormon fraternity, whose names are herewith subscribed, purpose to enter the service of the United States as volunteers, on the following terms:

1st. That we enrol to serve under the government of the United States for one year, on condition that the authorized representatives of the government in California pledge themselves, if we require it, to discharge us on the first day of March, 1848.

2d. That we, during the period of our service, have the same privileges, pay, and emoluments granted to us that other volunteers in the service enjoy.

3d. That, on our re-enlistment, we may have the privilege of garrisoning the town of San Diego, and not be sent lower down the coast than that post.

4th. That the authorities of California pledge themselves, on behalf of the government of the United States, at the period of our discharge, to furnish us with the rations and pay allowed by law to the Salt lake, into which Bear river empties, or to the bay of San Francisco, if preferred by us.

5th. That we shall all have the privilege of joining the battalion of Mormons, if there should be one raised.

As far as I have the authority, I agree to the foregoing stipulations.

J. D. STEVENSON,
Col. Comanding Southern Mil. Dist. of California.

CIUDAD DE LOS ANGELES, *July* 20, 1847.

True copy.

W. T. SHERMAN,
1st Lieut. 3d Art., A. A. A. G.

HEADQUARTERS TENTH MILITARY DEPARTMENT,
Santa Barbara, California, August 2, 1847.

SIR: Should any of the Catholic priests come to the mission of San Luis Rey, either to locate permanently or for the performance of any of their religious duties, you will not only cause them to be treated with great courtesy and kindness, but they are to have any of the apartments they desire, and any product of the mission or mission farms for their own use, and the entire management of the Indians, so far as it relates to their connexion with the mission and mission farms, the only object in placing you in charge of the mission and its property being to guard it from desecration and waste.

I am, sir, very respectfully, your obedient servant,
R. B. MASON,
Colonel 1*st Dragoons, Governor of California.*
Captain J. D. HUNTER, *Sub-Indian Agent, present.*

P. S.—Colonel Stevenson, at Los Angeles, commands the southern district, in which you are to be stationed, and may sometimes find it necessary to give you instructions; if so, I desire you will obey them.

HEADQUARTERS TENTH MILITARY DEPARTMENT,
Monterey, California, August 13, 1847.

SIR: Official intelligence has this day been received of the death of Major J. H. Cloud, paymaster United States army.

Colonel Mason directs that you secure all his effects, both public and private, and make an accurate inventory thereof, agreeably to the 94th article of war and paragraphs 115 and 116 of the general regulations.

All funds, books, papers, and property that appertain to the paymaster's department, you will turn over to paymaster William Rich, taking his receipt therefor.

I have the honor to be your most obedient servant,
W. T. SHERMAN, *A. A. A. Gen.*
Capt. H. M. NAGLE,
7th Regt. N. Y. Volunteers, Monterey, California.

HEADQUARTERS TENTH MILITARY DAPARTMENT,
Monterey, California, August 13, 1847.

SIR: I have the honor to acknowledge the receipt of your post returns for the months of May and June, 1847. Colonel Mason directs me to inform you that you need not make such returns in future, as your command is a detachment of Captain Brackett's company, and is accounted for by him on his post returns for Sonoma. You will please to send to Captain Brackett your blank post returns, and hereafter report to him the actual condition of your detachment monthly, in time to be entered on the post return of Sonoma of the same month.

Your certificate of disability for private A. J. Ward, 7th regiment New York volunteers, now acting as the hospital steward at Fort Sacramento, has also been received; and in answer thereto, Colonel Mason directs me to say that he cannot discharge private Ward from service. If physically incapacitated for the duties of a soldier, he can render service, as he now does, as hospital steward for your detachment—thus filling a place that otherwise might require one who is now in the actual performance of the duties of a soldier.

Private Ward has been transported to this country at the expense of the United States, and must render his services agreeably to his original contract.

I have the honor to be your most obedient servant,
W. T. SHERMAN,
1st Lieut. 3d Art., A. A. A. Gen.

Lieut. C. C. ANDERSON,
  Commanding, Sacramento, California.

HEADQUARTERS TENTH MILITARY DEPARTMENT,
Monterey, California, August 13, 1847.

SIR: Colonel Mason directs me to acknowledge the receipt of your letter of July 19, enclosing the resignation of Mr. James Ward as wagon and forage master of the army.

You can accept the resignation of Mr. Ward; and in case he held his appointment from the proper authority in Washington, his resignation necessarily creates a vacancy, which you may fill by appointing Mr. A. J. Grayson to the same office, referring his appointment to the proper authority for confirmation.

In case, however, that Mr. Ward did not have the appointment of wagon and forage master under the law referred to by you, you can secure the services of Mr. Grayson by employing him for special service in the quartermaster's department on the best terms you can make with him.

I have the honor to be your most obedient servant,
W. T. SHERMAN,
1st Lieut. 3d Art., A. A. A. Gen.

Capt. FOLSOM,
  A. Q. M., San Francisco, California.

HEADQUARTERS TENTH MILITARY DEPARTMENT,
Monterey, California, August 13, 1847.

SIR: I have the honor to acknowledge the receipt of your letter communicating the melancholy intelligence of the death of paymaster Cloud, United States army. The steps you have taken are approved; and you will send to Captain H. M. Nagle, 7th New York volunteers, as soon as convenient, the inventory you have made of the effects of Major Cloud, with all the property, public and private, that he had with him at the time of his death.

Your letter asking instructions about the public horses and cattle in the valley of the Sacramento has this day been received; and Colonel Mason was much astonished to learn that Lieutenant Colonel Fremont had given any orders relating to any public property, subsequent to his being relieved from duty in the Territory, conferring rights which he is forced not to recognise; yet Colonel Mason does not desire to interfere in the least with any horses, cattle, or other property in the Territory of California not clearly and publicly recognised as belonging to the United States. Horses or cattle taken from citizens before the hoisting of the American flag he can have nothing to do with, further than causing them to be restored to their proper owners. He therefore directs that you cause to be restored to the San Rafael mission all the horses, mares, and cattle now in charge of Mr. Shuddins, near Fort Sacramento, causing them to be properly handed over, and taking from the person who has actual charge of said mission the necessary evidence of such restoration of lost property.

That portion of the cattle in charge of Mr. Shuddins, or any other individual, that you may be assured belongs to General Vallejo, of Sonoma, taken from him either before or after the hoisting of the United States flag in that section of the Territory, you will likewise cause to be restored to General Vallejo, taking from him receipts, which you will hold as an offset to his claims against our government.

Lieutenant Colonel Fremont had no right whatever to give Mr. Redding, or other private individual, orders for public horses or cattle. Still, if he has done so, and Mr. Redding or other individuals have private possession of such property, you need not disturb it, but procure from Mr. Shuddins either Colonel Fremont's original order or an authenticated copy of it, with Mr. S.'s affidavit endorsed thereon that he has actually delivered upon it the stated number of horses or cattle known and held by him as public or United States property, which will be sufficient to charge Lieutenant Colonel Fremont with their value at the Treasury Department. Likewise procure a similar order, or copy of order, with a like endorsement, concerning the cattle and horses that Lieutenant Colonel Fremont's "majordomo" has received from the farm of Mr. Shuddins. In case Mr. Shuddins did not retain the order of Lieutenant Colonel Fremont, then let him make affidavit that he had made such delivery upon an order not now in his possession, and that the order called for it as public property.

If, however, these horses and cattle are not yet removed, you will take possession of them and dispose of them, as above directed, to the mission of San Rafael, General Vallejo, or retain them as the property of the United States. All horses and mares clearly and avowedly the property of the United States, for which payments have been made either by notes or money, or for which receipts have been given by any agent of the United States, you will take possession of, and dispose of according to Colonel Mason's letter of instructions to you of July 21, 1847.

I have the honor to be your most obedient servant,
W. T. SHERMAN,
1st Lieut. 3d Artillery, A. A. A. G.

Captain FOLSOM,
Asst. Quartermaster, San Francisco, California.

HEADQUARTERS TENTH MILITARY DEPARTMENT,
Monterey, California, August 16, 1847.

SIR: Colonel Mason has received your letter of July 26, on the subject of the pay accounts of Lieutenant Day, late of the New York volunteers, and directs me, in answer, to inform you that he believes that, without the affidavit of Lieutenant Day on the certificates referred to in paragraph 1,241, General Regulations of the Army, those accounts would not pass at the treasury. The oath of the attorney would not be sufficient, as he is not supposed to know the previous transactions that Lieutenant Day may have had with the disbursing departments of the army.

If, however, the accounts are sent to the United States, where the certificates of the Second and Third Auditors can be obtained, that Lieutenant Day is not indebted to the government, any paymaster then will cash them: in that way, they will serve the same purpose as a draft.

Colonel Mason is of opinion that, with your power of attorney, you can draw from the paymaster the amount due Lieutenant Day for his services as 1st sergeant, provided the muster-rolls show that such services were rendered, and that he has never drawn pay therefor.

I have the honor to be your most obedient servant,
W. T. SHERMAN,
1st Lieut. 3d Artillery, A. A. Adjt. General.

EDWARD GILBERT,
1st Lieut. N. Y. Vol., San Francisco, California.

HEADQUARTERS TENTH MILITARY DEPARTMENT,
Monterey, California, August 19, 1847.

SIR: Your communication of the 13th was received last night.

Send the prisoner charged with the Indian murders, under a proper guard, commanded by a commissioned officer, to Sonoma; he must be well and securely ironed. Direct Captain Brackett to receive him, and, with the one or two at Sonoma, in like manner securely ironed, to send to Sutter's Fort, under a guard, with a commissioned officer, where you will direct Lieutenant Anderson to securely keep them for trial and further orders.

Impress upon Lieutenant Anderson the necessity of himself looking to the irons and safe-keeping of the prisoners, as he will be held to a strict responsibility for their safety; and direct him to inspect the irons morning and evening himself, and not to delegate that duty to any one else.

I am, respectfully, your obedient servant,
R. B. MASON,
Colonel 1st Dragoons, commanding.

Major J. A. HARDIE,
Commanding, San Francisco, California.

HEADQUARTERS TENTH MILITARY DEPARTMENT,
Monterey, California, August 19, 1847.

SIR: Your communication of the 15th was received last night.

Major Hardie will give all the necessary orders for sending the prisoners charged with the Indian murders to Sutter's Fort for trial.

You had better send Mr. Grayson, (if he is in the employ of the quartermaster's department,) to pay the expenses of the trial, with instructions to be as economical as possible, and to pay no account without the approval of the court.

Enclosed is the account of Wall, approved.

The enclosed, addressed to General Vallejo and Captain Sutter, be pleased to forward, after Major Hardie and yourself have read them.

I am, respectfully, your obedient servant,
R. B. MASON,
Colonel 1st Dragoons, commanding.

Captain FOLSOM,
Assistant Quartermaster, San Francisco.

HEADQUARTERS TENTH MILITARY DEPARTMENT,
Monterey, California, August 16, 1847.

SIR: On my return from the south, I found your letter of the 10th instant at this place.

I request that you will raise a battalion of Mormon volunteers, to be mustered into the service of the United States for the term of twelve months, unless sooner discharged.

The battalion will consist of—

Field and staff.
- 1 lieutenant-colonel.
- 1 adjutant—a lieutenant of one of the companies, but not in addition.
- 1 sergeant major.
- 1 quartermaster's sergeant.

Three companies, each of which to consist of—
- 1 captain,
- 1 first lieutenant,
- 2 second lieutenants,
- 4 sergeants,
- 4 corporals,
- 2 musicians,
- 75 privates.

Should the number of privates, on being mustered, not fall below sixty-four effective men in a company, it will be received.

Some convenient point (to be hereafter designated) between Sutter's Fort and San Francisco will be named as the place of rendezvous.

The battalion will be inspected and mustered into service by an officer of the United States army, who will in every case be instructed to receive no man who is in years apparently over forty-five or under eighteen, or who is not of physical strength and vigor. To this end, the inspector will be accompanied by a medical officer of the army, and the volunteers will be submitted to his examination. It is respectfully suggested that public notice of these requirements will prevent much disappointment to the zealous and patriotic citizens of your fraternity who may be disposed to volunteer.

It may be proper to remark, that the law provides for the clothing (in money) and subsistence of the non-commissioned officers, musicians, and privates of volunteers who are received into the service of the United States.

In respect to clothing, the law requires that the volunteers shall furnish their own clothing; for which purpose it allows to each non-commissioned officer, musician, and private, three dollars and fifty cents per month during the time he shall be in the service of the United States, in order that the volunteers who shall be mustered into service under this requisition may be enabled to provide themselves with good and sufficient clothing; the commutation allowance for six months (twenty-one dollars) will be advanced to each non-commissioned officer, musician, and private, after being mustered into service, but only with the express condition that the volunteer has already furnished himself with six months' clothing— this fact to be certified to the paymaster by the captain of the company— or that the amount thus advanced shall be applied, under the supervision of his captain, to the object contemplated by law. In this latter case, the advanced commutation for clothing will be paid on the captain's certificate that he is satisfied it will be so applied.

When discharged, an allowance of fifty cents will be made for every twenty miles' distance from the place of discharge to the place of rendezvous.

The Mormon company at San Diego will be added to the three which it is proposed that you should raise—making the battalion to consist of four companies, the command of which you shall have, with the rank of lieutenant colonel; but should you not be able to organize three new companies, then your rank can only be that of major

The sergeant major and quartermaster's sergeant will be appointed by yourself, and should be good business men. The captains, lieutenants, and non-commissioned officers of companies to be elected by their respective companies; and I would suggest the extreme importance to the public service that the officers be judiciously selected.

The battalion will be armed and equipped either at San Francisco or this place; but the arms, &c., will not be given to the men when discharged, as was done when the Mormon battalion was recently discharged at Los Angeles.

When your people arrive in the country, you can inform me whether the companies can be raised, and at what time.

The pay and allowances will be the same as those received by the late Mormon battalion, unless Congress shall have changed them by some new law, of which we have no intelligence.

I am, sir, very respectfully, your obedient servant,
R. B. MASON, *Col. 1st Dragoons, commanding.*
Capt. HUNT, *late of Mormon Battalion, San Francisco, California.*

HEADQUARTERS TENTH MILITARY DEPARTMENT,
Monterey, California, August 23, 1847.

SIR: Your several letters of the 11th instant are received, and I am directed, in reply to the several subjects to which they relate, to inform you that your views are correct as to the assistance the military authorities should afford to the civil.

The civil officers would, without doubt, be most willing to shift upon military commanders the disagreeable labor of arresting and guarding their criminals; but this must not be permitted. Officers in command are only expected to aid the civil officers when the latter are unable to enforce their decrees or execute the laws without such aid; and even then a sound discretion should be exercised as to the nature and amount of assistance to be afforded.

It does not appear that the second alcalde had any just ground to offer the resignation of his office.

In regard to your inquiries as to the character of the land scrip referred to in department orders No. 34, of July 20, you will find, upon an inspection of that order, that it merely gives, verbatim, an extract from a newspaper published at New Orleans; nothing more is now known in relation to the subject, but in time full instructions will be received from the proper department that will convey all the information you ask for.

Your issue of a small supply of tools to the Indian agent is approved, but it is expected that in future the agent will be able to supply all his own wants from the resources of the property he has charge of.

I am, with respect, your obedient servant,
W. T. SHERMAN,
1st Lieut. 3d Artillery, A. A. A. General.
Colonel J. D. STEVENSON,
Commanding, Los Angeles, California.

P. S.—Colonel Mason directs me to add that you are not to infer from the above instructions that commanders of posts are prohibited from taking charge of civil prisoners. They can do so when convenient, and should do so when the general good requires it. He, however, remains the full judge of such necessity.
W. T. SHERMAN.

HEADQUARTERS TENTH MILITARY DEPARTMENT,
Monterey, California, August 24, 1847.

SIR: The American brig Thomas H. Benton sailed from this port the day before yesterday, and there is every reason to believe she carried away with her two deserters from this command—one, a private of the artillery company, named J. R. Barnes, about five feet ten inches high, dark hair and eyes, narrow chested, stooped shoulders, sallow complexion, supposed to be consumptive, and is said to have a brother on board the said brig Benton—Barnes is an American; the second, a sergeant of volunteers, named Chichester, of company E, 7th New York volunteers, stationed at Los Angeles, California; he was on extra duty at Monterey, an excellent mechanic and machinist, is about five feet eight or nine inches high, healthy and bronzed complexion, brown hair, clear eyes, stoops considerably, but is stout and muscular; he is known well by his company at Los Angeles.

If the brig Thomas H. Benton is at the port of Santa Barbara, Colonel Mason directs that you quietly endeavor to ascertain whether either or both of these men are on board; but at all events board her and search her hold, forecastle, cabins, pantries, every nook and corner and hiding-place in the vessel; and if you find either of the above described men, or good written evidence that either of them was carried in her from this port, you will cause the captain to pay you one thousand dollars ($1,000) as a fine imposed on him by Governor Mason. Should he (the captain) fail to pay you instantly the above sum, you will take the "ship's papers," and cause her to be stripped of her sails and running-gear—the whole to be taken on shore and kept under your care till you make a re-report upon the fact, and receive further instructions.

If the brig has sailed to leeward, despatch this same letter, by the bearer, to Colonel Stevenson or officer in command at Los Angeles, who is hereby required to adopt the same course prescribed if the brig is at San Pedro.

This letter is sent by especial despatch; and the bearer agrees to deliver it at Santa Barbara on Friday next for the sum of fifty dollars, ($50,) which sum you can cause to be paid him by the acting assistant quartermaster, if the contract has been complied with.

The bearer further agrees to carry the despatch on to Los Angeles for a further sum of twenty dollars ($20) by Sunday next, making in all twenty [seventy] dollars, which the acting assistant quartermaster at Los Angeles will pay him upon his arrival there on Sunday next.

I am, with great respect, your most obedient servant,
[W. T. SHERMAN,]
1*st Lieut.* 3*d Artillery, A. A. A. General.*

HEADQUARTERS TENTH MILITARY DEPARTMENT,
Monterey, California, August 25, 1847.

SIR: Your letter of August 11th, relating to an insult offered some of your camp-women, has been received; and yesterday a courier arrived from Santa Barbara, bearing a letter from the alcalde, Luis Carrillo, with copies of his correspondence with you, copies of which I enclose herewith.

These letters and papers show that, at the instance of Lieut. Huddart, of your command, the two men, Guerrera and Ruiz, were charged before the alcalde with having insulted the women, were arraigned, and a fair, open trial begun, and had proceeded so far as to prove, by the witness produced by the women themselves, that the only insult offered was in the use of words "asking a kiss," when the alcalde notified you that there was not sufficient testimony to warrant conviction; and you took the case out of his jurisdiction.

In reviewing these facts, the Colonel Commanding sees a desire on the part of the alcalde to do substantial justice, and, upon a fair, open trial, to make such a decree as the evidence would require.

His notifying you that the testimony was not enough to produce conviction, shows that he desired you to produce other and better. There does not, therefore, appear to be any reason for the interposition of martial law, as the acknowledged court was capable and willing to redress the grievance, if the proper testimony could be procured.

I am assured that the practice in Mexican courts is the same as our own; that a prisoner cannot give evidence in court in favor of himself, though his denial of the charge forces the plaintiff to establish every part of it by sworn facts. It is presumed you will find that, in this case, the alcalde has not departed from this well-established practice.

You will therefore discontinue your proceedings against Guerra and Ruiz, and notify the alcalde of it, that he may resume their trial.

The stealing a reáta from one of your men by a Californian is deemed too trifling a case to call for martial law. Release Señor Ruiz, and let the soldier sue him before the alcalde. Martial law was declared in Mexico as a matter of necessity. In California it is proclaimed as a preventive code, to come into full operation when the present courts are interrupted by accident or outbreak, and to supply the defects in the articles of war, so as to prevent soldiers from trampling upon the rights of citizens, which would necessarily produce disaffection. It was not designed, by the publication of orders No. 36, to interfere with the alcalde's jurisdiction in petty cases where soldiers are interested, but merely to make citizens amenable to military tribunals for high crimes against any person serving with the army of the United States.

Colonel Mason desires you to do all in your power to restore harmony, and to allay the ill-will that seemingly exists between your command and the citizens of Santa Barbara.

I have the honor to be your most obedient servant,

W. T. SHERMAN,
1st Lieut. 3d Artillery, A. A. A. General.

Capt. F. J. LIPPETT,
Commanding, Santa Barbara, California.

HEADQUARTERS TENTH MILITARY DEPARTMENT,
Monterey, California, August 25, 1847.

SIR: Governor Mason directs me to acknowledge the receipt of your communication of August 16, and to inform you that he has instructed Captain Lippett to discontinue proceedings against Juan Bautista Guerrera and José Antonio Ruiz, that you may resume your jurisdiction over these two men, and punish them as they deserve, if fairly convicted of having insulted the women.

Señor Ruiz is also ordered to be released, that he may be tried by you for having stolen the reata.

Your authority as alcalde, in all cases between citizen and citizen, is the same as it was under the Mexican law. But when a soldier is concerned, then the military law must have precedence, so long as war exists between the republic of Mexico and the United States, unless, in special cases, this precedence is yielded by the military governor.

In California Governor Mason is ready to yield the jurisdiction over minor cases to alcaldes, when he has reason to believe they are influenced by the proper motives of justice and probity.

Believing that you are thus influenced, he has given the orders before referred to.

I am, with much respect, your obedient servant,
W. T. SHERMAN,
1st Lieut. 3d Artillry, A. A. Adjt. General.
Don LUIS CARRILLO, *Alcalde of Santa Barbara.*

HEADQUARTERS TENTH MILITARY DEPARTMENT,
Monterey, California, August 28, 1847.

SIR: Mr. Thompson has presented to Colonel Mason his claim to a lot of ground in San Francisco, as also his correspondence with you upon the subject.

His title is not considered good, but it will be submitted to the United States government for their action when California shall become a Territory of the United States.

In the mean time, he can use the house on the lot, if not prejudicial to the interests of the public service at San Francisco.

Mr. Thompson says that the ground is at present so lumbered up with gun carriages, &c., that he cannot approach the house. As it is supposed you are now removing that property, it will be well to remove such of it first as will open a way to the house.

I have the honor to be your most obedient servant,
W. T. SHERMAN,
1st Lieutenant 3d Artillery, A. A. A. Gen.
Major J. A. HARDIE,
7th Reg't N. Y. Vol., commanding, San Francisco.

HEADQUARTERS TENTH MILITARY DEPARTMENT,
Monterey, California, September 6, 1847.

SIR: Your letter of the 2d instant reached Colonel Mason the evening before last; six days had then passed since the Indians had succeeded in driving off Captain Fisher's horses, and it was therefore too late to pursue them from this place. An expedition will start for the Tulares as soon as it can be fitted out, to look after these thieving Indians, and to adopt such measures as may check for a time their depredations.

The people of every neighborhood or district, however, the moment they hear of the Indians stealing or attempting to steal a lot of horses, should collect together, pursue and kill them, or at least show them that a pursuit was made. You may tell the people of your district, that if they catch Indians in the act of stealing or attempting to steal their horses, they should shoot them; but if they are merely loitering about, then to send them to the nearest alcalde, who will judge whether they be quiet Indians or hostile thieves.

Regulations are being now issued through all California for the Indians belonging to pueblos, settlements, or ranches, to receive from their employers, or the alcaldes of their districts, papers, which they must keep about their persons, so that all others who are found without such papers will be treated as horse-thieves and enemies.

I have the honor to be your most obedient servant,
W. T. SHERMAN,
1st Lieut. 3d Artillery, A. A. Adjt. General.
John Burton, *Alcalde, Pueblo de San José.*

Headquarters Tenth Military Department,
Monterey, California, October 7, 1847.

Sir: I returned from San Francisco yesterday, and found here Mr. Toler, with despatches from Washington, the receipt of which I have the honor to acknowledge. I am also informed by Commodore Shubrick that the sloop-of-war Preble is ready to sail for Panama, with Passed Midshipman Wilson, as bearer of despatches for the United States. I therefore avail myself of the opportunity to send you my letter of the 18th of September, with its several packages, and now have to communicate the result of my visit to San Francisco.

I found the town flourishing and prosperous, with a busy, industrious population of Americans, and refer you to the copies of my military correspondence for the steps adopted to give them a good town government. The bay of San Francisco, you are well aware, is a spacious, elegant harbor, susceptible of the most perfect defence; but as yet nothing has been done towards fortifying it, or even placing any of the heavy guns in position at the old fort. It is found almost impossible to get much work out of the volunteers; and all that I can now expect of the two companies of Major Hardie's command will be to improve their quarters at the old presidio. This they are at present engaged upon, using lumber made at the horse saw-mill, under direction of the assistant quartermaster, Captain Folsom. All this labor is done by the volunteers, so that the improvements will be made at very little expense to the government. The price of lumber at San Francisco is $50 per M.; but Captain Folsom says that he has it sawed and delivered, by the labor of the volunteers and his own machinery, at about $16. The mill is placed in the timber known as the Red woods, near the mission of San Rafael, on the west and north side of the bay, where any amount can be had. If the government designs to erect permanent structures to any extent in this country, it would be advisable to send out a steam-engine, with all the necessary frames and iron-work to adapt it to immediate use in connexion with the saw and grist mills now in possession of the quartermaster's department here. The site at present selected by Captain Folsom is well adapted, as easy water communication is had with the San Joaquin and Sacramento rivers, as well as the ports of the country south of San Francisco.

At San Francisco I found all the powder, arms, accoutrements, and perishable ordnance property well stored in a building prepared for the purpose at the presidio barracks; but the guns, mortars, carriages, shot, and shells are in the town in the open air, protected by paint alone.

The great difficulty of hauling such articles over the rugged hills between the town and presidio will prevent their being hauled to the latter place this season.

I did design to continue my tour of inspection to Sonoma and the Sacramento river, but was recalled by hearing of the arrival of the bearer of despatches at Monterey.

When on my way up to San Francisco, I was overtaken by Captain Brown, of the Mormon battalion, who had arrived from Fort Hall, where he had left his detachment of the battalion to come to California to report to me in person. He brought a muster-roll of his detachment, with a power of attorney from all its members to draw their pay; and as the battalion itself had been discharged on the 16th of July, Paymaster Rich paid to Captain Brown the money due the detachment up to that date, according to the rank they bore upon the muster-rolls upon which the battalion had been mustered out of service. Captain Brown started immediately for Fort Hall, at which place and in the valley of Bear river he said the whole Mormon emigration intended to pass the winter. He reported that he had met Captain Hunt, late of the Mormon battalion, who was on his way to meet the emigrants and bring into the country this winter, if possible, a battalion, according to the terms offered in my letter to him of the 16th of August, a copy of which you will find among the military correspondence of the department.

In my letter I offered Captain Hunt the command of the battalion, with the rank of lieutenant colonel, with an adjutant; but I find, by the orders lately received, that a battalion of four companies is only entitled to a major and acting adjutant. I will notify Captain Hunt of this change at as early a moment as I can communicate with him. I am pleased to find by the despatches that in this matter I have anticipated the wishes of the department.

Last season there was a great scarcity of provisions on the coast of California; but when the stores are received that are now on their way, there will be an ample supply for the coming winter. The crops in this country have been very fine this season, and at present wheat is plentiful and cheap at San Francisco. Beef is also plentiful. Beans can be purchased at the southern ports, and sugar imported from the Sandwich islands; but for all other subsistence stores we are dependent upon the South American ports or those of the United States. I have directed Captain Marcy, acting commissary of subsistence at this post, to supply the chief of his department with the market prices of all kinds of provisions, with such other facts as may enable his department to act with the proper economy. The want of good clothing for the regulars and volunteers is already felt in California; and unless a supply has already been despatched, many of the garrisons will be without shoes and proper clothing this winter. The price of such articles here is so exorbitant as to place them beyond the reach of the soldier. The volunteer clothing brought by sutler Haight has already been disposed of to citizens and soldiers, and there are no means of his renewing the supply except by sending to the United States. Justice to the soldier demands that he either be comfortably clad by the government, or that it should be within his power to clothe himself on the allowance provided for that purpose by law.

I respectfully recommend, if it has not already been done, that a large supply of infantry undress winter clothing be sent immediately to this country, to be distributed, so as to enable each volunteer to purchase for his own immediate use at cost prices. No summer clothing is needed, as the climate is too severe, summer and winter. Such articles as good blankets, cloth overcoats, caps, jackets, overalls, stockings, and shoes, with stout shirts and drawers, are the only ones that will ever be needed here.

General order No. 10, of 1847, promotes Lieutenant Loeser, 3d artillery, and orders him to join his company. I regret that at this moment his services cannot be spared, and I am compelled to retain him on duty with company F, 3d artillery, because the absence of Captain Tompkins, the death of Lieutenant Minor, and Lieutenant Sherman being detached as acting assistant adjutant general, has reduced the number of officers of that company to but two—Lieutenants Ord and Loeser. I trust that the two companies of regulars in this country will be kept with a full supply of officers, that an officer, upon being promoted, may be enabled to join the army in the field, and participate in the active operations to which he looks for distinction and experience.

Captain H. M. Nagle, 7th New York volunteers, with a strong detachment of his company, is now absent in pursuit of Indians in the valley of the San Joaquin. He has with him Lieutenant Burton's company of California volunteers, which is expected to return to Monterey before the end of this month; in which case I shall cause it to be mustered out of service and discharged on the 31st day of October.

Again I have to report the death, by sickness, of an officer of my command—Lieut. C. C. Anderson, 7th New York volunteers, who contracted a fever when on duty at Fort Sacramento, and died in consequence at San Francisco on the 13th of September. He was buried with military honors by the troops at San Francisco, under direction of Major Hardie. This death reduces the number of officers in Captain Brackett's company, 7th regiment New York volunteers, to one captain and one second lieutenant.

Commodore Shubrick will sail for the west coast of Mexico from this harbor next week; and having made application to me, I have directed Lieutenant Halleck, of the engineer corps, to accompany him, and shall give Lieutenant Colonel Burton, in command at La Paz, Lower California, authority to accompany Commodore Shubrick, should the latter design an attack upon any point or points of the west coast of Mexico, with orders, of course, to resume his position at La Paz as soon as the object is accomplished for which his command is desired. Colonel Burton will be directed to leave a sufficient number of men at La Paz to keep the flag flying.

It affords me much pleasure to assure the department that the most perfect harmony subsists between the members of the naval and land forces on this coast, and that the most friendly intercourse is kept up between the officers. I have had frequent occasions myself to ask assistance of Commodores Biddle and Shubrick, and my requests have been granted with promptness and politeness; and in return I have offered them all the assistance in my power. Our consultations have been frequent and perfectly harmonious, resulting, I hope, in the advancement of the common cause of our country.

I transmit herewith the post returns of Monterey for September, and copies of department orders and correspondence from September 13 to October 8; also, files of the Californian and Star from September 4 to October 2, 1847.

I have the honor to be your most obedient servant,
R. B. MASON,
Colonel 1st Dragoons, commanding.

To General R. JONES, *Adjutant General, Washington, D. C.*

HEADQUARTERS TENTH MILITARY DEPARTMENT,
Monterey, California, October 9, 1847.

SIR: I herewith transmit to you copies of all letters, &c., appertaining to the civil department of California up to this date, with the exception of some few that are so entirely unimportant that I deemed it not worth while to have them copied, or to trouble you with reading.

I am, respectfully, your obedient servant,

R. B. MASON,
Colonel 1st Dragoons, commanding.

Brig. General R. JONES,
Adjutant General U. S. Army, Washington.

NEW HELVETIA, *July* 12, 1847.

Mr. Samuel Smith, from the Upper Sacramento valley, has called upon me and made the following statement: That the citizens of that part of the country had sent him as their agent to inform me, as the sub-Indian agent of this district, that some two weeks since, Antonio Maria Armijo, (Californian,) Smith, and John Eggar, (foreigners,) citizens of the Sonoma district, visited an Indian rancheria, some sixty miles north of this post. They were received by the Indians kindly, and furnished with food, berries, &c. After remaining some half hour, they commenced an attack on the defenceless Indians—killed thirteen of their number, and took thirty-seven prisoners and carried them off as slaves. I immediately informed the alcalde of Sonoma of the transaction, and requested Mr. Smith to go before the alcalde of this district and make affidavit. Yesterday a chief of the "Yousumney" tribe, living on Consumney river, 20 miles from this place, made the following complaint to me: That two Californians, Rafael Altamiras (alias Rey) and Hixalto, came to his village on Saturday, the 10th instant, and claimed some horses that Lieutenant Riviere, of the United States navy, had left with them, and left the papers with them to that effect. They took the horses, and whipped the chief severely, and cut up his hat, and otherwise abused them. I immediately informed the alcalde of this district of the outrage, but they escaped. I this day also write to the alcalde of the Upper Pueblo, of which district they are citizens, on the subject.

You will confer a great favor on myself, as well as the suffering Indians, by giving me, in writing, my instructions as to how I am to act in these cases, as well as the general management of the Indians, as sub-Indian agent for this district.

I have the honor, sir, to be, respectfully, your obedient servant,

J. A. SUTTER,
Sub-agent for the Indians on Sacramento and San Joaquin rivers.

R. B. MASON,
Colonel 1*st Dragoons, Governor,*
Commander-in-chief of the land forces in California.

True copy:

W. T. SHERMAN,
First Lieutenant 3d Artillery, A. A. A. General.

HEADQUARTERS TENTH MILITARY DEPARTMENT,
Monterey, California, July 14, 1847.

SIR: Your communication of the 24th June and the accompanying copies of papers have been duly received. It gives me much gratification to learn that you have accepted and entered upon the duties of collector of customs and harbor-master at San Diego. Your salary will be at the rate of one thousand dollars per annum, provided revenue to that amount be collected and received in your office, the expenses of which being first paid.

I am, respectfully, your obedient servant,
R. B. MASON,
Colonel 1st Dragoons, Governor of California.

Don MIGUEL DE PEDRORENA,
Collector of Customs, San Diego, California.

HEADQUARTERS TENTH MILITARY DEPARTMENT,
Monterey, California, July 14, 1847.

SIR: Your communication of the 5th instant has been received. I will endeavor to visit San Francisco some time during the present month, and have adjusted the question concerning the survey of the 100-varas lots. If I cannot shortly visit your town, I will appoint commissioners to examine the question and make a report upon the subject.

I am, respectfully, your obedient servant,
R. B MASON,
Colonel 1st Dragoons, Governor of California.

GEORGE HYDE,
Alcalde, San Francisco, California.

Know all men by these presents, that I, Richard B. Mason, colonel 1st regiment United States dragoons, and governor of California, by virtue of authority in me vested, do hereby appoint John Foster an alcalde in the district of San Juan, embracing the ranches of San Juan, San Luis, and Pala, in Upper California.

Given at Monterey, the capital of California, this 14th day of July, 1847, and the 72d of the independence of the United States.
R. B. MASON,
Colonel 1st Dragoons, Governor of California.

HEADQUARTERS TENTH MILITARY DEPARTMENT,
Monterey, California, July 16, 1847.

CAPTAIN: I return you the account of Mr. J. F. Reed, sheriff: see my remarks thereon. The account should be supported by sub-vouchers, as in the case of account against the United States. You had better make out an account in form, &c., and send to him. The charge of $3 per day for himself and horse, I think, is rather high; the other charges are reasonable enough. There is no necessity for opening an account with the treasury touching the civil funds of California; that is a matter to be settled here. Make out a quarterly account and vouchers of the civil fund, and send them to this office.

I am, respectfully, your obedient servant,

R. B. MASON,
Colonel 1st Dragoons, Governor of California.

Captain FOLSOM,
Assistant Quartermaster, San Francisco, California.

ROBIDOUX
  vs.
LEASE.

The plaintiff in this cause came forward by his attorney on the 22d of June, 1847, and petitioned for a change of venue, on the ground that the recently appointed judge or alcalde, before whose court the cause then stood, had been employed as counsel in the case; but the petition did not disclose the fact that this judge had been the plaintiff's own counsel. That would have been a sufficient ground for the defendant to base an application upon for a change of venue, but not for the plaintiff, because any prejudices that the judge might have formed would very naturally have been in favor of his client, and not against him. The venue, however, was changed from San Francisco to Monterey.

On the 13th of the present month, the plaintiff again came forward and petitioned that the venue be changed a second time. To this latter petition the counsel on both sides have filed their arguments, much of which is so entirely foreign to the question before me that I deem it only necessary to state that, in all criminal cases, a change of venue is only allowed to the defendant; in other cases, neither party is ever granted more than one change of venue. Were this rule not to prevail, there would be no end to the expense, the vexation, and delay that litigating parties might cause each other. The rule will be adhered to; the venue will not be changed.

R. B. MASON,
Colonel 1st Dragoons, Governor of California.

MONTEREY, CALIFORNIA, *July 21, 1847.*

HEADQUARTERS TENTH MILITARY DEPARTMENT,
Monterey, California, July 21, 1847.

SIR: I have this moment received your letter of the 12th instant. I very much regret to hear that such great outrages have been committed upon the Indians as those reported in your above-mentioned letter. I beg that you will use every exertion to cause the guilty persons to be arrested, for which purpose you will call on the military officer near you for all the assistance in his power to afford. The good citizens of the country, as they value its peace and safety, should also render what assistance they can to arrest those men and bring them to condign punishment. When arrested, I will organize a tribunal for their trial, and, if sentence of death is passed upon them, will have it executed. The safety of the frontier shall not be put at hazard by a few lawless villains.

The Indians that have been captured you must at once seize, by any means in your power, and restore them to their people: tell them that these atrocious acts have been committed by lawless scoundrels, and are entirely condemned by the authorities and all good men of the country, and that the perpetrators of the outrages shall be made a public example of.

Very respectfully, your obedient servant,

R. B. MASON,
Colonel 1st Dragoons, Governor of California.

Mr. J. A. SUTTER,
Sub-Indian Agent, New Helvetia, California.

Know all men by these presents, that I, Richard B. Mason, colonel 1st dragoons United States army, and governor of California, by virtue of authority in me vested, do hereby appoint Jacob R. Snyder land surveyor in the middle department of Upper California.

Done at Monterey, the capital of California, this 22d day of July, 1847, and the 72d of the independence of the United States.

R. B. MASON,
Colonel 1st Dragoons, Governor of California.

HEADQUARTERS TENTH MILITARY DEPARTMENT,
Monterey, California, July 22, 1847.

SIR: Mr. Nash, the late alcalde at Sonoma, arrived here the night before last in the United States ship Dale. Yesterday morning I had an interview with him, at which he expressed himself in terms of regret at the course he had pursued; and he has given me his word that he will immediately give up to you all the books, papers, and records of the alcalde's office, and render an account of all lots disposed of by him, all funds and obligations for funds arising from the sale of lots or otherwise, appertaining to the town of Sonoma, that have come into his possession. I think there will be no further trouble in this matter. Mr. Nash has made me every promise that I could possibly require of him, and seems to be now sensible of the error committed.

I am, respectfully, your obedient servant,

R. B. MASON,
Colonel 1st Dragoons, Governor of California.

Mr. L. W. BOGGS,
Alcalde, Sonoma, California.

Know all men by these presents, that I, Richard B. Mason, colonel 1st regiment dragoons United States army, and governor of California, by virtue of authority in me vested, do hereby appoint Jacob R. Snyder land surveyor in the United States department of Upper California.

Done at Monterey, the capital of California, this 22d day of July, 1847, and the 72d of the independence of the United States.

R. B. MASON,
Colonel 1st Dragoons, Governor of California.

HEADQUARTERS TENTH MILITARY DEPARTMENT,
Monterey, California, July 15, 1847.

SIR: There is wanted in San Francisco an efficient town government, more so than is in the power of an alcalde alone to put in force. There soon may be expected a large number of whalers in your bay, and a large increase of your population by the arrival of emigrants; it is therefore highly necessary that you should, at an early day, have an efficient town police, proper town laws, town officers, &c., for the enforcement of the laws for the preservation of order, and for the proper protection of persons and property.

I therefore desire you call a town meeting for the election of six persons, who, when elected, shall constitute the town council, and who, in conjunction with the alcalde, shall constitute the town authorities until the end of the year 1848.

All the municipal laws and regulations will be formed by the council, but executed by the alcalde in his judicial capacity, as at present. The first alcalde will preside at the meetings of the council, but shall have no vote, except in cases where the votes are equally divided.

The town council (not less than *four* of whom shall constitute a quorum for the transaction of business) to appoint all the necessary town officers, such as treasurer, constables, watchmen, &c., and to determine their pay, fees, &c. The town treasurer to enter into ample and sufficient bonds, conditioned for the faithful performance of his duties, the bonds to be fully executed to the satisfaction of the council before the treasurer enters upon his duties.

The second alcalde shall, in case of the absence of the first alcalde, take his place and preside at the council, and then perform all the proper functions of the first alcalde. No soldier, sailor, or marine, nor any person who is not a "bona fide" resident of the town, shall be allowed to vote for a member of the town council.

AUGUST 13.

I had written the above, when a press of business came upon me which caused me to lay it aside for the time. I was then unexpectedly called to the south, which has caused a delay in this matter. Since my return, I see by the Californian of the 31st July that you have organized a council, &c., &c. Now, the council can either stand as it is, or an election be held, as may be deemed advisable. Whatever may be most agreeable to the good people of your town, cannot but be satisfactory to me.

I am, respectfully, your obedient servant,

R. B. MASON,
Colonel 1st Dragoons, Governor of California

Mr. GEORGE HYDE,
First Alcalde, San Francisco, California.

HEADQUARTERS TENTH MILITARY DEPARTMENT,
Monterey, California, July 17, 1847.

SIR: I have the honor to acknowledge the receipt of your communication of the 27th ultimo.

When the proper civil tribunals are established in the country, a ready means will be afforded for the redress of such grievances as those complained of by Clement Panand. It is not within the province of my power to afford relief in the way of an amount for damages, &c.

Enclosed is a paper from Mr. Colton, the alcalde, touching the case of the flour, mentioned by Panand.

I have the honor to be, sir, with high respect and esteem, your obedient servant,

R. B. MASON,
Colonel 1st Dragoons, Governor of California.

Mr. J. S. MOERENHOUT,
Consul of France, Monterey, California.

Know all men by these presents, that I, Richard B. Mason, colonel 1st regiment dragoons United States army, and governor of California, by virtue of authority in me vested, do hereby appoint Don Pedro C. Carrillo collector of the customs and harbor-master at the port of Santa Barbara, in Upper California.

Given at Santa Barbara, this 1st day of August, 1847, and the 72d year of the independence of the United States.

R. B. MASON,
Colonel 1st Dragoons, Governor of California.

HEADQUARTERS TENTH MILITARY DEPARTMENT,
Monterey, California, August 13, 1847.

SIR: On my return from the south, I received your letter of the 24th July, in which you informed me that you had been appointed by Captain Montgomery, when he commanded in the northern district, an inspector of hides and tallow in that district, &c., and that you still hold this appointment. The appointment never having been revoked, you are still recognised as the inspector of hides and tallow, according to the tenor of the appointment you received, a copy of which be pleased to forward to me.

I am, respectfully, your obedient servant,

R. B. MASON,
Colonel 1st Dragoons, Governor of California.

E. WARD PELL, *San Francisco, California.*

Know all men by these presents, that I, Richard B. Mason, colonel 1st regiment United States dragoons, and governor of California, by virtue of authority in me vested, do hereby appoint Lieutenant Henry W. Halleck, United States army, secretary of the Territory of California.

Done at Monterey, the capital of California, this 13th day of August, 1847, and the 72d of the independence of the United States.

R. B. MASON,
Colonel 1st Dragoons, Governor of California.

STATE DEPARTMENT OF THE TERRITORY OF CALIFORNIA,
Monterey, August 16, 1847.

SIR: I am directed by the governor to acknowledge the receipt of your letter of the 3d of June, calling his attention to certain land claims.

It is not the intention of the existing government to interfere in any respect with the land titles established by the government of Mexico, or the former legal authorities of this Territory. It is suggested, however, that it may be well for yourself and Mr. Black to employ some regularly-appointed surveyor to lay off your lands, in accordance with your title deeds, and to deposite certified copies of said surveys and papers in some office of record, in order that all questions of title may be examined and definitively settled whenever the proper tribunals shall be established for that purpose.

With respect to your claims to lands in Monterey and Yerba Buena, you may rest assured that the existing government will take no measures which shall prejudice in any way your titles to said lands.

Very respectfully, your obedient servant,

H. W. HALLECK,
*Lieutenant of Engineers, and Secretary of State
for the Territory of California.*

Captain STEPHEN SMITH,
Bodega, California.

STATE DEPARTMENT OF THE TERRITORY OF CALIFORNIA,
Monterey, August 16, 1847.

SIR: Representations have been made to the governor of the Territory, of differences between yourself and Captain Stephen Smith respecting your claims to certain lands. It is not the intention of the existing government to interfere in any respect with the land titles established by the government of Mexico, or the former legal authorities of this Territory. It is suggested, however, that it may be well for yourself and Captain Smith to employ some regularly-appointed surveyor to lay off your lands in accordance with your title deeds, and to deposite certified copies of said surveys and papers in some office of record, in order that all questions of titles may be examined and definitively settled whenever the proper tribunals shall be established for that purpose.

Very respectfully, your obedient servant,

H. W. HALLECK,
*Lieutenant of Engineers, and Secretary of State
for the Territory of California.*

Mr. JAMES BLACK,
Near Bodega, California.

STATE DEPARTMENT OF THE TERRITORY OF CALIFORNIA,
Monterey, August 16, 1847.

SIR: I am directed by the governor to acknowledge the receipt of your letters of the 26th of May and 16th of July, 1847. The absence of the governor from the capital has prevented an earlier reply to the last of these two letters.

The articles mentioned by you as having been given up by the Indian captain, Cucusuy, should be delivered to their rightful owners, on your receiving satisfactory proof of ownership. The same course will be pursued in all cases where stolen property is given up by the Indians, or taken from them by your orders.

No further military force can be sent to Sonoma, but it is hoped that the garrison now there will be found sufficient to deter the hostile tribes from further depredations in that quarter. It is thought, by sending messages to the leaders of the Indians spoken of in your letter of the 16th ultimo as having made a hostile demonstration near the lakes, or by obtaining a consultation with them yourself, you may be able to satisfy them of the kind intentions of our government. * * *

[The remainder of this letter the same as the following circular to Captain Sutter.]

Very respectfully, your obedient servant,
H. W. HALLECK,
Lieutenant of Engineers, and Secretary of State for the Territory of California.

Señor Don MARIANO G. VALLEJO,
Sub-agent of Indian Affairs, &c., &c., Sonoma, California.

STATE DEPARTMENT OF THE TERRITORY OF CALIFORNIA,
Monterey, August 16, 1847.

SIR: I am directed by the governor to express to you his entire approbation of your conduct as sub-Indian agent, in seeking to bring to justice the whites who committed the outrages on the Indians mentioned in your letter of the 12th of July, and also to say that he fully approves of the measures proposed in your letters of the 18th and 27th of May, for conciliating the tribes of wild Indians in your district.

To the instructions already given you by General Kearny, I am now directed to add the following

CIRCULAR.

Your duties as sub-Indian agent have reference more particularly to the "Gentiles" or wild Indians, but they will also embrace the "Neophytes" or tame Indians of the missions and ranches. The latter will be subject to all municipal regulations established by the alcaldes within their respective *alcaldias* or districts, and also to all local regulations which you may deem proper to establish for the government of these Indians—such regulations being in all cases reported to the governor for his approval. You will also regard yourself as the protector of the Indians from the ill treatment of their employers, and will take the proper measures to arraign before some alcalde, for trial and punishment, all persons who may be guilty of such maltreatment, or of any improper conduct towards the Indians of your district. In this matter much is left to your own discretion and good sense; and from your knowledge of the character and condition of these Indians, the governor expects that you will do much to induce them to pursue a more honest and industrious course of conduct.

It is thought by having a consultation with the leaders of the hostile tribes, or by sending them messages, you may be able to satisfy them of the kind intentions of our government towards their people, and persuade them to a more pacific policy. You will endeavor to convince these Indians that the new government wishes peace with them; that it is willing to forgive all past offences, but at the same time is determined to inflict severe punishment for all depredations which they may in future commit on the inhabitants of the country, whether native Californians or new settlers. Let them understand that while the government will punish them for their depredations, it will also protect them and their property from injury by the whites. Tell them that if any ill disposed person should do them injury they must complain of it to you, and not themselves attempt to inflict punishment, or to retaliate upon the offenders. The government will always be ready to do ample justice to the Indians, and will redress all their wrongs; but it cannot permit them to take this matter into their own hands.

In all cases of offence on the part of the whites against the Indians, or of the Indians against the inhabitants of the country, you are the authorized agent of the government for seeing that the culprits are brought to justice. In ordinary cases the offenders should be arraigned before one of the alcaldes of your district for his action in the premises; but in extraordinary cases you will retain the offenders in custody, and immediately report to the governor for his instructions.

You are authorized to call upon any military officer near you for whatever assistance you may require to enable you to carry into effect these or any other instructions which you may receive from the proper authorities.

It is desirable to collect some correct information respecting the location, numbers, and character of the several Indian tribes within your district; and, from your acquaintance with the chiefs of these tribes, it is supposed you will be able to communicate much that will be valuable and interesting, not only to the authorities of the Territory, but also to the general government at Washington. All statistics of these tribes, their manner of subsistence, their government, their mode of carrying on war, their military weapons and accoutrements—in fine, facts of any kind respecting their history or present condition will be highly acceptable.

In all cases where stolen property is given up by the Indians, or taken from them by your orders, such property will be restored to the rightful owners on your receiving satisfactory proofs of ownership.

It is to be regretted that the present state of the finances of the Territory will not authorize the purchase of presents to be given by the Indian agents to the friendly chiefs and tribes; but, a supply of such goods having been asked from the general government at Washington, it is hoped that some may be received in the course of the year.

You are requested to write frequently to the governor, communicating freely your views and opinions respecting the best measures to be adopted for the government of the Indians and for the security of their quiet and happiness.

Very respectfully, your obedient servant,
H. W. HALLECK,
Lieutenant of Engineers, and Secretary of State
for the Territory of California.

Captain J. A. SUTTER,
Sub-agent of Indian Affairs, &c., New Helvetia, California.

HEADQUARTERS TENTH MILITARY DEPARTMENT,
Monterey, August 16, 1847.

SIR: It appears from a letter of William Richardson, collector of customs and harbor-master of the port of San Francisco, dated July 12, that he is unable to collect certain duties of Messrs. Ward & Smith, except in *"government orders,"* (which are understood to be due-bills given by officers and other persons for claims against the United States.) The moneys collected for customs belong to the civil government of the Territory, and cannot properly be used for the payment of the general debts of the United States government.

To prevent further difficulties of this kind, it is respectfully suggested that some port regulations be established requiring all duties to be paid immediately on the entry of goods at the custom-house. The collectors have already been instructed by the governor of the Territory to receive nothing but *specie, treasury notes*, and *drafts* for customs and fees; but it is supposed to belong to the naval commander-in-chief, rather than the territorial governor, to establish regulations respecting the time of payment, &c.

Will you have the kindness to communicate a copy of such regulations as you may deem proper to establish.

Very respectfully, your obedient servant,
R. B. MASON,
Colonel 1st Dragoons, Governor of California.

W. Branford Shubrick,
Commander-in-chief of the naval forces.

Know all men by these presents, that I, Richard B. Mason, colonel 1st regiment United States dragoons, and governor of California, by virtue of authority in me vested, do hereby appoint Don Mariano G. Vallejo and J. A. Sutter, both citizens of California, and sub-Indian agents, special commissioners or judges to hold a court at or near Sutter's Fort, on the Sacramento, at such early day as may be most convenient, for the trial of Antonio M. Armijo, Smith, (commonly called "growling Smith,") and John Eggar, each and severally charged with the murder, as well as the capturing and carrying off in slavery, of several peaceable Indians, some time about the latter part of June, or early in July, 1847.

Done at Monterey, California, this 19th day of August, 1847, and the 72d of the independence of the United States.
R. B. MASON,
Colonel 1st Dragoons, Governor of California.

Know all men by these presents, that I, Richard B. Mason, colonel 1st dragoons United States army, and governor of California, by virtue of authority in me vested, do hereby appoint J. D. Hunter a sub-Indian agent for the Indians in the lower district of Upper California.

Given at Santa Barbara, Upper California, this 1st day of August, 1847, and the 72d of the independence of the United States.
R. B. MASON,
Colonel 1st Dragoons, Governor of California.

Headquarters Tenth Military Department,
Monterey, California, August 19, 1847.

Gentlemen: I herewith enclose you a commission for you to hold a special court for the trial of Armijo, Smith, and Eggar, each and severally charged with committing the outrages upon the Indians north of Sutter's Fort not long since.

I desire that you will cause a jury of twelve good men to be empannelled for their trial. The jury, after having pronounced upon their guilt or innocence, will, if guilty, pronounce sentence.

I desire that you see the accused persons have a full, fair, and impartial trial; that the jury, witnesses, and interpreters be all properly sworn; and that a full and fair record be made of each trial, which you will be pleased to forward to me for my further action, together with your views and recommendations in the respective cases.

Enclosed are the charges upon which the prisoners are to be tried, copies of which be pleased to furnish them in due season, to prepare themselves for trial.

I am, respectfully, your obedient servant,
R. B. MASON,
Colonel 1st Dragoons, Governor of California.
General M. G. VALLEJO, and
Captain J. A. SUTTER,
Sub-Indian Agents, Upper California.

CIRCULAR.

STATE DEPARTMENT OF THE TERRITORY OF CALIFORNIA,
Monterey, August 19, 1847.

SIR: You have been appointed collector of customs and harbor-master for the port of ———.

The commander-in-chief of the naval forces having been authorized by the President of the United States to establish port regulations, to prescribe the conditions under which American and foreign vessels may be admitted into the ports of California, and to regulate the import duties, you will be governed in respect to these matters by such rules and regulations as that officer may deem proper to establish.

The governor of the Territory directs that you receive for customs and fees nothing but specie, *treasury notes,* and *drafts,* which at the end of every quarter you will turn over to the authorized receiver, and settle with him all your accounts. The receipts of such authorized receiver will be for you full and sufficient vouchers. The receiver has been directed, after settling and auditing your accounts at the end of each quarter, to pay to you the amount of your quarterly salary, provided revenue to that amount be collected and received in your office, the authorized expenses of the office being first paid.

In case of any attempt to smuggle, you will immediately give information to the nearest naval and military officers, and report the circumstances to the governor for his instructions.

You will make out, at the end of each quarter, quarterly returns of all imports and exports; a quarterly return of all vessels arriving at and sailing from the port; a quarterly account current of customs; and a quarterly abstract of disbursements, with accompanying vouchers. These papers will be made out according to the accompanying blank forms, in duplicate, one copy of which will be filed in your office, and the other turned over to the authorized receiver, to be transmitted by him to the governor of the Territory.

Enclosed herewith is a copy of a "circular" of this date to the receiver of customs.
Very respectfully, your obedient servant,
H. W. HALLECK,
*Lieutenant of Engineers, and Secretary of State
for the Territory of California.*

CIRCULAR.

STATE DEPARTMENT OF THE TERRITORY OF CALIFORNIA,
Monterey, August 19, 1847.

SIR: You have been appointed to settle and audit the accounts of the collector and harbor-master of the port of ———.

You will settle the accounts of said collector at the end of every quarter, receiving from him all funds in his hands arising from customs. Before auditing these accounts, you will compare them with the entries on the custom-house books of the port, and see that the proper amount of duties have been collected on all goods entered at the custom-house. After having audited the accounts of the collector at the end of each quarter, you will pay him the amount of his quarterly salary, provided funds to that amount, collected and received by you from the revenues of the port, remain in your hands after the authorized quarterly expenses of the collector's office have been paid.

When the same officer is appointed to settle and audit the accounts of two or more collectors, the receipts and disbursements for each port will be kept separate and distinct, so that if there be not sufficient funds for the full payment of the collectors, each collector may be paid the money actually accruing from the receipts of his office, as specified in the letter of his appointment. Where there are not sufficient funds at the end of any one quarter for paying the full quarterly salary of the collector, the deficiency will be made up at the end of the next following quarter in which there shall be sufficient funds derived from the custom-house revenues remaining in your hands for that purpose.

In case the collector should fail at the end of each quarter to settle his accounts, or to turn over to you all public moneys in his hands, you will withhold the payment of his salary, and immediately report the circumstance to the governor of the Territory for his instructions.

The funds received from the collector of customs will be kept by you separate and apart from all other public funds in your possession. They are to be used for the civil government of the Territory, and will be paid out only upon the written order of the governor.

You will transmit, at the end of every quarter, an account current of the civil funds in your possession, and an abstract of disbursements, with the proper vouchers, for all your expenditures. You will also transmit the quarterly reports and other papers of the collector, seeing in all cases that they are made out according to the instructions received by him from the proper authorities.

Enclosed herewith is a copy of a circular to the collectors of customs, and also blank forms for returns, &c.
Very respectfully, your obedient servant,
H. W. HALLECK,
*Lieutenant of Engineers, and Secretary of State
for the Territory of California.*

STATE DEPARTMENT OF THE TERRITORY OF CALIFORNIA,
Monterey, August 20, 1847.

SIR: It appears from the records of this office that Captain Richardson was appointed collector of the port of San Francisco on the 28th of September, 1846. You will please ascertain if his accounts have been settled, and his salary paid from that date. John Vioget is one of Captain Richardson's securities for the amount of twenty thousand dollars on his bonds. Will you make the proper inquiries to ascertain for what amount Mr. Vioget is reputed good, and report to the governor?

After reading the enclosed papers for the collector of the port, you will turn them over to Captain Richardson. Please to impress upon his mind the importance of immediate and strict compliance with the directions therein contained.

Very respectfully, your obedient servant,
H. W. HALLECK,
Lieutenant of Engineers, and Secretary of State
for the Territory of California.

Captain J. L. FOLSOM,
Assistant Quartermaster, San Francisco, California.

STATE DEPARTMENT OF THE TERRITORY OF CALIFORNIA,
Monterey, August 20, 1847.

SIR: The governor of the Territory directs that you will immediately make out and turn over to Captain Folsom your quarterly returns and other papers for the quarter ending June 30, 1847, in accordance with the accompanying "circular" and blank forms. Your quarterly returns and accounts will hereafter be made out and forwarded immediately after the close of every quarter.

Very respectfully, your obedient servant,
H. W. HALLECK,
Lieut. of Engineers, and Secretary of State
for the Territory of California.

WM. RICHARDSON,
Collector, &c., &c., San Francisco, California.

STATE DEPARTMENT OF THE TERRITORY OF CALIFORNIA,
Monterey, August 20, 1847.

SIR: I am directed by the governor to acknowledge the receipt of your letter of the 10th instant, with your account current of customs for the second quarter of 1847, and the enclosed vouchers.

The governor directs that you will examine the accounts of the collector of the port of San Pedro back to the date of his first appointment after our occupation of the country, in order to ascertain for what purposes the funds of the custom-house have been expended, and see if he has turned over to you all moneys due the government. You will report to the governor the result of your examination.

After reading the enclosed papers for the collector of the port, you will turn them over to Mr. Alexander. Please to impress upon his mind the importance of immediate and strict compliance with the directions therein contained.

     Very respectfully, your obedient servant,
         H. W. HALLECK,
    Lieut. of Engineers, and Secretary of State
       for the Territory of California.
Lieut. J. W. DAVIDSON,
 A. A. Quartermaster, &c., Los Angeles, California.

  STATE DEPARTMENT OF THE TERRITORY OF CALIFORNIA,
       Monterey, August 20, 1847.

SIR: I am directed by the governor to acknowledge the receipt of your letter of July 16, enclosing the quarterly accounts and returns of the collector of the port of Santa Barbara. These papers are satisfactory, except that there is no return of imports and exports. You will see that he makes out one immediately.

After reading the enclosed papers for the collector, you will please turn them over to him, and endeavor to impress upon his mind the importance of immediate and strict compliance with the directions therein contained.

     Very respectfully, your obedient servant,
         H. W. HALLECK,
    Lieut. of Engineers, and Secretary of State
       for the Territory of California.
Captain FRANCIS J. LIPPETT,
 Santa Barbara, California.

  STATE DEPARTMENT OF THE TERRITORY OF CALIFORNIA,
       Monterey, August 20, 1847.

SIR: I am directed by the governor of the Territory to say to you that your accounts and returns for the last quarter are satisfactory, except that you make no returns of imports or exports. You will please make out such returns and turn them over to Captain Lippett.

Your quarterly accounts and returns will hereafter be made out and forwarded immediately after the close of every quarter, in accordance with the accompanying "circular" and blank forms.

     Very respectfully, your obedient servant,
         H. W. HALLECK,
    Lieut. of Engineers, and Secretary of State
       for the Territory of California.
Don PEDRO C. CARRILLO,
 Collector, &c., &c., Santa Barbara, California.

  STATE DEPARTMENT OF THE TERRITORY OF CALIFORNIA,
       Monterey, August 21, 1847.

SIR: The governor requests that you will furnish him with the names of all persons owning or claiming land within the limits of the survey which I received from you this morning, and the amount of land owned

or claimed by each individual; and also, that you will give your opinion of the character of the title or claim in each case.
Very respectfully, your obedient servant,
H. W. HALLECK,
*Lieut. of Engineers, and Secretary of State
for the Territory of California.*
WALTER COLTON, *Alcalde, &c., Monterey, California.*

STATE DEPARTMENT OF THE TERRITORY OF CALIFORNIA,
August 23, 1847.

SIR: I am directed by the governor to acknowledge the receipt of your letter of August 5, asking for a new district, with an alcálde, &c.

In accordance with your request, the governor has consulted Mr. Larkin on the subject, and they are both of the opinion that the matter had better be postponed for the present. It is quite possible that the increase of population in the district of Sonoma may render it necessary to establish a new district in the course of another year; but for the present it is deemed advisable to establish no new court, unless the state of public affairs absolutely requires it.
Very respectfully, your obedient servant,
H. W. HALLECK,
*Lieut. of Engineers, and Secretary of State
for the Territory of California.*
R. SEMPLE, Esq., *Benicia, California.*

STATE DEPARTMENT OF THE TRRRITORY OF CALIFORNIA,
August 24, 1847.

SIR: In reply to your letter of the 19th instant, the governor directs that you do not interfere in the land question now in dispute between Mr. Forbes and Mr. Cook. All questions of land titles, unless they can be settled by arbitration, or some other amicable arrangement between the parties, must remain as they are until the proper judicial tribunals can be established for investigating and settling them.

This order is in no way to affect the just rights of either of the aforesaid parties.
Very respectfully, your obedient servant,
H. W. HALLECK,
*Lieut. of Engineers, and Secretary of State
for the Territory of California.*
JOHN BURTON, Esq., *Alcalde of Pueblo de San José, California.*

STATE DEPARTMENT OF THE TERRITORY OF CALIFORNIA,
Monterey, August 26, 1847.

SIR : It appears from a letter just received from Lieutenant Carnes, that the collector of the port of Santa Barbara has called on him for payment of the collector's salary for the last two quarters.

You were appointed by Lieutenant Colonel Burton to settle and audit the accounts of the collector of Santa Barbara, and receive from him the revenues of the customs; and the governor directs me to say that you have not been authorized to confer this duty upon any other person, and that you will still be held responsible for the expenditure and safe-keeping of said funds.

In addition to the instructions sent you on the 19th and 20th of this month, the governor now directs that you will ascertain the date of Pedro C. Carrillo's first appointment as collector, and see that his accounts are settled back to that date. It appears that said Carrillo paid himself last quarter $188: of course, no such account can in future be passed. There is also another for $15, for 100 blank clearances. Please to report the facts in this case.

The salary of the collector covers the making out of all his papers, and he cannot be allowed any pay for blanks. This item will, therefore, be regarded as part payment of his salary for the last quarter.

Very respectfully, your obedient servant,
H. W. HALLECK,
*Lieutenant of Engineers, and Secretary of State
for the Territory of California.*
Captain F. J. LIPPETT, *New York Volunteers,
Santa Barbara, California.*

STATE DEPARTMENT OF THE TERRITORY OF CALIFORNIA,
Monterey, August 27, 1847.

SIR: You will procure the publication of the enclosed orders of the governor in each of the San Francisco papers: a single insertion will be sufficient. The expense of advertisement to be paid from the civil funds.

Very respectfully, your obedient servant,
H. W. HALLECK,
*Lieutenant of Engineers, and Secretary of State
for the Territory of California.*
Captain J. L. FOLSOM, *Assistant Quartermaster,
San Francisco, California.*

STATE DEPARTMENT OF THE TERRITORY OF CALIFORNIA,
Monterey, August 27, 1847.

SIR: The accompanying "circular" and blank forms are furnished for your instructions as collector.

In examining your accounts for the 2d quarter of 1847, I find that you have made no return of imports for that quarter. You will please make out one immediately and send it to the governor: your returns of exports, of customs collected, and also of vessels arriving at and clearing from the port of Monterey, do not include the month of April in that quarter. You will supply the deficiency, so that this office may be in possession of the above information for the full quarter.

Hereafter your papers will be made out according to the enclosed instructions and blank forms.

Very respectfully, your obedient servant,
H. W. HALLECK,
*Lieutenant of Engineers, and Secretary of State
for the Territory of California.*
T. H. GREEN, *Collector, Monterey, California.*

HEADQUARTERS TENTH MILITARY DEPARTMENT,
Monterey, August 27, 1847.

SIR: Your communication of this day's date is before me, enclosing the correspondence between yourself and Major Hardie at San Francisco, relative to your claim to a certain lot in that town, which has been reserved for government purposes. You present no title papers, nor make any reference to where they are recorded. I therefore cannot touch the subject, in the manner in which it is at present presented.

I am, sir, very respectfully, your obedient servant,
R. B. MASON,
Colonel 1*st Dragoons, Governor of California.*
A. B. THOMPSON, *Monterey, California.*

HEADQUARTERS TENTH MILITARY DEPARTMENT,
Monterey, California, August 27, 1847.

SIR: Your communication of the 23d instant is before me, asking my interference in the case between yourself and Mr. West, concerning the attachment of your property near Sonoma.

Any appeal from the judicial acts of the alcalde at Sonoma must come before me officially authenticated from that court. I cannot act upon a mere *ex parte* statement; I must have the subject so presented to me from the court as to enable me to act understandingly.

I am, sir, very respectfully, your obedient servant,
R. B. MASON,
Colonel 1*st Dragoons, Governor of California.*
A. B. THOMPSON, *Monterey, California.*

STATE DEPARTMENT OF THE TERRITORY OF CALIFORNIA,
August 30, 1847.

SIR: The governor directs me to acknowledge the receipt of your letter of the 7th instant, relating to the suit of Castro *vs.* German.

No election has been taken in this case since the decree and order of General Kearny, nor does Governor Mason intend, at present, in any respect to interfere with that decision.

Very respectfully, your obedient servant,
H. W. HALLECK,
Lieutenant of Engineers, and Secretary of State
for the Territory of California.
GEO. HYDE, Esq., *Alcalde of San Francisco, California.*

STATE DEPARTMENT OF THE TERRITORY OF CALIFORNIA,
Monterey, August 30, 1847.

SIR: In transmitting your appointment as alcalde of the pueblo of San José, the governor directs me to say to you that he hopes the growing interests of your town, and the great importance of having some competent and efficient person to watch over these interests, and to assist in preserving the quiet and tranquillity of the country, will be a sufficient inducement for you to accept this office. You have been highly recommended to the governor as the most suitable person in your district for the office of magistrate, as he has every reason to believe that his confidence in you will not be misplaced.

In the administration of your office, you will be governed by the laws and usages of the country, as they have heretofore existed, until other laws can be established.

You will please to exhibit to Mr. Burton your appointment, and give him the enclosed order to turn over to you all public papers and funds belonging to his office. If, however, you should deem it proper to decline this appointment, you will immediately return the enclosed papers without presenting them.

Very respectfully, your obedient servant,
H. W. HALLECK,
*Lieutenant of Engineers, and Secretary of State
for the Territory of California.*
WM. FISHER, Esq., *Pueblo of San José, California.*

[Appointment declined by Mr. Fisher, and therefore cancelled.]

STATE DEPARTMENT OF THE TERRITORY OF CALIFORNIA,
Monterey, September 6, 1847.

SIR: In order to enable him to act understandingly upon matters connected with the mission of Santa Inez, the governor directs that the renters of that mission immediately furnish him with copies of the contract or agreement by which they occupy said mission, and also a full amount of all rents paid, with the proper receipts for the same.

Very respectfully, your obedient servant,
H. W. HALLECK,
*Lieutenant of Engineers, and Secretary of State
for the Territory of California.*
Messrs. JOSE MARIA COBANBIAS, JOAQUIN, and CARRILLO.

STATE DEPARTMENT OF THE TERRITORY OF CALIFORNIA,
Monterey, September 6, 1847.

SIR: The governor directs me to acknowledge the receipt of your letter of the 26th August, and to say to you that you shall receive a more definitive answer to your petition as soon as the contracts of the renters of the mission of Santa Inez can be examined. These renters have been ordered to furnish to the governor a copy of each contract, for his instruction.

Very respectfully, your obedient servant,
H. W. HALLECK,
*Leiutenant of Engineers, and Secretary of State
for the Territory of California.*
ANGEL, JUAN BAUTISTA, and ANDRES,
Alcaldes of Santa Inez.

STATE DEPARTMENT OF THE TERRITORY OF CALIFORNIA,
Monterey, September 6, 1847.

SIR: The governor directs me to acknowledge the receipt of your letter of the 26th August, enclosing certain papers purporting to be a title to a piece of land in or near the mission of Santa Inez. The title to which you refer is of no value, Captain José Maria Flores having had no proper authority to make such grant; but as you are in possession of said land, you may continue to hold it (provided no other person presents a better claim) until the proper tribunals are organized for the investigation of questions of that character. Your papers are enclosed herewith.

Very respectfully, your obedient servant,
H. W. HALLECK,
Lieutenant of Engineers, and Secretary of State
for the Territory of California

JOAQUIN AQUILA, *Santa Inez.*

STATE DEPARTMENT OF THE TERRITORY OF CALIFORNIA,
Monterey, September 7, 1847.

SIR: In reply to your letter of the 18th ultimo, respecting instructions given by you to the collector of San Pedro, the governor directs me to say, that as soon as he can have a consultation with Commodore Shubrick, some general regulations on the subject will be made, which shall be uniform throughout the Territory. In the mean time the regulations made by you for San Pedro are approved.

It having been reported that the occupants of the mission of San Buenaventura have sold, without proper authority, cattle, horses, and other property belonging to that mission, the governor directs that you procure a copy of the contract, or agreement, by which these occupants hold possession of the mission, and also a full account of all rents paid by them, with the proper receipts for the same; you will also examine into the present state of this mission and of the mission property, as compared with the inventories given by the occupants at the time of making the contract, and report what measures you may deem best calculated to secure the just rights of all concerned.

The same course will be pursued with respect to the missions of San Fernando, San Juan Capistrano, and (if rented) the missions of San Gabriel and San Diego. It is reported that certain archives belonging to the mission of San Luis Rey were taken in January last from that mission to San Juan Capistrano. As it is desirable to collect in this office all the archives belonging to the missions of California, you are requested to use your best endeavors to procure all papers which may be likely to give information respecting their present or former condition.

Enclosed herewith is an order to the occupants of the mission above mentioned to furnish you with copies of their contracts, and such other information as may be required.

Copies of instructions for the sub-Indian agents, and of regulations for the government of the Indians, will be forwarded by the earliest opportunity.

Very respectfully, your obedient servant,
H. W. HALLECK,
Lieutenant of Engineers, and Secretary of State
for the Territory of California.

Col. J. D. STEVENSON, *commanding, Los Angeles, California.*

STATE DEPARTMENT OF THE TERRITORY OF CALIFORNIA,
Monterey, September 6, 1847.

To the occupants of the missions of San Buenaventura, San Fernando, San Gabriel, San Juan Capistrano, and San Diego:

The governor directs you, and each of you, to furnish Colonel J. D. Stevenson, commanding the southern district of California, or such person as he may designate for that purpose, copies of all contracts or agreements by which you hold possession of any mission or mission property, and any other information that may be required for fully understanding the conditions of such tenure, and the present state of the missions.

Very respectfully, your obedient servant,
H. W. HALLECK,
*Lieutenant of Engineers, and Secretary of State
for the Territory of California.*

STATE DEPARTMENT OF THE TERRITORY OF CALIFORNIA,
Monterey, September 10, 1847.

SIR: I have to acknowledge the receipt of your letter of the 5th instant, enclosing a communication of Captain Brackett, respecting the case of Sr. Armijo.

You will please to inform Captain Brackett that the governor approves the course pursued by him, under the circumstances, in admitting Sr. Armijo to bail.

Very respectfully, your obedient servant,
H. W. HALLECK,
*Lieutenant of Engineers, and Secretary of State
for the Territory of California.*

Major J. A. HARDIE,
*Commanding Northern Military District,
San Francisco, California.*

STATE DEPARTMENT OF THE TERRITORY OF CALIFORNIA,
Monterey, September 14, 1847.

SIR: Mr. J. W. Weeks having been appointed alcalde of the pueblo of San José, your term of office will consequently cease on the receipt of this letter, and the governor directs that you then turn over to Mr. Weeks all public papers and funds belonging to your office.

Very respectfully, your obedient servant,
H. W. HALLECK,
*Lieut. of Engineers, and Secretary of State
for the Territory of California.*

JOHN BURTON, Esq.,
Alcalde of San José, California.

STATE DEPARTMENT OF THE TERRITORY OF CALIFORNIA,
Monterey, September 15, 1847.

SIR: I am directed by the governor to acknowledge the receipt of your letter of the 7th instant, respecting the trial of Armijo and others. You will see from the enclosed order that the venue is changed to Sonoma, and that L. W. Boggs, esq., has been appointed, with yourself and Captain Sutter, as an additional commissioner or judge. This has been deemed necessary, in order to provide for cases that might otherwise arise of difference of opinion between the other two. Captain B. will be directed to conduct the trial on the part of the government. You will please give the requisite notice to all persons concerned of the time and place of trial, as directed in the enclosed order. The governor is desirous that the matter may be definitely settled without any unnecessary delay.

Very respectfully, your obedient servant,
H. W. HALLECK,
Lieut. of Engineers, and Secretary of State
for the Territory of California.

Don M. G. Vallejo

State Department of the Territory of California,
Monterey, September 15, 1847.

Sir: I am directed by the governor to acknowledge the receipt of your letter of the 7th instant, and also that of the 3d instant, through Major Hardie. Your course in admitting Armijo to bail is, under the circumstances, approved. You will perceive, from papers this day sent to General Vallejo and Governor Boggs, that the trial of the prisoners charged with Indian murders, &c., will take place at Sonoma, on the 25th of October next. The governor directs that in these trials you act as prosecutor on the part of the government and people, and see that justice is done to all the parties concerned. It is desirable that the court should not go into unnecessary formalities, but seek to bring the whole matter to as early a termination as may be compatible with a just and fair trial.

Very respectfully, your obedient servant,
H. W. HALLECK,
Lieut. of Engineers, and Secretary of State
for the Territory of California

Capt. J. E. Brackett,
Commanding, Sonoma, California.

State Department of the Territory of California,
Monterey, September 18, 1847.

Sir: Enclosed herewith are copies of custom-house and harbor regulations, which, of course, supersede the temporary arrangements communicated in your letter of the 18th of August. The colonel consents to the commutation of the rations of the men employed as guards at San Pedro, on account of the distance of the port from the military post; but no commutation will be allowed for any other post in your district.

Very respectfully, your obedient servant,
H. W. HALLECK,
Lieut. of Engineers, and Secretary of State
for the Territory of California.

Col. J. D. Stevenson,
Commanding, &c., Los Angelos, California.

STATE DEPARTMENT OF THE TERRITORY OF CALIFORNIA,
Monterey, September 18, 1847.

SIR: I am directed by the governor to acknowledge the receipt of your letter of blank date, and say to you that the existing government has no intention of interfering with your title to the mission of San Miguel; but as the title seems incomplete, and as there are other claimants to the property, it has been deemed best to make a temporary arrangement between yourself and the priest, until the subject could be satisfactorily examined by the proper authorities.

Very respectfully, your obedient servant,
H. W. HALLECK,
*Lieut. of Engineers, and Secretary of State
for the Territory of California.*

WILLIAM REED,
San Miguel, California.

STATE DEPARTMENT OF THE TERRITORY OF CALIFORNIA,
Monterey, September 18, 1847.

SIR: You are requested to procure, if possible, the records and papers of the mission of San Francisco Solano (Sonoma) and forward them to this office.

It is possible that General Vallejo may have old records and papers containing statistical information respecting the other missions, which he would be willing to deposite in this office for safe-keeping; if so, please forward them by the earliest opportunity.

Very respectfully, your obedient servant,
H. W. HALLECK,
*Lieut. of Engineers, and Secretary of State
for the Territory of California.*

Capt. BRACKETT,
Commanding, &c., Sonoma, California.

STATE DEPARTMENT OF THE TERRITORY OF CALIFORNIA,
Monterey, September 18, 1847.

SIR: You are requested to procure, if possible, the records and papers of the mission of San Francisco d'Asis, (also called Dolores,) and of the mission of San Rafael, and forward the same to this office for safe-keeping.

Very respectfully, your obedient servant,
H. W. HALLECK,
*Lieut. of Engineers, and Secretary of State
for the Territory of California.*

Capt. J. L. FOLSOM,
Assistant Quartermaster, San Francisco, California.

While Lieutenant Warner is engaged on ordnance duty, Mr. Bestor will be employed in the civil department, at the rate of $100 per month, (including all allowances,) to be paid out of the civil funds of the Territory; it being understood that Mr. Bestor resumes his duties with Lieutenant Warner as soon as his services may be required for topographical surveys.

          R. B. MASON,
     Colonel 1st Dragoons, Governor of California.
MONTEREY, CALIFORNIA, *September 20, 1847.*

  STATE DEPARTMENT OF THE TERRITORY OF CALIFORNIA,
       Monterey, September 23, 1847.

SIR: In the absence of the governor, I have the honor to acknowledge the receipt of your letter of the 17th instant.

By referring to articles 5 and 15 of Commodore Shubrick's instructions of the 15th September, you will find that the difficulties mentioned in your letter have already been provided for. All vessels, *not American,* engaged in the coast trade, pay the same duties as when coming from a foreign port.

    Very respectfully, your obedient servant,
         H. W. HALLECK,
   Lieut. of Engineers, and Secretary of State
      for the Territory of California.
Don PEDRO C. CARRILLO,
  Santa Barbara, California.

  STATE DEPARTMENT OF THE TERRITORY OF CALIFORNIA,
       Monterey, September 24, 1847.

SIR: I have the honor to acknowledge your letter of the 24th instant, accepting the appointment of alcalde of the pueblo of San José. The governor is now absent; but the moment he returns, I will ask his instructions respecting the town council, and also respecting the cutting of timber on the public lands.

    Very respectfully, your obedient servant,
         H. W. HALLECK,
   Lieut. of Engineers, and Secretary of State
      for the Territory of California.
J. W. WEEKS, Esq.,
  Alcalde of San José, California.

Know all men by these presents, that I, Richard B. Mason, colonel first dragoons United States army, and governor of California, by virtue of authority in me vested, do hereby appoint Chester S. Lyman a surveyor of land for and in the middle department of Upper California.

Done at Monterey, the capital of California, this 20th day of September, 1847, and the 72d of the independence of the United States.
          R. B. MASON,
    Colonel 1st Dragoons, and Governor of California.

Know all men by these presents, that I, Richard B. Mason, colonel first dragoons United States army, and governor of California, by virtue of authority in me vested, do hereby appoint Minor F. Leavenworth second alcalde for and in the district of San Francisco.

Done at San Francisco, this second day of October, 1847, and the 72d of the independence of the United States.

R. B. MASON,
Colonel 1st Dragoons, and Governor of California.

CIRCULAR.

STATE DEPARTMENT TERRITORY OF CALIFORNIA,
Monterey, August 16, 1847.

SIR: Your duties as sub-Indian agent have reference more particularly to the "Gentiles" or wild Indians, but they will also embrace the "Neophytes" or tame Indians of the missions or ranches. The latter will be subject to all municipal regulations established by the alcaldes within their respective *alcaldias* or districts, and also to all local regulations that you may establish for the government of these Indians—such regulations to be reported for the approval of the governor. You will also regard yourself as the protector of the Indians from the ill-treatment of their employers, and will take proper measures to arraign before some alcalde all persons who may be guilty of such maltreatment, or of any improper conduct towards the Indians of your district. In this matter much is left to your discretion and good sense; and from your knowledge of the character and condition of the Indians, the governor expects that you will do much to induce them to pursue a more honest and industrious course of conduct.

In all cases of offence on the part of the whites against the Indians, or of the Indians against the inhabitants of the country, you are the authorized agent of the government for seeing that the offenders are brought to justice. In ordinary cases, the offenders should be arraigned before one of the alcaldes of your district for his action in the premises; but in extraordinary cases, you will retain the offenders in custody, and immediately report to the governor for his instructions.

You are authorized to call upon any military officer near you for whatever assistance you may require to enable you to carry into effect these or any other instructions you may receive from proper authority.

Very respectfully, your obedient servant,
H. W. HALLECK,
Lieutenant of Engineers and Secretary of State.
SUB-AGENT OF INDIAN AFFAIRS,
District of ——.

HEADQUARTERS TENTH MILITARY DEPARTMENT,
San Francisco, California, September 27, 1847.

SIR: A surgeon's certificate of disability has been received at this office in the case of Acting Ordnance Sergeant J. C. Low, now under your command, together with a letter from Sergeant Low to Colonel J. D. Stevenson, urging his claim to discharge, and asking to be paid as ordnance sergeant.

From the certificate of disability, signed by Assistant Surgeon Parker, it appears that the disease that now affects Sergeant Low was upon him at the time he engaged to serve the United States: this he knew, and still palmed himself upon the government, subjecting it to the great expense of transporting him here to California, where his place cannot be filled. Sergeant Low must therefore abide by his contract—must remain in the service and render his best efforts in some sedentary capacity, such as clerk, or of his own present position, where little bodily labor will hereafter be required.

In relation to his pay as ordnance sergeant, you are aware that such appointments are conferred by the Secretary of War, who, again, is limited by law to certain persons who have served eight years in the army, four of which in the capacity of a non-commissioned officer. Sergeant Low has no such appointment, and is not, therefore, entitled to the pay. His appointment is only that of an acting ordnance sergeant, and such appointment is not recognised by law so as to warrant the payment of money.

You will please communicate the above to Sergeant Low, as the decision of Colonel Mason on his application.

I have the honor to be your most obedient servant,
W. T. SHERMAN,
First Lieut. 3d Artillery, A. A. A. General.

Major J. A. Hardie,
Commanding, San Francisco, California.

HEADQUARTERS TENTH MILITARY DEPARTMENT,
San Francisco, California, September 27, 1847.

SIR: Governor Mason directs me, in reply to your letter to him of the 11th instant, to say to you that the President of the United States has conferred upon the commander of the Pacific squadron the power to regulate the duties upon all imports into the ports of California, the military commander only receiving the duties when collected, and causing them to be properly disbursed. Commodore Shubrick has already made port regulations, and he alone has power to remit them when they conflict with the interests of any class of citizens or merchants. Colonel Mason will take pleasure in laying your letter before Commodore Shubrick when he returns to Monterey, and has no doubt the Commodore will make such decision in this case as will comport with the best interests of the government.

Your letter refers to the shipment of the lumber from one American port to another—an error you could not have committed, had you reflected that every port in California must still be regarded as Mexican until the Congress of the United States change their nationality.

The port of San Francisco is not an American port, but a Mexican one, held by the American government by right of conquest, and must remain so until further action is had by the Congress of the United States.

I have the honor to be your most obedient servant,
W. T. SHERMAN,
First Lieut. 3d Artillery, A. A. A. General.

R. M. SHERMAN, Esq., for
E. & H. GRIMES,
San Francisco, California.

HEADQUARTERS TENTH MILITARY DEPARTMENT,
San Francisco, California, September 30, 1847.

SIR: Governor Mason directs me to acknowledge the receipt of your letter of the 25th instant, and to assure you that he fully appreciates the motives of humanity and kindness that have influenced your conduct to the sick and abandoned sailors at San Francisco, but that it is not in his power to use the funds derived from the customs for any other purpose than that of defraying the civil expenses of the government of California.

With great respect, your obedient servant,

W. T. SHERMAN,
First Lieut. 3d Artillery, A. A. A. General.

Dr. T. M. LEAVENWORTH, *San Francisco, California.*

HEADQUARTERS TENTH MILITARY DEPARTMENT,
San Francisco, California, September 30, 1847.

SIR: You will be pleased neither to grant nor to give any deed for any town lots or other land to the southward of the Rincon point, and eastward of a line commencing at the northwest corner of the government reserve at the said Rincon point, and running south eleven degrees west (S. 11° W.) with the true meridian. The land eastward of the above-named line is intended for the use of the United States government, the southern boundary of which will be more particularly described when the town surveys are more fully completed.

I have the honor to be your most obedient servant,

W. T. SHERMAN,
First Lieut. 3d Artillery, A. A. A. General.

GEORGE HYDE, Esq.
Alcalde, San Francisco, California.

HEADQUARTERS TENTH MILITARY DEPARTMENT,
San Francisco, California, September 30, 1847.

SIR: I have the honor to inform you that I have this day ordered Captain J. L. Folsom, United States army, to perform the duties of collector and harbor master of the port of San Francisco, California. Your duties as collector, &c., will therefore cease with the present month, and you will please turn over to Captain Folsom all funds, books, papers, boats, or whatever else you may have belonging to the office of collector of customs and harbor-master.

I am, sir, very respectfully, your obedient servant,

W. T. SHERMAN,
First Lieutenant 3d Artillery, A. A. A. General.

WM. RICHARDSON, Esq.,
Collector of the Port of San Francisco, California.

HEADQUARTERS TENTH MILITARY DEPARTMENT,
San Francisco, California, October 1, 1847.

GENTLEMEN: The letter of your committee of this day's date has been received; and, in answer, I have to inform you—

First. That the jurisdiction of the present town council of San Francisco is confined to the limits of the town survey, the boundaries of which I have instructed the alcalde to have marked as soon as convenient.

Second. The duties of the council are prospective, not retrospective. They cannot impair the obligation of contracts entered into by the previous town authorities, nor take jurisdiction of the action or conduct of such authorities further than to modify or repeal any law or ordinance created by said authorities, and now in force, which they may deem inconsistent with the interests of the community. These instructions, together with those contained in my letter of the 15th July, 1847, authorizing the election of the town council, are deemed sufficiently explicit to enable the council to begin a system of policy for the future that will develop the resources and protect the interests of the citizens of San Francisco. Whatever expenses may be contemplated, or improvements made, it is strongly recommended that the town be kept perfectly free of debt.

Since my arrival here, I have received three petitions from the citizens, through the hands of a committee, for the removal of Geo. Hyde, esq., from his office of alcalde of the town. The committee, Messrs. Ward, Brannan, and Ross, also handed me distinct charges, signed by themselves, and herewith handed to you, against Mr. H., of a serious nature, that demand investigation. This is due to Mr. Hyde himself, and to the citizens of the town. I have selected you, gentlemen, to perform this duty of making a thorough investigation of these charges, and to report to me the facts of the case, with your opinion thereon. You have just been chosen by the people of this town to regulate their public affairs and to guard their interests. To whom, then, could I so well confide this duty? You must feel the importance of scrutinizing the charges against the chief magistrate of our town; but, while the interests of the community require an examination, the respect due to his office demands that Mr. Hyde be allowed every privilege and facility to explain any facts, or produce any testimony, that his case may call for. You are hereby authorized to call upon Mr. Hyde for a full exhibition of his accounts and general administration of the affairs of the town since they have been under his direction, that you may examine and report thereon.

Relying upon your integrity and patriotism, I am, gentlemen, your most obedient servant,

R. B. MASON,
Colonel 1st Dragoons, Governor of California.
To the TOWN COUNCIL ELECT *of San Francisco.*

HEADQUARTERS TENTH MILITARY DEPARTMENT,
Monterey, October 6, 1847.

SIR: Governor Mason directs me to acknowledge the receipt of your resignation of the office of captain of the California battalion of mounted riflemen, and to inform you that that battalion was discharged by Lieutenant Colonel Fremont about the 27th of April last, and that of necessity your commission ceased with the existence of the battalion. The battalion was likewise discharged in a manner not in accordance with the laws of the United States, and cannot receive pay until further action is had by the government. He regrets, therefore, that he cannot at this time order you to be paid; but assures you he fully appreciates your services and friendship, to which Commodore Stockton bears such high testimony.

I am, sir, very respectfully, your obedient servant,
W. T. SHERMAN,
First Lieutenant 3d Artillery, A. A. A. General.
Don Santiago E. Arguillo, *of San Diego, California.*

Headquarters Tenth Military Department,
Monterey, California, October 11, 1847.

Sir: Commodore Shubrick has been pleased to apply to Colonel Mason for your services and those of your command in Lower California, to assist him in carrying on the military operations of this season against the west coast of Mexico.

In consequence, it is ordered that, if compatible with the safety of that portion of California, you leave at La Paz or San José such officers and men of your present command as will insure the safety of our flag there, and with the balance embark and co-operate with the naval forces in any attack that they may make against Mazatlan or other ports on the west coast of Mexico. The instructions from the War Department are explicit that our sovereignty must be maintained; and in adopting your measures in obedience to the above instructions, you are expected, upon consultation with the naval commander, to insure this before embarking upon the present expedition.

The colonel commanding expects that no efforts will be spared on your part to secure that unity of action and feeling so essential to all military combinations. This must in a great measure result from your own good sense and judgment; but in a connexion with the subject, I am directed to refer you to an extract of the instructions of the Navy Department to Commodore Shubrick of August 17, 1847, and to paragraphs 24, 25, and 26, Army Regulations, (edition of 1825,) copies of which are herewith enclosed to you, and which have been received and made obligatory upon the army and navy by the orders of the President, through the Navy and War Departments.

When on board of any armed vessel, your command will be as passengers, not marines; but the most perfect discipline will still be kept up; and in the event of the ship finding herself in action, you and your command will not fail to show yourselves at least as efficient as any equal number of marines whatever.

You will continue to render your reports the same as though you were still on shore, reporting those left at La Paz as on detached service.

Very respectfully, your obedient servant,
W. T. SHERMAN,
Acting Assistant Adjutant General.
Lieut. Col. Burton.

Headquarters Tenth Military Department,
Monterey, California, October 20, 1847.

Sir: Your letter of the 5th instant, transmitting the proceedings of the military comission in session at Los Angeles, has been received; and in answer to your inquiries as to the powers of a military commission, I am directed by Colonel Mason to say that the court of military commission is a novel one, created by General Scott in his orders No. 20, dated Tampico, February 19, 1847. This order sets forth the necessity for such a tribunal, and is so clear and logical as to leave no doubt as to its character and powers. The commission is strictly military in its composition, in its form of trial, mode of passing sentence and executing punishment, and has power to try in any enemy's country for atrocities beyond reach of the rules and articles of war, which in the United States would be punished by the ordinary or civil courts of the land.

The second paragraph of the above mentioned order enumerates many crimes, by way of illustrating this class, over which the commission have jurisdiction; but these are not all, as the first paragraph in general terms embraces all crimes of magnitude not otherwise provided for. In awarding sentence, the commission is not required to follow the statutes of any one State, but is merely required not to exceed in severity " the punishment for like cases in any one of the States of the United States of America." This you see is a limit, *not* a rule, although it seems the commission at Los Angeles has governed its proceedings by the statutes of New York, and awarded to private John Smith, 1st dragoons, a sentence of imprisonment in a State prison, where, strictly speaking, there is not such a thing within thousands of miles. This would completely defeat the ends of justice, and shield from punishment many who richly deserve it. The commission should try a prisoner by the laws of war—the unwritten supplemental code, as it is termed by General Scott—and not by the statutes of any particular State, and should merely limit the amount of punishment by that which would be inflicted for a like offence in any one of the States of the Union: for instance, when the civil statute would imprison a person for five years, the commission would sentence him to confinement for a period *not exceeding* five years, leaving to the revenue officer to select the place of confinement.

I send herewith certified extracts from the statutes of Missouri, and digest of the laws of Texas, defining and punishing the crime of burglary. These are the only law books I have access to, that treat of the subject; and I also regret that it is not in my power to send you the proceedings of other military commissions that would serve as precedents to yours, and show the custom in like cases. A Vera Cruz newspaper received here some time ago, but not on hand now, contained the order promulgating the proceedings of a military commission that had tried two persons—one a negro, citizen of the United States—for having committed a rape upon a Mexican woman; he was sentenced to be hung, and was accordingly executed by order of General Scott: the other a volunteer soldier, for having committed *theft*, in taking by force from a woman a comb and ten dollars, for which he was sentenced to one month's imprisonment. This was ordered to be carried into effect at the castle of St. Juan de Ulua. No particular statutes seem to have been followed, and the commission awarded sentences just in themselves, and such as could be executed. It is conceived advisable for all military courts and commissions to aim at substantial justice, avoiding as much as possible learned technicalities and distinctions. Theft and larceny are the same in substance, although, for convenience, lawyers have adopted the latter, dividing it into grand and petit. This distinction is not made by General Scott, as he seems to have aimed at crimes by the names by which they are known to the world at large. The charges against Stokely have not, therefore, been changed.

The negro boy, Pete Beggs, is certainly amenable to martial law, and should be tried, unless some pledge has been made him to induce him to confess against his accomplices, or unless Captain Smith prefers to punish the boy himself, to the satisfaction of the gentleman he robbed; otherwise you will please prefer proper charges against him, and cause him to be arraigned before the commission. I cannot see, by the laws before quoted, that any distinction is made between a slave and a free person in punishment for burglary or larceny; but in the State of Texas, for grand larceny (stealing above the value of twenty dollars) the statute prescribes a punishment of thirty-nine lashes on the bare back, and imprisonment not exceeding five years.

I send you back the proceedings of the commission, that the sentence awarded private Smith may be reconsidered, and that it may resume the business that still remains before it.

I have the honor to be your most obedient servant,
W. T. SHERMAN,
First Lieutenant 3d Artillery, A. A. A. General.
Assistant Surgeon J. S. GRIFFIN,
Judge Advocate, Military Commission, Los Angeles, California.

HEADQUARTERS TENTH MILITARY DEPARTMENT,
Monterey, California, October 20, 1847.

SIR: I am directed by Colonel Mason to call your attention to general orders Nos. 16 and 17, of 1847, copies of which you will receive from Los Angeles. These authorize you to accept the services of individual volunteers, so as to increase the strength of your company to one hundred privates. Those whom you enlist should be enrolled for "during the war with Mexico," and their names, with the appropriate dates and remarks, entered upon the next muster rolls of your company. Volunteers so enrolled will be entitled to the same pay, allowances, bounties, and pensions, as are provided for those already in service.

I have the honor to be your obedient servant,
W. T. SHERMAN,
First Lieutenant 3d Artillery, A. A. A. General.
Captain F. J. LIPPETT,
Commanding, Santa Barbara, California.

HEADQUARTERS TENTH MILITARY DEPARTMENT,
Monterey, California, October 21, 1847.

MAJOR: Your letter of the 17th, addressed to Lieutenant Sherman, acting assistant adjutant general, has been received. The man you speak of as having stabbed the mate of the ship Vesper must be turned over to the alcalde for trial.

It will never do to let such atrocious crimes be committed on board of ships in the California ports, and go unpunished, because there happen to be no higher courts than those of the alcaldes in the country; but I learn from good authority that the alcaldes have always tried such cases, and, where the laws punished with death, the governor either sent the case to Mexico for final orders, or ordered the execution himself. This case, of course, is not punishable with death, and it will be very proper for the alcalde to try it; and if the man is found guilty, he should receive a sentence proportionate to his guilt.

I am, sir, very respectfully, your obedient servant,
R. B. MASON,
Colonel 1st Dragoons, commanding.
Major HARDIE, *commanding, San Francisco, California.*

HEADQUARTERS TENTH MILITARY DEPARTMENT,
Monterey, California, October 14, 1847.

CAPTAIN: Lieutenant Halleck has laid before me your letter of the 8th instant, asking to be relieved from the duties of collector, &c.

The President has assigned these duties to the officers of the army and navy, and you will see by the instructions that go up by this mail that I am in for it here, as well as yourself at San Francisco. Major Hardie must give you all the assistance that his command can afford, to aid you in the discharge of these duties. The instructions make you and himself the joint collectors.

Very respectfully, your obedient servant,
R. B. MASON,
Colonel 1st Dragoons, Governor of California.
Captain J. L. FOLSOM,
Assistant Quartermaster, San Francisco.

HEADQUARTERS TENTH MILITARY DEPARTMENT,
Monterey, California, October 14, 1847.

SIR: I have received your communication of the 8th instant, relating to the seizure of the goods and boats of W. H. Leidsdorff.

I have referred the subject to Commodore Shubrick, who thinks that the boats and goods were very properly seized, and are clearly a good prize; but that the matter should not be pushed, if Captain Leidsdorff can make it appear—as no doubt he can, by the evidence of Mr. Smith, to whom he refers—that he bought the goods just as the ship was getting under way, and that he took them with the understanding and expressed intention of paying the duties on shore. Neither the commodore nor myself supposes for a moment that Mr. Leidsdorff intended to avoid the payment of the duties; but, from the loose manner in which Mr. Richardson performed the duties, we presume that Mr. Leidsdorff was not at the moment aware, or did not at the time think, of the necessity of having the collector's permit to land the goods, and that they and the boats would be liable to seizure and confiscation without it.

You have acted very properly in seizing the goods, and in referring the matter here.

If Mr. Leidsdorff shows, by Mr. Smith, that he took the goods from the ship under the circumstances above stated, and with the understanding with the captain that he, Leidsdorff, was to pay the duties on shore, you are authorized to restore the goods and boats upon the duties being paid.

This evidence is required, not because either the commodore or myself doubts the word of Mr. Leidsdorff, but because it is thought best not to let this matter pass by in a manner so as to suffer it hereafter to be brought up as a precedent.

So much of the instructions relating to the customs, revenue, &c., (fresh ones go up by the mail which takes this,) as it is necessary for ship-masters and merchants to know, had better be published; and that will take from all the plea of not knowing what is made obligatory on them, as well as the officers of the customs.

I am, respectfully, your obedient servant,
R. B. MASON,
Colonel 1st Dragoons, Governor of California.

Captain J. L. FOLSOM,
Assistant Quartermaster, San Francisco.

CIRCULAR.

HEADQUARTERS TENTH MILITARY DEPARTMENT,
Monterey, California, October 14, 1847.

SIR: After a full and free consultation with Commodore Shubrick, and with his full concurrence touching the subject, I transmit herewith to you, for your guidance and government, printed instructions recently received from the War and Navy Departments, relative to the customs and collection of duties in the ports of Mexico and California, by which you will find that these duties are to be performed by army and naval officers.

It has been deemed most to the interest of the United States, by their present authorities in California, that the rates of duties directed to be collected in the ports of Mexico should not go into effect in this Territory; therefore there will be no change made in the rate or scale of duties as established by Commodore Shubrick in his instructions to the different collectors, dated September 15, 1847. They will be collected and reported to the department in the manner prescribed by the said printed instructions, but are to be disbursed, as heretofore, by order of the governor, on account of the civil government here. As no fees are to be charged for boarding vessels, for clearances, &c., it has been deemed proper to increase the tonnage duties from ten to fifteen cents per ton, in lieu thereof. The quartermaster at your post, or any other officer you may choose to direct, will perform the duties of custom-house officer, under your authority and direction, as directed by the printed instructions transmitted herewith, you receiving the amount of duties due, as ascertained by the quartermaster or other officer to whom you may have assigned the custom-house duties, and yourself paying it over to the disbursing officer, as the aforesaid printed instructions require.

Some erasures and interlineations are made in the printed instructions, beginning at page 9, so as to make them the better conform to the policy to be pursued in the California ports. Articles 1, 2, 3, 4, 6, 8, 9, 11, 13, and 15, in the instructions of the 15th of September last, are either annulled or provided for by the printed instructions.

You will take all proper measures to guard the revenue against frauds: for instance, you may prohibit the landing of any article before sunrise or after sunset; you may put a lock or seal upon the hatches and bulkheads at night, so as to prevent any access to the cargo, &c., &c. Should the lock or seal be broken, you may impose a penalty of one dollar per ton, registry measurement, upon the vessel, &c., &c.

When persons are called in to appraise the cargo, or any part thereof, that may be landed, the expense of the appraisement shall be paid, one-half out of the revenue, and the other by the captain of the vessel, the supercargo, consignee, or owner, as the case may be.

No freight, box, package, goods, wares, or merchandise, will be permitted to go on board of any ship or vessel after her clearance has been endorsed and signed on the manifest of her outward cargo. (See article 18, printed instructions.) Any box, package, goods, wares, or merchandise so put on board, or attempted to be put on board, after the clearance is signed on the manifest of the outward cargo, shall be confiscated.

I am, respectfully, your obedient servant,

R. B. MASON,
Colonel 1st Dragoons, Governor of California.

Major J. H. HARDIE,
   7th Regiment New York Volunteers, com'g, San Francisco.
Captain J. L FOLSOM,
   Assistant Quartermaster U. S. Army, San Francisco.
Colonel J D. STEVENSON,
   7th Regiment New York Volunteers, com'g, Los Angeles.
Captain DAVIS,
   Commanding, San Diego.
Captain LIPPETT,
   7th Regiment New York Volunteers, com'g, Santa Barbara.

P. S.—Whale ships pay no tonnage or revenue duty, unless they land or sell portions of their cargo for the purposes of trade.

HEADQUARTERS TENTH MILITARY DEPARTMENT,
Monterey, California, October 15, 1847.

SIR: The President of the United States having directed that the customs in the ports captured from the enemy shall be collected by the army and navy officers, your duties, therefore, as the collector of this port, cease this day.

You will be pleased to turn over to Lieutenant Commandant Lanman, United States navy, all the books and papers appertaining to the custom-house. Close your accounts up to this date, and turn over all funds derived from the customs to Captain Marcy, acting quartermaster.

I am, respectfully, your obedient servant,

R. B. MASON,
Colonel 1st Dragoons, Governor of California.

Mr. T. H. GREEN,
   Monterey, California.

STATE DEPARTMENT OF THE TERRITORY OF CALIFORNIA,
Monterey, October 15, 1847.

SIR: I have the honor to acknowledge the receipt of your letter of the 4th instant, in relation to taking a census of California. The object of the governor, as stated in the "circular" to which you refer, is not to take a census of California, but merely to obtain an approximate estimate of the population, &c., of the country. This, it is thought, may be obtained with sufficient accuracy by dividing the country into a number of districts, and consulting the opinions of one or more intelligent men in each district. By making inquiries of this kind, it is supposed that you may be able by the close of the year to forward to this office a tolerably accurate estimate of the population, &c., of the country south of the Santa Clara river. Nothing further than this is intended.

There are no funds that can at present be appropriated to the taking of a census.

Very respectfully, your obedient servant,
H. W. HALLECK,
Lieut. of Engineers, and Secretary of State for the Territory of California.

Colonel J. D. STEVENSON,
Commanding, &c., Los Angeles.

HEADQUARTERS TENTH MILITARY DEPARTMENT,
Monterey, Caifornia, October 15, 1847.

SIR: I have the honor to acknowledge the receipt of your communication of this date, together with its enclosures.

I herewith enclose to you the printed instructions concerning the collection of customs in the ports captured from the enemy, recently received from the War and Navy Departments. Those issued by Commodore Shubrick, as well as those issued jointly by the commodore and myself on the 15th of September, ultimo, will be handed to you by Mr. Green, the late collector of this port.

It has been deemed most to the interest of the United States, by their present authorities in California, that the rates of duties directed to be collected in the ports of Mexico should not go into effect in this Territory; therefore there will be no change made in the rate or scale of duties as established by Commodore Shubrick in his instructions to the different collectors, dated September 15, 1847. They will be collected and reported to the department in the manner prescribed by the said printed instructions, but are to be disbursed, as heretofore, by order of the governor, on account of the civil government here. As no fees are to be charged for boarding vessels, for clearances, &c., it has been deemed proper to increase the tonnage duties from ten to fifteen cents per ton in lieu thereof.

Some erasures and interlineations are made in the printed instructions, beginning at page 9, so as to make them the better conform to the policy to be pursued in the California ports. Articles 1, 2, 3, 4, 6, 8, 9, 11, 13, and 15, in the instructions of the 15th September last, are either annulled or provided for by the printed instructions.

When persons are called in to appraise the cargo, or any part thereof, that may be landed, the expense of the appraisement shall be paid, one-half out of the revenue, and the other by the captain of the vessel, the supercargo, consignee, or owner, as the case may be.

No freight, box, package, goods, wares, or merchandise, will be permitted to go on board of any ship or vessel after her clearance has been endorsed and signed on the manifest of her outward cargo. (See article 18, printed instructions.) Any box, package, goods, wares, or merchandise so put on board, or attempted to be put on board, after the clearance is signed on the manifest of the outward cargo, shall be confiscated.

It would afford me, my dear sir, great pleasure to release you from the keeping the accounts and records, if in my power; but really they are so few and so simple, that I know you will find not the least trouble or difficulty in getting along with them.

Your kind offer of co-operation, so characteristic of your profession, I accept and most heartily reciprocate.

However foreign these new duties that we have to perform may be to our respective branches of the public service, and however many the difficulties that may at this time suggest themselves to us, yet with that hearty co-operation which you propose and I so cordially reciprocate, and with a "long pull, a strong pull, and a pull *both* together," every obstacle and difficulty will be readily overcome.

I am, respectfully, your obedient servant,
R. B. MASON,
Colonel 1st Dragoons, Governor of California.
Lieut. Com. LANMAN, *U. S. Ship Warren, Monterey.*

HEADQUARTERS TENTH MILITARY DEPARTMENT,
Monterey, California, October 20, 1847.

COLONEL: I enclose some new instructions, touching the collection of customs, by which you will see that it is made the duty of the officers of the army and navy to collect and account for the revenue. I am at a loss to know how it is to be done at San Pedro, that port being twenty-odd miles from your post. You must, however, make the best arrangement you can; and, if you find that it cannot be properly done by yourself and officers, or so well done as at present, I see no other way than to keep in the present collector, he turning over the revenue, *as soon as collected,* to the quartermaster, who must account for it monthly, as the new regulations prescribe; copies of his monthly statement to the Secretary of War to be sent to this office. The strictest watch must be kept up to guard the revenue and protect it from fraud. I leave it to you to give such additional instructions to the collectors in your district as circumstances may call for, having that object in view. Captain Lippett and Captain Davis are the collectors at their respective posts.

The same mail that brings you this will take the instructions to San Diego.

I am having printed some blank forms and extracts from the regulations, such as are necessary for the information of ship-masters and merchants, and will send them to you as soon as they are received.

I am, respectfully, your obedient servant,
R. B. MASON,
Colonel 1st Dragoons, commanding.
Colonel J. D. STEVENSON,
Commanding, &c., Los Angeles.

HEADQUARTERS TENTH MILITARY DEPARTMENT,
Monterey, California, October 20, 1847.

SIR: Recent instructions from the President of the United States make the officers of the army and navy the collectors of the customs in California, and I very much regret that these instructions deprive you of the office of collector at San Diego. You, who have been so staunch a friend to the United States' interests in this country, deserve the thanks and patronage of the government, and I will take pleasure in mentioning your name in the most favorable manner to our authorities at Washington.

Should any change in the above-mentioned instructions be made by the department in Washington, or any circumstances arise in California by which I can restore to you the appointment of collector at San Diego, or in any other manner be serviceable to you, it will afford me much pleasure.

The instructions referred to will be shown to you by the commanding officer at your post, to whom be pleased to turn over all books, papers, property, and funds appertaining to the customs in your possession.

I am, respectfully, your obedient servant,
R. B. MASON,
Colonel 1st Dragoons, Governor of California.
Don Miguel DE PEDRORENA, *San Diego.*

NOTE.—This same letter was addressed to Don Pedro Carrillo, Santa Barbara.

HEADQUARTERS TENTH MILITARY DEPARTMENT,
Monterey, California, October 26, 1847.

SIR: Your communication, without date, reporting the trial and conviction, by a jury of twelve good and lawful men, of Chute, for manslaughter in the first degree, is received.

A similar case was tried here, not long since, I am informed, by the alcalde of this place, and the accused was found guilty and sentenced by him to seven years at hard labor on the public works. I see no reason why you should not pass on Chute a sentence not exceeding in severity the one just named.

If you have no good place of confinement, or any public work at which he might be placed at the pueblo, he might, after sentence is passed on him, be sent here, where there is a good calaboose, &c.

I am, respectfully, your obedient servant,
R. B. MASON,
Colonel 1st Dragoons, Governor of California.
JAMES W. WEEKS, *Alcalde, Pueblo de San José.*

HEADQUARTERS TENTH MILITARY DEPARTMENT,
Monterey, California, October 26, 1847.

SIR: I enclose the manifest, and a translation thereof, of the brig "Keone Ana," from Lima. This manifest appears, from its date, to have been made out at this port. The captain must produce the manifest and invoice called for in the 2d and 7th articles of the printed instructions. They of course will not be in exact accordance with those articles, as it is supposed they might not have been known at Lima when he sailed; but still he must necessarily have papers made out and signed by the custom-house officers, and others there corresponding to them, and he must produce them. The value of the articles at the port of shipment, mentioned in the 7th article, is of no moment here, as we charge duties by the valuation at the port where the goods are sold or landed. I am satisfied, by his presenting a manifest made out here, and not the one nor the invoice made out at the port from whence he sailed, that it is necessary to watch him close, and keep an account of everything he lands.

I am, rsepectfully, your obedient servant,

R. B. MASON,
Colonel 1st Dragoons, Governor of California.

Lieut. Com. LANMAN,
United States Ship Warren, Monterey.

HEADQUARTERS TENTH MILITARY DEPARTMENT,
Monterey, California, October 28, 1847.

SIR: Your letter of the 18th, and Lt. Gilbert's communication of the same date to you, have been received.

You will observe, by reference to my letter of the 14th, that I referred the subject-matter of yours of the 8th to Commodore Shubrick: this I did because it was appertaining to that branch of the service which, under previous instructions, the President had placed under the direction of the commodore, (see port regulations, revenue, &c.,) and my letter was the result of the conference we had upon the subject. As the recent instructions (the printed ones) from Washington make it the duty of the army and navy officers to collect the revenue, I think that, upon all questions that may arise in the discharge of those duties that require a decision from a superior officer, reference must be made to the senior army or naval officer on the California station, according as the revenue may be collected in the port by the one or the other of the officers of the army or navy, under the supervision of their respective chiefs.

The commodore and myself were of the opinion that the boats and goods of Mr. Leidsdorff were properly seized, &c., simply on the ground of landing without a permit; but we were not disposed to push the matter, if the goods were bought and landed upon the spur of the occasion, as was stated, and with the full intention of reporting the fact and paying the duties; but as it appears that most of the articles so landed were not on the ship's manifest, and that other parts of the cargo, from the same ship, had been previously landed without a permit and payment of duties, and which have since been found in Mr. Leidsdorff's store, the complexion of the whole affair becomes so materially changed, that, upon a careful reconsideration, I must direct the rigid rule to be applied, and the goods to be confiscated. But I cannot find any regulation that will confiscate the boats. The 7th article of the printed regulations confiscates goods landed or attempted to be landed without a permit, but it is silent about the boats in which the goods may be so landed. The boats in question, therefore, must be returned, as we cannot point to any regulation under which to confiscate them. Lt. Gilbert's claim to one-half of the goods seized is utterly inadmissible: as well might he claim the reward for apprehending a deserter. He is an officer specially put on duty in connexion with the collection of customs, and it is his special duty to look out for and detect any violation of the revenue laws—for the performance of which service, his pay and emoluments as a commissioned officer in the army are all that he is entitled to. The regulation on that subject never was intended to apply to a commissioned officer—only to enlisted soldiers, sailors, or citizens, who give to the revenue officers such information as enables them to seize and confiscate the goods, &c. It is true the regulations make no exception of the commissioned officer, nor does the regulation that offers thirty dollars reward for the apprehension of the deserter except the commissioned officers; but who ever heard of one claiming it? and if it was claimed, what disbursing officer would pay it? and if he did pay it, would it not very properly be charged to his account at the treasury?

I am, respectfully, your obedient servant,

R. B. MASON,
Colonel 1st Dragoons, Governor of California.

Captain J. L. FOLSOM,
Assistant Quartermaster U. S. A., San Francisco.

P. S.—A negative answer is given to your question, "Is it necessary to go before the alcalde to complete the forfeiture of the goods?"

HEADQUARTERS TENTH MILITARY DEPARTMENT,
Monterey, California, October 28, 1847.

SIR: The points presented in your letter of the 22d instant, relative to additional duties at the different ports in California, and duties on lumber, have been anticipated in the instructions sent to you to be printed.

I will give a special license to vessels under a foreign flag, that are owned by citizens of the United States now residing in California, as also to citizens of California who actually reside in the country and own vessels under such flag, to trade on this coast, until the subject can be referred to the authorities at Washington and a decision had thereon.

The growth, produce, or manufactures of California, shipped from one port in California to another port in California, will be free of duty. If it is not too late, have this printed with the other instructions.

I am, respectfully, your obedient servant,

R. B. MASON,
Colonel 1st Dragoons, Governor of California.

Captain J. L. FOLSOM,
Assistant Quartermaster U. S. A., San Francisco.

HEADQUARTERS TENTH MILITARY DEPARTMENT,
Monterey, California, October 28, 1847.

SIR: I cannot give the alcalde at the pueblo de San José instructions to retry the case you mention, as it has already been tried and decided by his predecessor in office. Were I to do so, there would be no end to suits. Every one who was cast in a trial would be for having his cause tried over again, whenever a new alcalde came into office.

I am, respectfully, your obedient servant,

R. B. MASON,
Colonel 1st Dragoons, Governor of California.

J. J. VIRJET, *San Francisco.*

Know all men by these presents, that I, Richard B. Mason, colonel 1st dragoons and governor of California, by virtue of authority in me vested, do hereby appoint Andrew Hœppener second alcalde for and in the town and district of Sonoma, in Upper California.

Done at Monterey, the capital of California, this 28th day of October, 1847, and the 72d of the independence of the United States.

R. B. MASON,
Colonel 1st Dragoons, Governor of California.

HEADQUARTERS TENTH MILITARY DEPARTMENT,
Monterey, California, October 29, 1847.

SIR: Your communication of the 18th instant has been duly received. I will appoint any one alcalde at San Luis Obispo that the good people of that district will sign a petition for.

I am, respectfully, your obedient servant,

R. B. MASON,
Colonel 1st Dragoons, Governor of California.

J. MARIANO BONILLA,
Alcalde, San Luis Obispo.

HEADQUARTERS TENTH MILITARY DEPARTMENT,
Monterey, California, November 1, 1847.

Sir: I received your communication of the 5th instant, and the depositions in the case of the Indian, Anastacio Ruiz, charged with killing another Indian named Guadalope.

You will send the prisoner back to Don P. E. Duarte, at San Vicente, with the enclosed communication to his address, which is left open for your perusal. Seal it and send it to him when you send the prisoner.

I am, respectfully, your obedient servant,

R. B. MASON,
Colonel 1st Dragoons, Governor of California.

Lieutenant ROBT. CLIFF,
Alcalde, San Diego.

HEADQUARTERS TENTH MILITARY DEPARTMENT,
Monterey, California, November 1, 1847.

SIR: Your communication of the 17th of August of the present year to the first magistrate of the first instance at San Diego, and all the depositions in the case of the Indian, Anastacio Ruiz, charged with the murder of another Indian named Guadalope, have been sent to me for my decision.

It does not appear from these papers that Anastacio Ruiz has been subjected to any *legal trial*, where his guilt or innocence could be passed upon, but simply depositions taken, and nothing more; nor does it appear that the accused was present at the taking of said depositions, or had any opportunity of interrogating the deponents, or allowed to call any witnesses whereby to exculpate himself. A man charged with any crime is entitled to all these privileges before he can be found guilty and punished. I shall direct the prisoner to be returned to you: you will then cause twelve good men to be summoned for his trial, the prisoner to be allowed to object to any four of them, without assigning any cause, if he thinks proper to do so. He may then object to any other of those remaining, by assigning good and sufficient cause why they should not sit on his trial. Any of the men being thus objected off, their places must be supplied by others, until there are twelve impartial men obtained, who, after being duly sworn, will hear all the testimony both for and against the prisoner; the prisoner to be present, and to be allowed the benefit of the counsel and advice of any one he chooses, and to hear all that is said both for and against him, and to interrogate the witnesses, so as to bring out the whole truth. The alcalde to preside at the trial. If the twelve men unanimously find the prisoner guilty of the murder of Guadalope with malice aforethought, then he should feel the full penalty of the law, which is death; but if he killed him in a sudden affray, in the heat of passion, upon great provocation, then he is not subject to the punishment of death, but to imprisonment and labor on the public works for a term not exceeding seven years, according to the nature and degree of the offence. If he killed Guadalope in self-defence, or in the defence of any member of his family, then he should be found "not guilty," and acquitted.

I am, respectfully, your obedient servant,

R. B. MASON,
Colonel 1st Dragoons, Governor of California.

Don E. P. DUARTE,
First Magistrate, &c., San Vicente, Lower California.

HEADQUARTERS TENTH MILITARY DEPARTMENT,
Monterey, California, November 1, 1847.

SIR: In examining your returns of customs, &c., collected at the port of Santa Barbara for the second quarter, ending June 30, 1847, I find a discrepancy in the amount that you return as having received for anchorage dues, visits, and clearances.

It appears from these returns, that the Peruvian barque Joven Guypuzcoana, which registers 201 tons, cleared twice: her tonnage dues, at five cents per ton, would therefore amount to $20 10. The Danish brig Matiedor, of 130 tons, at the same charge, should have paid $6 50; and the Hawaiian schooner Mary Ann, of 57 tons, $2 85; making in the aggregate $29 45, which should have been properly charged for tonnage dues. Instead of this, your return of the total amount received for the same item is $12 90, a deficiency of $16 55.

Again, you return the total amount of fees received for visits and clearances at $10. It appears from the same returns that there were four clearances and three visits, which would have made the proper charge for this $14; another deficiency of $4.

By these calculations, you should have collected $43 45; whereas you have charged yourself with but $22 90 as the total amount received for the above-stated items. The deficiency, $20 55, you will please turn over to Captain Lippett, the commanding officer at Santa Barbara.

I am, respectfully, your obedient servant,
R. B. MASON,
Colonel 1st Dragoons, Governor of California.
Don PEDRO CARRILLO,
 Santa Barbara, California.

HEADQUARTERS TENTH MILITARY DEPARTMENT,
Monterey, California, November 3, 1847.

SIR: Your letter of the 9th September was not received until the 28th of October.

You inform me that the Sandwich island brig "Keone Ana" had paid all her duties, amounting to $1,676 51, by giving bonds payable in 60, 80, and 120 days. I regret that you had not received instructions in time to have prevented your taking bonds for the payment of duties. The instructions sent to your predecessor in office, Don Santiago Arguillo, by General Kearny, and dated April 26, 1847, should have been turned over to you by that officer.

I am informed by Don José Domingo Yudast that he paid you on account of those bonds $973 25, on the 31st August, as per your receipt, (copy enclosed,) and that he left funds in the hands of a Mr. Cot, in Los Angeles, to pay the balance due on the bonds, without waiting for them to become due, and that he is certain the money has been paid over to you before this time.

In your return for the third quarter of the present year, you do not charge yourself with having received any part of the money due on the bonds. The $973 25 received on the 31st August, as per your receipt, you will be pleased to turn over to Lieutenant Cliff, as also the balance, if received from Mr. Cot. I shall send Lieutenant Cliff, by this mail, instructions as to the disposition he is to make of the funds he received from you.

I am, respectfully, your obedient servant,
R. B. MASON,
Governor of California.
Don MIGUEL DE PEDRORENA,
 San Diego, California.

HEADQUARTERS TENTH MILITARY DEPARTMENT,
Monterey, California, November 3, 1847.

SIR: The Sandwich island brig "Keone Ana," that was recently at Santa Barbara, was charged one hundred and four dollars and some cents duties. This amount must be refunded, as she paid all the duties on her cargo at San Diego, which should not have been done; but as it was done, it necessarily exempts her from paying her duties over again. Don Pedro received the duties, and I presume has paid them over to you. You will therefore pay over to the captain of the "Keone Ana," or his order, the amount received from that brig on account of "duties"—not the tonnage duties.

I am, respectfully, your obedient servant,
R. B. MASON,
Colonel 1st Dragoons, Governor of California.
Captain F. J. LIPPETT,
7th Regiment New York Volunteers,
Santa Barbara, California.

P. S.—The growth, produce, or manufactures of California, shipped from one port in California to another port in California, will be free of duty.

HEADQUARTERS TENTH MILITARY DEPARTMENT,
Monterey, California, November 3, 1847.

SIR: All funds derived from the collection of customs at San Diego you will turn over to Lieutenant Davidson, acting assistant quartermaster at Los Angeles, by the first safe opportunity after receiving them.

I am, respectfully, your obedient servant,
R. B. MASON,
Colonel 1st Dragoons, Governor of California.
Lieutenant ROBERT CLIFF,
Mormon company, San Diego, California.

HEADQUARTERS TENTH MILITARY DEPARTMENT,
Monterey, California, November 3, 1847.

SIR: In *addition* to the printed instructions for collecting the revenue at San Diego, sent to you with my circular of the 14th of October, you will be governed by the following, viz: The growth, produce, or manufactures of California, shipped from one port in California to another port in California, will be free of duty.

I am, respectfully, your obedient servant,
R. B. MASON,
Colonel 1st Dragoons, Governor of California.
Captain D. C. DAVIS,
Commanding, San Diego, California.

HEADQUARTERS TENTH MILITARY DEPARTMENT,
Monterey, California, November 3, 1847.

SIR: In *addition* to the printed instructions for collecting the revenue sent to you with my circular of the 14th October, you will please be governed by the following, viz: The growth, produce, or manufactures of California, shipped from one port in California to another port in California, will be free of duty.

I am, respectfully, your obedient servant,
R. B. MASON,
Colonel 1st Dragoons, Governor of California.
Colonel J. D. STEVENSON,
7th Regiment New York Volunteers,
Commanding Southern District, California.

HEADQUARTERS TENTH MILITARY DEPARTMENT,
Monterey, California, November 5, 1847.

SIR: I have received your communication of the 3d instant, together with its enclosures, as also the two lists of the day previous, showing the result of the two elections for the town council for the Pueblo de San José.

The object and intention of our election was to choose six persons to aid the alcalde in the government of *the town,* and *the town only.* They were to make such laws, regulations, &c., for the town, as might be deemed necessary to secure a good police, suppress vice, and afford a proper protection to persons and property within the *limits* of *the town;* consequently, no person was eligible to be elected a town councilman unless he was an *actual resident of the town,* and no one was entitled to vote for a town councilman unless he was also an actual resident of the town.

The second election was unauthorized, as there could be but one election under the authority given. The first election must therefore stand good; but should there be one or more persons elected who are not actual and bona fide residents of the town, they cannot serve as town councilmen, and their places must be supplied by holding a new election.

Independent of the second election being held without the proper warrant, it is observed that several of the judges of the election are returned as members elect. This is altogether unusual; no one can be both a candidate and a judge of the election at the same time.

Your letter of the 29th of October has been referred to the alcalde, Mr. Colton. The subject-matter must be arranged between you, as it is an affair that I do not think I should interfere with.

I am, respectfully, your obedient servant,
R. B. MASON,
Colonel 1*st Dragoons, Governor of California.*

JAMES W. WEEKS,
Alcalde, Pueblo de San José.

HEADQUARTERS TENTH MILITARY DEPARTMENT,
Monterey, California, November 8, 1847.

SIR: I have received your communication of the 28th instant. I fully concur with you in the views therein expressed.

I have spoken to Mr. Green (indeed he read your letter) on the subject of the schooner Mary Ann's clearance. He states that the list of goods he signed were put on board her, and that those goods had paid the duties.

I wish you to collect all the evidence you can touching Richardson's delinquencies, as I intend, so soon as proper courts are established, to put his bonds in suit. In the mean time his salary must be withheld, even though he does settle such accounts as the books may show. Find out from Captain Davis and others what amount of duties they have paid. I understand from Mr. Larkin, that Davis has paid in the last year something like $5,000 duties to Richardson.

I enclosed you some papers yesterday received from Mr. Leidsdorff concerning the goods you seized. You are on the spot, and must necessarily know better than I can from ex parte affidavits and statements all the circumstances of the case. Mr. Leidsdorff says that he was ignorant of the existence of the police regulations for the harbors, &c., as you will see by his letter of the 1st instant. The regulations were signed by the commodore and myself on the 15th of September, and sent off by the first opportunity to the collectors at San Francisco and other ports, and must have arrived in San Francisco on the 19th of that month, and were as well known there at the time the goods were seized as they were in the other ports, and just as well as were the regulations for the increase of duties from 15 to 20 per cent., signed by Commodore Shubrick, issued and sent to the collectors at the same time with the police regulations. In no other way have the instructions or regulations heretofore been published other than by sending them to the collectors of the different ports. I do not deem it necessary to give any additional instructions touching the case, unless you should have something to communicate after having read the papers herewith enclosed from Mr. Leidsdorff.

Please say to Mr. Leidsdorff, that being much pressed with business at present, I have not time to answer his letter of the first instant, and therefore desire that you will show him so much of this as concerns him.

The brig Elizabeth arrived here yesterday from San Francisco.

I observe some informality in her papers from the custom-house. You did not endorse on the manifest of her outward cargo, in addition to the certificate that the manifest had been deposited with the United States authorities, that she had "permission" to sail for her port of destination, according to "*form* 8." Again, on her manifest, there purports to be from 1 to 55 boxes, marked M, containing goods as per certificate. Enclosed is a copy of one of these certificates or bills. It does not show to whom the goods belong, nor does it give the *mark* or *number* of the box which contains them, so that we do not know in which of the 55 boxes to look for the articles. The certificate or bill should have contained the *name* of the *owner* or consignee, and given the *mark* and *number* of the box.

Make the shipper give the name of the consignee, and number and marks of boxes, in future, on such bills and certificates.

I have received the printed copies of the extracts from the "police regulations" for the harbors, &c. By reference to the instructions for printing, you will observe that it was my intention to have these "police regulations" and the extracts from the printed instructions from Washington form a little pamphlet, all under the head of " extracts from the regulations for collecting the tariff of duties on imports and tonnage, &c.," and not to have them separate. However, it is too late now to remedy it. Please have the forms and the other extracts from the regulations from Washington sent down as soon as possible.

I am, respectfully, your obedient servant,

R. B. MASON,
Colonel 1st Dragoons, Governor of California.

Capt. J. L. FOLSOM,
Assistant Quartermaster U. S. A., San Francisco.

HEADQUARTERS TENTH MILITARY DEPARTMENT,
Monterey, California, November 10, 1847.

SIR: I have received your communication, without date, relative to the ship "Confederacion" and her cargo. Beef, pork, bread, flour, butter, cheese, sugar, and rice, were admitted into the ports of California free of duty between the 1st of March and the 1st September last. Any of these articles not *entered* at the custom-house, and landed prior to the latter date, must pay duties, though the ship may have arrived on the coast or in port before that latter date.

All goods, merchandise, &c., not *entered* at a custom-house, and landed before the 15th of October ultimo, must pay the 20 per cent. duties.

Ships or vessels under foreign flags can go from port to port in California to sell the imported cargo, and take in cargo for exportation, but cannot carry freight or cargo from one port in California to another port in California, to be there sold, landed, or reshipped.

I am, respectfully, your obedient servant,
R. B. MASON,
Colonel 1st Dragoons, Governor of California.

RICHARD CARSON,
Supercargo Chilian ship Confederacion.

HEADQUARTERS TENTH MILITARY DEPARTMENT,
Monterey, California, November 10, 1847.

SIR: I send herewith a copy of my letter of this date to Richard Carson, the supercargo of the Chilian ship Confederacion, for your information and guidance; also, a copy of correspondence between the Secretary of the Treasury and E. D. Brigham & Co., of Boston; H. S. Wetmore, of New York; and Marcus Morton, the collector of Boston; brought here by the barque Amita, under the official seal of the Boston custom-house. This correspondence contains some useful information. Take a copy of it and then return it to me.

I am, respectfully, your obedient servant,
R. B. MASON,
Colonel 1st Dragoons, Governor of California.

Capt. J. L. FOLSOM,
Assistant Quartermaster U. S. A., San Francisco.

HEADQUARTERS TENTH MILITARY DEPARTMENT,
Monterey, California, November 11, 1847.

GENTLEMEN: I have the honor to acknowledge the receipt of your communication of the 30th of October, remitting the record of the trial of Armijo, Smith, and Eatson, recently tried at Sonoma by a special court upon the charge of murder; as also an account of fees, charges, &c., consequent upon the trial. I regret that I cannot fully approve of the account of fees, &c. I really think them exorbitantly high, and know that the account, as it stands, would be rejected at the treasury, and charged to the disbursing officer, or rather to myself, if I were to order its payment, as it is now presented, it being so far beyond any charges of the kind allowed in the United States. I have access only to the laws of the States of Missouri and Texas, in each of which, jurors are allowed one dollar per day for each day's attendance; in this case I am willing to double that, and make it two dollars per day. In Missouri, a juror is allowed a mileage of five cents; in Texas, I cannot find that any mileage is allowed.

In the former State, a sheriff is allowed for summoning a grand jury $4, a petit jury 50 cents, &c., and no mileage unless for taking a convict to the penitentiary, or removing a prisoner out of his county.

I know that these fees are not in accordance with California prices, and only mention them to show the very great disparity. There was a jury of twelve empannelled in this place not long since; they were allowed a per diem for each day's attendance of $2. The fees and charges in these trials will be looked to in future as precedents; and if paid as now presented, similar fees would be expected in all future causes. Such charges would be ruinous to litigating parties, and when regular courts are established, and the country divided into counties, their treasuries could not meet such demands—one or two trials would exhaust them. I must, therefore, be careful that I do not establish a ruinous precedent. After consulting several persons here who have been long in the country, I have, in relation to the trials at Sonoma, established the fees, &c., as you will find on the next page, which will be paid by Captain Folsom, assistant quartermaster, at San Francisco. The distance charged for mileage must be substantiated by the oath of the claimant taken before either of the special judges or an alcalde—the per diem by the certificate of either of the judges or the clerk of the court. No allowance can be made in the way of fees to Captain Brackett, because the United States are entitled to the services of all their officers in California, in a civil as well as a military capacity, without any other pay than that arising from their military commissions. I cannot order Mr. Green's charge of $200 as "attorney for the government" to be paid. I did not appoint Mr. Green a prosecuting attorney to attend the court at Sutter's; and if I had, his charge is exorbitant, and the record shows that he did not appear in court. I quote from the record of the 31st of August—the first and only day's proceedings at Sutter's—which says, "there being no prosecutor present, and it being thought necessary to allow time for summoning the witnesses and jury, it was therefore ordered that the sheriff," &c. The court then adjourned to the 18th of October.

Fees allowed in the trials at Sutter's and Sonoma.

SHERIFFS.

Mileage	$0 08
Each summons to witness or juror	1 00
Per diem, each, attending court	2 00

JURORS AND WITNESSES.

Mileage	8
Per diem each day's attendance on court	2 00

INTERPRETER.

Per diem	3 00

CLERK.

Mileage..$0 08
Per diem for each day attending court and making up record...... 2 50

JUDGES.

Per diem for each day's attendance and travel to and from court—a
  day's travel 30 miles.................................... 8 00

I am, respectfully, your obedient servant,
                              R. B. MASON,
              Colonel 1st Dragoons, Governor of California.
L. W. BOGGS,
M. G. VALLEJO,
    Sonoma, California.

HEADQUARTERS TENTH MILITARY DEPARTMENT,
            Monterey, California, November 11, 1847.

SIR: I enclose you the bill of fees, charges, &c., accruing upon the late trials by a special court at Sonoma, in the murder cases recently tried there. I cannot think of ordering the payment of these exorbitant demands. After consulting with several persons here, who have been long in the country, I have determined to authorize the following fees, &c. to be paid by you out of the civil fund arising from the customs, viz:

SHERIFFS.

Per diem for each day's attendance in court.....................$2 00
Mileage... 8
For each summons to juror or witness............................ 1 00

JURORS AND WITNESSES.

Per diem for each day's attendance in court..................... 2 00
Mileage... 8

INTERPRETER.

Per diem.. 3 00

CLERK.

Per diem for each day's attendance in court and making up record 2 50
Mileage... 8

JUDGES.

Per diem for each day's attendance, and travel to and from court—a
  day's travel 30 miles... 8 00

The distance charged for mileage must be substantiated by the oath of the claimant, taken before either of the special judges or an alcalde—the per diem by the certificate of either of the judges or clerk of the court.

No allowance can be made to Captain Brackett for fees. The United States are entitled to the services of all their officers in California, in a civil as well as a military capacity, without any other pay than that arising from their military commission. The charge Captain Brackett makes of $16 for expenses of express to this place is reasonable and proper—the express came on public business.

I cannot order Mr. Green's charge of $200 as "attorney for the government." I did not appoint Mr. Green a prosecuting attorney to attend the court at Sutter's; and if I had, his charge is exorbitant, and the record shows that he did not appear in court. I quote from the record of the 31st of August—the first and only day's proceedings at Sutter's—which says, "there being no prosecutor present, and it being thought necessary to allow time for summoning the witnesses and jury, it was therefore ordered that the sheriff," &c. The court then adjourned to the 18th of October.

I have written to Governor Boggs and General Vallejo, the special judges that sat on the trial, that you would pay the fees, &c., according to rates above mentioned, and informed them as to the manner the claims for mileage and per diem must be substantiated.

I am, respectfully, your obedient servant,
R. B. MASON,
Colonel 1st Dragoons, Governor of California.

Captain J. L. FOLSOM,
Assistant Quartermaster U. S. A., San Francisco.

[No. 22.] HEADQUARTERS TENTH MILITARY DEPARTMENT,
Monterey, California, November 11, 1847.

SIR: A small schooner will sail on the 13th instant for the Guayaquil river, South America, where several passengers will land and take the next steamer for Panama. To one of these passengers, a Mr. King, former commissary to Lieutenant Colonel Frémont's battalion, I will intrust a small mail to be carried to the city of Washington.

I have the honor again to report that peace and tranquillity prevail in California, and that no change whatever has taken place in the disposition of the garrisons since my last letter. By the storeship Lexington that arrived here on the 28th of October, reports were received from Lieutenant Colonel Burton, at La Paz, Lower California. He has quietly occupied that town since the 21st of July, but not in sufficient force to enable him to extend his authority far into the country. He reports that there is constant communication between Guaymas and Mulege, a small town in California, north of La Paz, and that the sloop-of-war Dale had sailed to the latter place to prevent the landing or collection of any arms or military stores. I do not anticipate any difficulty in holding La Paz by a small force, so as to afford the government, in the event of negotiations for peace, the influence a military occupation of Lower California would give us. If a garrison is to be kept for any length of time in that section of California, I must modify the recommendation contained in my letter of October 7, as to the kind of clothing required by the troops in this department, so as to furnish the garrisons in Lower California, in great part, with summer clothing. Lieutenant Colonel Burton likewise reports much insubordination in his command, and that the company officers have little or no control over their men. A similar state of things exists among some of the companies in Upper California, and for that reason, in my late orders to them, I have laid stress upon the fact that without an *honorable* discharge, no volunteer or regular soldier will be entitled to the bounty provided for them by the act of Congress approved February 11, 1847; and I shall cause such records to be kept as will enable the officer who is called upon to discharge the volunteers to grant honorable discharges only to such soldiers as are fairly entitled to them. I think this will have a good effect upon the volunteer regiment.

There are three or four vessels under foreign flags—mostly Sandwich Island flags (one Peruvian)—that are owned by citizens of the United States, or by citizens of California who are well disposed towards us; all actual residents of the country that have heretofore been engaged in the coasting trade from port to port. The owners of these vessels have large debts upon the coast, and if now they are to be shut out from the coasting trade, it will be ruinous to them. I have promised to give these vessels a special license to continue in the trade, as heretofore, until the matter is referred to the department for orders. This I shall do, subject in the mean time to the concurrence of Commodore Shubrick, who is at present absent from the coast. Some of the ports or points on this coast, where it is customary to land goods, have no military posts near them. San Pedro, for instance, is twenty-five miles from the nearest garrison, and it is not, therefore, possible to comply fully with the instructions from the department of April last. In relation to this point see my instructions to Colonel Stevenson of the 20th of October.

A great deal of smuggling has been done in California, and will doubtless continue, as the numerous coves, bays, &c., afford every opportunity for landing goods and merchandise. One or two good revenue cutters would, however, stop this effectually. The commodore and myself have made known that any one who would give information of goods, &c. being smuggled, should have one-half of the goods seized upon such information.

Since the departure of the commodore on the 16th ultimo for Mazatlan, I have taken the responsibility to instruct the different officers intrusted with the collection of the military contribution not to exact duties on lumber brought into a port of California, nor on the growth, produce, or manufacture of California, brought from one port of California direct to another. I have been induced to do this for the following reasons:

The great scarcity and high prices of lumber, ($50 per M. without duties.) Our own emigrants purchase nine-tenths of the lumber now consumed in the country. Hides, the principal article of trade, are collected at various points on the coast and taken to certain establishments at San Francisco and San Diego, where they are landed, cured, and prepared for exportation. Surely, upon these a duty should not be collected under the circumstances. And, again: wheat taken from San Francisco to the southern ports of Santa Barbara, San Pedro, and San Diego, should pay no duty as a military contribution, because the great wheat-growing country lies on the Sacramento and waters of San Francisco bay, settled almost entirely by our own people. In any point of view the duty on the produce of California, taken from port to port along the coast, will be more oppressive to our own people than to the Californians themselves. I know that it is not the desire of the President to check the prosperity of the country in its infancy whilst not in arms against us; to destroy by a single blow its commerce; and to shut out to our poor emigrants, who have toiled their way here, the simple articles of manufacture they stand in need of to make their presence here useful to themselves and to their government. California has very few resources in itself at present developed. Not a yard of cloth is made here, nor a tool of any kind; all are brought from Europe and the United States. The high duties imposed upon these articles by Mexico were seldom collected, and yet, from its geographical position, prices were and are still so high that the owner of leagues of land, thousands of cattle, and hundreds of horses, could command about him fewer of the comforts of civilized life than are enjoyed by the poorest class of citizens in the United States. Under such a state of things no country could flourish; and a more liberal policy was clearly laid down in the Secretary of War's letter of the 3d of June, 1846, to Colonel (now Brigadier General) S. W. Kearny, in which he says duties should be reduced " to such a rate as may be barely sufficient to maintain the necessary civil officers without yielding any revenue to the government. You may assure the people of these provinces that it is the wish and design of the United States to provide for them a free government, with the least possible delay, similar to what exists in our Territories. They will be then called on to exercise rights of freemen," &c. Promises and assurances, based upon these instructions, have gone forth to the people of California as a solemn pledge on the part of our government. It was believed, and received by the people generally as a pledge; but some of our enemies among them have asserted that these promises were made by us to delude them into subordination, after which the same high duties and restrictions on commerce would be restored. Now these persons pass for prophets, because, after nearly a year of quiet and tranquillity, high duties are again ordered to be laid, with restrictions upon the coast trade, that will in a great measure prevent the expected competition and reduction of prices; this, too, with the avowed declaration on the part of our government to treat the Californians as open enemies, subject to military contribution. After the peaceable policy indicated in the Secretary's letter, and the pledge made to the people of California in compliance with it, it will be a breach of good faith to re-establish high duties, with the addition of excluding from the coast trade vessels owned by citizens of California, and causing duties to be paid on articles from port to port, carried coastwise—some of the ports being not more than twenty-five or thirty miles apart. I would most urgently recommend that these duties and restrictions be withdrawn, and the more liberal policy first begun be adhered to of collecting no military contributions from the small commerce of this country, but only such duties as will maintain the necessary civil officers.

I am not insensible of the high responsibility I have taken in relation to the tariff and the trade between the ports of California. I am satisfied, even to conviction, that if the President could see with his own eyes the condition of things in California, I should be fully justified in all that I have done. In conclusion, I beg leave to mention the names of Don Pedro Carrillo, of Santa Barbara, and Don Miguel Pedrorena, of San Diego, who have recently lost their offices by reason of the revenue being now collected by the military, as warm friends of the interests of the

United States in this quarter, and who stood by our authorities in all the disturbances of the country when the United States flag was hoisted.

I transmit herewith copies of all department orders issued up to this date; copies of the civil and military correspondence of the department; also the original papers, of which the subjoined is a list:*

1. Department return for July and August.
2. Post return of Monterey for October.
3. Return of company C, 1st dragoons, for September.
4. Muster roll of Captain Davis's company of Mormons.
5. Enlistment of private Steans, company C, 1st dragoons.
6. Duplicate certificates of disability for private James Burkins, company F, 3d artillery.
7. Muster roll of company F, 3d artillery.
8. Muster roll of company I, 7th New York volunteers.
9. Muster roll of hospital steward.
10. Proceedings of G. C. M. at Los Angeles, California.
11. Proceedings of G. C. M. at Monterey, California.

I have the honor to be, very respectfully, your obedient servant,
R. B. MASON,
Colonel 1st Dragoons, commanding.

General R. JONES,
Adjutant General, Washington, D. C.

[No. 23.] HEADQUARTERS TENTH MILITARY DEPARTMENT,
Monterey, California, November 12, 1847.

SIR: Since closing my letter of yesterday, a mail has arrived from the southern part of Upper California, bringing no intelligence of importance, except the views expressed by Colonel Stevenson as to the practical application of the new revenue system to the ports of San Pedro and San Diego. I enclose his original letter, and would call your special attention to it. I would also call your attention to the fact that company C, 1st dragoons, stationed at Los Angeles, has but one officer (Captain A. J. Smith) on duty with it—Lieutenant Davidson being constantly engaged in his staff duties of acting assistant quartermaster and commissary, and Lieutenant Stoneman being so sick that Assistant Surgeon Griffin reports that a sea voyage is indispensably necessary for his restoration to health. I will, in consequence, grant him a sick leave of two months, to go to the Sandwich islands, or Mazatlan, whither he proposes to go.

I enclose, herewith—
1. Muster roll of company C, 1st dragoons, for September and October.
2. Return of company C, 1st dragoons, for October.
3. Enlistment of Thomas Dooly, company C, 1st dragoons.
4. Post return of Los Angeles, California.
5. Original letter from the vice-consul of Spain, in California, dated

---

* Copies of these not considered as required.

October 29, 1847, complaining of the imprisonment of José Noviega, a Spanish subject, by the order of Colonel Fremont.
I have the honor to be your obedient servant,
R. B. MASON,
Col. 1st Dragoons, Governor of California.
Gen. R. JONES, *Adjt. Gen., Washington, D. C.*

HEADQUARTERS SOUTHERN MIL. DIST., CALIFORNIA,
Ciudad de los Angeles, November 2, 1847.

SIR: I have the honor to acknowledge the receipt of your communication, enclosing instructions from the Secretary of the Treasury for the government of collectors of the revenue on this coast. The port of San Pedro being twenty-seven miles from this post, it will be impossible for me to perform the duties of collector without almost entirely abandoning my military duties. With the three companies stationed here I have eleven officers—one doing duty as acting assistant quartermaster and commissary, one adjutant, and three sick with the prevailing disease of the country, and one with consumption, (Lieut. Merrick,) who will, probably, never again do any duty; thus reducing me to five officers for duty. If I should assign to one the duties of collector at San Pedro, he would be compelled to reside there permanently. I should thus lose the services of another at this post; and, besides all this, I am quite sure that I have not an officer that I could with propriety assign to that duty, who is capable of performing it. Under all these circumstances, I shall avail myself of your permission (if I should deem it best for the public interest) to permit the present collector to retain his office. He is a most worthy and capable man, and I am quite sure the public interest will be benefited thereby. I shall therefore turn over to him all the instructions forwarded to me, and shall from time to time examine into his affairs, and give him such advice and instructions as I may deem necessary for the preservation of the public interest.

Your communication also advises me that Captain Davis will hereafter act as collector at San Diego. I must confess that I regret the change you have made. The late collector is a most worthy man, capable in every respect, has a high character for integrity, and, from the commencement of the war on this coast, has been one of our most useful and active friends, and for some time held a commission in the California battalion: he has, I have no doubt, most faithfully performed his duty as collector. Captain Davis is a most excellent and worthy man, but in my judgment entirely unfit for a collector. He is perfectly ignorant of mercantile matters, and can scarcely write his name; and I am fully persuaded that the public interest will greatly suffer by the change. The other officers of his command are no better qualified, except, perhaps, Lieutenant Clift, who is acting assistant quartermaster and commissary, and alcalde of the town. He is the most competent, but not by any means fitted for the station. I have deemed it my duty to give you freely my opinion of the capacity and fitness of the officers at San Diego for the office in question, that you may be the better able to judge of the propriety of the change.

I have the honor to be, very respectfully, your obedient servant,
J. D. STEVENSON,
Col. Comd'g S. M. D.
Col. R. B. MASON, *1st U. S. Dragoons, Governor of California.*

Vice Consulado de Espana en Californias.

El infrascrito Ve. consul de S. M. la Reina de España en Californias, tiene el honor de dirigirse por la primera vez al Exmo. Señor Gobernadór R. B. Mason para ocupár la atencion de S. E. sobre un asunto, de una naturaleza muy desagradable pero que es del debír del que suscribe sometér.

El 13 de Junio del año pasado, á consecuencia de ciesto movimiento politico occurrido en Sonoma (que no toca al infrascrito calificár) fué puesto en vigoroso prision el ciudadano español Don José Noviega, en la fortaleza de "Nueva Helvecia," por orden del S. Coronel Frémont y trasmitida al S. Murphy para su ejecution: el hallarse Noviega en aquellos puntos, fué para solicitár indios á su servicio para las cosechas de semillas que estaban proximas á lerantarse. Ignorando este desgraciado las razonels que pudiesén existir contra él para un tál procedimiento, con la calma que es propia de una conciencia limpia se atrevió, á frequentár; cual era el motivo de su prision? despues de varias amenazas le fué contestado que *"por ser Mexicano,"* á lo que replicó que era una gratuita suposicion; enfin toda observacion fué imítil. Al cabo de 29 dias de la prision mas injusta, con las privaciones mas inicuas, fué con dueido Noviega al embarcadero mas immediato y puesto á bordo de una lancha que llevaba una bandera blanca, con un oso y una estrella dibujados en el centro. Despuer de muchos trabajos, y despues de una ausencia de 50 dias llegó al seno de su familia, la que lo contaba finado, por las noticias que habian circulado de su desgracicuda suerte.

Esto es el hecho. La ausencia de Noviega de su rancho en el tiempo mas precioso del año para los trabajos lampestres leha occasionado un atrazo de bartante consideracion, pues á su regreso encontró sus siembras en totál abandono y sus bienes mueblas con mucho que branto; documentos existen en este Ve. consulado que acreditán los justos resentimiento de Noviega.

El infrascrito, descansa enteramente en que el gobierno de los Estados Unidos por sus instituciones sábias y liberales no dejará impune una arbitrarieday como la referida, y que los perpucios santo personales como de intereses inferidos á Noviega serán indemnizados con legalidad.

Por ahora, el infrascrito, se reducirá, á lo que ha sometido á S. E. el S. gobernadór, y se reserra haiér valér el derecho que asiste á su nacional, para la devida indemnizacion y ultrajé cometido, cuyo monto presenhará cuando fueré necesario.

A la primera vista pareierá sál vez á S. E., extemporanéo el reclamo, puro permitaséle al que suscribe, adventor á S. E. que no quizo presentár un asunto de esta naturaleza sobre datos frivólos, y per lo mismo le fué preciso lerciorarse de la veracidar de los hechos: esto demanda tiempo y tambien necesario esperár que el goberino se estableciese sobre bases que ofreciesen garantias.

Sérváse S. E. el S. Gobernadór R. B. Mason aceptár los seguridades del alto aprecio con que lo distingue el infrascrito, el que ruega á Dios que la vida, de S. E. Mr. Arños. Santa Barbara, Octubre 29 de 1847.

CESAREO LATAILLADE,
Vice Consul.

Exmo. Señor Gobernadór R. B. Mason.

[No. 24.] HEADQUARTERS TENTH MILITARY DEPARTMENT,
Monterey, California, November 13, 1847.

SIR: Will you please to inform me as soon as possible whether Captain Wm. G. Marcy, Surgeon Perry, and Assistant Surgeon W. C. Parker, are competent to sit as members of a general court martial for the trial of volunteers, or does the 97th article of war exclude them, because they are commissioned by the President and Senate? Again, can either of these officers, or a regular officer, be appointed the judge advocate of a court martial for the trial of volunteers?

At the last moment before the departure of Mr. King, I feel it my imperative duty to urge you to despatch to this country more staff officers, especially quartermasters. Major Swords should at once return, or some officer of equal rank and experience, with two assistant quartermasters; one of whom to be stationed at the Ciudad de los Angeles with Colonel Stevenson, and the other in Lower California with Lieutenant Colonel Burton. The necessity for the services of such officers will be great, so long as military possession is held of the country, and indispensably necessary now, as the revenue is collected by military officers. Captain Folsom is at San Francisco, and, with the custom-house duties on his hands, has as much business as he can possibly attend to.

I want very much an experienced quartermaster at these headquarters, to perform not only the duties of the post, but to exercise a general control over the affairs of his department in the two Californias. Major Swords left here with the understanding that he was, to return immediately with his family. The peculiar circumstances under which we are placed, the interests of the service, both in an economical and military point of view, imperatively require that these officers should be men of experience, and of the *regular army*, familiar with the duties of the department and the wants of the service.

I have the honor to be, very respectfully, your obedient servant,
R. B. MASON,
Colonel 1st Dragoons, commanding.

General R. JONES,
Adjutant General, Washington, D. C.

I, Richard B. Mason, colonel 1st regiment dragoons United States army, and governor of California, to all who shall see these presents, greeting:

Be it known that leave and permission are hereby granted to Elliot Libbey, master of the schooner called the Commodore Shubrick, lying at present in the port of Monterey, to engage in all lawful commerce, upon the authority of this paper, until a proper register can be obtained for said schooner from the government of the United States—the said Elliot Libbey having made oath before me that the said schooner belongs to Joseph S. Buchel and Henry D. Cooke, citizens of the United States.

Both of said citizens, Buchel and Cooke, are personally known to the undersigned. They are citizens of the United States, having recently purchased the said schooner Commodore Shubrick, and are hereby authorized to hoist on board of her the United States flag, with all the rights and privileges of United States vessels engaged in lawful commerce.

The said vessel being schooner-rigged, carrying two masts, with single deck, having a square stern, built at the Society Islands, and of the burden of about sixty tons.

Given at Monterey, the capital of California, this 11th day of November, A. D. 1847, and of the independence of the United States the seventy-second.

R. B. MASON,
Colonel 1*st Regiment Dragoons U. S. Army,*
Governor of California.

I, Richard B. Mason, colonel of the 1*st regiment dragoons United States army, and governor of California, to all who shall see these presents, greeting:*

Be it known that leave and permission are hereby granted to William S. McKinney, master of the brig Primavera, lying at present in the port of Monterey, to engage in all lawful commerce, upon the authority of this paper, until a proper register can be obtained for said brig from the government of the United States—the said William McKinney having made oath before me that the said brig belongs to Edward A. King, a citizen of the United States. The said King is personally known to the undersigned. He is a citizen of the United States, has recently purchased the said brig Primavera, and is hereby authorized to hoist on board of her the United States flag, with all the rights and privileges of a United States vessel engaged in lawful commerce.

The said vessel being brig-rigged, carrying two masts, with single deck, having square stern, built in the East Indies, and of the burden of about one hundred and eighty tons; length eighty feet, breadth twenty feet, depth ten feet six inches.

Given at Monterey, the capital of California, this thirteenth day of November, A. D. 1847, and of the independence of the United States the seventy-second.

R. B. MASON,
Colonel 1*st Regiment Dragoons U. S. Army,*
Governor of California.

HEADQUARTERS TENTH MILITARY DEPARTMENT,
Monterey, California, November 16, 1847.

Among the papers which from time to time I have received from your reverence, I cannot find any one which conveys to you the right to sell any part or portion of the mission lands.

I was under the impression that your reverence informed me, when I last had the pleasure of seeing you at this place, that you had furnished me with a copy of such paper; but I cannot find it.

The title given by Micheltorena, dated June 10, 1844, expressly prohibits the sale, &c. Will your reverence be pleased to inform me if the Mexican government ever confirmed that title; and, if it did, be pleased to furnish me, if in your power, with a copy of such confirmation, together with a copy of the authority which invests you with the power to sell.

I am, reverend father, your obedient servant,
R. B. MASON,
Colonel 1st Dragoons, Governor of California.
To the Rev. Father JOSE MARIA REAL.

HEADQUARTERS TENTH MILITARY DEPARTMENT,
Monterey, California, November 17, 1847.

The undersigned has the honor to acknowledge the receipt of the note addressed to him on the 29th ultimo, from the vice-consul of her Catholic Majesty the Queen of Spain.

That note has already been forwarded to the United States government at Washington; but the undersigned would suggest to the vice-consul, that before his government can take any steps towards causing reparation to be made to Don José Noviega for the outrages and injuries complained of, it will be necessary for them to be put in possession of whatever evidence that may be, to substantiate the complaint.

The vice-consul must be fully aware that it is not in the power of the undersigned to make to Don José Noviega any reparation for the outrages complained of. Lieutenant Colonel Fremont, against whom the complaint is made, is not in California, and the undersigned can do no more than forward the complaint to his government—which he has promptly done—and to suggest to the vice-consul that it will be necessary to substantiate the complaint by evidence.

The undersigned offers to the vice-consul the assurance of his esteem and consideration.

R. B. MASON,
Colonel 1st Dragoons, Governor of California.
Don CESAREO LATAILLADE,
Vice Consul de España, Santa Barbara, California.

HEADQUARTERS TENTH MILITARY DEPARTMENT,
Monterey, California, November 15, 1847.

SIR: I am in the receipt of your communication of the 2d instant. It is not proper that I should take any action touching the mercantile concerns or claims of a firm in Mazatlan.

I am, respectfully, your obedient servant,
R. B. MASON,
Colonel 1st Dragoons, Governor of California.
Mr. C. M. FLUGGE,
Los Angeles, California.

CIRCULAR TO COLLECTORS OF CUSTOMS AT THE POSTS IN CALIFORNIA.

HEADQUARTERS TENTH MILITARY DEPARTMENT,
Monterey, California, November 17, 1847.

The printed *extract* from the regulations for collecting the tariff of duties on imports and tonnage is herewith sent to you in that shape for the information of ship-masters and merchants. You will therefore give one copy to the master of each vessel arriving in your port. A vessel arriving in your port a second time need not be furnished with another copy.

The monthly statement of revenue collected, required to be sent to the War Department, will be forwarded through this office, and you will observe in the printed form of the monthly statement that the column of "*value of imports*" means the value at the port of entry; and for the manner of filling up that form, see the form as filled up in the printed pamphlet sent you a short time since.

I am, respectfully, your obedient servant,
R. B. MASON,
Colonel 1st Dragoons, Governor of California.

HEADQUARTERS TENTH MILITARY DEPARTMENT,
Monterey, California, November 19, 1847.

SIR: Your communication of yesterday is before me; in reply to which, I have to say that the product or manufacture of Mexico will be admitted into the ports of California, if brought in American vessels from the ports in Mexico that are in the possession of the United States forces; if such products or manufacture are brought in vessels belonging to any other nation, the vessels are liable to seizure and confiscation.

I am, respectfully, your obedient servant,
R. B. MASON,
Colonel 1st Dragoons, Governor of California.
ROBT. WALKINSHAM,
Monterey.

HEADQUARTERS TENTH MILITARY DEPARTMENT,
Monterey, California, November 20, 1847.

SIR: I have received your letter of the 16th instant, and also communications from various citizens, who, I am told, are among the most respectable in Pueblo, complaining and protesting against the election of Mr. Reed and Mr. Murphy, and denying that they are residents of the town or Pueblo de San José, and that they were declared to be residents by a considerable number who were not themselves known as residents.

The persons elected as town councilmen should be elected by the votes of persons who reside *within the limits of the town*, as marked by the *town plat*. No one who resides outside of these limits can be a town councilman, or vote for a town councilman, any more than he can vote in San Francisco for a town councilman.

A mere *transitory residence*, a mere sojourning in the pueblo for the time being, cannot constitute such a residence as to make a man eligible to be elected a town councilman, or to vote for one. He must have resided within the limits of the town a reasonable length of time previous to the election; or rather, his residence must have been of *such a character* as to plainly indicate his intention of becoming, and being in fact, a bona fide resident—such, for instance, as keeping house, going into business, opening shops, and working at his trade, &c., &c.

Suppose there was a poll tax laid upon each actual and bona fide resident of the town; would those who were mere transitory residents, or temporary sojourners, insist upon paying the tax, and being considered as actual residents of the place? or would they refuse to pay it, upon the ground of being mere transitory persons, and not actual permanent residents of the town? or would those who reside *outside* the limits of the town, as marked by the town plat, insist upon being subjected to the tax as residents of the town? or would they refuse to pay upon the ground of not residing within the limits of the town, as marked by the town plat?

It is very easy, it appears to me, to distinguish the bona fide from the pretended residents of a place. The votes of all those who reside within the limits of the town, as *marked by the town plat*, and are residents thereof *in good faith*, and not mere temporary sojourners or transient persons, must be taken as legal votes, *and all others rejected*, and the *six persons* who received a majority of such legal votes are declared to have been duly elected. I appoint you and Mr. Ruchel, of your town, and such third person as you two may choose, to examine this subject, and to decide which six persons received a majority of the legal votes of the town of San José; and such six persons are declared to have been duly elected, provided they were bona fide residents of the town.

I earnestly hope the committee, thus constituted, will decide the matter *fairly* and *equitably*, with the sole view to the better government of the town, apart from anything like partisan feeling.

I am, respectfully, your obedient servant,
R. B. MASON,
Col. 1st Dragoons, Governor of California.

JAMES M. WEEKS,
Alcalde, San José.

Know all men by these presents, that I, Richard B. Mason, colonel 1st dragoons United States army, and governor of California, by virtue of authority in me vested, do hereby appoint Julian Urgua an alcalde within the district of San Juan Bautista.

Given at Monterey, the capital of California, this twenty-second day of November, A. D. 1847, and of the independence of the United States the seventy-second.

R. B. MASON,
Col. 1st Dragoons, Governor of California.

HEADQUARTERS TENTH MILITARY DEPARTMENT,
Monterey, California, November 22, 1847.

SIR: Your communication of the 21st of the present month has been received, informing me that Julian Urgua had been elected in your place, &c.

The election was unauthorized. When you were last at this place, and spoke to me on the subject of a new alcalde, I said to you that *I would appoint* any person whom the people would *sign a petition* for. No petition has come in. The election being unauthorized, is null and void; but nevertheless, I enclose to you the appointment of alcalde for Julian Urgua, which be pleased to deliver to him.

R. B. MASON,
Col. 1st Dragoons, Governor of California.

Señor JOSE MARIA SANCHEZ,
San Juan Bautista.

I, Richard B. Mason, colonel 1*st regiment dragoons United States army, and Governor of California, to all who shall see these presents, greeting:*

Be it known, that leave and permission are hereby granted to E. Gray, master of the schooner Antonita, lying at present in the port of Monterey, to engage in all lawful commerce upon the coast of California, upon the authority of this paper; the said E. Gray having made oath before me that the said schooner belongs to Charles Rousillon and Peter Sainlerran, both citizens and residents of California, and was built in California this present year. He is hereby authorized to hoist the American flag on board of said schooner, with all the privileges of an American vessel engaged in lawful commerce on the coast of California. The said schooner is of the burden of thirty-four tons, or thereabouts, forty feet long above deck, six feet eight inches deep, and twelve feet and four inches wide, being flat built.

Given at Monterey, the capital of California, this twenty-third day of November, A. D. 1847, and of the independence of the United States the seventy-second.

R. B. MASON,
Col. 1st Dragoons, Governor of California.

HEADQUARTERS TENTH MILITARY DEPARTMENT,
Monterey, California, November 24, 1847.

SIR: The Catholic priest of Santa Cruz has this day called upon me, and complained that the alcalde has been granting or selling certain lots of land belonging to the mission of that place. By the decree of General Kearny of the 22d of March last, certain missions, of which Santa Cruz was one, and all the lands, &c., appertaining thereto, were put under the charge of their respective priests. These missions and mission lands cannot in any way be incumbered or disposed of by any of the authorities in California. An alcalde cannot grant or dispose of lands, unless when a town has been authorized to be laid off by the proper authorities, and the lots are authorized to be sold for the benefit and improvement of the place. If any town has been authorized to be laid off at Santa Cruz, be pleased to furnish me with a copy of such authority, and also with a copy of the town plot.

I am, respectfully, your obedient servant,
R. B. MASON,
Colonel 1st Dragoons, Governor of California.
WM. BLACKBURN, *Alcalde, Santa Cruz.*

HEADQUARTERS TENTH MILITARY DEPARTMENT,
Monterey, California, November 24, 1847.

SIR: Your letter of the 6th instant, enclosing the copy of one from Captain J. D. Hunter of the 1st instant, is before me.

I enclose to you a blank appointment for an alcalde, to be filled up for Mr. John Sharnon, the person recommended by Captain Hunter, if you think him a proper man; if not, fill the blank with the name of the most competent person you can find.

Enclosed is a letter to José Antonio Pico, which, after reading and filling up the blank with the name of the mission, seal and send to him.

I am, with much respect, your obedient servant,
R. B. MASON,
Colonel 1st Dragoons, Governor of California.
Col. J. D. STEVENSON,
Commanding Southern Military District, Los Angeles.

Know all men by these presents, that I, Richard B. Mason, colonel 1st regiment dragoons United States army, and governor of California, by virtue of authority in me vested, do hereby appoint John Sharnon an alcalde within the district of San Diego, at or near San Luis Rey.

Given at Monterey, the capital of California, this 24th day of November, A. D. 1847, and of the independence of the United States the 72d.
R. B. MASON,
Colonel 1st Dragoons, Governor of California.

HEADQUARTERS TENTH MILITARY DEPARTMENT,
Monterey, California, November 24, 1847.

SIR: I am informed that you have in your possession certain property belonging to the mission of ———. I desire you at once to turn all such property over to Captain J. D. Hunter, sub-Indian agent, who is in charge of San Luis Rey. I further desire that you will furnish me with an inventory of all the mission property that is now, or may have been at any time, in your possession, and that you will inform me when you obtain it.

With much respect, your obedient servant,
R. B. MASON,
Colonel 1st Dragoons, Governor of California.
JOSE ANTONIO PICO.

HEADQUARTERS TENTH MILITARY DEPARTMENT,
Monterey, California, November 24, 1847.

SIR: I am in the receipt of your letter of the 11th of the present month. In relation to the disputes about the boundaries of certain farms on the Contra Costa, the only way in the present condition of affairs in California is for the parties concerned to enter into articles of writing, binding themselves to abide the decision of arbitrators (the arbitration to be laid before the alcalde) for the permanent settlement of their lines or boundaries. If this cannot be done, let them agree to enter into an arbitration for the temporary settlement of the boundaries until such time as the proper law courts are established, it being understood that such temporary settlement is not to prejudice the claim or right of either party, when the cause comes before the proper court having the judicial power to try the same.

I am, respectfully, your obedient servant,
R. B. MASON,
Colonel 1st Dragoons, Governor of California.

J. W. WEEKS,
 Alcalde, Pueblo de San José.

HEADQUARTERS TENTH MILITARY DEPARTMENT,
Monterey, California, November 25, 1847.

SIR: I have your letter of the 13th instant, and the one enclosed, addressed to yourself, from Padre Real. I know not what are the privileges that his reverence enjoys, nor do I know to what "competent judge" he refers, who alone can take "judicial cognizance" against him; but it is very evident that if his reverence departs from his calling as a Catholic priest, and enters into a bargain or contract with a citizen of the country, he places himself, and must necessarily stand upon the same footing with that citizen, and that citizen has the same recourse against the padre for a breach of contract, as the padre would have against him, or as one citizen has against another in similar cases. Were this not the case, it would be useless to enter into an agreement or contract. An agreement or contract, verbal or written, necessarily implies a reciprocity: it must be equally obligatory upon both parties. One party failing to comply with his stipulated obligations, the other has the right to appeal to the civil laws of the land to compel the delinquent to conform to his agreement, and that delinquent cannot plead privileges not accorded to him in the contract or agreement into which he has entered.

I am, respectfully, your obedient servant,
R. B. MASON,
Colonel 1st Dragoons, Governor of California.

JAMES W. WEEKS,
 Alcalde, Pueblo de San José.

CIRCULAR.

HEADQUARTERS TENTH MILITARY DEPARTMENT,
Monterey, California, November 27, 1847.

Vessels sailing from port to port for the purpose of collecting and taking in cargo for exportation from California to the United States ports, or the ports of any foreign country in amity with the same, will not be subjected to tonnage or revenue duty, unless they land freight, or sell or land for sale portions of their cargo.

R. B. MASON,
Colonel 1st Dragoons, Governor of California.

HEADQUARTERS TENTH MILITARY DEPARTMENT,
Monterey, California, November 29, 1847.

GENTLEMEN: Your communication of the 23d October is before me. I cannot, with the information with which I am at present possessed, recognise you as the legal purchasers of the mission of Santa Ynez.

The authority given by the departmental assembly of April 3, 1846, to sell the missions, expressly required that they should be sold at *public auction,* the *customary notice* being *previously given.* This was not done: the mission was not sold at public auction, but, on the contrary, you yourselves say that you entered into a contract with the government by which you became the purchasers; and if you became the purchasers on the 15th of June, 1846, how is it that you continued to pay rent during all that year, and part of 1847? For this and other reasons, I declare there has been no legal sale, and the obligations under which you stood previous to the 15th of June, 1846, as the renters of said mission, to be in full force and effect. You will, therefore, without delay, pay up the amount due according to the terms of the contract by which you became the renters of the mission of Santa Ynez, a copy of which contract you will send to this office, as also copies of the receipts for the amount of rent paid since the 1st of January, 1846.

You sent a statement of the amount paid, but I wish a copy of the receipt given by the padre Jurieno.

I am, respectfully, your obedient servant,

R. B. MASON,
Colonel 1st Dragoons, Governor of California.

JOSE M. COVARUBIA,
J. CARRILLO,
Santa Ynez.

HEADQUARTERS TENTH MILITARY DEPARTMENT,
Monterey, California, November 29, 1847.

VERY REVEREND SIR: I have the honor to acknowledge the receipt of your letter of the 18th instant. The absence of Lieutenant Halleck, the secretary of the Territory, to Mazatlan, has been the reason why the subject to which your letter refers has not been brought to a conclusion at an earlier date. I will take up the subject and write to the renters of Santa Ynez by the same mail which will convey to you and will inform your reverence of the result of the matter.

I am, with high respect, your obedient servant,

R. B. MASON,
Colonel 1st Dragoons, Governor of California.

Very Rev. Friar JOSE MARIA DE JESUS GONZALES,
Governor of the Bishopric of California, Santa Barbara.

PROCLAMATION.

From and after the first day of January, eighteen hundred and forty-eight, if any person shall sell, exchange, give, barter, or dispose of, or in any way connive at selling, exchanging, giving, bartering, or disposing of any spirituous liquor or wine to an Indian, such person shall, upon conviction before an alcalde, forfeit and pay the sum of not less than fifty nor more than one hundred dollars, and be imprisoned for not less than three nor more than six months. One half of all fines recovered under this proclamation shall go to the benefit of the informer, and the other half to the benefit of the town or jurisdiction where the prisoner may be confined; and in all prosecutions arising under this proclamation, indians shall be competent witnesses.

Done at Monterey, the capital of California, this twenty-ninth day of November, eighteen hundred and forty-seven, and of the seventy-second of the independence of the United States.

R. B. MASON,
Colonel 1st Dragoons, Governor of California.

HEADQUARTERS TENTH MILITARY DEPARTMENT,
Monterey, California, December 1, 1847.

SIR: The record, papers, &c., of the case of Garner V. S. Farnham, I request you will to-day put under a seal, and hand them to Mr. Colton, the alcalde of this town, that he may send them to the alcalde at San Luis Obispo, by the mail which closes to-night, and which will leave here early to-morrow morning.

I am, respectfully, your obedient servant,

R. B. MASON,
Colonel 1st Dragoons, Governor of California.

Mr. J. RICORD, *Monterey.*

HEADQUARTERS TENTH MILITARY DEPARTMENT,
Monterey, California, November 30, 1847.

SIR: Your letter of the 22d instant is before me. The Indians you speak of as belonging to the mission of San Miguel, if belonging in fact to that mission, can be put in possession of the land that was granted to them by Micheltorena in 1844.

I am, respectfully, your obedient servant,
R. B. MASON,
Colonel 1st Dragoons, Governor of California.

JOSE MARIANO BONILLA,
Alcalde, San Luis Obispo.

HEADQUARTERS TENTH MILITARY DEPARTMENT,
Monterey, California, December 1, 1847.

SIR: I am in the receipt of a letter, dated 14th November, from Mr. J. J. Warner, complaining of the Indians committing depredations on his stock, &c.; also, a letter from Colonel Stevenson, of the 16th November, enclosing a communication from Mr. Warner, and papers, concerning his claim to the land on which the Indians reside, &c., &c.

Things must remain as at present until the time arrives when the proper tribunals, to be established in the country, shall set at rest all these disputed land questions. In the interim, however, you will, *after consulting with Mr. Warner*, establish regulations among the Indians of whom Mr. Warner speaks, for their better government, and for the protection of Mr. W.'s property—letting the chiefs know that, if they desire the friendship and protection of the American government, they must not only abstain from committing depredations upon the property of Mr. Warner and all other citizens of California, but they must endeavor, as far as practicable, to prevent other Indians from committing the same. It will be well to establish some kind of police among the Indians, by making them appoint alcaldes, from among themselves, for their own better government, and for preventing offences against the peace and good order of the neighborhood, &c., &c.

I deem it important, as a military measure, to sustain Mr. Warner in that position, and to keep up a good understanding with these Indians; and I therefore desire that you use every effort to conciliate them, and get them, as far as practicable, to gain a comfortable subsistence by cultivating the soil, and to abandon their depredatory habits. In your intercourse with them assure them that it is the wish of the United States to take all the red people by the hand, and treat them as friends, &c., &c.; but if they continue to destroy the stock of the people of the country, we shall treat them as enemies.

I am, respectfully, your obedient servant,
R. B. MASON,
Colonel 1st Dragoons, Governor of California.

Captain J. D. HUNTER,
Sub-Indian Agent, San Luis Rey.

HEADQUARTERS TENTH MILITARY DEPARTMENT,
Monterey, California, December 3, 1847.

SIR: I have to acknowledge the receipt of your communication of the 2d instant, and, in reply thereto, to state that there are no courts as yet established in California, other than the alcalde's court.

I am, respectfully, your obedient servant,
R. B. MASON,
Colonel 1st Dragoons, Governor of California.
Dr. WM. H. MCKEE, *Monterey.*

HEADQUARTERS TENTH MILITARY DEPARTMENT,
Monterey, California, December 3, 1847.

Sir: From the conversations had with you since my first note of this morning, it appears that I did not fully comprehend the scope of the object of your letter of the 2d instant.

I do not think that I can with propriety appoint a special court in the case you ask for. From the application of such courts from other parts of the Territory, I am of the opinion that the precedent I have set of making such appointments is not a good one, and will not be resorted to in future, except in some extraordinary cases.

I am, respectfully, your obedient servant,
R. B. MASON,
Colonel 1st Dragoons, Governor of California.
Dr. W. H. MCKEE, *Monterey.*

HEADQUARTERS TENTH MILITARY DEPARTMENT,
Monterey, California, December 3, 1847.

SIR: Your communication of the 28th instant is before me. The distance of Major Hardie's station from the town of San Francisco renders it impracticable for him to attend in person to the collection of the customs; the whole duty, therefore, necessarily devolves upon you, and therefore I do not deem it necessary for him to countersign the monthly statement of collections.

This should be explained to the authorities at Washington when you forward your accounts. I do not deem it necessary, for the reason which you assign, to make the weekly statements of revenue received. I do not do it here.

The change you suggest in the form of the quarterly return of vessels, &c., is approved.

I am, respectfully, your obedient servant,
R. B. MASON,
Colonel 1st Dragoons, Governor of California.
Captain J. L. FOLSOM,
Assistant Quartermaster U. S. Army,
San Francisco.

P. S.—The monthly statements of revenue collected intended for the Secretary of War you will send through these headquarters.
R. B. M.

HEADQUARTERS TENTH MILITARY DEPARTMENT,
Monterey, California, December 14, 1847.

SIR: I have to acknowledge the receipt of your letter of the 22d November, enclosing a petition signed by yourself, two citizens, and a soldier, asking for a special court to quiet land titles in the town of San Francisco, and referring to a commission appointed last summer that sat in Sonoma, as a precedent. The circumstances that caused that commission to be appointed are not at all parallel with those presented in your petition, and I find even that precedent not a good one. Any court or commission that might be appointed to quiet a land title, their verdict or opinion could only be of temporary character—it could not forever set at rest the title, and, when the proper law courts are established in the country after it becomes finally surrendered to and forms a part of the United States territory, would open anew all such decisions; and so far from special courts quieting titles and stopping litigation, they would only engender more. It is better, upon the whole, not to stir land titles by the appointment of special courts, until they can be finally quieted by the competent courts having the proper power and jurisdiction.

It would not be proper to appoint another body to continue the investigation of the charges against Mr. Hyde. The gentlemen who have that business in hand are fresh from the people, and were elected by them with a special view to town affairs; and were I to take the matter out of their hands and place it in others, it would be establishing a very unsafe precedent, and would be an assumption of power that I could not sustain myself in exercising, for it would effectually defeat the election of the people, and I might as well be justified in appointing a special commission to repeal or pass some town ordinance which the people's representatives had declined doing.

I am, very respectfully, your obedient servant,
R. B. MASON,
Colonel 1st Dragoons, Governor of California.

C. E. PICKETT,
  San Francisco.

HEADQUARTERS TENTH MILITARY DEPARTMENT,
Monterey, California, December 6, 1847.

SIR: Your communication of the 12th instant has been received. I have no authority to rent or sell land in California.

Respectfully, &c.,
R. B. MASON,
Colonel 1st Dragoons, Governor of California.

JOSEPH A. RANSCH,
  San Francisco.

HEADQUARTERS TENTH MILITARY DEPARTMENT,
Monterey, California, December 6, 1847.

SIR: Julian Urgua does not wish to accept the appointment of alcalde. I will, as I informed you at the time you were in Monterey, appoint any one an alcalde for whom the people will sign a petition, provided the person will accept the office, which you should ascertain before sending in the petition. I request that you will attend to this affair.

I am, respectfully, your obedient servant,
R. B. MASON,
Colonel 1st Dragoons, Governor of California.

JOSE MARIA SANCHEZ,
San Juan Bautista.

HEADQUARTERS TENTH MILITARY DEPARTMENT,
Monterey, California, December 6, 1847.

CAPTAIN: The merchant-shippers and masters of vessels at your port do not correctly make out their *invoices* and *manifests*. The invoices do not, in many cases, describe the *number* and *marks* of the different boxes, packages, &c. The *boxes* and *packages*, and each article not boxed or in packages, *must be plainly marked and numbered*. These marks and numbers *must be expressed upon the invoice*, and the invoice must show the *actual contents of each box or package*, according to its respective number and mark, otherwise it is impossible to ascertain whether the goods are properly or fraudulently invoiced. *The marks and numbers on the invoice must correspond with the marks and numbers on the manifests.*

The column under the head of "quantity" on the manifest should express, when it is practicable to do so, the quantity or contents of the boxes or packages, in yards, pounds, arrobas, gallons, &c., and not simply the number of the packages, as has generally been the case. The shippers must be more particular in their invoices, otherwise I shall be obliged to seize the goods as being improperly invoiced, or send them back to the port from whence they come. For fear that I have not clearly expressed myself, I send you herewith a manifest and invoice correctly made out, and corresponding in every particular; by which you will see how easy it is for the shippers and masters to comply with the regulation. I think it would be well if you were to give to each of the masters of vessels and merchants in your port, as there are not so very many of them, a copy of the manifest and invoice I send you, and require them in their future shipments to conform strictly to the manner of marking them. You will observe on the manifest that the boxes, &c., are described with their *general contents*, whilst on the invoice the *contents of each box are particularized*—the numbers and marks exactly corresponding with those on the manifest, as also the exact money value. I find the better plan is not to give vessels a separate manifest for such cargo as they take in at port, unless they take in an entire cargo; but to enter on the manifest deposited in the custom-house such boxes, packages, &c., as they receive on board, according to their invoices, setting forth the name of the port, date, &c.

I am, respectfully, your obedient servant,
R. B. MASON,
Colonel 1st Dragoons, Governor of California.

Captain J. L. FOLSOM,
Assistant Quartermaster, San Francisco.

P. S.—Since writing the foregoing I have overhauled the manifest and invoices of the brig Henry, from San Francisco. Her invoices show no mark or number of the boxes, packages, &c., which constitute her cargo, nor the value of the articles; neither does her manifest show the number of any box or package. This informality in her papers gives us a great deal of perplexity here. I wish that in future you will suffer no manifest to pass from your office without seeing that *marks and numbers* are properly expressed thereon, and that the *marks and numbers* on the *invoices* correspond with those on the manifest. Give no vessel a clearance until the master presents to you the manifest and invoices properly made out and authenticated.

R. B. M.,
Colonel 1st Dragoons.

DECEMBER 7.

HEADQUARTERS TENTH MILITARY DEPARTMENT,
Monterey, California, December 9, 1847.

SIR: In your account current with the civil government of California for the month of October, 1847, you credit yourself with two sums—forty-two dollars and six dollars—and enter them as disbursements per voucher No. 1, and do. per voucher No. 2. These vouchers are not to be found among the papers received here relating to customs, &c., collected at the port of San Diego for the said month. As it is necessary that these accounts should be perfectly explicit, and that all vouchers referred to in the account current should accompany that document, you will be pleased to take the earliest opportunity to transmit to this office the vouchers for the above stated sums.

I am, respectfully, yours,
R. B. MASON,
Colonel 1st Dragoons, Governor of California.

Don Miguel PEDRORENA,
   San Diego.

CIRCULAR.

HEADQUARTERS TENTH MILITARY DEPARTMENT,
Monterey, California, December 10, 1847.

SIR: There are some three or four vessels, under foreign flags, that are owned by resident citizens of California. Such vessels will be permitted to continue in the coasting trade, from port to port, on the coast of California, until the pleasure of the President of the United States can be known—subject, however, in the mean time, to the concurrence of the officer commanding the United States naval forces in the Pacific, who is at present absent from the coast of California.

I am, respectfully, your obedient servant,

R. B. MASON,
Colonel 1st Dragoons, Governor of California.

To the COLLECTORS OF CUSTOMS
   in the ports of California.

419   [18]

Know all men by these presents, that I, Richard B. Mason, colonel 1st regiment dragoons United States army, and governor of California, by virtue of authority in me vested, do hereby appoint Stephen C. Foster alcalde for and in the town and jurisdiction of Ciudad de los Angeles, to take effect on the 1st day of January, 1848.

Given at Monterey, the capital of California, this tenth day of December, A. D. 1847, and of the independence of the United States the seventy-second.

R. B. MASON,
Colonel 1st Dragoons, Governor of California.

Know all men by these presents, that I, Richard B. Mason, colonel 1st regiment dragoons United States army, and governor of California, by virtue of authority in me vested, do hereby appoint Robert Cliff alcalde for and in the town and jurisdiction of San Diego.

Given at Monterey, the capital of California, this 10th day of December, A. D. 1847, and of the independence of the United States the seventy-second.

R. B. MASON,
Colonel 1st Dragoons, Governor of California.

HEADQUARTERS TENTH MILITARY DEPARTMENT,
Monterey, California, December 10, 1847.

SIR: I have this day appointed Mr. Stephen C. Foster alcalde for the district and pueblo de los Angeles, to take effect on the 1st day of January, A. D. 1848. You will, therefore, on that day deliver over to him all the books, papers, and records, appertaining to the office of alcalde, as also any property or funds that may properly belong to the same—taking care to give the proper inventories of all that you deliver over to your successor in office.

I am, respectfully, your obedient servant,

R. B. MASON,
Colonel 1st Dragoons, Governor of California.

ALCALDE,
Ciudad de los Angeles, California.

HEADQUARTERS TENTH MILITARY DEPARTMENT,
Monterey, California, December 10, 1847.

COLONEL: I enclose herewith the appointment of alcalde for Mr. Stephen C. Foster, and also a letter to the present alcalde at Los Angeles, which be pleased to hand to him.

I transmit by the same mail which takes this, the appointment of alcalde to Lieutenant Cliff, at San Diego.

I am, respectfully, your obedient servant,

R. B. MASON,
Colonel 1st Dragoons, Governor of California.

Col. J. D. STEVENSON,
Commanding Southern Mil. District, Los Angeles

HEADQUARTERS TENTH MILITARY DEPARTMENT,
Monterey, California, December 11, 1847.

COMMODORE: I have the honor herewith to enclose to you some printed copies of extracts from the instructions received from Washington, for collecting the military contributions in California, prepared for the information of ship-masters and merchants, in which are included the additional items and alterations agreed upon between us before you sailed from this port, as also some additional items of my own, made since your departure. Your absence from the coast must be my apology for giving instructions to the collectors upon matters which the President has confided to you; but I deemed them of sufficient importance to justify me in giving the orders, and hope they will meet your approbation.

I also enclose you a copy of my letter to the Adjutant General of the 12th of November, as a part of it refers to the subject of duties, &c., and changes which I have made upon my own responsibility.

I am, respectfully, your obedient servant,

R. B. MASON,
Colonel 1st Dragoons, Governor of California.

Commodore W. BRANFORD SHUBRICK,
*Commanding U. S. naval forces off Mazatlan,
and in the Pacific.*

HEADQUARTERS TENTH MILITARY DEPARTMENT,
Monterey, California, December 20, 1847.

SIR: Your two communications of the 29th November and the 12th December are before me.

The moneys arising from the customs must be kept and accounted for separate from the other public funds.

A copy of your quarterly account current to the War Department, now that the funds from the custom-house are settled there, need only be sent to this office. The monthly statement of revenue collected, intended for the War Department, comes through this office, that it may be entered in a book kept for that purpose, so that the amount collected in all the ports may be known here monthly.

You speak of your custom-house accounts being setted at the treasury. Perhaps it has escaped your observation (see page 4 of the printed regu'ations) that these accounts are settled at the War and Navy Departments, according as funds collected by army and navy officers, and not at the treasury.

I have carefully read over my letter to you of the 6th instant: I cannot see how you can construe it into a censure of your conduct; surely, none such was intended. It was only meant to impart such information as I had been enabled to gain during the short time I have been discharging the duties of custom-house officer, and to point out the errors of ship-masters and merchants in making out their manifests and invoices, and showing you that the only way to compel them to make them out properly was to withhold the clearance until they did so.

If Major Hardie's command cannot afford a proper clerk for the custom-house, you must hire one as a matter of course.
I am, respectfully, your obedient servant,
R. B. MASON,
Colonel 1st Dragoons U. S. A., Governor of California.
Captain J. L. Folsom,
Assistant Quartermaster, San Francisco.

Headquarters Tenth Military Department,
Monterey, California, December 20, 1847.

Sir: I am in the receipt of your letter of the 14th instant. The practice has been to sentence persons convicted of horse stealing to a fine and a certain length of time to hard labor on any sort of general or public work, the length of service to be according to the nature and degree of the offence; and in very aggravated cases, I think, in addition to the imprisonment and hard labor, a sentence of fifty lashes would have a salutary effect.
I am, respectfully, your obedient servant,
R. B. MASON,
Colonel 1st Dragoons U. S. A., Governor of California.
James W. Weeks,
Alcalde, San José.

Headquarters Tenth Military Department,
Monterey, California, December 20, 1847.

Sir: A copy of the quarterly account current of funds derived from the customs, which you are required to make *direct* to the Secretary of War, will be promptly forwarded to this office by the first *mail* after the expiration of the quarter.
I am, respectfully, your obedient servant,
R. B. MASON,
Colonel 1st Dragoons, Governor of California.
Lieutenant H. S. Carnes,
Acting Assistant Quartermaster, Santa Barbara.

Headquarters Tenth Military Department,
Monterey, California, December 20, 1847.

Sir: The quarterly account referred to in my letter of the 28th November, need only be a copy of the one you make direct to the Secretary of War, in accordance with the printed instructions from Washington.
I am, respectfully, your obedient servant,
R. B. MASON,
Colonel 1st Dragoons, Governor of California.
Lieutenant J. N. Davidson,
Acting Assistant Quartermaster, Los Angeles.

P. S.—Say to the collector at San Pedro, that a copy of his monthly statement of revenue collected, and a copy of his quarterly account, must be sent to this office.

R. B. MASON,
Colonel 1st Dragoons.

HEADQUARTERS TENTH MILITARY DEPARTMENT,
Monterey, California, December 20, 1847.

SIR: As you are required to account direct to the Secretary of War for all funds coming into your hands from the customs, you will forward to this office by the *first mail*, after the expiration of each quarter, a copy of your quarterly account current, showing the receipts and expenditures during the quarter, together with the balance on hand that may not have been turned over to Lieutenant Davidson.

I am, respectfully, your obedient servant,

R. B. MASON,
Colonel 1st Dragoons, Governor of California.

Lieutenant ROBERT CLIFF,
  Mormon Company, San Diego.

HEADQUARTERS TENTH MILITARY DEPARTMENT,
Monterey, California, December 20, 1847.

SIR: I have the honor to acknowledge the receipt of your letter of the 5th instant.

Your own certificates of election to the gentlemen composing your town council will be all sufficient. The powers of the council are the same as those given to the town council at San Francisco, which you will find in my letter of the 15th July last, published in the California and Star of the 4th September, and my letter of the 1st October, published in the California of the 6th, and the Star of the 16th, of the same month.

I am, very respectfully, your obedient servant,

R. B. MASON,
Colonel 1st Dragoons, Governor of California.

L. W. BOGGS,
  Alcalde, Sonoma.

HEADQUARTERS TENTH MILITARY DEPARTMENT,
Monterey, California, December 21, 1847.

SIR: I have received your letter of the 9th instant. Although it would afford me at all times much pleasure to extend to Mr. Forbes, the British vice consul, all courtesies and civilities in my power, I cannot find that he can claim as a matter of right to be exempt from the payment of duties on articles imported by himself into the country: on the contrary, ambassadors, and even sovereigns themselves, are subject to them. Vattel, page 484, paragraph 105, says: " The independency of the ambassador exempts him, indeed, from every personal imposition, capitation, or other duty of that nature, and in general from every tax relating to the character of the subject of the state; but as for duties laid on any kind of goods or provisions, the most absolute dependency does not exempt him from the payment of them; even sovereigns themselves are subject to them."

I am, very respectfully, your obedient servant,

R. B. MASON,
Colonel 1st Dragoons U. S. Army, Governor of California.

Captain WM. RICHARDSON,
Late Collector, San Francisco.

CIRCULAR.

HEADQUARTERS TENTH MILITARY DEPARTMENT,
Monterey, California, December 21, 1847.

You will use every effort in your power to carry into full effect the proclamation of the 29th of November last, prohibiting the sale of spirituous liquors or wine to Indians.

R. B. MASON,
Colonel 1st Dragoons, Governor of California.

To the ALCALDE and INDIAN AGENTS,
California.

HEADQUARTERS TENTH MILITARY DEPARTMENT,
Monterey, California, December 22, 1847.

SIR: I am in the receipt of your communication of the 20th instant, and its enclosure.

In cases where a jury cannot come to a decision, after being out a reasonable time, the practice is to empannel a new jury to try the case.

I return to you the papers enclosed in your letter of the 20th instant.

I am, respectfully, your obedient servant,

R. B. MASON,
Colonel 1st Dragoons, Governor of California.

JAS. W. WEEKS,
Alcalde, Pueblo de San José.

HEADQUARTERS TENTH MILITARY DEPARTMENT,
Monterey, California, December 22, 1847.

SIR: I have received through Major Hardie, at San Francisco, a petition from the people of your town, to have a military guard stationed at the pueblo. Before making up my mind on the subject, I wish to know whether proper quarters can be obtained for them, and at what cost; also, at what price beef can be had. I will thank you for any information you can give me on the subject.

I am, respectfully, your obedient servant,
R. B. MASON,
Colonel 1st Dragoons, Governor of California.

Jas. W. Weeks,
Alcalde, Pueblo de San José.

Headquarters Tenth Military Department,
Monterey, California, December 22, 1847.

Sir: I have the honor to acknowledge the receipt of your letter of the 25th November, enclosing an account of $171, for services rendered in rescuing emigrants from the California mountains. It would give me much pleasure, I assure you, if it were in my power to order the account paid. I hoped before now to have received from our government at Washington full instructions in relation to all outstanding debts and claims against the United States in California, that will enable me to have them settled and paid off, but at present it is entirely out of my power to touch them.

I am, respectfully, your obedient servant,
R. B. MASON,
Colonel 1st Dragoons, Governor of California.

Mr. M. D. Ritchey,
Sonoma, California.

Headquarters Tenth Military Department,
Monterey, California, December 23, 1847.

I beg leave to remind your reverence that I have not received the document you hold, which you informed me authorized you to sell the mission lands, and which you were to send me.

Upon examining such laws as are within my reach, I find them so particular in forbidding the sale of mission lands, that I fear you labor under some misapprehension as to the legal powers you possess to sell those lands.

I hope to be favored by the return of mail with the document you promised to furnish me.

I am, reverend father, your obedient servant,
R. B. MASON,
Colonel 1st Dragoons, Governor of California.

To the Rev. Father Jose M. Real.

Headquarters Tenth Military Department,
Monterey, California, December 24, 1847.

Sir: Your letter of the 17th instant is before me. The first part of it is already answered by previous instructions.

For your information and guidance, as well as that of Captain Lippett, I enclose you a copy of a post order (No. 54) of November 1st, that I found necessary to issue here, relating to the officers and soldiers purchasing articles from vessels in the harbor. That the revenue may not be defrauded, soldiers must be restricted in their purchases to a reasonable amount. It is not reasonable to suppose that a private soldier could or would buy for his own individual use $400 worth of comestibles; and the natural inference is, that they were bought for other purposes.

This subject must in future be clearly looked to; and, whilst the soldier is permitted to purchase any imported article for his own individual use and consumption, and not intended for sale or transfer to others, free of duty, the revenue must be guarded by not permitting him to buy in larger quantities than his own personal comfort and wants may seem reasonably to require.

I am, respectfully, your obedient servant,
R. B. MASON,
Col. 1st Dragoons, Governor of California.

Lieut. H. S. CARNES,
Act'g Asst. Quartermaster, Santa Barbara.

HEADQUARTERS TENTH MILITARY DEPARTMENT,
Monterey, California, December 26, 1847.

SIR: I yesterday received your letter of the 21st instant, in relation to the goods seized from the schooner Mary Ann. I did not view your letter of the 28th October as presenting the case for decision, but merely as mentioning the occurrence of the seizure, &c. I do not deem it at all necessary that every seizure should receive confirmation from me before the goods are sold: the regulations are plain, and explicitly point out when the collector is authorized to seize and sell goods. He may with propriety suspend the sale when the owner of the goods protests against the seizure, and wishes himself to refer the matter to higher authority; though, strictly speaking, the regulations do not appear to have looked to higher authority, but to have made the collector the sole judge.

I have no recollection of receiving any letter from Captain Patty on the subject, and cannot find that one has been received.

I am, respectfully, your obedient servant,
R. B. MASON,
Col. 1st Dragoons, Governor of California.

Capt. J. L. FOLSOM,
Asst. Quartermaster, San Francisco.

HEADQUARTERS TENTH MILITARY DEPARTMENT,
Monterey, California, December 26, 1847.

SIR: I enclose you, herewith, Captain Marcy's receipt for $250, it being the amount paid on the invoice of goods brought from San Francisco in the brig Henry, and landed at Santa Cruz, which was exacted from the brig (because there was no evidence that the duties had been previously paid) under a promise to refund, upon satisfactory evidence being produced from you that the duties had been paid.

Your certificate, upon the invoice enclosed to me by Mr. C. L. Ross, is that evidence; and I request that you will turn the amount of the written receipts over to Mr. Ross, or the person to whom it properly belongs. Take his receipt for the same, and enclose it to me.

I am, respectfully, your obedient servant,
R. B. MASON,
Col. 1st Dragoons, commanding.

Capt. J. L. FOLSOM,
   Asst. Quartermaster, San Francisco.

PROCLAMATION.

No citizen of the province of Sonora will be permitted to enter California unless coming upon official business with the United States authorities, and then only under the protection of a flag of truce.

All Sonorenians in Upper California south of Santa Barbara will, within ten days after the publication of this proclamation in the Ciudad des los Angeles, report in person to Colonel Stevenson, United States army, commanding at that post, and make known their business and date of arrival in the country. All who fail to report to Colonel Stevenson, as above directed, will be arrested and treated as enemies and spies.

All Sonorenians in California north of Santa Barbara will, in like manner, report in person to the undersigned at Monterey, before the 15th day of January, 1848, or be subjected to similar penalties.

Done at Monterey, the capital of California, this 27th day of December, 1847, and of the independence of the United States the seventy-second.
R. B. MASON,
Col. 1st Dragoons, Governor of California.

HEADQUARTERS TENTH MILITARY DEPARTMENT,
Monterey, California, December 28, 1847.

SIR: I have to acknowledge the receipt of your communication of the 1st instant.

I have referred the whole subject connected with your cattle contract with Lieutenant Colonel Fremont to the United States government at Washington, by forwarding copies of all the papers that have come into my hands concerning the same, and therefore can take no action upon this subject, in this country, without instructions from Washington. It has not been my intention to cast any censure upon you as the contractor; nor am I aware of having done so, as you seem to suppose in your above-mentioned letter of the 1st instant.

I am, respectfully, your obedient servant,
R. B. MASON,
Col. 1st Dragoons, Governor of California.

Mr. EULOJIO DE CELIS, *Los Angeles.*

HEADQUARTERS TENTH MILITARY DEPARTMENT,
Monterey, California, December 28, 1847.

SIR: I have to acknowledge the receipt of your two communications of the 22d instant, in relation to the goods found on board the brig Henry, to be landed at Santa Cruz, a place where there was no custom-house; and there being no evidence that the duties had been paid, they were, as a matter of course, demanded here—a promise being given to refund, upon satisfactory evidence being produced that the duties had been paid. That being the milder course, the more rigid one was to have seized the goods, and if they exceeded in value one thousand dollars, to have confiscated the brig. And whether the duties had been paid or not, the goods were subject to seizure, if they had been landed at Santa Cruz without a permit from the collector here; and therefore, before allowing them to be landed, it was necessary to ascertain if the duties had been paid.

In answer to your interrogatories relative to the tonnage duties, it is proper to make your protests at the port complained of.

I am, respectfully, your obedient servant,
R. B. MASON,
Col. 1st Dragoons, Governor of California.

Mr. C. L. ROSS, *San Francisco.*

HEADQUARTERS TENTH MILITARY DEPARTMENT,
Monterey, California, December 29, 1847.

SIR: I am in the receipt of a letter on the subject of the sale of the brig Primavera, dated Juzgudo de los Angeles, 2d December, from José Salaraz, at present alcalde at Los Angeles, but whose term of office will have expired before this reaches you. I see no grounds on which to change any instructions that I have given in that cause.

I am, respectfully, your obedient servant,
R. B. MASON,
Col. 1st Dragoons, Governor of California.

STEPHEN C. FOSTER,
Alcalde, Ciudad de los Angeles.

HEADQUARTERS TENTH MILITARY DEPARTMENT,
Monterey, California, December 29, 1847.

COLONEL: I am in the receipt of your letter of the 19th instant. It would have been well if you had prohibited the election you speak of. Foster has been appointed alcalde, as you doubtless are aware of before this, and must be sustained in his position. The election was held without my authority; and you must, in my name, declare it null and void.

I am, respectfully, your obedient servant,
R. B. MASON,
Col. 1st Dragoons, Governor of California.

Col. J. D. STEVENSON,
Commanding Southern Military District, Los Angeles.

In all cases that are now, or may hereafter come before an alcalde's court, when the amount involved shall exceed one hundred dollars, the same shall be decided by a jury, which shall consist of six good and lawful men.

Done at Monterey, the capital of California, this 29th day of December, A. D. 1847, and of the independence of the United States the seventy-second.

R. B. MASON,
Colonel 1st Dragoons, Governor of California.

HEADQUARTERS TENTH MILITARY DEPARTMENT,
Monterey, California, December 29, 1847.

SIR: I have received your letter of the 18th instant. I have given no such instructions to the alcalde as those spoken of in your said letter, and, in order to set the question at rest, I have published the enclosed proclamation bearing date this day. You are hereby authorized to appoint a subaltern alcalde at the mission Dolores.

I am, respectfully, your obedient servant,

R. B. MASON,
Colonel 1st Dragoons, Governor of California.

GEORGE HYDE,
Alcalde, San Francisco.

Know all men by these presents, that I, Richard B. Mason, colonel 1st dragoons United States army, and governor of California, by virtue of authority in me vested, do hereby appoint Stephen Cooper an alcalde at Benicia city, at present in the district of Sonoma.

Given at Monterey, the capital of California, this third day of January, A. D. 1848, and of the independence of the United States the seventy-second.

R. B. MASON,
Colonel 1st Dragoons, Governor of California.

HEADQUARTERS TENTH MILITARY DEPARTMENT,
Monterey, California, January 3, 1848.

SIR: Dr. Semple, of Benicia city, is very desirous of having a new district (to be called the Benicia district) cut off from the Sonoma district, and to be bounded as follows, viz: Commencing at the mouth of Trappa river; thence up that river to the head of tide-water; thence due east to the top of the dividing ridge between the Trappa and Sacramento rivers; thence northwards on the top of said ridge to the northern boundary of the Sonoma district; thence due east to the Sacramento river; thence down that river and the bay of Suison to the place of beginning.

The Doctor tells me that it would be much more convenient for the people living in the proposed new district to come into Benicia on business with an alcalde, &c., &c., than to go to Sonoma. You will do me the favor to give me your views on the subject, and tell me whether the new district will in any way affect the district of Sonoma; and, if so, in what way.

I am, respectfully, your obedient servant,

R. B. MASON,
Colonel 1st Dragoons, Governor of California.

L. M. BOGGS,
Alcalde, Sonoma.

HEADQUARTERS TENTH MILITARY DEPARTMENT,
Monterey, California, January 3, 1848.

REVEREND SIR: I have the honor to acknowledge the receipt of your letter of the 29th December, and its accompanying document, purporting to give you authority to sell mission lands, bearing date 25th May and 16th June, 1846, signed by José Castro, and addressed to yourself.

This document certainly could give you no authority to sell any part of the mission lands after the 7th of July, 1846, the day on which the United States flag was hoisted in California, if indeed it could have conferred such authority before. Since that date, the mission lands can only be disposed of by virtue of authority from the United States government. I am therefore obliged to declare, and do hereby declare all sale of any part of the mission lands made by your reverence to be alleged null and void; and that the purchasers of such lands hold no legal title to them whatever, by virtue of any sale made by your reverence.

I am, respectfully, your obedient servant,

R. B. MASON,
Colonel 1st Dragoons, Governor of California.

Rev. Padre Fr. JOSÉ MA. R. S. DEL REAL,
Minister of the Mission of Santa Clara.

NOTE.—Copy of the above letter sent to the alcalde, Pueblo de San José, with instructions to make it public at the pueblo and Santa Clara, and their respective vicinities.

HEADQUARTERS TENTH MILITARY DEPARTMENT,
Monterey, California, January 5, 1848.

CAPTAIN: Since my letter to you of the 28th October on the subject of Lieutenant Gilbert's claim to a share of the merchandise seized from the English barque Janet, my opinion has undergone an entire change. This change has been wrought by my reading in Gordon's Digest of the Laws of the United States that the revenue officers in the United States would, under similar circumstances, be entitled to a share of the condemned goods. (See Gordon's Digest of the Laws of the United States, edition of 1837, note to page 584, and pages 585 and 586.) I think one-half of the amount of the proceeds of the said goods would be allowed to yourself and Lieutenant Gilbert, for you are equally entitled to a share, in your accounts with the War Department. When I directed that your monthly statement of revenue collected intended for the Secretary of War should pass through these headquarters, I did not expect that it would be the means of causing a separation in your accounts. I will, therefore, consider those you have sent me as copies only of those you will send to the Secretary, and only require of you copies in future.

I am, very respectfully, your obedient servant,

R. B. MASON,
Colonel 1st Dragoons, Governor of California.

Captain J. L. FOLSOM,
Assistant Quartermaster, San Francisco.

HEADQUARTERS TENTH MILITARY DEPARTMENT,
Monterey, California, January 6, 1848.

SIR: I have received yours of the 28th of December, resigning your appointment of alcalde of the district of San José, and must request that you will continue in the office until I can get some suitable person to supply your place. Can you recommend any properly qualified person who will accept the office?

I am, respectfully, your obedient servant,

R. B. MASON,
Colonel 1st Dragoons, Governor of California.

JAS. W. WEEKS,
Alcalde, Pueblo de San José.

The following named Indians of the mission of San Buenaventura, viz: Bernabi, Platon, Equicio, Mateo, Manano, and Pio, having represented that one José Moraga has prohibited them from planting and sowing on certain lands of said mission, which they have satisfactorily shown that they have resided on and cultivated for a number of years; this, therefore, is to authorize the said Indians to continue to reside on and cultivate said lands until the above mentioned José Moraga can show a legal right to dispossess them.

Done in Monterey, the capital of California, this 7th day of January, A. D. 1848, and of the independence of the United States the 72d.

R. B. MASON,
Colonel 1st Dragoons, Governor of California.

HEADQUARTERS TENTH MILITARY DEPARTMENT,
Monterey, California, January 9, 1848.

SIR: I have to acknowledge the receipt of your letter of the 31st of December, and its enclosure, showing a statement of Don Pedro's account for salary received as collector of the customs at Santa Barbara during a part of the year 1847.

I herewith transmit to you a copy of his account for the 2d quarter of the last year. By referring to Lieutenant Halleck's letter of the 26th of August, you will find that $5 for printing blanks was disallowed, which would make $90 27 that Don Pedro has been overpaid.

You must be held accountable for this overpayment, and pay the amount to Lieutenant Carnes, acting assistant quartermaster, and look to Don Pedro to reimburse you.

No returns are required under the instructions given previous to the reception of those from Washington.

All manifests, permits to lands, &c., should be carefully preserved, in case they should be called for.

I am, respectfully, your obedient servant,

R. B. MASON,
Colonel 1st Dragoons, Governor of California.

Captain F. J. LIPPETT,
New York Volunteers, commanding, Santa Barbara.

HEADQUARTERS TENTH MILITARY DEPARTMENT,
Monterey, California, January 10, 1848.

GENTLEMEN: Your communication of the 26th of December did not come to hand until last evening.

It is not within the province of my power to reverse the decision made by Commodore Shubrick in relation to the duties on the lumber brought into the port of San Francisco by the English barque Janet, which decision was enclosed to you in a letter of the 11th of October, by Lieutenant Halleck.

I am, respectfully, your obedient servant,

R. B. MASON,
Colonel 1st Dragoons, Governor of California.

Messrs. E. & H. GRIMES, *San Francisco.*

HEADQUARTERS TENTH MILITARY DEPARTMENT,
Monterey, California, January 10, 1848.

SIR: The making out of my custom-house accounts for the last quarter has brought the subject of accounts, the manner of making them, and the channel of transmittal to the War Department, more immediately to my attention than I before had time to give to the subject.

The regulations on the subject of the kind of accounts required are not very clear, except as to the making and transmittal of the monthly and weekly statements mentioned in the fifteenth article. From the letters of the Secretaries of War and Navy of April 3d, I infer that it is proper that all the accounts of the custom-house officers should be transmitted through this office for "approval" before going to the Secretary of War.

The Secretary of the Navy, in his letter, directs such a course in relation to the commodore and his officers; and the Secretary of War, in his, says "that the general instructions in the Naval Secretary's letter are applicable to the officers and persons connected with each branch of the public service." Nothing is said about quarterly accounts, though they must necessarily be made.

Your monthly and quarterly accounts to the Secretary of War will, therefore, be transmitted through these headquarters; and as I shall be able to obtain from them, before sending them off, all the information I require, you need make no copies for this office. Should you have sent off your accounts for the last quarter before this reaches you, send me a copy. I have given similar instructions to all the custom-house officers south of this, and furnished them with a form for their quarterly accounts current, and herewith send you a copy.

No returns are required from the custom-house, under instructions given previous to the reception of these printed ones from Washington, except the abstract of disbursements.

I am, respectfully, your obedient servant,
R. B. MASON,
Colonel 1st Dragoons, commanding.

Captain J. L. FOLSOM,
Assistant Quartermaster, San Francisco.

CIRCULAR.

HEADQUARTERS TENTH MILITARY DEPARTMENT,
Monterey, California, January 10, 1848.

A monthly statement of revenue collected, and a "quarterly account current," according to the "form" herewith sent, will be forwarded through these headquarters to the Secretary of War by the first mail that leaves your post after the end of each month and quarter to which they respectively refer. No copies of these accounts are required for this office, previous to the reception of these printed ones from Washington, except the abstract of disbursements.

R. B. MASON,
Colonel 1st Dragoons, Governor of California.

To the COLLECTORS
in the ports of California.

HEADQUARTERS TENTH MILITARY DEPARTMENT,
Monterey, California, January 10, 1848.

SIR: I enclose herewith a circular of this date, and the "form" of an account current, for the collector at San Pedro, which be pleased to forward to him as early as practicable. Examine and countersign his account at the close of each quarter. Impress upon him the importance of *promptness* and *correctness* in rendering and making out his accounts, and *punctuality* in paying over to you all money received from the customs, as soon as practicable after they come into his hands.

Enclosed also is the "form" of an account current for yourself in accounting for the funds received from the collectors at San Pedro and San Diego. This, with an abstract of disbursements, is, I believe, all the accounts that are required on account of the military contribution fund.

I am, respectfully, your obedient servant,
R. B. MASON,
Colonel 1st Dragoons, commanding.

Lieutenant J. W. DAVIDSON,
1st Dragoons, A. A. Quartermaster, Los Angeles.

HEADQUARTERS TENTH MILITARY DEPARTMENT,
Monterey, California, January 11, 1848.

GENTLEMEN: I beg leave to call your attention to my letter of the 29th of November last, and desire that the documents therein called for may be sent to this office by return mail.

I am, respectfully, your obedient servant,

R. B. MASON,
Colonel 1st Dragoons, Governor of California.

JOSE M. COVANUBIA and J. CARRILLO,
Santa Ynez.

HEADQUARTERS TENTH MILITARY DEPARTMENT,
Monterey, California, January 12, 1848.

SIR: I must call your attention to your want of correctness in making out your papers. In your monthly statement of revenue received for November, under the head of "date of arrival," instead of recording the *year* and *day of the month*, you write No. 1, No. 5, No. 27, opposite the names of vessels. Great care should be bestowed in examining papers, and seeing that they are correct in every particular before sending them off. The want of care and attention in this respect causes much delay and trouble at these headquarters.

In your letter of the 17th December you say, "private Stockton, mentioned above, bought $400 worth of comestibles, which he swore to me, on oath, were for his own private use, and not intended for resale. On the rest of his bill he paid duties regularly." The custom-house officers must not look to, nor have any transaction with, the purchasers of goods in collecting the duties; they must look to and collect the duties only from the owner or consignee.

Mr. Millens, not long since, presented a bill here for the payment of some articles purchased for the custom-house at San Diego—if my memory serves me right, by Don Pedro; please ask him what he did with the articles.

I am, respectfully, your obedient servant,

R. B. MASON,
Colonel 1st Dragoons, Governor of California.

Lieutenant H. S. CARNES,
New York Volunteers, Santa Barbara.

Know all men by these presents, that I, Richard B. Mason, colonel 1st regiment of dragoons United States army, and governor of California, by virtue of authority in me vested, do hereby appoint William R. Longley a second alcalde for the town and district of Monterey.

Done at Monterey, the capital of California, this thirteenth day of January, anno Domini eighteen hundred and forty-eight, and the seventy-second of the independence of the United States.

R. B. MASON,
Colonel 1st Dragoons, Governor of California.

HEADQUARTERS TENTH MILITARY DEPARTMENT,
Monterey, California, January 14, 1848.

SIR: I have received your letter of the 12th instant, and given it due consideration. It appears that the master of the Mary Ann had put on board of his vessel, the day before he landed the goods, the law concerning the permit to land; and if he did not regard it, he has no one to blame but himself. If these goods are released, it will be establishing an improper precedent, and one that will give us an infinite deal of trouble in future.

It is therefore not in my power to revoke what Captain Folsom has done in the matter.

Very respectfully, your obedient servant,
R. B. MASON,
Colonel 1st Dragoons, Governor of California.
Captain JNO. PATTY,
Monterey.

HEADQUARTERS TENTH MILITARY DEPARTMENT,
Monterey, California, January 14, 1848.

SIR: I am in the receipt of your letter of the 10th instant, asking for the grant of a lot, No. 188, to Mr. John Illig.

I do not feel that I possess the authority or power to make grants of land, under any circumstances, to individuals, and more especially where the land has been reserved for public uses.

I am, respectfully, your obedient servant,
R. B. MASON,
Colonel 1st Dragoons, Governor of California.
G. P. JONES, Esq.,
San Francisco.

HEADQUARTERS TENTH MILITARY DEPARTMENT,
Monterey, California, January 18, 1848.

SIR: I herewith enclose to you a copy of the papers which I have received from Mr. James W. Weeks, the alcalde at the Pueblo de San José, bearing date December 31, 1847, and January 12, 1848. From these papers you will see the propriety of my suspending the appointment you hold as a surveyor of land for and in the southern department of Upper California, and it is accordingly hereby suspended. You will, therefore, survey no more lands under the authority of that appointment, until you refute the charges mentioned in the said enclosed papers; and you are hereby required to appear without any unnecessary delay before the alcalde at the Pueblo de San José, for the purpose of answering to the said charges. You will please acknowledge the receipt of this letter, which I transmit to the alcalde at the Ciudad de los Angeles for delivery to you.

I am, respectfully, your obedient servant,
R. B. MASON,
Colonel 1st Dragoons, Governor of California.
JAMES D. HUTTON,
Land Surveyor, Southern Department, Upper California.

HEADQUARTERS TENTH MILITARY DEPARTMENT,
Monterey, California, January 18, 1848.

SIR: Your communication of the 12th instant, together with the deposition of Mr. Lyman of the 31st December, concerning the survey of Mr. Hutton, has been received.

It is proper to remark that Mr. H. had no appointment of surveyor at the time he surveyed the pueblo lands. His appointment of surveyor in the southern department bears date October 20, 1847.

I herewith transmit to you a copy of a letter I have this day written to Mr. Hutton, commanding him to appear before you to answer to the charges made against him.

I am, respectfully, your obedient servant,
R. B. MASON,
Colonel 1st Dragoons, Governor of California.

JAMES W. WEEKS,
  Alcalde, Pueblo de San José.

HEADQUARTERS TENTH MILITARY DEPARTMENT,
Monterey, California, January 18, 1848.

SIR: I request that you will inquire for Mr. James D. Hutton, and safely convey to him the package to his address, herewith enclosed. Should he be in or near Los Angeles, I desire that you will hand it to him in person.

Be pleased to inform me of the time when this package is delivered to Mr. Hutton.

I am, respectfully, your obedient servant,
R. B. MASON,
Colonel 1st Dragoons, Governor of California.

STEPHEN C. FOSTER,
  Alcalde, Cuidad de los Angeles.

HEADQUARTERS TENTH MILITARY DEPARTMENT,
Monterey, California, January 19, 1848.

SIR: I have received your letter of the 13th instant, enclosing the deed to the property purchased by Mr. Ricud, in which is asked my approval of your judicial decree relating thereto. This approval I cannot give, as real estate cannot be sold so long as there is movable property to satisfy the debts, or a part thereof; nor can the executor or heirs sell the fee simple title to land, when no such title was held by the deceased person himself; and when sold, it should always be sold to the highest and best bidder, after due notice of the time, place, and terms of sale being given.

I am, respectfully, your obedient servant,
R. B. MASON,
Colonel 1st Dragoons, Governor of California.

JAMES W. WEEKS,
  Alcalde, Pueblo de San José.

Know all men by these presents, that I, Richard B. Mason, colonel 1st regiment dragoons, and governor of California, by virtue of authority in me vested, do hereby appoint ―――― second alcalde for and in the town and jurisdiction of Ciudad de los Angeles.

Given at Monterey, the capital of California, the 22d day of January, A. D. 1847, and the 72d of the independence of the United States.

R. B. MASON,
Colonel 1st Dragoons, Governor of California.

HEADQUARTERS TENTH MILITARY DEPARTMENT,
Monterey, California, January 24, 1848.

SIR: Your letter of the 14th instant, transmitting your custom-house accounts for the War Department, is received. I examined them and found them correct, and have endorsed the account current and abstract of expenditure as follows: "Examined and approved. Monterey, January 23, 1848."

The form of the account current that I sent you with the circular of the 10th instant was not altogether correctly made. Make them in future as you have the one above mentioned for the Secretary of War; and I would suggest that you take your vouchers in triplicate, to guard against the many accidents that might befall them before reaching Washington. Let the caption of your account current read as follows: "The United States in account current with Lieutenant H. S. Carnes, New York volunteers, acting assistant quartermaster, on account of the military contribution fund derived from customs at the port of Santa Barbara, California."

I am, respectfully, your obedient servant,
R. B. MASON,
Colonel 1st Dragoons, Governor of California.

Lieutenant H. S. CARNES,
New York Volunteers, Acting Assistant Quartermaster,
Santa Barbara.

HEADQUARTERS TENTH MILITARY DEPARTMENT,
Monterey, California, January 24, 1848.

SIR: I have received your letter of 18th instant. You are right about the account current, &c. Continue to make them out as heretofore—though I do not see the necessity of making two accounts current, as you did for the fourth quarter of last year. I think one all-sufficient if supported by two abstracts of expenditures—one on account of the custom-house proper, and the other for the usual civic expenditures. I shall send no papers involving a pecuniary responsibility to Washington, unless put up in an *official mail*, and intrusted to a responsible bearer of despatches, as I am aware of the many accidents that might befall them, and would therefore suggest the propriety of taking vouchers in *triplicate*.

I am certain that an endorsement by me on the accounts of the expenditures of the funds derived from the customs, to this effect, "examined and approved," would go far to pass them at the War Department—

they do not go to the treasury. These accounts, upon reaching me, will always be acknowledged, and a copy of my remarks thereon furnished the disbursing officer. Should there be any vouchers requiring explanation, there will always be time to obtain it before an opportunity offers of sending it to Washington.

The caption of your account current would be better according to the following form:

"The United States in account current with Captain J. L. Folsom, assistant quartermaster, on account of the military contribution fund derived from customs at the port of San Francisco, California."

I am, respectfully, your obedient servant,
R. B. MASON,
Colonel 1st Dragoons, Governor of California.

Captain J. L. Folsom,
Assistant Quartermaster, San Francisco.

Headquarters Tenth Military Department,
Monterey, California, January 24, 1848.

Sir: I made an error in the form of the account current sent you and Mr. Alexander in my letter of the 10th instant. Make your account current as heretofore, and head it "the United States in account current with Lieutenant J. W. Davidson, acting assistant quartermaster, on account of the military contribution fund derived from customs at the ports of San Pedro and Santa Barbara, California." I would suggest that you take your vouchers in *triplicate*, to guard against the many accidents that might befall those sent to Washington.

I am, respectfully, your obedient servant,
R. B. MASON,
Colonel 1st Dragoons, commanding.

Lieutenant J. W. Davidson,
1st Dragoons, Acting Assistant Quartermaster, Los Angeles.

Headquarters Tenth Military Department,
Monterey, California, January 24, 1848.

Sir: I made an error in the form of the account current sent you with the circular of the 10th instant. Make the account current as heretofore, and head it as follows:

"The United States in account current with D. W. Alexander, on account of the military contribution fund derived from customs at the port of San Pedro, California."

I would suggest that you take your vouchers in triplicate, to guard against the many accidents that might befall those sent to Washington.

I am, respectfully, your obedient servant,
R. B. MASON,
Colonel 1st Dragoons, Governor of California.

D. W. Alexander,
Collector, &c., San Pedro.

HEADQUARTERS TENTH MILITARY DEPARTMENT,
Monterey, California, January 24, 1848.

SIR: The form of the account current sent to you with the circular of the 10th instant was not altogether correct. Make your account current after the form herewith enclosed. I would suggest that you take your vouchers in triplicate, to guard against the many accidents that might befall those sent to Washington.

I am, respectfully, your obedient servant,
R. B. MASON,
Colonel 1st Dragoons, commanding.

Lieutenant R. M. CLIFT,
Mormon Volunteers,
Acting Assistant Quartermaster, San Diego.

HEADQUARTERS TENTH MILITARY DEPARTMENT,
Monterey, California, January 24, 1848.

SIR: I have received your communication of the 11th instant and its enclosures. I approve of the course pursued by you in regulating the alcalde at Los Angeles.

Enclosed is the appointment for a second alcalde, with the name left blank for you to fill. I have not yet received from you the name of the person to fill the blank in the retained copy of the letter written to José Antonio Pico on the 24th of November last, and enclosed to you in my communication of the same date. Send up the name of the alcalde for whom blank appointments were sent to you on the 24th December.

Enclosed for your information is a letter received from Antonio Pico, which please return.

Very respectfully, your obedient servant,
R. B. MASON,
Colonel 1st Dragoons, commanding.

Colonel J. D. STEVENSON,
Commanding, &c., Los Angeles.

Know all men by these presents, that I, Richard B. Mason, colonel 1st regiment dragoons United States army, and governor of California, by virtue of authority in me vested, do hereby appoint John Price alcalde for and in the jurisdiction of San Luis Obispo.

Done at Monterey, the capital of California, the 25th day of January, A. D. 1848, and in the 72d year of the independence of the United States.
R. B. MASON,
Colonel 1st Dragoons, Governor of California.

HEADQUARTERS TENTH MILITARY DEPARTMENT,
Monterey, California, January 25, 1848.

SIR: I have received your communication of the 17th instant, and enclose herewith an appointment of alcalde for Mr. John Price.

I send this appointment not on account of the election that was held, for that was unauthorized.

I am, respectfully, your obedient servant,
R. B. MASON,
Colonel 1st Dragoons, Governor of California.

J. MARIA BONILLA,
San Luis Obispo, California.

HEADQUARTERS TENTH MILITARY DEPARTMENT,
Monterey, California, January 27, 1848.

SIR: In reply to your communication of the 22d instant, I have to say that the certificates of either of the special judges in the case of Armijo and others, as to the distance travelled by the witnesses and jurors, will be all-sufficient.

The consolidated account proposed to us by Messrs. Boggs & Vallejo would be the readiest way to settle those claims, if you think you could pass the voucher in that shape at Washington. I think you could not, as it is a rule there, I believe, never departed from, to pass no account without the receipt for the money from the claimant himself, or his authorized attorney.

I am, respectfully, your obedient servant,
R. B. MASON,
Colonel 1st Dragoons, commanding.

Captain J. L. FOLSOM,
Assistant Quartermaster, San Francisco.

[No. 31.]   HEADQUARTERS TENTH MILITARY DEPARTMENT,
Monterey, California, April 2, 1848.

SIR: I have the honor to enclose to you, herewith, department returns for the months of September, October, November, and December, 1847. These returns will exhibit the distribution of troops in the department to the end of last year, but since that time some changes have taken place.

The company of Mormons stationed at San Diego claimed and received their discharge on the 14th of March, 1848. Their place has been supplied by company "I," first New York volunteers. Company "D," of the same regiment, was detached on the 5th of March from Monterey to La Paz, to report to Lieutenant Colonel Burton, who it is believed will station it at San José. Lieutenant Colonel Burton's command was also strengthened by 114 recruits, so that it is believed he has at this time under his command 270 men. In order to avail myself of the services of Captain Naglee, I suspended him from the effects of his arrest, to await the action of the department upon the charges preferred against him, which were forwarded to you on the 2d of February last.

In my previous letters, I have detailed the steps adopted to raise volunteers upon the call of Commodore Shubrick, for the occupation of the city of Mazatlan, and to increase further the force in Lower California. My efforts thus far in Upper California have not resulted in getting any volunteers for that purpose. The Americans in this country alleged as a reason for their disinclination to volunteer, that they still remain unpaid for their services in the Fremont battalion, (see L. W. Hastings's letter, enclosed herewith,) and also that the wages are too small. I regard these rather as excuses than as reasons, and do not believe they would enlist even with better terms, unless on the occasion of an outbreak in Upper California. L. W. Hastings, esq., to whom I have offered the command of the battalion, if one is raised, is now on a tour among the American settlements on the Sacramento, but I must admit that I think his efforts will prove ineffectual.

Lieutenant Warner, of the topographical engineers, proceeded from here to Los Angeles, where he met Captain Hunt, of the old Mormon battalion, who was on the point of starting for the settlement at the Great Salt Lake. Hunt was of opinion that he could raise a battalion from among his people to serve in Upper California, but he was positive in his belief that they would not go to Lower California or Mazatlan. I have consented to receive three companies of Mormons, if they will hasten to San Francisco, so that I may detach the three companies of New York volunteers, now there, to the assistance of Lieutenant Colonel Burton. These cannot be looked for earlier than July next.

Major Hardie did not succeed in sailing for Oregon until the 3d of March, in the barque Anita, which was purchased by the quartermaster's department pursuant to my order. This barque is for the present under the command of acting master Woodworth, United States navy, who will bring the first detachment of volunteers that Major Hardie may succeed in forming in Oregon. I look for her return early in May, and shall despatch the volunteers at once to Mazatlan. Major Hardie is instructed to raise as many as 800 men, if he can do so, as I have almost relinquished all hopes of getting volunteers in California, or from the Mormons, in time to relieve the ships that will be compelled to leave Mazatlan as soon as the season of tempests sets in.

The expenses attending the calling into service of volunteers from Oregon will necessarily be heavy; and to be prepared to meet them, I have directed Captain Folsom, assistant quartermaster, and Captain Marcy, assistant commissary of subsistence, to get in California what specie they can, at par, by drafts on the quartermaster and commissary generals at Washington city. One year ago the scarcity of money was great here; and even at the Sandwich islands, specie could not be obtained on government drafts at less than 20 or 21 per centum discount. Now it is very different; there is little difficulty in negotiating small drafts at par. Major Rich, who returned from Mazatlan on the 29th of March, says he could have procured any amount of money, upon favorable terms, by drawing on the Paymaster General, so that no scarcity of funds is anticipated here. I am very much in want of disbursing officers; Captain Folsom is the only assistant quartermaster in the department, and I will be compelled to send Captain Marcy, the only assistant commissary, to Mazatlan, as disbursing officer there, for I do not regard it prudent to intrust any great amount of money into young and inexperienced hands, as will most likely be the case in selecting a volunteer subaltern for acting assistant quartermaster. I hope both an experienced quartermaster and paymaster are now on their way here. A paymaster in New York could pay troops in all the principal cities of Europe, and part of India, with more ease than one can pay in Upper and Lower California. Such is the difficulty of communication, Major Rich left this port on the 22d of October last to make a payment at La Paz, and did not return until the 29th of March. He was fortunate in getting back so soon, as the general probability was that he would have to return via the Sandwich islands.

I have the honor to be your obedient servant,
R. B. MASON,
Colonel 1st Dragoons, commanding.
ADJUTANT GENERAL U. S. ARMY,
Washington city, D. C.

[Extract.]

SAN FRANCISCO, *February* 13, 1848.

SIR: Your Excellency will, I hope, not deem it improper for me to remark that it will be difficult in the extreme to obtain the required number of volunteers, without having first paid them for their former services. I have been fully conversant with their views and determinations upon the subject ever since they were disbanded. Should public notice be given them to appear at a stated time and place for the purpose of being regularly mustered into and out of service, in order that they may receive the pay allowed them by law, there is no doubt but that all of the young men and many of the married men would receive their legal pay and re-enlist. This they would have done last spring, had the matter been properly explained to them; but they were assured by Colonel Fremont that if they accepted their legal pay, it would be a virtual relinquishment of all claims for further pay. It would be a great inducement for them to re-enlist if this proposition should be extended to those only who are willing to re-enter the service. Should they also be informed that the facts in reference to their re-enlisting should be fully represented at home, and that they would be just as likely to receive extra pay for their latter as for their former services, this would also afford an additional inducement.

I have the honor to be your Excellency's most obedient and humble servant,
L. W. HASTINGS.
His Excellency R. B. MASON.
Governor of California.

True extract from Mr. Hastings's letter on file in this office.
W. G. SHERMAN,
1st Lieutenant 3d Artillery, A. A. A. General
MONTEREY, *California, April* 17, 1848.

HEADQUARTERS TENTH MILITARY DEPARTMENT,
Monterey, California, April 15, 1848.

SIR: I herewith forward to you Captain Folsom's accounts of the military contribution fund, collected and disbursed in the port of San Francisco for the 2d, 3d, and 4th quarters of 1847, and for the 1st quarter of 1848; the accounts of Captain Marcy and myself for the 4th quarter of 1847, and the 1st quarter of 1848, collected and disbursed in Monterey, (my own for the 4th quarter of 1847 has already been forwarded;) the accounts of Lieutenant Davidson and Mr. Alexander for the 4th quarter of 1847, collected at San Pedro and disbursed at Los Angeles by Lieut. Davidson. I never have been able to get from the Mormon volunteer officer at San Diego any return at all of the military contribution fund collected at that port. But very little, however, has been received there. Not much commerce in that place. The paymaster has been instructed to withhold the officer's pay until he settles up.

I also enclose the accounts from San José and La Paz, Lower California. I beg leave to call your attention to that part of Lieutenant Colonel Burton's letter of the 14th of January (copy herewith enclosed) relating to the coasting trade. Pretty much the same thing exists here that he represents in Lower California, but not to the same extent, but sufficiently so to render it a matter of serious inconvenience and complaint on the part of the people along the coast, who cannot get their produce taken from port to port, the foreign vessels being excluded from the coasting trade, and the American vessels being too few in number. This state of things compels the people sometimes to pay as high as five dollars freight per barrel for sending the product of their vineyards a few hundred miles along the coast.

I am, very respectfully, your obedient servant,
R. B MASON,
Colonel 1st *Dragoons, commanding.*

Hon. SECRETARY OF WAR,
Washington city, United States.

LA PAZ, LOWER CALIFORNIA,
January 14, 1848.

SIR: I have the honor to transmit herewith the accounts of the collectors of La Paz and San José, Lower California, for the second and third quarters of 1847, and the accounts of the late collector of La Paz for part of the fourth quarter 1847; also my accounts with the civil government for the third and fourth quarters 1847. No accounts from the port of San José have been received, the disturbance in the country preventing it. The accounts for the second and third quarters 1847 from San José are in conformity to the first forms received from Monterey.

I request further instructions respecting the coasting trade in the Gulf of California. It has been carried on heretofore by small vessels and launches owned in the country. There are no American vessels to take their places; and if the instructions lately received are enforced, there will be no trade, and the American government will be a curse rather than a blessing to the country. The circumstances are such, that permission has been given to carry on this trade in the usual manner until further instructions can be received.

Surgeon Perry is now discharging the duties of collector for this port, and Lieutenant Haywood, United States navy, those of the port of San José.

In a commercial point of view, San José is a more important place than La Paz. It is near to Cape St. Lucas, and frequently visited by whale ships and other vessels bound to the Mexican coast. It has no harbor, and in some seasons of the year it is impossible to land upon its beach. La Paz is too far distant from the track of foreign vessels trading with the Mexican ports to enjoy the full advantages of its fine harbor. In time La Paz may be of some importance as a port of deposite and exchange, and is by far the best location for the capital of this country.

I am, sir, with much respect, your obedient servant,
HENRY S. BURTON,
Lieutenant Colonel New York Volunteers.
His Excellency Col. R. B. MASON,
U. S. Army, Governor of the Californias.

HEADQUARTERS TENTH MILITARY DEPARTMENT,
Monterey, California, January 28, 1848.

SIR: From intelligence received here yesterday from Commodore Shubrick, commanding the United States naval forces off Mazatlan—a copy of his communication is enclosed herewith—I deem it of the utmost importance to raise a corps of one thousand men to send to Lower California and Mazatlan, as early as practicable. I shall, therefore, despatch an officer—Major Hardie, of the army—to confer with your Excellency, and, if possible, to raise in Oregon an infantry battalion of four companies to be mustered into the service of the United States, to serve during the war, unless sooner discharged; or if it be impracticable to engage them for that period, then to engage them for twelve months from the time of being mustered into service, unless sooner discharged. The battalion will consist of—

Field and staff.—1 major; 1 adjutant—a lieutenant of one of the companies, but not in addition.

Non-commissioned staff.—1 sergeant major; 1 quartermaster's sergeant.
Four companies, each of which to consist of—
1 captain;
1 first lieutenant;
2 second lieutenants;
4 sergeants;
4 corporals;
2 musicians; and
100 privates.

Should the number of privates, on being mustered, not fall below sixty-four effective men in a company, it will be received.

In the United States the volunteer officers are appointed and commissioned in accordance with the laws of the States from whence they are taken: the officers from Oregon will therefore, of course, be appointed pursuant to the laws of Oregon, if there are any on that subject; and if not, in such manner as your Excellency may direct; in which case I would respectfully suggest that the company officers be elected by their respective companies, and that the major be appointed by yourself; and I would further respectfully suggest the extreme importance to the public service that the officers be judiciously selected.

The place of rendezvous for the several companies, as fast as they shall be organized, is necessarily left to yourself and Major Hardie.

The battalion will be inspected and mustered into service by Major Hardie, of the United States army, who will in every case be instructed to receive no man who is in years apparently over forty-five, or under eighteen, or who is not of physical strength and vigor. To this end the inspector will be accompanied by a medical gentleman, and the volunteers will be submitted to his examination. It is respectfully suggested that public notice of these requirements will prevent much disappointment to the zealous and patriotic citizens of Oregon who may be disposed to volunteer.

It may be proper to remark, that the law provides for the clothing (in money) and subsistence of the non-commissioned officers, musicians, and privates of volunteers who are received into the service of the United States.

In respect to clothing, the law requires that the volunteers shall furnish their own clothing, for which purpose it allows to each non-commissioned officer, musician, and private three dollars and fifty cents per month during the time he shall be in the service of the United States. In order that the volunteers who shall be mustered into service under this requisition may be enabled to provide themselves with good and sufficient clothing, the commutation allowance for six months (twenty-one dollars) will be allowed to each non-commissioned officer, musician, and private, after being mustered into service, but only with the express condition that the volunteer has already furnished himself with six months' clothing—this fact to be certified to the paymaster by the captain of the company—or that the amount thus advanced shall be applied, under the supervision of his captain, to the object contemplated by law. In this latter case the advance commutation for clothing will be paid on the captain's certificate that he is satisfied it will be so applied.

In respect to subsistence before arriving at the place of rendezvous, and for travelling home from the place of discharge, the allowance is fifty cents for every twenty miles distance.

The volunteers from Oregon will be discharged in California; or if they prefer it, they will be transported at the public expense back to the place of rendezvous.

I do not know how this call for volunteers will be met in Oregon, but I flatter myself with the assurance that it will receive the cordial support of your Excellency; and I am certain it will show that the citizens of Oregon have lost no patriotism by crossing the mountains, and that they will be equally prompt in coming to their country's standard as their brethren in the United States.

I am, respectfully, your obedient servant,

R. B. MASON,
Colonel 1st Dragoons, Governor of California.

To his Excellency GEORGE ABERNETHY,
Governor of Oregon.

HEADQUARTERS TENTH MILITARY DEPARTMENT,
Monterey, California, January 28, 1848.

SIR: From intelligence received here yesterday from Commodore Shubrick, who took Mazatlan on the 11th of November, it becomes of the greatest importance to send him a land force as early as practicable to enable the United States to hold that port and the ports of La Paz and San José, in Lower California, when the hurricane months (which commence in May) will oblige the fleet to leave that coast. Without the aid of this land force, the commodore writes that the United States flag at San José and Mazatlan will be hauled down. I am sure I can appeal with safety to the patriotism of the citizens of the United States in California to avert so unfortunate an occurrence.

I propose to raise in California an infantry battalion of at least three companies, with the least possible delay, and send them to the relief of our forces to the south.

The extracts from acts of Congress herewith enclosed, fully set forth the pay and allowances authorized by law; from which it will be seen distinctly what the law allows, and consequently any promise in the way of pay, &c. made by any one beyond that cannot be fulfilled. I am thus particular in order to prevent any expectation being created which cannot be realized, and which will result in disappointment.

I am desirous that the battalion should be engaged to serve during the war unless sooner discharged. If it cannot be engaged for that period, then for twelve months from the date of being mustered into service, unless sooner discharged. The companies to compose this battalion will rendezvous at the Presidio barracks, San Francisco, as soon as each one is raised, there to be mustered into service, armed and equipped, and sent off by sea to the south.

The companies will be inspected and mustered into service by an officer of the United States army, who will be instructed in every case to receive no man who is in years apparently over forty-five or under eighteen, or who is not of physical strength and vigor. To this end the inspector will be accompanied by a medical officer of the army, and the volunteers will be submitted to his examination. It is respectfully suggested that public notice of these requirements will prevent much disappointment to the zealous and patriotic citizens who may be disposed to volunteer.

The companies to elect their own officers. The major to command the battalion will be appointed by myself.

The foregoing gives you my views and wishes, and puts you in possession of the facts which render it of the utmost importance to the interests of the United States that a corps of one thousand men should be promptly organized for service in the south. May I then call on you to raise a company of infantry, and bring it as early as practicable into service? I am sure that, under this pressing necessity, you will cordially undertake to raise a company, and that neither my appeal to your own patriotism, nor that of our countrymen, will be unavailing. I shall send as soon as practicable an officer to Oregon with a view of raising a battalion there, as also one to the Mormon settlement at the Great Salt Lake, where I have every reason to expect success.

I command the means to pay in cash all expenses authorized by law, without contracting debts on account of the government, so that the patriotic citizens of the United States, in this country, who come to its standard, need not fear of being met now with "government orders," "government papers," &c., signed by this, that, and the other individual, in the way of pay.

Enclosed is also the form of a roll for the enrolment of the men before being mustered into service, copies of which it would be well to send, as also copies of the acts relating to pay, to such persons at different places as would likely be more successful in raising men, if they would not join the company themselves.

When the proper number for a company is obtained, give notice for them to rendezvous on a named day at the Presidio barracks, San Francisco, where Captain Folsom, of the army, will muster and receive them into service, from which time their pay will commence.

You will observe, by the act of Congress approved January 18, 1846, that each man is entitled to fifty cents for every twenty miles from his place of residence to the place of rendezvous, and the same from the place of discharge back to his place of residence.

I am, respectfully, your obedient servant,
R. B. MASON,
Colonel 1st Dragoons, Governor of California.

GRANVILLE P. SWIFT,
HENRY L. FORD,
Sacramento Valley.
BLUEFORD K. THOMPSON,
Pueblo de San José.

P. S.—If you cannot engage in this business yourself, please turn these papers over to some one who can. The companies will be received from any one who will raise them.

R. B. MASON,
Colonel 1st Dragoons.

HEADQUARTERS TENTH MILITARY DEPARTMENT,
Monterey, California, January 28, 1848.

SIR: By the enclosed copy of a circular to G. P. Swift, H. L. Ford, and B. K. Thompson, you will see the effort I am making to raise an infantry battalion in California for service in the south. The command I beg leave to offer to you, with the rank of major, and which I hope you may find it to your interest to accept; if so, you will be commissioned and mustered into service as soon as the third company is received.

Upon your knowledge and extensive acquaintance with the immigrants in this country I rely greatly for aid and assistance in raising the corps, and assure you that it is all-important to use the utmost despatch, for when our flag has been once raised, *it must never be struck.* Should you not accept the command, still I hope you will give me the aid of your influence in raising the men.

I shall be pleased to receive your reply at your earliest convenience.

I am, respectfully, your obedient servant,
R. B. MASON,
Colonel 1st Dragoons, Governor of California.

L. W. HASTINGS, Esq.,
San Francisco.

HEADQUARTERS TENTH MILITARY DEPARTMENT,
Monterey, California, January 28, 1848.

SIR: From intelligence received here yesterday from Mazatlan, it becomes all-important to raise a strong force for service in that quarter with the greatest despatch. Commodore Shubrick has taken the place, but will not be able to hold it after the hurricane season in those seas sets in—say after May next.

I am therefore setting to work to raise one thousand men in Oregon, California, and from the settlement on the Great Salt Lake. The object of this letter is to solicit the aid of your influence in encouraging and supporting the effort of raising a battalion in California.

I am now much pressed for time, and cannot write more; but I have written fully on the subject to Mr. L. W. Hastings, to whom I refer you, and request that he will show you all that I have written.

I am, respectfully, your obedient servant,
R. B. MASON,
Colonel 1st Dragoons, Governor of California.
Mr. SAMUEL BRANNAN, *San Francisco.*

HEADQUARTERS TENTH MILITARY DEPARTMENT,
Monterey, California, February 1, 1848.

SIR: I have the honor herewith to forward to you the accounts and vouchers of the military contribution collected from the customs in this port and Santa Barbara during the fourth quarter of the last year.

The instructions for collecting and accounting for this fund were received here in October. Before that time the citizen collectors accounted to and settled their accounts with the assistant quartermasters, who kept the fund distinct from other public moneys, and appropriated it to such civil purposes as I directed.

I am, respectfully, your obedient servant,
R. B. MASON,
Colonel 1st Dragoons, Governor of California.
To the Hon. SECRETARY OF WAR, *Washington.*

HEADQUARTERS TENTH MILITARY DEPARTMENT,
Monterey, California, February 3, 1848.

I send a military command, under Lieutenant Ord, of the army, for the purpose of arresting two horse thieves and recovering the horses that are reported to have been stolen from the neighborhood of Santa Cruz and San José, and hid way in the mountains.

I desire that you will cause as many of the citizens as you can to turn out and go with Lieutenant Ord and assist in recovering the stolen horses and arresting the thieves. Some exertions must be made by the citizens themselves, as I send the military to aid the civil authorities in recovering their lost property and bring the rogues to condign punishment.

Very respectfully, your obedient servant,
R. B. MASON,
Colonel 1st Dragoons, Governor of California.
To the ALCALDES
at *Santa Cruz and Pueblo de San José.*

HEADQUARTERS TENTH MILITARY DEPARTMENT,
Monterey, California, February 5, 1848.

SIR: I desire that you will confer with Padre José Prudencia Santillan, the minister of San Francisco and San Rafael, with the view of ascertaining if there be any lands appertaining to those missions which are not claimed by others, and which can be put in possession of Padre Santillan for the cultivation and use of the Indians of said mission.

It would be well for you, in company with the padre, to visit those missions, and, from actual observation, to possess yourself of all the necessary information as to what lands can be appropriated for the use of the Indians, without conflicting with other claimants. Not that I think any of the claims to the mission lands purporting to have been derived from Pio Pico in the last days of his authority can ever hold good, but that the time to investigate them has not yet arrived.

Learn, also, what movable property there is belonging to those missions, and in whose possession it is, that can be appropriated to the use of said Indians; and require them to give an inventory of the same, and hold it in readiness to be delivered up when I call for it.

After obtaining all the information, make a report to me, touching the quantity of land property, &c., that can be made available for the Indians.

I have the honor to be your obedient servant,

R. B. MASON,
Col. 1st Dragoons, Governor of California.

To the COMMANDING OFFICER,
San Francisco.

HEADQUARTERS TENTH MILITARY DEPARTMENT,
Monterey, California, February 7, 1848.

SIR: The long time that has elapsed since your return to California, and your non-arrival in Monterey, has given rise to rumors which create an excitement in the public mind, and has a tendency to disturb the tranquillity that happily has prevailed so long in California. Your presence in Monterey will quiet these rumors, so far as your name is connected with them, for I will frankly tell you, that I am informed there is a revolution in contemplation, with which it is said you are connected.

I will not believe that in returning to California, as you do, under a passport from myself, promising you the friendly reception of the United States authorities here, you would in any way violate your honor, which the acceptance of that passport has pledged; therefore I hope to see you in Monterey at your earliest convenience.

I am, respectfully, your obedient servant,

R. B. MASON,
Colonel 1st Dragoons, Governor of California.

Colonel JOSE CASTRO.

HEADQUARTERS TENTH MILITARY DEPARTMENT,
Monterey, California, February 7, 1848.

GENTLEMEN: I have received your communication of the 29th January and its enclosures.

Herewith are returned the four receipts of Friar José I. Ximeno for the rent of Santa Ynez for the year 1846.

I am, respectfully, your obedient servant,

R. B. MASON,
Colonel 1st Dragoons, Governor of California.

Messrs. COBAMBIA & CORILLA, *Santa Ynez.*

HEADQUARTERS TENTH MILITARY DEPARTMENT,
Monterey, California, February 8, 1848.

SIR: Your letter of the 28th January is before me. I cannot find on the files of this office either your letter or that of the late collector at Santa Barbara, enclosing instructions* from Commodore Biddle, touching the five dollars expended for blank clearances, to which you refer.

Lieutenant Halleck's letter to you of the 26th of August directed the facts to be reported respecting said sum; but, at the same time, "definitively directed" that "this item be regarded as part payment of his salary for the last quarter."

The amount of customs in your hands, (on the 3d quarter's return of 1847 you report $303 36,) turn over to Lieutenant Carnes.

I enclose you the appointment for Don Pedro C. Carrillo and Don Estavan Ardisson. The alcaldes throughout all California are appointed by myself, and it must be the same at Santa Barbara. The interest of the public service imperatively demands this course during the continuance of the war; and besides which, the late election at Santa Barbara is not deemed to have been in accordance with the law, or the customs heretofore established.

The alcaldes thus appointed must be sustained in the proper execution of the duties of their office.

I should have been glad to have sent the appointment to Don Pedro, but you tell me he positively declines acting under an appointment from myself, &c.

I am, respectfully, your obedient servant,

R. B. MASON,
Colonel 1st Dragoons, Governor of California.

Captain F. J. LIPPETT,
New York Volunteers, commanding, Santa Barbara.

Know all men by these presents, that I, Richard B. Mason, colonel 1st regiment of dragoons United States army, and governor of California, by virtue of authority in me vested, do hereby appoint Pedro C. Carrillo first alcalde for and in the town and jurisdiction of Santa Barbara, Upper California.

Given at Monterey, the capital of California, this 8th day of February, A. D. 1848, and seventy-second year of the independence of the United States.

R. B. MASON,
Colonel 1st Dragoons, Governor of California.

---

* If Don Pedro has such instructions touching the printing of blanks, send me a copy.

Know all men by these presents, that I, Richard B. Mason, colonel 1st regiment of dragoons United States army, and governor of California, by virtue of authority in me vested, do hereby appoint Estavan Ardisson second alcalde for the town and jurisdiction of Santa Barbara, Upper California.

Given at Monterey, the capital of California, this 8th day of February, A. D. 1848, and the seventy-second year of the independence of the United States.

R. B. MASON,
Colonel 1st Dragoons, Governor of California.

HEADQUARTERS TENTH MILITARY DEPARTMENT,
Monterey, California, February 9, 1848.

SIR: The messenger you sent to me has just informed me of your near approach to this place, where you will probably arrive to-morrow morning.

Your communication of the 2d instant from San Luis Obispo did not reach me until yesterday at half-past one o'clock. On the 7th instant, I had the honor to address you a note, apprizing you of the many rumors that were in circulation here with which your name was connected, but I learn from your messenger that the bearer of that note took the Ojibos road, and thus failed to meet you.

I congratulate you upon your return to California, and hope you may long live to enjoy the society of your family and friends, and beg leave to assure you of the kind feelings with which the United States authorities will receive you in Monterey.

I am, respectfully, your obedient servant,
R. B. MASON,
Colonel 1st Dragoons, Governor of California.

Colonel JOSE CASTRO.

HEADQUARTERS TENTH MILITARY DEPARTMENT,
Monterey, California, February 9, 1848.

SIR: Not desiring to impose the duties of alcalde upon you contrary to your wishes, I have appointed Mr. Charles White in your place, that you might retire from the office in accordance with the wishes you expressed in your letter of the 28th December. I thank you for continuing in the discharge of the duties until I could make another appointment.

Be pleased to turn over to Mr. White all the funds, records, books, papers, &c., appertaining to the office.

Enclosed herewith is the appointment of 1st alcalde for Mr. White, and the appointment of 2d alcalde for Mr. Dolores Pacheco, which be pleased to hand to them.

I am, respectfully, your obedient servant,
R. B. MASON,
Colonel 1st Dragoons, Governor of California.

JAMES W. WEEKS,
Pueblo de San José.

HEADQUARTERS TENTH MILITARY DEPARTMENT,
Monterey, California, February 9, 1848.

SIR: I have this day enclosed to Mr. Weeks the appointment of 1st alcalde for yourself, and that of the 2d alcalde for Dolores Pacheco.

When you have entered on your duties, I would suggest that you and the 2d alcalde consult together and appoint some suitable person "town treasurer," whose duty it should be to receive all moneys appertaining to the pueblo, and to disburse the same upon the written order of the alcalde, taking care to require from the treasurer good and sufficient bonds for the faithful performance of his duties before he enters upon them, and requiring him to render quarterly accounts of all moneys coming into his hands, with the necessary vouchers for his disbursements, &c.

I am, respectfully, your obedient servant,
R. B. MASON,
Colonel 1st Dragoons, Governor of California.

Mr. CHARLES WHITE,
1st Alcalde, Pueblo de San José.

Know all men by these presents, that I, Richard B. Mason, colonel 1st regiment of dragoons United States army, and governor of California, by virtue of authority in me vested, do hereby appoint Charles White 1st alcalde for and in the jurisdiction of the Pueblo de San José, Upper California.

Given at Monterey, the capital of California, this 9th day of February, 1848, and the 72d year of the independence of the United States.
R. B. MASON,
Colonel 1st Dragoons, Governor of California.

Know all men by these presents, that I, Richard B. Mason, colonel 1st regiment of dragoons United States army, and governor of California, by virtue of authority in me vested, do hereby appoint Dolores Pacheco 2d alcalde for and in the jurisdiction of Pueblo de San José, Upper California.

Given at Monterey, the capital of California, this 9th day of February, A. D. 1848, and the 72d year of the independence of the United States.
R. B. MASON,
Colonel 1st Dragoons, Governor of California.

HEADQUARTERS TENTH MILITARY DEPARTMENT,
Monterey, California, February 10, 1848.

SIR: Your communication of the 31st ultimo, enclosing one from Timothy Murphy, alcalde, San Rafael, of the 27th ultimo, is received.

It is impossible for me to make any decision in the case of the prisoner,

Garcia, until I have received the record of the trial referred to, which you have kept, and which should have been sent with your application for instructions on the subject.

I am, respectfully, your obedient servant,
R. B. MASON,
Colonel 1st Dragoons, commanding.

JAS. A. HARDIE,
*Major 1st New York Volunteers,
or Officer Commanding, San Francisco.*

HEADQUARTERS TENTH MILITARY DEPARTMENT,
Monterey, California, February 11, 1848.

SIR: I have reflected well upon the paper you handed me yesterday, appealing from the verdict of a jury, which was rendered against you in the alcalde court at San José, on the 28th of January, in the case of a disputed account of work done by yourself and one Honn.

Neither the *record* nor any of the *facts* are before me, upon which the jury rendered that verdict, and it is therefore entirely out of my power to take any action in the case at all.

I am, respectfully, your obedient servant,
R. B. MASON,
Colonel 1st Dragoons, Governor of California.

Mr. GEORGE BELLAMY, *Present.*

HEADQUARTERS TENTH MILITARY DEPARTMENT,
Monterey, California, February 12, 1848.

SIR: In the case of Honn *vs.* Bellamy, recently tried by a jury in your court, I am called on by Bellamy, and asked to give instructions that he may have a new trial, &c.

I can give no instructions touching the case, because I have none of the facts before me, on which the jury rendered their verdict. Until such facts are before me in an official shape, it would be manifestly improper for me to act in the case.

I am, respectfully, your obedient servant,
R. B. MASON,
Colonel 1st Dragoons, Governor of California.

To the ALCALDE
of Pueblo de San José, California.

From and after this date, the Mexican laws and customs now prevailing in California, relative to the "denouncement" of mines, are hereby abolished.

The legality of the denouncements which have taken place, and the possession obtained under them since the occupation of the country by the United States forces, are questions which will be disposed of by the American government after a definitive treaty of peace shall have been established between the two republics.

Done at Monterey, the capital of California, this 12th day of February, A. D. 1848, and the seventy-second year of the independence of the United States.

R. B. MASON,
Colonel 1st Dragoons, Governor of California.

HEADQUARTERS TENTH MILITARY DEPARTMENT,
Monterey, California, February 14, 1848.

SIR: 1 have received your letter of the 6th instant on the subject of the confiscated goods. For the reasons stated in my communication of the 5th January to Captain Folsom, I think the War Department will allow a portion of your claim, but not under the regulation to which you refer, because that regulation applies *only* to such persons upon whose information, lodged with the custom-house officer, he is enabled to seize and confiscate goods, &c., for a violation of the revenue laws.

I am, respectfully, your obedient servant,

R. B. MASON,
Colonel 1st Dragoons, commanding.

Lieutenant E. GILBERT,
New York Volunteers, San Francisco.

HEADQUARTERS TENTH MILITARY DEPARTMENT,
Monterey, California, February 14, 1848.

SIR: The Quartermaster's department of the army has purchased the American barque Anita. I wish to despatch her with all possible haste to Oregon for the battalion of volunteers that I am in hopes to organize there for service at Mazatlan. It will greatly facilitate and promote the interests of the public service if you can spare an officer from your ship to take charge of her until a competent shipmaster can be employed. Acting master Woodworth has expressed his willingness to take command of the Anita if it meets your approbation. I hope you may be able to spare Mr. Woodworth, for I assure you that it is of the utmost importance that the troops should be sent to Mazatlan as soon as it is possible to get them there. I must ask the further favor of such facilities as you can afford from the Warren in despatching the Anita as early as practicable.

I am, respectfully, your obedient servant,

R. B. MASON,
Colonel 1st Dragoons, commanding.

Lieutenant J. LANMAN,
United States Navy, commanding ship Warren, Monterey.

HEADQUARTERS TENTH MILITARY DEPARTMENT,
Monterey, California, February 19, 1848.

SIR: Yours of the 26th ultimo is received, enclosing the copy of an application from Captain Baristain, of the Central American brig Conception, for permission to reload his vessel with the same cargo she arrived with on this coast, and depart for the windward ports, according to her original clearance.

The facts set forth in the application (which you state are known to be true) are satisfactory, and I cannot conceive any impropriety in acceding to his request. Your course, therefore, in permitting her to clear for this port without any additional charge, has my approval, as I think, under the circumstances of the case, it would be unjust to subject her to a second payment of duties on the same goods.

I am, respectfully, your obedient servant,
R. B. MASON,
Colonel 1st Dragoons, commanding.

Colonel J. D. STEVENSON,
Commanding Southern District, California.

P. S.—Enclosed is a letter for Lieutenant Clift, at San Diego. Please appoint some one to succeed him, and to receive all the books, papers, funds, records, &c., appertaining to the alcalde's office; and I will send him the appointment upon learning his name.
R. B. MASON,
Colonel 1st Dragoons.

HEADQUARTERS TENTH MILITARY DEPARTMENT,
Monterey, California, February 19, 1848.

SIR: Your resignation of the office of alcalde of San Diego, contained in your letter of the 6th instant, is hereby accepted. You will, therefore, turn over all books, papers, &c., appertaining to said office, to such person as Colonel Stevenson may direct.

I am, respectfully, your obedient servant,
R. B. MASON,
Colonel 1st Dragoons, commanding.

Lieutenant ROBERT CLIFT,
Mormon Volunteers,
Acting Assistant Quartermaster, San Diego.

HEADQUARTERS TENTH MILITARY DEPARTMENT,
Monterey, California, February 19, 1848.

SIR: Yours of the 31st ultimo, in which you make application for a wagon to assist you in making repairs, &c., on the mission farm at Pala, is received. I have to say, in reply, that it is not in my power to send you a wagon, as I have none here that can be spared from the daily wants of the service.

I am, respectfully, your obedient servant,
R. B. MASON,
Colonel 1st Dragoons, Governor of California.

Captain J. D. HUNTER, *Sub-Indian Agent, Los Angeles.*

HEADQUARTERS TENTH MILITARY DEPARTMENT,
Monterey, California, February 19, 1848.

SIR: I have received yours of the 9th instant in relation to the property belonging to the mission of San Buenaventura.

You are authorized to make at any time you may deem proper an investigation in the particular case you refer to, viz: that of José Ormoss, and for the correction of abuses which it is too evident exist in reference to these matters. You will at your earliest convenience examine into all the missions south of Santa Barbara, and adopt such measures as in your judgment you may think will best tend to the preservation of the missions, and the security or recovery of the property that may have been fraudulently disposed of; a report of which you will afterwards make and forward here.

I have so constantly on hand such a multiplicity of business, that I have not been able to take up the subject of the missions, nor to examine all the papers relative thereto which you sent me, and which were received on the 26th of November and 9th of December. They are herewith returned to you, as they will be useful in your investigation of the subject. The person in charge of the mission of San Gabriel sold not long since, to Juan Ramirez, of Los Angeles, a valuable still for something like $200. The still was worth four or five times that amount.

Very respectfully, your obedient servant,
R. B. MASON,
Colonel 1st Dragoons, commanding.

Colonel J. D. STEVENSON,
Commanding Southern Military District, California.

HEADQUARTERS TENTH MILITARY DEPARTMENT,
Monterey, California, February 19, 1848.

SIR: I have received yours of the 11th instant, with the enclosed papers signed by José Castro, giving to Nicholas Leopez, as a reward for his services, a house in the old Presidio of Santa Barbara.

As that paper bears date subsequent to the hoisting of the United States flag in California, it can, of course, give no right. Castro, it must be evident, had no authority at that time to make such grant, and this claim, if based on no other ground, must be considered null and void.

In answer to your second communication, (also of the 11th instant,) and addressed to acting assistant adjutant general, I have to direct that the remission of duties in such cases as you mention cannot be claimed, any more than they could be if soldiers were to purchase from a store in Santa Barbara.

I am, respectfully, your obedient servant,
R. B. MASON,
Colonel 1st Dragoons, commanding

Lieutenant H. S. CARNES,
1st New York Volunteers, A. A. Quartermaster, Santa Barbara

HEADQUARTERS TENTH MILITARY DEPARTMENT,
Monterey, California, February 19, 1848.

SIR: I have to acknowledge the receipt of your communication of the 8th instant, enclosing a letter from José Antonio Pico in relation to certain property belonging to the mission of San Luis Rey, and a copy of your letter of appointment as auxiliary alcalde to Don Ylano Morillo, San Antonio.

You will continue to act in accordance with the views expressed in the said communication, all of which meets with my entire approval.

I am, respectfully, your obedient servant,
R. B. MASON,
Colonel 1st Dragoons, commanding.

Colonel J. D. STEVENSON,
Commanding Southern Military District, California.

HEADQUARTERS TENTH MILITARY DEPARTMENT,
Monterey, California, February 21, 1848.

SIR: Yours of the 23d ultimo has been received, enclosing the custom-house accounts of the collector at San Pedro for the 4th quarter of 1847, for the Secretary of War; as also your own for the same quarter. I have endorsed them "examined and approved," and will forward them to Washington by the first opportunity that offers.

No allowance can be made to the collector at San Pedro for office rent, as it is supposed that his salary is sufficient to cover this.

I am, respectfully, your obedient servant,
R. B. MASON,
Colonel 1st Dragoons.

Lieutenant J. W. DAVIDSON,
1st Dragoons, A. A. Quartermaster, Los Angeles.

HEADQUARTERS TENTH MILITARY DEPARTMENT,
Monterey, California, February 21, 1848.

SIR: Your custom-house accounts for the 4th quarter of 1847, transmitted by Lieutenant J. W. Davidson, have been received. I have endorsed them "examined and approved," and will forward them by the first opportunity that offers, to the Secretary of War at Washington.

I am, respectfully, your obedient servant,
R. B. MASON,
Colonel 1st Dragoons, Governor of California.

D. W. ALEXANDER,
Collector, &c., San Pedro.

P. S.—You are referred to form five of the printed regulations from Washington for the proposed manner of filling up the "monthly statement of revenue collected." It is improper to add the words "on anchorage" to the printed one "penalties paid," and insert in the column under their head the sums collected for tonnage duties. You will see that this item is placed in a line lower, in the column of "duty paid," and opposite the name "tonnage duty" is the column of consignee.

R. B. M.

HEADQUARTERS TENTH MILITARY DEPARTMENT,
Monterey, California, February 21, 1848.

SIR: Upon an examination of the account of sales made by the barque Anita, at Santa Barbara, I find a great abuse of the thirteenth article of the tariff regulations has been practised. Mr. Green, the consignee, informs me, on his arrival at Santa Barbara, Lieutenant Huddart boarded the barque and reported himself as the custom-house officer, and instructed him to sell any amount to the soldiers for which they had the means of paying; that he (Green) informed the lieutenant that at Monterey the troops were limited in their purchases; to which the lieutenant replied, Let them have what they can pay for, or words to that effect. The thirteenth article of the tariff regulations *only permits* officers and soldiers to purchase free of duty such articles as are required *"for their own actual individual use and consumption, and not as merchandise for resale."*

I transmit herewith a copy of the account of sales made to some of the men of your company, including the citizen-doctor hired to attend your sick, amounting to $1,247 48. Now, it is self-evident that a private soldier does not want, "for his own actual individual use and consumption," hundreds of yards of merchandise, barrels of rum, and thousands of cigars," &c., &c., as is set forth in the account of sales; and under what regulation is a hired citizen, picked up in the country, entitled to purchase free of duty to the amount of three hundred and twenty-five and a half yards of merchandise, besides various articles not necessary "for his own *individual* use and consumption," even if he came within the class of persons mentioned in the thirteenth article of the tariff regulations? No citizen, picked up and hired at a certain post to perform duties at that post and nowhere else, and not subject to orders which would place him on a footing with an officer, can by any possible stretching or twisting of the regulations be brought within the aforesaid thirteenth article. Dr. Ord (who I suppose is now at your post) comes within the thirteenth article, because he is a citizen of the United States, was specially employed to come to California as a physician to the troops, is liable to be ordered from post to post, and in that respect stands upon the footing of an officer, and is therefore equitably entitled to the benefits of the thirteenth article, though in fact not an officer or soldier. You, I believe, were not at Santa Barbara at the time of this transaction, and I therefore hold the officer charged with the collection of the revenue during your absence, and whose duty it was to have looked into this matter and not have permitted this gross abuse to have been practised, accountable for the amount of duties that ought to have been collected on this account of sales. You will therefore require them to pay over at once the duties due, to yourself, which you will turn over to Lieutenant Carnes, as in the case of other revenue collected; and in future you will suffer no soldier to make any purchase, duty free, from any ship or vessel, except upon the *written permission* of the commanding officer of the post, which permission must specify *each particular article* that is purchased, or to be purchased, duty free. The commanding officer must guard the revenue, and be the judge of what is, and how much is, necessary for the "actual individual use and consumption" of the soldier. An unreasonable quantity of any article cannot be purchased free of duty under the plea of its being for the "individual use and consumption" of the soldier; nor are spirituous or other liquors to be purchased from vessels by soldiers on any account. No clubbing together to make purchases should be tolerated: each man must buy on his own account for his own use, not to be transferred to another in way of sale. All proper articles, and in reasonable quantities, the soldier can freely purchase free of duty. The copy of the account of sales, before mentioned, plainly shows how loudly these stringent instructions are called for.

Lieutenant Carnes, in his letter of the 17th December, says that Stockton made oath before him that $400 of his purchase was "comestibles," and for his own use, and that *he paid* the duties on the balance of his bill. Even if they were "comestibles," the amount was *unreasonable*, and therefore liable to duties. The custom-house officer looks *to the seller* of the goods, and *not to the purchaser*, for the duties.

The account of sales to Stockton does not corroborate his statement on oath.

I transmit herewith the copy of a letter which appears to have been written by one of the men of your company to Sergeant Hesswood, of company B, a paragraph of which deeply affects the standing of Lieutenant Huddart, if true. This and other things mentioned in it require your notice and attention, especially the breaking up of the gambling and grog-shops said to be set up by Mason, Donelly, and Robertson. This you will *do at once*, and *do it effectually*. I have through many channels very unfavorable accounts of your company. I was told not long since, by a highly respectable shipmaster and citizen of the United States, that "the conduct of the volunteers at Santa Barbara was a disgrace to their country." I use his words.

I am, respectfully, your obedient servant,
R. B. MASON,
Col. 1st Dragoons, commanding.

Capt. F. J. LIPPETT,
New York Volunteers, commanding, Santa Barbara.

HEADQUARTERS TENTH MILITARY DEPARTMENT,
Monterey, California, February 22, 1848.

CAPTAIN: I have received a letter from Ira Johnson, of your company, asking for an order to the collector at San Pedro to release certain articles purchased from the captain of the ship Charles, which had been stopped there for the duties. Upon examination of the account of sales of the ship, made by Mr. Carter, I find that twenty men of your company, of whom Johnson was one, clubbed together and purchased the following articles:

240 caps, at 50 cents each	$120 00
24 pairs of boots, at $4 per pair	96 00
60 pairs of brogans, at $2 25 per pair	129 00
160 shirts, at $1 each	160 00
Total	505 00
Upon which, for duties, a deduction of twenty per cent. was made	101 00
	404 00

By reference to the tariff regulations, you will see that, by the 13th article, neither officers nor soldiers are allowed to buy any article free of duty, except "for their own actual individual use and consumption," and not as merchandise for resale. Now, as the above purchases are far beyond a reasonable allowance for the wants of twenty men, I shall require them to pay duty on

200 caps, at 50 cents each	$100 00
4 pairs of boots, at $4 per pair	16 00
20 pairs of brogans, at $2 25 per pair	45 00
40 shirts, at $1 each	40 00
	201 00
Amount of duties	40 20

which amounts to forty dollars and twenty cents. I shall instruct the collector to release the articles upon the payment of that amount of duties. This allows to each man, free of duty, two caps, one pair of boots, two pairs of brogans, and six shirts, and that is a liberal allowance for their "own actual individual use," as contemplated by the regulations.

Now that you are "ex-officio" collector at San Diego, you will permit the men of your command to purchase, free of duty, from vessels importing goods into California, such articles as they may require "for their own actual individual use and consumption, and not intended for resale," of which you must be the judge; for, while full justice is done to the men, the revenue must be guarded.

The following articles were purchased by the above mentioned twenty men, on which the duties have been paid:

Two shirts, one hundred and twenty pairs of shoes, six thousand cigars.

I have the honor to be your obedient servant,

R. B. MASON,
Colonel 1st Dragoons, commanding.

Captain W. E. SHANNON,
New York Volunteers, commanding, San Diego.

NOTE.—Two hundred and forty caps divided among twenty men, would give twelve to each man. Each man did not require twelve caps "for his own actual individual use," for which purpose he alone could purchase free of duty.

HEADQUARTERS TENTH MILITARY DEPARTMENT,
Monterey, California, February 22, 1848.

SIR: Private Ira Johnson, of the New York volunteers, has written to me on the subject of certain goods of his, detained by you in the custom-house of San Pedro.

I have made an examination of the matter, and find that on those articles, which were purchased at this port from the supercargo of the ship Charles, duties have been paid in part, but that there is still due on them $40 20.

You will therefore, upon the payment of this sum, release the goods you have properly detained.

I am, respectfully, your obedient servant,
R. B. MASON,
Colonel 1st Dragoons, Governor of California.

D. W. ALEXANDER,
Collector, &c., San Pedro.

HEADQUARTERS TENTH MILITARY DEPARTMENT,
Monterey, California, February 22, 1848.

SIR: I have received your letter of the 9th instant. I regret that it is not in my power at present to cause the accounts created by Colonel Fremont to be paid. I am daily expecting instructions concerning those claims. Should I receive them, I will lose no time in taking such steps towards them as my orders may require of me.

I am, respectfully, your obedient servant,
R. B. MASON,
Colonel 1st Dragoons, commanding.

Mr. ANTONIO JOSE COT,
Pueblo de los Angeles, California.

HEADQUARTERS TENTH MILITARY DEPARTMENT,
Monterey, California, February 22, 1848.

SIR: On the next page you will find the copy of a letter of the 12th instant from E. and H. Grimes, citizens of the United States, asking to import free of duty a threshing machine, to be used on their rancho, up the Sacramento.

From the last paragraph of the Secretary of War's letter to General Scott of the 3d of April, 1846, (a misprint—it should be 1847,) and the second paragraph of the one to General Taylor of September 22, 1846, (see both in the printed tariff regulations from Washington,) I think this a case that comes within the discretion therein given; and, besides, the more wheat there is grown in California, and the more facilities that can be given to prepare it for the mill, the cheaper we can get flour for the troops. You are therefore authorized to allow the Messrs. Grimes to enter the threshing machine free of duty.

I am, respectfully, your obedient servant,
R. B. MASON,
Colonel 1st Dragoons, commanding.

Captain J. L. FOLSOM,
Assistant Quartermaster U. S. Army, San Francisco.

HEADQUARTERS TENTH MILITARY DEPARTMENT,
Monterey, California, February 28, 1848.

SIR: I am in the receipt of your letter of the 16th instant and its enclosure.

By reference to the tariff regulations, you will find that the third article has already been so modified as to authorize the coastwise cargo to be free of duties if of the growth, &c. of California, and free of the coastwise duties thereon imposed, with the further modification of permitting vessels under foreign flags, owned in California, to engage in the coast trade. This is going as far as I can go, and perhaps further than I shall be justified in going, in setting aside the instructions of the President, without having first referred the subject to the department, as I shall do in the case you present.

I am, respectfully, your obedient servant,
R. B. MASON,
Colonel 1st Dragoons, commanding.

Colonel J. D. STEVENSON,
Commanding S. M. District, Los Angeles.

HEADQUARTERS TENTH MILITARY DEPARTMENT,
Monterey, California, February 28, 1848.

SIR: Your letter of the 19th instant is received. You made no return at the end of the fourth quarter of the last year, showing the disposition of the $303 36 reported on hand at the end of the third quarter, nor of the revenue collected and turned over to Lieutenant Carnes during the fourth quarter of 1847, (see last paragraph of article 7, and of second paragraph of article 14, of the printed tariff regulations from Washington.) These regulations make it *Lieutenant Carnes's duty to ascertain* the amount of duties that are to be paid. *You* receive them from the captain or consignee, and pay them over the next day to Lieutenant Carnes. You then must make quarterly returns, accompanied by Lieutenant Carnes's receipts, and a monthly statement of the revenue received. Lieutenant Carnes must also make the like quarterly returns, accompanied by the monthly statements, in order to show the amount that comes into his hands, and how it has been disbursed.

You will give this matter your early attention, and forward to this office an account current for the fourth quarter of 1847.

I am, respectfully, your obedient servant,
R. B. MASON,
Colonel 1st Dragoons, commanding.

Captain F. J. LIPPETT,
New York Volunteers, commanding, Santa Barbara.

HEADQUARTERS TENTH MILITARY DEPARTMENT,
Monterey, California, February 28, 1848.

SIR: Captain Lippett informs me that $313 36, the amount of customs being in his hands at the end of the third quarter of 1847, was turned over to you on the day it was received, and that he holds your receipt for the same.

In examining your account current for the fourth quarter of 1847, I cannot find that you have taken up this sum; and as Captain Lippett has rendered no account for the fourth quarter, I have nothing to show what disposition has been made of it.

A further discrepancy seems manifest from this examination. As you make no return of revenue received for October, I know not whether anything was paid in for that month, but suppose there was not; then from the " monthly statement of revenue received" for November and December, which were forwarded to this office, your account should stand thus:

Received from Carrillo	$4 00
As per monthly statement for November	565 49
Do do do for December	75 87
From Captain Lippett	303 36
Total to be accounted for	948 72
Deduct abstract of disbursements	70 62½
Amount due to the government	878 09½
Reported in account current for fourth quarter as due government	578 57½
Error	299 52

You will therefore take up this error, and charge yourself with the amount, $299 52, on the account current for the first quarter of the present year.

I am, respectfully, your obedient servant,
R. B. MASON,
Colonel 1st Dragoons, commanding.

Lieut. H. S. CARNES,
New York Volunteers,
Acting Asssistant Quartermaster, Santa Barbara.

Know all men by these presents, that I, Richard B. Mason, colonel 1st regiment of dragoons United States army, and governor of California, by virtue of authority in me vested, do hereby appoint John Sinclair alcalde for and in the district of country on the Sacramento river, near New Helvetia, Upper California.

Given at Monterey, the capital of California, this 28th day of November, A. D. 1848, and the 72d year of the independence of the United States.

R. B. MASON,
Colonel 1st Dragoons, Governor of California.

HEADQUARTERS TENTH MILITARY DEPARTMENT,
Monterey, California, February 28, 1848.

SIR: I enclose to you the appointment of alcalde for the district of country in which you now reside.

You are authorized to appoint some suitable person to act as sheriff, and one as constable.

I am, respectfully, your obedient servant,

R. B. MASON,
Colonel 1st Dragoons, Governor of California.

JOHN SINCLAIR, *Alcalde, Sacramento.*

HEADQUARTERS TENTH MILITARY DEPARTMENT,
Monterey, California, March 2, 1848.

SIR: I have received your communication of the 1st instant.

The courts, when established, will take cognizance of all cases within their jurisdiction, and which may not have been already finally settled, either by the consent of parties or by the courts; and should they determine that your case was finally settled by the arbitration to which it was referred, they will nevertheless have jurisdiction of any wrong that may have been committed in putting up landmarks contrary to their final decision.

I can take no further action in the case.

I am, respectfully, your obedient servant,

R. B. MASON,
Colonel 1st Dragoons, Governor of California.

IGNACIO CASTRO.

HEADQUARTERS TENTH MILITARY DEPARTMENT,
Monterey, California, March 2, 1848.

SIR: I have received your letter of the 20th ultimo, together with its enclosures, concerning Hands, Higgins, and Williams, who were brought here on the evening of the 23d by your order.

It does not appear from any of the papers accompanying them that they were charged with having committed any *specific* offence, nor has the jury found them guilty of any *overt act* for which they can be punished.

A man cannot be punished for "robbing on the highway and stealing horses" until it is actually proven that he has committed those acts.

It seems from the testimony of Beckwith that these men have been plotting mischief, and they will in all probability rob and steal when they can get an opportunity; but still I do not see how we are to punish men for what it is supposed they intend to do, and before it is legally proven that they have committed the crimes.

As there are at this time no other courts in the country but those of the alcaldes, and they possessing but limited powers, it of necessity sometimes devolves upon them to try offences of a grave character, but always by a jury. In such cases the jury should award, if they convict the prisoner, which, together with the record, shall be sent to me for approval, the prisoner awaiting the result in the place of trial.

No expenses can be paid for sending civil prisoners here, unless they are brought by express authority from this office.

The muskets that were in possession of these men, as mentioned in your letter, send to me by the mail-rider; he can bring one each trip.

I send back the horses on which you sent the prisoners to this place. Hands has enlisted in the regular army. One of the others is a deserter from San Francisco, and the third I shall send to Mazatlan in a vessel that leaves here in a few days.

I am, respectfully, your obedient servant,
R. B. MASON,
Colonel 1st Dragoons, Governor of California.

CHARLES WHITE,
First Alcalde, Pueblo de San José.

HEADQUARTERS TENTH MILITARY DEPARTMENT,
Monterey, California, March 2, 1848.

SIR: It was not until the 21st that I received the record of the trial of Garcia. As there are no other courts at this time in the country but those of the alcaldes, and these possessing but limited powers, it of necessity sometimes devolves upon them to try offences of a grave character, but always by a jury. In such cases, the jury should award a sentence if they convict the prisoner, which, together with the recorded testimony, should be sent to me for approval, the prisoner awaiting the result at the place of trial, or the nearest safe place of confinement, (if not admitted to bail,) to await sentence.

With these views I return to you the record, that you may re-assemble the jury, and have them award a sentence against the said Garcia.

I am, respectfully, your obedient servant,
R. B. MASON,
Colonel 1st Dragoons, Governor of California.

TIMOTHY MURPHY,
Alcalde, San Rafael.

HEADQUARTERS TENTH MILITARY DEPARTMENT,
Monterey, California, March 3, 1848.

SIR: Many of the New York volunteers recently arrived in this country have brought with them rifles, shot guns, powder, percussion caps, &c. Many of these articles they sold to the Californians before I knew the troops had such things in their possession. As soon as I learned these things, I had all the guns, &c., seized that I could lay my hands upon. Many of the articles are no doubt secreted, which you will be able to discover when the detachment lands at San Pedro. All such contraband articles you will seize, and keep possession of them until the war is over, when they will be returned to their respective owners, taking care to have each gun, package, &c., carefully marked with the owner's name.

I am, respectfully, your obedient servant,
R. B. MASON,
Colonel 1st Dragoons, Governor of California.

D. W. ALEXANDER,
Collector, &c., San Pedro.

HEADQUARTERS TENTH MILITARY DEPARTMENT,
Monterey, California, March 3, 1848.

SIR: In reply to so much of your letter of the 25th of February to Lieutenant Sherman, acting assistant adjutant general, as relates to the form of the account current sent you some time since, you will observe that the form is nothing more than to show how the accounts are in general to be made; and, among other items, it shows how funds that *may be* transferred from the customs to the commissary or quartermaster department are to be noted on the account current.

I am, respectfully, your obedient servant,
R. B. MASON,
Colonel 1st Dragoons, Governor of California.

Lieutenant H. S. CARNES,
New York Volunteers, A. A. Quartermaster, Santa Barbara.

HEADQUARTERS TENTH MILITARY DEPARTMENT,
Monterey, California, March 5, 1848.

SIR: I have received your several communications of the 13th of February. I approve of the steps you have taken to apprehend the Indian charged with stealing horses and cattle, and of the instructions given to the party sent in pursuit, "not to hurt the Indian, except it may be in self-defence." When the Indians come into the settlements and run off a band of horses, and are pursued and overtaken, they should be fired on and treated as enemies; but when any Indian merely kills or steals a bullock, if clearly convicted of the fact, he ought to be well (but not cruelly) flogged, like any other thief, whether he be white or red.

In relation to the costs attending the trial of Thompson, I regret that it is not in my power to do anything with them. Accounts created in different parts of the Territory without specific authority from this office cannot be liquidated; and, besides, Thompson had already been tried for this same murder at the Pueblo de los Angeles, and acquitted. So I am informed, though not officially.

I sent to you but a few days since, upon the recommendation of Mr. Sutter, the appointment of alcalde, and am sorry to learn, by one of your letters of the 15th ultimo, that you do not wish it. I am well aware of the difficulties that the alcalde has heretofore labored under. Those difficulties will soon be removed by the duties of alcaldes, prefects, judges, &c., being clearly defined and published, and the ways and means prescribed for raising the necessary funds to defray all proper civil expenses of the Territory. I therefore hope you will not refuse the appointment, and that the public may have the benefit of your experience as an alcalde in putting the new machine in motion.

I am, respectfully, your obedient servant,
R. B. MASON,
Colonel 1st Dragoons, Governor of California.

JOHN SINCLAIR,
Alcalde, Sacramento.

HEADQUARTERS TENTH MILITARY DEPARTMENT,
Monterey, California, March 5, 1848.

SIR: I last evening received your letter of the 22d February, together with the lease to certain lands on the waters of the "American fork," a tributary of the Sacramento, made by certain Indians of the Yalesummy tribe to yourself and Mr. James W. Marshall.

The United States do not recognise the right of Indians to sell or lease the lands on which they reside, or to which the tribe may have a claim, to private individuals. It would therefore be improper in me to sanction any lease of lands made by Indians to individuals, because, after the war, should the United States extinguish the Indian titles to these lands, they would find them encumbered with private claims, which certainly would not be recognised; for, as soon as the Indians' titles to any lands are extinguished, they are at once a part of the public domain.

I am, respectfully, your obedient servant,

R. B. MASON,
Colonel 1st Dragoons, Governor of California.

Captain J. A. SUTTER,
Sub-Indian Agent, New Helvetia.

P. S.—I return to you the lease, with an endorsement upon it.

HEADQUARTERS TENTH MILITARY DEPARTMENT,
Monterey, California, March 6, 1848.

SIR: I have the honor to acknowledge the receipt of your application of the 3d instant, to be put in possession of the orchard at the mission of San Juan.

General Kearny, my predecessor in office, by his decree of the 22d March last, put the mission of San Juan (gardens, orchard, &c., appertaining thereto) in the possession of the Catholic priest having charge of that mission. This possession, however, was not at all to operate to the prejudice of the claim of any one when the proper time arrives for the settlement of those claims. I cannot, therefore, with propriety, disturb that decree; but if the priest is willing for you to take the orchard, then so am I. It is believed to be of no use to him. It is not enclosed, and is open to pillage by every one.

I am, respectfully, your obedient servant,

R. B. MASON,
Colonel 1st Dragoons, Governor of California.

General JOSE CASTRO, *Monterey.*

HEADQUARTERS TENTH MILITARY DEPARTMENT,
Monterey, California, March 8, 1848.

SIR: Herewith you have a copy of my letter to Lieutenant Clift, at San Diego, concerning the settlement of his custom-house accounts, that you may look to this settlement when he is mustered out of service.

No returns have been received by him for either the last or present quarter; nor have any monthly statements been rendered of revenue received from the customs since he relieved the late collector.

I am, respectfully, your obedient servant,
R. B. MASON,
Colonel 1st Dragoons, commanding.

Lieutenant J. W. DAVIDSON,
1st Dragoons, A. A. Quartermaster, Los Angeles.

HEADQUARTERS TENTH MILITARY DEPARTMENT,
Monterey, California, March 8, 1848.

SIR: I wish to know the amount of funds in your possession due the government for customs collected at the port of San Diego, and with this view have been expecting for some time to receive your account current with the civil government of California for the 4th quarter 1847.

It appears from an examination of Pedrorena's account current, rendered up to November 4, 1847, (the day he vacated the office of collector,) that you receipted to him for $702 87$\frac{1}{2}$, which was the amount of funds returned by José Antonio Cot, on account of customs due the Keone Ana, as also for the balance, after settling his salary account, of $346 12. These two items, together with $348 12$\frac{1}{2}$, the amount of Fitch's note of hand which fell due on the 7th of December, and which it is supposed has been turned over to you, make $1,397 12, which should be accounted for on your account current for the 4th quarter of last year; together with whatever sums you received in that quarter after releasing Pedrorena.

You have never forwarded any monthly statement of revenue collected each month according to the printed forms. I desire that you will give this subject immediate attention, as here is the last month in the quarter, and no return has been received from you of the amount of customs that came into your hands during the last quarter.

I am, respectfully, your obedient servant,
R. B. MASON,
Colonel 1st Dragoons, commanding.

Lieut. ROBERT CLIFT,
Mormon Volunteers, A. A. Quartermaster, San Diego.

HEADQUARTERS TENTH MILITARY DEPARTMENT,
Monterey, California, March 9, 1848.

SIR: I am in the receipt of your letters of the 4th and 6th instant. I enclose you an advertisement, offering two hundred dollars for the apprehension and delivery of Beverly; and also an advertisement offering thirty dollars for the apprehension and delivery of each deserter from the army, whether volunteer or regular soldiers. The reward will be paid for Williams *alias* Martin, whom you sent here; but it is necessary to have Foster's receipt for the money, as he was the individual who delivered up the deserter to me. I enclose you a certificate for the delivery, upon which the reward will be paid into the hands of Foster upon his presenting it to the quartermaster at San Francisco or this place.

A person who actually and fully denounces a mine before the 12th of February is entitled to it; but the denouncement must have been full and complete in good faith before that date. Don Manuel Diaz, of this place, as the agent of Don Augustine Narvaez, complains that certain persons are digging on the lands of Narvaez in search of mines, and prays that they be stopped from such proceedings. No person has the right to dig for mines or commit any other trespass on the lands of another, without rendering himself liable to a prosecution for such trespass; and all magistrates shall use their authority, upon a just complaint being made to them, to arrest the progress of such trespasses.

I have mislaid the letter in which you speak of the sale of the school lands by the former alcalde, and of the writing, &c., recorded on the 13th of February, immediately after, on the record of the 17th instant. As I cannot reply to these subjects in a proper manner without having the letter before me, I must request that you will send me a copy of it.

I thank you for the information contained in your letter of the 4th, though I do not apprehend the least danger of an attack on the prison of Monterey. Such an attempt would afford me an excellent opportunity of making an example on the spot of some of the lawless characters with which this country is infested, and I shall always have ready a *halter* for the neck of any one who shall attempt in any way to subvert or overthrow the authority established in California by the United States.

I am, respectfully, your obedient servant,
R. B. MASON,
Colonel 1st Dragoons, Governor of California.
CHARLES WHITE, Esq.,
First Alcalde, Pueblo de San José.

HEADQUARTERS TENTH MILITARY DEPARTMENT,
Monterey, California, March 10, 1848.

SIR: Since writing my letter of yesterday I have found your mislaid letter of the 29th February.

An alcalde has no right or authority whatever to sell or in any other way to dispose of pueblo lands; and without touching the question of the legality of the late proceedings which resulted in the division of the lands of your pueblo, in which division some of them were set apart for the benefit of public schools, I say neither has he any power or authority to give, grant, or sell any of the lands so set apart. Any such gift, grant, or sale is utterly null and void, and of no sort of force or effect.

I remark what you say in relation to the sale of some of the pueblo lands alluded to above being entered on the records after transactions of a subsequent date to that which purports to be the sale. This evidently shows there has been something wrong; but in this case it is a matter of no moment, because any sale of those lands made by your predecessor in office, even if not antedated and recorded at the proper time, is utterly void, and of no sort of force or effect.

You will please enter this letter on your record, and file and preserve the original in your office. Also preserve on the files of your office my official letter of the 19th of January last, addressed to Mr. James W. Weeks, at that time alcalde in your town.

I am, respectfully, your obedient servant,

R. B. MASON,
Colonel 1st Dragoons, Governor of California.

CHARLES WHITE,
First Alcalde, Pueblo de San José.

HEADQUARTERS TENTH MILITARY DEPARTMENT,
Monterey, California, March 10, 1848.

SIR: I have the honor to acknowledge the receipt of your favor of the 4th instant. I will forward your letter to the department at Washington—an opportunity will offer in a day or two. Should it meet with the views of the authorities there, they will give me the necessary instructions for my government here.

I am, respectfully, your obedient servant,

R. B. MASON,
Colonel 1st Dragoons, Governor of California.

Mr. C. V. GILLESPIE,
San Francisco, California.

The bearer hereof, Antonio Chervis, a Mexican citizen, but at present a resident of Monterey, California, has permission to embark on board the schooner William, now lying in this port, and to proceed to the port of San Blas, with a view to a permanent residence in that place.

Given at Monterey, the capital of California, this 11th day of March, A. D. 1848, and of the independence of the United States the 72d.

R. B. MASON,
Colonel 1st Dragoons, Governor of California.

HEADQUARTERS TENTH MILITARY DEPARTMENT,
Monterey, California, March 14, 1848.

SIR: I am in receipt of your letter of the 1st instant. The charge of $16 for the express I supposed would have, like the other expenses of the trial of Armijo and others, been presented to Captain Folsom for payment. In my letter of the 10th November last, Captain F. had instructions to pay that charge.

I am, respectfully, your obedient servant,

R. B. MASON,
Colonel 1st Dragoons, commanding.

Captain J. E. BRACKETT,
N. Y. Volunteers, commanding, &c., Sonoma.

HEADQUARTERS TENTH MILITARY DEPARTMENT,
Monterey, California, March 14, 1848.

GENTLEMEN: I have the honor to acknowledge the receipt of your letter without date, in which you say, "having been by you intrusted with the affairs of Mr. George Hyde, would respectfully recommend his removal from office," &c.

By a reference to my letter of the 1st of October last to the town council, you will observe that the council were put in possession of distinct charges against Mr. Hyde, upon which they were requested to report the facts in the case, (that is, the result or conclusion of the council upon each charge from the hearing of the evidence, and therefore to be distinctly set forth as the council believe to be correct and true,) with their opinion thereon, (that is, from all the facts developed, whether Mr. H. was worthy of his office, or not.) Be pleased to furnish me with a report in that shape, and it shall receive my immediate attention.

I am, respectfully, your obedient servant,
R. B. MASON,
Colonel 1st Dragoons, Governor of California.

Messrs. HOWARD, JONES, PARKER, and LEIDESDORFF,
Members of the Town Council of San Francisco.

HEADQUARTERS TENTH MILITARY DEPARTMENT,
Monterey, California, March 16, 1848.

SIR: I return to you the affidavit and other papers in the case of Honn *vs.* Bellamy, enclosed to me in your letters of the 29th ultimo and 6th instant.

The case was not left to the arbitrary decision of an alcalde, as has generally been done in California, but was decided by a jury. There is no court to which an appeal can be made, because there is no higher court than the one before which the case was tried. This is to be regretted; but in the present state of affairs there is no remedy.

An intelligent jury of six men, in a mere matter of business and account of only a few weeks' standing between two men, can hardly be supposed to have erred much. Be pleased to show this letter to Mr. Bellamy, as I have no time to write to him.

I am, respectfully, your obedient servant,
R. B. MASON,
Colonel 1st Dragoons, Governor of California.

CHARLES WHITE, Esq.,
First Alcalde, Pueblo de San José.

HEADQUARTERS TENTH MILITARY DEPARTMENT,
Monterey, California, March 16, 1848.

GENTLEMEN: In my communication of the 14th requesting that each of the distinct charges against Mr. Hyde might be severally reported upon, I omitted to ask you to accompany the report with the *record* of the proceedings of the investigation, so that I might see the evidence given in upon each charge, when and by whom, for and against the accused. This is necessary, in order that I may be fully possessed of all the merits of the case before making up my opinion, so as to do justice to the complainants and the accused party.

I forward to Mr. Hyde a copy of your communication, to which mine of the 14th and this is a reply.

Very respectfully, your obedient servant,
R. B. MASON,
Colonel 1st Dragoons, Governor of California.
Messrs. HOWARD, JONES, PARKER, and LEIDESDORFF,
Members of the Town Council of San Francisco.

HEADQUARTERS TENTH MILITARY DEPARTMENT,
Monterey, California, March 16, 1848.

SIR: On the foregoing page you have the copy of a correspondence between myself and the town council of San Francisco, in which you are interested.

I am, respectfully, your obedient servant,
R. B. MASON,
Colonel 1st Dragoons, Governor of California.
Mr. GEORGE HYDE,
First Alcalde, San Francisco.

HEADQUARTERS TENTH MILITARY DEPARTMENT,
Monterey, California, March 18, 1848.

SIR: In compliance with the request contained in your note of the 8th instant, I herewith return to you your application to me of the 9th of February last, for the payment of three thousand dollars and interest, money loaned by you to Colonel Fremont, together with a copy of my reply thereto, dated on the 22d of the same month.

I am, respectfully, your obedient servant,
R. B. MASON,
Colonel 1st Dragoons, Governor of California.
Mr. ANTONIO JOSE COT,
Pueblo de los Angeles, California.

HEADQUARTERS TENTH MILITARY DEPARTMENT,
Monterey, California, March 18, 1848.

SIR: I am desirous to forward all the custom-house accounts and vouchers to the War Department, up to include the fourth quarter of the last year. I request you will forward me your vouchers to include that period, (I have the account current and abstract,) that I may examine and forward them, with those received from the other ports, by the mail which Lieutenant Carson will take to the United States.

If you can complete the accounts for the present quarter in time, I should like also to forward them with those of this port, and such others as may come in in season.

I am, respectfully, your obedient servant,
R. B. MASON,
Colonel 1st Dragoons, commanding.

Captain J. L. FOLSOM,
Assistant Quartermaster, San Francisco.

HEADQUARTERS TENTH MILITARY DEPARTMENT,
Monterey, California, March 18, 1848.

SIR: I am in the receipt of your letter of the 9th instant, in which you say you "had not received any orders relative to the amount a soldier was to purchase goods free of duty." The tariff regulations are so plain and explicit that none were necessary. The articles purchased by a soldier or officer must be for his "*own individual use and consumption, and not as merchandise for resale.*" Will an officer permit a soldier to buy, free of duty, five or six hundred yards of merchandise, because the soldier chooses to assert, or even to swear, that it is "for his own individual use and consumption?" or will he, in like manner, permit him to buy "*two barrels of rum*" for "his own individual use and consumption," when the army regulations prohibit sutlers from keeping the article at military posts, and when the invariable custom of the service does not allow the soldier to take one bottle of it in his quarters?

Deduct from $1,247 46 the *one hundred dollars' worth of rum* that private Stockton paid duties on, which leaves $1,147 46 worth of articles chargeable with duties. I can allow of no other deductions, as the large quantity purchased forbids the idea that the purchases were for any other purpose than a resale.

I am glad to hear that the statements made in Milford's letter are so stoutly denied, and am willing to believe that they were great falsehoods.

I am, respectfully, your obedient servant,
R. B. MASON,
Colonel 1st Dragoons, commanding.

Lieut. H. S. CARNES,
N. Y. Volunteers, A. A. Quartermaster, Santa Barbara.

HEADQUARTERS TENTH MILITARY DEPARTMENT,
Monterey, California, March 21, 1848.

SIR: Mr. Branch has called upon me, delivered your message, and reported the many serious depredations recently committed near San Luis Obispo by the Indians. He informs me that the people cannot pursue the Indians for the want of ammunition. You should organize a party, say twenty-five or thirty good men, and hold them in readiness to move at a moment's warning in pursuit of the Indians, where depredations are committed. I will deliver to your order twenty-five or thirty pounds of powder, and a proportionable quantity of lead, to be used by such organized party, when, in accordance to your instructions, they may be called on to go in pursuit of Indians who have committed depredations upon the ranchos and run off bands of horses. You must be responsible that this ammunition is not applied to improper purposes; that it is taken care of, and only used for the service for which it is intended.

I am, respectfully, your obedient servant,
R. B. MASON,
Col. 1st Dragoons, Governor of California.

Mr. JOHN PRICE,
Alcalde, San Luis Obispo.

HEADQUARTERS TENTH MILITARY DEPARTMENT,
Monterey, California, March 23, 1848.

SIR: I have the honor to acknowledge the receipt of your letter of the 20th instant.

The lands of the Presidio are believed to be claimed by private individuals, and they may possibly be confirmed to them. It would, therefore, be improper for the United States authorities, whilst they are in possession of the premises, to permit them to be used by any other individuals in a way which would tend to militate against the interests of the claimants in the event of their recovering the property, by the use and removal of materials valuable for brick-making or other building purposes.

I am, respectfully, your obedient servant,
R. B. MASON,
Col. 1st Dragoons, Governor of California.

Mr. C. L. ROSS,
San Francisco.

HEADQUARTERS TENTH MILITARY DEPARTMENT,
Monterey, California, March 23, 1848.

SIR: I acknowledge the receipt of your letter of the 12th instant. When I said, in my letter to you of the 5th of January, "I think one-half of the proceeds of said goods would be allowed to yourself and Lieutenant Gilbert, for you are equally entitled to a share, in your accounts with the War Department," I did not, by any means, intend it as a formal official decision in the case, but merely as the expression of my opinion that the department would allow the claim if presented, because if the identical same case had happened in the United States, one-half of the proceeds of the goods would have been equally divided between the collector, naval officer, and surveyor of the port, as you will see by a reference to the authority which I quoted. I wrote that letter, giving you my views, and the reasons and authority upon which I based them, that you might make the claim if you chose, either by making the charges in your account, or in any other way you might deem best; and that the whole ground might be before you pro and con, I called your attention to the latter part of article 19 of the printed regulations from Washington, which would seem to negative the opinion I had formed.

When Commodore Shubrick and myself framed the regulations, giving to the informer one-half the proceeds of confiscated goods, we meant by the "informer" some one who would come and give information to the custom-house officers, the possession of which information would enable him to seize smuggled goods, and without such information the goods would not have been seized. When goods are seized and sold in consequence of such information given, the regulation authorizes you to pay one-half of the proceeds to such informer; and when the officer may be of opinion that he is entitled to a part of the proceeds upon the ground that I think his claim rests as before stated, it is for the War Department to decide his claim, not me.

I am, respectfully, your obedient servant,
R. B. MASON,
Col. 1st Dragoons, commanding.

Captain J. L. Folsom,
Asst. Quartermaster, San Francisco.

Headquarters Tenth Military Department,
Monterey, California, March 24, 1848.

Sir: I have received your letter of the 20th instant, on the subject of the election of the town council of Santa Cruz.

The election is approved, and the four gentlemen chosen will act as the advisers and counsellors of the alcalde, and, in conjunction with him, make such regulations as will tend to preserve the quiet and good order of the town, suppress vice and protect the just rights of the persons and property of its inhabitants.

I am, respectfully, your obedient servant,
R. B. MASON,
Col. 1st Dragoons, Governor of California.

William Blackburn,
Alcalde, Santa Cruz.

Headquarters Tenth Military Department,
Monterey, California, March 25, 1848.

Sir: I have received your communication, of the 18th instant, concerning Castro's complaint.

I am fully aware of the difficulty of reconciling these land disputes, the boundaries being so indefinitely described. I send you a copy of the map embracing Yuigo's land, taken from the one on record in this office; that part embraced within the red lines agreeing as near as may be with Yuigo's title, and is supposed to embrace all the land that can be claimed by him. From the examination of the titles I should not suppose that his claim could by any means extend so far south as to reach the road to San Francisco. Try and settle this matter among the parties, if it be possible.

In relation to Narvaez, though he may not have had judicial possession given him of his land, yet that fact does not justify other persons in coming within the boundaries as described in his title, and digging for mineral, or committing any other trespass. The United States authorities are bound by every obligation of honor and duty to protect the Californians in all their just rights.

I am aware that the alcaldes have never been allowed fees by any law in California, though, I believe, of late years it has been customary, at least with some of the alcaldes, to charge them. I can see no objection to their charging a reasonable fee for their services, as their time is much employed in their official duties.

When persons have not been put in possession of lands that their deeds from the proper official authorities entitle them to, you can give them such possession, unless there appears some manifest cause why such possession should be withheld.

I am, respectfully, your obedient servant,
R. B. MASON,
Colonel 1st Dragoons, Governor of California.
CHARLES WHITE, Esq.,
First Alcalde, Pueblo de San José.

P. S.—I send you a translation of the title under which Castro claims.

HEADQUARTERS TENTH MILITARY DEPARTMENT,
Monterey, California, March 25, 1848.

GENTLEMEN: I have to acknowledge the receipt of your letter of the 18th instant, in reply to mine of the 14th, addressed to yourself and two other gentlemen of the town council of San Francisco.

From the tenor of the communication without date, signed by the four gentlemen of the council, it was natural to infer that all the charges against Mr. Hyde had been investigated, and in their judgment substantiated, as not the slightest intimation was given to the contrary; but it appears from your letter that only two of the charges underwent an examination. This shows how necessary it was that I should have been made acquainted with all the facts upon which the gentlemen formed their judgment, before being called upon to remove Mr. Hyde from office. I was left completely in the dark, and required to perform an official act, involving serious consequences to a public officer, with the merits of whose case I was entirely ignorant. The source from whence I should have derived the necessary information to have enabled me fully to understand the subject, makes no reference to the charges not examined into, nor to what extent the investiagtion was carried, nor how far the charges were proved or disproved.

Before I can approve the act of council, it is proper I should know all the circumstances of the case, the sufficiency of the testimony upon which they formed their judgment, and whether that testimony was in any way weakened or counterbalanced by any offered by the accused. In fact, I should know all that influenced the gentlemen in forming their determination—should know all that was urged both for and against the accused party. Without this knowledge, how is it possible for me to act understandingly in the matter? I am informed by one of the members, that there has been no meeting of the council to investigate the charges since some time in December, and that the report was made without his knowledge.

The foregoing and other reasons render it, in my judgment, improper to remove Mr. Hyde from office. Every man must be deemed innocent until his guilt is clearly established.

I am, gentlemen, your most obedient servant,
R. B. MASON,
Colonel 1st Dragoons, Governor of California.

Messrs. JONES and LEIDESDORFF,
San Francisco.

P. S.—You request, as the conclusion of the P. S. to your above-mentioned letter of the 18th, that it may be considered as a private communication, as there were but two of you to sign it. The letter relates solely to official matters, and gives much information touching the subject of which it treats. I can, therefore, only receive and reply to it as a letter on public business.

R. B. M.,
Colonel 1st Dragoons.

HEADQUARTERS TENTH MILITARY DEPARTMENT,
Monterey, California, March 27, 1848.

SIR: The resignation of your appointment as the first alcalde of the district of San Francisco is accepted, to take effect on the 31st of the present month.

I am, respectfully, your obedient servant,
R. B. MASON,
Colonel 1st Dragoons, Governor of California.

GEORGE HYDE, Esq.,
First Alcalde, San Francisco.

Know all men by these presents, that I, Richard B. Mason, colonel 1st regiment of dragoons United States army, and governor of California, by virtue of authority in me vested, do hereby appoint John Townsend first alcalde of the district of San Francisco, Upper California, vice Hyde, who resigned, to take effect on the 31st of the present month.

Given at Monterey, the capital of California, this 27th day of March, A. D. 1848, and the seventy-second year of the independence of the United States.

R. B. MASON,
Colonel 1st Dragoons, Governor of California.

HEADQUARTERS TENTH MILITARY DEPARTMENT,
Monterey, California, March 27, 1848.

SIR: I have the honor to acknowledge the receipt of your letter of the 14th of January, enclosing the accounts of the collectors at La Paz and San José, together with your own for the third and fourth quarters of the last year. I have endorsed on your abstract of expenditures, and on the accounts current, "examined and approved," and will forward them to the War Department by the express, Lieutenant Carson, mounted rifles, who will leave Los Angeles for the United States, via Santa Fe, on the 1st of May.

In relation to the coasting trade you must consult the commodore, and whatever, under the peculiar circumstances of the case, is thought most advantageous to our cause, will surely be approved.

During the continuance of hostilities in Lower California, every effort should be made to bring these people to their proper senses, their property captured, and their trade and communication—especially with the Mexican coast—destroyed and cut off whenever practicable. Those who are friendly or contribute aid to our cause, should of course be treated differently.

I am, respectfully, your obedient servant,
R. B. MASON,
Colonel 1st Dragoons, commanding.

Lieutenant Colonel H. S. BURTON,
New York Volunteers, commanding, Lower California.

HEADQUARTERS TENTH MILITARY DEPARTMENT,
Monterey, California, March 28, 1848.

SIR: I have to acknowledge the receipt of your letter of the 25th instant, asking that no duties be charged on a theodolite imported by you. It is not in my power to comply with your request, as it would establish a precedent injurious to the public interests, and cause numerous applications from others to be exempted from the payment of duties.

I am, respectfully, your obedient servant,
R. B. MASON,
Colonel 1st Dragoons, Governor of California.

Mr. C. S. LYMAN,
Pueblo de San José.

HEADQUARTERS TENTH MILITARY DEPARTMENT,
Monterey, California, March 28, 1848.

SIR: You have above, agreeably to your request, a copy of my letter of the 25th instant addressed to Messrs. Jones & Leidesdorff.

I am, respectfully, your obedient servant,
R. B. MASON,
Colonel 1st Dragoons, commanding.

Mr. GEORGE HYDE,
1st Alcalde, San Francisco district, Present.

HEADQUARTERS TENTH MILITARY DEPARTMENT,
Monterey, California, March 29, 1848.

SIR: On the next page you have a copy of the translation of a note addressed to me by the vice consul of Spain, dated on the 12th instant, respecting the brig Primavera.

I have to request that you will give the information he states he has called for.

I am, respectfully, your obedient servant,
R. B. MASON,
Colonel 1st Dragoons, Governor of California.

To the ALCALDES
at Los Angeles and Monterey.

HEADQUARTERS TENTH MILITARY DEPARTMENT,
Monterey, California, March 29, 1848.

SIR: Your account current and abstracts of disbursements of military contribution fund for the fourth quarter of the last year have been received, and endorsed by me "examined and approved," and will be forwarded to the War Department by Lieutenant Carson, mounted rifles, who will leave Los Angeles for the United States, via Santa Fe, about the 1st of May.

I am, respectfully, your obedient servant,
R. B. MASON,
Colonel 1st Dragoons, commanding.

Captain W. G. MARCY,
Acting Assistant Quartermaster, Present.

HEADQUARTERS TENTH MILITARY DEPARTMENT,
Monterey, California, March 29, 1848.

SIR: I herewith transmit to you the translation of some papers that I yesterday received from the Spanish consul at Santa Barbara, and also a copy of my reply thereto.

I am, respectfully, your obedient servant,
R. B. MASON,
Colonel 1st Dragoons, commanding.

Colonel J. D. STEVENSON,
New York Volunteers, commanding S. M. District, Los Angeles.

P. S.—Be pleased to return to me the translation above mentioned.

HEADQUARTERS TENTH MILITARY DEPARTMENT,
Monterey, California, March 29, 1848.

SIR: The undersigned has the honor to acknowledge the receipt of your note of the 14th instant, and the document accompanying it relating to the mission of San Buenaventura, and the calls of Colonel Stevenson upon Señor Amas to account for property, &c., appertaining to said mission.

Colonel Stevenson has authority to investigate the affairs of all the missions south of Santa Barbara, with a view to their preservation and the security or recovery of the property that may have been fraudulently disposed of. If Señor Amas has an honest title to the property he claims, he has nothing to fear from making an exhibition of it to Colonel Stevenson, and rendering such personal explanations as may be called for. Colonel S., when he has completed the duty assigned him concerning the mission, will make a full report to me; in the interim Señor Amas must confer with the Colonel, and show him by what title he claims to hold the mission of San Buenaventura and the property appertaining thereto.

The Juzgado at Los Angeles and this place have been instructed to give to you the information asked for in relation to the brig Primavera.

Be pleased to accept the assurances of my high esteem and consideration.

R. B. MASON,
Colonel 1st Dragoons, Governor of California.
To Don Cesareo Lataillade,
Vice Consul of Spain for Ca'ifornia, Santa Barbara.

Headquarters Tenth Military Department,
Monterey, California, March 30, 1848.

Sir: I herewith enclose to you a copy of the letter asked for in your communication of yesterday.

I am, respectfully, your obedient servant,

R. B. MASON,
Colonel 1st Dragoons, Governor of California.
George Hyde, Esq.,
1st Alcalde, San Francisco District, Present.

Headquarters Tenth Military Department,
Monterey, California, March 30, 1848.

Sir: On the next page you have the copy of a letter that 1 have just received from Don Manuel Dias, complaining that Mr. William Fisher continues to trespass on the lands of Don Augustine Narvaez, and will not attend to your orders.

You will be pleased to report to me the facts in this case, and what steps you have taken, together with the orders you have given to Mr. Fisher.

I am, respectfully, your obedient servant,

R. B. MASON,
Colonel 1st Dragoons, Governor of California.
Charles White, Esq.,
1st Alcalde, Pueblo de San José.

Know all men by these presents, that I, Richard B. Mason, colonel 1st regiment of dragoons United States army, and governor of California, by virtue of authority in me vested, do hereby appoint Elam Brown an alcalde for the section of country lying along the Contra Costa, and embracing the settlement in the valley of the San Joaquin—vice Estradillo, whose term of office has expired.

Given at Monterey, the capital of California, this 30th day of March, A. D. 1848, and the seventy-second year of the independence of the United States.

R. B. MASON,
Colonel 1st Dragoons, Governor of California.

HEADQUARTERS TENTH MILITARY DEPARTMENT,
Monterey, California, April 1, 1848.

SIR: Since writing my letters of the 29th of March, I have received yours of the 22d of the same month, the answer to which has been anticipated by my reply to the Spanish consul, a copy of which was enclosed with my letter of the 29th ultimo.

Amas has been here, and I have directed him to go to you, show his papers, and answer such questions as you might ask him; and told him that, if he were the proper owner of the mission and mission property, he had nothing to fear; but that if it came fraudulently into his possession, it would be restored to the mission, &c.

I am, respectfully, your obedient servant,

R. B. MASON,
Colonel 1st Dragoons, commanding.

Colonel J. R. STEVENSON,
New York Volunteers, commanding Southern Military District, Los Angeles.

HEADQUARTERS TENTH MILITARY DEPARTMENT,
Monterey, California, April 1, 1848.

SIR: I have to acknowledge the receipt of your communication of the 28th of March. I do not see how these conflicting titles to land can be settled before the proper law courts are established in the country, unless the interested parties themselves settle them by compromise or by arbitration.

I am, respectfully, your obedient servant,

R. B. MASON,
Governor of California.

Mr. S. A. WRIGHT,
Santa Cruz, California.

HEADQUARTERS TENTH MILITARY DEPARTMENT,
Monterey, California, April 1, 1848.

SIR: I have to acknowledge the receipt of your communication of the 29th of March. It will not be in my power to make any grants, temporary or otherwise, conferring rights or privileges to public lands, it being beyond the scope of my authority.

I am, respectfully, your obedient servant,
R. B. MASON,
Colonel 1st Dragoons, Governor of California.

Messrs. JAMES and CAROLAN MATHEWS,
Santa Cruz, California.

HEADQUARTERS TENTH MILITARY DEPARTMENT,
Monterey, California, April 4, 1848.

SIR: Your communication of the 27th of March was not received until after the ship Barnstable left here.

I will send you the powder and lead by the first opportunity. I think you had better send a pack horse for it.

I am, respectfully, your obedient servant,
R. B. MASON,
Colonel 1st Dragoons, Governor of California.

JOHN M. PRICE,
Alcalde, San Luis Obispo.

HEADQUARTERS TENTH MILITARY DEPARTMENT,
Monterey, California, April 5, 1848.

SIR: Your letter of the 20th ultimo, reporting the arrest of Benjamin Foxon, charged with the murder of Augustine Davilla on the morning of the 22d of March, near the mission of Santa Ynez. has been received.

As there are at this time no regularly organized courts in California before whom Foxon can be arraigned and tried, and that so atrocious a crime as murder may not go unpunished, I enclose a commission appointing yourself and Estavan Ardisson judges to hold a special court for the trial of the said Foxon on the charges herewith trasmitted. You will cause a jury of *twelve* good men to be empannelled for his trial. It would be well to summon eighteen or twenty jurors, so that if any are objected to, there may be others on the spot to supply their places. A list of the jurors summoned should be given to the prisoner two days before he is put upon his trial. Be careful to have each juror and witness and interpreter properly sworn, and see that the prisoner has a fair and impartial trial. If found guilty by the unanimous voice of the jury, the court will pronounce sentence upon him; which, together with the whole record, will be forwarded to me.

The record should accurately present each day's proceedings of the court, and should show that each juror, witness, and interpreter was duly sworn. The testimony given in should be entered, as near as can be, in the very words of the witness, who should accurately state, as near as he can, the *day, month, year,* and *place* where the alleged murder was committed.

The trial will take place at Santa Barbara on Monday, the 1st day of May next, or as soon thereafter as practicable. Mr. Dent, of this place, will be sent down to conduct the prosecution on the part of the Territory.

You will appoint some one sheriff for the occasion, and also appoint the clerk of the court, and cause the jurors and witnesses to be summoned in due season. If the prisoner is acquitted, the costs will be paid by the acting assistant quartermaster at Santa Barbara. If he is convicted, and unable to pay the costs of the prosecution, they will be paid as above.

I am, respectfully, your obedient servant,
R. B. MASON,
Colonel 1st Dragoons, Governor of California.
Don Pedro C. CARRILLO,
1*st Alcalde, Santa Barbara.*

I, Richard B. Mason, colonel 1st regiment of dragoons United States army, and governor of California, by virtue of authority in me vested, do hereby appoint Don Pedro C. Carrillo and Don Estavan Ardisson judges to hold a special court at Santa Barbara on Monday, the 1st day of May, 1848, or as soon thereafter as practicable, for the trial of Benjamin Foxon, charged with the murder of Augustine Davilla.

Given at Monterey, the capital of California, this 5th day of April, 1848, and the 72d year of the independence of the United States.
R. B. MASON,
Colonel 1st Dragoons, Governor of California.

HEADQUARTERS TENTH MILITARY DEPARTMENT,
Monterey, California, April 5, 1848.

SIR: The cost of the prosecution that will be incurred on the coming trial of Benjamin Foxon, charged with murder, will be paid if acquitted, by you, out of the military contribution fund, according to the rates mentioned below. If the prisoner is convicted and unable to pay the costs, they will in that case be paid by you—the court to certify to the correctness of the bill of costs before you pay.

JUDGES

Will be allowed for each day the court is actually in session - $8 00

SHERIFF.

For summoning each juror and witness - - - - 50
For each mile travelling in summoning jurors and witnesses - 6
For each day's attendance on the court - - - - 1 00

JURORS AND WITNESSES.

For each day's attendance on court - - - - 50
For each day occupied in travelling to and from the court by the most direct route, reckoning a day's travel at 35 miles - 50

For each mile travelling to and from the court by the most direct
    route - - - - - - - - - $0 06

CLERK OF THE COURT.

For each day the court is in actual session - - - 2 50
    I am, respectfully, your obedient servant,
            R. B. MASON,
                Colonel 1st Dragoons, Governor of California.
Lieutenant H. S. CARNES,
    1st New York Volunteers,
        A. A. Quartermaster, Santa Barbara.

HEADQUARTERS TENTH MILITARY DEPARTMENT,
    Monterey, California, April 5, 1848.

SIR: In reply to that part of your letter of the 24th ultimo as to Colonel Stevenson's authority for sending into your jurisdiction for certain persons, and his requiring you to send Badillo to the pueblo, I have to reply that Colonel Stevenson is the supreme authority in the southern district of Upper California, and as such is responsible to me for the peace and quiet of that part of the country, and for the protection of the persons and property of its inhabitants; and that it is fully within the scope of his authority and power to summon any persons to appear before him whose presence he requires, and this he may do by sending direct to the person or persons, or instruct the alcalde to send them. Badillo must, therefore, not refuse to obey the summons of Colonel Stevenson.
    I am, respectfully, your obedient servant,
            R. B. MASON,
                Colonel 1st Dragoons, Governor of California.
Don PEDRO C. CARRILLO,
    1st Alcalde, Santa Barbara.

HEADQUARTERS TENTH MILITARY DEPARTMENT,
    Monterey, California, April 5, 1848.

SIR: Amas has been here to see the French consul, who is temporarily in charge of the consulate of Spain.

In a conversation with the consul, he informed me that from the strong order you gave Amas, and the threat of imprisonment, he was afraid to go to the pueblo, and requested me to write and ask that no violence might be used towards Amas. I replied to the consul, that whilst you would thoroughly investigate the manner in which the mission property had been disposed of, I was sure you would do nothing improper in the matter, and that I would write according to his request.
    I am, respectfully, your obedient servant,
            R. B. MASON,
                Colonel 1st Dragoons, commanding.
Colonel J. D. STEVENSON,
    New York Volunteers,
        Commanding S. M. District, Los Angeles, California.

HEADQUARTERS TENTH MILITARY DEPARTMENT,
Monterey, California, April 7, 1848.

SIR: I understand that you have in your possession the original decree of the departmental assembly, annulling the sales of the mission made by Don Pio Pico. I desire that you will send said decree to me through the hands of Don Manuel Jomeno, without unnecessary delay.

I am, respectfully, your obedient servant,
R. B. MASON,
Colonel 1st Dragoons, Governor of California.

Don RAYNUMDA CAULLO, *Santa Barbara, California.*

HEADQUARTERS TENTH MILITARY DEPARTMENT,
Monterey, California, April 8, 1848.

SIR: The jury before which Garcia was tried have decided that he be put under bonds to keep the peace, and not again molest or disturb the family of Mr. William Richardson; and that in the event of his not being able to give good and sufficient bonds, he is prohibited from going into the San Rafael district. You will therefore release Garcia from confinement, that he may give bonds to you to the amount of five hundred dollars, conditioned for the purposes above stated. If he goes into the San Rafael district without giving such bonds, he will be liable to be again arrested.

I am, respectfully, your obedient servant,
R. B. MASON,
Colonel 1st Dragoons, Governor of California.

Captain J. B. FRISBEE,
Commanding, San Francisco, California.

HEADQUARTERS TENTH MILITARY DEPARTMENT,
Monterey, California, April 12, 1848.

SIR: I have to acknowledge the receipt of your letter of the 3d instant, relative to your arrest and imprisonment, on the 7th of January, by Don Pablo Guena, then acting as alcalde.

It has been the practice in all cases since I have been in California, for an alcalde, when his term of service expired, to continue in the discharge of the duties of his office until he was relieved by his successor duly appointed, during which time all of the official acts have been recognised and acquiesced in by the parties concerned. Viewing these cases as precedents, I am inclined to believe that you could not maintain an action against Don Pablo for his official acts during the time to which you allude.

I am, respectfully, your obedient servant,
R. B. MASON,
Colonel 1st Dragoons, Governor of California.

Don JOSE CARRILLO, *Santa Barbara.*

HEADQUARTERS TENTH MILITARY DEPARTMENT,
Monterey, California, April 12, 1848.

SIR: I have to acknowledge the receipt of your letter of the 2d instant, asking that I would reverse the decision made by the umpire in the case of the horse race to which you refer.

I must inform you that I have made it a rule not to entertain nor make any decision or order upon subjects of that character. I decline taking any action in such matters, and leave them to be settled by the parties themselves.

I am, respectfully, your obedient servant,
R. B. MASON,
Colonel 1st Dragoons, Governor of California.
Don G. ARDISSON, *Santa Barbara.*

HEADQUARTERS TENTH MILITARY DEPARTMENT,
Monterey, California, April 12, 1848.

SIR: The eight articles of regulation which were published by yourself and the second alcalde, bearing date the 19th of last month, for the promotion of good order, police, &c. in and about Santa Barbara, have been translated by Mr. Hartwell, and are approved by me.

You may rely upon the support of the United States authorities to sustain you in all proper acts as the chief civil magistrate in the jurisdiction of Santa Barbara; and whilst I urge you to be vigilant, firm, impartial, and decisive in the discharge of your official duties as an alcalde, I recommend at the same time as mild and conciliating a course to be pursued as the ends of justice will permit.

I am, respectfully, your obedient servant,
R. B. MASON,
Col. 1st Dragoons, Governor of California.
Don PEDRO C. CARRILLO, *First Alcalde, Santa Barbara.*

HEADQUARTERS TENTH MILITARY DEPARTMENT,
Monterey, California, April 13, 1848.

SIR: I have to acknowledge the receipt of your letter of the 8th instant. It is not in my power to comply with your request. I have so many applications of a similar character, that I am obliged to refuse them all. In the one or two instances in which I have remitted the duties on importations, I may, when the custom-house officers' accounts are settled at the treasury, be called on to make good the amount of duties thus remitted. Were I to accede to all the applications that are made, I should stand committed to the treasury for thousands of dollars. The remission of duties by my order is nothing more than *assuming the debt myself*, if the amount is disallowed at the treasury. This I cannot do; nor should it be asked of me.

I am, respectfully, your obedient servant,
R. B. MASON,
Col. 1st Dragoons, Governor of California.
Mr. THOMAS DOUGLASS, *San Francisco.*

I, Richard B. Mason, colonel of the first regiment of dragoons United States army, and governor of California, to all who shall see these presents, greeting:

Be it known that leave and permission are hereby granted to William C. Hinckley, master of the schooner called the "Providence," lying at present in the port of Monterey, to engage in all lawful commerce, upon hte authority of this paper, until a proper register can be obtained for said schooner from the government of the United States—the said William C. Hinckley having made oath before me that the said schooner belongs to Robert A. Parker, a citizen of the United States. The said Parker is personally known to the undersigned. He is a citizen of the United States, has recently purchased the said schooner Providence, and is hereby authorized to hoist on board of her the United States flag, with all the rights and privileges of a United States vessel engaged in lawful commerce. The said schooner has two masts, quarter galleries, and a billet-head; is single-decked, is fifty-five feet in length and sixteen feet breadth of beam, is eight feet depth of hold, and measures 61 93-95 tons or thereabouts, and was built at New South Wales.

Given at Monterey, the capital of California, this 14th day of April, A. D. 1848, and seventy-second year of the independence of the United States.

          R. B. MASON,
      Col. 1st Dragoons, Governor of California.

    HEADQUARTERS TENTH MILITARY DEPARTMENT,
      Monterey, California, April 14, 1848.

SIR: I herewith enclose to you your custom-house accounts for the 4th quarter of 1847 and the 1st quarter of 1848: the pencil marks thereon will indicate the errors. The opportunity is lost of sending them to Washington by Carson.

  I am, respectfully, your obedient servant,
          R. B. MASON,
      Col. 1st Dragoons, commanding.
Capt. F. J. LIPPETT, *N. Y. Vols., comd'g at Santa Barbara.*

    HEADQUARTERS TENTH MILITARY DEPARTMENT,
      Monterey, California, April 14, 1849.

SIR: Your letter of the 7th instant is received. I cannot see why there was not time enough between the last of March and the 7th of April to make out your accounts and transmit them. The opportunity is thus lost, for the want of promptness on your part, of forwarding them to Washington by Carson.

The amount due as duties on the merchandise sold from the Anita, of which you speak, must be taken up on your account. It is deemed to be in your hands, as you are responsible for it.

  I am, respectfully, your obedient servant,
          R. B. MASON,
      Col. 1st Dragoons, Governor of California.
Lieut. H. S. CARNES, *A. A. Quartermaster, Santa Barbara.*

Know all men by these presents, that I, Richard B. Mason, colonel of the first regiment of dragoons United States army, and governor of California, by virtue of authority in me vested, do hereby appoint Don Juan Bandini first alcalde for and in the district of San Diego, Upper California.

Given at Monterey, the capital of California, this 15th day of April, A. D. 1848, and the seventy-second year of the independence of the United States.

          R. B. MASON,
      Col. 1st Dragoons, Governor of California.

Know all men by these presents, that I, Richard B. Mason, colonel of the first regiment of dragoons United States army, and governor of California, by virtue of authority in me vested, do hereby appoint E. L. Brown second alcalde *"supliénte"* for and in the district of San Diego, Upper California.

Given at Monterey, the capital of California, this 15th day of April, A. D. 1848, and the seventy-second year of the independence of the United States.

R. B MASON,
Col. 1st Dragoons, Governor of California.

HEADQUARTERS TENTH MILITARY DEPARTMENT,
Monterey, California, April 15, 1848.

SIR: I have the honor to acknowledge the receipt of your letter of the 4th instant, enclosing one from Mr. Flugge and yourself on the subject of the coasting trade. You speak of the "heavy port charges imposed upon vessels authorized to navigate the coast." I think they are unusually light, having long since been reduced from one dollar to fifteen cents per ton, and that is the only port charge that exists. I am well aware of the inconvenience that is felt along the coast, arising from the exclusion of the foreign vessels; the subject has been presented to the department, and we must await its orders. I have already made so many modifications of the President's regulations in favor of the people of California, that I cannot assume a further responsibility until I hear from Washington upon what has already been done. Every favor that is granted "under the peculiar circumstances of the case" embarrasses me a great deal. Every vessel upon the coast seizes hold of it as a precedent upon which to claim that similar indulgences should be granted to them; and not only that, but they claim other indulgences and immunities, and say, "We don't see why we should be denied the privilege we ask, when you granted such privileges to such a vessel;" and in this way I am unceasingly beset.

I am, respectfully, your obedient servant,

R. B. MASON,
Colonel 1st Dragoons, commanding.

Col. J. D. STEVENSON,
New York Volunteers, comd'g S. M. Dist., Los Angeles.

HEADQUARTERS TENTH MILITARY DEPARTMENT,
Monterey, California, April 15, 1848.

SIR: Your accounts of the military contribution fund derived from the customs for the second, third, and fourth quarters of 1847, and the first quarter of 1848, have been examined and approved by me, and will be forwarded to the War Department by Lieutenant Carson, of the mounted rifles, who will leave Los Angeles about the first of next month for Washington city.

I am, respectfully, your obedient servant,

R. B. MASON,
Colonel 1st Dragoons, commanding.

Captain J. L. FOLSOM,
Assistant Quartermaster U. S. A., San Francisco.

HEADQUARTERS TENTH MILITARY DEPARTMENT,
Monterey, California, April 17, 1848.

SIR: Señor Narvaez complains, through his agent Don Manuel Diaz, that his land, or part of it, is claimed by Mr. Fisher, and that upon a representation of Mr. Fisher, you have stopped certain works upon said land, carried on by his (Narvaez) authority. Narvaez has sent me his title-papers—please direct Mr. Fisher to send his. In the mean time, if Narvaez has all along been in possession or occupancy of the land in question, the works will be allowed to progress.

I am, respectfully, your obedient servant,
R. B. MASON,
Colonel 1st Dragoons, Governor of California.

CHARLES WHITE, Esq.,
Alcalde, Pueblo de San José.

[No. 36.] HEADQUARTERS TENTH MILITARY DEPARTMENT,
Monterey, California, August 16, 1848.

SIR: I have the honor to enclose you, herewith, copies of reports made by Lieutenant Colonel Burton, and the officers under his command, the originals of which were received by me on the 15th of June last. These give a history of the suppression of the insurrection in the peninsula, which, in its entire management, reflects high credit upon all concerned. I can only draw your attention to the report of Lieutenant Heywood's defence of San José; of Captain Steele's rescue of the American prisoners of war at San Antonio; and of Lieutenant Colonel Burton's attack upon the enemy at Todos Santos.

I regret exceedingly that these creditable military operations should have been stained by an act of cruelty on the part of any officer; but I cannot pass over, without comment, the facts stated by Lieutenant Colonel Burton, in his report of the 16th of April. Captain Naglee, of the New York volunteers, in command of a mounted party, was left, after the fight at Todos Santos, to pursue the broken forces of the enemy. In this pursuit he captured several prisoners, whom he conducted to La Paz, the headquarters of Lieutenant Colonel Burton. When within sight of that place, he caused two of his prisoners to be shot. By Lieutenant Colonel Burton's letter of April 16, you will see that Captain Naglee was informed that he could not execute a prisoner without the sanction of a council of war; and yet, when within sight of his commanding officer, where a council of war could easily have been assembled, to dispose of these prisoners as they deserved, they were shot dead by order of Captain Naglee. In his report to Lieutenant Colonel Burton, you will observe that Captain Naglee makes no mention of having executed these prisoners, further than stating that they were "afterwards ordered to be shot." After reflecting upon these facts, I determined to disavow the act on the part of the government of the United States, as one of cruelty, not sanctioned by the laws of war, and at direct variance with the humane principles that have governed our conquering armies. I have ordered the arrest of Captain Naglee, to await the decision of the President of the United States in his case. (See my orders No. 39, of June 15, 1848.) I could not prefer charges against Captain Naglee for this exercise of authority, and then order his trial, as such course would have been in violation of the first section of the act of Congress approved May 29, 1830. I could, therefore, only order the necessary reports to be sent to you, to be laid before the President for his action. Now, however, that peace is secured, Captain Naglee must be mustered out of service with his company, without answering for an act that stands as a stain upon the fair fame of the army. You will remember that Captain Naglee was arrested by me for a similar act of cruelty on a former occasion. (See letter No. 28, of February 2, 1848.)

Lieutenant Halleck, of the engineers, who, upon the application of Commodore Shubrick, in October last, accompanied him to Mazatlan, after rendering good service, crossed over to La Paz, and was most active in the military operations there; his name is most favorably mentioned by the different commanders. He is now at these headquarters, and has supplied the topographical sketches that are enclosed with this.

I have the honor to be your most obedient servant,
R. B. MASON,
Colonel 1st Dragoons, commanding.
General R. JONES,
Adjutant General, Washington, D. C.

BARRACKS, LOWER CALIFORNIA,
San José, February 20, 1848.

SIR: I continue my report from the 22d ultimo, from which time my force consisted of 27 marines and 15 seamen, of whom 5 were on the sick report, besides some twenty volunteers, Californians, who at least served to swell the numbers. From that date the enemy were continually in sight of us, intercepting all communication with the interior, and driving off all the cattle from the neighborhood. A party of our men who went out to endeavor to obtain cattle, were driven in and narrowly escaped being cut off. We succeeded in obtaining a few cows, however, which were very necessary to us in the reduced state of our provisions, as, in addition to our garrison, we were obliged in humanity to sustain some fifty women and children of the poor, who sought our protection in the greatest distress. I found it necessary, as soon as our fresh beef was consumed, to put all hands on half allowance of salt provisions. We had no bread. On the 4th of February the enemy closed around us more, and commenced firing upon all who showed themselves at our port-holes or above the parapets. On the morning of the 6th the enemy appeared to be a little scattered, a considerable force being seen riding about some distance from the town, and at the same time a strong party of them posted at the lower end of the street were keeping up an annoying fire upon us. I judged this a favorable opportunity to make a sortie upon them, and, taking 25 men with me, closed with them and dislodged them, driving them into the hills without the loss of a man on our part, and returned to the cuartel. On the morning of the 7th it was reported to me that the enemy had broken into the houses on the main street, and there was some property exposed which might be secured. I took a party of men and went down and brought up a number of articles belonging to the Californians who were in the cuartel; some distant firing took place, but no injury was sustained. On the same day, hearing there were some stores of rice and tobacco in a house some 300 yards down the main street, I determined upon an effort to obtain them, and sallied out with 30 men: these were immediately fired upon from several different quarters, and some fighting ensued, resulting in the death of one of my volunteers—shot through the heart. We charged down the end of the street, and drove the enemy to the cover of a cornfield at the outside of the town, where they were considerably reinforced, and recommenced a hot fire; but we were enabled to save a part of the articles which we were in search of, though we found that the enemy had anticipated us in this object, having forced the building from the rear. On the afternoon of the following day Ritchie's schooner, having provisions for us from La Paz, came in sight and achored, but a canoe which was enticed towards the shore by a white flag displayed by the enemy was fired upon, and the schooner immediately got under way. On the 10th the enemy had entire possession of the town: they had perforated with port-holes all the adjacent houses and walls, occupying the church, and, hoisting their flag on Galindo's house, ninety yards distant, held a high and commanding position, which exposed our back yard and the kitchen to a raking fire, which from this time forth was almost incessant from all quarters upon us, the least exposure of person creating a target for fifty simultaneous shots. The enemy appeared to have some excellent rifles, among other arms; and some of them proved themselves tolerably sharp shooters, sending their balls continually through our port-holes. On the 11th the fire was warm, but on our part it was rarely that we could get sight of them. In the afternoon of this day we had to lament the death of Passed Midshipman McLanahan, attached to the United States ship Cyane: a ball striking him in the right side of the neck, a little below the thyroid cartilege, lodged in the left shoulder. He died in about two hours. He was a young officer of great promise, energetic, of much forethought for his age, and brave to temerity. All lamented his untimely fate, and all bear willing testimony to his worth. On the morning of the 12th, at daylight, we discovered that the enemy had thrown up a breastwork upon the sand, about 150 yards to the northeast of the cuartel, and entirely commanding our watering place. We fired several round shot at it, with little effect. We succeeded in getting in some water at night, but at great hazard, the enemy being in strong force, and kept a close watch upon us. Their force was over three hundred, speaking within bounds. I immediately commenced digging a well in the rear of Mott's house, which is the lowest ground. I found that we had to go through rock, and judged we should have to dig about twenty feet. I thought it imprudent to blast, as the enemy, suspecting our intention, would throw every obstacle in our way. The men worked cheerfully on this and the succeeding day against all difficulties. Our situation was becoming now an imminently critical one, having with the greatest economy but four days' water. On the 14th we continued digging for water. We found that the enemy had thrown up a second breastwork more to the westward, giving them a cross-fire upon our watering place: there was a continual fire kept up upon the cuartel during the day. At 3 o'clock 30 minutes p. m., a sail was reported in sight, which proved to be the United States ship Cyane. She anchored after sundown. It was of course a joyful sight to us to see friends so near; but I was apprehensive that they could render us but litte assistance, the enemy being so vastly superior in numbers. The enemy continued their firing upon us during the night. On the 15th at daylight we became aware that the Cyane was landing men. They soon commenced their advance, which for a few moments was opposed only by a scattering fire; then the enemy opened upon them in earnest. They had concentrated nearly their entire force near San Vincente. We saw the flash of musketry through all the hills above the village. There was the odds of three to one against our friends. Steadily they came on, giving back the enemy's fire as they advanced. There was still a party of the enemy occupying the town, firing upon us. I took thirty men and sallied out upon them, drove them from cover, killed one and wounded several of them, and marched out to join the Cyane's men, who, with Captain Dupont at their head, had now drawn quite near to us. There were small detached parties of the enemy still hovering about them, and firing at them, but the main body of the enemy had been broken, and retired to "Las Animas," distant two miles. The march of the Cyane's men to our relief, through an enemy so vastly their superior in numbers, well mounted and possessing every advantage in knowledge of the ground, was certainly an intrepid exploit, as creditably performed as it was skilfully and boldly planned, and reflects the greatest honor on all concerned. It resulted most fortunately for us in our harassed situation. They had but four wounded: this cannot be termed anything but the most remarkably good luck, considering the severe fire that this heroic little band were exposed to. The loss of the enemy we have not positively ascertained: we hear of 13 killed, with certainty, and general report says 35; wounded not known. Of the total loss of the enemy in their attack upon the cuartel, I cannot speak with certainty: we have found several graves, and know of a number wounded, one of whom we have in the cuartel a prisoner. I suppose their total loss to be not far from 15 killed, and many wounded; I am sure it could not be less than this. Our own total loss was 3 killed and 4 slightly wounded. After the death of Passed Midshipman McLanahan, there remained but one officer to my assistance, Passed Midshipman George A. Stevens, to whom, for his coolness and indefatigable zeal at a time when so much devolved upon him, I am most happy to accord the highest credit; and at the same time I must honorably mention the conduct of a volunteer, Eugene Gillispie, esq., who, although suffering from illness, never deserted his post, and was with me in the sortie of the 7th. The non-commissioned officers and men went through privation, unceasing watchfulness, and danger, without a murmur. I cannot express too highly my satisfaction in their conduct. Captain Dupont immediately upon his arrival here, becoming aware of our situation as regards provisions, took measures for our supply. The day after the battle of San Vincente he despatched a train, which brought us by hand (the enemy having driven off all the mules and horses) a quantity of stores and articles of which we stood most in need, among the rest bread, and has since been unceasing in his exertions for our relief. I cannot too earnestly express the obligations which we are under for the prompt and efficient assistance which Captain Dupont, his officers, and crew have rendered us.

I am, sir, respectfully, your obedient servant,

CHAS. HEYWOOD,
Lieutenant U. S. Navy, com'g, San José.

Lieut. Col. HENRY S. BURTON,
U. S. Army, com'g troops in Lower California.

True copy:

W. T. SHERMAN,
First Lieutenant 3d Artillery, A. A. A. General.

UNITED STATES BARRACKS,
La Paz, California, March 10, 1848.

SIR: I have the honor to continue my report of January 16, 1848.

From the arrival of the United States sloop of-war Cyane at this place on the 8th of December, 1847, until the time of her departure, and the arrival of the United States storeship Southampton, February 11, 1848, nothing of particular importance occurred in this portion of Lower California; the enemy having removed the main body of their force to invest San José, leaving a few outposts on the roads leading to this place for the purpose of cutting off all our communications with the interior of the country.

On the 8th of February I received a communication from the commander of the Mexican forces, which is herewith enclosed, with my reply, marked A.

The arrival of the Cyane at San José was very opportune, as the gallant little garrison of that place was closely invested, and in a distressed condition.

The report of Lieutenant Heywood, United States navy, commanding at San José, is herewith transmitted, marked B. I cannot omit this opportunity of expressing my own gratification, and that of my command, with the cordial co-operation, whenever necessary, of Captain Dupont and his officers during the time the Cyane was here.

About the 13th of February we began to collect horses and saddles for the purpose of mounting a portion of this command.

On the night of the 26th of February Lieutenant Young, with a small party, surprised an outpost of the enemy, about seven leagues distant, and captured three men.

On the night of the 28th of February Lieutenant Matsell, with a small party, surprised another outpost, about six leagues distant, and captured two more.

Captain Steele endeavored to surprise another outpost a few nights afterwards; but the enemy receiving information of his movements, in spite of his precautions, were not to be found.

I regret to report that on the night of the 22d of February privates Wm. Sutphan, company A, and Maguire, company B, being intoxicated, endeavored to break into the house of a French resident of this place, and that one of them fired a musket into the house, and instantly killed a man in the act of opening a door. Application was made to confine those men on board the Southampton, which was declined, not having a proper place in which to confine prisoners of this character. Private Sutphan made his escape on the night of the 24th of February, and has not been heard of since.

Enclosed herewith are the charges preferred against both, and I have the honor to request that a military commission may be ordered to this place for the trial of private Maguire, and such other prisoners as may be brought before it.

I have the honor to be your obedient servant,
H. S. BURTON,
Lieutenant Colonel 1st N. Y. Volunteers, commanding.
To Lieut. W. T. SHERMAN,
First Lieut. 3d Artillery, A. A. A. General

True copy:
W. T. SHERMAN,
1st Lieutenant 3d Artillery, A. A. A. General.

HEADQUARTERS UNITED STATES BARRACKS,
La Paz, Lower California, March 20, 1848.

SIR: I have the honor to report that on the evening of the 15th inst. Captain Steele, New York volunteers, commanding a party of first New York volunteers, accompanied by Lieutenant Halleck, United States engineers, Surgeon Perry, two foreigners, residents in the country, and three friendly Californians, acting as guides, aggregate 34, left this place with orders to attack an outpost of the enemy, about five leagues distant; or if, from information received on the route, it should prove practicable, to make a forced march upon San Antonio, the enemy's headquarters, and endeavor to rescue the American prisoners of war at that place.

The forced march upon San Antonio was made with great success; the enemy was surprised, several killed and wounded, two Mexican officers and one soldier taken prisoners, several arms and a small quantity of ammunition destroyed, the official correspondence and the flag of the enemy captured, one ambuscading party of the enemy defeated, and the command safe in La Paz within 30 hours from the time it started. Our loss was but of one man killed—that of H. Hipwood, sergeant in B company. Several of the men had their clothes pierced by the enemy's shot; a ball entered the saddle of Captain Steele, and the horses of Lieutenant Halleck and private Melvin, of B company, were wounded in those engagements. All engaged in the expedition acquitted themselves with great credit; and particular praise is due to Captain Steele, who commanded the troops, and to Lieutenant Halleck, by whose advice and assistance the expedition was undertaken, and so successfully executed.

Enclosed herewith is Captain Steele's report.

I am, sir, very respectfully, your obedient servant,
HENRY S. BURTON,
Lieutenant Colonel N. Y. Volunteers.
Lieut. W. T. SHERMAN,
Acting Assistant Adjutant General,
Tenth Military Department, Monterey, California.

True copy:
W. T. SHERMAN,
First Lieutenant 3d Artillery, A. A. A. General.

La Paz Barracks,
Lower California, March 20, 1848.

Sir: I have the honor to report that, in compliance with your order, I took command of the mounted force destined for an incursion into the interior. On the 15th, and between the hours of 9 and 10 p. m., we started. On examination, I found our whole force to consist of 27 non-commissioned officers and privates, three officers, (Surgeon Alexander Perry, Acting Lieutenant Scott, B company, and myself,) Lieutenant Halleck, United States engineers, who kindly volunteered his valuable experience and services, and Messrs. Herman, Ehrenberg, and Taylor, residents of this place, and three guides, Californians—(aggregate 34.) On conferring with the officers, we were unanimous in the conclusion to proceed with all possible speed direct to San Antonio, (the headquarters of the enemy,) instead of attacking the advanced party at the ranche of Noviellas, with the principal object of rescuing the American prisoners of war confined there, and doing all else we could.

We took the route by the ranche of the Tuscalamas. Proceeding cautiously, we passed an outpost of some 50 men, without being observed by them, and reached the top of the mountain, overlooking and eight miles distant from San Antonio, at daylight on the following morning, where we captured one of the "enemy's pickets," and quickening our speed, we descended and passed up the arroyo to the east of the town, and, arranging the men, we charged into the town at full speed. A small party having been previously detailed to secure the persons of the officers of the enemy: the rest were directed against the building occupied as a cuartel for the soldiers; and not finding any there, one of the liberated captives directed my attention to a building on the other side of the arroyo, to the east of the town, distant from the Plaza about 150 yards, and commanding it, (to which I afterwards learned the soldiers had been removed but the day previous, thereby deranging all our previous plans of attack,) from which, with a small force of the enemy drawn up in front, a brisk fire of musketry opened upon us.

Having first gained our object in rescuing our men, besides taking two of their officers prisoners, I ordered the men to dismount and rally under cover of the church on the east side of the Plaza.

The party sent to secure the officers were unsuccessful in securing the commandant—(he escaped in his night clothes, having just arisen from his bed)—but the second in command, Captain Calderon, and the Adjutant Lieutenant Arsse, were taken, their flag and the private and public papers secured. When a sufficient number of our men had rallied, we sallied out and charged the enemy in position, and drove them in all directions to the adjacent hills, killing three of their number and wounding seven or eight. The rout of their force being complete, which we learned amounted to some 50 men, and being too tired to pursue them, we collected all the arms they abandoned, (some 30,) their trumpet, bullet moulds, &c., destroyed them and left them in the Plaza, as it was impracticable to carry them with us.

I have to record the loss of one of our number, Sergeant Thomas M. Hipwood, of B company, who fell dead in the charge, pierced by a bayonet and two balls. "A better and a truer man never fell in his country's service or the performance of his duty; and his loss will ever be lamented by those who knew his worth."

Pantaloons, cravats, hats, horses, saddles, attest the numerous narrow escapes, but none wounded.

Not more than half an hour elapsed before we were on our way back. We halted at a ranche after travelling some 10 miles, (owing to the accession of our number of men, and but one or two horses, many had to walk that distance,) for the first time, to refresh. In two hours we were on our way again, but little recruited in strength. Proceeding slowly, we reached the mountain pass of Trincheras a little before sunset, and were just entering an arroyo, bordered by elevated banks and a thick growth of underbrush, when a fierce fire of musketry opened upon us in front; a dismount and rally in front was but the work of an instant, the men standing fire like veterans. I ordered the advance guard to deploy to the right and left, who drove them from tree to tree and hill to hill, while the main body proceeded slowly, leading their horses, until we had passed the dangerous ground, when we mounted and took a different road, diverging to the right, which would make the distance much further, but the travelling much safer.

There was none wounded on our side. One of the captives, Captain Chalderon, received a severe wound from a rifle ball in the right breast from the fire of the enemy, which did not prevent his riding, however; the horses received several wounds, but not so as to disable them. The loss on the part of the enemy was some five or six killed and wounded. We continued our march, proceeded some three miles further, when our rear guard was attacked; but on firing one musket at them they scampered off, and scarcely a charge ensued. We proceeded cautiously, but our horses were getting now so fatigued that they would lie down, and it was with the greatest perseverance and exertion that we continued advancing, but finally arrived at the barracks on the morning of the 17th at 2 a. m.

Having accomplished the extraordinary distance of 120 miles (the route we took) in less than 30 hours on the same horses, with but little food or refreshment, stopping but once to feed, through the most rocky country and the roughest road that can be travelled, and by men, many of them, totally unused to riding, and without any previous preparation, I cannot express in terms too commendatory the coolness and bravery displayed by the men of my command. Acting Lieutenant Scott, B company, Sergeant Peasley, A company, and Sergeant Denneston, B company, were conspicuous.

To Surgeon Alexander Perry, Lieutenant Halleck, United States engineers, most sincere thanks are due for their counsel and assistance. And to Mr. Herman Ehrenberg, "my volunteer aid," to say that he fully sustained that reputation for gallantry, coolness, and bravery that has been awarded to him on former occasions, is enough.

And to Luz, Morano, and to Juan de Dios Talamantis, our Californian guides, I am greatly indebted; their bravery and fidelity deserve to be duly appreciated. Respectfully, your obedient servant,

SEYMOUR G. STEELE,
Captain 1st New York Regiment, commanding.

Lieutenant Colonel HENRY S. BURTON,
United States Army, commanding U. S. forces, &c.

True copy: W. T. SHERMAN,
1st Lieutenant 3d Artillery, Acting Assistant Adjutant General.

UNITED STATES BARRACKS,
La Paz, California, April 13, 1848.

SIR: I have the honor to acknowledge the receipt of your letter of March 1, 1848, and to report the arrival of the army storeship " Isabella" at this place on the 22d of March, 1848, with Captain Naglee's company (D) New York volunteers, and 114 recruits for the detachment of New York volunteers stationed at this place.

The rescue of the prisoners of war on the 15th ultimo caused great excitement among the enemy, and tended very much to disorganize their forces, and the important arrival of the re-enforcements to my command determined me to take the field as soon as possible; accordingly, I left this place on the morning of the 26th instant with 217 officers and men; Lieutenant Halleck, United States engineers, acting chief of staff, and Passed Midshipman Duncan, United States navy, temporarily attached to the mounted portion of Captain Naglee's command.

The afternoon of the 27th a party of 15 men captured, in San Antonio, Pineda, the commander of the Mexican forces, with his secretary, Serrano.

The morning of the 29th, having received information that the enemy had concentrated their forces in Todos Santos, we pressed on with all speed, fearing they might evade us, by retreating towards Magdalena bay. The morning of the 30th, about 10 o'clock, having received accurate information respecting the enemy, Captain Naglee with 45 mounted men was despatched to intercept the road leading from Todos Santos to Magdalena bay, and, if practicable, to attack the enemy in the rear at the same time our main body made its attack in front.

The road leading from Todos Santos to La Paz, for some distance before reaching the first named place, passes through a dense growth of chaparal, (very favorable for an ambush,) and in this the enemy made their arrangements to receive us. We left the road about five miles from Todos Santos and marched along a ridge of high land on the north side of the river, having full view of the enemy's operations.

They then took possession of a commanding hill directly in our route, between 3 and 4 miles from Todos Santos, with their Indians in front. Companies A and B, under the direction of Lieutenant Halleck, were deployed as skirmishers in such a manner as to expose the enemy to a cross-fire. The enemy opened their fire at long distance, but our force advanced steadily, reserving their fire until within good musket range, when it was delivered with great effect, and the enemy retreated very rapidly, after a short but sharp engagement. At this time, Captain Naglee being near Todos Santos, and hearing the firing, attacked the enemy in rear, and after a severe action completed their dispersion. Our men and horses being too much fatigued by their long march to pursue the scattered enemy, we marched on to Todos Santos.

The loss of the enemy in this engagement cannot be ascertained with any accuracy; we know of 10 killed and eight wounded. Our loss was nothing: one man and the horse of Acting Lieutenant Scott were slightly wounded, the enemy, as usual, firing too high.

Our officers and men fully sustained the character they won on the 16th and 27th of November last.

My warmest thanks are due to Lieutenant Halleck, for his assistance as chief of staff, and I present him particularly to the notice of the colonel commanding, for the able manner in which he led on the attack on the 30th ultimo.

Captain Naglee also deserves particular notice for the energetic and successful manner in which he fulfilled his instructions. A copy of his report is herewith enclosed.

On the 31st ultimo Captain Naglee, with fifty mounted men of his company, was ordered to pursue the enemy in the direction of Magdalena bay. He returned to La Paz on the 12th instant, having pursued the enemy very closely, capturing five prisoners and some arms.

Lieutenant Halleck started for San José with a party of mounted men, consisting of 1 officer and 25 non-commissioned officers and privates, on the 5th instant, for the purpose of communicating with Captain Dupont, commanding United States sloop-of-war Cyane. He returned here on the 11th instant, having captured 10 prisoners on his march, and taken a number of arms.

From him I learn that the naval force at San José have thirty-odd prisoners, and among others "Mauricio Castro," the self-styled political chief of Lower California. Lieutenant Selden, with a party from the Cyane, made a most opportune march on Santiago, where he captured a number of the enemy who had fled from the field of Todos Santos. Castro, who commanded the enemy's forces in the action of the 30th, was arrested near Maria Flores by the civil authorities and delivered up to Lieutenant Selden.

During the stay of our main body at Todos Santos 14 prisoners were captured; among them two sons of the reverend padre Gabriel Gonzales, officers of the Mexican forces.

We left Todos Santos on the 5th instant, and arrived at this place on the 7th. The result of this short campaign has been the complete defeat and dispersion of the enemy's forces.

We have captured their chief and 6 officers, and 103 non-commissioned officers and privates; and others are daily presenting themselves to the civil authorities in different parts of the country.

The captured arms have been given to those rancheros known to be friendly to the interests of the United States, for their protection.

I am, sir, with much respect, your obedient servant,
HENRY S. BURTON,
Lieutenant Colonel New York Volunteers.

Lieutenant W. T. SHERMAN,
Act. Asst. Adjt. Gen. Tenth Mil. Dept.

True copy:
W. T. SHERMAN,
First Lieut. 3d Artillery, A. A. A. General.

TODOS SANTOS, *March* 30, 1848.

I have the honor to report, that, after receiving your verbal order at 10 o'clock a. m. this day, "to select the men" from "those of my company that were mounted whose horses would be able to carry them more expeditiously to the junction of the road, by the arroyo Muelle, at its mouth, with the road from Todos Santos, in the direction of Magdalena bay, one league and a half from Todos Santos, and there ascertain whether the enemy had passed towards Magdalena bay, and, if so, to follow them; or, if still remaining at Todos Santos, to attack them, or not, at my discretion," I selected 45 men, and at 1 p. m. arrived at the point designated, where I received information that the whole of the Mexican forces, numbering from 200 to 300, were lying in position on the main road leading out to Todos Santos, and about half a league from it. I immediately despatched a courier to you with this information, adding my determination to attack him in the rear about the time you should approach from the front. The men and horses were then allowed one hour's rest—the latter having been fifty-six hours without feed. At 2 p. m. we again mounted, at 3 passed through Todos Santos, and passed as rapidly as our horses could bear us towards the point occupied by the enemy, who had been informed of our approach. When half a league without Todos Santos, we discovered a body of cavalry posted, partly concealed among a heavy growth of cactac, at the foot of a steep ridge, and a body of Indians and Mexicans in line along its summit—in all about 120. The detachment was ordered into line within 50 yards of the first, and whilst forming, and before it could be dismounted, received the fire of those at the foot of the ridge, who retired towards those at the summit, where they were joined by a large number who came precipitately from the other side. The detachment, after leaving a guard of 10 men with the horses, was marched by a steep, rocky path half way up the side hill, it being the only approach, and there deployed to the right and left, and charged upon the summit. The enemy continued their fire until we had approached to within 50 yards and commenced firing, when they broke and run. They were pursued until they were completely routed, and until fearing my command were becoming too much scattered among the immense cactac with which the surface of the whole country is covered. They were recalled, and we returned to this place by 5½ p. m.

A number of the bodies of the enemy were found, but it is impossible to say what was their loss. A number of their horses and a quantity of their baggage was captured.

Our thanks are due to First Lieutenant George H. Pendleton, of my company, and to Passed Midshipman James M. Duncan, of the United States navy, for the very satisfactory manner that they performed every duty.

Of the men, I could not in justice to them say less than that volunteers never behaved better.

I have the honor to be, very respectfully, your obedient servant,
HENRY M. NAGLEE,
Captain 1st New York Regiment,
Commanding Detachment.
To Lieut. Col. H. S. BURTON, *Commanding.*

A true copy:
W. T. SHERMAN,
First Lieut. 3d Artillery, A. A. A. General.

LA PAZ, LOWER CALIFORNIA, *April* 16, 1848.

SIR: Enclosed herewith I send you Captain Naglee's report of his operations from the 30th of March, 1848, when he left Todos Santos, until the 14th instant, when his whole command arrived here, with a copy of my instructions to him; attached also is a copy of General Scott's general orders No. 372, of 1847.

Before leaving Todos Santos, Captain Naglee held much conversation with Lieutenant Halleck and with me respecting the fourth article of those general orders; and he was distinctly told, particularly by Lieutenant Halleck, that if he took any *prisoners*, they could not be *shot* without the sanction of a council of war; and that he (Captain Naglee) could not, under the circumstances, order such council.

From San Ilarius, April 8, 1848, Captain Naglee reported to me, and I considered the report, approving of the course he had thus far pursued, and directing him to return to La Paz.

On the 11th of April, 1848, I received a communication from Captain Naglee, which is herewith enclosed, with my reply. Captain Naglee did not receive the reply, as the courier could not find him.

When within a mile or less of La Paz, the two prisoners—Juan José Brulé, a Mayo Indian, and Antonio Keyes, a Californian and a resident of La Paz—were shot by order of Captain Naglee—in my opinion, in direct violation of General Scott's order No. 372, and of my instructions to him. The case is thus laid before the colonel commanding, for his decision and opinion as to the course to be pursued respecting it.

I am, sir, very respectfully, your obedient servant,
HENRY S. BURTON,
Lieutenant Colonel New York Volunteers.

Lieutenant W. T. SHERMAN,
Act. Asst. Adjt. Gen. Tenth Mil. Dept.

A true copy:
W. T. SHERMAN,
First Lieut. 3d Artillery, A. A. A. General.

[Unofficial.]

CARISALO, *April* 11, 1848.

SIR: We arrived here yesterday at 3 p. m., intending to push on to La Paz, but our animals are so tired that I am compelled to remain here until this afternoon, and will hope to get to La Paz during to-morrow morning.

I have no other news to communicate except that the country has been well cleared of its cursed vermin, and that there are not half a dozen Taquies south of Punification. I have five prisoners with me, but shall shoot two of them when near La Paz, in sight of the ruin that they have caused. I have sent with this a note to Lieutenant Penrose for one hundred and fifty rations of hard bread and one hundred and fifty rations of coffee. Mr. Pendleton will not get here before to-night, and will not be able to leave here before to-morrow evening.

Very respectfully, your obedient servant,

H. M. NAGLEE.

Lieutenant Colonel H. S. Burton,
  Commanding, La Paz.

A true copy:

HENRY S. BURTON,
Lieutenant Colonel New York Volunteers.

True copy:

W. T. SHERMAN,
First Lieutenant 3d Artillery, A. A. A. General.

La Paz, Lower California, *April* 11, 1848.

Sir: In your unofficial note of to-day, you mention your intention of *shooting* two of your *prisoners* when near La Paz, in sight of the ruin they have caused. I am under the impression that your instructions will not admit of this course. You will therefore bring all of your prisoners to La Paz.

I am, sir, with much respect, your obedient servant,

HENRY S. BURTON,
Lieutenant Colonel N. Y. Volunteers, commanding.

Captain H. M. Naglee,
 New York Volunteers.

A true copy:

W. T. SHERMAN,
First Lieutenant 3d Artillery, A. A. A. General.

Headquarters First Detachment N. Y. Volunteers,
Todos Santos, March 31, 1848.

Sir: You will leave this place this afternoon at four o'clock, with the mounted men from your company, for the ranche of "Cunano," distant about fifty miles, on the road to Magdalena bay, for the purpose of intercepting any of the enemy's forces which may move in that direction. On arriving at that place, you will be guided in the course then to be pursued by such information as you may obtain—it being the object to follow and cut up the scattered forces of the enemy wherever they may be found. And even before reaching "Cunano," you will be at liberty to change your direction, if, in your opinion, circumstances justify you in doing so. If you should not again join the main body, you will proceed to La Paz, after having accomplished, so far as you may be able, the object indicated above. The movements of the main body will depend entirely upon the information respecting the enemy's position; but it is hoped that you may be able to communicate to headquarters anything you may learn of the enemy's operations. In your treatment of the Taquies you will be governed by general orders No. 372 of 1847, of General Scott's, regarding them as robbers and murderers, who are bound by no civilized rules of warfare.

I am, sir, very respectfully, your obedient servant,
HENRY S. BURTON,
Lieut. Colonel 1st New York Volunteers, commanding.
Captain H. M. NAGLEE,
1st New York Volunteers.

The undersigned would respectfully report, that he received the above order at 4 o'clock p. m., on the 31st of March, and at 5 o'clock p. m., with 50 men, left Todos Santos to pursue the enemy. We had scarcely commenced our march, when it was discovered that the guide upon whom we were most trusting for our information, and who resided at "Cunano," had not joined us. The interpreter was sent back to advise you of this fact, but nevertheless this guide did not join us. When near the mouth of the arroyo Muelle, we were informed that José Rosa Merina, a Mexican officer, with 16 men, and Colegial, the Taqui chief, with 26 Indians, had gone towards "Carisalle" to wait for others to join them. We were informed that the distance to Cunano was 55 miles, by a heavy, sandy road, without a habitation or drop of water. We had but 3 days' provisions; and the animals, although they had rested 24 hours, had filled themselves with the stocks of the green corn and sugar cane, and were not in a condition to travel the road to "Cunano." I therefore concluded to take the road to "Carisalle," and thence by the road to "Aripes," near La Paz, where I could order in advance an additional supply of provisions, and proceed to San Ilarius and "Aqua Colorado," where all of the enemy must necessarily pass who were retreating towards "Mulige."

On the morning of the 1st of April we reached "Carisalle," 36 miles from "Todos Santos," but were disappointed in learning that the forces above referred to had passed during the night without stopping, and a few hours afterwards, whilst the men were sleeping, a small party of cavalry made their appearance, and were pursued, but they ran into the cactac, and it was impossible to follow them. At 6 p. m. we were mounted, and followed the trail of the previous night for about 6 miles, when it left the road and entered the cactac, and we afterwards learned they had been advised of our pursuit, and changed their route.

On the morning of the 2d we arrived at the "Aripes," and were here detained unnecessarily 24 hours, waiting for a detachment that had been despatched in advance for provisions. They returned on the 3d, and reported the capture of two Mexican soldiers at Refugio. During the 3d we passed through "Rodrigues, El Caxon de los Reys," and at midnight reached "Los Reys."

On the evening of the 4th we arrived at Guadalupe, and leaving 25 men with Lieutenant Pendleton, with the remainder we pressed forward for "San Ilarius." When within 9 miles of that place, we were informed that a party of 50 Taquies had passed from "San Ilarius" to "La Junta," and we at once turned in that direction. At 4 a. m. of the 5th, after having searched all the places where the Indians would have stopped, we approached the last hut, and the only one of the four in "La Junta" that had not been deserted, and discovered the fires of the Indians, which were 200 yards from the house, and on the other side of a lagoon, around which it was necessary to pass. We dismounted, and, with 15 men, were in the act of surrounding them, when one of the guides discharged his musket, which awakened the Indians; we charged in upon them, but it was too dark to use powder and ball, and they made their escape. We, however, succeeded in capturing all their horses, arms, and ammunition, and in taking two prisoners, which were afterwards ordered to be shot.

In consequence of the outrages that this band of Indians were committing, and the impossibility of my overtaking them, (for I could not obtain fresh horses,) I considered some extraordinary effort absolutely necessary to drive them out of the country, and at the same time to reassure the "rancheros," who were so much intimidated by the diabolical acts of these villains that many of them had left their houses, and concealed their families, and the little property they could carry with them, in the mountains. I therefore called upon the authorities and rancheros (see the copy attached) to arrest them in their flight, and sent a detachment of a sergeant and nine men, in company with Don Juan de Dios and Don Questis, responsible Mexican friends, to pursue the Indians as far as "Punification."

It being impossible for our tired horses to go further, suffering for the want of food, barely living upon sprouts of the mosquit tree, and there being no water at the places I have named—frequently 30 and 50 miles apart—and learning that a number of Mexican officers, with 30 to 40 men, were concealed near San Antonio, I determined to return, and on the 6th I ordered Lieutenant Pendleton to take the road by "Agua Colorado," whilst I took that to "San Ilarius," and to meet at "Conéja" where the roads join.

On the 7th I learned that two Mexican soldiers were concealed about the premises of Don Juan Gomez De Ayer, a Portuguese, living at San Ilarius. He denied any knowledge of them until he was placed in arrest and ordered to be taken to La Paz, when he had them produced; one of them had been wounded at San José.

On the morning of the 8th we reached Conéja, 40 miles, and Lieutenant Pendleton joined me, and brought one prisoner that one of his patrols had taken near Agua Colorado. On the 9th we entered Cunano, 18 miles. Here, as at Conéja, both on the Pacific coast, we found a little very brackish water, and some salt grass of two years standing, there having been no rain during that time. We learned that there had passed in all about 90 persons during the 2d and 3d; that none had passed since; that the greater part of these had been driven from the other roads in consequence of our close pursuit; and they were so much pressed, knowing they would receive no quarter, that many of them had thrown away their arms.

On the morning of the 10th we entered Carisalle, 45 miles, without water or grass, and hearing of the surprise of the Mexicans near San Antonio, by Lieutenant Selden, of the Cyane, we rested our tired men and animals during the 11th, and on the 12th returned to La Paz, and Lieutenant Pendleton and Sergeant Roach on the 14th; the former bringing three and the latter two prisoners.

Although not so fortunate as to come in close contact with many of the enemy, we have at least succeeded in preventing any reunion, and in keeping them moving towards Loretto and Mulige, towards which points they have proceeded with the most astonishing rapidity. Since the evening of the 31st of March we have passed over all the road and searched all the ranchos between Todos Santos and La Paz, and as far north as Punification, and cleared that part of the country with the ruin that threatened to destroy its vitality.

During the pursuit we have travelled 350 miles over a road—or rather a path, for there are nothing but narrow mule paths in any of Lower California—through a worthless waste of sandy, rocky country, literally covered with the cactac, and various species of leafless thorn bushes, so closely matted together that none but a Californian with his leather clothes and armor can pass through them. The sun was so hot that we could not travel under it, and there was not water except at the places named, which was frequently so brackish that the thirst was increased more than diminished; at these places we found one and never more than two miserable huts, in which the occupants barely existed upon some milk and meat, and the cattle so exceedingly poor that they could hardly sustain their frames.

My command suffered much from the burning sun, dust, and the want of their full rations, living upon nothing but hard bread and fresh beef, and more than half the time upon the latter alone.

I have the honor to be, very respectfully, your obedient servant,
HENRY M. NAGLEE,
Captain 1st New York Regiment, com'g Detachment.
To HENRY S. BURTON,
Lieut. Colonel 1st New York Regiment, com'g, &c.

A true copy:

W. T. SHERMAN,
First Lieutenant 3d Artillery, A. A. A. General.

To all whom it may concern:

Know ye that authority is hereby given, and the authorities and rancheros are hereby required to arrest, and in the arrest to use any force that may be required, even to the taking of life, in order to bring to immediate punishment a number of banditti, who are known by the name of Taquies, and who have committed robbery, arson, murder, and rape, and are now committing the most infamous crimes through the whole country, and in consequence of which they have been declared outlaws, and their lives forfeited. Any prisoners that may be taken will be delivered to the nearest United States forces, and any lives that may be necessarily taken under this authority will be reported to the commanding officer of the United States forces at La Paz.

Given under my hand at Junta, Lower California, this fifth day of April, A. D. 1848.

HENRY M. NAGLEE,
Capt. 1st N. Y. Regiment, com'g detachment N. Y. Vols
To the AUTHORITIES and RANCHEROS
at Cayote, Punification, &c., to Mulige.

LA PAZ, *Lower California, April* 17, 1848.

SIR: I have the honor to send you herewith (in duplicate) returns for this post for the months of January, February, and March, 1848, and a copy of the written orders issued during the same period.

I am happy to report that the defeat and dispersion of the enemy on the 30th ultimo has been complete, and seems to have concluded the insurrection here.

The southern part of the peninsula is perfectly quiet. It is rumored that a party of the enemy has reunited at Mulige, but not in sufficient force to be effective. The present force in Lower California is thought to be sufficient to keep the country quiet, provided our squadron can prevent communication with the coast of Mexico, for the purpose of bringing over arms, ammunition, and men.

To-morrow nine prisoners of war, among them Manuel Pineda, the late Mexican commander in this country, and the reverend padre Gabriel Gonzales, with his sons, will be sent to Mazatlan. I have requested Commodore Shubrick to send the padre and his son to Monterey, if there is no prospect of a speedy declaration of peace between the United States and Mexico.

Lieutenant Halleck has charge of all the papers referring to these persons.

On the 15th instant Captain Naglee, with his company, embarked on board the United States ship Southampton, destined to garrison San José. Governed by the following portion of your letter of March 1, 1848: "Of these one officer and 114 recruits are assigned to your command, to be assigned to companies A, B, and D, in such a manner as you may think proper," I assigned 60 recruits to company D, making it 100 strong, for the purpose of garrisoning San José with one company of sufficient strength.

I have not the act for raising volunteers with me to refer to, and a doubt has arisen in my mind respecting the number of men allowed to each company.

I have the pleasure of sending to department headquarters, by Lieutenant Halleck, the Mexican flag captured at San Antonio, by Captain Street's command, on the 16th instant.

I am, sir, with much respect, your obedient servant,
HENRY S. BURTON,
Lieutenant Colonel New York Volunteers.

Lieut. W. T. SHERMAN,
A. A. A. General, Tenth Military Department.

A true copy:

W. T. SHERMAN,
First Lieutenant 3d Artillery, A. A. A. General.

[No. 37.] HEADQUARTERS TENTH MILITARY DEPARTMENT,
Monterey, California, August 17, 1848.

SIR: I have the honor to inform you that, accompanied by Lieutenant W. T. Sherman, 3d artillery, acting assistant adjutant general, I started on the 12th of June last to make a tour through the northern part of California. My principal purpose, however, was to visit the newly-discovered gold placer in the valley of the Sacramento.

I had proceeded about forty miles when I was overtaken by an express, bringing me intelligence of the arrival at Monterey of the United States storeship Southampton, with important letters from Commodore Shubrick and Lieutenant Colonel Burton. I returned at once to Monterey, and despatched what business was most important, and on the 17th resumed my journey. We reached San Francisco on the 20th, and found that all, or nearly all, its male population had gone to the mines. The town, which a few months before was so busy and thriving, was then almost deserted. On the evening of the 24th, the horses of the escort were crossed to Sansolito in a launch, and on the following day we resumed the journey, by way of Bodega and Sonoma, to Sutter's Fort, where we arrived on the morning of the 2d of July. Along the whole route mills were lying idle, fields of wheat were open to cattle and horses, houses vacant, and farms going to waste. At Sutter's there was more life and business. Launches were discharging their cargoes at the river, and carts were hauling goods to the fort, where already were established several stores, a hotel, &c. Captain Sutter had only two mechanics in his employ—a wagon-maker and blacksmith—whom he was then paying ten dollars per day. Merchants pay him a monthly rent of one hundred dollars per room, and whilst I was there a two-story house in the fort was rented as a hotel for five hundred dollars a month.

At the urgent solicitation of many gentlemen, I delayed there to participate in the first public celebration of our national anniversary at that fort, but on the 5th resumed the journey and proceeded twenty-five miles up the American Fork, to a point on it now known as the lower mines, or Mormon diggings. The hill sides were thickly strewn with canvass tents and bush arbors. A store was erected, and several boarding shanties in operation. The day was intensely hot; yet about two hundred men were at work in the full glare of the sun, washing for gold, some with tin pans, some with close-woven Indian baskets, but the greater part had a rude machine known as the cradle. This is on rockers six or eight feet long, open at the foot, and at its head has a coarse grate and sieve; the bottom is rounded, with small cleets nailed across. Four men are required to work this machine; one digs the gravel in the bank close by the stream, another carries it to the cradle and empties it on the grate, a third gives a violent rocking motion to the machine, whilst a fourth dashes water on from the stream itself. The sieve keeps the coarse stones from entering the cradle, the current of water washes off the earthy matter, and the gravel is gradually carried out at the foot of the machine, leaving the gold mixed with a fine heavy black sand above the first cleets. The sand and gold, mixed together, are then drawn off through auger holes into a pan below, are dried in the sun, and afterwards separated by blowing off the sand. A party of four men thus employed at the lower mines averaged a hundred dollars a day. The Indians, and those who have nothing but pans or willow baskets, gradually wash out the earth and separate the gravel by hand, leaving nothing but the gold mixed with sand, which is separated in the manner before described. The gold in the lower mines is in fine bright scales, of which I send several specimens.

As we ascended the south branch of the American Fork, the country became more broken and mountainous, and at the saw-mill, twenty-five miles above the lower washings, or fifty miles from Sutter's, the hills rise to about a thousand feet above the level of the Sacramento plain. Here a species of pine occurs, which led to the discovery of the gold. Captain Sutter, feeling the great want of lumber, contracted, in September last, with a Mr. Marshall, to build a saw-mill at that place. It was erected in the course of the past winter and spring—a dam and race constructed; but when the water was let on the wheel, the tail race was found to be too narrow to permit the water to escape with sufficient rapidity. Mr. Marshall, to save labor, let the water directly into the race, with a strong current, so as to wash it wider and deeper. He effected his purpose, and a large bed of mud and gravel was carried to the foot of the race. One day Mr. Marshall, when walking down the race to this deposite of mud, observed some glittering particles at its upper edge: he gathered a few, examined them, and became satisfied of their value. He then went to the fort, told Captain Sutter of his discovery, and they agreed to keep it secret until a certain grist-mill of Sutter's was finished. It however got out, and spread like magic. Remarkable success attended the labors of the first explorers, and in a few weeks hundreds of men were drawn thither. At the time of my visit, but little more than three months after its first discovery, it was estimated that upwards of four thousand people were employed. At the mill there is a fine deposite, or bank of gravel, which the people respect as the property of Captain Sutter, although he pretends to no right to it, and would be perfectly satisfied with the simple promise of a pre-emption, on account of the mill which he has built there, at considerable cost. Mr. Marshall was living near the mill, and informed me that many persons were employed above and below him, that they used the same machines as at the lower washings, and that their success was about the same, ranging from one to three ounces of gold per man daily. This gold too is in scales, a little coarser than those of the lower mines. From the mills Mr. Marshall guided me up the mountain, on the opposite or north bank of the South Fork, where, in the beds of small streams, or ravines, now dry, a great deal of the coarse gold has been found. I there saw several parties at work, all of whom were doing very well. A great many specimens were shown me, some as heavy as four or five ounces in weight; and I send three pieces, labelled No. 5, presented by a Mr. Spence. You will perceive that some of the specimens accompanying this hold, mechanically, pieces of quartz, that the surface is rough, and evidently moulded in the crevice of a rock. This gold cannot have been carried far by water, but must have remained near where it was deposited from the rock that once bound it. I inquired of many people if they had encountered the metal in its matrix, but in every instance they said they had not, but that the gold was invariably mixed with washed gravel, or lodged in the crevices of other rocks. All bore testimony that they had found gold in greater or less quantities in the numerous small gullies or ravines that occur in that mountainous region. On the 7th of July I left the mill and crossed to a small stream emptying into the American Fork, three or four miles below the saw-mill. I struck this stream (now known as Weber's creek) at the washings of Suñal & Co. They had about thirty Indians employed, whom they pay in merchandise. They were getting gold of a character similar to that found in the main fork, and doubtless in sufficient quantities to satisfy them. I send you a small specimen, presented by this company, of their gold. From this point we proceeded up the stream about eight miles, where we found a great many people and Indians; some engaged in the bed of the stream, and others in the small side valleys that put into it. These latter are exceedingly rich, and two ounces were considered an ordinary yield for a day's work. A small gutter, not more than a hundred yards long by four feet wide and two or three feet deep, was pointed out to me as the one where two men, William Daly and Perry McCoon, had, a short time before, obtained in seven days $17,000 worth of gold.

Captain Weber informed me that he knew that these two men had employed four white men and about a hundred Indians, and that, at the end of one week's work, they paid off their party and had left with $10,000 worth of this gold. Another small ravine was shown me, from which had been taken $12,000 worth of gold. Hundreds of similar ravines, to all appearances, are as yet untouched. I could not have credited these reports had I not seen, in the abundance of the precious metal, evidence of their truth. Mr. Neligh, an agent of Commodore Stockton, had been at work about three weeks in the neighborhood, and showed me, in bags and bottles, over $2,000 worth of gold; and Mr. Lyman, a gentleman of education and worthy of every credit, said he had been engaged, with four others, with a machine, on the American Fork, just below Sutter's saw-mill, that they worked eight days, and that his share was at the rate of fifty dollars a day; but, hearing that others were doing better at Weber's place, they had removed there, and were then on the point of resuming operations.

I might tell of hundreds of similar instances; but to illustrate how plentiful the gold was in the pockets of common laborers, I will mention a simple occurrence which took place in my presence when I was at Weber's store. This store was nothing but an arbor of bushes, under which he had exposed for sale goods and groceries suited to his customers. A man came in, picked up a box of seidlitz powders, and asked its price. Captain Weber told him it was not for sale. The man offered an ounce of gold, but Captain Weber told him it only cost fifty cents, and he did not wish to sell it. The man then offered an ounce and a half, when Captain Weber *had* to take it. The prices of all things are high; and yet Indians, who before hardly knew what a breech-cloth was, can now afford to buy the most gaudy dresses.

The country, on either side of Weber's creek, is much broken up by hills, and is intersected in every direction by small streams or ravines, which contain more or less gold. Those that have been worked are barely scratched, and, although thousands of ounces have been carried away, I do not consider that a serious impression has been made upon the whole. Every day was developing new and rich deposites, and the only apprehension seemed to be that the metal would be found in such abundance as seriously to depreciate in value.

On the 8th of July I returned to the lower mines, and on the following day to Sutter's, where, on the 10th, I was making preparations for a visit to the Feather, Yubah, and Bear rivers, when I received a letter from Commodore A. R. Long, United States navy, who had just arrived at San Francisco from Mazatlan, with a crew for the sloop-of-war Warren, and with orders to take that vessel to the squadron at La Paz. Captain Long wrote to me that the Mexican Congress had adjourned without ratifying the treaty of peace, that he had letters for me from Commodore Jones, and that his orders were to sail with the Warren on or before the 20th of July. In consequence of these, I determined to return to Monterey, and accordingly arrived here on the 17th of July. Before leaving Sutter's, I satisfied myself that gold exists in the bed of the Feather river, in the Yubah, and Bear, and in many of the small streams that lie between the latter and the American Fork; also, that it had been found in the Cosumnes, to the south the American Fork. In each of those streams the gold is found in small scales, whereas in the intervening mountains it occurs in coarse lumps.

Mr. Sinclair, whose rancho is three miles above Sutter's, on the north side of the American, employs about fifty Indians on the North Fork, not far from its junction with the main stream. He had been engaged about five weeks when I saw him, and up to that time his Indians had used simply closely-woven willow baskets. His nett proceeds (which I saw) were about $16,000 worth of gold. He showed me the proceeds of his last week's work—fourteen pounds avoirdupois of clean washed gold.

The principal store at Sutter's Fort, that of Brannant & Co., had received in payment for goods $36,000 worth of this gold from the 1st of May to the 10th of July; other merchants had also made extensive sales. Large quantities of goods were daily sent forward to the mines, as the Indians, heretofore so poor and degraded, have suddenly become consumers of the luxuries of life. I before mentioned that the greater part of the farmers and rancheros had abandoned their fields to go to the mines; this is not the case with Captain Sutter, who was carefully gathering his wheat, estimated at 40,000 bushels. Flour is already worth at Sutter's $36 a barrel, and soon will be fifty. Unless large quantities of breadstuffs reach the country, much suffering will occur; but as each man is now able to pay a large price, it is believed the merchants will bring from Chili and Oregon a plentiful supply for the coming winter.

The most moderate estimate I could obtain from men acquainted with the subject was, that upwards of four thousand men were working in the gold district, of whom more than half were Indians, and that from $30,000 to $50,000 worth of gold, if not more, was daily obtained. The entire gold district, with very few exceptions of grants made some years ago by the American authorities, is on land belonging to the United States. It was a matter of serious reflection with me how I could secure to the government certain rents or fees for the privilege of procuring this gold; but upon considering the large extent of country, the character of the people engaged, and the small scattered force at my command, I resolved not to interfere, but permit all to work freely, unless broils and crimes should call for interference. I was surprised to learn that crime of any kind was very unfrequent, and that no thefts or robberies had been committed in the gold district. All live in tents, in bush houses, or in the open air, and men have frequently about their persons thousands of dollars' worth of this gold; and it was to me a matter of surprise that so peaceful and quiet a state of things should continue to exist. Conflicting claims to particular spots of ground may cause collisions, but they will be rare, as the extent of country is so great, and the gold so abundant, that for the present there is room and enough for all; still the government is entitled to rents for this land, and immediate steps should be devised to collect them, for the longer it is delayed the more difficult it will become. One plan I would suggest is to send out from the United States surveyors, with high salaries, bound to serve specified periods; a superintendent to be appointed at Sutter's Fort, with power to grant licenses to work a spot of ground, say 100 yards square, for one year, at a rent of from $100 to $1,000, at his discretion; the surveyors to measure the grounds and place the renter in possession.

A better plan, however, will be to have the district surveyed and sold at public auction to the highest bidder, in small parcels, say from 20 to 40 acres. In either case there will be many intruders, whom for years it will be almost impossible to exclude.

The discovery of these vast deposites of gold has entirely changed the character of Upper California. Its people, before engaged in cultivating their small patches of ground and guarding their herds of cattle and horses, have all gone to the mines, or are on their way thither; laborers of every trade have left their work-benches, and tradesmen their shops; sailors desert their ships as fast as they arrive on the coast, and several vessels have gone to sea with hardly enough hands to spread a sail; two or three are now at anchor in San Francisco with no crews on board. Many desertions, too, have taken place from the garrisons within the influence of the mines; 26 soldiers have deserted from the post of Sonoma, 24 from that of San Francisco, and 24 from Monterey. For a few days the evil appeared so threatening that great danger existed that the garrisons would leave in a body; and I refer you to my orders of the 25th of July to show the steps adopted to meet this contingency. I shall spare no exertions to apprehend and punish deserters; but I believe no time in the history of our country has presented such temptations to desert as now exist in California. The danger of apprehension is small, and the prospect of higher wages certain; pay and bounties are trifles, as laboring men at the mines can now earn in *one day* more than double a soldier's pay and allowances for a month, and even the pay of a lieutenant or captain cannot hire a servant. A carpenter or mechanic would not listen to an offer of less than fifteen or twenty dollars a day. Could any combination of affairs try a man's fidelity more than this? And I really think some extraordinary mark of favor should be given to those soldiers who remain faithful to their flag throughout this tempting crisis. No officer can now live in California on his pay. Money has so little value, the prices of necessary articles of clothing and subsistence are so exorbitant, and labor so high, that to hire a cook or servant has become an impossibility, save to those who are earning from thirty to fifty dollars a day. This state of things cannot last forever; yet, from the geographical position of California, and the new character it has assumed as a mining country, prices of labor will always be high, and will hold out temptations to desert. I therefore have to report, if the government wish to prevent desertions here on the part of men, and to secure zeal on the part of officers, their pay must be increased very materially. Soldiers both of the volunteer and regular service discharged in this country should be permitted at once to locate their land warrants in the gold district. Many private letters have gone to the United States giving accounts of the vast quantity of gold recently discovered, and it may be a matter of surprise why I have made no report on this subject at an earlier date. The reason is, that I could not bring myself to believe the reports that I heard of the wealth of the gold district until I visited it myself. I have no hesitation now in saying that there is more gold in the country drained by the Sacramento and San Joaquin rivers than will pay the cost of the present war with Mexico a hundred times over. No capital is required to obtain this gold, as the laboring man wants nothing but his pick, shovel, and tin pan, with which to dig and wash the gravel; and many frequently pick gold out of the crevices of rock with their butcher knives in pieces from one to six ounces.

Mr. Dye, a gentleman residing in Monterey, and worthy of every credit, has just returned from Feather river. He tells me that the company to which he belonged worked seven weeks and two days, with an average of fifty Indians, (washers,) and that their gross product was 273 pounds of gold. His share, one-seventh, after paying all expenses, is about 37 pounds, which he brought with him and exhibits in Monterey. I see no laboring man from the mines who does not show his two, three, or four pounds of gold. A soldier of the artillery company returned here a few days ago from the mines, having been absent on furlough twenty days; he made by trading and working during that time $1,500. During these twenty days he was travelling ten or eleven days, leaving but a week, in which he made a sum of money greater than he receives in pay, clothes, and rations during a whole enlistment of five years. These statements appear incredible, but they are true.

Gold is believed also to exist on the eastern slopes of the Sierra Nevada; and when at the mines, I was informed by an intelligent Mormon that it had been found near the Great Salt lake by some of his fraternity. Nearly all the Mormons are leaving California to go to the Salt lake, and this they surely would not do unless they were sure of finding gold there in the same abundance as they now do on the Sacramento.

The gold "placer" near the mission of San Fernando has long been known, but has been but little wrought for want of water. This is a spur that puts off from the Sierra Nevada, (see Fremont's map,) the same in which the present mines occur. There is, therefore, every reason to believe that in the intervening space of five hundred miles (entirely unexplored) there must be many hidden and rich deposites.

The placer gold is now substituted as currency of this country; in trade it passes freely at $16 per ounce; as an article of commerce its value is not yet fixed. The only purchase I made was of the specimen No. 7, which I got of Mr. Neligh at $12 the ounce. That is about the present cash value in the country, although it has been sold for less. The great demand for goods and provisions made by this sudden development of wealth has increased the amount of commerce at San Francisco very much, and it will continue to increase.

I would recommend that a mint be established at some eligible point on the bay of San Francisco, and that machinery, and all the apparatus and workmen, be sent by sea. These workmen must be bound by high wages, and even bonds, to secure their faithful services; else the whole plan may be frustrated by their going to the mines as soon as they arrive in California. If this course be not adopted, gold to the amount of many millions of dollars will pass yearly to other countries, to enrich their merchants and capitalists. Before leaving the subject of mines, I will mention that on my return from the Sacramento I touched at New Almoden, the quicksilver mine of Mr. Alexander Forbes, consul of her Britannic Majesty at Tepic. This mine is in a spur of mountains 1,000 feet above the level of the bay of San Francisco, and is distant in a southern direction from the Pueblo San Jose about twelve miles. The ore (cinnabar) occurs in a large vein dipping at a strong angle to the horizon. Mexican miners are employed in working it, by driving shafts and galleries about six feet by seven, following the vein.

The fragments of rock and ore are removed on the backs of Indians in raw-hide sacks. The ore is then hauled in an ox wagon from the mouth of the mine down to a valley well supplied with wood and water, in which the furnaces are situated. These furnaces are of the simplest construction, exactly like a common bake-oven, in the crown of which is inserted a whaler's trying kettle; another inverted kettle forms the lid. From a hole in the lid a small brick channel leads to an apartment or chamber, in the bottom of which is inserted a small iron kettle. This chamber has a chimney.

In the morning of each day the kettles are filled with mineral, (broken in small pieces,) mixed with lime; fire is then applied, and kept up all day. The mercury, volatilized, passes into the chamber, is condensed on the sides and bottom of the chamber, and flows into the pot prepared for it. No water is used to condense the mercury.

During a visit I made last spring, four such ovens were in operation, and yielded in the two days I was there 656 pounds of quicksilver, worth at Mazatlan $1 80 per lb. Mr. Walkinshaw, the gentleman now in charge of this mine, tells me that the vein is improving, and that he can afford to keep his people employed even in these extraordinary times. This mine is very valuable of itself, and becomes the more so, as mercury is extensively used in obtaining gold. It is not at present used in California for that purpose, but will be at some future time. When I was at this mine last spring, other parties were engaged in searching for veins; but none have been discovered that are worth following up, although the earth in that whole range of hills is highly discolored, indicating the presence of this ore. I send several beautiful specimens, properly labelled. The amount of quicksilver in Mr. Forbes's vats on the 15th of July was about 25,000 pounds.

I enclose you herewith sketches of the country through which I passed, indicating the position of the mines, and the topography of the country in the vicinity of those I visited.

Some of the specimens of gold accompanying this were presented for transmission to the department by the gentlemen named below; the numbers on the topographical sketch, corresponding to the numbers on the labels of the respective specimens, show from what part of the gold region they were obtained:

1. Captain J. A. Sutter.
2. John Sinclair.
3. William Glover, R. C. Kirby, Ira Blanchard, Levi Fairfield, Franklin H. Ayer; Mormon diggings.
4. Chas. Weber.
5. Robert Spence.
6. Sernal & Co.
7. Robert D. Neligh.
8. C. E. Picket; American Fork, Columa.
9. E. C. Kemble.
10. T. H. Green, from San Fernando, near Los Angeles.
A. Two ounces purchased from Mr. Neligh.
B. Sand found in washing gold, which contains small particles.
11. Captain Frisbie; Dry diggings, Weber's creek.
12. Cosumnes.
13. Cosumnes; Hartnell's ranch.

14. A small specimen, supposed to be platina, found mixed with the finer particles of the gold.

I have the honor to be your obedient servant,
R. B. MASON,
Colonel 1st Dragoons, commanding.

General R. JONES,
Adjutant General U. S. A., Washington, D. C.

[No. 38.] HEADQUARTERS TENTH MILITARY DEPARTMENT,
Monterey, California, August 18, 1848.

SIR: I have the honor herewith to enclose you a copy of a letter from Lieutenant Colonel Burton, which was received here on the evening of the 6th instant.

The instructions asked for by him were anticipated, and are contained in a letter addressed by my order, dated June 17, 1848, sent him by the United States storeship Southampton, on the 6th of July, a copy of which letter you will find among the military correspondence sent you by this opportunity.

I enclose herewith the original petitions from citizens of the towns of La Paz and San José, Lower California, one of which is addressed to the Congress of the United States. Many of these people assisted our garrisons there, and dread the consequences of their conduct, since it is known that Lower California is to be given back to Mexico. I must say in their behalf, that, by active assistance, and by neutrality, they have contributed much towards upholding our authority in the peninsula; for Lieutenant Colonel Burton had at La Paz only 112 men, and it was not in my power to reinforce him until the 20th of March last, so that it is doubtful whether he could have held his post without such aid. This consideration entitles them to a favorable hearing of the Congress of the United States.

The mutineers referred to by Lieutenant Colonel Burton will, most probably, come to Monterey, and will necessarily have to be discharged and let loose in the country, to swell the number of bad men already here. The man, Lawson, charged with murder, will also have to be discharged, as a military commission cannot now be assembled, and, as the act was committed in Mexican territory, the man is not liable to be tried by the courts of the United States.

I enclose you herewith charges preferred by Lieutenant Colonel Burton against two of his officers, Lieutenants Buffum and Lemon, of the United States volunteers. These officers reached Monterey in the ship Southampton, June 13, and were, by my order, assigned temporarily to the companies under the immediate command of Colonel Stevenson. They, too, must be mustered out of service with their companies, without trial.

I have the honor to be your most obedient servant,
R. B. MASON,
Colonel 1st Dragoons, commanding.

Brigadier General R. JONES,
Adjutant General U. S. A., Washington city.

LA PAZ, LOWER CALIFORNIA,
June 27, 1848.

SIR: Enclosed herewith, I send you, by special express to San Diego, the accompanying documents from Mexico, directed to Colonel Mason. Official news of the ratification of a treaty of peace with Mexico has reached me, through Commodore Jones, and I am anxiously awaiting instructions respecting my movements from deptartment headquarters.

I request instructions, also, respecting those inhabitants of Lower California who have taken up arms in our favor, during the late disturbances in the country, relying upon the assurances that Lower California would never revert to the republic of Mexico, made to them by Commodore Shubrick, in his proclamation issued at San José, November, 1847, and contained in the statement of the President of the United States, in his annual message of 1847, that it "should never be given up to Mexico."

These assurances were received in good faith ; and among the better class of population in the country great pleasure was evinced at the prospect of receiving, in Lower California, a just and permanent government.

As nothing is said, in this treaty of peace, respecting persons in the situations of these inhabitants of Lower California, they are left to the mercy of Mexico; and many have appealed most earnestly to the agents of the United States in the country for protection, saying that their property will be confiscated, their lives and those of their families endangered, if they remain in the country after the American troops leave, and requesting that means of transportation may be furnished them for the removal of their families and effects to Upper California, Oregon, or such other of the United States as they may select for their future residence.

Enclosed herewith, I send two communications, which will exhibit, in some measure, the state of feeling in the jurisdictions of La Paz and San José.

On the 8th of May last I sailed for Mazatlan, via San José, for the purpose of procuring a vessel of war to proceed to Mulige and disperse the remnant of the enemy's force reunited at that place after the action of Lodos Santos. The news from Mexico, at that time, was of such a nature that Commodore Jones thought there was no urgent necessity for this movement, and it would be advisable to await further information from Mexico. Two days after my arrival in Mazatlan, I was taken sick with fever and ague, and detained until the 8th of June, when I sailed for Cape St. Lucas. After a passage of ten days I arrived in San José. I reached this place on the 23d instant, after a detention of ten days in San José. I regret to report that I found this command in a great state of excitement.

On my arrival in Mazatlan I found a party of ten men, to whom I had given a leave of absence for fifteen days, (previous to my departure for Mazatlan,) for the purpose of visiting some of the islands in the harbor of La Paz, with a small sloop.

Immediate measures were taken to send these men back to the place, and they arived here on the 28th of May. These men, hearing the news of peace in Mazatlan, appear to have returned here with an idea that they were released from further military rule, and immediately commenced an excitement, which soon became beyond the control of the officers.

On the 3d instant, Captain Steele sent a small vessel to Mazatlan, requesting assistance from Commodore Jones, who sent the Independence to this place immediately. The Independence arrived on the 18th instant.

On the 2d of June, Captain Steele, then commanding, addressed a communication to department headquarters, enclosing charges against the leaders, and requesting a general court-martial for their trial. On the 5th of June, Captain Steele again addressed Commodore Jones and department headquarters, reporting another outbreak, and the command setting order at defiance. On my arrival I found the ringleaders at liberty, and the excitement somewhat abated.

The next day ten of the most prominent of the command in the late troubles were sent on board the Independence as prisoners; and on the 26th three more. The command is more quiet, and I anticipate no disturbance.

On the 25th instant some sailors from the Lexington were permitted to come on shore on liberty, and had a drunken frolic in the quarters of one of the married men, named Lawson. Both man and wife became intoxicated; a quarrel ensued; and about half-past 10 o'clock in the evening the man shot his wife with his musket. She died a short time after.

The man is in irons on board the Independence. Enclosed herewith are charges preferred against him.

As there is a prospect of a speedy removal from this place, I would request that the court-martial applied for by Captain Steele may be convened after our arrival in Upper California, and not at this place.

It will be advisable not to detail any of the company officers in the command upon the court.

It will be necessary to try the case of private Macguire, referred to in my application for a military commission, March 10, 1848, at this place, as the principal witnesses in it are Californians; such is not the case with private *Lawson*.

I have the honor to acknowledge the receipt of your communications of March 18, April 26, and May 2, 1848.

Musician Farley, referred to in yours of March 18, is at this post, and will be returned to Monterey by the first opportunity.

The board of survey ordered in yours of April 18, 1848, to examine into the claims of those friendly to our flag who have sustained damages during the attack upon this place and San José, will be formed as soon as Commodore Jones arrives here. He is daily expected from Guaynas.

I send enclosed herewith the return of this post (in duplicate) for April, 1848, with copies of the written orders issued during that month. The return and orders for May have been forwarded to department headquarters via Mazatlan.

I am, sir, with much respect, your obedient servant,

H. S. BURTON,
Lieutenant Colonel N. Y. Volunteers.

Lieutenant W. T. SHERMAN,
A. A. A. General 10th Military Department, Monterey.

A true copy of the original on file in this office.

W. G. SHERMAN,
First Lieutenant 3d Artillery, A. A. A. General.

HEADQUARTERS TENTH MILITARY DEPARTMENT,
Monterey, California, August 17, 1848.

Muy Honorable Congreso de los Estados Unidos:

Señor como que los Fines de la Sosiedad jamas podran dirigirse á la Dicha de ernos y a la adbursidad de otros de hay a qui los Hombres no deben estipular tombenciones, ni aser pactos que no se dirigan al vien comun y á una felicidad solida.

¿Como podremos llaman Patriotas a los perturbadores de nuestra sosiego, y á los Raptores de nuestras esearos vienes? La esperansia nos a echo sentir el quyo de la siranid que profesan los militares de nuestra nacion, y non estremesemos al recordar su echos. En ningun punto se dieron a conaser mas que aqui en donde disembolbieron toda la Rapasidad de su genio y dieron a salier quienes eran. Pero vien notorio es quienes fueron las que formaron la rebolucion y no deran que ningun Hombre de vien sequiera sus malba dos Huestes.

Las Hombres de bein del pais señor estan por el orden y aspiran á la felicidad de esta peninsula, y como la esperansia nos ha echo ver que despues de mas de tresientos años de desenbierta jamas si a tratado de protijirta ni ilustrar la ni por los españoles in por los Miguraros? Podremos esperar en lo subresibo algun vien cuando á los que no hemos sido adictos a los ladrones nos llaman tracidores y venan nuestro esterminio? ¡No lo permeta Dios que buelbamos a esperimentar mas rigores de nuestra mal sistemada republica! Dichasas nasatros si el Gobierno de los Estados Unidos nos admite bajo de su protusion y agrega a sus Estados este (por tantos años) desgraciado continento. Na señor asi lo deseamos y prosternados ante la V. M. N. impetramos esta gracia, los que subscribirnos a nombre de los pueblos.

San Jose, del cabo, Mayo 13, 1848.

JOSE MIGUEL CHOSADO, *Alcalde.*
NORATO ALVAREZ, *Regidor.*
JOSE IGNO. DUARTO.

HEADQUARTERS TENTH MILITARY DEPARTMENT,
Monterey, California, August 18, 1848.

SIR: I transmit herewith copies of letters, &c., pertaining to the civil government of California up to this date.

Very respectfully, your obedient servant,

R. B. MASON,
Colonel 1*st Dragoons, commanding.*

General R. JONES,
Adjutant General, Washington, D. C.

HEADQUARTERS TENTH MILITARY DEPARTMENT,
Monterey, California, April, 1848.

SIR: I am in the receipt of your letter of the 10th instant, reporting the arrest of Canfield, Barnes, and others, charged with passing counterfeit gold coin purporting to be the coin of the United States.

I do not think they can be properly tried by a military commission, as you suggest. I do not wish to try before military courts any cases that are not clearly such as military courts should take cognizance of. 'Tis true there are no civil courts in California above those of the alcalde, but one can be created for these special cases; and I have therefore appointed Stephen C. Foster and ———— special judges, to hold a court at Los Angeles for the trial of those men charged with passing the counterfeit coin. The name of the judge is left blank in the appointment, that you may fill it with the name of some suitable person in the lower country. Please appoint some one to conduct the prosecution on the part of the Territory, and give to him such information as may be in your power relative to trials by jury.

I am, respectfully, your obedient servant,

R. B. MASON,
Colonel 1st Dragoons, commanding.

Colonel J. D. STEVENSON,
New York Volunteers, commanding Southern Military Department, Los Angeles, California.

HEADQUARTERS TENTH MILITARY DEPARTMENT,
Monterey, California, April, 1848.

SIR: Colonel Stevenson has reported the arrest of Canfield, Barnes, and others, charged with passing counterfeit gold coin purporting to be the coin of the United States. I herewith endorse an appointment of judge for yourself and ————, to hold a special court for the trial of said persons. The court will be held at Los Angeles, on such day as you may appoint, after consulting with Colonel Stevenson. You will cause the prisoners to be tried by a jury of twelve impartial men. It would be well to summon eighteen or twenty jurors, so that, if any are objected to, there may be others on the spot to supply their places. A list of the jurors summoned should be given to each of the prisoners at least two days before they are put upon their trial. Be careful to have each juror, witness, and interpreter properly sworn, and that fact entered on the record; and see that the prisoners have a fair and impartial trial. If found guilty, the court will pronounce sentence, which, together with the whole record, will be forwarded to me. The record should present each day's proceedings; the testimony given in should be entered, as near as can be, in the words of the witness, who should accurately state, as near as he can, the day, month, year, and place where the counterfeit coin was passed, together with all the circumstances attending the same.

Colonel Stevenson will appoint some one to prosecute the cases on the part of the Territory; you will appoint a sheriff and a clerk for the occasion. Be pleased to examine well the Mexican law on the subject of passing counterfeit coin. I am told it is very severe.

The quartermaster at Los Angeles has instructions relative to paying the costs of the prosecutions.

I am, very respectfully, your obedient servant,

R. B. MASON,
Colonel 1st Dragoons, Governor of California.

STEPHEN C. FOSTER,
Alcalde, Cuidad de los Angeles.

HEADQUARTERS TENTH MILITARY DEPARTMENT,
Monterey, California, April 18, 1848.

SIR: The costs of the prosecution that will be incurred in the coming trial of Canfield, Barnes, and others, for passing counterfeit gold coin, will be paid, if acquitted by you, out of the military contribution fund, according to the rates mentioned below. If they are convicted, the costs must be paid by themselves, and the amount stopped in the paymaster's hands, as they are not yet paid off. The court must certify to the correctness of the bill of costs before you pay.

THE JUDGE

Will be allowed, for each day the court is actually in session.......$5 00

PROSECUTING ATTORNEY.

For each case...30 00

SHERIFF.

For summoning each juror and witness......................	50
For each mile travelling in summoning jurors and witnesses......	6
For each day's attendance on the court........................	1 00

JURORS AND WITNESSES.

For each day's attendance on court...........................	50
For each day occupied in travelling to and from the court by the most direct route, reckoning a day's travel at 35 miles..........	50
For each mile travelling to and from the court by the most direct route...	6

CLERK OF THE COURT.

For each day the court is in actual session...................... 2 50

I am, respectfully, your obedient servant.
R. B. MASON,
Colonel 1st Dragoons, commanding.
Lieutenant J. W. DAVIDSON,
1st Dragoons, A. A. Quartermaster,
Los Angeles, California.

I, Richard B. Mason, colonel of the 1st regiment of dragoons United States army, and governor of California, by virtue of authority in me vested, do hereby appoint Stephen C. Foster and ———— judges, to hold a special court at Cuidad de los Angeles, on such a day as may be appointed by said judges, for the trial of Ruel Barnes, C. C. Canfield, Samuel Myers, and others, of the company of Mormon volunteers, late in the service of the United States, charged with passing counterfeit gold coin purporting to be the coin of the United States.

Given at Monterey, the capital of California, this 18th day of April, A. D. 1848, and the 72d year of the independence of the United States.
R. B. MASON,
Colonel 1st Dragoons, Governor of California.

HEADQUARTERS TENTH MILITARY DEPARTMENT,
Monterey, California, April 19, 1848.

SIR: In obedience to your order of the 29th of October, which was received on the 11th instant, I have the honor herewith to forward to you a general account of all moneys derived from the collection of revenue that have passed through my hands, to include the month of March of the present year.

I am, respectfully, your obedient servant,

R. B. MASON,
Colonel 1st Dragoons, commanding.

Hon. SECRETARY OF WAR,
Washington city, D. C.

HEADQUARTERS TENTH MILITARY DEPARTMENT,
Monterey, California, April 21, 1848.

SIR: I have the honor to acknowledge the receipt of your communication of the 14th instant, together with the petition of the same date enclosed. I have no authority to make grants of land. My instructions confer no such power; nor could the President delegate any such to me, because the United States only holds the Californias as a military conquest, and no such authority can be rightfully exercised until the country becomes a part of the territory of the United States, and under her laws, and then only by an act of Congress. The precedent to which you refer me, I thought at the time, and have always thought, was one improperly exercised.

I am, respectfully, your obedient servant,

R. B. MASON,
Colonel 1st Dragoons, Governor of California.

R. SEMPLE, Esq.,
Benecia city, California.

HEADQUARTERS TENTH MILITARY DEPARTMENT,
Monterey, California, April 24, 1848.

SIR: I have received your letter of the 11th, and have given Yingo's and Castro's land case a complete consideration and have fully examined the records in this office concerning the same. Yingo petitioned for the land lying between the lines designating the limits of Castro's land and the land of the mission of Santa Clara, as shown upon the accompanying map, which is a copy of the official map here. The whole of the land asked for by Yingo was not granted; that only was granted lying within the said lines, marked in the accompanying map, which lines are *copied from the said official map on record here*, and these said lines correspond exactly with the reading of Yingo's title, "the boundaries being from *his house to the first spring of water, inclusive, called Los Animas.*" Thus it is clear that Yingo has no claim to land from his house in the direction of the Santa Clara land, nor beyond the spring Los Animas in the other direction: he is *tied fast down* to the land lying between his house and the spring; or, in other words, supposing the arrow on the map to correctly point to north, Yingo's land does *not extend to the westward of the spring, nor to the eastward of his house.* The book of land records estimates Yingo's to be " half of a league, little more or a little less." The land designated as that asked for by Yingo, as you will see by the note in the corner of the map, is three-fourths of a league in breadth, and one and a quarter in length; but only half a league was granted, a little more or less, that to be between the house and spring, and is marked on the official map by lines, from which the said red lines on the accompanying map are copied.

You speak of Castro's title being younger than that of Yingo's, which is the 14th of February, 1844. Castro claims under Estrada's title, which is the 1st of January, 1842—two years older than that of Yingo. But Yingo had only granted to him one half league, and that is marked by lines on the official map or record, which, in the copy, is shown by the red lines, and the land outside cannot be held by any one claiming under Yingo.

With the accompanying map I send the copy of the letters of Estrada, Yingo, and Castro.

I am, respectfully, your obedient servant,

R. B. MASON,
Colonel 1st Dragoons, Governor of California.

CHARLES WHITE, Esq.,
Alcalde, Pueblo de San José.

P. S.—An alcalde cannot hold a court for the final adjudication and settlement of land titles. In this case the official records clearly determine the matter, and confine Yingo, or rather those who claim under him, within the "red lines," beyond which they cannot go without being liable to be removed by the alcalde.

R. B. MASON,
Colonel 1st Dragoons, Governor of California.

HEADQUARTERS TENTH MILITARY DEPARTMENT,
Monterey, California, April 24, 1848.

SIR: I have, with great care, examined the question which you presented to me in the case of land claimed by Narvaez and Fisher. It appears, from the official record and map in this office, that, on the 30th of March, 1844, there were granted to Narvaez two leagues within the land called San Juan Bautista; this grant is clearly defined and marked on the northwest, southwest, and southeast, as is shown on the official map corresponding with the title papers, but it is undefined to the northeast. Thus it appears clear that the grant cannot extend into the hills of San Juan Bautista, if the two leagues of land called for are contained between the said hills and the boundaries, as designated on the map.

I am, respectfully, your obedient servant,

R. B. MASON,
Colonel 1st Dragoons, Governor of California.

Don MANUEL DIEZ, *Monterey, California.*

HEADQUARTERS TENTH MILITARY DEPARTMENT,
Monterey, California, April 28, 1848.

SIR: I herewith enclose to you some modifications of the tariff, ordered by the President, as proposed by the Secretary of the Treasury, of the 5th of November, 1847, together with his orders for the collection of an export duty on gold and silver, as also recommended by the Secretary of the Treasury, on the 16th of November, 1847. These documents were sent to me by Commodore Jones, from Callao, as you will see by the extracts from his letter accompanying the copies now sent you. The ad valorem duties now to be collected, according to the recommendations of the Secretary of the Treasury of the 5th of November, will render it necessary to closely examine vessels' invoices, and see that they are authenticated, as required by the 7th article of the regulations, and that all entries of merchandise are strictly made in conformity to " form" 3.

From Commodore Shubrick's letter to me of the 8th of February, and one of the same date from Hugh W. Green, collector at Mazatlan, to the commodore, sent to me by the commodore, with a copy of the printed tariff regulations from the Treasury Department of the 30th of March, 1847, including amendments made by the Secretary of the Treasury and those by the commodore's authority, it appears that the latter has thrown open the coasting trade to all vessels. This I did not discover until your letter of the 21st relative to the Chilian barque Natalia brought me to look closer into the subject. This accounts for the Natalia being cleared by the collector at Mazatlan for San Francisco. I send you herewith one of the printed regulations from Washington of the 30th of March, 1847, corrected in red ink, copied from one Commodore Shubrick sent me, embracing the modifications of the 5th of November, 1847, and those made by the commodore. I have been obliged to make this correction upon an old corrected copy; but the red ink will distinguish the present changes from the old blank marks. All articles of merchandise now stand tariffed *as in the print*, except where the red marks indicate a change.

The regulation of the import trade, you recollect, was assigned to the senior naval officer by the Secretary of the Navy's letter to Commodore Stockton, dated November, 1846. Lumber and the growth and produce of California, carried from port to port in California, will still continue free from duty, except it come from Lower California, where the people are in arms against us. Have some copies of Mr. Walker's recommendations to the President of the 5th and 16th of November printed, and send them to me for distribution as soon as possible. Send some to the islands, &c., when an opportunity offers. Have also some blank forms of No. 3 printed, so as to meet this change to the *ad valorem* duties.

Goods imported into California from the United States and other countries—via the Sandwich islands, for instance—and then reshipped and brought here, must pay duties according to the invoices from the latter port, and not according to the invoices from the original port. Having once been introduced into the foreign port, they must pay duties according to the valuation, &c., as shown by the *properly-authenticated invoices* from that port. I mention this because a vessel arrived here some time since from the Sandwich islands with goods, some or all of which had been brought from the United States, and, expecting to pay *ad valorem* duties, came prepared with two sets of invoices—one set from the United States, and one set from the island—the intention being to enter by the United States invoice, and sell by the one from the islands. I did not learn all this until after she had sailed. Others will doubtless attempt the same thing.

I am, respectfully, your obedient servant,
R. B. MASON,
Colonel 1st Dragoons, commanding.

Captain J. L Folsom,
Assistant Quartermaster U. S. Army, San Francisco.

A copy of the above letter has been furnished to the commanding officers at Santa Barbara and San Diego, and to the collector at San Pedro, for their information and government.
R. B. MASON,
Colonel 1st Dragoons, commanding.

Headquarters Tenth Military Department,
Monterey, California, April 28, 1848.

Sir: I enclose to you a communication, dated on the 10th instant, from H. A. Green and the attorney of Mr. West, from which it would appear that the trial he speaks of took place some months since, and an appeal was granted, when there were not courts to appeal to, though granted under an impression that there would soon be; and, as there are yet no such courts, I see no other way than to dismiss the appeal, or try it anew before a jury, if it was not so tried in the first instance. I know nothing of this affair beyond what is contained in Mr. Green's letter. The above are, therefore, mere suggestions, leaving you to dispose of the case as you think proper, knowing more of it than I do.

I am, respectfully, your obedient servant,
R. B. MASON,
Colonel 1st Dragoons, Governor of California.

L. H. Boggs,
Alcalde, Sonoma, California.

Headquarters Tenth Military Department,
Monterey, California, April 29, 1848.

Sir: I have to acknowledge the receipt of your letter of the 17th instant. An affidavit from yourself and the alcalde referred to in your said letter as to the facts therein set forth, together with the certificates of Captains Hunter and Davis, herein returned to you, will, I think, with the accounting officers, give you a credit for such property as you can clearly make appear was stolen during your absence; but the law has placed the settlement of accounts of officers in the quartermaster and commissary's departments in other hands than mine, and therefore they are beyond the scope of my power or authority.

I am, respectfully, your obedient servant,
R. B. MASON,
Colonel 1st Dragoons, commanding.

Robert Clift,
Late lieutenant in Mormon company,
Care of Lieutenant Davidson, Los Angeles, California.

HEADQUARTERS TENTH MILITARY DEPARTMENT,
Monterey, California, April 29, 1848.

SIR: I have examined the papers you handed me two days since, and have borne in mind the verbal representations you made on presenting them, but I do not see that I can take any action in the matter. When parties agree to submit their cases to the decision of arbitrators, they are bound to abide by whatever decision is made, whether that decision be right or wrong. The very fact of the parties referring their case to arbitrators for final and amicable settlement, shows that confidence was reposed in their integrity and judgment, and that the parties stand pledged to abide the verdict. Were I to exercise a stretch of power that in fact I do not possess, as to molest or disturb the decision of your abitrators, I should be establishing a precedent fraught with evil consequences.

I am, respectfully, your obedient servant,
R. B. MASON,
Colonel 1*st Dragoons, Governor of California.*

Mr. J. F. REED, *present.*

HEADQUARTERS TENTH MILITARY DEPARTMENT,
Monterey, California, April 29, 1848.

SIR: I have read the papers, dated on the 15th of the present month, that you sent me. I have enclosed them to Colonel Stevenson, at Los Angeles, who will see that your case is attended to.

Go to the Pueblo de los Angeles, and see him on the subject.

I am, respectfully, your obedient servant,
R. B. MASON,
Colonel 1*st Dragoons, Governor of California.*

JUAN DE JESUS OSIA,
San Diego, California.

HEADQUARTERS TENTH MILITARY DEPARTMENT,
Monterey, California, May 3, 1848.

SIR: I have received no reports or returns from the custom-house in San Diego since you have commanded that port. The custom-house regulations are plain and explicit. Perhaps it may be that the Mormon officers did not turn over to you the regulations, &c., appertaining to that branch of the service. I was not able to get from them a single report or return from the custom-house whilst they were at San Diego.

I send you herewith a corrected copy of the regulations, a copy of the alterations of the tariff of the 5th and 16th of November, 1847, and the President's orders thereon, together with a copy of my letter of the 28th of April to Captain Folsom, for your information and government. You will also find here the necessary blanks for the use of the custom-house, as also a manuscript quarterly account current and abstract of expenditures, showing the manner of making out those accounts and accounting for the funds derived from the customs.

I beg that you will study the regulations well, and strictly comply with all their requirements. The quarterly accounts current are for the War Department, and are to be transmitted through this office. At the end of each month *you must see* that the disbursing officer sends *promptly* to this office a "statement of revenue collected" during the month, according to the printed form. You will see, by reading the regulations, that the disburing officer ascertains the amount of duties due, and the commanding officer receives them and on the next day pays them over to the disbursing officer, and that they countersign each other's accounts.

The disbursing officer keeps the funds arising from the customs *separate* and apart from the funds belonging to the commissary and quartermaster's department, and expends them *only* upon orders from this office. Keep and regularly file all manifests, entries of merchandise, and permits to land the same.

Very respectfully, your obedient servant,
R. B. MASON,
Colonel 1st Dragoons, Governor of California.
Captain WILLIAM E. SHANNON,
New York Volunteers, commanding,
San Diego, California.

HEADQUARTERS TENTH MILITARY DEPARTMENT,
Monterey, California, May 6, 1848.

GENTLEMEN: On the 4th instant I received your communication of that date, and have attentively examined its contents. It is couched in such general terms, especially upon points where it ought to have been specific, in giving particular information, in order to a full and correct understanding of the controversy, with a view to my complying with the requests you make, that, were I now to make the decision or executive order you require, I should do it in the dark, and without the necessary information.

You say that "on the 17th of December last Cook denounced a quicksilver mine on his own ranch. Shortly thereafter he conveyed that mine to your company; and that on the 2d of February Alcalde Weeks gave Cook possession," &c.

According to the mining laws then existing, Cook, as an individual denouncer, could only acquire two appurtenances, "if in a new vein in a known mountain"—that is, in a mountain known to contain the mineral; or *three* appurtenances "if the discovery be absolutely new mineral mountains"—an appurtenance being 200 varas in length in direction of the vein, and varying from 100 to 200 varas in breadth, according to the inclination or angle the vein forms with the horizon.

You represent Cook as an individual denouncer, and as such conveying to your company; the company, then, under Cook's denouncement, only holds what Cook would have held under that denouncement had he not conveyed to your company, which, under the most favorable circumstances, was "three appurtenances." Now, does the "given space of land" (a very general and indefinite term) containing the hole Cook had dug "embrace no more than the two or three appurtenances," as above referred to; and does Sunal's claim fall within those appurtenances? Did Alcalde Weeks, in granting possession to Cook of the "given space of land containing the hole he had dug," grant no more or larger quantity than the mining laws authorized him to grant; or did he exceed his power, and by so doing give possession of a greater quantity of land than the mining laws authorized him to give an individual denouncer, and thus embrace the claim which Sunal makes?

From the manner in which you represent the subject in your letter, and the clearness and explicitness of the mining laws, it appears to me that the case must be decided according as the above questions are answered in the affirmative or negative. I do not see that the fee-simple title you speak of can affect a denouncement made prior to the 12th of February—the day on which the mining law relating to the denouncement of mines was abolished.

I enclose to you an extract of the mining laws concerning the denouncement of mines, as translated by Mr. Hartnell. If an accurate survey and plat be made of the possession given on the 2d of February to Cook in consequence of his denouncement on the 17th of December, according to the *boundaries* as *established* and *marked* on *the day possession was given*, it will at once be seen whether such possession contains a greater number of "appurtenances" than the alcalde was authorized to put Cook in possession of, and the question will at once decide itself, supposing the denouncer had complied with all the requirements of the law.

I am, respectfully, your obedient servant,
R. B. MASON,
Colonel 1st Dragoons, commanding.

ALRIGO & LARKIN,
Monterey, California.

HEADQUARTERS TENTH MILITARY DEPARTMENT,
Monterey, California, May 8, 1848.

SIR: Your letter of the 29th April is before me. Notes and accounts contracted in the United States cannot legally be enforced and collected in California during the continuance of the war, but can be as soon as the United States Congress shall organize a territorial goverment in this country and extend her laws over the same. Mr. Elam Brown was appointed on the 30th of March "an alcalde for the section of country lying along the Contra Costa and embracing the settlements in the valley of the San Joaquin, *vice* Estridilla, whose term of office has expired." Brown, therefore, possesses the same powers that Estridilla did. If he was within the jurisdiction of the Pueblo San José, and subordinate to the court there, then so is Brown. I do not know the extent of the jurisdiction of the pueblo to the northward.

The talk you had with the Indian José Jesus, as stated in your above mentioned letter, was a very proper one. Should any Indian prisoners be brought in and delivered up to you, you will immediately inform me of it.

I am, respectfully, your obedient servant,
R. B. MASON,
Colonel 1st Dragoons, Governor of California.

Mr. CHARLES WHITE,
Alcalde, Pueblo San Jose.

HEADQUARTERS TENTH MILITARY DEPARTMENT,
Monterey, May 8, 1848.

SIR: I acknowledge the receipt of your letter of the 24th of April. When Amas was here some time since, he exhibited a paper purporting to be an acknowledgment of the priest that he was satisfied in full for whatever claims he had on account of dues from the mission of San Buenaventura. If it be the fact that he has given such acknowledgment, and has received the consideration, he can have no further claim on the mission, though his successors may have.

You will no doubt be guarded and circumspect in recovering the property justly belonging to the mission that has "been fraudulently disposed of," in order to guard against any future disputes, and at the same time to avoid doing any wrong to the holders of the property that may be supposed to belong to the mission; or, in other words, for the sake of greater security, the fraudulent disposition of the property should be well established before it is wrested from the present holders. This will be the most prudent course, though by it some of the property may not be recovered. From the property clearly belonging to the mission thus recovered and restored, I think it nothing but just that the reasonable expenses incurred in its recovery should be paid, in the manner you suggest.

I have the honor to be your obedient servant,
R. B. MASON,
Col. 1st Dragoons, commanding.

Col. J. D. STEVENSON,
1st New York Regiment, com'g Southern Military District.

HEADQUARTERS TENTH MILITARY DEPARTMENT,
Monterey, California, May 8, 1848.

SIR: Your custom-house accounts, accompanying your letter to the Secretary of War of the 6th April, have been examined by me, and appear correct, except that the account does not show for what length of service Carrillo received the sums of one and two hundred dollars on account of his salary as collector. You should have made out a formal account, viz: "The Military Contribution Fund to Pedro C. Carrillo Dr., for services as collector at the port of Santa Barbara from the ———— to ————, at the rate of ———— dollars per annum." Then the usual receipt for the money should follow the account, which should contain the order for payment. Carrillo's informal receipts are herewith returned to you. An abstract of expenditures should accompany your quarterly accounts, made out similar to form 8 of the quartermaster's department, and endorsed on the quarterly account, as is shown in form 6.

I am, respectfully, your obedient servant,
R. B. MASON,
Col. 1st Dragoons, commanding.

Lieut. H. S. CARNES,
Acting Assistant Quartermaster, Santa Barbara, California.

HEADQUARTERS TENTH MILITARY DEPARTMENT,
Monterey, California, May 8, 1848.

SIR: Your custom-house accounts for the fourth quarter of 1847 and the first quarter of the present year have been examined by me. I have endorsed upon them "Examined and approved May 8, 1848," and will forward them to the Secretary of War by the first safe opportunity. See what I have said to Lieutenant Carnes in my letter of this date about an abstract of disbursements, &c., and comply with it in future.

I am, respectfully, your obedient servant,
R. B. MASON,
Col. 1st Dragoons, commanding.

Capt. F. J. LIPPETT,
Commanding, Santa Barbara, California.

HEADQUARTERS TENTH MILITARY DEPARTMENT,
Monterey, California, May 15, 1848.

SIR: I did not receive until last night, on my return to this place, your letter of the 9th instant. My letter to Captain Folsom, of the 28th ultimo, on the subject of the modification of the tariff, (as contained in the copies you were kind enough to send me,) an official copy of which I sent to the collector at San Pedro for his guidance, will enable him to enter the Olga as you desire.

I am, respectfully, your obedient servant,
R. B. MASON,
Colonel 1st Dragoons, Governor of California.

Mr. HENRY MELLUS,
Los Angeles, California.

HEADQUARTERS TENTH MILITARY DEPARTMENT,
Monterey, California, May 16, 1848.

SIR: Padre Gomez, the Catholic priest at San Luis Obispo, through his friend, Don Manuel Zimena, complains that, at the instance of Vicente Feliz, you have taken from him a pair of mill-stones that have been in his possession for three years, and which he acquired by purchase.

Whilst I do not doubt at all the correctness of your motive in taking these stones from the priest, yet, from the circumstances of the case, and all the information I can gain, I am of opinion they should be returned to him, which I desire you will do; and this will relieve me from any responsibility in the transaction.

I am, respectfully, your obedient servant,
R. B. MASON,
Colonel 1st Dragoons, Governor of California.

JOHN PRICE,
Alcalde, San Luis Obispo, California.

HEADQUARTERS TENTH MILITARY DEPARTMENT,
Monterey, California, May 17, 1848.

SIR: I have to acknowledge the receipt of your letter dated the 10th of this month—evidently a mistake, as I received it on the 10th.

The grant made by General Vallejo, in 1837, of lot number 52, to Juan Castinado, is good.

The United States stand pledged to protect the Californians in the possession of their property. The commissioners, as you say, had no power to look into any grant made by the Mexican authorities. Castinado held this grant before our flag was raised in California, and that is sufficient for us. Your town council, or any other authority, has no right to dispute his title or possession to it. Be pleased to lay this letter before the council for their information and guidance.

I am, respectfully, your obedient servant,
R. B. MASON,
Colonel 1*st Dragoons, commanding.*

L. W. BOGGS,
Alcalde, Sonoma, California.

HEADQUARTERS TENTH MILITARY DEPARTMENT,
Monterey, California, May 17, 1848.

SIR: The schooner Louisa arrived here a few days since from your port. She brought *two manifests*, and one other paper, setting forth merchandise shipped on board. These three documents purported to show the amount of the cargo. All that was contained on those three papers should have been put on *one* properly-made-out manifest. I desire that in future you will suffer no vessel to leave your port with more than *one manifes'*, and that *one* must show the *whole amount* of the *en'ire cargo*.

I am, respectfully, your obedient servant,
R. B. MASON,
Colonel 1*st Dragoons, commanding.*

D. W. ALEXANDER,
Collector, San Pedro, California.

HEADQUARTERS TENTH MILITARY DEPARTMENT,
Monterey, California, April 17, 1848.

SIR: I received your letter of the 2d instant late in the afternoon of the 6th, together with the papers which accompanied it, concerning the quicksilver mines denounced in your office on the 17th of December and on the 5th of February last—the former by Cook, Beldon, Alrigo, Ricord, and others; the latter by Pedro Sainsevan and partners. Two days previous to the reception of your letter, I received one dated on the 4th instant, signed by Messrs. Alrigo and Larkin, though written by Mr. Ricord, as he informed me, in which it is stated that the mine denounced on the 17th of December was denounced by Mr. Cook, and shortly thereafter transferred to their company, and that the one denounced on the 5th of February was denounced by Jose Sunal. Alrigo and Larkin "ask for an executive order for Sunal to desist from digging within their proper limits, and that the right of Sunal to be put in possession be deferred until the creation of certain tribunals;" and state that the denouncement of Cook on the 17th of December, and the possession obtained under it on the 2d of February, were prior to Sunal's denouncement, which was on the 5th of February. The other party, those interested in the denouncement of the 5th of February, claim to be the lawful and rightful owners of that mine, and demand possession of it under the 4th article, title 6, of the mining laws, and assert that the party claiming under the denouncement of the 17th of December have no right to possession, because neither their excavations nor measurements of possession were made in accordance with the requirements of the aforesaid fourth article of the mining laws.

I availed myself of the opportunity which a visit to your part of the country last week afforded me, to personally examine and minutely inspect and measure both of those mines, denounced on the 17th December and the 5th of February last. There were three excavations at the mine pointed out to me as the one denounced on the 17th of December—all three within a few paces of each other. In one of the excavations, over which was erected a windlass, a man named Cash was at work; and near the two excavations lowest down the hill, stood a small cabin and Mr. Taylor's tent. This was on the 11th instant. The deepest of these three excavations, measuring in the most favorable manner from the upper side of the hill, did not exceed fifteen feet, though one of the interested parties state that one of the excavations was of the depth required by the mining laws when possession was given, on the 2d of February, but that it since "caved in." I examined that spot which is said to have "caved in" with great care. It had the appearance of having been purposely filled up. It was dug in rock, not in earth; and, in my mind, it was as much impossible for that rock to have "caved in," as it would be for an auger hole to "cave in" that had been bored in a large solid block of sound timber. Neither myself nor those with me could discover the slightest trace of quicksilver ore in either of these excavations, though some specimens were shown to us, said to have been taken, I believe, from the hole said to have "caved in."

The mine denounced on the 5th of February was, if I mistook not the points of the compass, in a direction west of north from the three excavations just spoken of, and distant, I should judge, some four hundred yards or more, and was between sixty and seventy feet in length under ground. In this hole there was a very well defined vein of quicksilver ore, about two or two and a half inches wide.

Article 4, title 6, of the mining laws requires that he who discovers a mine or vein shall present himself in writing to the magistrate of the place, expressing his name and those of his partners, if he have any, the place of his birth, his residence, profession, and employment, and the most characteristic marks or indications of the place, mountain, or vein, which he wishes to have adjudicated to him. In the denouncement of the 17th of December, neither the place of birth, residence, profession, and employment, nor any of the characteristic marks or indications of the place, mountain, or vein, were made known in writing to the magistrate, or, in other words, set forth in the denouncement—all of which are positive and absolute requirements of the law; and the entire non conformity with the law, in failing to set forth these peremptory requirements, renders the denouncement illegal, and therefore null and void.

The aforesaid article (4th) requires an excavation of one and a half varas in diameter at the mouth, and ten in depth, to be made in the run or veins of the spot recorded, before those who denounce can be entitled to be put into the legal possession of the number of appurtenances allowed by law; and not then, unless such excavation be made within ninety days. In this case, the parties denouncing on the 17th of December are put in possession by the alcalde at the expiration of forty-eight days, when it is not in proof that their excavation was in conformity to law, but, on the contrary, it was the alcalde's opinion, not of sufficient depth; for he says, "the excavation was going on, and that there was sufficient time to finish them (it) before the ninety days"—that is, before the expiration of the ninety days allowed by law—and that he did not measure the depth. In a statement made on the 12th instant, the alcalde who gave the possession estimates the depth at twenty or twenty-two feet, but made no measurement. Here the imperative requirements of the law are set aside, or not complied with, and therefore, on that ground, the possession given on the 2d of February was not legal. The said 4th article further requires the magistrate to examine the course and direction of the vein, its breadth, and other circumstances, taking an exact account of all this, in order to add to it the corresponding entry of record, with the certificate of possession. Not one of these indispensable and imperative requirements of the law has been complied with—the non-compliance with each and every one of which presents so many separate grounds of illegality of the possession given on the 2d of February.

The mining laws give to the denouncer of a new vein in a "known mountain"—that is, a mountain known to contain the named mineral—"two appurtenances;" and to those who work in company, four new appurtenances—an appurtenance being 200 Spanish varas in length, and from one hundred to two hundred varas in breadth, according to the dip or inclination of the mineral vein. This denouncement of the 17th of December, being a new vein, if any, in mountains known to contain quicksilver ore, entitled the party to but two appurtenaces; but working in company entitled them to "four new appurtenances," making six in all, (though it is said by Mr. Walkinshaw, a practical miner of great experience and intelligence, that in Mexico the law is so construed, and such the invariable practice there, that a company is only entitled to four appurtenances in all.) Now, an appurtenance being two hundred varas long, and its greatest width, under the most favorable circumstances, two hundred varas wide, it follows that six appurtenances cannot contain more than 240,000 square varas. The magistrate put the party in possession on the 2d of February of a given space of land, including the hole they had dug, measuring, if I remember rightly your reading from your record when I was at the Pueblo on the 12th, 600 varas one way by 800 varas the other, making the area to contain 480,000 square varas—just 240,000 square varas more than he was authorized by law to put them in judicial possession of, even supposing that they had fulfilled all the requirements of the law to entitle them to possession. The possession given on the 2d of February was therefore illegal, the magistrate greatly exceeding his judicial powers and authority. The judicial acts of a magistrate can only confer rights on one party, or take them from another, so long as he confines himself within the limits the law has assigned to him. As soon as he steps beyond those limits, his judicial acts are at once stripped of all binding force and effect, and have no more legal force than if performed by any other individual.

The reservation made by the magistrate on the 2d of February in the certificate of possession, that the measurement was good only for what the laws designate on the subject, amounts to nothing. It was his business to have ascertained what the law did designate or allow, and his duty to have the appurtenances measured and marked according to law; and this he did not do. There are other instances where the law has not been complied with in giving this possession, but it is useless to follow them; enough has been shown to render the possession so given illegal, and utterly null and void.

But we will for a moment suppose that all the steps taken subsequent to the denouncement were legal, and that the requirements of the law were adhered to both on the part of the magistrate and the denouncer, so far as relates to the excavation made, and the possession given is concerned: still the denouncement of the 17th of December is of itself defective and illegal, because the plain and imperative requirements of the law were not adhered to or complied with.

The denouncement—the foundation upon which the whole work is erected—being defective and illegal, and swept away, the whole superstructure built thereon must fall with it. The denouncement made on the 17th of December last by the parties first above named, and the possession given under it on the 2d of February, both being so entirely illegal and at variance with the law, they cannot militate against the party claiming under the denouncement of the 5th of February; and the only question that now remains to be ascertained is, Have they denounced this mine in a proper manner, found mineral, and made their excavation according to law, and within ninety days from the 5th of February?

I have not the denouncement of the 5th of February by me to refer to, and therefore only speak of it from recollection, which tells me that all the requirements of the law were fulfilled in said denouncement. I measured, on the 11th instant, the excavation made by those who made that denouncement of the 5th February, and found it more than one and a half varas in diameter at its mouth, and about sixty-five or six feet in length under ground, but not in a perpendicular direction.

If, upon examination of the denouncement you have upon record of the 5th February, it is found to be in accordance with the mining laws, the party claiming under it is entitled to the judicial possession of the legal number of appurtenances. I herewith return to you the papers that were enclosed with your letter of the 2d instant.

I am, respectfully, your obedient servant,

R. B. MASON, *Colonel 1st Drag., com'g.*

CHARLES WHITE, *Alcalde, Pueblo de San José.*

HEADQUARTERS TENTH MILITARY DEPARTMENT,
Monterey, California, May 20, 1848.

SIR: Mr. William A. Leidsdorff, a citizen of the United States, died intestate, in San Francisco, on the morning of the 18th instant, possessed, it is said, of a large, valuable property. It is all-important that his estate should at once be placed in safe and responsible hands. As you have never resigned or been deprived of your consular commission, I think it your duty, under the general consular instructions from the State Department, to take charge of said estate.

I am, respectfully, your obedient servant,
R. B. MASON, *Colonel 1st Drag., com'g.*

Mr. Thomas O. Larkin, *U. S. Consul, Monterey, California.*

HEADQUARTERS TENTH MILITARY DEPARTMENT,
Monterey, California, May 21, 1848.

Sir: I send Mr. Hartnell, the government interpreter, to San Francisco, to attend to the correctly printing of the Spanish translation of some laws, &c., that I intend to publish. The Spanish printing heretofore done in San Francisco has generally been so full of errors that it is important that Mr. Hartnell should attend to the proof-sheet of this himself. I desire that you will have a number of copies, both in Spanish and English, struck off and stitched together, so that they can be distributed in that way together. Send me, if it be possible, one or more copies so as to reach me before the arrival of the Anita, and an English copy without the Spanish, if the latter will cause any delay. I hope, by the printer using his utmost exertions, that he may get this printing done before the sailing of the Anita. I wish the manuscript copy returned to me, and not a copy of the printing retained in the printer's office, or be suffered to go abroad.

The soldier who goes up with Mr. Hartnell has commutation of rations to bring him back: send him back immediately. The horses Mr. Hartnell rides are public: please have them taken care of until he is ready to return.

I am, respectfully, your obedient servant,
R. B. MASON,
Colonel 1st Dragoons, commanding.

Captain J. L. Folsom, *A. Q. M., San Francisco, California.*

HEADQUARTERS TENTH MILITARY DEPARTMENT,
Monterey, California, May 23, 1848.

Sir: It has been suggested to me that the great number of persons now flocking to the newly-discovered gold region on the Sacramento, for the purpose of obtaining gold by the process of "washing," renders it immediately necessary that some wholesome laws or regulations should be made with a view to the security of personal rights and the prevention of disputes among those engaged in that business. It has been further suggested, that this gold region should be laid off in numbered lots, with marked boundaries; that, under certain regulations, a person should be secured in the quiet possession of his lot, so long as he chooses to work on it; that he could give it up at pleasure, and thus leave it open for another to enter upon it, and obtain any other vacant lot; that there should be a public agent in that quarter to survey and mark those lots, and put persons in possession of them, decide disputes, &c., &c.; that, to cover the expenses of the agent, the surveyors, &c., persons applying for a lot should be required to pay a certain fee for his certificate of possession, &c As you are about visiting the gold region, I will thank you to obtain for me what information you can upon this subject, and, in conjunction with some of the most influential and best informed citizens engaged in that business, draw up and submit to me a project of such regulations as will, in your judgment, be most productive of good, and tend most to preserve harmony, prevent trespasses, disputes, litigations, &c.

I am, respectfully, your obedient servant,

R. B. MASON,
Colonel 1st Dragoons, Governor of California.

Major J. R. SNYDER, *Monterey, California.*

HEADQUARTERS TENTH MILITARY DEPARTMENT,
Monterey, California, May 25, 1848.

SIR: I am in the receipt of your letter of the 22d instant, on the subject of the threatened Indian hostilities, and the removal of Captain Brackett's company from Sonoma. The condition of the garrisons in Lower California is such that they must be strengthened. The measures taken and the whole plan of operations proposed at La Paz and San José will be defeated and broken up by Captain Brackett's company remaining at Sonoma. This the interests of the public service will not permit. The number of American citizens, to say nothing of the Californians north of the bay of San Francisco, is sufficient to meet any Indian troubles that may arise in that quarter. I have no fear of not finding plenty of men in the country to turn out and put them down, if there is really danger to be apprehended. I have arms and ammunition in sufficient quantities to place in their hands for that purpose. I shall, however, apprehend no real danger from the Indians, however rife the rumor may be, so long as the inhabitants refuse to turn out and meet it, or leave their families to go to work at the mines. I cannot believe that in time of real danger men will abandon their families to merciless savages, and go off to hunt gold dust.

The inhabitants of the country must rely principally upon themselves to put down Indian aggressions. I will furnish the powder and lead, and such force as can be spared from San Francisco—from the force now there protecting public property; but the people must make some effort to protect themselves until the arrival of the 500 troops now on their way here from Santa Fe.

I have sent orders to the commanding officer at San Francisco to hold his disposable force in readiness to make a campaign in the Indian country, if it becomes necessary, in company with the inhabitants north of the bay, whom I shall expect to turn out and organize in one or more companies, for the protection of themselves, their families, and property; but, in the meantime, Captain Brackett's company must embark for Lower California. With this view, Major Hardie has been directed to visit Sonoma, and has discretionary authority to organize and arm the citizens north of the bay, should the Indians by any movements or acts of aggression render it necessary.

I am much pleased to learn that you will visit those Indians and use your efforts to pacify them. I am sure that your well-known prudence, judgment, and knowledge of Indian character will render those efforts eminently successful.

I received on the 20th of last month a letter from you, without date, offering the resignation of your commission as sub-Indian agent, and stating that the Indians did not wish the whites to occupy their lands. I should have acknowledged the receipt of that at an earlier day, but for the difficulties of finding some one to fill your place.

The Indians are right in pressing their wish that the whites should not intrude on their lands. Upon proper application of the Indian agents, these intruders shall be removed.

I am, respectfully, your obedient servant,

R. B. MASON,
Colonel 1st Dragoons, commanding.

General M. G. VALLEJO,
Sub-Indian Agent, Sonoma, California.

HEADQUARTERS TENTH MILITARY DEPARTMENT,
Monterey, California, May 25, 1848.

SIR: The recent intelligence from Sonoma, though I cannot credit it to the full extent, induces me to countermand your late orders to sail for Lower California in the Anita. I have now to direct that you at once proceed to Sonoma, and make yourself well acquainted with all the facts concerning the reported hostile intentions of the Indians to the northward of that place, as reported to me by General Vallejo, sub-Indian agent, and L. W. Boggs, alcalde, at Sonoma.

You are hereby clothed with authority to organize the American settlers and other foreigners and Californians north of the bay into one or more companies, and to arm and equip them from the ordnance stores at the Presidio, with a view of making a campaign against the Indians, should their conduct or any act of hostility on their part render, in your judgment, such a step necessary; and you can draw for such campaign such of the force from the two companies at San Francisco as can be prudently spared from guarding the public stores.

I can offer no pay to the citizens who turn out for their own safety and protection to put down any Indian disturbance, but will furnish them with arms and ammunition and such other assistance as is in my power. But, if you can raise a company of one captain, one first lieutenant, two second lieutenants, four sergeants, four corporals, and two musicians, and from 50 to 100 privates, to be mustered into the service of the United States for one year, to serve in Upper California, unless sooner discharged, do so, and muster them in accordingly. I have written to Captain John Garett on the subject of raising this company, and I offered him the command of it. See him on the subject. The other officers will be elected by the men.

Strong petitions and remonstrances are made by the people of Sonoma against Captain Brackett's company being withdrawn from that place; but Brackett must sail, as ordered, and the people must rely upon their own exertions, when furnished with arms and ammunition, to protect themselves against the Indians. There are now 500 troops on their way here from Santa Fe. When they arrive, I shall be able to replace Brackett's company at Sonoma.

The papers, rolls, and instructions relating to pay, &c., of volunteers, which you took to Oregon, are applicable to the company now proposed to be raised on the bay of San Francisco.

Let me caution you to be very guarded in receiving and crediting reports and rumors about this Indian disturbance, always bearing in mind that the people north of the bay are exceedingly anxious to keep Brackett's company there, and would, in all probability, kick up a disturbance with the Indians, if in no other way their object could be effected.

I have the honor to be your obedient servant,
R. B. MASON,
Colonel 1st Dragoons, commanding.
Major JAMES A. HARDIE,
Commanding West Military District,
San Francisco, California.

HEADQUARTERS TENTH MILITARY DEPARTMENT,
Monterey, California, May 26, 1848.

SIR: I am in the receipt of your communication of the 22d instant, which informs me that the case of the mill-stones was regularly tried and decided by proof in your juzgado. That being the case, it is certainly not my intention to disturb that decision. My communication of the 16th was written under the impression, as therein expressed, that you had taken them from the priest at the instance of Vicente Feliz, by which I meant to convey the idea that they had been taken upon the representation of Feliz, without due course of trial; and it was under that view of the case that I desired them to be returned.

I am, very respectfully, your obedient servant,
R. B. MASON,
Colonel 1st Dragoons, commanding.
JOHN M. PRICE, *Alcalde of San Luis Obispo, California.*

HEADQUARTERS TENTH MILITARY DEPARTMENT,
Monterey, California, May 31, 1848.

SIR: Your communication of the 16th instant is before me. The subject which you present, of the want of a proper jail, and the funds to erect one, has been anticipated, and will be fully met in some laws which a few days since were sent to San Francisco to be printed.

I think it will be very proper in you to rent out the municipal lands you speak of, and appropriate the funds to municipal purposes.

There are a large pile of mission records here; but whether those of which you speak are among them, I know not. Mr. Hartnell is now absent at San Francisco; when he returns, I will direct him to examine them and inform you accordingly.

I propose to have constructed a good and secure prison at the Angeles, Santa Barbara, (at this place there is one,) Pueblo de San José, Sonoma, and at Sutter's Fort, and will appropriate $1,000 towards the construction of each one, (the plan of the building to be submitted to me for approval,) the balance of the cost to be raised by the citizens.

These prisons should be planned with a view of quartering the keeper, proper ventilation, and the security of the prison apartments, and the separation of prisoners according to crime, solitary confinement, &c.

I should be glad to receive a well-drawn plan and specifiation, with estimates of cost, &c.

I am, very respectfully, your obedient servant,
R. B. MASON,
Colonel 1st Dragoons, commanding.
STEPHEN C. FOSTER, *Alcalde, Los Angeles, California.*

HEADQUARTERS TENTH MILITARY DEPARTMENT,
Monterey, California, June 1, 1848.

SIR: I received last night your letter of the 29th instant, with its enclosure, on the subject of the administration of the estate of the late W. A. Leidsdorff, who, it appears, was not a citizen of the United States, but a naturalized citizen of the republic of Mexico; and, therefore, it only remains for the courts of the country to proceed in the matter according to the laws and customs of the country.

You, as the alcalde, and at this time the highest judicial officer in the district where Mr. Leidsdorff died, should take the necessary steps to put the estate in the hands of competent and safe men, who should be required to give bond and good security in at least double its estimated value, conditioned for the proper management, accountability, and settlement of the same, according to such laws as are now, or may be created touching such matters.

Inventories and appraisements of every species and article of property of the deceased should immediately be made, under oath, by two competent and respectable persons appointed by your court, and deposited in your office.

There are now in progress of printing some laws touching the settlement of estates, &c.; and therefore the bond spoken of above should be expressly conditioned that the accountability, settlement, &c., should be in accordance with such laws as are now, or may be hereafter, applicable to such accountability and settlement.

I am, respectfully, your obedient servant,
R. B. MASON,
Colonel 1st Dragoons, commanding.

JOHN TOWNSEND,
1st Alcalde, San Francisco, California.

HEADQUARTERS TENTH MILITARY DEPARTMENT,
Monterey, California, June 1, 1848.

SIR: I received last night your letter of the 26th instant. The copy of the tariff regulations corrected in red ink was made from one sent me by the commodore. The discrepancies which you point out, I presume, were oversights, as you say, in making the alterations.

I send you herewith a little book with the tariff of duties alphabetically arranged, compiled by one of the custom-house clerks in New York. You will find it more convenient than the printed tariff you have. I have corrected it in pencil, or at least believe I have, in accordance with the Secretary of the Treasury's letter to the President of the 5th of November. If I have not in the corrections fully complied with that letter, you must supply the omissions yourself.

Your views in relation to the seagoing vessels trading in the bay, &c., are approved.

I have the honor to remain your obedient servant,
R. B. MASON,
Colonel 1st Dragoons, commanding.

Captain J. L. FOLSOM,
Assistant Quartermaster, San Francisco, California.

HEADQUARTERS TENTH MILITARY DEPARTMENT,
Monterey, California, June 2, 1848.

CAPTAIN: You have now been in command of the post of San Diego for three months, and yet I have received no returns from the custom-house at that port, though you acknowledge in your letter of the 30th of April that you had "the printed forms and regulations," which give all the data upon which to make the returns required.

The business in this office is retarded and kept back for months and months in consequence of the want of promptness and correctness of some of the officers in rendering and making their returns.

I send you herewith a little book with the tariff of duties alphabetically arranged, compiled by one of the custom-houses clerks in New York. You will find it, in determining the amount of duties to be paid, more convenient than the printed one you have. I have corrected it in pencil, or at least believe I have, in accordance with the Secretary of the Treasury's letter to the President of the 5th of November. If I have not in the corrections fully complied with that letter, you must supply the omissions yourself.

I am, respectfully, your obedient servant,
R. B. MASON,
Colonel 1st Dragoons, commanding.

Captain WM. E. SHANNON,
Commanding, San Diego, California.

P. S.—Send up at once the returns due for the quarter ending 31st of March, showing the amount received from the Mormon officer, &c., and also the monthly statements of revenue received during each month since you have commanded at San Diego.

HEADQUARTERS TENTH MILITARY DEPARTMENT,
Monterey, California, June 2, 1848.

CAPTAIN: I herewith send you a little book with the tariff alphabetically arranged, compiled by one of the custom-house clerks in New York. You will find it, in determining the amount of duties to be paid, more convenient than the printed tariff you have. I have corrected it in pencil, or at least believe I have, in accordance with the Secretary of the Treasury's letter to the President of the 5th of November. If I have not in the corrections fully complied with that letter, you must supply the omissions yourself.

I am, respectfully, your obedient servant,
R. B. MASON,
Colonel 1st Dragoons, commanding.

Captain F. J. LIPPETT,
Santa Barbara, California; and
DAVID W. ALEXANDER,
San Pedro, California.

HEADQUARTERS TENTH MILITARY DEPARTMENT,
Monterey, California, June 5, 1848.

SIR: I have the honor to acknowledge the receipt of your communication of the 28th ultimo and its enclosures, Nos. 1, 2, 3, and 4, relating to the complaint made to you by Mr. Cambuston on account of my proclamation of the 12th of February taking effect at the Pueblo de San José from the day of its date, when the said proclamation was not received at the pueblo until several days thereafter. A statute, when duly made, takes effect from its date, when no time is fixed, and this is now the settled rule. It was so declared by the Supreme Court of the United States in Mathews *vs.* Zane, and it was likewise so adjudged in the circuit court in Massachusetts in the case of the "brig Ann."—(See Kent's Commentaries, vol. 1, page 454, an eminent legal writer.) I again quote from the same author: "There is a good deal of hardship in the rule as it now stands, both here and in England, for a statute is to operate from the very day it passes, if the law does not establish the time.

"It is impossible in any State, and particularly in such a wide-spread dominion as that of the United States, to have notice of the existence of the law until some time after it has passed.

"It would be no more than reasonable and just that the statute should not be deemed to operate upon the persons and property of individuals, or impose pains and penalties for acts done in contravention of it, until the law was duly promulgated. The rule, however, is deemed to be fixed beyond the power of judicial control; and no time is allowed for the publication of the law before it operates, when the statute itself gives no time.

"Thus, in the case of the brig Ann, the vessel was libelled and condemned for sailing from Newburyport, in Massachusetts, on the 12th of January, 1808, contrary to the act of Congress of the 9th of January, 1808, though it was admitted the act was not known in Newburyport on the day the brig sailed."

That part of my proclamation of the 12th of February complained of, is in these words: "From and after this date, the Mexican laws and customs now prevailing in California, relating to the 'denouncement' of mines, are hereby abolished."

Now, this proclamation deprives no one of his property; it does not "operate upon the persons and property of individuals, or impose pains or penalties for acts done in contravention of it." It merely prevents persons from possessing themselves of that which at its date did not belong to them. I therefore decline making any alterations touching the operation of this proclamation in California.

Be pleased, Mr. consul, to accept the assurance of my most respectful consideration.

R. B. MASON,
Colonel 1st Dragoons, Governor of California

To J. S. MOERENHOUT,
Consul of France, Monterey, California.

HEADQUARTERS TENTH MILITARY DEPARTMENT,
Monterey, California, June 8, 1848.

SIR: In my communication of the 8th of May, I returned to you the informal receipts of Pedro C. Carrillo, and called your attention to the proper manner of making his accounts. The mail arrived to-day from the south, but did not bring up the account of Carrillo properly made out, nor any letter from you accounting for the delay. I beg that you will be more prompt in future, and not again suffer a mail to pass by when there is a communication, document, voucher, &c., to be forwarded to these headquarters, without sending it up.

I am, respectfully, your obedient servant,
R. B. MASON,
Colonel 1st Dragoons, commanding.

Lieut. H. S. CARNES,
New York Volunteers, Santa Barbara, California.

HEADQUARTERS TENTH MILITARY DEPARTMENT,
Monterey, California, June 9, 1848.

SIR: Mr. Foster has written to me in relation to some contingent expenses of the court recently held at Los Angeles, for the trial of Canfield, Myers, Burrows, and others—such as pay for the services of an interpreter and stationery. These are proper charges, and you are authorized to pay them. Fees for witnesses summoned on the part of the defendants are not to be paid by you unless in the case of an acquittal. The convicted party always pays his own witnesses.

I am, respectfully, your obedient servant,
R. B. MASON,
Colonel 1st Dragoons, commanding.

Lieutenant J. W. DAVIDSON,
First Dragoons, A. A. Quartermaster,
Los Angeles, California.

HEADQUARTERS TENTH MILITARY DEPARTMENT,
Monterey, California, June 11, 1848.

SIR: I have received your letter of the 30th of May and its enclosures.

I shall leave here to-morrow for the north, to be absent some three or four weeks; consequently, will not be here when the record of Barnes's trial arrives. I will, however, attend to it immediately on my return. I have written to Lieutenant Davidson on the subject of the contingent expenses of the court.

I am, respectfully, your obedient servant,
R. B. MASON,
Colonel 1st Dragoons, commanding.

S. C. FOSTER,
Alcalde, Los Angeles, California.

HEADQUARTERS TENTH MILITARY DEPARTMENT,
Monterey, California, June 11, 1848.

SIR: There appears a difficulty about some mills and millstones between Padre Gomez and Vincente Felis; and it appears that the said mills and millstones were at one time the property of the mission of San Luis Obispo, and that they were disposed of by you.

I desire that you will, by the return of the mail, send me a copy of the authority, if it exists, in writing, by which you are authorized to dispose of said property; and, if you had no such written authority, you will communicate to me, by letter, by what or whose authority you did dispose of that property.

I am, respectfully, your obedient servant,
R. B. MASON,
Colonel 1*st Dragoons, Governor of California.*

MARIANO BONILLO,
San Luis Obispo, California.

HEADQUARTERS TENTH MILITARY DEPARTMENT,
Monterey, California, June 11, 1848.

COLONEL: I have received your three letters of the 30th ultimo, and their enclosures.

It would have been better to have referred to these headquarters the case of Ortega's resignation, which should have been in writing, as a verbal one is hardly admissible. Officers other than myself accepting resignations, or removing civil officers, unless in some extraordinary case that admits of no delay, produces confusion; for the civil officers know there can be but one source of authority for such matters: when there appears to be two, they yield a reluctant obedience, if not a direct refusal.

Your communication of the 16th of May, to Francisco Ortega, directing him not to carry into effect the sentence against Mrs. Elville, for selling liquor to Indians without referring to you for your approbation, has been sent to me. I am so desirous of breaking up the practice of selling liquor to Indians, that I must cause the civil magistrates to be sustained in all cases where they inflict penalty for this offence: a remission of penalty imposed in one instance, will be a precedent for others; and as I have so rigidly sustained the magistrates in all cases up to this time, I am unwilling to relax in a single instance, even though it might be a hard case. I must, therefore, request that you will recall your instructions in the case of Mrs. Elville, and let the law take its course.

As the mails are very regular, and but little delay can arise, it will be best to refer to these headquarters when you wish a civil magistrate removed from office, or any decision of theirs reversed: they are very naturally tenacious upon those points, and are sure to complain when they think their prerogatives encroached upon; and as a reference here would not cause much delay, it had better be done in future, both for the sake of harmonizing with the civil magistrates, and taking from them any grounds of complaint, that they are not sustained in enforcing the proclamations and laws. I hope you will not construe anything I have said above into a want of confidence in yourself; I know that you have but one object in view, and that is the best interest of the public service at large, but you will readily perceive that there can be but one authority to remove from office, remit punishments, reverse decisions, &c., without producing great confusion and dissatisfaction. It is, therefore, better to refer to this office such questions touching the administration of civil affairs, as also such instructions as you may, from time to time, wish given to the alcaldes; except in cases that will admit of no delay, which of course should be reported.

Ortega is one of those subordinate alcaldes, if I may so express it, that it has been the practice of alcaldes of large districts to appoint at prominent points, remote from themselves; they are mere assistants to the first alcaldes, and have not the power and jurisdiction of alcaldes proper.

I will remove Ortega at once, and appoint Callaghan a subordinate alcalde, with special instructions to co-operate with you in your management of the mission of San Buenaventura.

In one of your letters of the 3d instant you acknowledge the receipt of one from me of the 15th of that month. I do not find a letter of that date recorded in my book; perhaps the clerk omitted to record it, or perhaps you have made a mistake in the date. My recorded letters to you in the month of May bear date on the 8th and 30th.

I shall leave here to-morrow for San Francisco, and other places north, and shall be absent about three weeks.

I am, respectfully, your obedient servant,

R. B. MASON,
Col. 1st Dragoons, commanding.

Colonel J. D. STEVENSON,
Commanding Southern Military District,
Los Angeles, California.

HEADQUARTERS TENTH MILITARY DEPARTMENT,
Monterey, California, June 11, 1848.

SIR: I herewith enclose to you the appointment of a subaltern alcalde for the mission of San Buenaventura, in the district and jurisdiction of Santa Barbara. You stand in relation to the first alcalde of that district and jurisdiction as did your predecessor; but you are to co-operate zealously, to the extent of your power, with Colonel Stevenson in carrying out his views in the management of the affairs of the mission.

I have specially to call your attention to my proclamation of the 29th of November, 1847, and to direct that you rigidly enforce it, without regard or respect to persons; suffer no one to escape who violates its provisions.

I am, respectfully, your obedient servant,

R. B. MASON,
Colonel 1st Dragoons, commanding.

ISAAC CALLAGHAN,
Sub-alcalde, Santa Barbara, California.

Copy furnished to Colonel Stevenson, Los Angeles, California.

Know all men by these presents, that I, Richard B. Mason, colonel 1st dragoons and governor of California, by virtue of authority in me vested, do hereby appoint Isaac Callaghan a subordinate alcalde for the mission of San Buenaventura, in the district and jurisdiction of Santa Barbara, vice Ortega, removed.

Given at Monterey, California, this 11th day of June, 1848, and the seventy-second year of the independence of the United States.

R. B. MASON,
Colonel 1st Dragoons, and Governor of California.

HEADQUARTERS TENTH MILITARY DEPARTMENT,
Monterey, California, June 11, 1848.

SIR: In reply to that part of your letter of the 2d instant relative to keeping in confinement the civil prisoners, I have only to say that, situated as is the civil magistrate of Santa Barbara, he must be sustained and assisted by the military, or his authority and efforts to preserve order and sustain the laws will be entirely defeated. You must therefore continue, as heretofore, to receive his prisoners; and I trust that they may not be allowed to escape, at least so frequently as they have done, which, I think, they could not if the guard were vigilant and attentive to their duties. When I was last at your post, I frequently observed the grossest negligence on the part of your sentinels and guard. I hope this has been corrected, and that you will rigidly enforce the strictest letter of the regulations in respect to guard duties; prisoners cannot well escape even from tents, much less from a guard-house, if the guard are on the alert, and strict in the discharge of their duties.

I am inclined to think that your company has been too long at Santa Barbara, and that your men would improve in their guard duties by an exchange with one of the companies at regimental headquarters.

I am, respectfully, your obedient servant,

R. B. MASON,
Col. 1st Dragoons, commanding.

Captain F. J. LIPPETT,
Commanding, Santa Barbara, California.

HEADQUARTERS TENTH MILITARY DEPARTMENT,
Monterey, California, June 16, 1848.

SIR: I have just learned that Rodereguez, of Santa Cruz, was not long ago tried before you for selling spirituous liquor to an Indian, found guilty and fined; that some time afterwards you reopened the case and had it decided by arbitrators. If this was so, then the whole proceeding subsequent to the fine being imposed was wrong *in toto*, and entirely beyond the scope of your authority. Having once decided the case, and imposed the fine, you no longer had any jurisdiction over it, nor could you appoint an arbitrator in a case in which the Territory was concerned. By referring to the proclamation of the 29th of November last, you will find that when the accused person is convicted, the alcalde has no *discretion* as to the minimum amount of the *fine* and *imprisonment*. If convicted, the law *fixes* that minimum at *fifty dollars and the three months' imprisonment*.

An alcalde cannot lessen that amount of punishment by inflicting the fine and not the imprisonment. They must both go together. The proclamation makes all such cases alone triable "before an alcalde." Therefore, arbitrators and all other tribunals are excluded.

e pleased to make to me a report on this case as early as you can, as I leave town to-morrow.

Respectfully, your obedient servant,
R. B. MASON,
Colonel 1st Dragoons, commanding.
Mr. LONGLEY,
Second Alcalde, Monterey, California.

HEADQUARTERS TENTH MILITARY DEPARTMENT,
Monterey, California, June 16, 1848.

SIR: The undersigned has the honor to inform the consul of France that he has received instructions from the Secretary of War to institute a board of officers to examine into certain transactions which Mr. Pageot, the minister of France to the United States, has laid before the Secretary of State in the way of complaint, which complaint is founded upon representations made by the consul of France to his government of "certain proceedings of Colonel Fremont, the military governor of California, towards him, and the arbitrary and violent acts committed by officers of the United States against Frenchmen in that Territory."

The board will assemble in Monterey on Monday next.

I have the honor to be, sir, with great respect,
R. B. MASON,
Colonel 1st Dragoons, Governor of California.
Mr. J. S. MOERENHOUT,
Consul of France, Monterey, California.

HEADQUARTERS TENTH MILITARY DEPARTMENT,
Monterey, California, June 17, 1848.

SIR: I acknowledge the receipt of your letter of yesterday's date in reply to my note of the same day.

The board of arbitrators in Rodereguez's case was entirely irregular and illegal. They had not, and could not have, any cognizance of the case whatever, for reasons assigned in my note of yesterday. Their action in the case is therefore null and void, and of no legal force or effect.

You will proceed to collect the fine imposed on Rodereguez, being found guilty. The law also imposed an imprisonment of three months; but, under all the circumstances of the case, that is hereby remitted.

Very respectfully, your obedient servant,
R. B. MASON,
Colonel 1st Dragoons, Governor of California.
WILLIAM R. LONGLEY,
Second Alcalde, Monterey, California.

HEADQUARTERS TENTH MILITARY DEPARTMENT,
Monterey, California, June 17, 1848.

SIR: I send the barque Anita, belonging to the United States quartermaster department, to Oregon, with a liberal supply of arms and ammunition, to be delivered to you. The officers of the army, who are accountable for this property, will send by the barque receipts therefor, which, upon the arrival of the property, be pleased to sign and return to them.

I much regret that it has been entirely out of my power to furnish you with any assistance of troops, or send you the arms and ammunition at an earlier day, as no vessel could be chartered or freighted.

The Anita, since her return from Oregon, has been undergoing repairs at San Francisco, and I am hourly expecting her here with troops and provisions for the garrison in Lower California; but from recent intelligence from that quarter the Anita will be stopped here, and the ordnance stores put on board of her for Oregon.

A treaty of peace between the United States and Mexico has been ratified by our Senate, and returned to Mexico for their ratification. Having undergone some alterations in the Senate, it is supposed by many to be very doubtful whether the Mexican Congress will ratify it. In the interim there is an armistice.

The boundary line runs up the Rio Grande to the southern boundary of New Mexico, thence along that boundary west till it strikes the first branch of the Gila; thence down that river to its union with the Colorado; thence to a point of the Pacific ocean one league south of San Diego. So we give up Lower California. Should Mexico ratify the treaty, we shall hear of it in a few weeks, when all the New York volunteers will be discharged, their term of service expiring with the war. There will be left in California only one company of dragoons and one company of artillery, not enough to guard the public property at San Francisco, Monterey, and Los Angeles.

I am, respectfully, your obedient servant,
R. B. MASON,
Colonel 1st Dragoons, Governor of California.
To his Excellency GEORGE ABERNETHY,
Governor of Oregon.

HEADQUARTERS TENTH MILITARY DEPARTMENT,
San Francisco, June 23, 1848.

SIR: I must call your attention to the large amount still due from you as the late collector of this port on account of the customs, and beg you will make immediate payment to Captain Folsom of the balance due; otherwise I shall be obliged to take measures to collect the amount due, as shown by your last account current form your bondsmen.

I am, respectfully, your obedient servant,
R. B. MASON,
Colonel 1st Dragoons, Governor of California.
W. A. RICHARDSON,
Late Collector at San Francisco, California.

HEADQUARTERS TENTH MILITARY DEPARTMENT,
San Francisco, June 23, 1848.

GENTLEMEN: I have the honor to acknowledge the receipt of your memorial of the 22d instant, asking that Lieutenant Gilbert may be appointed first alcalde " of this district, in the absence of Mr. John Townsend, the present or late incumbent." If Mr. Townsend's absence is to be of long continuance, it is certainly necessary, under the peculiar circumstances at present existing, that an appointment of a first alcalde should be made, and I would with great pleasure make the appointment you ask were Lieutenant Gilbert not employed upon other public duties which could not be properly discharged at the same time with those of an alcalde; the duties of one would essentially interfere with the duties of the other. Should the length of Doctor Townsend's absence continue so as to inconvenience the interests of the town or district, I will, with pleasure, appoint any civilian that the citizens may wish.

I am, respectfully, your obedient servant,
R. B. MASON,
Colonel 1*st Dragoons, Governor of California.*

W. D. M. HOWARD,
S. BRANNIN,
H. RICHARDSON, and others,
San Francisco.

STATE DEPARTMENT OF THE TERRITORY OF CALIFORNIA,
Monterey, July 18, 1848.

SIR: Your letter of June 16th has been received, and I am directed by the governor to say, in reply to your question, that the duties are to be levied *ad valorem* on the invoices, and not on the gross amount of sales, as formerly. This question might have been readily settled by referring to Colonel Mason's letter to Captain Folsom, April 28, (a copy of which was sent to the commanding officer at Santa Barbara,) and to the printed pamphlet forwarded to Captain Lippett on the 2d of June; and I am directed to say that those instructions are deemed sufficiently full and explicit.

Very respectfully, your obedient servant,
H. W. HALLECK,
Lieutenant of Engineers, and Secretary of State.

Lieut. HENRY S. CARNES,
Collector, &c., Santa Barbara, California.

STATE DEPARTMENT OF THE TERRITORY OF CALIFORNIA,
Monterey, July 19, 1848.

SIR: I have to acknowledge the receipt of your letter of June 26th, enclosing your monthly statements of revenue collected for April and May; also, your letter of June 25, with your account current and abstract of expenditures for the quarter ending March 31st, and your monthly statement of revenue collected for March; also, your letter of June 11, in answer to which I am directed by the governor to say, that as the exemption from duties by the tariff is limited to soldiers and military officers by the express orders of the President of the United States, he cannot assume the responsibility of changing such limitation.

It would afford him great pleasure to give Señor Bandini every assistance in his mining operations; but under existing circumstances he cannot feel himself justified in suspending the regulations made by the President respecting the landing and sale of gunpowder: not that he has any want of confidence in the intentions of Señor Bandini, but at the present time it is necessary to take every precaution to guard against accidents.

Very respectfully, your obedient servant,
H. W. HALLECK,
Lieutenant of Engineers, and Secretary of State.

Capt. WM. E. SHANNON,
Commanding, &c., San Diego, California.

STATE DEPARTMENT OF THE TERRITORY OF CALIFORNIA,
Monterey, July 19, 1848.

SIR: I am directed by the governor to acknowledge the receipt of your letter of June 29th, relative to the affairs of the alcalde of Santa Barbara, and to inform you that orders have been sent to that officer in accordance with your recommendation.

Very respectfully, your obedient servant,
H. W. HALLECK,
Lieutenant of Engineers, and Secretary of State.

Col. J. D. STEVENSON,
Commanding, &c., Los Angeles, California.

STATE DEPARTMENT OF THE TERRITORY OF CALIFORNIA,
Monterey, July 19, 1848.

SIR: It is stated by Colonel Stevenson that the town of Santa Barbara owes the acting assistant commissary of subsistence the sum of $97 66 for the support of the civil prisoners confined by the alcalde of that place. This money must be paid to the United States out of the municipal funds of the town.

The other towns of California have raised, by means of fines, the labor of prisoners, the license for grog-shops, billiard tables, &c., funds sufficient to cover their municipal expenses; and when any deficiency arises, it is paid by a town tax. The alcalde of Santa Barbara must resort to similar means to raise money to defray the necessary expenses of his office. He should endeavor to employ his prisoners in such a way as to earn their own subsistence, and to pay the guard required to secure them.

The United States officers cannot be called upon to defray such municipal expenses. The civil authorities must, under all ordinary circumstances, not only take care of their own prisoners, but also attend to the execution of all civil processes. The interference of the military is to be called for only when forcible resistance is made to the execution of the law, and never for such purposes as the serving of civil processes and the collection of debts. It must be remembered that the military are not the agents of the municipal officers of California, and cannot properly be called upon to act in that capacity, although they will always be ready to lend all necessary aid and assistance to the civil officers in the execution of their duties.

For the present, a prison should be rented by you; and as soon as the labor of your prisoners can be made available for that purpose, or a sufficient municipal fund can be raised, you should construct or purchase a suitable building for a jail, which should be the property of the town.

If you think of any new sources of municipal revenue, you will please to report them to the proper authorities for their approval.

Very respectfully, your obedient servant,
H. W. HALLECK,
Lieutenant of Engineers, and Secretary of State.

Pedro C. Carrillo,
Alcalde, &c., Santa Barbara, California.

Headquarters Tenth Military Department,
Monterey, California, July 19, 1848.

Sir: On the 8th of May I addressed a letter to Lieutenant Carnes, returning to him an informal voucher for the payment of $300, made to Pedro C. Carrillo on account of services as collector at Santa Barbara. On the 8th of the following month I again addressed Lieutenant Carnes, reminding him that he had not returned to me the corrected voucher of the payment made to Carillo, and required him to be more prompt in his correspondence, transmission of vouchers, &c. To neither of these letters have I received any reply.

You will place this letter in the hands of Lieutenant Carnes, who is hereby ordered to hand to you, for transmission to me, by the *first mail from the south*, the corrected voucher called for, together with his reasons, in writing, why the letters of the 8th of May and the 8th of June have not been attended to. Should Lieutenant C. fail to do this in time for the *first mail* from the south, you will release him from duty, and place him in arrest.

I am, respectfully, your obedient servant,
R. B. MASON,
Colonel 1*st Dragoons, commanding.*

Capt. F. J. Lippett,
Commanding, Santa Barbara, California.

State Department of the Territory of California,
Monterey, July 20, 1848.

The proceedings of the special court convened at Santa Barbara, California, by virtue of an order of the 5th of April last, for the trial of Benjamin Foxon, have been approved by the governor. Benjamin Foxon having been found guilty by a jury of twelve impartial men of the crime of manslaughter, or "homicide simple," was sentenced by said court to four years' imprisonment. This sentence will be carried into execution by the commanding officer of Santa Barbara.

Copies sent to Captain Lippett and Pedro C. Carrillo.

By order of the governor:

H. W. HALLECK,
Lieutenant of Engineers, and Secretary of State.

STATE DEPARTMENT OF THE TERRITORY OF CALIFORNIA,
Monterey, July 20, 1848.

SIR: Your letters of the 16th and 30th of June have been received. In the case of the Indian Juan José the governor has remitted a part of the fine imposed; and the alcalde has been directed to make preparations, as soon as possible, for having his prisoners guarded by civil officers, except when otherwise specially directed, and to ask for military assistance only in cases where the civil officers are unable to execute the laws.

Very respectfully, your obedient servant,

H. W. HALLECK,
Lieutenant of Engineers, and Secretary of State.

Captain F. J. LIPPETT,
Commanding, &c., Santa Barbara, California.

STATE DEPARTMENT OF THE TERRITORY OF CALIFORNIA,
Monterey, July 20, 1848.

The proceedings of the special court convened at Los Angeles, California, by virtue of an order of the 18th of April last, for the trial of Ruel Barnes, C. C. Canfield, Samuel Myers, and others, have been approved by the governor. Ruel Barnes having been found guilty by a jury of twelve impartial men of the crime of knowingly passing counterfeit coin, was sentenced by the said court to five years' hard labor in such place of detention as the governor might direct; at the same time, from the palliating circumstances which appeared upon the trial, as well as the youth of the prisoner, the court recommended him to mercy. In consequence of this recommendation of the court, the governor is pleased to mitigate the sentence to one year's confinement to hard labor, to date from the 23d of May, 1848. The sentence will be carried into execution under the direction of the commanding officer at Los Angeles.

By the governor:

H. W. HALLECK,
Lieutenant of Engineers, and Secretary of State.

Copy sent to Col. STEVENSON and STEPHEN C. FOSTER.

STATE DEPARTMENT OF THE TERRITORY OF CALIFORNIA,
Monterey, July 20, 1848.

SIR: The petition of the Indian Juan José, your own statement to Captain Lippett, and the testimony of various persons in Santa Barbara, have all been examined by the governor; and I am directed by him to call your attention to some irregularities of proceeding in the case of this Indian. Although his statements were in some respects improbable, nevertheless the persons accused by him of having sold the liquor should have been subjected to a proper trial, in order that their innocence or guilt might be fully established. If there were good reasons to suspect Francisco Vadillo of being the guilty person, he also ought to have been arraigned and regularly tried. In future, it will be necessary for you to arraign, try, and if proved guilty, commit all persons accused of selling liquor to Indians, in the manner directed in the governor's proclamation of the 29th of December last.

Very respectfully, your obedient servant,
H. W. HALLECK,
Lieutenant of Engineers, and Secretary of State.

Don PEDRO C. CARRILLO,
Acalde of Santa Barbara, California.

STATE DEPARTMENT OF THE TERRITORY OF CALIFORNIA,
Monterey, July 21, 1848.

SIR: Your letter and accompanying papers announcing the return of Don Pio Pico have been received. You will require Don Pico to immediately report himself to you, and to give his written parole of honor that he will take no part whatever in the existing war between the United States and Mexico, either by bearing arms himself or by inducing others to do so, or by giving the Mexicans any aid or assistance of whatsoever character. Should he refuse to give such parole, he will be held as a prisoner of war. He must of course be treated with all the respect due to his rank and character; but, at the same time, a strict watch must be kept upon his conduct.

By order of the governor:
H. W. HALLECK,
Lieutenant of Engineers, and Secretary of State.

Colonel J. D. STEVENSON,
Commanding, &c., Los Angeles, California.

STATE DEPARTMENT OF THE TERRITORY OF CALIFORNIA,
Monterey, July 21, 1848.

SIR: I have to acknowledge the receipt of your letter of the 12th instant, enclosing certain papers relating to the cargo of the "Joven Guipuscuana." The governor directs that the vessel be entered according to the original invoices, paying on them the duties required by the present tariff. As these tariff regulations must have been known at Lima even before they reached this country, the governor does not feel himself justified in remitting the fine required by the tariff, (vide page 14 of Bibby's pamphlet,) and which will be imposed accordingly by the collector at San Pedro. If the invoices are not verified as required by the tariff regulations, the one-quarter additional duties will also be imposed. (Vide article 10, page 17, of Bibby's pamphlet.) The collector must retain her original manifest and require of her a new one, (vide articles 1 and 18 of the tariff regulations,) setting forth the amount of cargo with which she leaves your port. This ought to have been done at Santa Barbara, where the penalties incurred should have been imposed.

Very respectfully, your obedient servant,

H. W. HALLECK,
Lieutenant of Engineers, and Secretary of State.

Colonel J. D. STEVENSON,
Commanding, &c., Los Angeles, California.

STATE DEPARTMENT OF THE TERRITORY OF CALIFORNIA,
Monterey, July 21, 1848.

SIR: I have to acknowledge the receipt of your letter of the 11th instant relating to police regulations at Santa Barbara, and also your letter of the same date, and the accompanying papers, relating to the military contribution imposed on that town. Your proceedings are entirely approved. In imposing this contribution, it was known that many innocent persons would be made to suffer for the acts of others; but, as it was impossible to distinguish between individuals, all were required to pay their quota. The contribution was upon the *town*, not upon *individuals*, and no one should consider himself as individually suspected of the crime, because, as a citizen of Santa Barbara, he is made to pay for the acts of that town. At the time of imposing this contribution, the governor had every reason to believe that the gun had been removed by some of the inhabitants of Santa Babara; but, as you think otherwise, he now directs that the money be retained in deposite by the acting assistant quartermaster, to be paid back again to the town as soon as proof is sent to headquarters that the act was not committed by any of the inhabitants, or, if by them, as soon as the guilty individuals are made known. The governor hopes that the people of Santa Barbara will assist him in his efforts to discover the real perpetrators of the act; but in the mean time each one must pay over his own part of the contribution, for all the citizens of a town are responsible for the acts of that town till the guilty individuals are pointed out. This is the law in many civil cases, and always the rule in war.

Very respectfully, your obedient servant,

H. W. HALLECK,
Lieutenant of Engineers, and Secretary of State.

Colonel J. D. STEVENSON,
Commanding, &c., Los Angeles, California.

STATE DEPARTMENT OF THE TERRITORY OF CALIFORNIA,
Monterey, July 22, 1848.

SIR: It appears from information received at this office that the "Joven Guipuscuana" arrived at the port of Santa Barbara from Callao on the 9th of June last, with a manifest not certified to as required by the tariff regulations, (vide page 14 Bibby's pamphlet;) that the penalty required by the regulations was not imposed; and that the vessel was allowed to sail with her original manifest, which ought to have been retained and a new one given, as required by articles 1 and 18 of the tariff regulations. (See also articles 7 and 10.) The governor directs me to call your attention to that part of his letter of April 28 to Captain Folsom relating to the verification of invoices, (a copy of which was furnished you,) and to say that he is unable to account for so manifest a neglect of duty on the part of the collector of the port of Santa Barbara, as not to impose upon the "Guipuscuana" the penalty she incurred.

Very respectfully, your obedient servant,
           H. W. HALLECK,
   Lieutenant of Engineers, and Secretary of State.
Captain F. J. LIPPETT,
  Commanding, &c., Santa Barbara, California.

STATE DEPARTMENT OF THE TERRITORY OF CALIFORNIA,
Monterey, July 22, 1848.

SIR: Your letter of the 11th instant relating to the missions of San Buenaventura and Santa Barbara has been received. It appears from the contract (a copy of which is in this office) entered into by Nicholas A. Dew and Daniel A. Hill, that they have rented the mission of Santa Barbara for nine years from the 1st of January, 1846; for which they are to pay $1,200 per annum. With the mission are also rented all its self-movable property and appurtenances, of which there was given an "inventory of delivery." The governor directs that you will endeavor to procure the original or certified copies of these inventories and of the bonds given by the renters; and also to ascertain whether they have complied with the requisitions of the decree of the departmental assembly of May 28, 1845, and of the governor's regulations of October 28, of the same year, with respect to the preservation of the public property and the payment of the rents. The results of your examination will be communicated to the governor for his action in the case.

Very respectfully, your obedient servant,
           H. W. HALLECK,
   Lieutenant of Engineers, and Secretary of State.
Colonel J. D. STEVENSON,
  Commanding, &c., Los Angeles, California.

STATE DEPARTMENT OF THE TERRITORY OF CALIFORNIA,
Monterey, July 25, 1848.

SIR: Your letter of July 11 enclosing a copy of your decision in the case of James McKinley *vs.* Chas. W. Flugé has been received. It was proper and just under the circumstances that the trial should be conducted in the English language, and your decision in the case is fully approved by the governor.

Very respectfully, your obedient servant,
           H. W. HALLECK,
   Lieutenant of Engineers, and Secretary of State
STEPHEN C. FOSTER, Esq ,
  First Alcalde, &c., Los Angeles, California.

STATE DEPARTMENT OF THE TERRITORY OF CALIFORNIA,
Monterey, July 25, 1848.

SIR: The commanding officer at Santa Barbara has been directed by the governor to restore to you the alcalde's staff of office, the key of the juzgado, and the saddle claimed by José Carrilo and one of the soldiers of Captain Lippett's command, the saddle to be disposed of by you according to justice. Cases of offences committed by soldiers against the persons or property of citizens are to be tried only by military commissions, and cannot be taken cognizance of by the civil tribunals; but in all matters of trade or traffic between citizens and soldiers, military officers will, except in very extraordinary cases, allow the civil law to take its ordinary course.

Very respectfully, your obedient servant,
H. W. HALLECK,
Lieutenant of Engineers, and Secretary of State.
Don PEDRO C. CARRILLO,
First Alcalde, Santa Barbara, California.

STATE DEPARTMENT OF THE TERRITORY OF CALIFORNIA,
Monterey, July 25, 1848.

SIR: I have to acknowledge the receipt of your letter of the 17th instant, with the accompanying papers. It appears from these papers that, on the morning of the 15th instant, the first alcalde of Santa Barbara caused a saddle claimed as the property of José Carrillo to be taken from the house of one Badillo and carried to the juzgado for judicial decision in the case; that, without waiting for this decision, you immediately ordered the alcalde to deliver this saddle into the hands of Sergeant Mullory, " to remain in your possession until proof was furnished you that no officer or soldier of your command had any just claim upon it;" that the alcalde, being at dinner at the time, promised to attend to the matter on his return to the juzgado; that soon afterwards, and while the alcalde was engaged in the judicial examination of the case, you sent a sergeant and file of men with peremptory order that, if the property was not immediately given up, the alcalde be brought as a prisoner to the guard-house and kept in confinement until the saddle was delivered over to you; that, after receiving this saddle, you informed the alcalde that it would be given over by you to the person judged entitled to it by any civil court or magistrate after a fair trial, provided the alcalde did not sit as a judge on the case himself, he being a near relation of one of the parties claiming the property; that thereupon the alcalde resigned his office, turning over to you his staff and the key of the juzgado.

The governor, upon a full examination of these papers, directs me to say to you that he regards your proceedings as too hasty, being calculated to interfere with the due administration of justice, and to give unnecessary offence to a civil officer of the territorial government. He therefore orders that you immediately restore to the alcalde of Santa Barbara his staff of office, the key of the juzgado, and the saddle in dispute.

It is made obligatory, by the orders of the government, upon all military officers to pursue a mild and conciliatory course towards the civil magistrates and people of this country, and threats of imprisonment or an armed force should not be resorted to, except under very aggravated circumstances, or in case of absolute necessity.

Cases of offences committed by soldiers against the persons or property of citizens can be tried only by military commissions; but, in matters of trade or traffic between citizens and soldiers, commanding officers (except in extraordinary cases, to be immediately reported to headquarters) will allow the civil law to take its ordinary course.

Very respectfully, your obedient servant,
H. W. HALLECK,
Lieutenant of Engineers, Secretary of State.

Captain F. J. LIPPETT,
Commanding, Santa Barbara, California.

STATE DEPARTMENT OF THE TERRITORY OF CALIFORNIA,
Monterey, July 25, 1848.

SIR: I am directed, by the governor, to furnish you with such information from this office as may be deemed useful for your guidance in the management of the affairs of the missions in your district.

By the Mexican law of August 17th, 1833, the missions of Upper and Lower California were secularized and made the property of the government. Each mission was to constitute a parish, and be placed under the charge of a parish priest of the secular clergy, with a fixed salary.

The churches of the several missions, with the sacred vessels, ornaments and other appurtenances, and such adjacent buildings as the government may deem necessary, were to be assigned for the use of the parish. The most appropriate building of each mission was to be assigned for the habitation of the curate, with a lot of ground not exceeding 200 varas square. The remaining edifices were to be designated for court-houses, preparatory schools, workshops, &c. A lot of ground was also to be laid out in each parish for a burial ground. All the expenses of this law were to be provided for out of the product of the estate, capitals, and revenues at present recognised as the pious fund of the missions of California.

The governor of California at first declined acting upon this law of secularization; but afterwards, on the 9th of April, 1834, he issued his provisional regulations converting three of these missions into pueblos.

By these regulations, the duties of the priests were confined to the spiritual affairs of the missions, while the territorial government assumed to itself the administration of all their temporal affairs. To each head of family, and to all over the age of 21 years, even when having no family, was to be assigned a lot of land not exceeding 400 varas square, nor less than 100, out of the common lands of the missions. Common lands, and, when convenient, municipal lands also, were to be assigned to each pueblo; one-half of the stock, seeds, and agricultural implements of the missions, was to be distributed to individuals in the same way. All other lands and property to remain at the disposal of the governor. The fiscal affairs of these new pueblos were to be under the direction of ayuntamientos, while the legal matters were to be decided by the primary judges of the nearest town.

The emancipated Indians were to assist in the cultivation of the common grounds of the new pueblos, but were prohibited from selling any of the lots or stock assigned them by the government. All contracts made by them were declared null and void, and the property sold by them was to be reclaimed by the government as national, the purchasers losing their money. If the Indians died without heirs, their property reverted to the nation.

In the extraordinary session of the legislative body at Monterey, November 3, 1834, these regulations were confirmed, except the one relating to the personal services of the Indians to the priests, and other regulations framed marking out the different curacies, defining the salaries of their priests, &c.

The whole direction of the temporal affairs of these missions was transferred from the priests to civil officers called administrators, who were stationed in each mission. Their duties were to manage, under the general direction of the government, the property of their establishments for the benefit of the Indians, while the padres were to devote themselves to their spiritual labors. These administrators were to make no sales without the express orders of the government.

Governor Alvarado's regulations of January 17, 1839, declare null and void all debts contracted by these administrators without the previous consent of the government. On the 1st of March, 1840, he made new regulations for the missions, replacing the administrators by mayordomos, and defining the powers of the latter over these establishments. Both of these sets of regulations seem designed merely to carry out the provisions of the previous laws and decrees. On the 29th of March, 1843, Governor Micheltorena ordered the missions of San Diego, San Luis Rey, San Juan Capistrano, San Gabriel, San Fernando, San Buenaventura, Santa Barbara, Santa Ynez, La Purissima, San Antonio, Santa Clara, and San José, to be delivered up to the priests, to be managed by them in the same manner as formerly.

The mission lands which had been granted previous to that date, in accordance with the law, were not to be reclaimed; but all the cattle property, and utensils of the missions, which had been let out, were to be restored to these establishments. One-eighth part of the total annual produce of every description of the missions was to be paid into the public treasury for the support of the government troops and civil officers.

By a decree of the departmental assembly of May 28, 1845, it was directed that the missions of Monterey, San Juan Bautista, San Juan Capistrano, and San Francisco, (Solano,) be considered as pueblos, they having already been made such, and that their premises (except the reservations which have been mentioned) be sold at public auction. That if the Indians of the missions of San Rafael, Dolores, (San Francisco Asi,) La Solidad, San Miguel, and La Purissima, did not, after one month's public notice by proclamation, unite for the purpose of occupying and cultivating the said missions, they be declared unoccupied, and be disposed of as the assembly and departmental government may deem best for the general good.

The remainder of the missions, as far as San Diego inclusive, to be rented out at the option of the government, care being taken to secure their prosperity. The principal edifice of the mission of Santa Barbara not to be included in the renting of the missions—one-half of the total rent of this mission to be invested for the benefit of the church and the maintenance of its ministers, and the other half for the benefit of its Indians.

Of the rents of the other missions, one-third to go to the priests and church, one-third to be for the benefit of the Indians, and one-third towards education and public beneficence, as soon as the legal debts of each mission are paid.

On the 28th of October, 1845, Governor Pico advertised for sale to the highest bidder the aforementioned missions of San Rafael, Dolores, La Solidad, San Miguel, and La Purissima, and directed that of the existing premises of San Luis Obispo, Carmelo, (Monterey,) San Juan Bautista, and San Juan Capistrano, edifices be selected for the curates' houses, court-houses, and school-houses, and the church and its appurtenances and the remainder of the edifices sold at public auction; and in the same manner the personal property, such as grain, goods, &c., of these missions.

The public sale of San Luis Obispo, La Purissima, San Juan Capistrano, to take place on the first four days of the following December, and of San Rafael, Dolores, San Juan Bautista, Carmelo, and San Miguel, on the 23d and 24th of the following January, notice being previously posted up in the towns of the department.

The missions of San Fernando, San Buenaventura, Santa Barbara, and Santa Ynez, to be rented to the highest bidder for the term of nine years. All the lands, out-door property, implements of agriculture, vineyards, orchards, workshops, and other property of these missions, to be included in said renting, except the principal edifice of the mission of Santa Barbara, the churches and their appurtenances, court-houses, curates' houses, and places for schools, and the small portions of lands occupied by certain Indians in each of the respective missions.

The proceeds of the rents of these missions to be divided into three parts, as already mentioned. The renting of the missions of San Diego, San Luis Rey, San Gabriel, San Antonio, Santa Clara, and San José, to take place in the same manner as those aforementioned, as soon as the difficulties respecting their debts are arranged. The government reserves to itself the right of taking care that these establishments prosper, in virtue of which it will prevent their destruction, ruin, or decline, should it be necessary during the period of their renting.

The renters of the missions are to pay punctually and quarterly the amount of their rents. They may pay to the respective padres, prefects, or their authorized agents, the third part of the rents destined for the ministers and religious worship, (of Santa Barbara one-half of the rent to be so paid.) These renters are to deliver back with improvement, at the expiration of the nine years, whatever they may receive on rent, except the stills, movables, and implements of agriculture, which must be returned in a serviceable state. They are to return the number of cattle which they receive, and of the same description, and of such an age as not to embarrass the procreation of the following year. They are to give bonds to the satisfaction of the government before they receive these establishments, conditioned on the fulfilment of the obligations of the renters, and the payment of such damages as the government may find against them.

A decree of the departmental assembly of April 3d, 1846, authorizes the departmental government to proceed with the missions of San Gabriel, San Luis Rey, San Diego, and others in similar circumstances, in the manner directed by the laws respecting bankruptcies, and that if it found necessary, in order to prevent their total ruin, they may be sold at public auction, the customary notice being previously given. A portion of the lands and other property of these missions may be set apart for the maintenance of the padres and the expenses of the public worship—this property being delivered as a sale at a perpetual interest of 4 per cent., the proceeds being applied to these objects. This act is no way to interfere with what has already been done under the previous decrees of the assembly. Six months at furthest are allowed for its fulfilment.

The foregoing is a brief summary of the substance of all the decrees and laws in my possession relating to the missions of California. I am at present engaged in examining and arranging the government archives; and if any further information on this subject be found, it will be immediately communicated to you.

It appears from the documents already referred to, that since the 17th of August, 1833, the missions of California have been regarded as public property and held at the disposal of the government; that the departmental assembly, basing their authority on the Mexican law of secularization, have authorized, upon certain specified conditions, the sale of some of the missions and the renting of others; that the departmental governors under this authority have advertised certain of their missions for sale and others for rent, with the conditions and reservations specified in the laws; that the lands set apart for the priests in each mission cannot exceed 200 varas square, and that granted to any individual cannot exceed 400 varas square; that the lands granted to Indians are merely for the use of themselves and their descendants, and that they can in no way dispose of them, but when abandoned they revert to the government; that all sales of mission property by the Indians are null and void; that the civil agents and administrators of the missions could not dispose of mission property or contract debts in the name of the missions without previous authority of the government; that the leases of the missions are not made in conformity to law unless bonds have been previously given to the satisfaction of government, conditioned for the fulfilment of the obligations of the renters; that the renters of the missions are bound by certain regulations respecting the care and preservation of the mission property; that the rents are to be paid punctually and quarterly, and that only one-third of these rents (in Santa Barbara one-half) can be paid over to the priests, prefects, or their authorized agents, the other two-thirds to be paid into the public treasury and expended for certain specified objects; that the government has reserved to itself the right to take such measures as may be necessary to prevent *the " destruction, ruin, or decline"* of the *missions during the period of their renting*.

It is therefore evident that the missions and the mission property which have not been sold in accordance with the provisions of these laws and decrees are still the property of the government, and may be disposed of accordingly; and that if the renters of the missions are found injuring or destroying them, the government may take such measures as may be deemed necessary to prevent their destruction, ruin, or decline.

Very respectfully, your obedient servant,
H. W. HALLECK,
Lieutenant of Engineers, and Secretary of State.

Colonel J. D. STEVENSON,
 Commanding, &c., Los Angeles, California.

HEADQUARTERS TENTH MILITARY DEPARTMENT,
Monterey, California, July 26, 1848.

SIR: I enclose you a letter from Robert Clift to myself of the 14th of June, which I found here on my late return from the gold mines.

From the copy of Mr. Canfield's quarterly account current for the first quarter of the present year, it appears that he turned over to Robert Clift $560, and from Pedrorena's account rendered up to the 4th of November, 1847, (see my letter to Lieutenant Clift of the 8th of March last—copy herewith,) he received from Pedrorena, together with $348 12½ on account of Fitche's note, $1,397 12—making in all $1,957 12. Mr. Clift made no reply to my several letters calling on him for a rendition of his custom-house accounts. I wish you to ask him why he never replied to them, particularly to the one of the 8th of March. I wish you to get such a settlement out of him as you can.

I am, very respectfully, your obedient servant,
R. B. MASON,
Colonel 1st Dragoons, commanding.

Lieutenant DAVIDSON,
A. A. Quartermaster, Los Angeles, California.

HEADQUARTERS TENTH MILITARY DEPARTMENT,
Monterey, California, July 25, 1848.

Whereas many citizens have gone to the gold mines of the Sacramento without making proper provisions for the families they have left behind them, and whereas many soldiers, tempted by the flattering prospects of sudden wealth, have deserted their colors to go to the same region, regardless of their oaths and obligations to the government, endangering the safety of the garrisons and thereby the tranquillity of the country, it is made known that unless families are guarded and provided for by their natural protectors, and unless citizens lend their aid to prevent desertions from the garrisons of the country, the military force now in California will be concentrated in the gold region to the exclusion of all unlicensed persons. Persons employed at the mines are reminded that up to this time they have enjoyed the high privilege of digging gold on government land without charge or without hindrance; in return for this privilege they are bound to assist in appprehending deserters, and in giving notice to the nearest military officer where any are concealed. A dragoon force will soon be at the mining district, and will traverse it in every direction to arrest deserters from the army and navy, and to apprehend such citizens as employ or harbor them, for these citizens are as culpable as the deserters themselves, and if arrested will be tried by a military commission and punished according to the laws of war. Should the officer in command of this force receive the cordial aid and support of the citizens, he will be enabled to check the serious evil which now threatens the safety of the country; but if citizens are not willing to lend their aid and assistance, but one alternative remains, that of taking military possession of the mining district.

It is hoped that there are enough of reflecting men at the mines to see how much the prosperity of California will be retarded, unless they pursue the course that is pointed out to them. It is desirable to develop the riches and wealth of California; but the military safety of the country must be secured at all hazards.

R. B. MASON,
Colonel 1st Dragoons, Governor of California.

HEADQUARTERS TENTH MILITARY DEPARTMENT,
Monterey, California, July 28, 1848.

SIR: In reply to your letter of the 20th of June, I have to say that I have sought for the Mexican laws on the subject of usury, and can find nothing on the subject except what is found in Febreno Mexicana, vol. 3, page 275, to which I refer you. I learn from the best business and mercantile men, and old inhabitants, that custom, for the last ten or fifteen years, has established the rate of interest at 12 per centum per annum, or agreement to the contrary, and that for the same period the custom has been, both among the mercantile and all other classes, to pay and receive greater rates of interest that may have been agreed upon between the contracting parties, and which was expressed in writing, either in the shape of contract, bond, or note. Long custom would therefore seem to have established interest at the above named rates.

I am, respectfully, your obedient servant,
R. B. MASON,
Colonel 1st Dragoons, Governor of California.

W. D. M. HOWARD,
San Francisco, California.

HEADQUARTERS TENTH MILITARY DEPARTMENT,
Monterey, California, July 28, 1848.

GENTLEMEN: I have the honor to acknowledge the receipt of your communication of yesterday's date. Under the circumstances you mention, and which are so well known to me—the almost entire absence of gold and silver coin—I have no hesitation in saying, that if the California grain gold, now in such abundant quantities in the country, can be wrought into convenient shapes, so as to answer as a substitute for gold and silver coin, I will order it to be received at the custom house, in payment of duties, at its intrinsic value.

I am, respectfully, your obedient servant,
R. B. MASON,
Colonel 1st Dragoons, Governor of California.

To WALTER COLTON, TALBOT H. GREEN, J. S. RUCKLE, THOMAS O. LARKIN, C. WOOSTER, MILTON LITTLE, D. SPENCER, JOSE ABRIGO.

HEADQUARTERS TENTH MILITARY DEPARTMENT,
Monterey, California, July 28, 1848.

SIR: Your letter of the 18th instant has been duly received, together with its enclosures, asking my advice and authority in reference to a bond and mortgage on a valuable landed property, belonging to the estate of the late Mr. Leidesdorff.

I would certainly advise the paying off of the debt at once, and thereby stop the interest and relieve the property from the mortgage, if it is certain the estate will be able to pay all of its creditors; but if there be not assets sufficient, then they must receive a *pro rata* amount, and this they could not do if the debt in question be paid in full now. Other and older creditors, perhaps to a larger amount, might be prejudiced thereby. As soon as I can get the laws, now being printed in San Francisco, a court will be organized for that district, if I can find a suitable person for the judge, having jurisdiction to all that relates of administrators and the settlement of the estates of deceased persons.

I am, respectfully, your obedient servant,
R. B. MASON,
Colonel 1st Dragoons, Governor of California.

W. D. M. HOWARD,
San Francisco, California.

STATE DEPARTMENT OF THE TERRITORY OF CALIFORNIA,
Monterey, California, July 28, 1848.

SIR: I am directed to ask your explanation of the matter referred to in the enclosed extract from a protest of Jules Chavon, captain of the Adelaide, at the same time calling your attention to the second modification in the Secretary of the Treasury's letter of June 10th, 1847. (Vide Bibby's pamphlet, page 1.)

Very respectfully, your obedient servant,
H. W. HALLECK,
Lieut. of Engineers, and Secretary of State.

Captain J. L. FOLSOM,
Collector, San Francisco, California.

STATE DEPARTMENT OF THE TERRITORY OF CALIFORNIA,
Monterey, July 29, 1848.

SIR: I am directed by the governor to acknowledge the receipt of your letter of the 25th instant, and to say, in reply to your inquiries, that if the governor's instructions relative to inventories and appraisements, in the administration of the estate of the late H. A. Leidesdorff, have not been executed by the first alcalde, it will be your duty, in his absence, to see that these instructions are fully carried out.

Herewith are enclosed the papers which accompanied your letter.

Very respectfully, your obedient servant,
H. W. HALLECK,
Lieut. of Engineers, and Secretary of State.

H. W. LEAVENWORTH,
Second Alcalde, San Francisco, California.

Know all men by these presents, that I, Richard B. Mason, colonel 1st dragoons United States army, and governor of California, by virtue of authority in me vested, do hereby appoint Charles V. Gillespie notary public in and for the district of San Francisco.

Done at Monterey, the capital of California, this 29th day of July, A. D. 1848, and the 73d year of the independence of the United States.

R. B. MASON,
Colonel 1st Dragoons, Governor of California.

STATE DEPARTMENT OF THE TERRITORY OF CALIFORNIA,
Monterey, July 29, 1848.

SIR: I have the honor to enclose herewith your appointment of notary public in and for the district of San Francisco.

Very respectfully, your obedient servant,

H. W. HALLECK,
Lieutenant of Engineers, and Secretary of State.

C. V. GILLESPIE,
San Francisco, California.

Custom-house and port regulations for the harbors of California.

In the absence of the commander-in-chief of the Pacific squadron, the undersigned, in virtue of authority in him vested, orders and establishes the following regulations for the police of the harbors of California, and for the better enforcement of the orders of the President of the United States respecting the collection of military contributions:

1. The collector shall visit all merchant vessels immediately on their arrival, and make the master of each vessel acquainted with such regulations as may be established from time to time for the police of the harbor.

2. Any disputes which may arise between the masters of merchant vessels in relation to anchorage or moorings shall be decided by the collector.

3. If the master of any merchant vessel shall refuse or fail to obey the directions of the collector as to the anchorage or mooring of his vessel, he shall be fined not exceeding thirty dollars, or imprisoned not exceeding one week, for each offence.

4. If any master of a merchant vessel shall receive, or connive at being received on board his vessel, any deserter from the army or navy, or if such deserter shall be found concealed on board his vessel, the vessel itself shall be confiscated, and the master shall be tried by a military commission, and punished according to the laws of war.

5. If any person belonging to a merchant vessel, other than the master, shall receive, or connive at being received on board, any deserter from the army or navy, such person shall be tried by a military commission, and punished according to the laws of war.

6. Any person who shall entice any sailor or other person belonging to any vessel on the coast of California to desert, or who shall aid or abet in such desertion, or who shall knowingly receive or conceal, or assist in concealing such deserter, shall, on conviction before any judge, alcalde, or other civil magistrate, who may be authorized to issue warrants or try

cases, be subject to a fine not exceeding five hundred dollars, and imprisonment not exceeding sixty days.

7. If any master of a vessel shall be detected in landing, or attempting to land anywhere in California, any goods or merchandise without permit from a collector, he shall be fined for every such offence in the sum of five hundred dollars, and the goods or merchandise so landed, or attempted to be landed, and the boat or boats through which such landing is effected or attempted, shall be seized, forfeited, and sold by the nearest collector.

8. If any person or persons other than the master of a vessel shall be detected in landing, or attempting to land anywhere in California, any goods or merchandise without permit from a collector, he or they shall be fined in the sum of one hundred dollars, and the goods or merchandise so landed, or attempted to be landed, and the boat or boats through which such landing is effected or attempted shall be seized, forfeited, and sold by the nearest collector.

9. In case goods or merchandise are landed or attempted, without permit from a collector, at a point distant from any port of entry, it shall be the duty of the nearest alcalde or other civil magistrate to seize, confiscate, and sell such goods and boats, and impose the penalties designated in the two preceding articles, in the same manner as is directed for the collector of a port.

10. On the arrival of any vessel whose cargo is subject to duty, the collector will notify the nearest commanding military officer, who, on receiving such notice, will immediately detail one or more non-commissioned officers or privates as a guard for such vessel. This guard will be instructed to allow no cask, box, package, or other article of merchandise to be removed from the vessel without a permit signed by the collector. These permits will be returned from day to day by the guard to the collector, for file in the custom-house.

11. Masters of vessels will be responsible for the conduct of their men while on shore or at liberty, and will be held accountable for the payment of any fines or forfeitures imposed on them for violations of law, or riotous or improper conduct.

12. The collectors will require the masters of all vessels when clearing at the custom-house to make oath to the correctness of their manifests, and that to the best of their knowledge and belief no gold or silver is on board, or about to be exported in their vessel, other than that set forth in their manifest.

13. All shippers and supercargoes will be required to make oath that their invoices and papers set forth truly and correctly the amount of all goods, merchandise, or other property shipped on board the vessel about to be cleared. A similar oath may, at the option of the collector, be administered to any passenger or other person about to sail in such vessel. All baggage belonging to passengers will be examined at the custom-house before it is suffered to go on board, and the keys thereof be withheld until the custom-house guard is withdrawn from the vessel.

14. All gold and silver not mentioned in the manifest, and found on board of any vessel about clearing from port in California, or concealed in passengers' baggage, or otherwise secreted for the purpose of defrauding the revenue, will be seized and confiscated, together with the box, trunk, or package, and all the contents of the same in which it may be

found; and should the amount of gold or silver so found on board of any vessel exceed in value one thousand dollars, the vessel will be seized and confiscated.

15. Any collector who may have just and reasonable grounds for suspecting a vessel of having gold or silver on board for the purpose of defrauding the revenue by exporting the same without paying the export duty, will detain and search such vessel, even, if necessary, to the unloading and examining of her entire cargo.

16. A similar examination will be made by any collector who may have satisfactory reasons for believing that any vessel trading in the ports of California has goods or merchandise on board not mentioned in her manifest. And all such goods or merchandise, and the vessel upon which they may be found, will be subjected to the penalties mentioned in the article 12th of the tariff regulations.

17. The personal baggage of all passengers or other persons arriving in the ports of California will be inspected at the custom-house, and any dutiable goods or merchandise which may be found in the possession of any such passengers or other persons and not on the manifest will be confiscated, together with the box, trunk, or package in which it may be found.

18. Any master of a vessel who, after his clearance has been granted, shall communicate, or allow any other person to communicate, from his vessel with the shore, or with any other vessel in port, will be subjected to a fine of five hundred dollars; and the boat or boats through which such communication is effected will be confiscated. And any other person other than the master of a vessel who shall make such communication shall be subjected to a fine of one hundred dollars and the confiscation of the boat or boats as aforesaid.

19. Any person who shall visit a vessel arriving in a port of California before she has a custom-house guard or inspector on board, or before her manifest and papers are deposited at the custom-house, will be subjected to a fine of one hundred dollars and the confiscation of the boat or boats used for such visit. Any person guilty of either of the offences mentioned in this and the foregoing article will be imprisoned until said fines are paid.

20. The proceeds of all fines and confiscations imposed by military commissions or otherwise for offences designated in articles 4, 5, and 6 of these regulations shall go for the exclusive benefit of the informer—the necessary expenses of court having previously been paid; and in all other cases of fines or confiscations under these regulations, one-half of the proceeds shall go for the benefit of the informers.

21. All other custom-house and port regulations for the ports of California, so far as they conflict with these regulations, are hereby repealed.

Done at Monterey, California, this 26th day of July, 1848.

R. B. MASON,
Colonel 1st Dragoons, and Governor of California.

STATE DEPARTMENT OF THE TERRITORY OF CALIFORNIA,
Monterey, California, August 1, 1848.

SIR: I have to acknowledge the receipt of your letter of the 28th of July, enclosing a copy of the proceedings of a suit instituted by you before the alcalde of San Francisco against Captain Dring for receiving deserters from the United States navy on board his vessel, the Jenet.

The governor has examined these proceedings, and approved so much of them as relates to the fine imposed in the case of Hutchinson, but disapproving of the decision of the alcalde in the case of the other sailor brought into court and identified as a deserter from the public service. The 4th article of the police regulations of September 15, 1847, has all the force of a positive law; and any master of a vessel who receives a deserter from the public service, or even if the deserter be found concealed on board his vessel, is liable to the specified penalties. Ignorance of the law, or an unconscious or unintentional violation of it, cannot exempt any person from its penalties; nor can the government be required to prove an *intention* and *design* on the part of the master—the fact itself is sufficient. The master, however, may prove his good intentions, and this proof may influence the court in the amount of the fine imposed between the specified limits; but when the fact of a deserter from the public service being concealed on board a vessel, or of the master of a vessel receiving such deserter or conniving at his being received, is proved in evidence, the alcalde *must* impose upon the master of such vessel the prescribed penalties—he has then no discretion except in the *amount* of the fine. The decision in this case is, therefore, disapproved; but it is not deemed necessary that you should prosecute the matter any further.

I am, respectfully, your obedient servant,
H. W. HALLECK,
Lieutenant of Engineers, and Secretary of State.

Major JAMES A. HARDIE,
Commanding, &c., San Francisco.

STATE DEPARTMENT OF THE TERRITORY OF CALIFORNIA,
Monterey, California, August 1, 1848.

SIR: In reply to your letter of July 28th, relative to the settlement of the estate of the late William A. Leidesdorff, I am directed to inform you that as soon as the printing of the laws can be completed, a court will be organized which can take cognizance of this matter. The organization of a court will be made with the least possible delay.

Will you recommend some suitable person for first judge or prefect of the San Francisco district? The governor wishes you to hurry the printing as much as possible.

Very respectfully, your obedient servant,
H. W. HALLECK,
Lieut. of Engineers, and Secretary of State.

Major JAMES A. HARDIE,
Commanding, &c., San Francisco, California.

STATE DEPARTMENT OF THE TERRITORY OF CALIFORNIA,
Monterey, August 1, 1848.

SIR: I have to acknowledge the receipt of your letter of July 27th. Several of your inquiries are answered in the custom-house and port regulations dated July 26th, and in the governor's letter of July 31, 1848.

All gold dust received by you in payment of duties, or on deposite, should be entered on your accounts as such, and carried out at the deposite value; that is, your account for so many dollars and cents in cash, and so many in gold dust, at so much per ounce.

From the difficulty, or rather the impossibility of ascertaining the value of this gold dust, the governor authorizes you to receive the export duty in *kind;* that is, taking the required per centage out of each lot of gold dust exported.

Your decision in case of the English brig "Tepic" is approved, and the barrel of wine will be given up. You will institute a thorough examination of the Chilian brig, Seis de Junia, as directed in the custom-house regulations, and subject her to such penalties as she may have incurred under the tariff regulations. The value of goods and merchandise not included in the manifest, and forfeited to the use of the United States, as directed in article 12th, tariff regulations, will be determined by the proceeds of the sales of the confiscated articles, and if these proceeds exceed the sum of one thousand dollars, the tariff regulations make it imperative upon the collector to seize and confiscate the vessel. In all cases of confiscation, you should be careful to preserve the evidence upon which you act, so as to be prepared to meet any appeal to the authorities at home.

Very respectfully, your obedient servant,
H. W. HALLECK,
Lieut. of Engineers, and Secretary of State.

Captain J. L. FOLSOM,
Collector, &c., San Francisco.

STATE DEPARTMENT OF THE TERRITORY OF CALIFORNIA,
Monterey, August 3, 1848.

SIR: I have to acknowledge the receipt of your letter of the 25th of July, with the enclosed papers. The governor authorizes you to turn over to the quartermaster and commissary departments eight thousand dollars of the military contribution funds now in your hands. As acting assistant quartermaster and commissary you will sign the receipts, the same as if the money were received from any other person.

Please to send the enclosed to Mr. Alexander, so that, if possible, the missing papers may be sent for the mail to Washington.

Very respectfully, your obedient servant,
H. W. HALLECK,
Lieut. of Engineers, and Secretary of State.

Lieut. J. W. DAVIDSON,
Acting Assistant Quartermaster, Los Angeles, California.

STATE DEPARTMENT OF THE TERRITORY OF CALIFORNIA,
Monterey, California, August 3, 1848.

SIR: Your custom-house papers and returns for the first quarter of 1848 have all been received, except your abstract of disbursements and the accompanying vouchers.

Please to forward them by the very first opportunity, so that they may go to Washington by the next express.

Very respectfully, your obedient servant,
H. W. HALLECK,
Lieut. of Engineers, and Secretary of State.

D. W. ALEXANDER,
Collector, &c., San Pedro, California.

STATE DEPARTMENT OF THE TERRITORY OF CALIFORNIA,
Monterey, August 4, 1848.

SIR: I have to acknowledge the receipt of your letter of July 22d, and the enclosed papers, relating to the mission of San Buenaventura. The governor approves of the renting of this mission and mission property in accordance with the conditions specified in the enclosed draught of a lease. He authorizes you to direct the acting assistant quartermaster to purchase of the mission a number of horses and mules, or such other property as may be required for government use, sufficient to cover the expenses of collecting this property. This should be done before the contract is entered into. The receipts for these purchases, as also an account of all the expenditures of the money, should be sent to this office. In inventory marked 3, it is stated that a number of sheep, cattle, &c., have been delivered to V. Noniago and others. If these have been sold, the receipts should be forwarded, and also an account of the expenditures. If not sold, why were they so delivered? The governor refers you to the letter of July 25th from this office, and wishes you to be cautious, in proceeding with the missions, not to go counter to the territorial laws; and also to see that these laws and regulations are complied with by the renters. So long as they observe these conditions they should not be molested; but when they are found injuring or destroying mission property, they must be regularly removed from the possession. The papers enclosed in your letter are returned herewith.

Very respectfully, your obedient servant,
H. W. HALLECK,
Lieutenant of Engineers, and Secretary of State.

Colonel J. D. STEVENSON,
Commanding, &c., Los Angeles, California.

STATE DEPARTMENT OF THE TERRITORY OF CALIFORNIA,
Monterey, August 4, 1848.

SIR: The governor directs me to acknowledge the receipt of your letter of July 19, and to inform you that he accepts your resignation as alcalde of San Luis Rey.

Very respectfully, your obedient servant,
H. W. HALLECK,
Lieut of Engineers, and Secretary of State.

J. B. CHARHAUNEA,
San Luis Rey.

STATE DEPARTMENT OF THE TERRITORY OF CALIFORNIA,
Monterey, California, August 4, 1848.

SIR: The governor has received your letter of July 28th, and directs me to refer you to my letter of July 21st to Colonel Stevenson, (a copy of which will be shown you by Captain Lippett,) for an explanation of the grounds upon which the contribution was levied on the town of Santa Barbara. As that explanation cannot fail to satisfy you that the measure was fully authorized by the customs of war in such cases, and that no imputation was cast, or intended to be cast, upon any individual, the governor declines accepting your resignation of the office of second alcalde of the jurisdiction of Santa Barbara.

Very respectfully, your obedient servant,
H. W. HALLECK,
Lieutenant of Engineers, and Secretary of State.

E. ARDISSON,
Second Alcalde, Santa Barbara, California.

STATE DEPARTMENT OF THE TERRITORY OF CALIFORNIA,
Monterey, August 4, 1848.

SIR: You will please hand the enclosed letter to Mr. Ardisson and to show him my letter to Colonel Stevenson of July 21, respecting the contribution imposed on Santa Barbara.

Very respectfully, your obedient servant,
H. W. HALLECK,
Lieutenant of Engineers, and Secretary of State.

Captain F. J. LIPPETT,
Commanding, &c., Santa Barbara, California.

HEADQUARTERS TENTH MILITARY DEPARTMENT,
Monterey, California, August 8, 1848.

GENTLEMEN: In my letter of the 28th of July, replying to yours of the day previous, you were informed that "if the California grain gold could be brought into convenient shapes, so as to answer as a substitute for gold and silver coin, I would order it to be received at the custom-house in payment of duties, at its intrinsic value." By a reference to the act of Congress, approved August 6, 1846, you will see that it would be manifestly illegal in me to do so. I was not aware of all the requirements and prohibitions of that act, at the date of my letter above mentioned.

I am, respectfully, your obedient servant,
R. B. MASON,
Colonel 1st Dragoons, Governor of California.

Messrs. WALTER COLTON, T. H. GREEN, J. S. RUCKLE, T. O. LARKIN, C. WOOSTER, MILTON LITTLE, J. SPENCE, and J. ABRIGO.

PROCLAMATION.

To the people of California.

The undersigned has the pleasure to announce the ratification of a treaty of peace and friendship between the United States of America and the Mexican republic, by which Upper California is ceded to the United States.

The boundary separating this country from Lower California "consists of a straight line drawn from the middle of the Rio Gila, where it unites with the Colorado, to a point on the coast of the Pacific ocean distant one marine league due south of the southernmost point of the port of San Diego."

By the conditions of this treaty, those residing within the limits of this territory thus ceded, who may wish to become citizens of the United States, are absolved from all further allegiance to the Mexican republic, and will at the proper time (to be judged of by the Congress of the United States) be incorporated into the Union, and admitted to the enjoyment of all rights and privileges granted by the constitution to American citizens. Those who wish to retain the character of Mexicans will be at liberty to do so, and also to retain their property in this territory, or to dispose of it and remove the proceeds thereof wherever they please; but they must make their election within one year from the 30th day of May last, and those who remain after the expiration of that year without declaring their intentions to retain such character will be considered to have elected to become citizens of the United States. In the mean time they will be protected in the free enjoyment of their liberty and property, and secured in the free exercise of their religion. They, however, are reminded that, as war no longer exists, and as Upper California now belongs to the United States, they owe a strict obedience to the American authorities, and any attempt on their part to disturb the peace and tranquillity of the country will subject them to the severest penalties.

The undersigned has received instructions from Washington to take proper measures for the permanent occupation of the newly acquired territory. The Congress of the United States (to whom alone this power belongs) will soon confer upon the people of this country the constitutional rights of citizens of the United States; and, no doubt, in a few short months we shall have a regularly organized territorial government: indeed, there is every reason to believe that Congress has already passed the act, and that a civil government is now on its way to this country, to replace that which has been organized under the rights of conquest. Such territorial government will establish all local claims and regulations which, within the scope of its legitimate powers, it may deem necessary for the public welfare. In the mean time the present civil officers of the country will continue in the exercise of their functions as heretofore, and when vacancies exist or may occur, they will be filled by regular elections held by the people of the several towns and districts, due notice of such elections being previously given. The existing laws of the country will necessarily continue in force till others are made to supply their place. From this new order of things there will result to California a new destiny. Instead of revolutions and insurrections, there will be internal tranquillity; instead of a fickle and vacillating policy, there will be a firm and stable government, administering justice with impartiality, and punishing crime with the strong arm of power. The arts and sciences will flourish, and the labor of the agriculturist, guided by the lamp of learning, will stimulate the earth to the most bountiful production. Commerce, freed from the absurd restrictions formerly imposed, will be greatly extended; the choked up channels of trade will be opened, and the poisoned fountains of domestic faction forever dried up. Americans and Californians will now be one and the same people, subject to the same laws, and enjoying the same rights and privileges; they should therefore become a band of brothers, emulating each other in their exertions to develop the wealth and resources, and to secure the peace, happiness, and permanent prosperity of their common country.

Done at Monterey, California, this seventh day of August.

R. B. MASON,
Colonel 1st Dragoons, Governor of California.

STATE DEPARTMENT OF THE TERRITORY OF CALIFORNIA,
Monterey, August 7, 1848.

SIR: In reply to your letter of July 30, I am directed to inform you that no authority has been granted to exempt vessels "landing lumber" from the regular tonnage duty.

Very respectfully, your obedient servant,

H. W. HALLECK,
Lieutenant of Engineers, and Secretary of State.

Colonel J. D. STEVENSON,
Commanding, &c., Los Angeles, California.

STATE DEPARTMENT OF THE TERRITORY OF CALIFORNIA,
Monterey, August 7, 1848.

SIR: Colonel Mason directs that the moneys collected from the citizens of Santa Barbara as a military contribution, imposed for the disappearance and concealment at that place of a gun belonging to the brig Elizabeth, will be turned over to the first alcalde of Santa Barbara, to be held by him as a municipal fund, and used for the purchase or erection of a prison, &c., as was suggested to the alcalde in a former communication from this office.

The alcalde will receipt to you for this money, and be held accountable that it is properly expended for the purpose designated. You will show him this letter.

Very respectfully, your obedient servant,

H. W. HALLECK,
Lieutenant of Engineers, and Secretary of State.

Captain F. J. LIPPETT,
Commanding, &c., Santa Barbara, California.

STATE DEPARTMENT OF THE TERRITORY OF CALIFORNIA,
Monterey, August 9, 1848.

SIR: You will receive by the same express which brings you this, a notification of the ratification of a treaty of peace, by which Upper California is ceded to the United States. Colonel Mason directs that you will continue to perform the duties of collector of the port of San Francisco until further orders. You will hire such assistance as may be required for the performance of these duties, and pay for it out of the proceeds of the customs. The tariff of duties for the collection of military contributions will immediately cease, and the revenue laws and tariff of the United States will be substituted in its place. You will also, in making out your accounts, observe, as far as you may be able, the forms used in the custom-house and Treasury Department of the United States. No more gold dust will be received in payment or in pledge of payment of duties; the revenue must be collected in the same currency as in any other port of the United States. You will be relieved from these duties as soon as a successor can be appointed. Will you recommend some suitable citizen who will accept the office? As the duties of collector will be far less arduous than formerly, it is thought that a salary of about —— dollars will be sufficient. Bonds must be given by the collector for the sum of ten or fifteen thousand dollars. It is supposed that you will be able to procure a copy of the present tariff of the United States from some of the merchants of San Francisco. If not, one will be sent you from this place.

Very respectfully, your obedient servant,
H. W. HALLECK,
Lieutenant of Engineers, and Secretary of State.
Captain J. L. FOLSOM,
Collector, &c., San Francisco, California.

STATE DEPARTMENT OF THE TERRITORY OF CALIFORNIA,
Monterey, July 26, 1848.

SIR: Your letter of the 16th instant is received, and the governor has accepted your resignation of the office of 1st alcalde of the jurisdiction of San José.

Very respectfully, your obedient servant,
H. W. HALLECK,
Lieutenant of Engineers, and Secretary of State.
CHARLES WHITE,
First Alcalde, San José, California.

Know all men by these presents, that I, Richard B. Mason, colonel first regiment dragoons United States army, and governor of California, by virtue of authority in me vested, do hereby appoint William Byrne first alcalde for and in the jurisdiction of the Pueblo de San José, Upper California.

Given at Monterey, the capital of California, this 26th day of July, A. D. 1848, and the 73d year of the independence of the United States.
R. B. MASON,
Colonel 1st Dragoons, Governor of California.

STATE DEPARTMENT TERRITORY OF CALIFORNIA,
Monterey, August 7, 1848.

SIR: It is reported that the first alcalde of the district of San Francisco has removed from the district, and that the office is now vacant. Unless that officer has returned and resumed his duties, you will give due notice of an election to supply his vacancy, as is directed in the governor's proclamation of this date.

Very respectfully, your obedient servant,
H. W. HALLECK,
Lieutenant of Engineers, and Secretary of State.

W. J. LEAVENWORTH,
Second Alcalde, San Francisco.

STATE DEPARTMENT TERRITORY OF CALIFORNIA,
Monterey, August 7, 1848.

SIR: The governor directs that you will give due notice for the election of four subordinate alcaldes of the Sacramento district. That district will be considered as including the whole country west and northwest of the district of Sonoma. It is suggested that these subordinate alcaldes be located at or near four most prominent places in the district. They will have concurrent jurisdiction, but will all be subordinate to the first alcalde of the district. You will please to report to this office the names of the persons so elected.

Very respectfully, your obedient servant,
H. W. HALLECK,
Lieutenant of Engineers, and Secretary of State.

JOHN SINCLAIR,
First Alcalde, Sacramento district, California.

STATE DEPARTMENT TERRITORY OF CALIFORNIA,
Monterey, August 12, 1848.

SIR: I am directed by the governor to acknowledge the receipt of your letter of June 12, and to inform you that his answer has been delayed on account of the absence of Mr. Hartnell, the government translator from Monterey. As it appears that the Indian Geronimo has already suffered a pretty long imprisonment for his offence, the governor is of opinion that it would be as well not to prosecute the matter any further. If you are also of that opinion, you will release the prisoner.

The several subordinate alcaldes of your district have concurrent jurisdictions among themselves, but are all subordinate to the first alcalde, and must conform to his decisions.

Very respectfully, your obedient servant,
H. W. HALLECK,
Lieutenant of Engineers, and Secretary of State.

Don JUAN BONDINI,
First Alcalde, San Diego district.

STATE DEPARTMENT TERRITORY OF CALIFORNIA,
Monterey, August 14, 1848.

SIR: I am directed to acknowledge the receipt of your communication of June 12, complaining of the judicial conduct of Alcalde Colton, Monterey, and asking for the interference of the governor. Such interference is now unnecessary, inasmuch as peace exists between the United States and the republic of Mexico; and the proper courts will now be established in this country, to which all matters of litigation can be referred.

Very respectfully, your obedient servant,
H. W. HALLECK,
Lieutenant of Engineers, and Secretary of State.

To Don GREGORIO DE AJURIA.

STATE DEPARTMENT TERRITORY OF CALIFORNIA,
Monterey, August 14, 1848.

SIR: In reply to your letter of July 31, I am directed to say to you that, as Upper California will now become a Territory of the United States, with a regularly-organized territorial government, of course the standard weights and measures of the United States will become the legal weights and measures of this country.

Whether Congress has yet organized such government, or whether the Treasury Department has yet forwarded to this country such standard weights and measures, it is not now possible to say; but the presumption is, that both the government and the weights are by this time on their way to California.

Gold is always bought and sold by troy weight.

Very respectfully, your obedient servant,
H. W. HALLECK,
Lieutenant of Engineers, and Secretary of State.

R. SEMPLE, Esq., *Benicia.*

STATE DEPARTMENT TERRITORY OF CALIFORNIA,
Monterey, August 14, 1848.

SIR: I am directed by Governor Mason to acknowledge the receipt of your communication of July 3, enclosing the protest and papers of Jules Chanons. As the penalty for non-verified invoices was imposed by the custom-house officers, under an order of the President of the United States, the governor does not consider himself authorized to remit it. With reference to the claims for surplus duties imposed on brandy in the port of San Francisco, it appears from the enclosed custom-house papers that no such duties were imposed, and that the claim is entirely unfounded.

I have the honor, sir, to be, with high respect, your obedient servant,
H. W. HALLECK,
Lieutenant of Engineers, and Secretary of State.

Mr. J. S. MOERENHOUT,
Consul of France.

571 [18]

STATE DEPARTMENT TERRITORY OF CALIFORNIA,
Monterey, August 14, 1848.

SIR: I am directed by Governor Mason to acknowledge the receipt of your communication of August 3, relating to a fine imposed on Captain Dring, of the barque "Janet." Previous to the receipt of your letter, the governor, at the request of Major Hardie, examined the proceedings of the alcalde's courts of San Francisco, and, finding that the fine had been imposed in a regular course of law, declined to interfere.

The misfortunes of Captain Dring are certainly greatly to be regretted; but no private sympathy would justify an executive officer in interrupting the ordinary course of law in a case like this.

I have the honor, sir, to be, with high respect, your obedient servant,
H. W. HALLECK,
Lieutenant of Engineers, and Secretary of State.

JAMES ALEXANDER FORBES,
British Vice Consul, Santa Clara, California.

STATE DEPARTMENT TERRITORY OF CALIFORNIA,
Monterey, August 15, 1848.

SIR: The governor requests that you will give due notice of an election for a subordinate alcalde in and for the valley of Nossa, in the district of Sonoma.

The several subordinate alcaldes of your district will have concurrent jurisdiction among themselves; but all are subordinate to the first alcalde, and must conform to his decisions.

Very respectfully, your obedient servant,
H. W. HALLECK,
Lieutenant of Engineers, and Secretary of State.

L. W. BOGGS,
First Alcalde, District of Sonoma.

STATE DEPARTMENT TERRITORY OF CALIFORNIA,
Monterey, August 15, 1848.

SIR: The governor directs me to reply to so much of your letter of the 9th instant as relates to the appointment of an alcalde in the Nossa valley. If the petition you mention was ever received by the governor, it has been lost, for there is no paper of the kind on file at this office. Directions have been sent to Governor Boggs to hold an election in the Nossa valley for a subordinate alcalde, in accordance with the governor's proclamation of the 7th of August.

Very respectfully, your obedient servant,
H. W. HALLECK,
Lieutenant of Engineers, and Secretary of State.

J. GARNET, Esq.,
San Francisco, California.

STATE DEPARTMENT TERRITORY OF CALIFORNIA,
Monterey, August 18, 1848.

VERY REVEREND SIR: Enclosed herewith is an inventory of the movable and self-moving property belonging to the mission of San Diego, now in the hands of Philip Crostwait. The governor directs that this property be delivered to your reverence, to be disposed of as your reverence may deem proper. It had better be taken care of immediately, for if neglected for a few months it will entirely disappear.

I have the honor to be your reverence's most obedient servant,
H. W. HALLECK,
Lieutenant of Engineers, and Secretary of State.
To the Very Reverend JOSE MARIA DE JESUS GONZALES,
Governor of the Bishopric of California, Santa Barbara.

STATE DEPARTMENT TERRITORY OF CALIFORNIA,
Monterey, August 18, 1848.

SIR: I have to acknowledge the receipt of your letter of August 9, and the enclosed inventory of property belonging to the mission of San Diego. You will perceive from the enclosed copy of a letter of this date to Padre Gonzales, that Colonel Mason has directed the property to be placed at his disposition.

Your letter of August 9, and the accompanying papers, relative to the ranch of San Marcos, belonging to the mission of Santa Barbara, are also received, and your course in this matter fully approved. The act of the alcalde of Santa Barbara, in giving possession to this property, is decided by the governor to be utterly null and void—no alcalde in this Territory having any power whatever to dispose of public lands or other public property, or to give any legal force whatever to any claim or titles to such lands or other property.

Very respectfully, your obedient servant,
H. W. HALLECK,
Lieutenant of Engineers, and Secretary of State.
Colonel J. D. STEVENSON,
Commanding Southern Military District, Los Angeles, California.

STATE DEPARTMENT TERRITORY OF CALIFORNIA,
Monterey, August 18, 1848.

SIR: It is reported that you have recently put Dr. R. Den in judicial possession of the ranch or farm of San Marcos, belonging to the mission of Santa Barbara. The governor therefore directs me to inform you that this act of yours is utterly null and void—no alcalde in California having authority to give any legal force whatever to any existing claims or titles to the missions or other public lands in this Territory.

Very respectfully, your obedient servant,
H. W. HALLECK,
Lieutenant of Engineers, and Secretary of State.
DON PEDRO C. CARRILLO,
1st Alcalde, Santa Barbara.

HEADQUARTERS TENTH MILITARY DEPARTMENT,
Monterey, California, August 19, 1848.

SIR: I have the honor to acknowledge the receipt, on the 6th instant, by an overland express sent from La Paz, Lower California, by Lieutenant Colonel Burton, of the Secretary of War's letter of March 15, 1848. Accompanying this was one dated City of Mexico, May 24, 1848, signed by George W. Lay, A. D. C., informing me that the letter of the Secretary of War was intrusted to the United States commissioners, Messrs. Sevier and Clifford, and that General Butler desired me to "consider the transmission by them of this communication as equivalent to the official notification from himself."

The letter of the commissioners, dated City of Queretaro, May 30, 1848, informs me "that peace is *definitively settled* between the United States and the republic of Mexico," and "that the amendments made by our Senate have been acceded to by the Mexican government, and of course constitute a part of the treaty."

I was therefore officially informed, on the evening of the 6th instant, that the war with Mexico was at an end, and that Upper California was ceded to the United States. I accordingly issued orders for the discharge of the regiment of New York volunteers, and all others whose periods of service end with the war, and also that the collection of revenue as military contribution should forthwith cease. A proclamation was then issued to the citizens of California, a copy of which you will find among my civil correspondence, dated August 7, 1848. Orders had previously been issued to Lieutenant Colonel Burton to embark his command for Upper California, in the event of his receiving official intelligence of a treaty of peace, duly ratified, whereby Lower California is given back to Mexico, and the upper province retained. The first part of the Secretary's instructions were therefore anticipated, and I have now only to fulfil the latter part, viz: "to take proper measures with a view to its (Upper California's) permanent occupation."

The above are the only instructions I have received from the department to guide me in the course to be pursued, now that war has ceased, and that the country forms an integral part of the United States. For the past two years no civil government has existed here, save that controlled by the senior military or naval officer; and no civil officers exist in the country, save the alcaldes appointed or confirmed by myself. To throw off upon them or the people at large the civil management and control of the country, would most probably lead to endless confusions, if not to absolute anarchy; and yet what right or authority have I to exercise civil control in time of peace in a Territory of the United States? or, if sedition and rebellion should arise, where is my force to meet it? Two companies of regulars, every day diminishing by desertions, that cannot be prevented, will soon be the only military force in California; and they will be of necessity compelled to remain at San Francisco and Monterey, to guard the large depots of powder and munitions of war, which cannot be removed. Yet, unsustained by military force, or by any positive instructions, I feel compelled to exercise control over the alcaldes appointed, and to maintain order, if possible, in the country, until a civil governor arrive, armed with instructions and laws to guide his footsteps.

In like manner, if all customs were withdrawn, and the ports thrown open free to the world, San Francisco would be made the depot of all the foreign goods in the north Pacific, to the injury of our revenue and the interests of our own merchants. To prevent this great influx of foreign goods into the country duty-free, I feel it my duty to attempt the collection of duties, according to the United States tariff of 1846. This will render it necessary for me to appoint temporary collectors, &c., in the several ports of entry, for the military force is too much reduced to attend to those duties.

I am fully aware that, in taking these steps, I have no further authority than that the existing government must necessarily continue until some other is organized to take its place; for I have been left without any definite instructions in reference to the existing state of affairs. But the calamities and disorders which would surely follow the absolute withdrawal of even a show of authority, impose on me, in my opinion, the imperative duty to pursue the course I have indicated, until the arrival of despatches from Washington (which I hope are already on their way) relative to the organization of a regular civil government. In the mean time, however, should the people refuse to obey the existing authorities, or the merchants refuse to pay any duties, my force is inadequate to compel obedience.

I must call your attention to my letter No. 19, of September 18, 1847, wherein these very dangers and difficulties were foreseen; and certainly the department was fully advised of the fact that nearly the entire force at my command were entitled to their discharges immediately upon the reception of official information of the ratification of a treaty of peace.

I do not anticipate any rebellion or revolution on the part of the Californians, although the southern district must be entirely abandoned by the military force now there; and, in fact, the minds of all men are so intently engaged upon getting gold, that for the present they have not time to think of mischief; but if, upon your receipt of this, measures have not already been adopted for giving this country a suitable government, I would earnestly recommend that it be done as soon as possible. Since writing my letter No. 19, above referred to, my mind has not changed as to the kind and character of force that should be stationed in California, only that since the discovery of these rich gold deposites the pay of troops sent to the country should be sufficient to prevent their deserting; for, so sure as men come here at seven dollars a month, they will desert, with the almost absolute certainty of being able to make ten or twenty dollars a day at the mines.

I have the honor to be your most obedient servant,
R. B. MASON,
Colonel 1st Dragoons, commanding.

General R. JONES,
Adjutant General, Washington, D. C.

HEADQUARTERS SOUTHERN MILITARY DISTRICT,
Los Angeles, California, July 20, 1848.

SIR: By the last mail I informed you of the arrival of Don Pio Pico in this district. I subsequently learned that he had passed through San Diego without presenting himself to Captain Shannon, or in any manner reporting his arrival. Immediately after his arrival rumors reached me of conversations had by him with his countrymen, in which he stated that he had returned with full powers to resume his gubernatorial functions, and that he had only to exhibit his credentials to you to have the civil government turned over to him. I found the people becoming very much excited, and some rather disposed to be imprudent. I sent for Jose Ant. Carrillo and some others in the town, who were giving currency to these reports, and informed them that I should hold them responsible for any imprudent or indiscreet act of their countrymen, and that, at the first appearance of any disrespect to the American authorities, I should arrest and confine them in the guard-house. This had the effect to check all excitement here; but as Don Pio removed up the country, the same excitement began to spread among the rancheros. In the mean time, his brother Andreas informed me that he, Don Pio, would come in and report to me in person in a few days, as soon as he had recovered from the fatigue of his journey. On Saturday, the 15th instant, he reached the ranch of an Englishman named Workman, some eighteen miles from here. This man has ever been hostile to the American cause and interest, and is just the man to advise Pico not to come in and report to me. On Sunday and Monday I was advised that many Californians had visited Pico at Workman's, and that the same story had been told them of his having returned to resume his gubernatorial functions, &c., and also that he should not report to me, but go direct to San Fernando, from whence he would communicate with you. The moment I became satisfied that he intended to adopt this course, I issued an order (copy enclosed) requiring him to report to me immediately in person. I sent my adjutant with a detachment of men to the ranch of Workman to deliver to Don Pio in person a copy of this order, with instructions to bring him in by force, in case he refused or even hesitated to obey. The adjutant returned here at 12 o'clock on Monday with information that the Don had left for San Fernando. I immediately despatched Lieutenant Davidson with a detachment of dragoons and a copy of the order, with instructions similar to those given Adjutant Bonnycastle. About 5 o'clock on Tuesday morning I received a visit from a gentleman named Reed, living at the mission of San Gabriel, who informed me that Don Pio Pico had arrived at his house quite late in the evening of Monday, on his way to San Fernando. Reed inquired if he did not intend reporting to me in person; he answered in the negative; when Reed assured him, if he attempted to pass my post without reporting, I would cause him to be arrested, and that he was aware of my being displeased at his passing through San Diego without reporting to the commandant of that post. Don Pio Pico, upon receiving this information, became alarmed, and requested Reed to come in and see me, to say he intended no disrespect, and would come and report at any hour I would name. Reed is a highly respectable man, and has ever been friendly to the American cause; and I gave him a copy of the order I had issued in regard to Don Pio, requesting him to deliver it, and say to Don Pio he could come in at any hour he chose, within twenty-four hours. Accordingly, about 8 p. m. the same evening, the ex-governor came in. He was unaccompanied even by a servant, evidently desiring it should not be known he was in town. I received him kindly, told him I had no desire to treat him harshly, but that the American authorities must be respected, and if he had not come in I should certainly have arrested him. He informed me that he left Guaynas on the 22d of May, crossed to Mulige, which he left for California on June 3, and arrived at San Diego July 6. He says that when he left Guaynas nothing had been heard of the action of the Mexican Congress upon the treaty, but it was generally supposed it would be ratified. He says the Mexican government did not answer any of his communications; and the moment he saw the armistice published in a newspaper, he determined to return home, as he supposed he could return with credit, under the stipulations of the armistice. He brings with him no other authority for his return, and says he desires to live peaceably, and attend to his private affairs. He denies ever having said that he came back with powers to resume his gubernatorial functions, and that he rebuked such of his friends as he had seen for their last attempt at a revolution, and advises that they remain quiet and obey the laws, as no part of the people of the conquered Mexican territory have been treated as kindly as the Californians have been by the American authorities. He thanked me for my personal kindness to his family and countrymen in general, and said if I would permit him he would go to San Fernando, from whence he would answer that part of my order which required a written communication from him. I gave him permission to leave, and offered him an escort, which he thanked me for, but declined. Don Pio Pico is about five feet seven inches high, corpulent, very dark, with strongly-marked African features; he is no doubt an amiable, kind-hearted man, who has ever been the tool of knaves; he does not appear to possess more intelligence than the rancheros generally do; he can sign his name, but I am informed cannot write a connected letter; hence, as he informed me, he would be compelled to send for his former secretary before he could answer my order or communicate with you, which he advised me he intended doing. I have promised to take charge of and forward any communication he may choose to make you. He left town on Wednesday morning very early, as obscurely as he had entered it; and those who advised him to assume the bombastic tone he did upon his first arrival have done him irreparable injury, for he is now ridiculed by many who before entertained a high respect for him.

I have the honor to be, very respectfully, your obedient servant,
J. D. STEVENSON,
Colonel 1st New York Regiment, commanding S. M. District.
Colonel R. B. MASON,
1st U. S. Dragoons, Governor of California.

P. S.—Since writing the above, I have received the enclosed note from Don Pio Pico, enclosing a communication to your excellency. In the note of Don Pio to me, you will perceive that he is no sooner arrived at San Fernando than he claims to have returned to California as its Mexican governor, to carry out the provisions of the armistice. I shall not answer his note until I have heard from you; but I shall keep an eye on him, and if I find he is preaching sedition, I will bring him in here at short notice.

J. D. STEVENSON,
Colonel, commanding.

True copy:
W. T. SHERMAN,
First Lieutenant 3d Artillery, A. A. A. General.

HEADQUARTERS TENTH MILITARY DEPARTMENT,
Monterey, California, August 23, 1848.

SIR: I have the honor to inform you that on the 30th of April I received a letter from Governor George Abernethy, of Oregon, dated April 3, 1848, informing me that the people of that Territory were engaged in a war with the Indian tribes of that country, and that ammunition of all kinds was very scarce. He requested that a supply should be sent him; and by the first opportunity thereafter, viz: the brig Henry, which sailed from San Francisco last month, I caused to be sent two navy six-pounders suited to blockhouses, one six-pounder brass gun, with caisson, harness, &c., complete, and 500 rounds of fixed ammunition for the same, with twenty barrels of cannon powder, 100 rifles, 500 muskets, with accoutrements, 85,000 cartridges, three barrels of musket powder, and 1,000 pounds of rifle and musket-balls. I have requested Governor Abernethy to take charge of these important stores, and to send receipts for the same to the officers here, who are responsible for the property. The mere fact of these munitions of war being in Oregon will restrain the Indians on the frontier, and give confidence to the existing authorities of that Territory.

In consequence of the exposed condition of many rancheros in California, I have likewise issued to them, in small quantities, powder and lead for the protection of their lives and property against the Indians, who at times are very troublesome and commit many depredations upon their stock and other property. Also, in a few instances, I have caused to be issued to persons who can be trusted a few old Spanish muskets and carbines that were captured at the outset of the war.

Don Pio Pico, the Mexican governor of California, returned from Mexico in the early part of July, passing through Lower California, the post of San Diego, and mission of San Gabriel, to that of San Fernando, the residence of his brother Don Andreas Pico. He brought no passport, and failed to report himself to the commanding officers at San Diego and Los Angeles, until Colonel Stevenson very properly compelled him to come to Los Angeles and report in person. Colonel Stevenson directed him also to report by writing; and I enclose you a translated copy of his letter to me of July 22, with a copy of Colonel Stevenson's letter of July 20. These letters were received by me on the 3d of August; and as Pico's presence in the country, with such absurd pretensions, might have led to seditious acts, I forthwith despatched a courier to Los Angeles with orders for Colonel Stevenson to arrest him and send him here by sea, whence I proposed shipping him to Oregon or some foreign country.

The treaty of peace was received three days afterwards, and was immediately communicated to Colonel Stevenson, with directions to restore Pio Pico to liberty.

I would most respectfully recommend that speedy measures be taken to fortify the entrance of the bay of San Francisco. It was impossible to repair the old fort or to construct any new works with the volunteer garrison; and at this moment the guns, mortars, shot, and shells are lying in the town of San Francisco, not twenty yards from the place where they were first disembarked. To hire labor in this country is out of the question, as any laboring man can command from ten to twenty dollars a day, since the discovery of the gold mines. It would be more economical to ship men especially for this purpose from the United States, bound in such a manner as to secure their services after their arrival here.

The present redoubt at Monterey is sufficiently strong for some years at least, as there is very little commerce carried on in this port; but the bay of San Francisco is daily becoming of more importance, and its entrance should be fortified as soon as possible. The survey and plans are already in the chief engineer's office, having been sent by Lieutenant Halleck in May, 1847.

I have the honor to be your most obedient servant,
R. B. MASON,
Colonel 1st Dragoons, commanding.

Brig. General R. Jones,
Adjutant General U. S. Army, Washington.

[Translation.]

Most Excellent Sir: As Mexican Governor of California, I have come to this country with the object that the armistice agreed upon in the city of Mexico, on the 29th of last February, by the generals in chief of the forces of the United Mexican States and those of the United States of the North, be observed herein. In making this declaration to your excellency, the just principle on which it is founded fills me with confidence; and from the favorable information which I possess respecting the qualifications which adorn your excellency, I trust that my mission to California will produce its due effect.

For which reason, and in due observance of the before-mentioned armistice, I have the honor to address myself to your excellency, requesting that you will be pleased to expedite your orders to the end that, in the places in California occupied by the forces of the United States of America, no impediment be placed in my way towards the establishment of constitutional order in a political, administrative, and judicial manner.

It is my desire that the Mexicans and Americans look upon and consider themselves with the most sincere fraternity; and, in accordance with this principle, I feel disposed to co-operate with your excellency in surmounting any difficulties which may arise in the business which occupies us.

This opportunity offers me means of protesting to your excellency the assurances of my distinguished consideration and high respect.

God and Liberty! San Fernando, July 22, 1848.
PIO PICO.

His Excellency R. B. Mason,
Governor and Commander-in-chief of the forces of the United States in California, Monterey.

I, the undersigned, do hereby certify the foregoing to be a correct translation of the original document.
W. E. P. HARTNELL,
Government Translator.

Monterey, *August* 19, 1848.

[No. 41.] HEADQUARTERS TENTH MILITARY DEPARTMENT,
Monterey, California, August 25, 1848.

SIR: I have the honor to acknowledge the receipt, on the 14th of June, of two letters from the Secretary of War, dated October 13 and 27, 1847, with their respective enclosures. By reference to department special orders No. 21, of June 16, you will perceive that a board of officers, consisting of Lieutenants Ord and Loeser, 3d artillery, were ordered to assemble at this place, to examine into the facts complained of by the French minister. The board has been in session since the 19th of June last, and has experienced much difficulty in getting the proper witnesses.

Their report will be forwarded to you as soon as it is completed.

The quartermaster's barque Anita is now here awaiting the arrival of Major Rich, paymaster, to proceed down the coast. Captain A. J. Smith, 1st dragoons, is also here, and will go in the Anita to the ports of Santa Barbara, San Pedro, and San Diego, mustering out of service, as he goes, the companies of New York volunteers stationed near those ports. Major Rich will pay these companies at the same time. Vague rumors have also reached me that the battalion of volunteers ordered from Santa Fe are on their way to California, and that they are in a wretched condition. Nothing authentic on this subject has been received, and but little credit is attached to the rumor; still, as I am officially advised that the commanding officer in Santa Fe was ordered, in January last, to despatch such a battalion, I have ordered the Anita to carry down the coast 15,000 rations for this battalion, should it arrive. The companies of the 1st New York volunteers stationed at San Francisco and Sonoma, viz: C, H, & K, have been discharged. The four companies in the southern military district of Upper California, viz: E, F, G, and I, will be mustered out before the middle of September, and the remaining three companies of the regiment, viz: A, B, and D, at present supposed to be at sea on their way from La Paz to Monterey, will be discharged upon their arrival here. After which, there will remain in California but two companies of regulars—F, 3d artillery, and C, 1st dragoons. The former, stationed here, has now present two commissioned officers and 44 non-commissioned officers and privates; absent two commissioned officers and 11 privates; aggregate, 62. Scarcely a day passes, however, that some one or more do not desert. The dragoon company has an aggregate of 83. That company has lost none by desertion in consequence of the gold mania; but as now it is to be brought to San Francisco, it is feared its ranks will be reduced as rapidly as has been the case with the artillery company here. There will be 50 able-bodied soldiers fit for duty in California.

At the present moment there is not a vessel of war on the coast of California; but, now that the war is over, I presume Commodore Jones will either come himself or despatch a portion of the squadron to this port. I am hourly expecting a vessel from the squadron, but do not believe she will remain long, as the danger of losing the crew will be so great that the officers in command will be forced to leave the coast and proceed to some foreign port.

The crews of some of the merchant vessels now in San Francisco have committed acts of outrage and mutiny; but there are no means of arresting the criminals, or punishing them when arrested. I enclose you the letter of Major Hardie and Captain Folsom on this subject, marked A and B. A detachment of twenty dragoons, commanded by Lieutenant Stoneman, which arrived last evening from Los Angeles, will be sent up to San Francisco at once; and, to illustrate the scarcity of saddles and horse equipments in this country, I will merely mention that Lieutenant Stoneman's party will have to be dismounted, so that Captain Smith may take the saddles back to Los Angeles, to enable him to bring up the remainder of his company by land. Even then Captain Smith will not be able to mount more than forty men. I have long been expecting the horse equipments referred to in your letter of the 28th of October, 1847.

My latest letter from you is dated January 20, brought out by Paymaster Hill, the receipt of which I acknowledged in my letter of May 19, 1848, sent by Mr. Chouteau, via Santa Fe.

I send by this mail, in seperate packages—

1. Proceedings of general court-martial held in this department.
2. Department orders from No. 37 to ——, inclusive ; also, orders No. 25, of 1847, previously omitted and referred to in your letter of January 20, 1848.
3. Special orders from No. 16 to ——, inclusive.
4. Military correspondence from May 22 to ——, inclusive.
5. Department returns for January, February, and March. These may be slightly erroneous, in consequence of errors in post returns that would require too much time to have corrected. They can, however, vary but little from the truth.
6. Post returns of Monterey for May and July.
7. Post returns of Los Angeles, June and July ; of La Paz, January, February, and March.
8. Muster roll of company C, 1st New York volunteers, sent here for transmittal.
9. Copy of letter from Commodore Shubrick, to which I invite your attention.
10. Claims of Jose Miguel Choza to a share in the prize ship Admittance.
11. Report on the defences of Lower California.
12. From newspapers, Californian, for May 17 and 24 ; July 15, and August 14, 1848.

I have the honor to be your most obedient servant,
R. B. MASON,
Colonel 1st Dragoons, commanding.

General R. JONES,
Washington city, D. C.

UNITED STATES SHIP INDEPENDENCE,
Mazatlan, May, 3, 1848.

GOVERNOR: I have received your letter of March 20, and learn with great regret that you have so little prospect of getting volunteers for service here. It is so important to hold Mazatlan, that I shall strain every nerve to do so.

With a prospect of peace before us, in the course of the summer, it would occasion me a degree of mortification of which you, as a soldier, may form some conception, but which I want words to express, to be obliged to abandon the Vera Cruz of the Pacific; but I can only use the means I have, and must look to facts for my justification. When I said three hundred men could hold Mazatlan, I intended to be understood to mean in addition to the force that the squadron could supply. With five hundred, all told, on shore, and a ship (a frigate or sloop-of-war) in the offing, I should feel easy about the terms of the place.

I expected, and had good reason for the expectation, to have had the Ohio, the Preble, and one other sloop-of-war here long before this. In that case I could have spared seamen and marines enough from the squadron to make the garrison; but now I have only this ship and the Dale available—the terms of service of the crews of the Congress and Cyane expiring early in the summer.

I still hope to get some assistance from you, or that the ratification of the treaty of peace may allow us to leave the coast. At the recommendation of Colonel Burton, I send to you, in charge of Lieutenant Halleck, Padre Gabriel Gonzales and his son, Villiano. The other prisoners I have allowed to go on shore here or in California on parole.

The reports of Colonel Burton will have informed you of the state of affairs in Lower California. I think we may feel assured, if the treaty of peace should not be ratified, and hostilities are renewed, that the Lower Californians have had such a lesson as will make them cautious how they give us more trouble.

And now, Governor, let me take this occasion to express, in the warmest manner, my sense of the prompt, zealous, and judicious aid which I have, at all times and in every way, received from you in the execution of the duties of my command.

If your means had been commensurate with your disposition, I should have wanted nothing; but you have aided me to the extent of your power, and no one could do more.

I have the honor to be, Governor, your obedient servant,
W. BRANFORD SHUBRICK,
Commanding Pacific Squadron.
Colonel R. B. MASON,
U. S. Army, Governor of California, Monterey, U. C.

I herewith enclose copies in English and Spanish of the armistice agreed upon by the commissioners of the United States and those of Mexico.

H. LA REINTRIE, *Secretary.*

[Translation.]

PORT OF SAN JOSÉ, *April* 12, 1848.

SIR: I have the honor to inform your excellency that three days after leaving your port I arrived happily at San José, where I found my family in perfect health; and I have the pleasure to offer myself and the whole of my family at your disposal, in order that your superior goodness may dispose thereof.

Most excellent sir, yesterday the American prize " Admittance," bound from Monterey, left this port, as I am informed, to be sold, with her cargo, in your place.

In my representation to your excellency, presented under date of the 9th ultimo, I reminded you in one of its paragraphs that I considered myself entitled to a share in that prize, for the reasons on which I therein found myself; and every one tells me that, the prize of that vessel having been made whilst she was at anchor in this port, during the time that I was captain in the port, (which I have proved to your excellency that I was until the 9th of November last,) I am entitled to an officer's share, unless the laws of the United States have changed.

My friend, Don Thomas Mott, whom I asked several times in this port respecting the affair, last year, after the Admittance left for Monterey, gave me repeated assurances and hopes that I might certainly depend on having a share in that prize, and he even caused me to give him a memorial to be forwarded by him to Commander John P. Montgomery, in order that this gentleman might accompany it along with the other proceedings of the case instituted by him, and I did so, giving the memorial to Don Thomas, for which reason I called your attention submissively in my first letter relating to this prize; and your excellency, in your esteemed answer of the 11th, does not tell me anything calculated to undeceive my well or ill-founded hopes of a share in this prize; and therefore, as the proceedings respecting said prize now fall into your worthy hands, I address you in this present petition, in order that you may be pleased, in the name of justice, to take it into consideration and to bear me in mind, in case that any part thereof belong to me, or, if not, that you would undeceive me, whereby I shall receive favor and justice.

Praying God to preserve your important life many years, your obedient, humble servant, &c.,

JOSE MIGUEL CHOZA.

Most Excellent Señor Commodore.

La Paz, *April* 12, 1848.

Sir: In compliance with the instructions of the commanding general of the department to make a "reconnoissance of the coast of California, with reference to the location of works of military defence," I reported in my last upon so much as relates to the upper province, and I now submit a few remarks on the military defence of the peninsula of Lower California.

I. *General description of the coast and harbors.*—The principal ports of the coast of Lower California, visited by whaling and merchant vessels, are San Quintin, Magdalena, San José, La Paz, Escondido, (near Loreto,) and Mulige.—(Vide general map of Lower California.) There are some other points at which vessels occasionally touch for supplies and trade, but they are comparatively of little commercial or military importance. The port of San Quintin, in latitude 30° 23′, is represented as affording a secure anchorage for vessels of every description, and to be sufficiently commodious for the reception of a numerous fleet. The extensive bay of Magdalena has acquired considerable notoriety from its being resorted to every winter by large numbers of whaling vessels. Its size gives it the character of an inland sea, its waters being navigable for the distance of more than a hundred miles. It furnishes several places of safe and commodious anchorage. The bay of San José, near Cape Saint Lucas, is much frequented by coasting vessels, and occasionally visited by whalers and men-of-war. Being the outlet of a fertile valley, extending some forty or fifty miles into the interior, it is probably the best place in the peninsula for supplying shipping with water and fresh provisions. It is, however, a mere roadstead, affording no protection whatever during the season of southeasters.

La Paz is the seat of government and the principal port of Lower California, and its extensive bay affords excellent places of anchorage for vessels of any size, and is sufficiently commodious for the most numerous fleets.—(Vide plan No. 1.) The principal pearl fisheries are in this immediate vicinity, and also the most valuable mining districts. It is the outlet of the fertile valley of the Todos Santos, and of the produce of the whole country between Santiago and Loreto. The cove or estero opposite the town of La Paz furnishes spacious and safe anchorage, which may be reached by vessels drawing not more than 18 or 20 feet of water; and the cove of Pichilingue, at the southeastern extremity of the bay, and about six miles from the town, affords an excellent anchorage for vessels of any size; but the inner bay can be reached only by small merchant vessels. The bar, however, between the two is only a few yards in extent; and if the importance of the place should ever justify it, the channel might be made deeper without difficulty or great expense. The adjacent country being barren and mountainous, and the roads to the interior exceedingly difficult, this place can never be the outlet of much agricultural produce. But as the island of Carmen, nearly opposite the entrance to this bay, contains an almost inexhaustible supply of salt, very easy of access, it is possible that the trade in this article may eventually give considerable importance to the port of Escondido.

The bay of Mulige contains several places of anchorage, but none of them are deemed safe for large vessels, or even for small vessels, at all seasons of the year. There are also several other ports in the gulf further north which are occasionally visited by coasting vessels, but it is not known that any of them are likely to be of much commercial or military importance.

II. *Proposed system of defence.*—It is not supposed that, under existing circumstances, any military post will be necessary on the western coast of the peninsula; nor is it probable that, for many years, any place there will become of sufficient importance to justify the construction of military works for its defence. It is true that the whale fishery on this coast has become, from the amount of shipping engaged in it, an object of the highest consideration; but our having ports of refuge at San Francisco or San Diego, and at La Paz, strong enough to resist a naval coup de main, will, it is believed, afford sufficient security to these whalers in case of a war with a maritime power.

On our arrival here, in October last, it was deemed desirable to establish a small military post at San José, for the double purpose of giving protection to the friendly inhabitants against a band of Mexican freebooters who had crossed the gulf from Guaynas to Mulige and Loreto, and of preventing the further introduction of men and munitions from the opposite coast. The old mission building was found well adapted to the purpose in view, and with a few repairs and improvments served as an admirable protection for the little garrison in the several attacks which it afterwards sustained from greatly superior forces. It will probably be necessary to continue this post during the war with Mexico, or at least so long as there is any danger of the enemy's sending troops from the opposite coast to again disturb the tranquillity of the peninsula; but it is not deemed advisable to establish at this place any works of permanent defence, the character of the port not being such as to warrant expenditures for this purpose. The defences of the cuartel or mission building are deemed sufficient for all purposes of temporary occupation.

Should the war with Mexico continue, and the naval forces be again withdrawn from the gulf, it may be necessary to establish temporarily a small military post at Mulige; but no permanent garrison will be required either at that place or Escondido, unless perhaps hereafter the commercial importance of the latter port should justify such a measure.

La Paz is, therefore, the only port in Lower California which it will be necessary, for the present, to occupy with a permanent military force, or to secure by means of fortifications. For temporary purposes, the site of the old cuartel is well suited for the construction of defensive barracks, inasmuch as it commands the town, and may readily be secured against an attack from the side.—(Vide plan No. 1.) The buildings at present occupied as barracks are not judiciously located. A permanent work on Punta Colorada will completely close the entrance to Pichilingue cove, and its heavy guns will reach the entrance to the channel of La Paz; but to give the requisite security to the latter, a small battery will be necessary on Punta Priéta. The topographical features of both these points are favorable for the construction of small fortifications. Stone of good quality for building purposes is found in the immediate vicinity, and good lime may be procured at the distance of only a few miles. Quarries have been opened in the "Calaveras," and the stone, though soft and easily worked, is found to be in this climate of a very durable character. La Paz is not difficult to defend against a naval attack, and the proposed fortifications may be constructed in a short time and without a very large expenditure of money. The commercial character of the place, its military importance as connected with the defence of the peninsula, its great value as a naval depot and port of refuge for our commercial and military marine in case of war with any naval power, will, it is believed, fully justify the expenditures necessary for securing this port against a maritime attack.

III. *Commercial and military importance of Lower California.*—Thus far in my report I have proceeded on the supposition that it is the intention of our government to retain the whole of California in any treaty of peace with Mexico; but doubts have recently been expressed on the policy of retaining this peninsula, on account of its being of little or no value to the United States. As the guerrilla forces which were sent over from Mexico the past summer, during the absence of our squadron from this coast, to regain possession of Lower California and force the inhabitants to their allegiance to the Mexican government, have been defeated and completely dispersed, leaving our own troops in undisputed possession of the Territory, nothing but a conviction of the utter worthlessness of the country could now induce our government to consent to its abandonment. On this subject I beg leave to add a few remarks:

The peninsula of California lies between $22°\ 50'$ and $32°\ 30'$ north latitude, being about 700 miles in length and varying from 50 to 100 miles in breadth. An irregular chain or broken ridge of mountains extend from Cape St. Lucas to the frontiers of Upper California, with spurs running off on each side to the gulf and ocean. Between these spurs are numerous broad plains covered with stunted trees, and during the rainy months with a thin but nutricious grass. In the dry season this grass is parched up like hay, but from its nutricious character it affords abundant food for the herds of cattle and horses which constitute the principal wealth of rancheros. The dryness of the soil prevents the growth of trees of any considerable magnitude, except on the borders of a few mountain streams. This timber, though far from being plentiful, is exceedingly durable and much esteemed in ship-building. The greatest height of the mountains is estimated at five thousand feet; many of them are piles of mere broken rocks, while others are covered with grass, shrubbery, and small trees. The plains are sandy and mostly unproductive—not, however, from any natural barrenness in the soil, but from a deficiency of water. There are but few durable streams in the whole country, and streams of good water are extremely scarce. But in the plains and most of the dry beds of rivers water can be obtained by digging wells only a few feet in depth; and wherever irrigation has been resorted to by means of these wells, the produce of the soil, from its remarkable fertility, has abundantly rewarded the labor of the agriculturist. Much of this soil is of volcanic origin, having been washed from the mountains by the action of heavy rains, and the produce extracted by means of irrigation from these apparently barren and unprolific sands is something most marvellous. The general aspect of the country on the coast is exceedingly barren and forbidding, but I have seen no instance where the soil is properly cultivated that the labor bestowed on it is not well rewarded. The growth of vegetation is exceedingly rapid, and the soil and climate are such as to produce nearly all the tropical fruits in great perfection. But the inhabitants are disinclined to agriculture, and most of them live indolent and roving lives, subsisting principally upon their herds. Notwithstanding the unfavorable character of the country, it is capable, in the hands of an industrious and agricultural people, of supporting a population much more numerous than the present. In the time of the missions, when very small portions of the soil were cultivated, and even these but rudely, by the Indians, the four districts of San José, Santiago, San Antonio, and Todos Santos contained a population of 35,000 souls, whereas the present population of the same districts is only 7,000.

The agricultural products of Lower California are maize, sugar-cane, potatoes, dates, figs, grapes, quinces, lemons, and olives. A considerable quantity of hides, beef, cheese, soap, sugar, figs, raisins, &c., is annually exported to Mexico and Upper California, flour and merchandise being received in exchange. The vegetable market of Mazatlan is also in part supplied from the valley of San José.

But the value of Lower California does not result from its being either a grazing or agricultural country. Its fisheries, mines, commerce, and the influence of its geographical position, are matters of much higher importance than its agricultural productions.

The whole coast of the peninsula abounds with fish; clams and oysters are found in great plenty and of every variety. The islands of the gulf abound with seal, and the whaling grounds on the Pacific coast are of great value. During the past year Magdalena bay alone has, at one time, contained as many as twenty-eight sail, all engaged in this fishery. The pearl fishery is also exceedingly valuable. Formerly, when it was conducted with system and regularity, the annual produce of a single vessel with thirty or forty divers, between the months of July and October, usually amounted to about $60,000; and now, badly as the fishery is conducted, the annual exportation of pearls amounts to between forty and fifty thousand dollars. Tortoise and pearl shells are also articles of exportation.

Lower California contains valuable mines of gold, silver, copper, and lead; but, for the want of capital, very few of these are worked, and this in the rudest manner possible. Nevertheless, the labor expended on them is well rewarded; and there can be no doubt that with capital and suitable means they would yield very handsome profits. The salt mines on Carmen island are capable of supplying the whole coast of Mexico and California; already the duties on this article amount to a considerable sum.

The commerce of the peninsula is now very limited, being principally confined to a coasting trade with the ports of Mexico. The whole population of the country is but little more than ten thousand, and the annual imports and exports are estimated at $300,000. But in our hands this commerce, freed from the absurd restrictions imposed by Mexico, will soon receive a very great extension. La Paz will become the principal depot of American goods for the western coast of Mexico; and in a few years most foreign goods intended for this coast will also be deposited in the warehouses of Lower California, to be transferred to the ports of Mexico at such times and in such quantities as the demands of the market may require. In the present variable state of Mexican trade, resulting from an irregular and fluctuating tariff, which differs for each port and changes with every change of general or state administration, it is frequently necessary to transfer vessels with their cargoes from one port to another, or to keep them for weeks at sea, standing off and on, so as to enable the agents to arrange the rate of duties at the custom-house before landing the cargoes. Sometimes the consignees are obliged to send their vessels to the Sandwich islands or Valparaiso until a change of administration will enable them to avoid the exorbitant demands of some petty governor or collector of customs. Moreover, the principal commercial ports of this coast (Mazatlan and San Blas) are inaccessible to merchant vessels for four months of each year, and during that time are visited only by small coasters. But, with Lower California in our possession, merchant vessels of whatever character, at all seasons and in all winds, can find a refuge in La Paz, and their cargoes despatched in such quantities and to such points of the opposite coast as circumstances may justify. This place in a few years will be what Mazatlan now is, and Mazatlan experience the fate of San Blas and Acapulco.

The importance, however, of this port results mainly from its geographical position, and the influence it is likely to exert as a military and naval depot upon our commercial interests in the Pacific. The port of San Francisco, in Upper California, should be well fortified, and every care taken to make it a harbor of refuge for our merchant and military marine, in case of a maritime war; but it must be remembered that that place is nearly fifteen hundred miles from the nearest port of Mexico, and that it is very far north of some of the best whaling grounds in the Pacific, and too distant to afford much protection to our commerce with Central America, although its position gives it a controlling influence over the commerce of Sandwich islands, Upper California, and Oregon. In the same way a well-fortified naval station at La Paz, from its immediate proximity to the coast of Mexico, would have a most beneficial influence on our commercial and whaling interest in this part of the Pacific. The great value, in time of maritime war, of such *key* points as La Paz, and the commanding influence exercised by them in the protection of commerce, have become settled principles in military defence; and England shows her appreciation of their truth, and the wisdom of her own policy, in establishing stations at points like St. Helena, Cape of Good Hope, Gibraltar, Malta, Corfu, and Bermuda.

Again, the growing commerce of California and Oregon, and the political importance of our possessions on the Pacific, render it necessary that we should have some means of rapid communication between them and the seat of government at Washington. This communication must be effected by the isthmus of Panama or of Tehuantepec. In either case steamers bound to Upper California and the Columbia river must have one or more intermediate depots of fuel; and in time of war it is important that these depots be established in our own rather than in a hostile territory. A glance at the map will show that La Paz is nearly equi distant from the extremities of this line; and that Tehuantepec, La Paz, and San Francisco divide into four equal parts the whole distance from Panama to Oregon. Moreover, as this ocean is peculiarly suited to steam navigation, a large part of the commerce of the Pacific must eventually be carried on in steam vessels; and in all probability not many years will elapse before a portion of our naval force in these waters is of the same character. Under this supposition, the importance of our possessing some naval depot and harbor of refuge and repair south of Upper California is too manifest to require argument or illustration.

But whatever may be thought of the value of this peninsula or of the gulf as a natural boundary between us and Mexico, instead of an imaginary line drawn from the Colorado to the Pacific, thus separating a kindred people, and exposing the governments of the two Territories to continual collisions, the propriety of retaining Lower California is, in my opinion, now no longer an open question. When this country was first taken possession of by the forces of the United States, the people were promised the protection of our government against Mexico, and guarantied the rights secured by our constitution; and in November, 1847, they were assured by the commander-in-chief of the Pacific squadron, (with the approbation of the Secretary of the Navy,) that this Territory would be *permanently* retained by the American government; and again, by the President of the United States, in his annual message of December, 1847, that it "should never be given up to Mexico." Acting under these assurances, all the most respectable people of the Territory not only refused to take part with the Mexican forces which were sent to attempt the recapture of that country from the Americans, but many of them actually took up arms in our defence, and rendered most valuable services in ridding the peninsula of the guerrilla hordes sent over from Mexico for the purpose of effecting our expulsion. In this conflict, some who thus sided with us lost their lives, many their property, and all have exposed themselves to the vengeance of the Mexican government. But these losses and dangers they have willingly encountered, in the hope of obtaining the better government of the United States. They have regarded these promises as made in good faith, and have been guided in their conduct by the assurances thus held out to them by the agents of the American government; and now, for the United States to voluntarily surrender this country to the republic of Mexico, and leave these Californians exposed to the loss of life and confiscation of property, for having sided with us, under the assurances thus held out to them, would not only be in itself a breach of national faith, but would make us appear in the eyes of the world guilty of the most deliberate and cruel deception.

          H. WAGER HALLECK,
            Lieutenant of Engineers.

Colonel R. B. MASON,
 Commanding Tenth Military Department.

        SAN FRANCISCO, CALIFORNIA,
          August 14, 1848.

SIR: I have the honor to call your attention to the fact that the deficiency of force to support the civil organization at this place is likely to be productive of the most serious consequences. The lower classes of the community here are of the most lawless kind; and when the regiment of volunteers are disbanded, and the number of the evil-disposed become swelled by disorganizers freed from the restraints of discipline, there will be no security here for either life or property. Disorders of the worst kind are of daily occurrence among the crews of the shipping; and there are no means of repressing disturbances or enforcing order. Under this view of the state of affairs, I have the honor to express a hope that as soon as the squadron arrives here a vessel of war will be despatched to this post. The support of the navy is the only thing now to be relied on here to protect the citizens and to secure the safety of the public interests.

 I am, sir, respectfully, your obedient servant,
          JAS. A. HARDIE,
  First Lieutenant 3d Artillery, Major 1st N. Y. Volunteers.

Colonel R. B. MASON,
 1st U. S. Dragoons, Monterey, California.

         QUARTERMASTER'S OFFICE,
        San Francisco, August 14, 1848.

SIR: The Anita takes down fifteen thousand (15,000) rations for the use of the troops below; but as I do not know to whom they are to go, my invoices are put into the hands of the captain of the Anita, and he has instructions to take receipts from the officers to whom they are delivered. Please to give the necessary orders, so that I may obtain receipts for the stores. I shall be unable to forward the invoices of the stationery, as you desire. There is no stationery here, and there has not been an assortment for months past. I have sent to Valparaiso for it. Such as can be obtained is sent.

I have given an order for several thousand bushels of barley to be brought from Chili. The arrangement was made before the late news from Mexico; but it will not cost more than $1 37 per bushel aside from the duties, and the supply will not be more than sufficient for the animals kept in service, provided the horses of the dragoons and artillery are kept in good condition and fit for active duty. Since our force is so small here, I suppose this will be the case, as it will be important to make the command as efficient as possible. I have also sent for some other stores—as ready-made horse shoes and nails, stationery, and sperm candles—all of which will be required even with our reduced force.

The most mortifying state of things prevails here at this time. Government, both civil and military, is abandoned. Offences are committed with impunity; and property, and lives even, are no longer safe. If something is not done soon, our institutions will inevitably be disgraced. Last night the crew of the Chilian brig Corred rose upon their officers, with arms in their hands, and, after driving them into the cabin, the vessel was robbed, and the men escaped up the Sacramento in the long-boat; one man was badly cut with a knife. Acts of disgraceful violence occur almost daily on board the shipping, and we have no power to preserve order. To-morrow morning the volunteers will be mustered out of service, and we shall be utterly without resource for the protection of public property. Robberies and pillage will no doubt occur, and it is impossible to be responsible for consequences. My office is left with a large amount of money and gold dust in it, and the volunteers are discharged without pay. If it is possible to send a vessel of war here, it should be done at once. This is now a United States port, and we are bound by our treaties to protect the commerce in it. We collect port charges, &c., from both foreign and American vessels, and in return we are under the most imperative obligation to protect trade. This we cannot do at present, and our utterly powerless condition and the lawless transactions in this port and its neighborhood are a constant theme for reproach to our flag. I repeat that a man-of-war should come here at once, if it is possible. There are now seven or eight vessels in port, and we learn of eight or ten others on their way from the islands alone.

I am, sir, respectfully, your obedient servant,
J. L. FOLSOM,
Captain and Assistant Quartermaster.

Lieutenant W. T. Sherman,
3d U. S. Artillery, A. A. A. General.

Headquarters Tenth Military Department,
Monterey, California, May 22, 1848.

Sir: Colonel Mason learned with profound regret the death of W. A. Leidsdorff, esq., communicated to him in your letter of the 18th instant. The steps adopted by Major Hardie and yourself to secure the papers and property of the deceased met Colonel Mason's full approbation; and he wishes you to retain such necessary charge of those papers and effects until called for by T. O. Larkin, esq., consul for the United States government for California, to whom, under the circumstances, the administration of the estate belongs. Mr. Larkin will, in a few days, come to San Francisco in person to attend to this business. You will please afford him any facilities in your power for the proper settlement of the affairs of this estate, and will please notify the alcalde of San Francisco of Mr. Larkin's office and authority in the matter, together with Colonel Mason's wish that he extend to him every assistance consistent with his office in the proper administration of said estate.

I have the honor to be your obedient servant,
W. T. SHERMAN,
First Lieutenant 3d Artillery, A. A. A. General.

Captain J. L. FOLSOM,
Assistant Quartermaster, San Francisco, California.

HEADQUARTERS TENTH MILITARY DEPARTMENT,
Monterey, California, May 24, 1848.

SIR: Your letter of May 22 is this moment received, and Colonel Mason directs me to convey to you his surprise that, whilst under orders, you should enter upon the Indian expedition. That may delay the departure of the Anita, and cause serious consequences to troops in Lower California, who depend upon you for assistance. If you are now absent from Sonoma, you will forthwith return, and hold yourself in readiness to embark for San Francisco when the Anita is reported ready for sea.

I have the honor to be your obedient servant,
W. T. SHERMAN,
First Lieutenant 3d Artillery, A. A. A. General.

Captain BRACKETT,
*Commanding Co. C, 1st N. Y. Volunteers,
Sonoma, California.*

HEADQUARTERS TENTH MILITARY DEPARTMENT,
Monterey, California, May 25, 1848.

SIR: Colonel Mason orders that you turn over to the assistant quartermaster, Captain W. T. Marcy, for transportation to Sonoma, California, one hundred pounds rifle powder and four hundred pounds of musket balls.

I invoice the same to L. W. Boggs, esq., alcalde of Sonoma, California.

I have the honor to be your obedient servant,
W. T. SHERMAN,
1st Lieutenant 3d Artillery, A. A. A. General.

First Lieut. E. O. C. ORD,
Commanding Monterey Redoubt, California.

HEADQUARTERS TENTH MILITARY DEPARTMENT,
Monterey, California, May 27, 1848.

SIR: By order of Colonel Mason, I return to you the records of the case of private Patrick Ford, of company "E," first New York volunteers, arraigned by the general court-martial at Los Angeles, on the 5th instant, for a violation of the 9th article of war, when the court determined not to proceed to his trial until the action of the reviewing officer should be made known.

The prisoner's plea in bar of trial is not considered good, as it is well established that alleged punishment before trial forms no reason why the matter of accusation should not be investigated by the proper tribunal. De Hart, page 144, gives it as his clear opinion " that the court cannot reject a charge on this ground," viz: previous confinement and punishment. "It may be sufficient reason for them to affix a mitigated, or declare no punishment at all; but when matter legally cognizable by a court-martial is referred to them for investigation by competent authority, they are bound to act upon it and proceed with the trial."

The court may very properly take evidence concerning the amount and nature of punishment he has already received, so as to give it as much or as little weight as it deserves.

The court will therefore proceed with the trial of private Patrick Ford, of company " C," 1st New York volunteers; and, upon the assembling of the court, you will submit this letter as containing the views and decision of the colonel commanding.

I have the honor to be your obedient servant,
W. T. SHERMAN,
First Lieutenant 3d Artillery, A. A. A. General.
Lieutenant E. WILLIAMS,
1st New York Volunteers, Los Angeles, California.

HEADQUARTERS TENTH MILITARY DEPARTMENT,
Monterey, California, May 31, 1848.

SIR: I have the honor to enclose to you herewith an order laying a military contribution on the town of Santa Barbara, in consequence of the disappearance on the 5th of April last of the gun belonging to the brig Elizabeth.

This is the first contribution ever imposed in California, and will require much prudence and care in its collection. All citizens of California, native or naturalized, must pay their respective shares; for it is impossible, under the law of nations, to favor those foreigners who by long residence are so identified with the country that their interests cannot be separated.

Colonel Mason says you can exempt from the effects of this tax such Americans as, during the late revolution, contributed aid to the American arms and cause.

I have the honor to be your obedient servant,
W. T. SHERMAN,
First Lieutenant 3d Artillery, A. A. A. General.
Colonel J. D. STEVENSON,
Commanding Southern Military District, California.

HEADQUARTERS TENTH MILITARY DEPARTMENT,
Monterey, California, May 31, 1848.

SIR: Colonel Mason directs me to acknowledge the receipt of your two letters of the 16th instant, with their enclosures, and to say to you that he has, at your request, issued orders enforcing the proper application of the clothing money allowed by law to volunteer soldiers. See special order No. 16, sent you by this mail.

The defence of the settlements against the incursions of the horse-thief Indians is a matter of great importance, but is necessarily subordinate to the general safety and tranquillity of the country. Colonel Mason says that after the military contribution laid upon Santa Barbara is collected, you may deposite with the alcaldes or trustworthy Americans residing at the principal groups of ranches in your district a small supply of arms and ammunition, to enable the people to defend their property.

The number of men and arms enrolled at any one point should not exceed twenty five or thirty; and these are not to be used for a compaign against the Indians, unless especially ordered by you; but such party may pursue and inflict punishment upon any band of Indians engaged in stealing, or who are fresh from an incursion among the settlements.

When, in your judgment, it becomes necessary to make a campaign against the Indians, you can fit out a suitable party from your own command, and may permit Don Andreas Pico, or any other good man, to take along as many of his countrymen, or of the organized parties, as you may deem prudent—the whole to be commanded by one of your own officers who is responsible for his acts.

I have the honor to be your obedient servant,
W. T. SHERMAN,
First Lieutenant 3d Artillery, A. A. A. General.
Colonel J. D. STEVENSON,
Commanding Southern Military District,
Los Angeles, California.

HEADQUARTERS TENTH MILITARY DEPARTMENT,
Monterey, California, May 31, 1848.

SIR: Don Cesario Latarllade, consul of Spain, and resident of Santa Barbara, when in Monterey, a few days since, presented what appears to be a decree of the honorable assembly of California, made in its session of October 30, 1846, at the city of Los Angeles, California, annulling in toto all sales of missions and mission property made anterior to that date by Senor Don Pico, as governor. This decree is signed on the 31st of October, 1846, by A. Botello and Jose Ma. Flores.

The above paper appears to be a genuine and original decree, and will have an important bearing in settling the future titles to missions and mission property. Colonel Mason desires that you will endeavor, if possible, to find a similar decree bearing these signatures, as only a copy of this can be retained here, Don Cesario desiring the original to take with him to Mexico.

I have the honor to be your obedient servant,
W. T. SHERMAN,
First Lieutenant 3d Artillery, A. A. A. General.

Col. J. D. STEVENSON,
 Commanding Southern Military District,
  Los Angeles, California.

HEADQUARTERS TENTH MILITARY DEPARTMENT,
Monterey, California, June 1, 1848.

SIR: Your letter of the 29th ultimo was received last evening, and Colonel Mason directs me to inform you that your recommendation that Quartermaster Sergeant George G. Belt, of the 1st New York volunteers, be discharged, that he may be appointed wagon and forage master, will be referred to Colonel J. D. Stevenson, to whose regiment staff Sergeant Belt belongs, and that, if it meets his approval, then Sergeant Belt shall be discharged. I enclose you orders No. 37, of yesterday's date, which you will please cause to be inserted several times in one of the newspapers of San Francisco.

I have the honor to be your obedient servant,
W. T. SHERMAN,
First Lieutenant 3d Artillery, A. A. A. General.

Captain J. L. FOLSOM,
 Acting Quartermaster, San Francisco, California.

HEADQUARTERS TENTH MILITARY DEPARTMENT,
June 5, 1848.

SIR: I enclose herewith, for your inspection, a copy of a map exhibiting the boundaries to land selected by the engineer officers as necessary for the military defence of Monterey and its harbor. Colonel Mason wishes you to furnish him with copies of all deeds or titles to land recorded in your office that by any construction would be in whole or in part within the boundaries marked; likewise, copies of the deeds to Spence, Little, Castro, and Jinero, which are believed to be along the northern and western boundaries.

Colonel Mason desires, further, that you will inform him what are considered by yourself the limits of the town of Monterey; what law or decree fixes or defines such limits; who has the right to sell or deed away lots or parcels of land within these limits; and what law or decree confers the right on an alcalde to sell the title of a Mexican fort or battery. Answers to these questions are necessary, that the claims against the present fort lands may be properly defined and understood.

I have the honor to be your obedient servant,
W. T. SHERMAN,
First Lieutenant 3d Artillery, A. A. A. General.

WALTER COLTON,
 First Alcalde, Monterey, California.

HEADQUARTERS TENTH MILITARY DEPARTMENT,
Monterey, California, June 10, 1848.

SIR: Colonel Mason will start on a tour to the Sacramento on Monday next, and will leave orders for the Anita, when she arrives from San Francisco, to sail for San José, in Lower California, to land Captain Brackett's company, and thence to La Paz, to report to you. Should you desire to send any men or provisions to that point, you can use the Anita for that purpose.

Colonel Mason wishes the Anita, after leaving La Paz, to communicate with the Commodore at Mazatlan, and then to return to Monterey.

The Anita has been detained at San Francisco longer than was anticipated, on account of an extraordinary excitement which has seized the people of San Francisco, drawing all the working population to the gold mines at the Sacramento. So great was and is still the excitement, that Captain Folsom could employ men only at the most exorbitant rates, and then they would not work as rapidly as he expected.

The latest intelligence received from you is of the 16th January last, brought by Major Rich; but a late arrival at San Francisco from the islands brings intelligence of the arrival there of the Isabella from Mazatlan.

By this arrival papers have been received from the city of Mexico, stating that a treaty of peace had been negotiated on the 2d of February last between the United States and Mexico, which treaty had been laid before the Senate by the President of the United States. If such a treaty be in existence, it will doubtless influence the leaders of the insurrection in Lower California to cease their hostilities, of which they must be somewhat tired. On that account you should be none the less watchful to maintain the two points of La Paz and San José.

Such a cessation of hostilities will only be regarded as a truce, as no respect will be given to a treaty unless properly ratified and officially communicated.

A letter from the Adjutant General of January 20, 1848, received here on the 18th May, gives notice that 500 men, half of whom are to be mounted, are ordered to California from Santa Fe. Doubts are entertained that these troops cannot come this season, as an express has reached us from Santa Fe, which place he left on the 12th of May, at which time the order had not been received there, and General Price had gone with 1,500 of his best troops towards Chihuahua, leaving behind at Santa Fe barely enough men for service there. Admitting that the order of the Adjutant General to General Price should have reached Santa Fe immediately after the departure of this express, it could not have overtaken General Price before he got to Chihuahua, and then the season would be too far advanced for him to despatch these 500 men back to Santa Fe, and thence to California, as it is impossible for infantry or even horsemen to cross the deserts in the summer season. Could Colonel Mason feel assured that these troops would reach California this summer, he would increase your command still further.

No intelligence has reached us from Salt Lake since my last letter to you.

Upper California remains peaceful and quiet.

I enclose you herewith department orders from 21 to 37, special orders 15, 16, and 17, and post orders No. 34.
I have the honor to be your obedient servant,
W. T. SHERMAN,
First Lieutenant 3d Artillery, A. A. G.
Lieut. Col. H. L. BURTON,
Commanding Lower California.

HEADQUARTERS TENTH MILITARY DEPARTMENT,
Monterey, California, June 11, 1848.

SIR: I have been contemplating for some time a visit to the Sacramento, but have been waiting for the departure of the Anita for Lower California.

My last letter informed you that, in consequence of the failure to get volunteers in Oregon or California, I should send to San José, in Lower California, Captain Brackett's company of New York volunteers as soon as certain repairs were made to the government barque Anita. At that time I did not think it would require more than two or three weeks to complete these repairs; but such extravagant stories have been circulated about the richness of the gold mines lately discovered in the valley of the Sacramento river, that the greater part of the laboring population of San Francisco have gone thither, and Captain Folsom has found great difficulty in retaining at extravagant wages a few carpenters to work on the vessel. The same cause has led to the desertion of many soldiers at San Francisco, and to a part of the Anita's crew; and the quartermaster at San Francisco says that it is impossible to have any sailors at all, and that he will have to depend upon the few sailors that are found among the volunteer soldiers to sail her to Monterey.

It is probable, after the Anita reaches the gulf of California, she will be very short-handed; and if you can give to Acting Master Woodworth a suitable crew, I will feel under obligations to you, and will cause Captain Folsom, at San Francisco, to replace them by a hired crew as soon as possible.

If the Anita does not arrive from San Francisco to-day, I shall be compelled to start, and leave written orders for Acting Master Woodworth to proceed to San José, there to land Captain Brackett's company and stores; thence to La Paz, after which to communicate with you, and return to Monterey.

By the ship Matilda, which arrived here on the 18th of May, we have dates from the United States to the 29th of January last. A letter from the Adjutant General of the army informs me that orders have been sent to Brigadier General Price, commanding in New Mexico, to send to California five hundred men, half of whom to be mounted. An overland courier, who left Santa Fe on the 12th of March, informs me that when he left such orders had not reached the commanding officer at Santa Fe; that General Price at that date was at the Paso del Norte, on his way to Chihuahua, with 1,500 of his best troops, having left behind at Santa Fe barely enough men to hold that place. It is therefore almost certain that the order of the Adjutant General did not overtake General Price until he was in the city of Chihuahua, when the season would have been too far advanced to admit of troops marching back to Santa Fe and thence to California. For these reasons, I do not expect this battalion from Santa Fe this summer. No intelligence has been received at the Great Salt Lake as to whether they will come into California as volunteers or not.

My latest dates from you are to the 13th of March, and I am exceedingly anxious for later intelligence from Mazatlan.

I have the honor to be your obedient servant,
R. B. MASON,
Colonel 1st Dragoons, commanding.
Commodore W. B. SHUBRICK,
Or officer commanding naval forces at Mazatlan, Ca'ifornia.

HEADQUARTERS TENTH MILITARY DEPARTMENT,
Monterey, California, June 15, 1848.

SIR: Colonel Mason directs me to acknowledge the receipt of your letter of May 6, enclosing a copy of your report of February 20, 1848. The duplicate of this report was received by the same opportunity, through Lieutenant Colonel Burton, commanding La Paz, Lower California.

Colonel Mason thanks you and your brave little command for so gallant a defence, made under circumstances calculated to try the stoutest hearts; and he trusts that the lustre you have shed upon the common fame of our arms will compensate you for privations and perils so severe, and so patiently endured.

He will take great pleasure in sending your report to the Secretary of War, with the expression of his high approval of your course during your eventful defence of San José, Lower California.

I have the honor to be your obedient servant,
W. T. SHERMAN,
1st Lieutenant 3d Artillery, A. A. A. Gen.
Lieut. CHARLES HAYWOOD,
U. S. Navy, ship Independence, Mazatlan, California.

HEADQUARTERS TENTH MILITARY DAPARTMENT,
Monterey, California, June 16, 1848.

SIR: In consequence of recent intelligence from Lower California, company "C," 1st New York volunteers, now on board the Anita, will not go to San José, Lower California, but will return to San Francisco. You will please, upon your arrival at Monterey, take on board certain ordnance stores in charge of Captain W. G. Marcy, acting assistant quartermaster, and without unnecessary delay return to San Francisco, where Captain Brackett will disembark his company, and where Captain Folsom has other ordnance stores, invoiced to the governor of Oregon.

With these you will proceed to Oregon city; and upon the governor signing the receipts sent by you for the ordnance property, you will deliver it to him, and then return with despatch to San Francisco.

I have the honor to be your obedient servant,
W. T. SHERMAN,
1st Lieut. 3d Art., A. A. A. Gen.
Acting Master WOODWORTH,
Com'g U. S. barque Anita, California.

HEADQUARTERS TENTH MILITARY DEPARTMENT,
Monterey, California, June 17, 1848.

COMMODORE: As I informed you in my letter of the 11th instant, I started on Monday last towards the Sacramento, and had proceeded fifty miles, when I was overtaken by an express, advising me of the arrival here of the United States ship Southampton with important despatches from Mazatlan. I immediately returned, but shall to-day or to-morrow resume my tour.

In consequence of Lieutenant Colonel Burton's report that the insurrection in Lower California is put down, and that with his present force he can hold the two places of La Paz and San José, I have countermanded my orders for the additional company of New York volunteers to go to San José. The army barque Anita will not, therefore, at this time come to Mazatlan and Lower California, but will sail for the Columbia river, to carry to the governor of Oregon certain ordnance stores, for which he stands much in need.

By the Southampton, I received from Commodore Shubrick a copy of the armistice, concluded on the 9th of March, suspending hostilities during the pending negotiation for a treaty of peace, with the information that a treaty of peace had already been ratified by the President and Senate of the United States, and that a Congress was on the point of assembling in Queretaro, Mexico, to decide upon this treaty.

I am not in possession of the treaty of peace which has been accepted by the government of the United States, but am informed that by it Upper California is retained, and the lower provinces given back. If such has been the case, it will be necessary to transport the volunteer troops now serving at La Paz and San José to Monterey, California, to be there discharged. As the government has promised to discharge these volunteers in American territory, should a treaty of peace be signed and ratified by both governments, will you please let one of your vessels transport to Monterey the troops now in Lower California, numbering two hundred and sixty-eight officers and men, with probably fifteen or twenty women? I have instructed Lieutenant Colonel Burton, in the event of his evacuating Lower California, to make this request of you, and, if you cannot comply with his request, to charter transport vessels.

I have the honor to be your obedient servant,
R. B. MASON,
Colonel 1st Dragoons, commanding.
To Commodore T. A. C. JONES,
Com'g U. S. naval force in the Pacific,
Mazatlan, California.

HEADQUARTERS TENTH MILITARY DEPARTMENT,
Monterey, California, June 17, 1848.

SIR: As I informed you in my letter of the 10th instant, Colonel Mason started on a tour towards San Francisco on Monday last, and on Wednesday was overtaken by an express, advising him of the arrival of the Southampton, with important despatches from yourself and the commodore, at Mazatlan. Colonel Mason at once returned to this place, but will resume his tour to-morrow.

By the Southampton were received your letters of the 10th and 20th of

March, and of the 13th, 16th, and 17th of April last, with their respective enclosures.

Orders No. 38, herewith enclosed, assembled a general court-martial at La Paz, before which you can arraign any offenders; but any sentence awarded by such a court must, of necessity, be approved and ordered to be executed by the colonel commanding.

To punish crimes not embraced by the articles of war, and of too serious a character to be tried by a military commission of three members, you can resort to a council of war, such as are referred to in General Scott's general orders 372, of December 13, 1847. Your position, far removed from department headquarters and of very difficult communication, is regarded by Colonel Mason as one of the extreme cases referred to in the sixth paragraph of that order. A council of war should be composed of from three to thirteen members; their proceedings should be recorded, revised, approved or disapproved by yourself, and the sentence executed by your order. They are governed by no written code, nor limited by any fixed boundaries, but derive their powers from necessity, the customs of war, and good sense of the members. Colonel Mason thinks that privates Stephen and McGuire may be very properly arraigned before such a tribunal and punished as they deserve; I therefore enclose to you the charges against these men.

Orders No. 39 contain the decision of the colonel commanding in the case of Captain Nagle, and he regrets exceedingly that the very creditable military operations that led to the suppression of the insurrection in Lower California should be stained by an act of cruelty.

The responsibility must fall upon Captain Nagle; and it is much to be regretted that the scarcity of officers in this department, and their scattered positions, should make it impossible to assemble at once a tribunal competent to try and dispose of this inexplicable case. Orders No 40 direct Captain Brackett's company to resume its post at Sonoma. They are known now to be on board the government barque Anita, which is hourly looked for from San Francisco.

This vessel, instead of coming to La Paz, as I informed you, will now be despatched to the Columbia river, to carry to the governor of Oregon certain arms and ordnance stores, for which he stands much in need. When she returns from Oregon, she will probably come to La Paz, unless in the mean time events occur there which may render such a step unnecessary.

The destination of the Anita has been changed because you report your ability to maintain peace and quiet in the southern part of the peninsula with your present force, and the intelligence brought from Mazatlan renders it almost certain that Lower California will be soon given up by our government. Should you receive, officially, a treaty of peace between the two republics of the United States and Mexico, duly ratified by both governments, you will apply to the commander of the naval forces in the gulf of California for transportation for your command to Monterey, California, at which point the companies under your charge will be discharged, provided that Upper California is retained and that lower province given up. This is in compliance with the conditions of the enrolment of this regiment, as communicated to Colonel J. D. Stevenson, in a letter of the Secretary of War, dated June 26, 1846, "that the men of this regiment must explicitly understand that they may be discharged, without a claim for returning home, wherever they may be serving at the termination of the war, provided that it is in the territory of the United States, or may be taken to the nearest and most convenient territory belonging to the United States and there discharged." Should the naval commander not be able to furnish transportation for all the forces in Lower California, you will charter suitable transports.

The field guns and all arms and ammunition should be brought away; but other stores, supplies, and provisions should be sold, if it be more to the interest of the United States than to transport them, at heavy cost, to Monterey. In this matter you will exercise your discretion.

Lieutenant Halleck says, that he thinks you did not retain a copy of Captain Nagle's report. I have therefore caused a copy to be made, and send you the original. Colonel Mason notices the fact in this report that Captain Nagle makes no mention of his having executed the two prisoners.

Captain Brackett's company was reduced before leaving Sonoma, by desertions, to 23 men rank and file, from 60 on his rolls when his company was ordered to Lower California. This is attributed solely to what is known as the gold-mines excitement. Had it, therefore, come to Lower California, it could have been of little service to you.

I take great pleasure in communicating to you Colonel Mason's great satisfaction at hearing of your dispersing the enemy's forces at Todos Santos, and of the previous rescue of the American prisoners at San Antonio, by the party under the immediate command of Captain Steele, first New York volunteers. These operations were alike creditable in their conception and execution.

Colonel Mason wishes you to convey to the officers and men under your command his thanks for their gallantry and good conduct displayed on those occasions.

I have the honor to be, very respectfully, your obedient servant,
W. T SHERMAN,
1st Lieut. 3d Artillery, A. A. A. General.
Lieut. Colonel H. S. BURTON,
Commanding in Lower California.

HEADQUARTERS TENTH MILITARY DEPARTMENT,
Monterey, California, July 18, 1848.

SIR: The great excitement now prevailing in the country caused by the quantity of gold recently discovered in the valley of the Sacramento renders it absolutely impossible to hire a crew for the barque Anita, belonging to the quartermaster's department of the army, and, unless you can spare me men enough from the Warren to man her, she must be dismantled and laid up, and her services, just now so much required, entirely lost to the government. I therefore respectfully ask for as many men as, in your judgment, may be necessary to navigate her, if they can be possibly spared from your ship.

The interests of the service imperatively require a public vessel on this coast; but with two guns and a naval crew on board of the Anita, in the present condition of affairs, she will answer all the purposes, so far as Upper California is concerned, of a man-of-war.

I am, very respectfully, your obedient servant,
R. B. MASON,
Colonel 1st Dragoons, commanding.

Captain A. R. LONG,
U. S. N., com'g sloop-of-war Warren, Monterey, California.

HEADQUARTERS TENTH MILITARY DEPARTMENT,
Monterey, California, July 19, 1848.

COMMODORE: On the 10th instant, at Sutter's Fort, I received a note from Commander Long, informing me of his arrival at San Francisco, and that he possessed letters for me from yourself, which he did not desire to send by the messenger who brought me this. I forthwith started for Monterey, where, on the 17th instant, at the hands of Commander Long, I received your letters of the 15th and 26th of May.

The affairs in Upper California are so stable, that I do not consider the presence of a man-of-war necessary on the coast; but I think it advisable that a frequent communication should be kept up between us, in the manner you propose.

In my last letter I informed you that a strong excitement in relation to the gold washings on the Sacramento river had led to many desertions from the volunteer companies. The same cause led to the desertion of many men from the Warren; and I fear for some time it will be unsafe fo vessels to remain in our ports, as the prices of labor are so exorbitantly high that all occupations are abandoned, save those of digging gold and selling goods to those so employed.

Believing my presence necessary at the Sacramento, on the 17th of June I started for the mines, taking San Francisco, Bodega, and Sonoma in my way, so that it was not until the 5th of July that I reached the Mormon diggings on the American Fork of the Sacramento river, about twenty-five miles from Sutter's Fort. There were employed a couple of hundred of men, washing the sand and gravel deposites of the river in pans, baskets, or rude machines. A man there employed could, by easy labor, earn his gold ounce daily, and many were actually getting from twenty-five to thirty dollars' worth a day. At this point may be said to commence the placers, although gold exists in the bed of the stream to its very mouth; but at this point (the Mormon diggings) the particles of gold have sufficient size to be separated easily from the sand. I went up the river about twenty-five miles further, and found parties of people, foreigners, natives, and wild Indians, at work. In the valleys, and in the ravines, to the right and left, the precious metal is found in greater or less abundance. The truth would seem miraculous to one who has not seen with his own eyes.

It was my purpose to extend my visit to other rivers—the Bear, the Yubah, and Feather—but I was recalled by your letters; still the American Fork may be taken as a fair sample of the rivers that discharge the waters of the western slope of the Sierra Nevada.

The general opinion is, that now there are about four thousand people employed, and that from $30,000 to $50,000 worth of gold is daily extracted. I certainly saw enough to justify such a conclusion.

I consider the mines on the placers so extensive and so important that I shall, as soon as possible, despatch a messenger to the United States with my report on the subject, and with enough specimens to carry convictions of its truth. Of course, this discovery very much increases the value of California as a conquest, and, treaty or no treaty, settles the question of the destiny of the country.

The present and temporary difficulties and dangers involved in this extraordinary state of things must be met as they arise.

Now that Captain Long has been so kind as to furnish me with an officer and crew from the Warren for the army barque Anita, I will place a gun or two on board of her, and she will answer all the purposes of a sloop of war, so far as Upper California is concerned.

Hoping to have the pleasure of seeing you soon,

I am, very respectfully, your obedient servant,

R. B. MASON,
Colonel 1st Dragoons, commanding.

Commodore A. C. JONES,
Commanding Pacific Squadron, Mazatlan, California.

HEADQUARTERS TENTH MILITARY DEPARTMENT,
Monterey, California, July 20, 1848.

COLONEL: I desire that you will, immediately on the receipt of this, order Sergeant Falls, of Captain Smith's company of the 1st dragoons, to repair forthwith to this post preparatory to going to the United States as bearer of despatches. A schooner will sail from here for Valparaiso in about three weeks from this time, in which he will take passage; from the latter port he will take the English steamer for Panama; and please direct the quartermaster to furnish Sergeant Falls with horses, that he may come to this place in company with the bearer of this. The mail riders will be instructed to take the horses back to Los Angeles; they can be turned over to the quartermasters there.

I have just returned to Monterey, after a month's absence; from all I can learn, there is no prospect of peace.

Very respectfully, your obedient servant,

R. B. MASON,
Colonel 1st Dragoons, commanding.

Colonel J. D. STEVENSON,
Comd'g S. M. Dist., Los Angeles, California.

HEADQUARTERS TENTH MILITARY DEPARTMENT,
Monterey, California, July 21, 1848.

SIR: I have the honor to acknowledge the receipt of your communication of this date, and very much regret that the military force here is so small that it is entirely out of my power to furnish you a guard for the naval store, now that the marine guard has been withdrawn. The public property in charge of the military is necessarily so scattered, for the want of proper storehouses and other conveniences, that I am obliged to keep up from one company, with which this post is garrisoned, three different and distinct guards; this, together with the details necessary in the quartermaster's department, the details for hospital attendants, cooks, mail riders, and details to meet various contingencies, which almost daily arise, call for a larger force than this one company is able to supply.

I beg you to be assured that it would give me pleasure to furnish you with a guard, if the company here had the strength to afford it.

I would suggest to you to get some family to live in that part of the storehouse recently occupied by the marine guard, or to hire some trusty watchman; in these times you will have to pay high, but it cannot be avoided.

I am, very respectfully, your obedient servant,
R. B. MASON,
Colonel 1st Dragoons, commanding.

Mr. CHAS. T. BOTTS,
U. S. naval store, Monterey, California.

HEADQUARTERS TENTH MILITARY DEPARTMENT,
Monterey, California, July 24, 1848.

SIR: In answer to your letter of the 16th of June, (which I did not receive till my return to Monterey on the 18th instant,) I have the honor to inform you that there are on file in this office, charges against privates Shreve, Carpenter, McSpadden, and John C. Lee. A general court-martial will be ordered for their trial as soon as officers can possibly be spared for such duty.

The charges against private John G. Smith not being capital, are sent you to be tried by a garrison court.

Colonel Mason has received the petition in favor of private C. R. O. Lee, but cannot consent to remit any part of his sentence.

I have the honor to be your obedient servant,
W. T. SHERMAN,
First Lieut. 3d Artillery, A. A. A. General.

Captain F. J. LIPPETT,
Commanding, Santa Barbara, California.

HEADQUARTERS TENTH MILITARY DEPARTMENT,
Monterey, California, July 25, 1848.

SIR: I have the honor to enclose you an order, assembling a military commission at Los Angeles, California, on the 4th of August, of which commission you are the judge advocate.

Enclosed are approved charges against Jose Sugards Rivo, Esteban Sylvos, and Saturnine Palmer, of company C, 1st dragoons; other charges of a similar character are probably in the hands of Colonel Stevenson, and Colonel Mason directs that you receive from him any charges that bear his written approval, and that you arraign the persons charged, before this military commission, in the same manner as though they came to you from this office.

I have the honor to be, very respectfully, your obedient servant,
W. T. SHERMAN,
First Lieut. 3d Artillery, A. A. A. General.

Assistant Surgeon R. MURRAY,
Judge Advocate Mil. Com., Los Angeles, California.

HEADQUARTERS TENTH MILITARY DEPARTMENT,
Monterey, California, July 25, 1848.

SIR: Colonel Mason directs me to return to you the original proceedings of the general court-martial constituted at Los Angeles, California, by department orders No. 23, current series, in the case of private Patrick Ford, of company E, first New York volunteers, where the court adhere to their first decision to support the prisoner's plea in bar of trial on the ground that he had been previously punished for the offence he stood charged with.

This decision is so adverse to the well-established practice of courts-martial, that Colonel Mason cannot pass it over in silence; for, at some future time, it might be quoted as a precedent and lead to dangerous results.

For instance: a murderer, confined in a guard-house for security, gets the officer of the guard to punish him more than the ordinary prison rules justify; is afterwards arraigned for trial, and pleads in bar of trial that he has already been punished; would any court, civil or military, permit a murderer thus to avoid trial? And, yet, is not this the very parallel of Ford's case? Has he not avoided trial by pleading simple punishment, which he has received by command of an officer, and not as the sentence of a proper military tribunal? The court is again referred to De Hart, the very pages they refer to in their record, page 6, and more especially to his opinion clearly expressed in page 144, "that a court cannot reject a charge on this ground. It may be sufficient reason for them to affix a mitigated or declare no punishment at all; but when matter legally cognizable by a court-martial is referred to them for investigation by competent authority, they are bound to act upon it and proceed to trial."

This remark is exactly applicable to the case of Ford: when the evidence of both prosecution and defence is in possession of the court, they can determine what allowance to make for the punishment he has already received. Colonel Mason, therefore, orders that you reassemble the court-martial, of which you are the president, as soon as the military commission adjourns which is to assemble at Los Angeles on the 4th proximo, and to convey to the members this (his) order, that they proceed to the trial of private Patrick Ford, upon the charges already on record, which were submitted to them by competent authority.

I have the honor to be your obedient servant,
W. T. SHERMAN,
First Lieut. 3d Artillery, A. A. A. General.

Colonel J. D. STEVENSON,
Commanding, Los Angeles, California.

HEADQUARTERS TENTH MILITARY DEPARTMENT,
Monterey, California, July 25, 1848.

SIR: Colonel Mason directs me to acknowledge the receipt of your letter of the 10th July, (enclosing one of Lieutenant Buffman, asking for certain witnesses in the event of his trial,) and to inform you that the condition of affairs at present will not admit of the course you suggest.

It is expected these gentlemen will have a fair opportunity of meeting these charges against their character before returning to civil life.

I have the honor to be, very respectfully, your obedient servant,
W. T. SHERMAN,
First Lieut. 3d Artillery, A. A. A. General.
Colonel J. W. DAVIDSON,
Commanding, Los Angeles, California.

HEADQUARTERS TENTH MILITARY DEPARTMENT,
Monterey, California, July 25, 1848.

SIR: Your letter of the 13th of June was not received by me until the 18th instant, in consequence of an absence from Monterey up to that date. I have referred that letter, with its enclosed copy of special orders No. 66, dated War Department, Adjutant General's office, Washington, August 3, 1846, to Colonel Mason, who directs me to say that, although your furlough expires on the 3d of August next, your services in your present capacity cannot be dispensed with; and, until other orders are received from the War Department, you will continue on duty as the major of the 1st regiment of New York volunteers.

I have the honor to be, very respectfully, your obedient servant,
W. T. SHERMAN,
First Lieut. 3d Artillery, A. A. A. General.
To Major JAS. A. HARDIE,
Commanding, San Francisco, California.

HEADQUARTERS TENTH MILITARY DEPARTMENT,
Monterey, California, July 25, 1848.

SIR: Your letter of the 13th of June, enclosing a copy of the proceedings of a board of survey held at Los Angeles, California, on the 10th of June, 1848, has been received and laid before Col. Mason, who says that you will break up the gun-carriage condemned by that board, and take up the iron on your return as "scrap iron," sell at public auction the whole of the carriages and the harness, and turn over to Lieutenant Davidson the funds arising from said sale, taking his receipts therefor.

I have the honor to be your obedient servant,
W. T. SHERMAN,
First Lieut. 3d Artillery, A. A. A. General.
Ordnance Sergeant HEATHCOTE,
Los Angeles, California.

HEADQUARTERS TENTH MILITARY DEPARTMENT,
Monterey, California, July 25, 1848.

SIR: Ordnance Sergeant Heathcote is this day ordered to sell at public auction certain condemned ordnance stores at the post of Los Angeles, California, and to turn over to you the funds arising from said sale.

Colonel Mason directs that you receipt for and enter those funds to credit of the civil fund of California.

I have the honor to be, very respectfully, your obedient servant,
W. T. SHERMAN,
First Lieut. 3d Artillery, A. A. A. General.

To Lieut. J. W. DAVIDSON,
A. C. S. & A. A. Quartermaster, Los Angeles, California.

HEADQUARTERS TENTH MILITARY DEPARTMENT,
Monterey, California, July 27, 1848.

SIR: Your letter of the 10th instant, with its enclosure, is received, and Colonel Mason directs me to say to you that it is not in his power to accept your resignation: your commission was conferred upon you by the governor of New York, who is the proper person to accept its resignation.

You will please render post returns for Sonoma for the month of June, even if you had not returned to the post at the end of the month. It is important to keep up a military history of the posts so long as troops occupy them. I send you the returns of Sonoma for January, February, March, April, and May, which contain errors I have noted in pencil marks. Please correct them and return them to this office.

Muster rolls should be sent direct to the Adjutant General, with a letter of advice, and not to this office.

I have the honor to be your most obedient servant,
W. T. SHERMAN,
First Lieutenant 3d Artillery, A. A. A. General.

Captain J. E. BRACKETT,
Commanding company E, 1st New York Volunteers,
San Francisco, California.

HEADQUARTERS TENTH MILITARY DEPARTMENT,
Monterey, California, August 2, 1848.

SIR: The amount of labor at the custom-house at San Francisco is daily becoming more onerous, and the revenues collected are increasing so rapidly that it is impossible for Captain Folsom to acquit himself of the heavy responsibilities now resting on him, unless he receives a great deal of assistance.

This assistance must of necessity come from the military garrison, and Colonel Mason directs that Lieutenant Gilbert of company H, 1st New York volunteers, be detailed to assist Captain Folsom in the performance of the duties of collector of the port of San Francisco; and, if Captain Folsom desires it, Lieutenant Roach, of company C, be also detailed for the same duty.

He also wishes you to furnish, upon Captain F.'s application, such non-commissioned officers and men as may be necessary to guard the revenues from fraud.

The details will fall heavily upon your reduced command, and you are accordingly authorized, at any moment you think proper, to break up the post of Sonoma, leaving a non-commissioned officer and from six to ten men to assist the alcalde of the town.

The detail of Lieutenant Gilbert will leave Captain Frisbee without a subaltern. You can assign one of the lieutenants of Captain Dimmick's company to Frisbee, until other officers arrive from the United States.

Colonel Mason wishes you to consult with the assistant quartermaster as to the propriety of breaking up the town guard altogether, and to protect the public property by detailing, on extra duty, three or four good men to work at the storehouse by day and to sleep there at night.

I have the honor to be your most obedient servant,
W. T. SHERMAN,
First Lieutenant 3d Artillery, A. A. General.
Major JAMES A. HARDIE,
Commanding Northern Military District,
San Francisco, California.

HEADQUARTERS TENTH MILITARY DEPARTMENT,
Monterey, California, August 2, 1848.

SIR: Your letter of the 25th of July was received on the 31st ultimo, and has been laid before Colonel Mason, who directs me to inform you that he cannot possibly relieve you from the duties of collector of the port of San Francisco.

He is fully aware of the heavy additional labor and responsibility imposed upon you by that office, but the number of disbursing officers at his command is so small that no other than yourself can be stationed at San Francisco. But Colonel Mason is willing to give you every assistance possible, in the way of details of officers and soldiers, but he cannot sanction the payment to them of any fee, " charge, commission, or compensation of any kind" for the performance of those duties, as it would be in direct violation of the latter part of the 19th paragraph of the regulations for collecting the revenue.

He is satisfied that soldiers should be paid for such extra duties, and he will recommend to the department that a suitable daily allowance be made to soldiers employed in duties pertaining to the collection of revenues, and that this regulation should have a retrospective effect, so as to compensate those who have heretofore been employed as guards, clerks, &c.

Major Hardie will be instructed to detail Lieutenant Gilbert as your assistant, and also Lieutenant Roach, if you request him to do so; and he will be directed to detail, upon your application, a sufficient number of non-commissioned officers and privates from his command to act as sentinels, guards, clerks, &c., at the custom-house of San Francisco, even if it be necessary to break up the post of Sonoma.

Major Hardie is also directed to consult you as to the propriety of breaking up the town guard, and giving you a sufficient number of trustworthy men, on extra duty, to sleep by night at the storehouse in the town, and to work, subject to your orders, during the day. When orders No. 40 were issued, removing company H from San Francisco to Sonoma, it was not contemplated that it would take Lieutenant Gilbert from your office, as he still remained under the command of Major Hardie, and, therefore, liable to be detailed under special orders No. 22, of September, 1847.

Lieutenant George Stoneman, first dragoons, will be on the Sacramento towards the latter part of this month, with twenty five men and about sixty horses and mules. It is designed to keep those horses in fine order, so that Lieutenant Stoneman may act with energy; and Colonel Mason wishes you to send to some point on the Sacramento, below Sutter's, a quantity of hay and grain, with enough lumber, nails, &c., to build a shed for this command.

Lieutenant Stoneman will take with him from here one or more wagons, so as to haul his lumber to a suitable point for the prosecution of his plan of operations, and likewise to transport his provisions. He will be instructed to draw on you for subsistence, and will communicate with you, by letter, as to the best mode of drawing these provisions—most probably by monthly returns, to be delivered at certain times at Sutter's embarcadero, when he can have his wagons there to receive them. No provisions need be sent in advance, or until he communicates with you.

I have the honor to be your obedient servant,
W. T. SHERMAN,
First Lieutenant 3d Artillery, A. A. A. General.
Captain J. L. FOLSOM,
Assistant Quartermaster, San Francisco, California.

HEADQUARTERS TENTH MILITARY DEPARTMENT,
Monterey, California, August 3, 1848.

SIR: I have the honor, herewith, to return the post returns of San Francisco for April, May, and June, which contain certain errors noted in pencil. Please cause them to be corrected and sent to this office. Unless the post returns are absolutely correct, it is impossible to make out proper department returns, which have to be rendered monthly to the Adjutant General of the army, from department headquarters.

I have the honor to be your most obedient servant,
W. T. SHERMAN,
First Lieutenant 3d Artillery, A. A. A. General.
Major JAMES A. HARDIE,
Commanding, San Francisco, California.

HEADQUARTERS TENTH MILITARY DEPARTMENT,
Monterey, California, August 3, 1848.

SIR: Your letter of the 20th of July, with its enclosure of June, has this moment been received, and the same mail brings to Colonel Mason a letter from Don Pio Pico, in which he styles himself the Mexican governor of California.

Colonel Mason directs that you cause Pio Pico to be forthwith arrested and confined securely in Los Angeles, and that he be not permitted to confer with any of his countrymen.

If an opportunity offers to send him here by sea, you will send him on board the vessel in charge of a commissioned officer, who will be ordered not to permit him to land to communicate with any person at Santa Barbara. The officer will accompany him (Pico,) until he delivers him to the commanding officer at this post; or, if the vessel be bound to San Francisco, then to the commanding officer of that post.

Colonel Mason desires that you keep this matter a profound secret until Pico is safely arrested and confined, confiding it to no one save the officer sent to execute the arrest.

I have the honor to be your most obedient servant,
W. T. SHERMAN,
First Lieutenant 3d Artillery, A. A. A. General.
Colonel J. D. STEVENSON,
Commanding Southern Military District.

P. S.—I enclose approved charges against the deserters from your command, which Colonel Mason orders to be laid before the general court martial now in session at Los Angeles. A few examples may at this critical moment stop desertions. The descriptive list of Ford and Krienan has been sent to San Francisco. This is sent you by an express.
W. T. SHERMAN,
First Lieutenant, and A. A. A. General.

HEADQUARTERS TENTH MILITARY DEPARTMENT,
Monterey, California, August 5, 1848.

SIR: You are hereby authorized to employ Mr. Charles P. Wilkins as a clerk in the quartermaster's department at Los Angeles, California, dating from the time of his first reporting to you for duty, at the same rate of pay as is allowed to a wagon and forage master of the army. When Mr. Wilkins receives from Washington his appointment which he lost in Santa Fe, whatever sum he may have received as clerk must be deducted from the whole amount due him as wagon and forage master.

By order of Colonel Mason:
W. T. SHERMAN,
First Lieutenant 3d Artillery, A. A. A. General.
Lieutenant J. W. DAVIDSON,
Acting Assistant Quartermaster, Los Angeles, California.

HEADQUARTERS TENTH MILITARY DEPARTMENT,
Monterey, California, August 7, 1848.

SIR: If you arrive at San Francisco in time to be present when the volunteers stationed there are discharged, Colonel Mason wishes you to pay them off, and then hasten to Monterey in the Anita, if possible. The Anita will await your arrival here, so that you may go down the coast in her. I enclose you department orders No. 50 of this date.

I have the honor to be your obedient servant,
W. T. SHERMAN,
First Lieutenant 3d Artillery, A. A. A. General.
Major WM. RICH,
Assistant Paymaster U. S. A., San Francisco, California.

HEADQUARTERS TENTH MILITARY DEPARTMENT,
Monterey, California, August 7, 1848.

SIR: Last night, by an express from Lower California, was received official intelligence of the ratification of a treaty of peace between the republics of the United States and Mexico. The regiment of New York volunteers are in consequence to be discharged; and you will accordingly proceed with your detachment to San Francisco, and report to the commanding officer. You will give public notice in the Pueblo de San José of the fact that peace now exists, and that Upper California is ceded to the United States.

Your obedient servant,
W. T. SHERMAN,
First Lieutenant 3d Artillery, A. A. A. General.
To the COMMANDING OFFICER
N. Y. Volunteers, San José, California.

HEADQUARTERS TENTH MILITARY DEPARTMENT,
Monterey, California, August 7, 1848.

SIR: I have the honor herewith to enclose you department orders No. 50, which imposes on you the duty of discharging from the service of the United States the three companies of volunteers now under your command. This duty, you must be aware, must be in virtue of your commission of first lieutenant third artillery. Too much care cannot be taken in completing these rolls, which remain as important records, and I enclose you a copy of general orders No. 18 of April 22, 1847, for your guidance. Major Rich is now believed to be on board the barque Olga, at sea, bound for San Francisco. It is hoped that he may arrive to pay these companies at the time of discharge; but, should he be not in San Francisco, you will nevertheless discharge these volunteers, and Major Rich will pay them on the rolls as soon as he arrives.

A detachment of dragoons ordered from Los Angeles for the purpose of arresting deserters will, upon its arrival here, be sent to the presidio to guard the magazine.

I have the honor to be your obedient servant,
W. T. SHERMAN,
First Lieutenant 3d Artillery, A. A. A. General.
Major J. A. HARDIE,
Commanding Northern Military District,
San Francisco, California.

HEADQUARTERS TENTH MILITARY DEPARTMENT,
Monterey, California, August 8, 1848.

SIR: When Colonel Mason was at Sutter's Fort some days ago, he was informed that there was at Los Angeles a small Russian field-piece belonging to Captain Sutter. If such a piece be among those still remaining at your post, and if you can recognise it as the former property of Captain Sutter, you will please cause it to be placed on board the United

States barque Anita when she comes to San Pedro, that Colonel Mason may restore it to its proper owners.

I have the honor to be your obedient servant,
W. T. SHERMAN,
First Lieutenant 3d Artillery, A. A. A. General.

Colonel J. D. STEVENSON, *Commanding, Los Angeles, California.*

HEADQUARTERS TENTH MILITARY DEPARTMENT,
Monterey, California, August 8, 1848.

SIR: I have the honor to acknowledge the receipt of your letters of the 24th ultimo, and to convey to you Colonel Mason's answers thereto. Lieutenant Davidson has not made any estimate of funds this year, and his summary statements for the past months of December, January, February, March, April, and May were not received here until the 18th of July. His abstract of provisions on hand at the expiration of the second quarter 1848 is not yet received. The estimate for funds and requisitions for provisions have not been made with the punctuality required by orders. However, as all the posts in southern military district are to be abandoned as soon as your regiment is discharged, it will not be necessary to send down the coast more provisions than may be required for their immediate use. Fifteen thousand rations will come down in the Anita, to meet the wants of the battalion of volunteers which is reported to be near San Diego from Santa Fe. This battalion of volunteers was hardly expected, or provisions would have been sent long since for their use. Instead of quartering this battalion at San Luis Rey, as you propose, Colonel Mason wishes to bring them nearer Los Angeles—say to San Gabriel—for the care of subsistence, and so that they may be mustered out of service at the same time with the companies of your regiment.

As Don Eulojoi de Celis relinquishes his claim to the title of the house now occupied by company "C," 1st dragoons, Colonel Mason says you may consider Williams the legal owner; and you will order the acting assistant quartermaster to pay him (Williams) the rent due since the time it was first occupied by the dragoons company.

I have the honor to be your obedient servant,
W. T. SHERMAN,
First Lieutenant 3d Artillery, A. A. A. General.

Colonel J. D. STEVENSON,
Commanding Southern Military District, California.

HEADQUARTERS TENTH MILITARY DEPARTMENT,
Monterey, California, August 8, 1848.

SIR: I have the honor to acknowledge the receipt of your letter of July 24, and to inform you that Mrs. Kelly draws her rations regularly as any other camp woman at this post.

I enclose you department orders Nos. 50, 51, and 52.

I have the honor to be your obedient servant,
W. T. SHERMAN,
First Lieutenant 3d Artillery, A. A. A. General.

Captain W. E. SHANNON, *Commanding, San Diego, California.*

HEADQUARTERS TENTH MILITARY DEPARTMENT,
Monterey, California, August 8, 1848.

SIR: I have the honor to acknowledge the receipt of your letter of July 30th, sent by Sergeant Falls, and to convey to you Colonel Mason's approval of the terms of your letter addressed to Don Pio Pico, from Los Angeles, July 27, 1848.

Before this can reach you my letter of the 3d instant will have been received, ordering Don Pio Pico to be arrested, and, if possible, to be sent to Monterey or San Francisco by water. If he be still confined at Los Angeles, you will restore him to liberty, and inform him that he is released in consequence of the reception of a treaty of peace, duly ratified by the governments of the United States and Mexico, the 4th article of which stipulates that all prisoners of war "shall be restored as soon as practicable after the exchange of the ratification of this treaty."

Had it not been for this, you may inform Pico, he would have been sent to Oregon or some other foreign country.

The manner in which he entered California might have subjected him to the treatment of a spy; and his subsequent conduct, after his conversation with you, together with his absurd pretensions to the government of the country, made him merit harsher treatment than he now receives. You will please inform him that Upper California is now American territory, and that he is at liberty to leave it or not, as he pleases; but so long as he continues in Upper California he must be cautious how he acts towards our authorities, civil or military.

I have the honor to be your obedient servant,
W. T. SHERMAN,
1st Lieut. 3d Artillery, A. A. A. General.
Colonel J. D. STEVENSON,
Commanding S. M. District, Los Angeles, California.

HEADQUARTERS TENTH MILITARY DEPARTMENT,
Monterey, California, August 8, 1848.

SIR: In order that no unnecessary delay may attend the movement of the Anita, as pointed out in orders No. 50, dated the 7th instant, Colonel Mason wishes you to direct the serviceable ordnance and ordnance stores to be hauled to San Pedro ready for embarcation.

Should there be any small arms, muskets, rifles, or carbines at your post, which were taken during the war from the people of your district, you will please restore them, if possible, to the original owners, or deposite them in the hands of the alcalde, or some responsible person, to be reclaimed and given up when applied for.

Guns, which are of no use and not worth transporting to San Francisco, will be made unserviceable by breaking off one or both trunnions.

The field battery, with all its ammunition and appurtenances, will be put on board the Anita.

In like manner, all tools and serviceable quartermaster property will be securely boxed and sent to San Pedro, ready for embarcation.

Captain Smith will be instructed to select, upon his arrival at Los Angeles, such wagons and means of transportation as he may require for moving his company of dragoons by land to Monterey, and cause the balance to be sold at public auction.

You may give notice of such intention, so that persons desirous of purchasing wagons, carts, harness, &c., may be prepared to bid.

These instructions are sent you that you make the preparations in advance for abandoning the post of Los Angeles, and for the proper disposition of government property in that quarter.

Whatever provisions may be on hand when the place is evacuated will also be sold at auction.

Colonel Mason says you may issue a small quantity of powder and ball to trustworthy individuals for the defence of their property and lives; but as the articles are no longer contraband, there will be no difficulty in purchasing plenty of them in a short time.

I have the honor to be your obedient servant,
W. T. SHERMAN,
1st Lieut. 3d Artillery, A. A. A. General.
Colonel J. D. STEVENSON,
Commanding S. M. District, Los Angeles, California.

HEADQUARTERS TENTH MILITARY DEPARTMENT,
Monterey, California, August 9, 1848.

SIR: Should this letter reach you at, or before you reach Santa Barbara, you will turn back with your detachment, and rejoin your company at Los Angeles.

This change is in consequence of the receipt of the treaty of peace, which requires the discharge of all the volunteers in the country.

I have the honor to be, very respectfully, your obedient servant,
W. T. SHERMAN,
1st Lieut. 3d Artillery, A. A. A. General.
Lieut. GEORGE STONEMAN,
Commanding detachment 1st Dragoons, en route from Los Angeles to Monterey.

This was enclosed, addressed to Captain Lippett, Santa Barbara.

HEADQUARTERS TENTH MILITARY DEPARTMENT,
Monterey, California, August 11, 1848.

SIR: Colonel Mason directs that the contract entered into on the 13th day of July, 1846, at Fort Columbus, New York, between Captain C. Q. Tompkins, on the part of the United States, and Dr. James L. Ord, be annulled from and after the day in which company F, New York volunteers, is mustered out of the service of the United States. You will pay Dr. Ord whatever may be due him on said contract up to the day before mentioned.

I have the honor to be your obedient servant,
W. T. SHERMAN,
1st Lieut. 3d Artillery, A. A. A. General.
Lt. H. S. CARNES,
1st New York Volunteers, A. A. Quartermaster at Santa Barbara, California.

HEADQUARTERS TENTH MILITARY DEPARTMENT,
Monterey, California, August 11, 1848.

SIR: I have the honor to enclose, herewith, department orders No. 50, of the 7th instant, requiring you to muster out of service all the volunteers now in the southern military district of Upper California; and also to superintend the disposition of the public property in that quarter.

The United States barque Anita is under orders for Monterey, and you will hold yourself in readiness to take passage in her to Santa Barbara, San Pedro, and San Diego.

Upon arriving at each of the military garrisons in the southern district, you will cause to be sent on board of the Anita all arms and accoutrements, ammunition, ordnance, and ordnance stores of the United States manufacture, and all other serviceable guns, if the Anita wants them for ballast.

Provisions, carts, wagons, harness, tents, camp equipage, and bulky quartermasters' stores, not needed when the posts are evacuated, you will order to be sold at public auction. Such articles as tools, scales, weights and measures, and other articles easy to be carried to the port and placed on board of the Anita, you will order to be sent to San Francisco; serviceable horses and mules will also be retained, and brought by land to Monterey—unserviceable ones sold. As many citizens may feel insecure in consequence of the withdrawal of all military force, you are authorized to leave with the alcalde, or other trusty citizen, a few arms and some ammunition, taking his receipt for the same. The arms will be delivered out of those which were taken from the citizens of California during the past war, and may be distributed to persons who can be trusted, who stand in need of such protection. The disbursing officers must be careful to leave behind them no unsettled accounts; and, that there be no scarcity of funds, Captain W. G. Marcy will be instructed to turn over to you ten thousand dollars, with which you may supply deficiencies, should any exist. When these officers have closed their money account, you will receipt to them for any balances on hand, upon their delivering the same to you. Acting assistant quartermasters and commissaries, commanders of companies, or any other officer who may ship on board the Anita property for which they are accountable, will send therewith invoices to Captain Folsom, at San Francisco, accompanied by a letter advising him to what place he shall send his receipt. When these conditions are fulfilled, you will muster and discharge the company or companies, as required by department orders No. 50.

I enclose you, herewith, a copy of general orders No. 18, dated Adjutant General's office, April 22, 1848, for your guidance, and the monthly reports of men "tried" and "confined" in the companies you are to discharge, that you may judge who are and who are not entitled to an honorable discharge.

Having completed this business, you will direct Acting Master Woodsworth to proceed to San Francisco; and you will then join your company at Los Angeles, and conduct it by land to the vicinity of Monterey, where you will encamp it, and report in person to these headquarters. You will bring with you all the public horses and mules that are at any of the military posts, or that are distributed along the road for express or other purposes. You will also give general notice that the express mail is discontinued south of Monterey.

I have the honor to be, your obedient servant,
W. T. SHERMAN,
1st Lieut. 3d Artillery, A. A. A. General.

Captain A. J. SMITH,
1st Dragoons, Monterey, California.

HEADQUARTERS TENTH MILITARY DEPARTMENT,
Monterey, California, August 16, 1848.

SIR: I have the honor to acknowledge the receipt of your letter of August 11, with the enclosed copies of correspondence between the Secretary of War and the governor of the State of New York, in relation to the conditions of enrolment of the regiment of New York volunteers, now serving in California.

Colonel Mason directs me to say to you that he has no instructions concerning the discharge of this regiment of volunteers, and they will be paid by Major Rich according to the laws of Congress and instructions of his department. He, however, is not aware of any law or enactment of Congress that entitles officers of this regiment to mileage, or any other allowance, to the place of enrolment. If any such law exist, the paymaster will know of it, and will act accordingly.

If you or any other officer know of the existence of a law of Congress providing transportation in kind, or any allowance of money in lieu thereof, to a commissioned officer of volunteers when discharged, you will please transmit an authenticated copy of the same to this office for future reference; none such has ever been received from the War Department at these headquarters.

The cases of Doctors Perry and Parker differ but little from those of other officers in service under the same act, approved May 13, 1846, modified by the fifth section of the act approved June 18, 1846, as contained in general orders No. 22, of May 29, 1847. The services of all terminate with the war, and the claims of each for pay and allowances must be based on a law of Congress. These officers have, therefore, only to produce to the paymaster the law, and the evidence of service under the law, when they will be paid. The paymaster is the proper person to settle all such questions.

I have the honor to be, your most obedient servant,
W. T. SHERMAN,
First Lieutenant 3d Artillery, A. A. A. General.

Captain J. L. FOLSOM,
Assistant Quartermaster, San Francisco, California.

HEADQUARTERS TENTH MILITARY DEPARTMENT,
Monterey, California, August 21, 1848.

SIR: I have the honor to acknowledge the receipt of your letter of August 8; in answer to which Colonel Mason says you will direct Lieutenant J. W. Davidson, A. A. C. S. at Los Angeles, to pay the outstanding debts in the commissary's department at San Diego, left unpaid by Lieutenant Clift, upon the claimant's producing proper evidence of their being just and true.

Colonel Mason wishes you to call Lieutenant Davidson's particular attention to the letters addressed to him on the 8th of March last, and the 26th of July, to neither of which have answers been received.

I have the honor to be, very respectfully, your obedient servant,
W. T. SHERMAN,
First Lieutenant 3d Artillery, A. A. A. General.
Colonel JOHN D. STEVENSON,
Commanding S. M District, California.

HEADQUARTERS TENTH MILITARY DEPARTMENT,
Monterey, California, August 21, 1848.

SIR: The Anita has arrived here from San Francisco, and at the time of her departure you had not arrived at that post. It is all-important that you should go down the coast in this vessel in company with Captain A. J. Smith, so as to pay off the companies of New York volunteers upon the day of their discharge. Colonel Mason wishes you, therefore, to prepare the muster and pay rolls of discharge of the volunteer companies lately mustered out of service at San Francisco by Major James A. Hardie, and to turn over to Major Hardie a sum of money sufficient to enable him to pay off on the rolls previously prepared by yourself.

Lest you should not have with you enough funds for the above mentioned purpose, orders will be given to Captain Folsom to transfer "temporarily" to you whatever amount of money you may require, to be replaced by the same amount when you return to San Francisco.

Having made arrangements as above, you will hasten with all due speed to Monterey, to embark in the Anita.

I have the honor to be, very respectfully, your obedient servant,
W. T. SHERMAN,
First Lieutenant 3d Artillery, A. A. A. General.
Major W. RICH,
Paymaster, San Francisco, California.

HEADQUARTERS TENTH MILITARY DEPARTMENT,
Monterey, California, August 21, 1848.

SIR: I send you herewith, for correction, your returns of the post of San Diego for the months of March and May, 1848. No returns have been received for the month of April, which deficiency you will please to supply. Those for June and July are received, and are correct. Please be careful to make a correct return for the month in which the post is evacuated.

I have the honor to be your obedient servant,
W. T. SHERMAN,
First Lieutenant 3d Artillery, A. A. A. General.
Captain W. E. SHANNON,
Commanding, San Diego, California.

HEADQUARTERS TENTH MILITARY DEPARTMENT,
Monterey, California, August 21, 1848.

SIR: Your letter of the 12th instant is received, and, in answer, I am directed by Colonel Mason to inform you that orders have already been issued to sell, at public auction, all provisions that may remain at the post of Santa Barbara at the time your company is mustered out of service. This will afford your men the opportunity they ask for of obtaining supplies for their journey to the gold mines.

I have the honor to be, very respectfully, your obedient servant,
W. T. SHERMAN,
First Lieutenant 3d Artillery, A. A. A. General.

Captain F. J. LIPPETT, *Commanding, Santa Barbara, California.*

HEADQUARTERS TENTH MILITARY DEPARTMENT,
Monterey, California, August 21, 1848.

SIR: I have the honor to acknowledge the receipt of your letter of the 16th instant, and to inform you that Colonel Mason fully appreciates the motives that have influenced the volunteer soldiers lately under your command to ask some evidence of their honorable discharge. A certificate that a man *had been* discharged by yourself is not believed to be, strictly speaking, either a "discharge" or certificate in lieu of discharge, either of which is prohibited by the 221st paragraph General Regulations, edition of 1847.

If, therefore, you will give each man honorably discharged by youself a paper setting forth that fact, with the name, rank, period of service, and date of discharge of its bearer, it will meet Colonel Mason's full approval.

There is no vessel of war now at Monterey, and it is therefore, at this time, impossible to comply with the request contained in your letter of the 14th instant. The application will be referred to Commodore Jones.

I have the honor to be, very respectfully, your obedient servant,
W. T. SHERMAN,
First Lieutenant 3d Artillery, A. A. A. General.

Major JAMES A. HARDIE,
First N. Y. Volunteers, commanding, San Francisco, California.

HEADQUARTERS TENTH MILITARY DEPARTMENT,
Monterey, California, August 21, 1848.

SIR: The Anita arrived here last evening from San Francisco; and from Captain Woodworth we learn, up to the time of his departure, the 19th instant, the barque Olga had not arrived, and, therefore, that Major Rich was not yet at San Francisco. It is all-important that Major Rich should come to Monterey as soon as possible; and to facilitate his departure from San Francisco, I have conveyed to him orders to make out the pay-rolls for the companies discharged by yourself, and to turn over to you the funds necessary to pay on said rolls. Colonel Mason wishes you to take charge of such money, and pay it out in the name of Major Rich, taking receipts as usual on the pay-rolls.

I have the honor to be, very respectfully, your obedient servant,
W. T. SHERMAN,
First Lieutenant 3d Artillery, A. A. A. General.

Major JAMES A. HARDIE, *Commanding, San Francisco, California.*

HEADQUARTERS TENTH MILITARY DEPARTMENT,
Monterey, California, August 23, 1848.

SIR: Should Major Rich, acting assistant paymaster United States army, apply to you for funds to complete the payment to the companies of New York volunteers, lately mustered out of service by Major James A. Hardie, Colonel Mason directs that you deliver to him whatever he may require out of the military contribution fund, to be replaced by the Major when he returns to San Francisco.

I have the honor to be your most obedient servant,
W. T. SHERMAN,
First Lieutenant 3d Artillery, A. A. A. General.
Capt. J. L. FOLSOM,
Assistant Quartermaster, San Francisco, California.

HEADQUARTERS TENTH MILITARY DEPARTMENT,
Monterey, California, August 25, 1848.

SIR: I have the honor to inform you that in consequence of the quantity of gold obtained in this country, cash is in great demand. Drafts cannot be negotiated except at a ruinous discount, and it will be necessary to transmit funds for the service of the quartermaster's department here. The disbursements will be heavy in consequence of the small garrisons, and necessity of hiring laborers at tremendous wages.

At the present moment the assistant quartermaster at San Francisco is hiring guards for his storehouses at from fifty to one hundred and twenty dollars a month. The services of laboring men cannot be commanded at a lower price.

I have the honor to be, very respectfully, your obedient servant,
R. B. MASON,
Colonel 1st Dragoons, commanding.
Major General JESUP,
Quartermaster General U. S. Army, Washington, D. C.

HEADQUARTERS TENTH MILITARY DEPARTMENT,
Monterey, California, August 25, 1848.

SIR: Colonel Mason directs me to return you the proceedings of the general court-martial in session yesterday at the Monterey Redoubt, California, with the enclosed extract from orders No. 35, of May 27, 1848, and to direct you to reassemble the court, that it may cause the judge advocate to make the record as pointed out in said orders, which directs that no blank pages be left; and yet the records of your court, which consist of five sheets of paper, have four blank pages.

Your most obedient servant,
W. T. SHERMAN,
First Lieutenant 3d Artillery, A. A. A. General.
To Capt. W. G. MARCY,
President General Court-martial,
Monterey Redoubt, California.

HEADQUARTERS TENTH MILITARY DEPARTMENT,
Monterey, California, August 26, 1848.

SIR: Your several letters of the 20th instant are just received, and I am directed to convey to you by the return of the express the answers of Colonel Mason, as follows:

The women, wives of soldiers, will be given a free passage to San Francisco in the government barque Anita, as also such sick men as may, in the opinion of the medical officer, be unable to come up by land.

If Colonel Mason were to remit the corporal punishment awarded by the general court-martial to privates Earl and Hutcheson of company E, he could not with propriety in a similar instance order the execution of the same sentence of a regular soldier. He cannot consent to make so wide a difference; and therefore cannot change orders No. 56 of yesterday's date, herewith sent you.

You are aware that the arms given the Mormons at the time of their discharge were in fulfilment of an agreement made with them at the time of their enrolment. No such stipulation was made to your regiment, and General Kearny left no record of the promise he made you verbally to that effect; nor did he even mention it in conversation with Colonel Mason. If the arms now in the hands of your men be given them, for all time to come the soldiers stationed in California can sell their muskets, and citizens will freely buy of them, knowing that those so bought cannot be distinguished from those given to your regiment. For this reason, even in the United States, government arms of late patterns, bearing the inspector's mark, are never sold. At present there are no percussion muskets or rifles properly in the hands of citizens of California; and if, at any future time, such are seen by a government officer, they can be identified and seized. This, of course, could not be done were Colonel Mason to permit each man of your regiment to retain his musket. The dangers to their lives for the want of fire-arms will not be at all great in that part of California where they are certain to go. For these reasons, he cannot comply with your urgent request to the effect that the men of your regiment retain their arms and accoutrements.

But as to provisions, he is waiting the arrival of Major Rich, to learn from him whether he is instructed to pay your men the travelling allowance to the place of enrolment. If such payment be made, each man will have enough money to meet all his wants till he arrives at such point of California as he may select to reside or work in. Should, however, the paymaster's instructions not warrant such allowances to your men, then Colonel Mason will order the commissary to issue enough provisions to subsist them during their journey to Monterey or San Francisco. Full instructions on this subject will go down the coast in the Anita, which is only waiting the arrival here of Major Rich to take her departure for Santa Barbara.

In consequence of the great danger to life and property described by you, the orders heretofore given to Captain Smith are countermanded; and his company will remain at Los Angeles.

I have the honor to be your obedient servant,
W. T. SHERMAN,
First Lieutenant 3d Artillery, A. A. A. General.

Colonel J. D. STEVENSON,
Commanding S. M. District, Los Angeles, California.

HEADQUARTERS TENTH MILITARY DEPARTMENT,
Monterey, California, August 29, 1848.

SIR: I have the honor to inform you that specie is now so scarce in California, that drafts on the subsistence department cannot be negotiated except at a ruinous discount.

I have the honor to be your most obedient servant,
R. B. MASON,
Colonel 1st Dragoons, commanding.

General GEO. GIBSON,
Commissary General of Subsistence,
Washington, D. C.

[No. 42.]   HEADQUARTERS TENTH MILITARY DEPARTMENT,
Monterey, California, August 28, 1848.

SIR: The schooner Lambay-acana has just arrived from San Francisco, bound for Valparaiso. I shall forthwith despatch Lieutenant Loeser, 3d artillery, as bearer of despatches, in this vessel, so that, if possible, he may meet the British steamer of October at Payta, and reach Washington before the month of December of this year.

My letters Nos. 36, 37, 38, 39, 40, and 41, herewith sent, will give you an idea of the state of affairs here; but words cannot convey the full effect of gold mines upon the changed condition of the people of this country—none can withstand their powerful influence. The ship Isaac Walton, that arrived at this port on the 27th instant from New York, laden with navy stores, has already lost a great part of her crew by desertion; and it will cost more to land her cargo in Monterey than her entire freight from New York. At San Francisco, many vessels are reported to be without a soul on board; and the schooner Lambay-acana, that conveys this, has but three or four men before the mast.

Up to this date 33 of the artillery company have deserted. It is represented that much sickness prevails at the mines from the effects of exposure; the sickly season will end in October. Troops sent to this country must be paid better than those now here, else there is no use of sending them at all. Those now here who stand faithful to their colors should be rewarded.

I enclose you copies of letters received on the 25th instant from Colonel J. D. Stevenson, at Los Angeles, California, to show the effects upon the people of that district produced by the order to discharge the garrisons at Santa Barbara, Los Angeles, and San Diego. In consequence of the well-grounded fears therein described, I have ordered C company 1st dragoons to remain in Los Angeles until further orders. A detachment of that company, 19 strong, under command of Lieutenant Stoneman, has been sent to San Francisco, to guard the magazine there. The remainder of the company, about 60 strong, will be all the troops south of Monterey. If these detachments are much reduced by desertion, I will be forced to abandon Los Angeles altogether, and in that case will feel myself compelled to issue to the inhabitants arms and ammunition to defend their lives and property against the Indians. This will be a dangerous alternative; but it would be inhuman to expose an unarmed people, owing their allegiance to our government, to the mercy of ruthless Indians. Should, unfortunately, any rebellion take place in California, or should the Indians make incursions in the southern districts of this Territory, no future promise of pay, however great, would call a hundred men from the mines to carry on an expedition against them. The late tariff so effectually excluded powder and ammunition, that not an ounce of either can be bought at any price.

Major Rich has just arrived from San Francisco, where he paid off the volunteers lately stationed there. He will at once proceed down the coast, to pay off the garrisons in that quarter.

I have the honor to be your most obedient servant,
R. B. MASON,
Colonel 1st Dragoons, commanding.

To Brigadier General R. JONES,
Adjutant General U. S. Army,
Washington, D. C.

HEADQUARTERS SOUTHERN MILITARY DISTRICT CALIFORNIA,
Los Angeles, California, August 20, 1848.

SIR: I have the honor to acknowledge the receipt of your several communications of the 8th, and proclamation of the 7th instant, together with department orders Nos. 50 and 52, announcing the conclusion of a treaty of peace between the United States and Mexico, and containing instructions for the disbanding of the 1st regiment New York volunteers under my command. Earnestly as all have desired such an event, the very sudden and unexpected termination of our service has surprised us all, and found many a poor fellow, who has served his country faithfully for more than two years, without a dollar beyond the small amount of pay that will be due them at the time of their discharge; and if they pay the few small debts they owe here, they will not have money sufficient to buy a pair of shoes; and I know that many, if not all at this post, possess so high a sense of honor that they would go barefooted rather than leave in debt to any one in the town. Thank God, all here have acted honorably and fairly to the people of the country, and I trust they will do so to the end. Yet, hard as their case is, they do not complain of the want of anything but the means of defence; for when they are disbanded, not ten men will have either a gun or pistol; and I assure you great fears are entertained, and not without just cause, that they will be wanted, as well for their defence against Indians as against some miserable wretches of the country, who already threaten not only to attack all Americans, but the families of the people of the country who have been friendly to us. My men complain that the Mormons retained their arms, and were allowed transportation to the Salt Lake, for seven months' service, and supplied with twenty rounds of cartridges each, while they, who have served more than two years and travelled thousands of miles of the ocean to come here in the service of their country, are to be discharged without an arm for their defence, or a dollar of commutation; and some of them (the last recruits) had their arms taken from them at Monterey, which, unless you have sent them down in the Anita, they will in all human probability never receive. Soon after I arrived in this country, in a frank conversation with General Kearny on this very subject, he assured me that my men should be allowed to retain their arms, as he had no doubt if it had been suggested to the authorities at home before sailing, it would have been authorized, as they were intended for, and would become, permanent residents of the country. He said he made the stipulation with the Mormons, and he felt authorized to make it with me for my men; and the day he left here for the United States he assured me that he would leave such instructions with you as would insure it. A very large number of my men here must remain until they can raise the means of reaching the upper country, or go up on foot; which would be a most toilsome and perilous journey, unarmed as they will be. Under these circumstances, I have deemed it my duty to present you their most earnest appeal that you will allow them to retain their arms, and that fifteen days' rations of such stores as are at the post may be served out to them on the day they are disbanded. They would not ask this favor of the government if they could in any manner dispose of the land or money scrip. I present this their petition most cheerfully, because I feel that they more than deserve it at the hands of their government; for no soldiers, either regulars or volunteers, have ever surpassed them in correct, honorable, and manly deportment, or in a most faithful and diligent discharge of the duty required of them as soldiers.

I have the honor to be, very respectfully, your obedient servant,
J. L. STEVENSON,
Colonel 1st New York Regiment,
Commanding Southern Military District.

Colonel R. B. MASON,
  1st United States Dragoons, Govervor of California.

A true copy:
W. T. SHERMAN,
1st Lieut. 3d Artillery, A. A. A. General.

HEADQUARTERS SOUTHERN MILITARY DISTRICT,
Los Angeles, California, August 20, 1848.

SIR: The sudden discharge of the volunteers in this town, and the removal of the dragoons to the northward after that event shall take place, has created the strongest excitement in this section of the country. For months past the Indians have frequently come boldly into the country and shot down people in the road and in the fields, and taken from them their horses and property, and the greatest fears are entertained. And I assure you, upon my honor, that I consider their fears far from groundless, that when all the troops shall evacuate this district of country, there will not be sufficient power to prevent their even coming into the town, robbing the stores and dwelling-houses, and violating the women with impunity; for the few citizens who remain in the town are entirely without arms, and all the arms left here by Fremont's battalion are perfectly worthless and unfit for service unless repaired, which could not be done here if double the value of the arms were paid for it. Forty-five old muskets were selected by the alcalde and repaired at the expense of the town, and these are all the arms I can leave here that are fit for service under your last instructions, and the ammunition you authorize me to issue will be useless without arms. I cannot express the pain and distress exhibited by the people at the idea of being left thus exposed to the ravages of the Indians, and, perhaps, the worthless of their own countrymen. The very best and most reputable of the people of the town and neighborhood are left; and by far the largest portion of them were the firm and fast friends of the Americans in 1846, and they complain—and in my opinion justly, too—that, after all the sacrifices they have made for us, they are now to be abandoned to the mercy of all who choose to do them injury; our government first taking from them their arms to awe their soldiers, and then abandoning them to the mercy of the savage and the worthless portion of the community, without the means of protecting their wives and daughters from insult and violence.

This, sir, is no imaginary picture. 'Tis a true state of the case, upon my honor; and I ask you, as the representative of our government at home, to protect this people, who, by the treaty of peace, have become incorporated into, and made to form a portion of, the United States: from the dangers that surround them, protect them as far as you can. Soldiers you cannot give, but arms and ammunition you can give, and I beg of you, in the name of humanity, as well as for the honor of our country, that you will do so. I know the people well, and know to whom arms can be safely issued; and if you will authorize it, I will place them in such hands as will protect the lives and property as well from the savage as from those who may be disposed to disturb the peace of the country.

I have the honor to be, very respectfully, your obedient servant,

J. D. STEVENSON,
Colonel 1st New York Regiment,
Commanding Southern Military District.

Colonel R. B. MASON,
1st United States Dragoons, Governor of California.

A true copy: W. T. SHERMAN,
1st Lt. 3d Art., A. A. A. General.

[No. 44.] HEADQUARTERS TENTH MILITARY DEPARTMENT,
Monterey, California, September 12, 1848.

SIR: I have the honor to inform you that the ship "Huntress" arrived at this port on Sunday last, the 10th inst., having on board Capt. R. Ingalls, assistant quartermaster, Lieutenant M. Norton, 1st New York volunteers, and 46 recruits for the two companies of regulars serving in California. These recruits are in a lamentable condition, the scurvy having broken out on board, causing the death of four men and seriously affecting the health of the rest.

They disembarked yesterday, and twenty are now in hospital, thirteen sick in quarters, and the remaining thirteen reported for duty are too feeble for military duty.

I would suggest the propriety of causing in future all transport ships bound for California to touch at one or more intermediate ports on the way. The charter of the Huntress required her to come direct to Monterey, without stopping unless absolutely necessary.

Her trip was remarkably good; and still Captain Ingalls reports, that had the voyage been protracted two weeks longer, he would have lost the greater part of his command.

The Huntress had on board a large supply of clothing for the volunteers; but as their term of service has expired, it will not be needed. I have ordered Captain Folsom, at San Francisco, to receive it and store it as well as possible. The charter of this ship requires her cargo to be landed at the end of her tackles; and as she has no launch, it is impossible to discharge her here. I, in consequence, have directed Capt. Marcy to contract with the master for the delivery of the entire cargo at San Francisco, where there are more facilities for landing and where the stores will be more secure. I would again respectfully renew the recommendation contained in my letter of April 10, that all ships chartered for this coast be required to have suitable launches, and to land their cargoes if required to do so; for, with the exception of San Francisco and San Diego, the harbors of California are open roadsteads, in which it is impossible to keep launches or lighters. Had the captain of the Huntress been so disposed, he might have laid here at great cost to the government, as it would have been impossible for us to discharge his ship under the circumstances. Captain Ingalls is ordered to San Francisco to superintend the delivery of the stores to Captain Folsom, after which he will return and report to me at Monterey.

The New York volunteer regiment being partly mustered out of service, and the whole being under orders for discharge, I have discharged from service Lieutenant Norton, the officer of that regiment, who came from New York on duty with these recruits.

I have the honor to enclose you duplicate copies of my letters Nos. 37, 39, and 42, sent to Washington in charge of Lieut. Loeser, 3d artillery, who sailed for Pata, Peru, on the 30th ult.; and I will merely add, that the state of the country has not materially changed since that date.

The artillery company here continues to diminish in numbers by desertion. This morning's report shows one officer for duty, one officer extra duty, 13 non-commissioned officers and privates for duty, 5 sick, 13 extra or daily duty, 3 confined, 9 on furlough, and 4 on detached service—a total of 47 enlisted men. No reports have been received from the dragoon company since my last letter.

The reports from the gold mines continue full as flattering as ever, but much sickness has resulted from the great exposure and heat of the summer, causing many citizens to return to the cool climate of the seacoast.

I have the honor to acknowledge the receipt of your letters of April 13th and 18th; one of February 8th, to Major General Jesup; special orders No. 11, and general orders Nos. 6, 9, 10, 13, and 16, of 1848. By the post returns already sent you, you will perceive that my file of orders is very incomplete.

I have no news of the squadron, but am expecting daily some part of it with Lieut. Col. Burton's command from Lower California.

I am, sir, very respectfully, your obedient servant,
R. B. MASON,
Colonel 1st Dragoons, Governor of California.
Brigadier General R. JONES,
Adjutant General U. S. A., Washington.

[No. 45.] HEADQUARTERS TENTH MILITARY DEPARTMENT,
San Francisco, November 24, 1848.

SIR: I embrace the opportunity which presents itself by a gentleman who leaves here to-morrow for the United States, via the isthmus of Panama, to address you a few lines. Nothing of importance has occurred in the administration of the civil affairs of California since my last communication (No. 44) of the 12th of September, reporting the arrival of the ship Huntress, with recruits and army stores, and forwarding you duplicates of my letters Nos. 37, 39, and 42. The whole of the New York volunteers have been mustered out of service. Lieutenant Colonel Burton's command arrived at Monterey on board of Commodore Jones's squadron, and was discharged at that place. A large number of the people of Lower California, who had taken an active part in our cause, was also brought by the same conveyance. I ordered the assistant commissary and acting assistant quartermaster to feed and quarter them for two months; and Commodore Jones promptly caused them to be paid from the military contribution fund, collected under his orders, for their lost property, &c. The recruits brought by the Huntress have nearly all deserted; just so fast as they recovered sufficiently from the scurvy to leave the hospital, they went off. Company C, 1st dragoons, and company F, 3d artillery, are very much weakened from the same cause. I learn, unofficially, that a large party, say twelve men, of the former company, took their horses, saddles, arms, and accoutrements, and went off in a body to the gold mines.

So long as the gold mines continue to yield the great abundance of metal they now do, it will be impossible to keep soldiers in California; and it is of no use to send them here. Soldiers will not serve for seven and eight dollars per month when laborers and mechanics are getting from fifty to one hundred. At the very time the recruits were deserting from Monterey, there was a ship in the harbor which had lost all her men; and her captain was offering one hundred dollars per month for sailors, and could not get a crew.

Gold continues to be found in increased quantities, and over an increased extent of country. I stated to you in my letter No. 37 that there was more gold in the country drained by the Sacramento and San Joaquin rivers than would pay all the cost of the war with Mexico one hundred times over; if I had said five hundred times over, I should have been nearer the mark. Any reports that may reach you of the vast quantities of gold in California can scarcely be too exaggerated for belief. In my last-mentioned letter, (No. 37,) I suggested that the gold district be surveyed, and sold in small parcels, &c. A better plan, I think, would be not to sell at all, but to throw the mines open to all who choose to work them, and collect a rent by charging them a small per centage upon the gold, coined at a mint to be established here, which shall have been taken from the mines in California I cannot too strongly recommend a territorial government to be organized in California at the earliest moment possible, if it has not already been done. There is no security here for life or property; and, unless a civil government is specially organized, anarchy and confusion will arise, and murder, robbery, and all sorts of crime will be committed with impunity in the heterogeneous and mixed community that now fills California.

I am, rsepectfully, your obedient servant,

R. B. MASON,
Colonel 1st Dragoons, commanding.

Brigadier General R. JONES,
Adjutant General U. S. A., Washington.

[No. 46.] HEADQUARTERS TENTH MILITARY DEPARTMENT,
San Francisco, California, November 24, 1848.

SIR: The war being over, the soldiers nearly all deserted, and having now been from the States two years, I respectfully request to be ordered home. I feel the less hesitancy in making this request, as it is the second only that I recollect ever to have made, in more than thirty years' service, to be relieved from any duty upon which I have been placed: the first was asking to be relieved from the recruiting service, in 1832, that I might join my company in the Black Hawk war.

I am, respectfully, your obedient servant,

R. B. MASON,
Colonel 1st Dragoons, commanding.

Brigadier General R. JONES,
Adjutant General U. S. A., Washington.

[No. 47.] HEADQUARTERS TENTH MILITARY DEPARTMENT,
Monterey, California, December 27, 1848.

SIR: I have the honor, herewith, to enclose you a copy of the muster and descriptive roll of the detachment of recruits which arrived here on the 10th of September, on board the ship Huntress, and to report that but *twelve* men remain of the original number. The original roll will be sent you by the first safe opportunity.

On the 12th instant a courier arrived here from Los Angeles, bringing a letter from Captain Smith, commanding that post, reporting the arrival at Los Angeles of a Mr. Lane, sutler to Major Graham's command, which he left November 22d, on the east bank of the Rio Colorado, engaged in rafting their property across that river. Mr. Lane brought a letter from Lieutenant Evans, adjutant to the command, requiring of the commissary of San Diego certain subsistence stores, which were immediately despatched from Los Angeles, to meet them on their way in.

The command is reported two hundred and seventy-seven strong, with two hundred teamsters and two quartermaster's men, ninety two wagons, over a thousand mules, horses, &c. The horses are reported very much reduced, and mules broken down.

The subsistence stores at Los Angeles, though ample for its small garrison, could not supply so large a body of men more than three weeks, and it became imperatively necessary to send thither a further supply as early as possible. A courier was despatched to San Francisco on the 13th instant, with orders for Captain Folsom to despatch to San Pedro seventy thousand rations, and a letter to Commodore Jones, requesting him to furnish, if possible, one of the smaller ships of his squadron, to convey these stores down the coast. I have learned, in answer, that the commodore had despatched, on the 19th instant, the storeship Southampton, so that full supplies will reach Major Graham before the stores already at Los Angeles are exhausted. For the present I shall keep Major Graham's command in the southern district, at some eligible point for recruiting his animals; but, in the spring, propose stationing a part of the force within striking distance of the gold placer. Captain Smith's company is ordered to San Francisco.

I was in hopes that the news of the discovery of the gold mines in this country, together with its effects on the troops stationed here, would have reached the department before any more were ordered out, for every day adds to my conviction that no soldier should be sent to California for some years to come, unless Congress provide them pay bearing some proportion to the amount they can make in the country, and, at the same time, devise some laws by which deserters, and those who entice them away, employ them, and purchase from them their arms, accoutrements, clothing, and other public property, which they steal and carry off, can be more summarily and severely punished; the present laws being entirely inadequate, as long experience has proven. Troops are needed here, and greatly needed; but of what use is it to send them, with the positive certainty of their running off to the gold mines as soon as they arrive. taking with them whatever public property they can lay their hands on? To arrest them is impossible, as they receive every encouragement to desert, and every facility to elude pursuit. I cannot but apprehend that Major Graham's men will desert nearly as fast as the horses recover strength to travel, for the wages in the country continue as extravagant as when I last wrote, and the gold mines hold out fully as tempting a prospect as ever. At this season of the year the operatives in that quarter are checked by cold weather and snow in the mountains; but, with spring the gold fever will break out with renewed violence. It will also be difficult to keep troops mounted in this country, on account of the scarcity of suitable horses and all kinds of grain or forage—horses even now so scarce and dear, that it is difficult to buy enough for the quartermaster's department.

The entire regiment of New York volunteers has been mustered out of service—companies C and K on the 15th of August, and H on the 25th of August, by Lieutenant James A. Hardie, 3d artillery, at San Francisco, California; company F, September 8, 1848, at Santa Barbara, Upper California; staff companies E and G, September 18, 1848, at Los Angeles, California, and company I, September 25, 1848, at San Diego, by Captain A. J. Smith, 1st dragoons; and companies A, B, and D on the 23d and 24th of October, 1848, at Monterey, California, by Captain H. S. Burton, 3d artillery. The field officers of the regiment were mustered out at Monterey, by Captain Burton, on the 26th of October. The mustering officers were directed to transmit two copies of each roll to your office— one endorsed for the Commissioner of Pensions. Another copy has been deposited in this office, so that reference can be made to it without consuming the time required to communicate with Washington. In like manner have been retained at these headquarters copies of the muster-rolls of discharge of Burton's company of California volunteers and of the Mormon companies discharged here. The volunteers have in many cases asked for individual discharges, separate from that given by the muster-rolls. Such discharges would be in violation of the 221st paragraph of general regulations, and is therefore prohibited; but I have given my consent for the mustering officer to furnish, at the request of a volunteer, a certificate that the bearer (setting forth his rank, &c.) *had been honorably discharged.* Such a paper could not be regarded as a duplicate discharge, and would serve to distinguish him who had honestly served his time from the many deserters now at large in the country, as also from those who were *dishonorably* discharged from service.

This regiment, you are aware, had been strung from Sonoma in the north to San José, in Lower California, during their whole time of service in this quarter. The companies stationed at La Paz (Steel's and Matsell's) held that town for many weeks against four times their numbers; and the very moment they were re-enforced by Naglee's company with additional recruits, they took the field under the command of Lieutenant Colonel Burton, routed the enemy, completely dispersed him, and restored peace to the peninsula. Colonel Burton speaks highly of the courage and coolness of his men and officers under fire; and I refer you to his report for individual acts of gallantry. Lieutenant Colonel Burton, throughout his whole conduct whilst in command of the forces in Lower California, completely executed his instructions, which were based upon the orders from the War Department; and as his reports and copies of his instructions are already in your office, I need only add my present approval of his conduct. He is now on duty at this place, in command of his company F, 3d artillery.

Colonel J. D. Stevenson, since April, 1847, has been in command of the district of country embracing Santa Barbara, Los Angeles, and San Diego, has by energy and good management maintained most excellent discipline amongst his men, and has preserved harmony amongst the population of that district, which is composed mostly of the native Californians. This required peculiar tact and firmness—qualities possessed by him in a peculiar degree. I will warrant that at no previous time in that district were life or property so secure, the magistrates of the country so effectually supported, and industry so encouraged, as during the past two years; one common cry of regret arose at the order for their disbandment; the little petty causes of complaint were forgotten in the remembrance of the more substantial advantages they had enjoyed under the protection of the military. Subalterns and men are entitled to share with their commander the honor due for this creditable state of feeling on the part of a people nominally conquered. That part of California lying on the bay of San Francisco has been under the command of the major of this regiment, James A. Hardie, who has effectually aided the civil authorities, dispelled the fears of the threatened Indian incursions, and guarded the heavy depôt at San Francisco—duties which were performed to the best advantage with the limited force at his command. His officers and men were generally attentive to their duties, and anxious to serve the United States. Major Hardie is still in command at San Francisco as first lieutenant 3d regiment of artillery. About the time of the disbanding of the three companies from Lower California at this place, some of the individuals of those companies committed gross acts of pillage upon public and private property, took forcible possession of a public building belonging to the town authorities, which they occupied for some days, and wantonly injured to a considerable extent.

Since my letter No. 44, I have made a visit to the gold mines, which I found as prosperous as ever. I went to the Stanislaus, a river that drains a country which a twelvemonth ago could only be visited by armed parties, but now known as one of the richest gold placers of the whole district. People are still working where the gold was originally discovered, as well as in the whole range of country lying between the American and Stanislaus rivers.

Now that the war with Mexico is over, I feel it due to the officers of the army who have served and still serve under my command, to draw your attention to the services they have rendered to the government. With the exception of Captain Burton and Lieutenant Halleck, they have not had the good fortune to be engaged in action. But this should not stand in their way of advancement. They have obeyed the orders of their government, and, by careful and strict attention to their appropriate duties, have maintained quiet and order among the worst elements of society. Heavy and responsible duties devolved upon Captain Folsom as assistant quartermaster and collector of customs at San Francisco, and they have been well performed. Captain Smith and Lieutenant Davidson of the dragoons, Lieutenants Ord and Loeser of the artillery, have been faithful and constant on duty with their respective companies. Lieutenant Davidson has also been on duty as chief officer of the quartermaster's department at Los Angeles, and in the southern district of Upper California—an arduous and responsible trust, which he has satisfactorily performed. Lieutenant Sherman, 3d artillery, has performed the duties of assistant adjutant general since May 31, 1847. I take great pleasure in bearing witness to his ability and talents; to his untiring zeal and industry, and close and constant application to all and every official duty.

Lieutenant Halleck has been employed in the civil department as secretary of the Territory of California, in his proper profession as an engineer officer at Mazatlan, and as chief of Lieutenant Colonel Burton's staff in the military operations in the field in Lower California, and has acquitted himself with great credit in every situation. Lieutenant Warner, topographical engineers, has been employed in the ordnance department here, as well as in making surveys of the country, and has shown himself an active and excellent officer. Assistant surgeons Griffin and Murray have been constantly on duty at their respective posts, and have been unremitting in their attentions to the sick.

Should it be contemplated to order the two companies of regulars to the United States, I would suggest the propriety of giving the few men who still remain the option of being discharged in this country, even before the expiration of their term of enlistment. No country could possibly hold out better prospects to the laboring man than California now does, and a discharge, honorably obtained, would be some reward to those who have proven faithful to their oaths.

I regret to report that several most horrible murders have of late been committed in this country. The entire occupants of the mission of San Miguel—men, women, and children—in all ten persons, were murdered about two weeks ago, and there is no doubt the murders were committed by white men. Murders and robberies have been committed in the mineral district, and I am informed that three men were hung in Pueblo de San José, on the 18th instant, for assault with intent to kill. The case is represented to be this: Two men were returning from the mines, having about their persons the gold which they had dug, amounting, it is said, to 23 pounds. They were met by six men, who inquired, as usual, where they had been working, and with what success. The two men shortly after encamped, and were assaulted: one was shot through the arm, the ball striking his breast; the other begged for mercy, and gave up his gold. This occurred on the road between the San Joaquin river and the Pueblo de San José. The two men succeeded in reaching the latter place, and made their complaint to the alcalde, giving such a description of the six men, that they were identified and arrested.

Only three of the six had made the assault, and the evidence against them was so clear, that a jury, regularly empannelled, sentenced them to death by hanging. The sentence was executed on Monday last. You are perfectly aware that no competent civil courts exist in this country, and that strictly speaking there is no legal power to execute the sentence of death; but the necessity of protecting their lives and property against the many lawless men at large in this country, compels the good citizens to take the law into their own hands. I shall not disapprove of the course that has been taken in this instance, and shall only endeavor to restrain the people, so far as to insure to every man charged with a capital crime an open and fair trial by a jury of his countrymen.

Upon hearing of the murder of Mr. Reed's family at the mission of San Miguel, I despatched Lieutenant Ord with a couple of men to that mission to ascertain the truth, and, if need, to aid the alcalde in the execution of his office. As it was reported that five men had been found, with strong evidence of guilt, I told Lieutenant Ord to inform the alcalde that if the evidence were clear and positive, and the sentence of the jury were death, he might cause it to be executed without referring the case to me. This course is absolutely necessary, as there are no jails or prisons in the country, where a criminal can be safely secured. This state of affairs must illustrate the absolute necessity of establishing a territorial government here as early as practicable. Common humanity demands it.

I would respectfully recommend that the military posts in California be placed on the list of double ration posts, and that it take retrospective effect as far back as is consistent with law. This would be just to the commanding officers who have been subjected to the heavy expenses of living in this country. I shall send this letter to Mazatlan, with a note, requesting Mr. Bolton to forward it to Vera Cruz overland; copies of orders, letters, and other papers of record, will be kept until some opportunity offers by way of Panama.

The latest dates from the department are to the 18th of April, brought out by the ship Huntress; and to illustrate how completely we are cut off from any communication with the United States, I will merely mention that Major Graham's command received orders and marched across the continent, bringing the first intelligence of their coming.

I have the honor to be, your obedient servant,

R. B. MASON,
Colonel 1st Dragoons, commanding.

Brigadier General R. JONES,
Adjutant General U. S. Army, Washington city, D. C.

[No. 51.]   Headquarters Tenth Military Department,
Monterey, California, March 8, 1849.

General: I have the honor to acknowledge the receipt, on the 29th of January, of your communications of April 13 and July 6, and on the 23d ultimo your instruction of October 2, and communications of October 13 and December 1; the instructions of the Secretary of War of October 9, covering a joint resolution of the houses of Congress, dated June 16; a copy of the communication of the Secretary of State to Mr. Van Voorhees, of October 7; of the circular of the Secretary of the Treasury of the same date, and printed forms from the Pension Office, and his communication of October 12, covering a communication from the governor of Oregon to the President of the United States; a copy of the Secretary of War's instructions to Brevet Major General Smith, dated November 15; of your instructions to Brevet Brigadier General Riley, dated October 5, and to Brevet Captain Andrews, 3d artillery, dated October 2, 1848.

Very respectfully, General, your obedient servant,
R. B. MASON,
Colonel 1st Dragoons, commanding.

General R. Jones,
Adjutant General U. S. A., Washington, D. C.

[No. 54.]   Headquarters Tenth Military Department,
Monterey, California, March 28, 1849.

General: I have the honor to transmit, herewith, returns of this department for January and February, 1849.

Very respectfully, General, your obedient servant,
R. B. MASON,
Colonel 1st Dragoons, commanding.

General R. Jones,
Adjutant General U. S. A., Washington, D. C.

Know all men by these presents, that I, R. B. Mason, colonel 1st dragoons, and governor of California, in virtue of authority in me vested, do hereby appoint Miguel Pedrorena temporary collector and harbor-master of the port of San Diego, California, with the salary of one thousand dollars per annum, provided that that sum is collected in said port over and above the expenses of the custom-house of the port.

Given at Monterey this 7th day of August, 1848.
R. B. MASON,
Colonel 1st Dragoons, Governor of California.

State Department, Territory of California,
Monterey, August 7, 1848.

Sir: You will continue to hold the office of collector and harbor-master of the port of San Pedro as heretofore, until orders are received from the Treasury Department at Washington.

The collection of military contributions will cease from this date, and all duties and port charges will hereafter be levied in accordance with the tariff laws and custom-house regulations of the United States, in the same manner as in any other American port. I enclose herewith a copy of the American tariff of 1846, custom-house information, &c.

Very respectfully, your obedient servant,
H. W. HALLECK,
Lieutenant of Engineers, and Secretary of State.
D. W. ALEXANDER,
Collector, &c., San Pedro.

STATE DEPARTMENT, TERRITORY OF CALIFORNIA,
Monterey, August 7, 1848.

SIR: Enclosed herewith you will receive the appointment of temporary collector and harbor-master of the port of San Diego.

The governor is aware that the amount of duties to be collected in your port under the present tariff will be very small, and he regrets that he has no more lucrative appointment at present within his gift. He hopes, however, that, as soon as a regular territorial government is organized, you will receive some more suitable reward for the services you have rendered our government.

The governor has already presented your name in the most favorable manner to the authorities at Washington, and he will take pleasure in again mentioning you as a person most eminently deserving the thanks and patronage of the government.

With respect to the losses which you mention in your letter of the 6th instant, as having been incurred during the early military operations, I am directed to say that it is believed the Congress of the United States has already made appropriations, and commissioners may soon be expected in this country to adjust all such claims.

In the mean time, it is recommended to you to procure the proper certificates of your losses, and to have your papers in readiness to lay before such commissioners on their arrival.

Very respectfully, your obedient servant,
H. W. HALLECK,
Lieutenant of Engineers, and Secretary of State.
Don MIGUEL DE PEDRORENA, *San Diego.*

Know all men by these presents, that I, R. B. Mason, colonel 1st dragoons, and governor of California, in virtue of authority in me vested, do hereby appoint Edward Gilbert temporary collector and harbor-master of the port of San Francisco, California, with the salary of two thousand dollars per annum, provided that that sum is collected in said port, over and above the expenses of the custom-house of the port.

Given at Monterey, this 7th day of August, 1848.
R. B. MASON,
Colonel 1st Dragoons, Governor of California.

STATE DEPARTMENT, TERRITORY OF CALIFORNIA,
Monterey, August 17, 1848.

SIR: It appears, from the records of this office, that Captain Lippett has refunded to the government the sum of $90 27, as money overpaid to you. If you have not already settled with Captain Lippett for this overpayment, the governor directs that you will do so immediately.

Very respectfully, your obedient servant,
H. W. HALLECK,
Lieutenant of Engineers, and Secretary of State.

Don PEDRO C. CARRILLO,
Santa Barbara.

STATE DEPARTMENT, TERRITORY OF CALIFORNIA,
Monterey, August 17, 1848.

SIR: It appears, from your letter of August 11, that Señor Aguire claims for overcharges of duties on goods landed in the port of Santa Barbara, from the Joven Guipuscuana, the collector having charged duties on the sale prices of the goods, instead of on the invoice prices, as directed in the tariff regulations. The governor directs me to say that repeated instructions have been sent to the collector of Santa Barbara to charge duties on the invoice prices, and not on the amount of sales, as was done previous to the operation of the tariff regulations for the collection of military contributions, and that you will return to Señor Aguire the difference between the amount of duties collected and the amount which ought to have been charged according to the tariff regulations then in force in California.

Very respectfully, your obedient servant,
H. W. HALLECK,
Lieutenant of Engineers, and Secretary of State.

Lieutenant H. S. CARNES,
Collector, &c., Santa Barbara, California.

STATE DEPARTMENT, TERRITORY OF CALIFORNIA,
Monterey, August 21, 1848.

SIR: The governor directs me to acknowledge the receipt of your letter of the 17th of August, asking permission for the British schooner "William" to discharge her cargo, and also to receive her outward cargo, at the embarcadero of Santa Clara, and to say to you that he does not feel himself authorized to allow vessels to enter, or to receive outward cargoes, in any other ports than those designated as ports of entry by the senior naval officer on this coast. Even if he possessed this authority, it would be impossible for him to do so at the present time, as, from the difficulty of procuring custom-house employés in San Francisco, no proper officer could be sent to superintend the discharge of the vessel.

Very respectfully, your obedient servant,
H. W. HALLECK,
Lieutenant of Engineers, and Secretary of State.

ROBERT WALKINGSHAW, Esq.,
New Almaden, California.

STATE DEPARTMENT TERRITORY OF CALIFORNIA,
Monterey, August 21, 1848.

SIR: I have to acknowledge the receipt of your letter of the 11th instant relative to the prisoner Foxon. On being relieved from further duty at Santa Barbara, you will turn over to the alcalde of that jurisdiction all civil prisoners in your charge. You will endeavor to impress the civil authorities of that place with the importance, now that the troops are to be withdrawn, of their using every exertion to preserve the order and quiet of the jurisdiction.

Captain A. J. Smith will be authorized to receive and receipt for all customs collected at your port as "military contributions." Should there be no collector for that port when your company is discharged from service, you will seal up all custom-house books and papers, and place them in charge of the alcalde, to be kept by him until further orders. Your custom-house accounts will be examined by Captain Smith, and forwarded to this office.

Very respectfully, your obedient servant,
H. W. HALLECK,
Lieutenant of Engineers, and Secretary of State.
Captain F. J. LIPPETT,
Commanding, &c., Santa Barbara.

STATE DEPARTMENT TERRITORY OF CALIFORNIA,
Monterey, August 21, 1848.

SIR: Captain A. J. Smith, 1st dragoons, will be authorized to receive and receipt for all customs collected at your port as military contributions. Should there be no collector for that port when your company is discharged from service, you will seal up all custom-house papers and books, and place them in charge of the alcalde, to be kept by him until further orders. Your accounts will be examined by Captain Smith, and forwarded to this office.

Very respectfully, your obedient servant,
H. W. HALLECK,
Lieutenant of Engineers, and Secretary of State.
Captain W. E. SHANNON,
Commanding, &c., San Diego.

STATE DEPARTMENT TERRITORY OF CALIFORNIA,
Monterey, August 21, 1848.

SIR: I enclose herewith an appointment of collector and harbor-master of the port of San Francisco. The governor is aware that the salary attached to this office is much less than the prices at present paid in California for similar services; but it is hoped that the prospect of a permanent appointment from Washington may induce you to accept the appointment. You will be required to give good and satisfactory bonds, to the amount of fifteen thousand dollars, before entering upon the duties of your office. Your regular monthly and quarterly papers will be made out and submitted, for examination and approval, to the quartermaster of that port, who will endorse and forward them to Washington through this office. The nett proceeds of the customs will also be turned over to the quartermaster as above at the end of every month, and the receipts of that officer will be good and sufficient vouchers in the settlement of your accounts.

Very respectfully, your obedient servant,
          H. W. HALLECK,
    Lieutenant of Engineers, and Secretary of State.
EDWARD GILBERT, Esq.,
  San Francisco.

STATE DEPARTMENT TERRITORY OF CALIFORNIA,
      Monterey, August 21, 1848.

SIR: Enclosed herewith you will receive a letter and appointment for Mr. Gilbert, which you will please to read and hand to him; and on his giving bonds to your satisfaction for the sum of fifteen thousand dollars, you will put him in possession of all the books and papers of the office. You will hereafter act as receiver of customs for that port, and at the end of every month will examine the books and returns of the collector, and receive from him the proceeds of customs.

His salary will commence upon his entering upon the duties of his office, and will be paid by you either monthly or quarterly, as was done previous to the collection of "military contributions." The returns and papers of the collector will be endorsed by you and forwarded to Washington through this office.

Very respectfully, your obedient servant,
          H. W. HALLECK,
    Lieutenant of Engineers, and Secretary of State.
Captain J. L. FOLSOM,
  Collector, &c., San Francisco.

STATE DEPARTMENT TERRITORY OF CALIFORNIA,
      Monterey, August 23, 1848.

SIR: I am directed by the governor to acknowledge the receipt of your letter, dated August 16, asking that the bill of costs in the case of Dring, master of the "Janet," be paid out of the public funds, and also how you are to proceed to collect the fine imposed on the said Dring.

All costs legally taxed in this case must be charged against the convicted person, and collected in the same manner as the fine. If you will refer again to the fourth article of the regulations under which Captain Dring was convicted, you will see that it is directed that the convicted person be "imprisoned until the fine is paid." It is the duty of the magistrate to see that the law is executed in all its provisions.

Very respectfully, your obedient servant,
          H. W. HALLECK,
    Lieutenant of Engineers, and Secretary of State.
T. M. LEAVENWORTH,
  2d Alcalde, San Francisco.

HEADQUARTERS TENTH MILITARY DEPARTMENT,
Monterey, California, August 23, 1848.

SIR: Your communication of yesterday's date is before me; and, for the reasons therein set forth, your salary, from and after the thirty-first day of this present month, will be at the rate of two thousand dollars per annum.

The assistant commissary is authorized to sell you, from time to time, such articles of subsistence stores as may be necessary for the actual consumption of your own family.

I am, respectfully, your obedient servant,
R. B. MASON,
Colonel 1*st Dragoons, Governor of California.*

Mr. W. E. P. HARTNELL,
Government Translator and Interpreter, present.

STATE DEPARTMENT TERRITORY OF CALIFORNIA,
Monterey, August 23, 1848.

SIR: You will please to read the enclosed letter and hand it to the 2d alcalde of San Francisco. He reports the bill of costs, in the case referred to, to be $29. If this bill be legally taxed, it must be collected from the convicted person in the same manner as the fine.

You will please to report what is done in the case.

Very respectfully, your obedient servant,
H. W. HALLECK,
Lieutenant of Engineers, and Secretary of State.

JAMES A. HARDIE,
Commanding, &c., San Francisco.

STATE DEPARTMENT TERRITORY OF CALIFORNIA,
Monterey, August 26, 1848.

SIR: I am directed by the governor to acknowledge the receipt of your letter of the 20th instant, and to inform you that a military force will be continued in Los Angeles, and that you will be retained as government interpreter and translator for the southern military district. The governor is exceedingly desirous that you continue in the performance of the duties of first alcalde of your district, as heretofore. The resignation of an American alcalde at the present juncture will be likely to produce very erroneous impressions among the ignorant and excitable people of this country; and it is the imperative duty of Americans, under such circumstances, to make every personal sacrifice, and to use every exertion in their power, to preserve the peace and quiet of the country. From your influence with the people of your district, and the confidence which they will place in your decisions and opinions, it is of the utmost importance that you remain firm in your position. The civil authorities will continue to receive every possible assistance from the military; but, in the present reduced state of our garrisons, this aid will necessarily be limited, and the peace and quiet of California, and the security of life and property, must mainly depend upon the friendship and energy of the civil magistrates, assisted as they will be by all good citizens.

For these reasons, the governor cannot consent to accept your resignation, and he hopes that you will find it for your interest, as well as your duty, to continue in the performance of the office of first magistrate of your district.

Very respectfully, your obedient servant,
H. W. HALLECK,
Lieutenant of Engineers, and Secretary of State.
STEPHEN C. FOSTER,
First Alcalde, Los Angeles.

Know all men by these presents, that I, R. B. Mason, colonel first dragoons, and governor of California, in virtue of authority in me vested, do hereby appoint Edward H. Harrison temporary collector of the port of San Francisco, California, with the salary of two thousand dollars per annum, provided that that sum is collected in said port over and above the expenses of the custom-house of the port.

Given at Monterey, this 3d day of September, 1848.
R. B. MASON,
Colonel First Dragoons, and Governor of California.

STATE DEPARTMENT TERRITORY OF CALIFORNIA,
Monterey, September 3, 1848.

SIR: I enclose herewith an appointment of collector of the port of San Francisco. You will be required to give good and satisfactory bonds, to the amount of fifteen thousand dollars, before entering upon the duties of your office. Your regular monthly and quarterly papers will be made out and submitted for examination and approval to the quartermaster at San Francisco, who will endorse and forward them to Washington through this office. The proceeeds of the customs, after the payment of all the necessary and proper expenses of the custom-house, will be turned over to the quartermaster, as above, at the end of every month, and the receipts of that officer will be good and sufficient vouchers in the settlement of your accounts.

Very respectfully, your obedient servant,
H. W. HALLECK,
Lieutenant of Engineers, and Secretary of State.
EDWARD HARRISON, Esq.,
San Francisco, California.

STATE DEPARTMENT TERRITORY OF CALIFORNIA,
Monterey, September 3, 1848.

SIR: I have the honor to acknowledge the receipt of your letter of the 27th ultimo, relating to permits granted by you for vessels to trade on the bay of San Francisco; also, your communication of August 31, enclosing a letter from Mr. Gilbert, who declines the office of collector of that port with a less salary than three thousand dollars per annum, and unless he be given full authority to "appoint and pay such deputy collector, clerks, appraisers, inspectors, weighers, and gaugers, as may be necessary to conduct the business of the custom house," &c. In the settlement of the accounts of the collector, you were fully authorized to allow all necessary and proper expenses connected with that office, and the collector was directed to turn over to you only the nett proceeds after all such expenses were deducted. But Mr. Gilbert demands to have the entire and unlimited control of all the expenditures of the custom-house, the appointment of such officers and the payment of such salaries as he may choose, and the hire of such boats, warehouses, &c., as he may see fit to rent. Such demands are certainly very unusual, and rather extravagant. He requires more power to be placed in his hands than that possessed by the collector of the port of New York, and a salary larger than that paid in some of the principal ports of the United States. In all the disbursements of public money, it is requisite to have proper checks; and, in requiring your endorsement and approval of the expenditures of the collector of San Francisco, it was intended merely to keep those expenditures within proper limits. Such checks are required of all public officers, either in the army, navy, or revenue service.

With respect to the extravagant prices which you mention as being obliged to pay for clerks in the custom-house, the governor directs me to say that he has just employed a good clerk in this office for $75 per month, and that he has no doubt clerks may be hired in San Francisco in the course of a few months upon very reasonable terms.

Very respectfully, your obedient servant,
H. W. HALLECK,
Lieutenant of Engineers, and Secretary of State.

Captain J. L. Folsom,
United States Army, San Francisco.

State Department Territory of California,
Monterey, September 4, 1848.

Sir: It appears from the papers this day laid before the governor, that the election held by you on the 29th ultimo for the office of first alcalde of the district of San Francisco was not held in accordance with the instructions given.

In the first place, *due* notice was not given in all parts of said district, for it appears that the notice was given only in the town of San Francisco; that but six days were allowed to elapse between the date of the notice and the time of election; and that (if the statement of a number of respectable citizens can be relied on) only two days intervened between the giving of the notice and the day of election.

In the second place, you limit the elective franchise to resident citizens of San Francisco, whereas all the resident citizens of the other parts of the district had an equal right to vote at the said election.

Thirdly, you make a distinction between recently-discharged soldiers and other persons who have recently arrived in San Francisco, allowing the former to be entitled to vote, and the latter not, "unless they have purchased property and occupy it"—whereas no such distinction can be made, both being voters if actual residents of the district, and neither when not such actual residents. Property qualifications cannot be required in the exercise of the elective franchise, unless there is a special law or regulation to that effect.

Fourthly, you say that Mexicans citizens, although absolved from allegiance, cannot vote under the proclamation of the governor, dated August 7, 1848. No such ground is taken or intended to be taken in that proclamation. All citizens of this Territory continue to retain that character until they give notice of their intention "to preserve the character of citizens of the Mexican republic;" and there is nothing in the government proclamation depriving them of the rights pertaining to their citizenship in California.

The governor, therefore, declares the election held on the 29th ultimo to be null and void, and directs that a new one be held.

Due notice must be given in all parts of the district at least three weeks prior to the day of election—the first alcalde being for the *district* and not for the *town* of San Francisco alone.

The following-named persons are appointed judges and inspectors of election, viz: W. D. M. Howard, E. V. Gillespie, H. H. Dimmick, Jas. C. Ward, and W. S. Clark.

They will give the proper notice and decide upon the election; any three of their number are empowered to act in the absence of the others; votes will be received only from actual and *bona fide* residents of the district.

By direction of the governor:
H. W. HALLECK,
Lieutenant of Engineers, and Secretary of State.

T. M. LEAVENWORTH, Esq.,
San Francisco, California.

HEADQUARTERS TENTH MILITARY DEPARTMENT,
Monterey, California, September 5, 1848.

SIR: The barque Callao has been admitted to entry in this port—Mr. Huttman having given bond, according to law, for the production within eight months of the invoice of the cargo, properly authenticated, before the United States consul, &c.

A vessel entering a port in California, and landing a part of her cargo, may proceed to other ports in California and land the remainder, without the payment in other ports of any additional tonnage duties, or those denominated "light money." Her entrance and clearance and other fees in the other ports will, of course, be paid.

I am, respectfully,
R. B. MASON,
Colonel 1st Dragoons, &c.

To the COLLECTOR
of the port of San Francisco.

STATE DEPARTMENT TERRITORY OF CALIFORNIA,
Monterey, September 7, 1848.

SIR: I am directed to acknowledge the receipt of your letter of the 5th instant, proposing to the governor the following questions:

First. Can American goods, so bonded in warehouses in Chili, Peru, &c., be reshipped into American bottoms, and brought into California free of duty?

Second. Can American goods, so bonded in warehouses, be brought in foreign bottoms into California free of duty?

As a reply to the first of these questions, I enclose you herewith a copy of so much of the act of 2d March, 1799, as relates to this subject, by which it appears that goods of American growth and manufacture, which have been exported from the United States, may be returned again, under certain conditions, free of duty. It is believed that this law is still in force; at least it is not known that it has ever been repealed.

With respect to the second question, the governor is of opinion that to bring goods so bonded in Chili, Peru, &c., in a foreign vessel, to a port in California, free of duty, would be an interference with the coasting trade, which, by law and treaty stipulations, is reserved exclusively to vessels of the United States. It would evidently be unlawful for a foreign vessel to receive the cargo or any part of a cargo of a coasting vessel, during her voyage, and carry it to an American port; and it is believed that it would be equally improper for a foreign vessel to receive American goods which have been put in depot in the usual route between any two ports of the United States, and to enter them in an American port, with the same privileges as a coasting vessel of the United States.

The subject, however, will be referred to the Secretary of the Treasury by the earliest opportunity for his decision in the case.

Very respectfully, your obedient servant,
H. W. HALLECK,
Lieutenant of Engineers, and Secretary of State.

Mr. F. HUTTMAN,
San Francisco, California.

Know all to whom it may concern:

Whereas José Antonio Aguirre, a naturalized citizen of the United States, resident in Santa Barbara, California, and sole owner of the American-built barque "Joven Guipuzcouna," of which James Chapman, a native citizen of the United States, resident in California, is master, has made due application for the re-registry of said vessel, according to the requisitions of the laws:

Now, therefore, I, Richard B. Mason, colonel 1st dragoons, and governor of California, in virtue of authority in me vested, do hereby authorize the said barque "Joven Guipuzcouna," owned and commanded as aforesaid, to wear the American flag, and to enjoy all the immunities and privileges pertaining thereto, both with respect to coast trade and foreign commerce.

The said barque has one deck and three masts; her length is one hundred and eight feet; her breadth twenty feet; her depth ten feet; she measures two hundred and one tons, has no figure head, has a plain stern, and was built in Rhode Island in the year eighteen hundred and thirty-eight, her original name being the "Roger Williams."

This sea-letter or license shall be good for one year from this date, or until the decision of the Treasury Department of the United States on the aforesaid application for re-registry shall be made known to the owner or master of the said vessel.

Given at Monterey, California, this ninth day of September, anno Domini one thousand eight hundred and forty-eight, and of the independence of the United States the seventy-third.

R. B. MASON,
Colonel 1st Dragoons, and Governor of California.

STATE DEPARTMENT TERRITORY OF CALIFORNIA,
Monterey, September 10, 1848.

SIR: In reply to your letter of the 5th instant, recommending that a box of liquors and a piece of silk sent as a present by the admiral of the French squadron to Mr. Wm. Richardson and family be admitted free of duty, as Mr. Richardson has always been most friendly disposed towards the American government, and as these articles were received during the operation of the "military contribution" tariff, the governor directs me to say that they may be received, as you recommend, free of duty.

I have to acknowledge the receipt of your letter of the 6th instant, relating to the landing of certain cordage from the American schooner Honolulu, whose voyage had been changed in order to proceed to Oregon, and recommending that permission be given to transfer this cordage to some vessel going to the Sandwich islands, the place from which it originally came. Considering the circumstances under which this cordage was landed, during the operation of the military contributions tariff, the governor can see no objection to the permit for reshipment, as you recommend.

Very respectfully, your obedient servant,
H. W. HALLECK,
Lieut. of Engineers, and Secretary of State.
Captain J. L. FOLSOM,
U. S. Army, San Francisco.

HEADQUARTERS TENTH MILITARY DEPARTMENT,
Monterey, California, July 31, 1848.

GENTLEMEN: Your communication of the 22d, together with its enclosure, has been received.

I will instruct the collector at San Francisco to receive gold dust in payment of duties at the custom-house, with the privilege reserved to the payer of redeeming one half by a payment to the collector in gold or silver coin any time within ninety days, and the other half by a like payment any time within 180 days. This, however, is to be a mere temporary arrangement, owing to the present scarcity of coin in the country. It would give me pleasure to comply fully with the wishes expressed by the public meeting held at San Francisco on the night of the 21st instant, by making the whole redeemable at 180 days, but it would have the effect of entirely cutting off the receipts of any available funds in the custom house for six months to come That is a longer period than it will be prudent to dry up the only source of revenue that the country affords, and would be too wide a departure from my instructions, which are very positive to collect the duties "exclusively in gold and silver coin," before the goods, wares, and merchandise leave the custody of the collector, or in other words before they are suffered to go into the market. I am willing to allow the goods to go at once into the market, and to wait three and six months for the duties, although I am ordered to collect them in cash, provided the gold dust is taken at a rate low enough to make it certain that the merchant will redeem it at the stipulated time, and, if he does not, that there will be no doubt that the duties can be realized at once by putting it up at auction, if the money be immediately required. You will readily perceive the situation in which I am placed. A large amount of duties will be received at San Franciso. Should some ten or twenty thousand dollars of this gold dust received at the custom-house, reckoning at the rate per ounce at which it will be received, fail to be redeemed at the stipulated time, and I should be forced by the want of funds to throw suddenly this large amount into market to be sold for cash, and it should not bring this sum, I at once become and am held personally and individually responsible and accountable to the department at Washington for the loss sustained in consequence of the departure from my orders and instructions.

I am very sure that none of the merchants of your town would desire to see me assume a risk of becoming pecuniarily involved by departing from my instructions for their accommodation; and therefore I feel, by departing from my orders in this instance, in permitting goods, wares, and merchandise to go at once into the market, and waiting three and six months before the duties can be realized, that the precautions I take to guard both the public and myself from any loss are not unreasonable or greater than the occasion calls for.

I shall strongly recommend, in my first communication to the department, the immediate establishment of a mint in Upper California.

I am, respectfully, your obedient servant,
R. B. MASON,
Colonel 1st Dragoons, and Governor of California.
W. D. M. HOWARD, C. V. GILLESPIE, and JAMES C. WARD,
San Francisco, California.

STATE DEPARTMENT TERRITORY OF CALIFORNIA,
Monterey, September 10, 1848.

SIR: I am directed by the governor to acknowledge the receipt of your letter of the 7th. and to inform you that a sea-letter or other document may be given to an unregistered vessel *owned by citizens of the United States.*—Vide Gordon's Digest, art. 1,788.

In order that a vessel may receive a new registry, she must belong exclusively to citizens resident of the United States, and be an American bottom. For conditions, &c., vide Gordon's Digest, art. 1,361, 70.
Very respectfully, your obedient servant,
H. W. HALLECK,
Lieutenant of Engineers, and Secretary of State.
Mr. C. L. Ross,
San Francisco, California.

STATE DEPARTMENT TERRITORY OF CALIFORNIA,
Monterey, September 10, 1848.

SIR: In reply to your letter of September 7, the governor directs me to say that the provisions of the first section of the act of March 1, 1817, will not be enforced against vessels which actually sailed from the ports of California during the war for cargoes expressly for this market, and which have not in the mean time been engaged in other trade.

As soon as the time of redemption of the gold dust in your hands received in deposite as security of the payment of duties expires, you will give due notice, and sell it at public auction. In order that there may be no loss to the revenue, you will bid it in at the value for which it was deposited. If it sells for more, the surplus, after the expenses of sale are deducted, will be paid over to the depositors.

The gold dust received in payment of duties, with the privilege of redemption, of course becomes the property of the United States if not redeemed at the expiration of the time specified, without any sale.

Respectfully, your obedient servant,
H. W. HALLECK,
Lieutenant of Engineers, and Secretary of State.
Captain J. L. FOLSOM,
San Francisco, California.

HEADQUARTERS TENTH MILITARY DEPARTMENT,
Monterey, California, September 14, 1848.

SIR: I have just received a communication from the merchants of San Francisco on the subject of the manner in which the ad valorem duties are estimated in your port, and enclosing me a copy of the fifth section of "An act for regulating the collection of duties on imports and tonnage," passed March 1, 1823.

I enclose you herewith a copy of the fifteenth section of an act of Congress of the 4th of July, 1832, and a copy of the eighth section of the bill reducing the duties on imports, and for other purposes, passed July 29, 1846. These are believed to be the latest laws upon the subject, and of course repeal the fifth section of the act of March 1, 1823. Any duties, therefore, collected under the 5th section of this latter act, should be refunded.

Very respectfully, your obedient servant,
R. B. MASON,
Colonel 1st Dragoons, Governor of California.
COLLECTOR *of San Francisco, California.*

STATE DEPARTMENT TERRITORY OF CALIFORNIA,
Monterey, September 15, 1848.

SIR: I am directed by the governor to acknowledge the receipt of your letter of the 10th instant, and to inform you that he has no intention or desire to oblige you to retain your office of alcalde; but, under existing circumstances, he deems it the duty of every civil officer, where the personal sacrifice is not too great, to remain at his post, and to use every exertion to preserve order. The civil magistrates will continue to receive from the military all the assistance which it may be proper and possible to render; but in the present reduced state of our garrisons it will not be possible to make detachments for the interior towns, and the peace and quiet of the country will depend upon the firmness of the alcaldes, assisted as they should be by all good citizens.

If it would be compatible with your other engagements to retain the office of first alcalde of your district until a new territorial government is formed, the governor would be pleased to have you do so, in which case you will return the letter accepting your resignation, in order that it may be cancelled on the records.

Very respectfully, your obedient servant,
H. W. HALLECK,
Lieutenant of Engineers, and Secretary of State.
CHAS. WHITE, Esq., *San José.*

HEADQUARTERS TENTH MILITARY DEPARTMENT,
Monterey, California, September 16, 1848.

GENTLEMEN: I have this morning received a memorial from certain of the citizens of the town of San Francisco, dated on the 8th instant, requesting that an election might be held for two town councilmen to supply the vacancies caused by the resignation of Mr. Glover and the death of Mr. Leidsdorff. You will be pleased to hold an election to fill the aforesaid vacancies on the same day that the election takes place for the first alcalde, which I believe is on the 3d of October, proximo. The town council have the authority, under my letter of the 15th of July, 1847, to Alcalde Hyde, to appoint all the necessary police officers for the town, and to determine their pay, &c. The jurisdiction of police officers extends to the shipping in the harbor precisely the same as it does over any part of the town, and the town council have the same authority to pass laws for the preservation of the peace and the maintenance of good order among the shipping in port that they have on shore.

It may be proper, however, to observe, that no local laws can supersede or interfere with the general regulations for the collection of the customs; nor can any municipal officer interfere in the execution of the duties or arrangements of the revenue officer.

The duplicate of this communication, herewith enclosed, be pleased to present to the town council, at their next session, for their information and guidance.

I am, gentlemen, very respectfully, your obedient servant,
R. B. MASON,
Colonel 1st Dragoons, Governor of California.
To W. D. M. HOWARD, C. V. GILLESPIE, K. H. DIMMICK, JAS. E. WARD, and W. S. CLARK.

P. S.—I do not deem it necessary to enclose a copy of the memorial above mentioned, as it is signed by four of the gentlemen to whom this is addressed.

STATE DEPARTMENT TERRITORY OF CALIFORNIA,
Monterey, September 19, 1848.

SIR: I have to acknowledge the receipt of your letter of the 16th, relating to the admission of the French brig New Perseverance and the British brig Tepic.

It is believed, and that belief is confirmed by the positive assurances of the French consul, that American vessels are permitted to enter French ports with cargoes not from ports of the United States. The New Perseverance is therefore entitled to enter her cargo.

With respect to the British brig Tepic, the governor directs your attention to his decision, as communicated on the 10th instant: "That the provisions of the first section of the act of March 1, 1817, will not be enforced against vessels which actually sailed from the ports of California during the war for cargoes expressly for this market, and which have not in the mean time been engaged in other trade." If, however, official news of the peace should have reached the port of lading previous to the departure of the vessel, she ought not to be permitted to enter. But, before prohibiting the entrance of the vessel, the collector should satisfy himself that the official or at least very authentic news of peace was actually received: mere reports or rumors of peace should not be deemed sufficient to effect the prohibition. The policy in this respect should be a liberal one.

It is believed that the retaliatory law of March 1, 1817, is only applicable to English vessels.

Mr. H. Grimes has petitioned to have his furniture admitted free of duty. For the decision in this case you are referred to the tariff of 1846, words " household furniture, old and new."

You will be pleased to communicate to the parties concerned the governor's decision as above.

Very respectfully, your obedient servant,
W. H. HALLECK,
Lieutenant of Engineers, and Secretary of State.

E. H. HARRISON,
Collector, San Francisco, California.

[Confidential.]

STATE DEPARTMENT TERRITORY OF CALIFORNIA,
Monterey, July 26, 1848.

SIR: It is highly probable that the persons who obtained grants or deeds of sales for land from Pio Pico, just as he was leaving the country, will now, on hearing of his return to California, endeavor to obtain from him certificates that these grants or deeds of sale were not antedated. I refer particularly to deeds of sales of land by Pio Pico which are dated at Los Angeles about the 25th of June, 1846, whereas it is believed he was not in that place between about the middle of June and the latter part of July. Some of these titles purport to be recorded on the corresponding book of records, which book has been abstracted from the territorial archives. There are reasons for suspecting that this volume of records is now in the hands of some one of the holders of these antedated titles, and that it is so retained in order to get Pico, on his return to this country, to enter these titles upon the records, or, if they have destroyed the book, to get his certificates that they were entered according to the dates they bear. Something will undoubtedly be sought for from Pico to strengthen their unjust claims to government property.

It is thought that, if you can establish a friendly intercourse with Don Pio before he can have any communication with these holders of fraudulent titles, you may obtain from him a statement of the real facts of the case. The matter should be acted on with promptness, and will require much care and discretion in its management.

Very respectfully, your obedient servant,
H. W. HALLECK,
Lieutenant of Engineers, and Secretary of State.
Colonel J. D. STEVENSON,
Commanding Southern Military District, Los Angeles.

STATE DEPARTMENT TERRITORY OF CALIFORNIA,
Monterey, ——————.

SIR: I have to acknowledge the receipt of your letters of the 12th instant, relating to business of the custom-house.

The collector has full authority to allow the correction of clerical errors in invoices; and as you are satisfied of there being such an error in the invoice of Messrs. Starkey & Jamon, the governor is of opinion that you ought to refund to the parties the amount of over-payment of duties.

If you are satisfied that the articles of female clothing which you mention as belonging to Mrs. Grimes were actually brought to this coast previous to the reception of the official news of peace, and that they are not for sale, it would seem proper that they be allowed to pass free of duty. You say that most of them are old, and altogether of little value. It would therefore seem that they are of the character of personal baggage, rather than merchandise.

Very respectfully, your obedient servant,
H. W. HALLECK,
Lieutenant of Engineers, and Secretary of State.
Captain J. L. FOLSOM,
United States Army, San Francisco, California.

STATE DEPARTMENT TERRITORY OF CALIFORNIA,
Monterey, September 26, 1848.

SIR: I am directed by the governor to again call your attention to the settlement of your custom-house accounts.

The time has now arrived when it is absolutely necessary that this matter should be definitely settled; no further delay or procrastination in this matter can be admitted. The amount due from you must be paid over at once.

Very respectfully, your obedient servant,
H. W. HALLECK,
Lieutenant of Engineers, and Secretary of State.
Wm. Richardson,
Bay of San Francisco, California.

State Department Territory of California,
Monterey, September 26, 1848.

Sir: I enclose you herewith a letter for Mr. Richardson, relating to his custom-house accounts. You will please see that it is delivered to him, and call on him to pay over to you the amount due from him to the government. Should he fail to do so, you will report the fact, in order that proceedings may be instituted to embargo his property and that of his bail.

Very respectfully, your obedient servant,
H. W. HALLECK,
Lieutenant of Engineers, and Secretary of State.
Captain J. L. Folsom,
San Francisco, California.

State Department Territory of California,
Monterey, September 26, 1848.

Sir: On your arrival here in October last, you informed Colonel Mason that some law books had been sent to him from Washington for the use of the United States authorities here, and that they had been left on the route, from some cause, but would probably arrive in the next vessel. These books have never come to hand, and are very much needed.

Will you have the goodness to inform me where the books were left and in whose charge. Any other information that may be in your possession, which will tend to their recovery, will be thankfully received.

Very respectfully, your obedient servant,
H. W. HALLECK,
Lieutenant of Engineers, and Secretary of State.
H. Foller, Esq.,
San Francisco, California.

State Department Territory of California,
Monterey, September 26, 1848.

Sir: I am directed to acknowledge the receipt of your letter of the 20th instant, asking, for reasons given, a reversal of the decision in the alcalde's court of San Francisco in the case of Merrills *vs.* Harris. In all probability, regular judicial courts have already been organized by Congress for this Territory, and the proper officers may be expected to arrive here in a very short time. You can then appeal from the alcalde to a higher court, should you wish to do so. In the mean time, the governor is unwilling to interefere in matters of litigation, especially where trial has been had by a jury.

Very respectfully, your obedient servant,
H. W. HALLECK,
Lieutenant of Engineers, and Secretary of State.

Henry Harris,
  San Francisco, California.

State Department of the Territory of California,
Monterey, September 26, 1848.

Sir: In reply to your letter of the 20th, I have to inform you that the governor is of the same opinion with yourself—that the iron bottles imported in the "Cayuga," if taken from the warehouse and used in the country, cannot be considered as entitled to drawback.

It is not the intention to erect at the present time any new storehouses, and goods cannot be warehoused beyond the amount of accommodation afforded by the public stores. It is hoped that we may receive some act of Congress on the subject in the course of a very short time. It is known that, just at the present time, the most enormous wages are demanded for clerk hire, &c.; but it is hoped, after a little time, services may be procured at more reasonable rates. In the mean time, you *must* have assistance; and the only restriction which it is intended to impose in this respect is, that you will not increase the number of your employés beyond what is absolutely necessary, and that you hire them at as cheap rates as you can.

Your own certificate, countersigned by Captain Folsom, will be deemed sufficient evidence of the necessity of the service and the propriety of the wages paid.

Very respectfully, your obedient servant,
H. W. HALLECK,
Lieutenant of Engineers, and Secretary of State.

E. H. Harrison, Esq.,
  Collector, &c., San Francisco.

State Department of the Territory of California,
Monterey, September 25, 1848.

Sir: I am directed by the governor to acknowledge the receipt of your letter of the 20th instant, asking for information relative to the registering and licensing of vessels on the coast of California.

1. The governor has determined, under existing circumstances, that he will not register any vessel, but will forward all applications for registry or re registry to the authorities at Washington; and if, in his opinion, the vessel is entitled to registry, he will grant a sea-letter or license, which will enable her to wear the American flag, and to engage in trade as an

American vessel. In order to the registry of a vessel, the owner, or one of the owners, shall take and subscribe to an oath, declaring, according to the best of his knowledge and belief, her name and burden; the time when and the place where she was built; declaring also his own name and place of abode, (or, if more than one owner, the name and abode of each;) and that he or they so swearing are citizens of the United States; and *that there is no subject of any foreign State, directly or indirectly, by way of trust, confidence, or otherwise, interested in such vessel, or in the profits thereof;* and that the master is also a citizen of the United States. If the master be within the district when the application for the registry is made, he himself must make oath to the fact of his citizenship. If the master or owner is a naturalized *citizen*, this fact, and when he became so, must be stated. None but American bottoms, or vessels adjudged to be forfeited for breach of the laws of the United States, can be registered; moreover, they must belong exclusively to citizens resident in the territory of the United States, or, if residing abroad, to a consul or other public agent, or an agent or partner in some house of trade or copartnership, consisting of citizens of, and actually carrying on trade within, the United States. If the owner be a naturalized citizen of the United States, and reside more than one year in the country from which he originated, or more than two years in any other foreign country, unless he be a consul or other public agent, he cannot register. But this last prohibition does not prevent the registering anew any vessel before registered, in case of *bona fide* sale thereof to a citizen (whether native or naturalized) resident in the United States, and exhibiting satisfactory proof of his citizenship; and if such citizen, now actually resident in the territory of the United States, can register anew a vessel purchased by him, it is inferred that he may register anew any American bottom owned by him previous to his resuming such residence.

In all applications of this kind, the facts must be clearly stated and sworn to, and the application be accompanied by the necessary proof, to enable the governor to judge of the probability of her receiving a new register, and whether, under the circumstances, a sea-letter should be granted. It may be proper to remark in this place that, in case any matter of fact alleged in the application, and sworn to, be not true, the vessel and tackle, and furniture, &c., shall be forfeited. (*Vide* Gordon, Book IX, chap. II.)

2. It appears that an unregistered vessel, which is owned exclusively by citizens of the United States, may, under certain circumstances, receive a sea-letter or other document proving her to be American property, and that, with such document, she shall be entitled to certain privileges of trade; but that, on the entry of every such vessel from every foreign place, oath shall be made that such sea-letter or document contains the name or names of all the owners of such vessel, (or, in case any part has since been sold, the fact must be stated on the oath,) *and that no foreign citizen or subject has any share, by way of trust, confidence, or otherwise, in such vessel.*

If such oath is refused, she shall not be entitled to privileges specified. (*Vide* Gordon, chap. XIII, sec. 1.) It is believed that the schooner Star comes under the provisions of this act, and that her consular license does not exempt her from duty when she enters an American port, unless the foregoing oath be given. When Louisiana and Florida became a part of the territory of the United States, provision was made by acts of Congress for the registry, enrolment, and license of vessels belonging to the inhabitants of the respective Territories, and it is presumed that a similar act has already been passed with respect to California. Again: there are sometimes special instances where vessels are in justice entitled to registry, but do not come within the requisitions of the law. In all such cases a special act of Congress is required to authorize the registry; and more or less such acts are passed at every session. But some time must elapse before the action of Congress respecting the registry of vessels belonging to the citizens of California can be known here; and, until a regular mail is established between this coast and the Atlantic States, no inconsiderable delay must be experienced in learning the result for an application for a special act of registry.

It would seem exceedingly rigorous and unjust that vessels thus situated should be shut up in port for so many months, especially when they are so much needed for carrying on the commerce of the country. The governor has accordingly decided that, where vessels are owned exclusively by citizens of California, he will, on application, accompanied by the proper proof, being made, through him, to the proper authorities in Washington, for registry, or re-registry, grant sea-letters or other documents for their protection, till such time as the result of such application can be known. In all cases, however, the vessels must exclusively be the property of citizens of the United States or of California, and now actually resident within the territory of the United States. If any citizen or subject of any foreign State, directly or indirectly, by way of trust, confidence, or otherwise, be in any way interested in such vessel, or in the profits thereof, no such sea-letter or license will be granted.

3. It may be proper to remark here, that, without a register, a vessel in foreign trade is not entitled to all the privileges and benefits of a ship of the United States; but in other respects she is recognised by law. The extent of her privileges depends upon the character of the document given, and the nature of the authority granting it.

A license to coast would not authorize a vessel to engage in foreign trade; nor a license for a foreign voyage authorize a vessel to engage in the coast trade of the United States. But, under existing circumstances, and until the action of Congress shall be known, the governor has decided to consider Upper California as a single district, and to allow all American vessels to trade from one port to another. A foreign vessel entering at one port will be allowed to discharge any portion of her cargo in another port. The coast of Upper California will, in respect to coasting and foreign trade, be regarded in the same light as the northern frontier of the United States.

The effect of a sea letter, license, or other document, in giving protection to a vessel in time of war, depends upon the competency of the authority which issues them. As a general rule, this document, in order to afford protection, must proceed from the sovereign authority of the State; but this authority, says Wheaton, "may be vested in military or naval officers, or in certain civil officers, either expressly or by inevitable implication. From the nature and extent of their general trust, such documents are to be interpreted by the same rules of liberality and good faith as other acts of the sovereign power."

It has been decided in the British courts of admirality, that an instrument granted by a consul cannot protect the property of an enemy beyond the consular district, and on the high seas. Neither does an admiral or other naval commander possess authority to give protection beyond the limit of his own station; nor can a minister resident in a foreign country give protection to the vessel of a belligerent found on the high seas. The authority to exempt the property of enemies from the effect of hostilities can only be exercised, says Wheaton, "either by those who have a special commission granted to them for the particular business, and who, in legal language, are called *mondatories*, or by persons in whom such a power is vested in virtue of any situation to which it may be considered incidental." What would be the exact extent of the protection afforded in time of war by a license or sea-letter proceeding from the existing government of California, it is not now easy to decide; but in time of peace, and to all American vessels, there can be no doubt that such document will serve as a safe conduct on the high seas, and will confer full authority to trade within the specified limitations of time, persons, and places.—(Vide Wheaton, part iv., chap. ii.)

Very respectfully, your obedient servant,
H. W. HALLECK,
Lieutenant of Engineers, and Secretary of State.
E. H. Harrison, Esq.,
Collector, San Francisco, California.

State Department Territory of California,
Monterey, September 23, 1848.

Sir: I have to acknowledge the receipt of your letter of the 2d instant, with the enclosed papers. Mr. Alexander's abstract of disbursements and vouchers for the first quarter were never received. I wrote to you on this subject, and also Mr. Alexander, on the 3d of August, but have received no answer. Your account current for that quarter proves that Mr. Alexander's accounts are correct; but as the accounts will probably be settled in different offices in Washington, it is necessary that Mr. Alexander's own papers should be accompanied by your receipts for the money he turned over to you. For neither the first nor the second quarter of this year has he forwarded such papers. Please to see Mr. A., and have the proper vouchers forwarded; for, otherwise, there may be delay and difficulty in settling his accounts in Washington.

Very respectfully, your obedient servant,
H. W. HALLECK,
Lieutenant of Engineers, and Secretary of State.
Lieut. J. W. Davidson,
U. S. Army, Los Angeles, California.

State Department of the Territory of California,
Monterey, October 4, 1848.

Sir: Messrs. E. & H. Grimes have applied for permission to remove the brig "Euphemia" from San Francisco to the embarcadero near Sutter's Fort, for the purpose of converting her into a store vessel. The governor sees no objection to this; but no vessel can be licensed to engage in the coast trade unless she be owned exclusively by American citizens, as stated in my letter of September 25.

Very respectfully, your obedient servant,
H. W. HALLECK,
Lieutenant of Engineers, and Secretary of State.

E. H. HARRISON, Esq.,
  Collector, San Francisco, California.

STATE DEPARTMENT OF THE TERRITORY OF CALIFORNIA,
Monterey, October 31, 1848.

SIR: I have the honor to acknowledge the receipt of your letter of this morning, enclosing a communication from William Anderson, of Santa Cruz, in which he refuses to answer to your summons in the case of Graham *vs.* Anderson, and denies your jurisdiction over persons in the town of Santa Cruz. You ask if an armed force cannot be employed to compel him to obey your citation.

You, as first alcalde of Monterey, have jurisdiction over the entire district, which includes the mission and town of Santa Cruz. The local alcaldes have concurrent jurisdiction among themselves, but are all subordinate to the first alcalde. There can be, therefore, no doubt that a suit can be instituted before you against any person resident within the district, and that such person is legally bound to obey your citation. This would be the case, even if there were a subordinate alcalde at the place of residence of the person so summoned; and the propriety of the rule is still more manifest in a case like the present, where there is no regularly-appointed alcalde at hand, and where the defendant in the case himself claims to be the acting magistrate.

If Mr. Anderson refuses to appear at the appointed time, I think you could with propriety proceed with the case, and give judgment according to the evidence produced.

Mr. Anderson's letter is enclosed herewith.

Very respectfully, your obedient servant,
H. W. HALLECK,
Lieutenant of Engineers, and Secretary of State.

FLORENCIO SERRANO,
  1st Alcalde, Monterey.

To all who may see these presents:

Be it known, that whereas Charles Walters, a resident of the Territory of California, owner and captain of the brigantine "El Placer," formerly the "Manuel Adolfo," which vessel was captured by the United States ship Cyane, and regularly sold at public auction at the town of La Paz, California, has this day signified, in writing, his intention to continue his residence in California as a citizen of the United States: Now, therefore, I, R. B. Mason, colonel 1st dragoons, and governor of California, in virtue of authority in me vested, do hereby grant the said brigantine "El Placer" this sea-letter, authorizing the said brigantine to wear the American flag, and to engage in all lawful trade both with foreign countries and on the coast of California.

This sea-letter shall continue in force one year from this date, or until due notice is given to the captain or owners of said vessel of the decision of the competent authorities at Washington in this case.

Said "El Placer" is brigantine-rigged, is of sixty tons burden, and copper bottom, and is commanded by Charles Walters.

Given at Monterey, California, this fifteenth day of November, A. D. eighteen hundred and forty-eight.

For R. B. MASON,
Colonel 1st Dragoons, and Governor of California.
H. W. HALLECK,
Lieutenant of Engineers, and Secretary of State.

HEADQUARTERS TENTH MILITARY DEPARTMENT,
Monterey, October 5, 1848.

SIR: I have to acknowledge the receipt of your letter of the 25th ultimo, informing me that you had granted letters of administration to J. S. Ruckel, of San Francisco, on the estate of the late Thomas J. Farnham. Whether the deceased had made San Francisco his place of residence or not, the fact that he did during his last illness, and but a short time before his death, request J. S. Ruckel to administer upon his estate, as is proven by the affidavit of one of his attendants during his illness, is deemed all-sufficient to put the matter at rest, and Mr. Ruckel is fully authorized, as the legal administrator, to take charge of the estate and manage the same, where any part of the same may be found in Upper California—he first giving the proper bonds in your office for the faithful administration of the same.

Full inventories of every species of property belonging to the said estate must be required to be promptly furnished for file in your office.

I am, &c.,
R. B. MASON,
Colonel 1st Dragoons, Governor of California.
T. M. LEAVENWORTH,
or First Alcalde, San Francisco.

HEADQUARTERS TENTH MILITARY DEPARTMENT,
Camp on the San Joaquin river, October 11, 1848.

License is hereby given to Jacob Bonsell, a citizen of the State of Pennsylvania, at present residing in California, to keep a ferry on the San Joaquin river, where the main road at this time crosses said river, leading from Livermore's ranch to Sutter's Fort; this license to continue in force until further orders.

R. B. MASON,
Colonel 1st Dragoons, Governor of California.

HEADQUARTERS TENTH MILITARY DEPARTMENT,
New Helvetia, October 24, 1848.

SIR: Your communication of the 18th has been duly received; but the one of the 2d ultimo, therein mentioned, has never come to hand. I had prepared a code of laws, and a judicial organization; and, although they were sent to the press in due season, I did not succeed in getting them printed before I received official notification of the ratification of the treaty of peace between the two republics, owing to the stopping of the presses upon the discovery of the gold mines, &c.

As I am very certain that Congress has already organized a territorial government for California, and that we shall now, in the course of a very short time, receive the official intelligence of the appointment of the civil officers, a proper organization could not be put in operation now before we receive the new government.

I am well aware of the want in California of a regular organized government, and I have every reason to believe we shall have it in the course of a very short time.

Although some murders have been committed and horses stolen in the "placer," I do not find that things are worse here, if, indeed, they are so bad, as they were in our own mineral regions some years ago, when I was stationed near them.

In the present excitement of gold digging, I find it impossible to get men to do anything else. I shall be absent from here about ten days, when I propose paying a visit to your neighborhood, when I hope to have the pleasure of seeing you.

I am, very respectfully, your obedient servant,
R. B. MASON,
Colonel 1st Dragoons, Governor of California.

L. W. HASTINGS,
Coloma, California.

HEADQUARTERS TENTH MILITARY DEPARTMENT,
New Helvetia, California, October 24, 1848.

SIR: I have offered a reward of five hundred dollars for the apprehension and delivery of Peter Raymond, charged with the murder of Von Pfister. Should he be apprehended and delivered to you, please cause him to be well and securely ironed, and give a certificate of his being delivered to you, that the person entitled to the reward may receive it from Captain Folsom, at San Francisco.

The first alcalde of the Sacramento district, so soon as the aforesaid Raymond shall be apprehended, is hereby authorized to summon a jury, and hold a special court for the trial of Raymond for the murder of said Von Pfister.

Please turn this document over to your successor in office.

I am, respectfully, your obedient servant,
R. B. MASON,
Colonel 1st Dragoons, Governor of California.

JOHN SINCLAIR,
1st Alcalde Sacramento district, California.

HEADQUARTERS TENTH MILITARY DEPARTMENT,
San Francisco, California, November 25, 1848.

SIR: I have the honor to acknowledge the receipt of your note of the 15-27th October, and beg leave to assure you that whatever is in my power with propriety to do to forward the views of Captain Harder and the Russian American Company, in relation to the business you mention, it will give me pleasure to perform.

At this time, however, there are no properly-organized courts of law in California fully competent to take cognizance of important cases, having not yet received a government and code of laws from the American Congress. This circumstance may cause some delay in bringing the affairs of your company with Mr. Sutter to a close, but I hope that difficulty will be soon removed.

I have the honor to be, with high respect, your obedient servant,
R. B. MASON,
Colonel 1st Dragoons, Governor of California.
To his Excellency M. TEBENKOFF,
Governor of the Russian American Colonies, Sitka.

HEADQUARTERS TENTH MILITARY DEPARTMENT,
Monterey, California, December 1, 1848.

SIR: The purser of your ship made a requisition on Captain Folsom for one hundred thousand dollars, which I directed Captain Folsom to comply with from the civil fund; but upon a more careful reference to the amount reported on hand, I find that all the funds in his hands, derived from the customs, up to the end of November, will probably not amount to that sum; and as it would not be well to leave myself entirely bare of the military fund at San Francisco, I have this day directed Captain Folsom to retain the amount he had on hand at the end of July, (say about thirty-six thousand dollars,) and to turn over to the purser all the remaining funds received from the customs, to include the last month. Should the purser have received from Captain Folsom all the funds in his possession derived from the customs, I must beg the favor of you to cause to be refunded to Captain Folsom the sum of about thirty-six thousand dollars.

I am, very respectfully, your obedient servant,
R. B. MASON,
Colonel 1st Dragoons, commanding.
Commodore THOS. AP C. JONES,
Commanding United States naval forces in the Pacific.

STATE DEPARTMENT OF THE TERRITORY OF CALIFORNIA,
Monterey, December 2, 1848.

SIR: I am directed by the governor to acknowledge the receipt of your letter of October 9, and to say that he fully approves of the proceedings in the election of an alcalde to supply the place of Don Juan Bandine, which election was held on the 3d of October. Don Juan Maria Marron will therefore be recognised as the 1st alcalde of the San Diego district.

The governor is of opinion that, under existing circumstances, the receipts of the custom-house at San Diego will not justify the appointment of an inspector with a fixed salary, as you propose; but should the commerce of your port become sufficient to authorize the appointment of additional officers, such appointment will then be made.
Very respectfully, &c.,
H. W. HALLECK,
Lieutenant of Engineers, and Secretary of State.
Don MIGUEL DE PEDRORENA,
Collector, &c., San Diego, Upper California.

HEADQUARTERS TENTH MILITARY DEPARTMENT,
San Francisco, California, November 25, 1848.

SIR: In reply to your letter of the 7th instant, (not yet received, but a copy of which you have just shown me,) I have to say that you were right in seizing the goods you mention. As the value of them is not great, I have no objection to their being restored to the owner, upon his paying the proper duties. He not attempting to introduce the goods into the country without the knowledge of the custom-house officer, it may be possible, though perhaps not probable, he did not premeditate a fraud; and I do not deem the amount of sufficient value to detain and bring him before a court.
I am, respectfully, your obedient servant,
R. B. MASON,
Colonel 1st Dragoons, commanding.
Captain J. L. FOLSOM,
Assistant Quartermaster, San Francisco.

STATE DEPARTMENT OF THE TERRITORY OF CALIFORNIA,
Monterey, December 5, 1848.

SIR: I am directed by Governor Mason to acknowledge the receipt of your letter of November 7, asking for instructions respecting the disposition of your custom-house accounts. By referring to my communication to you, dated September 3, 1848, you will find that it is directed that the quartermaster at San Francisco " endorse and forward your accounts to Washington *through* this office;" and, in the letter of instructions to Captain Folsom, dated August 21, it is stated " the returns and papers of the collector will be endorsed by you and forwarded to Washington *through this office.*" A copy of your bond should also have been sent here for file.
Very respectfully, your obedient servant,
H. W. HALLECK,
Lieutenant of Engineers, and Secretary of State.
E. H. HARRISON, Esq.,
Collector, San Francisco, California.

STATE DEPARTMENT OF THE TERRITORY OF CALIFORNIA,
Monterey, December 2, 1848.

SIR: I am directed by the governor to acknowledge the receipt of your letter of ―――― 2, and the enclosed paper. This answer has been delayed on account of the absence of the governor in the northern part of this Territory. The governor is fully aware of the long and valuable services which you have rendered to the United States, and of your devotion to our cause, and he hopes the time is not far distant when you will be rewarded for your services; but he regrets to say that, under present circumstances, while waiting for instructions from Washington, he has no office at his disposal. The appointment of collector of customs at San Diego was made before the receipt of your letter.

Very respectfully, your obedient servant,
H. W. HALLECK,
Lieutenant of Engineers, and Secretary of State.

Don SANTIAGO ARGUILLO,
San Diego, California.

HEADQUARTERS TENTH MILITARY DEPARTMENT,
Monterey, California, December 7, 1848.

SIR: I have the honor to acknowledge the receipt of your communication of October 25, and the documents which accompanied it, concerning the loss of your schooner "Julia" and other property, which I will forward to the United States government, with the following endorsement: "Respectfully referred to the United States government, and their most favorable consideration requested."

Very respectfully, your obedient servant,
R. B. MASON,
Colonel 1st Dragoons, commanding.

Don FRANCISCO LOPE DE URIZA,
Monterey, California.

HEADQUARTERS TENTH MILITARY DEPARTMENT,
Monterey, California, December 9, 1848.

SIR: I have this moment received your note of this date, as also the notes of to-day from Captain Burton and Lieutenant Ord, addressed to you, on the subject of the sentence passed by your court on Guild. I see no grounds on which I can interpose to save him from the sentence awarded: not one single mitigating or extenuating circumstance attending the theft with which he was charged is offered. Within a short time past, houses have been forcibly entered in this town, property taken by force in broad daylight from the owners, and the public stores pillaged; and, now that an example is about to be made of one of the many depredators, I should feel that I was encouraging such open robberies were I to interfere and shield this convicted man from the punishment awarded him.

I am, respectfully, your obedient servant,
R. B. MASON,
Colonel 1st Dragoons, Governor of California.

FLORENCIO SERRANO, *First Alcalde, Monterey.*

HEADQUARTERS TENTH MILITARY DEPARTMENT,
Monterey, California, December 17, 1848.

SIR: Your note of this day, asking to be absent for six months from your duties of sub-Indian agent, is received. The leave asked for is granted, with the understanding that Mr. William Williams will take charge of the mission of San Luis Rey, so that it will sustain no damage, and act as sub-agent for you during your absence.

I am, respectfully, your obedient servant,
R. B. MASON,
Colonel 1st Dragoons, Governor of California.

Captain J. D. HUNTER,
  Sub-Indian Agent.

STATE DEPARTMENT OF THE TERRITORY OF CALIFORNIA,
Monterey, December 18, 1848.

SIR: The governor has received and duly examined a communication of J E. Brackett, esq., attorney of defendants in the case of Elias Barnett *vs.* E. F. Bale and K. L. Kilburn, tried in the alcalde's court, district of Sonoma, on the 3d of April last, asking for a new trial or stay of the proceedings, and also the accompanying papers, intended to sustain the appeal. It appears, from the record of the court, that the case was submitted to the jury by consent of the parties, and that the verdict was returned for the plaintiff. A new trial is now asked by the defendants—1st, on the ground that "the alcalde had no jurisdiction, because the case concerned the title to land." It appears, from the record of the court, that this is not a case in any way affecting the validity of land titles, but merely the execution of a contract to give a title for certain lands; and that the verdict of the jury and action of the court had reference only to the validity and execution of the contract. 2d, " that the verdict was contrary to law;" and, 3d, "that it was contrary to evidence." The jury in this case (under the instructions of the court) were the proper judges of the law and evidence bearing upon the points at issue; and, in the absence of sufficient proof that the trial was an unfair one, or that there was any illegality in the proceedings, the governor declines interfering with the decision of the jury or the action of the court.

By direction of the governor:
H. W. HALLECK,
Lieutenant of Engineers, and Secretary of State.

A. HŒPPENER,
  Second Alcalde, District of Sonoma.

HEADQUARTERS TENTH MILITARY DEPARTMENT,
Monterey, December 18, 1848.

SIR: 1 have to acknowledge the receipt of your letter of August 2, and accompanying papers, relating to your claim for damages, house rent, &c., in San José, Lower California, occupied for a time by the United States forces. These papers were referred to Captain Burton, late lieutenant colonel, and commanding in that country, for his report on the case; and as I do not consider myself authorized to decide upon your claim, I have delivered this day to Mr. T. H. Green, your agent, at his request, both the papers and the report of Colonel Burton.

Very respectfully, your obedient servant,
R. B. MASON,
Colonel 1st Dragoons.

J. T. MOTT, *Mazatlan, Mexico.*

STATE DEPARTMENT OF THE TERRITORY OF CALIFORNIA,
Monterey, December 19, 1848.

SIR: I am directed by the governor to acknowledge the receipt of your letter of the 30th ultimo, giving information of reported Indian depredations near Clear Lake, some 60 miles from Sonoma, and asking what measures it is your duty as sub-Indian agent to take in such cases.

As there are frequent rumors of this kind, which, upon investigation, turn out to be untrue, or at least generally exaggerated, it is made one of the principal duties of the Indian agency to ascertain the real facts in such cases, and to communicate them to the superior authorities for their information and guidance.

The present reduced state of the garrisons in the northern part of this Territory renders it impossible for the governor to send out detachments of troops into the Indian country; and if the Indians commit depredations upon the frontier ranchos, the people should arm themselves and punish the depredators. In such cases the sub-Indian agent should see that no unjust punishments are inflicted, and that pretended robberies be not made a pretext for maltreating and murdering the natives.

The governor hopes that ere long the military force in this country will be increased sufficiently to enable him to afford greater security to the rancheros on the extreme frontiers.

Very respectfully, your obedient servant,
H. W. HALLECK,
Lieutenant of Engineers, and Secretary of State.

Gen. M. G. VALLEJO, *Sub-Indian Agent.*

HEADQUARTERS TENTH MILITARY DEPARTMENT,
Monterey, December 28, 1848.

SIR: I enclose herewith a copy of a letter from the governor of Oregon, acknowledging the receipt of the ordnance stores sent from this place, and giving information of the state of Indian affairs; also, copies of petitions of the owners of the barque "Joven Guipuzcouna" and the brigantine "El Placer" for registry and sea-letters.

In the absence of the commander-in-chief of the Pacific squadron, I have issued sea-letters to the aforementioned vessels, to continue in force one year from their date, or until due notice is given to the captains or owners of the decision of the competent authorities at Washington in these cases. If Congress has not already acted on this subject, it is highly important that a law be immediately passed to authorize the registry and license of vessels similarly situated.

In my letter of the 19th of August last, I informed the department that it would be necessary, in the reduced state of the military forces in California, to employ civilians to take charge of the custom-houses; it, however, has been found so difficult to procure suitable persons to perform these duties for anything like reasonable salaries, that I have been obliged in some instances to continue the collection of the revenue by military officers, and I doubt whether for some time to come suitable collectors of customs can be procured on this coast for anything like the salaries and fees now authorized by law.

I have the honor to be your obedient servant,
R. B. MASON,
Colonel 1st Dragoons.

Brigadier General R. JONES,
Adjutant General of the Army, Washington, D. C.

STATE DEPARTMENT OF THE TERRITORY OF CALIFORNIA,
Monterey, December 20, 1848.

SIR: Mr. Alexander, the collector at San Pedro, has given notice that the impossibility of procuring the necessaries of life in San Pedro will render it necessary for him to remove to Los Angeles, and that he therefore wishes to be relieved from the duties connected with the custom-house.

It is hoped that an arrangement may be made with Mr. Alexander, by permitting him to reside in Los Angeles during the winter, and to visit San Pedro whenever a vessel arrives in port, to secure the continuance of his services—he having always performed his duties to the entire satisfaction of the government. But if no such arrangement can be made, the commanding officer at Los Angeles will appoint some suitable person to take his place; and in case no such person can be found, the governor directs that some officer will be temporarily detailed to collect the revenue on vessels arriving at that port.

If Mr. Alexander has not occupied a public building as his office, he will be entitled to reasonable office rent, which will be paid to him by the quartermaster of the port out of the civil funds.

Very respectfully, your obedient servant,
H. W. HALLECK,
Lieutenant of Engineers, and Secretary of State.
COMMANDING OFFICER, *Los Angeles.*

HEADQUARTERS TENTH MILITARY DEPARTMENT,
Monterey, California, December 23, 1848.

SIR: I have the honor to acknowledge the receipt of your note of this date, and will, as you request, give to the authorities at Yerba Buena

(San Francisco) the information of Mr. Jourdain's having been appointed by you consular agent of the French republic at that place.

I have the honor to be, sir, with high respect, &c.,
R. B. MASON,
Colonel 1st Dragoons, commanding.

J. S. MOERENHOUT,
Consul of the French Republic, Monterey.

STATE DEPARTMENT OF THE TERRITORY OF CALIFORNIA,
Monterey, December 28, 1848.

SIR: I have to acknowledge the receipt of your letter of the 18th instant, asking for information as to your responsibility in examining the accounts of the collector of San Francisco.

Previous to the enforcement of the "military contribution tariff," and when civilians performed the duties of collectors in California, it was deemed necessary that some military officer, at each post, should have a general supervision of accounts of the collector, in order to check any extravagant expenditures or improper use of the public money; and on returning to this system of collecting the revenue, at the close of the war, the governor deemed it necessary to establish the same check as before, and your relations towards the new collector became the same as they had been towards Mr. Richardson.

The great length of time required in communicating with Washington renders it absolutely necessary that some one here should supervise the accounts of the collector, and immediately report anything that he may think improper or incorrect. The extent of this examination must depend on the circumstances of the case, and should, in all cases, be sufficient to satisfy the officer of the correctness of the collector's accounts, for otherwise he cannot endorse them with his approval. From your position in San Francisco, it is presumed that you will be able to judge whether the expenditures of the collector for clerk hire, &c., are *just and necessary;* if so, you will approve the accounts, and if not, you will forward them, with your reasons for not approving them.

The nature and extent of your duties were pointed out in my letters of August 21 and September 3. In the latter it is stated that you will allow all necessary and proper expenses connected with the collector's office, and that, in requiring your endorsement and approval of the expenditures of the collector, it was intended merely to keep those expenditures within proper limits.

Very respectfully, your obedient servant,
H. W. HALLECK,
Lieut. of Engineers, and Secretary of State.

Captain J. L. FOLSOM,
United States Army, San Francisco.

STATE DEPARTMENT OF THE TERRITORY OF CALIFORNIA,
Monterey, December 28, 1848.

SIR: Colonel Mason directs me to acknowledge the receipt of your letter of December, and to say that, if it should be determined to appoint a collector for Santa Barbara, your name will be considered in connexion with the office.

In the mean time, I am instructed to call your attention to some irregularities in your custom-house papers.

You would have been written to on this subject before, had your address been known at this office.

In your account current for the second quarter of 1848, you credit yourself with $900 transferred to quartermaster's department, April 20; also, same date, $300 transferred to subsistence department; but no receipts from those departments, as vouchers, have been received. Your civil accounts for that quarter are therefore deficient $1,200.

Again, in your account current for the third quarter of 1848, you credit yourself with $282 34, as cash paid on account of trial of Foxon, and with $1,361 53½, as cash turned over to quartermaster's department; but for neither of these sums have you forwarded any vouchers, and your civil account for that quarter are therefore deficient $1,643 87½.

The governor does not doubt but that you have paid out and turned over the money precisely as stated in your accounts current; but it is necessary that you should furnish *proof* of this to the auditing officer, and the only proper proof is the receipt of the persons to whom the money has been paid, or of the officers to whom it was transferred.

If any of this money was transferred to yourself as acting assistant quartermaster, or commissary, you should have made out the receipt to yourself as collector, and have signed them in precisely the same manner as if the money had been received from any other person. In no other way can your accounts be properly settled in Washington.

Very respectfully, your obedient servant,
H. W. HALLECK,
Lieut. of Engineers, and Secretary of State.
Lieut. HENRY S. CARNES, *Santa Barbara.*

STATE DEPARTMENT OF THE TERRITORY OF CALIFORNIA,
Monterey, December 28, 1848.

SIR: I am directed by Colonel Mason to call your attention to the fact that your custom-house accounts are deficient in a voucher for $143 70, collected in the month of July last. This amount is taken up on Lieutenant Carnes's accounts, which show that the money was turned over to him; but you should forward, as *proof* of this, his receipt for that sum, as otherwise there will be a difficulty in auditing your accounts in Washington. Every payment or transfer of public money should be accompanied with the proper voucher. If you will forward the receipt for that sum, it will be sent to Washington, with your accounts for last quarter, by the first safe conveyance that occurs.

Very respectfully, your obedient servant,
H. W. HALLECK,
Lieut. of Engineers, and Secretary of State.
Captain F. J. LIPPETT, *San Francisco.*

HEADQUARTERS TENTH MILITARY DEPARTMENT,
Monterey, California, January 1, 1849.

SIR: I have the honor to acknowledge, late last night, the receipt of your letter of the 27th of December, together with its enclosures.

I herewith return you a duplicate of the paper marked "A," as you requested, signed by myself, having also signed the one you sent me, and placed it on file here.

I fully agree with you in "doubting the expediency of enforcing any more stringent revenue rules and regulations than the several acts of Congress provide for;" and that it is "not advisable to enforce with much rigor the provision of the laws of the United States, as expressed in the articles 4, 7, and 8 of the series of regulations proposed by Mr. Harrison." Indeed, I think, under the peculiar position of things in California, that the revenue officers should be as indulgent as possible, and as liberal in the construction and application of the revenue laws as the nature of each case, as it may arise, will permit; for, in the absence of the proper courts, it will be difficult to enforce many of the provisions, and, until we hear from the department at Washington on the subject of the collection of customs in California, the best policy is not a too stringent application of those laws and regulations, especially in matters not touching frauds upon the revenue.

Upon another perusal of your letter and accompanying papers, after writing the foregoing, it occurs to me that it would not be proper to say anything about foreign vessels entering the ports of Oregon. That country has now a regularly-organized territorial government, and we can no more say what vessels shall enter those ports upon the footing of coasters than we can say relative to the port of New York. The constituted authorities there may possibly choose to differ with us; at all events, leave them to settle that matter themselves. I would therefore suggest that in the "*form* of the special license proposed to be issued, for a limited period," the words "within the territorial limits of the United States on the Pacific coast" be stricken out, and the words "of Upper California" be inserted.

This will not prevent foreign vessels from going into the Oregon ports, if the authorities there choose to admit them; and if they exclude them, (which is by no means anticipated before the regular establishment of custom-house and revenue offices,) no license granted by any of the United States authorities here will be of any service to them.

I am, sir, very respectfully, your obedient servant,

R. B. MASON,
Colonel 1st Dragoons, commanding.

Commodore THOS. AP. C. JONES,
Commanding U. S. naval forces in the
Pacific ocean, San Francisco.

STATE DEPARTMENT OF THE TERRITORY OF CALIFORNIA,
Monterey, January 2, 1849.

SIR: I have to acknowledge the receipt of your letter of December 28, 1848, relating to compensation as collector, the proceeds of confiscated goods, and the sale of certain goods seized for false entry.

With respect to pay for service as collector, Colonel Mason thinks that the officers who have been thus employed should in justice be paid for such services; but he thinks it manifestly improper to introduce any such charge in the accounts, with the latter part of article 19 of the printed instructions from Washington, and the act of Congress approved August 22, 1842, (page 274 Military Laws,) before them. He thinks the proper course would be to make the claim direct to the Secretary of War.

With respect to the proceeds of confiscated goods, I am directed to refer you to Colonel Mason's letter of March 23, 1848.

Under the circumstances you mention, the governor agrees with you that it will be best to sell the goods seized from Signor Bonjiovanni.

Very respectfully, your obedient servant,
H. W. HALLECK,
Lieutenant of Engineers, and Secretary of State.
Captain J. L. FOLSOM,
U. S. Army, San Francisco, California.

STATE DEPARTMENT OF THE TERRITORY OF CALIFORNIA,
Monterey, January 2, 1849.

SIR: I am directed by Governor Mason to acknowledge the receipt of your letter of November 15, 1848, giving notice of the appointment of George Frail Allen, esq., as his Hawaiian Majesty's consul for the ports of California, and to inform you that he will be recognised in that capacity until he obtain the necessary *exequatur* from the proper authorities at Washington.

I have the honor to be your obedient servant,
H. W. HALLECK,
Lieutenant of Engineers, and Secretary of State.
Hon. R. C. WYLLIE,
Minister, &c., &c., Honolulu.

STATE DEPARTMENT OF THE TERRITORY OF CALIFORNIA,
Monterey, January 2, 1849.

SIR: I have to acknowledge the receipt of your letter of December 21, relating to the appointment of post physician for the port of San Francisco.

By referring to Colonel Mason's letter to the town council of San Francisco, dated September 16, 1848, you will perceive that that body is authorized to appoint all police officers, regulate their pay, &c., and that the jurisdiction of such officers extends to all the shipping in the harbor.

The question of appointing a post physician rests entirely with the local authorities of that place.

Very respectfully, your obedient servant,
H. W. HALLECK,
Lieutenant of Engineers, and Secretary of State.
Dr. ALEX. PERRY,
U. S. Army, San Francisco, California.

HEADQUARTERS TENTH MILITARY DEPARTMENT,
Monterey, California, January 16, 1849.

SIR: Your letter of the 5th instant was received last night, enclosing Mr. Shillaber's letter of advice and draft for $5,000 on Mr. Gleason, which

Mr. S. is under the impression is in the hands of the quartermaster of this place.

I have this morning shown your communication and the letter of advice and draft to Captain Marcy, who states he knows nothing of the matter, having never heard of it before. I return you the above-mentioned papers addressed to Mr. Gleason, who left here for San Francisco some days since.

I have received a letter from Mr. Harrison, in which he says, in consequence of the dilapidated state of the building, the room that he now occupies (for a custom-house) is in part inundated with water and rendered unfit for the purpose for which it is intended, &c.

I desire you will have the room properly repaired, it being a public building, and to pay for the same out of the custom-house funds.

I am, respectfully, your obedient servant,
R. B. MASON,
Colonel 1st Dragoons, commanding.

Captain J. L. FOLSOM,
Assistant Quartermaster, San Francisco.

HEADQUARTERS TENTH MILITARY DEPARTMENT,
Monterey, California, January 16, 1849.

SIR: I am in the receipt of your letter of the 9th instant, and have this day instructed Captain Folsom to have the custom-house office repaired. Daily expecting instructions from Washington on the subject of the collection of customs, &c., I do not think it prudent at this time to rent a building, or incur any expense in that branch of the public service that can possibly be avoided.

I desire that you will send to me monthly a statement of revenue collected, made out and filled up after the form enclosed, which is the one that has heretofore been used. Send monthly statements for the back months since you have been in office.

I am, respectfully, your obedient servant,
R. B. MASON,
Colonel 1st Dragoons, commanding.

Mr. E. HARRISON,
Collector, San Francisco.

STATE DEPARTMENT OF THE TERRITORY OF CALIFORNIA,
Monterey, January 17, 1849.

SIR: I have to acknowledge the receipt of your letter of the 1st instant, relating to your duties in examining and endorsing the papers of the collector of San Francisco.

In the letter of the 28th ultimo from this office, it was stated that your relations towards the new collector were the same as they had been towards Mr. Richardson, and that, if you should not be satisfied with the correctness of his accounts and the justness of his expenditures, you would report the fact to this office.

The same duties as those required of you have been performed by Lieutenant Davidson for the ports of San Diego and San Pedro, during the most part of the last two years, and are now performed by Colonel Mason for the collector of this place; and as you have already had several months' experience in examining the accounts of the former collector, it is thought that you may be able to continue the performance of these duties without any very serious inconvenience to yourself, until some other system can be put into operation. And Colonel Mason now directs me to say that he cannot excuse you from these duties, as he knows, from a year's experience in collecting the customs here, that the duties required of you can be performed, when the collector presents his accounts made up for transmission, in any one fore or after noon, and that they involve no keeping of accounts on your part correlative with those of the collector himself. Colonel Mason deems the instructions which have already been sent to you on this subject as sufficiently clear and explicit.

Very respectfully, your obedient servant,
H. W. HALLECK,
Lieutenant of Engineers, and Secretary of State.

Captain J. L. FOLSOM,
U. S. Army, San Francisco, California.

STATE DEPARTMENT OF THE TERRITORY OF CALIFORNIA,
Monterey, January 21, 1849.

GENTLEMEN: The governor has just received the petition of the inhabitants of San Juan Bautista, giving notice of the depredations by the Indians upon the ranchos in that vicinity, and asking that powder and lead may be furnished them for the defence of their lives and property against these depredators, there being no military munitions in the country for sale. They also ask for the election of a local alcalde for the town of San Juan Bautista.

The governor therefore requests that you, gentlemen, will give due notice and act as inspectors for such election, and he will issue to the person whom you may select as your alcalde a quantity of powder and lead sufficient for the protection of the people of San Juan and its vicinity, until such stores can be purchased in the country.

It will be remembered that all the subordinate alcaldes of the district have concurrent jurisdiction among themselves, and are subject to the decisions of the first alcalde of Monterey.

The governor regrets that he has not at present a disposable military force to send in pursuit of the Indians; but he hopes that in a short time the force in this country may be sufficient to prevent any renewal of these depredations.

Very respectfully, your obedient servant,
H. W. HALLECK,
Lieutenant of Engineers, and Secretary of State.

Messrs ANGEL LEBRIJA,
MANUEL LARIOS,
JON. VARQUER,
San Juan Bautista.

STATE DEPARTMENT OF THE TERRITORY OF CALIFORNIA,
Monterey, January 22, 1849.

GENTLEMEN: Representations having been made to the governor that the offices of first and second alcaldes of the district of Santa Barbara are vacant, he requests that you will give due notice for an election of alcaldes and such other local or municipal officers as may be wanting in the district, and that you will act as judges and inspectors of such election.

Very respectfully, your obedient servant,
H. W. HALLECK,
Lieutenant of Engineers, and Secretary of State.

Messrs. Don CARLOS CARRILLO,
Don PABLO NOVIEGA,
HENRY S. CARNES,
Santa Barbara, California.

STATE DEPARTMENT OF THE TERRITORY OF CALIFORNIA,
Monterey, California, January 22, 1849.

SIR: I am directed by Colonel Mason to acknowledge the receipt of your letter of 1st instant informing him that the attempt to hold an election in Los Angeles for alcalde had entirely failed, the people having declined to vote, and that in consequence you have continued to act in that capacity. Your resignation was never formally accepted, it being expected that you would continue to act until your successor was elected. You are therefore entitled to the same pay as before; for as no successor has been elected to supply your place, your relations to the government will continue the same, so long as you perform the same duties; and the governor hopes that under the peculiar circumstances you will be induced to continue to act as the first magistrate of your district.

Very respectfully, your obedient servant,
H. W. HALLECK,
Lieutenant of Engineers, and Secretary of State.

S. C. FOSTER,
First Alcalde, Los Angeles, California.

STATE DEPARTMENT OF THE TERRITORY OF CALIFORNIA,
Monterey, January 22, 1849.

SIR: I have the honor to enclose herewith a letter for the first alcalde of your district, S. J. Foster, esq.; and I am directed by Colonel Mason to say, that the quartermaster is authorized to pay him, out of the civil funds in his hands, as government interpreter, the same salary as heretofore; the payment to begin at the time at which his salary ceased, under the supposition that his resignation had taken effect, and it will continue so long as he acts as interpreter and alcalde.

Very respectfully, your obedient servant,
H. W. HALLECK,
Lieutenant of Engineers, and Secretary of State.

Major L. P. GRAHAM,
commanding, &c., Los Angeles, California.

HEADQUARTERS TENTH MILITARY DEPARTMENT,
Monterey, California, January 23, 1849.

SIR: I have the honor to acknowledge the receipt of the certificate of election for first and second alcaldes of the "pueblo de San José," dated December 12, 1848; also, a report of the trial of Freer, Campbell, and Davis, for highway robbery, &c.; also, your letter (without date) giving notice of the execution of these prisoners; and also, a bill of costs for jurors in the aforementioned trial; all of which papers have been put on file here.

With respect to the payment of costs of the jurors, &c., it is not within the scope of my powers or authority to order the disbursement of the public moneys in paying the costs of trials not strictly legal. I know, in this case, that necessity and circumstances, and the violent outrages of late so frequently committed upon society, compelled the good citizens of the pueblo to rise and promptly make a public example of those robbers, for the sake of their own safety and that of society in general. The country affording no means—jails or prisons—by which the persons of these lawless men could have been secured and society protected, it is not much to be wondered that, after the many atrocities so recently committed upon unoffending citizens, the strict bounds of legal proceedings should have been a little overstepped.

I am, very respectfully, your obedient servant,
R. B. MASON,
Colonel 1st Dragoons, Governor of California.
Captain K. H. DIMMICK,
First Alcalde, Dist. Pueblo de San José.

HEADQUARTERS TENTH MILITARY DEPARTMENT,
Monterey, California, January 24, 1849.

SIR: I am in the receipt of your letter of the 31st December. Great credit is due to yourself and the citizens of Santa Barbara for promptness, and energy, and perseverance in pursuing and apprehending that band of outlaws who have been committing such horrid acts of barbarity through the country—murders of men, women, and children—no less than twelve in the short space of a week or two.

I am of the opinion that a very proper disposition has been made of the money, &c., found in their possession; and that it would be equally proper to pay, from the balance in your hands, for the loss and damage of the private arms that were broken or destroyed in the fight which resulted in their capture. I would most cheerfully apply a portion of the public funds at my disposal to the relief of the wife and children of Señor Rodriguez, who was killed in apprehending those men; but such an application is beyond the reach of my power and authority.

I am, respectfully, your obedient servant,
R. B. MASON,
Colonel 1st Dragoons, Governor of California.
Don CESAREO LATAILLADE,
Santa Barbara, California.

STATE DEPARTMENT OF THE TERRITORY OF CALIFORNIA,
Monterey, February 3, 1849.

SIR: I have to acknowledge the receipt of your letter of the 22d ultimo, asking permission to purchase chain and anchors for buoying out certain rocks in the bay of San Francisco. Colonel Mason approves of these purchases, and authorizes you to pay the expenses from the civil funds in your hands.

Your letter of the 23d ultimo, transmitting custom-house and military contribution accounts for the 3d quarter of 1848, has been received. In reference to the change which you advise in the management of the custom-house affairs, Colonel Mason directs me to say that he is daily expecting instructions from Washington on this subject, and that until he receives such instructions he cannot undertake to make any change.

Colonel Mason directs that you turn over from the civil funds $50,000 to the quartermaster's department and $20,000 to the subsistence department, taking the proper receipt for the same.

Very respectfully, your obedient servant,
H. W. HALLECK,
Lieutenant of Engineers, and Secretary of State.
Captain J. L. FOLSOM,
San Francisco, California.

STATE DEPARTMENT OF THE TERRITORY OF CALIFORNIA,
Monterey February 6, 1849.

SIR: I enclose you herewith a copy of a letter of January 21, in which the governor authorizes the inhabitants of the mission or town of San Juan Bautista to hold an election for a local alcalde to reside in that place. This election of a civil magistrate is not to interfere in any way with your jurisdiction; you will still continue as one of the alcaldes of the district, with the same powers and faculties as heretofore.

Very respectfully, your obedient servant,
H. W. HALLECK,
Lieutenant of Engineers, and Secretary of State.
Sor. D. JOSE MARIA SANCHEZ,
Alcalde, San Juan Bautista, California.

STATE DEPARTMENT OF THE TERRITORY OF CALIFORNIA,
Monterey, February 6, 1849.

SIR: Your letter of the 1st instant, transmitting the register of the brig Eveline, has been received. The register and letter will be forwarded to Washington, as addressed. The commanding officer of the Pacific squadron, when present, properly has charge of all matters afloat, such as granting sea-letters, &c., and this matter ought to have been referred to Commodore Jones; but to save the trouble of sending the vessel again to San Francisco, and as the case is a clear one, the proper document will be issued at this place.

Very respectfully, your obedient servant,
H. W. HALLECK,
Lieutenant of Engineers, and Secretary of State.
E. H. HARRISON, *Collector, &c., San Francisco.*

STATE DEPARTMENT OF THE TERRITORY OF CALIFORNIA,
Monterey, February 7, 1849.

SIR: Colonel Mason directs that you report to this office—

1st. The whole amount of civil funds received from customs between the 1st of June, 1847, and December 31, 1848.

2d. The whole amount expended (excepting amount turned over to quartermaster and commissary's department) for the same period.

3d. The amount of civil funds on hand December 31, 1848.

Very respectfully, your obedient servant,
H. W. HALLECK,
Lieutenant of Engineers, and Secretary of State.

To Captain J. L. FOLSOM,
Captain W. G. MARCY,
Lieutenant J. W. DAVIDSON.

To all whom it may concern:

Whereas Thomas O. Larkin and Jacob Leese, citizens of the United States resident in California, sole owners of the American built vessel "Eveline," of Boston, whereof John B. B. Cooper is at present master, and is a citizen of the United States, have this day made oath to these facts, and that no foreign citizen or subject has any share by way of trust, confidence, or otherwise, in said vessel:

Therefore, this said vessel "Eveline" is hereby authorized to wear the American flag, and to enjoy all the privileges and immunities pertaining thereto, both with respect to coast trade and foreign commerce.

The said vessel is a brig, has a square stern, no galleries, and a billet-head; has one deck and two masts; and that her length is eighty-six feet two inches, her breadth twenty-three feet nine and three-quarter inches; and that she measures one hundred and ninety-six and twenty-nine ninety-fifths tons.

This sea-letter or license shall be good for one year from this date, or until the decision of the proper authorities, on her application for a new register, shall be made known to the owner or master of said vessel.

Given under my hand and seal at the port of Monterey, this —— day of February, 1849.

HENRY S. BURTON, *Collector.*

R. B. MASON,
Governor of California.

HEADQUARTERS TENTH MILITARY DEPARTMENT,
Monterey, California, February 20, 1849.

CAPTAIN: I have just received from the alcalde of this district a communication of to-day's date, of which the enclosed is a translation.

You will furnish him the armed force he asks, for the security of the prisoner, as long as he desires it. You will judge whether it will be most convenient for you to guard the prisoner where he is at present, or to take him to your own guard-house. The guard is furnished solely for the safe-keeping of the prisoner, and is to take no part in carrying the sentence into execution—that belongs entirely to the civil authorities.

I am, respectfully, your obedient servant,
R. B. MASON,
Colonel First Dragoons, commanding.

Captain H. S. BURTON,
Third Artillery, commanding, Monterey, California.

STATE DEPARTMENT OF THE TERRITORY OF CALIFORNIA,
Monterey, California, February 26, 1849.

SIR: I have the honor to acknowledge the receipt of your communication of the 14th instant, and the enclosed statement of civil funds.

Colonel Mason authorizes the proposed transfer of $10,000 to the purser of the Dale, and also the payment of ten dollars to Mr. Toler for the translation of official papers. If you deem it necessary for the use of your office, no objection is made to your subscribing to the "Alta California;" but Colonel Mason has great doubts of the account being passed in Washington.

Very respectfully, your obedient servant,
H. W. HALLECK,
Brevet Captain, and Secretary of State.

Captain J. L. FOLSOM,
United States Army, San Francisco, California.

HEADQUARTERS TENTH MILITARY DEPARTMENT,
Monterey, California, February 21, 1849.

SIR: I have the honor to request that you will deliver to the officer who hands you this note, all official records and papers now in your possession belonging to the archives of the government of California.

Very respectfully, your obedient servant,
R. B. MASON,
Colonel First Dragoons, commanding.

Señor DON PIO PICO,
Los Angeles, California.

STATE DEPARTMENT OF THE TERRITORY OF CALIFORNIA,
Monterey, California, February 24, 1849.

SIR: I am directed by Governor Mason to acknowledge the receipt of your letter of February 9th, and to reply as follows to the questions proposed by you in relation to the collection of customs:

In the instructions just received from Washington, it is assumed that, by the treaty of peace with Mexico, California has become a part of the Union; that the constitution of the United States is extended over this Territory, and is in full force throughout its limits.

The position of California, in her commercial relations, both with respect to foreign countries and to other parts of the Union, is, therefore, the same as that of any other portion of the territory of the United States. There, however, being as yet no collection districts established by Congress in California, no foreign dutiable goods can be introduced here. Vessels having on board dutiable goods which they wish to land in California, must enter them in some regular port of entry of the United States, and there pay the duties prescribed by law. Any such vessels presenting themselves in a port of California, without having so entered their dutiable goods, ought properly to be warned away and refused admission; and when the goods are entered at a regular custom-house, they can be brought here only in American bottoms. Such is the course required by a strict interpretation of the law; but, as this would subject such vessels to great inconvenience and expense, the authorities having charge of this matter have resolved to present to them the following alternative: *To pay here all duties and fees, and to execute all papers prescribed by the revenue laws of the United States;* and, upon their doing so, their goods will be admitted. But, without the execution of such papers, and the payment of such duties and fees, they cannot be allowed to enter or to land their cargoes; and any attempt to import into this Territory foreign dutiable goods, without the payment of duties, will subject them to all penalties of the law—both vessels and goods will be seized and sent for adjudication in the United States court established in Oregon.

This view of the subject presents a ready reply to the questions proposed in your letter. No vessel can demand as a right to enter any foreign dutiable goods here, and you will not be liable to prosecution for refusing such entry; and by a voluntary payment of her duties here, in preference to going to a regularly established port of entry, such vessel binds herself to abide by the revenue laws of the United States, in the absence of all instructions to the contrary.

Your books and papers should be kept, so far as possible, in accordance with the regulation of the Treasury Department of the United States, transmitting your accounts to this office in the manner already directed.

Very respectfully, your obedient servant,
H. W. HALLECK,
Brevet Captain, and Secretary of State.

E. H. HARRISON, Esq.,
Collector, San Francisco.

STATE DEPARTMENT OF THE TERRITORY OF CALIFORNIA,
Monterey, February 21, 1849.

SIR: Colonel Mason directs that you will have the enclosed note delivered to Don Pio Pico by an officer who will receive and receipt for any official papers that may be turned over to him. A written answer to that note will re required of Señor Pico.

You will also please to call upon the person (believed to be M. Temple) who claims to own the island of Alcatraces, in the bay of San Francisco, and request a copy of his title. I enclose you a copy of a confidential letter to Colonel Stevenson, dated July 26, 1848. Colonel Mason wishes

you to forward any information which you may obtain on the subjects mentioned in these letters.
Very respectfully, your obedient servant,
H. W. HALLECK,
Lieutenant of Engineers, and Secretary of State.
Major L. P. GRAHAM,
Commanding, &c., Los Angeles.

HEADQUARTERS TENTH MILITARY DEPARTMENT,
Monterey, California, February 26, 1849.

COMMODORE: General P. F. Smith, United States army, arrived here on the 23d instant with important instructions from Washington. The substance of these instructions, as far as they relate to the collection of revenue, is embodied in the enclosed letter, copies of which will be immediately sent to the collectors of the different ports of California. It is reported here that several vessels have just arrived in San Francisco with dutiable goods on board, which they intend to land without the payment of duties. If they attempt this, I request that the naval forces at San Francisco may seize both goods and vessels, and send them to Oregon for adjudication. A judge of admiralty is now aboard the steamer California, and will go immediately to his district in that Territory.

General Smith will go to San Francisco in the steamer, where he will inform you more fully of the character of the orders received here by the recent mail.

I am, sir, very respectfully, your obedient servant,
R. B. MASON,
Colonel 1st Dragoons, commanding.
Commodore THOS. AP C. JONES,
*Commanding United States naval forces
in the Pacific ocean, San Francisco.*

STATE DEPARTMENT OF THE TERRITORY OF CALIFORNIA,
Monterey, February 28, 1849.

SIR: On examination of your accounts for the 3d quarter of 1848, they are not found to contain any receipt from Captain Folsom for the $21,942 97 turned over to him during that quarter. Will you please to forward the receipts, so that they may be sent to Washington with the account.

Very respectfully, your obedient servant,
H. W. HALLECK,
Brevet Captain, and Secretary of State.
E. H. HARRISON, Esq.,
Collector, San Francisco, California.

STATE DEPARTMENT OF THE TERRITORY OF CALIFORNIA,
Monterey, March 2, 1849.

SIR: I have to acknowledge the receipt of your letter of the 31st of December, enclosing your custom-house accounts for the 4th quarter

of 1848. I find, upon examination, that the amount charged for your salary from August 7 to December 31 is $427 33; whereas you should have charged for 25 days in the month of August, $68 49, and for the last 4 months of 1848, $333 33—making a total of $401 82. You will, therefore, deduct from your salary for this quarter $25 51, which was overcharged in your accounts for the last quarter.
 Very respectfully, your obedient servant,
         H. W. HALLECK,
       Brevet Captain, and Secretary of State.
Don Miguel DE PEDRORENA,
 Collector, San Diego, California.

   STATE DEPARTMENT OF THE TERRITORY OF CALIFORNIA,
        Monterey, March 2, 1849.

 SIR: Governor Mason directs that, on the arrival of United States troops at the mission of San Luis Rey, the sub-Indian agent at that place will turn over to the commanding officer all public property and official papers in his possession. His pay will cease on the day of his being relieved from the duties of his office by the arrival of the troops.
 Very respectfully, &c., your obedient servant,
         H. W. HALLECK,
       Brevet Captain, and Secretary State.
Captain J. D. HUNTER,
 Sub-Indian Agent, San Luis Rey, California,
  or his representative, Mr. William Williams.

   STATE DEPARTMENT OF THE TERRITORY OF CALIFORNIA,
        Monterey, March 3, 1849.

 SIR: I have to acknowledge the receipt of your letter of the 6th ultimo, with the enclosed papers. Your civil accounts for the third and fourth quarters of 1848, and for the first quarter of 1849, have been endorsed by Colonel Mason "examined and approved," and will be forwarded to Washington by the earliest opportunity.
 Your account current for the second quarter of 1848 was received in August last, but as it contained no abstract of disbursements as voucher, it has not been sent to Washington. You will please to forward them to this office by the next mail, in order that your civil accounts may be settled.
 Very respectfully, your obedient servant,
         H. W. HALLECK,
       Brevet Captain, and Secretary of State.
Lieut. J. W. DAVIDSON,
 U. S. Army, San Francisco, California.

HEADQUARTERS TENTH MILITARY DEPARTMENT,
Monterey, California, March 6, 1849.

This is to certify that Emeterio Fillamil, a native of Bolivia, under date of the 4th of March of the present year, made known to the undersigned his intention and wish to become a citizen of the United States, and to reside in California.

R. B. MASON,
Col. 1st Dragoons, Governor of California.

STATE DEPARTMENT OF THE TERRITORY OF CALIFORNIA,
Monterey, California, March 13, 1849.

SIR: I am directed by the governor to acknowledge the receipt of your letter of the 2d instant, giving official notice of an election held in San Luis Obispo on the 18th ultimo, to fill the vacancy caused by the expiration of your term of office as alcalde of that district. The governor approves of the election of Don Miguel Abila; and you will therefore, on the receipt of this, recognise him as your successor in that office.

Very respectfully, your obedient servant,

H. W. HALLECK,
Brevet Captain, and Secretary of State.

JOHN MICHAEL PRICE, Esq.,
Alcalde, San Luis Obispo, California.

HEADQUARTERS TENTH MILITARY DEPARTMENT,
Monterey, California, March 15, 1849.

This is to certify that William Jones, "by birth an Englishman," under date of the 14th of March of the present year, made known to the undersigned his intention to become an American citizen, "with a view of fixing his residence permanently in this Territory."

R. B. MASON,
Col. 1st Dragoons, Governor of California.

STATE DEPARTMENT OF THE TERRITORY OF CALIFORNIA,
Monterey, March 17, 1849.

SIR: The commanding officer of the division (General Smith) suggests that where vessels have entered and paid their duties at San Francisco, they be allowed to discharge their cargoes at such points on the bay as they may choose. As all matters concerning port regulations in California were by the President assigned to the commanding officer of the naval forces, (and it is not known that these instructions have been changed since the end of the war,) Governor Mason directs that you will consult Commodore Jones on this subject, and act in accordance with his views. It will be necessary that a custom-house officer accompany each vessel to its place of discharge, to see that the revenue laws are not infringed.

Very respectfully, your obedient servant,

H. W. HALLECK,
Brevet Captain, and Secretary of State.

E. H. HARRISON, Esq.,
Collector, San Francisco, California.

HEADQUARTERS TENTH MILITARY DEPARTMENT,
Monterey, California, March 18, 1849.

SIR: I have the honor to acknowledge the receipt of your note of the 5th of February, in reply to mine of the 24th of January, in which I could only express the opinion therein mentioned.

I can give no command relative to the money and property of the persons referred to, as it is not subject to my authority to say in what manner it should be disposed of.

I am, respectfully, your obedient servant,
R. B. MASON,
Colonel 1st Dragoons.

Señor D. C. LATAILLADE,
Santa Barbara, California.

HEADQUARTERS TENTH MILITARY DEPARTMENT,
Monterey, California, March 19, 1849.

SIR: I have the honor to acknowledge the receipt of your communication of the 14th instant. I have this day given to the alcalde of the San Francisco district instructions to take the proper steps to have your wishes carried into effect.

I am, sir, with high respect and esteem, your obedient servant,
R. B. MASON,
Col. 1st Dragoons, Governor of California.

Mr. J. S. MOERENHOUT,
Consul of France, Monterey, California.

HEADQUARTERS TENTH MILITARY DEPARTMENT,
Monterey, California, March 19, 1849.

SIR: I transmit to you herewith a translation of a communication received on the 15th instant from the French consul, Mr. Moerenhout, dated Monterey, 14th March, 1849. I desire you will take proper steps to carry into effect the wishes of the French consul, as he is the only authorized person in whose hands the papers and effects found in California belonging to deceased Frenchmen should be deposited.

I am, respectfully, your obedient servant,
R. B. MASON,
Col. 1st Dragoons, Governor of California.

M. T. LEAVENWORTH,
1st Alcalde, district of San Francisco, California.

STATE DEPARTMENT OF THE TERRITORY OF CALIFORNIA,
Monterey, March 19, 1849.

SIR: Your letter of the 7th instant is received; and Colonel Mason directs me to reply to so much of it as relates to civil matters. All your quarterly papers relating to civil funds should be forwarded to Washington through this office, where they will be examined and endorsed. The monthly statements are for information here, and do not go to Washington. The civil funds can be expended only on the orders of the governor; and the accounts are to be sent directly to this office.

Very respectfully, your obedient servant,
H. W. HALLECK,
Brevet Captain, and Secretary of State.

Captain E R. KANE,
U. S. Army, Los Angeles, California.

HEADQUARTERS TENTH MILITARY DEPARTMENT,
Monterey, California, March 24, 1849.

This is to certify that Herrumann Wohler, a native of Germany, has this day made known to the undersigned that he was in "California" prior to the ratification of the treaty of peace between the United States and Mexico; "that he intends" establishing himself permanently in this Territory, "and gives notice of his intention and desire to become a citizen of the United States."

R. B. MASON,
Col. 1st Dragoons, Governor of California.

STATE DEPARTMENT OF THE TERRITORY OF CALIFORNIA,
Monterey, March 26, 1849.

SIR: I have to acknowledge the receipt of your letter of the 24th instant, resigning your office of alcalde of Santa Cruz.

The governor requests that you will give the proper notice, and hold an election to supply the vacancy made by your resignation.

Very respectfully, your obedient servant,
H. W. HALLECK,
Brevet Captain, and Secretary of State.

WM. BLACKBURN, Esq.,
Alcalde, Santa Cruz, California.

HEADQUARTERS TENTH MILITARY DEPARTMENT,
Monterey, California, March 26, 1849.

SIR: I have the honor herewith to transmit to you the accounts for the collection and disbursement of customs collected in Upper and Lower California from the following named officers, viz: Lieutenant Colonel Burton, New York volunteers, for the 2d, 3d, and 4th quarters 1848; Colonel Mason, 1st dragoons, for the 3d quarter 1848; Captain Folsom, assistant quartermaster, for the 3d quarter 1848; Mr. Harrison, collector at San Francisco, for the 3d quarter 1848; Captain Lippett, New York volunteers, for the 2d and 3d quarters 1848; Captain Marcy, acting assistant quartermaster, for the 2d and 3d quarters 1848; Lieutenant Carnes, New York volunteers, 2d quarter 1848; Mr. Alexander, collector at San Pedro, for the 1st, 2d, and 3d quarters 1848; Lieutenant Davidson, 3d and 4th quarters 1848, and 1st quarter 1849; Lieutenant Canfield, Mormon company, 4th quarter 1847, and 1st quarter 1848; Lieutenant Clift, Mormon company, 4th quarter 1847, and 1st quarter 1848; Lieutenant McGee, 1st quarter 1848; M. Pedrorena, collector at San Diego, 3d and 4th quarters 1848; Surgeon Perry, United States army, 2d quarter 1848; Lieutenant Pendleton, New York volunteers, 3d quarter 1848; Captain Steele, New York volunteers, 2d and 3d quarters 1848; Captain Naglee, New York volunteers, 2d and 3d quarters 1848; and a statement from Lieutenant Colonel Burton and Lieutenant Pendleton of the amount collected at La Paz and San José, Lower California, after the 30th of May, 1848.

I am, respectfully, your obedient servant,
R. B. MASON,
Colonel 1st Dragoons, commanding.
To the Hon. the SECRETARY OF WAR,
Washington, D. C.

CIRCULAR.

To alcaldes, Indian agents, and others.

STATE DEPARTMENT OF THE TERRITORY OF CALIFORNIA,
Monterey, March 31, 1849.

Representations having been made that the Indians of the southern missions of this Territory, freed from the restraint formerly imposed upon them by the military and ecclesiastical authorities of the country, have contracted habits of indolence and vice, and are now reduced to a state of great destitution and want, trusting mainly to charity and theft for the means of subsistence, their condition calls not only for our commiseration, but for some active measure to protect society from their vices and to save the Indians themselves from total destruction. It would hardly be possible, even if it were desirable, to restore the missions to their former condition, or to give over to the priests the same control which they formerly exercised over the neophytes; but it is believed that if the local authorities will unite with the priests in their endeavors to subject the Indians to wholesome restraints, much may be accomplished towards inducing them to pursue a more honest and industrious course of conduct. It is, therefore, the wish of the governor that all magistrates and other civil authorities lend their aid and assistance to the mission priests, in all proper endeavors to ameliorate the condition of these Indians, by inducing them to cultivate their lands and to observe such local regulations as may be conducive to morality and good order.

By the laws of California the mission Indians have the right to elect their own alcaldes, who, with the advice and assistance of the mission priests, make all the necessary regulations for their own internal government. In case of any violation of law, they are liable to trial and punishment by the alcaldes of the nearest towns in the same manner as the whites, but in their own internal government they should not be interfered with, and the civil authorities should give to the missionaries and Indian alcaldes their countenance and assistance in promoting industry, decency, morality, and good order among the neophytes. Such a course is not only required by the existing laws of the country, but is the one best calculated to secure the welfare of the Indians and the good of society.

It is also represented that the occupants of some of the missions have claimed and appropriated to their own use the books, ornaments, and other appurtenances of the mission churches, and have otherwise encroached upon the property reserved for the use of the priests. By the laws of secularization enacted by the supreme government of Mexico, the churches of the several missions, with the sacred vessels, ornaments, and other appurtenances, were assigned for the use of the parishes, and the most appropriate building of each mission given for the habitation of the curate, with a lot of ground not to exceed two hundred varas square. Such was and is the supreme law, and until it be changed by competent authority no local or territorial officer can dispose of them or include them in any sale or renting of the missions. The governor, therefore, directs all magistrates to assist in the recovery and restoration of the books and other appurtenances of the churches, and that the priests be secured in the possession of the house and garden in each mission appropriated for their use and occupation.

By order of the governor:

H. W. HALLECK,
Brevet Captain, and Secretary of Sta'e.

STATE DEPARTMENT OF THE TERRITORY OF CALIFORNIA,
Monterey, April 2, 1849.

SIR: It is represented that you have taken tiles from the roofs of good and substantial houses in the mission of San Antonio, and removed them to the rancho of Los Ojitos for the purpose of covering a new building. The permission of the governor was merely to take some tile from old and uninhabited mission buildings for the purpose of re-roofing the house said by you to have been burnt by order of Lieutenant Colonel Fremont, and you are hereby prohibited from taking any other tile than those mentioned, or to use them for any other purpose than the one designed in the governor's order.

Very respectfully, your obedient servant,

H. W. HALLECK,
Brevet Captain, and Secretary of State.

Don MARIANO SOBERANEZ,
Rancho of the Ojito, California.

STATE DEPARTMENT OF THE TERRITORY OF CALIFORNIA,
Monterey, March 31, 1849.

SIR: It has been represented that insomuch as your residence is some distance from the mission or town of San Luis Obispo, there is great need of a subordinate alcalde to reside in the mission itself. The governor,

therefore, requests that you will give the proper notice and hold an election for a local alcalde, who shall reside in the mission or town.
Very respectfully, &c.,

H. W. HALLECK,
Brevet Captain, and Secretary of State.

Don MIGUEL ABILA,
Alcalde of the jurisdicton of San Luis Obispo, California.

HEADQUARTERS TENTH MILITARY DEPARTMENT,
San Francisco, California, April 9, 1849.

SIR: I have the honor to acknowledge the receipt of your communication of the 5th instant, together with the credentials submitted to my inspection, which are herewith returned.

As I shall soon be relieved from all civil and military duties in California, by Brigadier General Riley, now daily looked for, I deem it most proper not to make, at this time, the appointment you solicit, but will hand over your application to the General when he relieves me, to whom you had better submit the credentials above mentioned.

I am, respectfully, your obedient servant,

R. B. MASON,
Colonel 1st Dragoons, commanding.

Mr. S. P. HAREN, *Present.*

HEADQUARTERS TENTH MILITARY DEPARTMENT,
San Francisco, California, April 9, 1849.

SIR: Your communication addressed to General Smith, erroneously dated 9th April, asking for the appointment of "notary public for the district of San Francisco," has been referred to me as governor of California.

As I shall soon be relieved from all civil and military duties in California, by Brigadier General Riley, now daily looked for, I deem it most proper not to make at this time the appointment you solicit, but will hand over your application to the General when he relieves me.

I am, &c.,

R. B. MASON,
Colonel 1st Dragoons, commanding.

Mr. M. SCOTT, jr., *Present.*

List of reports from General Smith.

Report to the Secretary of War, January 7, 1849.
Report to the Secretary of War, January 18, 1849.
Report to the Secretary of War, January 26, 1849.
Report to the Secretary of War, February 15, 1849.
Report to the Adjutant General, March 15, 1849.
Report to the Adjutant General, April 5, 1849.

Report to the Adjutant General, April 9, 1849.
Report to the Secretary of War, April 16, 1849.
Report to the Adjutant General, April 29, 1849.
Report to the Adjutant General, May 1, 1849.
Report to the Adjutant General, May 21, 1849.
Report to the Adjutant General, June 19, 1849.
Report to the Secretary of War, June 20, 1849.
Report to the Adjutant General, June 29, 1849.
Report to Lieutenant Colonel Freeman, August 26, 1849.

PANAMA, *January* 7, 1849.

DEAR SIR: Just as I was leaving New Orleans, your letter enclosing one to your son came to hand. I will take great pleasure in doing everything to meet your wishes in relation to him.

The situation of affairs in California is really most extraordinary. No accounts we had are exaggerated. Captain Fleurian de Langle, of the French brig of-war Genie, now here, says that he learned at Valparaiso and Lima that there had been brought to those places, from California, to be run into bars, gold to the amount of nine millions of francs, (near $1,800,000.) The British consul tells me he has forwarded 15,000 ounces from this place, across the isthmus; and Lieutenant Wood, of the British navy, commanding the Pandora, now here, says that the truth is beyond the accounts we have heard. These gentlemen also say that hundreds of people from the western coast of South America are embarking for the gold region, and most of the clerks in the commercial places here quit their employments for the same object.

It will evidently be impossible to prevent the troops, when they arrive, from deserting, and there will be no force to control the crowd of adventurers that will arrive.

The sale of the land cannot be properly made, until surveys are prepared and the actual value of each tract known: in the mean time all is disorder. But the only power capable of regulating the search for gold, will be the self-interest of those engaged in it; and to secure the proper direction of this, some recognised right must be accorded. Not to throw away entirely the proprietary interest of the government in these lands and mines, and at the same time to avoid the delay of public surveys, I would propose that a temporary land office be established in the region, and that parties desiring to seek for gold should themselves survey and locate tracts, and lease them for five years at a fixed rate of rent; those persons will be interested in keeping out intruders, and in the five years the lands can be examined, surveyed, and sold.

I am partly inclined to think it would be right for me to prohibit *foreigners* from taking the gold, unless they intend to become citizens. I cannot decide until I arrive there and learn the disposition of the people.

No preparation was made here by the steamboat company for transporting passengers across the isthmus, or affording them any information or aid in relation to it. The roads are almost impassable even for mules, and the number of boats in the river and animals on the roads are entirely insufficient. The public property in charge of the quartermaster has been lying a week at Cruces, waiting for thirty or forty mules to carry it; and the trouble, vexation, and exposure in getting it up the river Chagres to this place, brought on Captain Elliott, the senior quartermaster, an attack of cholera, of which he died on the night of the 5th, and was buried the next day at Cruces, in the church-yard. Major Fitzgerald has taken charge of the property, but he is now sick here of a similar attack.

I have directed all the public property and officers' baggage now there to be brought at once to this place, which is more healthy. The greater part of it will be carried on men's backs. They are now asking $20 apiece for mule loads of one-third of the ordinary weight—the usual price being from $4 to $5 for full loads. I will not attempt to describe the roads or paths. Under these circumstances, I think it will not be wise to send anything by this route, except a messenger with a very small trunk, until other arrangements are made. The resources of the isthmus are entirely unequal to the business now thronging to it.

Flour is to-day at $40 a barrel, and the inhabitants of the town are alarmed at the prospect of pestilence and famine. Mr. Burch, a very fine young man, a mechanic, from Washington, is one of the victims of the cholera at Cruces.

So much for the present state of affairs; for the future, I am entirely of opinion that the route across the isthmus, either this or Tehuantepec, must have a good harbor at each end. By a good harbor, I mean one where a ship can lie alongside of a wharf in smooth water. If goods are to be put into lighters, and from them to other carriages, either by land or water, the expense of freight is quadrupled; and if the vessel must be out at sea, there is not only expense, but delay and risk.

This, in my opinion, is a fatal objection to Chagres: there are thirteen feet water on the bar, but the entrance has a short turn between rocks, immediately under the cliff on which the old fort at Chagres stands; this cliff obstructs the breeze at the most critical moment, and vessels must wait for a particular wind to enter. The pilot of our boat (the Falcon) would not bring her in, because, although there was water enough, she was too long to turn the point of rocks. Once in the mouth of the river, freight must be carried some distance up before the ground is high enough for a road; this requires lighters.

Puerto Bello, a perfect harbor, one of the best in the world, is forty-two miles from this place; the road formerly ran there. The walls of old buildings still remain, of which good storehouses could be made. A vessel-of-war of the largest class can enter and lie alongside a wharf in security. At Panama the harbor is imperfect, but may be made good by docks, as there is an average rise and fall of eighteen feet in the tide, and the shape of part of the bay renders the work easy.

I would propose that a road be graded from Puerto Bello to Panama. It will be about sixty miles long if made for a railroad, but be made wide enough to be macadamized and used as a carriage road. This can be done, as the route has been examined; if the trade requires it, rails can be laid afterwards. A carriage road of this kind, after having been well located by *good* engineers, can be made by the natives; others will die. A railroad can only be made by good mechanics, which the country does not furnish.

The great opposing element here is *rain*. The quantity that falls during three fourths of the year is inconceivable. The examination made by Mr. Stevens for Howland & Aspinwall was made in the dry season;

and I am informed here—but do not vouch for the fact, as the truth is hard to get at—that part of the road he has located is now at the bottom of a lake, sixty feet under water. Before *anything* is done, the route must be examined by *scientific engineers* in the wet season—viz: from May to December—and especially in the fall, when the waters have accumulated. No works can be relied on until those who place them have witnessed the extraordinary fall of water and most rapid and exuberant vegetation.

My baggage and papers are still on the road; but I seize an opportunity that offers to write on this subject, in order that any legislation on it may admit of the choice of different routes and different means, to be decided on *good* and *exact* information.

With sincere respect, your obedient servant,

PERSIFOR F. SMITH,
Brevet Major General U. S Army.

Hon. W. L. Marcy,
Secretary of War.

As I was about leaving New Orleans, I received an order directing accounts to be rendered of moneys collected in Mexico.

Money was collected and disbursed under my authority in the city, for public purposes, of which accurate accounts were kept. These were in my trunks of papers sent from Vera Cruz, and I have brought them along, for the purpose of obeying the order. When they arrive, I will hasten to comply with it. I have had no access to my baggage since it went on board of the Falcon, at New Orleans. It has consequently been impossible to come within the ten days' limitation of the order.

Yours, most respectfully,

PERSIFOR F. SMITH,
Brevet Major General U. S. Army.

We have no news of the steamer from Cape Horn.

Panama, *January* 18, 1849.

Sir: Since I had the honor of addressing you last from this place, I have been detained waiting for the steamer, which arrived yesterday. Her voyage has been very satisfactory to those interested in her, and the passengers speak in high terms of all the arrangements on board; so that it may be confidently expected that the branch of the service between this and the mouth of the Columbia river will be most promptly and effectually performed as soon as the damage done to the other boat shall have been repaired, and she and the Oregon arrived at their stations.

But very little use can be made of this route for any other purpose but carrying intelligence, until the road be made across the isthmus. I have already expressed the opinion that Chagres will not answer for one of the termini: it is not a good port. Another vessel has been lost in attempting to enter it, since I last wrote. As a road from this to Puerto Bello crosses the Chagres river where it is navigable, it may be well to make the road between this and that crossing first, and use it and the river and port of Chagres until the rest of the way is finished to Puerto Bello. But I am certain that no commerce on it will be secure until that harbor be reached, unless another project be adopted of making a breakwater in Simon bay, which will make it a good harbor.

Every one of my party has been attacked with fever since coming up the river, except myself; all have recovered except Lieutenant Gibbs, who is now better, but not free from the fever entirely.

I learn from many sources that there is a great emigration of people of all nations to California, and that many are going off with large quantities of gold. On my arrival there I shall consider every one, not a citizen of the United States, who enters on public land and digs for gold, as a trespasser, and shall enforce that view of the matter if possible, depending upon the distinction made in favor of American citizens to engage the assistance of the latter in carrying out what I propose.

All are undoubtedly trespassers; but, as Congress has hitherto made distinctions in favor of early settlers, by granting pre-emptions, the difficulties of present circumstances in California may justify forbearance with regard to citizens, to whom some favor may be hereafter granted. But an indiscriminate rush of adventurers of all nations will give a very bad foundation for society; and such a class will be very apt to put themselves under the lead of any one whose views are opposed to the formation of a regular government, and to submission to the laws of the United States.

No confidence can be placed in the regular troops, and, unfortunately, most of the men of the 2d infantry are recruits, and the order directing all who had not three years to serve to remain and be replaced by five-years men removed most of the non-commissioned officers, so that little dependence can be placed on them. To carry out the views of the government when they are known, or its interests as far as I can foresee them, great dependence must be placed on the well-disposed citizens who may be found there; and, to engage their co-operation, their own interests must be involved to at least some extent.

The mere loss of so much gold carried off I do not estimate so great a misfortune as the introduction of the worst kind of population, and the probability of their combining together to resist the introduction and the regular administration of laws and government.

With all the expedients that may be adopted on the spot, nothing can effectually answer the end but the organization of a regular government by Congress. Of this, I suppose, there is no hope this session. I am only afraid that, before the next, some evil past remedy may come into existence, and render the organization of a government, when it shall be provided, difficult, if not impossible.

From the difficulty expected in getting transportation across the isthmus, I required of the quartermaster, Captain Elliott, to provide transportation for the officers under orders on the route. In explanation of all this, I have written to General Jesup to-day. My aid, Mr. Gibbs, being sick, and having no one to help me, I cannot copy the letter in time to have it ready for Lieutenant Lenman, of the navy, to whom I commit this.

May I beg leave to refer you to that letter for that purpose, as well as my relation to other points.

The California will not probably leave for eight days. The number of passengers now here, bound for California, is about four hundred.

From all I can learn of California, I do not see how it is possible to live there. I foresee the greatest difficulties even in the ordinary affairs of life.

The stories you will hear of the most extraordinary state of affairs there, while strictly true, will be incredible.

With the sincerest respect, your obedient servant,

PERSIFOR F. SMITH,
Brevet Major General United States Army.

Hon. W. L. MARCY,
Secretary of War.

PANAMA, *January* 26, 1849.

SIR: We are still here, waiting on the steamer. She has been here since the 17th; but I cannot learn when she will be ready to go.

There will be a great deal of distress among many persons who have arrived here from the United States. There they were told the expenses of crossing the isthmus would be from 18 to 25 dollars. It has cost many $250; and, instead of finding the boat ready to receive them, they have spent nearly a month at most expensive rates of living. But I see no way the government can relieve them, unless some of its agents be authorized to employ these people and transport them to California, in case there should be public works or employments there authorized by law.

I am sorry *any* troops are going there; the men will all desert. Some of the oldest and most trusty marines, with their non-commissioned officers, have deserted from the British men-of-war in a body—a thing, these officers say, hitherto unknown.

The only thing to depend on there will be the emigrants from the United States. Those who are here are of a very good class; but I am informed that ships loaded with all the rabble of the Pacific ports are on their way there. All that is necessary to give a proper direction to the love of order and law so general among our citizens, is the regular institution of proper tribunals for enforcing the law. If Congress will not (and I suppose they will not) organize a government for the Territory, would this not annex California for the present as a judicial and collection district to Oregon, and so grant subordinate officers of the revenue at San Francisco, and let terms of court be held in each Territory every six months, for three months each, beginning with California? for Judge Bryants will probably be still there when the news of such a law arrives.

What an excellent appointment his was! I wish he were to remain in California. I wrote to the consul here, desiring him to communicate it to the other consuls on the South American coast, that the laws of the United States forbid trespassing on the public lands, and that, on my arrival in California, I would enforce this law against persons not citizens—alluding to the bands of plunderers organizing all along the coast for taking possession of the mines. I will do all I can to enforce the law; but that will be confined, at the furthest, to arresting them, if I have the means, and confining them until courts are organized to try them.

I have been and am still confined by an inflammation of the eye, from which I suffered after entering the city of Mexico, and write with great pain. As soon as I am able, I will report officially through the adjutant general. As I have done this (relating to trespasses) without instructions, the governor is not answerable for it, and can disavow it without difficulty, if it be found fault with on good reasons. I have not, however, forbidden any one from going to California; I have only threatened foreigners with the law, if they infringe it.

The value of California and Oregon has not begun to be appreciated in the United States. Their commerce with the countries of this ocean will in 20 years astonish the world. It will produce as great an effect in developing the resources of the old Spanish colonies (now republics) as it will in any other particular—resources which the remote position of these countries hitherto has permitted, if not caused, to lie hidden. The importance they will assume in future demands of our government that the ministers and consuls sent to the Pacific coasts and seaports should be men capable, not only of foreseeing the improvement, but of so connecting it with us that we may lose none of the advantages it may offer us.

I hope liberal appropriations may be made for exploring these Territories, (Oregon and California,) and for making a good wagon road or two in each. One may very easily be made from San Diego to San Francisco, and from San Diego over to the mouth of the Gila; one from San Francisco northward to the headwaters of the Willamette, with a branch off northeast; and one direct to the Columbia river; and one over the mountains eastward from San Francisco towards the Salt Lake.

In establishing posts for collecting revenues, or posts of any kind, on the bay of San Francisco, it would be well not to designate the particular point on the bay, but to leave that to be selected, subject to the approval of the government. I learn from our own and foreign officers that there are many points on the bay far more proper than the town of San Francisco; but that people interested there are active in getting an additional value given to their property, by getting the public establishments there.

It has one great defect: that it is nearly cut off from the main land, instead of having its rear open to the country dependent on it.

Nearly all the officers who came here have been sick with fevers taken in the Chagres river. They are all recovering, except Lieutenant Williamson, of the topographical engineers, who is still confined to his bed.

With the sincerest respect, your obedient servant,

PERSIFOR F. SMITH,
Brevet Major General U. S. Army.

Hon. W. L. MARCY,
Secretary of War.

My aid, Lieutenant Gibbs, having been very sick, having no clerk, and suffering much from my eyes, I have not been able to copy my letters. May I ask the favor that some one who has time may copy for me this and the preceding letters addressed to you and the quartermaster general, and send me the copies.

I shall be able hereafter to have Mr. Gibbs's services for that purpose.

P. S.—The gentleman who carries this may go to Washington--Mr. Thorn. He has lived many years in South America, and can give a great deal of useful information.

MAZATLAN, *February* 15, 1849.

SIR: The steamer California, the first of the Pacific mail line, arrived here this morning, fourteen days from Panama. We have about 350 passengers on board.

I find that large numbers of persons from the coasts of South and North America, on the Pacific, are flocking to California to seek for gold. Many expeditions are fitting out in Mexico by people of large capital for the same purpose, and all have the intention of bringing the gold away. The amount of that metal already collected is variously estimated at from four to nine millions of dollars. I do not think it can exceed four and a half millions; but of that, four millions have gone to other countries than the United States; and those who go from these parts have no design of remaining.

I shall endeavor to enforce the laws against trespassers on public lands, at least as far as regards such persons. But to do this I must rely upon the co-operation of those who are citizens of the United States. And I can do no more than arrest offenders and hold them until tribunals are constituted to try them.

The troops who are coming out will all desert immediately on their arrival. If I can have the means of communicating with them before their arrival, I shall post the largest part of them at San Diego, as being further from the scene of attraction and nearest the frontier.

All vessels going to San Francisco lose their crews. We saw a brig in San Blas, yesterday, which pays $300 a piece to her men to come there and return to San Francisco, and only procured them because the rainy season and showers had driven the people from the gold mines.

Every thing will be, of course, in great confusion there, and I find some persons going out armed with Colonel Benton's letter to set up a government for themselves.

I conceive myself armed with no civil authority, but shall deem it my duty to see that the laws of the United States are not infringed if I can prevent it. But nothing effectual can be done to secure the interests of the United States until a territorial government be organized and laws passed to dispose of the public lands. There are a great many false and insufficient titles to land in existence in California; and in the organization of the land office and appointment of officers, great care must be exercised to prevent the loss of the greater part of the public lands there. Just as the American flag was hoisted there, many improper grants were made by the local authorities, which were never confirmed, and could not be.

We expect to start this evening and to arrive at San Francisco in twelve days.

With respect, your obedient servant,
PERSIFOR F. SMITH,
Brevet Major General United States Army.

To the Hon. SECRETARY OF WAR.

[No. 1.] HEADQUARTERS PACIFIC DIVISION,
San Francisco, California, March 15, 1849.

SIR: On the 28th of February last I arrived at San Francisco in the steamer California from Panama; it was not until the 10th instant that I was able to procure quarters on shore. One month was spent in Panama waiting for the steamer.

I saw Colonel Mason at Monterey as we passed, and learned from him the arrival of Brevet Major L. P. Graham's command, of about 270 men, at the Pueblo de Los Angeles.

The force in this department consists of his command, of Captain Burton's company 3d artillery at Monterey, and of Captain Smith's company 1st dragoons at the Presidio of this place. The larger portion of these latter corps have deserted to go to the mines, and it is presumed that nearly all the rest will follow as soon as the season permits them to live on the hills where the gold is found.

The rate of pay paid to the enlisted men is so much inferior to that earned by common laborers here, that the temptations cannot be resisted; and to employ the men still remaining in searching for the others, would be to lose them also.

As some inducement to stay, in order to secure protection to the public property, I have authorized the quartermaster to give the same wages to soldiers who have leave of absence from their commanding officers as he gives to laborers. But I yesterday saw the latter refuse eight dollars a day. This is not more owing to the scarcity of labor than to the extreme plenty of gold and the facility with which it is procured.

I think it probable that the troops expected to arrive will be affected in the same manner as those now here; for, though the influx of population will be great, the quantity of gold taken will be greater in proportion, so that little benefit can be expected from them.

I propose to place the greater part of the 2d infantry in the southern part of the Territory, as furthest removed from the mines, and near the frontiers; its headquarters at San Luis Rey, where the buildings of the mission are most commodious, and the country most abundant in supplies of forage and food; to garrison San Diego, Warner's Pass, the outlet to Lower California, and Sonora; and as soon as possible to establish a post at the mouth of the Gila, not only to facilitate travelling to and from New Mexico, but to prepare for the boundary commission. San Luis Rey is well situated to communicate with these places, and to supply them. But the post at the Gila should be supplied by the gulf of California as soon as the proper kind of vessels can be procured, viz: those of light draught. A company of artillery will be stationed at Monterey, where there is a temporary work, and one near the entrance of this harbor, to control the vessels trading at these places. I have directed some of the heavy artillery now here to be placed in the old battery commanding the entrance of this bay. No work will be done except laying the platforms, as the site of this fortification will most probably have to be cut down in regularly fortifying the harbor.

I shall put two companies of infantry and one of cavalry at some point near the bay, above the district infected by fogs in the summer—the point to be established in a visit I shall make in a few days. From their position, they can be moved either by land or water towards the mines, and among the Indians north of San Francisco, some of whom it is represented are dissatisfied with the treatment received from the whites.

I would recommend that no great expense be incurred for storehouses, or other permanent constructions of the kind, until the whole neighborhood be examined. The harbor at Yerba Buena is a very inconvenient one—the sea too rough three days out of seven to load or unload vessels; and the town of San Francisco is situated at the extremity of a long point cut off from the interior by an arm of the bay more than thirty (30) miles long, having no good water and few supplies of food.

The road along the bay—the only one reaching this place—is intersected by streams that render it now nearly impassable.

I am without any returns from department headquarters since my arrival.

I have no observations to make in relation to the gold region of this country, as all my knowledge on this subject is derived from others, and principally from officers who have communicated directly to the War Department. But from what I have seen here, I have no doubt that everything thus communicated has been, if anything, short of the truth, as new discoveries are daily adding to the extent of the mining district, and to its productiveness.

Referring to the President's message, and to the letters of the Secretary of State to Mr. Voorhies of the 7th of October last, and that of the Secretary of War to Colonel Mason, dated October 9, 1848, and the circular of the Secretary of the Treasury, dated October 7, 1848, to the collectors of the customs, I have assumed as the opinion and decision of the government that the government existing in Upper California on the 30th of May last was a government *de facto*, which must from necessity be presumed to have existed and to continue with the consent of the people; for, as the " full and exclusive power of legislating for the Territory is in Congress," the only other alternative would be anarchy, until Congress shall act: that the laws of Mexico formerly in force in California, and not repealed on that day, nor contrary to the laws, constitution, and treaties of the United States, remain in vigor: and that by the treaty with Mexico California became part of the United States, and subject to the laws of the United States. I therefore recognise this government *de facto* as the government of California, and its acts as lawful, and recognise the force of Mexican laws remaining in vigor, and cannot recognise any other government or laws until established by Congress or its authority. Consequently, the laws of the United States in relation to trespassers on public lands, in cutting timber, mining, &c., are in force, and should be executed. But as Congress have made distinctions in favor of citizens who brave the difficulties of emigration and the wilderness, and settle on public lands, bringing their value into notice, and settling an uninhabited country, these penal laws should not be enforced against them until the pleasure of the government be known. But as to bands of foreigners, who, without any intention of settling in the country, have flocked here by thousands solely to gather gold from the public lands and carry it away, where none of it will ever come to the United States, these reasons for consideration do not apply; and I shall, as soon I can, endeavor to enforce these laws, depending on the citizens of the United States for aid in doing it. I enclose a copy of a letter I addressed to our consul in Panama, with a view of advising foreigners of the offences they were about committing.

It is evident, our revenue laws being in force here, dutiable goods cannot be brought in unless they pay duties, nor landed but at a port of entry; and, there being no port of entry in the Territory, and no collectors appointed, all such goods must be sent away. But as many vessels come from Europe—a long and expensive voyage—and there is no port of entry or collector yet on the Pacific, except those in Oregon, and those not yet ready, and as the people of this Territory are suffering for the want of supplies, I have instructed Colonel Mason, that, though no duties can be exacted from any vessel, or on any goods, yet, if the parties interested prefer it, rather than go away, to their entire ruin, and the inconvenience of the people here, they may deposite the amount of duties and fees payable in ports of entry, subject to such disposition as Congress may make of them, and land their goods.

I have also concurred with Commodore Jones in permitting foreign-built launches, owned by American citizens, fit for the navigation of the bay, to convey passengers and goods to the interior, as many persons are in great suffering here, having no houses to cover them, and there are no small vessels of the proper class built in the United States to carry them; and in permitting foreign-built vessels to be taken to the interior, to be dismantled and used as warehouses, the scarcity and price of lumber rendering it impossible to build. Lumber sells at $600 per thousand feet.

All those modifications of laws, however necessary, can only be temporary. It would, however, be just, before enforcing rigidly our revenue and navigation laws, that other nations should have due notice of this peculiar state of affairs here, which cuts off their commerce with the United States.

The steamers running between this place and Panama are not provided with coal. On our arrival here in the California, we had not two hours' fuel; and there are no depots this side of Panama. The crew of that ship, engineers, second and third mates, and servants, have all deserted for the mines; and she now lies here, with the captain, first mate, and purser on board. No dependence, therefore, can be placed on the punctuality of this line; and if the route across the isthmus has not been improved, as soon as the rainy season comes on, in May, it will no longer be passable for officers to reach this place by Panama and the steamers.

For the troops and public stores many public buildings will be necessary. These should all be prepared in the United States, and sent around the cape, with persons to put them up, engaged by the contractors who furnish them.

Mechanics cannot be kept here who are brought out by the quartermaster's department. The wages of a good carpenter here are more than the pay of the major general commanding the army.

I would earnestly recommend that the commissary's department be instructed to send here, and sell at the prices of the eastern States, all the articles of food necessary and usual for the officers and their families. They will all undoubtedly be ruined here, but they should not also be starved.

After I shall have visited the country, I shall report in detail, from my own observation, in relation to all points of interest. I enclose, besides the letter to the consul at Panama, copies of division orders from 1 to 5 inclusive, special orders Nos. 1 and 2, and copies of all letters written since my arrival here.

I have the honor to be your obedient servant,
PERSIFOR F. SMITH,
Brevet Major General, commanding.

To Brig. Gen. R. JONES,
Adjutant General U. S. Army, Washington city, D. C.

HEADQUARTERS THIRD DIVISION,
Panama, New Grenada, January 14, 1849.

SIR: By direction of Brevet Major General Smith, I have the honor hereby to inform you that you are authorized to retain in service of the quartermaster's department Messrs. R. M. Heath and Lloyd Brooke until their arrival in California, or as long as may be deemed convenient to the public service—said agents having proceeded from the United States in the employ of the late Captain E. G. Elliott, assistant quartermaster, their services being highly important to the service, and no means being available at hand for their return.

I am, very respectfully, your obedient servant,
ALFRED GIBBS,
Lieutenant Riflemen, Aid-de-camp, and A. A. A. Gen.

To Brevet Major FITZGERALD,
Assistant Quartermaster U. S. Army.

HEADQUARTERS THIRD DIVISION,
San Francisco, California, March 6, 1849.

SIR: We arrived here the morning after leaving Monterey, and I have found everything here entirely on the extreme of speculation. Labor cannot be procured but at the most exorbitant prices, and materials hardly at all. Nevertheless, some work must be done towards mounting some pieces at the entrance of the harbor, and preparing for the troops coming by sea. I propose to mount six pieces at the point, viz: four 32-pounders and two 8-inch howitzers, to repair the buildings at the Presidio, and to find quarters, if possible, for a troop of horse at Sonoma.

When the necessary orders are given for these, I will give at once a copy to Captain Folsom, that he may begin at once his preparations; for the work must be done by hired laborers. It will be well for Captain Smith to give short leaves of absence to his men, and for the quartermaster to hire them. This would be some encouragement for them to remain. They have already begun to desert.

I have said to Mr. Harrison, the collector, that as this is not a port of entry established by law, there is no obligation to prevent foreign vessels from discharging at other points on the bay, where the inhabitants think commerce will eventually establish itself; that, as much may depend upon the start given to a plan at the beginning by restrictions put upon its rivals, it is best to be perfectly impartial, to afford an equal chance to all, and thus to allow a free choice to those engaged in trade to select a spot for its depot, and to furnish to Congress evidence upon which it can found its legislation in fixing the ports of entry.

To avoid multiplicity of accounts and modes of collection, there can be of course but one custom-house and one collector, which are established and must remain at San Francisco; so that all vessels must enter and pay their duties here: but an inspector of the revenue can accompany each vessel to its place of discharge, and see that the laws of the United States are not infringed. Those vessels that go up the north branch of the bay can anchor near Sansolito until they are entered and the duties paid, and then go up without coming round this way. As there is no law making this a port of entry, I presume Mr. Harrison can regulate this matter himself.

I imagine it will be found necessary to bring some more troops in this neighborhood than I at first expected. Two companies of the second infantry will be stationed somewhere near above the influence of the fogs; the company of artillery at the Presidio; the cavalry at Sonoma.

They will require some additional inducements beyond their pay to prevent them from deserting. Such may be given by authorizing the quartermaster to employ them on the public works.

If we can thus keep them through the mining season, they will remain next winter; and in the spring circumstances may be altered.

The headquarters of the second infantry will probably be best at San Luis Rey, as you suggested, with posts at San Diego, Warner's Pass, and the mouth of the Gila. You will want a company probably at Monterey. Will you be good enough to let me hear from you on these points, and I will issue an order and send it to San Diego to meet General Riley, in case he arrives there first.

With respect, your obedient servant,
PERSIFOR F. SMITH,
Brevet Major General, commanding.

Colonel R. B. MASON,
 1st *Regiment Dragoons, commanding*
  Tenth Military Department, Monterey, California.

HEADQUARTERS THIRD DIVISION,
San Francisco, California, March 7, 1849.

SIR: You will please cause a government horse, now in charge of 1st Lieutenant W. T. Sherman, 3d artillery, acting assistant adjutant general, to be foraged and kept for Lieutenant Sherman's service at the Presidio of San Francisco.

I have the honor to be your obedient servant,
PERSIFOR F. SMITH,
Brevet Major General, commanding.

Captain J. L. FOLSOM.

HEADQUARTERS THIRD DIVISION,
San Francisco, California, March 9, 1849.

SIR: General Smith directs that you deliver to John Adair, esq., collector of customs for the district of Oregon, thirty-six (36) blankets, taking his receipt for the same.

I have the honor to be your obedient servant,
W. T. SHERMAN,
1st Lieutenant 3d Artillery, A. A. A. General.

Captain J. L. FOLSOM,
 Assistant Quartermaster, San Francisco, California.

PANAMA, *January* 19, 1849.

SIR: The laws of the United States inflict the penalty of fine and imprisonment on trespassers on the public lands. As nothing can be more unreasonable or unjust than the conduct pursued by persons, not citizens of the United States, who are flocking from all parts to search for and carry off gold from the lands belonging to the United States in California, and as such conduct is in direct violation of law, it will become my duty, immediately upon my arrival there, to put those laws in force, and to prevent their infraction in future, by punishing, by the penalties provided by law, all those who offend.

As these laws are probably not known to many about starting to California, it would be well to make it publicly known that there are such laws in existence, and that they will be in future enforced against all persons, not citizens of the United States, who shall commit any trespass on the lands of the United States in California.

Your position as consul here, and being in communication with our consuls on the coast of South America, affords you the opportunity of making this most generally known; and I shall be much obliged to you if you will do it.

With sincere respect, your obedient servant,

PERSIFOR F. SMITH,
Brevet Major General, commanding.

WM. NELSON, Esq.,
United States Consul at Panama.

[No. 3.]

HEADQUARTERS THIRD DIVISION,
San Francisco, April 5, 1849.

GENERAL: Since my last communication, no troops have arrived to change the strength of the force here; but the steam transport Edith arrived on the 21st of March, and reports that the transports Iowa and Massachusetts, the former having General Riley with a part of the 2d infantry, and the latter having the command of artillery for Oregon on board, left Valparaiso about the 8th of February. The former is expected here every day, and the Edith is held in readiness to convey the troops south to the position they are to occupy.

There will be great difficulty in establishing and maintaining a post at the mouth of the Gila, until more knowledge is acquired of the navigation of the head of the gulf of California and the lower part of the Colorado. Transportation by land from San Diego is impossible for large quantities of stores.

In the gulf, the winds blow in the winter almost invariably from the northward; and in the summer, when they come occasionally from southward, it is in violent gales, with severe squalls and thunder, rendering it very dangerous to be in the gulf then. In other words, it is always difficult to run up the gulf, but almost always easy to run south. These circumstances render the employment of steam vessels very advantageous. If the navigation of the gulf permits the Edith to be used, she will answer, having both sails and steam. If she draws too much water, others of lighter draught could be procured. I mention this now, as the boundary commission will commence their labors on this end of the line, and will be on the Gila next season. I should have observed that the Colorado is supposed to be navigable only for boats drawing three or four feet.

I see no reason for posting troops on any other point out of reach of the ports on the Pacific. The Indians in the interior do not make it necessary, and it would be useless to place them near the mines to maintain order there. Nothing but the establishment of a regular civil government, to be carried on by those most interested in the existence of good order, will answer that end.

Such detachments as go to the southern part of the Territory will accordingly be placed, as heretofore mentioned, in healthy and convenient positions, and those on this bay at such points as will combine good climate, convenience of supply, and facility of movement. I propose, when such a point is found, to have removed all the public stores there, both from this place and Monterey, leaving the heavy ordnance and stores.

The town of San Francisco is no way fitted for military or commercial purposes; there is no harbor, a bad landing place, bad water, no supplies of provisions, an inclement climate, and it is cut off from the rest of the country, except by a long circuit around the southern extremity of the bay. In time of war, enemies' troops could be landed for many miles south of the entrance of the bay on the sea beach, and thus cut it off by a short line across the peninsula on which it stands. There are points on the bay, more inland, having good harbors and landings, good water, and open to the whole country in rear, and accessible without difficulty to ships of the largest class. One of these should be the point at which the future depots should be established; and I propose to go to-morrow in the Edith, in company with Commodore Jones and other officers of the army and navy, to examine the straits of Karquinez, said to combine most advantages. I hope to return and report the result of our examination before the next mail boat leaves, (on Monday, 9th,) but at any rate by the succeeding boat, a few days afterwards.

I hope that in fixing the port of entry, capital, or other public places, the law will leave to the President the selection; otherwise, private interests, already involved in speculation here, will, by misrepresentation, lead to a very bad choice.

If Congress has not provided by law for the government of this Territory, or its admission as a State, I would be very glad that the government would officially promulgate its views as to the civil authority now exercised here. Some important questions of law, involving both life and property, are now depending; and judges and jurors, without experience in these difficult questions, are called upon to act under great responsibility.

It appears to be the opinion of merchants in many of the ports of the Pacific—and they allege in support of it the advice of some of our consuls—that in virtue of the circular of the Secretary of the Treasury of October 30, as the Treasury Department could not collect duties on imports in California, their goods, though dutiable, could be imported without paying duty. I have held that this was not the construction proper to be given to the circular, but only that the law had not provided the means of collecting duties here, that law being still in force which prohibits certain goods being introduced into the United States, unless they pay duties as prescribed; that consequently no dutiable goods can be landed in California until they shall have paid their duties elsewhere—the effect of which would be, that they could not be admitted at all from foreign ports.

Under the circumstances, which showed a very hard case, I thought it proper that the parties should be allowed to deposite the amount of duties and land the goods; but, lest this should be construed as giving them a right for the future, and as the President may think proper to put an end even to this indulgence, I have addressed a circular to all our consuls on these seas, warning them of this possibility—a copy of which is enclosed.

I was directed, when coming here, by the Secretary of War, to do all I could to facilitate the arrival of the civil officers of government in Oregon, as the public service required their presence there. The steamer in which we came here could go no further north, and there was no possible way of those gentlemen getting there, except on a small vessel about sailing, on which there were no accommodations.

Commodore Jones kindly sent carpenters from the fleet to put up some berths, and, on General Adair's (the collector's) representation, that no bedding could be procured, I directed the quartermaster to issue him the necessary number of blankets for the voyage, and take his receipt for them. I respectfully ask that this may be approved, and the amount charged to General Adair. The quartermaster could not tell him the price of the blankets when he took them.

As the rainy season has ended, people are again repairing to the mines. New discoveries further south are said to have been made; and it is now pretty certain that the whole slope of the Sierra Nevada, comprised within the head waters of the San Joaquin to the south and those of the Sacramento to the north, contains gold. These two rivers, forming, as it were, a bracket, join to enter the bay of San Francisco; and their tributaries from the east, in their beds, expose the deposites of gold as they descend from the mountains. It is on the banks and branches of these streams that adventurers are now at work; but some excavations elsewhere, to a depth equal that worn by the creeks, have disclosed quantities similar to those most generally found. There appears to be a line parallel to the summit of the main ridge, and some distance down the slope, at which the product of gold is at its maximum; but whether this be from the quantity deposited, or from the different position as relates to the surface, or from the difficulty of working it, I have not the means of knowing.

The gold is found in small particles: the largest I have seen, but such are rare, weighs 71 ounces troy. The appearance invariably is as though it had been spurted up when melted through crevices and fissures in drops, which have often the form of the leaves and gravel on which they have fallen. I speak of this as an appearance, not as a theory or hypothesis. The extent ascertained within which gold is thus found is at least 400 miles long by 40 wide; in almost every part of which, where the surface is depressed by the beds of rivers, gold has been obtained without digging more than ten feet below the surface, and very seldom that much.

It is impossible to furnish any grounds for estimating the number of people engaged in mining, or the amount they have produced. Persons engaged in trading with the miners say they amount to about 10,000, but I cannot say with what reason. They can better judge of the amount produced, which the lowest estimate places at $4,000,000. More than

3,000 persons have been added to the miners up to this time—chiefly from Mexico and South America.

When the mines were first discovered, all the ports of South America on the Pacific, and of the Sandwich islands, sent the merchandise collected and stored there to be sold here. They realized enormous profits, before any competition from our eastern States could meet them; and these goods were generally owned by European houses, who thus became possessed of the first fruits of the mines, which were shipped to Europe on their account; and it is thus that so little gold has reached the United States.

When the merchandise now on its way from our Atlantic States arrives, and is sold, the current will set that way; but the profits will be much diminished by competition, and still more by the enormous expenses here for labor, storage, &c. These are almost incredible; the ordinary wages for the poorest laborer is $6 per day; many receive $10.

The extent and richness of the gold region have not been exaggerated; and the exorbitant prices paid for labor, rent, and subsistence, have hardly been fully set forth. But all the estimates of the amount actually produced are but mere suppositions, which may surpass or may fall short of the truth.

I have already directed that the men to whom their commanding officers may give short leaves of absence may be employed by the quartermasters at the usual rates here. This will be an encouragement to the men and an advantage to the public service, as labor is hard to get. But I doubt the propriety of yielding to the current of gold-seeking, and allowing large bodies of the men to go to the mines. It may be permitted to reward good conduct, as any other indulgence is; but to make it general, would be either to acknowledge the right of the men to modify their obligations as they please, or to confess our inability to enforce their fulfilment. For the sake of principle and preciseness, it would be better to adhere to what is right now, though the effect here in this particular instance would be the desertion of the men.

I am, with respect, your obedient servant,
PERSIFOR F. SMITH,
Brevet Major General, commanding 3d Division.
Brigadier General R. Jones,
Adjutant General.

CIRCULAR.

Headquarters Pacific Division,
San Francisco, California, April 1, 1849.

The treaty concluded with Mexico on the 30th of May last brought Upper California within the United States, and of course within the operation of all its laws. But the means of enforcing some of these laws have not been provided by Congress. Thus, as the Secretary of the Treasury, in his circular of the 30th of October last, observes, "although Congress have recognised California as part of the Union, and legislated for it as such, yet it is not brought by law within the limits of any collection district, nor has Congress authorized the appointment of any officers to collect the revenue." The laws of the United States are in force here, and consequently the revenue and navigation laws are; though at this moment some part of the machinery necessary to their complete action is wanting.

Now, the law declares that certain goods shall only enter upon having paid the duties prescribed by the tariff; and when the secretary says that the department is unable to collect duties on such, the proper inference is not, as many seem to think, that the goods can enter without paying duties, but that, being unable to pay the duties here, as required by law, they cannot be admitted at all.

As many cargoes had been shipped under the wrong impression that they could enter, and there was no American port of entry on the Pacific to which they could resort to comply with the law, a case of extreme hardship was presented, which appeared to authorize such a modification as would allow the cargoes to be entered, on depositing the duties, to await the action of Congress on this subject. And so, from the want of American vessels on the coast, and from the unwillingness of the few in this ocean to frequent these ports, where the men desert to the gold mines, an absolute necessity of some means of transportation existed, which could only be supplied by using foreign vessels that came from the neighboring coasts.

But both of these modifications of law can be but temporary. There can be no hardship in enforcing the law on those who are fully aware of its provisions and their effect; and time will doubtless do away with the scarcity of American vessels of small class here. There will be then no reasons for indulgence, and the suspension of the strict enforcement of the law will cease. Even before that time, the government at Washington, thinking itself empowered to allow of any such suspension, may revoke the indulgence granted, and require a strict adherence to the law, whatever may be the inconvenience to individuals.

I think it would be proper, then, to notify all persons designing to come here from your port, or its neighborhood, that they can have no right to count upon any other than the strictest construction of the law, as in all other ports of the United States, both as regards cargoes and vessels; and particularly that dutiable goods cannot be entered here at all, unless Congress shall have made provision for appointing the necessary officers.

It would be well also to inform all adventurers coming here to search for gold, that trespassing on the public lands is punishable by fine and imprisonment; that, although the position of affairs here, incident to the change of government, has hitherto prevented action under these laws, yet they will be enforced as soon as the means are organized.

I should like to be informed of the date of your receipt of this communication, to be enabled to judge of the degree of indulgence proper to award to those claiming it.

PERSIFOR F. SMITH,
Brevet Major General, commanding Division.

To UNITED STATES CONSULS,
Valparaiso, Callao, Panama, Canton, Singapore, Manilla, Sidney, Tahiti, Sandwich Islands, and all other ports of the Pacific ocean.

[No. 4.]   HEADQUARTERS THIRD DIVISION,
San Francisco, April 9, 1849.

GENERAL: I mentioned in my communication of the 5th instant that I designed examining the northern branch of the bay before the departure of the steamer with the mail for Panama. Accordingly, on Friday last, the 6th instant, I left this in the morning at 7 o'clock in the steamer Edith, and ran down to Sansolito, near the mouth of the harbor, where the fleet lies, and took on board Commodore Jones and several other officers. We left Sansolito about a quarter before 9 a. m., with the beginning of the flood-tide, but the wind ahead, and anchored at the upper end of the straits of Karquinez about half-past 11 o'clock a. m. The distance of this point from Sansolito is about twenty-one miles, and from the sea twenty-four—showing that, with a fair wind, a vessel could easily come in from sea and reach this point in one tide. We had soundings carefully taken the whole distance, and found nothing less than five fathoms—this result corresponding with the depth marked on the Wilkes chart of the exploring expedition. The channel is in general from two to five miles wide, except in Racoon straits, (between the island Los Angeles and the main,) and the points San Pedro and San Pablo, the entrance to the bay of San Pablo. The officers of the navy, those of the joint commission of engineers and navy officers, (all of whom, except Lieutenant Leadbetter, were present,) the officers on the coast survey, and such staff officers as were present, were all of opinion that there was a perfectly good and sufficient beating channel without obstruction for vessels of-war of the largest class from sea to the upper end of the straits of Karquinez. The coves in the bay of San Francisco, within a line drawn through the projecting points which bound them, are shoal, though in some of them the line curves a little inward and affords anchorage protected from all winds, except that which blows directly into the cove; but there is no point entirely covered from all winds, except in the straits of Karquinez, and consequently no point at which vessels can lie and discharge their cargoes at all times. On Saturday morning we attempted to pass across the S—— bay, (the expanse of water lying between the straits of Karquinez and the mouth of the river above,) and, after going from seven to nine miles, we got aground and were obliged to return. We were not in the best channel, and have reason to believe that at least three fathoms can be taken up to the junction of the San Joaquin and Sacramento; beyond that point the evidence is unsatisfactory.

As the channel through S—— bay will not admit of vessels of-war of the largest class at all times, I presume that an important naval establishment can only be located below it, or at the upper end of Karquinez straits. As you enter the bay from the straits, turning round to the left, there is a bold shore and seven fathoms water; and the low mud islands with which the bay is interspersed form a breakwater which prevents any heavy sea breaking on the shore. Commodore Jones thinks this the best point for a naval establishment.

The straits are about five miles long and from one to two broad. Near the lower end the land is bold and high on both sides; halfway up on the north side, the hills recede from the water, leaving a very favorable site for a town larger than is likely to exist anywhere here for a century to come; and on this inclined plane a town is now laid out, called Benicia. Between the plat of this town and the upper end of the straits, a distance of about one mile, a large vessel can lie near enough the bank to unload at several points, and in the whole extent by a small expense for wharves. As this line forms with that designated by Commodore Jones for the front of the navy yard very nearly a right angle, having across the base a line of heights very appropriate for defence, it seems to me the best location for the depots of public stores. On the opposite side of the straits the land does not sink until near the upper end, where flats along shore present a near approach to the bank.

The road to the upper Sacramento from the southern country crosses here during the season of high water, when the valley of San Joaquin is overflowed; and this point has at all times a free communication with all parts of the Territory. The objections to this place are, that there is no wood near the site, whereas the south side of the straits has some scattered trees on its hills, and that there is no stream of fresh water on it. The wells, however, furnish much better water than is got at San Francisco, and as good as is generally found, from December until June, when the rivers are high. At low water, the water of the straits is fresh; we found it at that time perfectly good.

As the expense of landing stores at San Francisco is enormous, and difficult everywhere else on the coast where lighters are necessary, I propose, if the land can be procured without expense to the United States, to establish immediately the quartermasters' depots at those points, so as to have the stores now coming out landed there; there are no warehouses here to be had, and they can be built there cheaper than here, on account of the expense attending the landing of the lumber here.

As this point (straits of Karquinez) has, in my opinion, so many advantages over any other, on the waters of the bay, for commercial, naval, and military purposes, I would respectfully suggest that the laws to be proposed for establishing ports of entry, depots, admiralty courts, &c., should not name the points of location, but should leave them to be selected by the President, and thus the commissioners now here be asked to examine and report immediately, in time for the action of the next session of Congress. At present there are no public establishments, and but temporary commercial ones at any place; but if commerce be once fixed, it will be hard to remove it against the private interests of those who desire it to remain, even under great disadvantages. The difficulties attending the shipping coming to this port have prevented the mail steamers from running regularly; and it is not probable that one can return here before the 10th of June: two are now here.

It is of so much importance to know what legislation has been made by Congress in relation to this Territory, that, as that will be known by our consul at Mazatlan by the 25th instant, if the Edith should be obliged to carry down south the troops destined for that port, I will direct her to proceed to San Blas, Mazatlan, and bring the intelligence.

I cannot find a copy of the Laws of the United States in California, and they are of the greatest necessity. I applied for them coming out here, and understood that the War Department would order them to be purchased. Some laws, especially navigation laws, cannot be enforced, for want of knowing the phraseology of the statute.

I have the honor herewith to enclose division special orders Nos. 3, 4, and 5, copies of letters since the date of letter No. 1, circular issued to consuls at the principal foreign ports of the Pacific, and the letters addressed to me by a committee of the self-styled district legislature, with my reply.

With respect, your obedient servant,
PERSIFOR F. SMITH,
Brevet Major General, commanding Department.
Brigadier General ROGER JONES,
Adjutant General.

HEADQUARTERS PACIFIC DIVISION,
San Francisco, March 19, 1849.

SIR: I am directed to acknowledge the receipt of your letter of the 13th instant and its enclosure. The instructions conveyed by you to Brevet Brigadier General Riley, or senior officer of the transport ship first arriving at San Diego, meet the general's approval, except that he wishes two companies of the 2d infantry to disembark at San Francisco, and to take post at some point near the bay, hereafter to be selected. The objections to this step urged by yourself are fully appreciated by the general; yet he deems the necessity for an armed force north of the bay of San Francisco so imperative, that it is necessary to try the experiment. It is hoped that the commanding officer of this battalion, by freely using the provisions of division order No. 5, already sent you, may retain a sufficient number of good men, whose presence will have a good effect upon the citizens who reside north of the bay. Should all, however, desert, it will be demonstrated beyond the shadow of a doubt that no reliance can be placed upon soldiers in California, and that, under existing circumstances, the government should not attempt to keep up a military establishment in California. The general, therefore, desires that you will modify your orders and instructions accordingly, and suggests that you send to this place duplicates of those orders and instructions, in the event the ships should first make the port of San Francisco.

I have the honor to be your most obedient servant,
W. T. SHERMAN,
First Lieutenant 3d Artillery, A. A. A. General.
Colonel R. B. MASON,
Com'g Tenth Military Department, Monterey, California.

HEADQUARTERS PACIFIC DIVISION,
San Francisco, California, March 22, 1849.

SIR: The government steam propeller "Edith" arrived here last evening forty-one days from Valparaiso, Chili. The captain reports that the mail steamer Oregon sailed from Valparaiso for Panama on or about the 3d of February; and that the United States steam propeller "Massachusetts," with two companies of the 1st artillery on board, was at Valparaiso on the 7th of February—the day on which the Edith sailed— and was to sail for the Columbia river in two or three days after the ship "Iowa," with General Riley on board; and a detachment of the 2d infantry was also at Valparaiso, and was on the point of sailing for San

Francisco. She is therefore at least forty days at sea, and may be looked for in ten or twelve days. The Edith came up principally under sails, and had very fine weather. Another of the transports, having a portion of the 2d infantry on board—the ship Rhone—was daily looked for at Valparaiso, having sailed from Rio Janeiro about the 20th December last. The two will probably be in this port in a short while. It it therefore probable that General Riley will be here in a few days. It is thought that it will conduce much to the good of the public service if you could likewise be here, so that Generals Riley and Smith and yourself, in consultation, might devise the best measures for the distribution and disposition of the troops en route for California, without the delay that necessarily attends communication by express. The general directs me to suggest this to you only, as he does not wish to put you to the trouble of coming here unless you can do so conveniently. The general wishes you to order Captain Ingall to San Francisco, to report at division headquarters, when he will be ordered to Oregon for duty in the eleventh military department. Ordnance storekeeper F. B. Schaffer arrived here in the Edith, and has reported at these headquarters. He is ordered to report by letter to you; but, as his appointment contemplates his assignment to duty at San Francisco, the general will direct him verbally to receipt to First Lieutenant J. A. Hardie, 3d artillery, for the ordnance and ordnance stores now at this depot, it being understood that Lieutenant Hardie is under orders from your headquarters that will take him from the post for some weeks. Both these officers being on duty in the tenth department, the necessary written orders for the transfer of property will emanate from you.

The bearer of this express will report to you, and can be detained to come up with you, in case you determine to come; otherwise, he will return with your answer.

The Edith brings no troops, and is loaded with quartermasters' stores —mostly clothing for the 2d regiment of infantry.

I have the honor to be your most obedient servant,
W. T. SHERMAN,
First Lieutenant 3d Artillery, A. A. A. General.
Colonel R. B. MASON,
Com'g Tenth Military Department, Monterey, California.

HEADQUARTERS PACIFIC DIVISION,
San Francisco, California, March 23, 1849.

SIR: General Smith desires that you will communicate to him, as soon after the expiration of the present quarter as is convenient, the following information:

I. Number of immigrants arrived and landed at the port of San Francisco from American or foreign bottoms from the 1st of October, 1848, to March 31, 1849, classifying, if possible, the nations to which they belong, and the port from which they came.

II. Tabular statement of the usual form exhibiting the quantity and kind of dutiable goods and merchandise imported into California then in the custom-house at San Francisco, from the 1st of October, 1848, until the 31st of March, 1849, with the amount of duties collected thereon;

also, whether imported in American or foreign bottoms, and the quantity and kind of free goods imported during the same period, separating those brought from the United States from foreign free goods.

I have the honor to be your most obedient servant,
W. T. SHERMAN,
First Lieutenant 3d Artillery, A. A. A. General.

E. W. HARRISON, Esq.,
Collector of Customs, San Francisco, California.

HEADQUARTERS PACIFIC DIVISION,
San Francisco, March 24, 1849.

SIR: General Smith directs, in the event of the steam propeller Massachusetts coming into the bay of San Francisco, that you permit no soldier to leave her; and if you have control over the crew, that you permit none of them to communicate with the shore, except such as may absolutely be required to row the boat or boats you may send to communicate with officers or persons on shore. These precautions are absolutely necessary to prevent desertion; and the general advises that you do not come to the usual anchorage, but that you lay at Sansolito, where the squadron now is, and where you can obtain the necessary supplies of wood, water, and provisions. Be prepared, after communicating with the general, to go to sea, as any long delay may result seriously.

I am, very respectfully, your obedient servant,
W. T. SHERMAN,
1st Lieut. 3d Artillery, A. A. Adjutant General.

To Brevet Major J. S. HATHAWAY,
1st Regiment Artillery, or officer commanding Battalion Artillery on board Massachusetts.

HEADQUARTERS PACIFIC DIVISION,
San Francisco, California, March 24, 1849.

SIR: It is represented to General Smith that during the month of July, 1848, companies A and B, 1st regiment New York volunteers, were required to embark at Santa Barbara for La Paz, and that the men were unable to convey with them their private baggage, which in consequence was stored in the public buildings then used as the quarters of camp F, of the same regiment, which remained as the garrison of Santa Barbara. That baggage was left in September last in charge of Messrs. Thompson & Scott, with directions only to be given up upon the order of one of the officers of camp A and B, New York volunteers, or that of an officer of the army.

General Smith deems it just to these men, who never returned to Santa Barbara, that their baggage should be delivered to them; and he accordingly directs that you take the necessary measures to have brought to San Francisco the baggage referred to, and that upon its receipt you will cause it to be stored until the owners of property claim and carry off their respective parts.

It is also represented that the companies of dragoons now at Los Angeles are in want of clothing, that you have on hand a large supply, and that you are on the point of despatching a vessel to San Pedro. The general directs that you send a supply of such articles as they probably need, invoiced in such a manner that the assistant quartermaster in that quarter may receipt for a part or the whole, according to the wants of the command.

I am, sir, very respectfully, your obedient servant,
W. T. SHERMAN,
1st Lieut. 3d Artillery, A. A. Adjutant General.

To Captain J. L. Folsom,
A. Quartermaster, San Francisco, California.

Headquarters Pacific Division,
San Francisco, March 24, 1849.

Sir: I have to acknowledge the receipt of your communication of the 22d instant.

I have seen Commodore Jones on the subject of the entry of the cargo of the brig "Richard and William." We are of the opinion that it will be proper to allow the cargo to be landed and entered, under the same forms and conditions as that of the brig "Alert."

I am, sir, very respectfully, your obedient servant,
PERSIFOR F. SMITH,
Brevet Major General, commanding.

To E. H. Hamilton,
Collector of Customs, port of San Francisco.

Official:
W. T. SHERMAN,
1st Lieut. 3d Artillery, A. A. Adjutant General.

Headquarters Third Division,
San Francisco, March 24, 1849.

Dear Sir: I have had occasion to call up the question of the establishment of the district legislature, in answering a communication from a committee here. I have no doubt that their functions must be confined to regulating the interior police of the district, and that a new organization of the different branches of the government is beyond their control. I expect Colonel Mason, and General Riley, who relieves him, to arrive in a few days, when such views may be taken as will set the matter at rest as to the course the officers of government may be obliged to take. I will beg you, in the mean time, to be good enough to suspend further action, if possible, in relation to a change, and that you would continue the functions of alcalde until I have an opportunity of again communicating with you, which will be very shortly. It is my earnest desire that whatever may be done in this matter should not only be legal, but acceptable to all our fellow-citizens.

With sincere respect, your obedient servant,
PERSIFOR F. SMITH,
Brevet Major General, commanding.

Governor L. W. Boggs.

HEADQUARTERS PACIFIC DIVISION,
San Francisco, March 26, 1849.

SIR: General Smith desires me to acknowledge the receipt of your letter of this morning, and to inform you that, in his opinion, you are still the alcalde and chief magistrate of the district of San Francisco, notwithstanding any law, enactment, or resolution of the district legislature to the contrary. And he advises you to retain possession of your office, books, and papers.

The immediate commander of this department, Colonel Mason, is charged with the control of the civil affairs of California, and will apply whatever correction the circumstances you have reported may call for.

He is expected here in the course of a few days, and upon his arrival your letter will be submitted to him.

I am, sir, with much respect, your obedient servant,
W. T. SHERMAN,
1*st Lieut.* 3*d Artillery, A. A. A. General.*

T. M. LEAVENWORTH,
1*st Alcalde district of San Francisco.*

HEADQUARTERS THIRD DIVISION,
San Francisco, California, March 27, 1849.

SIR: As you desire me to say in writing what I have already answered verbally to your communication of the 27th of February last, in which you ask me to give you such instructions as will enable you to bring the wrongs of which you complain (as committed by Colonel Mason) before the proper tribunal, I now repeat, that the matter seems to me to be entirely a personal one, and not a proper one for my interference as superior military officer in this division.

Respectfully, your obedient servant,
PERSIFOR F. SMITH,
Brevet Major General, commanding Third Division.

CHARLES T. BOTTS, Esq.

HEADQUARTERS PACIFIC DIVISION,
San Francisco, California, March 27, 1849.

SIR: General Smith directs that you immediately instruct the person having charge of the government horses at the Certa Madera, near San Rafael, to deliver to the officer of the navy sent by Commodore Jones in pursuit of deserters such number of public horses as he may require in executing his orders.

By order of Brevet Major General Smith:
W. T. SHERMAN,
First Lieutenant Third Artillery, A. A. A. General.

Captain J. L. FOLSOM,
Assistant Quartermaster, San Francisco, California.

HEADQUARTERS THIRD DIVISION,
San Francisco, California, March 27, 1849.

SIR: General Smith directs that you cause four horses to be delivered to Acting Lieutenant Woodworth, United States navy, to-morrow morning, to enable that officer to pursue certain deserters from the United States ship Ohio.

By order of General Smith:
W. T. SHERMAN,
First Lieutenant Third Artillery, A. A. A. General.

Captain A. J. SMITH,
First United States Dragoons, commanding, San Francisco.

HEADQUARTERS PACIFIC DIVISION,
San Francisco, California, April 5, 1849.

SIR: General Smith directs that you cause the steam propeller Edith, now lying in this harbor, to be in readiness, by daylight to-morrow morning, to take on board himself, Commodore Jones, and the joint board of army and navy officers who have been appointed to inspect the harbors and ports of the Pacific coast, and who are now here.

It is deemed important that these gentlemen should have an opportunity of examining the northern branch of the bay of San Francisco, before the departure of the mail steamer Oregon for Panama. The Edith will probably be absent four days, and you will please instruct the captain to be prepared to steam up the bay. Direct Captain Conillard to report in person to General Smith, this afternoon, for orders and information concerning the proposed trip.

The general further thinks the Edith should not leave the bay of San Francisco and go to Santa Cruz until after the arrival of the ship Iowa, which is daily expected.

I have the honor to be your obedient servant.
W. T. SHERMAN,
First Lieutenant 3d Artillery, A. A. A. General.

Captain J. L. FOLSOM,
Assistant Quartermaster, San Francisco, California.

SAN FRANCISCO, *March* 20, 1849.

SIR: In pursuance of a resolution passed by the district legislature, the undersigned beg leave to present to your notice the enclosed papers, viz:

I. A copy of the Alta Californian of the 15th of February, 1849, containing proceedings of a convention of the citizens of the town and district of San Francisco, held on the 12th of February.

II. A certificate of a judge of the election held on the 21st of February, stating who were elected justices of the peace and members of the legislative assembly.

III. A certificate of a justice of the peace that the members of the assembly were sworn in by him.

IV. A copy of proceedings at the first meeting of the legislature.

V. A copy of a resolution passed by the assembly on March 6, 1849.
VI. A letter addressed to you by the committee.

Desiring that you will give the above your earliest consideration, we beg leave to subscribe ourselves, with high respect, your most obedient servants,

JAMES CREIGHTON,
GEORGE HYDE,
HENRY A. HARRISON,
THOMAS J. ROACH,
TALBOT H. GREEN,
Committee.

To Major General P. F. Smith,
Commanding Pacific Divison.

No. I.

A public meeting of the citizens of the town and district of San Francisco was held in the public square on Monday afternoon, the 12th instant, in accordance with previous notice.

The meeting was organized by calling Mr. Norton to preside, and S. W. Perkins to act as secretary.

The chairman, after reading the call of the meeting, opened it more fully by briefly but succinctly stating its object; when Mr. Hyde, on being invited, after some preliminary remarks, submitted the following plan of organization or government for the district of San Francisco:

Whereas we, the people of the district of San Francisco, perceiving the necessity of having some better defined and more permanent civil regulations for our general security than the vague, unlimited, and irresponsible authority that now exists, do, in general convention assembled, hereby establish and ordain:

Article I.

Section 1. That there shall be elected by ballot a legislative assembly for the district of San Francisco, consisting of fifteen members, citizens of the district, eight of whom shall constitute a quorum for the transaction of business; and whose power, duty, and office shall be to make such laws as they in their wisdom may deem essential to promote the happiness of the people, provided they shall not conflict with the constitution of the United States, nor be repugnant to the common law.

Section 2. Every bill which shall have passed the legislative assembly shall, before it becomes a law, be signed by the speaker and the recording clerk.

Section 3. It shall keep a journal of its proceedings, and determine its own rules.

Section 4. The members of the legislative assembly shall enter upon the duties of their office on the first Monday of March.

Article II.

Section 1. That for the purpose of securing to the people a more efficient administration of law and justice, there shall be elected by ballot three justices of the peace, of equal though separate jurisdiction, who shall be empowered by their commission of office to hear and adjudicate all civil and criminal issues in this district, according to the common law, as recognised by the constitution of the United States, under which we live.

Section 2. That there shall be an election held, and the same is hereby ordered, at the Public Institute, in the town of San Francisco, on Wednesday, the 21st of February, 1849, between the hours of eight a. m. and 5 p. m., for fifteen members of the legislative assembly for the district of San Francisco, and three justices of the peace, as hereinbefore prescribed.

Section 3. That the members of the said legislative assembly, and the three justices of the peace elected as hereinbefore prescribed, shall hold their office for the term of one year from the date of their commissions, unless sooner superseded by the competent authorities from the United States government, or by the action of a provisional government now invoked by the people of this Territory, or by the action of the people of this district.

Section 4. Members of the legislature and justices of the peace shall, before they enter upon the duties of their respective offices, take and subscribe the following oath:

I do solemnly swear that I will support the constitution of the United States and government of this district, and that I will faithfully discharge the duties of office of ———, according to the best of my ability.

Mr. Harris moved the adoption of the plan entire, which was seconded; when Mr. Buckalew moved to supersede the plan of government presented by submitting the subject to a committee to be appointed by the meeting, and whose duty it should be to report to an adjourned meeting Thereupon an animated discussion ensued. Mr. Buckalew's motion having been seconded, was lost by vote; when the question recurred on the original motion of Mr. Harris, which was carried almost unanimously.

On motion of Mr. Hyde, it was

Resolved, That the judge of the election to be held on the 21st instant shall meet at the Public Institute, in the town of San Francisco, on the 22d instant, at 10 o'clock a. m., to present to the justices of the peace their commissions, and administer to them their oath of office.

On motion of Mr. Per Lee, it was determined that every white male resident of the age of twenty-one years or upwards shall be entitled to vote at the said election.

On motion of Mr. Roach, it was

Resolved, That the persons who were elected on the 27th of December last to serve as a town council for the year 1849, and those who were elected for the same purpose on the 15th of January, 1849, be, and are hereby, requested to tender their resignations to a committee selected by this meeting to receive the same.

Messrs. Ellis, Swasey, Long, Buckalew, and Hyde were elected such committee.

On motion, it was

Resolved, That these proceedings be published in the "Alta Californian."

On motion, the meeting then adjourned.

WYDEN NORTON, *President*.

T. W. PERKINS, *Secretary*.

No. II.

SAN FRANCISCO, *March* 23, 1849.

I do hereby certify, that at an election held for justices of the peace and for members of the district legislature, on the 21st day of February, 1849, Wyden Norton, Heron R. Per Lee, and William M. Stewart, were elected justices of the peace. Stephen A. Wright, Alfred J. Ellis, Henry A. Harrison, George C. Hubbard, George Hyde, Isaac Montgomery, William M. Smith, Andrew J. Grayson, James Creighton, Robert A. Parker, Thomas J. Roach, William F. Swasey, Talbot H. Green, Francis J. Lippitt, and George Hawk Lemon were elected to the district legislature.

W. GILLESPIE,
One of the judges, and Inspector of Election.

No. III.

I hereby certify that I administered the oath of office to the members of the legislature of the district of San Francisco, on the 5th of March, 1849.

H. R. PER LEE, *Justice of the Peace.*
SAN FRANCISCO, *March* 20, 1849.

No. IV.

MONDAY EVENING, *March* 5, 1849.

The legislative assembly of the district of San Francisco met the first time at the Public Institute. Present: Messrs. Creighton, Ellis, Grayson, Green, Harrison, Hubbard, Hyde, Lemon, Lippitt, Montgomery, Parker, Roach, Smith, Swasey, and Wright.

The oath of office was administered to the aforesaid members elect by his honor Judge H. R. Per Lee.

Mr. Hyde was then appointed chairman pro tempore.

The members then proceeded to elect, by ballot, their officers, Messrs. Roach and Smith having been appointed tellers, who, after counting the votes, declared Francis J. Lippitt duly elected as speaker to the house, and J. Howard Ackerman clerk. Accordingly, Mr. Lippitt took the chair.

On motion, a committee of three were appointed to draw up rules of proceeding, to report at a special meeting to be held on Tuesday evening, at 7 o'clock. Messrs. Harrison, Hyde, and Roach, committee.

Mr. J. Cade was appointed sergeant-at-arms, and Mr. E. Gilbert printer for the house.

On motion, a special committee of three were appointed to act in connexion with the judges of the district, to report a code of laws as soon as practicable.

On motion, Mr. Lippitt was added to the committee. Messrs. Hyde, Harrison, and Creighton, committee.

The following resolution was presented by Mr. Hyde, which, after some discussion, was carried unanimously:

Resolved, That Mr. Frank Ward be appointed the treasurer of the district of San Francisco, to act temporarily until properly superseded by law, and who shall be empowered to receive all bonds, mortgages, notes, and money or moneys now in the hands of any officers existing under the late authority, and report the amount to this house.

Moved by Mr. Smith, and seconded, that a suitable place be provided in which the magistrates elect may hold a court.

On motion, a committee of three were appointed to confer with the judges on the subject. Messrs. Parker, Wright, and Ellis, committee.

On motion, the meeting adjourned until Friday evening, 7 o'clock.

FRANCIS J. LIPPITT, *Speaker*.

True copy from the minutes:
J. HOWARD ACKERMAN, *Clerk*.

No. V.

Resolved, That Messrs. Creighton, Green, Hyde, Harrison, and Roach be a committee to wait upon Major General Persifor F. Smith, commanding the third or Pacific military division, and Commodore Thomas Ap C. Jones, commander-in-chief of the naval forces on the Pacific station, and lay before those gentlemen a true statement of the affairs of this district, which have impelled the people to organize this legislative assembly, and to appoint judges and other ministerial officers, to enact suitable laws, to establish principles of justice and equity, and give protection to life, liberty, and property; and to solicit from the above-mentioned high officers of the government of the United States such recognition and concurrence in our proceedings as will strengthen, and, if need be, sustain the exercise of the high conservative powers which have been delegated by the people of this district.

FRANCIS J. LIPPITT, *Speaker*.

A true copy from the minutes of the meeting held by the legislative assembly.

J. HOWARD ACKERMAN, *Clerk*.

MARCH 6, 1849.

No. VI.

SAN FRANCISCO, *March* 10, 1849.

SIR: The undersigned, a committee appointed by the legislative assembly of the district of San Francisco, now in session, have the honor to address you this letter in pursuance of, and in accordance with, the tenor of a resolution passed by that body.

The committee, recognising you as the highest military authority of the United States government in this Territory, would respectfully invite your attention to the following facts and reasons, by which the people of this district were impelled to adopt the government now existing, with a view to obtain the aid and concurrence of your authority, if required, in the execution of its laws—the object aimed at in its establishment being the protection of public property and private right:

Before the occupation of this Territory by the United States naval forces of the Pacific squadron, the civic relations of California, in a great measure, were abandoned, and the country existing in a state of war. When taken possession of by the American troops, although the *"former usages"* were declared to be in force, yet for some reason they were not promulgated to the people. The consequence was, that many ministerial and judicial offices, necessary for the efficient administration of law and justice, became vacant, and have never been revived. The single office of alcalde, however, was retained by the military authorities during the war. This office, of Spanish creation, having its power, duty, and jurisdiction limited and defined by law, was, by necessity, in the absence of that law, tacitly permitted to obtain and exercise a most extensive and unlimited jurisdiction, wholly incompatible with the dictates both of reason and justice, and the increased necesities of the people. The right of appeal from the jurisdiction and decision of the officer holding it was sometimes obtained, of course, to the military governor; and sometimes this right was denied or evaded.

Upon the ratification of peace and its official announcement by Governor Mason, it is believed he withdrew from all connexion with the civic relations of the Territory. Consequently, for present security, and in lieu of any legislative action by the United States Congress, the office of alcalde was continued "by the presumed consent of the people," and without any alteration, except that the right to appeal, sometimes exercised under martial law, and therefore recognised by it, became imperative. The jurisdiction, power, and duty of the office, partially limited by martial law, without it, became unlimited and irresponsible. The tenure, duty, and property of the office, existing under martial law, without any defined or prescribed rules, was continued so, and the people left without any law, in the adjudication of every civil and criminal issue, *except the mere will of this single officer.* Although elected by the people, being the only judicial officer in the Territory, and having all the public records, both of the Mexican and recent authorities in his hands, without any controlling or superior tribunal either to investigate or punish for any crime or misdemeanor commited by him, or even to compel him to discharge his obligations with his fellow-citizens as a private individual, the impropriety of such a state of things was soon perceived and felt to be a most serious evil.

From the foregoing statement it can readily be perceived that the transition from the right use of power to the abuse of it was easy; and the committee regret to say, that the power of the office has been abused for the purpose of gratifying personal malice, and to promote self-aggrandisement, to the great injury of the people, without their possessing the means to redress it.

During the four or five months succeeding the official announcement of the ratification of peace in this Territory, the people patiently submitted to this loose state of affairs, in the hope that relief would soon be extended to them from the government at home, or by the creation of a provisional government, already invoked by them. The prospect of obtaining relief from the action of Congress soon faded away, and the time necessary to be employed in framing and organizing the provisional government was found to be too protracted to secure the advantages sought for. An event soon occurred rendering the necessity of immediate action indispensable.

Accordingly, on the 12th day of February, A. D. 1849, after due notice, a convention of the people of the district of San Francisco, numbering four or five hundred, assembled in Portsmouth square, in their primary capacity, to discuss the propriety and means of creating some defined organization of the district, until superseded by competent authority. After a session of three hours, and an animated debate on a proposition introduced, a plan of organization was unanimously adopted.

The committee would respectfully refer you to the accompanying newspaper, (the Alta Californian,) containing the official statement of the proceedings of the convention; and also the accompanying papers, containing the names of the persons elected to office, and the number of votes cast for them, under this organization, showing an unexampled unanimity of sentiment among the people. The committee would likewise refer you to the accompanying official returns of the election of the officers, and of their having been duly qualified according to the provisions of the law, and signed by the judges of the election.

From all the foregoing, it will be perceived that, although the Mexican law was in force, at least partially, before the occupation of this Territory by the United States forces, and after that event declared to be in force, yet it was never promulgated to the people. The judicial magistrates, in nearly every instance, being Americans, the various offices necessary to administer it were dispensed with during the war, and have never been restored. The only judicial office existing, the alcalde, never could, and never did, administer that law; but all the civil and criminal issues that came before him for adjudication were determined according to his notions of right and wrong, directed and enforced by his mere will. This single will, therefore, was the law, without the right of an appeal; and hence the Mexican law has never been actually in force, recognised, or in use in this Territory, from the occupation by the United States troops up to the present moment.

The committee are of opinion that this is also the view of the subject taken by the President of the United States and by Congress; for if the Mexican law had been in use, there must necessarily have been a government organized *de facto*, requiring an executive power to see that the law was duly administered. It would have been the duty of the President to have nominated, and the duty of the Senate to have ratified a nomination for that purpose. Besides, stipulations would have been made in the treaty with Mexico securing this action, had it been contemplated. No such stipulations, however, were made, and no governor, so far as the committee can ascertain, has been appointed; on the contrary, the language employed by the President, in two messages to Congress, assumes quite a different position: he asserts that "the temporary governments which had been established over New Mexico and California by our military and naval commanders, by virtue of the rights of war, have ceased to derive any obligatory force from that source of authority, and, having been ceded to the United States, all government and control over them, under the authority of Mexico, had ceased to exist. * * * The inhabitants, by the transfer of their country, had become entitled to the benefits of our laws and constitution, and yet were left without any regularly-organized government."

The President also, in his last annual message, has declared that he "*advised*" the people of this Territory to conform and submit, for a short time, to the "only government which remained," and "was established by the military authorities during the war." Strange to say, this advice has never reached the people until this time. However, the spirit of it has been fulfilled. The President, regarding this to be a *de facto* government, which it was not, offered this advice upon the "presumed consent of the people." To a certain degree the people, without any knowledge of this advice having been given, have consented and abode by it until the system became too oppressive to bear with. As the President has merely advised, and left the matter to the consent of the people, it clearly shows that the consent of the people must first be obtained before it can be *de facto* in force; and that, without that consent being given, they have the right to create any government they may think necessary for their protection. Hence you will perceive, sir, that the organization of the people of this district was within the reach of their power, and will be, and is, sustained by the united opinion and action of the President and both houses of Congress.

The committee, therefore, in conclusion, and according to instructions, in behalf of the people of this district, deem it their duty to inform you of this organization, of the motives impelling them to undertake it, of the means by which it was accomplished, and of the purposes for which it was ordained; and would apply to you, as the highest military authority of the United States in this Territory, to know whether you will extend to the government of this district the necessary aid, when it may be required, for the purpose of preserving order, and of protecting the property, lives, and liberty of its people. This duty the committee believe devolves upon you, as the representative of the government of the United States, and respectfully solicit your acquiescence in the premises.

Resolved, That the foregoing is the sense of this legislative assembly in reference to the premises.

Passed unanimously.

With the highest respect, the committee have the honor to subscribe themselves your most obedient servants,

JAMES CREIGHTON,
GEORGE HYDE,
HENRY A. HARRISON,
THOMAS J. ROACH,
TALBOT H. GREEN,
Committee.

Major General PERSIFOR F. SMITH,
Commanding Pacific Division.

REPLY.

HEADQUARTERS THIRD DIVISION,
San Francisco, California, March 27, 1849.

GENTLEMEN: I have the honor to acknowledge the receipt of your letter of the 20th instant, with its several enclosures.

The object stated in the resolution referred to in your letter, is to obtain from Commodore Jones and myself such "recognition and concurrence in (your) proceedings as will strengthen, and, if need be, sustain the exercise of the high conservative powers which have been delegated by the people of this district."

The powers alluded to are as follows, viz: "To organize (this) legislative assembly, and to appoint judges and other ministerial officers, and to enact suitable laws to establish principles of justice and equity, and to give protection to life, liberty, and property."

These include all the sovereign powers of government; and as my recognition and concurrence would only be asked on the presumption that your proceedings are constitutional and legal, this is equivalent to asking my opinion on those points.

I shall confine myself to stating the opinion of the President of the United States and those of his cabinet on the subject of the legal and constitutional effect of the events in California and Mexico on the state of law and government in Upper California, and which opinions have been officially promulgated and laid before Congress as the decision of the Executive on these points, and to which I must conform, as I believe them well founded.

1st. That, at the conclusion of the treaty with Mexico, on the 30th of May, 1848, the military government existing here was a government *de facto*.

2d. That it must of necessity continue until Congress provide another, because, if it cease, anarchy must ensue—thus inferring that no power but Congress can establish any government.

3d. That Congress has full and exclusive power of legislating for Territories.

4th. And that, though the existence of a state of war no longer affords a foundation for a military government *as such*, yet, as a government *de facto*, the consent of the people *must be presumed*, because no society can intentionally fall into a state of anarchy; and such is the necessary result—the "only alternative"—if the government *de facto* be abrogated before Congress provide another.

I have no doubt but that the citizens who have joined in this movement have been actuated by the purest and most patriotic motives, and that the government they have devised would be conducted to insure the respect and gratitude of all under it. But, unless it be well founded, and secure in a validity which can carry it safely through all the searching examinations of future judicial scrutiny, all must be aware that every step taken in prosecution of it is only weaving up an endless thread of litigation in every commercial and domestic relation. I have not replied to the arguments accompanying your letter, for the position assumed by the Executive seems to me self-evident. But I would respectfully suggest to you and your fellow-citizens, whether an opinion on a point of constitutional law, the result of the deliberations of such jurists as Mr. Buchanan, Governor Marcy, Judge Mason, Mr. Walker, and Judge Toucey, and published to the world by the President of the United States in his annual message, is not entitled to some weight, in at least postponing your further action in this matter until it could be reconsidered by the Executive.

I assure you, and your fellow-citizens, that I feel the greatest interest in the welfare of your rising community, and would at once lay down any of my personal opinions on matters of expediency to your superior knowledge of what will best suit the wishes of the people. But in relation to fundamental principles, I would be doing them great injustice if I did not use every effort to prevent the confusion and intricacy that will inevitably result from establishing even the best government on a false basis.

I must also remark, that it strikes me that the chief ground of your present action is the misconduct (alleged) of some of the officers of the existing government. Let me assure you that any definite charge will be thoroughly examined, as it will be seen that there is not only the disposition, but the law and the power, to remove and to punish any officer clearly proved to be guilty.

In conclusion, I will state that I do not deem it inconsistent with the principles above stated, that the inhabitants of each district should have and exercise the free right to establish such interior regulations for police and security as they may think fit, and are not adverse to existing laws; and that such regulations should receive the aid of all authorities, civil and military, in their enforcement.

With much respect, your obedient servant,

PERSIFOR F. SMITH,
Brevet Major General, commanding division.

To Messrs. JAMES CREIGHTON, GEORGE HYDE, HENRY A. HARRISON, THOMAS J. ROACH, TALBOT H. GREEN, *Committee.*

HEADQUARTERS THIRD DIVISION,
San Francisco, April 16, 1849.

SIR: It is, no doubt, a matter of great interest to the government to have some accurate information relative to the actual product and probable wealth of the gold mines in Upper California. But there are no means of collecting facts in an authentic form in the country where the gold is found. The enormous expense attending a visit and residence there can only be incurred by some one who partakes of the advantages of laboring or trading there, and is utterly beyond the means of any whom I am authorized to send.

The estimate of the amount produced up to the 1st of this month, which I have stated in my report to the Adjutant General at about four millions, was founded on a comparison of the calculations of different persons who have been at the mines, and of those who trade with the miners. I mentioned in the report that I was collecting some facts which might fix the amount with more certainty.

These facts are set forth in the enclosed documents from the person acting as collector of the revenue here; being, first, a statement of the quantity and value of goods, wares, and merchandise, imported into the port of San Francisco district, California, from October 1st, 1848, to 31st March, 1849; and, second, a statement of gold dust exported from the port of San Francisco from October 1st, 1848, to 31st March, 1849.

By the first it appears that the amount of goods received at this port was, during the six months mentioned, $1,089,801 85. Though some of these remain unsold because they do not suit the market, yet that amount is more than balanced by the amount of gold dust not yet brought into market. The goods which have been sold here average 200 per cent.

on the invoice value, though the whole amount would not give that rate, as some are unsold. The amount of goods sold would then be in even numbers $3,200,000. Now every part of this has been paid for in gold dust, for all other business has been abandoned which formerly gave a foundation for commerce. And if the amount carried out by those who first procured it be estimated $1,000,000, as it generally is, it would show a probable yield of the mines of $4,250,000. A small trade has been carried on at Monterey and some of the southern ports. As this result is only approximative, it need not be calculated.

By the second statement, it appears that the amount actually exported and declared in the custom-house in the same period, is $2,842,040. This amount carried out by individuals, without being declared, by sea, and to Oregon and Sonora by land, is estimated at $1,000,000; and there is here and near the mines about $800,000; making in all about $4,642,000. The estimate of what is here and at the mines is pretty accurate. If that taken out without being declared be reduced one-half—and no one puts in lower than $600,000—there will still remain something near the result of the first calculation, viz: $4,250,000 for the six months ending 1st April. But the period of low water from June to December is that of greatest product in the mines; and this year the force at work there will be at least quadrupled, (if half we hear be true, it will be decupled,) and will have the advantage of better tools and machinery. So that, supposing the gold most easily got has already been gathered, the product of the next 12 months will be from $12,000,000 to $20,000,000. And if it be not a scattered deposite on the surface, but the indications of deeper and extra veins, the amount must be still greater.

Two important consequences may follow a very large production of gold, viz: a very large increase of the circulating medium of the commercial world, with a corresponding decrease of its value, and, consequently, a rise in the nominal value of all other articles; and, secondly, a change in the relative value of gold and silver.

I cannot believe that either of these evils will be felt very suddenly, or to a great extent, demanding special measures of prevention. As to the second, it may be said that if gold becomes cheaper, silver will be relatively worth more than it now is, and its production increased; for there are some discoveries of silver in South America as wonderful as the gold here. This discovery of the American silver mines, and the immense addition of that metal to the circulation of the world, were many years in changing materially the state of the markets. Several hundred millions were produced before the effect was very apparent. But refer to the state of agriculture and manufactures at that time, see in how few channels money could be directed with profit, and it is evident that a comparatively small surplus would soon find obstructions and choke up the way for its own progress.

Now, ten times the same amount, instead of waiting inactive for investment, would be instantly absorbed by the thousand demands of modern industry and enterprise for capital, and, instead of overflowing and ruining the existing channels of trade and commerce, would open many new ones in proportion to the power of supplying them. So far from foreseeing any evil in the augmentation of gold from these mines, I believe it will only give new life and activity to our country where we have land, enterprise, industry, and skill, awaiting only for capital to make them

productive; and thus a far greater benefit will ensue than if one-half of the gold went into the public treasury.
With respect, your obedient servant,
PERSIFOR F. SMITH,
Brevet Major General, commanding division.
Hon. SECRETARY OF WAR.

[No. 5.] HEADQUARTERS PACIFIC DIVISION,
San Francisco, California, April 29, 1849.

SIR: I have the honor herewith to send copies of division orders Nos. 6 and 7, and special orders Nos. 6, 7, 8, 9, 10, and 11. Also, an enclosed surgeon's certificate of ordinary disability in the cases of Sergeant Fanning, privates Griffith, Lomer, and Eversfield, all of the 2d regiment of dragoons. They were referred to me from department headquarters No. 10; and were it not for the fact that a steamer is on the point of starting for Panama, I should act on them. They are forwarded to your office in pursuance with the provisions of the paragraphs 223 and 224, General Regulations; but it is most respectfully suggested that the regulation be so modified as to permit the commanders of the 10th and 11th military departments to discharge upon certificates of disability without referring them to Washington.

Communication with general headquarters from California and Oregon is, and must continue for some time, precarious.

I have the honor to be, your most obedient servant,
PERSIFOR F. SMITH,
Brevet Major General, commanding division.
Brig. Gen. R. JONES,
Adjutant General, Washington, D. C.

[No. 6.] HEADQUARTERS THIRD DIVISION,
San Francisco, May 1, 1849.

GENERAL: Part of General Riley's regiment has arrived since my last report. The general depot has been established at Benicia, on the straits of Karquinnes, and two companies stationed there for its protection. The lease of the warehouses here, occupied by the quartermasters, expires next month, and others could not be hired under $20,000 per annum, if for that. I authorized him to buy a vessel for a sum not exceeding this, to be used as a warehouse and for quarters for two companies, until lumber could be collected and temporary buildings put up. I beg the Quartermaster General may be advised of the change in the location, in order that all stores may be shipped for "Benicia, bay of San Francisco."

Two of the small transports here have been ordered to Oregon for lumber; and Captain Ingalls, acting assistant quartermaster, will go to make preparations for receiving and quartering the regiment of mounted riflemen in this Territory. No returns have been received from Oregon, nor have I any intelligence yet of the arrival of Major Hathaway's command, and I do not, therefore, make a division return. A small vessel from the mouth of Columbia river reports that it was said an American steamer had arrived at Victoria, in Admiralty inlet, and was taking in coal.

The immigrants from Oregon and the Indians on the upper part of the Sacramento river have had disputes, and some on each side have been murdered. General Riley will send a command of infantry into this neighborhood.

The people in some parts of this Territory are organizing local legislatures and appointing judges, &c.; the object in view is to try certain suits, in which the government is interested, before the establishment of the United States court. I shall in no case, unless absolutely driven to it, employ military force to resist or overthrow these usurpations; but I respectfully ask that the Attorney General may be directed to advise General Riley what course to pursue to arrest any judicial proceedings, by such illegal tribunals—whether by applying for a writ of prohibition or other writs, and in what manner, &c. There will be serious difficulties here if Congress has not legislated for the Territory.

With respect, your obedient servant,
PERSIFOR F. SMITH,
Brevet Major General, commanding department.
Brigadier General ROGER JONES,
Adjutant General.

HEADQUARTERS THIRD DIVISION,
San Francisco, May 21, 1849.

GENERAL: I take advantage of the sailing of a vessel for San Blas to communicate with your office. The steamers have not commenced running regularly, and no one of them is expected here before the 12th of June. A mail will not probably leave here before the 20th of June. We have no instructions from the departments later than those the receipt of which has been heretofore acknowledged.

All of the 2d infantry, except the companies on the Mary and Adeline, have arrived. Many men have deserted, and some have been retaken. Nearly all the dragoons have, it is said, deserted from the southern posts. I have no official information on this subject.

The enormous expense attending the landing and shipment of goods here will be obviated by having the depot removed to Benicia, on the straits of Karquinnes, where the general depot is established. Brevet Colonel Casey is there with two companies. Two are sent up the San Joaquin, under Major Miller, and two are destined to the upper Sacramento, under Brevet Major Kingsbury. Some disturbances have taken place there with the Indians. About four thousand persons have come to the mines from Sonora; most of them are established on the upper San Joaquin.

I have heard, but not officially, that Major Hathaway's command is in the Columbia river. There has been no mail carried between this and Oregon. It is reported here that an amendment to the civil appropriation bill provides a temporary government for California. If it does not, specific instructions to the governor *de facto*, General Riley, will be necessar to remove the difficulties and embarrassments now existing in civil affairs. Mercantile affairs are languishing from the large importations of goods, which must be sacrificed. Labor is still high and scarce.

I wish to submit to the department the propriety of allowing me, when officers are ordered home, (not for any pressing duty,) to permit them to take various routes—through Russia, by way of China, or across the southern part of the continent; the observations of intelligent officers on what they may see will be invaluable, and the time requisite will not much extend beyond that necessary now. The Russian officers here assert, that from Sitka the journey or voyage to St. Petersburg will not exceed forty days. It is not proposed to increase the allowance for transportation beyond that now made by the mail route.

As there are actually no mail routes here or in Oregon, and it has been hitherto impossible to count upon the arrival or departure of the steamboats, and as the troops in this division are not all arrived, it is impossible to have returns ready to send when a mail goes. So soon as these things are regulated, returns will be forwarded in order.

It is very probable that long since, instructions have been sent as to the collection and disposition of the revenue; but, should this not be the case, and the course at present pursued continued here, coin will accumulate in the hands of the depositary here, to the great inconvenience of commerce and risk of the government. To ship the coin would be ruinous to the merchants here, and very expensive. Under these circumstances, unless otherwise ordered, after waiting some time, I will direct such part of the funds as will not be required here to be used in purchasing gold, to be sent to the mint.

Your obedient servant,
PERSIFOR F. SMITH,
Brevet Major General, commanding division.
Brigadier General R. JONES,
Adjutant General.

HEADQUARTERS PACIFIC DIVISION,
San Francisco, June 19, 1849.

GENERAL: Since my last communication, I have the report of Brevet Major Hathaway of his arrival, with his command, (two companies of artillery,) in the Columbia river. No difficulty was found in entering the mouth of the river; the Massachusetts went in without a pilot. At this season, little or no danger is to be apprehended from the sea on the bar. When south winds prevail, it will be impassable for weeks together. Astoria is represented as very unfit for a military post or residence, and a point higher up recommended; but as the custom house is established there by law, and the troops may be necessary for its protection, no change will be made, unless it prove very unhealthy there, and the post can be removed without inconvenience.

I purpose visiting Oregon in August, and to be able to furnish detailed information on all these points from my own observation. In the mean time, a post is to be established near Tusqually, on Puget's sound. The garrison of the "Presidio," two and a half miles from this towards the entrance of the bay, is the only body of troops near this place. That place is properly called the "Presidio of San Francisco." This town is properly "Yerba Buena"—the people have assumed for it the name of San Francisco, and it is generally known as such; but it is not a military post—has had no garrison; and now the stores are all removed from it to "Benicia," a place on the straits of Karquinnes, where is established the general depot for this division, and a military post garrisoned by two companies of infantry. A small company of dragoons is posted at Sonoma, a day's ride west-southwest from Benicia, whence it can visit, if necessary, the country bounded by the Sacramento (latitude 42) and the ocean—said to be thickly inhabited by Indians. I am about to move my headquarters to Sonoma. A post is being established on the upper Sacramento, and on the upper San Joaquin; and San Diego and Monterey have garrisons. The troops which sailed in the "Mary Adeline," and which put back into the Chesapeake, have not yet arrived.

As correct and minute information in relation to this country is, no doubt, much desired by government, I shall take the liberty, when officers are returning to the Atlantic States under orders to report to their respective corps, to order them, unless some specific duties are pointed out, to report to you at Washington, that an opportunity may be afforded of questioning them personally. Some of them have been over a great part of the territory, and have not wasted their opportunities of gaining valuable knowledge.

The steamers from Panama have never been to Oregon, and have not regularly stopped at the ports south of this, so that we have but occasional communication with other parts of the coast, and consequently have no regular returns from the two departments up to the last of May. A field return of the division, formed on the latest returns received, is all that can yet be furnished. Desertions still take place, but I hope will not continue; many desire to return. I will not make any offer of pardon which they may or may not accept; but, should any come back, I would encourage such conduct by clemency towards them.

High prices of rent and labor still continue, and adventurers of all classes and nations still flock in. Further examination does not diminish the prospect of a continuation, for some years at least, at the same rate of production as heretofore; and though many are disappointed, yet the good fortune of a few is sufficient to keep alive the hopes of all; and nearly every one who arrives goes directly to the mines, so that the numbers there are constantly increasing.

I have no doubt that, when the immigrants by the plains arrive, there will be a population of over one hundred thousand souls in California.

L. Jarvis (2d July) died a few days since at Sonoma, of disease of the bowels, contracted in Mexico.

Some of the New York volunteers, discharged some months since, ask for transportation home, under the order of the Secretary of War. Will the department please to say as to what time, and under what circumstances, this privilege is to be continued to them. Those who have always been endeavoring to get home, would seem to be entitled to it; but those who at first chose to remain, and now, having completed their business, change their minds, seem to me to be concluded by their first elections.

I hear of no late disorders in this Territory, and the people seem in-

clined to meet in convention to form a State constitution, in conformity with General Riley's recommendation in his proclamation.
With respect, your obedient servant,
PERSIFOR F. SMITH,
Brevet Major General, commanding department.
Brevet Major General R. JONES,
Adjutant General.

HEADQUARTERS PACIFIC DIVISION,
San Francisco, June 20, 1849.

SIR: I have the honor to acknowledge the receipt of your communication, by the hands of the Hon. T. Butler King.

With the view of affording him every possible opportunity of acquiring information relative to California, its present situation, its capabilities and prospects, I have prepared the means of making a journey over the most part of the Territory that is inhabited—going from the upper part of the Sacramento along the foot of the Sierra Nevada to the upper waters of the San Joaquin, and returning by a route nearer the coast, after visiting the country north of this bay, near the sea. Several officers of the staff will accompany us; and an experienced geologist, Dr. Tyson, of Maryland, has promised to go along. Commodore Jones will also be of the party, if he finds he can be spared from the court. We shall leave as soon as the steamer is despatched.

It is hoped that the character of the country, its capability of cultivation, its products in minerals and timber, will be so far ascertained as to furnish all the data necessary for legislation.

If the country, as I think it will, prove capable of sustaining a large population and of furnishing them with most of the materials necessary for all branches of industry, its situation on the Pacific, its excellent harbor, and uninterrupted navigation, will give birth to a commerce of the highest class, independent of the advantage given by the possession of gold mines; so that, whether these continue to be productive or not, the future importance of California will be the same. The crowd of gold seekers increases every day; yet the ratio of their gains continues about the same as at first, showing as yet no diminution of the quantity of gold in the "placers."

The history of discoveries similar to this shows that, after a period of from ten to twenty years, such deposites are so far exhausted as to furnish only the ordinary profit to labor; but in this case the extent of the deposites is so unprecedented that its limit is yet to be known. Some years may first elapse before the usual period of gradual exhaustion begins. As the annual product may be estimated safely at ten millions as the minimum, it is clear that even twenty years of production will furnish a capital sufficient to develop all other resources of the country, and give vigor to a commerce unrivalled; and consequently no effort should be left untried to furnish legislation with all the lights necessary to clear the way for so interesting a future. Nothing on my part will be spared to enable the government, at the earliest moment, to provide for all the political or commercial wants of a people who are to take so important a position in the world as those of California.

Under the hope that some act of the last Congress had provided, or at least defined, the government of California, it was thought prudent to await intelligence of the close of the session; and then, if nothing had been done at Washington, to put in action the authority of the laws already existing here, and at the same time to propose to the people of California to form a State constitution, and present it at the next session of Congress—when their admission into the Union as a State would at once solve so many difficulties, and, while it removed a cause of disagreement at home, would give them an opportunity of legislating for themselves.

The steamer Edith had been sent to Mazatlan for the necessary intelligence; and on her arrival, with information that no other than a revenue law had been passed, General Riley issued a proclamation for the election of the necessary executive and judicial officers under the existing laws, recommending at the same time the election of delegates to a convention to form a State constitution.

Mr. King arrived at the time these proclamations were about being issued, and it was matter of great congratulation that the government by anticipation had approved of the latter measure.

Every means will be used to give the people of California an opportunity of expressing their wishes on this point, and of bringing the matter to a happy conclusion.

To insure this, I may find it necessary to postpone my visit to Oregon, unless some pressing and unforeseen necessity arises.

No opposition has been manifested to the project of forming a State—*that* has met with universal approbation; but some small factions here expressed dissatisfaction that the measure did not proceed from them. Its obvious utility will drown their censure.

During the military occupation of California, sums were collected as military contributions. After the news of peace, a revenue conformably to the tariff was collected. On my arrival, the acting collectors were instructed not to exact duties, but to receive them as deposites at the door of the treasury, awaiting the action of Congress. The revenue laws (without our knowledge) were extended over California at the same time, (March 11,) and all the sums thus collected are now deposited in the hands of the quartermaster. They amount to near half a million. The military contribution, under a late law, can be paid into the treasury; but the revenue collected after the peace, and up to March 10, is not money collected according to law. The money collected since is due by law, but not collected according to law while the collector is yet absent. As the money will finally go into the treasury in some way or other, it is desirable that some disposition should at once be made of it; and I would suggest that all the disbursing officers authorized to draw should cash their drafts here out of this fund, and send the drafts home, to remain subject to final action. This would transmit the fund to Washington, and furnish the disbursing officers here, without expense: drafts at par on Mexican Pacific ports, cause two or three per cent. loss in export duty, freight, &c.

The emoluments attached to military office were no doubt intended to provide the officers with all the necessaries of life, while the *pay proper* was intended as compensation for service. In the course of experience, it was found that these could not always be drawn in kind. An officer in a boarding-house, for example, could do nothing with his rations, fuel, &c., &c., and the whole were calculated, together with his quarters, in the sum he paid for board and lodging. From this arose the practice of commuting these emoluments; and the sum fixed on had reference to what the officer would have to pay if he furnished himself, and was, perhaps, an equitable arrangement, and would meet the wants of any reasonable and economical man, being founded on the actual price at the time and place. But these prices are totally inadequate here; they will not furnish the articles they are intended to represent.

The salary of the Secretary of War would not half pay the rent of the quarters to which a general officer is entitled by the regulations, and not much more than pay the hire of his servants.

It seems to me fair, and I would respectfully suggest, that the commutation here be brought back to be what was originally intended—a fair alternation for the supply furnished, and that the disbursing departments should from time to time fix the rate according to an average of prices, so that when circumstances oblige an officer to take the commutation, it may bear some relation to the article it is intended to represent.

In the hope of preventing desertion, I have authorized the quartermasters to employ soldiers to labor at a rate approaching to that current at the place, the soldiers having short furloughs for the purpose; and as other laborers were not to be had at lower prices than the additional emolument, this is economy for the government.

But it would be better that it should be the subject of some general regulation. In the Atlantic States the pay, clothing, subsistence, quarters and medical attendance a soldier receives are equal, if not superior, to the average daily wages of a laborer. Here they are not one-tenth—the soldier receiving a little over fifty cents a day, and the laborer from six to ten dollars.

The high rate of labor here would seem (for it is likely to last some years) to render all heavy public works here unadvisable; yet the necessity of securing the harbors and public establishments increasing every day with their increase of value, renders some system immediately necessary.

If the system of fortification for each place be at once adopted, and only the water batteries at the entrance executed, the others might be postponed, and in the mean time security attained.

By the construction of many large steamships in the Atlantic States, where prices are still the same, as coal is no doubt plenty in Oregon, these vessels could run in the Pacific as packets to China and South America, and always anticipate the arrival of an enemy on our coast; so houses, barracks, storehouses, and everything that requires labor in its construction, may be prepared in the Atlantic States and transported here, thus diffusing the advantages of the gold mines here over the whole country.

With sincere respect, your obedient servant,
PERSIFOR F. SMITH,
Brevet Major General, commanding division.

Hon. W. H. CRAWFORD,
Secretary of War.

[18]

HEADQUARTERS PACIFIC DIVISION,
Sonoma, June 29, 1849.

SIR: I have the honor to acknowledge your communication of the 26th of March last, calling for certain muster-rolls and other information with respect to the New York and California volunteers, and to state in answer, that, in consequence of the want of the requisite information at my headquarters, your letter was referred to the commander of the 10th department—his reply to which is herewith enclosed.

Very respectfully, your obedient servant,

PERSIFOR F. SMITH,
Brevet Major General, commanding department.

Brevet Major General R. JONES,
Adjutant General, Washington.

HEADQUARTERS TENTH MILITARY DEPARTMENT,
San Francisco, June 16, 1849.

COLONEL: I have the honor to state, in reply to your communication of the 14th instant, that a part of the information required by the instructions of the Secretary of War of October 9 has already been forwarded to Washington, and the reason of the failure to furnish the muster-rolls of Colonel Fremont's battalion has been reported to the Adjutant General. The original muster-rolls of the New York regiment are printed with the department record, and copies of the missing rolls will be forwarded upon my return to Monterey.

Very respectfully, Colonel, your obedient servant,

B. RILEY,
Brevet Brigadier General, commanding department.

Lieutenant Colonel J. HOOKER,
A. A. G., Headquarters Third Division,
San Francisco, California.

HEADQUARTERS PACIFIC DIVISION,
Sonoma, California, August 26, 1849.

SIR: At the time of the departure of the last mail for the Atlantic States I had not yet returned from a journey through the mining districts in the mountains at the western part of the Sierra Nevada, and was not in communication with San Francisco until after the steamer had left. As the return for this department for May only reached division headquarters three days ago, and nothing of any moment had transpired in the division, there was nothing of importance to communicate.

The two last companies of the 2d infantry arrived in July. They have since lost many men by desertion.

The points occupied by troops in this department now, are San Diego, Monterey, the Presidio of San Francisco, Benicia, (the general depot,) Camp Stanislaus on the river Stanislaus, about twenty-five miles SSE. from Stockton; and Major Kingsbury, with a command, is directed to occupy a point about thirty miles NNW. from Sutter's Fort. It is uncertain when he will reach it.

San Diego and Monterey are harbors; the Presidio of San Francisco, 2½ miles from the town, is near the entrance of the bay, where there is a small dilapidated work. Benicia, about 26 or 30 miles from the sea, accessible to the largest ships, just below the junction of the Sacramento and San Joaquin rivers, is the general depot.

The other two posts on the upper waters of those two streams were intended to have an influence on the mining districts and the neighboring Indians, but principally as auxiliary depots, from which expeditions could be supplied when about marching towards the mountains. They lie beyond the immense marshes surrounding the rivers, and which are often impassable, and from these posts any part of the mines, mountains, or country beyond can be reached by troops at any season—though during the latter part of the rainy season the difficulties of travelling anywhere in the country, (except on the bays and large rivers,) are almost insurmountable. The cost and difficulty of transportation, and other causes, have hitherto prevented the complete establishment of these posts.

General Riley proposes to increase the number of posts. I do not think this advisable, except placing one near the Oregon frontier between the Sacramento and the sea, when the country shall have been explored. It is preferable to have a column or two moving through the country—small scattered posts are the graves of activity and enterprise.

I have sent Captain Warner, topographical engineers, with an escort to make an accurate examination of what is indicated as the best route from Humboldt's river to the Sacramento. He is directed to ascertain if this route, especially the pass through the mountains, be practicable for a railroad. The season remaining for this purpose is very short.

There are very few houses in the country, and the expense of all kinds of labor is so enormous that it is difficult to build: nevertheless I have directed the erection of temporary quarters and storehouses at the general depot, to cover, if possible, the garrison and stores before the rains. For the other posts, frame, or rather iron buildings should be sent from the Atlantic. None of the apparently exaggerated reports of the price of labor here reach the truth.

I start to-morrow for Oregon, and expect to be here again the 10th of October. As my examination of the mining country will not be complete until I have visited the country near latitude 40 and 41, I postpone a general report until my return.

I have to regret exceedingly that the Edith and Massachusetts have been transferred to the navy. The prevailing winds here are constant from the northwest, and sailing-vessels go northward with great difficulty. They dare not approach an unknown part of the coast to examine it, as it is rocky, without anchorage, and a lee shore.

Your obedient servant,
PERSIFOR F. SMITH,
Brevet Major General, commanding division.
Brevet Lt. Col. W. G. FREEMAN,
A. A. G., Headquarters of the Army.

Official:

W. G. FREEMAN,
Assistant Adjutant General.

HEADQUARTERS OF THE ARMY,
New York, October 18, 1849.

[18]

List of reports from General Riley.

ON CIVIL AFFAIRS.

Report, with correspondence, June 30, 1849.
Report, with correspondence, August 30, 1849.
Report, with enclosure, August 30, 1849.
Report, with correspondence, October 1, 1849.
Report, with correspondence, October 31, 1849.

ON MILITARY AFFAIRS.

Report to the Adjutant General, February 12, 1849.
Report to the Adjutant General, April 10 & 13, 1849.
Report to the Adjutant General, April 21, 1849.
Report to the Adjutant General, April 25, 1849.
Report to the Adjutant General, with enclosures, April 30, 1849.
Copies of correspondence, June 2, 1849.
Report to the Adjutant General, June 11, 1849.
Report to the Adjutant General, June 19, 1849.
Report to the Adjutant General, June 19, 1849.
Report to the Adjutant General, June 30, 1849.
Copies of correspondence, June 30, 1849.
Report to the Secretary of War, August 30, 1849.
Report to the Commanding General, September 20, 1849.
Report to the Commanding General, October 15, 1849.
Report to the Adjutant General, October 31, 1849.
Report to the Adjutant General, November 1, 1849.

Executive Department of California,
Monterey, June 30, 1849.

GENERAL: I have the honor to transmit herewith copies of all civil correspondence and papers since the 13th of April last, at which time I relieved Colonel Mason from his duties as governor of California.

It was (with the advice of Colonel Mason) my intention, on assuming the direction of civil affairs in this country, to complete the organization of the existing government; at the same time to call a convention for forming a State constitution, or plan of Territorial government, to be submitted to Congress for its approval. But on further consultation it was deemed best to postpone all action on this subject, until I could ascertain what had been done in Congress. On the first instant I received reliable information by the steamer "Edith" that that body had adjourned without organizing any Territorial government for this country; and accordingly, on the 3d instant I issued my proclamation to the people of California, defining what was understood to be the legal position of affairs here, and pointing out the course it was deemed advisable to pursue in order to procure a new political organization better adapted to the character and present condition of the country. The course indicated in my proclamation will be adopted by the people, almost unanimously, and there is now little or no doubt that the convention will meet on the first of September next and form a

State constitution, to be submitted to Congress in the early part of the coming session.

A few prefer a territorial organization, but I think a majority will be in favor of a State government, so as to avoid all further difficulties respecting the question of slavery. This question will probably be submitted, together with the constitution, to a direct vote of the people, in order that the wishes of the people of California may be clearly and fully expressed. Of course, the constitution or plan of territorial government formed by this convention can have no legal force till approved by Congress.

On the receipt of the treaty of peace with Mexico, doubt was entertained by a portion of the people here respecting what constituted the legal government and laws of the country. A few contended that all government and all laws in California were at an end, and that therefore the people, in their sovereign capacity, might make such government and laws as they should deem proper. Accordingly, in two of the northern districts, local legislative assemblies were organized, and laws enacted for the government of the people of these districts. The members of the Sonoma assembly, however, soon became convinced of their error, and that body was dissolved. But in San Francisco the assembly continued its sessions, making laws, creating and filling offices, imposing and collecting taxes, without the authority and in violation of law, and finally went so far as to abolish the office of alcalde, whose records and papers were seized and forcibly removed from his custody. On receiving official information of these facts, I issued my proclamation of the 4th instant. Since then I have made a personal visit to San Francisco, and find that the more respectable members of the so-called district assembly are convinced of the impropriety of the course pursued by that body, and in a very short time I think all the difficulties will be amicably arranged. These difficulties arose in part from a misapprehension as to what constituted the legal government of the country, and in part from the unpopularity of the first alcalde of that district, against whom serious charges had been made. Unfortunately, there was at the time no legal tribunal for investigating these charges; and, there being no other magistrate in that district, I could not, with propriety, remove him from office. A new election, however, will soon be held to supply his place; and on the organization of the "superior court," the charges against him can be properly investigated.

The publication of a portion of the instructions received from Washington respecting the government of this country, and the disposition manifested by the authorities here to enforce the existing laws, have done much to remove the erroneous opinions which were for a time entertained by a portion of the people of California. The civil government of this country has been, and will continue to be, administered on the principle laid down by the Supreme Court of the United States, viz: on the transfer of the ceded territory, it has never been held that the relations of the inhabitants with each other undergo any change. Their relations with their former sovereign are dissolved, and new relations are created between them and the government which has acquired their territory. The mere act which transfers their country transfers the allegiance of those who remain in it; and the law which may be denominated political is necessarily changed, although that which regulates the intercourse and general conduct of individuals remains in force until altered by the newly-created power of the State.

The treaty is the law of the land, and admits the inhabitants of [California] to the enjoyment of the privileges, rights, and immunities of citizens of the United States. It is unnecessary to inquire whether this is not their condition, independent of stipulation. They do not, however, participate in political power; they do not share in the government till [California] shall become a State. In the mean time, [California] continues to be a Territory of the United States, governed by virtue of that clause of the constitution which empowers Congress to make all needful rules and regulations respecting the territory and other property belonging to the United States.

When we take into consideration the great mass of floating population of the United States and of other countries—people of all nations, kindreds, and tongues—which has been suddenly thrown into this country, it must be acknowledged that everything has, thus far, remained remarkably quiet, and that the amount of crime has been much less than might, under the circumstances, have reasonably been expected. It is to be feared, however, that during the coming winter, when large numbers of the miners collect in the towns, public order may be occasionally disturbed. But it is believed that in the mean time a more complete organization of the existing government will be effected, so as to enable the authorities to enforce the laws with greater regularity and efficiency.

Rumors have reached me that there is no very amicable feeling existing between the Americans and foreigners in the gold regions, and that the former are disposed to forcibly expel the latter from the placer districts. I shall soon visit the valleys of the Sacramento and San Joaquin, and hope to be able to report upon the true state of affairs there by the August steamer. As Congress has declined passing any laws restricting the working of the placers, I shall not deem myself authorized to interfere in this matter, any further than may be necessary to preserve the public tranquillity. Indeed there is much reason to believe that Congress has pursued the best policy, under the circumstances, in leaving the placers open to all; for it would be exceedingly difficult to enforce any regulations not absolutely required by the necessity of the case, and it is more than probable that any attempt at this time to rent out the mineral lands, or to tax their products, would involve a great expense, and it is quite possible that such an attempt would lead to very serious difficulties. Of the large numbers who have been attracted to this country by the flattering prospect of sudden wealth, and with the intention of returning to their former homes to enjoy their gains, many foreigners as well as Americans are becoming established in business, and will make California their permanent place of residence. It is therefore well worthy of serious consideration whether the present system may not prove equally beneficial with that of a more exclusive policy. It certainly conduces much towards developing the resources of the country, extending its commerce, and rapidly augmenting its wealth and population. As soon as I have made a personal examination of the gold regions, I shall be prepared to express my views on this subject; but I cannot omit the present occasion to urge upon the government the importance of establishing a mint in California, with the least possible delay.

Information, not official, has been received, that the revenue laws of the United States have been extended over this country, and that a collector and deputies may soon be expected to take charge of the collection of revenue in this district. On their arrival, all custom-houses and customhouse property will be turned over to them, and the temporary collectors employed by my predecessor and by myself will be discharged. The moneys collected during and since the war, under the direction of the governor of California, and not required for defraying the expenses of the civil government, will be kept as a separate and distinct fund, subject to the disposition of Congress. The grounds upon which this revenue has been collected since the declaration of peace, are fully stated in a letter to the collector of San Francisco, dated the 24th of February last. It may be proper to add, that the course pursued by my predecessor was rendered absolutely necessary by the peculiar circumstances of the case. The wants of the country rendered it imperative upon him to permit the landing of foreign goods in this Territory; and had this been done without the collection of duties, large amounts of dutiable goods would have been placed in depôt on this coast, to the manifest injury of the revenue and prejudice to our own merchants. The importers have sold their goods at such prices as to cover the duties paid, and still leave them enormous profits; and to now return these duties to the importers would be a virtual gift, without in any way benefiting the people of California. But, to expend this money in objects of public utility in the country, would confer a lasting benefit upon all. I would therefore recommend that such portions of these moneys as may be left, after defraying the expenses of the existing civil government, be given to California as a "school fund," to be exclusively devoted to purposes of education. No difficulty has been experienced in enforcing the tariff of 1846, and the revenue has been collected at a very moderate expense, considering the peculiar circumstances of the times.

All officers of the civil government of California will be paid, out of the "civil fund" arising from the customs, the salaries fixed by law, and I would recommend that those officers of the army and navy who have been employed as collectors and receivers of customs in California, both during and since the war, be allowed a fair per centage on the money which they have collected and disbursed. Two and a half per cent. on the amount collected, with the restriction contained in section 2 of the act of March 3, 1849, is deemed a fair allowance for collecting these customs, and two and a half per cent. on the amount actually expended is deemed ample compensation for keeping and accounting for the same. It would be more just and proper to make the allowance for the *actual expenditures* than for receiving and keeping these moneys; because, if the reversed rule were established, officers who have received large sums, and within a few days transferred them to others, with no other trouble than merely passing receipts, would be entitled to a higher pay than those who have had all the trouble of expending this money in small sums, and in keeping and rendering accounts of these expenditures.

As soon as these "civil funds" can be collected from the officers now holding them, it is proposed to place them in the hands of some officer, or other responsible person, who will act as treasurer for the civil government, with a fixed compensation for his services. On the arrival of the regular collector and deputies, appointed according to law, a full statement will be made of all the moneys which have been collected in California, and the papers and accounts connected with the expenditure of this civil fund will be sent to Washington, as heretofore, in order that all officers who shall receive or expend the same may be held to a strict accountability.

I am, sir, very respectfully, your obedient servant,

B. RILEY,
Brevet Brig. Gen. U. S. A., and Governor of California.

Major General R. JONES,
Adjutant General of the Army, Washington, D. C.

STATE DEPARTMENT OF THE TERRITORY OF CALIFORNIA,
Monterey, April 17, 1849.

SIR: Representations have been made to the governor that various individuals have interfered with Father Gomez in the possession of certain buildings and other property granted by Governor Micheltorena, July 15, 1844, to the parish priest of San Luis Obispo. He therefore directs that you will use your official authority to protect the said priest in the possession of the lands, buildings, and other property so granted, till the proper tribunals shall be organized to decide upon the validity of land titles; it being understood that this order shall in no way affect the titles of any claimants.

It is also represented that a dispute has arisen between Father Gomez, Vicente Felis, and Mariano Buillo, respecting the ownership of a certain mill and mill-stones. The governor requests that, as the magistrate of this district, you will endeavor to settle this matter upon principles of justice and equity.

By order of the governor:

H. W. HALLECK,
Brevet Captain, and Secretary of State.

Don Miguel ABILA,
Alcalde of the jurisdiction of San Luis Obispo, California.

STATE DEPARTMENT OF THE TERRITORY OF CALIFORNIA,
Monterey, April 20, 1849.

SIR: I am directed by the governor to acknowledge the receipt of your communication, of the 18th instant, informing him that you had resigned the office of alcalde of this jurisdiction, and that Don Ignacio Esquer had been elected in your place; Señor Esquer will, therefore, be recognised as the alcalde of the jurisdiction of Monterey.

Very respectfully, your obedient servant,

H. W. HALLECK,
Brevet Captain, and Secretary of State.

Señor Don FLORENCIA LENANO,
Late Alcalde of the jurisdiction of Monterey, California.

STATE DEPARTMENT OF THE TERRITORY OF CALIFORNIA,
Monterey, April 20, 1849.

SIR: I am directed by General Riley to acknowledge the receipt of your letter of yesterday, and to inform you that you are recognised as the alcalde of the jurisdiction of Monterey.

Very respectfully, your obedient servant,
H. W. HALLECK,
Brevet Captain, and Secretary of State.

Don IGNACIO ESQUER,
Alcalde of the jurisdiction of Monterey.

STATE DEPARTMENT OF THE TERRITORY OF CALIFORNIA,
Monterey, April 21, 1849.

SIR: I am directed by General Riley to call your attention to the fact that no monthly statements have ever been rendered by you, nor have your custom-house papers and accounts for the 4th quarter of 1848 and 1st quarter of 1849 yet been received at this office.

The governor directs that you submit your accounts to the quartermaster immediately after the close of each quarter; and if not examined by him within a reasonable time, you will withdraw them and send them to this office, reporting the fact that the quartermaster had failed to examine them as has already been directed.

By order of Governor Riley:
H. W. HALLECK,
Brevet Captain, and Secretary of State.

E. H. HARRISON,
Collector, San Francisco, California.

STATE DEPARTMENT OF THE TERRITORY OF CALIFORNIA,
Monterey, April 24, 1849.

SIR: Your letter of the 23d has been received and laid before the governor, who is of opinion that a sutler's appointment gives him no exemption except so far as his sales to officers and soldiers are concerned. In so far as he engages in trade with others, he will be subject to the same municipal duties as other traders. His position as sutler is not intended to give, in matters of business, any monopoly or exemption from taxes and municipal duties not enjoyed by other citizens.

Very respectfully, your obedient servant,
H. W. HALLECK,
Brevet Captain, and Secretary of State.

Don IGNACIO ESQUER,
Alcalde of Monterey.

STATE DEPARTMENT OF THE TERRITORY OF CALIFORNIA,
Monterey, April 28, 1849.

SIR: I am directed to call your attention to the fact that your monthly returns (or summary statements) of civil funds are greatly in arrears, and to say to you that hereafter these returns will be rendered promptly at the end of every month.

This communication will be turned over to the officer who relieves you. By order of Governor Riley:

H. W. HALLECK,
Brevet Captain, and Secretary of State.

Captain J. S. FOLSOM,
U. S. Army, Monterey, California.

STATE DEPARTMENT OF THE TERRITORY OF CALIFORNIA,
Monterey, April 30, 1849.

SIR: I am directed by the governor to inform you that he has approved of the election held March 4th, for the district of Santa Barbara, at which you were elected alcalde, and certain others as regidors and sindicos.

I have also to inform you that the governor will order to be paid over to the town of Santa Barbara the sum of five hundred dollars and fifty cents, to be expended in the purchase or erection of a suitable building for a jail. This money accrued from a military contribution levied on the town of Santa Barbara during the war, and it will be paid over to the sindico as soon as proper evidence is given that a suitable jail has been purchased or erected.

A letter was received at this office some time since from Nariso Fabrigut, claiming remuneration for a house occupied as alcalde's office. The alcalde is the proper person to settle such questions.

Very respectfully your obedient servant,

H. W. HALLECK,
Brevet Captain, and Secretary of State.

Don RAYMUNDO CARRILLO,
Alcalde of Santa Barbara, California.

Know all men by these presents, that I, Bennet Riley, brevet brigadier general United States army, and governor of California, by virtue of authority in me vested, do hereby appoint Jabez Halleck collector and harbor-master for the port of Monterey, with a salary of one hundred and fifty dollars per month.

Done at Monterey, California, this first day of May, in the year of our Lord eighteen hundred and forty-nine.

B. RILEY,
Brevet Brigadier General, and Governor of California.

Official:

H. W. HALLECK,
Brevet Captain, and Secretary of State.

STATE DEPARTMENT OF THE TERRITORY OF CALIFORNIA,
Monterey, May 3, 1849.

SIR: I am directed by Governor Riley to acknowledge the receipt of your letter of the 14th, tendering your resignation as first alcalde of the district of Sonoma.

The governor sincerely regrets to receive your resignation, and hopes you may find it compatible with your interests to continue to act as first magistrate of your district for a few months longer. This is now one of the highest judicial offices in California, and, under the present circumstances, it is important that it be filled by men of high character and influence, whose opinions and decisions will receive the confidence of the people. It is to be feared that if an election should take place at the present time, a suitable person may not be selected for the office. The governor is aware that this office is to you one of no honor, and of little or no profit; but he hopes you will continue to give your aid and the influence of your name in maintaining public order and in executing the laws. If, however, you find it impossible to continue in office, you will consider your resignation as accepted, and, after giving due notice, hold an election to fill the vacancy.

General Riley directs me to present you his assurances of high consideration and personal regard, and hopes that while he continues to fill the office of governor of California, you will communicate with him fully respecting affairs in your district.

Very respectfully, your obedient servant,
H. W. HALLECK,
Brevet Captain, and Secretary of State.

Hon. L. W. Boggs,
  1st Alcalde, District of Sonoma, California.

The first alcalde of the district of San Francisco having reported the escape of a prisoner named Passenger, during his transfer from San Francisco to Sonoma for trial, under the charge of having committed a rape,

Now, therefore, I, Bennet Riley, brigadier general U. S. army, and governor of California, do hereby offer a reward of five hundred dollars for the apprehension and safe delivery of said Passenger into the custody of the first alcalde of the district of Sonoma.

Given at Monterey, California, this third day of May, in the year of our Lord eighteen hundred and forty-nine.

B. RILEY,
Brevet Brigadier General, and Governor of California.

Official:
H. W. HALLECK,
Brevet Captain, and Secretary of State.

State Department of the Territory of California,
Monterey, May 3, 1849.

Sir: The governor has received your letter of April 30, in which you state that you had been directed to send a prisoner named Passenger from San Francisco to the district of Sonoma, and that he had effected his escape during the transfer. The only authority in California for directing the transfer of civil prisoners from one district to another for trial is vested in the governor; and it does not appear, from the records of this office, that any such direction has been given in this case. The governor, therefore, requests that you will inform him from whom you received such direction.

Agreeably to your request, the governor will offer a reward for the apprehension of the prisoner.

By order of Governor Riley:
H. W. HALLECK,
Brevet Captain, and Secretary of State.

J. M. LEAVENWORTH,
First Alcalde, District of San Francisco, California.

Know all men by these presents, that I, Bennet Riley, brevet brigadier general United States army, and governor of California, do hereby appoint Joshua B. Haven notary public in and for the district of San Francisco.

Done at Monterey, California, this third day of May, eighteen hundred and forty-nine.

B. RILEY,
Brevet Brigadier General, and Governor of California.

Official:

H. W. HALLECK,
Brevet Captain, and Secretary of State.

STATE DEPARTMENT OF THE TERRITORY OF CALIFORNIA,
Monterey, May 3, 1849.

SIR: I am directed by the governor to acknowledge the receipt of your letter of the 30th ultimo, and to say that it affords him great pleasure to be able to forward you the appointment of notary public in and for the district of San Francisco.

Very respectfully, your obedient servant,
H. W. HALLECK,
Brevet Captain, and Secretary of State.

J. B. HAVEN,
San Francisco, California.

CIRCULAR.

STATE DEPARTMENT OF THE TERRITORY OF CALIFORNIA,
Monterey, May 3, 1849.

The instructions from this office to the collector of San Francisco, dated February 24, 1849, (copies of which have been sent to the other collectors,) contain the views of the governor respecting the collection of customs in California. Those views will continue to be carried out in every particular. The custom-house books and papers will be kept as near as possible in accordance with the regulations of the Treasury Department, and the accounts sent to this office for transmission to Washington. Monthly summary statements of revenue collected will be made out and forwarded to this office at the end of every month; and the quarterly accounts and papers will, at the end of every quarter, be submitted to the quartermaster of the nearest post for his examination; and if there should be no such officer in the vicinity, or he should fail to examine the accounts within a reasonable time, they will be sent directly to this office.

As all matters relating to port regulations in California were assigned by the President to the commander-in-chief of the Pacific squadron, (and it is not known that these instructions have been changed,) the collector will on such subjects act in accordance with the views of the commanding naval officer. Such instructions have heretofore been communicated by the commodore through the governor; but if they shall be sent directly to the collectors, they will nevertheless be obeyed. In all other matters relating to the collection and disbursement of the revenue in California, the collectors (until further instructions) will be subject only to the order of the governor; and no orders, unless emanating from him, or communicated through him, will be recognised or obeyed; and all officers having or receiving these civil funds will be held to a strict accountability, and no portion of them will be paid out or transferred or loaned to any military fund, without a written order of the governor communicated through the proper channel. The difficulties which have occurred in keeping these civil funds separate from the appropriation for military purposes, and the frequent delays in making out accounts and returns—difficulties attributed to the fact that orders have been received and acted on which did not emanate from the governor, or were not communicated through the proper channels—render it necessary that these instructions be rigorously enforced. The military officers appointed to receive the revenue from the collectors will render to this office monthly summary statements at the end of every month, and their quarterly papers at the end of every quarter.

Such portion of the civil funds as may be required for that purpose will be expended to pay the expenses of the civil government of California, and the remainder held subject to orders from Washington.

By order of Governor Riley:

H. W. HALLECK,
Brevet Captain, and Secretary of State.

Know all men by these presents, that I, Bennet Riley, brevet brigadier general United States army, and governor of California, in virtue of authority in me vested, do hereby appoint Jabez Halleck notary public and commissioner of deeds in and for the district of Monterey.

Done at Monterey, California, this 3d day of May, in the year of our Lord eighteen hundred and forty-nine.

B. RILEY,
Brevet Brigadier General, and Governor of California.

Official:

H. W. HALLECK,
Brevet Captain, and Secretary of State.

STATE DEPARTMENT OF THE TERRITORY OF CALIFORNIA,
Monterey, May 5, 1849.

SIR: Your letters of April 20 and 24, (erroneously directed to General Smith,) have been referred to Brigadier General Riley, commanding 10th military department, and governor of California, who directs me to present you his thanks for the information they contain.

A military force has been ordered to the Sacramento valley, as you suggest, to assist in maintaining public order, and in checking the mutual encroachments of the whites and Indians. Copies of your letters, and also of instructions to sub-Indian agents, dated August 16, 1847, have been sent to the commanding officer in the Sacramento district, who will render you every necessary assistance in carrying out the instructions of the government towards the Indians.

Very respectfully, your obedient servant,

H. W. HALLECK,
Brevet Captain, and Secretary of State.

Captain J. A. SUTTER,
Sub-Indian Agent, Sacramento city, California.

STATE DEPARTMENT OF THE TERRITORY OF CALIFORNIA,
Monterey, May 6, 1849.

GENTLEMEN: By a decree of the governor, of this date, you have been named commissioners to examine into certain complaints against the 1st alcalde of the district of San Francisco. You are empowered to call for persons and papers, to administer oaths, and examine witnesses. You will assemble in the town of San Francisco as soon as practicable after the receipt of your appointment; and before entering upon the investigation, you will each take an oath faithfully and truly to perform the duties assigned to you. You will give to the alcalde (J. M. Leavenworth, esq.) due notice of the time and place of your meeting. A full record of your proceedings will be signed by each commissioner and transmitted to the governor, with your opinion whether there are sufficient grounds to justify the governor in exercising the power vested in him of removing from office. It may not be necessary to investigate all the charges that may be preferred against said alcalde; for if the commissioners, upon a thorough investigation of any one complaint, find that there are sufficient grounds for removal, they will close their proceedings and report to the governor for his action in the premises. Full trial for mal-administration of office may be had before a higher tribunal which shall possess power to inflict the proper punishment. One of the charges which you are called to investigate, is that of permitting the escape of a man named Passenger, (or Passanger,) who was charged with the crime of rape. Any other complaints made against said alcalde for official misconduct will be received by you, and, if necessary, fully investigated. You will be entitled to $10 per diem for every day you are in session. The fees of sheriff or constable for summoning witnesses, and witnesses for attendance on court, will be such as are usually charged by the alcalde's court in San Francisco.

These expenses will be paid by the quartermaster in San Francisco, on the proper certificates signed by the commissioners.

By order of Governor Riley:

H. W. HALLECK,
Brevet Captain, and Secretary of State.

Messrs. J. H. GREEN,
  JAMES C. WARD,
  H. A. HARRISON,
Commissioners, &c., San Francisco.

STATE DEPARTMENT OF THE TERRITORY OF CALIFORNIA,
Monterey, May 6, 1849.

GENTLEMEN: The governor requests that, if the office of 2d alcalde of the town of San Francisco be vacant, you will immediately give notice, and act as judges and inspectors of election for filling the vacancy. As the election is for the town only, it is not deemed necessary that the notice should be given for more than two days, provided it be made sufficiently public. The same cautions should be observed, as heretofore directed, in receiving votes. In the absence of the others, any three of your number are empowered to act.

By order of Governor Riley:

H. W. HALLECK,
Brevet Captain, and Secretary of State.

Messrs. W. D. M. HOWARD, S. A. WRIGHT, J. TOWNSEND, J. MONTGOMERY, EDWARD GILBERT, FRANK WARD, and T. J. ROACH.

Know all men by these presents, that I, Bennet Riley, brevet brigadier general United States army, and governor of California, by virtue of authority in me vested, do hereby appoint J. H. Green, James C. Ward, and H. A. Harrison, commissioners with full powers to investigate complaints against J. M. Leavenworth, esq., the 1st alcalde of the district of San Francisco.

Given at Monterey, California, this 6th day of May, in the year of our Lord eighteen hundred and forty-nine.

B. RILEY,
Brevet Brig. Gen., commanding Tenth Military Department, and Governor of California.

Official:

H. W. HALLECK,
Brevet Captain, and Secretary of State.

Know all men by these presents, that I, Bennet Riley, brevet brigadier general United States army, and governor of California, by virtue of authority in me vested, do hereby suspend J. M. Leavenworth, esq., from the exercise of all the duties and functions of his office as 1st alcalde of the district of San Francisco. The duties and powers of this office will, until further instructions, be performed by the 2d alcalde of the town of

San Francisco. The above suspension will take effect on the receipt by the alcalde of a copy of this decree.

Given at Monterey, California, this 6th day of May, in the year of our Lord eighteen hundred and forty-nine.

B. RILEY,
Brevet Brig. Gen. commanding 10th Military Department, and Governor of California.

Official:
H. W. HALLECK,
Brevet Captain, and Secretary of State.

PROCLAMATION.

The undersigned has been directed by the Secretary of War, while exercising the functions of governor of California, to assist the civil authority of the country, with the military forces under his command, in executing the laws and maintaining public tranquillity. It is desirable that a portion of these forces should be employed in maintaining order in the gold districts, and also in restraining the Indian horse-thieves, who, in the absence of the rancheros from the southern districts, are driving the horses to the mountains and committing numerous robberies and murders; but in order to accomplish these objects, it is absolutely necessary that the civil authorities and all good citizens lend their aid and assistance to the naval and military commanders, by arresting deserters and restoring them to their ships and garrisons.

Tempted by the flattering prospect of sudden wealth in the gold regions, and forgetful of their oaths and obligations to government, sailors and soldiers desert their colors, and leave their ships and military stores without the means of security and defence. The crews of merchant vessels, also yielding to the same seductive hopes, leave their vessels helpless and exposed to destruction by the elements. Very few of these merchant vessels which enter our ports are able to proceed on their voyages, and the owners are obliged to cover by the price of their cargoes the detention and loss of the vessels which bring them, thus severely taxing the productive industry of the country to pay for the neglect of the civil authorities to compel men to fulfil the obligations which they have voluntarily contracted. The civil authorities, however, can do little towards enforcing the laws without the countenance and assistance of the people themselves. The evils resulting from this state of things are daily increasing, and if allowed to continue, the discovery of the gold placers, instead of benefiting California, will prove her greatest curse. It is hoped, therefore, that all good citizens will give to the civil and military authorities their cordial aid and co-operation in the execution of their duties and the maintenance of public order.

Given at Monterey, this 6th day of May, in the year of our Lord eighteen hundred and forty-nine.

B. RILEY,
Brev. Brig. Gen. U. S. Army, commanding 10th M. Dept., and Governor of California.

Official:
H. W. HALLECK,
Brevet Captain, and Secretary of State.

STATE DEPARTMENT OF THE TERRITORY OF CALIFORNIA,
Monterey, May 9, 1849.

SIR: I have to acknowledge the receipt of your letter of the 8th instant. You say that one of your predecessors, Mr. Colton, sold town lands to various individuals, but left no record in your office of the governor's orders with respect to such sales, nor any plans to indicate what lands have been sold and what are still saleable, and that, under these circumstances, you wish the advice of the governor before proceeding to make any further sales.

Your letter has been laid before Governor Riley, who directs me to reply as follows:

1. Neither Governor Kearny nor Governor Mason gave to alcalde Colton any power to sell lands. Governor Mason directly questioned the power of the alcalde to make such sales, and demanded of him his authority for so doing; to which the said alcalde repied, in effect, that the limits of the town were understood to be half a league from the church, but that he had no record of these limits, or of their extension; that it was the custom at least, if not the law, for the alcalde, with the advice of the ayuntamiento, to sell the lands within the town limits.

2. The most recent law that can be found in the government archives, and which is believed to be still in force, gives to the ayuntamiento power to sell out as *solares* the municipal lands *(proprios)* which have been regularly granted to the town. But the common lands (*egidos*) cannot be sold without special authority, nor can any town sell land without the limits of the grant made for the town, for all such lands belong to the government, and cannot be sold without the authority of Congress. The alcalde, being the executive officer of the town, may, it is believed, with the consent of the ayuntamiento, make sales and sign deeds in the name of the town; but it is thought he cannot sell without such consent.

If there are no regidors and sindicos in the town of Monterey, the governor requests that you give due notice, and hold an election for filling the vacancies; and that when the ayuntamiento is formed, you will take their advice in this matter of land sales. But you are hereby forbidden to make any sales of land beyond the recognised limits of the town, or which has been occupied or designated for military purposes, the laws especially reserving all such for the use of the general government.

3. The law requires that the alcalde shall register in his office all sales of town lands, and that he shall keep a plan of the town, upon which shall be designated the land belonging to each individual. If the alcalde of Monterey has no such plan, the governor would strongly advise that no further sales be made until the town is properly surveyed and a plan formed; for otherwise innumerable difficulties will necessarily occur in the adjustment of titles, and the town authorities be liable to prosecution for damages for selling the same land to two or more individuals. However important it may be to raise funds for the expenses of the town, it is still more important that the proceedings of the municipality be conducted according to law, and in such a manner as not to infringe upon the rights of government or the claims of individual citizens.

This letter will be laid before the ayuntamiento, and filed in the office of the alcalde.

By order of Governor Riley: H. W. HALLECK,
Brevet Captain, and Secretary of State.

Señor Don IGNACIO ESQUER, *Alcalde at Monterey.*

STATE DEPARTMENT OF THE TERRITORY OF CALIFORNIA,
Monterey, May 10, 1849.

SIR: If you have on hand or can procure them in San Francisco, I wish you would send to this office about three months' supply of blank entries, clearances, &c., for the use of the custom-houses at this place, San Pedro, and San Diego; the same to be paid for out of the proceeds of customs in your hands.

Very respectfully, your obedient servant,
H. W. HALLECK,
Brevet Captain, and Secretary of State.

E. H. HARRISON, Esq.,
Collector, San Francisco.

STATE DEPARTMENT OF THE TERRITORY OF CALIFORNIA,
Monterey, May 11, 1849.

SIR: Your letter of April 17th, with the accompanying documents and papers, was received yesterday, and immediately laid before the governor, who, after taking legal advice, directs me to reply as follows:

1. It appears from the above mentioned letter and documents that J. J. Warner was arraigned before alcalde S. C. Foster, of the district of Los Angeles, on the charge of theft, and on the 21st of February was admitted to bail to appear before said court on the 20th of the following April; that at the time specified in the bond, viz: the 20th of April, the case was called up, but the prisoner failed to appear; that it was then adjourned to the following day, at which time, the prisoner being still absent, the court proceeded to take testimony; the prisoner's bondsman, Mr. Abel Sternes, appearing as counsel for the accused, and cross-questioning the witnesses; that on the 29th of April the prisoner presented himself, but the alcalde refused to confine him, on the ground that the offence was committed out of his district; whereupon the commanding officer at Los Angeles took the accused into custody; that the alcalde did not collect the amount of the bond for fear of pecuniary responsibility; whereupon the whole subject was referred to the governor, for his action in the premises.

2. The treaty of peace, by which Upper California has become a part of the Union, left this Territory with an existing government and existing laws. This *de facto* government must continue with its full powers until legally changed; and the existing laws must also continue in force until changed or modified by competent authority.

3. In the absence of positive law, we must be governed by custom and general usage in this country, and in the absence of both law and precedent, the laws and usages of other States and Territories, in like cases, should be referred to, to guide our decisions.

4. The first alcalde of each district has been recognised by former governors of California as being, in the absence of a higher judicial authority, *ex officio juez de primera justancia*, and as having jurisdiction in criminal cases. All other alcaldes of the same district had concurrent jurisdiction among themselves, but are subordinate to the first alcalde.

5. Starting from these premises, it is concluded that criminal proceedings may be instituted in any district of California, no matter whether the

offence was committed in that district or not. And when the proceedings are so commenced, either the prosecutor or the accused may ask for a change of *venue* to any other district, and the governor may, for sufficient reasons, order such change; but if no such change is asked for or ordered, the trial must proceed, and a verdict be given.

6. It does not appear from the records of the court in the case that any change of venue was asked for, or that any question was raised by the prisoner or his counsel as to the jurisdiction of the alcalde. But even supposing that the change of venue had been asked for, and the alcalde's jurisdiction questioned, the fact could in no way avoid the security given for the prisoner's appearance at the time specified. Where a prisoner fails to appear as specified in the bond, and where the bondsman does not at the time satisfy the court that the absence of the accused is due to unavoidable causes, it is the duty of the court to enter judgment on the bond, and to collect the amount forfeited. This, however, does not exempt the prisoner, if afterwards taken into custody, from trial and punishment.

7. The governor, on a review of the facts of the case, as presented in the record of the court and accompanying papers, directs that the alcalde proceed with the trial of the prisoner, J. J. Warner, and that if good and sufficient reasons are not given to show that said bond should not be forfeited, he also proceed to enter judgment on the same, and to collect the amount due. The money so collected will be held by the alcalde as a district fund, to be expended by him in the purchase, erection, or repair of a jail in the town of Los Angeles.

8. The practice of trial by jury, in criminal cases, was introduced into California previous to the treaty of peace, and it is believed that such practice is now in accordance with usage and not contrary to law, and, when desired, should be permitted.

9. The governor regrets that so much time has been occupied in disposing of this case, for it is due both to the people and the accused that the question of the prisoner's guilt should be decided without unnecessary delay. The frequent occurrence of thefts of this kind renders it important that the guilty should be immediately brought to trial and summarily punished.

Very respectfully, your obedient servant,

H. W. HALLECK,
Brevet Captain, and Secretary of State.

Major J. C. GRAHAM,
U. S. A., commanding at Los Angeles, California.

STATE DEPARTMENT OF THE TERRITORY OF CALIFORNIA,
Monterey, May 11, 1849.

SIR: Your letter of March 25th was received yesterday, and also duplicate receipts for $900, turned over by you to the quartermaster's department April 20, 1848; for $300, turned over to commissary's department same date; and for $1,361 55½, turned over to quartermaster's department September 8, 1848. One copy of these receipts will be forwarded to Washington, and the other retained in this office. Should the receipt for $282 34, paid by you in the case of Foxon, be found among the custom-house papers deposited by Captain Lippett at Santa Barbara, it will also be sent to Washington. Unless that receipt can be procured, I fear the accounting officer will charge the amount to you.

Very respectfully, your obedient servant,

H. W. HALLECK,
Brevet Captain, and Secretary of State.

Lieut. H. S. CARNES,
Late Collector, Santa Barbara, California.

STATE DEPARTMENT OF THE TERRITORY OF CALIFORNIA,
Monterey, May 15, 1849.

GENTLEMEN: The governor has received your communication of the 1st instant, in behalf of the town of San Diego, and directs me to reply as follows:

However extensive the powers of the governor of California for making grants of land previous to the cession of this country to the United States, there can be no doubt that such power is now very limited, if not entirely abrogated. By the treaty of peace Upper California became a part of the Union, and all lands which had not previously been granted for towns, colonies, or to individuals, became a part of the public domain, and can be disposed of only by authority of Congress; but what had been previously granted in accordance with law, remains, as before, the property of the persons or corporations to which it was given. Whatever lands, therefore, were legally given to the town of San Diego previous to the treaty of peace, still continue the property of that town, and may be disposed of in accordance with the existing laws of the country. It must be remembered, however, that the general government of Mexico reserved to itself whatever lands might be required for fortifications, arsenals, and other public structures; this reserved right now belongs to the government of the United States, and it is believed that no territorial or municipal authority can interfere with or limit this right. A board of engineer and naval officers has already been appointed by the President to designate such lands as may be required for military purposes in California; and it is believed that this board will very soon visit the port of San Diego to mark out the reservations required by government at that place.

The most recent law that can be found in the government archives, respecting town lands, gives to the ayuntamiento power to sell out in *solares* the municipal lands *(proprios)* which have been regularly granted to the town; but the common lands *(egidos)* cannot be sold without special authority. The alcalde being the executive officer of the town, may, it is believed, with the consent of the ayuntamiento, make sales and sign deeds in the name of the town; but without such consent, it is thought he can make no sales of the kind.

If there is now no town council at San Diego, the governor requests that the alcalde give due notice and hold an election for a sindico and the usual number of regidors; and that, when the ayuntamiento is formed, this matter be submitted to that body for its action. Great caution should be taken not to dispose of lands beyond the recognised limits of the town, for all sales beyond such limits will be null and void. The law requires that the alcalde will register in his office all sales of town lands, and that he shall keep a plan of the town, upon which shall be designated the land belonging to each individual. If the alcalde of San Diego has no such plan, the governor would strongly advise that no further sales be made until the town is properly surveyed and a plan formed; for otherwise, innumerable difficulties will necessarily occur in the adjustment of titles, and the town authorities be liable to prosecution for damages, for selling the same land to two or more individuals. However important it may be to raise funds for the expenses of the town, it is still more important that the proceedings of the municipality be conducted according to law, and in such a manner as not to infringe upon the rights of government or the claims of individual citizens.

This letter will be laid before the ayuntamiento and filed in the office of the alcalde.

By order of Governor Riley :

H. W. HALLECK,
Brevet Captain, and Secretary of State.

Señors JUAN MA. MARRON, MIGUEL DE PEDRORENA, JOSE MA. BAUDINE, JOSE MA. ESTUDILLO, SAN JAGO E. ARGUITTO,
San Diego, California.

STATE DEPARTMENT OF THE TERRITORY OF CALIFORNIA,
Monterey, May 15, 1849.

SIR : I am directed to acknowledge the receipt of your letter of the 4th instant, and to inform you that you have permission to turn over from the civil funds to the quartermaster's department the sum of one hundred thousand dollars, taking the proper receipts for the same. This transfer is to be regarded as a loan, and is to be restored to the civil fund as soon as the quartermaster's department may have the means available for doing so.

By order of Govenor Riley :

H. W. HALLECK,
Brevet Captain, and Secretary of State.

Brevet Major FITZGERALD,
Assistant Quartermaster, San Francisco, California.

STATE DEPARTMENT OF THE TERRITORY OF CALIFORNIA,
Monterey, May 15, 1849.

SIR : Your letter of April 28th has been received and laid before the governor, who directs me to reply as follows :

The laws of California which existed previous to the treaty of peace with Mexico (and do not conflict with the constitution of the United States) are still in force, and will continue in force till changed by proper authority ; and all civil officers will be supported in the exercise of the powers conferred upon them by these laws. It is expected that the next steamer will bring information of the organization of a government for this Territory, and the passage of new laws, which will be sent to you the moment they are received. Justices of the peace in the United States do not receive salaries, but are paid from the fees of their office. In all the northern districts of California the fees of office have been found sufficient for the remuneration of the alcaldes, whose official duties do not usually very materially interfere with their private business. In my letter of April 30, I informed you that the governor has assigned the sum of $500 50 for the purchase or construction of a jail in Santa Barbara. This money will be paid to the sindico, as stated in that letter.

The municipal funds required by each town must be raised by the ayuntamiento by direct taxation from licenses for stores, grog-shops, &c.; such is the course pursued by all the northern towns of California.

Very respectfully, your obedient servant,
H. W. HALLECK,
Brevet Captain, and Secretary of State.

Don RAYMUNDO CARRILLO,
1st Alcalde, district of Santa Barbara, California.

STATE DEPARTMENT OF THE TERRITORY OF CALIFORNIA,
Monterey, May 15, 1849.

REVEREND SIR: Your letter of the 10th instant has been received, and its contents communicated to the governor.

The first alcalde of San Luis Obispo is deemed the proper judge to decide what houses and lands were granted to the parish priest by Governor Micheltorena, July 15, 1844, and to which you are now entitled to possession by the governor's order of April 17. The power of the alcalde is limited to the act of *possession*, the question of *ownership* being reserved for the decision of a higher tribunal, which it is hoped may be organized in the course of a few months.

Very respectfully, your obedient servant,
H. W. HALLECK,
Brevet Captain, and Secretary of State.

Reverend Father Friar JOSE MIGUEL GOMES,
Parish Priest, San Luis Obispo, California.

STATE DEPARTMENT OF THE TERRITORY OF CALIFORNIA,
Monterey, May 15, 1849.

SIR: Your letters of April 20 and May 10 have been received, and laid before the governor.

The alcalde is deemed the proper judge to decide to what lands and buildings the parish priest is entitled to possession under titles given by Governor Micheltorena, July 15, 1844. It must be observed that the power of the alcalde is limited to the act of *possession*, the question of *ownership* being reserved for the decision of a higher tribunal, which it is hoped may be organized in the course of a few months.

It was represented to the governor in March last that there was great need of a local alcalde, who should reside in the town of San Luis Obispo, and you were accordingly requested to hold an election for filling such office. It was not the intention of the governor to limit the choice of the people in any respect, and if they prefer giving their votes for any citizen residing without the town, they should have full liberty to do so.

The governor authorizes you to send to Monterey the prisoner Ildefonso, sentenced to five years' labor in this presidio, if you can find a safe opportunity for doing so. Perhaps arrangements may be made with the mail rider to conduct the prisoner to this place the next time he brings the mail from the south. The difficulties that have recently occurred in the placer district, between the whites and Indians, have rendered it necessary to concentrate all the available military forces in that region, and the governor regrets that under existing circumstances he will be unable to comply with your request to station troops at San Luis Obispo.

Very respectfully, your obedient servant,

H. W. HALLECK,
Brevet Captain, and Secretary of State.

Don MIGUEL ABILA, 1*st Alcalde of the*
Jurisdiction of San Luis Obispo, California.

STATE DEPARTMENT OF THE TERRITORY OF CALIFORNIA,
Monterey, May 17, 1849.

SIR: Your letter of April 16, erroneously directed to General Smith, has been referred to Brigadier General Riley, commanding tenth military department, and governor of California.

The enclosed extract from orders No. 16 will afford an answer to your inquiries respecting the interference of military officers with the civil authorities of the country; and my letter of the 11th instant to Major Graham (a copy of which has been sent to you) will give you the governor's views respecting the case of Warner.

As the people have neglected to elect a first alcalde for your district, there can be no doubt that you legally hold over till such election is made. If you should now wish to resign, the proper course to be pursued is for you to give due notice and hold an election to fill the vacancy so created. If there is no ayuntamiento in the town of Los Angeles, the governor requests that you give notice and hold an election for the several municipal officers recognised by the laws of California. The governor's views respecting the sale of municipal lands are fully expressed in a letter from this office, dated May 15, to certain gentlemen of San Diego, a copy of which is enclosed.

It is deemed highly probable, from information just received, that the bill before Congress at the last session for organizing a territorial government has become a law. If, on the arrival of the next steamer, this should not prove to be the case, the governor has it in contemplation to call a general election, and to complete, so far as possible, the organization of the government as recognised by the existing laws of California. These laws, so far as they do not conflict with the constitution and such laws of the United States as have been extended over this Territory, are still in force, and must continue in force until changed by the proper authority.

It is greatly to be regretted that any differences or bad feelings should have arisen between the civil and military authorities in your district, especially at a time when the condition of the country rendered it the imperious duty of all good men to do everything in their power to preserve the public tranquillity.

By order of Governor Riley:

H. W. HALLECK,
Brevet Captain, and Secretary of State.

S. C. FOSTER, 1*st Alcalde, District of Los Angeles, California.*

STATE DEPARTMENT OF THE TERRITORY OF CALIFORNIA,
Monterey, May 17, 1849.

SIR: I have to acknowledge the receipt of your letter of the 15th, enclosing a copy of the proceedings of the court in the case of Antonio Valencia. These papers will be placed on file in this office.

It is believed that under the existing laws in California, the first alcalde of each district has jurisdiction in criminal cases. But whatever may be the ultimate decision of this question, there can be no doubt that, under existing circumstances, cases will sometimes arise where the exercise of such power is absolutely necessary for the security of life and property.

Very respectfully, your obedient servant,
H. W. HALLECK,
Brevet Captain, and Secretary of S ate.

K. H. DIMMICK,
1st Alcalde, District of San José, California.

STATE DEPARTMENT OF THE TERRITORY OF CALIFORNIA,
Monterey, May 17, 1849.

SIR: I have to acknowledge the receipt of your letter of the 12th inst., enclosing monthly summary statements of civil funds in your possession for the months of January, February, March, and April, 1849.

Very respectfully, your obedient servant,
H. W. HALLECK,
Brevet Captain, and Secretary of State.

Captain J. L. FOLSOM,
U. S. Army, San Francisco, California.

STATE DEPARTMENT OF THE TERRITORY OF CALIFORNIA,
Monterey, May 17, 1849.

SIR: Your custom-house accounts for the 4th quarter of 1848, and monthly summary statements to 31st March, 1849, were received on the 2d May, after the departure of the steamer. Your accounts have been examined and found correct, and will be sent to Washington by next mail.

Very respectfully, your obedient servant,
H. W. HALLECK,
Brevet Captain, and Secre ary of State.

E. H. HARRISON, Esq.,
Collector, San Francisco, California.

STATE DEPARTMENT OF THE TERRITORY OF CALIFORNIA,
Monterey, May 19, 1849.

SIR: For a reply to your letters of the 15th instant, which are just received, I would refer you to mine of the same date.

It is believed that Congress has already passed a law for the settlement of land titles in the country, and for the organization of higher courts. While awaiting the organization, the governor will use every means in his power to support the existing authorities of the country. But, as has already been said, the Indian difficulties of the north will prevent him from sending troops at this time to San Luis Obispo. The people of your district ought to unite with you in enforcing the laws, and in maintaining your legal authority.

Very respectfully, your obedient servant,

H. W. HALLECK,
Brevet Captain, and Secretary of State.

Don Miguel Abila,
   1st Alcalde of the jurisdiction of San Luis Obispo, California.

State Department of the Territory of California,
Monterey, May 22, 1849.

Sir: Your letter of this date is received, and I am directed by the governor to inform you that he approves of the election held on the 20th instant, at which Messrs. Osio, Spence, Abijo, and Watson were chosen regidores, and Sanchez as syndico procurador of the town of Monterey.

Very respectfully, your obedient servant,

H. W. HALLECK,
Brevet Captain, and Secretary of State.

Don Ygnacio Ezquer,
   Alcalde of Monterey, California.

State Department of the Territory of California,
Monterey, May 22, 1849.

Sir: Representations have been made to the governor that you have put the parish priest of San Luis Obispo in possession not only of the buildings and property granted to said priest by Micheltorena, in 1844, but also of other buildings and property sold to Mr. John Wilson, in 1845. If so, it is believed that you have exceeded your powers, and mistaken the intention of the governor. In his letter of April 17, he merely directed you to use your official authority to protect said priest in the possession of the property granted to him by Governor Micheltorena—not to interfere in the possession of other property, which has since been granted to other individuals. The power of the alcalde in such matters is of a very limited character, and he ought to be very careful not to exceed it, for he may thus render himself liable to damages. If there is any difficulty in making a division of the property, of which each claimant is entitled to the possession, he should call in other good men to assist him in forming his decision. Any arrangement of this kind that may be made will, of course, only be of a temporary character; for the proper court will soon be formed to decide definitively upon all such questions of title. Great care should be taken that justice be done to both parties, and that no feelings of partiality be allowed to affect the decision. If possible, you should induce the parties to come to an amicable arrangement, so as to avoid all litigation.

In your correspondence you seem to be under the impression that the governor had ordered you to put the priest in possession of the mission buildings. Such was not the case. You were merely requested to protect him in his lawful possessions until the titles of the other claimants can be properly investigated.

Your attention is again called to the necessity of holding an election for another alcalde in your district; and if the notice for such an election has not already been given, the governor requests that you will give it immediately. There will be associated with you, as judges and inspectors of such election, the following persons, viz: William Dana, John M. Price, Julian Estrada, and John Wilson.

By order of Governor Riley:

H. W. HALLECK,
Brevet Captain, and Secretary of State.

Don Miguel Abila,
  1st Alcalde of San Luis Obispo, California.

State Department of the Territory of California,
Monterey, May 23, 1849.

Sir: The governor directs that you will stay the execution of the sentence and fine imposed by you on Don Mariano Bonillo until the affair can be properly investigated. This order is not to be considered as deciding, in any respect, upon the merits of the case, or the correctness of your judgment.

By order of Governor Riley:

H. W. HALLECK,
Brevet Captain, and Secretary of State.

Don Miguel Abila,
  1st Alcalde of San Luis Obispo, California.

State Department of the Territory of California,
Monterey, May 26, 1849.

Sir. I am directed by Governor Riley to acknowledge the receipt of your letter of the 16th instant, and to say that he has approved of the election held by the people of Santa Cruz, at which you were chosen alcalde for that town and district.

With respect to the "duties and powers of the town council," they will, until further orders, confine themselves to attending to the internal police of the town and district.

Very respectfully, your obedient servant, (in the absence of the Secretary of State,)

W. E. P. HARTNELL,
Government Translator.

Mr. J. L. Majors,
  Alcalde, Santa Cruz, California

Know all men by these presents, that I, Bennet Riley, brevet brigadier general United States army, and governor of California, in virtue of power in me vested, do hereby appoint Stephen C. Massett notary public and commissioner of deeds in and for the city of "New York of the Pacific," district of San Joaquin, California.

Given at Monterey, California, this 23d day of May, A. D. 1849.

B. RILEY,
Brevet Brigadier General U. S. A., Governor of California.

Know all men by these presents, that I, Bennet Riley, brevet brigadier general United States army, and governor of California, in virtue of authority in me vested, do hereby restore T. M. Leavenworth, esq., to the full exercise of his duties and functions as first alcalde of the district of San Francisco.

Done at Monterey, California, this 1st day of June, in the year of our Lord 1849.

B. RILEY,
Brevet Brigadier General, and Governor of California.

Official:

H. W. HALLECK,
Brevet Captain, and Secretary of State.

MONTEREY, CALIFORNIA, *June* 1, 1849.

SIR: I have to acknowledge the receipt of yours of the 29th ultimo, and, in accordance with your request, enclose herewith your account current and abstract C for the fourth quarter of 1848. General Riley will act upon the matter of your salary the moment the law is officially received: in the mean time, he leaves it optional with you to receive the amount of salary authorized by Colonel Mason, or to wait till the new law is officially received.

Very respectfully, your obedient servant,

H. W. HALLECK,
Brevet Captain, and Secretary of State.

E. H. HARRISON,
Collector, San Francisco, California.

HEADQUARTERS TENTH MILITARY DEPARTMENT,
Monterey, California, June 2, 1849.

COMMODORE: I have received information from a reliable source that several Peruvian or Chilian vessels have recently landed passengers and freight in the bays of San Simeon and San Luis Obispo, (between this port and Santa Barbara,) in violation of the revenue laws of the United States. I have therefore to request that the naval forces under your command may take measures to seize said vessels and goods, and to prevent repetition of the offence. Captain Wilson, of San Luis Obispo, now in San Francisco, will give you more particular information with respect to this matter.

I am, sir, very respectfully, your obedient servant,
B. RILEY,
Bt. Brig. Gen. U. S. A., com'g 10*th Military Dept,*
and Governor of California.

Commmodore THOS. AP. C. JONES,
Com'g U. S. naval forces in the Pacific ocean.

STATE DEPARTMENT OF THE TERRITORY OF CALIFORNIA,
Monterey, June 2, 1849.

SIR: I am directed by Governor Riley to reply as follows to so much of your communication of the 16th ultimo as relates to the powers and duties of the ayuntamiento or town council of the town of Santa Cruz.

The laws of California, as they existed on the 1st of June, 1848, which are not inconsistent with the provisions of the constitution or the laws of Congress applicable to this country, as a part of the territory of the United States, are still in force, and must continue in force till changed by competent authority. The powers and duties of town councils in California (except so far as they may be modified by the constitution and laws of Congress) are the same as they were previous to the conquest of the country. As the laws touching this subject may not be of convenient reference, I subjoin a few of their provisions.

The number of members of each town is regulated by the approbation of the governor, but can in no case exceed six alcaldes, twelve regidores or councilmen, and two syndicos.

They are charged with the police and good order of the town, the construction of roads, the laying out, lighting, and paving of streets, the construction and repair of bridges, the removal of nuisances, the establishment of public burying-grounds, the building of jails, the support of town paupers, the granting of town licenses, the examination of weights and measures, and the management and disposition of all municipal property. The council appoints its own secretary, who, as well the members of the council, before entering upon their respective duties, must take the usual oath of office. Each member of the council is bound to assist the alcaldes in executing the laws, and is individually liable for any mal-administration of the municipal funds. A full account of the receipts and expenditures of the council must be kept, and at the end of each year submitted to the prefect of the district, who, after his examination, transmits them to the governor, for file in the government archives. In case of the death of any member of the town council, the vacancy may be supplied by a special election; but if such vacancies occur within three months of the close of the year, it will not be filled until the regular annual election. In case of the suspension of the members of the council, those of the preceding year may be reinstated with their full powers.

Very respectfully, your obedient servant,
H. W. HALLECK,
Brevet Captain, and Secretary of State.

J. G. MAJORS,
Alcalde, Santa Cruz, California.

Know all men by these presents, that I, Bennet Riley, brevet brigadier general United States army, and governor of California, by virtue of authority in me vested, do hereby appoint Frederick Billings a commissioner of deeds in and for the district of San Francisco, California.

Given at Monterey, California, this second day of June, in the year of our Lord one thousand eight hundred and forty-nine.

B. RILEY,
Brevet Brigadier General U. S. A., and Governor of California.

Official: H. W. HALLECK,
Brevet Captain, and Secretary of State.

PROCLAMATION.

To the people of the District of San Francisco.

Whereas proof has been laid before me that a body of men styling themselves "the legislative assembly of the district of San Francisco" have usurped powers which are vested only in the Congress of the United States, by making laws, creating and filling offices, imposing and collecting taxes, without the authority of law, and in violation of the constitution of the United States and of the late treaty with Mexico: Now, therefore, all persons are warned not to countenance said illegal and unauthorized body, either by paying taxes or by supporting or abetting their officers.

And whereas due proof has been received that a person assuming the title of sheriff, under the authority of one claiming to be a justice of the peace in the town of San Francisco, did, on the 31st of May last, with an armed party, violently enter the office of the 1st alcalde of the district of San Francisco, and there forcibly take and carry away the public records of said district from the legal custody and keeping of said 1st alcalde: Now, therefore, all good citizens are called upon to assist in restoring said records to their lawful keeper, and in sustaining the legally-constituted authorities of the land.

The office of justice of the peace in California, even where regularly constituted and legally filled, is subordinate to that of alcalde; and for one holding such office to assume the control of, and authority over, a superior tribunal, argues an utter ignorance of the laws or a wilful desire to violate them, and to disturb the public tranquillity. It is believed, however, that such persons have been led into the commission of this rash act through the impulse of the moment, rather than any wilful and settled design to transgress the law; and it is hoped that on due reflection they will be convinced of their error, and unite with all good citizens in repairing the violence which they have done to the laws. It can hardly be possible that intelligent and thinking men should be so blinded by passion, and so unmindful of their own interests and the security of their property, after the salutary and disinterested advice and warnings which have been given them by the President of the United States, by the Secretaries of State and of War, and by men of high integrity and disinterested motives, as to countenance and support any illegally-constituted body in their open violation of the laws, and assumption of authority which in no possible event could ever belong to them.

The office of alcalde is one established by law, and all officers of the United States have been ordered by the President to recognise and support the legal authority of the person holding such office; and whatever feelings of prejudice or personal dislike may exist against the individual holding such office, the office itself should be sacred. For any incompetency or mal-administration the law affords abundant means of remedy and punishment—means which the executive will always be found ready and willing to employ to the full extent of the powers in him vested.

Given at Monterey, California, this 4th day of June, in the year of our Lord 1849.

B. RILEY,
Brevet Brig. Gen. U. S. A., and Governor of California.

Official:

H. W. HALLECK,
Brevet Captain, and Secretary of State.

Know all men by these presents, that, T. M. Leavenworth, esq., having tendered his resignation of the office of 1st alcalde of the district of San Francisco, which is accepted, to take effect on the legal election of a successor; and it being represented that certain municipal offices in the town of San Francisco are vacant, and that it is highly important that they be filled with the least possible delay: Now, therefore, I, Bennet Riley, brevet brigadier general United States army, and governor of California, and by virtue of authority in me vested, do hereby appoint R. A. Parker, Frederick Billings, John Servine, W. S. Clark, Stephen Harris, B. R. Buckalew, William H. Tillinghurst, A. J. Grayson, and J. P. Haven, judges and inspectors, to give notice and hold a special election to fill the above-named vacancies in the said district and town. In the absence of the others, any three of these judges and inspectors are empowered to act.

Given at Monterey, California, this 5th day of June, in the year of our Lord 1849.

B. RILEY,
Brevet Brig. Gen., and Governor of California.

Official:

H. W. HALLECK,
Brevet Captain, and Secretary of State.

State Department of the Territory of California,
Monterey, June 5, 1849.

Gentlemen: I am directed to send you the enclosed appointment as judges and inspectors, to give notice and hold a special election for filling certain vacancies in the district and town of San Francisco.

The growing importance of your town, and the immense amount of business transacted there, render it important for the security of property and of the rights of citizens that it should not be kept without regular and legally constituted officers for the administration of justice and the management of the affairs of your municipality. It is therefore hoped that an election will be held, with no more delay than may be necessary in order to have the notice generally known in the town and district.

It is the opinion of all eminent legal authorities which have been consulted, that all laws of California which existed at the time this country was annexed to the United States, and which are not inconsistent with the constitution, laws, and treaties of the United States, are still in force, and must continue in force till changed by competent authority. The powers and duties of all civil officers in California, except so far as they may have been modified by the act of annexation, are therefore the same as they were previous to the conquest of the country. As the laws touching the subject of town councils (ayuntamientos) may not be of convenient reference, I am directed to subjoin a few of their provisions. The number of members for each town cannot exceed 6 alcaldes, 12 councilmen, (regidores,) 1 collector, and 1 treasurer, (or 2 syndicos;) to change, however, from their number previously established, requires the assent of the governor. For the town of San Francisco, such assent is hereby given for any number not exceeding the provisions of the law.

The council is charged with the police and good order of the town, the construction of roads, the laying out, lighting, and paving of streets, the construction and repair of bridges, the removal of nuisances, the establishment of public burying-grounds, the building of jails, the support of town paupers, the granting of town licenses, the examination of weights and measures, the levying of municipal taxes, and the management and disposition of all municipal property. The council appoints its own secretary, who, as well as the members, before entering upon their respective duties, must take the usual oath of office. Each member of the council is bound to assist the alcaldes in executing the laws, and is individually liable for any mal-administration of the municipal funds, provided he voted for such mal-administration. A full account of the receipts and expenditures of the council must be kept, and at the end of each year submitted to the prefect or sub-prefect of the district, who, after his examination, will transmit them to the governor, for file in the government archives. In case of the death or removal of any member of the council, the vacancy may be supplied by a special election; but if such vacancy occur within three months of the close of the year, it will not be filled till the regular annual election. In case of the suspension of the members of the council, those of the preceding year may be reinstated, with their full powers.

As questions are frequently asked respecting town lands, I am directed to say that the most recent law on the subject that can be found in the government archives gives to the council (ayuntamiento) power to sell out in building lots (solares) the municipal lands (proprios) which have been regularly granted to the town; but the common lands (egidos) so granted cannot be sold without special authority. All public lands without the limits of the town form a part of the public domain, and can be disposed of only by authority of Congress.

The laws require that the results of elections be transmitted to the governor for his approval, and placed on file in this office. This is not always a useless form, for in some cases it is necessary to accompany legal papers with certificates of the governor or secretary of state that certain officers have been duly elected and qualified—which certificates cannot be given unless the requisite evidence of election is deposited in the government archives.

By order of Governor Riley:

H. W. HALLECK,
Brevet Captain, and Secretary of State.

Messrs. R. A. PARKER, FREDERICK BILLINGS, JOHN SERVINE, W. S. CLARK, STEPHEN HARRIS, B. R. BUCKALEW, WILLIAM H. TILLINGHURST, A. J. GRAYSON, J. P. HAVEN, *San Francisco.*

STATE DEPARTMENT OF THE TERRITORY OF CALIFORNIA,
Monterey, June 4, 1849.

SIR: Your letter of the 6th ultimo, erroneously addressed to General Smith, has been referred to Brigadier General Riley, commanding tenth military department, and governor of California, who directs me to reply as follows:

With respect to the administration of the estate of which you speak, it is sufficient to remark that the law should be allowed to take its accustomed course; and that, if the alcalde has illegally interfered to change such administration, or to deprive you of your rights and liberties, he has rendered himself liable to the penalties of the law. The governor does not consider himself competent (even if he possesses the power) to decide, with the information before him, upon so complicated and important a case; and the whole matter, if not amicably settled between the parties interested, can be brought before the proper courts, which will, without doubt, be established in the course of a very short time.

Very respectfully, your obedient servant,

H. W. HALLECK,
Brevet Captain, and Secretary of State.

Don ANTONIO JOSÉ COT,
Los Angeles, California.

PROCLAMATION.

To the people of California.

Congress having failed at its recent session to provide a new government for this country to replace that which existed on the annexation of California to the United States, the undersigned would call attention to the means which he deems best calculated to avoid the embarrassments of our present position. The undersigned, in accordance with instructions from the Secretary of War, has assumed the administration of civil affairs in California, not as a military governor, but as the executive of the existing civil government. In the absence of a properly-appointed civil governor, the commanding officer of the department is, by the laws of California, *ex officio* civil governor of the country; and the instructions from Washington were based on the provisions of these laws. This subject has been misrepresented, or at least misconceived, and currency given to the impression that the government of the country is still *military*. Such is not the fact. The military government ended with the war, and what remains is the *civil* government recognised in the existing laws of California. Although the command of the troops in this department and the administration of civil affairs in California are, by the existing laws of the country and the instructions of the President of the United States, temporarily lodged in the hands of the same individual, they are separate and distinct. No military officer other than the commanding general of the department exercises any civil authority by virtue of his military commission; and the powers of the commanding general as *ex officio* governor are only such as are defined and recognised in the existing laws. The instructions of the Secretary of War make it the duty of all military officers to recognise the existing civil government, and to aid its officers with the military force under their control. Beyond this, any interference is not only uncalled for, but strictly forbidden. The laws of California not inconsistent with the laws, constitution, and treaties of the United States are still in force, and must continue in force till changed by competent authority. Whatever may be thought of the right of the people to temporarily replace the officers of the existing government by others appointed by a provisional territorial legislature, there can be no question that the existing laws of the country must continue in force till replaced by others made and enacted by competent power. That power, by the treaty of peace, as well as from the nature of the case, is vested in Congress. The situation of California in this respect is very different from that of Oregon. The latter was without laws, while the former has a system of laws, which, though somewhat defective and requiring many changes and amendments, must continue in force till repealed by competent legislative power. The situation of California is almost identical with that of Louisiana; and the decisions of the Supreme Court in recognising the validity of the laws which existed in that country previous to its annexation to the United States, where not inconsistent with the constitution and laws of the United States, or repealed by legitimate legislative enactments, furnish us a clear and safe guide in our present situation. It is important that citizens should understand this fact, so as not to endanger their property and involve themselves in useless and expensive litigation by giving countenance to persons claiming authority which is not given them by law, and by putting faith in laws which can never be recognised by legitimate courts.

As Congress has failed to organize a new territorial government, it becomes our imperative duty to take some active means to provide for the existing wants of the country. This, it is thought, may be best accomplished by putting in full vigor the administration of the laws as they now exist, and completing the organization of the civil government by the election and appointment of all officers recognised by law; while at the same time a convention, in which all parts of the Territory are represented, shall meet and frame a State constitution, or a territorial organization, to be submitted to the people for their ratification, and then proposed to Congress for its approval. Considerable time will necessarily elapse before any new government can be legitimately organized and put in operation; in the interim, the existing government, if its organization be completed, will be found sufficient for all our temporary wants.

A brief summary of the organization of the present government may not be uninteresting. It consists, first, of a governor, appointed by the supreme government: in default of such appointment, the office is temporarily vested in the commanding military officer of the department. The powers and duties of the governor are of a limited character, but fully defined and pointed out by the laws. Second, a secretary, whose duties and powers are also properly defined. Third, a territorial or departmental legislature, with limited powers to pass laws of a local character. Fourth, a superior court (tribunal superior) of the Territory, consisting of four judges and a fiscal. Fifth, a prefect and sub-prefects for each district, who are charged with the preservation of public order and the execution of the laws: their duties correspond, in a great measure, with those of district marshals and sheriffs. Sixth, a judge of first instance for each district: this office is, by a custom not inconsistent with the laws, vested in the first alcalde of the district. Seventh, alcaldes, who have concurrent jurisdiction among themselves in the same district, but are subordinate to the higher judicial tribunals. Eighth, local justices of the peace. Ninth, ayuntamientos, or town councils. The powers and functions of all these officers are fully defined in the laws of this country, and are almost identical with those of the corresponding officers in the Atlantic and western States.

In order to complete this organization with the least possible delay, the undersigned, in virtue of power in him vested, does hereby appoint the 1st of August next as the day for holding a special election for delegates to a general convention, and for filling the offices of judges of the superior court, prefects, and sub-prefects, and all vacancies in the offices of first alcalde, (or judge of first instance,) alcaldes, justices of the peace, and town councils. The judges of the superior court, and district prefects are, by law, executive appointments; but, being desirous that the wishes of the people should be fully consulted, the governor will appoint such persons as may receive the plurality of votes in their respective districts, provided they are competent and eligible to the office. Each district will therefore elect a prefect and two sub-prefects, and fill the vacancies in the offices of first alcalde, (or judge of first instance,) and of alcaldes. One judge of the superior court will be elected in the districts of San Diego, Los Angeles, and Santa Barbara; one in the districts of San Luis Obispo and Monterey; one in the districts of San José and San Francisco; and one in the districts of Sonoma, Sacramento, and San Joaquin. The salaries of the judges of the superior court, the prefects and judges of first instance, are regulated by the governor, but cannot exceed, for the first, $4,000 per annum; for the second, $2,500; and for the third, $1,500. These salaries will be paid out of the civil fund which has been formed from the proceeds of the customs, provided no instructions to the contrary are received from Washington. The law requires that the judges of the superior court meet within three months after its organization, and form a tariff of fees for the different territorial courts and legal officers, including all alcaldes, justices of the peace, sheriffs, constables, &c. All local alcaldes, justices of the peace, and members of town councils elected at the special election, will continue in office till the 1st of January, 1850, when their places will be supplied by the persons who may be elected at the regular annual election, which takes place in November, at which time the election of members to the territorial assembly will also be held.

The general convention for forming a State constitution or a plan for territorial government will consist of thirty-seven delegates, who will meet in Monterey on the first day of September next. These delegates will be chosen as follows:

The district of San Diego will elect two delegates; of Los Angeles, four; of Santa Barbara, two; of San Luis Obispo, two; of Monterey, five; of San José, five; of San Francisco, five; of Sonoma, four; of Sacramento, four; of San Joaquin, four. Should any district think itself entitled to a greater number of delegates than that above named, it may elect supernumeraries, who, on the organization of the convention, will be admitted or not, at the pleasure of that body.

The places for holding the election will be as follows: San Diego, San Juan Capistrano, Los Angeles, San Fernando, San Buenaventura, Santa Barbara, Nepoma, San Luis Obispo, Monterey, San Juan Bautista, Santa Cruz, San José de Guadalupe, San Francisco, San Rafael, Bodega, Sonoma, Benicia. (The places for holding elections in the Sacramento and San Joaquin districts will be hereafter designated.) The local alcaldes and members of the ayuntamientos, or town councils, will act as judges and inspectors of elections. In case there should be less than three such judges and inspectors present at each of the places designated on the day of election, the people will appoint some competent persons to fill the vacancies. The polls will be open from 10 a. m. to 4 p. m., or until sunset, if the judges deem it necessary.

Every free male citizen of the United States and of Upper California, 21 years of age, and actually resident in the district where the vote is offered, will be entitled to the right of suffrage. All citizens of Lower California who have been forced to come to this Territory on account of having rendered assistance to the American troops during the recent war with Mexico should also be allowed to vote in the districts where they actually reside.

Great care should be taken by the inspectors that votes are received only from *bona fide* citizens, actually resident in the country. These judges and inspectors, previous to entering upon the duties of their office, should take an oath faithfully and truly to perform these duties. The returns should state distinctly the number of votes received for each candidate, be signed by the inspectors, sealed, and immediately transmitted to the secretary of state, for file in his office. The following are the limits of the several districts:

1st. The district of San Diego is bounded on the south by Lower California, on the west by the sea, on the north by the parallel of latitude including the mission of San Juan Capistrano, and on the east by the Colorado river.

2d. The district of Los Angeles is bounded on the south by the district of San Diego, on the west by the sea, on the north by the Santa Clara river, and a parallel of latitude running from the head waters of that river to the Colorado.

3d. The district of Santa Barbara is bounded on the south by the district of Los Angeles, on the west by the sea, on the north by Santa Inez river and a parallel of latitude extending from the head waters of that river to the summit of the coast range of mountains.

4th. The district of San Luis Obispo is bounded on the south by the district of Santa Barbara, on the west by the sea, on the north by a parallel of latitude including San Miguel, and on the east by the coast range of mountains.

5th. The district of Monterey is bounded on the south by the district of San Luis, and on the north and east by a line running east from New Year's Point to the summit of the Santa Clara range of mountains, thence along the summit of that range to the Arroya de los Leagas and a parallel of latitude extending to the summit of the coast range, and along that range to the district of San Luis.

6th. The district of San José is bounded on the north by the straits of Karquinez, the bay of San Francisco, the arroya of San Francisquito, and a parallel of latitude to the summit of Santa Clara mountains, on the west and south by the Santa Clara mountains and the district of Monterey, and on the east by the coast range.

7th. The district of San Francisco is bounded on the west by the sea, on the south by the districts of San José and Monterey, and on the east and north by the bay of San Francisco, including the islands in that bay.

8th. The district of Sonoma includes all the country bounded by the sea, the bays of San Francisco and Suisun, the Sacramento river, and Oregon.

9th. The district of Sacramento is bounded on the north and west by the Sacramento river, on the east by the Sierra Nevada, and on the south by the Cosumnes river.

10th. The district of San Joaquin includes all the country south of the Sacramento district, and lying between the coast range and the Sierra Nevada.

The method here indicated to attain what is desired by all, viz: a more perfect political organization, is deemed the most direct and safe that can be adopted, and one fully authorized by law. It is the course advised by the President, and by the Secretaries of State and of War of the United States, and is calculated to avoid the innumerable evils which must necessarily result from any attempt at illegal local legislation. It is therefore hoped that it will meet the approbation of the people of California, and that all good citizens will unite in carrying it into execution.

Given at Monterey, California, this third day of June, in the year of our Lord eighteen hundred and forty-nine.

B. RILEY,
*Brevet Brigadier General U. S. Army,
and Governor of California.*

Official:

H. W. HALLECK,
Brevet Captain, and Secretary of State.

San Francisco, California,
June 17, 1849.

Sir: Information has just been received that a boy by the name of Juan Vanerde, charged with the crime of robbery, has fled to Monterey for the purpose of taking passage on some vessel bound to a Mexican port. Governor Riley wishes you to make every effort in your power to ap ehend the said Vanerde, and to secure him till the charges can be pr perly investigated. If Vanerde has gone south, please forward this to the alcaldes of the southern district.

Very respectfully, your obedient servant,
H. W. HALLECK,
Brevet Captain, and Secretary of State.

Don YGNACIO,
   1st *Alcalde district of Monterey, California.*

SAN FRANCISCO, CALIFORNIA,
June 18, 1849.

SIR: I have the honor to acknowledge the receipt of your communication of the 15th instant, stating that Mr. William Richardson, formerly collector of this port, has offered to pay $5,000 of the amount still due from him in Peruvian money of the coinage of 1848, accompanying the same with consular and other certificates of the value of this coin. Although there may be some doubt as to the exact value of this coin, nevertheless, as Mr. Richardson is unable to meet the payment in any other funds, and as the bonds given for the security of this payment are irregular, Governor Riley authorizes you to receive the coin as offered. In order to secure the government against any possible loss in case this coin should be found of less than its nominal value, you should state in your receipts the character of the funds paid in, and also that the bonds will be surrendered the moment it is ascertained that the coin is of the requisite degree of purity, and can be paid out at its nominal value; or, if preferred, this can be endorsed on the bonds themselves. It is highly important that Mr. Richardson's accounts should be settled with the least possible delay.

Very respectfully, your obedient servant,
H. W. HALLECK,
Brevet Captain, and Secretary of State.

Captain J. L. FOLSOM,
   U. S. A., San Francisco, California.

SAN FRANCISCO, CALIFORNIA,
June 18, 1849.

SIR: Your letter of the 14th instant, to General Smith, and accompanying papers, have been referred to Governor Riley for reply.

General Riley has given no instructions, either civil or military, to any individual, to fence in the lot claimed by Mr. Thompson in this town, or to interfere in any way with the rights or possessions of any one in said property. He has no power to decide upon the validity of Mr. Thompson's claims, nor has he any intention to interfere with the rights secured to Mr. Thompson by Colonel Mason's instructions of August 28, 1847. If such interference has been attempted, it was without his authority.

Very respectfully, your obedient servant,
H. W. HALLECK,
Brevet Captain, and Secretary of State.

E. P. JONES, Esq.,
   San Francisco, California.

SAN FRANCISCO, CALIFORNIA,
June 18, 1849.

SIR: I am directed by Governor Riley to reply to so much of your letter of June 4 as relates to the payment of expenses incurred in the transfer of a man named Passenger from San Francisco to Sonoma, and of sending an express from San Francisco to Monterey with important information to the governor.

On proof being presented that the transfer of Passenger to another district was made "by order of Governor Mason," the quartermaster at San Francisco will be authorized to pay all just and proper expenses incurred in the execution of said order, taking the proper vouchers for the same.

The quartermaster at San Francisco is hereby authorized to pay from the civil funds in his hands what he shall deem proper and just for the express which, in his absence, you sent to Monterey, on or about the 1st instant, with despatches relative to the magistracy of your district.

By order of Governor Riley:
H. W. HALLECK,
Brevet Captain, and Secretary of State.

T. M. LEAVENWORTH, Esq.,
1st Alcalde district of San Francisco, California.

SAN FRANCISCO, CALIFORNIA,
June 21, 1849.

SIR: I am directed by Governor Riley to acknowledge the receipt of your letter of the 19th instant, and to say that you misapprehend the purport of my letter to you of the 18th instant. It is expressly said in that letter that Governor Riley "has no power to decide upon the validity of Mr. Thompson's claim, nor has he any intention to interfere with the right secured to Mr. Thompson by Colonel Mason's instructions of August 28, 1847." By looking again at Colonel Mason's instructions, you will find that, so far from acknowledging Mr. Thompson's claim to the fifty-varas lot in question, he expressed the opinion that it was *not* valid, and merely allowed him the temporary use of the hide-house, with a road to the beach. The question of title must rest exactly where Colonel Mason left it, till it can be settled by competent authority; and General Riley would advise Mr. Thompson to make a representation of the case to the Secretary of War, with all the accompanying papers, so that the question may be settled with the least possible delay. General Riley will take pleasure in forwarding such a representation, and will recommend it to the immediate attention of the Secretary.

Very respectfully, your obedient servant,
H. W. HALLECK,
Brevet Captain, and Secretary of State.

E. P. JONES,
San Francisco, California.

SAN FRANCISCO, CALIFORNIA,
June 18, 1849.

SIR: I am directed by Governor Riley to acknowledge the receipt of your letter of the 14th instant, stating that the alcalde of this district has been endeavoring to take from you your property without any legal measures. If the alcalde has given judgment against you, you have only to give notice in due form of an appeal to a higher tribunal; in which case the judgment will be stayed, provided the amount at issue is sufficient to entitle you to carry it to a higher court. It is hoped that a tribunal will soon be organized in a legal manner, which will investigate any charges you may make against the alcalde. The governor is unwilling to interfere in this matter on *ex parte* statements; and if it is desired he should exercise his authority in ordering the judgment to be stayed till the matter can be properly investigated by a higher tribunal, it will be necessary to lay before him a copy of the proceedings in the case.

Very respectfully, your obedient servant,
H. W. HALLECK,
Brevet Captain, and Secretary of State.

DON JOSE DOMINGO PEROTTA,
District of San Francisco, California.

HEADQUARTERS TENTH MILITARY DEPARTMENT,
San Francisco, California, June 19, 1849.

GENERAL: I have the honor to enclose herewith printed copies of manuscripts of the 3d and 4th instant, as governor of this Territory. Copies of all official papers and correspondence connected with the civil government of the country will be forwarded by the regular mail steamer of the 1st proximo, for the information of the government at Washington.

Very respectfully, your obedient servant,
B. RILEY,
Brevet Brig. Gen. U. S. A., and Governor of California.

Major General R. JONES,
Adjutant General of the Army, Washington, D. C.

Know all men by these presents, that I, Bennet Riley, brevet brigadier general United States army, and governor of California, by virtue of authority in me vested, do hereby appoint Addison H. Flint a land surveyor in the district of San Francisco, California.

Given at San Francisco, California, this 21st day of June, in the year of our Lord one thousand eight hundred and forty-nine.

B. RILEY,
Brevet Brig. Gen. U. S. A., and Governor of California.

Official:

H. W. HALLECK.

Know all men by these presents, that I, Bennet Riley, brevet brigadier general United States army, and governor of California, by virtue of authority in me vested, do hereby appoint Edward A. King harbor master for the port of San Francisco. The fees of office, where not otherwise provided for by law, will be the same as those of the harbor-master of the port of New York.

Given at San Francisco, California, this 19th day of June, in the year of our Lord one thousand eight hundred and forty-nine.

B. RILEY,
Brevet Brig. Gen. U. S. A., and Governor of California.

Official:

H. W. HALLECK,
Brevet Captain, and Secretary of State.

Know all men by these presents, that I, Bennet Riley, brevet brigadier general United States army, and governor of California, by virtue of authority in me vested, do hereby appoint N. Wise and J. Walsh wardens for the port of San Francisco. When called upon to perform the duties of their office, their fees, where not otherwise provided for by law, will be the same as the fees of wardens of the port of New York.

Given at San Francisco, California, this 19th day of June, A. D. 1849.

B. RILEY,
Brevet Brig. Gen. U. S. A., and Governor of California.

Official:

H. W. HALLECK,
Brevet Captain, and Secretary of State.

Know all men by these presents, that I, Bennet Riley, brevet brigadier general United States army, and governor of California, by virtue of authority in me vested, do hereby appoint A. C. Peachy a notary public in and for the district of San Francisco, California.

Given at San Francisco, California, this 21st day of June, A. D. 1849.

B. RILEY,
Brevet Brig. Gen. U. S. A., and Governor of California.

Official:

H. W. HALLECK,
Brevet Captain, and Secretary of State.

Know all men by these presents, that I, Bennet Riley, brevet brigadier general United States army, and governor of California, by virtue of authority in me vested, do hereby appoint W. M. Eddy a land surveyor in the district of San Joaquin, California.

Given at San Francisco, California, this 22d day of June, A. D. 1849.

B. RILEY,
Brevet Brig. Gen. U. S. A., and Governor of California.

Official:

H. W. HALLECK,
Brevet Captain, and Secretary of State.

SAN FRANCISCO, CALIFORNIA,
June 22, 1849.

SIR: Governor Riley directs that you will turn over to Captain Ringgold, United States navy, the anchors and cables purchased with moneys from the "civil funds" for planting buoys in the bay of San Francisco. Captain Ringgold will receipt to you for the same, and when required for the purpose for which they were originally intended, will return them to the harbor-master of this port.

Very respectfully, your obedient servant,
H. W. HALLECK,
Brevet Captain, and Secretary of State.

Major E. H. FITZGERALD,
United States Army, San Francisco, California.

To the people of California.

The following are designated as places of election of delegates, judges, alcaldes, &c., on the 1st of August next. In the district of San Joaquin: the placer above Hick's rancho, Stockton, Jamestown, Sullivan's camp, Carson's creek, and near the crossings of the Towalamne and Merced rivers; in the district of Sacramento: Sutter's Fort, Mormon island, Culloma mills, Weber's creek, North Fork, Juba and Feather rivers; in the district of San José: San José mission and Martinez landing. It is highly important that all parts of the Territory should be represented in said convention, and all good citizens are earnestly requested to unite in carrying this recommendation into execution.

It may not be improper here to remark, that the instructions from Washington, received by the steamer "Panama," since the issuing of the proclamation of the 3d instant, fully confirm the views there set forth; and it is distinctly said in these instructions that "the plan of establishing an independent government in California cannot be sanctioned, no matter from what source it may come."

Given at San Francisco, California, this 22d day of June, A. D. 1849.
B. RILEY,
Brevet Brig. Gen. U. S. A., and Governor of California.

Official:

H. W. HALLECK,
Brevet Captain, and Secretary of State.

EXECUTIVE DEPARTMENT OF CALIFORNIA,
Monterey, August 30, 1849

GENERAL: I have the honor to transmit, herewith, copies of civil papers and letters issued by me since my despatch of June 30, and to continue my report on the civil affairs of this country from this date.

Accompanied by Captain Halleck, secretary of state for California, and Major Canby, Captain Wescott, and Lieutenant Derby, of my military staff, I left this place on the 5th July for the purpose of inspecting the military posts in the interior, and of learning from personal observation the actual state of affairs in the mineral regions, and also of allaying, so far as I could, the hostile feeling which was said to exist between the Americans and foreigners who were working in the gold placers. My report on the state of the troops and a more detailed account of my tour will be forwarded with my military papers.

Passing the mission of San Juan Bautista, we crossed the coast range of mountains near the ranche of Señor Pacheco, and struck the San Joaquin river near the mouth of the Merced; and, after visiting Major Miller's camp on the Stanislaus, we proceeded to examine the principal placers on the tributaries of that river and of the Tualumne. These washings or diggings have been among the richest and most productive in California.

They are situated within a circuit of some twelve or fifteen miles, and are known as Jamestown, Wood's creek, Sonorenian camp, Sullivan's creek, Curtis's creek, French creek, Carson's creek, and Angelo creek. Some of these have become places of considerable business, particularly the Sonorenian camp, which presents the appearance of a city of canvass houses.

Passing the Stanislaus river in the mountains, we proceeded to Major Kingsbury's camp near the mouth of the American river, crossing in our route the Calaveras, Moquelume, Seco, and Cosumnes rivers; all of which have rich washings near their sources and on their bars and islands. From Major Kingsbury's camp we ascended the American river to Cullamo hills, where the first placer was discovered by Captain Sutter's employees in the spring of 1848. From Cullamo we crossed the country to Stockton, a new town on an estero some distance above the mouth of the San Joaquin, and thence proceeded to Colonel Cazey's camp at the straits of Carquinnes; returning via San Francisco to Monterey, which place we reached on the afternoon of the 9th instant.

We found the country at this season dry and parched by the sun, the heat of which became very great the moment we crossed the coast range of mountains. The thermometer ranges as high as 113° Fah. in the shade, and above 140° Fah. in the sun. A great portion of the valley of the Joaquin is so barren as scarcely to afford subsistence for our animals, and can never be of much value for agricultural purposes. There, however, is some excellent land on the east side of that river, bordering its large tributaries. A considerable portion of the valleys of the Moquelume, Seco, Cosumnes, and American rivers is also well adapted to agriculture; and the broad plains lying between them furnish abundant pasture for raising stock. But the amount of good arable land, as compared with the extent of country which we passed over, is small, and I am inclined to believe that the richness and extreme fertility of certain localities have led to erroneous conclusions respecting the general character of the country. Certain it is that while there may be found sufficient arable lands to support, if well cultivated, a numerous population, here is also a very great extent of rough and mountainous country and sandy and barren plains which are of little value. The great difficulty to be encountered in agricultural pursuits in some portions of California is the want of water for irrigation; but possibly this difficulty may be overcome in part by resorting to artesian wells. If so, much of the public land which is now unsaleable may be brought into market, and the settlement of the country greatly accelerated. I would, therefore, suggest whether it may not be advisable for our government to direct some experiments to be made at the public expense in sinking wells of this character, for even if unsuccessful as a means of irrigation, their construction will greatly assist in determining the geological character of the country. At present nearly all agricultural labors are suspended in the general scramble for gold; but the enormous prices paid for fruit and vegetables in the towns will undoubtedly induce many, during the coming year, to turn their attention to the cultivation of the soil. The failure on the part of Congress, at its last session, to authorize the sale of public lands in California, has proved detrimental to the agricultural interest of the country.

A large number of those who have recently emigrated to California are desirous to locate themselves permanently in the country, and to cultivate the soil, but the uncertainty which exists with respect to the validity of land titles in California, and to what actually constitutes the public domain, serves as a serious check to the forming of new agricultural settlements; moreover, speculators are purchasing up fraudulent and invalid titles to large tracts of the public domain, and selling them off in parcels, and at enormous profits, to those who have recently arrived in the country, and who are necessarily ignorant of the real state of the case. All the mission lands in California were secularized, or made government property, by a law of Mexico, dated August 17th, 1833, and the territorial government of California, under the authority of the Mexican laws, leased and sold a portion of these lands and mission property. Another portion of this property, however, still remained unsold when the Americans took possession of the country, and it has since been left in the hands of government agents for preservation. Erroneously supposing that these lands are subject to pre-emption laws, some of the recent emigrants have attempted to settle upon them.

But I cannot deem myself justifiable in permitting this, for I do not conceive that lands which have been under cultivation for half a century, and now belong to government, can be subject to the pre-emption claims of private individuals, in the same manner as the uncultivated lands of the public domain. It is, however, important for the interest of the country that these mission lands be brought into market with the least possible delay, and also that provision be made by law for the settlement and sale of other public lands in California. And as disputes are almost daily occurring between individuals respecting the extent of their several claims, and the validity of their titles, I would urge upon our government the necessity of immediately taking measures for the speedy and final settlement of these titles upon principles of equity and justice. This is absolutely essential for the peace and prosperity of the country.

For information connected with this subject, I beg leave to call attention to the report of Captain Halleck, secretary of state for California, which was forwarded to Washington by my predecessor, in the early part of April last.

Before leaving Monterey I heard numerous rumors of irregularities and crimes among those working in the *placers;* but, on visiting the mining regions, I was agreeably surprised to learn that everything was quite the reverse from what had been represented, and that order and regularity were preserved throughout almost the entire extent of the mineral districts. In each little settlement, or tented town, the miners have elected their local alcaldes and constables, whose judicial decisions and official acts are sustained by the people, and enforced with much regularity and energy. It is true, that in a few instances certain local questions have produced temporary excitements and difficulties, but none of these have been of a very important character, or led to serious results. Alcaldes have probably in some cases, and under peculiar circumstances, exercised judicial powers which were never conferred upon them by law; but the general result has been favorable to the preservation of order and the dispensation of justice.

The old *placers* are still exceedingly productive, and new ones are almost daily discovered in the smaller streams running from the western slope of the Sierra Nevada into the great valleys of the Sacramento and San Joaquin rivers.

I am satisfied, however, from personal observation, that very exaggerated accounts have been sent to the United States respecting the ease with which the precious metal is extracted from the earth, and that many who come to this country with the expectation of acquiring sudden wealth, with little or no labor, will be sadly disappointed. It is true that the reward of labor in the mines is very high; but it should not be forgotten that gold *digging* and gold washing in that climate require strong constitutions and great physical exertions, and very few need expect to acquire fortunes by working the *placers*, without severe labor and fixed habits of industry and temperance. The yield of different localities is, of course, very different, some of the *placers* being exceedingly rich, while the product of others is scarcely sufficient to pay the expenses of working. But I think the general averages per diem, for those actually employed in washing for gold, will not vary much from an ounce or an ounce and a half per man; some make much more than that sum, while those who are less fortunate fall much short of it. The actual number of persons working the *placers* will not vary much from ten thousand. The entire population now in the mining district is much greater than that number; but many are engaged in mercantile pursuits and in transporting goods and provisions, while others employ much of their time in "prospecting," or looking for newer and richer localities.

I also found that the reports which had reached me of hostilities between Americans and foreigners, in the mining districts, were greatly exaggerated, and that, with a few individual exceptions, everything had remained quiet and orderly. In some of the northern *placers* a party of Americans and Europeans, urged on by political aspirants, who seem willing to endanger the peace and tranquillity of the country, in order to promote their own personal interest, have assumed the authority to order all Mexicans and South Americans from that part of the Territory. Their orders were quietly submitted to by the foreigners, a portion of whom removed to the mines further south, where the American population manifested a very decided disposition to afford them protection should they be further molested. The more intelligent and thinking portion of Americans regard this measure as illegal and injudicious, and will discountenance any repetition of movements so well calculated to disturb the public tranquillity, and to create bitter and exasperated feelings, where it is evidently our policy to cultivate those of the most friendly character. Some of the English, Irish, and German emigrants, in the northern *placers*, assisted in this movement against the Mexicans, Peruvians, and Chilians, and probably exerted themselves much more than any of our own citizens to create a prejudice and excitement against the Spanish race. They were probably actuated by pecuniary interest. The great influx of people from the southern portion of this continent was diminishing the price of labor in the towns near the northern rivers, and the large number of pack animals brought from Lower California and Sonora was producing a corresponding reduction in the expenses of transportation.

For example, the price of a pack mule in some parts of the mining districts a few months ago was about $500, whereas they can now be purchased for less than $150. The cost of transportation from the principal landing on the San Joaquin river to the Sonorenian camp was $75 per hundred, whereas at the present time it is only about $7.

This has reduced the prices of provisions in the *placers* one and two hundred per cent. Some of the merchants who had large stocks of goods in the mines, and those who were engaged in transportation at the prices formerly paid, have suffered by the change, and it is natural that they should feel incensed against that class of foreigners who have contributed most to effect it.

But it is thought by others that the great majority of the laborers and consumers in the mining districts have been benefited by this change, and that it would be injurious to the prosperity of the country to restore things to their former state by the expulsion and prohibition of foreigners from the mines.

Americans, by their superior intelligence and shrewdness in business, generally contrive to turn to their own benefit the earnings of the Mexicans, Chilians, and Peruvians in this country, and any measure of exclusiveness which is calculated to diminish the productive labor of California would be of exceedingly doubtful policy.

When applied to by the different parties for my opinion on the question of expelling foreigners, I have uniformly told them that no persons, native Americans or foreigners, have any legal right to dig gold in the public lands; but that, until the government of the United States should act in the matter, they would not be molested in their pursuits; that I could not countenance any class of men in their attempts to monopolize the working of the mines, and that all questions touching the temporary right of individuals to work in particular localities, of which they were in actual possession, should be left to the decision of the local judicial authorities.

I cannot close my remarks on this subject without again calling the attention of government to the importance of establishing a mint in California at the earliest moment.

This measure is called for by every consideration of natural policy and of justice to the mercantile mining population of California.

General Kearny, during his administration of affairs in this country, appointed, by virtue of his authority as governor of California, two sub-Indian agents, who have ever since been continued in office, and their services found of great utility in preserving harmony among the wild tribes, and in regulating their intercourse with the whites.

They have been paid from the "civil fund" very moderate salaries, which will be continued until arrivals of agents regularly appointed by the general government. Notwithstanding every effort on the part of those agents and of the officers of the army here, it has not been possible at all times to prevent aggression on the part of the whites, or to restrain the Indians from avenging these injuries in their own way.

In the month of April last, the agent in the Sacramento valley reported that a body of Oregonians and mountaineers had committed most horrible barbarities on the defenceless Indians in that vicinity.

Those cruel and inhuman proceedings, added, perhaps, to the execution of a number of chiefs some year and a half since by a military force sent into the San Joaquin valley by my predecessor, (the facts of which were reported to Washington at the time,) have necessarily produced a hostile feeling on the part of the natives, and several small parties of whites, who, in their pursuit of gold, ventured too far into the Indian country, have been killed.

My correspondence with the Indian agents and military officers established in the Sacramento and San Joaquin valleys will inform you of the measures taken to prevent a repetition of these difficulties.

I would respectfully recommend that at least three sub-Indian agents be appointed for this country, and stationed in the valleys of the Sacramento and San Joaquin.

These agents should receive ample pay in order to enable them to defray the expenses of living in that part of the country, and should be men of the highest moral character; for otherwise they would not resist the temptation to engage in illicit trade with the natives, or to employ them for the individual benefit of the agents in washing for gold.

The election called by me for the 1st instant was held on that day, and has been attended with the most happy results.

Every district has elected its local officers, and appointed delegates to meet in general convention at this place on the 1st proximo, to form a State constitution or plan of territorial government, which will be submitted to the people for their ratification, and transmitted to Washington for the action of Congress.

Most of the local and judicial officers named in my proclamation of the 3d of June have already entered upon their duties, and the interest which was taken by the people in every part of the country in this election, and the zeal manifested by those elected and appointed to office, afford strong hopes that the existing government will be able to preserve order and secure the administration of justice until a new one shall be put into regular and successful operation.

In my former despatch I mentioned that the civil officers of the existing government would be paid their regular salaries from the "civil funds," which had been formed, under the direction of the governor of California, mainly out of the proceeds of the temporary custom-houses established by my predecessors on this coast.

It will also be necessary to use a portion of this fund in the immediate construction of jails for the security of civil prisoners.

The want of such jails has already led to the most serious inconveniences; prisoners have so frequently effected their escape, that, on several occasions, the people have risen in masses and executed criminals immediately after trial, and without waiting for the due fulfilment of all the requisitions of the laws.

In many cases it has been found necessary to confine civil prisoners on board vessels of war, and in the guard-houses of the garrison; but in towns, at a distance from the coast and the military posts, the difficulty of retaining prisoners in custody has led, in some instances, to immediate and summary executions.

This evil calls for an immediate remedy, which will be afforded, so far as the means at my disposal will admit.

I beg leave, in this place, to add a few remarks on the use which has been, and will continue to be, made of this "civil fund."

In the instructions from Washington to General Kearny, in 1846, for his guidance in California, the establishment of port regulations on this coast was assigned to the commander of the *Pacific squadron*, while it was said "the appointment of temporary collectors at the several ports appertains to the civil governor of the province."

It was also directed that the duties at the custom-houses be used for the support of the necessary officers of the civil government. This division of duties and this disposition of the proceeds of the customs were continued during the whole war.

On the receipt of the Treasury Department regulations respecting the collection of military contributions in Mexico, officers of the army and navy were made collectors at some of the ports, but at others the civil collectors appointed by the governor of California were retained.

At the close of the war, Governor Mason, for reasons already communicated, determined to continue the collection of revenue in the country, on the authority which had previously been given to him, until Congress should act in the matter, or orders to the contrary be received from Washington. He therefore, as governor of California, again appointed civil collectors in the ports where military officers had temporarily performed those duties, and collected the customs on all foreign goods, in accordance with the provisions of the tariff of 1846, while the commander of the Pacific squadron continued the direction of all matters relating to port regulations. A double necessity impelled the governor to this course. The country was in pressing need of these foreign goods, and Congress had established no port of entry on this coast. The want of a more complete organization of the existing civil government was daily increasing, and, as Congress had made no provisions for supporting a government in this country, it was absolutely necessary to create a fund for that purpose from the duties collected on these foreign goods. It is true that there were no laws authorizing the collection of these duties; but at the same time the laws forbade the landing of the goods till the duties *were* paid. Governor Mason, therefore, had no alternative but to pursue the course which he adopted. He immediately communicated to Washington his action in the case; and as the receipt of his despatch was acknowledged without any dissent being expressed, it must be presumed that his course met the approbation of the government. When I assumed command in this country as civil governor, I was directed to receive these communications and instructions from Governor Mason for my guidance in the administration of the civil affairs of this Territory. I have accordingly continued the collection of the revenue and added the proceeds to the "civil fund," using that fund for the necessary expenses of the civil government. The expenses of employing civil officers in this country are very great; and as I have no authority to lay taxes, this fund forms my only means of carrying on the government. The necessity of employing these officers, and of paying them the full salaries authorized by law under the existing state of affairs, is too obvious to require comment. I have pledged myself to pay these salaries from the "civil fund," unless forbidden to do so by direct orders from Washington; and that pledge will be fulfilled. This "civil fund" was commenced in the early part of 1847, and has been formed and used in the manner pointed out in the early instructions to the governor of this Territory. This money has been collected and disbursed by the "governor of California" and by those appointed by him in virtue of his office. He is, therefore, the person responsible for this money, both to the government and to the parties from whom it is collected, and it can be expended only on his orders. None of the military departments of the army, nor any army officer simply in virtue of his commission, can have any control, direct or indirect, over it. It is true that some of this money has, from time to time, as the wants of the service required, been transferred to the different military departments; but this transfer was in the form of a *loan*, and the money so transferred will be returned to the "civil fund" as soon as arrangements can be made for that purpose. The increased expenditures for the support of the existing government will soon render this restoration absolutely necessary; especially as the transfer of the custom-houses to the regular collectors appointed by the general government will now cut off all further means of supplying the civil treasury. These collectors have not yet arrived, but are daily expected. Detailed accounts of the expenditure of this "civil fund," with the accompanying vouchers, will be transmitted to Washington as heretofore.

Very respectfully, your obedient servant,
BENNET RILEY,
Brevet Brig Gen. U. S. Army, and Governor of California.
Major General R. JONES,
Adjutant General of the Army, Washington, D. C.

STATE DEPARTMENT OF CALIFORNIA,
Monterey, July 1, 1849.

SIR: I enclose you herewith copies of papers received by Governor Riley, through General Smith, from Mr. M. Bartley, of Mansfield, Ohio, who asks for information respecting the estate of John Hofsteeter, deceased. The original papers are on file in this office.

The governor will be most happy to communicate to the brother of the deceased any information you may be able to furnish touching this subject.

Very respectfully, your obedient servant,
H. W. HALLECK,
Brevet Captain, and Secretary of State.
Captain J. A. SUTTER,
Sacramento City, California.

STATE DEPARTMENT OF CALIFORNIA,
Monterey, July 1, 1849.

SIR: I have to acknowledge the receipt of your three letters of June 12, and one of May 30.

As Governor Riley is on the point of leaving this place to visit the northern districts, I am unable to reply at this time to your inquiries; I, however, enclose you a Spanish translation of acts V and VI, amendments to the constitution of the United States, relating to the right of trial by jury.

Very respectfully, your obedient servant,
H. W. HALLECK,
Brevet Captain, and Secretary of State.

Don JOSE C. LUGO,
Alcalde, Los Angeles, California.

Know all men by these presents, that, whereas information has been laid before me that proceedings have been instituted in the alcalde's court of San Francisco to change the administration of the estate of Mr. Leidesdorff, deceased; and whereas said initiatory proceedings are apparently wanting in regularity, and of doubtful propriety, if not illegal;

Now, therefore, I, Bennet Riley, brevet brigadier general United States army, and governor of California, by virtue of power in me vested, do hereby order and direct that said alcalde's court stay all further proceedings with respect to such change of administration until further orders from superior authority, and leave said administration in the hands of the administrator who held it previous to the commencement of the aforesaid proceedings.

This order shall in no way be considered or construed to justify or confirm the proceedings of the present administrator, or to exempt him from the penalties which he already has or in future may incur by illegal acts of administration, as stated and charged in the petition of P. Barry, esq., (filed June 27, 1849, in the alcalde's court,) its only object being to suspend and stay proceedings till legal and competent authority can investigate the facts of the case, so as to secure the rights of the administration, creditors, and heirs of the said estate.

If, previous to the receipt of this order to the aforesaid alcalde's court, it should have changed the administration of the said estate, such change will be immediately countermanded and annulled, and everything restored to the position occupied when these proceedings for change were first instituted.

Given at Monterey, California, this first day of July, A. D. 1849.
B. RILEY,
Brevet Brig. Gen. U. S. A., and Governor of California.

STATE DEPARTMENT OF CALIFORNIA,
Monterey, July 1, 1849.

SIR: I have the honor to acknowledge the receipt of your letter of May 15, reporting the trial, sentence, and execution of the Indian Juan Antonio; also your letter of May 14, respecting the "Leandry estate;" also your letter of May 22, reporting the result of an election, held May 6, of certain officers of the district and town of Los Angeles.

Very respectfully, your obedient servant,
H. W. HALLECK,
Brevet Captain, and Secretary of State.

S. C. FOSTER, Esq., *Los Angeles, California.*

STATE DEPARTMENT OF CALIFORNIA,
Monterey, July 1, 1849.

SIR: I have the honor to acknowledge the receipt of your letter of June 20, asking for copies of letters to you by C. V. Gillespie, touching the estate of the late William A. Leidesdorff, which you say were sent to Governor Mason in July or August, 1848. I have examined the files of civil correspondence for the year 1848, and find no letters answering your description. There are, however, letters on file from Mr. Howard to you, dated about that time, touching the aforementioned estate.

Are not those the letters to which you have reference? If so, copies will be furnished as you request.

Very respectfully, your obedient servant,
H. W. HALLECK,
Brevet Captain, and Secretary of State.

T. M. LEAVENWORTH, Esq.,
Alcalde, San Francisco, California.

STATE DEPARTMENT OF CALIFORNIA,
Monterey, July 1, 1849.

SIR: I am directed by Governor Riley to acknowledge the receipt of your letter of June 15, and to say that the priest has no right to sell houses in the mission of Santa Cruz, unless he should possess a regular title to such property in the same manner as any other private individual.

You will, therefore, forbid all sales of mission or other public property by said priest.

Very respectfully, your obedient servant,
H. W. HALLECK,
Brevet Captain, and Secretary of State.

J. L. MAJORS, Esq.,
Alcalde, Santa Cruz, California.

STATE DEPARTMENT OF CALIFORNIA,
Monterey, July 1, 1849.

SIR: I have the honor to acknowledge the receipt of your letter of May 28, giving notice of the escape of the Indian " Ildefonso;" also your letter of June 1, giving information of the landing of certain foreign goods at San Luis Obispo.

Very respectfully, your obedient servant,
H. W. HALLECK,
Brevet Captain, and Secretary of State.

Don MIGUEL ABILA,
Alcalde, San Luis Obispo, California.

STATE DEPARTMENT OF CALIFORNIA,
Monterey, July 3, 1849.

SIR: I am directed by Governor Riley to acknowledge the receipt of your petition and the accompanying papers.

If the alcalde's court at San José has exceeded its powers, your proper course of redress will be to bring the case before the superior tribunal, which it is hoped will be organized in August next.

As no attempt has been made by that court to forcibly execute its sentence upon your person, or to seize your property, the governor does not perceive at present any necessity for his official interference.

Very respectfully, your obedient servant,
H. W. HALLECK,
Brevet Captain, and Secretary of State.

THEODORE ROBBS, *Sonoma.*

STATE DEPARTMENT OF CALIFORNIA,
Monterey, July 3, 1849.

SIR: I am directed by General Riley to acknowledge the receipt of your letter of June 25, and to enclose you an extract from a Mexican law believed to be still in force respecting possession of property.

A translation of the laws of 1837, respecting the jurisdiction of courts in California, will soon be published. The main features of that law are believed to be still in force.

General Riley is on the point of leaving for Sutter's Fort, and has no time to write you more at length.

Very respectfully, your obedient servant,
H. W. HALLECK,
Brevet Captain, and Secretary of State.

L. W. BOGGS, Esq.,
Alcalde, Sonoma.

CIRCULAR.

EXECUTIVE DEPARTMENT OF CALIFORNIA,
Monterey, July 2, 1849.

The persons who may receive the plurality of votes respectively in each of the four judicial districts of California for judges of the superior court of this Territory, are requested to meet at Monterey immediately after the election of the 1st of August next, for the purpose of forming a tariff of fees and duties, to be collected by primary judges, (*de primera instancia,*) alcaldes, advocates, clerks, and other judicial officers; to form rules of their own tribunal; and to determine upon the times and places for holding their court. The absolute necessity of having some judicial authority superior to the present alcalde's courts renders it important that this superior tribunal should be organized with the least possible delay.

B. RILEY,
Brevet Brig. Gen. U. S. A., and Governor of California.

STATE DEPARTMENT OF CALIFORNIA,
Monterey, July 2, 1849.

MAJOR: I am directed by General Riley to acknowledge the receipt of your letter of June 4, respecting certain property belonging to the mission of San Diego.

Governor Mason, in August last, authorized the turning over of this property to Padre Gonzales, of Santa Barbara; but if neither the padre nor his agents take possession of it, and it is likely to be lost or injured from neglect, you are authorized to dispose of it by sale, turning over the proceeds to Captain Lyon, as "civil funds."

Very respectfully, your obedient servant,
H. W. HALLECK,
Brevet Captain, and Secretary of State.

Major S. P. HEINTZELMAN,
Commanding, San Diego, California.

CIRCULAR.

STATE DEPARTMENT OF CALIFORNIA,
Monterey, July 2, 1849.

Official information having been received that a collector and deputy collectors of customs, for the district of California, have been appointed according to law, and are now *en route* for their respective stations, it is therefore directed that, on their arrival, and the presentation of their appointments, the temporary collectors appointed by the authority of the governor of California cease their functions; and that they, and all other officers of this department, turn over to said collectors and their deputies all books and other custom-house property in their possession, taking the necessary receipt for the same.

So much of these moneys as may be requisite for that purpose will be expended by the order of the governor, to defray the expenses of the existing civil government of California, and the remainder held subject to such disposition as Congress may direct.

By order of the governor:
H. W. HALLECK,
Brevet Captain, and Secretary of State.

Know all men by these presents, that I, Bennet Riley, brevet brigadier general United States army, and governor of California, by virtue of authority in me vested, do hereby appoint and commission Major Robert Allen treasurer of California, with the salary of two thousand five hundred dollars per annum.

This appointment will have a retrospective effect to the first of July last, at which time Major Allen took charge of the "civil funds."

Given at camp near Benicia, California, this 3d day of August, in the year of our Lord 1849.

B. RILEY,
Brevet Brig. Gen. U S. A., and Governor of California.

Know all men by these presents, that I, Bennet Riley, brevet brigadier general United States army, and governor of California, by virtue of authority in me vested, do hereby appoint and commission J. W. Geary as judge of first instance in and for the district of San Francisco, to date from the 1st of August, 1849.

Given under my hand and seal, at San Francisco, California, this 6th day of August, in the year of our Lord eighteen hundred and forty nine.

B. RILEY,
Brevet Brig. Gen. U. S. A., and Governor of California.

Know all men by these presents, that I, Bennet Riley, brevet brigadier general United States army, and governor of California, by virtue of authority in me vested, do hereby appoint and confirm Horace Hawes as prefect of the district of San Francisco, to date from the 1st of August, 1849.

Given under my hand and seal, at San Francisco, California, this 7th day of August, in the year of our Lord eighteen hundred and forty nine.

B. RILEY,
Brevet Brig. Gen. U. S. A., and Governor of California.

STATE DEPARTMENT OF CALIFORNIA,
Monterey, August 10, 1849.

SIR: Your letter of July 4th has just been received, and I am directed to inform the ayuntamiento of Santa Barbara that the governor cannot excuse Mr. Daniel Hill from performing the duties of 1st register of that town, unless Mr. Hill should give good and sufficient reasons for declining an office imposed on him by the laws of the country and the wishes of his fellow-citizens. If Mr. Hill should persist in refusing to perform the duties of his office, he will subject himself to all the penalties of the laws.

Very respectfully, your obedient servant,
H. W. HALLECK,
Brevet Captain, and Secretary of State

Don RAYMUNDO CARRILLO,
Alcalde, Santa Barbara, California.

STATE DEPARTMENT OF CALIFORNIA,
Monterey, August 10, 1849.

SIR: I am directed by the governor to acknowledge the receipt of your letter of July 4th, and to inform you that he fully approves of the appointment of Antonio Maria de la Guerra as secretary of the Ylustre Ayuntamiento, with the salary of $30 per month.

Very respectfully your obedient servant,
H. W. HALLECK,
Brevet Captain, and Secretary of State.

Don RAYMUNDO CARRILLO,
Alcalde, Santa Barbara, California.

[18]

STATE DEPARTMENT OF CALIFORNIA,
Monterey, August 10, 1849.

REVEREND SIR: I am directed by the governor to acknowledge the receipt of your reverence's letter of May 28, giving information of the arrival of an impostor named Brignole, who falsely represented himself as bishop, apostolic legate, &c. It is said that Brignole was some time since arraigned before the alcalde of one of the northern districts, under the charge of being an impostor, since which time he has not been heard of, but is supposed either to have left the country or to have thrown off his assumed character of bishop.

I have the honor to be your reverence's most obedient servant,

H. W. HALLECK,
Brevet Captain, and Secretary of State.

Very Reverend JOSE MARIA DE JESUS GONZALES,
Governor of the Bishopric of California,
Santa Barbara, California.

STATE DEPARTMENT OF CALIFORNIA,
Monterey, August 10, 1849.

GENTLEMEN: I am directed by the governor to acknowledge the receipt of your letter of the 7th instant, and to say that it would give him great pleasure to afford every facility in his power for increasing the circulating medium in your city, and to supply the want of coin; but as it is quite certain, from information just received, that the new collectors will arrive in a very few days with instructions direct from the government at Washington, he deems it improper to make any changes in the regulations now established for the custom-houses in California. Any changes he might make could not continue more than a few days; for the moment the new collectors arrive, the entire control of the revenue will pass to other hands.

I am, gentlemen, very respectfully, your obedient servant,

H. W. HALLECK,
Brevet Captain, and Secretary of State.

Messrs. WRIGHT & Co.,
San Francisco, California.

STATE DEPARTMENT OF CALIFORNIA,
Monterey, August 10, 1849.

SIR: I am directed by the governor to acknowledge the receipt of your communication of the 7th ultimo, enclosing the proceedings of a meeting of the citizens of Santa Barbara. The governor is much pleased to learn that his plan of calling a general convention for forming a State government for California has met the approval of so respectable a body of his fellow-citizens. It was hardly to be expected that the number of delegates designated in his proclamation would be entirely satisfactory to all portions of the Territory; indeed, it was impossible at the time to obtain any satisfactory data respecting the relative population of the several districts, and it was therefore provided in the proclamation that each district should elect as many *additional* delegates as it should see fit, leaving it for the convention itself to decide how many of these ought to be received. When the regular delegates shall assemble, they can, on consultation, form a just estimate of the relative population of the district, and fix the final number of delegates accordingly. This was the most just and fair plan that could be devised. The relative population of the several districts is changing almost daily, and is now quite different from what it was at the time of issuing the proclamation. The population of the northern districts has probably nearly doubled within the last three months; and they will undoubtedly demand in convention a greater representation than that designated by the governor. It is hoped, however, that when the delegates assemble, they may, by a mutual spirit of conciliation and forbearance, make some satisfactory arrangement by which all parts of the country shall be duly and properly represented. With respect to the limits of the several districts, it is only necessary to remark that the governor followed, in his proclamation, as nearly as possible the old boundaries. He was unable at the time to ascertain what were the exact limits of the district of Santa Barbara, as defined by the departmental assembly, and he therefore fixed upon the rivers of Santa Ynez and Santa Clara as the most natural boundaries. This arrangement, however, was intended to be only of a temporary nature, as it is supposed that the convention will make a new political division of the Territory, and increase the number of districts. Please to assure the people of your district that the governor has no intention to make any permanent changes in the limits of their district; and that, so far as it may depend upon him, the older residents of the country shall have full security and protection in all their former rights and privileges. The changes complained of were the result of unavoidable circumstances, and were intended to be only of a temporary character.

With every assurance of respect, I am, sir, very respectfully, your obedient servant,

H. W. HALLECK,
Brevet Captain, and Secretary of State.

Don PABLO DE LA GRANA, *Santa Barbara.*

STATE DEPARTMENT OF CALIFORNIA,
Monterey, August 10, 1849.

SIR: I am directed by the governor to acknowledge the receipt of your letter of July 20, accompanying a petition of the citizens of Santa Cruz, dated July 10. According to the title given by General Micheltorena to Dodero on the 18th March, 1844, he has the privilege of carrying the water of the three springs to his mill; but, after passing through said mill, the water belongs to the community, under the direction of the respective magistrate; and neither Dodero nor any other person shall divert the natural course of the water, either before or after it passes the mill. The alcalde of Santa Cruz should therefore take the proper measures to protect the citizens of that place in the rights secured to them in the aforesaid title.

Very respectfully, your obedient servant,

H. W. HALLECK,
Brevet Captain, and Secretary of State

J. L. MAJORS, *Santa Cruz, California.*

STATE DEPARTMENT OF CALIFORNIA,
Monterey, August 11, 1849.

GENTLEMEN: I am directed by the governor to acknowledge the receipt of your letter of the 8th instant, and to inform you that he cannot make any loan of the public funds in his possession. He, however, will direct Major R. Allen, the treasurer of the "civil funds," to pay over to the municipality of San Francisco the sum of ten thousand dollars, ($10,000,) on the following conditions, viz: 1st. That said municipality give to the treasurer of California proper pledges and security that this money shall be expended in the erection or purchase of a suitable building or buildings for a district jail and court-house, and that an equal sum has been raised and appropriated by the said municipality for the same purpose. 2d. That the treasurer of California shall be satisfied that the treasurer of San Francisco has given good and sufficient bonds for the safe-keeping and proper expenditure of this money. 3d. That none of this money be expended by the town treasurer, except on the orders of the town council, signed by its legally-constituted officers.

Very respectfully, your obedient servant,
H. W. HALLECK,
Brevet Captain, and Secretary of S ate.

Dr. JOHN TOWSEND and others,
Committee Town Council of San Francisco, California.

STATE DEPARTMENT OF CALIFORNIA,
Monterey, August 11, 1849.

SIR: I am directed by the governor to inform you that he received yesterday your letter of June 14 and 15, communicating the information that the Chilian brig "Imperial" had put into the port of Santa Barbara in distress, and been condemned as unseaworthy; that you had permitted the cargo to be landed, and warehoused on deposite; that you had permitted a few articles to be sold, and collected the duties thereon, to the amount of $94 50, and had received duties from a passenger in said vessel to the amount of $300 75, both of which sums you hold at the disposal of the government. The governor will immediately despatch a custom-house agent to Santa Barbara to collect the duties on the cargo of the condemned vessel. An agent cannot be permanently stationed at that place till after the arrival of the new collector of customs for California, who, it is supposed, will bring from Washington full instructions touching the revenue on this coast.

Very respectfully, your obedient servant,
H. W. HALLECK,
Brevet Captain, and Secretary of State.

Don RAYMUNDO CARRILLO,
Alcalde, Santa Barbara, California.

STATE DEPARTMENT OF CALIFORNIA,
Monterey, August 11, 1849.

SIR: I am directed by the governor to acknowledge the receipt of your communication of yesterday, and to inform you that your resignation should first be presented to the prefect of the district; and, should he not accept it, you then have the right of appeal to the governor.

Very respectfully, your obedient servant,

H. W. HALLECK,
Brevet Captain, and Secretary of State.

Rafael Sanchez,
Syndico, Monterey, California.

State Department Territory of California,
Monterey, August 13, 1849.

Sir: The governor directs that you will make inquiries as to the probable cost of erecting buoys at the following points in the bay of San Francisco, viz: on Blossom rock; on the bar near Yerba Buena point; on the sunken rock off the Presidio; and on the bar or rock in the channel above Angel island. You are requested to consult with Captain Ringgold, United States navy, (who is now engaged upon a survey of the bay and its tributaries,) and report for what sum the work can probably be done by contract. The anchors and chains purchased by Captain Folsom for this purpose, and which the quartermaster was authorized to loan to Captain Ringgold, will be used in the proposed work. An early answer is requested.

Very respectfully, your obedient servant,

H. W. HALLECK,
Brevet Captain, and Secretary of State.

Captain E. A. King,
Harbor-master, San Francisco, California.

State Department Territory of California,
Monterey, August 13, 1849.

Reverend Sir: I am directed by the governor to acknowledge the receipt of your reverence's letter of July 23, complaining that a Protestant minister did, on the 9th of July, in Monterey, before the very eyes of the governor, solemnize a marriage in which one of the contracting parties was a Catholic, such act being in violation of Governor Mason's prohibitory order of August 23, 1847.

The governor was absent from Monterey from the 5th of July to the 9th of August, and consequently had no official information of the marriage alluded to, until he received the communication of your reverence.

The order of Governor Mason above referred to was one issued under the laws of war, and before California became a part of the territory of the United States, and it ceased to have any force on the ratification of the treaty of peace. Indeed, it was evidently intended to be only of a temporary character, and to continue only during the military occupation of the country. Neither Governor Mason nor Governor Riley has claimed authority to make any new laws for California since the war, that power being vested in Congress alone; and even Congress is prohibited in the constitution from making any laws respecting an establishment of religion, or prohibiting the free exercise thereof. The governor has, therefore, no power either to enforce or to renew the order of Colonel Mason above referred to.

The governor directs me to express to you his high regard and consideration, and to thank you for the very liberal and generous sentiments expressed in your letter.

While it will always be his earnest endeavor to protect the Catholics of California in the rights and privileges secured to them by the laws of the land, he cannot consent to interfere in matters touching religious opinions, for by so doing he would evidently violate the spirit of the constitution of the United States, which makes all religious denominations equal before the laws.

He would, however, suggest to your reverence, as a friend rather than in his official character, whether the dispensation already given by the Roman Pontiff for the solemnization of marriages in the United States is not applicable to California without any new order. California is now a part of the territory of the United States, and must, it is believed, be regarded as such in all its civil and religious relations. If this view be correct, does it not relieve your reverence from all difficulty and responsibility respecting marriages between Catholics and Protestants?

I have the honor to be, very respectfully, your reverence's most obedient servant,

H. W. HALLECK,
Brevet Captain, and Secretary of State.
Very Reverend F. Jose Maria de Jesus Gonzales,
Governor of the Bishopric of California, Santa Barbara.

State Department Territory of California,
Monterey, August 13, 1849.

Sir: I am directed by the governor to acknowledge the receipt of your letter of July 30, and to inform you that he can take no measures towards renting the missions of San José and Santa Clara until a full examination is made into the affairs of these establishments, and the tenor by which the priest claims to hold them.

Very respectfully, your obedient servant,

H. W. HALLECK,
Brevet Captain, and Secretary of State.
J. B. Steinberger, Esq.,
San Francisco, California.

State Department Territory of California,
Monterey, August 13, 1849.

Major: I enclose herewith an extract from a circular from this department, dated February 24, and also a copy of a circular dated July 2, 1849.

As "Treasurer of California" you will strictly observe the instructions contained in these circulars, respecting the keeping, expenditure, and accountability of the "civil fund" of this Territory.

All your quarterly returns and papers will hereafter be rendered to this office in duplicates, one copy of which will be forwarded to Washington, and the other retained in this office for the information of the governor.

Until the arrival of the new collector appointed under the laws of Congress, it is made your duty to receive at the end of every month from the temporary collector of San Francisco all the proceeds of the customs, and to examine and audit his accounts.

As charges of a serious character have recently been made respecting the management of the custom-house affairs at San Francisco, and the official conduct of some of its subordinate officers, the governor directs that you will immediately make a thorough examination of the custom-house affairs at that place, and official conduct of all the employés of that establishment, and he authorizes you to associate with yourself for this examination two other persons of suitable character and capacity, to each of whom you will pay the sum of ten dollars per day for every day they are so employed.

All the books of the custom-house will be submitted to your inspection, and you are empowered by the governor to administer oaths and send for persons and papers.

A full report of your proceedings will be made out and signed by yourself and the other members of the commission, and sent to this office for the information of the governor.

Arrangements will be made by you for the payment at San Francisco and Monterey of the salaries of the civil officers of California at least every quarter, and due notice given of the times and places of such payments.

Very respectfully, your obedient servant,
H. W. HALLECK,
Brevet Captain, and Secretary of State.

Major ROBERT ALLEN,
Treasurer of California, San Francisco, California.

STATE DEPARTMENT OF CALIFORNIA,
Monterey, August 13, 1849.

GENTLEMEN: Your letter of March 12, addressed to General Mason, has just been received by General B. Riley, the present governor of California, who directs me to say, in reply, that the Congress of the United States has, as yet, passed no laws for the sale of public lands, or for the working of the mines in California; but it is supposed that these matters will receive the early attention of that body at its coming session.

Our government has always pursued the most liberal policy towards foreigners settling in the country, and the public and the mineral lands have been brought into market on such terms as to place them within the means of the smallest capitalist; and it is presumed that the same liberal course will be pursued in enacting laws for California.

The vast mineral wealth and agricultural resources of California, and the rapid increase of the population, enable her to offer greater attractions to new settlers than almost any other country.

Very respectfully, your obedient servant,
H. W. HALLECK,
Brevet Captain, and Secretary of State.

Messrs. JOHN McDOUGALD,
  WILLIAM E. CORMACK,
  ROBERT MITCHELL, and others,
    Aukland, New Zealand.

STATE DEPARTMENT OF CALIFORNIA,
Monterey, August 13, 1849.

SIR: I am directed by the governor to acknowledge the receipt of your communication of July 15, respecting the conduct of the captain of the steamer California, and to inform you that your letter has been referred to the Postmaster General of the United States.

Very respectfully, your obedient servant,
H. W. HALLECK,
Brevet Captain, and Secretary of State.

Don MIGUEL PEDRORENA,
San Diego, California.

STATE DEPARTMENT OF CALIFORNIA,
Monterey, August 13, 1849.

SIR: I am directed by the governor to acknowledge the receipt of your letter of July 4, asking, on the part of the ayuntamiento, his orders respecting the construction of a jail in Santa Barbara.

As soon as the ayuntamiento shall have made arrangements for the purchase or erection of a suitable building for a jail and court-room, and raised money for that purpose, the governor will assign to Santa Barbara, from the "civil fund," a corresponding sum, not to exceed $6,000.

The governor requests that the ayuntamiento will take immediate measures for the accomplishment of this object, either by subscription or a municipal tax, and report to him the amount of money so collected, in order that he may make the assignment required.

Very respectfully, your obedient servant,
H. W. HALLECK,
Brevet Captain, and Secretary of State.

Don RAYMUNDO CARRILLO,
Alcalde, Santa Barbara, California.

Know all men by these presents, that I, Bennet Riley, brevet brigadier general United States army, and governor of California, by virtue of authority in me vested, do hereby appoint Hopeful Toler a notary public and translator in and for the district of San Francisco.

Given under my hand, at Monterey, California, this 13th day of August, in the year of our Lord 1849.

B. RILEY,
Brevet Brig. Gen. U. S. Army, and Governor of California.

STATE DEPARTMENT OF CALIFORNIA,
Monterey, August 13, 1849.

MAJOR: I am directed by the governor to acknowledge the receipt of your communication of July 8, respecting the claim of Señor Arguillo to the mission of San Diego. The United States being in possession of that mission, it cannot be delivered up till the title of the claimant is properly established; and it is hoped that a proper tribunal for deciding upon those claims will soon be established.

Very respectfully, your obedient servant,
H. W. HALLECK,
Brevet Captain, and Secretary of State.

Major L. P. HEINTZELMAN,
Commanding at San Diego, California.

Know all men by these presents, that I, Bennet Riley, brevet brigadier general United States army, and governor of California, by virtue of authority in me vested, do hereby appoint H. F. Page a notary public in and for the district of San Francisco.

Given under my hand, at Monterey, California, this thirteenth day of August, in the year of our Lord eighteen hundred and forty-nine.
BENNET RILEY,
Brevet Brigadier General United States Army,
and Governor of California.

Know all men by these presents, that I, Bennet Riley, brevet brigadier general United States army, and governor of California, by virtue of authority in me vested, do hereby appoint John McVickar a notary public in and for the district of San Francisco.

Given under my hand, at Monterey, California, this thirteenth day of August, in the year of our Lord eighteen hundred and forty-nine.
BENNET RILEY,
Brevet Brigadier General United States Army,
and Governor of California.

Know all men by these presents, that I, Bennet Riley, brevet brigadier general United States army, and governor of California, by virtue of authority in me vested, do hereby appoint and commission William Shaw a notary public and commissioner of deeds in and for the district of Sacramento.

Given under my hand, at Monterey, California, this thirteenth day of August, in the year of our Lord eighteen hundred and forty-nine.
BENNET RILEY,
Brevet Brigadier General United States Army,
and Governor of California.

STATE DEPARTMENT OF CALIFORNIA,
Monterey, August 14, 1849.

This is to certify that John Mackay this day filed in this office his written declaration of intention to become a citizen of the United States, and to renounce forever all allegiance to all and any prince, potentate, state, and sovereignty.

H. W. HALLECK,
Brevet Captain, and Secretary of State.

STATE DEPARTMENT OF CALIFORNIA,
Monterey, August 14, 1849.

This is to certify that Randolfa Westhoff this day filed in this office his written declaration of intention to become a citizen of the United States, and to renounce forever all allegiance to all and any prince, potentate, state, and sovereignty.

H. W. HALLECK,
Brevet Captain, and Secretary of State.

STATE DEPARTMENT OF CALIFORNIA,
Monterey, August 14, 1849.

This is to certify that Hipolito Adler this day filed in this office his written declaration of intention to become a citizen of the United States, and to renounce forever all allegiance to all and any prince, potentate, state, and sovereignty.

H. W. HALLECK,
Brevet Captain, and Secretary of State.

Know all men by these presents, that I, Bennet Riley, brevet brigadier general United States army, and governor of California, by virtue of authority in me vested, do hereby appoint and commission R. M. May as judge of first instance of the district of San José, to date from the first of August, 1849.

Given under my hand and seal, at Monterey, California, this thirteenth day of August, in the year of our Lord eighteen hundred and forty-nine.

BENNET RILEY,
Brevet Brigadier General U. S. Army,
and Governor of California.

Know all men by these presents, that I, Bennet Riley, brevet brigadier general United States army, and governor of California, by virtue of authority in me vested, do hereby appoint and commission Antonio Ma. Pico a prefect of the district of San José, to date from the first day of August, 1849.

Given under my hand and seal, at Monterey, California, this thirteenth day of August, in the year of our Lord eighteen hundred and forty nine.

BENNET RILEY,
Brevet Brigadier General U. S. Army,
and Governor of California.

Know all men by these presents, that I, Bennet Riley, brevet brigadier general United States army, and governor of California, by virtue of authority in me vested, do hereby appoint and commission David Spence as prefect of the district of Monterey, to date from the first day of August, 1849.

Given under my hand and seal, at Monterey, California, this tenth day of August, in the year of our Lord eighteen hundred and forty-nine.

BENNET RILEY,
Brevet Brigadier General U. S. Army,
and Governor of California.

STATE DEPARTMENT TERRITORY OF CALIFORNIA,
Monterey, August 10, 1849.

SIR: I am directed by the governor to inform you that your letter of June 1, respecting the trial and sentence of the Indian "Saco," was not received till last evening. As the time of suspension of the execution has long since expired, no occasion now exists for any interference on the part of the executive.

The organization of the *superior tribunal,* and the publication of the laws of California (a translation is now in press) respecting the powers of jurisdiction of the several courts, will hereafter remove all doubts respecting the right of appeal in criminal cases.

The commissions for prefect and judges of first instance for your district will be made out as soon as we receive the election returns from Bodega and San Rafael.

The prefect commissions the sub-prefects, and submits his appointments to the governor for his approbation. The prefect also decides upon the election of all town officers, subject to an appeal to the governor. I think the sheriffs of districts should be commissioned by the district courts.

The question of whether yourself or Major Cooper should be commissioned as judge of first instance, will be left for further consideration.

The first alcalde may be judge of first instance, but is not necessarily so, the governor having a right to appoint any other person.

Very respectfully, your obedient servant,
H. W. HALLECK,
Brevet Captain, and Secretary of State.

Governor L. W. BOGGS,
Sonoma, California.

Know all men by these presents, that I, Bennet Riley, brevet brigadier general United States army, and governor of California, by virtue of authority in me vested, do hereby appoint and commission Frederick Billings fiscal of the superior tribunal, or attorney general of California, to date from the 1st of August, 1849.

Given under my hand and seal, at Monterey, California, this thirteenth day of August, in the year of our Lord eighteen hundred and forty-nine.

BENNET RILEY,
Brevet Brig. Gen. U. S. Army, and Governor of California.

Know all men by these presents, that I, Bennet Riley, brevet brigadier general United States army, and governor of California, by virtue of authority in me vested, do hereby appoint Theodore Griswold a notary public in and for the district of San Francisco.

Given under my hand, at Monterey, California, this 17th day of August, in the year of our Lord eighteen hundred and forty-nine.

BENNET RILEY,
Brevet Brig. Gen. U. S. Army, and Governor of California.

Know all men by these presents, that I, Bennet Riley, brevet brigadier general United States army, and governor of California, by virtue of authority in me vested, do hereby appoint and commission Peter H. Burnett judge or minister of the superior tribunal of California, to date from the 1st day of August, 1849.

Given under my hand and seal, at Monterey, California, this 13th day of August, in the year of our Lord eighteen hundred and forty-nine.

BENNET RILEY,
Brevet Brig. Gen. U. S. Army, and Governor of California.

STATE DEPARTMENT TERRITORY OF CALIFORNIA,
Monterey, August 17, 1849.

MAJOR: On the return of General Riley to this place, he was informed that some of the men under your command had removed from this office half a dozen candlesticks belonging to the civil government, and shipped them to Benicia.

You are requested to inquire into this matter, and, if this property has been so removed, to return it to Monterey without delay.

By order of the governor:

H. W. HALLECK,
Brevet Captain, and Secretary of State.

Major W. SEAWELL,
2d Infantry, commanding at Benicia.

Know all men by these presents, that I, Bennet Riley, brevet brigadier general United States army, and governor of California, by virtue of authority in me vested, do hereby appoint and commission William G. Dana prefect of the district of San Luis Obispo, to date from the first day of August, 1849.

Given under my hand and seal, at Monterey, California, this twentieth day of August, in the year of our Lord eighteen hundred and forty-nine.

BENNET RILEY,
Brev. Brig. Gen. U. S. Army, and Governor of California.

Know all men by these presents, that I, Bennet Riley, brevet brigadier general United States army, and governor of California, by virtue of authority in me vested, do hereby appoint and commission H. A. Pefft a notary public and commissioner of deeds in and for the district of San Luis Obispo.

Given under my hand, at Monterey, California, this 20th day of August, in the year of our Lord eighteen hundred and forty nine.

BENNET RILEY,
Brevet Brig. Gen. U. S. Army, and Governor of California.

State Department Territory of California,
Monterey, August 17, 1849.

Sir: I am directed by the governor to acknowledge the receipt of your letter, as attorney for debts, in the case of Elias Barnet and E. F. Bole and R. L. Kilburn, asking for new trial, for reasons given.

The governor is of opinion that there are sufficient reasons given why the judge of first instance of the district of Sonoma should grant a new trial; or the case may be brought up before one of the benches of the superior tribunal, the organization of which court will be completed as soon as the election returns are received.

The circumstances under which a new trial or an appeal may be had are explained in the laws organizing courts for California, a translation of which is in press, and will be ready for delivery in a few days. That publication will render it unnecessary for any action of the executive in this case, as it will be seen that the superior tribunal has power to order the case up for new trial or decision, if litigants appeal from the decision of the judge of first instance.

Very respectfully, your obedient servant,
H. W. HALLECK,
Brevet Captain, and Secretary of State.

J. E. Brackett, Esq.,
Attorney for Bole and Kilburn, Sonoma, California.

State Department of California,
Monterey, August 20, 1849.

Sir: I have the honor to acknowledge the receipt of your communication of the 8th instant, with the accompanying papers, all of which have been laid before the governor.

It is a matter of regret to the governor that any person in Mr. Bellamy's position should have assumed to himself power which could never have belonged to him, and still more, that any officer of the army should in any way have connected himself with the transaction.

Both have been notified of the governor's decided disapproval of the course; and it is to be hoped that the more thorough organization of the courts which has just taken place may prevent any further irregularities of this kind. I enclose you herewith copies of my letter of this date to Mr. Bellamy, and of one from Major Canby to Lieutenant Derby.

The governor has directed a thorough examination to be made into the affairs of the missions of Santa Clara and San José; his action on that

matter will be postponed till after he learns the result of this examination.
With assurances of high respect, I have the honor to be your obedient servant,
H. W. HALLECK,
Brevet Captain, and Secretary of State.
J. ALEXANDER FORBES,
Vice Consul to H. B. M., Santa Clara, California.

STATE DEPARTMENT OF CALIFORNIA,
Monterey, August 20, 1849.

CAPTAIN: On the 22d of March, 1847, General Kearny, then governor of California, directed that the missions of San José and Santa Clara, with the houses, grounds, gardens, and vineyards around and near them, should be left in the charge of the Catholic priests, who should be held responsible for the preservation of said missions and property till the various questions of titles and claims would be properly investigated.

This property has since that time been left in the charge of the priest of Santa Clara, as the agent of the government, for its preservation.

But it is now reported that he has been unfaithful to his trust; that various persons, under different pretexts, have been allowed to trespass upon this property; and that many of the buildings have been seriously injured: moreover, that said priest has recently made a formal transfer of his trust to a private citizen, for a term of years, and for which he is to receive a valuable consideration.

And it is also known that he at one time attempted to sell and convey away portions of the real estate of those missions.

It is also charged that he is entirely unfit and incompetent to continue in charge of this property, and to preserve it from trespassers.

The governor therefore directs that you will immediately proceed to San José and Santa Clara, for the purpose of inspecting these establishments, and ascertaining the facts relating to the priest's management of this property.

I enclose herewith various papers relating to this subject, which you will return to this office as soon as you have completed your inspection.

The title to all the property of these missions (with a few reservations) was vested in government; and where they have not been legally conveyed by government to private individuals, they are still public property, and will be held as such.

The priests have, since 1833, been regarded as tenants at will, and liable to be removed at the pleasure of the government.

The laws also provide for the renting of this property, and designate the disposition to be made of the proceeds of this rent.

On your return to this place you will report whatever information you may obtain respecting these missions, and also whether, under the circumstances, it will not be advisable to remove the priest of Santa Clara from his charge as government agent, and to rent the property to some responsible citizens, in accordance with the laws of the country.

You will be allowed, from the "civil funds," your necessary expenses, and a per diem of $6 for the time you are actually and necessarily engaged in this inspection.

Very respectfully, your obedient servant,

H. W. HALLECK,
Brevet Captain, and Secretary of State.

Captain G. C. WESCOTT,
United States Army, Monterey.

STATE DEPARTMENT OF CALIFORNIA,
Monterey, August 20, 1849.

SIR: I am directed by the governor to acknowledge the receipt of your letter of the 14th instant, asking for an approval of your course in your recent difficulty with Mr. Forbes. As the governor believes that your course in that case was evidently illegal, and that you assumed powers which never properly belonged to you, he must decline acceding to your request.

Nor does he deem it necessary for him to interfere officially in the affair, when the question can easily be settled by a resort to the proper judicial tribunal.

Very respectfully, your obedient servant,

H. W. HALLECK,
Brevet Captain, and Secretary of State.

GEORGE W. BELLAMY,
Santa Clara.

Know all men by these presents, that I, Bennet Riley, brevet brigadier general United States army, and governor of California, by virtue of authority in me vested, do hereby appoint and commission Stephen Cooper judge of first instance of the district of Sonoma, to date from the first day of August, 1849.

Given under my hand and seal, at Monterey, California, this twenty-first day of August, in the year of our Lord eighteen hundred and forty-nine.

B. RILEY,
Brevet Brig. Gen. U. S. A., and Governor of California.

Know all men by these presents, that I, Bennet Biley, brevet brigadier general United States army, and governor of California, by virtue of authority in me vested, do hereby appoint and commission Charles P. Wilkins prefect of the district of Sonoma, to date from the first of August, 1849.

Given under my hand and seal, at Monterey, California, this twenty-first day of August, in the year of our Lord eighteen hundred and forty-nine.

B. RILEY,
Brevet Brig. Gen. U. S. A., and Governor of California.

STATE DEPARTMENT OF CALIFORNIA,
Monterey, August 22, 1849.

CAPTAIN: Governor Riley directs that you will immediately transfer to Major R. Allen, "civil treasurer," all "civil funds" in your possession, taking his receipt for the same.

Very respectfully, your obedient servant,

H. W. HALLECK,
Brevet Captain, and Secretary of State.

Captain E. K. KANE,
Assistant Quartermaster, Monterey.

STATE DEPARTMENT OF CALIFORNIA,
Monterey, August 22, 1849.

MAJOR: I am directed by Governor Riley to acknowledge the receipt of your accounts of the civil funds for the month of July, and to call your attention to the facts therein stated, that you have transferred, without his order or approbation, from this fund to the quartermaster's department, $35,124 79, and to Major Fitzgerald $500.

This transfer is in direct violation of the instructions which have heretofore been issued to all persons holding these "civil funds," and the governor will hold you strictly responsible as civil treasurer that the money be immediately restored.

By order of Governor Riley:

H. W. HALLECK,
Brevet Captain, and Secretary of State.

Major ROBERT ALLEN,
Civil Treasurer, Benicia.

STATE DEPARTMENT OF CALIFORNIA,
Monterey, August 22, 1849.

MAJOR: General Riley directs me to call your attention to the facts that no monthly summary statement of "civil funds" in your possession, nor quarterly accounts and papers, have been received from you since your arrival in this country; nor have you acknowledged the receipt of my order or circular, which has been sent to you by his direction, in relation to this "civil fund." Nevertheless, it is known that you received, both at Monterey and at San Francisco, considerable sums of this money.

By order of Governor Riley:

H. W. HALLECK,
Brevet Captain, and Secretary of State.

Major E. H. FITZGERALD,
Assistant Quartermaster, Benicia.

STATE DEPARTMENT OF CALIFORNIA,
Monterey, August 22, 1849.

SIR: I am directed by the governor to acknowledge the receipt of your letter of the 4th instant, relating to the murder of an Indian in Sonoma, and to thank you for your prompt attention in giving him the informtion.

As the judicial tribunals in your district are now organized, it is deemed proper that you immediately lay the facts of the case before Judge Cooper, the *juez de primera instancia* of Sonoma district, for his action in the premises.

Very respectfully, your obedient servant,

H. W. HALLECK,
Brevet Captain, and Secretary of State.

General M. G. VALLEJO,
Sub-Indian Agent, Sonoma, California.

STATE DEPARTMENT OF CALIFORNIA,
Monterey, August 22, 1849.

MAJOR: In compliance with your request of the 18th instant, I transmit herewith copies of reports from Captains Folsom and Marcy, and Lieut. Davidson, from which you will be able to ascertain the amounts due the "civil fund" from the military departments of the government.

The sum of $6,200 transferred by Captain Folsom to Captain Marcy was for civil purposes, and has been accounted for by him as such.

The $10,000 transferred to Major Hardie was for raising troops in Oregon, but very little of it was so expended; nor, so far as is shown by the records of this office, has it ever been restored to the "civil fund."

The $70,000 transferred to Purser Forest was for paying the expenses of bringing emigrants from Lower California. The loan was made to the navy at the request of Commodore Jones, but how much of it was expended is not known. Nor is it known that any arrangements have been made for refunding the sum of $3,500 transferred to Major Rich, and the sum of $200 transferred to Lieutenant Warren. All these items should, therefore, be charged on your books as due the "civil funds."

It appears from Lieutenant Davidson's accounts, enclosed herewith, that he transferred $10,804 50 to the quartermaster and commissary's departments; but, as his accounts have been sent to Washington, I do not know how much to each, nor the dates of the transfer. As Lieutenant Davidson is in your vicinity, you can get these items from him. It appears from the enclosed copy of a letter from Captain Ingall that he has received $896 70 of "civil funds" from the collector of San Pedro.

It does not appear from the records of this office that any authority or permission was ever given for the transfer; nor was it known here that the money had been so transferred till the receipt of Captain Ingall's letter on the 21st of June last.

In addition to the items mentioned in Captain Marcy's report, that officer has loaned from the "civil funds" the following sums:

1848.
August	17.	To Captain Lanman, United States navy	-	$50	00
September	30.	To Captain Lanman do do	-	60	00
October	13.	To Captain Lanman do do	-	500	00
August	30.	To S. E. Woodworth	-	100	00
April	12.	To Colonel R. B. Mason	-	2,500	00

None of this money has ever been returned or accounted for, and it should therefore appear on your books as due the "civil funds." The amount of "civil funds" in the hands of Lieutenant Davidson, December 31, has been paid over to Captain Kane.

Very respectfully, your obedient servant,

H. W. HALLECK,
Brevet Captain, and Secretary of State.

Major R. ALLEN,
   Treasurer, Benicia.

STATE DEPARTMENT OF CALIFORNIA,
Monterey, August 24, 1849.

SIR: The governor has received your official communication of yesterday, and directs that you give the proper notice and hold an election for regidor, in place of David Spence, appointed prefect of the district.

Very respectfully, your obedient servant,

H. W. HALLECK.
Brevet Captain, and Secretary of State.

Don YGNACIO EZQUER,
   Alcalde, Monterey, California.

EXECUTIVE DEPARTMENT OF CALIFORNIA,
Monterey, August 30, 1849.

SIR: I have the honor to acknowledge the receipt of your letter of June 26; and in reply to that part of it which relates to the civil affairs of this country, I would respectfully refer you to my civil despatches Nos. 1 and 2 to the Adjutant General of the army, and my letter of this date to the assistant adjutant general of the Pacific division, copies of which are enclosed herewith.

I beg leave to call your attention particularly to the views which I have expressed in these communications respecting the "civil fund" formed from the duties collected on imports into California previous to the time when the general government assumed control over these revenues. Unless this fund be left at my disposal, it will be utterly impossible for me to carry on the government; and as no military authority over civil affairs in this country is or can be exercised, anarchy will necessarily ensue.

Very respectfully, your obedient servant,

B. RILEY,
Brevet Brig. Gen. U. S. A., and Governor of California.

Hon. GEO. W. CRAWFORD,
   Secretary of War.

EXECUTIVE DEPARTMENT OF CALIFORNIA,
Monterey, August 30, 1849.

COLONEL: I have the honor to acknowledge the receipt of your letter of the 12th instant, communicating the views of General Smith respecting my acts and duties as governor of California.

I must beg leave to dissent from some of these views, and to offer a few remarks in defence of the course which I have pursued in the administration of civil affairs in this country.

In the instructions issued from Washington to General Kearny in 1846, for his guidance in California, the establishment of port regulations was assigned to the commander of the Pacific squadron, while it was said "the appointment of temporary collectors at the several ports appertains to the civil governor of the province." It was also directed that the duties at the custom-houses should be used for the support of the necessary officers of the civil government. This division of duties and this disposition of the proceeds of the customs were continued during the whole war, except that for a part of one year the duties of collectors in some of the ports were performed by army and navy officers, while in others the civil collectors appointed by the governor of California were retained. On the reception of the treaty of peace, Governor Mason, for reasons which have been communicated to government, determined to continue the collection of revenues in this country, on the authority which has been given him, until Congress should act in the matter, or orders to the contrary should be received from Washington. He, therefore, as governor of California, again appointed collectors in the ports where military officers had performed those duties, and collected the customs on all foreign goods as directed in the tariff of 1846—the commodore of the Pacific squadron continuing the direction of all matters relating to port regulations.

A double necessity impelled the governor to this course: the country was in pressing need of these foreign goods, and Congress had established no port of entry on this coast; the want of a more complete organization of the existing civil government was daily increasing; and as Congress had made no provision for supporting a territorial government in this country, it was absolutely necessary to create a fund for that purpose from duties collected on these foreign goods. It is true there was no law of Congress authorizing the collection of those duties, but at the same time the laws forbade the landing of the goods till the duties were paid. Congress had declined to legislate on the subject, and both the President and Secretary of the Treasury acknowledged the want of power of the Treasury Department to collect revenue in California. The governor of California, therefore, assumed the responsibility of collecting this revenue for the support of the government of this country—a responsibility which he was fully justified in assuming by the necessity of the case, by the instructions which he had received from Washington, (and which had never been countermanded,) and by the existing laws of the country. It is not pretended that the governor of California could derive any authority, either from the laws of this country or the instructions of the President, to collect revenue here, *after Congress* assumed the control of it. But in the interim between the signing of the treaty of peace and the extension of the revenue laws over this country, it is a fair presumption that the temporary regulations established here by executive authority respecting foreign commerce continued in force, so far as they conflicted with no provision of the constitution, treaties, or laws of the United States; at any rate, such was the course which Governor Mason determined to pursue, and, as this determination was immediately communicated to Washington, and the receipt of his despatch acknowledged, without one word of dissent being expressed, it is to be presumed that his action in the case met the approval of the government. The executive departments, though well informed of the course which the governor of California was pursuing in reference to the collection and disposition of this money, refrained from any interference, and, in all their orders, letters, and circulars, they most carefully avoided expressing the slightest disapprobation, or even doubt, as to the propriety of that course. Congress was fully aware that Governor Mason was collecting revenue here for the support of the civil government, and yet that body declined passing any laws for appointing collectors on this coast till the very close of the session, and even then no cognizance was taken of the moneys which had been or might be collected previous to the appointment and due instalment of these officers. The reason of this is obvious: as Congress had failed to organize a territorial government here, all were aware that the existing government must continue in force, and that it must have some means of support; such means were found in the neglected revenues of this coast, and employed for that object, and no one felt disposed to interfere or to turn these revenues into the general treasury, until a fund was established sufficient for the more immediate and urgent wants of California. On no other supposition can we account for the action of Congress and of the authorities at Washington. It cannot for a moment be supposed that they would direct the continuance of a government here without the means of defraying its expenses; nor that they would tax, through the custom-houses, the people of this infant colony, and at the same time deprive them of all the benefits of a government. Such a course might accord with the policy of the despotic powers of the Old World, but it could never be attempted with impunity in our country.

On assuming command in this country as civil governor, I was directed to receive from Governor Mason all his instructions and communications, and to take them for my guidance in the administration of civil affairs. Upon an examination of these instructions, and a full consultation with Governor Mason, I determined to continue the collection of the revenue till the general government should assume that power, and to add the proceeds to the "civil fund"—using that fund for the necessary expenses of the civil government. Indeed, I had no other course left for me to pursue. This fund formed my only means of defraying the expenses of the government, which were already great. These expenses are daily increasing, and, as I have no power to impose taxes in this country, I cannot carry on the government without the moneys belonging to this "civil fund." Under existing circumstances, the necessity of employing civil officers, and of paying them the full salaries allowed by law, is too obvious to require comment. I have pledged myself to pay these salaries from that fund, unless forbidden to do so by direct orders from Washington; and I shall redeem my pledge.

This "civil fund" was commenced in the early part of 1847, and has been formed and used in the manner pointed out in the early instructions to the governor of this Territory. The money has been collected and disbursed by the "governor of California," and by those appointed by him in virtue of his office. He is, therefore, the person responsible for this money, both to the government and the parties from whom it was collected; and it can be expended only on his orders. Not a cent of this money has been collected under the authority of any department of the army; nor can any such department, or any officer of the army, simply in virtue of his military commission, have any control, direct or indirect, over it. It is true, some of this money has, from time to time, as the wants of the service required, been transferred to the different military departments; but this transfer was in the form of a *loan*, and the money so transferred is still due the "civil fund," and should be returned. The increased expenditures for the support of the civil government as it is now organized, and the pressing necessity of constructing prisons for the security of civil prisoners, will soon render this restoration absolutely essential in order to carry on the government, especially as the transfer of the custom-houses to the regular collectors appointed by the general government will now cut off all further means of supplying the civil treasury.

Entertaining these views of the correctness of the course which has been pursued by my predecessor and by myself respecting this "civil fund," I was not a little surprised at the ground assumed in your communication, that the collectors in California "are agents of the *military* authority of the department," and that "disbursing officers [of the army] are allowed to draw on this deposite [the civil fund] for all expenses for which there are appropriations by law."

No collectors in California now hold, or have ever held, any appointments, commissions, or authority from any military department; nor have they ever received any orders or instructions from such sources. All their powers have been derived from the governor of California, and they have been subject to his orders only. No disbursing officer of the army or of the general government has ever been allowed to draw upon this "civil fund," except in character of civil agent, or as a *loan* to a military department. And I am both surprised and mortified to learn that, at this late hour, an attempt is to be made to remove this money from my control, and to place it at the disposition of officers who have had no responsibility in its collection, and who of right can exercise no authority over it. Under the peculiar situation of the country, with an immense floating population collected together from all parts of the world, I thought my position as governor of California sufficiently embarrassing without having new obstacles placed in my way by any attempts to deprive me of the only means at my disposal for carrying on the government.

If I mistake not, the opinion that the governor of California has no control over the "civil fund" is of recent origin. I am told that the civil order of General Mason, as *governor of California*, dated February 23, to the collector at San Francisco, was shown to General Smith on that day, and received his approbation; and that division orders No. 2, of the same date, were issued at the request of Governor Mason, for the purpose of showing the people of California that the course which had been adopted respecting the revenue on this coast accorded with the views of the general of the division. Moreover, that when informed that all the temporary collectors in California held their authority from the *governor*, the General expressed no wish or desire that the system should be changed. Granting that the military authorities here had a right to assume entire control of the revenue on this coast, although the President of the United States (if I mistake not) has clearly asserted that no such powers could be exercised by officers of the general government without the authority of Congress, it is nevertheless plain that no such power *has* ever been exercised. If such a course was intended by

General Smith's orders of February 23, these instructions were never properly carried into execution; nor until the receipt of your letter had I any intimation that such a course was at all desired. The commanding general of the division was certainly aware that this whole revenue matter was managed by officers holding their authority from me as governor of California, and that when money was wanted by the military departments, application was made to me to authorize the loan or temporary transfer from the "civil funds." If, however, it now be the General's wish to assume a military control of the collection of duties on imports into California, I will immediately discharge the collectors appointed by the governors of California, and surrender the entire direction of the matter to such military department or military officers as he may direct. But for the money which *has already been collected* by the civil officers under my authority, I alone am responsible; and until further instructions from Washington, I shall continue to hold it, subject to my orders only, and to expend, as heretofore, such portions of it as may be required for the support of the existing civil government. No military officer or military department will be allowed to exercise any control over it. Let me not be understood as claiming for California any authority whatever over the duties on imports *after* that power was assumed and exercised by the general government. But I do say, that when the general government declined exercising that power, and voluntarily and knowingly permitted the proceeds of such duties to be devoted to the support of the existing civil government, it would be both unjust and ungenerous for military officers to attempt to embarrass the civil authorities by taking from them their only means of carrying on that government.

I have but a few words to add respecting that part of your letter which refers to the relations of the civil government with Indian affairs and the public lands.

General Kearny, some two years and a half ago, in virtue of his authority as governor of California, appointed two sub-Indian agents, and immediately communicated these appointments to Washington. The general government was also informed that these agents were paid from the "civil fund," and would be retained in office until the arrival of agents appointed by the proper authority at Washington.

No military officer has any control over these agents of the civil government, nor can they interfere in any way with the duties of the military officers. I have never claimed to exercise any authority as civil governor over lands properly belonging to the public domain; it, however, is a question still undecided, whether the missions of California belong to the general government, to the government of California, or to the church. The direction and preservation of this property have for many years been vested in the governor of California, and this system will be continued till the general government shall see fit to assume control over it. The rents of these missions are paid into the "civil fund," and expended as directed by the laws of California; but the leases are so conditioned as to cease whenever the agents of the United States shall be authorized to take possession of this property in the name of the general government. The authorities at Washington have been informed of this course; and as no dissent has ever been expressed, it is presumed it meets their approbation.

I beg leave to remark, in conclusion, that while I shall always be most happy to receive the advice and suggestions of the commanding general of the division respecting my duties as civil governor of California, I must nevertheless be permitted to decide upon the measures of my own government; for as no military officer can be held accountable for my civil acts, so no such officer can exercise any control whatever over those acts.

Very respectfully, your obedient servant,
B. RILEY,
Brevet Brig. Gen. U. S. Army, and Governor of California.

Brevet Lieutenant Colonel J. HOOKER,
Com'g Department, Ass't Adj. General Pacific Division.

EXECUTIVE DEPARTMENT OF CALIFORNIA,
Monterey, October 1, 1849.

GENERAL: Enclosed herewith are copies of all civil papers issued since the date of my last civil despatch.

The convention called by my proclamation of June 3 assembled at this place on the 1st ultimo, and has nearly completed its labors in forming a constitution to be submitted to the people for their ratification. It has been determined by the unanimous vote of this convention (at least I am so informed) that the new government organized under this constitution, should it be ratified by the people, shall go into operation as soon as may be convenient after such ratification, and without waiting for the approval of Congress and the admission of California into the Union. I have strong doubts of the legality of such a course, under the decision of the Supreme Court of the United States; but if it should be the wish of the people of California to put the new government into operation without awaiting the action of Congress, I shall deem it my duty, under the circumstances, to surrender my civil powers into the hands of the new executive, unless special orders to the contrary are received from Washington.

In my civil despatch of August 30 I explained the character of the "civil funds" now in my hands, and the use which would be made of them in defraying the expenses of the existing government; and I now ask for instructions as to the disposition to be made of such portions of these funds as may be left when this government shall be superseded by that organized by the constitution now forming by this convention. Many have expressed the opinion that these funds should be turned over to the new government to enable it to go immediately into successful operation. However strongly of the opinion that this money belongs, in justice, to the people of California, I nevertheless shall not deem myself authorized to turn over this money till instructed to do so by direct orders from Washington. I hope that the views of the government touching this matter may be sent to me without delay.

I send herewith a copy of a report of Brevet Captain Wescott respecting the missions of San José and Santa Clara. The temporary arrangement made for the care and management of this property, will be seen in the copies of civil papers transmitted with this despatch.

Very respectfully, your obedient servant,
B. RILEY,
Brevet Brig. Gen. U. S. Army, commanding Department,
and Acting Governor of California.

Major General R. JONES,
Adjutant General U. S. Army, Washington, D. C.

[18]

STATE DEPARTMENT OF CALIFORNIA,
Monterey, August 30, 1849.

MAJOR: In compliance with the directions of Governor Riley, I enclose herewith, for your information, a copy of his letter of this date to Brevet Lieutenant Colonel Hooker respecting the " civil fund " of California.

Very respectfully, your obedient servant,

H. W. HALLECK,
Brevet Captain, and Secretary of State.

Major R. ALLEN,
Civil Treasurer, Benicia, California.

STATE DEPARTMENT OF CALIFORNIA,
Monterey, August 30, 1849.

SIR: I am directed by the governor to acknowledge the receipt of your letter of the 27th instant, and to inform you, in reply, that the resolutions of the ayuntamiento which you communicated are fully approved. This approval, however, will not be construed as yielding to the town any rights or titles which the government of California or the United States may possess to lands within the limits of the proposed survey.

The governor would respectfully call the attention of the ayuntamiento to the law requiring that the communications of the subordinate authorities of the district pass through the hands of the prefect.

Very respectfully, your obedient servant,

H. W. HALLECK,
Brevet Captain, and Secretary of State.

Don IGNACIO ESQUER,
Alcalde, &c., Monterey, California.

Know all men by these presents, that I, Bennet Riley, brevet brigadier general United States army, and governor of California, by virtue of authority in me vested, do hereby appoint and commission Pacificus Ord judge or minister of the superior tribunal of California, to date from the first day of August, 1849.

Given under my hand and seal at Monterey, California, this thirtieth day of August, in the year of our Lord eighteen hundred and forty-nine.

B. RILEY,
Brevet Brigadier General U. S. A., Governor of California.

Know all men by these presents, that I, Bennet Riley, brevet brigadier general United States army, and governor of California, by virtue of authority in me vested, do hereby appoint and commission Ignacio Esquer judge of first instance of the district of Monterey, to date from the first day of August, 1849.

Given under my hand and seal at Monterey, California, this thirtieth day of August, in the year of our Lord eighteen hundred and forty-nine.

B. RILEY,
Brevet Brigadier General U. S. A., Governor of California.

Know all men by these presents, that I, Bennet Riley, brevet brigadier general United States army, and governor of California, by virtue of authority in me vested, do hereby appoint and constitute Henry M. Naglee captain in the first California Guards.

Given under my hand and seal at Monterey, California, this 8th day of September, in the year of our Lord eighteen hundred and forty-nine.

B. RILEY,
Brevet Brigadier General U. S. A., and Governor of California.

Know all men by these presents, that I, Bennet Riley, brevet brigadier general United States army, and governor of California, by virtue of authority in me vested, do hereby appoint and constitute William O. H. Howard first lieutenant in the first California Guards.

Given under my hand and seal at Monterey, California, this 8th day of September, in the year of our Lord eighteen hundred and forty-nine.

B. RILEY,
Brevet Brigadier General U. S. A., and Governor of California.

Know all men by these presents, that I, Bennet Riley, brevet brigadier general United States army, and governor of California, by virtue of authority in me vested, do hereby appoint and constitute Myrin Norton first lieutenant in the first California Guards.

Given under my hand and seal at Monterey, California, this 8th day of September, in the year of our Lord eighteen hundred and forty-nine.

B. RILEY,
Brevet Brigadier General U. S. A., and Governor of California.

Know all men by these presents, that I, Bennet Riley, brevet brigadier general United States army, and governor of California, by virtue of authority in me vested, do hereby appoint and constitute Hall McAllister second lieutenant in the first California Guards.

Given under my hand and seal at Monterey, California, this 8th day of September, in the year of our Lord eighteen hundred and forty-nine.

B. RILEY,
Brevet Brigadier General U. S. A., and Governor of California.

Know all men by these presents, that I, Bennet Riley, brevet brigadier general United States army, and governor of California, by virtue of authority in me vested, do hereby appoint and commission Lewis Dent judge or minister of the superior tribunal of California, to date from the first day of August, 1849.

Given under my hand and seal at Monterey, California, this third day of September, in the year of our Lord eighteen hundred and forty-nine.

B. RILEY,
Brevet Brigadier General U. S. A., and Governor of California.

Know all men by these presents, that I, Bennet Riley, brevet brigadier general United States army, and governor of California, by authority in me vested, do hereby appoint and commission W. E. Shannon judge of first instance, in and for the district of Sacramento, to date from the first day of August, 1849.

Given under my hand and seal at Monterey, California, this third day of September, in the year of our Lord eighteen hundred and forty-nine.

B. RILEY,
Brevet Brigadier General U. S. A., and Governor of California.

STATE DEPARTMENT OF CALIFORNIA,
Monterey, September 3, 1849.

SIR: I have the honor to transmit, herewith, by the direction of the governor, all the returns, &c., which have been received up to this date, of the election of delegates in the several districts, for the general convention. These papers are numbered from 1 to 51, inclusive: as they are originals, and contain the votes for district and town officers, as well as for delegates to the convention, it is hoped that they will be preserved with care, and returned to this office as soon as your honorable body shall have completed its organization.

It appears from these returns that the following regular delegates are elected from the several districts, viz:

From San Diego.—Miguel Pedrorena, and Henry Hill.

From Los Angeles.—S. C. Foster, J. A. Carrillo, M. Dominguez, and A. Stearnes.

From Santa Barbara.—De Laguerra, and J. M. Covarubias.

From San Luis Obispo.—H. A. Tefft, and J. M. Covarubias.

From Monterey.—H. W. Halleck, T. O. Larkin, C. T. Botts, P. Ord, and L. Dent.

From San José.—J. Aram, K. H. Dimmick, J. D. Hoppé, and E. Brown.

From San Francisco.—E. Gilbert, M. Norton, W. M. Gwinn, J. Hobson, and W. M. Stewart.

From Sonoma.—J. Walker, R. Semple, L. W. Boggs, and M. G. Vallejo.

From Sacramento.—J. R. Snyder, W. E. Shannon, W. S. Sherwood, and J. A. Sutter.

From San Joaquin.—It appears, from the returns from this district, that in the town of Stockton the election (for reasons stated in the report of the judges and inspectors of election) was held on the 16th instead of the 1st of August. Counting all the votes polled in the district, including the town of Stockton, it appears that the four delegates elected are, J. M. Hollingsworth, S. Haley, B. S. Lippincott, and C. L. Peck; but if only the votes polled on the 1st of August are to be counted, i. e. if the vote of Stockton is excluded, the four delegates elected are, J. M. Hollingsworth, T. L. Vermule, M. Fallon, and B. F. Moore.

This question is left for the decision of your honorable body, which is deemed the proper judge of the elections, returns, and qualifications of its own members.

As the relative population of the several districts have materially changed since the issuing of the proclamation of June 3, calling for the election of delegates to this convention, the governor would respectfully recommend that additional delegates be received from some of the larger and more populous districts. It should, however, be recommended, that at the time of holding the election, (on the 1st August last,) many of the legal voters were absent from the middle and southern portions of the country, so that the number of votes actually polled will not serve as a perfect criterion by which to judge of the true relative population of the different districts. It is hoped that, by mutual concessions, all these questions may be amicably arranged, and that a spirit of harmony and good will may prevail in your councils. You have an important work before you—the laying of the corner-stone of the State structure; and the stability of the edifice will depend upon the character of the foundation which you may establish. Your materials are good: let it never be said that the builders lacked skill in putting them together.

By order of the governor:

H. W. HALLECK,
Brevet Captain, and Secretary of State.

Hon. K. H. DIMMICK,
Chairman of the Convention.

STATE DEPARTMENT OF CALIFORNIA,
Monterey, September 4, 1849.

SIR: I have the honor to acknowledge the receipt of your communication of the 1st instant, and to inform you that the military storekeeper has been directed to furnish you with the arms and ammunition asked for.

Very respectfully, your obedient servant,

H. W. HALLECK,
Brevet Captain, and Secretary of State.

Don IGNACIO ESQUER,
Alcalde, &c., Monterey, California.

STATE DEPARTMENT OF CALIFORNIA,
Monterey, September 5, 1849.

SIR: I am directed by the governor to acknowledge the receipt of your letter of August 28. The governor is not certain that he has any power to make, or authorize the making of, new political *districts* in California, but the people in any town or district are deemed to be authorized by law to form a municipal organization whenever their population is such as to require it.

The prefect of the district is the proper authority to determine upon the election of municipal officers of the several towns of this district, subject to an appeal to the governor; but where no such appeal has been made, and no question raised, no action of the governor is required.

Very respectfully, your obedient servant,

H. W. HALLECK,
Brevet Captain, and Secretary of State.

GILBERT A. GRANT, Esq.,
Vernin, Sacramento District, California.

EXECUTIVE DEPARTMENT OF CALIFORNIA,
Monterey, September 5, 1849.

COLONEL: Instructions have this day been sent to Major R. Allen, treasurer of the "civil fund," to loan to Major H. Leonard, for the use of the pay department, the sum of $30,000. This transfer will be made from the civil fund now in the hands of Major Allen, as it cannot be spared from the civil fund south of San Francisco, without embarrassing the payments of the expenses of the civil government in the middle and southern districts.

The substance of your letter of August 29 has already been replied to in my communication of the 30th ultimo.

Very respectfully, your obedient servant,
H. W. HALLECK,
Brevet Captain, and Secretary of State.

Lieut. Col. J. HOOKER,
Assist. Adjutant General, San Francisco, California.

Know all men by these presents, that I, Bennet Riley, brevet brigadier general United States army, and governor of California, by virtue of authority in me vested, do hereby appoint and commission Joaquin Carrillo prefect of the district of Santa Barbara, to date from the first of August, 1849.

Given under my hand and seal at Monterey, California, this 6th day of September, in the year of our Lord eighteen hundred and forty-nine.
B. RILEY,
Brevet Brigadier General United States Army,
and Governor of California.

Official:
H. W. HALLECK,
Brevet Captain, and Secretary of State.

Know all men by these presents, that I, Bennet Riley, brevet brigadier general United States army, and governor of California, by virtue of authority in me vested, do hereby appoint and commission Manuel Abrita judge of the first instance in and for the district of San Luis Obispo, to date from the 1st day of August, 1849.

Given under my hand and seal at Monterey, California, this 6th day of September, in the year of our Lord eighteen hundred and forty-nine.
B. RILEY,
Brevet Brigadier General United States Army,
and Governor of California.

Official:
H. W. HALLECK,
Brevet Captain, and Secretary of State.

Know all men by these presents, that I, Bennet Riley, brevet brigadier general United States army, and governor of California, by virtue of authority in me vested, do hereby appoint and commission Raymundo Carrillo judge of the first instance in and for the district of Santa Barbara, to date from the first day of August, 1849.

Given under my hand and seal at Monterey, California, this 6th day of September, in the year of our Lord eighteen hundred and forty-nine.
B. RILEY,
Brevet Brigadier General United States Army,
and Governor of California.

Official: H. W. HALLECK,
Brevet Captain, and Secretary of State.

STATE DEPARTMENT OF CALIFORNIA,
Monterey, September 6, 1849.

SIR: I am directed by the governor to acknowledge the receipt of your communication of the 28th ultimo, and to inform you that any letters which he may receive addressed to you will be forwarded at your request.

Very respectfully, your obedient servant,
H. W. HALLECK,
Brevet Captain, and Secretary of State.

S. HERMAN,
San Francisco, California.

STATE DEPARTMENT OF CALIFORNIA,
Monterey, September 6, 1849.

SIR: I am directed by the governor to acknowledge the receipt of your communication of the 31st ultimo, conveying the information of your intention to leave California on the 1st of October next, in accordance with the instructions of your government.

The governor begs leave to assure you of his most distinguished consideration.

Very respectfully, your obedient servant,
H. W. HALLECK,
Brevet Captain, and Secretary of State.

DON CARLOS VAREAS, &c., &c.,
San Francisco, California.

STATE DEPARTMENT OF CALIFORNIA,
Monterey, September 6, 1849.

SIR: The governor directs me to acknowledge the receipt of your communication of the 31st ultimo, conveying the official information that the consulate, in your absence, is to be left in charge of Don Guilliman Gobinet; and to assure you of his distinguished consideration.

Very respectfully, your obedient servant,
H. W. HALLECK,
Brevet Captain, and Secretary of State.

DON CARLOS VAREAS, &c., &c.,
San Francisco, California.

STATE DEPARTMENT OF CALIFORNIA,
Monterey, September 4, 1849.

SIR: I am directed by the governor to acknowledge the receipt of your petition in relation to the conduct of the alcalde of the "Sonorenian camp."

Now that the "supreme tribunal" of California is fully organized, the executive does not conceive it to be his duty to interfere in a case like this. The case can either be carried up before that court, or you can arraign the alcalde before that tribunal for mal-administration of justice.

Very respectfully, your obedient servant,
H. W. HALLECK,
Brevet Captain, and Secretary of State.
JUAN JOSE NEEDA, *Present.*

STATE DEPARTMENT OF CALIFORNIA,
Monterey, September 5, 1849.

MAJOR: The governor authorizes you to loan, from the "civil fund" now in your hands, to Major H. Leonard, for the use of the pay department, the sum of thirty thousand dollars, taking from him the proper drafts on the Paymaster General for the refunding of the same.

Very respectfully, your obedient servant,
H. W. HALLECK,
Brevet Captain, and Secretary of State.
Major R. ALLEN,
Civil Treasurer, Benicia, California.

STATE DEPARTMENT OF CALIFORNIA,
Monterey, September 5, 1849.

This is to certify that Francisco Mila this day filed in this office his written declaration of intention to become a citizen of the United States, and to renounce forever all allegiance to all and any prince, potentate, state, and sovereignty.

H. W. HALLECK,
Brevet Captain, and Secretary of State.

STATE DEPARTMENT OF CALIFORNIA,
Monterey, September 5, 1849.

This is to certify that Manuel Mallen this day filed in this office his written declaration of intention to become a citizen of the United States, and to renounce forever all allegiance to all and any prince, potentate, state, or sovereignty.

H. W. HALLECK,
Brevet Captain, and Secretary of State.

STATE DEPARTMENT OF CALIFORNIA,
Monterey, August 30, 1849.

SIR: I am directed by the governor to acknowledge the receipt of your letter, (without date,) and the enclosed papers.

The governor will excuse you from performing the duties of regidor in time for you to make your arrangements for leaving the country; but for the present, it will be necessary for you to perform the duties of that office as required by the laws of California.

Very respectfully, your obedient servant,
H. W. HALLECK,
Brevet Captain, and Secretary of State.

MILTON LITTLE, Esq.,
Monterey, California.

Know all men by these presents, that I, Bennet Riley, brevet brigadier general United States army, and governor of California, by virtue of authority in me vested, do hereby appoint and commission J. M. Covarubias judge or minister of the supreme tribunal of California, to date from the 1st day of August, 1849.

Given under my hand and seal, at Monterey, California, this 3d day of September, 1849.

B. RILEY,
Brevet Brig. Gen. U. S. Army, and Governor of California.

Know all men by these presents, that I, Bennet Riley, brevet brigadier general United States army, and governor of California, by virtue of authority in me vested, do hereby appoint and commission G. D. Dickerson prefect of the district of San Joaquin, to date from the 1st of August, 1849.

Given under my hand and seal, at Monterey, California, this 30th day of August, in the year of our Lord eighteen hundred and forty-nine.

B. RILEY,
Brevet Brig. Gen. U. S. Army, and Governor of California.

Know all men by these presents, that I, Bennet Riley, brevet brigadier general United States army, and governor of California, by virtue of authority in me vested, do hereby appoint and commission George G. Belt judge of first instance of the district of San Joaquin, to date from the 1st of August, 1849.

Given under my hand and seal, at Monterey, California, this 30th day of August, in the year of our Lord eighteen hundred and forty-nine.

B. RILEY,
Brevet Brig. Gen. U. S. Army, and Governor of California.

Know all men by these presents, that I, Bennet Riley, brevet brigadier general United States army, and governor of California, by virtue of authority in me vested, do hereby appoint and constitute D. L. Bayly second lieutenant in the first California Guards.

Given under my hand and seal at Monterey, California, this 8th day of September, in the year of our Lord 1849.

B. RILEY,
Brevet Brig. Gen. U. S Army, and Governor of California.

Know all men by these presents, that I, Bennet Riley, brevet brigadier general United States army, and governor of California, by virtue of authority in me vested, do hereby appoint and constitute S. R. Gerry surgeon in the first California Guards.

Given under my hand and seal at Monterey, California, this 8th day of September, in the year of our Lord 1849.

B. RILEY,
Brevet Brigadier General United States Army.

EXECUTIVE DEPARTMENT OF CALIFORNIA,
Monterey, September 11, 1849.

GENTLEMEN: I have the honor to acknowledge the receipt of your communication of yesterday, respecting the mode of providing for the payment of the expenses of the convention now in session.

I consider myself authorized by the Executive of the United States to use the "civil funds" now in my hands for defraying the necessary expenses of the civil officers of the existing government.

The necessary expenses of the convention will be paid by me from this fund, as far as I may have the means at my disposal; but, as these means may be limited, and as I am held responsible to the government of the United States for the expenditure of the money, I cannot say beforehand whether I shall feel authorized to pay all, or, if not all, what proportion of the expenses incurred by the convention.

Very respectfully, your obedient servant,
B. RILEY,
Brevet Brig. Gen. U. S. Army, and Governor of California.

Messrs. C. T. BOTTS, E. O. CROSBY, T. O. LARKIN, ELAM BROWN, R. M. PRICE, *Committee.*

STATE DEPARTMENT OF CALIFORNIA,
Monterey, September 11, 1849.

CAPTAIN: I enclose herewith your commission as captain of the first California Guards. The commissions of the other officers of this corps have been sent to their address. The captain of the corps is authorized by the governor to sign the warrants of the non-commissioned officers.

So much of your communication as relates to the issue of clothing, arms, &c., will be replied to by the assistant adjutant general of the department.
Very respectfully, your obedient servant,
H. W. HALLECK,
Brevet Captain, and Secretary of State.
Captain H. M. NAGLEE,
San Francisco, California.

EXECUTIVE DEPARTMENT OF CALIFORNIA,
Monterey, September 13, 1849.

SIR: I have the honor to acknowledge the receipt of your note, (without date,) with a copy of a resolution of the committee, asking if I can place at the disposition of the convention, on or before the first day of October next, the sum of $70,000. I have no authority to place any of the public money now under my control at the disposition of any other person; but, as stated in my letter of the 11th instant, I shall consider it my duty to pay, so far as my means will allow, all the necessary expenses of the convention. I cannot, however, now say positively whether I shall have money enough at my disposal for the accomplishment of this object. In order that your committee may judge of this contingency for yourselves, I enclose a copy of my letter of August 30 to Lieutenant Colonel Hooker.
Very respectfully, your obedient servant,
B. RILEY,
Brevet Brig. Gen. U. S. A., and Governor of California.
Hon. C. T. BOTTS, *Chairman, &c.*

To all whom it may concern:

Whereas proof has been laid before me that the Reverend Padre Real, who was placed in charge of the missions of Santa Clara and San José by a decree of Brigadier General Kearny, governor of California, dated March 22, 1847, has shamefully neglected his duty as the agent of the government charged with taking care of said missions and mission property, and preserving them from waste; and has manifestly exceeded his powers and authority as agent in selling and leasing said mission and mission property:

Now, therefore, I, Bennet Riley, brevet brigadier general United States army, and governor of California, by virtue of authority in me vested, do hereby remove the said Father Real from the agency of the aforesaid missions, and do declare all leases, sales, or conveyances made by said priest of mission lands and mission property since the 7th day of July, 1847, to be null and void.

The Reverend Father Estanislas Lelret will, until further orders, be recognised as the successor of Father Real in the aforesaid agency, and will conform himself to the instructions which will be given to him respecting the management and care of said lands, tenements, and other property.

Given at Monterey, California, this 17th day of September, in the year of our Lord 1849.

B. RILEY,
Brev t Brigadier General United States Army,
and Governor of California.

Know all men by these presents, that I, Bennet Riley, brevet brigadier general United States army, and governor of California, by virtue of authority in me vested, do hereby appoint and commission Stephen C. Foster prefect of the district of Los Angeles, to date from the 1st day of September, 1849.

Given under my hand and seal at Monterey, California, this 18th day of September, 1849.

B. RILEY,
Brevet Brigadier General United States Army,
and Governor of California.

Know all men by these presents, that I, Bennet Riley, brevet brigadier general United States army, and governor of California, by virtue of authority in me vested, do hereby appoint and commission Augustin Olivera judge of first instance in and for the district of Los Angeles, to date from the first day of September, 1849.

Given under my hand and seal, at Monterey, California, this 18th day of September, in the year of our Lord 1849.

B. RILEY,
Brevet Brigadier General United States Army,
and Governor of California.

Know all men by these presents, that I, Bennet Riley, brevet brigadier general United States army, and governor of California, by virtue of authority in me vested, do hereby appoint and commission ———— judge of first instance in and for the district of San Diego, to date from the 1st day of September, 1849.

Given under my hand and seal at Monterey, California, this 18th day of September, in the year of our Lord 1849.

B. RILEY,
Brevet Brigadier General United States Army,
and Governor of California.

EXECUTIVE DEPARTMENT OF CALIFORNIA,
Monterey, September 19, 1849.

GENTLEMEN: I have the honor to acknowledge the receipt of yours of the 17th, asking for information respecting the mode of making out the accounts of the affairs of the convention. Such accounts should in all cases be certified by the president of the convention *as just and true, and authorized by the convention;* then, on receiving my written approval, they will be paid by the civil treasurer, or his agents. Captain Kane will furnish you with blank form of accounts.

Very respectfully, your obedient servant,

B. RILEY,
Brevet Brigadier General United States Army,
and Governor of California.

Messrs. E. O. CROSBY, J. P. WALKER, E. BROWN, T. O. LARKIN, J. ARAM, *Committee, &c.*

STATE DEPARTMENT OF CALIFORNIA,
Monterey, September 20, 1849.

GENTLEMEN: The governor has examined the project, submitted to him, of an ordinance of the council of San Francisco imposing taxes, &c., for the support of the government of that town, and directs me to return it to you with the following remarks:

The provisions of articles 1, 2, 3, 4, 5, 6, 7, 8, as amended in manuscript, are believed to be in strict accordance with the laws and customs of the country.

The governor cannot, at present, give any definite information respecting the power of ayuntamientos to tax real estate. It is said that the law authorizing this in Mexico was suspended in its operation in California. The archives will be examined for further information on this subject.

The governor is of opinion that the prefect has no power to *veto* ordinances passed by town councils. It is made his duty to exercise, in the administration and expenditure of municipal funds, such supervision as may be granted to him by the ordinances of ayuntamientos; and in case they exceed their authority, he must report the fact to the governor.

Very respectfully, your obedient servant,

H. W. HALLECK,
Brevet Captain, and Secretary of State.

Captain SIMMONS, Mr. HARRISON, and others.

STATE DEPARTMENT OF CALIFORNIA,
Monterey, September 22, 1849.

SIR: I am directed by the governor to enclose you herewith, as a reply to your letter of August 31, a copy of his decree of the 17th instant, relative to the missions of San José and Santa Clara.

Very respectfully, your obedient servant,

H. W. HALLECK,
Brevet Captain, and Secretary of State.

J. B. STEINBERGER, Esq.,
San Francisco, California.

[18]

STATE DEPARTMENT OF CALIFORNIA,
Monterey, September 22, 1849.

SIR: I am directed by the governor to enclose you herewith a copy of the harbor-master's letter of August 24, and to offer you the superintendence of the improvements proposed in that letter. The immediate establishment of these buoys is deemed absolutely necessary for the safety of the shipping in the bay of San Francisco; and as Congress has made no provision for these improvements, the governor has determined to provide for the expenses out of the "civil fund," now in his hands. These expenditures must be limited to the sum of ten thousand dollars, exclusive of *your own* pay as superintendent, which will be two hundred and fifty dollars per month. These improvements should be made with the least possible delay.

Very respectfully, your obedient servant,
H. W. HALLECK,
Brevet Captain, and Secretary of State.

Captain C. RINGGOLD,
San Francisco, California.

Know all men by these presents, that, on the recommendation of the supreme court of California, I, Bennet Riley, brevet brigadier general United States army, and governor of California, by virtue of authority in me vested, do hereby appoint and commission Wm. B. Almond a judge of first instance, with civil jurisdiction only, in and for the district of San Francisco, to date from the 1st day of October, 1849.

Given under my hand and seal at Monterey, California, this 21st day of September, in the year of our Lord eighteen hundred and forty-nine.

B. RILEY,
Brevet Brig. Gen. U. S. A., and Governor of California.

Know all men by these presents, that, on the recommendation of the supreme court of California, I, Bennet Riley, brevet brigadier general United States army, and governor of California, by virtue of authority in me vested, do hereby appoint and commission James S. Thomas a judge of first instance, with civil jurisdiction only, in and for the district of Sacramento, to date from the first day of October, 1849.

Given under my hand and seal at Monterey, California, this 21st day of September, in the year of our Lord eighteen hundred and forty-nine.

B. RILEY,
Brevet Brig. Gen. U. S. A., and Governor of California.

STATE DEPARTMENT OF CALIFORNIA,
Monterey, September 24, 1849.

SIR: On the recommendation of the superior court of California, the governor has appointed Wm. B. Almond a judge of first instance, for the

district of San Francisco, with civil jurisdiction only. His commission takes effect the 1st day of October next; after which time your jurisdiction will, in conformity to the laws, be confined to criminal matters only.
Very respectfully, your obedient servant,
H. W. HALLECK,
Brevet Captain, and Secretary of State.

Hon. J. W. GEARY,
Judge of First Instance, San Francisco, California.

STATE DEPARTMENT OF CALIFORNIA,
Monterey, September 25, 1849.

SIR: I am directed by the governor to forward, for your official action, the enclosed papers for juzgado of Los Angeles.
Very respectfully, your obedient servant,
H. W. HALLECK,
Brevet Captain, and Secretary of State.

Hon. LEWIS DENT,
Judge of the Superior Court, Monterey, California.

STATE DEPARTMENT OF CALIFORNIA,
Monterey, September 25, 1849.

SIR: You are appointed by the governor to examine the books and accounts of the collector of this port from the time he entered upon the duties of his office to the 30th September, and to audit the same, or report to this office any irregularities you may find in the same, or any neglect of duty on the part of the collector or his employés. You are empowered to send for persons and papers, and to administer oaths.
Very respectfully, your obedient servant,
W. H. HALLECK,
Brevet Captain, and Secretary of State.

H. S. BURTON,
Monterey, California.

Know all men by these presents, that I, Bennet Riley, brevet brigadier general United States army, and governor of California, by virtue of authority in me vested, do hereby appoint and commission Hall McAllister attorney for the district of San Francisco, with a salary of two thousand dollars per annum. This commission will take effect the 1st day of October next.

Given under my hand and seal, at Monterey, California, this 25th day of September, in the year of our Lord eighteen hundred and forty-nine.
B. RILEY,
Brevet Brig. Gen. U. S. A., and Governor of California.

Official.

STATE DEPARTMENT OF CALIFORNIA,
Monterey, September 25, 1849.

SIR: On the recommendation of the superior court of California, the governor has appointed James S. Thomas a judge of first instance for the district of Sacramento, with civil jurisdiction only. His commission takes effect on the first day of October next; after which time, your jurisdiction will, in conformity with the laws, be confined to criminal matters only.

Very respectfully, your obedient servant,
H. W. HALLECK,
Brevet Captain, and Secretary of State.

Hon. W. E. SHANNON,
Judge of First Instance, Sacramento district.

STATE DEPARTMENT OF CALIFORNIA,
Monterey, September 26, 1849.

MAJOR: You were authorized on the 5th instant to loan from the "civil fund," to the pay department, the sum of thirty thousand dollars. If that sum was not turned over to Major Leonard before he left for Oregon, the governor requests that you will furnish Captain Kane with instructions to deliver one-third of it to the paymaster at this place.

Very respectfully, your obedient servant,
H. W. HALLECK,
Brevet Captain, and Secretary of State.

Major R. ALLEN,
Civil Treasurer, San Francisco, California.

EXECUTIVE DEPARTMENT OF CALIFORNIA,
Monterey, October 31, 1849.

GENERAL: The convention which assembled at this place on the 1st of September has completed its labors, and the constitution formed by that body was submitted on the 12th instant to the people for their approval, and I have no doubt of its being ratified by the almost unanimous vote of the qualified electors of this country. A printed copy of this constitution is enclosed herewith. You will see by examining the schedule that it is contemplated to put the new government into operation on or soon after the 15th day of December next; and I shall then surrender my civil powers to whosoever may be designated under the constitution as the executive of the new State. Whatever may be the legal objections to putting into operation a *State* government previous to its being acknowledged or approved by Congress, these objections must yield to the obvious necessities of the case; for the powers of the existing government are too limited, and its organization too imperfect, to provide for the wants of a country so peculiarly situated, and of a population which is augmenting with such unprecedented rapidity.

I have deemed it my duty to pay from the "civil funds" the current expenses of the convention, and also the salaries of officers as authorized by that body. In the absence of any legislative assembly, I have regarded this convention as representing the wishes of the people of California in the matter of public expenditures. It is true that the salaries and payments authorized by the convention were high, and by some may be considered extravagant; but in deciding upon their justice, we must take into consideration the peculiar state of the country, and the high prices paid here for everything, even including the necessaries of life. It, however, will continue to be my aim, as it has been heretofore, to keep the expenditures from the "civil funds" within the limits of the strictest economy; nevertheless, the expenses of a civil government in this country are now, and will be for years to come, very large.

The whole country remains remarkably quiet, and the civil officers encounter no serious difficulties in enforcing the laws. It is therefore hoped and believed that the powers of the existing government will be found sufficiently ample to preserve the public tranquillity until it shall be replaced by a more perfect organization under the constitution.

For my views with respect to the proper disposition to be made of the mineral and agricultural lands in this country, with respect to the importance of immediately establishing a mint in California, and the use which should be made of the "civil funds" which have accrued from the customs collected here by the governor of California previous to the assumption by the general government of the control of this matter, I would respectfully refer you to my former civil despatches. The attention which I have given to these subjects since writing those despatches has only tended to confirm the opinions there expressed.

This despatch and the accompanying papers will be delivered to you by Mr. J. McHenry Hollingsworth, late lieutenant of the regiment of New York volunteers disbanded in this country. He has, in accordance with the instructions of the Secretary of War, been furnished by the quartermaster's department with transportation to the place of his enlistment. Mr. Hollingsworth has proved himself a faithful and trustworthy officer, and merits in every respect the confidence of the government.

Very respectfully, your obedient servant,
B. RILEY,
Brevet Brig. Gen. U. S. A., and Governor of California.

Major General R. JONES,
Adjutant General of the Army, Washington, D. C.

STATE DEPARTMENT OF CALIFORNIA,
Monterey, October 2, 1849.

MAJOR: I have the honor to acknowledge the receipt of your letter of the 29th ultimo, enclosing summary statement of "civil funds" for August. That letter has been submitted to General Riley, who directs me to express to you his surprise at your question, Whether or not you were to continue to loan the "civil funds" to the quartermaster's department? In all the instructions which have been given respecting this fund, it has been expressly stated that none of this money could be expended or loaned without the direct order of the governor.

Very respectfully, your obedient servant,
H. W. HALLECK,
Brevet Captain, and Secretary of State.

Major R. ALLEN,
United States Army, San Francisco, California.

STATE DEPARTMENT OF CALIFORNIA,
Monterey, October 3, 1849.

SIR: I am directed by the governor to acknowledge the receipt of your letter of the 29th ultimo, and to say, in reply, that the appointments of sheriffs and clerks will be left, as heretofore, to the courts.
Very respectfully, your obedient servant,
H. W. HALLECK,
Brevet Captain, and Secretary of State.

Wm. B. ALMOND,
Judge of First Instance, San Francisco, California.

STATE DEPARTMENT OF CALIFORNIA,
Monterey, October 3, 1849.

SIR: I am directed by the governor to acknowledge the receipt of your letter of the 27th ultimo, and to say, in reply, that the appointments of sheriffs and clerks will be left, as heretofore, to the courts.
Very respectfully, your obedient servant,
H. W. HALLECK,
Brevet Captain, and Secretary of S ate.

R. M. MAY,
Judge of First Instance, San José, California.

STATE DEPARTMENT OF CALIFORNIA,
Monterey, October 3, 1849.

SIR: I have the honor to acknowledge the receipt of your letter of September 29, and the enclosed copy of the record in the case of the people of Upper California *vs.* Joseph Daniel.

It is not believed to be required either by the laws or usages in California that the governor should approve the sentence of the courts of first instance. All appeals and references from this court should be made, not to the executive, but to the superior tribunal. The governor, therefore, directs me to return herewith the copy of the record in this case, for such action as may be deemed necessary and proper.
Very respectfully, your obedient servant,
H. W. HALLECK,
Brevet Captain, and Secretary of State.

Hon. J. W. GEARY,
Judge of First Instance, San Francisco, California.

EXECUTIVE DEPARTMENT OF CALIFORNIA,
Monterey, October 4, 1849.

The bearer, William C. Jones, esq., being on public business, all civil officers of the government of California are requested to allow him to examine the archives of the different public offices.
B. RILEY,
Brevet Brigadier General, and Governor of California.

STATE DEPARTMENT OF CALIFORNIA,
Monterey, October 4, 1849.

SIR: I have the honor to acknowledge the receipt of your letter of August 29, appealing to the governor in certain cases tried before the alcalde of Sonoma. Appeals of this kind should not be made to the governor, but to the superior tribunal, which is now completely organized and in session.

Very respectfully, your obedient servant,
H. W. HALLECK,
Brevet Captain, and Secretary of State.

Capt. J. E. BRACKETT, *Sonoma, California.*

Know all men by these presents, that I, Bennet Riley, brevet brigadier general United States army, and governor of California, by virtue of authority in me vested, do hereby appoint and commission Charles C. Moore a notary public in and for the district of San Francisco.

Given under my hand and seal, at Monterey, California, this 4th day of October, in the year of our Lord eighteen hundred and forty-nine.
B. RILEY.
Brevet Brig. Gen. U. S. A., and Governor of California.

Official:

H. W. HALLECK,
Secretary of State, and Brevet Captain.

Know all men by these presents, that I, Bennet Riley, brevet brigadier general United States army, and governor of California, by virtue of authority in me vested, do hereby appoint and commission Thomas Filden a notary public in and for the district of San Francisco.

Given under my hand and seal, at Monterey, California, this 4th day of October, in the year of our Lord eighteen hundred and forty-nine.
B. RILEY,
Brevet Brig. Gen. U. S. A., and Governor of California.

Official:

H. W. HALLECK,
Brevet Captain, and Secretary of State.

Know all men by these presents, that I, Bennet Riley, brevet brigadier general United States army, and Governor of California, by virtue of authority in me vested, do hereby appoint and commission Charles J. Brenham a notary public in and for the district of San Francisco.

Given under my hand and seal, at Monterey, California, this 4th day of October, in the year of our Lord eighteen hundred and forty-nine.
B. RILEY,
Brevet Brig. Gen. U. S. A., and Governor of California.

Official:

H. W. HALLECK,
Brevet Captain, and Secretary of State.

Know all men by these present, that I, Bennet Riley, brevet brigadier general United States army, and governor of California, by virtue of authority in me vested, do hereby appoint and commission Julius R. Rose a notary public in and for the district of San Francisco.

Given under my hand and seal, at Monterey, California, this 4th day of October, in the year of our Lord eighteen hundred and forty-nine.

B. RILEY,
Brevet Brig. Gen. U. S. A., and Governor of California.

Official :

H. W. HALLECK,
Brevet Captain, and Secretary of State.

STATE DEPARTMENT OF CALIFORNIA,
Monterey, October 4, 1849.

GENTLEMEN: I am directed by the governor to acknowledge the receipt of your letter of September 30. As the revenue laws of the United States are now extended over California, the governor does not consider himself authorized to interfere in their execution. The collector of San Francisco is the proper person to decide whether you are entitled to the drawback of $381, and the governor leaves the question for such action as he may deem proper.

Very respectfully, your obedient servant,

H. W. HALLECK,
Brevet Captain, and Secretary of State.

Messrs. E. MICKLE & Co.,
San Francisco, California.

STATE DEPARTMENT OF CALIFORNIA,
Monterey, October 4, 1849.

SIR: I am directed by the governor to acknowledge the receipt of your letters of September 11 and 17.

The governor cannot consent to pay the prefect's clerk any higher salary than that authorized by law. The question of appointing an additional judge of first instance in the district of San Francisco had been acted on by the superior tribunal previous to the receipt of your letter.

Very respectfully, your obedient servant,

H. W. HALLECK,
Brevet Captain, and Secretary of State.

Hon. H. HAWES,
Prefect of San Francisco, California.

STATE DEPARTMENT OF CALIFORNIA,
Monterey, October 4, 1849.

SIR: I am directed by the governor to acknowledge the receipt of your letter, (without date,) and to say, in reply, that, as Congress has failed to pass any laws respecting the occupation and sale of public lands in California, he has no power to secure you in any "exclusive right or privilege" to the ferry or crossing mentioned in your letter.

Very respectfully, your obedient servant,
H. W. HALLECK,
Brevet Captain, and Secretary of State.

WILLIAM KNIGHT, Esq.,
Knight's Crossing, Stanislaw river, California.

STATE DEPARTMENT OF CALIFORNIA,
Monterey, October 4, 1849.

SIR: I am directed by the governor to acknowledge the receipt of your letter of September 4, respecting the making out the boundaries of a piece of land to which you hope to have a pre-emption right. As Congress has passed no laws on this subject applicable to California, the governor is unable to give you any directions with respect to the survey and possession of the land in question. Congress will, no doubt, at its coming session, pass the necessary laws respecting pre-emption claims to public lands in this country.

Very respectfully, your obedient servant,
H. W. HALLECK,
Brevet Captain, and Secretary of State.

W. S. SWART, Esq.,
Toulumme, mouth of Wood Creek, California.

STATE DEPARTMENT OF CALIFORNIA,
Monterey, October 4, 1849.

GENTLEMEN: I am directed by the governor to acknowledge the receipt of your letter of September 20, and to say, in reply, that it is neither usual nor necessary for the executive to commission the officers of a district, except the first judge and prefect. Where vacancies occur in the local offices, they should be filled by election, and the returns of said election sent to the prefect of the district for his approval. But if the prefect should refuse to approve them, then an appeal may be made to the governor. Mr. Crosby is the prefect of Sacramento district, and Mr. Dickenson of San Joaquin district.

Very respectfully, your obedient servant,
H. W. HALLECK,
Brevet Captain, and Secretary of State.

J. B. DONALEN and FRANCIS J. RUSSELL,
Dry Diggings, California.

Know all men by these presents, that I, Bennet Riley, brevet brigadier general United States army, and governor of California, by virtue of authority in me vested, do hereby appoint and commission R. H. Linton a notary public in and for the district of San Francisco.

Given under my hand and seal, at Monterey, California, this fourth day of October, in the year of our Lord eighteen hundred and forty-nine.

B. RILEY,
Brevet Brigadier General U. S. Army,
and Governor of California.

Official:

H. W. HALLECK,
Brevet Captain, and Secretary of State.

STATE DEPARTMENT OF CALIFORNIA,
Monterey, October 6, 1849.

MAJOR: I am directed by Governor Riley to return your accounts of the "civil funds," and call your attention to a charge of $6 25 as sub-treasurer of civil fund. Such charge is unauthorized, and General Riley cannot pass your accounts in their present shape. When Major Allen received the appointment of civil treasurer, all of the civil funds were transferred to him, and the different officers who held portions of this fund allowed to charge 2½ per cent. on their actual expenditures. Such charges have been approved by the governor, and it has been recommended to the authorities at Washington that they be allowed. You are requested to make out your accounts in accordance with that rule.

Very respectfully, your obedient servant,

H. W. HALLECK,
Brevet Captain, and Secretary of State.

Major E. H. FITZGERALD,
San Francisco, California.

STATE DEPARTMENT OF CALIFORNIA,
Monterey October 8, 1849.

SIR: Your letter of the 6th instant has been received and laid before the governor, who directs me to say, in reply, that the legality of Colonel Mason's decree of February 14, 1848, and its effects upon the title to the mine mentioned by you, are proper subjects for judicial decision, and that, therefore, he cannot interfere in any way in the matter.

Very respectfully, your obedient servant,

H. W. HALLECK,
Brevet Captain, and Secretary of State.

Hon. JAMES ALEXANDER FORBES,
&c., &c., Santa Clara, California.

STATE DEPARTMENT OF CALIFORNIA,
Monterey, October 8, 1849.

MAJOR: It appears from Major Fitzgerald's accounts that Captain J. L. Folsom has retained the sum of $9,789 72 from the "civil funds," for which he has rendered no account. As no authority was given him to retain any of this fund, the amount will be charged to him on your books. It appears from the same accounts that $86,460 34 was transferred to the quartermaster's department on the 30th of June last. It should be charged accordingly.

Very respectfully, your obedient servant,

H. W. HALLECK,
Brevet Captain, and Secretary of State.

Major R. ALLEN,
Treasurer, &c., San Francisco, California.

STATE DEPARTMENT OF CALIFORNIA,
Monterey, October 10, 1849.

SIR: I am directed by the governor to acknowledge the receipt of a letter, signed by your secretary, enclosing bills from the "Placer Times" for $500 against the civil government for publishing copies of "laws of California." As no order or authority was ever given by the governor for such publication, the bills cannot be paid; and I am therefore directed to return them herewith.

Very respectfully, your obedient servant,

H. W. HALLECK,
Brevet Captain, and Secretary of State.

Hon. H. HAWES,
Prefect of San Francisco, California.

STATE DEPARTMENT OF CALIFORNIA,
Monterey, October 10, 1849.

SIR: I am directed by the governor to acknowledge the receipt of your letter, enclosing election returns for Sacramento city, all of which have been referred to Mr. Crosby, the prefect of the district, for his action.

Very respectfully, your obedient servant,

H. W. HALLECK,
Brevet Captain, and Secretary of State

Hon. J. S. THOMAS,
Sacramento city, California.

STATE DEPARTMENT OF CALIFORNIA,
Monterey, October 10, 1849.

MAJOR: You are authorized by the governor to loan from the "civil funds" to the quartermaster's department, for the use of Major McKinstry, the sum of fifteen thousand dollars, and to the topographical department,

for the use of Lieutenant Derby, the sum of three thousand dollars, taking the proper drafts for the same.
Very respectfully, your obedient servant,
H. W. HALLECK,
Brevet Captain, and Secretary of State.
Major ALLEN,
Civil Treasurer, San Francisco, California.

STATE DEPARTMENT OF CALIFORNIA,
Monterey, October 10, 1849.

SIR: I am directed by the governor to acknowledge the receipt of your affidavit of October 1, in the matter of E. A. King, harbor-master of San Francisco; and to inform you that it has been referred to the commission appointed to investigate the affairs of the custom-house at San Francisco.
Very respectfully, your obedient servant,
H. W. HALLECK,
Brevet Captain, and Secretary of State.
ELISHA ELY, Esq.,
San Francisco, California.

Know all men by these presents, that I, Bennet Riley, brevet brigadier general United States army, and governor of California, by virtue of authority in me vested, do hereby appoint and commission K. H. Dimmick a notary public and commissioner of deeds in and for the district of San José.
Given under my hand and seal, at Monterey, California, this 11th day of October, in the year of our Lord eighteen hundred and forty-nine.
B. RILEY,
Brevet Brigadier General U. S. A., and Governor of California.

Official:

H. W. HALLECK,
Brevet Captain, and Secretary of State.

PROCLAMATION.

To the people of California.

The delegates of the people, assembled in convention, have formed a constitution, which is now presented for your ratification. The time and manner of voting on this constitution, and of holding the first general election, are clearly set forth in the schedule. The whole subject is therefore left for your unbiased and deliberate consideration.
The prefect (or person exercising the functions of that office) of each district will designate the places for opening the polls, and give due no-

tice of the election, in accordance with the provisions of the constitution and schedule.

The people are now called upon to form a government for themselves, and to designate such officers as they desire to make and execute the laws. That their choice may be wisely made, and that the government so organized may secure the permanent welfare and happiness of the people of the new State, is the sincere and earnest wish of the present executive, who, if the constitution be ratified, will, with pleasure, surrender his powers to whomsoever the people may designate as his successor.

Given at Monterey, California, this 12th day of October, in the year of our Lord eighteen hundred and forty-nine.

B. RILEY,
Bvt. Brig. General U. S. Army, and Governor of California.

Official:

H. W. HALLECK,
Brevet Captain, and Secretary of State.

STATE DEPARTMENT OF CALIFORNIA,
Monterey, October 12, 1849.

MAJOR: I send you herewith a copy of the governor's proclamation of to-day, and of the constitution just formed by the convention. They will be printed together, in pamphlet form, for general circulation among the people. No effort should be spared to have them printed and circulated with the least possible delay.

I enclose you a copy of proposals for printing by the proprietors of the " Alta Californian;" but, if you can get it done with equal expedition and at less expense by any other press, you will do so. These proposals were made with the understanding that the constitution would be printed in the two languages in parallel columns; but it was afterwards determined to print them separately, viz: 8,000 copies in the English, and 2,000 in the Spanish language. You may therefore be able to expedite the printing by contracting with separate presses for the printing, that is, with one for the English and the other for the Spanish. Mr. Tefft has been employed by Captain Kane to take this to San Francisco, and to assist you in superintending the printing. As soon as the work is completed, you will deliver to him the copies intended for the districts south of San José, including that district. In distributing the printed copies of the constitution, you will be guided by the ratio of representation as fixed in the schedule; but in dividing the Spanish and English copies, a larger proportion of the latter should be sent to the northern districts, and most of the former to the south. Extra copies should be retained, on the first distribution, at San Francisco, to be sent south by the steamer, and north by other conveyances, so as to provide for the contingency of the loss of any of those first sent out. Every care should be taken to make the distribution as general as possible, previous to the time of holding the first election.

The Spanish translation will leave here on the 14th by express. You can make your contract accordingly for the printing. I will write you again by the express.

Very respectfully, your obedient servant,
H. W. HALLECK,
Brevet Captain, and Secretary of State.

Major R. ALLEN,
Civil Treasurer, San Francisco, California.

Know all men by these presents, that I, Bennet Riley, brevet brigadier general United States army, and governor of California, by virtue of authority in me vested, do hereby appoint and commission Edward M. Howison a notary public in and for the district of San Joaquin.

Given under my hand and seal, at Monterey, California, this 13th day of October, in the year of our Lord eighteen hundred and forty-nine.
B. RILEY,
Bvt. Brig. General U. S. Army, and Governor of California.

Official:

H. W. HALLECK,
Brevet Captain, and Secretary of State.

Know all men by these presents, that I, Bennet Riley, brevet brigadier general United States army, and governor of California, by virtue of authority in me vested, do hereby appoint and commission John McDougal a notary public and commissioner of deeds in and for the district of Sacramento.

Given under my hand and seal, at Monterey, California, this 13th day of October, in the year of our Lord eighteen hundred and forty-nine.
B. RILEY,
Bvt. Brig. General U. S. Army, and Governor of California.

Official:

H. W. HALLECK,
Brevet Captain, and Secretary of State.

STATE DEPARTMENT OF CALIFORNIA,
Monterey, October 14, 1849.

MAJOR: I send you by the express of to-day a translation of the proclamation and constitution, which will be printed in accordance with the directions contained in my letter of the 12th. Mr. Houston has been employed by Captain Kane to distribute the constitution in the districts of Sonoma and Sacramento, and Mr. Kennedy in the districts of San José and San Joaquin. As stated in my former letter, Mr. Tefft will bring to this place the copies intended for this and the southern districts, and will leave at San José the copies intended for that district. Every exertion should be made to get them in circulation as soon as possible.

Very respectfully, your obedient servant,
H. W. HALLECK,
Brevet Captain, and Secretary of State.

Major R. ALLEN,
Civil Treasurer, San Francisco, California.

P. S. Employ some competent person to correct the proof of the Spanish copy.

STATE DEPARTMENT OF CALIFORNIA,
Monterey, October 11, 1849.

SIR: I am directed to acknowledge the receipt of your letter of September 30, in relation to hospital dues collected at San Francisco. It is presumed that the new collector, who is daily expected, will bring instructions touching that subject; but in order to provide for the contingency of the non-arrival of such instructions, a copy of your letter will be forwarded to Washington by the next steamer, calling to it the immediate attention of the government.

Very respectfully, your obedient servant,
H. W. HALLECK,
Brevet Captain, and Secretary of State.

E. H. HARRISON, Esq.,
Collector, San Francisco, California.

STATE DEPARTMENT OF CALIFORNIA,
Monterey, October 11, 1849.

SIR: I am directed to acknowledge the receipt of your letter of September 30, on the propriety of your transferring the registers of vessels on the sheriff's bill of sale. The governor can give no direction in this matter, but is of opinion, from what information he can obtain on this subject, that such transfer would, to say the least, be of very doubtful propriety, if not entirely contrary to law.

Very respectfully, your obedient servant,
H. W. HALLECK,
Brevet Captain, and Secretary of State.

E. H. HARRISON, Esq.,
Collector, San Francisco, California.

PROCLAMATION.

To the people of California.

The delegates of the people, assembled in convention, have formed a constitution, which is now presented for your ratification. The time and manner of voting on this constitution, and of holding the first general election, are clearly set forth in the schedule. The whole subject is therefore left for your unbiased and deliberate consideration.

The prefect (or person exercising the functions of that office) of each district will designate the places for opening the polls, and give due notice of the election, in accordance with the provisions of the constitution and schedule.

The people are now called upon to form a government for themselves, and to designate such officers as they desire to make and execute the laws. That their choice may be wisely made, and that the government so organized may secure the permanent welfare and happiness of the people of the new State, is the sincere and earnest wish of the present executive, who, if the constitution be ratified, will, with pleasure, surrender his powers to whomsoever the people may designate as his successor.

Given at Monterey, California, this twelfth day of October, in the year of our Lord eighteen hundred and forty-nine.

B. RILEY,
Brevet Brig. General U. S. Army, and Governor of California.

Official: H. W. HALLECK,
Brevet Captain, and Secretary of State.

Constitution of California.

We, the people of California, grateful to Almighty God for our freedom, in order to secure its blessings, do establish this constitution:

ARTICLE 1.—*Declaration of Rights.*

SECTION 1. All men are by nature free and independent, and have certain inalienable rights, among which are those of enjoying and defending life and liberty, acquiring, possessing, and protecting property, and pursuing and obtaining safety and happiness.

SEC. 2. All political power is inherent in the people. Government is instituted for the protection, security, and benefit of the people; and they have the right to alter or reform the same, whenever the public good may require it.

SEC. 3. The right of trial by jury shall be secured to all, and remain inviolate forever; but a jury trial may be waived by the parties in all civil cases, in the manner prescribed by law.

SEC. 4. The free exercise and enjoyment of religious profession and worship, without discrimination or preference, shall forever be allowed in this State; and no person shall be rendered incompetent to be a witness on account of his opinions on matters of religious belief; but the liberty of conscience hereby secured shall not be so construed as to excuse acts of licentiousness, or justify practices inconsistent with the peace or safety of this State.

SEC. 5. The privilege of the writ of *habeas corpus* shall not be suspended, unless when, in cases of rebellion or invasion, the public safety may require its suspension.

SEC. 6. Excessive bail shall not be required, nor excessive fines imposed, nor shall cruel or unusual punishments be inflicted, nor shall witnesses be unreasonably detained.

SEC. 7. All persons shall be bailable by sufficient sureties, unless for capital offences, when the proof is evident or the presumption great.

SEC. 8. No person shall be held to answer for a capital or otherwise infamous crime, (except in cases of impeachment, and in cases of the desertion of militia when in actual service, and the land and naval forces in time of war, or which this State may keep with the consent of Congress in time of peace, and in cases of petit larceny under the regulation of the legislature,) unless on presentment or indictment of a grand jury; and in any trial, in any court whatever, the party accused shall be allowed to appear and defend in person and with counsel, as in civil actions. No person shall be subject to be twice put in jeopardy for the same offence; nor shall he be compelled, in any criminal case, to be a witness against himself, nor be deprived of life, liberty, or property, without due process of law; nor shall private property be taken for public use without just compensation.

SEC. 9. Every citizen may freely speak, write, and publish his sentiments on all subjects, being responsible for the abuse of that right; and no law shall be passed to restrain or abridge the liberty of speech or of the press. In all criminal prosecutions or indictments for libels, the truth may be given in evidence to the jury; and if it shall appear to the jury that the matter charged as libellous is true, and was published with good motives and for justifiable ends, the party shall be acquitted; and the jury shall have the right to determine the law and the fact.

SEC. 10. The people shall have the right freely to assemble together to consult for the common good, to instruct their representatives, and to petition the legislature for redress of grievances.

SEC. 11. All laws of a general nature shall have a uniform operation.

SEC. 12. The military shall be subordinate to the civil power. No standing army shall be kept up by this State in time of peace; and in time of war no appropriation for a standing army shall be for a longer time than two years.

SEC. 13. No soldier shall in time of peace be quartered in any house, without the consent of the owner; nor in time of war, except in the manner to be prescribed by law.

SEC. 14. Representation shall be apportioned according to population.

SEC. 15. No person shall be imprisoned for debt in any civil action on *mesne* or final process, unless in cases of fraud; and no person shall be imprisoned for a militia fine in time of peace.

SEC. 16. No bill of attainder, *ex post facto* law, or law impairing the obligation of contracts, shall ever be passed.

SEC. 17. Foreigners who are or who may hereafter become *bona fide* residents of the State, shall enjoy the same rights in respect to the possession, enjoyment, and inheritance of property, as native-born citizens.

SEC. 18. Neither slavery nor involuntary servitude, unless for the punishment of crimes, shall ever be tolerated in this State.

SEC. 19. The right of the people to be secure in their persons, houses, papers, and effects, against unreasonable seizures and searches, shall not be violated; and no warrant shall issue but on probable cause, supported by oath or affirmation, particularly describing the place to be searched and the persons and things to be seized.

SEC. 20. Treason against the State shall consist only in levying war against it, adhering to its enemies or giving them aid and comfort. No person shall be convicted of treason, unless on the evidence of two witnesses to the overt act, or confession in open court.

SEC. 21. The enumeration of rights shall not be construed to impair or deny others retained by the people.

ARTICLE 2.—*Right of Suffrage.*

SECTION 1. Every white male citizen of the United States, and every white male citizen of Mexico who shall have elected to become a citizen of the United States under the treaty of peace exchanged and ratified at Queretaro on the 30th day of May, 1848, of the age of twenty-one years, who shall have been a resident of the State six months next preceding the election, and the county or district in which he claims his vote thirty days, shall be entitled to vote at all elections which are now or hereafter may be authorized by law: *Provided*, That nothing herein contained shall be construed to prevent the legislature, by a two-thirds concurrent vote, from admitting to the right of suffrage Indians or the descendants of Indians, in such special cases as such a proportion of the legislative body may deem just and proper.

SEC. 2. Electors shall in all cases, except treason, felony, or breach of the peace, be privileged from arrest on the days of the election, during their attendance at such election, going to and returning therefrom.

SEC. 3. No elector shall be obliged to perform militia duty on the day of election, except in time of war or public danger.

SEC. 4. For the purpose of voting, no person shall be deemed to have gained or lost a residence by reason of his presence or absence while employed in the service of the United States; nor while engaged in the navigation of the waters of this State, or of the United States, or of the high seas; nor while a student of any seminary of learning; nor while kept at any almshouse, or other asylum, at public expense; nor while confined in any public prison.

SEC. 5. No idiot or insane person, or person convicted of any infamous crime, shall be entitled to the privileges of an elector.

SEC. 6. All elections by the people shall be by ballot.

ARTICLE 3.—*Distribution of Powers.*

The powers of the government of the State of California shall be divided into three separate departments: the legislative, the executive, and judicial; and no person charged with the exercise of powers properly belonging to one of these departments shall exercise any functions appertaining to either of the others, except in the cases hereinafter expressly directed or permitted.

ARTICLE 4.—*Legislative Department.*

SECTION 1. The legislative power of this State shall be vested in a senate and assembly, which shall be designated the Legislature of the State of California; and the enacting clause of every law shall be as follows: "The people of the State of California, represented in senate and assembly, do enact as follows."

Sec. 2. The sessions of the legislature shall be annual, and shall commence on the first Monday of January next ensuing the election of its members, unless the governor of the State shall, in the interim, convene the legislature by proclamation.

Sec. 3. The members of the assembly shall be chosen annually by the qualified electors of their respective districts, on the Tuesday next after the first Monday in November, unless otherwise ordered by the legislature; and their term of office shall be one year.

Sec. 4. Senators and members of assembly shall be duly qualified electors in the respective counties and districts which they represent.

Sec. 5. Senators shall be chosen for the term of two years, at the same time and places as members of assembly; and no person shall be a member of the senate or assembly who has not been a citizen and inhabitant of the State one year, and of the county or district for which he shall be chosen, six months next before his election.

Sec. 6. The number of senators shall not be less than one-third, nor more than one-half, of that of the members of assembly; and at the first session of the legislature after this constitution takes effect, the senators shall be divided by lot, as equally as may be, into two classes; the seats of the senators of the first class shall be vacated at the expiration of the first year, so that one-half shall be chosen annually.

Sec. 7. When the number of senators is increased, they shall be apportioned by lot, so as to keep the two classes as nearly equal in number as possible.

Sec. 8. Each house shall choose its own officers, and judge of the qualifications, elections, and returns of its own members.

Sec. 9. A majority of each house shall constitute a quorum to do business; but a smaller number may adjourn from day to day, and may compel the attendance of absent members in such manner and under such penalties as each house may provide.

Sec. 10. Each house shall determine the rules of its own proceedings, and may, with the concurrence of two-thirds of all the members elected, expel a member.

Sec. 11. Each house shall keep a journal of its own proceedings, and publish the same; and the yeas and nays of the members of either house, on any question, shall, at the desire of any three members present, be entered on the journal.

Sec. 12. Members of the legislature shall, in all cases except treason, felony, and breach of the peace, be privileged from arrest, and they shall not be subject to any civil process during the session of the legislature, nor for fifteen days next before the commencement and after the termination of each session.

Sec. 13. When vacancies occur in either house, the governor, or the person exercising the functions of the governor, shall issue writs of election to fill such vacancies.

Sec. 14. The doors of each house shall be open except on such occasions as, in the opinion of the house, may require secrecy.

Sec. 15. Neither house shall, without the consent of the other, adjourn for more than three days, nor to any other place than that in which they may be sitting.

Sec. 16. Any bill may originate in either house of the legislature; and all bills passed by one house may be amended in the other.

Sec. 17. Every bill which may have passed the legislature shall, before it becomes a law, be presented to the governor. If he approve it, he shall sign it; but if not, he shall return it, with his objections, to the house in which it originated, which shall enter the same upon the journal and proceed to reconsider it. If, after such reconsideration, it again pass both houses, by yeas and nays, by a majority of two-thirds of the members of each house present, it shall become a law, notwithstanding the governor's objections. If any bill shall not be returned within ten days after it shall have been presented to him, (Sunday excepted,) the same shall be a law, in like manner as if he had signed it, unless the legislature, by adjournment, prevent such return.

Sec. 18. The assembly shall have the sole power of impeachment; and all impeachments shall be tried by the senate. When sitting for that purpose, the senators shall be upon oath or affirmation; and no person shall be convicted without the concurrence of two-thirds of the members present.

Sec. 19. The governor, lieutenant governor, secretary of state, comptroller, treasurer, attorney general, surveyor general, justices of the supreme court, and judges of the district courts shall be liable to impeachment for any misdemeanor in office; but judgment in such cases shall extend only to removal from office, and disqualification to hold any office of honor, trust, or profit, under the State; but the party convicted or acquitted shall, nevertheless, be liable to indictment, trial, and punishment, according to law. All other civil officers shall be tried for misdemeanors in office in such manner as the legislature may provide.

Sec. 20. No senator, or member of assembly, shall, during the term for which he shall have been elected, be appointed to any civil office of profit, under this State, which shall have been created, or the emoluments of which shall have been increased, during such term, except such office as may be filled by elections by the people.

Sec. 21. No person holding any lucrative office under the United States, or any other power, shall be eligible to any civil office of profit under this State: *Provided*, That officers in the militia, to which there is attached no annual salary, or local officers and postmasters whose compensation does not exceed five hundred dollars per annum, shall not be deemed lucrative.

Sec. 22. No person who shall be convicted of the embezzlement or defalcation of the public funds of this State, shall ever be eligible to any office of honor, trust, or profit under this State; and the legislature shall, as soon as practicable, pass a law providing for the punishment of such embezzlement, or defalcation, as a felony.

Sec. 23. No money shall be drawn from the treasury but in consequence of appropriations made by law. An accurate statement of the receipts and expenditures of the public moneys shall be attached to and published with the laws at every regular session of the legislature.

Sec. 24. The members of the legislature shall receive for their services a compensation to be fixed by law, and paid out of the public treasury; but no increase of the compensation shall take effect during the term for which the members of either house have been elected.

Sec. 25. Every law enacted by the legislature shall embrace but one object, and that shall be expressed in the title; and no law shall be revised or amended by reference to its title; but, in such case, the act revised, or section amended, shall be re-enacted and published at length.

Sec. 26. No divorce shall be granted by the legislature.

Sec. 27. No lottery shall be authorized by this State, nor shall the sale of lottery tickets be allowed.

Sec. 28. The enumeration of the inhabitants of this State shall be taken, under the direction of the legislature, in the years one thousand eight hundred and fifty-two and one thousand eight hundred and fifty-five, and at the end of every ten years thereafter; and these enumerations, together with the census that may be taken under the direction of the Congress of the United States in the year one thousand eight hundred and fifty, and every subsequent ten years, shall serve as the basis of representation in both houses of the legislature.

Sec. 29. The number of senators and members of assembly shall, at the first session of the legislature holden after the enumerations herein provided for are made, be fixed by the legislature, and apportioned among the several counties and districts to be established by law according to the number of white inhabitants. The number of members of assembly shall not be less than twenty-four, nor more than thirty-six, until the number of inhabitants within this State shall amount to one hundred thousand; and after that period, at such ratio that the whole number of members of assembly shall never be less than thirty, nor more than eighty.

Sec. 30. When a congressional, senatorial, or assembly district shall be composed of two or more counties, it shall not be separated by any county belonging to another district; and no county shall be divided in forming a congressional, senatorial, or assembly district.

Sec. 31. Corporations may be formed under general laws, but shall not be created by special act, except for municipal purposes. All general laws and special acts passed pursuant to this section may be altered from time to time or repealed.

Sec. 32. Dues from corporations shall be secured by such individual liability of the corporators and other means as may be prescribed by law.

Sec. 33. The term corporations, as used in this article, shall be construed to include all associations and joint-stock companies having any of the powers or privileges of corporations not possessed by individuals or partnerships. And all corporations shall have the right to sue, and shall be subject to be sued, in all courts, in like cases as natural persons.

Sec. 34. The legislature shall have no power to pass any act granting any charter for banking purposes, but associations may be formed under general laws for the deposite of gold and silver ; but no such association shall make, issue, or put in circulation, any bill, check, ticket, certificate, promissory note, or other paper, or the paper of any bank, to circulate as money.

Sec. 35. The legislature of this State shall prohibit by law any person or persons, associations, company or corporation, from exercising the privileges of banking, or creating paper to circulate as money.

Sec. 36. Each stockholder of a corporation or joint-stock association shall be individually and personally liable for his proportion of all its debts and liabilities.

Sec. 37. It shall be the duty of the legislature to provide for the organization of cities and incorporated villages, and to restrict their power of taxation, assessment, borrowing money, contracting debts, and loaning their credit, so as to prevent abuses in assessments and in contracting debts by such municipal corporations.

SEC. 38. In all elections by the legislature, the members thereof shall vote *viva voce,* and the votes shall be entered on the journal.

ARTICLE 5.—*Executive Department.*

SECTION 1. The supreme executive power of this State shall be vested in a chief magistrate, who shall be styled the governor of the State of California.

SEC. 2. The governor shall be elected by the qualified electors at the time and places of voting for members of assembly, and shall hold his office two years from the time of his installation and until his successor shall be qualified.

SEC. 3. No person shall be eligible to the office of governor (except at the first election) who has not been a citizen of the United States and a resident of this State two years next preceding the election, and attained the age of twenty-five years at the time of said election.

SEC. 4. The returns of every election for governor shall be sealed up and transmitted to the seat of government, directed to the speaker of the assembly, who shall, during the first week of the session, open and publish them in presence of both houses of the legislature. The person having the highest number of votes shall be governor; but in case any two or more have an equal and the highest number of votes, the legislature shall, by joint vote of both houses, choose one of said persons, so having an equal and the highest number of votes, for governor.

SEC. 5. The governor shall be commander in-chief of the militia, the army, and navy of this State.

SEC. 6. He shall transact all executive business with the officers of government, civil and military, and may require information in writing from the officers of the executive department, upon any subject relating to the duties of their respective offices.

SEC. 7. He shall see that the laws are faithfully executed.

SEC. 8. When any office shall, from any cause, become vacant, and no mode is provided by the constitution and laws for filling such vacancy, the governor shall have power to fill such vacancy by granting a commission, which shall expire at the end of the next session of the legislature, or at the next election by the people.

SEC. 9. He may, on extraordinary occasions, convene the legislature by proclamation, and shall state to both houses, when assembled, the purpose for which they shall have been convened.

SEC. 10. He shall communicate, by message to the legislature, at every session, the condition of the State, and recommend such matters as he shall deem expedient.

SEC. 11. In case of a disagreement between two houses with respect to the time of adjournment, the governor shall have power to adjourn the legislature to such time as he may think proper; provided it be not beyond the time fixed for the meeting of the next legislature.

SEC 12. No person shall, while holding any office under the United States, or this State, exercise the office of governor, except as hereinafter expressly provided.

SEC. 13. The governor shall have the power to grant reprieves and pardons, after conviction, for all offences, except treason and cases of impeachment, upon such conditions, and with such restrictions and limitations, as he may think proper, subject to such regulations as may be provided by law relative to the manner of applying for pardons. Upon conviction for treason, he shall have the power to suspend the execution of the sentence, until the case shall be reported to the legislature, at its next meeting, when the legislature shall either pardon, direct the execution of the sentence, or grant a further reprieve. He shall communicate to the legislature, at the beginning of every session, every case of reprieve or pardon granted, stating the name of the convict, the crime of which he was convicted, the sentence and its date, and the date of the pardon or reprieve.

SEC. 14. There shall be a seal of this State, which shall be kept by the governor, and used by him officially, and shall be called "The great seal of the State of California."

SEC. 15. All grants and commissions shall be in the name and by the authority of the people of the State of California, sealed with the great seal of the State, signed by the governor, and countersigned by the secretary of state.

SEC. 16. A lieutenant governor shall be elected at the same time and places and in the same manner as the governor; and his term of office, and his qualifications of eligibility, shall also be the same. He shall be president of the senate, but shall only have the casting vote therein. If, during a vacancy of the office of governor, the lieutenant governor shall be impeached, displaced, resign, die, or become incapable of performing the duties of his office, or be absent from the State, the president of the senate shall act as governor, until the vacancy be filled, or the disability shall cease.

SEC. 17. In case of the impeachment of the governor, or his removal from office, death, inability to discharge the powers and duties of the said office, resignation, or absence from the State, the powers and duties of the office shall devolve upon the lieutenant governor for the residue of the term, or until the disability shall cease. But when the governor shall, with the consent of the legislature, be out of the State in time of war, at the head of any military force thereof, he shall continue commander-in-chief of all the military force of the State.

SEC. 18. A secretary of state, a comptroller, a treasurer, an attorney general, and surveyor general, shall be chosen in the manner provided in this constitution; and the term of office and eligibility of each shall be the same as are prescribed for the governor and lieutenant governor.

SEC. 19. The secretary of state shall be appointed by the governor, by and with the advice and consent of the senate. He shall keep a fair record of the official acts of the legislative and executive departments of the government; and shall, when required, lay the same, and all matters relative thereto, before either branch of the legislature; and shall perform such other duties as shall be assigned him by law.

SEC. 20. The comptroller, treasurer, attorney general, and surveyor general shall be chosen, by joint vote of the two houses of the legislature, at their first session, under this constitution; and thereafter shall be elected at the same time and places and in the same manner as the governor and lieutenant governor.

SEC. 21. The governor, lieutenant governor, secretary of state, comptroller, treasurer, attorney general, and surveyor general, shall each at stated times, during their continuance in office, receive for their services a compensation, which shall not be increased or diminished during the term for which they shall have been elected; but neither of these officers shall receive for his own use any fees for the performance of his official duties.

ARTICLE 6.—*Judicial Department.*

SECTION 1. The judicial power of this State shall be vested in a supreme court, in district courts, in county courts, and in justices of the peace. The legislature may also establish such municipal and other inferior courts as may be deemed necessary.

SEC. 2. The supreme court shall consist of a chief justice and two associate justices, any two of whom shall constitute a quorum.

SEC. 3. The justices of the supreme court shall be elected at the general election, by the qualified electors of the State, and shall hold their office for the term of six years from the first day of January next after their election; provided that the legislature shall, at its first meeting, elect a chief justice and two associate justices of the supreme court, by joint vote of both houses, and so classify them that one shall go out of office every two years. After the first election, the senior justice in commission shall be the chief justice.

SEC. 4 The supreme court shall have appellate jurisdiction in all cases when the matter in dispute exceeds two hundred dollars; when the legality of any tax, toll, or impost or municipal fine is in question; and in all criminal cases amounting to felony, or questions of law alone. And the said court, and each of the justices thereof, as well as all district and county judges, shall have power to issue writs of habeas corpus, at the instance of any person held in actual custody. They shall also have power to issue all other writs and process necessary to the exercise of their appellate jurisdiction, and shall be conservators of the peace throughout the State.

SEC. 5. The State shall be divided, by the first legislature, into a convenient number of districts, subject to such alterations, from time to time, as the public good may require; for each of which a district judge shall be appointed by the joint vote of the legislature, at its first meeting, who shall hold his office for two years from the first day of January next after his election; after which, said judges shall be elected by the qualified electors of their respective districts, at the general election, and shall hold their office for the term of six years.

SEC. 6. The district courts shall have original jurisdiction, in law and equity, in all civil cases where the amount in dispute exceeds two hundred dollars, exclusive of interest. In all criminal cases not otherwise provided for, and in all issues of fact joined in the probate courts, their jurisdiction shall be unlimited.

SEC. 7. The legislature shall provide for the election, by the people, of a clerk of the supreme court, and county clerks, district attorneys, sheriffs, coroners, and other necessary officers; and shall fix by law their duties and compensation. County clerks shall be *ex officio* clerks of the district courts in and for their respective counties.

SEC. 8. There shall be elected, in each of the organized counties of this State, one county judge, who shall hold his office for four years. He shall hold the county court, and perform the duties of surrogate, or probate judge. The county judge, with two justices of the peace, to be designated according to law, shall hold courts of sessions, with such criminal jurisdiction as the legislature shall prescribe, and he shall perform such other duties as shall be required by law.

Sec. 9. The county courts shall have such jurisdiction, in cases arising in justices' courts, and in special cases, as the legislature may prescribe, but shall have no original civil jurisdiction, except in such special cases.

Sec. 10. The times and places of holding the terms of the supreme court, and the general and special terms of the district courts within the several districts, shall be provided for by law.

Sec. 11. No judicial officer, except a justice of the peace, shall receive, to his own use, any fees or perquisites of office.

Sec. 12. The legislature shall provide for the speedy publication of all statute laws, and of such judicial decisions as it may deem expedient; and all laws and judicial decisions shall be free for publication by any person.

Sec. 13. Tribunals for conciliation may be established, with such powers and duties as may be prescribed by law; but such tribunals shall have no power to render judgment to be obligatory on the parties, except they voluntarily submit their matters in difference, and agree to abide the judgment, or assent thereto in the presence of such tribunal, in such cases as shall be prescribed by law.

Sec. 14. The legislature shall determine the number of justices of the peace to be elected in each county, city, town, and incorporated village of the State, and fix by law their powers, duties, and responsibilities. It shall also determine in what cases appeals may be made from justices' courts to the county court.

Sec. 15. The justices of the supreme court, and judges of the district court, shall, severally, at stated times during their continuance in office, receive for their services a compensation, to be paid out of the treasury, which shall not be increased or diminished during the term for which they shall have been elected. The county judges shall also severally, at stated times, receive for their services a compensation, to be paid out of the county treasury of their respective counties, which shall not be increased or diminished during the term for which they shall have been elected.

Sec. 16. The justices of the supreme court and district judges shall be ineligible to any other office during the term for which they shall have been elected.

Sec. 17. Judges shall not charge juries with respect to matters of fact, but may state the testimony and declare the law.

Sec. 18. The style of all process shall be, "The people of the State of California;" all the prosecutions shall be conducted in the name and by the authority of the same.

Article 7.—*Militia.*

Section 1. The legislature shall provide by law for organizing and disciplining the militia in such manner as they shall deem expedient, not incompatible with the constitution and laws of the United States.

Sec. 2. Officers of the militia shall be elected, or appointed, in such manner as the legislature shall, from time to time, direct; and shall be commissioned by the governor.

Sec. 3. The governor shall have power to call forth the militia to execute the laws of the State, to suppress insurrections, and repel invasions.

Article 8.—*State debts.*

The legislature shall not, in any manner, create any debt or debts, liability or liabilities, which shall singly, or in the aggregate, with any previous debts or liabilities, exceed the sum of three thousand dollars, except in case of war, to repel invasion, or suppress insurrection, unless the same shall be authorized by some law for some single object or work, to be distinctly specified therein; which law shall provide ways and means, exclusive of loans, for the payment of the interest of such debt or liability as it falls due, and also pay and discharge the principal of such debt or liability within twenty years from the time of the contracting thereof, and shall be irrepealable until the principal and interest thereon shall be paid and discharged; but no such law shall take effect until, at a general election, it shall have been submitted to the people, and have received a majority of all the votes cast for and against it at such election; and all money raised by authority of such law shall be applied only to the specific object therein stated, or to the payment of the debt thereby created; and such law shall be published in at least one newspaper in each judicial district (if one be published therein) throughout the State, for three months next preceding the election at which it is submitted to the people.

Article 9.—*Education.*

Section 1. The legislature shall provide for the election, by the people, of a superintendent of public instruction, who shall hold his office for three years, and whose duties shall be prescribed by law, and who shall receive such compensation as the legislature may direct.

Sec. 2. The legislature shall encourage, by all suitable means, the promotion of intellectual, scientific, moral, and agricultural improvement. The proceeds of all lands that may be granted by the United States to this State for the support of schools, which may be sold or disposed of, and the five hundred thousand acres of land granted to the new States, under an act of Congress distributing the proceeds of the public lands among the several States of the Union, approved in the year of our Lord eighteen hundred and forty-one, and all estates of deceased persons who may have died without leaving a will, or heir, and also such per cent. as may be granted by Congress on the sale of lands in this State, shall be, and remain, a perpetual fund, the interest of which, together with all the rents of the unsold lands, and such other means as the legislature may provide, shall be inviolably appropriated to the support of common schools throughout the State.

Sec. 3. The legislature shall provide for a system of common schools, by which a school shall be kept up and supported in each district at least three months in every year; and any school district neglecting to keep up and support such a school may be deprived of its proportion of the interest of the public fund during such neglect.

Sec. 4. The legislature shall take measures for the protection, improvement, or other disposition of such lands as have been, or may hereafter be, reserved or granted by the United States, or any person or persons, to this State, for the use of a university; and the funds accruing from the rents or sale of such lands, or from any other source, for the purpose aforesaid, shall be, and remain, a permanent fund, the interest of which shall be applied to the support of said university, with such branches as the public convenience may demand, for the promotion of literature, the arts and sciences, as may be authorized by the terms of such grant; and it shall be the duty of the legislature, as soon as may be, to provide effectual means for the improvement and permanent security of the funds of said university.

ARTICLE 10 —*Mode of amending and revising the constitution.*

SECTION 1. Any amendment or amendments to this constitution may be proposed in the senate or assembly, and if the same shall be agreed to by a majority of the members elected to each of the two houses, such proposed amendment or amendments shall be entered on their journals, with the yeas and nays taken thereon, and referred to the legislature then next to be chosen, and shall be published for three months next preceding the time of making such choice. And if, in the legislature next chosen as aforesaid, such proposed amendment or amendments shall be agreed to by a majority of all the members elected to each house, then it shall be the duty of the legislature to submit such proposed amendment or amendments to the people, in such manner and at such time as the legislature shall prescribe; but if the people shall approve and ratify such amendment or amendments, by a majority of the electors qualified to vote for members of the legislature, voting thereon, such amendment or amendments shall become part of the constitution.

SEC. 2. And if at any time two-thirds of the senate and assembly shall think it necessary to revise and change this entire constitution, they shall recommend to the electors, at the next election for members of the legislature, to vote for or against the convention; and if it shall appear that a majority of the electors voting at such election have voted in favor of calling a convention, the legislature shall at its next session provide by law for calling a convention, to be holden within six months after the passage of such law; and such convention shall consist of a number of members not less than that of both branches of the legislature.

ARTICLE 11.—*Miscellaneous provisions.*

SECTION 1. The first session of the legislature shall be held at the Pueblo de San José; which place shall be the permanent seat of government, until removed by law: *Provided, however*, That two-thirds of all the members elected to each house of the legislature shall concur in the passage of such law.

SEC. 2. Any citizen of this State who shall, after the adoption of this constitution, fight a duel with deadly weapons, or send or accept a challenge to fight a duel with deadly weapons, either within this State or out of it, or who shall act as second, or knowingly aid or assist in any manner those thus offending, shall not be allowed to hold any office of profit, or to enjoy the right of suffrage, under this constitution.

SEC. 3. Members of the legislature, and all officers, executive and judicial, except such inferior officers as may be by law exempted, shall, before they enter on the duties of their respective offices, take and subscribe the following oath or affirmation: " I do solemnly swear, (or affirm, as the case may be,) that I will support the constitution of the United States, and the constitution of the State of California; and that I will faithfully discharge the duties of the office of ——— according to the best of my ability." And no other oath, declaration, or test shall be required as a qualification for any office or public trust.

SEC. 4. The legislature shall establish a system of county and town governments, which shall be as nearly uniform as practicable throughout the State.

SEC. 5. The legislature shall have power to provide for the election of a board of supervisors in each county; and these supervisors shall, jointly and individually, perform such duties as may be prescribed by law.

SEC. 6. All officers whose election or appointment is not provided for by this constitution, and all officers whose offices may hereafter be created by law, shall be elected by the people, or appointed, as the legislature may direct.

SEC. 7. When the duration of any office is not provided for by this constitution, it may be declared by law; and if not so declared, such office shall be held during the pleasure of the authority making the appointment; nor shall the duration of any office, not fixed by this constitution, ever exceed four years.

SEC. 8. The fiscal year shall commence on the first day of July.

SEC. 9. Each county, town, city, and incorporated village shall make provision for the support of its own officers, subject to such restrictions and regulations as the legislature may prescribe.

SEC. 10. The credit of the State shall not in any manner be given or loaned to, or in aid of, any individual, association, or corporation; nor shall the State, directly or indirectly, become a stockholder in any association or corporation.

SEC. 11. Suits may be brought against the State in such manner and in such courts as shall be directed by law.

SEC. 12. No contract of marriage, if otherwise duly made, shall be invalidated for want of conformity to the requirements of any religious sect.

SEC. 13. Taxation shall be equal and uniform throughout the State. All property in this State shall be taxed in proportion to its value, to be ascertained as directed by law; but assessors and collectors of town, county, and State taxes, shall be elected by the qualified electors of the district, county, or town in which the property taxed for State, county, or town purposes is situated.

SEC. 14. All property, both real and personal, of the wife, owned or claimed by her before marriage, and that acquired afterwards by gift, devise, or descent, shall be her separate property; and laws shall be passed more clearly defining the rights of the wife in relation as well to her separate property as to that held in common with her husband. Laws shall also be passed providing for the registration of the wife's separate property.

SEC. 15. The legislature shall protect by law, from forced sale, a certain portion of the homestead and other property of all heads of families.

SEC. 16. No perpetuities shall be allowed except for eleemosynary purposes

Sec. 17. Every person shall be disqualified from holding any office of profit in this State who shall have been convicted of having given or offered a bribe to procure his election or appointment.

Sec. 18. Laws shall be made to exclude from office, serving on juries, and from the right of suffrage, those who shall hereafter be convicted of bribery, perjury, forgery, or other high crimes. The privilege of free suffrage shall be supported by laws regulating elections, and prohibiting, under adequate penalties, all undue influence thereon from power, bribery, tumult, or other improper practice.

Sec. 19. Absence from this State on business of the State, or of the United States, shall not affect the question of residence of any person.

Sec. 20. A plurality of the votes given at any election shall constitute a choice, where not otherwise directed in this constitution.

Sec. 21. All laws, decrees, regulations, and provisions, which from their nature require publication, shall be published in English and Spanish.

Article 12.—*Boundary.*

The boundary of the State of California shall be as follows:

Commencing at the point of intersection of the 42d degree of north latitude with the 120th degree of longitude west from Greenwich, and running south on the line of said 120th degree of west longitude until it intersects the 39th degree of north latitude; thence running in a straight line in a southeasterly direction to the river Colorado, at a point where it intersects the 35th degree of north latitude; thence down the middle of the channel of said river to the boundary line between the United States and Mexico, as established by the treaty of May 30, 1848; thence running west and along said boundary line to the Pacific ocean, and extending therein three English miles; thence running in a northwesterly direction, and following the direction of the Pacific coast to the 42d degree of north latitude; thence on the line of said 42d degree of north latitude to the place of beginning. Also all the islands, harbors, and bays, along and adjacent to the Pacific coast.

SCHEDULE.

Section 1. All rights, prosecutions, claims, and contracts, as well of individuals as of bodies corporate, and all laws in force at the time of the adoption of this constitution, and not inconsistent therewith, until altered or repealed by the legislature, shall continue as if the same had not been adopted.

Sec. 2. The legislature shall provide for the removal of all causes which may be pending when this constitution goes into effect, to courts created by the same.

Sec. 3. In order that no inconvenience may result to the public service from the taking effect of this constitution, no office shall be superseded thereby, nor the laws relative to the duties of the several officers be changed, until the entering into office of the new officers to be appointed under this constitution.

Sec. 4. The provisions of this constitution concerning the term of residence necessary to enable persons to hold certain offices therein mentioned, shall not be held to apply to officers chosen by the people at the first election, or by the legislature at its first session.

Sec. 5. Every citizen of California declared a legal voter by this constitution, and every citizen of the United States a resident of this State on the day of election, shall be entitled to vote at the first general election under this constitution, and on the question of the adoption thereof.

Sec. 6. This constitution shall be submitted to the people for their ratification or rejection, at the general election to be held on Tuesday, the thirteenth day of November next. The executive of the existing government of California is hereby requested to issue a proclamation to the people, directing the prefects of the several districts, or, in case of vacancy, the sub-prefects, or senior judge of first instance, to cause such election to be held, on the day aforesaid, in their respective districts. The election shall be conducted in the manner which was prescribed for the election of delegates to the convention, except that the prefect, sub-prefect, or senior judge of first instance, ordering such election in each district, shall have power to designate any additional number of places for opening the polls, and that, in every place for holding the election, a regular poll-list shall be kept by the judges and inspectors of election. It shall also be the duty of these judges and inspectors of election, on the day aforesaid, to receive the votes of the electors qualified to vote at such election. Each voter shall express his opinion, by depositing in the ballot-box a ticket, whereon shall be written or printed "for the constitution," or "against the constitution," or some such words as will distinctly convey the intention of the voter. These judges and inspectors shall also receive the votes for the several officers to be voted for at the said election, as herein provided. At the close of the election, the judges and inspectors shall carefully count each ballot, and forthwith make duplicate returns thereof to the prefect, sub-prefect, or senior judge of first instance, as the case may be, of their respective districts; and said prefect, sub-prefect, or senior judge of first instance, shall transmit one of the same, by the most safe and rapid conveyance, to the secretary of state. Upon the receipt of said returns, or on the tenth day of December next, if the returns be not sooner received, it shall be the duty of a board of canvassers, to consist of the secretary of state, one of the judges of the superior court, the prefect, judge of first instance, and an alcalde of the district of Monterey, or any three of the aforementioned officers, in the presence of all who shall choose to attend, to compare the votes given at said election, and to immediately publish an abstract of the same in one or more of the newspapers of California. And the executive will also, immediately after ascertaining that the constitution has been ratified by the people, make proclamation of the fact; and thenceforth this constitution shall be ordained and established as the constitution of California.

Sec. 7. If this constitution shall be ratified by the people of California, the executive of the existing government is hereby requested, immediately after the same shall be ascertained, in the manner herein directed, to cause a fair copy thereof to be forwarded to the President of the United States, in order that he may lay it before the Congress of the United States.

Sec. 8. At the general election aforesaid, namely, the thirteenth day of November next, there shall be elected a governor, lieutenant governor, members of the legislature, and also two members of Congress.

Sec. 9. If this constitution shall be ratified by the people of California, the legislature shall assemble at the seat of government on the fifteenth day of December next; and, in order to complete the organization of that body, the Senate shall elect a president *pro tempore,* until the lieutenant governor shall be installed into office.

Sec. 10. On the organization of the legislature, it shall be the duty of the secretary of state to lay before each house a copy of the abstract made by the board of canvassers, and, if called for, the original returns of election, in order that each house may judge of the correctness of the report of said board of canvassers.

Sec. 11. The legislature, at its first session, shall elect such officers as may be ordered by this constitution to be elected by that body, and, within four days after its organization, proceed to elect two senators to the Congress of the United States. But no law passed by this legislature shall take effect until signed by the governor after his installation into office.

Sec. 12. The senators and representatives to the Congress of the United States, elected by the legislature and people of California as herein directed, shall be furnished with certified copies of this constitution, when ratified, which they shall lay before the Congress of the United States, requesting, in the name of the people of California, the admission of the State of California into the American Union.

Sec. 13. All officers of this State, other than members of the legislature, shall be installed into office on the fifteenth day of December next, or as soon thereafter as practicable.

Sec. 14. Until the legislature shall divide the State into counties and senatorial and assembly districts, as directed by this constitution, the following shall be the apportionment of the two houses of the legislature, namely: the districts of San Diego and Los Angeles shall, jointly, elect two senators; the districts of Santa Barbara and San Luis Obispo shall, jointly, elect one senator; the district of Monterey, one senator; the district of San José, one senator; the district of San Francisco, two senators; the district of Sonoma, one senator; the district of Sacramento, four senators; and the district of San Joaquin, four senators. And the district of San Diego shall elect one member of assembly; the district of Los Angeles, two members of assembly; the district of Santa Barbara, two members of assembly; the district of San Luis Obispo, one member of assembly; the district of Monterey, two members of assembly; the district of San José, three members of assembly; the district of San Francisco, five members of assembly; the district of Sonoma, two members of assembly; the district of Sacramento, nine members of assembly; and the district of San Joaquin, nine members of assembly.

Sec. 15. Until the legislature shall otherwise direct, in accordance with the provisions of this constitution, the salary of the governor shall be ten thousand dollars per annum; and the salary of the lieutenant governor shall be double the pay of a State senator; and the pay of members of the legislature shall be sixteen dollars per diem while in attendance, and sixteen dollars for every twenty miles travel by the usual route, and in returning therefrom. And the legislature shall fix the salaries of all officers other than those elected by the people at the first election.

Sec. 16. The limitation of the powers of the legislature, contained in article 8th of this constitution, shall not extend to the first legislature elected under the same, which is hereby authorized to negotiate for such amount as may be necessary to pay the expenses of the State government.

R. SEMPLE,
President of the Convention, and delegate from Benicia.
WM. G. MARCY,
Secretary.

J. Aram.	B. S. Lippincott.
C. T. Botts.	M. M. McCarver.
E. Brown.	John McDougal.
J. A. Carrillo.	B. F. Moore.
J. M. Covarubias.	Myron Norton.
E. O. Crosby.	P. Ord.
P. De La Guerra.	Miguel Pedrorena.
L. Dent.	A. M. Pico.
M. Domirguez.	R. M. Price.
K. H. Dimmick.	Hugo Reid.
A. J. Ellis.	Jacinto Rodriguez.
S. C. Foster.	Pedro Sansevaine.
E. Gilbert.	W. E. Shannon.
W. M. Gwinn.	W. S. Sherwood.
H. W. Halleck.	J. R. Snyder.
Julian Hanks.	A. Stearns.
L. W. Hastings.	W. M. Steuart.
Henry Hill.	J. A. Sutter.
J. Hobson.	Henry A. Tefft.
J. McH. Hollingsworth.	S. L. Vermule.
J. D. Hoppe.	M. G. Vallejo.
J. M. Jones.	J. Walker.
T. O. Larkin.	O. M. Wozencraft.
Francis J. Lippett.	

STATE DEPARTMENT OF CALIFORNIA,
Monterey, October 17, 1849.

MAJOR: Captain Kane, on the 15th instant, turned over from the "civil fund" to Major H. Hill the sum of $15,500, and holds Major Hill's receipts to Major Leonard for that amount. Captain Kane will send these receipts to you, in order that you may get from Major Leonard drafts on the pay department for that amount. The civil fund should not be loaned to the military departments simply on receipts; drafts on the heads of the departments in Washington should be required in all cases.

Very respectfully, your obedient servant,
H. W. HALLECK,
Brevet Captain, and Secretary of State.

Major R. ALLEN,
Civil Treasurer, San Francisco, California.

STATE DEPARTMENT OF CALIFORNIA,
Monterey, October 17, 1849.

COLONEL: The governor has taken the advice of such delegates of the convention as were most likely to understand such subjects, as to the propriety of appointing harbor-masters in places other than ports of entry and delivery, and the opinion expressed by all is, that such is not the practice in the States. If, however, it should prove upon further inquiry that it is usual to make such appointments, and a harbor-master is required at " New York of the Pacific," it will afford him pleasure to make an appointment as you request.

Very respectfully, your obedient servant,

H. W. HALLECK,
Brevet Captain, and Secretary of State.

Colonel J. D. STEVENSON,
San Francisco, California.

Know all men by these presents, that I, Bennet Riley, brevet brigadier general United States army, and governor of California, by virtue of authority in me vested, do hereby appoint and commission Henry A. Schoolcraft a notary public in and for the district of Sacramento, California.

Given under my hand and seal at Monterey, California, this 17th day of October, in the year of our Lord eighteen hundred and forty-nine.

B. RILEY,
Brevet Brig. Gen. U. S. Army, and Governor of California.

Official:

H. W. HALLECK,
Brevet Captain, and Secretary of State.

STATE DEPARTMENT OF CALIFORNIA,
Monterey, October 19, 1849.

SIR: The governor has deemed proper to direct the prefect of Santa Barbara to excuse you from the further performance of the duties of regidor of that town.

Very respectfully, your obedient servant,

H. W. HALLECK,
Brevet Captain, and Secretary of State.

DANIEL HILL, Esq., *Santa Barbara, California.*

STATE DEPARTMENT OF CALIFORNIA,
Monterey, October 19, 1849.

SIR: The governor has decided that, for reasons given in the papers enclosed in the communication of the acting alcalde of August 29, Daniel Hill be excused from the duties of regidor of Santa Barbara.

Very respectfully, your obedient servant,

H. W. HALLECK,
Brevet Captain, and Secretary of State.

Don JOAQUIN CARRILLO,
Prefect of Santa Barbara, California.

[18]

STATE DEPARTMENT OF CALIFORNIA,
Monterey, October 19, 1849.

SIR: Your letter of August 11, enclosing a communication from George W. Vincent respecting the appointment of a branch pilot at San Francisco, was duly received. The governor was unwilling to act in this matter till he should ascertain what time it was proposed to put in operation the new government under the constitution; and now that the existing government is so very soon to be superseded, he deems it best to leave the subject of organizing branch pilots for the several ports of California to the legislature which is to assemble in December next.

Very respectfully, your obedient servant,
H. W. HALLECK,
Brevet Captain, and Secretary of State.

Captain E. A. KING,
Harbor-master, San Francisco, California.

STATE DEPARTMENT OF CALIFORNIA,
Monterey, October 19, 1849.

SIR: I am directed by the governor to acknowledge the receipt of your letter (without date) complaining of the conduct of the sub-prefect of the district. The letter has been referred to the prefect, who will take the proper measures to investigate the official conduct of said sub-prefect.

Very respectfully, your obedient servant,
H. W. HALLECK,
Brevet Captain, and Secretary of State.

PATRICK BRIEN,
San Juan Bautista, California.

STATE DEPARTMENT OF CALIFORNIA,
Monterey, October 19, 1849.

SIR: I am directed by the governor to acknowledge the receipt of your letter of the 3d instant, enclosing a petition of the citizens of Sonoma for a special election to fill certain vacancies in town offices. If any such vacancies exist the prefect should give due notice, and hold an election for filling them.

Very respectfully, your obedient servant,
H. W. HALLECK,
Brevet Captain, and Secretary of State.

Hon. C. P. WILKINS,
Prefect of Sonoma, California.

STATE DEPARTMENT OF CALIFORNIA,
Monterey, October 19, 1849.

SIR: An appointment as prefect of the district of San Diego was made out and forwarded to you some time in August last, but no copy was re-

tained in this office. The appointment was dated about the 18th of August, and had a retrospective effect to the first of that month. If you have received it, please send a copy to this office.
Very respectfully, your obedient servant,
H. W. HALLECK,
Brevet Captain, and Secretary of State.
Jose Antonio Estridillo,
Prefect of San Diego, California.

Know all men by these presents, that I, Bennet Riley, brevet brigadier general United States army, and governor of California, by virtue of authority in me vested, do hereby appoint and commission Robert A. Wilson a notary public in and for the district of San Francisco, California.

Given under my hand and seal, at Monterey, California, this 17th day of October, in the year of our Lord 1849.
B. RILEY,
Brevet Brig. Gen. U. S. A., and Governor of California.

Official: H. W. HALLECK,
Brevet Captain, and Secretary of State.

State Department of California,
Monterey, October 19, 1849.

Sir: Your letter of the 6th instant has been laid before the governor, who directs me to say, in reply, that the adobic building occupied as the custom-house never has belonged, and does not now belong, to the municipal authorities of San Francisco. It was constructed by the collector of the port of San Francisco out of the proceeds of the customs in California, and was, until the treaty of peace, the property of the general government of Mexico. It is now the property of the government of the United States, and cannot be turned over to the authorities of the town of San Francisco without orders direct from the Secretary of the Treasury, or by an act of Congress.
Very respectfully, your obedient servant,
H. W. HALLECK,
Brevet Captain, and Secretary of State.
Hon. J. W. Geary,
Judge of First Instance, San Francisco, California.

State Department of California,
Monterey, October 19, 1849.

Reverend Sir: By the governor's decree of the 17th ultimo you were appointed to succeed the Reverend Father Real in the agency of the missions of Santa Clara and San José. You will be required to keep an account of all property turned over to you by the said Father Real, and also of the receipts and expenditures arising from the property thus placed temporarily under your management and care, subject at all times to the inspection of the governor or such persons as he may appoint for that purpose.

Very respectfully, your obedient servant,
H. W. HALLECK,
Brevet Captain, and Secretary of State.

Rev. Father ESTANISLAS LEHET,
Santa Clara, California.

STATE DEPARTMENT OF CALIFORNIA,
Monterey, October 19, 1849.

SIR: I have to acknowledge the receipt of your letter of the 15th instant, with the accompanying papers, all of which have been laid before the governor. If it be true that San Juan Bautista has been regularly organized into a pueblo, there can be no legal objection to the holding of a special election at that place for forming an ayuntamiento, in accordance with the provisions of the law; but the governor can give to such ayuntamiento no power to grant or sell land which has not been given to that body by the existing laws of the country. The ayuntamiento can grant in salaries such land as has been regularly ceded to the town for municipal purposes, and no more. All other lands belong either to the government or to private individuals; and all sales or grants of such lands by the ayuntamiento will be null and void: no act either of the governor or of subordinate authorities can make them valid. All grants, sales, or rents, by the priest, of lands or other property belonging to the mission of San Juan Bautista, are utterly null and void, the priest having no legal authority to dispose of said property.

The prefect of the district has full authority to designate the buildings which were directed in the law of secularization to be reserved for the use of the priest, for municipal purposes, a school-house, &c.

By order of the governor:
H. W. HALLECK,
Brevet Captain, and Secretary of State.

Hon. DAVID SPENCE,
Prefect of Monterey, California.

Know all men by these presents, that, inasmuch as the legal tribunals recognised by the existing laws of California are now fully organized, I do therefore revoke my order of July 1, 1849, staying all further proceedings with respect to a change in the administration of the estate of Mr. Leidsdorff, deceased, leaving the whole matter to be disposed of by the proper tribunal, in accordance with the laws governing in such cases.

Given at Monterey, California, this 19th day of October, in the year of our Lord 1849.

B. RILEY,
*Brevet Brigadier General United States Army,
and Governor of California.*

Official:

H. W HALLECK,
Brevet Captain, and Secretary of State.

STATE DEPARTMENT OF CALIFORNIA,
Monterey, October 20, 1849.

SIR: I am directed by the governor to acknowledge the receipt of your communication of the 15th instant, resigning your appointment as judge of the superior tribunal. Your resignation is hereby accepted, to take effect on the 1st day of November next.

Very respectfully, your obedient servant,

H. W. HALLECK,
Brevet Captain, and Secretary of State.

Hon. LEWIS DENT,
Judge of Superior Tribunal, Stockton,
San Joaquin district, California.

PROCLAMATION.

In conformity with the custom of other States and Territories, and in order that the people of California may make a general and public acknowledgment of their gratitude to the Supreme Ruler of the Universe for his kind and fostering care during the past year, and for the boundless blessings which we now enjoy, it is recommended that Thursday, the 29th day of November next, be set apart and kept as a day of thanksgiving and prayer.

Given at Monterey, California, this 24th day of October, in the year of our Lord 1849.

B. RILEY,
Brevet Brigadier General United States Army,
and Governor of California.

By the governor:

H. W. HALLECK,
Brevet Captain, and Secretary of State.

Know all men by these presents, that I, Bennet Riley, brevet brigadier general United States army, and governor of California, by virtue of authority in me vested, do hereby appoint and commission Mariano Malarin a judge of first instance in and for the district of Monterey, with exclusive jurisdiction of civil cases, to date from the 1st of November, 1849.

Given at Monterey, California, this 24th day of October, in the year o our Lord eighteen hundred and forty-nine.

B. RILEY,
Brevet Brig. Gen. U. S. A., and Governor of California.

Official:

H. W. HALLECK,
Brevet Captain, and Secretary of State.

HEADQUARTERS TENTH MILITARY DEPARTMENT,
Monterey, California, October 25, 1849.

CAPTAIN: The commanding general has just received from Lieutenant Sherman, aid-de-camp, information leaving little doubt in his mind that Captain Warner, topographical engineers, has been murdered by the Indians of the upper Sacramento. He accordingly directs that you proceed immediately with all the effective men of your troop, and those recently transferred to company E, if they are still with you, to the scene of this murder, for the purpose of apprehending and chastising its perpetrators.

The information received is indefinite as to time and place, but it is supposed that you will be able to gather the particulars on your route.

Under the apprehension that your troops may be too weak to penetrate far into the Indian country, the commanding general will immediately send instructions to Lieutenant Wilson, 1st dragoons, to meet you with his troop at or near Captain Day's camp, or Bear creek.

In the absence of particular information, the commanding general can give you no definite instructions; but he desires that your arrangements be made to move as expeditiously as possible, and that every effort be made to secure the perpetrators of this outrage.

If it should not be possible to secure the individual murderers, hold the tribe or band to which they belong responsible, and inflict upon it such punishment as will not readily be forgotten.

You will call, by the general's orders, upon the officers of the quartermaster's department for any supplies or funds that may be needed to facilitate your movements.

Very respectfully, your obedient servant,
EDWARD R. S. CANBY,
Assistant Adjutant General.

Captain A. J. SMITH,
1st Dragoons, commanding, &c., Sonoma, California.

STATE DEPARTMENT OF CALIFORNIA,
Monterey, October 26, 1849.

SIR: I have to acknowledge the receipt of your letter of October 22, asking for arms and ammunition for the use of the municipal authorities of San José. The governor will give the necessary orders to the military officers to send you the articles asked for.

Very respectfully, your obedient servant,
H. W. HALLECK,
Brevet Captain, and Secretary of State.

Don ANTONIO M. PICO,
Prefect of San José, California.

STATE DEPARTMENT TERRITORY OF CALIFORNIA,
Monterey, October 26, 1849.

SIR: I am directed by the governor to acknowledge the receipt of your letter of the 18th instant, resigning your office as judge of the superior tribunal.

Your resignation is hereby accepted, to take effect on the 1st of November next.

Very respectfully, your obedient servant,
H. W. HALLECK,
Brevet Captain, and Secretary of State.

Hon. PETER H. BURNETT,
 San José, California.

Know all men by these presents, that I, Bennet Riley, brevet brigadier general United States army, and governor of California, by virtue of authority in me vested, do hereby appoint and commission Kembal H. Dimmick a judge of the superior tribunal of California, to date from the 1st day of November next; vice Burnett, resigned.

Given under my hand and seal, at Monterey, California, this 26th day of October, in the year of our Lord eighteen hundred and forty-nine.
B. RILEY,
Brevet Brig. Gen. U. S. Army, and Governor of California.

Official:
H. W. HALLECK,
Brevet Captain, and Secretary of State.

Know all men by these presents, that I, Bennet Riley, brevet brigadier general United States army, and governor of California, by virtue of authority in me vested, do hereby appoint and commission Richard A. Maupin a judge of the superior tribunal of California, vice Lewis Dent, resigned; to date from the first day of November next.

Given under my hand and seal, at Monterey, California, this twenty-sixth day of October, in the year of our Lord eighteen hundred and forty-nine.
B. RILEY,
Brevet Brig. Gen. U. S. A., and Governor of California.

Official:
H. W. HALLECK,
Brevet Captain, and Secretary of State.

To all to whom these presents shall come, greeting:

I, the undersigned, secretary of state for California, hereby request all whom it may concern to permit safely and freely to pass Juan de Dios Talamentes, a citizen of California, entitled by the provisions of the treaty of Guadalupe Hidalgo to all the rights, privileges, and immunities of a citizen of the United States of America, and in case of need to give him all lawful aid and protection.

Given under my hand and seal of the department of state, at Monterey, California, this twenty-sixth day of October, in the year of our Lord [L. S.] eighteen hundred and forty-nine.
H. W. HALLECK,
Brevet Captain, and Secretary of State.

Description.—Age, 22 years; stature, 5 feet 7 inches English; eyes, dark; nose, Roman; mouth, medium; chin, ordinary; hair, very dark; complexion, dark.

Signature of the bearer:
JUAN DE DIOS TALAMENTES.

State Department of California,
Monterey, October 26, 1849.

Major: You are authorized by the governor to loan from the "civil fund" to the quartermaster's department one hundred thousand dollars, for which you will take the proper drafts on that department in Washington.

Very respectfully, your obedient servant,
H. W. HALLECK,
Brevet Captain, and Secretary of State.

Major R. Allen,
Civil Treasurer, San Francisco, California.

To all to whom these presents shall come, greeting:

I, the undersigned, secretary of state for California, hereby request all whom it may concern to permit safely and freely to pass Luis Mareno, a citizen of California, entitled by the provisions of the treaty of Guadalupe Hidalgo to all the rights, privileges, and immunities of a citizen of the United States of America, and in case of need to give him all lawful aid and protection.

Given under my hand and seal of the department of state, at Monterey, California, this twenty-sixth day of October, in the year of our Lord eighteen hundred and forty-nine.

[L. S.]
H. W. HALLECK,
Brevet Captain, and Secretary of State.

Description.—Age, 22 years; stature, 5 feet 8 inches English; forehead, ordinary; eyes, dark; nose, straight; mouth, medium; chin, ordinary; hair, very dark; complexion, dark.

Signature of the bearer:
his
LUIS + MARENO.
mark.

State Department of California,
Monterey, October 27, 1849.

Sir: I have to acknowledge the receipt of your communication of the 24th instant, and the accompanying papers, all of which have been referred by the governor to the superior court, for such action as that body may deem necessary and proper.

Very respectfully, your obedient servant,
H. W. HALLECK,
Brevet Captain, and Secretary of State.

Don Antonio Ma. Pico, *Prefect of San José, California.*

Know all men by these present, that, on the recommendation of the superior tribunal of California, I, Bennet Riley, brevet brigadier general United States army, and governor of California, by virtue of authority in me vested, do hereby appoint and commission J. T. Richardson a judge of first instance, with exclusive civil jurisdiction, in and for the district of San José, to date from the first day of November, 1849.

Given under my hand and seal, at Monterey, California, this twenty-ninth day of October, in the year of our Lord eighteen hundred and forty-nine.

           B. RILEY,
  Brevet Brig. Gen. U. S. A., and Governor of California.

Official:
           H. W. HALLECK,
    Brevet Captain, and Secretary of State.

      STATE DEPARTMENT OF CALIFORNIA,
        Monterey, October 29, 1849.

SIR: On the recommendation of the superior tribunal of California, the governor has appointed J. T. Richardson a judge of first instance for the district of San José, with exclusive civil jurisdiction. His commission takes effect on the first day of November next, after which time your jurisdiction will, in accordance with the laws, be confined to criminal matters only.

Very respectfully, your obedient servant,
           H. W. HALLECK,
    Brevet Captain, and Secretary of State.

Hon. R. M. MAY,
 Judge of First Instance, San José, California.

       On Military Affairs.

    HEADQUARTERS SECOND INFANTRY,
    On board U. S. Transport Ship "Iowa,"
     Valparaiso, Chili, February 12, 1849.

GENERAL: I have the honor to report my arrival at this port on the 7th instant, with the headquarters and first battalion second infantry, (companies C, G, and I,) after the uncommonly short passage of thirty-seven days from Rio Janeiro.

At this place we have dates from California as late as the 8th of December last; and from the accounts given here, it would seem that the extraordinary news received in the United States in September and October last, in regard to the mineral wealth of that country, is correct in every particular; if in anything those accounts were erroneous, it is that they fall far short of the reality, as to the quantity of gold the country contains, and the care with which it is procured. The towns along the coast, it is said, are completely deserted; provisions are very high, and labor cannot be obtained at any price, nearly all the inhabitants having gone off to the gold region.

The troops stationed in California have lost many men by desertion; and if the current reports are to be relied on, very few, if any, remain to garrison the different posts.

In consequence of the state of affairs in California, I think that the interests of the service render it proper that I should make the port of Monterey, with my regiment, instead of San Francisco or San Diego. I have accordingly given instructions to the commanding officer of the troops on board the transport Rome, (now here,) and left orders for the troops which are to follow, to rendezvous at Monterey. The temptation for the men to desert will, I think, be much less at Monterey than at San Francisco; and we will be near enough the latter place to obtain with little trouble (if it can be obtained) the requisite transportation for the distribution of the regiment along the coast. In addition to these reasons, there are, I understand, quarters more than sufficient at Monterey for the comfortable accommodation of my whole regiment, which is not the case either at San Francisco or San Diego; and from the latter place there will be difficulty and great delay in obtaining transportation for the distribution of my command. For these causes, and on the advice of the officers of the United States storeship Lexington, (now here, and just from California,) I have thought it advisable to disembark my whole command at Monterey.

Not less than $450,000 in California gold has arrived at this place within the last three months; and the Lexington, which arrived here on the 9th instant, bound for the United States, brought gold to the amount of $350,000, part of which has been sold here.

Some seventeen vessels in the last two months have sailed from this port with emigrants and provisions for California; but the liability to be laid up by the desertion of crews may in future, to some extent, operate against vessels there. If such be the case, unless there is a speedy change in the state of affairs there, no doubt there will be much suffering for the want of provisions during the coming fall and winter, particularly as a large emigration from the United States (overland) may be expected this spring; and the cultivation of the soil has been entirely neglected in California since the discovery of its inexhaustible wealth in gold.

The very high price of provisions and all the necessaries of life in California will render it impossible for officers to live on the pay at present allowed them by the government; and I would earnestly beg that the attention of the government may be called to the matter, as one of the greatest importance to the officers serving there, many of whom, encouraged by the liberality of the department in furnishing transportation for their families, have brought them out with them.

The health of the troops on board of this transport has been exceedingly good since we left New York, having lost but one man by ordinary death since our embarcation in November last. One man (private Carey, of company C) was accidently drowned on the 10th January last off the coast of Patagonia.

The "Rome," with companies D and H, 2d infantry, under the command of Major Heintzelman, arrived here on the 9th instant. The steamship "Massachusetts" made this port on the same day with this transport. The "Edith" preceded us two days.

I shall leave here to-morrow, and I trust to be in California at furthest by the middle of April.

I am, general, very respectfully, your obedient servant,
B. RILEY,
Brevet Brigadier General, commanding

Brigadier General R. Jones,
Adjutant General U. S. A., Washington, D. C.

Headquarters Second Infantry,
On board the Transport Ship "Iowa," at Sea, April 10, 1849.

General: Herewith I have the honor to enclose regimental returns of the second infantry for the months of February and March, 1849.

I am, sir, very respectfully, your obedient servant,
B. RILEY,
Lieut. Col., Bvt. Brig. Gen., commanding.

Bvt. Brig. Gen. R. Jones,
Adjt. Gen. U. S. Army, Washington, D. C.

Monterey, *April* 13, 1849.

P. S.—I arrived here last evening, after a passage of 56 days from Valparaiso—all well. The steamer is just in, and I have only time to report my arrival, as she leaves in a few minutes. The "Rome" arrived here six days before me.
B. R.

Headquarters Second Infantry,
Monterey, April 21, 1849.

General: I have the honor to report my arrival at this post on the 12th instant, with the first battalion 2d infantry, (companies C, G, I,) after a passage of 56 days from Valparaiso. The transport "Rome," with companies D and H, under the command of Major Heintzelman, arrived here six days before me.

I have the honor to be, very respectfully, your obedient servant,
B. RILEY,
Brevet Brig. Gen. U. S. Army, com'g the 10th Mil. Dept.
and 2d Infantry.

Brig. Gen. R. Jones,
Adjt. Gen. U. S. Army, Washington, D. C.

[No. 1.] Headquarters Tenth Military Department,
Monterey, California, April 25, 1849.

General: I have the honor to report, that the troops assigned to this department by general orders No. 49, which have reached this country, have been distributed as follows:

Two companies of the 2d infantry, D and H, have been ordered (department orders No. 11) to San Diego. One of these companies will form the infantry part of the escort, required by general orders No. 65, of 1848, for the commissioners appointed to run the boundary line between Mexico and the United States; the other company constitutes the garrison of San Diego. Company D sailed for its destination on the 16th instant. Company H, detained by the want of transportation, sails to-morrow. Both companies have been filled up to the standard of 64 privates. Company M, 3d artillery, which arrived at this port on the 16th instant, has been ordered to the Presidio of San Francisco, and sailed for that place on the morning of the 18th instant, after landing the recruits sent out for the general service. In accordance with instructions from the headquarters of the division, companies C and G, 2d infantry, have been sent to the bay of San Francisco, and sailed on the 20th instant. I am not yet advised what position they will occupy. Company I, 2d infantry, has been retained at this place, with a view to reinforce the garrison of San Diego, if, as there is much reason to apprehend, it should be much reduced by desertions.

Thirty-six of the recruits for the general service have been assigned to company F, and six to company M, 3d artillery; twelve of the 2d infantry recruits, which arrived, under the command of Lieutenant Gardner, of that regiment, on the 24th instant, to company D, nineteen to company H, and seven to company I, of the 2d infantry. The remainder in each of these detachments have been landed, and will be assigned and sent to companies as soon as practicable.

Accounts received from the south of an authentic, although not of an official character, represented the number of desertions from the dragoon commands at Los Angeles and San Luis Rey to have been so great as to render it necessary to transfer the musicians, farriers, and privates, from the 2d to the 1st dragoons, to enable me to furnish the company required for the escort of the commissioners. Department orders No. 14, and the instructions to Majors Graham, 2d, and Rucker, 1st dragoons, and to Captain Kane, assistant quartermaster, indicate the measures to be taken in carrying out the provisions of this order, and for the disposition of the public property at Los Angeles, the abandonment of which, as a military post, results necessarily from the determination above referred to. I have not yet received the reports of the commanders at Los Angeles and San Luis Rey, but expect them in time to be forwarded by the steamer which will leave this place about the 1st proximo. It is known, however, that the number of desertions has been so great, that it will be impossible to organize the dragoon command for the commissioners without making this transfer, and that the deserters have carried off with them a large amount of public property, including, in almost every instance, their horses, arms, and equipments.

The disposition I purpose to make of the troops yet to arrive is indicated in my communication to General Smith of the 6th instant. Although this differs materially from that determined upon before my arrival in this country, I am, with the light of additional information, more deeply impressed with the importance of keeping the troops as much concentrated and embodied as possible. It is believed to be impracticable at present to establish posts on the extreme frontiers or to retain a reputable force at a distance from the mines, where, indeed, the presence of troops, aside from all other considerations, is more necessary for the preservation of order than at any other point in the Territory. But for the disposition required by general orders No. 65, for the escort of the commissioners, I would concentrate all the military supplies on the bay of San Francisco and at this place, and all the troops in the mineral region, except the necessary guards for the depots.

This disposition will leave the inhabitants of the southern military district without protection from Indian depredations; but as the Indians are composed of many different tribes, speaking different languages, any combined action on their part is improbable, and the most that is to be apprehended will be occasional incursions for the purpose of stealing horses. I am satisfied that they will suffer less from this source than from deserters from any command that may be sent to the south for their protection.

To enable the inhabitants to protect themselves against the Indian horse-thieves, instructions will be given to the ordnance officers of the department to issue ammunition, in limited quantities, to farmers and other respectable persons, holding the alcaldes and other responsible individuals of each neighborhood responsible that the ammunition so issued does not fall into the hands of improper individuals.

Whether the disposition of the troops for the mines, as proposed in my communication to General Smith, will be preferable to their concentration at one point, I am yet unable to decide. If there be a suitable position on the San Joaquin from which troops can easily reach the Tulans or the valley of the Sacramento, I should give a decided preference to the concentration of all the troops in the department, except the depot guards, at one point. In this case, I have but little doubt that the greater part of our men can be retained. At least, a sufficient force can be kept on hand to make occasional detachments into the Indian country, if necessary, and to aid in the preservation of order. The importance of having a respectable body of troops in the neighborhood of the mixed population of the mines, and the restraint which its presence would impose upon the lawless and disorderly, must be so apparent that it is unnecessary to advert to it further. Beyond this, the occurrence of an emergency in that quarter which would require the presence of more troops than we now have in the country is not merely possible, but very probable. From the great number of foreign adventurers in the mines, between whom and the Americans there is no community of feeling, and the conflicting interests of all parties, it is scarcely to be hoped that a collision can be avoided.

The troops at the depots may be rendered more contented and the number of desertions diminished by granting furloughs for the purpose of visiting the mines, by permitting the men to labor for their own benefit when not required for military duties, and by such a system of exchange as will give all the troops an opportunity of visiting the mines. The practice of furloughs acted upon at this post, with the sanction of the department commander, has succeeded well, and there is no doubt that its application in other cases will be equally so. A visit to the mines, and the knowledge acquired thereby of the difficulties experienced on account of the scarcity of provisions and other necessaries, tend greatly to allay the gold fever; but the excitement is so universal that this knowledge must be enforced by experience, and but few will remain contented at a distance from the mines until they have seen for themselves.

The necessity for this disposition of the troops, it is hoped, will only be temporary; and that, before the commencement of another year, the excitement will be so far allayed that troops may be sent to the frontier, for the protection of the inhabitants, without, as at present, the inevitable danger that the men will desert, and the public property, transported to distant points at an immense expense, be lost by the absence of the proper guards.

In the mean time, I shall endeavor to have the necessary preliminary examination made with a view to the selection of positions for permanent military posts, particularly at the points indicated in Colonel Mason's communication to division headquarters of the 27th February, and other arrangements for the establishment of those posts, as soon as the state of affairs in this country will permit it.

To make these examinations, the services of topographical engineers are highly important, and the officers of that corps heretofore serving in this department have been transferred to division headquarters. I respectfully ask, if the officers of that corps assigned to this department by general orders No. 49 have not already left the United States, that they be sent out by the next steamer.

The services of *two* or *three* additional officers of the quartermasters's department, *one* of the subsistence, and *one* of the ordnance department, are very necessary, and I request that they may be ordered to report to me as soon as possible.

If, contrary to my expectation, the *placers* should continue to yield gold as abundantly for the future as they have done for the past, the continued concentration of the troops in the mineral region is, in my opinion, the only method by which we can hope to retain a respectable force embodied. No reasonable increase of pay will render men contented at a distance from the mines; nor, where the mania is so universal, can any restrictive measure be attended with success. The current cannot be stemmed, but it may be diverted and rendered subservient to many of our purposes here. The mines may be worked by the troops when not required for purposes purely military, reserving a sufficient per centage to reimburse the government for portions of the expenses of the military establishment in this country. For the depots, the interests of the service may be promoted by the enlistment of married men for service in this department.

These matters will be made the subject of another report, as soon as I am possessed of the requisite information. These suggestions are now made for the consideration of the authorities at home.

I have the honor to be, very respectfully, general, your obedient servant,
B. RILEY,
Bvt. Brig. Gen. U. S. A., com'g 10th Military Depart.
General R. Jones,
Adjutant General U. S. A., Washington, D. C.

Headquarters Tenth Military Department,
Monterey, California, January 1, 1849.

Sir: I have the honor herewith to enclose you orders No. 64, of 1848, with the circular of April 1, 1847. Duplicates of these papers were sen you by Captain Ingall, assistant quartermaster, who sailed from this port for San Pedro on the 30th ultimo, in the brig Euphemia.

The mail express referred to in the circular was in successful operation from April, 1847, until August, 1848, when it was partially discontinued in consequence of the reduction of the military force in the southern military district. The arrival of your command renders it necessary to re-establish it, to afford opportunities for frequent communication.

The country is now regarded safe enough for one man to travel without danger, if properly armed; and the assistant quartermaster here finds it best to hire a citizen specially as mail-rider, who, by experience, takes better care of his horses, and delivers his mail more punctually. Instead, therefore, of sending two soldiers, as prescribed in the circular, you can instruct your quartermaster to send but one, and that one a soldier or citizen, as you think best.

It is expected that Captain Ingall, assistant quartermaster, will, in a short time, be ordered to Monterey. Colonel Mason therefore desires that you impose on him no duty that would interfere with such expected orders.

I have the honor to be your most obedient servant,
W. T. SHERMAN,
1st Lieut. 3d Artillery, A. A. A. General.

Major L. P. GRAHAM,
Los Angeles, California.

HEADQUARTERS TENTH MILITARY DEPARTMENT,
Monterey, California, January 2, 1849.

SIR: Your letter of the 30th ultimo has just been received. Colonel Mason on the 1st of December instructed Captain Folsom to turn over to you the ordnance stores brought out in the "Undine," thinking that invoices from Captain Thornton accompanied the property. He has received but one invoice of these stores, which I herewith enclose to you. He wishes you receipt to Captain Thornton for this property.

I have the honor to be your obedient servant,
W. T. SHERMAN,
1st. Lieut. 3d Artillery, A. A. A. General.

Lieut. JAMES A. HARDIE,
Commanding, San Francisco, California.

HEADQUARTERS TENTH MILITARY DEPARTMENT,
Monterey, California, January 8, 1849.

SIR: Commodore Jones, in August last, delivered to Lieutenant Colonel Burton, 1st New York volunteers, and to the disbursing officers of the commissary and quartermaster's department at La Paz and San José, Lower California, the sum of two thousand three hundred dollars, ($2,300,) taking the receipts of those officers for the sums delivered to each, respectively.

Colonel Mason directs that you redeem those receipts, by paying to the commodore the sum above named, out of the military-contribution fund in your charge. Commodore Jones will turn over to you the original receipts still held by him, with his own endorsed thereon, according to the plan suggested by himself.

I have the honor to be, very respectfully, your obedient servant,
W. T. SHERMAN,
1st Lieut. 3d Artillery, A. A. A. General.

Captain J. L. FOLSOM,
Assistant Quartermaster, San Francisco, California.

HEADQUARTERS TENTH MILITARY DEPARTMENT,
Monterey, California, January 8, 1849.

SIR: I have the honor to acknowledge the receipt of your letter of the 1st instant, and have this day instructed Captain Folsom to refund to you from the military-contribution fund the sum of two thousand three hundred dollars advanced by you to the army disbursing officers in Lower California.

I enclose herewith a copy of a communication received from Mr. Botts, naval storekeeper, dated 27th September, asking for twelve hundred dollars on account of the Navy Department, which sum was turned over to him by Captain Marcy. (See my endorsement on Mr. B.'s letter.)

I do not know whether this money should properly be refunded by a purser or navy agent. I submit the subject to you for such action as you may think proper, merely suggesting that if a purser has any military-contribution fund in his possession, it might be paid by him.

I am, sir, very respectfully, your obedient servant,
R. B. MASON,
Colonel 1st Dragoons.

Commodore THOS. AP C. JONES,
Commanding U. S. naval forces in the Pacific.

HEADQUARTERS TENTH MILITARY DEPARTMENT,
Monterey, California, January 9, 1849.

SIR: On Friday last, the 5th instant—the regular day for the departure of the express from Monterey to San Francisco—there was no man here to convey the mail. Captain Marcy, acting assistant quartermaster here, was called upon for the reasons of this failure, and stated that the man hired to convey the express mail between San Francisco and Monterey is under your direct orders and control; that he arrived here from the north on his last regular day, December 27, 1848, and reported to Captain Marcy that you had ordered him to return to San Francisco by Sunday, the 31st ultimo, and that he accordingly left on the 29th ultimo. Captain Marcy further reports that the express between this and San Francisco has been irregular for some time past.

Colonel Mason deems it sufficient to call your attention to these facts to prevent their recurrence in future. The express must arrive and depart at the time fixed in orders; otherwise it will fail to connect here with the one from the south. The military express mail to and from San Francisco and Monterey is under your control; that from Monterey to

Dana's is under the control of the quartermaster here; and that from Dana's south under the control of the quartermaster at Los Angeles.

These officers are required to take the proper measures to insure the punctual arrival and departure of the express riders.

I have the honor to be your most obedient servant,
W. T. SHERMAN,
First Lieutenant 3d Artillery, A. A. A. General.
Captain J. L. Folsom,
Assistant Quartermaster, San Francisco, California.

HEADQUARTERS TENTH MILITARY DEPARTMENT,
Monterey, California, January 17, 1849.

SIR: I am directed to acknowledge the receipt of your letter of the 8th instant, concerning the sale by you of the public wagon and harness referred to in mine of the 30th ultimo.

It is beyond Colonel Mason's power or authority to give his sanction to the sale of that wagon and harness; and he therefore leaves the matter in the hands of the assistant quartermaster, who is responsible for the property.

I have the honor to be your most obedient servant,
W. T. SHERMAN,
First Lieutenant 3d Artillery, A. A. A. General.
Colonel J. D. Stevenson,
San Francisco, California.

HEADQUARTERS TENTH MILITARY DEPARTMENT,
Monterey, California, January 20, 1849.

SIR: I have the honor to acknowledge the receipt of your letters of January 10, 11, and 13, 1849.

Colonel Mason has given your proposition to erect government storehouses his attention. He approves of your suggestion, and authorizes you to plan and erect on the lot in the town of San Francisco reserved for that purpose a building of sufficient capacity for the probable wants of the quartermaster and commissary's department at that place, provided you can do so upon better terms than to continue renting as heretofore. No official notification has yet reached us that the steamer Massachusetts has been despatched for service in the quartermaster's department on this coast. You had, therefore, in your estimates, better rely upon getting lumber from the Certa Madera, Bodega, and Santa Cruz, than from Oregon; should, however, the Massachusetts arrive, it will be so much the better.

I have already addressed you on the subject of the express mail; but, to prevent further misunderstanding, I will repeat that the express between this place and San Francisco has never been changed in orders since its first establishment, in April, 1847. I again send you a copy of the original circular, with an endorsement of the days of its arrival and departure from San Francisco for some months to come. It is impossible to comply with your request that the man hired to carry this express between San Francisco and Monterey be permitted to arrive at the latter place and return at once to the former, so as to be employed by you in other duties, when not actually on the road. To keep up the connexion with the southern line, he must arrive and depart on the day fixed in the circular. The man, though hired by you, can be employed here, under the direction of the assistant quartermaster, during the days he is not on the road. Colonel Mason says he cannot give you an order for hiring a hospital steward for the Presidio of San Francisco, as recommended by Lieutenant Stoneman and Surgeon Perry. He knows that such an account would not be audited at the treasury. A surgeon ought to be able to take care of the sick in a detachment of sixteen officers and men. When Captain Smith arrives, he will probably be able to detail a suitable steward from his company.

I have the honor to be your most obedient servant,
W. T. SHERMAN,
1st Lieut. 3d Art., A. A. A. General.

Captain J. L. Folsom,
A. Q. M., San Francisco, California.

Headquarters Tenth Military Department,
Monterey, California, January 20, 1849.

Sir: Captain Folsom reports that it is the opinion of Surgeon Perry and Lieutenant Stoneman that a hospital steward is required at the Presidio of San Francisco; that no suitable man is in the command; and that one cannot be obtained for the compensation allowed by law.

The aggregate strength of the garrison is 16; but it is Colonel Mason's opinion that Surgeon Perry ought to be able to take care of the sick of that number of men, with the aid of a nurse. It is known that he resides in the town of San Francisco; and if there be much sickness among the men at the Presidio, you should require him to reside there, especially when deprived of the aid of a good steward.

Captain Smith's company will soon arrive at San Francisco, and will doubtless be enabled to furnish one.

I have the honor to be your obedient servant,
W. T. SHERMAN,
1st Lieut. 3d Art., A. A. A. General.

Lieutenant James A. Hardie,
San Francisco, California.

Headquarters Tenth Military Department,
Monterey, California, January 22, 1849.

Sir: Colonel Mason directs that you cause the two men now at this post belonging to company C, 1st dragoons, to report to Lieutenant J. W. Davidson, 1st dragoons, now here en route for San Francisco, for the purpose of going with him to San Francisco, there to join their company. He also directs me to remind you to report to Captain Smith, commanding company C, the changes that have taken place among the recruits belonging to his company since you have been in command of this post. (See paragraph 210, new regulations.) Also, give orders to the assistant quartermaster to furnish the necessary horses and saddles for their transportation.

I have the honor to be your obedient servant,

W. T. SHERMAN,
First Lieutenant 3d Artil'ery, A. A. A. General.

Captain H. S. BURTON,
  Commanding, Monterey, California.

HEADQUARTERS TENTH MILITARY DEPARTMENT,
Monterey, California, January 22, 1849.

SIR: Colonel Mason directs that you send to Captain A. J. Smith, commanding company C, 1st dragoons, a muster and descriptive roll, with account of pay and clothing of the recruits assigned to company C, 1st dragoons, on the 3d day of October, 1848, when you were in command of the post of Monterey. This roll and account should have been sent at the time the assignment was made. Colonel Mason also directs me to remind you to send to Captain Smith, at the same time, a report of the changes (if any) in that detachment of recruits that occurred subsequent to the time of their assignment and before you relinquished the command of the post of Monterey. (See paragraph 210, new regulations.) These papers must be sent by Lieutenant J. W. Davidson, 1st dragoons, now here en route for San Francisco, where he will join Captain Smith's company, C.

I have the honor to be your most obedient servant,

W. T. SHERMAN,
First Lieutenant 3d Artillery, A. A. A. General.

Lieutenant E. O. C. ORD,
  Third Artillery, Monterey, (redoubt,) California.

HEADQUARTERS TENTH MILITARY DEPARTMENT,
Monterey, California, January 22, 1849.

SIR: Orders have been conveyed to Captain Burton to cause two men of company C, 1st dragoons, now here, to report to you and accompany you by land to San Francisco, where you will cause them to join their company. Orders will be given for them to be provided with horses and saddles.

I have the honor to be your obedient servant.

W. T. SHERMAN,
First Lieutenant 3d Artillery, A. A. A. General.

Lieutenant J. W. DAVIDSON,
  First United States Dragoons, Monterey, California.

HEADQUARTERS TENTH MILITARY DEPARTMENT,
Monterey, California, January 23, 1849.

SIR: I have the honor to enclose to you special orders No. 3, granting a leave of absence for sixty days to Captain D. H. Rucker, the application for which was forwarded by you. Colonel Mason says that such applications should be "approved" or "disapproved" by you, instead of (as in this instance) being simply "forwarded."

I have the honor to be your most obedient servant,
W. T. SHERMAN,
First Lieutenant 3d Artillery, A. A. A. General.
Brevet Major L. P. GRAHAM,
Second Dragoons, commanding S. M. District,
Los Angeles, California.

HEADQUARTERS TENTH MILITARY DEPARTMENT,
Monterey, California, January 24, 1849.

SIR: I have the honor to acknowledge the receipt of your letters of December 15 and 27, 1848, with their enclosures, and to convey to you Colonel Mason's instructions on the various subjects embraced in them. There are no courts in California, civil or military, that can take cognizance of and punish for the crime of murder committed in a foreign country.

John Price, charged with the murder of Elise Martin at or near Chihuahua, Mexico, cannot be tried here; and however guilty, must escape punishment. You will cause him, (Price,) if a soldier, to be returned to duty; and if a citizen, to be set at liberty.

By your reports it is seen that you have with you 205 hired men of the quartermaster's and commissary's departments. These are far more than can be profitably employed at Los Angeles, and Colonel Mason directs that you dispose of them as follows:

By the first opportunity, by land or sea, send to San Francisco to report to Captain J. L. Folsom, assistant quartermaster, two (2) blacksmiths and six (6) teamsters. If the nature of the agreement with the teamsters and wheelwrights be such that they can be employed at work of other character, then send to Captain Folsom twenty teamsters instead of six, as before mentioned, and five wheelwrights.

Send to Monterey one blacksmith and four teamsters, and, after making these details, retain for service at Los Angeles such as you consider necessary for your command, and cause all the rest of the hired men to be paid off and discharged.

Captain Rufus Ingalls, assistant quartermaster, was sent to Los Angeles to afford his assistance in the important and multifarious duties that fell upon the quartermaster of your command, for a short time after your arrival in the country. Colonel Mason wishes you to order him to Monterey as soon as you can spare his services.

The colonel commanding directs me to add, that he wishes you to have all your wagons and harness repaired, all saddles and horse equipments kept in good order, and every attention paid to your animals, so as to be ready to move at short notice.

I have the honor to be your obedient servant,
W. T. SHERMAN,
1st Lieut. 3d Artillery, A. A. A. General.
Brevet Major L. P. GRAHAM,
Com'g Southern Military District, Los Angeles, California.

HEADQUARTERS TENTH MILITARY DEPARTMENT,
Monterey, California, January 24, 1849.

SIR: I have the honor to inform you that instructions have been sent to Brevet Major Graham, commanding in Los Angeles, to send to San Francisco, to report to you, two blacksmiths and six teamsters.

A great number (205) of hired men came out with his command, enlisted for twelve months from July 1, 1848, unless sooner discharged; but they are mostly teamsters, wheelwrights, &c. It is not known whether by their contract of enlistment they can be put upon other labor than that of teamsters, &c.; but if such a construction can be given to their contract, Major Graham is instructed to send twenty teamsters, instead of six, and five wheelwrights.

These men will be useful in building the storehouse referred to in my letter of January 20.

I have the honor to be your obedient servant,
W. T. SHERMAN,
1st Lieut. 3d Artillery, A. A. A. General.

Captain J. L. FOLSOM,
Assistant Quartermaster, San Francisco, California.

HEADQUARTERS TENTH MILITARY DEPARTMENT,
Monterey, California, January 24, 1849.

SIR: Colonel Mason directs that you report, as early as possible, the amount of public funds brought over to California by the quartermaster and commissary of your command.

I have the honor to be your obedient servant,
W. T. SHERMAN,
1st Lieut. 3d Artillery, A. A. A. General.

Major L. P. GRAHAM,
Com'g Southern Military District, Los Angeles, California.

HEADQUARTERS TENTH MILITARY DEPARTMENT,
Monterey, California, January 25, 1849.

GENTLEMEN: Your letter of July 25, 1848, did not reach Monterey until the 21st instant, and then was not accompanied by the accounts for commutation of fuel and quarters at Mazatlan, and the bill for commutation of quarters at Monterey, to which your letter refers.

An officer of the army, when travelling under orders, has certain allowances prescribed by the regulations, which are paid by an officer of the quartermaster's department upon presentation of proper vouchers. If you have Lieutenant Colonel Burton's order to proceed from La Paz, Lower California, to Mazatlan, and thence to Monterey, California, with your orders from Monterey to Los Angeles, you can still make your charge, and receive whatever allowance the army regulations contemplate. The assistant quartermaster at San Francisco can inform you whether the expenses incurred by you at Mazatlan and Monterey are such as are provided for by the quartermaster's department, either as actual expenses incurred by you in obeying your orders, or as commutation for quarters and fuel when necessarily delayed on the road.

The case does not call for an order from Colonel Mason.

I have the honor to be your obedient servant,
W. T. SHERMAN,
1st Lieut. 3d Art., A. A. A. General.

Messrs. E. G. BUFFUM and G. T. SÉMON,
Late Lieuts. N. Y. Vols., San Francisco, California.

HEADQUARTERS TENTH MILITARY DEPARTMENT,
Monterey, California, January 26, 1849.

SIR: Colonel Mason directs that you proceed up the valley of the Sacramento river as early as it is practicable to travel with horses or mules, to examine it about fifty or one hundred miles above Sutter's, with a view to the selection of a military post in that quarter. A good location as to water, timber, grass, and easy communication with San Francisco by water, is desired. You will examine different locations, as well as collect information concerning the general resources of that part of California. For the purpose of making the reconnoissance, you will hire two or more men, as you think proper, to accompany you, with the necessary horses and outfit.

Having completed this, you will then proceed to Sonoma, and thence to the lake country, lying some twenty or thirty leagues north of that place, there to make a similar reconnoissance for the like purpose.

Having completed these, you will return to department headquarters and report the result of your examination. It is not expected that you will make accurate surveys; but it is believed, with the limited means at your command, you can obtain the information and knowledge of that country which will be needed in posting the troops supposed to be en route for California from the United States.

I have the honor to be, very respectfully, your obedient servant,
W. T. SHERMAN,
1st Lieut. 3d Art., A. A. A. General.

Lieutenant W. H. WARNER,
Top. Eng., Sutter's Fort, California.

HEADQUARTERS TENTH MILITARY DEPARTMENT,
Monterey, California, February 2, 1849.

SIR: Intelligence has just been received that the United States ship Ohio is daily expected at San Francisco from Mazatlan, with a large and important mail from the United States.

Colonel Mason directs that, upon the arrival of the Ohio, you despatch the mail for these headquarters by a special courier, with orders to reach Monterey in the shortest practicable time.

I have the honor to be your obedient servant,
W. T. SHERMAN,
1st Lieut. 3d Art., A. A. A. General.

Captain J. L. FOLSOM,
Assistant Quartermaster, San Francisco.

HEADQUARTERS TENTH MILITARY DEPARTMENT,
Monterey, California, February 3, 1849.

SIR: In consequence of representations from Captain J. L. Folsom, Colonel Mason has made the following modification of the express mail now in operation between San Francisco and Monterey:

The express will leave San Francisco on Mondays of alternate weeks, arrive here on Wednesday evening, so as to connect with the express south of Monterey—stay here until Saturday morning, and then return to San Francisco. This will break the connexion of the return mail from the south at this place.

The change is made so as to give time, at Monterey and San Francisco, to answer letters by the return trip. Colonel Mason directs that you give the necessary orders for executing this change, and that you cause the express riders to start punctually on Saturday morning for San Francisco.

I have the honor to be your obedient servant,
W. T. SHERMAN,
1st Lieutenant 3d Artillery, A. A. Adjutant General.
Capt W. G. MARCY,
 Monterey, California.

HEADQUARTERS TENTH MILITARY DEPARTMENT,
Monterey, California, February 3, 1849.

SIR: I am directed to acknowledge the receipt of your letter of January 9, enclosing charges and specifications preferred against 1st Lieutenant C. J. Couts, 1st dragoons, by Captain D. H. Rucker of the same regiment. In the present state of affairs, Colonel Mason says he cannot, consistently with the interest of the service, order a general court martial for the trial of Lieutenant Couts, and he thinks it possible that such a court cannot be assembled until after the arrival of more troops in California.

Lieutenant Couts must therefore continue on duty until further orders in his case.

I have the honor to be your obedient servant,
W. T. SHERMAN,
1st Lieutenant 3d Artillery, A. A. Adjutant General.
Brevet Major L. P. GRAHAM,
 Commanding S. M. District,
  Los Angeles, California.

HEADQUARTERS TENTH MILITARY DEPARTMENT,
Monterey, California, February 3, 1849.

SIR: Agreeably to the application contained in your letter of the 27 ult., received yesterday, orders will be sent from Colonel Mason, through Lieutenant Halleck, for the transfer of $70,000 from the military contribution fund to the quartermaster's and commissary's departments.

Your letter of the 25th ult., concerning the failures of the express, has been laid before Colonel Mason, who directs me to say that he approves of your suggestion in regard to the departure and arrival of the express mail at San Francisco, and will give orders to Captain Marcy to cause your express rider to return from Monterey on the third day after his arrival here, so as to allow two days to answer letters brought down from San Francisco. You will be careful to despatch your express on alternate Monday, as heretofore, with orders to reach Monterey on Wednesday evening in time, by the regular express man who leaves here on Thursday mornings.

The effect of this change will be to break the connexion of the return from Los Angeles at this point, so that letters from San Francisco from any of the southern officers will necessarily be delayed here from Thursday evening of one week until Saturday morning of the following week.

The advantages, however, pointed out by you, of allowing ample time at San Francisco and Monterey for answering letters by return trip, will fully compensate for this interruption of letters south of Monterey, intended for persons north of this.

I am, with much respect, your obedient servant,
W. T. SHERMAN,
1st Lieutenant 3d Artillery A. A. Adjutant General.
Captain J. L. FOLSOM,
Assistant Quartermaster, San Francisco, California.

HEADQUARTERS TENTH MILITARY DEPARTMENT,
Monterey, California, February 3, 1849.

SIR: As you were the chief of Lieutenant Colonel Burton's staff in Lower California, about the month of March last, can you say whether Captain Naglee, New York volunteers, received—and if so, at what time— a copy of General Scott's order No. 372, 1847, by which Colonel Burton directed him to be governed?

Please be particular as to the circumstances of its delivery and receipt.

I am, respectfully, your obedient servant,
W. T. SHERMAN,
1st Lieutenant 3d Artillery, A. A. Adjutant General.
Lieutenant H. W. HALLECK,
Corps of Engineers, present.

HEADQUARTERS TENTH MILITARY DEPARTMENT,
Monterey, California, February 6, 1849.

SIR: Your letter of the 14th of January, addressed to Colonel Mason, was received last evening, and I am directed to inform you that it should have been addressed to me, as acting assistant adjutant general.

Orders, corresponding with your recommendation, went down by the last express, in regard to the discharge of the great number of teamsters and quartermaster's men who came out with Major Graham's expedition. It is believed that, with the funds now at Los Angeles, those men can be paid off and discharged.

Major Graham has also been instructed to order you to Monterey, when he can spare your services at Los Angeles.

I have the honor to be your most obedient servant,
W. T. SHERMAN,
Lieutenant 3d Artillery, A. A. A. General.

Captain R. INGALLS,
Quartermaster, Los Angeles, California.

HEADQUARTERS TENTH MILITARY DEPARTMENT,
Monterey, California, February 6, 1849.

SIR: I have the honor to send you herewith the following blanks for the company under your command:

20 muster and pay rolls,
12 ordinary muster-rolls,
20 blank discharges,
20 surgeon's certificates of ordinary disability,
10 certificates of pension,
10 descriptive lists of deserters.

These are the only blanks that can be sent you from this office—there being no company returns on hand.

I have the honor to be your obedient servant,
W. T. SHERMAN,
1st Lieutenant 3d Artillery, A. A. A. General.

COMMANDING OFFICERS
Companies A and E 1st Dragoons, and Companies D and E 2d Dragoons, Los Angeles, California.

HEADQUARTERS TENTH MILITARY DEPARTMENT,
Monterey, California, February 7, 1849.

SIR: I have the honor to acknowledge the receipt of your three letters of the 14th of January, with their respective enclosures. These have been laid before Colonel Mason, who directs me to call your attention to the 927th paragraph General Regulations, edition of 1847, which requires all official letters and documents to be endorsed before being sent to their address.

The additional charge and specification preferred against Lieutenant Couts, 1st dragoons, must be retained on file until further orders, subject to the decision of the colonel commanding, as contained in my letter of the 3d instant.

I enclose you herewith department orders No. 2, assembling a general court martial at Los Angeles, California, on the 20th instant, for the trial of private James Keogh, and such other enlisted men as you may order to be brought before it. Approved charges against Keogh, Gatz, Lovell, and Marcy are endorsed, and Colonel Mason says you can bring before this court any other cases that may arise before the court adjourns, provided they be of a serious nature, not cognizable by a garrison court martial.

By the express which arrived from the south on the 5th instant, were received reports from Captain Ingalls and Lieutenant Couts in relation to the affairs of the quartermaster's and commissary's departments at your post. The former reports that it will require $100,000 to pay off the public dues at Los Angeles up to the 30th of June, 1849. Captain Folsom has already sent down about $75,000, which has almost entirely exhausted the quartermaster and commissary funds in his possession. These heavy drafts were entirely unexpected, and may produce serious embarrassments, as drafts upon the departments at Washington cannot be cashed here now at any price. As the great number of quartermaster's men brought out with your expedition are to be discharged, it is believed your staff officers have in hand a sufficient sum of money to pay them off, with enough left to meet current expenses for some time to come. Colonel Mason wishes you to control the public expenses at Los Angeles, and to reduce all kinds of disbursements to the very lowest standard of economy, and see that not a cent is expended unless it is indispensably necessary. For instance, Lieutenant Couts reports his bread as far from being good, and flour "unfit for issue." It is known that this flour is a part of the same lot that is used at Monterey, and Colonel Mason says it must be used at your post, though it is not of good quality. Please to remind the assistant quartermaster and commissary at Los Angeles to send to this office, *monthly*, a summary statement of funds; and quarterly, a list or abstract of provisions or property, &c.; also that requisitions for funds or stores of any kind should be forwarded to this office, through you, that the necessary orders may be issued.

In your field returns which have been received at this office, the *absent* officers are not noticed. I am directed to say, that on your post returns the *absent officers* must be accounted for on the back of the return, to correspond with the figures on the face of the return.

I have the honor to be your obedient servant,

W. T. SHERMAN,
Lieutenant 3d Artillery, A. A. A. General.

Brevet Major L. P. GRAHAM,
Commanding Southern Military District,
Los Angeles, California.

HEADQUARTERS TENTH MILITARY DEPARTMENT,
Monterey, California, February 7, 1849.

SIR: Colonel Mason directs that you report the following facts for his information at your earliest convenience:

1. Total amount of the military contribution fund that has come into your hands, from June 1, 1847, until January 1, 1849.

2. Total amount of the military contribution fund transferred by you to the quartermaster's and commissary's departments, during the period above named.

3. Total amount of expenditures and disbursements on account of the quartermaster's department, during the above named period, exclusive of all sums transferred to and accounted for by other disbursing officers.

4. Total amount of expenditures and disbursements, on account of the

commissary's department, for the above-named period, exclusive of transfers to other disbursing officers.

I have the honor to be your most obedient servant,
W. T. SHERMAN,
1st Lt. 3d Art., A. A. A. General.

Captain J. L. FOLSOM,
Assistant Quartermaster, San Francisco, California.

A similar letter to the foregoing was addressed to Captain W. G. Marcy, A. C. S. and A. Quartermaster at Monterey.

HEADQUARTERS TENTH MILITARY DEPARTMENT,
Monterey, California, February 8, 1849.

SIR: Colonel Mason directs that you report, at your earliest convenience, the following facts:

1. Total amount of the military contribution fund that has come into your hands, from June 1, 1847, until January 1, 1849.
2. Total amount of the military contribution fund transferred by you to the quartermaster's and commissary's departments, during the period above named.
3. Total amount of expenditures and disbursements on account of the quartermaster's department, during the above-named period, exclusive of all sums transferred by you to other disbursing officers.
4. Total amount of expenditures and disbursements, on account of the commissary's department, for the above-named period, exclusive of transfers to other disbursing officers.

From your position at Los Angeles, it is supposed that you may be enabled to state, in general terms, the amount of receipts and expenditures of the disbursing officers at Santa Barbara and San Diego. If you can, Colonel Mason wishes you to do so, as he is desirous to ascertain, as nearly as possible, the amount of moneys received and expended in California, from June 1, 1847, until the end of the year 1848.

I have the honor to be your most obedient servant,
W. T. SHERMAN,
1st Lt. 3d Art., A. A. A. General.

Lieutenant J. W. DAVIDSON,
1st Reg. U. S. Dragoons, A. A. Q., Los Angeles, California, now at San Francisco.

HEADQUARTERS TENTH MILITARY DEPARTMENT,
Monterey, California, February 8, 1849.

SIR: At the suggestion of Captain J. L. Folsom, assistant quartermaster, Colonel Mason has directed the following change to be made in the mail express between San Francisco and Monterey:

Express to leave San Francisco on alternate Mondays, as heretofore, to arrive at Monterey on Wednesday evening, so as to connect with the express going south of this point—delays here two days, viz: until Saturday morning, when it returns to San Francisco, arriving there on Monday evening.

Instructions have gone to Captain Folsom accordingly.

I have the honor to be your obedient servant,

W. T. SHERMAN,
1st Lieut. 3d Art., A. A. A. General.

Captain A. J. SMITH,
1st Dragoons, commanding, San Francisco, California.

HEADQUARTERS TENTH MILITARY DEPARTMENT,
Monterey, California, February 20, 1849.

CAPTAIN: I have just received from the alcalde of this district a communication of to-day's date, of which the enclosed is a translation. You will furnish him the armed force he asks for the security of the prisoner, as long he desires it. You will judge whether it will be most convenient to guard the prisoner where he is, or to take him to your own guard-house. The guard is furnished solely for the safe-keeping of the prisoner, and is to take no part in carrying the sentence into execution—that belongs entirely to the civil authority.

I am, very respectfully, your obedient servant,

R. B. MASON,
Colonel 1st Dragoons, commanding.

Captain H. S. BURTON,
3d Art., commanding, Monterey.

HEADQUARTERS TENTH MILITARY DEPARTMENT,
Monterey, California, February 21, 1849.

SIR: Your letter of January 29th is this day received, and, in answer, I am directed to say to you that general orders No. 36, of July 7, 1848, herewith enclosed, continues you in service until you are "duly notified of your discharge." The exhibition of these orders to Major Hill, paymaster, will remove any doubt he may have entertained as to your position as an officer of the army.

Very respectfully, your obedient servant,

W. T. SHERMAN,
First Lieut. 3d Artillery, A. A. A. General.

Assistant Surgeon W. S. BOOTH,
U. S. A., Los Angeles, California.

HEADQUARTERS TENTH MILITARY DEPARTMENT,
Monterey, California, February 25, 1849.

SIR: By direction of Colonel R. B. Mason, I enclose you a copy of a letter from the Adjutant General, received on the 23d instant, and an extract from one received on the same day from the Secretary of War, calling for certain muster-rolls and information that Lieutenant Colonel Fremont states are in your possession.

These letters will exhibit to you the great importance of these rolls to establish the claims of the California battalion to pay for their services. Colonel Mason requests that you will, with all convenient despatch, forward to him the original rolls referred to, and any other information that would aid in establishing the claims referred to, which rolls and information he will transmit to the Adjutant General at Washington. Should the muster-rolls in your possession not be in duplicate, it would be advisable to have copies made for yourself, so that the originals might go to Washington.

Very respectfully, your obedient servant,
W. T. SHERMAN,
First Lieutenant 3d Artillery, A. A. A. General.

Major READING,
Late Paymaster, Fremont's Battalion.

HEADQUARTERS TENTH MILITARY DEPARTMENT,
Monterey, California, February 25, 1849.

SIR: Colonel Mason directs that upon the return of the government barque Anita to San Francisco, you load her with commissary stores, and despatch her to San Pedro; then to deliver to the commissary of the dragoon command, now at Los Angeles, the stores he may require; after which to proceed to San Diego, and there await the arrival of the troops from the United States, or further instructions from proper authority.

I have the honor to be your obedient servant,
W. T. SHERMAN,
First Lieutenant 3d Artillery, A. A. A. General.

Captain J. L. FOLSOM,
Assistant Quartermaster.

HEADQUARTERS TENTH MILITARY DEPARTMENT,
Monterey, California, February 27, 1849.

SIR: I proceed to suggest, in compliance with the wish expressed yesterday in conversation by the General, in relation to the points at which the troops now in the country, and those shortly to arrive, under Brevet Brigadier General Riley, should take post until the permanent positions for the military posts are selected. This cannot be done until the country is more thoroughly examined, with that particular view.

Two companies should occupy the Presidio barracks at San Francisco Captain Smith's company, 1st dragoons, now garrisons that. The company of the 3d artillery, soon to arrive, should at once take post there, though a much greater force is required for the purpose of repairing the old fort at the entrance of the harbor, and mounting as early as practicable a few heavy guns; but it is useless to attempt to keep such a force there, as the gold fever, the season for which is at hand, will take off nearly the whole of any force at that post. Company F, 3d artillery, now here, is sufficient for Monterey.

The whole of Brevet Brigadier General Riley's command should disembark at San Diego, and take post at the mission of San Luis Rey, distant about 39 miles, leaving a small force at San Diego. The two companies of the 1st dragoons now at Los Angeles should also take post at the mission of San Luis Rey, leaving Brevet Major Graham's command at Los Angeles.

The above-named mission will afford ample quarters and storehouses for the whole of this command, and the troops will be more out of the gold mania. From its position, detachments can easily be thrown into either Warner's or the Cajori pass, or further on, in the direction of the junction of the Colorado and Gila rivers, at or near which point, I think, it will be found necessary to establish a military post.

The Indians are troublesome and commit depredations upon the settlements in all parts of the country, particularly to the south. There should be a small post on the waters of the San Joaquin, east of San Luis Obispo, with a view to protection against the Indians; and also one in the Sacramento valley, some distance north of Sutter's Fort; but so long as the gold mines continue to yield in the abundance they now do, it will be impossible to keep soldiers in those valleys, and it will be useless to put them there.

I am, respectfully,
R. B. MASON,
Colonel 1st Dragoons, commanding.

Lieutenant A. GIBBS,
Mounted Rifles, A. A. A. General, 3d div'sion.

HEADQUARTERS TENTH MILITARY DEPARTMENT,
Monterey, California, February 28, 1849.

CAPTAIN: In acknowledging the receipt of your communication of the 7th instant, I am instructed by the colonel commanding the department to say that, under the peculiar circumstances existing in California, you will exercise a sound discretion in granting furloughs to your men—to such numbers, and for such periods, as shall be most consistent with the interests of the service.

Very respectfully, captain, your obedient servant,
ED. R. S. CANBY,
Assistant Adjutant General.

Captain A. J. SMITH,
1st Dragoons, commanding, &c., San Francisco.

HEADQUARTERS TENTH MILITARY DEPARTMENT,
Monterey, California, March 1, 1849.

SIR: The American steamship "California" arrived here on the 23d ult., and brought me a copy from the Adjutant General of your instructions of the 5th of October, and I hasten, by the first opportunity, to inform you that the whole of the 2d infantry are to disembark at San Diego, and to take post at the mission of San Diego, distant about thirty-nine miles, leaving such a force at San Diego as you may think proper. Never more than one company has garrisoned that post.

San Luis Rey will afford your command ample quarters and storehouses for everything, and it is the only place in California that can shelter so comfortably your whole regiment; and, besides, it is the most suitable point at which to locate the main depot and force in the south.

Brevet Major Graham, commanding at Los Angeles, will be directed to send to San Luis Rey, to await your arrival at San Diego, all the wagons and teams that he can spare. Captain Folsom, assistant quartermaster at San Francisco, has been instructed to send provisions and lumber, (if any can be obtained,) iron, nails, &c., to San Diego, suitable for making or repairing doors, windows, &c. He is also directed to send a number of new wagons and harness. Teams you will have to pick up in the lower country, and perhaps put ox-tongues to your wagons, and work oxen.

Should the transport-ship having on board company M, 3d artillery, and the detachment of fifty recruits, put into San Diego, please order her to San Francisco, touching at Monterey to land the recruits, and then proceeding to San Francisco to land company M. Should any vacancies exist in the companies of the 2d infantry, you had better fill them from these recruits, bearing in mind that the company at this place requires some thirty-odd to fill it up to sixty-four.

I am, sir, very respectfully, your obedient servant,
R. B. MASON,
Colonel 1st Dragoons, commanding.

Brevet Brig. Gen. RILEY, or
SENIOR OFFICER *of the transport first arriving at San Diego.*

HEADQUARTERS TENTH MILITARY DEPARTMENT,
Monterey, California, March 1, 1849.

CAPTAIN: The colonel commanding directs that you send by the barque Anita to San Diego, for the use of General Riley's command, *twenty* four-horse wagons and *ten* one-horse carts, with harness, &c., complete, from those now in store at San Francisco. You will also send a sufficient supply of scythes to enable the troops to cut grass for the public animals.

The colonel suggests (a suggestion only) that the master of the Anita be instructed to touch at Santa Cruz and take on a deck load of lumber for San Diego. If the vessel is not capable of carrying at one trip all the supplies required for San Pedro and San Diego, it will be advisable to load her with a portion of each, and make two trips.

Very respectfully, captain, your obedient servant,
ED. R. S. CANBY,
Assistant Adjutant General

Captain J. L. FOLSOM,
Assistant Quartermaster U. S. A.,
San Francisco, California.

[18]

CIRCULAR.

The colonel commanding the tenth military department requires, as soon as practicable, a list of all public property received from Colonel Fremont's battalion, or any agent or member thereof, with an estimate of the value of the articles at the time they were received. The list will also state the condition of the property as receipted for, serviceable or unserviceable, good or bad condition, according to the facts. Any horse, gun, or other article that may have been restored to the original owner, will be mentioned in the column of remarks.

Very respectfully,
ED. R. S. CANBY,
Assistant Adjutant General.

HEADQUARTERS TENTH MILITARY DEPARTMENT,
Monterey, California, March 1, 1849.

HEADQUARTERS TENTH MILITARY DEPARTMENT,
Monterey, California, March 7, 1849.

MAJOR: The colonel commanding the department directs that the squadron of 1st dragoons, now under your command at Los Angeles, be immediately sent to the mission at San Luis Rey. The quartermaster of the squadron will be instructed to take with him to San Luis all the public wagons that can be spared from Los Angeles. They will be placed at the disposition of General Riley for the transportation of his command from San Diego to the mission, upon his arrival at the former place, which it is supposed he will reach some time in the course of the month of April. The command need not take a large supply of subsistence stores to San Luis, as an abundant supply will be sent by sea to San Diego.

Instructions for the command of the squadron are sent herewith, under cover to you.

The express from your post, due at this place on the 1st instant, has not yet arrived. The colonel commanding desires that your attention be called to this subject, and that you give at Los Angeles such directions as will insure its regular arrival in future.

You will instruct your quartermaster to establish an express from San Luis Rey to Los Angeles, running in connexion with the regular expresses from Los Angeles to this place.

Very respectfully, major, your obedient servant,
ED. R. S. CANBY,
Assistant Adjutant General.

Brevet Major L. P. GRAHAM,
2d Dragoons, commanding, Los Angeles.

HEADQUARTERS TENTH MILITARY DEPARTMENT,
Monterey, California, March 7, 1849.

MAJOR: I am instructed by the colonel commanding the department to say that, on the arrival of your squadron at the mission of San Luis Rey, you will take all necessary measures to preserve the public property, buildings, gardens, and vineyards attached to the mission, and will instruct your quartermaster to use all the means under his control for the repair of such of the buildings as may be required as quarters, &c. for troops.

The greater part of the 2d infantry (probably *nine* companies) will be established at San Luis. They will debark at San Diego, and may be expected to arrive at that post in the months of April and May. Select quarters for your command with reference to this and to convenient stabling for your horses.

The quartermaster of your command will be instructed to take with him from Los Angeles all the wagons that can be spared from that post. These, with the wagons and carts that have been ordered from San Francisco to San Diego, will probably be sufficient for the movement of the 2d infantry to San Luis, and the transportation of the necessary supplies. You are desired to instruct your quartermaster to put his wagons, harness, &c. in good condition for this service, and to see that all the spare transportation at your post is placed at the disposition of General Riley, as soon as you hear of his arrival at San Diego.

If you should find, upon your arrival at San Luis, any priests belonging to the mission, or if any should arrive there subsequently, you will furnish them with suitable quarters, and treat them with all proper courtesy and respect. It is understood that there are attached to the mission a building and garden, intended for the exclusive use of the padres. If now occupied by them, they will be continued in possession, or put in possession if any should reach the mission subsequent to your arrival.

Supplies for the troops at San Luis Rey have been ordered by sea from San Francisco to San Diego.

Very respectfully, major, your obedient servant,
ED. R. S. CANBY,
Assistant Adjutant General.

Brevet Major D. H. RUCKER,
Commanding squadron 1st Dragoons.

Under cover to commanding officer at Los Angeles.

HEADQUARTERS TENTH MILITARY DEPARTMENT,
Monterey, California, March 13, 1849.

SIR: I have the honor to acknowledge the receipt, on the 10th instant, of the general's communication of the 5th instant. You will see by my letter of the 1st instant, (copy herewith,) addressed to Brevet Brigadier General Riley, or senior officer on board the transport ship first arriving at San Diego, as also by my letters of the 7th instant, severally addressed to Brevet Majors Graham and Rucker, (copies already forwarded to division headquarters,) the information communicated relative to the debarcation of the 2d infantry, should any of the ships having companies of that regiment on board first put into San Diego, their taking post at San Luis Rey, and the steps taken to furnish them with transportation and supplies.

The country should be well examined with a view to the selection of sites for the posts at Warner's pass, and at or in the vicinity of the mouth of the Gila river, before any detachment to garrison there is made from San Luis Rey. I am well aware of the necessity of stationing both cavalry and infantry north of the bay of San Francisco; but the only obstacle is the almost absolute certainty of losing seven-tenths of them by desertion from being brought within the direct influence of the gold mines.

The company of artillery now here should remain. Instructions will be sent to the collector at San Francisco in accordance with the general's suggestion.

Very respectfully, your obedient servant,
R. B. MASON,
Colonel 1st Dragoons, commanding.

Lieut. W. T. SHERMAN,
First Lieutenant 3d Artillery,
A. A. A. General third division.

HEADQUARTERS TENTH MILITARY DEPARTMENT,
Monterey, California, March 22, 1849.

SIR: I am directed by the colonel commanding the department to acknowledge the receipt of your communication of the 20th instant, making an application for a change of station from the post of Monterey to that of San Francisco, and asking that your limits may be extended from the latter to a circuit of 160 miles.

It is believed that your commanding officer, Captain Burton, has already awarded to you all the indulgences that an arrested officer can reasonably expect, and to comply with your wishes would be attaching no importance to the grave charge which now lies against you. It would be prejudicial to military discipline, in making the service bend to the wishes and convenience of an officer by sending him nominally to a post when his services are not required, and by granting him favors and indulgences which, at the present time, can be extended to no officer of the department.

Very respectfully, sir, your obedient servant,
ED. R. S. CANBY,
Assistant Adjutant General.

Lieut. M. R. STEVENSON,
Seventh Infantry, Monterey, California.

HEADQUARTERS TENTH MILITARY DEPARTMENT,
Monterey, California, March 22, 1849.

SIR: I last night received your letter of the 15th instant. I have directed Captain Burton to send you twenty-five pounds of powder and fifty pounds of lead or balls.

Upon the receipt of this powder and lead you will do us the favor to distribute it to the *farmers* and such *other persons* as will use it in *a proper manner* for the protection and defence of the settlement in the vicinity of San Luis Obispo, and along down in that quarter. Be careful into whose hands you place it; distribute it in small quantities, and, if any should be left, place it in the hands of the alcalde for future distribution, with whom please leave this letter for his guidance as to the persons to whom he should give it.

Very respectfully, your obedient servant,
R. B. MASON,
Colonel 1st Dragoons, commanding.
W. R. GARNER, *San Luis Obispo, California.*

HEADQUARTERS TENTH MILITARY DEPARTMENT,
Monterey, California, March 22, 1849.

SIR: I am instructed by Colonel Mason to say that, in the execution of the duties assigned you by department special orders No. 9, of this date, you will govern yourself, unless the plan should be changed by the authority of the division commander, by the plan and instructions prepared by Lieutenant Halleck, corps of engineers, under the instructions of General Kearny of May 4, 1847, for repairing and arming this battery, (San Joaquin,) and submitted by him to Lieutenant J. A. Hardie, 3d artillery, then major New York volunteers, and commanding at San Francisco.

These plans, &c., are supposed to be in your office, or in the possession of Lieutenant Hardie.

Very respectfully, sir, your obedient servant,
EDWARD R. S. CANBY,
Assistant Adjutant General.

COMMANDING OFFICER
Presidio of San Francisco, San Francisco, California.

HEADQUARTERS TENTH MILITARY DEPARTMENT,
Monterey, California, April 15, 1849.

MAJOR: Your several communications of the 25th ultimo have been received, and submitted to the commanding general.

Your application for leave of absence has been forwarded by him to division headquarters, with the following endorsement: "Major Graham being under orders from higher authority, (instructions from Adjutant General's office,) I cannot, as I would under other circumstances very gladly do, recommend that the indulgence applied for be granted." The applications for transfer have also been forwarded to division headquarters, with a recommendation that the necessary action should be taken there. Under the peculiar circumstances of the case, the surgeon's certificates of ordinary disability have been forwarded to division headquarters, with a like recommendation. The application of Sergeant Cady for discharge has been approved and forwarded.

We have accounts here (not official) of a number of desertions from your command, and particularly from that of Major Rucker, on the march to San Luis Rey, which the general hopes are greatly exaggerated. He has, however, directed the immediate transfer of the musicians, farriers, and privates of your command to the 1st dragoons, and tne abandonment of Los Angeles as a military post.

He desires that the measures necessary in consequence of these orders be taken with as little delay as practicable, and with a view to the best interests of the service. At this distance, and in the absence of more certain information, he cannot give you more definite instructions.

Captain Kane, after completing the duties necessarily devolving upon him in consequence of these orders, will be ordered by you to report at department headquarters.

The general desires that you advise him as early as possible of the receipt of these orders, and the measures you have taken in carrying them out. If any outrages have been committed upon the inhabitants in your neighborhood, please report all the information in relation to them that may be in your possession.

Very respectfully, major, your obedient servant,
ED. R. S. CANBY,
Assistant Adjutant General.

Major L. P. GRAHAM,
Commanding Squadron 2d Dragoons, Los Angeles.

HEADQUARTERS TENTH MILITARY DEPARTMENT,
Monterey, California, April 15, 1849.

MAJOR: I have the honor to enclose herewith, by direction of the commanding general, orders 11, 12, 13, and 14, current series.

The company required for the escort of the commissioners you will please equip and send to San Diego as soon as practicable. Accounts (of unofficial character) have reached this place with regard to desertions from your command, which the general hopes are greatly exaggerated. He, however, directs that, if the enlisted men transferred from the 2d dragoons be not enough to fill up both of the companies of your squadron, the company designated for the escort of the commissioners be first filled up and sent, as above directed, to San Diego.

The headquarters of the other company will remain until further orders at San Luis Rey. You will grant any reasonable indulgences to your men that will, in your estimation, have a tendency to prevent desertion. Secure the public property by paying liberally, under the provisions of division orders No. 5, the non-commissioned officers and men in charge of it.

The general directs that the receipt of these orders, and the measures you have taken in carrying them out, be reported to him as soon as practicable. For this purpose, you will please communicate with Major Graham, who will probably send an extra express to this post.

If any outrages have been committed upon the inhabitants of the country, you will please report all the information in relation to them that may be in your possession.

Very respectfully, major, your obedient servant,
ED. R. S. CANBY,
Assistant Adjutant General.

Major D. H. RUCKER,
Or officer commanding 1st *Dragoons, San Luis Rey*

HEADQUARTERS TENTH MILITARY DEPARTMENT,
Monterey, California, April 16, 1849.

SIR: I have bestowed an attentive consideration on the several communications on the files and records of this office from the general commanding the division, and Colonel Mason, recently commanding the department, relative to the temporary disposition of the troops in this Territory, and to the other sources of information within my reach. As this consideration has resulted in a conviction differing materially from that experienced by Colonel Mason, and assented to in great part by General P. Smith, I respectfully submit for his consideration a disposition of the troops intended for this department, which I hope will meet his approbation:

The companies "F" and "M," 3d artillery, are required for the depots at Monterey and San Francisco. The transport Fanny Forrester, which is hourly expected, will, accordingly, after landing the recruits for company "F," be ordered to proceed immediately with company "M" for San Francisco. Two companies of the 2d infantry and one of the 1st dragoons are required, and are now under orders, for service at or near San Diego; one company 2d infantry for the depot at that place; the company 1st dragoons, and other companies of the 2d infantry, for the escort required by general orders No. 65, 1848. Two companies of the 2d infantry, now in this harbor, will, under instructions from division headquarters of the 19th ultimo, be ordered to the bay of San Francisco. The 5th company of that regiment, now at this place, will be retained here for the present, with a view to reinforce the garrison of San Diego, if it should be greatly reduced, as there is much reason to apprehend it will be, by desertions.

The remainder of the troops I propose to distribute as follows: Three companies of the 2d infantry, on their arrival, and the company of the 1st dragoons now at the Presidio of San Francisco, at some healthy position in the immediate vicinity of the mines south of the junction of the San Joaquin and Sacramento rivers; the remaining companies of the 2d infantry, and one company of the 1st dragoons, if its organization can be retained, at or in the vicinity of the pass leading from the country in rear of San Luis Obispo to the Zulaces valley.

Information from the south, from authentic (although not official) sources, shows that, with very few exceptions, the dragoons of the squadron of the 1st regiment deserted upon being ordered to San Luis Rey. Many had previously deserted from Los Angeles, carrying with them their horses, arms, and equipments; and it is believed that the desertions at that place will be greatly increased when the order breaking up the companies of the 2d dragoons is received; so that I fear I shall not be able to organize from *four* companies of dragoons *one* required for the escort of the commissioners. It is known that these deserters had committed many outrages upon the property, and it is feared, upon the persons, of the inhabitants they encountered in their route to the mines. Unable to carry the means of subsistence with them, they have plundered from the ranches on the road. The gold mania is greater at a distance from the mines than in their immediate neighborhood. The experiment of preventing desertions by placing troops at a distance from the mines has been fully tried, and has signally failed; and the same result will attend any similar disposition of the troops in future, and will be attended with greater suffering to the inhabitants if the deserters be from the infantry, as they will be longer upon the road and have greater wants to supply than deserters from a mounted corps.

The disposition I have proposed will be an experiment, but one that should be tried, if only for the sake of preventing a repetition of the outrages unoffending people have suffered from those they have been led to suppose would protect them from Indian depredations and domestic violence. It is reasonable to suppose that troops stationed within the vicinity of the placer, with permission to work a portion of their time for their own benefit, will willingly devote the remainder to military duties, for the sake of the clothing, subsistence, and medical attendence furnished them by the government.

They can be placed in tents during the summer, and, with the abundance of timber on the slopes of the Sierra, can easily build quarters before the commencement of the rainy season. It is believed that the necessary supplies can be transported by water to within a very short distance of the posts to be established, and that the additional expense will not equal the value of property that has already been lost or destroyed by desertions.

The mass of the population will be in the mines, and the presence of troops in that neighborhood will have a salutary effect upon the lawless and turbulent of our own people, as well as upon the Indians of that region, if they should become troublesome. It is probable, too, that it may have a tendency to diminish desertions in commands that are necessarily stationed at a distance from the mineral region. Under present circumstances, if no other result be obtained than that of keeping embodied a respectable portion of the troops, it will be well worth the experiment; and it is my settled conviction that this result can be attained in no other way.

For the troops stationed at a distance from the mines, a system of periodical exchanges, well understood and uniformly acted upon; furloughs, granted to such numbers and for such lengths of time as may be most consistent with the interests of the service; a liberal use of the provision of paragraph 3, division orders No. 5; and permission to the enlisted men to labor for their own benefit when not employed for the government—will, it is believed, have a great tendency to render them contented, and diminish the number of desertions.

The Tulan Indians, emboldened by the absence of many of the male inhabitants of the country in the vicinity of San Luis Obispo, have become more daring in their incursions. Depredations are more frequent than formerly, and several murders have recently been committed; and it will be necessary to establish troops in that vicinity for the protection of the inhabitants. The remarks made above, intended for troops stationed in the vicinity of the northern placers, will apply also to a command stationed in the vicinity of the pass by San Luis Obispo. Mines recently discovered in the Sierra, east of that place, are now being successfully worked; and the troops stationed there, by being permitted to visit them, will be contented. Their presence will intimidate the Indians in that neighborhood, and detachments may be made to punish them, if necessary. Troops stationed in the south might be furloughed to visit the mines, when it would be impracticable for them to reach the upper mines in any reasonable length of time.

I have written hastily, with a view to obtain the general's views upon these matters as early as possible, and, if his concurrence is obtained, in order that suitable positions for the troops to occupy may be selected before their arrival in this country.

I have the honor to be, very respectfully, sir, your obedient servant,
B. RILEY,
Brevet Brigadier General, commanding 10th Mil. Department.

W. T. SHERMAN,
3d Art., A. A. A. Gen. 3d Division, San Francisco, California.

HEADQUARTERS TENTH MILITARY DEPARTMENT,
Monterey, California, April 17, 1849.

MAJOR: I am instructed by the commanding general to enclose herewith a communication for the United States commissioner, which you will please hand him on his arrival. It is unnecessary to request that the commissioners should be treated with all proper courtesy and respect during their stay at your post. You will cause them to be furnished with everything that may facilitate their operations while at San Diego, and after their surveys are commenced.

Communications are sent by this mail for the commanding officers at San Luis Rey and Los Angeles. The general directs that they be forwarded by a trusty person, immediately after their receipt, to San Luis Rey, and, if the garrison for that place has not arrived, to Los Angeles.

You are desired to use all practicable measures to prevent desertions, and are authorized to grant furloughs, and any other reasonable indulgence that in your estimation will have a beneficial effect. Secure the public property by paying liberally, under the provisions of division orders No. 5, current series, the non-commissioned officers and privates in charge of it. You will make reports of the state of your command, and of other matters of interest, as often as opportunities occur.

Very respectfully, major, your obedient servant,
E. R. S. CANBY,
Assistant Adjutant General.

Brevet Major S. P. HEINTZELMAN,
Commanding 2d Infantry, San Diego.

HEADQUARTERS TENTH MILITARY DEPARTMENT,
Monterey, California, April 17, 1849.

SIR: I have the honor to enclose for your information copies of department orders Nos. 1,112 and 1,113, current series.

The commanding officer at San Diego has been instructed to furnish you with all the facilities under his control during your stay at San Diego, and after your operations have been commenced.

I will be happy to receive any suggestions that may, in your estimation, tend to facilitate those operations.

I have the honor to be, very respectfully, sir, your obedient servant,

B. RILEY,
Brevet Brig. Gen., com'g Tenth Military Department.

Hon. JNO. B. WELLER,
U. S. Com'r, (care of Major Heintzelman, San Diego.)

HEADQUARTERS TENTH MILITARY DEPARTMENT,
Monterey, California, April 20, 1849.

MAJOR: As it is uncertain whether the supplies ordered to San Diego by the department instructions of February 25 and March 1 have yet reached that place, you are desired, if there should not be a sufficiency of supplies there, to communicate with Majors Graham and Rucker, and obtain from the posts of Los Angeles and San Luis Rey any supplies that may be needed for your command. It is not intended at present to send to the south more supplies than are needed for the commands of San Luis Rey and San Diego; and, in order to ascertain what supplies are already in that quarter, you will instruct the quartermaster and commissary of your command to report to this office, by the first opportunity after the receipt of this communication, what stores they now have on hand.

Captain Kane, assistant quartermaster United States army, has been instructed to send, after the removal of the public property from Los Angeles is completed, to San Luis Rey, the wagons and other means of transportation at Los Angeles, to be within reach of San Diego, if required there.

It is expected also that a considerable portion of the property at that place will be transferred to San Luis Rey, and the remainder to San Pedro, for embarcation for San Francisco, but may be sent to San Diego if it will be useful there. Please communicate with Major Graham as soon as possible, and advise him of your wants in this respect. It will be necessary, after the abandonment of Los Angeles, to send the express rider from your post through to Dana's ranch, instead of Los Angeles, as directed in department orders No. 10.

Very respectfully, major, your obedient servant,

E. R. S. CANBY,
Assistant Adjutant General.

Major S. P. HEINTZELMAN,
Second Infantry, commanding, San Diego, California.

HEADQUARTERS TENTH MILITARY DEPARTMENT,
Monterey, California, April 17, 1849.

CAPTAIN: If it be decided to send the public property at Los Angeles to San Pedro for embarcation for San Francisco, the commanding general directs that you give your attention to its embarcation before acting upon the orders which you will receive from Major Graham to repair to these headquarters.

One or more vessels will be sent very soon to San Diego with troops and supplies. By communicating with the quartermaster at that place, arrangements may be made for one of them to touch at San Pedro for the property there.

Wagons and other means of transportation should be sent with the transferred men to San Luis Rey, in order that it may be within reach of San Diego, if required by the commissioners or for other purposes.

Very respectfully, captain, your obedient servant,
E. R. S. CANBY,
Assistant Adjutant General.

Captain E. K. KANE,
Assistant Quartermaster U. S. A., Los Angeles.

[Under cover to commanding officer at Los Angeles.]

HEADQUARTERS TENTH MILITARY DEPARTMENT,
Monterey, California, April 20, 1849.

MAJOR: As it is not intended at present to send more supplies to the south than may be absolutely necessary for the commands at San Luis Rey and San Diego, Major Heintzelman, commanding at the latter place, has been instructed to communicate with Major Rucker and yourself, and obtain from San Luis Rey and your post the supplies needed for his command.

Some embarrassment is experienced by the general in giving instructions for the disposition of the public property at Los Angeles, from the want of the customary reports from the quartermaster and commissary of your command.

It is hoped that they will be able to forward them by the mail which leaves your post on the 6th proximo. In the mean time, I am instructed to say that it is desirable, as indicated in department orders No. 14, if there be a sufficiency of land transportation at Los Angeles, to send all the public property at that place to San Luis Rey.

If the reports in regard to the number of desertions from your command be true, the general apprehends that you will experience some difficulty in securing the public property at your post from loss; in this contingency, he desires you to exercise your discretion, with a view to the best interests of the service, in giving directions for the disposition of this property.

If the property be not sent to San Pedro, and cannot be immediately embarked, Mr. Alexander, the collector at that port, is suggested as a suitable person to be put in charge of it.

Very respectfully, major, your obedient servant,
E. R. S. CANBY,
Assistant Adjutant General.

Major L. P. GRAHAM,
Second Dragoons, Los Angeles, California.

HEADQUARTERS SECOND INFANTRY,
Monterey, California, April 21, 1849.

GENERAL: I have the honor to acknowledge the receipt of general orders No. 4, dated "War Department, Adjutant General's office, Washington, January 24, 1849," in regard to certificates of merit. All the recommendations for the 2d infantry that have been received at regiment headquarters have already been forwarded.

I have also to acknowledge the receipt of your letter of the 16th January, 1849, enclosing certificates of merit for privates Meridith Qualls and Vernon B. West, transferred from the 4th infantry to the 2d infantry.

I am, general, very respectfully, your obedient servant,

B. RILEY,
Brevet Brig. Gen. U. S. A., commanding
Tenth Military Dept. and 2d Infantry.

Brigadier General R. JONES,
Adjutant General U. S. A., Washington, D. C.

HEADQUARTERS TENTH MILITARY DEPARTMENT,
Monterey, California, May 4, 1849.

MAJOR: Your communication of the 1st instant, reporting the arrival of the battalion of the 2d infantry under your command, has been received and submitted to the commanding general, by whom I am directed to enclose department special orders No. 19, indicating the disposition to be made of the companies of your command.

The camp to be established at or near the main crossing of the San Joaquin will be a temporary one; but care will be taken in selecting a dry and healthy position, in the neighborhood of good water and abundance of wood. As soon as the necessary arrangements can be made, a topographical examination of that part of the country will be made, with a view to the selection of a more permanent position. In the mean time, you are desired to collect and report for the information of the commanding general all the information that may be useful in determining such a selection.

You are authorized to grant furloughs, so soon as your camp is established, to the men of your command, and any other reasonable indulgence that may in your estimation have a tendency to prevent desertions; and you will endeavor to secure the public property by paying liberally, under the provisions of division order No. 5, current series, the non-commissioned officers and men that may be placed in charge of it.

It is supposed here that your command and the necessary supplies can more readily reach the position to which you are ordered in launches than by any other means; but you are desired to consult with the assistant quartermaster at San Francisco, and to furnish him with any assistance that may be useful in manning the launches or vessels by which your command is sent up. The men so employed should be paid. Instructions more in detail will be furnished you in a few days.

If Major Seawell should not arrive by the next steamer, the command of the 2d infantry will be turned over to you, and the headquarters of the regiment established in some central position; until then, the interest of the service requires that you should remain in the position to which you are now assigned.

I have the honor to be, very respectfully, your obedient servant,
E. R. S. CANBY,
Assistant Adjutant General.

Major A. S. MILLER,
Second Infantry, commanding Battalion, &c., &c.,
San Francisco.

HEADQUARTERS TENTH MILITARY DEPARTMENT,
Monterey, California, May 5, 1849.

MAJOR: The principal object to be attained in establishing your company in the vicinity of Sutter's Fort will be the prevention of difficulties between the Americans and Indians of that neighborhood. These difficulties, resulting from alleged outrages by the Indians, have been followed by serious aggresssions on the part of the whites, which, if not prevented by the speedy interposition of some controlling force, will result in the most serious consequences. The nature of these difficulties is more fully explained by the reports of the Indian agent in that district, copies of which are herewith furnished you. I also enclose, for your information and government, an extract from the instructions heretofore given the agent, with whom it is desired that you should communicate freely and fully. The commanding general directs that you should use all the means under your control to effect this object; and for this purpose you will consider yourself invested with full discretionary powers to act as the best interests of the service and the country may require. Unauthorized interferences with the Indians by the whites must, if possible, be prevented; and, on the other hand, the Indians, through the agent, will receive assurances of protection, if their conduct be such as to warrant it. They will be advised to remain quiet in the pursuit of their ordinary occupations, and, when aggrieved, to make their complaints through their agent to the proper authorities; that any attempt to revenge themselves for any real or fancied injury will not be permitted; and that offenders in every instance will be sought out and severely punished. If any outrage be committed, you will require the offenders to be delivered up; and if this be not done promptly, you will hold the tribe or the rancheria to which the offenders belong responsible for their conduct.

The position you may occupy for your camp should be carefully selected, with reference to health, and the advantage of wood and water, and convenience to the landing place for your supplies.

The general desires that you will collect and report any information that may be useful in determining the selection of a position for a military post in the vicinity of Sutter's, or higher up on the Sacramento, indicating particularly the resources of the country, the number of Indians in that quarter, their disposition towards the Americans, &c., &c. So soon as your command is established, you will consider yourself authorized to grant furloughs to the men of your command, and any other reasonable indulgence that may in your estimation have a tendency to prevent desertions. Endeavor to secure the public property from loss by paying liberally, under the provisions of division orders No. 5, the non-commissioned officers and men in charge of it.

Instructions more in detail will be furnished you in a few days. Major Miller will be instructed to furnish you with copies of division and department orders forwarded to him by the mail. Your command will be reinforced, on the arrival of the transport Mary and Adeline, by another company. The general directs that you make frequent reports of the state of your command and of affairs in your neighborhood.

I have the honor to be, very respectfully, major, your obedient servant,
ED. R. S. CANBY,
Assistant Adjutant General.

Major J. J. B. KINGSBURY,
Commanding, &c., &c., Sutter's Fort.

HEADQUARTERS TENTH MILITARY DEPARTMENT,
Monterey, California, May 7, 1849.

MAJOR: The commanding general designs establishing a semi-monthly mail connecting the points occupied by troops in the northern military district of California with division and department headquarters.

This mail will leave the most distant military posts, Sutter's Fort, Stockton, Sonoma, &c., immediately after the first and middle (say 3d and 17th) of each month, and San Francisco for this place after the arrival of the mail from Sonoma, and for the posts above after the arrival of the mail for this place. It is supposed that this mail can be more economically transported to and from Benicia, Stockton, Sutter's Fort, and Sonoma, by water than by land; and you are desired to ascertain and report for the general's information what arrangements can be made for its transportation, as above suggested, that will insure regularity and as much despatch as possible. If the means of transportation employed in forwarding troops and supplies furnish you the necessary facilities, it will of course be proper to use them in preference to any other, as the means of carrying this mail should be kept as much as possible under the control of the officers of the quartermaster's department. It is designed to offer to citizens the opportunity of communicating by this mail on all the routes where the United States mail agents have not made arrangements for the transportation of mails.

Very respectfully, major, your obedient servant,
EDWARD R. S. CANBY,
Assistant Adjutant General.

Major E. H. FITZGERALD,
Assistant Quartermaster U. S. A., San Francisco.

HEADQUARTERS TENTH MILITARY DEPARTMENT,
Monterey, California, May 7, 1849.

MAJOR: The intimate contact between the whites and Indians in the neighborhood of your post has given rise to many collisions between them, in which it is extremely difficult to ascertain which party was originally in the wrong. To explain the nature of the difficulties now existing, I enclose copies of reports from the Indian agent of that district, and, also, for your information and government, an extract from the instructions heretofore given him.

The commanding general directs that you use the utmost exertions to preserve quiet and order in your neighborhood, and to prevent any collisions between the whites and Indians. For this purpose, you will consider yourself invested with full discretionary power to act as the interests of the service and the country may require. Unauthorized interference with the Indians by the whites must, if possible, be prevented; and, on the other hand, the Indians will receive, through their agent, assurances of protection, if their conduct be such as to merit it; they will be advised to remain quiet in the pursuit of their ordinary occupations, and, when aggrieved, to make their complaints to the proper authorities; that any attempt to revenge themselves for fancied or real injuries will not be permitted, and that the offenders will in every instance be sought out and severely punished.

If any outrages are committed, you will require the offenders to be delivered up; and if this be not done promptly, you will hold the tribe or rancheria to which they belong responsible for their conduct. The Indians most likely to give trouble in your quarter reside in the neighborhood of the Merced river and of the Tulans. If the state of your command will permit it, you will make occasional detachments in that direction for the purpose of overawing these Indians, or punishing them for any outrages they may commit.

Your command will be reinforced on the arrival of the Mary and Adeline by another company.

Very respectfully, your obedient servant,
EDWARD R. S. CANBY,
Assistant Adjutant General.

Major A. S. MILLER, 2d *Infantry.*

CIRCULAR.

HEADQUARTERS TENTH MILITARY DEPARTMENT,
Monterey, California, May 10, 1849.

All sums heretofore transferred from the military-contribution fund to officers of the pay, quartermaster's, and subsistence department, in California, will immediately be refunded. If the funds in the hands of any officer pertaining to the department in which he is serving should be insufficient to meet his indebtedness to the military-contribution fund, the fact will be reported promptly for the information and action of the commanding general.

By order of General Riley:
ED. R. S. CANBY,
Assistant Adjutant General.

[18]

HEADQUARTERS TENTH MILITARY DEPARTMENT,
Monterey, California, May 15, 1849.

CAPTAIN: The commanding general has learned, with much surprise, by a report from the commanding officer at San Diego, that the supplies ordered to that place by department instructions of February 25 and March 1 have not been received, and that the vessel sent down, after landing at San Pedro the supplies intended for the dragoon command at Los Angeles, returned to San Francisco; and he now directs you to report, for his information, why these instructions were not complied with.

Very respectfully, captain, your obedient servant,

E. R. S. CANBY,
Assistant Adjutant General.

Captain J. L. FOLSOM,
Assistant Quartermaster U. S. A., San Francisco.

HEADQUARTERS TENTH MILITARY DEPARTMENT,
Monterey, California, May 18, 1849.

MAJOR: The commanding general has been much disappointed in learning that the supplies ordered from San Francisco to San Diego, in February and March last, have not yet reached that place, and that the garrison would, after a few days, be (and probably now is) dependent upon the supplies at San Luis Rey. Believing that the supplies then ordered, if not already at San Diego, would reach that place soon after the arrival of the troops ordered there, but a limited supply was sent down with them; and the same reasons influenced Colonel Mason in directing that a small quantity of subsistence should be sent from Los Angeles to San Luis Rey.

The failure of these supplies to reach San Diego, besides subjecting the troops to much inconvenience from the want of many indispensable articles, will probably embarrass the quartermaster and commissary of that post in supplying the escort for the commissioners; and the general accordingly directs that a vessel be sent immediately to San Diego with such supplies of subsistence and quartermaster's stores as may be necessary for the immediate wants of the garrison and escort.

The supplies recently sent by Captain Folsom to San Pedro will be transferred to San Diego, as will also those sent from Los Angeles to San Pedro upon the abandonment of Los Angeles. The vessel to be sent down by you will be placed at the disposal of the acting quartermaster at San Diego until the transfer of this property is completed.

It is the intention of the commanding general that there should be at San Diego supplies for six months for the garrison of that place and the escort of the commissioners—say 300 persons; and you are desired to ascertain from Captain Folsom what supplies were sent to San Pedro, and if any have since been sent direct to San Diego, and govern yourself in the quantity now to be sent by the information you may receive from him.

I enclose, for your information, copies of the instructions to Captain Folsom, and a list of articles required by the quartermaster at San Diego.

If these articles on this list have not already been sent, they will now be furnished. The wagons and carts ordered from San Francisco, and those at Los Angeles and San Luis Rey, (already ordered to San Diego,) will probably meet the wants of the service in that kind of transportation; but as the route to be travelled by the commissioners may be impracticable for wagons, the general directs that one hundred pack-saddles be sent to the quartermaster at San Diego.

From five to eight hundred feet of lumber, suitable for doors, windows, &c., &c., will also be sent down. If any of the vessels sent out by the quartermaster's department for service on the Pacific coast are now at your disposal, the general directs that one of them be sent to San Diego, in preference to chartering a private vessel.

Very respectfully, major, your obedient servant,
E. R. S. CANBY,
Assistant Adjutant General.

Major E. H. FITZGERALD,
Assistant Quartermaster U. S. A., San Francisco.

HEADQUARTERS TENTH MILITARY DEPARTMENT,
Monterey, California, May 18, 1849.

CAPTAIN: The commanding general directs that you ascertain from Captain J. L. Folsom, assistant quartermaster, what subsistence stores have recently been sent to San Pedro and San Diego, and there put up and turn over to the assistant quartermaster at San Francisco, for transportation to San Diego, such stores as will, with those already sent, make a six-months supply for that post—say for 300 men.

Very respectfully, sir, your obedient servant,
E. R. S. CANBY,
Assistant Adjutant General.

Captain G. P ANDREWS,
3d Artillery, Depot Commissary, San Francisco.

HEADQUARTERS TENTH MILITARY DEPARTMENT,
Monterey, California, May 18, 1849.

COMMODORE: Some twenty-five or thirty deserters from the army, recently tried at this place, have been sentenced " to be sent to the Atlantic coast of the United States, to serve out, at hard labor, in confinement, the remainder of their term of service, at such station as the War Department may direct."

Believing that this sentence, if *carried out*, will produce an exceedingly beneficial effect in preventing many desertions hereafter, I am very anxious to see it carried into full effect, and the prisoners sent home.

It has been suggested to me that an opportunity will soon offer by the return of one of the vessels of your squadron to the Atlantic; and if there is no objection to these men being sent home in a vessel-of-war, I trust that authority will be given to have them thus transported. This mode of conveyance, whilst it will be the most *safe*, so far as the security of the prisoners is concerned, will also be the most economical to the government.

Can I ask of you the favor to allow me to hear from you on the subject, and as to whether an opportunity will soon offer of sending these men to the Atlantic coast by a vessel-of-war, and, if so, if there will be or not any objection to their being thus sent?

I have the honor to be, commodore, very respectfully, your obedient servant.

HEADQUARTERS TENTH MILITARY DEPARTMENT,
Monterey, California, May 18, 1849.

MAJOR: Your communications of the 12th instant have been received and submitted to the commanding general, and I enclose in another package order No. 21, establishing the expresses connecting the military stations in this department.

The general desires that this arrangement should go into effect on the first of next month, if the necessary arrangements can be made in time.

Orders go up by this mail, through Captain Halleck, for the transfer of $100,000 from the military contribution fund.

Very respectfully, your obedient servant,
E. R. S. CANBY,
Assistant Adjutant General.

Major E. H. FITZGERALD,
Assistant Quartermaster U. S. A., San Francisco.

HEADQUARTERS TENTH MILITARY DEPARTMENT,
Monterey, California, May 20, 1849.

MAJOR: Your communication of May 2 has been received and submitted to the commanding general, who is greatly surprised and disappointed in finding that the supplies ordered to San Diego in February and March last have not reached you. Orders were sent to assistant quartermaster at San Francisco to despatch a vessel with supplies for your command immediately. The supplies landed at San Pedro, and those to be sent to Los Angeles from that place, will also be transferred to your post; and, with this view, the general has instructed Major Fitzgerald to place the vessel sent down at the disposal of your quartermaster until the transfer of these supplies is completed. The articles required by Captain Lyon have been ordered, and will be sent from San Francisco. A small supply of lumber will also be sent down for your immediate wants. Requisitions for supplies should be sent to this office for the consideration and action of the commanding general; and you will please instruct your quartermaster to make an estimate in detail of all the supplies that are necessary for the comfort of your command. It is not intended that any permanent structures should be erected at San Diego until the position for a permanent fortification has been determined upon; and the improvements to be made at San Diego will at present be limited to such alterations and repairs in the quarters occupied by your command as may be necessary for the health and comfort of the troops.

Very respectfully, major, your obedient servant,
E. R. S. CANBY,
Assistant Adjutant General.

Major S. P. HEINTZELMAN,
Second Infantry, commanding, &c., &c., San Diego.

HEADQUARTERS TENTH MILITARY DEPARTMENT,
Monterey, California, May 20, 1849.

SIR: I enclose an extract from department orders No. 16, of the 8th instant, by which you will see that your company is to be stationed at a new post to be established near the main crossing of the San Joaquin river; and the commanding general directs that you make, as soon as possible, the necessary arrangements for abandoning San Luis Rey and moving your company to the post above referred to. The public property at your post will be sent to San Diego; and your company property not needed on the march will be packed and sent to that place for transportation to San Francisco, from which place it will be forwarded to you. Means of transportation will be greatly needed at San Diego; and the general directs that you turn over to the quartermaster at that place all now in your possession, except such as may be absolutely necessary for the transportation of the supplies and baggage needed on your march to this place. Tents and other articles of camp and garrison equipage will be supplied you from San Francisco; and you will please make your requisition by the return of this express, in order that it may be sent to Stockton by the time your company reaches this place. Your requisition should be sent to this office for the orders of the commanding general.

Very respectfully, your obedient servant,
ED. R. S. CANBY,
Assistant Adjutant General.

Lieutenant C. J. L. WILSON,
First Dragoons, commanding, &c., &c., San Luis Rey.

HEADQUARTERS TENTH MILITARY DEPARTMENT,
Monterey, California, May 21, 1849.

CAPTAIN: Your communication in relation to the want of supplies at San Diego has been received and submitted to the commanding general; and I am instructed to say in reply that a vessel has been ordered from San Francisco to your post with the supplies you require. The supplies now at San Pedro, and those to be sent from Los Angeles, will be transferred to San Diego. Major Fitzgerald has been instructed to place the vessel sent down with supplies at your disposal until the transfer of the stores from San Pedro is completed.

The post at San Luis Rey will be abandoned; and the commanding officer has been instructed to send the public property at that place to San Diego. He will also send such of his company property as will not be needed on the march to this place to San Diego, for shipment to San Francisco. You will please forward it by the first opportunity to the quartermaster at that place.

The means of transportation at Los Angeles and San Luis Rey, except such as will be absolutely necessary on the march of the company to this place, will be sent to San Diego. It is not known what amount of transportation is on hand at those places; but it is hoped it will be sufficient to meet the wants of the service in that respect. The list of articles sent by

you to Lieutenant Tully has been forwarded to the quartermaster at San Francisco, with instructions to furnish them.
Very respectfully, captain, your obedient servant,
ED. R. S. CANBY,
Assistant Adjutant General.

Captain N. Lyon,
Acting Assistant Quartermaster, &c., San Diego.

Headquarters Tenth Military Department,
Monterey, California, May 21, 1849.

Major: In consequence of the failure of supplies to reach San Diego, the commanding general directs that the property ordered from Los Angeles to San Pedro, there to be embarked for San Francisco, be now sent to San Diego.

If this communication should reach you before leaving Los Angeles, you are desired to give any directions that may be necessary to effect this object.
Very respectfully, major, your obedient servant,
E. R. S. CANBY,
Assistant Adjutant General.

Major L. P. Graham,
2d Dragoons, commanding, Los Angeles, &c.

Headquarters Tenth Military Department,
Monterey, California, May 21, 1849.

Captain: The commanding general has learned from San Diego that the supplies ordered from San Francisco to that place in February and March last have not been received; and in consequence he now directs that the property ordered from Los Angeles to San Pedro be embarked for San Diego, instead of San Francisco, as then directed.

The supplies recently sent to San Pedro by the Olya will also be transferred to San Diego; and the general desires that you make, before leaving for this place, such arrangements for facilitating the shipment of this property as may be in your power.

A vessel has been ordered from San Francisco to San Diego with supplies, and, after discharging her cargo, will be employed in the transfer of the property above referred to.

Company E, 1st dragoons, has been ordered to the placer, and will pass through this place. If you should not be able to leave before that time, it may be more convenient to come up with the company than alone. The steamer Oregon will touch at San Diego about the 5th of next month, and the Panama about a fortnight later.
Very respectfully, captain, your obedient servant,
ED. R. S. CANBY,
Assistant Adjutant General.

Captain E. R. Kam,
Asst. Quartermaster U. S. Army,
Los Angeles, California.

HEADQUARTERS TENTH MILITARY DEPARTMENT,
Monterey, California, June 1, 1849.

MAJOR: The general commanding the department wishes to send by the express which leaves for the south on the 8th instant, the orders, &c., now in the hands of the printer at San Francisco; and if an express should not leave your place on the 4th instant, as directed in department orders No. 21, he directs that one be sent through on the 5th, in order to connect with that going south from this place. The express for San Diego will be detained until the arrival of yours from San Francisco.

Very respectfully, major, your obedient servant,
ED. R. S. CANBY,
Assistant Adjutant General.

Major E. H. FITZGERALD,
Asst. Quartermaster U. S. Army, San Francisco.

HEADQUARTERS TENTH MILITARY DEPARTMENT,
Monterey, California, June 2, 1849.

SIR: The commanding general has received authentic information of the murder of several citizens of this Territory by Indians, on or near the river Los Reyes, and he in consequence directs, that after reaching the mission of San Miguel, you proceed with your company by the pass leading to the valley of the San Joaquin; from that place to the river above indicated, for the purpose of securing these murderers, or the perpetrators of any other outrages that may have been committed in that part of the country.

Some of the persons murdered are understood to be residents of San Luis Obispo, or its vicinity. They belonged to the Mr. Garner of this place, and it is probable that you may gain some useful information from the friends or relations of these persons, as you pass through San Luis Obispo.

The general directs that no exertions be spared in ferreting out these murderers, and if unsuccessful in your efforts, that you seize the chief or head men of the tribe or rancheria to which they belonged, and conduct them with you to the point at which your company is to be stationed. From Los Reyes you will proceed by the valley of the San Joaquin to the neighborhood of Stockton, where you will find, and report to, Major Miller, in accordance with the instructions heretofore sent you.

The result of your expedition will be reported promptly, for the information of the commanding general.

I enclose, for your information and government, extracts from the instructions heretofore issued in relation to intercourse with Indians. In accordance with these, it will be your duty to investigate the circumstances connected with any outrages of which you may be advised on your march down the San Joaquin, to seize the offenders, if possible, and to hold them until you receive the orders of the general.

Your baggage will be sent, under a small escort, to this place, to be forwarded to Stockton, and arrangements made at San Luis Obispo or San Miguel, as you may find most advantageous, for the transportation, on pack mules, of such subsistence as may be needed on your march.

The general desires that you will collect and report any information that may be useful with regard to these Indians—their numbers and haunts—the best position for the establishment of troops to operate against them, &c., &c.

Copies of this letter and the enclosed papers will be sent to the care of the alcaldes of San Luis Obispo and San Miguel, for fear that the express rider may miss you on his route down.

Very respectfully, sir, your obedient servant,

E. R. S. CANBY,
Assistant Adjutant General.

First Lieut. C. J. L. WILSON,
First Dragoons.

HEADQUARTERS TENTH MILITARY DEPARTMENT,
Monterey, California, June 2, 1849.

SIR: I have the honor to acknowledge the receipt, last evening, of your communication of May 23. I regret very much that any misconception should have arisen with regard to the organization of the division staff, especially as it has already been productive of serious embarrassments to the public service, and great mortification to myself. It is due, however, to myself to state that, until the receipt of your communication, no instructions, either written or verbal, had been received of the charges you assume to have been made, nor were they at all anticipated.

The senior quartermaster is still borne upon my returns, and the orders (not requisitions) sent to him, and to his successor, who stands in precisely the same position, by Colonel Mason and myself, were issued in the belief, then and now entertained, that they were still subject to the orders of the department commander.

A report from Captain Folsom, called for in consequence of his failure to comply with an order issued more than three months ago, gave me the first information I have received that any orders from department headquarters had been at all interfered with. Upon the orders, above referred to, were based many subsequent arrangements made by Colonel Mason and myself, all of which were known at division headquarters; and as no modification of them was either suggested or directed, it was reasonable to suppose that they were approved, and it was with equal surprise and mortification that I learned that they had, in effect, been countermanded. If no consideration for the public service required (and there were many that did) that these changes should have been made known to me, it was, at least, due in courtesy, and this course will be expected in future.

It is my intention, so soon as I am advised of the transfer of division headquarters from San Francisco, to establish a connexion with Benicia from San José, but the importance of San Francisco in a civil as well as a military point of view, renders it necessary that the communication with it should be regular and frequent.

The suggestion of the general in relation to the investigation of the circumstances connected with outrages that may be committed by, or upon Indians, is embraced in the duties of the agents of the several districts, and covered by instructions heretofore given them, but such orders will now be given as will insure prompt action at points remote from the agencies.

I have the honor to be, very respectfully, sir, your obedient servant,
E. R. S. CANBY,
Assistant Adjutant General.

The ASSISTANT ADJUTANT GENERAL,
Division Headquarters, San Francisco, California.

HEADQUARTERS TENTH MILITARY DEPARTMENT,
Monterey, California, June 2, 1849.

SIR: I have the honor to report, for the information of the commanding general, that I shall leave this place for the San Joaquin and Sacramento valleys, by the pass of San Miguel, as soon after the arrival of the steamer as possible, for the purpose of making such arrangements as may be necessary, or practicable, for the prevention of collisions between the whites and Indians of those neighborhoods.

It is very desirable that a topographical examination of that part of the country should be made at the same time, and as I cannot, from present paucity of officers in the department, detach a line officer for that purpose, I shall be much gratified if the interests of the service will permit the temporary detachment of one of the topographical officers now at Benicia for the purpose of accompanying me.

Very respectfully, your obedient servant,
·B. RILEY,
Brevet Brigadier General, commanding the Department.

ASSISTANT ADJUTANT GENERAL,
Division Headquarters.

[No. 8.]   HEADQUARTERS TENTH MILITARY DEPARTMENT,
Monterey, California, June 11, 1849.

GENERAL: The orders and military correspondence to be transmitted by the next mail will furnish you with a history of the operations in this department since the date of my despatch of April 25. The troops now in the department occupy, or are *en route* for, the stations assigned them by department orders No. 16, except company "I," 2d infantry, which has in confinement at this place seventeen or eighteen deserters sentenced to be sent to the "Atlantic coast of the United States," and the movement of that company has been delayed to await the answer to an application, made to the commander of our naval forces, for authority to send them home by some one of our naval vessels. If no opportunity should occur within a limited period they will be transferred, with the remainder of the company, to San Diego, where they may be usefully employed upon some public work at that place.

The route given company E, 1st dragoons, in my instructions of May 20, has been changed, (instructions to Lieutenant Wilson, 1st dragoons, of June 2,) in consequence of information received of several murders recently committed upon inhabitants of this territory engaged in mining upon the Los Reyes rivers.

The transport Mary and Adeline, with companies A and F, 2d infantry, has not yet arrived.

The exposed situation of isolated parties in the mineral region offers many temptations for the commission of outrages by the Indians. These, confined in the first instances to thefts, and occasionally outrages of a more serious character, have been made the pretence, by the lawless and disorderly of our own people, for the commission of outrages of the most unprovoked character, extending, in several instances, to the harmless and inoffensive Indians of the rancherias. The Indian agents of the several districts are clothed with ample powers to arrest and punish the perpetrators of these outrages, but in the absence of troops in the vicinity of their agencies, to aid them in the execution of their duties, their authority has in several instances been set at defiance by a few lawless men.

The establishment of troops on the San Joaquin and Sacramento rivers, by putting them in a condition to make their authority respected, will, it is hoped, diminish the number of these outrages, if it does not prevent them entirely.

For the purpose of establishing the troops in the mineral region, at the points best calculated to control the Indians and prevent unauthorized interference with them, I shall leave this place for the San Joaquin, and thence for the valley of the Sacramento, as soon as possible after the arrival of the next steamer. Being unable, at this time, to detach a line officer for topographical duty, I have applied to Major General Smith to detach temporarily one of the topographical engineers now on duty at division headquarters, for the purpose of making a topographical examination of the country through which it will be necessary to pass.

The difficulties to be apprehended in the mineral region are not confined to Indian disturbances. The ill feeling existing between the Americans and foreign adventurers continues to be fostered by designing persons; and although no serious collision has yet taken place, it is greatly to be feared that it may soon occur, and that many native Californians and good citizens will unavoidably be involved in it. I fear that the small force in that quarter will prove insufficient to preserve order.

It will be seen, from the department returns for March and April, that desertions have been quite frequent in the past two months. The evil, however, has not been so great as I anticipated. Orders Nos. 16 and 19, and my proclamation of May 6, indicate the measures I have taken with the view of diminishing this evil: how far they will be successful, is yet to be determined. In consequence of the difficulty in procuring printing, and in the transmission of information, these papers have only been partially distributed, and it will be some time before its operation can be fairly tested.

I deem it important to call the attention of the War Department to the inadequate force now in this department to meet present, to say nothing of anticipated emergencies. The force now in the mineral region is not sufficient to meet the necessities of the service in that quarter; and this force, inadequate as it is, could only be obtained by stripping other portions of the country of the troops needed for the protection of the property of their inhabitants. The estimate of the former department commander, based upon the anticipated wants of the service in a time of peace, was sufficiently limited. Since his requisition was made, the state of affairs in this country has entirely changed. The discovery of the gold placers has attracted hither thousands of foreign adventurers, many of them from the lowest classes of society, and has produced a state of affairs here that will require much stronger controlling force to preserve order than I can now command. Our relations with the Indians have also been materially changed. Although no combination appears to exist between the different tribes inhabiting the slopes of the Sierra Nevada, they are evidently hostile, and will seize every opportunity of committing outrages upon the inhabitants of the country.

The murder recently committed upon the party of Mr. Garner, long a resident of this country, by a body of Indians upon the river Los Reyes, was done, as was stated by the Indians, to revenge themselves for the aggressions committed by Americans upon the Indians of the Sacramento; indicating an evident understanding between different tribes speaking different languages, and separated by a distance of two hundred and fifty miles.

In a report made to the commander of the division, of this date, I have made an estimate of the force that I deem absolutely necessary in this department, until affairs assume a more settled condition. There are many difficulties in the way of keeping troops in this country—the danger of desertions, and the great expense of the military establishment; but, if measures be not taken speedily to maintain a respectable force here, the country will, in the end, be involved in expenses immensely greater than will be sustained by maintaining for the next two or three years a force that will effectually control the Indians, that part of our population disposed to commit aggressions upon them, and effectually to prevent collisions between the Americans and foreigners in this country.

In sending recruits to this country, I strongly advise that authority be given to enlist married men for service at the depots and posts that it may be necessary to establish at points at considerable distance from the mines.

I have not yet been able to obtain from Major Reading, paymaster of Colonel Fremont's battalion, the copies of muster-rolls of that battalion required by the instructions of the Secretary of War of October 9, 1848. He has repeatedly been written to, but no answer has been received. I learn, unofficially, that he is unwilling to furnish these rolls, for fear that it may prejudice the claims of members of the battalion for greater pay than was allowed by law. I shall probably see him in the course of the ensuing month, and will then endeavor to obtain the rolls, and forward the required copies.

I have the honor to be, very respectfully, general, your obedient servant,
B. RILEY,
Brevet Brig. Gen., commanding the Department.
General R. JONES,
Adjutant General U. S. A., Washington City.

[No. 10.]   HEADQUARTERS TENTH MILITARY DEPARTMENT,
San Francisco, California, June 19, 1849.

GENERAL: I have the honor to report that I came to this place on the 15th instant, at the request of Major General Smith, for the purpose of meeting the Hon. Thomas Butler King, and shall return to Monterey as soon as I have transacted the business on hand here.

Very few of the New York volunteers discharged in this country have applied for the transportation home, authorized by the instructions of the Secretary of War of October 9, 1848. It has, therefore, been deemed proper to limit the period in which they can avail themselves of the provisions of those instructions. If it should be intended to extend this limit, I desire that I may receive instructions to that effect before its expiration.

I have learned (unofficially) since my arrival at this place, that Colonel Abert's order, directing Brevet Major Linnard, topographical engineers, to report to me, has been countermanded; and I now respectfully repeat my application of April 25 for topographical engineers for service in this department. The want of these officers is severely felt. The number of medical officers in this department will be insufficient to meet the wants of the service, particularly in the unhealthy season of the year. I have not yet been able to supply the post at Sonoma; the escort of the commissioners are to discharge Assistant Surgeon Booth, 16th infantry. I request that three additional officers of the medical department be ordered to report to me.

I have the honor to report the death of First Lieutenant C. E. Jarvis, 2d infantry, on the 8th instant, at Sonoma, California, to which place he had been ordered for the benefit of his health. His disease was chronic dysentery, contracted while on duty in Mexico. He was an active, enterprising officer, and his death will be a severe loss to his regiment and to the service.

Very respectfully, general, your obedient servant,
B. RILEY,
Brevet Brig. Gen., commanding the Department.
Brevet Major General R. JONES,
Adj. Gen. U. S. A., Washington, D. C.

HEADQUARTERS TENTH MILITARY DEPARTMENT,
San Francisco, California, June 19, 1849.

GENERAL: I have the honor to enclose, herewith, printed copies of my proclamations of the 3d and 4th instant, as governor of this Territory.

Copies of all official papers and correspondence connected with the civil government of the country will be forwarded by the regular mail steamer of the 1st proximo, for the information of the government at Washington.

Very respectfully, your obedient servant,
B. RILEY,
Brevet Brig. Gen., and Governor of California.
Major General R. JONES,
Adj. Gen. of the Army, Washington, D. C.

[No. 13.]   HEADQUARTERS TENTH MILITARY DEPARTMENT,
Monterey, California, June 30, 1849.

GENERAL: I have the honor to report that, since my despatch No. 8, nothing of importance has occurred in this department, and that so far as accounts have been received, everything remains quiet on the frontier and in the mineral region.

The experience of every day convinces me in the opinion, heretofore expressed, that without great forbearance on the part of all engaged in the mines, a collision between the Americans and foreigners will inevitably take place. The unfortunate results of such a collision need only be adverted to, to be appreciated in their fullest extent. The similarity of language and appearance of the native Californians, and the mass of adventurers in the mines, will unavoidably involve the former in the consequences of any acts of aggression committed against the latter. Men inflamed by passion will not delay long enough to discriminate; and, from the insufficiency of the military force now in the department, I fear the commission of many outrages upon the unoffending inhabitants of this country, whom, by treaty stipulations as well as by every principle of justice, we are bound to protect in their rights and to treat with respect and kindness.

The occurrence of such an event will undoubtedly be seized by disorganizers for the purpose of carrying out their scheme of opposition to the government and of involving everything in this country in anarchy and confusion.

Great danger, too, is to be apprehended from the congregation of the miners in the towns on the seacoast, when driven from the mines by the inclemency of the rainy season; and for the purpose of preventing this evil, I shall, if possible, reenforce the garrison of San Francisco and Monterey, and establish commands (for the winter only) at San José and Los Angeles, the points at which this danger is most to be apprehended. If unable to make this arrangement, I shall endeavor to organize an armed police force in each of the above places, of sufficient strength to aid effectually the civil authorities in the preservation of order and tranquillity.

I deem it important to urge again upon the consideration of the proper authorities the immediate necessity of having an additional military force in this department. Aside from the considerations—and they are imperative—that demand an increased force for the protection of the frontier and the preservation of internal tranquillity, a compliance with the stipulations of the 11th article of the late treaty with Mexico will require a considerable force in the northeastern part of this department, and it is impossible, under present circumstances, to detach any command for that purpose.

I desire also to call your attention to the great want of officers, both line and staff, in this department. I have now under my control but one officer of the quartermaster's department; one of engineers, Brevet Captain Halleck, secretary of state, under orders for division headquarters, but retained by the consent of the commander of the division, Lieutenant Derby, topographical engineers, (temporarily detached from division headquarters,) an insufficiency of medical officers, and none of the subsistence department. The duties devolved by law upon officers of those corps are necessarily performed by officers of the line, and the necessity of involving these officers in the performance of staff duties materially impairs the efficiency of every command in the department. Four of the eight companies of infantry now in the department have each but one officer with them, and but one company in California has its full complement of officers. The evils resulting from such a state of affairs, under ordinary circumstances, are of the greatest magnitude; but, in this country, where troops are exposed to the greatest temptation to desert, and where the sympathies of the people are so far in favor of the soldiers, that it is almost impossible to apprehend deserters, it is absolutely necessary to the preservation of the discipline and efficiency of command, that they should be well officered. I trust, therefore, I shall not be deemed importunate in again urging that the staff officers heretofore applied for, and all officers of the 2d infantry now absent from their regiment, be at once ordered to report to me. I have never been placed in a position where the want of officers was so severely felt as here, or where the exertions of every officer were so necessary for the efficiency of the service.

In consequence of the want of officers I have ordered Lieutenant Slaughter, recently promoted to the 4th infantry, to continue on duty with the company to which he was formerly attached. This company ("H") has been designated for the escort of the commissioners, and has now but one of its officers with it.

The instructions of the Secretary of War, terminating the service of several officers of the volunteer staff on duty in this department, have been received from division headquarters, and communicated. Before leaving Washington for California I received the verbal instructions of the Secretary of War, "to relieve and discharge all officers that had been provisionally retained." Under these instructions Surgeon A. Perry and Captain W. G. Marcy, A. C. S., volunteer staff, were discharged—the former on the 14th, and the latter on the 30th of April last. Up to these periods these officers were employed in the performance of their appropriate duties, and as they could not have been relieved at an earlier period, I respectfully recommend that their terms of service be extended to the dates above given.

Your communication to Major General Smith, of March 26th, in relation to the rolls of the New York volunteers and California battalion, referred by him to me, was received at San Francisco on the 16th instant. Upon examination of the department record, after my return to this place, I found that the missing rolls of the New York volunteers were forwarded by the steamer Oregon, on the 14th of April. For fear they may miscarry, I have directed duplicate copies to be made, and if they can be got ready in season, will forward them by the next steamer. The cause of the delay in forwarding the rolls of the California battalion I reported in my despatch No. 8. I hope to obtain these in season to forward them by the August steamer.

My visit to the San Joaquin and Sacramento valleys has been delayed by the pressure of other business. I shall be able to leave on the first proximo; and as my time will be very limited, I shall confine myself to an examination of the country between the Merced and Los Reyes rivers, in the San Joaquin valley, and to the neighborhood of Feather river, a tributary of the Sacramento, with a view to the establishment of two or more military posts for the better protection of that frontier. Later in the season I shall visit the country south of this place, for the purpose of examining passes leading into the Indian country east of San Luis Obispo and Los Angeles, and also the passes leading from Sonora into the lower part of California. It is important that the whole of the Indian frontier should be examined before the commencement of the rainy season, and so soon as I have officers at my disposal I shall direct an examination of the entire country north of Sonora, and the country between the Sierra Nevada and the coast range from the headwaters of the San Joaquin, to the northern boundary of California.

Desertions continue to be frequent, and occur in the greatest numbers at the points most distant from the *placer* regions.

In consequence of the failure to receive the returns from two or three posts, I am unable to send you by the next steamer a return of the department for May.

I have the honor to be, very respectfully, general, your obedient servant,
B. RILEY,
Brevet Brigadier General, commanding the Department.
Brevet Maj. Gen. R. JONES,
Adjutant General U. S. Army, Washington, D. C.

HEADQUARTERS TENTH MILITARY DEPARTMENT,
Monterey, California. June 11, 1849.

SIR: I have for some time been collecting information for the purpose of making an estimate for an additional force in this department; and, although the information now in my possession is not so complete as I could wish, I am induced, by the importance of making the wants of the service in this respect known to our authorities at home as early as possible, to submit the estimate now.

For the purpose of controlling the Indians of the "lake country," north and east of Sonora, a post should be established some sixty or eighty miles north of that place, to be garrisoned by at least two companies of infantry. For the protection of the emigrant route from the United States, one company of cavalry should be established on the American Fork, eighty or one hundred miles above its confluence with the Sacramento; in the vicinity of the mineral region, above Sutter's Fort, *two* companies of infantry and one of cavalry; in the valley of the San Joaquin, between the Stanislaus river and the Tulares, three companies of infantry and one of cavalry; at the Cajori pass, east of the city of Los Angeles, for the protection of the inhabitants of the rich valley of Porcumcula from Indian depredations, one company of infantry and one of cavalry—this pass commands one of the approaches from Ceinua and the Gila river, and derives additional importance from that fact; at Warner's pass, (Aqua Caliente,) or Kaciha, the principal approach from Sonora and the Gila river, one company of cavalry and one company of infantry; at San Diego, one company of artillery; at the junction of the Gila and Colorado rivers, one company of cavalry or infantry; at San Diego, one company of artillery; at Monterey redoubt, one company of artillery; in the present unsettled state of affairs, the presidio of San Francisco should be garrisoned by not less than two companies of artillery.

For the command of the lower pass, Senora Viacita has some advantages over Warner's pass, but its neighborhood furnishes no resources either for building or sustaining a garrison, and it will probably be found most advantageous to establish the post at Warner's pass, in a fruitful country, which will, in a very few years, produce enough to sustain a small garrison. For the principal depot and Sonoma, the same garrisons as at present will be sufficient—two companies of infantry and one of cavalry. There should also be shows of military force at San Pedro, Santa Barbara, and San Luis Obispo, as well to prevent Indian incursions from the mountains as to prevent violation of the revenue laws. For these purposes, a company of infantry at each of the points above referred to will be sufficient. Several instances of smuggling have occurred between Monterey and San Pedro in the last two months; and, under the operations of the new revenues, it is believed that the temptation to engage in this unlawful trade will be greatly increased. The entire force that I deem necessary for the department will be six companies of cavalry, five companies of artillery, and fourteen companies of infantry, or, in numbers, seven hundred men, in addition to that assigned to the department by general orders No. 49, 1848.

It is unnecessary for me to remark upon the importance of having a force in the department sufficient for the protection of the frontier and the preservation of law and order; for however great may be the difficulty of retaining men, and the expenses of the military establishment, the failure to take sufficient and prompt measures for the accomplishment of these objects will entail upon our government difficulties and expenses immeasurably greater.

Very respectfully, Colonel, your obedient servant,
E. R. S. CANBY,
Assistant Adjutant General.

Lieutenant Colonel J. HOOKER,
Asst. Adjt. Gen., Headquarters Third Division.

HEADQUARTERS TENTH MILITARY DEPARTMENT,
Monterey, California, June 26, 1849.

MAJOR: If the transport Mary and Adeline, with companies "A" and "F," 2d infantry, should arrive in season, it will be desirable to detail one of this company for the escort directed in special orders No. 29 of this date, filling up the escort to the required strength in officers and men by details from other companies. It will be necessary to have active and efficient officers, as well as able-bodied men, for this duty, and it is important that the command should be organized and in readiness to commence as early as possible. Assurance may be given the non-commissioned officers and men of this escort that, upon the completion of this duty, they will be stationed in the vicinity of the mines and be furloughed, for the purpose of visiting them, or that they will receive such other indulgence as may be reasonable and proper.

Very respectfully, Major, your obedient servant,
E. R. S. CANBY,
Assistant Adjutant General.

Major W. SEAWELL,
Commanding 2d Infantry.

HEADQUARTERS TENTH MILITARY DEPARTMENT,
Monterey, California, June 27, 1849.

MAJOR: Your report and requisition of the 5th instant were received, and submitted to the commanding general on his return from San Francisco on the 25th instant; and I am instructed by him to say, that in anticipation of the wants of the commissioners, all the available transportation in the department was ordered to San Diego in April last. What quantity was sent in obedience to these instructions has not yet been reported, but it is supposed that there are now at that place for your purposes about fifty wagons.

Captain Kane, assistant quartermaster, reported at Los Angeles, on the 1st May, three serviceable ambulances, and General Riley supposes they have been sent, with the other means of transportation at Los Angeles and San Luis Rey, to San Diego. For fear that they have not been, your requisition is approved and sent to the depot quartermasters at Benicia, who will furnish them, if they have any on hand at that place. At the date of the last property-list from the depot there were none on hand, and it is doubtful whether any have been received since.

In consequence of the *gold* excitement, it is feared that you will experience difficulty in obtaining mules, but a few may probably be obtained by sending to Los Angeles and Aqua Caliente, (Warner's ranche,) from the Sonorenians passing through the country; and oxen will to the same extent supply their place with your supply-train. Pack-saddles were sent from this place by the quartermaster in May and June.

The general is anxious to facilitate the operations of the commissioners by the use of all the means under his control, and desires that you will communicate freely with him upon the subject.

Very respectfully, major, your obedient servant,
E. R. S. CANBY,
Assistant Adjutant General.

Major J. MCKINSTRY,
Assist. Quartermaster U. S. A., San Diego, California.

HEADQUARTERS TENTH MILITARY DEPARTMENT,
Monterey, California, June 29, 1849.

CAPTAIN: Your communication of the 19th instant, recommending that furloughs be given to certain non-commissioned officers of your company whose terms of service are about to expire, has been received, and submitted to the commanding general, who directs me to say that he does not feel authorized to grant furloughs for the length of time asked for; but as these non-commissioned officers may be usefully employed as assistants in a topographical survey about to be made, he will retain them in this country, and when that duty is completed grant them the usual furloughs.

Their descriptive lists and clothing accounts will be sent to this office, in order that they may be discharged here.

Very respectfully, your obedient servant,
E. R. S. CANBY,
Assistant Adjutant General.

Captain R. P. CAMPBELL,
2d Dragoons, Monterey.

HEADQUARTERS TENTH MILITARY DEPARTMENT,
Monterey, California, June 30, 1849.

MAJOR: I am instructed by the commanding general to acknowledge the receipt, on his return from San Francisco, of your report of the 3d instant.

Company I, 2d infantry, will sail for San Diego about the first proximo, and Major Heintzelman, 2d infantry, is instructed to fill up the infantry company of your escort to an efficient strength by transfers from the other companies of his command.

Under the supposition that company A, 2d infantry, will not be required immediately by you, two officers of that company have been placed upon the detail for a general court-martial ordered at San Diego. This detail will not interfere with your operations, as Major Heintzelman is instructed not to assemble the court if those officers should be required before its proceedings can be completed. General Riley will be pleased to receive any suggestions that may in your estimation tend to facilitate your operations.

If the companies of your command are not supplied with the necessary blanks for returns, &c., you will oblige me by making requisitions for them at your earliest convenience.

Very respectfully, major, your obedient servant,
E. R. S. CANBY,
Assistant Adjutant General.

Major W. H. EMORY,
U. S. A., commanding escort of commissioners,
San Diego, California.

HEADQUARTERS TENTH MILITARY DEPARTMENT,
Monterey, California, June 30, 1849.

MAJOR: Your several communications of May 24th and 31st, and June 1, 2, 4, and 5, have been received and submitted to the commanding general, who directs that the charges preferred against Lieutenant Sweeney, by Brevet Captains Hayden and Lyon, be returned for the endorsement required by paragraph 924 of general regulations. The endorsement is necessary to enable the commanding general to act understandingly where the interests of the "service or the officer are concerned;" and is peculiarly so when serious charges are preferred against an officer.

The applications of Lieutenants Sweeney and Slaughter have been approved and recommended until the result of the application for transfer is known. Lieutenant Slaughter will be continued on duty with the company to which he is now attached.

The artillery required by you, with the necessary equipments and ammunition, will be sent down with company I, 2d infantry, which leaves this place in the schooner Sylphide about the first proximo.

The general directs that the company designated for the escort of the commissioners be filled up to an effective strength by transfers from the other companies of your command.

The commutation of quarters should be regulated by the customary rents at San Diego, provided it does not exceed $15 per month for each room. This limit has been fixed by Major Vinton, the senior quartermaster on the Pacific coast.

For fuel, the commutation will, of course, be regulated by the market price.

The general desires that you will quiet any uneasiness that may exist in the minds of the inhabitants of your neighborhood by assuring them that he will use all the means under his control to give them an adequate protection. The necessity for having more troops in the south is fully felt, and has been represented to the proper authorities. He hopes to have it in his power in the course of a few months to establish troops in such positions as will effectually prevent the occurrence of the dangers which they apprehend.

Very respectfully, your obedient servant,
E. R. S. CANBY,
Assistant Adjutant General.

Major S. P. HEINTZELMAN,
2d Infantry, commanding, San Diego.

HEADQUARTERS TENTH MILITARY DEPARTMENT,
Sacramento City, July 22, 1849.

COLONEL: I have the honor to report, for the information of the commanding general, that, from a partial examination of the country south of this place, and from information collected at Monterey before leaving that place, and while upon the road, I am satisfied that the most important point for a military post in the San Joaquin valley will be at or near the junction of the Los Reyes river with its most southern branch, distant 120 to 140 miles from Monterey, and from 15 to 20 miles east of the Yuba lake.

The rapidly-increasing white population on the headwaters of the Merced, Stanislaus, and Tuolumne rivers, is driving the Indians from those rivers to the south, where they concentrate about the headwaters of the San Joaquin and Los Reyes rivers. The Indian population of these rivers, with the exception of two or three tribes, have given evidence of the most friendly disposition towards the Americans. The country bordering on these rivers is rich in minerals, and the population now in the southern mines is moving to the south, and the close contact that must result will inevitably lead to many aggressions committed by the one party upon the other. It is important that our own citizens be protected against Indian hostilities; and the dictates of policy, as well as humanity, require that the Indians should be secured against the aggressions of the whites.

The establishment of a military post on the Los Reyes river will give protection to the country east of the San Luis Obispo, which frequently suffers from the depredations of Indian horse thieves.

There will be much difficulty at present in supplying a post so remote from the coast; and, of the routes by which supplies may be sent, I am not yet able to decide which will be the best; but I expect, on my arrival at Benicia, to receive a report from Lieutenant Wilson, 1st dragoons, which will determine this point; and, when that report is received, I shall be able to report more definitively.

Very respectfully, your obedient servant,

B. RILEY,
Brevet Brigadier General.

Lieut. Col. J. Hooker,
Assistant Adjutant General, Headquarters, 3d Division.

Headquarters Tenth Military Department,
Monterey, California, August 9, 1849.

Colonel: I have the honor to acknowledge the receipt of your letter of June 21, and, in reply to so much of it as desires aid "to direct Major Kingsbury to proceed to his destination at or near Feather river without further delay," to state that, at the date of your letter, Major Kingsbury had received no instructions from *me*, nor from any other source *through* me, to establish himself on or near Feather river. He was ordered to establish his camp in the vicinity of Sutter's Fort, for the immediate object, suggested by the major general commanding the division, of "looking into certain Indian troubles that have recently occurred on the American fork;" and I did not intend he should go beyond that neighborhood until the selection of a position for a military post on the Upper Sacramento, ordered by the commander of this department in January last, could be made.

Before leaving San Francisco, Major Kingsbury had indicated, for the temporary encampment of his command, a point on the Cosumnes river, distant from Sutter's Fort 18 or 20 miles. His selection was approved by me, as it was the seat of the principal Indian disturbances referred to in the communication in division headquarters of May 4. He now reports that, previous to the receipt of your communication of July 10, he had no order to remove to Feather river, or any instructions going beyond those given him from department headquarters; and that, in encamping his command at Sutter city, he was governed by the advice of the Indian agent of that district, and the information communicated to him from me—that, so soon as the necessary arrangements could be made, a topographical examination of that part of the country would be ordered for the purpose of determining a more permanent position for his command. My recent visit to the Sacramento river was for the purpose of determining this position, when it was arrested by the selection announced in your communication to Major Kingsbury of July 10.

Very respectfully, your obedient servant,

B. RILEY,
Brevet Brigadier General, commanding.

Lieut. Col. J. Hooker,
Assistant Adjutant General U. S. A., Sonoma.

HEADQUARTERS TENTH MILITARY DEPARTMENT,
Monterey, California, August 9, 1849.

CAPTAIN: I am instructed by the commanding general to say that you will cause the government reserves at San Francisco to be properly marked out, and notice to be given in one or more papers published in that town, forbidding trespasses by the erection of buildings, or in any other manner whatsoever.

Mr. Thompson and Mr. Steineberger are the only persons authorized to occupy any portion of these lands; and without authority communicated to you through or from department headquarters, you will permit no one else to occupy them.

Very respectfully, sir, your obedient servant,
E. R. S. CANBY,
Assistant Adjutant General.

Capt. E. D. KEYES,
Commanding, &c., San Francisco.

HEADQUARTERS TENTH MILITARY DEPARTMENT,
Monterey, California, August 14, 1849.

MAJOR: I am instructed by the commanding general to enclose for your information a copy of a letter to the assistant quartermaster at San Francisco, in relation to the land on which the post office agent at San Francisco was authorized by you to erect a building. This portion of the reserve is covered by a grant to Mr. A. B. Thompson, given by the Mexican authorities in 1838, which, although not considered good, was recognised by Governor Mason, the former governor of California, himself, to the extent of "occupancy of the house, and right of way to the water."

The remainder of the reservation is in possession of Mr. Steineberger, under authority given him by the assistant quartermaster at San Francisco, which was not submitted to the commanding general of this department.

Mr. Allen's application to General Riley, and your conditional permission, have been forwarded to division headquarters disapproved.

Doctor E. Jones, mentioned in the enclosed communication, was the agent or assignee of Mr. Thompson, and the papers therein referred to are on file at the presidio of San Francisco.

Very respectfully, major, your obedient servant,
E. R. S. CANBY,
Assistant Adjutant General.

Major R. ALLEN,
Assstant Quartermas'er, San Francisco.

HEADQUARTERS TENTH MILITARY DEPARTMENT,
Monterey, California, August 9, 1849.

SIR: I am instructed by the commanding general, in reply to your communication of the 7th instant, to say that the ground on which you have commenced building is covered by a grant to Mr. A. B. Thompson, given by the Mexican authorities in 1838, which, although not considered good, has been recognised by Governor Mason and himself to the extent of "occupancy of the house, and right of way to the water," until his claim be submitted to the United States government.

Until this title matter is decided by the authorities at home, he has no disposition to interfere. The remainder of the reserve is already in the possession of Mr. Steineberger. It is proper to say that your application would not have been approved, as the reservation has been selected for military purposes by a board of engineer officers, and the selection approved by the Secretary of War.

Your application has been forwarded to division headquarters disapproved.

Very respectfully, your obedient servant,
E. R. S. CANBY,
Assistant Adjutant General.

R. T. P. ALLEN, Esq.,
Post Office Agent, San Francisco.

HEADQUARTERS TENTH MILITARY DEPARTMENT,
Monterey, California, August 10, 1849.

SIR: You will herewith receive a letter from the alcalde of Santa Barbara, giving information that a Chilian brig, the "Imperial," which put into that place in distress, has been condemned as unseaworthy, and her cargo landed and stored; and that the alcalde has allowed a small portion of these goods to be sold, and now holds the duties on them at the disposal of the government.

General Riley directs that you immediately proceed to Santa Barbara, and reserve the duties so collected by the alcalde; and also collect the duties and fees that may be due on the ship and balance of her cargo.

It has also been reported that other foreign vessels have recently landed passengers and freights in the ports of Santa Barbara and San Luis Obispo, in violation of the revenue laws of the United States. It will be your duty to inquire into these matters, and take such measures as may be found necessary to enforce the revenue laws; and, for this purpose, you are authorized to call in the assistance of the local magistrates of those districts. But should you meet on the way, or find at Santa Barbara, the collector or deputy collector appointed for the ports on this coast, you will turn the whole matter over to them, and immediately return to department headquarters.

You will probably find at Santa Barbara, among the custom-house papers, a MS. copy of the tariff of 1846, but as it may be possible that copy is lost, you will, if possible, procure one at this place, and take it with you as your guide in collecting the duties and fees.

As soon as you have completed these duties, you will immediately return to this post, and bring with you the moneys so collected, which will be paid over as "civil funds" to the quartermaster at this place.

Very respectfully, your obedient servant,
E. R. S. CANBY,
Assistant Adjutant General.

Lieutenant J. HAMILTON, *3d Artillery.*

HEADQUARTERS TENTH MILITARY DEPARTMENT,
Monterey, California, August 12, 1849.

MAJOR: Your communication of June 19, with its enclosures, and that of July 5, were received on the 10th instant, and have been submitted to the brigadier general commanding, by whom I am directed to say that he will keep the companies composing your command filled up to the standard authorized to companies serving in this department. Beyond that it is not in his power to go, without instructions from the War Department.

Your correspondence with the commission will be transmitted to the Secretary of War with the following endorsement:

"This correspondence is respectfully submitted to the Secretary of War, with information that under instructions from these headquarters of April 15, 18, and June 30, the companies of this escort have been filled up to an efficient strength, and that arrangements will be made to keep up this strength by transfer from other companies serving in this department. This force, in conjunction with that furnished by Mexico, I deem amply sufficient for protection in any operation west of Gila river. Beyond that river a greater force will probably be necessary; but it cannot be furnished from this department without serious detriment to the service, nor do I feel authorized, without further instructions from the War Department, in going beyond the instructions of general order No. 65.

"At the date of last report from San Diego, Major Emory's command had an aggregate present of 101, and the Mexican of 140."

By department special orders No. —, Lieutenant Slaughter, 4th infantry, was continued on duty with the company to which he was then attached. As this order may have failed to reach you, I enclose a duplicate.

The communication from Major McKinstry, to which you refer, in relation to the transportation to San Luis Rey, has not been received; nor is the commanding general in possession of any information in regard to it, except that communicated in your letter. The officer in command at San Luis Rey when it was abandoned has been directed to report what disposition has been made of the transportation at that place.

It has not been in General Riley's power to furnish a medical officer to your command. His inability to do so was reported some time since to the Adjutant General, and an additional number of officers applied for. The number of officers of the medical staff originally assigned to this department was reduced by the Surgeon General before the troops left the United States; and although General Riley has received no instructions to furnish a medical officer for your command, he would of course have done so if there had been one at his disposal. It is important that the commanding general should receive, as early as possible, a return of your command, in order that he may direct any transfer that may be necessary.

Very respectfully, major, your obedient servant,
E. R. S. CANBY,
Assistant Adjutant General.

Major W. H. EMORY,
  Topographical Engineers,
    Commanding escort of Commissioners.

HEADQUARTERS TENTH MILITARY DEPARTMENT,
Monterey, California, August 14, 1849.

MAJOR: I am instructed by the commanding general to enclose, for your information, a copy of a letter to the assistant quartermaster at San Francisco in relation to the land upon which the Post Office agent at San Francisco was authorized by you to erect a building. This portion of the reserve is covered by a grant to Mr. A. B. Thompson, given by the Mexican authorities in 1838, which, although not considered good, was recognised by Governor Mason (the former governor of California) himself, to the extent of "occupancy of the house and right of way to the water." The remainder of the reservation is in possession of Mr. Steineberger, under authority given him by the assistant quartermaster at San Francisco, which was not submitted to the commanding general of this department.

Mr. Allen's application to General Riley and your conditional permission have been forwarded to division headquarters disapproved. Dr. E. Jones, mentioned in the enclosed communication, was the agent or assignee of Mr. Thompson, and the papers therein referred to are on file in the presidio of San Francisco.

Very respectfully, your obedient servant,
E. R. S. CANBY,
Assistant Adjutant General.

Major R. ALLEN,
Assistant Quartermaster.

HEADQUARTERS TENTH MILITARY DEPARTMENT,
Monterey, California, August 15, 1849.

GENERAL: Your communication of December 8, 1848, to Governor Mason, in relation to the arrangement for supplying the officers of the quartermaster's department in California with funds, was turned over to me on the 19th of April last.

The funds, thus far, have not been sufficient to meet the current expenditures, and your department is greatly indebted to the "civil fund" of this Territory.

In advance of my annual estimate, to be transmitted by the next steamer, I have now the honor to request that arrangements may be made as soon as practicable for the remission of the sum of $500,000, to meet the indebtedness above referred to and the current disbursements until after my detailed estimate shall have been received and acted upon.

Very respectfully, general, your obedient servant,
B. RILEY,
Brev. Brig. Gen. U. S. Army, commanding, &c.

Major General T. S. JESUP,
Quartermaster General U. S. Army,
Washington, D. C.

HEADQUARTERS TENTH MILITARY DEPARTMENT,
Monterey, California, August 16, 1849.

MAJOR: Your communications of June 30 and July 1 and 5 were received on General Riley's return to this place, (a few days since,) and have been submitted to him. I am directed to say, in reply, that he designs visiting San Diego for purposes connected with your suggestions immediately after the adjournment of the convention that meets in this place on the 1st proximo. In the mean time, he directs that estimates be prepared and forwarded to headquarters for the lumber and other materials that will be required for building quarters for two companies of infantry, with the necessary storehouse and hospital.

The difficulty of procuring building materials in this country is so great, that the commanding general is not disposed to authorize any permanent buildings until materials can be sent out from the United States. If, however, quarters for your command cannot be obtained at San Diego, it will be necessary to put them under cover before the commencement of the rainy season. The best position for the erection of these quarters will be as near Punta Guij (already selected by a board of engineer officers for the construction of a fortification for the defence of the harbor of San Diego) as a suitable position can be found—reference being had to a good supply of water, convenient to the landing, and to a location that will not interfere with any work of a more permanent character. You are desired to collect information on these points, and any others that may be useful in aiding the commanding general in making a selection when he visits your post, and report them for his information.

No information has reached department headquarters with regard to building materials left at San Pedro, but instructions will be given to send any that are there to San Diego.

In consequence of a want of officers, a general court-martial cannot at present be convened at San Diego for the trial of the charges returned by you, but one will be assembled there at the earliest period that the interest of the service will permit.

It is a matter of great regret that the stores sent you from San Pedro and San Francisco should have proved insufficient. A six months' supply for 300 men was ordered by General Riley, and he now directs that you immediately estimate for any additional supply that may be required.

Very respectfully, your obedient servant,
E. R. S. CANBY,
Assistant Adjutant General.

Major S. P. HEINTZELMAN,
2d Infantry, San Diego, California.

HEADQUARTERS TENTH MILITARY DEPARTMENT,
Monterey, California, August 20, 1849.

CAPTAIN: Your communication of the 3d instant, in relation to quarters for your family during your absence from San Diego with the escort of the commissioners of the boundary survey, has been referred to the commanding officer at San Diego, with the following endorsement:

"The commanding general directs that, during the absence of Captain Hayden from San Diego, his family be furnished with the quarters and fuel to which he would be entitled if he were on duty at that post. The allowance to be in kind, or the commutation to be paid, as may be most convenient to the service."

Very respectfully, captain, your obedient servant,
E. R. S. CANBY,
Assistant Adjutant General.

Captain J. HAYDEN,
2d Infantry, Camp Riley, near San Diego, California.

HEADQUARTERS TENTH MILITARY DEPARTMENT,
Monterey, California, August 20, 1849.

MAJOR: Your communications of July 16, 25, and August 2d, 3d, and 12th, were received by the steamer on the 18th instant, and have been submitted to the commanding general, by whom I am directed to say, that the court-martial for which you apply will be ordered at the earliest practicable moment. Your requisition for supplies has been approved and forwarded.

The lumber ordered to your post is intended only for repairs; and, until the requisitions of paragraph 111, general orders No. 49, 1848, and VIII of department orders No. 16, current series, are first complied with, no authority can be given for the erection of buildings.

The commanding general will visit San Diego for this purpose as soon as it is possible to leave this place.

The military express from San Diego to Monterey is exceedingly important in connecting department headquarters with the intermediate places, and it will be continued until the establishment of the post office mail, now in contemplation, renders it no longer necessary.

Very respectfully, your obedient servant,
E. R. S. CANBY,
Assistant Adjutant General.

Major S. P. HEINTZELMAN,
2d Infantry, San Diego, California.

HEADQUARTERS TENTH MILITARY DEPARTMENT,
Monterey, California, August 20, 1849.

SIR: Your communication of yesterday in explanation of your interference in the matter complained of by Mr. Forbes, vice consul of her Britannic Majesty, has been received and submitted to the brigadier general commanding, by whom I am directed to say that the interference of a military force to aid the civil authorities in the exercise of their duties can only be called for when all the means under the control of the civil authorities have been unsuccessfully employed; and that when applied for, the requisition should come from the highest judicial authority in the district in which the alleged offence was committed. Even if properly clothed with the authority he attempted to exercise, Mr. Bellamy had no jurisdiction in the case; nor does it appear that efforts were made to execute the process by a civil posse, or that any reference of the case was ma'e to the first alcalde of the district. His conduct, therefore, is not approved; and your interference is deemed unnecessary, particularly when the whole matter might, without any difficulty or prejudicial delay, have been referred to higher judicial authority, or to the governor of the Territory. For the course to be pursued under similar circumstances, you are respectfully referred to the several paragraphs of department orders No. 16 and orders No. 17 of the 8th of May last.

Very respectfully, your obedient servant,

E. R. S. CANBY,
Assistant Adjutant General.

Lieutenant E. H. DERBY,
Topographical Engineer, Monterey, California.

HEADQUARTERS TENTH MILITARY DEPARTMENT,
Monterey, California, August 23, 1849.

COLONEL: Lieutenant Wilson, 1st dragoons, was instructed, on the 2d of June last, to proceed with his company to Los Reyes river, for the purpose of apprehending the perpetrators of some Indian murders that had recently been committed on or near that river. He was also directed to "report the result of his expedition promptly for the information of the commanding general;" to collect and report any information that might be useful with regard to the Indians—their numbers, haunts, the best position for the establishing of troops to operate against them.

In my communication to you of July 22, I repeated that I expected on my arrival at Benicia to receive a report from Lieutenant Wilson "that would determine this point"—the best route for supplying a command sent to that river—"and enable me to report more definitely than I now can." I was greatly disappointed in not finding Lieutenant Wilson's report at Benicia, and still more so that it was not received by the mail which arrived last night. Although it is exceedingly important that troops should be sent to the Los Reyes river before the mining population is established in that neighborhood, yet, from the imperfect knowledge of that region, and the ascertained fact that the whole neighborhood of the lake is at certain seasons of the year exceedingly unhealthy, I am greatly averse to the establishment of troops in that country until after the receipt of the information expected from Lieutenant Wilson, or until that neighborhood be properly examined for the selection of a healthy position. If the report of Lieutenant Wilson should not be satisfactory in this respect, I shall recommend that Major Miller's command remain in its present location until the commencement of the rainy season; and that it then be withdrawn and established in quarters on the coast during the winter. In the mean time, if topographical engineers should arrive by the next steamer, as I expect, I will cause the neighborhood to be thoroughly examined, and the necessary preparations to be made for the establishment of this post early in the spring.

Very respectfully, your obedient servant,

E. R. S. CANBY,
Assistant Adjutant General.

Lieutenant Colonel J. HOOKER,
Assistant Adjutant General U. S. A., Sonoma, California.

HEADQUARTERS TENTH MILITARY DEPARTMENT,
Monterey, California, August 23, 1849.

MAJOR: The commanding general, early in June last, instructed Lieutenant Wilson, 1st dragoons, to proceed with his company, "E," by the way of King's river, for the purpose of apprehending the perpetrators of some Indian murders recently committed on or near that river, to report the result of his expedition promptly, and to collect and report for the information of the commanding general any information that might be useful with regard to these Indians, their numbers and haunts, and the best positions for the establishment of troops to operate against them, &c. Unofficial information was received last night to the effect that Leutenant Wilson has been for some time at your camp, and the general was much disappointed in not receiving from him, by the mail of last night, the expected report. If this report has been sent, it has probably been lost, and you will direct Lieutenant Wilson to forward you a duplicate of his report. If it has not been made, you will cause it to be made out at once and forwarded with as little delay as possible. In either case, you will add to it any information that you think may be useful, particularly with regard to the points indicated in his instructions to you of May 4 and May 7.

It is apprehended, from the irregular communication with your command, that the provisions of department orders No. 21 have not been fully carried out. Your attention is called to this subject; and you are desired to give any orders that may be necessary to insure a regular and uninterrupted communication with department headquarters. A duplicate copy of department orders No. 30 is herewith enclosed. You are desired to acknowledge the receipt of this communication.

Very respectfully, your obedient servant,
E. R. S. CANBY,
Assistant Adjutant General.

Major A. S. MILLER,
Second Infantry, commanding, Camp Stanislaus.

HEADQUARTERS TENTH MILITARY DEPARTMENT,
Monterey, California, August 23, 1849.

CAPTAIN: Your communication of the 17th instant and its enclosures were received last night, and I am directed by the commanding general to say that his instructions of the 9th instant were not more definite because the papers in reference to the claim of Mr. Thompson, and the permission of Mr. Steineberger to occupy a position on the reserve, are (or should be) on file at your post, or in the assistant quartermaster's office in San Francisco. By the decisions of Generals Mason and Riley, former and present governors of California, "occupancy of the house" commonly known as "the Kanaha House," and a "right of way to the beach," are guarantied to Mr. Thompson "until his claim be submitted to the United States government" or "decided by the proper tribunals." Beyond this his title has not been and will not be recognised; and you are directed to apply to Mr. Billings, attorney general of California, for any assistance that may be necessary to protect the interests and rights of the United States to this property. The reservation at Rincon point, and any other public lands that there may be at San Francisco, are included in your instructions of the 9th instant.

Very respectfully, your obedient servant,

E. R. S. CANBY,
Assistant Adjutant General.

Captain E. D. KEYES,
Commanding, Presidio, San Francisco.

[No. 4.] HEADQUARTERS TENTH MILITARY DEPARTMENT,
Monterey, California, August 30, 1849.

COLONEL: I found, on my return to this place from a reconnoissance of a portion of the valleys of San Joaquin and Sacramento rivers, general orders No. 1 from the headquarters of the army; and, as I cannot have copied in season for transmission by the steamer of the 1st proximo the military correspondence at these headquarters, I respectfully submit, for the information of the commander-in-chief, a brief summary of reports heretofore made in relation to military affairs in this department.

My attention was directed, on my arrival in this country, to the unparalleled excitement in relation to the mineral regions; the imminent danger that our troops, as they arrived, would desert to the "*placers*," and, instead of giving protection to the parties, and aid in the preservation of order and tranquillity, would themselves become the very worst element of disorder; the great extent of Indian frontier to be guarded, and the difficulties then apprehended from the unsettled state of affairs in the mining districts. An attentive consideration of these subjects impressed me with the opinion that the policy most likely to prove advantageous to the service, would be the concentration of all the troops serving in this department, except the necessary guards for the depôts at one or more points in the immediate vicinity of the gold regions, from whence a portion of them might be permitted to visit the placers for the purpose of working them for their own benefit—the remainder to be held embodied in a proper state of discipline, in readiness for any emergency that might occur. After the expiration of the furlough of the first class, a second class to be furloughed, and so in succession with the remainder; the troops stationed at points so distant from the mines, that they could not be furloughed, to be relieved by exchange with commands that have been more favorably situated. The practice of granting furloughs, adopted at some of the posts in this country, with the sanction of the former department commander, had succeeded well, and the information received about the time of my arrival from the southern part of this department confirmed me in the opinion previously entertained, that the mania for gold-hunting would exist, in its most exaggerated form, at points most remote from the *placers*. I accordingly, immediately after relieving Colonel Mason in the command of the department, recommended the adoption of the policy above indicated. It is a matter of regret, that the emergencies of the service have been such that it could not be carried out to the extent recommended; for the experience of the past four months has convinced me that it is the only course that can be adopted, with reasonable hope of success, until the state of affairs in this country is materially changed. In addition to the mere question of expediency, Indian difficulties that were then occurring, and the threatening danger of a proximate collision between the different classes at work in the gold region, made it highly important that a strong military force should be established in the immediate vicinity of the mining region.

For the disposition of the troops in the department, and the measures taken to prevent desertions, &c., I respectfully refer to department order and special orders forwarded to you by this mail. These furnish you with a history of the operations in the department since my assumption of the command. The present disposition of the troops is the same as indicated in orders No. 16, except that company A, 2d infantry, re-enforced by details from other companies—in all, four officers and eighty men—has been detached, under instructions from the commander of the division, as an escort for Captain Warner, topographical engineers, and company E, 1st dragoons, when *en route* for the station, was diverted from that route, for the purpose of securing the perpetrators of some murders committed by Indians on or near Los Reyes river.

The difficulties apprehended from a collision between the different classes of the mining population have not yet occurred in the form which it was feared they would assume, and at present I do not apprehend any serious difficulty from that source. Some serious Indian disturbances have occurred on the American fork of the Sacramento, and a few isolated murders have occurred at other points; but at the date of the last report from the frontier, everything was quiet. The Indians of the Sierra Nevada, although in a great number, are of a degraded class, and are divided into so many different tribes, or rancherias, speaking different languages, that any combination on their part is scarcely to be apprehended. Their depredations heretofore have been confined generally to horse-stealing, and only occasionally have murders been committed by them. These, however, have been made the pretence, by the whites in their neighborhood, for the commission of outrages of the most aggravated character—in one or two cases involving in an indiscriminate massacre the wild Indians of the Sierra and the tame Indians of the ranchos. The commanders of detachments serving on the Indian frontiers are instructed to prevent any authorized interference with the Indians by the whites, and to support the Indian agents of their districts in the exercise of their appropriate duties. From the character of the mining population, and the nature of their occupations, unless a strong military force be maintained on that frontier, it will be impossible to prevent the commission of outrages upon the Indians; and they, in turn, will be avenged by murders committed upon isolated parties of whites. Unfortunately, the eagerness with which gold is sought after by detached parties of miners, gives many opportunities for the commission of such outrages. To seek after and apprehend the perpetrators in cases of this kind, a mounted force is absolutely necessary; and, although great difficulty will be experienced in obtaining forage and replacing horses that may be disabled, its services are so indispensably necessary, that I greatly regret my inability to supply more than one company on the Indian frontier until after the company now on duty with the commissioner of the boundary survey is relieved.

I have heretofore called the attention of the War Department and the division commander to the insufficiency of the force assigned to this department by general order No. 49 of 1848. As it may not be possible, with the present military establishment, to order any additional force to this country without the action of Congress, I respectfully invite the attention of the commanding general to the views heretofore expressed on this subject. A topographical sketch of a portion of this department is herewith enclosed, upon which I have indicated the positions or neighborhoods in which I deem it important that troops should be established. The amount and character of the force required in my report to division headquarters, of June 11, is also enclosed.

The embarrassments under which the service has labored will be so readily appreciated at home, that it is unnecessary to refer to them here except to say that, great as these embarrassments have been, they have been greatly increased by the want of line and staff officers.

In consequence of the extraordinary prices of labor, and the consequent enormous expenditures in this country, young officers of the line should not be, in justice to the service and themselves, as they have unnecessarily been, encumbered, in addition to their company duties, with money and property responsibilities to a very great amount. Experienced officers of the quartermaster's department are required at San Francisco, San Diego, and with the commands on the upper Sacramento and San Joaquin rivers. 1 have now but one officer, Captain Kane, of that department, under my control; and he is necessarily detained at department headquarters in the preparation of my estimates for the service of the ensuing year. Quarters must soon be erected at several of the posts in this department; and I cannot spare line officers for this duty, without destroying their efficiency with their companies, even were it proper to do so. There are no topographical engineers on duty in this department, and, in consequence of the want, I have been able to perform very little of the duty devolved upon me by the 111th paragraph general orders No. 49, of 1848. A reconnoissance of a portion of the valleys of the Sacramento and San Joaquin rivers, undertaken for the purpose of determining the position to be occupied, as recommended in my report to division headquarters of April 16, to the War Department of the 25th of the same month, has strengthened my opinion of the importance of giving the country a most thorough examination before any military posts are permanently located in the interior. The whole district of country lying between the coast range and the Sierra Nevada is exceedingly sickly at certain seasons of the year. The common timber of the country (oak) is not fit for building purposes; and I was greatly disappointed in finding that south of the Sacramento river, pine fit for lumber exists only on the spur of the mountains in small quantities, and in places difficult of access. Stone, as a building material, is scarce; and at several of the points where it may be desirable to establish military posts, grain for forage is out of the question, and grass can only be found in exceedingly limited quantities. I expressed a hope in my despatches to the War Department of June 30, that I would be able to make an examination of the country along the western slope of the Sierra Nevada, from the source of the San Joaquin to the southern boundary of California; but the season is now so far advanced that I fear I shall not be able to accomplish more than the determination of a position to be occupied in the neighborhood of Los Reyes river. It is of great importance that this point should be determined as soon as possible; for the new discoveries of gold constantly being made in that direction, are attracting thither a large portion of the mining population. The rapidly increasing population of the northern *placers* is gradually forcing the Indians to the south, and congregating them on the waters of the Lake Buena Vista, (Tula.) This position should be occupied, if possible, before the miners have become established in Los Reyes and the neighboring rivers; and the necessary examinations and arrangements will be made as soon as it is possible to do so.

Since my application (April 25) for officers of the quartermaster's department was made, two officers of that corps, Majors Allen and Fitzgerald, whom I had supposed would be available for duty in this department, have been permanently separated from it; and the number then applied for should be increased by two.

Two of the medical officers in this department are now prostrated by disease; and as their places cannot be supplied here, there should be at least three in this department, in addition to those actually required for duty at the different posts in the department, to meet emergencies of this kind.

The ordnance depots at Monterey and San Francisco are under the charge of military store-keepers. It is important, for the preservation of this property in a serviceable condition, that they should be under the supervision of an experienced ordnance officer.

With the exception of the assistant quartermaster above referred to, the officers above enumerated have heretofore been applied for; but as none have been reported to me, I will state in detail what officers are absolutely required with this command:

Four officers of the quartermaster's department, in addition to Captain Kane now on duty here;

Two topographical engineers;

Three additional medical officers;

One officer of the ordnance department;

One officer of the subsistence department.

The irregular communication with some of the interior posts, creates a good deal of embarrassment by delaying the department returns. In consequence of this I am unable to furnish a later return than for June. The transport Mary and Adeline, with companies A and F, 2d infantry, reached San Francisco on the 8th ultimo. The detachment of dragoons, on their march to the department with the collector of this district and the Arkansas emigrants, have not yet arrived. During the months of July and August, so far as reports have been received, there were but few desertions, except from the company detailed for the escort of Captain Warner, topographical engineers: 34 men, more than half the whole number reported, have deserted from this company. The entire force in the department at this time does not probably exceed 650, (aggregate;) and consequently more than 400 recruits are now required to fill up these companies to the standard authorized for this department.

A detailed report of my reconnoissance in the valleys of the San Joaquin and Sacramento will be forwarded by the next steamer. I have delayed it in order to embody in it information in regard to the country in the neighborhood of the Tula, which I am in the daily expectation of receiving.

The want of company officers is very much felt; and I request that authority may be given me to break up the companies whose captains are permanently absent, transferring the officers to other companies, as their services may be needed.

I have the honor to be, very respectfully, colonel, your obedient servant,

B. RILEY,
Brev't Brigadier General U. S Army, commanding.

Lieut. Col. W. G. Freeman,
Assistant Adjutant General U. S. army,
Headquarters of the Army, New York.

Headquarters Tenth Military Department,
Monterey, California, August 30, 1849.

Sir: I have the honor to acknowledge the receipt, on the 18th instant, of your communication of June 26.

The policy adopted in relation to the subjects embraced in that communication has been fully reported in my despatches to the Adjutant General, and in the military correspondence transmitted through him for the information of your department. I deem it important, however, in connexion with this subject, to make some suggestions with reference to the policy to be pursued in future.

The greatest difficulties that have been encountered, thus far, in the efforts to prevent desertion, have grown out of the strong sympathy felt by the great mass of citizens of this country for the apparent hardships experienced by our men in being obliged to serve for a sum that in this country is really nominal, while all around them are reaping an extraordinary remuneration for their labor, and the consequent indisposition to render the military authorities any aid whatever in apprehending deserters.

It is thought that the passage of a law increasing, in a very considerable degree, the penalties imposed upon citizens who may entice soldiers to desert or harbor them after desertion, and the forfeiture, for the benefit of the United States, of any property that may be acquired by citizens from deserters, will have a beneficial effect—particularly by rendering it hazardous to engage in any occupation or have any business transactions with them.

This sympathy may be still further weakened, if the difficulties under which the soldiers labor in California be rendered less apparent, by some increase of pay and some allowance in the shape of bounty lands.

For desertion in this country, I respectfully recommend the restoration of the war penalty. The temptations to desert here are undoubtedly unparalleled; but so, also, are the difficulties and dangers that may result from the abandonment of the duties which the soldier has voluntarily contracted to perform, and so should be the obligation to perform them faithfully. I can see no difference between desertion now and desertion in the face of an enemy; nor any good reason why the extreme penalty of the law should not be restored. But if this be thought inexpedient, I would recommend, in its stead, disqualification as a citizen; the forfeiture, for the benefit of the United States, of all property that may be in the possession of a deserter at the time of desertion, or is acquired thereafter; confinement at hard labor upon any of the public works, or in any penitentiary of the country for a number of years, at the discretion of the court that tries, but extending beyond the period of his enlistment.

Although no reasonable increase of pay will have the effect of preventing desertions, a slight increase will have a beneficial effect for the reasons above stated, and in rendering the men more contented in their situations here. I recommend an increase of from three to five dollars per month, the increase to be retained until the expiration of the soldier's term of service; and that a bounty of 320 or 640 acres of land be given to all soldiers who may serve faithfully the full period of their enlistments. This last provision should be retrospective, and should embrace all who have served faithfully in California since the discovery of the gold *placers*.

In my despatch of April 25, I suggested, for the consideration of the authorities at home, the plan of employing a portion of the force in this country in working the mines for their own benefit, reserving, of the amount collected, a sufficient per centage to reimburse the government for the extraordinary expense of the military establishment in this country. I am satisfied, however, from an examination of a portion of the mineral region and a more detailed investigation of the subject, that this plan would not be at all *practicable* without a much greater force in this country than we now have. Another suggestion, made in the same despatch, will, I think, operate advantageously, and I respectfully recommend that authority be given for the enlistment of married men for service at the depots, and such of the interior posts as it may be necessary to establish at points so remote from the placers, that furlough cannot be given without prejudice to the service.

It is probable that the operations of the commissioners of the boundary surveys will, from necessity, be suspended during the rainy season. Should this be the case, I request that authority may be given me to establish the companies composing the escort at Los Angeles, until operations are resumed next spring. Troops will be greatly needed there for the preservation of order, and it will be difficult to organize a sufficient police force to effect this object.

I have been unable to complete my estimate for supplies for the service of the ensuing year in season for transmission by the steamer of the 10th proximo; but I deem it proper to state now that the cost of building material and labor is so great in this country, that I am satisfied that buildings for barracks and storehouse may be sent from the Atlantic coast at less than one-fourth of the cost of buildings here, and any estimate will be based upon this view of the case. If this suggestion be approved, I respectfully request that such directions may be given in advance as will facilitate the operations of the quartermaster's department in furnishing those supplies, where the estimates are received.

By the next steamer, plans and detailed estimates for the necessary barracks and storehouse will be transmitted through the Adjutant General for your approval.

I have the honor to be, very respectfully, sir, your obedient servant,

B. RILEY,
Brevet Brig. Gen. U. S. A., commanding
Tenth Military Department.

Hon. Geo. W. Crawford,
Secretary of War, Washington, D. C.

[No. 5.] HEADQUARTERS TENTH MILITARY DEPARTMENT,
Monterey, California, September 20, 1849.

COLONEL: I have the honor to transmit herewith a copy of a topographical sketch by Lieutenant Derby, topographical engineers, of the country traversed by me on a recent reconnoissance of a portion of the San Joaquin and Sacramento valleys, and to submit, for the information of the commanding general, some remarks upon the character of the country lying between the coast range and the Sierra Nevada, and between the confluence of Feather river on the north and the Lake Buena Vista on the south. These remarks are based upon my own observations, and upon information obtained from the reports made by officers of my command, made in accordance with instructions heretofore given by me.

My original intention, as indicated in my report to division headquarters of June 2d, was to have proceeded by the pass of San Miguel to the lake country east of San Luis Obispo, for the purpose of determining the proper position for the establishment of a military command, to prevent the incursions of the Tulare Indians, (recommended in my report of April 25,) and to give protection to the mining interests north of the lake. Information of the hostile attitude assumed by the Indians in that neighborhood, and my inability to take an escort, determined me to proceed to the valley of the San Joaquin by Pacheco's pass.

I accordingly left this place on the 5th of July, accompanied by Captain Halleck, secretary of state, Major Canby, Captain Westcott, and Lieutenant Derby. Passing by the mission of San Juan Bautista and through Pacheco's pass, I crossed the San Joaquin river at the lower mouth of the Merced, the Tuolumne near its mouth, and the Stanislaus river at Taylor's ferry, about thirty miles in a southeasterly direction from the town of Stockton. Pacheco's pass was found to be of easy practicability for mules, but exceedingly difficult for wagons. As a route for sending supplies from the coast into the interior, considerable labor must be expended upon it before it can be made a feasible one. The pass of San Juan, a few miles to the south, is less difficult for wagons, but presents the additional disadvantage of being without water during the season of the year best suited to land transportation. The country in the immediate vicinity of my route was found to be exceedingly barren, and singularly destitute of resources, except a narrow strip on the borders of the stream; it was without timber and grass, and can never, in my estimation, be brought into requisition for agricultural purposes. The timber on the banks of the San Joaquin, Tuolumne, and Stanislaus rivers is composed almost entirely of the holly-leafed oak, a species of white oak, willow, and sycamore. The timber is low, dwarfish, apparently hard to work, and unfit for building purposes.

Major Miller was encamped with two companies of the 2d infantry at Taylor's ferry, in an apparently healthy situation, with fine water, and an abundance of fire-wood. This command was established in its present position for the purpose of preventing conflict between the Indians and whites, and to be at hand should a collision (as was then much apprehended) occur between the Americans and foreigners who had congregated in great numbers upon the waters of the Stanislaus, Tuolumne, and Merced rivers. The necessity of keeping troops in this position to meet Indian difficulties will probably not exist much longer. The rapidly increasing mining population is gradually forcing the Indians to the south, and another season will find them so surrounded by the whites that the presence of troops, unless it be to protect the Indians, will be no longer required. The danger of the occurrence of the last-mentioned difficulty has also, in a great measure, passed away.

I was disappointed in finding that company E, 1st dragoons, had not joined Major Miller's command; and I was, in consequence, reluctantly obliged to defer my proposed examination of the country in the neighborhood of the Lake Buena Vista until able, at some future time, to obtain a mounted escort.

From Major Miller's command I proceeded through the mineral region on the headwaters of the Tuolumne and Stanislaus rivers to the Sacramento, crossing, on my route, the Calaveras, Mokelumne, Seco, and Cosumnes rivers, for the purpose of examining the valley of the Sacramento river for the distance of eighty or one hundred miles above its confluence with the American. The selection of a military post in that neighborhood had been ordered by the commander of this department in January last, but the survey was suspended by the transfer of the topographical engineer in this department to division headquarters.

Upon my arrival at Major Kingsbury's camp, I found that the major general commanding the division had already selected a position for his command on Bear creek, a tributary of Feather river. and distant about 30 miles from Sutter's Fort. The country between the Stanislaus and the Sacramento is, a portion of it, exceedingly hilly ground, and dry, arid plains, unfit for cultivation, except in particular localities on the borders of the stream, constituting an infinitely small portion of the surface of the country. The timber is generally larger, but of the same kinds as on the western sides of the San Joaquin, and the same destitution of resources obtains as on that side of the valley. As you ascend the lower slope of the Sierra Nevada, pine of an indifferent quality becomes common, but exists in situations where it is difficult of access, and not in sufficient quantity to meet the demands created by the rapidly increasing population of the country. It cannot, therefore, be depended upon in the erection of quarters in the interior; and, as before stated, the oak of the country is unfit for building purposes. For the erection of the walls of the buildings adobes may be used; and in the fabrication of these, Indian labor may economically be called into requisition. That portion of that valley of the Sacramento is far better suited to agricultural purposes than the valley of the San Joaquin, and I learn from others that this advantage becomes more apparent as you proceed to the north.

The position occupied by Major Kingsbury was selected for temporary occupation, under instructions from department headquarters, for the purpose of putting an end to outrages that were then being committed by the whites upon the Indians of that neighborhood. In its new position this command may readily be supplied from Benicia, the greater part of the distance being by water transportation.

The country lying between Stanislaus and King's river, or Lake Fork, presents the same general features, barren hills and arid plains, with narrow strips of arable land on the borders of the streams running from the Sierra Nevada.

In the neighborhood of the lake these streams are densely populated with Indians, divided into many independent tribes or rancherias, speaking different languages and exceeding difficult to control. Many of these rancherias prefer to be friendly to the Americans, and will probably continue so, unless induced to become hostile by aggressions committed upon them. They subsist chiefly by hunting and fishing, or upon the seeds of several grasses, or upon acorns; and upon the appearance of an enemy, abandon their villages and take refuge in the mountains. No disposition that can be made of troops will give security, unless they be stationed in some controlling position in their midst. Although it will be difficult to supply a garrison in that vicinity, unless the San Joaquin should be found navigable to a much greater distance than it is now believed to be, it will be more economical in the end than any other course that can be adopted.

The three routes by which supplies may be sent are from Benicia, by the river and valley of the San Joaquin, from Monterey by Pacheco's pass, and the pass of San Miguel. The best of these can only be selected after a careful examination of all.

Very respectfully, colonel, your obedient servant,
B. RILEY,
Bvt. Brig. Gen. U. S. Army, com'g the Department.
Lieut. Col. W. G. FREEMAN,
Assistant Adjutant General U. S. Army.

[No. 8.]   HEADQUARTERS TENTH MILITARY DEPARTMENT,
Monterey, California, October 1, 1849.

COLONEL: I have the honor to report that no material changes have occurred in this department since my report of August 30. So far as reports have been received, everything remains quiet on the northern and eastern frontier.

To the south the incursions of the Indian horse-thieves have been more frequent than usual, but they have been confined, as heretefore, to driving off the horses and cattle of the rancheros. So far as I have learned, no murders have been committed. Complaints are also made, no doubt justly, that many robberies have been committed upon the inhabitants of the lower country by parties of Sonorans, (driven by the Americans from the northern mines,) on their passage out of the country, and the emigrants by the Gila complain greatly of the thefts and hostilities committed upon them by the river Indians. The Indians engaged in these depredations are principally the Tulare, Mohaves, and the Yumas; the latter are the most warlike Indians of this frontier.

The points at which troops should be stationed to control these Indians have already been reported, and measures are being taken to make the necessary establishments at the earliest possible periods. With the insufficient force now in the department, it is impossible to give entire security against the depredations of the horse-thieves, with whom there are many of the renegade Christian Indians, acquainted with the interior of the country and the pasture grounds of the rancheros. In this emergency Colonel Mason adopted the policy of issuing arms and ammunition to such of the inhabitants as were most exposed to these depredations—a policy that I have felt constrained to continue from the same necessity. An officer of some experience in this country will be sent to the south by the next steamer, to superintend the issue of arms and ammuniton to such of the inhabitants as may most need them. This officer is also charged with the duty of making the preliminary examination of the country in the vicinity of the Cajori pass, with the view to the establishment of a command at that point as soon as possible; and Major Emory has been requested to furnish any information that may be useful in determining the selection of a point at or near the mouth of the Gila river, for occupation as early as possible in the spring.

To give greater protection to the emigrants to this country by the Gila river, a post of considerable strength should be established at the Pino's village. I have already reported to the War Department my inability, from the force assigned to this country, to make any establishment east of the Colorado.

Much difficulty is apprehended in the management and control of the Indians in this country, from the fact that there is no recognised Indian country, and that in consequence it will be impossible, without the intervention of Congress, to regulate the intercourse and traffic with the Indians in such a manner as to prevent a too intimate contact of the whites and Indians, and collisions between federal and State authorities. Reports received about the first of this month from the emigrants by the northern route, represented them to be suffering greatly from destitution; and arrangements were immediately made for sending out relief to them. Information was received from General Smith that he had charged Major Rucker, 1st dragoons, with this duty; all the means of transportation that could be collected in the neighborhood was sent to the Upper Sacramento, and placed at the disposal of the officer charged with this duty. Subsequent information from the emigrants represents that the first accounts were greatly exaggerated, and they are coming over in much better condition than was at first apprehended.

Instructions have been sent to the commanding officer at San Diego to send to Warner's pass to meet the emigrants by the Gila river, if he should learn that they are arriving in a destitute condition.

I am still unable to send complete department returns. The returns for one or two months from some of the commands have failed to reach here, and the express from the south, due for nearly a month, has not yet arrived. The express rider has probably deserted and carried the mail with him.

Brevet Major Kingsbury, 2d infantry, has been arrested, and in order to relieve him in the command of his company, I have been obliged to detach my aid-de-camp, Captain Westcott, who will probably be promoted to that company.

The want of officers in this department is so great that I shall be obliged to retain the officers in command of the escort with the collector and the Arkansas emigrants, now on their march to this country. The same reasons will prevent the selection (although greatly needed) of an aid-de-camp until after the arrival of other officers.

Major McKinstry, assistant quartermaster, who has reported to me in arrest, under instructions from Major Emory, commanding the escort of the boundary commission, has been assigned to temporary duty in this department; his arrest being suspended until the instructions of the War Department can be received.

Assistant Surgeon W. S. Booth will be continued in service until the arrival of other medical officers. The reported illness of three of the medical officers now in this department renders this necessary.

Very respectfully, Colonel, your obedient servant,

B. RILEY,
Brevet Brigadier General U. S. A., commanding Department.

Lieut. Col. W. G. FREEMAN,
Assistant Adjutant General, Headquarters of the Army.

[No. 28.] HEADQUARTERS TENTH MILITARY DEPARTMENT,
Monterey, California, October 31, 1849.

GENERAL: I have the honor to acknowledge the receipt, this morning, from your office, of general orders Nos. 36, 38, and 42; your communication of August 14th, enclosing instructions from the War Department of the same date to the commanders of the 8th and 9th military departments; of August 20th, in relation to Lieutenant Stevenson, 7th infantry; certificates for discharge in the cases of privates O'Brien, of company "E," 1st dragoons, and Tillett, of company "F," 3d artillery; and letter of promotion for Lieutenant N. H. Davis, 2d infantry.

Very respectfully, your obedient servant,

B. RILEY,
Brevet Brigadier General U. S. A., commanding Department.

Major General R. JONES,
Adjutant General U. S. A., Washington, D. C.

[No. 30.] HEADQUARTERS TENTH MILITARY DEPARTMENT,
Monterey, California, November 1, 1849.

GENERAL: Lieutenant M. R. Stevenson, 7th infantry, after being discharged from the volunteer service, was assigned to duty at Monterey redoubt by Colonel Mason, under the authority of your instructions to him of April 13, 1848.

A general court martial was assembled at this place in February of this year for his trial, upon charges preferred by Captain H. S. Burton, 3d artillery; but the court adjourned without completing the case, and the proceedings were referred by Colonel Mason to the Secretary of War, transmitting them through division headquarters. In your letter of acknowledgment of June 23, this despatch (No. 52) is mentioned as missing, and was so reported by me to division headquarters on the 6th of August last. Lieutenant Stevenson has been constantly since his assignment borne upon the post returns of Monterey redoubt.

Very respectfully, General, your obedient servant,

B. RILEY,
Brevet Brig. Gen. U. S. A., commanding Department.

Major General R. JONES,
Adjutant General U. S. A., Washington, D. C.

DEPARTMENT OF THE NAVY.

NAVY DEPARTMENT, *January* 23, 1850.

SIR: I have the honor to acknowledge the receipt of the resolution of the Senate of the 17th instant, and referred by you to this department, requesting the President of the United States to communicate certain information in reference to the appointment of a civil and military governor for the Territory of California, and the organization of a government for said Territory. In answer thereto, I herewith transmit all the information in this department called for by said resolution.

I have the honor to be, very respectfully, your obedient servant,
WM. BALLARD PRESTON.

To the PRESIDENT.

NAVY DEPARTMENT, *April* 2, 1849.

SIR: This will be handed to you by the Hon. T. Butler King, if there should be, in his opinion, occasion for so doing. The object of this letter is to impress upon you the desire of the President that you should, in all matters connected with Mr. King's mission, aid and assist him in carrying out the views of the government as expressed in his instructions from the Department of State, and that you should be guided by his advice and counsel in the conduct of all proper measures within the scope of those instructions.

I am, sir, very respectfully, your obedient servant,
WM. BALLARD PRESTON.

Commodore THOS. AP C. JONES,
Commanding U. S. naval forces, Pacific ocean.

NAVY DEPARTMENT, *April* 3, 1849.

SIR: I have the honor to request that you will be pleased to furnish for the use of this department the articles named in the within enclosed memorandum.

I am, sir, very respectfully, your obedient servant,
WM. BALLARD PRESTON.

Hon. GEO. W. CRAWFORD,
Secretary of War.

NAVY DEPARTMENT, *April* 3, 1849.

SIR: You will be pleased to furnish for the Navy Department, if in your power, the articles named in the enclosed memorandum. Should you be unable to supply all, you will name those you cannot furnish, and state where they can be purchased. The articles are wanted with despatch.

I am your obedient servant,
WM. BALLARD PRESTON.
Lieutenant M. F. MAURY,
Superintendent of the U. S. Observatory.

NAVY DEPARTMENT, *April* 3, 1849.

SIR: You will be pleased to furnish this department with the articles named in the within-enclosed memorandum.

Very respectfully, your obedient servant,
WM. BALLARD PRESTON.
Commodore CHARLES WILKES,
Washington.

Memorandum.

1 Gunter's chain.
1 spy-glass, strapped.
1 small lot selected drawing-paper and pencils, (in travelling case.)
1 12-inch ivory protracter.
4 Lawson's maps of Upper California.
2 box sextants.
2 pocket prismatic compasses.
2 pocket ordinary compasses.
1 sextant and artificial horizon.
1 pocket chronometer.
1 case mathematical instruments.
1 Bowditch's Navigator.
1 Nautical Almanac, 1849.
4 sets charts of Upper California, Oregon, and Rio Sacramento, by Exploring Expedition, on tracing paper.
Sets of Fremont's and Emory's Survey, with notes.
Small lot of drawing-paper, blank-books, note-books, stationery, &c.

The above, it is believed, can be furnished readily from the Hydrographical Bureau.

8 Colt revolvers, large size, holsters, &c.
4 Colt revolvers, small size, holsters, &c.
4 rifles, with necessary equipments.
4 saddles, bridles, blankets, &c.
4 tents, small size.
1 set camp equipage.
4 elastic beds, blankets and equipments.

The most of the above can be supplied by War Department.
Respectfully submitted.
CADWALADER RINGGOLD,
United States Navy

Hon. WM. B. PRESTON,
Secretary of the Navy, Washington.

Navy Department,
April 3, 1849.

Sir: I intrust to your care important despatches addressed to Commodore Thomas Ap C. Jones, commanding the United States naval forces in the Pacific.

You will sail from New York in the first steamship bound to the port of Chagres. Upon your arrival at Chagres, you will proceed without delay across the isthmus to Panama, and take passage in the first steamer bound to San Francisco, and make the best of your way in her to that point, or wherever else Commodore Jones may be found upon the coast of California, and deliver the despatches addressed to him into his own hands.

If, upon your arrival at Panama, it should appear that any circumstance had delayed the arrival of the mail steamer at that port, you will, after waiting a reasonable time, proceed to make your way by the earliest opportunity to San Francisco.

After performing the services with which you have been charged, you will rejoin the Hon. Mr. King, and co-operate with him in fulfilling the object of his mission, under whose direction you will return home.

I am, very respectfully, your obedient servant,
WM. BALLARD PRESTON.

Lieutenant Cadwalader Ringgold,
United States Navy, Washington.

[Confidential.]

Navy Department,
April 3, 1849.

Sir: The department, being desirous to send out, without delay, a bearer of despatches to California, begs to call into requisition your kind offices in securing a passage for three gentlemen, to proceed from New York, across the isthmus. The urgency of the case makes it all-important they should leave New York in the first steamer for Chagres, to join your next steamship from Panama to San Francisco. You will therefore be pleased to secure three through tickets, so as to insure against the possibility of any delay in their reaching their destination at the earliest moment.

I am, sir, respectfully, your obedient servant,
WM. BALLARD PRESTON.

W. H. Aspinwall, Esq., *New York.*

Navy Department,
April 3, 1849.

Sir: You will pay to Lieutenant Cadwalader Ringgold the sum of one thousand dollars, for travelling expenses to California.

I am, very respectfully, your obedient servant,
WM. BALLARD PRESTON.

Wm. H. Le Roy, Esq.,
Navy Agent, New York.

NAVY DEPARTMENT,
April 3, 1849.

SIR: You will advance to Lieut. Cadwalader Ringgold five months' pay, and charge to his account.

I am, respectfully, your obedient servant,
WM. BALLARD PRESTON.

JOSEPH WHITE, Esq.
Navy Agent, Baltimore.

NAVY DEPARTMENT,
April 3, 1849.

SIR: I transmit enclosed an order to Purser Rodman M. Price, at San Francisco, disbursing agent on the west coast. Should you find it necessary, you can present the same and receive the funds to enable you to pay your travelling expenses home.

I am, respectfully, your obedient servant,
WM. BALLARD PRESTON.

Lieutenant CADWALADER RINGGOLD,
United States Navy, Washington.

NAVY DEPARTMENT, *April* 3, 1849.

SIR: You will be pleased to pay to Lieutenant Cadwalader Ringgold the sum of six hundred and fifty dollars, for his travelling expenses home from California.

Very respectfully, your obedient servant,
WM. BALLARD PRESTON.

Purser R. M. PRICE,
U. S. Navy, San Francisco, Alta California.

NAVY DEPARTMENT, *April* 3, 1849.

SIR: Enclosed I transmit a duplicate order of this date, the original of which has been placed in the hands of Lieutenant Cadwalader Ringgold for delivery, should it become necessary for him to receive the amount to enable him to defray his travelling expenses home.

I am, respectfully, your obedient servant,
WM. BALLARD PRESTON.

Purser RODMAN M. PRICE,
U. S. Navy, San Francisco, California.

NAVY DEPARTMENT, *April* 3, 1849.

SIR: It is important that the Hon. T. Butler King, and the gentlemen forming his party, should meet with the least possible delay on their way

to California. You will therefore be pleased to afford them every possible facility your ship will offer to convey them to their place of destination.
I am, respectfully, your obedient servant,
WM. BALLARD PRESTON.
COMMANDING OFFICER PACIFIC SQUADRON,
Or the commander of any single ship which may be at Panama.

NAVY DEPARTMENT, *April* 7, 1849.

SIR: 'This despatch has been intrusted to the care of Lieutenant Cadwalader Ringgold, United States navy, who will place it into your hands.

The Hon. T. Butler King, of Georgia, has been designated by the President, and sent out to California, to be intrusted with the performance of most important duties for the interest of that country. Should you be called upon by that gentleman in reference thereto, you will be pleased to co-operate with, and render him all the assistance in your power, to enable him to accomplish the object of his mission, as expressed in his instructions from the State Department.

I am, very respectfully, your obedient servant,
WM. BALLARD PRESTON.
Commodore THOS. AP C. JONES,
Commanding U. S. naval forces in the Pacific.

[No. 59.] SAN FRANCISCO, *June* 16, 1849.

SIR: I have the honor to acknowledge the receipt of your letter of the 7th of April, handed to me on the 5th instant by Lieutenant Ringgold of the navy, in company with the Hon. T. Butler King. A more acceptable visiter than Mr. King could hardly have been sent to California; nor could his arrival here have been more opportune, being himself the bearer of the first authentic intelligence of the failure of all efforts in Congress to extend the laws of the United States over this Territory. Mr. King will doubtless report by the first steamer the state and condition of affairs here as he found them. It is very gratifying to that portion of the army and navy serving on this station, to find that the measures they have adopted for the security of persons and property, and for the collection of duties on foreign imports, are approved by Mr. King, as we hope they will be by the President.

Among other temporary measures touching the collection of duties and inland trade, some of which have already expired by their own limitation, is one still in operation, as indicated by the enclosed blank license, called into existence by the following circumstances: The new town of San Francisco (Yerba Buena by Wilkes's chart) is situated among sandhills, near the extremity of a narrow peninsula of some sixty miles in length, washed by the Pacific ocean on the west, and the southern arm of the bay of San Francisco on the east. The greater portion of this peninsula being for the most part extremely sterile, is but sparsely inhabited; consequently nine-tenths of the immense amount of goods entered at the port or town of San Francisco are transhipped in launches and bay-craft up the Sacramento and San Joaquin rivers, for distribution among the various gold-diggings. The want of American built craft, adapted to the bay and river trade, was manifested in the high price of freight from San Francisco to Sutter's Fort and up the San Joaquin river, which had reached the enormous price of $—— per 100 lbs.; and even at this rate the amount of tonnage in the trade was altogether insufficient to send forward the necessaries of life to meet the great flood of immigration pouring into the gold region from all quarters. There was neither time, materials, nor laborers at hand to build, nor was there time for suitable vessels to be sent from the Atlantic States; so that the only remedy was to permit citizens of the United States owning foreign vessels, built at the Sandwich islands and in Mexican ports, to embark in it at once, and until the pleasure of the Executive should be known.

The question now is as to the continuation of those licenses. Under this license, tonnage to about twelve hundred in thirty-one vessels has been added to the trade; and yet the freight is six and a half to seven dollars on a barrel of flour from San Francisco to Sutter's Fort, and the *storage* on flour at San Francisco is now *three dollars per barrel per month*. These prices are not likely to be much reduced until suitable steamers take the place of sail-craft, now exclusively employed on the above lines of transportation, or until Congress shall establish a custom-house at the more convenient port of Benicia, on the straits of Karquines.

I have the honor to be, with great respect, your obedient servant,
       THOS. AP C. JONES,
   Commander-in-chief U. S. naval forces, Pacific ocean.
The Hon. Wm. Ballard Preston,
  Secretary of the Navy.

[No. 65.]   San Francisco, *September* 1, 1849.

Sir: The steam propellers Edith and Massachusetts have been transferred from the War to the Navy Department—the former to the squadron, and the latter to the joint commission. The Edith was in a very unserviceable condition—that is, her propelling machinery, which has been repaired at a very considerable cost, ($3,500;) and she is now in charge of Lieutenant McCormick, with two engineers hired for the occasion, and has gone to leeward upon a requisition of the Hon. T. B. King, to bring the members elect from San Diego, Los Angeles, and Santa Barbara, to Monterey, where the convention for forming a State constitution will this day meet.

Lieutenant Meade arrived here in the July steamer, but without the engineers and other officers appointed to accompany him. As soon as the Edith returns to this place, Lieutenant Meade will be put in command; but she will not be able to leave the port again until the arrival of the Falmouth, with the officers and engineers ordered out for that vessel.

I have no information from the Bureau of Equipment, &c., that any coal is on the way here; the steamers will be of but little use without fuel, and coal can be purchased here only in small parcels, and at high prices—from $30 to $40 per ton.

I regret exceedingly to inform you that Mr. King is lying dangerously ill in this town, of dysentery, which is very prevalent here. He was attacked a fortnight ago, and, although the worst symptoms have been somewhat subdued, Dr. Bowie, of the navy, is not entirely free from apprehension of a fatal termination; should such be the case, the public, and California in particular, would sustain a loss which could not be speedily replaced.

I have the honor to be, most respectfully, your obedient servant,
THOS. AP C. JONES,
Commander-in-chief U. S. naval forces, Pacific ocean.
Hon. WM. BALLARD PRESTON,
Secretary of the Navy.

P. S.—Since the above was written, Dr. Bowie has called in to say that Mr. King's symptoms are much more favorable, and that he thinks him doing very well.

T. AP C. J.

[No. 66.] FLAG-SHIP OHIO,
San Francisco, September 12, 1849.

SIR: The enclosed copy of a letter from Lieutenant James McCormick will inform you of the shipwreck and total loss of the United States steam-propeller "Edith." My letter (No. 65) of the 1st of September informed you of the object for which the Edith was despatched to leeward, which will be better understood by the accompanying copy of a letter from the Hon. T. Butler King, to me addressed. I am pleased to say that, notwithstanding the loss of the "Edith," the object of her visit below has not been defeated, as all the members elected to the convention from the southern districts, with a single exception, were in attendance at Monterey when the convention organized for business on Monday, the 3d instant, and, by last accounts, were proceeding harmoniously in their great work.

I have the honor to be, most respectfully, your obedient servant,
THOS. AP C. JONES,
Commander-in-chief U. S. naval forces, Pacific ocean.
Hon. WM. B. PRESTON,
Secretary of the Navy.

SAN FRANCISCO, *August* 13, 1849.

SIR: In carrying into effect the views and policy indicated in the letter of the Secretary of the Navy, which I had the honor to deliver to you on my arrival in this place, it has become necessary that I request you to despatch the steamer Edith, as soon as practicable, to St. Diego, touching at the intermediate ports, and to return to Monterey by the 1st proximo. Please to have her supplied with stores, &c., to accommodate some twenty persons in her cabin. As she is now, I am informed, undergoing repairs, I must beg that you will not hesitate to employ such force as will insure her being ready for sea, if possible, by Saturday next.

I have the honor to be, with very great respect and esteem, your most obedient servant,

T. BUTLER KING.

Commodore T. AP C. JONES, &c., &c., &c.

U. S. Steam Propeller Edith, *August* 26, 1849.

Sir: I am under the painful necessity of reporting this vessel on Point Conception. On Friday night last, near 10 o'clock, surf was discovered close aboard; all haste was used to alter the course, but without availing anything. She struck frequently and heavily; but the bottom being sand, she was a long time before any leak was made. Yesterday, finding it impossible to get off, and the hold having three feet of water in it, I thought it prudent to cut away the masts. In the afternoon she leaked so fast that both the pumps and the engine pumps could not keep her free.

I shall now in a few moments despatch Mr. Carnes with Major Garnet to arrange an express to carry this. This I hope you will consider only the announcement of this disaster. When I have time I will draw up a more detailed report. I will proceed to get on shore all that I can. I think there is only a remote hope that the vessel might be saved by the use of the balzas now on board the Fredonia. We have now under the stern about ten feet of water; at the bows six to seven; but it is rather low tide. If she was got off she might be towed to some port to the southward and repaired, provided the balzas could be kept under her. The boiler and engine can be got out by the use of the above article. I think she may be considered a wreck.

I suppose you will expect to hear how those under my command acted. I have only to say, well; they have obeyed all orders cheerfully and with alacrity. As for myself, I am greatly mortified at the result, but I am cheered by the knowledge of having done my duty; nothing but circumstances over which I had no control, brought about this disaster. We had no sun, and from that circumstance had to depend on dead reckoning. I considered myself in the middle of the passage.

I suppose it would appear out of the way to appear over-ready in asking that the loss may be made the subject of investigation before a proper court; but I do ask inquiry, and as soon as possible.

I have no time to write more now, as I wish to despatch Mr. Carnes to Santa Barbara, and then go on with the duty of discharging.

Very respectfully, &c.,

JAS. McCORMICK,
Lieutenant U. S. Navy.

Com. Thos. Ap C. Jones,
Commander-in-chief, Pacific squadron.

[No. 78.] Flag Ship Savannah,
San Francisco, October 31, 1849.

Sir: The failure of the United States mail-steamers to bring forward the mails from Panama has become so *habitual* as to destroy all confidence in that channel of communication with the Navy Department, as may be inferred by reference to my several acknowledgments of letters—some, for instance, of June dates reaching me before others of February and March; and I have good reason to suppose that mine to the department may not have been more regular in their transit: consequently, I have determined to employ a special messenger, as I much desire to keep the department fully posted in relation to naval operations in this quarter, that you may be at all times prepared to answer any calls that Congress may make concerning what is doing or has been done by the navy out here.

Mr. Beale, of the navy, the bearer hereof, is also bearer of a treaty just concluded by Mr. Eames, our commissioner for the Sandwich Islands, with Dr. Judd, one of the King of the Sandwich Islands' ministers of state, who has been sojourning here for a month, on his way to Washington, London, and Paris, charged with high diplomatic functions to those courts. I also send herewith a printed copy of the constitution formed by the convention which recently assembled at Monterey for that purpose. The constitution is now before the people, and is well received; it will probably be adopted.

I have the honor to be, very respectfully, your obedient servant,
THOS. AP C. JONES,
Commander-in-chief, Pacific squadron.

Hon. Wm. Ballard Preston,
Secretary of the Navy.

[Confidential.]

San Francisco, *June* 19, 1849.

Sir: I have the honor to report my arrival at this place on the 4th instant, in company with Mr King. I found Commodore Jones here, with his flag on board the sloop Warren, to whom I immediately delivered the despatches in person, with which you intrusted me.

I am happy to state that, in my humble opinion, Mr. King's arrival evidently gave great satisfaction, and a committee of the citizens promptly called upon him, and requested he would meet the citizens publicly, and express his views in regard to the affairs respecting the Territory, &c. A very respectable meeting soon followed, and received and welcomed Mr. King. Resolutions were adopted recommending a convention for the purpose of forming and adopting a constitution and State government, and measures taken to confer with all portions of the Territory. From present appearances, I have no doubt every measure in conformity with the wishes of the President and cabinet, and the best interests of the republic, will be secured in due season. I consider the arrival of Mr. King most opportune and fortunate, and an impetus, confidence, and direction given to affairs, which will greatly promote the important objects confided to him. It is clear that the strong arm of the general government, and salutary laws, must at the earliest possible moment be extended over this immense and magnificent land, in order to prevent bloodshed, confusion, and a sad state of affairs. Foreigners are flocking in, goods smuggled in along the coast, and jealousy and deep hostility engendered between these hordes of intruders and our interprising and adventurous countrymen. A large fleet of merchantmen are at anchor here, exceeding a hundred sail, requiring an effective squadron to regulate and keep them in order.

By the mail from Monterey, we learn that the people have responded favorably to the resolutions originating here, in public meeting, and every sign is favorable.

I will address you again by the steamer of July 1, and apprize you of all matters of interest in connexion with the Territory.

I am, sir, with great respect, your obedient servant,
         CADWALADER RINGGOLD,
             United States Navy.

Hon. WM. BALLARD PRESTON,
 Secretary of the Navy, Washington.

[Confidential.]

          SAN FRANCISCO, *August* 31, 1849.

SIR: The departure of the steamer Panama to-morrow affords me the occasion of again addressing you. I regret to inform you of the very severe illness of the Hon. T. B. King, who was assailed two weeks since with a violent attack of dysentery. For a length of time he was in great danger, with but slender hope of recovery. The skill of Dr. Bowie, of the navy, has prevailed, and Mr. King is now out of danger, and will, it is hoped, recover.

The moment for the assembling of the convention is at hand, and the delegates with great unanimity are in attendance. Major Garnett left here a week ago in the Edith for San Diego, for the purpose of conveying the southern delegates to Monterey, while Mr. King and myself were to have proceeded down to Monterey in company with those from the northern districts. It is a matter of universal regret that Mr. King cannot be present when the convention organizes, as great respect and importance are attached to his opinions, and his counsel sought very extensively.

The prospect of a successful accomplishment of the duties that become good citizens, no one seems to doubt. The delegates are generally selected from among the common sense class of the community; and if I judge from the resolute tone and manner of many of those who have passed through, they are resolved to act promptly and prudently, and with a just sense of duty to the Union and themselves. All seem impressed with exalted ideas of public duty and a strong desire to assemble in good feeling, execute the high trust confided to them, and return without unnecessary delay to their homes. Territorial government has its advocates, on the plea of the inability of a State situated as California is to support herself. The great majority, I think, are in favor of State government, and I trust the results of the convention will fully confirm my opinions.

I am, sir, with great respect, your obedient servant,
         CADWALADER RINGGOLD,
            United States Navy.

Hon. WM B. PRESTON.

P. S.—Mr. King is recovering slowly, and now no fears whatever are entertained; he will, I trust, yet be able to attend at Monterey during the session of the convention. He charges me to say to you, and to ask you to say also to the honorable Secretaries of State and War, that his severe illness will account for the omission of any communications from him by the steamer which leaves to-morrow.
                  C. R.

DEPARTMENT OF THE POST OFFICE.

Post Office Department,
January, 1850.

To the Presid'nt of the United States:

In compliance with the resolution of the Senate of the United States of the 17th ultimo, I have the honor to report that the third section of the act of 14th August, 1848, authorizes the Postmaster General to employ an agent to make arrangements for the establishment of post offices and for the transmission of the mails in California; and that, in pursuance of said authority, the Postmaster General, on the 1st of November, 1848, appointed William Van Voorhees the agent for that Territory, to whom the following instructions were addressed:

Post Office Department,
November 1, 1848.

Being authorized by an act of Congress, approved 14th August, 1848, to employ an agent in making arrangements for the establishment of post offices and for the transmission, receipt, and conveyance of letters in California, I hereby appoint you such agent. The duties with which you are to be charged will not be confined to any one branch of the department. They will embrace whatever may appertain to the operations of the contract, appointment, and fiscal bureaus of this department in California.

A route having been created by law, and the same being put in operation by the employment of steamships extending along the whole coast of California, your first duty will be to proceed to the selection of suitable persons for postmasters at San Diego, San Pedro, Santa Barbara, San Luis Obispo, and Monterey, and at such other points on the Pacific, at which the United States steam mail packets shall touch, as may need such appointments.

For San Francisco a postmaster has already been appointed, Samuel Yorke At Lee, esq., who will repair, by the first opportunity, to that place. Of course, you will not take steps for appointing postmasters at any of the above-named places on finding that such appointment would be inexpedient or unnecessary by reason of not having a mail supply or from any other cause. On making such selection you will report the same to the department at Washington for appointment, in the mean time placing the nominee in the performance of the duties of his office by a temporary letter of appointment, signed by yourself, to cease on receiving a commission from the Postmaster General, or official information that the appointment has been refused. With your report of the nomination of any postmaster, you will forward his bond, duly executed by himself and sureties, and certified by you to be sufficient, and filled with such an amount as you shall deem adequate for the case. You will also cause him to be duly sworn on entering upon his duties. You will furnish him with proper blanks for post bills, accounts of mails sent, accounts of mails received, quarterly returns, and whatsoever else may be necessary to enable him properly to discharge his duties of postmaster, and to keep and render full and faithful accounts.

You will also instruct each postmaster how to perform his duties, and especially that he render his acounts for each quarter immediately after the expiration thereof to the Postmaster General of the United States at Washington. The collection of the balances arising at each office is a duty that will demand your utmost care and vigilance.

Before selecting postmasters for offices not receiving their mails by the government packets, you will ascertain by what road and from what point on the coast the same is to be supplied; and as no route into the interior of California has yet been created by act of Congress, you will have to make the supply of each office situated in the interior, conditioned upon the expense thereof being defrayed out of the net proceeds of such office. This restriction will necessarily keep the post-route arrangements which you may create upon an economical footing. With or without this restriction, the observance of economy in this respect is important; otherwise one or two points might absorb all the means which could arise in California for the support of mail service, leaving the others destitute. At present no more can be contemplated than semi-monthly or weekly transportation by the cheapest mode of conveyance, unless the same can be obtained at any favorable terms within the yield of the offices. You will bear in mind that no contract can be made for a longer period than four years, that the quarterly periods are for three months, commencing on the 1st of January, 1st of April, 1st of July, and 1st of October, and that arrangements, accounts, and settlements should be made to conform to these divisions of time, unless the circumstances be such as to render it impossible. On making such arrangements, you will immediately report the same to the department at Washington, for such order and contracts as the Postmaster General may make in the premises, in the mean time giving a letter of authority to perform the duties required.

Whether the compensation is restricted to the proceeds of the office or not, you will first determine in your mind a limit for that compensation by the rate per mile per annum. Horseback conveyance of the mails on the present routes in the United States, for weekly conveyance, will vary from three to six dollars per mile per annum. There may be some few instances, in the cotton-growing regions, where the wealth of the country is considerable, but the population very sparse, where the compensation will rise perhaps as high as ten dollars per mile per annum for weekly horseback conveyance.

You will make the contracts at the lowest offers the competition will produce, and not rise above the scale of prices indicated by the foregoing remark; the distance is to be counted but one way.

You will make provision in the contract that payment is not to be made until service is performed and certified to, and in every instance of omission there is to be an abatement of price.

A proper supervision is to be established and maintained, to insure performance, or deduction of pay. William Nelson, esq., United States consul at Panama, will be the mail agent of the United States for the Pacific mail. You will promptly advise him by the earliest opportunity of every office put in operation upon the coast, with those in the interior, depending on them respectively for their supply, so that he may properly *bag* the mails for those places.

You will prepare before leaving the United States, and take on with you, an adequate supply of all the blanks needed by youself and the postmasters in California; also, mail-locks and bags of different kinds needed for that service. The iron lock and key belonging to it will be used for the interior mails; the brass lock and key for the mails conveyed by the steam packets. Hereafter, as the system enlarges in California, further discrimination in the mails may be made by placing the brass lock upon the most important interior routes. At present, the iron lock is deemed sufficient.

You will make report by every mail of the condition and progress of the business under your charge, and will be careful at the expiration of each quarter to render those official returns which will show the state of all pecuniary arrangements of the department in California, and the indebtedness and credits of each party, whether postmasters, contractors, or others; and to keep the Postmaster General advised from time to time of the state and progress of settlements in the country, and what routes should be created by law to furnish them with the mails.

The postage for California is 40 cents on each single letter (which is a letter not exceeding half an ounce in weight) between any place in California and any place on the Atlantic coast, and 12½ cents between any place on the Pacific. Double, treble letters, and so on, will be chargeable with double, treble, and the like increase of rates.

C. JOHNSON, *Postmaster General.*

WM. VAN VOORHEES, Esq.

The following reports were received from Mr. Van Voorhees, 21st June, 1849:

SAN FRANCISCO, CALIFORNIA, *March* 13, 1849.

DEAR SIR: Mr. Robinson, agent for Messrs. Howland & Aspinwall, having arranged with the captain of the brig "Laura Ann" to take a mail for the States to Panama, I embrace the only opportunity since my arrival to report that the mail steamer "California" reached San Francisco on the morning of the 28th ultimo, after a protracted voyage of twenty-eight days from Panama. Owing to the diminished supply of coal on board—insufficient, it was apprehended, to take the ship to San Francisco, if she were delayed to touch at San Diego and Santa Barbara—those places were omitted, and the mails in my charge to be delivered there were brought on, and are now in my possession here, no opportunity having offered to send them down. At Monterey the mails were delivered to Captain William G. Marcy, who received, opened, and distributed them, without, however, consenting to enter permanently upon the duties of the office. He nevertheless executed his bond as postmaster, which will be sent to the department hereafter, but with the understanding that he should probably relinquish the office in a short time. In case he concludes to do so, it will be found difficult to secure the services of another. No one in California seems at present disposed to take upon himself the trouble of public office, though it yield five times the compensation which may be expected from the post office at California. Young men, for example, daily relinquish places in the custom-house here with salaries of from four to eight dollars per diem; and, indeed, to engage anybody permanently in any business, at any reasonable salary, is exceedingly difficult. Eight and ten dollars per day are demanded and received for the most common services, and even these sums are respectfully declined during the mining season, which is just opening. With this state of things existing, you can readily see the difficulties to be encountered in organizing the department in the Territory of California. I am credibly informed that *teamsters* from Sutter's Fort to the mines may command $200, and often as much as $400 per month. Horses I know to be worth—and very ordinary horses, too—from $200 to $300. To contract with a Californian, therefore, to convey the mails, the department may well calculate a heavy "debit balance" over and above the proceeds of the post offices supplied at the rates of postage now established for the Territory.

The postmaster for San Francisco not having arrived, and the demand for intelligence from the States absolutely requiring it, it was deemed best to have the mails opened and distributed. For this purpose, Mr. C. L. Ross, a merchant of some considerable standing, was selected by me to take charge of them until the arrival of *Mr. Dallas*, to whom he was directed to pay over such postages as he may have collected, and deliver the office, should he (Dallas) consent to take it, which I am inclined to think is extremely questionable. The compensation afforded postmasters under the existing system in the States will be found wholly inadequate here, if the office is conducted separately from other business. All expenses are exorbitant: boarding $17 50 per week; washing, from $6 to $8 per dozen; fuel from $30 to $40 per cord; and office rent inordinately high. Nothing is more common than $100 per month for a small room, scarcely sufficient for an office, to say nothing of lodging apartments for the officers. The cheap desk or case, for which the department usually allows from $5 to $10 in the States, can be had here for not less than from $25 to $30; and so in proportion for all other necessary office furniture. With this office, however, in connexion with some other business, I apprehend no very serious difficulty in respect to obtaining a postmaster; for there are a number of merchants in the place who, having established themselves, will not hesitate to take charge of it in view of the benefit to be derived in the way of calling custom to their counters. So also with the offices at Stockton, Sutter's Fort, and perhaps the mines. Postmasters, I think, may be readily had for these, if their supply can be arranged; but at San Diego, Santa Barbara, Sonoma, Benicia, San José, Pueblo de los Angeles, &c., they will be rather more difficult to secure.

I am unable to state with any degree of accuracy at what time the steamer California may be expected to start upon her return voyage to Panama. Without coal or crew, the prospect of her speedy departure is certainly not the most flattering. Her crew have all, I believe, together with engineers, second and third mates, deserted or otherwise left her; and to hire others, especially engineers, is not an easy matter. I do not see that the other two steamers will be in any better condition upon their arrival, so that there is no guessing when the Pacific line of steamers shall commence operations. It is to be hoped, however, some arrangement will be made to establish the line. If nothing else can be done, they might be put in command of regular naval officers, and manned by the government.

In the course of a day or two I shall set out for the upper country, where most of the inhabitants of California, particularly at this season, "do congregate," and where it is very desirable to establish offices, if arrangements to supply them may be effected. As speedily as practicable I shall endeavor to collect all the information to be had relative to the establishment of post offices and post roads in the Territory, and communicate the same to the department without unnecessary delay. In the mean time it will give me pleasure to attend to any further instructions from the department.

I have the honor to be, very respectfully, your obedient servant,

W. VAN VOORHEES,
Special Agent.

To the POSTMASTER GENERAL.

SAN FRANCISCO, CALIFORNIA,
March 14, 1849.

DEAR SIR: In addition to my report of yesterday, I have the honor to add that the mails therein mentioned for Santa Barbara and San Diego (at neither of which places has an office yet been established or postmaster appointed) I authorized to be opened and distributed here. This was considered expedient and advisable; first, because it was believed (and so turns out) that the most important communications they contained were of an official character, addressed to officers connected with the army in California, the greater part of whom it was known did not now reside there; and, secondly, because I have not been able to select any person to take charge of the mails at either of those points, owing to the failure of the steamers to touch there on their passage up.

Until necessary arrangements are made for the conduct of other officers than those provided for by the department at Washington, of which I will advise the department immediately upon effecting them, I would beg to suggest, that the postmasters at Washington city and New York be directed to mail all letters for California (except Monterey) to this office. Persons who would probably be written to at San Diego, Los Angeles, Santa Barbara, &c., from the States, and who, perhaps, resided there some six or eight, or even two or three months since, are now as likely to be found here, or "parts adjacent," as there—indeed more so, for in the *neighborhood of the mines* congregate, I may venture to say, fully two-thirds, if not a greater proportion, of the citizens and residents of California. But were this not the case, it would be decidedly better, it seems to me, that the mails for points not yet provided for be kept at this office, from whence they may be forwarded to their destination so soon as proper officers have been appointed to receive them, rather than deliver them, as required now to do, if made up directly for such places, to persons irregularly and temporarily selected for the purpose.

In respect to such official letters as may be intended for officers of the army stationed at the above mentioned points, they could be sent, if necessary, to Monterey, and thence over the country by military express, (see the accompanying letter from Major Canby) or by the steam packets upon their return trip, when the line shall be put regularly into operation.

The office at San Francisco bids fair to be of the first importance. If the now rapidly growing prospects of the town, its advancing commerce and increasing wealth and population continue, it must soon be second to few offices in the Union. In the absence of other and better accommodation, it is now kept in the counting-room of C. L. Ross, esq., but at no distant period it must unquestionably become of quite too much consequence to be thus "*cabined.*" What better arrangement can be made for it, unless the department authorizes the rent or purchase of a house for the purpose, I cannot well see. As stated in my report of yesterday, the emoluments and commissions afforded postmasters under the existing system in the States, considering the exorbitant expenses incurred here for fuel, office rent, and *living*, are not sufficient to induce the acceptance of the office *by anybody unconnected with other business.* Merchants may be had to take it in charge, but it is accepted by them as a sort of secondary auxiliary business, promotive of other *private* and more important concerns. Properly conducted, it requires, or soon will require, the *undivided* attention of some efficient and capable officer; and I do not think it possible, under the state of things existing here at present, to secure the services of such upon such conditions, unless some more increased compensation be in some way provided. But in relation to this I shall report more fully hereafter.

I have the honor to be your obedient servant,
W. V. VOORHIES,
Special Agent Post Office Department.
To the Postmaster General.

"Assistant Adjutant General's Office,
"*Monterey, California, March 9,* 1849.

"Dear Sir: Please send me, by the first opportunity, any letters or packages that may be in your hands for General Riley, or for officers, &c., of the 2d infantry. The regiment will debark at San Diego, and I will have an opportunity of sending them south by the military express which runs *from this place to the South Fork nightly.*

"Very respectfully, your obedient servant,
"ED. R. S. CANBY,
"*Assistant Adjutant General.*
"Mr. W. Van Voorhies,
"*U. S. Mail Agent, San Francisco, California.*"

Referred to in my communication of this date.
W. V. VOORHIES.

Mr. Van Voorhies was, on the 30th of March, 1849, superseded by the appointment of R. T. P. Allen, esq., to whom the following instructions were given:

Post Office Department,
March 31, 1849.

Being authorized by an act of Congress approved the 14th of August, 1848, to extend mail facilities to the Territory of California, I have, by letter of appointment dated the 30th instant, selected you as *special agent* for that purpose, vice W. Van Voorhies, removed. You will, accordingly, so soon as practicable, proceed, by way of the isthmus of Panama, to California, and relieve Mr. Voorhies, receiving of him the public property in his possession, and giving him a receipt for the same.

Your duties will embrace whatever may appertain to the operations of the *contract, appointment,* and *fiscal* bureaus of the department in California; and the efficiency of the mail service in that Territory will mainly depend upon your energy, industry, and integrity.

It will be your first duty to see that post offices are established, and suitable persons selected for postmasters, at San Diego, San Pedro, Santa Barbara, San Luis Obispo, Monterey, and San Francisco, and at such other points on the Pacific, at which the United States steam packet shall touch, as may need such appointments. Should you find that a post office is inexpedient or unnecessary at any of the above-named points, you will, of course, govern yourself accordingly.

On selecting a postmaster, you will place him in charge of the duties of his office, under a letter of *appointment* signed by yourself, until his commission may issue from the Postmaster General, or official information be received that it has been refused.

You will cause each postmaster, before entering on the discharge of his duties, to be duly sworn, and see that he executes his bond, with good and sufficient sureties, for such amount as you may deem adequate in the case.

You will furnish him with proper blanks for post bills, accounts of mails sent, accounts of mails received, quarterly returns, and whatever else may be found necessary to enable him properly to discharge his duties of postmaster, and to keep and return full and faithful accounts.

You will also instruct each postmaster how to perform his duties, and especially that he render his accounts for each quarter, immediately after the expiration thereof, to you, and through you to the Postmaster General of the United States at Washington, to be forwarded after the returns shall have been examined and registered at your office.

The collection of balances due from postmasters will demand your utmost care and vigilance.

As no route into the interior of California has yet been established by act of Congress, all offices not supplied by government packets will be *special*, and will, in general, depend for their supply of mail on the net proceeds of the offices severally; and, in extending the mail system into the interior of the Territory, you will have strict regard to *economy*, that the expense of the service may not exceed the means arising from it and properly applicable to it. At present, no more can be contemplated than semi monthly or weekly transportation, by the cheapest mode of conveyance.

You will bear in mind that no contract can be made for a longer period than four years; that the quarterly periods are for three months, commencing on 1st January, 1st April, 1st July, and 1st October; and that arrangements, accounts, and settlements should be made to conform to these divisions of time, unless circumstances be such as to render such conformity impracticable.

You will make your contracts for transportation of the mails at the lowest offers the competition will produce, recollecting that the distance is to be counted but one way; and you will make provision in the contract that payment is not to be made until service is performed and certified to, and, in every instance of omission, there is to be an abatement of price. A proper supervision is to be established and maintained, to insure performance or deduction of pay.

William Nelson, esq., United States consul at Panama, is the mail agent of the United States for the Pacific mails. You will promptly advise him, by the earliest opportunity, of every office put in operation upon the coast, with those in the interior depending upon them respectively for their supplies, so that he may properly *bag* the several mails.

You will prepare, before leaving the United States, and take with you, an adequate supply of all the blanks needed by yourself and the postmasters in California; also, mail keys, locks, and bags of different kinds needed for that service. The iron lock and key belonging to it will be used for the interior mails—the brass lock and key for the mails conveyed by the steam packets. Hereafter, as the system enlarges in California, further discrimination in the mails may be made by placing the brass lock upon the most important interior routes.

You will make frequent reports of the condition and progress of the business under your charge, and will, as soon as practicable after the expiration of each quarter, render those official returns which will show the state of all pecuniary arrangements of the department in California, and the indebtedness and credits of each party, whether postmasters, contractors, or others; and you will keep the Postmaster General advised, from time to time, of the state and progress of settlements in the country, and what routes should be created by law to furnish them with the mail.

The postage for California is 40 cents on each single letter, (which is a letter not exceeding half an ounce in weight,) between any place in California and any place on the Atlantic coast, and 12½ cents between any places on the Pacific. Double and triple letters, &c., will be charged with corresponding rates.

You will cause all contracts to be executed in triplicate, and postmasters' bonds in duplicate, and retain one copy of each in your office, transmitting the others to the department in Washington for file, as required by law and regulations.

You are authorized, when, in your judgment, the good of the service requires it, to remove a postmaster, and to withdraw from him the post office property; but you will, on exercising this power, report the fact to the Postmaster General, with your reasons for such removal. You are also authorized to annul a contract for the violation of its stipulations as expressed in the instrument; but you will be careful to report every exercise of this power to the department, stating your reasons therefor. You are also hereby empowered to dismiss a mail carrier from the service, when, in your opinion, the good of the service requires such action—the reasons to be reported as above.

The authority is hereby conferred on you to exercise the power of the department, in the first instance, to make deductions, and impose fines for omissions, failures, and delinquencies in the performance of mail service; the same to be reported to the department at Washington for ratification, record, and report.

You are hereby directed to bring suit in the proper courts for balances due to the United States by postmasters, when, in your opinion, the good of the service requires prompt action in the premises; and you will do and perform all needful acts in arranging, directing, and superintending all post office business whatsoever in California, and in regard to the transmission of the mails to and from the same; and postmasters and all other persons in the service of the department are expected and required to render you all practicable aid, and to obey all lawful directions given by you, as fully as if they had been given by myself.

The terms of the third section of the act of the 14th of August, 1848, do not require the Postmaster General to appoint an agent for each of the Territories therein mentioned, but merely authorize him to employ not exceeding two agents for Oregon and California.

It is now deemed expedient to place the whole of the mail arrangements within and between these Territories under the general superintendence and control of one individual, in order that they may be conducted with unity and harmony. You will therefore assume the principal charge of the mail business in both Territories, with the authority hereby conferred on you to continue the present agent for Oregon as your assistant, or to supersede him, and to employ another, should you, for the advantage of the public interest, consider it advisable and proper to do so.

In case of the removal by you of the present incumbent of the Oregon agency, you will forthwith report the fact to the department, together with the name of the person whom you may appoint as his successor, in order that a commission may be sent to him. In the interval, you are empowered to give him a temporary commission; or, should you find occasional or temporary assistance sufficient, you may of your own authority engage it, and commission the person employed accordingly.

J. COLLAMER,
Postmaster General.

R. T. P. ALLEN, Esq.

The following is the first report received at the department from Mr. Allen:

PANAMA, *May* 17, 1849.

SIR: In obedience to your instructions, I sailed from New York, in the steamer Falcon, April 19, for the scene of my distant service. We arrived at Charleston, Savannah, and Havana, on the days indicated in your advertisement; were delayed near five hours off Charleston bar awaiting the mail, and two days at Havana coaling. The Isthmus did not bring us the New Orleans mail until the 26th, one day after her time. Leaving Havana on Friday, the 27th, we reached Chagres on Wednesday, the 2d of May, and immediately sent the mail to the post office, as required by the authorities there. I will here mention that the Falcon is a noble steamer and well adapted to the service, but entirely unable to keep up the monthly communication required by law; and hence no regularity can be attained in the transmission of the Pacific mails until additional steamers are put on the line.

Many letters and papers were put on board the Falcon for various points on both coasts after the regular mail, a portion being prepaid to the clerk of the steamer. I also noticed that a number of bags of newspapers were shipped as merchandise. I name the facts as interfering materially with the resources of the department, and as needing correction. Indeed, many packages of mailable matter will always, legally or otherwise, be carried by these steamers, unless we have an agent on board.

I desired the captain of the Falcon to wait at Chagres some days, that I might report to you from Panama by her, and also that, if possible, a Pacific mail might be taken home in her; but being told that he could not delay longer than the 6th or 7th instant, I at once gave up the thought of communicating by that trip, and proceeded leisurely up the river, and across the hilly country to this place.

Immediately on my arrival I had an interview with Senor Arosemana, the "intendente" (law interpreter) of this province, and explained to him at length my views of the postal convention, in regard to the unity of a mail, whether of one or many bags. I then directed our consul to write an official note to the governor on the subject, explaining those views as of our government, (not deeming it advisable to demand *here* permission to transport the mail as merchandise,) and demanding a reduction in their charge. A favorable answer has been returned, so far as the authorities *here* are concerned, and the matter referred to the chief executive for final decision; so that, until the existing convention be modified, our mails will pay thirty dollars for the first hundred of gross weight, and twelve dollars for each additional hundred pounds.

The importance of this admission will be seen, when I name that they had charged for the mail of the Falcon ($1,250) twelve hundred and fifty dollars tax, whereas the charge paid will be less than one-tenth of that sum. I have directed this to be paid, but still under *protest*, as we claim the right to carry our mails across as merchandise.

I have been informed by the intendente, within a day or two, that a law has been enacted by this government passing all merchandise across the isthmus free of toll of every kind. Whether this law may not be made to bear on the transmission of the mails, is worthy of inquiry.

As, independent of the terms of our postal convention, newspapers pass the isthmus *free*, I have directed Mr. Nelson to send to the post office for weighing as *mail* the bags containing *correspondence* alone, in the letter pouches.

My attention was called to a bag, about to be shipped on one of our steamers, marked "L. & Co.'s *express mail*," and I directed the consul, whom I have appointed sub-agent for the service of the isthmus, (see letters of appointment and instructions, herewith transmitted,) not to permit it to be shipped, or the letters and papers to be forwarded in the steamers, except in the regular mail. Under my instructions, this mail matter will be placed in the mail, and charged as though it had been mailed in New York.

The mail pouches crossing the isthmus *should be of leather;* the India-rubber pouches will not stand the service—those sent by the Falcon being worn out before they arrived at Panama.

I observe a tendency on the Atlantic side to make the mail service a secondary matter, and *to run for passengers*. This needs correction. Had the Falcon waited one day more, she would have carried back the Oregon's mail, and important despatches for our government from California. The loss of a mail for want of a single day's delay has now occurred twice during her short period of service. She should be ordered always to wait until a messenger can go to Panama and return—this at the least. The Panama mail contains many letters not prepaid; these are issued here by the post office for the New Granadian charge simply. It also contains letters for the coast of South America, for forwarding which, in the British mail, provision should be made.

In view of the entire field, I deem a confidential agent here, with ample powers, as indispensable to the efficiency of the service. I would not advise a separate mail agent on board the steamers; this would be objectionable in many points of view: it would require a large expenditure in the first place, unnecessarily; and there would almost invariably arise a jealousy of feeling between him and the officers of the ship, productive constantly of unpleasant results, and ever working to the disadvantage of the service. I would strongly recommend, therefore, the appointment of the captains of the steamships as mail agents, with a small salary to compensate them for the additional trouble the supervision of the mails would give them—say five hundred dollars per annum. This would identify them with the mail service, and *they* (who have controlling power on board the steamers) would feel an interest and pride in the efficiency of that service; and I am entirely satisfied that the department would save annually more than their salaries in the prevention of frauds of various kinds, and in the increased correspondence arising from offering facilities to passengers and others to mail letters. I recommend, then—

1st. A resident agent in Panama, fully empowered to superintend the mail service on the isthmus.

2d. Let the contract for the transportation from Chagres to Panama be as heretofore; and if the great increase of service demanded since the bid was made require additional compensation, let it be given. The natives cannot be trusted for the *promptness* necessary to this service.

3d. Appoint the captains of the mail steamers on both oceans mail agents, duly sworn, with powers and duties similar to the travelling route agents on the railroads of the States.

4th. Give instructions that the steamers carry no mailable matter not in the mails.

5th. Fix the day of departure, on either side of the isthmus, at the first of each month. We will try to bring the California steamers to Panama by the 20th, and start them regularly on the first of the succeeding month. We must *aim* at regularity, or have confusion worse confounded in the entire line, and a constant recurrence of such misadventures as the last failure in connecting.

6th. Let the letters be put in *leather* pouches and labelled "*correspondence*," or "*letters;*" and the newspapers in unsealed canvass bags, labelled "*newspapers.*"

7th. Let the steamer agents be directed to collect the *small lett r bags* into a large canvass bag, and to mark it accordingly.

8th. I suggest that steps be taken immediately to terminate the present "postal convention." Our mails should pass *free*, as the service is not rendered for which the payment provided for in the present convention was a "*consideration.*"

9th. I suggest that you direct the various postmasters to receive letters for ports in South America, charging postage in advance to Panama, and from Panama to those ports twenty-five cents extra—a total of fifty-five cents on the single letter, prepaid in all cases.

I am, sir, very respectfully, your obedient servant,

R. T. P. ALLEN,
Special Agent California and Oregon.

Hon. Jacob Collamer.

Second report received at the department from Mr. Allen.

Mail Agency Office, *San Francisco, June* 23, 1849.

Sir: Having been delayed in Panama in the discharge of duties pertaining to my office, and by illness, I did not arrive at this place until the 13th instant, and on the 15th resumed the duties of my office, surperseding Messrs. Voorhies and Bronson, leaving the latter, however, in office as assistant. (He has since returned to the States.)

I have, until this date, been engaged in establishing my office in this place, and collecting such information, from the various sources accessible to me, as might guide me in extending the proper facilities of the mail system to the people of California. There exists at present a very general spirit of dissatisfaction among all classes of people here with the absence of these facilities; and I shall feel it an imperative duty, acting under the advice of the governor and of Hon. T. B. King, to extend to the various parts of the Territories the benefits of the service.

The unexampled productiveness of the mining districts has greatly enhanced the price of labor, and, as a consequence, of rents and of real estate generally. While the laborer can realize an ounce of gold per day (on the average) in the mines, he cannot be hired here for a great deal less; and while carpenters get $18 per day, and service of every kind is in proportion, the cost of living must be very great. Boarding and lodging rates at about $25 per week, and all expenses are proportionably high. I know gentlemen who pay $200 per month (more than my entire income) for their cooks; and one man gets, as I have been well assured, $6,000 per annum for driving a wagon for one firm, with the privilege reserved of hauling for other houses when not engaged in the service of his employers; and ordinary clerks are receiving $300 to $500 per month.

You will readily perceive, therefore, that the expenses of the department here must greatly exceed those of the department at home for similar services; and it can scarcely be expected that the income arising from postages here will meet the necessary expenditures of the department, conducted however economically. You may rest assured that I will not permit unnecessary expenditures, and that in extending the system into the interior I will conduct everything on the most economical plan.

Each mail from the East has, for the last two months, brought about six thousand letters. Considering the great number of emigrants now "en route" from the States, the ensuing mails may be expected to bring a greatly increased number; so that I think we may safely estimate an average of ten thousand letters per month, which will yield an income of nearly $50,000 per annum—say $40,000 as nett income, applicable to current expenses; while the amount of service that seems absolutely indispensable cannot be procured for less than $80,000 to $100,000 per annum.

It will be necessary to make special provision for the post office in this place, as the duties of the office will occupy the postmaster's entire time, not permitting him to engage in any other business, while his entire commissions will not pay the rent of his office.

I would suggest for your consideration the propriety of purchasing, or erecting, a permanent building for the post office, &c., in this town, or wherever the distributing office for the Territory is to be permanently located.

True economy would certainly demand some such course, to save the enormous rents to which the department is now liable. In order that you may be well advised of the state of things here, I would respectfully refer you to the reports of General Riley, and other officers of the government, to be found on file in the proper offices, and to H. D. Cooke, esq., to whom I have committed my despatches, that he might give you information of the state of affairs here more fully than I can do in this report. Mr. Cooke has been in this Territory several years, and is every way reliable.

I shall leave this place on Monday, the 25th instant, for the purpose of examining at what places the establishment of a post office may be necessary, and at the conclusion of that tour I shall have the honor of reporting to you the result of the exploration.

Since my arrival here I have had opportunity of communicating with some of the first citizens of Oregon, and have, acting on information derived from them, established post offices at Portland, Oregon city, and Salem, on the Willamette river, and appointed postmasters at those several points.

As the postmaster of Astoria has absented himself for a long period from his office, (is now in this Territory at the mines,) I have removed him, and appointed General John Adair, of Astoria, in his place. So soon as I receive the acceptance of these several officers, I will formally communicate their appointments to you, that their commissions may issue.

I transmit herewith a report from my predecessor, which I have caused to be placed on record in this office, and have the honor to remain,

Very respectfully, your obedient servant,
R. T. P. ALLEN,
Special Agent California and Oregon.

Hon. JACOB COLLAMER.

Third report received at the department from Mr. Allen.

AGENCY OFFICE, *San Francisco, August 2, 1849.*

DEAR SIR: I have been so constantly engaged in the "out-door" duties of my office, that I have been unable to prepare an *official report* in time for this steamer—shall doubtless be able to prepare one in time for the next. Enclosed you have a notice designed to inform the public of the locality of post offices. At present, nearly all the letters arriving remain in this office many weeks before being called for.

I have advertised for proposals for carrying the mail to these several offices, and will endeavor to get the lines in operation "on regular contracts" by the first of October.

The last mail brought near *eighteen thousand* letters. If correspondence increases in anything like this ratio, the receipts will more than cover all liabilities for transportation, &c., unless, *as at present*, a large portion of the letters come prepaid. The extraordinary state of things here will render instructions for the support of this office *necessary*, as no responsible man can be found to take the office for the emoluments accruing under the present laws. I crave instructions that will enable me to make this office effective, and to transport the mail into the interior so far as may seem *necessary*, and on such other points as may seem to you proper.

I have not heard from Mr. Moore since informed by the prints that he had left New York for Chagres.

I am, sir, very respectfully, your obedient servant,
R. T. P. ALLEN,
Special Agent California and Oregon.

Hon. Jacob Collamer.

Fourth report received at the department from Mr. Allen.

Mail Agency Office,
San Francisco, August 29, 1849.

Sir: As indicated in my report of the 23d of June, I left this place on the 25th of that month for the purpose of selecting proper sites for the post offices in the interior.

A pleasant sail of four hours in San Francisco and San Pablo bays brought me to Benicia, a mapped town on the straits of Karquinez, containing now about forty houses, where I landed and took horses for the Upper Sacramento. Benicia is selected for a post office, with a view to the supply of the army and naval depot established there, and of the valleys of Mopa and Sonoma—the latter having been selected as the headquarters of the Pacific division by Major General Smith.

From Benicia I travelled along the base of the hills on the North Suisun bay, crossing several small but beautiful valleys, a distance of seventy-five miles, to Vernon, at the mouth of Feather river. This village is established for the commercial supply of the mining districts of Bear creek, and Juba and Feather rivers—its location being doubtless well chosen for the object in view. I selected it as being, among existing points on the river, best adapted for the postal supply of the regions named.

After a day's delay at this point, I passed up Feather river, through a most beautiful country, twenty miles, to Sutter's upper farm, on the west bank of the river. The country bordering the Feather river is by far the most fertile and most beautiful I have seen in California.

Crossing Feather river at Sutter's, I crossed the barren, arid plains twenty miles to the foot of the hills—visited the lower mines of the Juba, and, finding no grass for our animals, passed immediately to the crossing of Bear creek at Johnson's ranch, a distance of fifteen miles. At this point, being fifteen miles from the mouth of Feather river, it is in contemplation, I believe, to establish a military station. Passing thence the same day twenty-five miles further, we encamped at the "dry diggings" of the North Fork of American river, and the next day, visiting the mouth of the North Fork, in the vicinity of Mormon island, passed down the

American river to Sacramento city, at its mouth, encamping one night on the road.

This is a thriving town, rapidly building up, and promises well to be a place of much importance. Here I established a post office for the supply of the vicinity, and of the mining district of the American and its branches.

From Sacramento city I passed through the plain lying to the east of the Sacramento and Joaquin rivers to Stockton, another thriving town, located on a slough about three miles from the latter river, and sixty miles from Sacramento city. We crossed in this space several beautiful streams marked on the map; and, locating a post office at Stockton for the supply of the district watered by the branches of the Joaquin, I returned by water to San Francisco.

The entire region passed over in this journey, with the exception of narrow strips bordering the Sacramento and its upper and western tributaries, is not at all adapted to agriculture, and but ill so to grazing, and is only valuable for its mineral resources.

The entire valley of the Joaquin, and of the lower Sacramento, doubtless formed, at no very distant epoch, a lake, of which Suisun bay, still rapidly filling up, is the remnant.

Since my return from Stockton, I have remained so far as possible in this place, being unwilling to leave the office here for any considerable length of time, pending the arrival of Mr. Moore, and being mostly occupied in the duties pertaining to the establishment of post offices, appointment of postmasters, formation of temporary contracts, inviting bids for permanent ones, &c.

Finding myself thus fully occupied in the upper portion of the Territory, I despatched J. Ross Brown, esq., with a commission as temporary special agent, and instructions to proceed southward as far as San Diego, establishing post offices at San José, Santa Barbara, Los Angeles, San Diego, and such other points on the main southern route as might appear to him necessary.

I shall be able, from present indications, to provide the necessary mail service for the Territory on much more reasonable terms than I had supposed possible; and, should we be able to get the letters out of the offices, the revenue will be amply sufficient for the service.

Soon after my arrival at this place, John W. Geary, esq., the then incumbent in office here, tendered his resignation; and, there being presented to me an eminent (whig) gentleman of Tennessee, as willing to accept the office temporarily, who was every way suitable to the post, I accepted his resignation, and gave the gentleman alluded to (W. P. Bryan, esq.) a letter of temporary appointment, to continue in force until the arrival of Mr. Moore, taking from him bonds in the sum of $5,000.

I have established post offices at the following points, viz:

Benicia, supplied weekly by water from San Francisco.
Sacramento city, supplied weekly by water from San Francisco.
Stockton, supplied weekly by water from San Francisco.
San José, supplied weekly by water from San Francisco.
Vernon, supplied weekly by water from Sacramento city.
Culloma, supplied weekly on horseback from Sacramento city.
Sonoma, supplied weekly on horseback from Benicia.

And have appointed the following named gentlemen postmasters at the several points indicated, viz:

Charles W. Hayden, to be postmaster at Benicia.
Henry E. Robinson, to be postmaster at Sacramento city.
William Hipkins, to be postmaster at Stockton.
Gilbert A. Grant, to be postmaster at Vernon.
Jacob P. Little, to be postmaster at Culloma.
L. W. Boggs, to be postmaster at Sonoma.
J. D. Happe, to be postmaster at San José.

These gentlemen are men of great respectability, and every way worthy the appointments they have received. I respectfully recommend that commissions be forwarded them in due time.

I rejoice that you have thought proper to relieve me of a portion of my duties by your instructions to Mr. Moore, because it will enable me to be absent for a longer period at a time from my office, and thus more efficiently to discharge the out-door duties of my agency.

Bids for the mail service for one year from the first of October next will be received, according to advertisement, until the first day of September, when the lettings will be made, according to law.

In my report from Panama in May last, I had the honor to recommend a system for the transportation of the mail on both oceans, as well as on the isthmus. From information given me by Mr. Moore, I see that nothing has been done towards securing a speedy and safe transit of the isthmus; while, from facts reported by him, speedy action would seem to have become imperatively necessary. I would respectfully urge that the mails cannot be safely intrusted to the care of the natives. An agent should always accompany the mail across the isthmus, and also on the steamers on each side; and I would recommend that the steamers be required to have a mail room as an office for the agent, and for keeping and assorting the mails.

No care seems to be now taken of the mails, especially on the Atlantic side. They are stowed away in a dark corner below, and are constantly liable to be overlooked. Thus the last Havana mail was carried to Panama and returned; and Mr. Moore informs me that at Chagres they were thrown ashore and left exposed all night, one of the bags wet and another broken open: his servant put them under cover and took care of them, himself not being permitted to accompany the mail on shore.

The clerk of the Falcon had in his possession letters and packages left with him to be forwarded in April, which Mr. Moore mailed in July. He is not, I should think, a suitable person to have charge of so important a service. It would seem, indeed, that neither the officers nor owners of the Falcon have any regard to the good of the public service, but make it entirely subsidiary to other ends.

I am not advised of the terms of the Pacific Steamship Company's contract; will you cause a copy of it to be forwarded to me?

I have the honor to forward herewith a letter from John W. Geary, the late postmaster at San Francisco, (C;) also, copies of a correspondence between the undersigned and Commodore Jones, marked A 1, 2, 3; and of a letter to Brigadier General Riley, with his answer thereto, and a letter to Jacob B. Moore, marked B 1, 2, 3; which will explain themselves, and are forwarded because it is probable your attention may be called to the matters to which they relate by others.

I have received, since the commencement of this report, the acceptances of the persons appointed to the post offices in Oregon. I would respectfully ask that commissions be sent to them as follows, viz: to John Adair, as postmaster at Astoria; to Thomas Smith, as postmaster at Portland; to George S. Curry, as postmaster at Oregon City; to J. B. McLane, as postmaster at Salem. The India-rubber mail bag is entirely unfit for this service. I would respectfully request you to cause an assortment of the smaller leather pouches, say fifty in all, to be sent to the office in this place, for use in this Territory and Oregon. There are no "distribution blanks" among those heretofore sent to the Pacific coast; a full assortment is greatly needed for the post office in this place; they should be sent in quantity by the first steamer.

Jesse D. Carr, esq., an attaché of the custom house here, has presented a claim, on which I need instructions from the department. It appears that the postmaster at New Orleans confided to his care a mail of eight bags for this coast, which Mr. Carr receipted for and brought to Panama at his own expense; he now asks to be reimbursed in the sum of two hundred dollars, ($200.) This mail was turned over to our consul at Panama, as shown by his receipt, without passing through the New Granadian post office, and of course without paying the usual toll to that government. It is proper to add, that he did not come from New Orleans to Chagres in the mail steamer. The matter will be left in "*statu quo*" until instructions are received to cover the case. So little care is taken of the mail on the steamers, and in the transit of the isthmus, that I have thought it proper, pending a permanent arrangement, to commit it to the care of a special agent, who will deliver also a budget to the department at Washington. This agent will be entitled to no compensation other than the free passage secured to mail agents.

Having received information that J. Ross Brown, the temporary special agent whom I sent southward, has gone no further than Monterey, (having been detained there by sickness,) I have recalled him, and will, so soon as the steamer leaves, proceed in person to establish the southern offices. For this purpose I will leave San Francisco early next week, and remain in the field on the southern route until the middle of October or the first of November.

Judging from information derived from Mr. Moore, I think it probable that the authorities on the isthmus do not adhere to the arrangement, made during my stay in Panama, diminishing the tax on our mails by counting *all the bags as one mail*, and that Messrs. Howland & Aspinwall decline carrying them across the isthmus according to their proposition to your predecessor. I earnestly commend this matter to your early attention. The mails should by all means cross the isthmus in charge of an American, and the old postal convention with New Granada should be terminated.

At the commencement of the ensuing rainy season, when I will be unable to travel in the interior for several months, and shall have completed mail arrangements for both Territories, I will visit the isthmus, and, probably, report to you in person the condition of the service, as, during the season indicated, such an absence from the Territory as the expedition would require would not be detrimental to the interests of the service, and my presence in Washington and on the isthmus might be of material advantage to it in many respects.

Owing to the inadequate compensation of postmasters, I find it very difficult to procure proper persons to serve in offices where there is so much business as to interfere with the incumbent's ordinary avocations. This is the case at Sacramento city, where a very large amount of mail matter will be distributed. I enclose a letter (marked D) from the postmaster at that place, and solicit instructions on the subject. Can I in any case authorize a postmaster to employ a clerk? Can I, where it appears necessary to use a separate building, authorize one to be rented? On examination, it will appear that in all cases clerk hire and office rent would each exceed the postmaster's entire commissions.

I am, sir, very respectfuly, your obedient servant,
R. T. P. ALLEN,
Special Agent for California and Oregon.
Hon. JACOB COLLAMER.

The following instructions were addressed by the Postmaster General to Mr. Allen:

POST OFFICE DEPARTMENT, *May* 16, 1849.

SIR: Mr. Jacob B. Moore having been appointed and commissioned as postmaster at San Francisco, in California, and having duly executed and filed his bonds to the United States for the faithful performance of the duties of said office, the special instructions given you in reference to the post office at San Francisco are, by said appointment, suspended, and are therefore revoked. You will, however, furnish Mr. Moore, out of the supplies taken with you for the offices in California, all blanks, stationery, mail pouches, sacks, &c., which may be required for the use of his office; and also render him any aid in the due enforcement of the laws of the United States regulating the Post Office Department which he may from time to time require, and your instructions warrant. As the post office at San Francisco is a distributing office, you will report to Mr. Moore all offices which you may establish under your instructions, with the names of the postmasters, and also the names of all contractors and mail carriers whom you may employ, and the routes over which they travel, the times of arrival and departure, the distance from point to point, the mode of conveyance stipulated, &c., and the compensation allowed to each, in order that he may be enabled, according to law, to report to the inspection office at Washington, from time to time, the condition of the service.

And you will also file in the office at San Francisco copies of all contracts which you may make for the transportation of the mails.

You will instruct each and every postmaster in California and Oregon to render their quarterly accounts to the department, through the postmaster at San Francisco, and to deposite with him the nett proceeds of their respective offices, or to pay the same to the contractors or others engaged in the service, on his order. The instructions addressed to you on the 31st March last are therefore so modified as to conform to the above.

You will find Mr. Moore ready to co-operate with you in the best mode of arranging the mail service, and establishing post offices at proper points; and, as he has had experience in the department, and is well ac-

quainted with the post office system, you will consult with him on those matters, and all others touching the interest of the department.
Respectfully,

J. COLLAMER,
Postmaster General.

Col. R. T. P. ALLEN,
Special Agent, &c., San Francisco, California.

The following additional instructions were addressed by the Postmaster General to Mr. Allen:

POST OFFICE DEPARTMENT,
December 10, 1849.

SIR: Your letter of appointment of the 31st March last specified it to be your first duty to see that post offices were established, and suitable persons were selected for postmasters, at San Diego, San Pedro, San Luis Obispo, Monterey, and San Francisco, and such other points on the Pacific, at which the United States steam packets shall touch, as may need such appointments. It appears that such appointment has been much needed at San Diego, but it does not appear that any has as yet been made.

You were also instructed that, as no route into the interior of California had yet been established by act of Congress, all post offices not supplied by government vessels would be special—that is depend for their supply of mail on nett proceeds of the offices severally. And you were enjoined, that in extending the mail system into the interior of the Territory you must have a strict regard to economy, that the expense of the service may not exceed the means arising from it and properly applicable to it.

The last mail from San Francisco brings accounts against this department for fourteen weeks' transportation of the mail from San Francisco to Sacramento city, and thence to Culloma, at the amount of $9,800, being at the rate of $36,400 per annum; also, accounts for eight weeks' transportation of the mail from San Francisco to Monterey, and from San Francisco to Stockton, at $4,000, which is at the rate of $26,000 per annum. Said accounts recite that the service was performed as per contract with you, as the special agent of this department for California. There is nothing to show that the offices above named yield at the rate of $62,400 per annum—an amount that is believed to be vastly beyond the nett proceeds of those offices, to which nett proceeds you are instructed to limit the cost of your mail arrangements.

The only knowledge or intimation that the department has of such contracts being made is contained in these accounts, which, however, come through a channel that induces full reliance on the correctness of their statements; whereas your letter of appointment requires that you should, as soon as practicable after the expiration of each quarter, render those official returns which will show the state of all pecuniary arrangements in California, and the indebtedness and credit of each party, &c., &c., and that you cause all contracts to be executed in triplicate—one of which you were to file in the office in San Francisco, as per instructions of the 16th of May, 1849, and the two others in each case were to be transmitted to Washington, to be filed in the department and the Auditor's office, as required by law. No contract, or duplicate thereof, in the foregoing or any other case, has been received from you for file as aforesaid; nor any account of contract arrangements or expenditures whatever.

The department has received information through different channels, but unofficial, that you have entered into new contracts for a term of one year from the first of October, 1849, at amounts in the aggregate exceeding $50,000 per annum. But no report is received from you to show officially whether such be the fact or not; detailing, as your report should, the advertisement put before the public, the bids received, and that those accepted were, in the language of your instructions, the lowest that competition could produce; and shewing, moreover, that the amounts you had engaged to pay were within the means arising from the service itself—that is, the nett proceeds of the offices—agreeably to the limitations prescribed in your instructions.

I desire it to be distinctly understood that payments cannot be made for mail transportation service at San Francisco or here, until the contracts in triplicate are executed and placed on file, one in the office at San Francisco and the other in Washington, which can easily be done, before any payment can become due, at the expiration of the first quarter; and that a contract for any service, made at a higher amount than the lowest bid, or made for an amount beyond what is well understood to be the revenue of the route, cannot be considered as authorized by this department.

In my letter to you of the 16th of May, after speaking of the experience in the department of J. B. Moore, esq., the newly-appointed postmaster of San Francisco, and his acquaintance with the post office system, I directed that you should consult with him in the arrangement of the mail service, and the establishment of post offices, and all other matters touching the interests of the department. I trust that this instruction will be faithfully observed. Mr. Moore will make payment, so far as his means will go, not upon your order as such, but upon the contract, duly filed, agreeably to the instructions of May last, and upon your certificate of the performance of service, setting forth the amount to be deducted for failures and delinquencies, if any.

By the instructions of March last, the general superintendence of Oregon was placed in your charge, in addition to the special agency of California; and you were instructed to continue the present agent in Oregon as your assistant, or to supersede him, and employ another, as you should think best; and, in case of his removal, you were forthwith to report the name of a suitable person as his successor, that a commission might be sent to him; during the mean time, to give him full authority and instructions to act at once in the business.

Great complaint is made that nothing whatever has been done in the way of providing any mail arrangements for Oregon; and, although the then special agent had returned to the States, as appears by your letter of June 23, yet no report of a successor has been made by you.

To recur again to the contracts which it is said you have made, I have to remark that, if they are of the character stated, the sanction of this department must be withheld—not only because they are beyond the limitations prescribed in the instructions, but beyond the limitations prescribed by law, because, as the letter of 31st March informed you, no routes in the interior of California had yet been established by act of Congress.

The expediency of establishing a route parrallel to the one created by

act of Congress, and used by the steam ship, is not perceived; nor the propriety of drawing on the postmaster of San Francisco for your salary, until an account is duly made up and sent to this department for audit.
Respectfully, &c.,
J. COLLAMER,
Postmaster General.

Col. R. T. P. ALLEN,
Special Agent, &c., San Francisco, California.

The foregoing copies, respectfully submitted to the President, present all the correspondence between the Post Office Department and its agent in California.
J. COLLAMER,
Postmaster General.

MAP OF FORT HILL

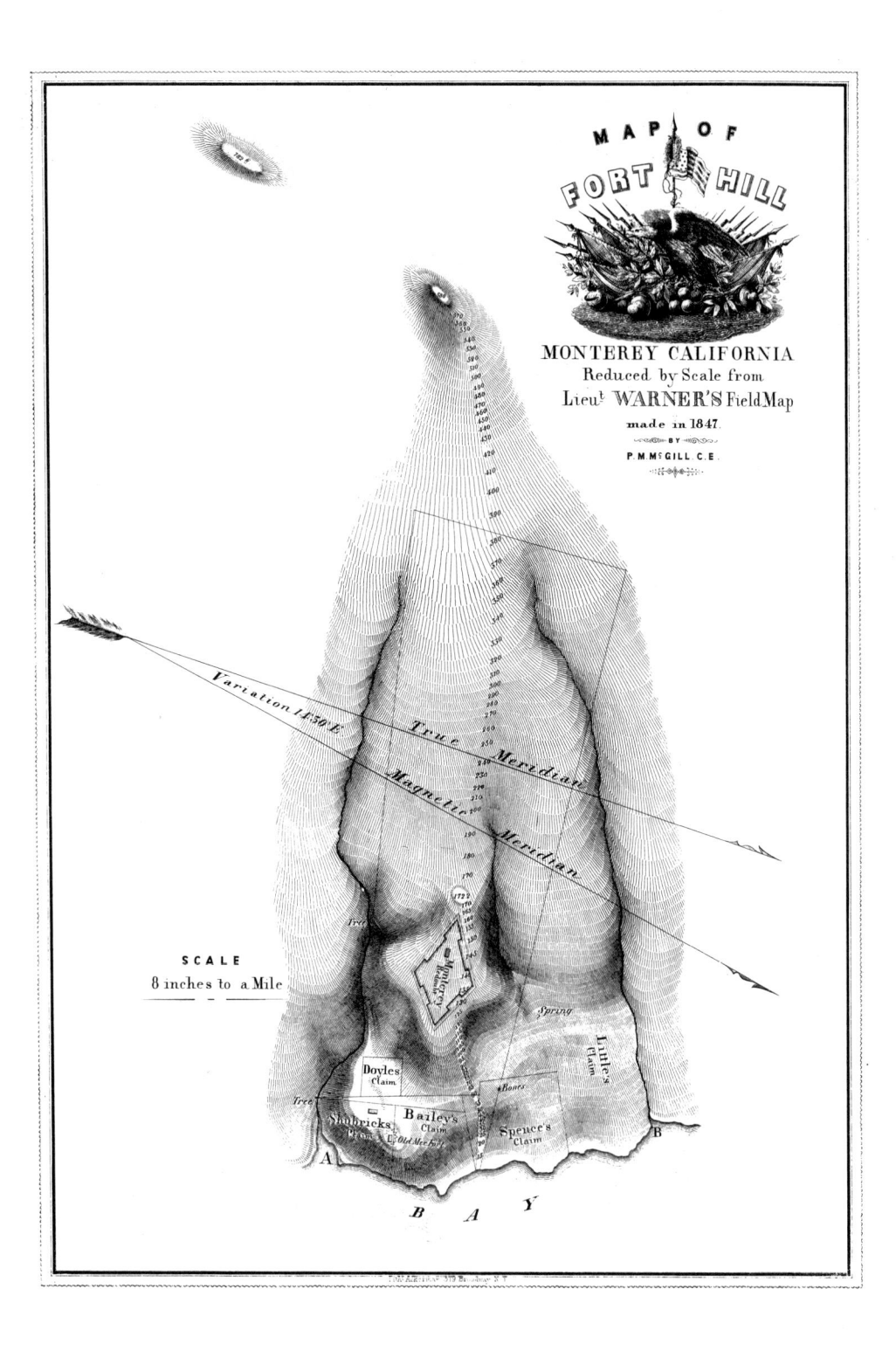

MONTEREY CALIFORNIA
Reduced by Scale from
Lieut WARNER'S Field Map
made in 1847.
BY
P. M. McGILL. C.E.

SCALE
8 inches to a Mile

190. Riley.

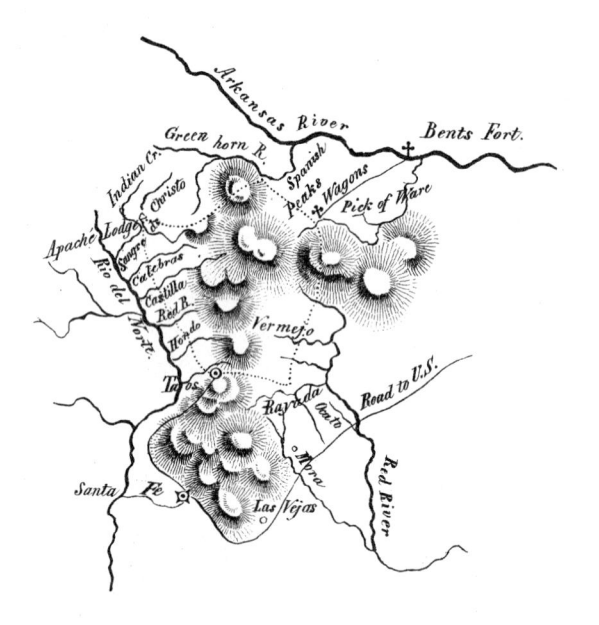

Plan of the Route of the Expedition of Major Beall,
1st Drag's for the Relief of the Wagons of Mr F.X.
Aubrey against the Apaché Indians.
  N.B. The Route is designated by dotted lines.

H. R. WIRTZ MED. STAFF. U.S.A

Ackerman Lithr, 379, Broadway, N.Y.

Yerba buena

Loma alta

Sausalito

Presidio

Punta del Castillo

N.E.

N.W.   S.E.

S.W.

Punta de lobos

Plan No. 2.

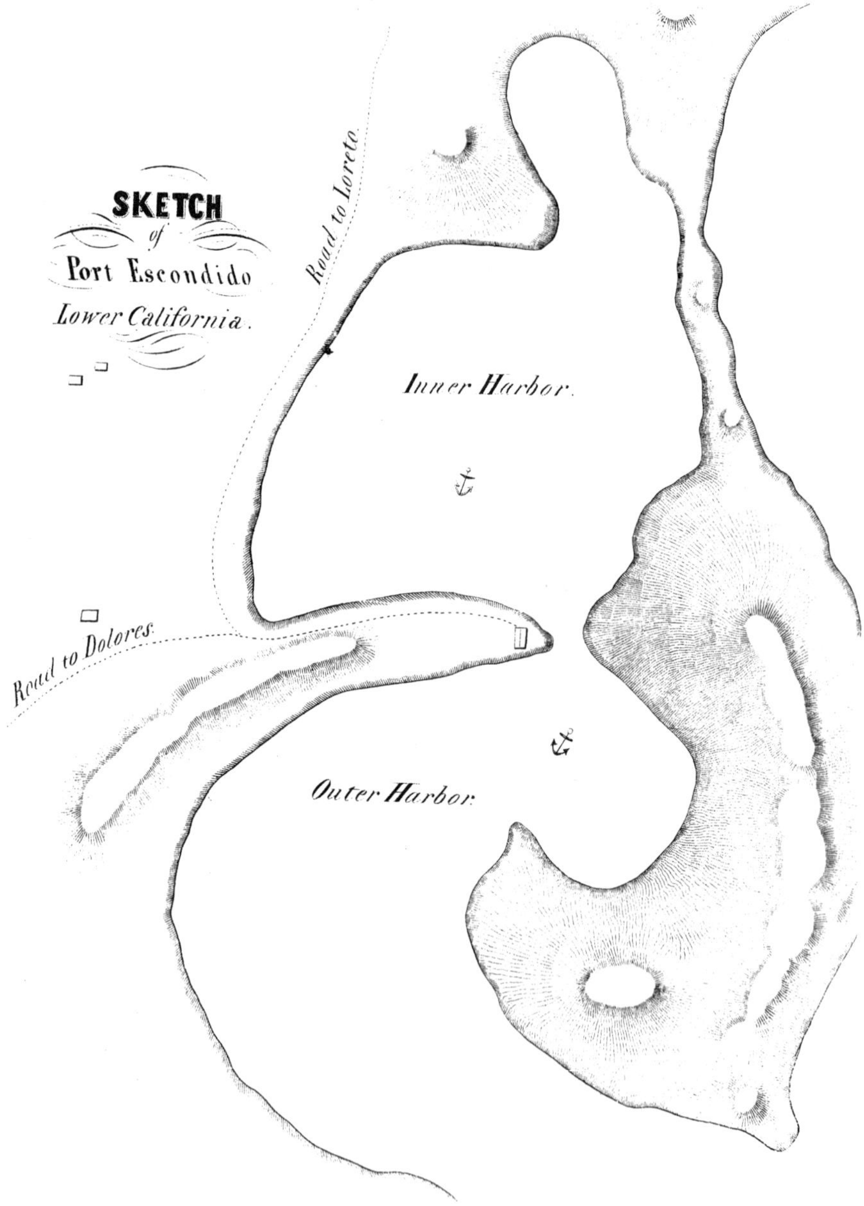

Ackerman Lith. 379 Broadway, NY

THE CHICANO HERITAGE

An Arno Press Collection

Adams, Emma H. **To and Fro in Southern California.** 1887

Anderson, Henry P. **The Bracero Program in California.** 1961

Aviña, Rose Hollenbaugh. **Spanish and Mexican Land Grants in California.** 1976

Barker, Ruth Laughlin. **Caballeros.** 1932

Bell, Horace. **On the Old West Coast.** 1930

Biberman, Herbert. **Salt of the Earth.** 1965

Casteñeda, Carlos E., trans. **The Mexican Side of the Texas Revolution (1836).** 1928

Casteñeda, Carlos E. **Our Catholic Heritage in Texas, 1519-1936.** Seven volumes. 1936-1958

Colton, Walter. **Three Years in California.** 1850

Cooke, Philip St. George. **The Conquest of New Mexico and California.** 1878

Cue Canovas, Agustin. **Los Estados Unidos Y El Mexico Olvidado.** 1970

Curtin, L. S. M. **Healing Herbs of the Upper Rio Grande.** 1947

Fergusson, Harvey. **The Blood of the Conquerors.** 1921

Fernandez, Jose. **Cuarenta Años de Legislador:** Biografia del Senador Casimiro Barela. 1911

Francis, Jessie Davies. **An Economic and Social History of Mexican California** (1822-1846). Volume I: Chiefly Economic. Two vols. in one. 1976

Getty, Harry T. **Interethnic Relationships in the Community of Tucson.** 1976

Guzman, Ralph C. **The Political Socialization of the Mexican American People.** 1976

Harding, George L. **Don Agustin V. Zamorano.** 1934

Hayes, Benjamin. **Pioneer Notes from the Diaries of Judge Benjamin Hayes, 1849-1875.** 1929

Herrick, Robert. **Waste.** 1924

Jamieson, Stuart. **Labor Unionism in American Agriculture.** 1945

Landolt, Robert Garland. **The Mexican-American Workers of San Antonio, Texas.** 1976

Lane, Jr., John Hart. **Voluntary Associations Among Mexican Americans in San Antonio, Texas.** 1976

Livermore, Abiel Abbot. **The War with Mexico Reviewed.** 1850

Loyola, Mary. **The American Occupation of New Mexico, 1821-1852.** 1939

Macklin, Barbara June. **Structural Stability and Culture Change in a Mexican-American Community.** 1976

McWilliams, Carey. **Ill Fares the Land:** Migrants and Migratory Labor in the United States. 1942

Murray, Winifred. **A Socio-Cultural Study of 118 Mexican Families Living in a Low-Rent Public Housing Project in San Antonio, Texas.** 1954

Niggli, Josephina. **Mexican Folk Plays.** 1938

Parigi, Sam Frank. **A Case Study of Latin American Unionization in Austin, Texas.** 1976

Poldervaart, Arie W. **Black-Robed Justice.** 1948

Rayburn, John C. and Virginia Kemp Rayburn, eds. **Century of Conflict, 1821-1913.** Incidents in the Lives of William Neale and William A. Neale, Early Settlers in South Texas. 1966

Read, Benjamin. **Illustrated History of New Mexico.** 1912

Rodriguez, Jr., Eugene. **Henry B. Gonzalez.** 1976

Sanchez, Nellie Van de Grift. **Spanish and Indian Place Names of California.** 1930

Sanchez, Nellie Van de Grift. **Spanish Arcadia.** 1929

Shulman, Irving. **The Square Trap.** 1953

Tireman, L. S. **Teaching Spanish-Speaking Children.** 1948

Tireman, L. S. and Mary Watson. **A Community School in a Spanish-Speaking Village.** 1948

Twitchell, Ralph Emerson. **The History of the Military Occupation of the Territory of New Mexico.** 1909

Twitchell, Ralph Emerson. **The Spanish Archives of New Mexico.** Two vols. 1914

U. S. House of Representatives. **California and New Mexico:** Message from the President of the United States, January 21, 1850. 1850

Valdes y Tapia, Daniel. **Hispanos and American Politics.** 1976

West, Stanley A. **The Mexican Aztec Society.** 1976

Woods, Frances Jerome. **Mexican Ethnic Leadership in San Antonio, Texas.** 1949

Aspects of the Mexican American Experience. 1976
Mexicans in California After the U. S. Conquest. 1976
Hispanic Folklore Studies of Arthur L. Campa. 1976
Hispano Culture of New Mexico. 1976
Mexican California. 1976
The Mexican Experience in Arizona. 1976
The Mexican Experience in Texas. 1976
Mexican Migration to the United States. 1976
The United States Conquest of California. 1976
Northern Mexico On the Eve of the United States Invasion:
    Rare Imprints Concerning California, Arizona, New Mexico, and Texas, 1821-1846. Edited by David J. Weber. 1976